Oh My Goddess!

OMNIBUS 3

ああっ女神さまっ

STORY AND ART BY
Kosuke Fujishima

TRANSLATION BY
Dana Lewis AND Toren Smith

LETTERING AND TOUCHUP BY
Susie Lee AND Betty Dona
WITH Tom2K

CHAPTER 43
Belldandy's
Tempestuous Heart 5

CHAPTER 44
The Queen of Vengeance 37

CHAPTER 45
The Man Who
Invites Misfortune 75

CHAPTER 46
Thank You 113

CHAPTER 47
Goodbye and Hello 145

CHAPTER 48
The Forgotten Promise 182

CHAPTER 49
Lunchbox with Love 217

CHAPTER 50
Meet Me by the Seashore............ 255

CHAPTER 51
No, Sweetie............................ 295

CHAPTER 52
Ninja Master......................... 329

CHAPTER 53
Law of the Ninja..................... 363

CHAPTER 54
Together for Never.................... 399

CHAPTER 55
Can't Stop Being Jealous............. 437

CHAPTER 56
It's Lonely at the Top................. 473

CHAPTER 57
Tainted God........................... 509

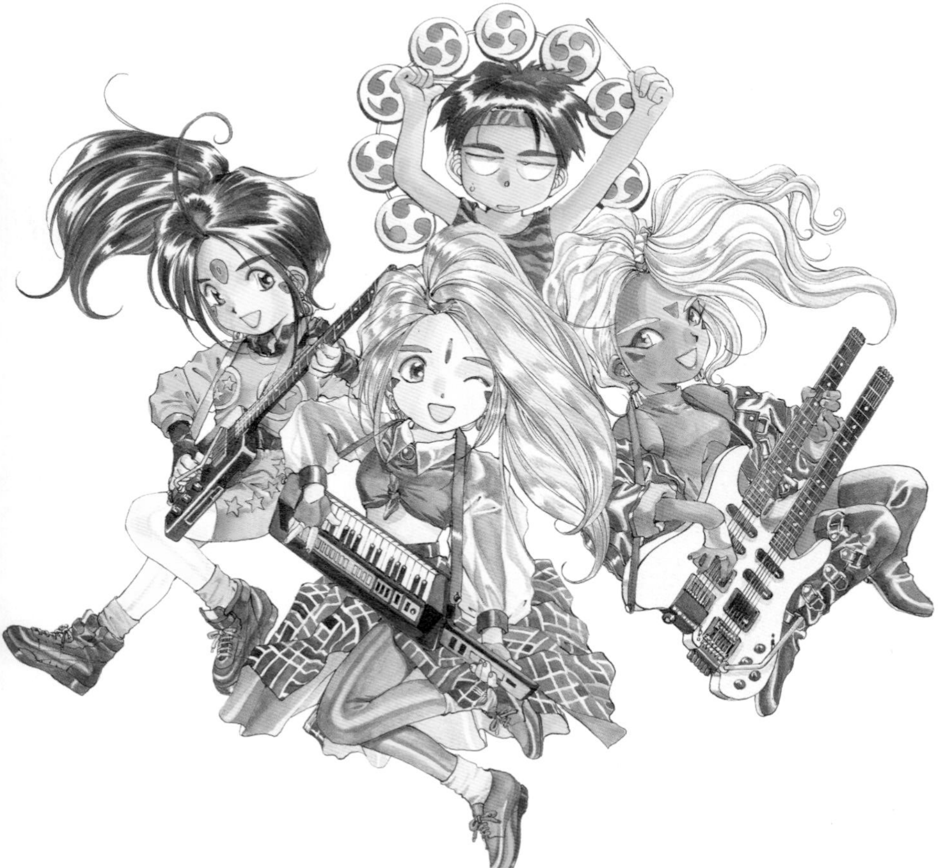

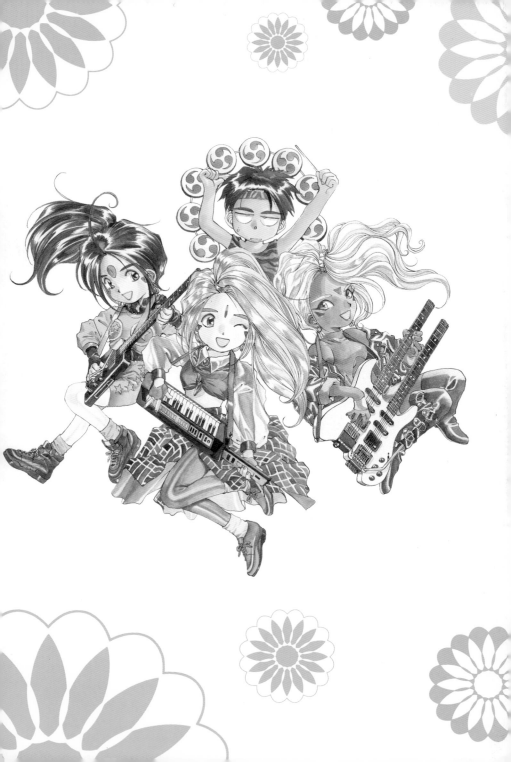

CHAPTER 43

Belldandy's Tempestuous Heart

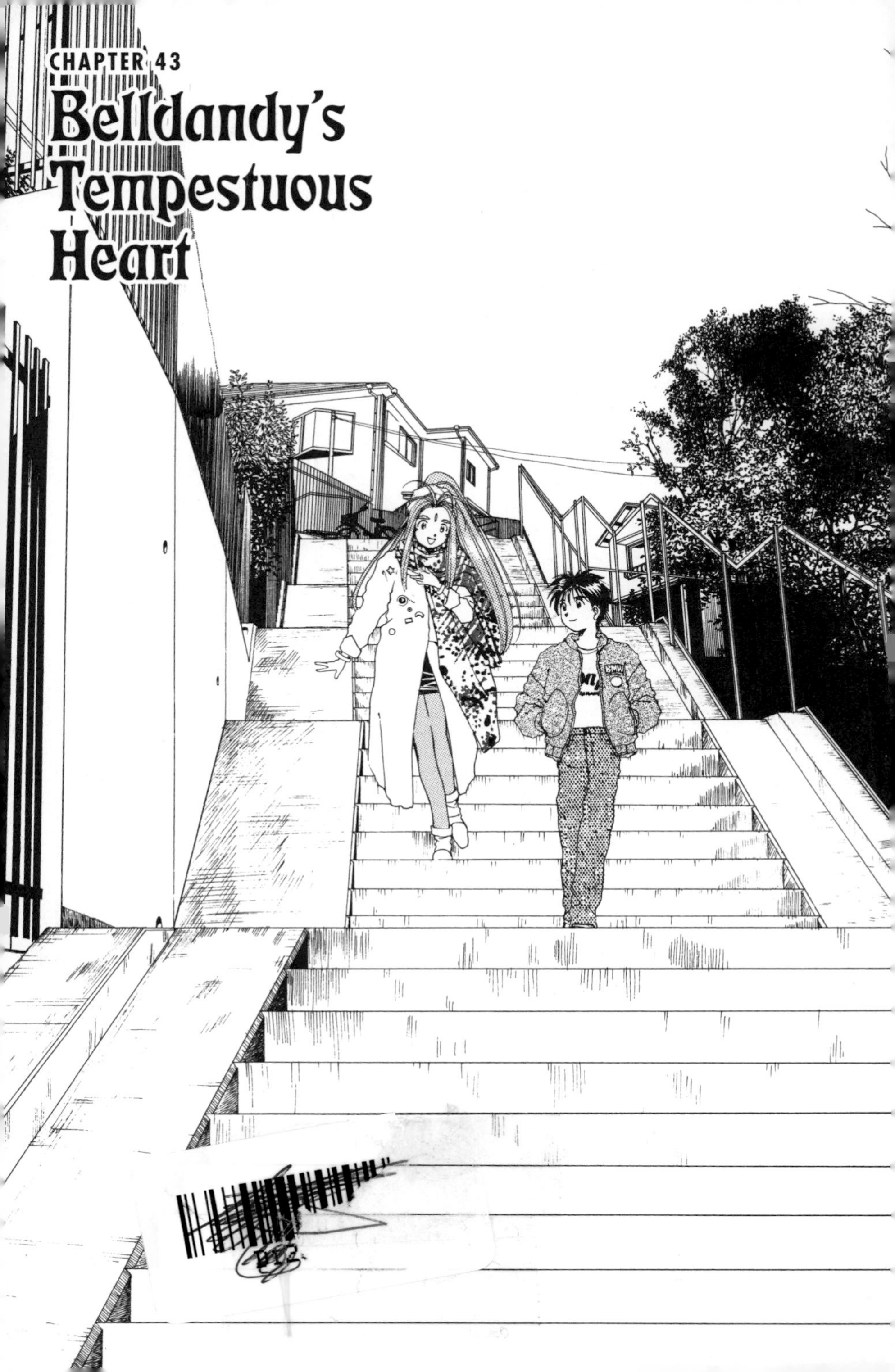

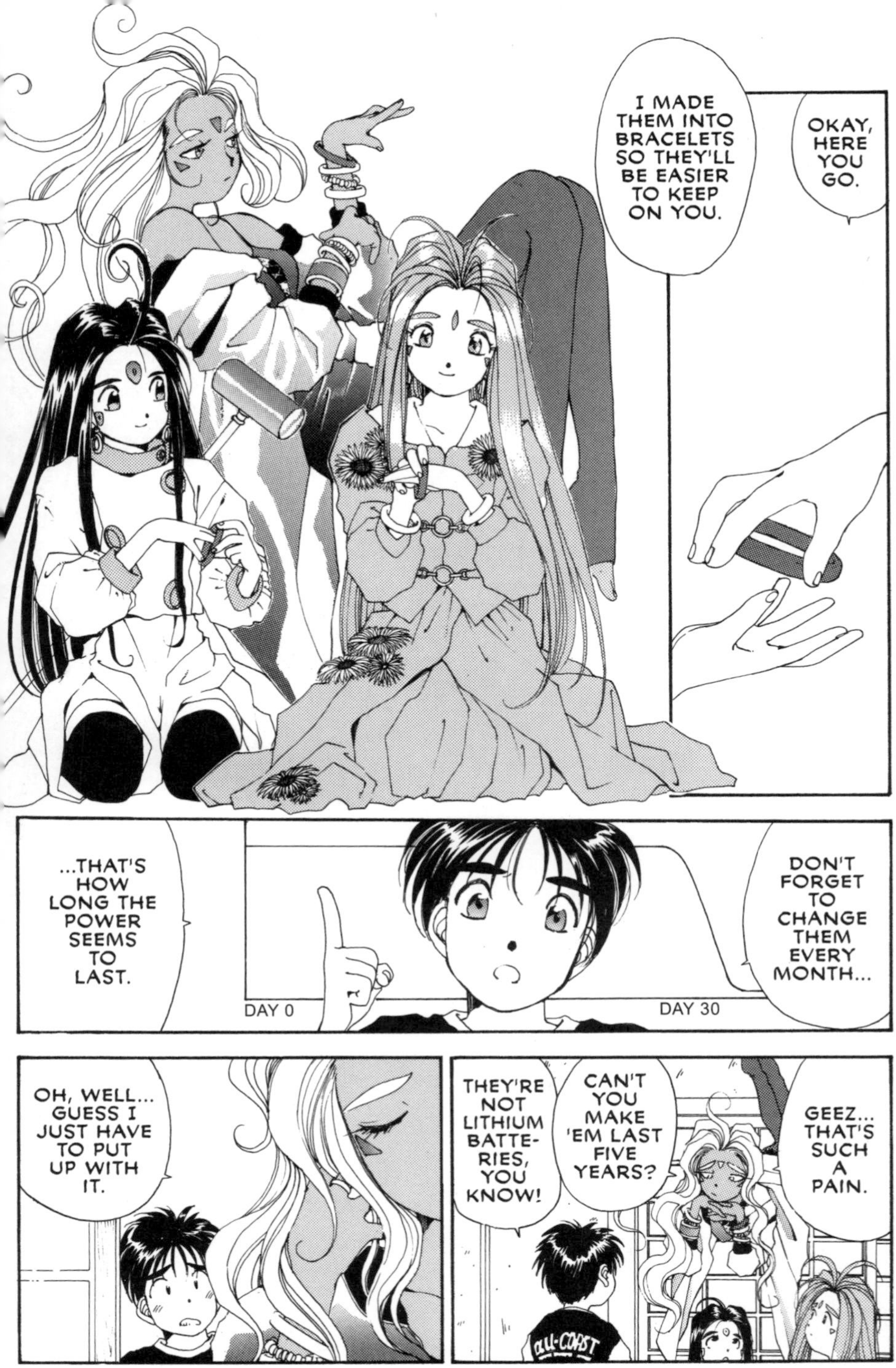
OKAY, HERE YOU GO.
I MADE THEM INTO BRACELETS SO THEY'LL BE EASIER TO KEEP ON YOU.
DON'T FORGET TO CHANGE THEM EVERY MONTH...
DAY 30
DAY 0
...THAT'S HOW LONG THE POWER SEEMS TO LAST.
GEEZ... THAT'S SUCH A PAIN.
CAN'T YOU MAKE 'EM LAST FIVE YEARS?
THEY'RE NOT LITHIUM BATTE-RIES, YOU KNOW!
OH, WELL... GUESS I JUST HAVE TO PUT UP WITH IT.

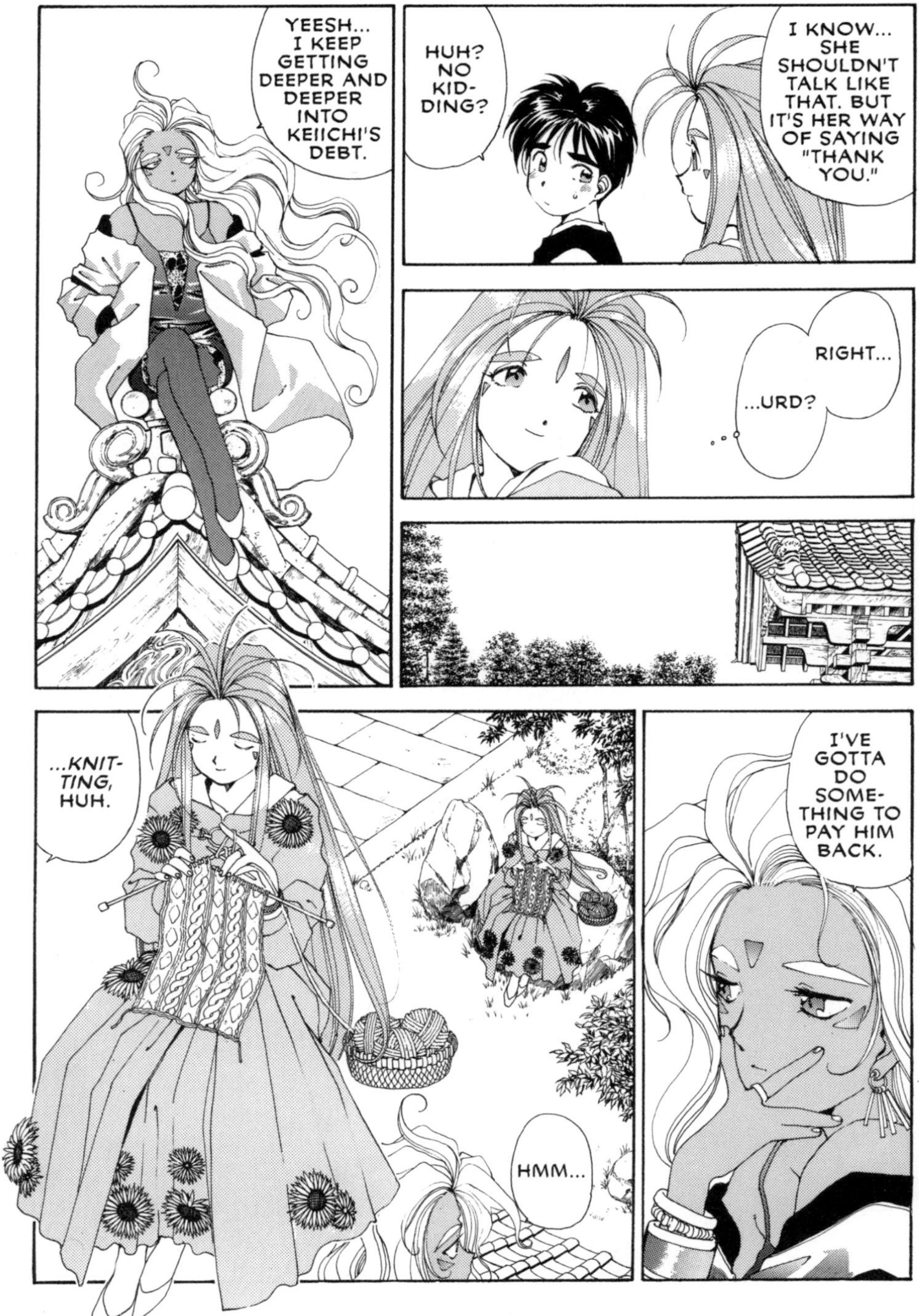
I KNOW... SHE SHOULDN'T TALK LIKE THAT. BUT IT'S HER WAY OF SAYING "THANK YOU."
HUH? NO KID-DING?
RIGHT...
...URD?
YEESH... I KEEP GETTING DEEPER AND DEEPER INTO KEIICHI'S DEBT.
I'VE GOTTA DO SOME-THING TO PAY HIM BACK.
HMM...
...KNIT-TING, HUH.

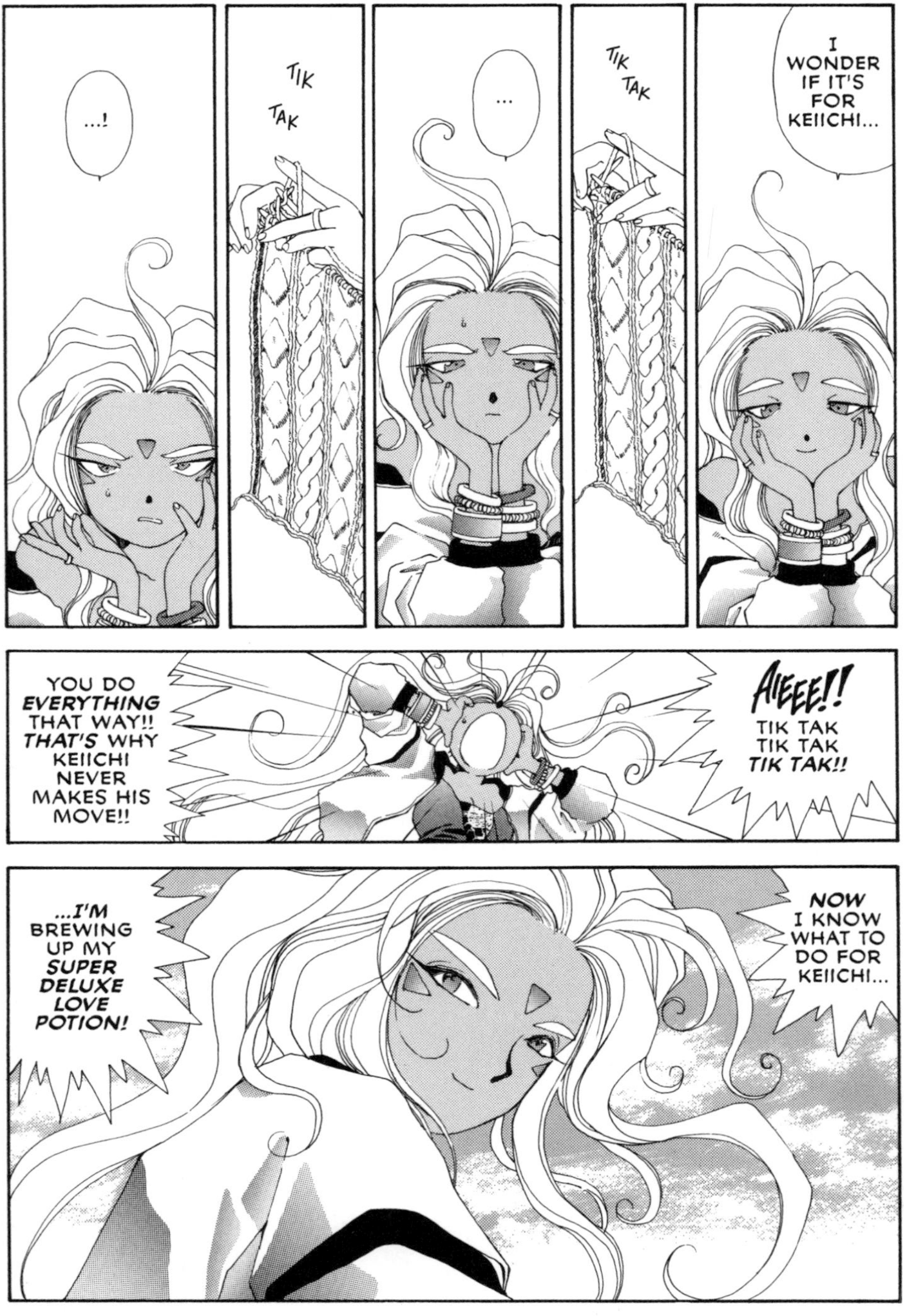
I WONDER IF IT'S FOR KEIICHI...
TIK TAK
...
TIK TAK
...!
AIEEE!!
TIK TAK TIK TAK *TIK TAK!!*
YOU DO *EVERYTHING* THAT WAY!! *THAT'S* WHY KEIICHI NEVER MAKES HIS MOVE!!
NOW I KNOW WHAT TO DO FOR KEIICHI...
...I'M BREWING UP MY *SUPER DELUXE LOVE POTION!*

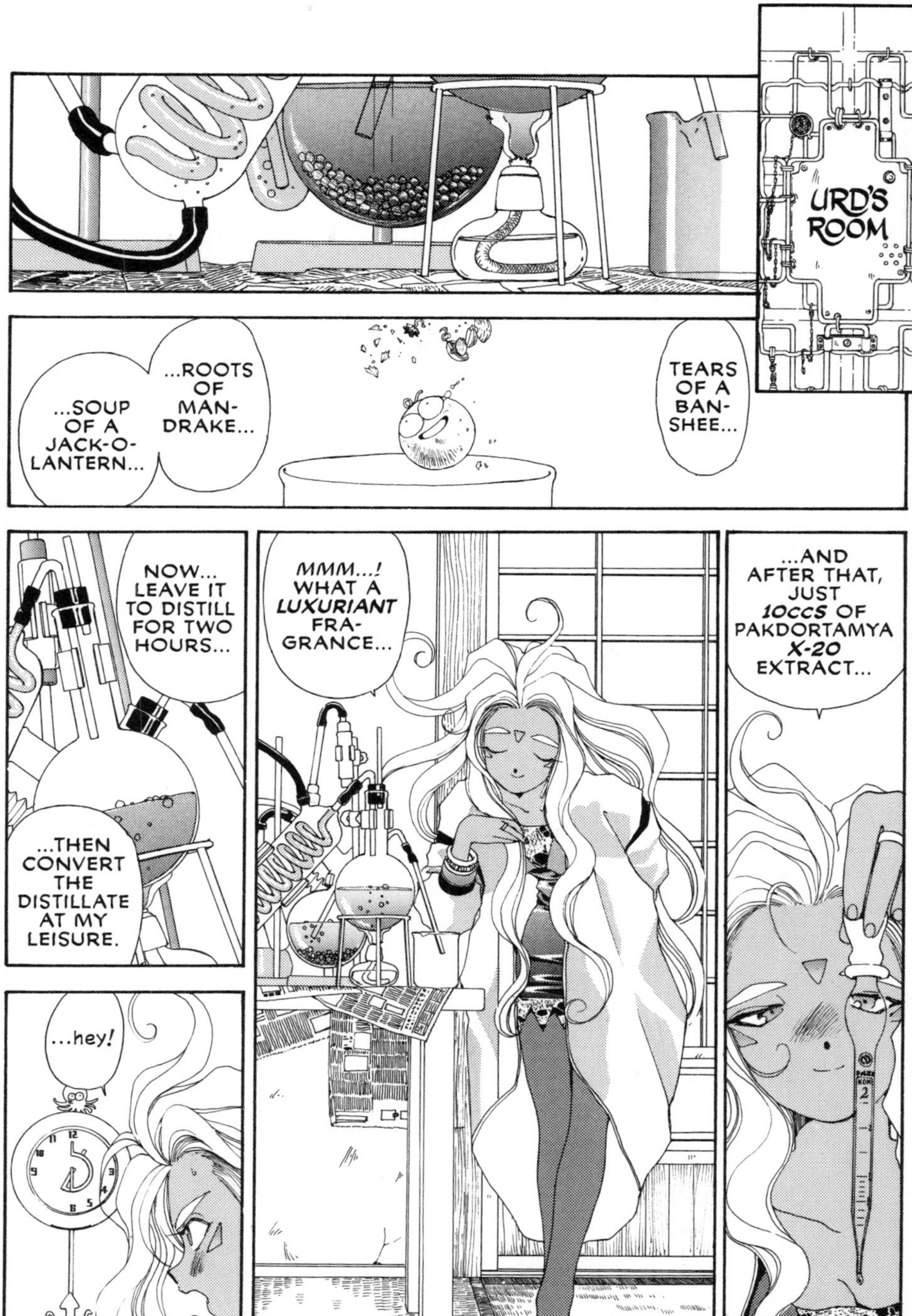
URD'S ROOM
TEARS OF A BAN-SHEE...
...ROOTS OF MAN-DRAKE...
...SOUP OF A JACK-O-LANTERN...
...AND AFTER THAT, JUST 10CCS OF PAKDORTAMYA X-20 EXTRACT...
MMM...! WHAT A LUXURIANT FRA-GRANCE...
NOW... LEAVE IT TO DISTILL FOR TWO HOURS...
...THEN CONVERT THE DISTILLATE AT MY LEISURE.
...hey!

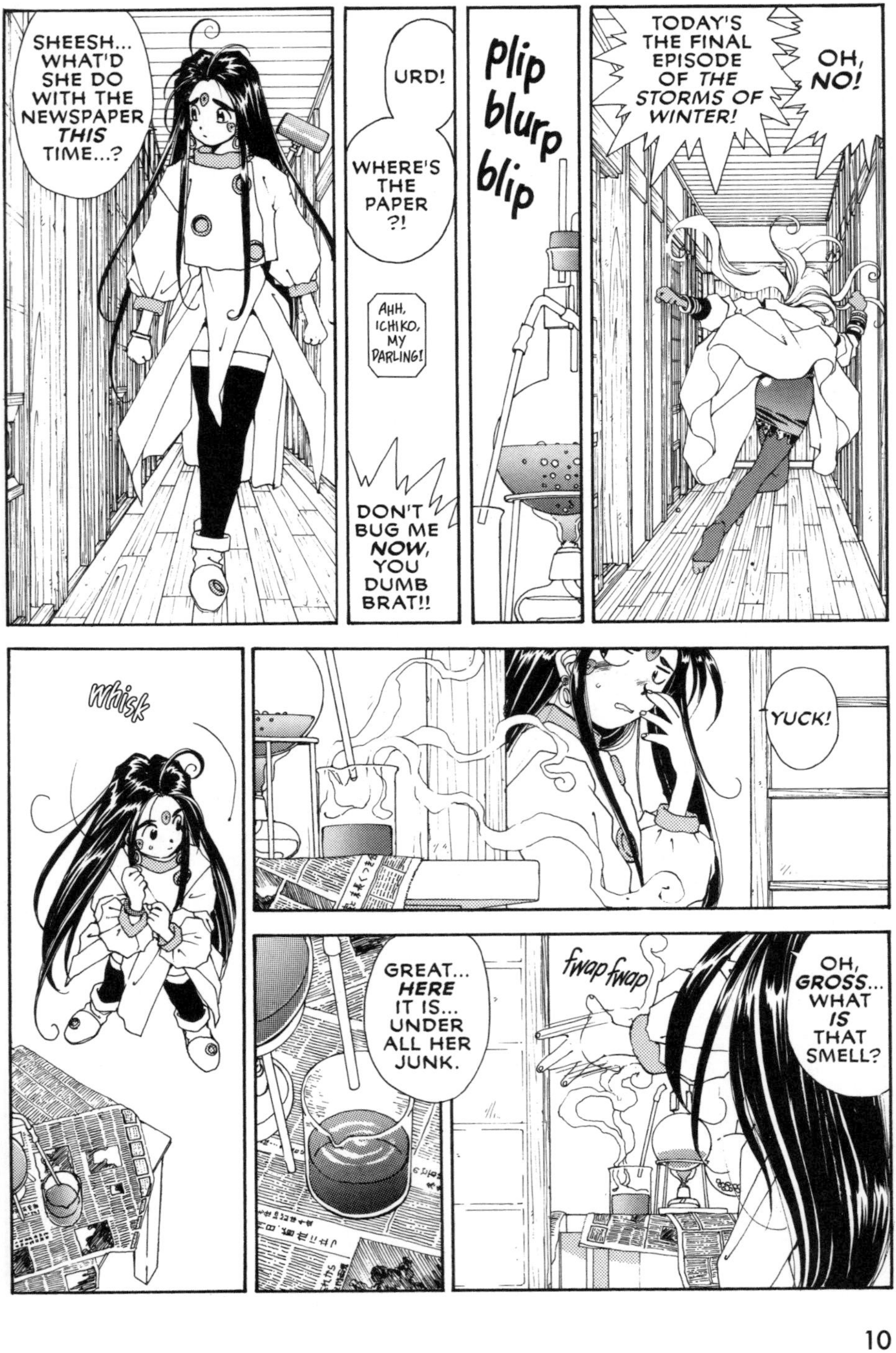
OH, NO!
TODAY'S THE FINAL EPISODE OF THE STORMS OF WINTER!
plip blurp blip
URD!
WHERE'S THE PAPER ?!
AHH, ICHIKO, MY DARLING!
DON'T BUG ME NOW, YOU DUMB BRAT!!
SHEESH... WHAT'D SHE DO WITH THE NEWSPAPER THIS TIME...?
YUCK!
OH, GROSS... WHAT IS THAT SMELL?
fwap fwap
GREAT... HERE IT IS... UNDER ALL HER JUNK.
whisk

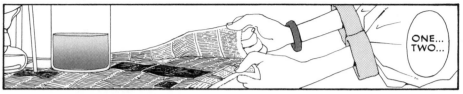

ONE...
TWO...

SKULD
MAGIC
SUPREME!

FWAP

...THREEE!!

um...

drip
drip

MAGNIFI-
CENT...

...IF
I DO
SAY
SO
MY-
SELF.

GACK!

N-
N--

--NOW
WHAT
DO
I
DO?

11

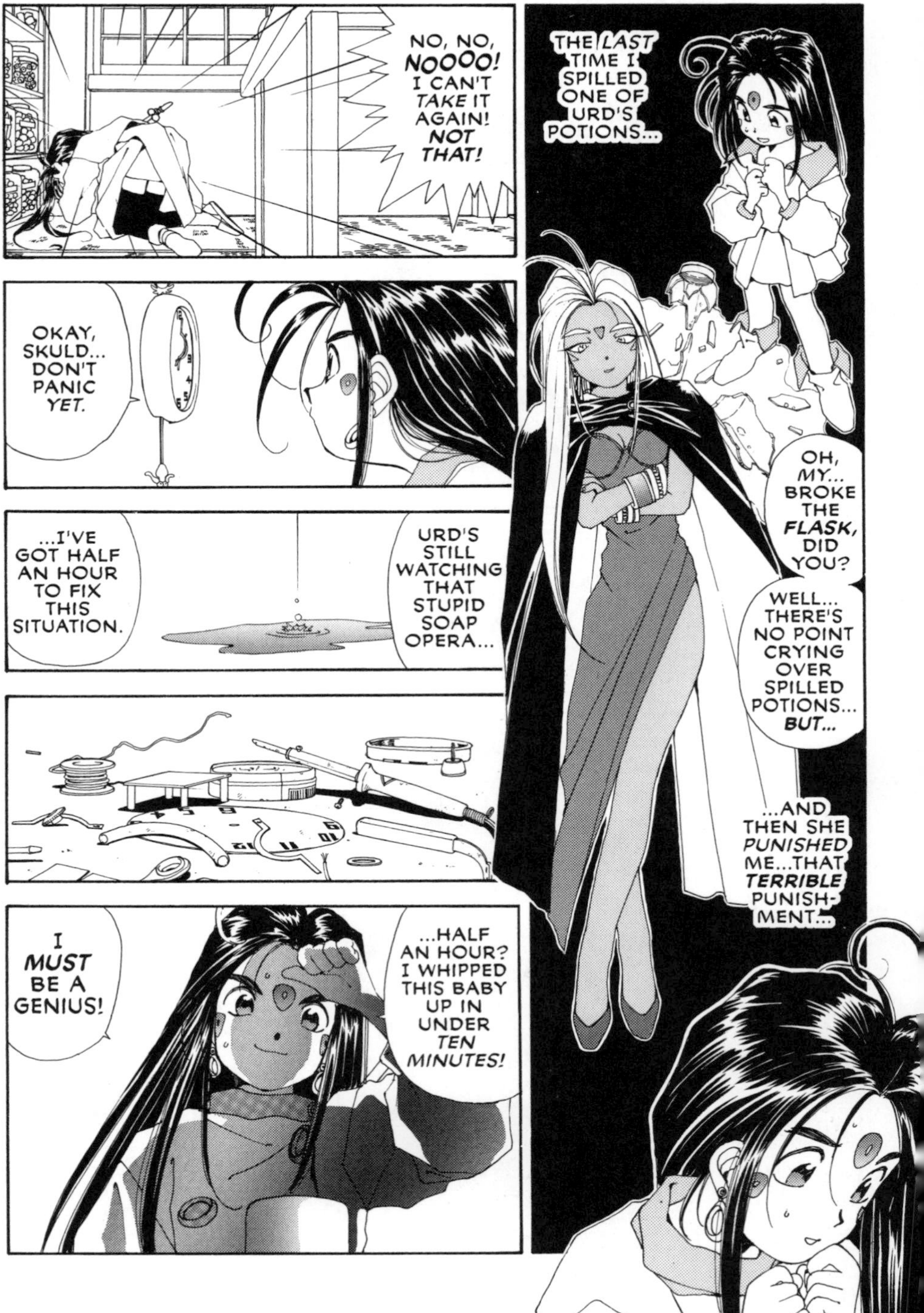
THE *LAST* TIME I SPILLED ONE OF URD'S POTIONS...
OH, *MY*... BROKE THE ***FLASK,*** DID YOU?
WELL... THERE'S NO POINT CRYING OVER SPILLED POTIONS... ***BUT...***
...AND THEN SHE *PUNISHED* ME...THAT ***TERRIBLE*** PUNISHMENT...
NO, NO, ***NOOOO!*** I CAN'T *TAKE* IT AGAIN! ***NOT THAT!***
OKAY, SKULD... DON'T PANIC *YET.*
URD'S STILL WATCHING THAT STUPID SOAP OPERA...
...I'VE GOT HALF AN HOUR TO FIX THIS SITUATION.
...HALF AN HOUR? I WHIPPED THIS BABY UP IN UNDER *TEN MINUTES!*
I ***MUST*** BE A GENIUS!

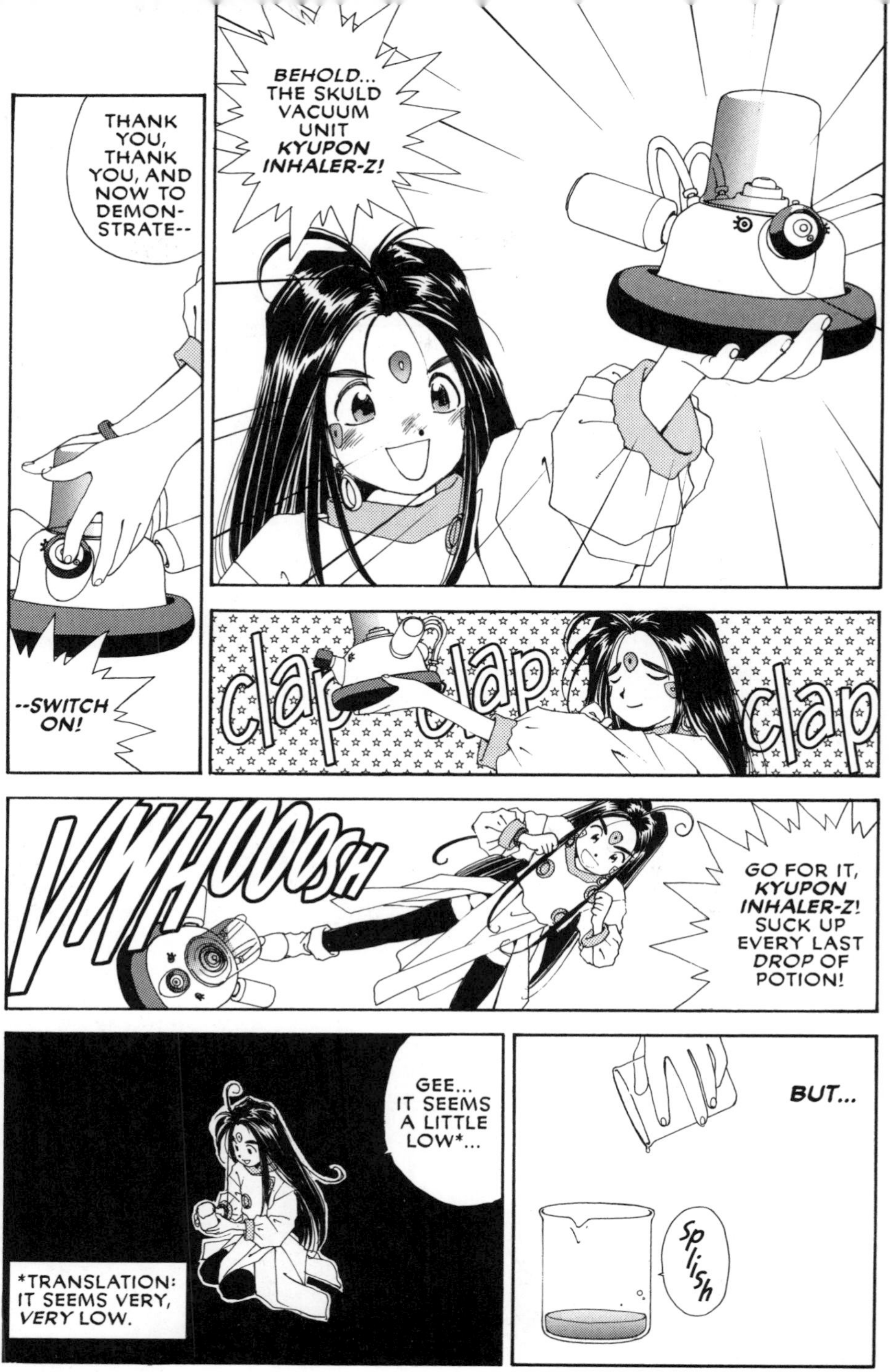
BEHOLD... THE SKULD VACUUM UNIT *KYUPON INHALER-Z!*
clap clap clap
THANK YOU, THANK YOU, AND NOW TO DEMON-STRATE--
--SWITCH ON!
VWHOOOSH
GO FOR IT, *KYUPON INHALER-Z!* SUCK UP EVERY LAST *DROP* OF POTION!
BUT...
Splish
GEE... IT SEEMS A LITTLE LOW*...
*TRANSLATION: IT SEEMS VERY, *VERY* LOW.

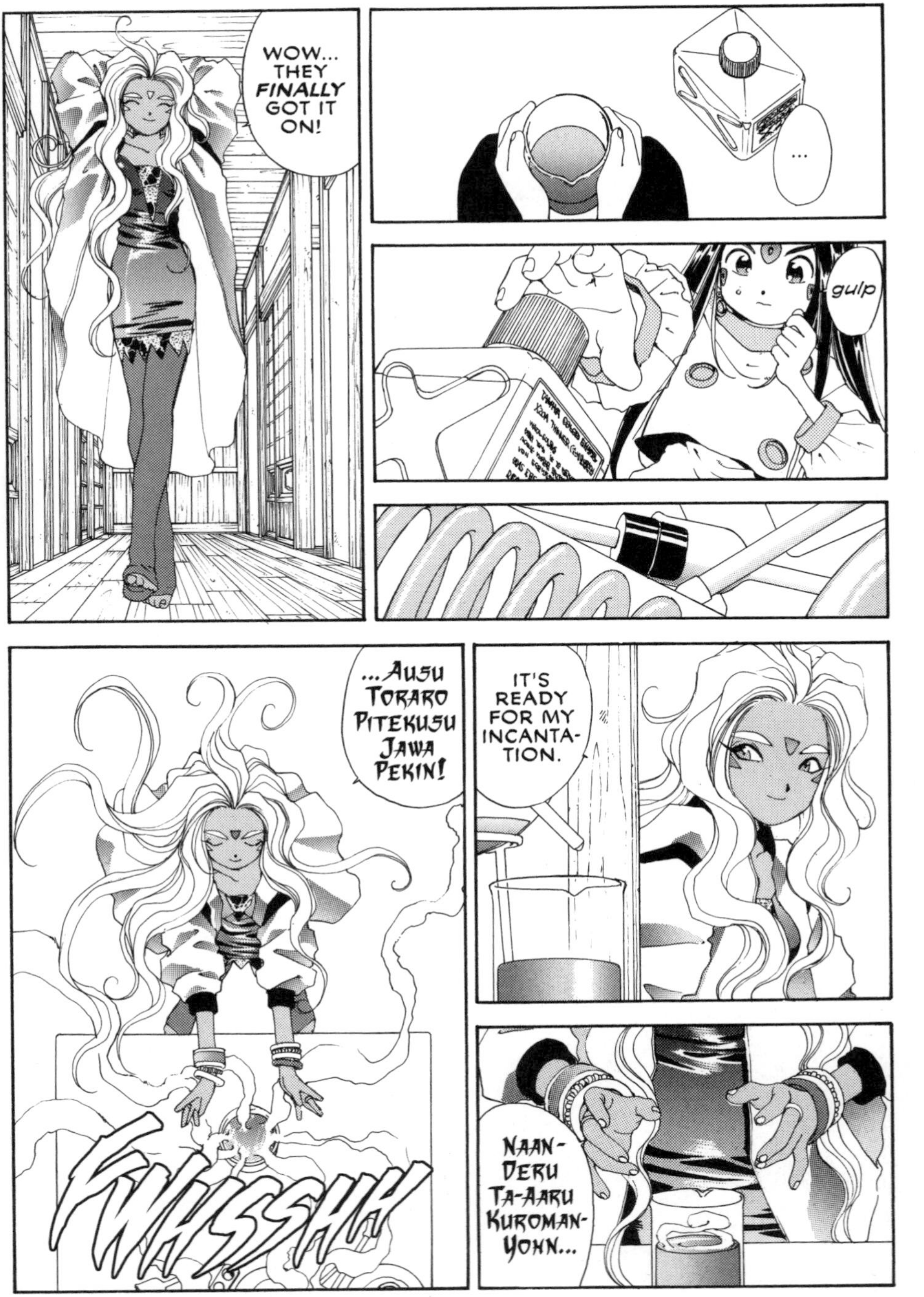
...
gulp
WOW... THEY FINALLY GOT IT ON!
IT'S READY FOR MY INCANTATION.
NAAN-DERU TA-AARU KUROMAN-YOHN...
...AUSU TORARO PITEKUSU JAWA PEKIN!
FWASSHA

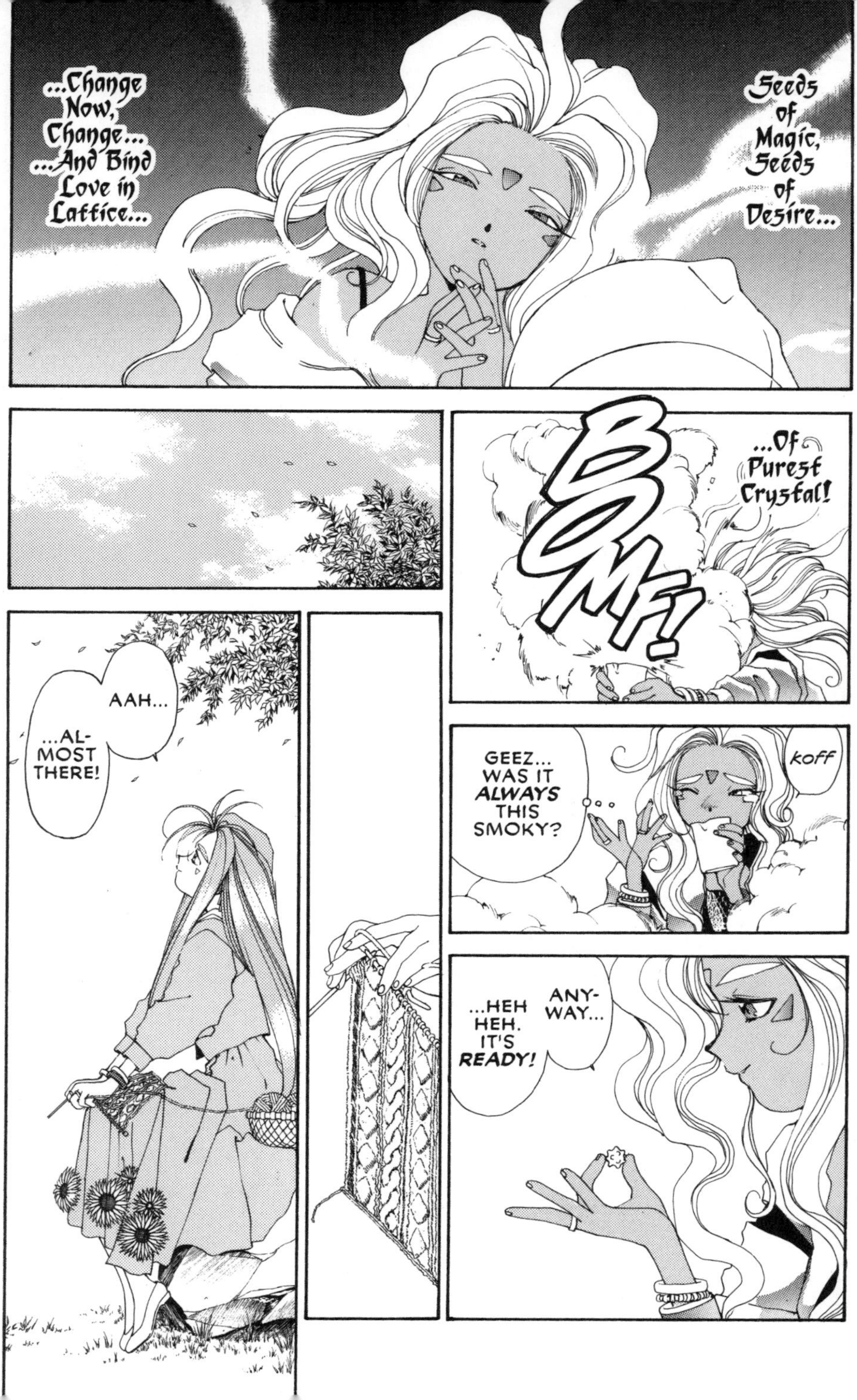

Seeds of Magic, Seeds of Desire...
...Change Now, Change... ...And Bind Love in Lattice...
...Of Purest Crystal!
BOMF!
koff
GEEZ... WAS IT *ALWAYS* THIS SMOKY?
ANY-WAY...
...HEH HEH. IT'S *READY!*
AAH...
...AL-MOST THERE!

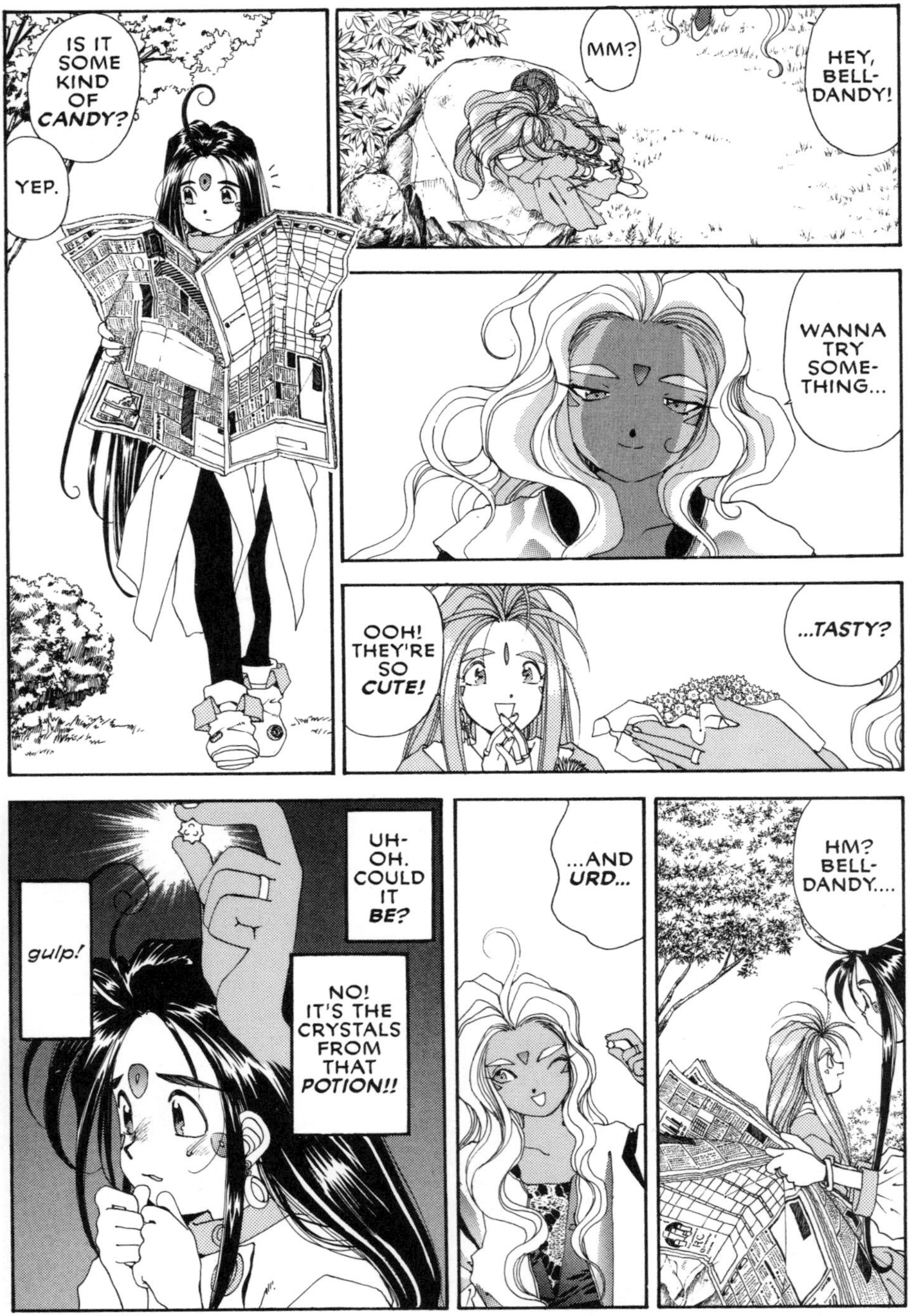
HEY, BELL-DANDY!
MM?
WANNA TRY SOME-THING...
...TASTY?
OOH! THEY'RE SO CUTE!
IS IT SOME KIND OF CANDY?
YEP.
HM? BELL-DANDY....
...AND URD...
UH-OH. COULD IT BE?
NO! IT'S THE CRYSTALS FROM THAT POTION!!
gulp!

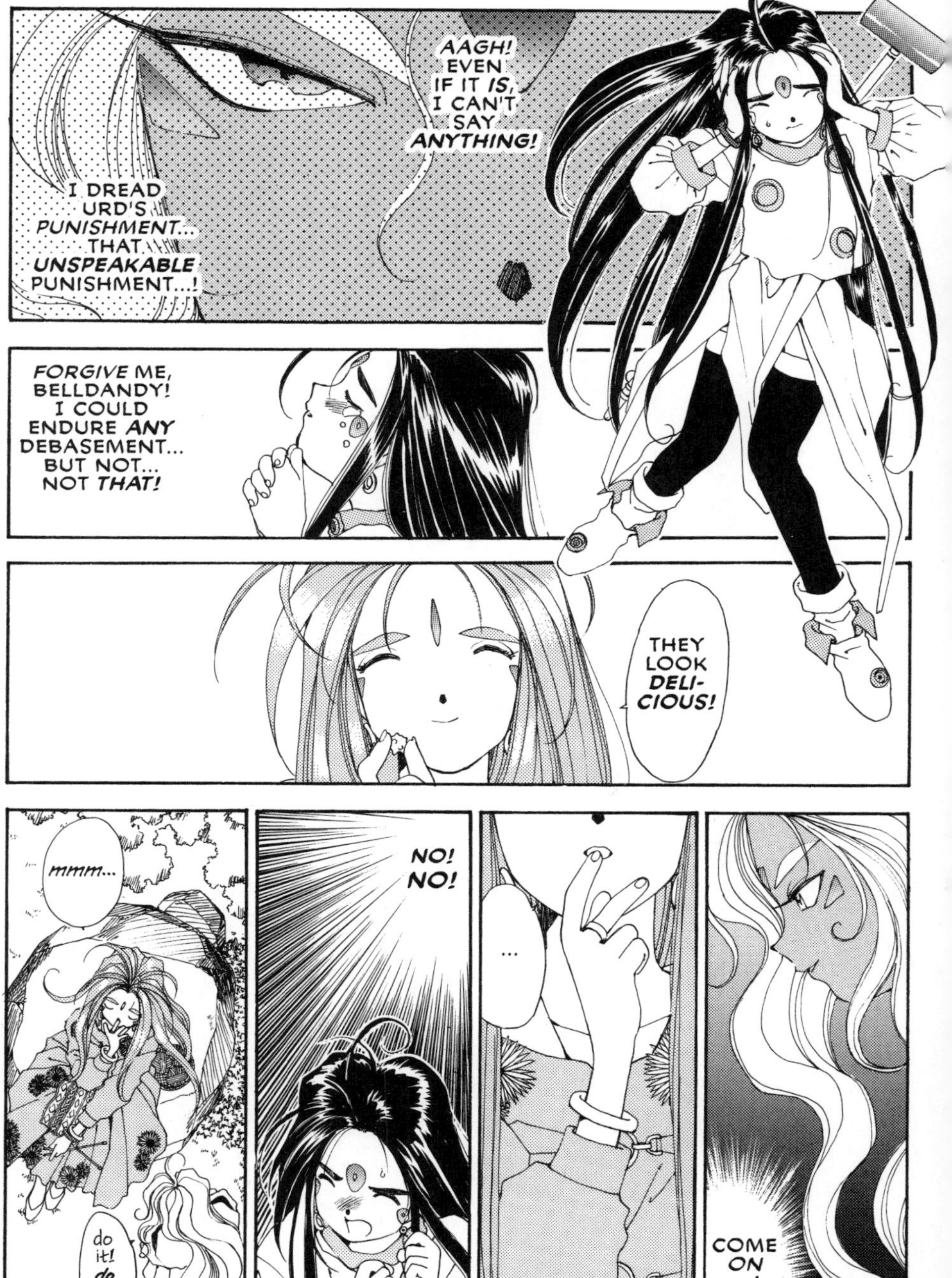
AAGH! EVEN IF IT IS, I CAN'T SAY ANYTHING!
I DREAD URD'S PUNISHMENT... THAT UNSPEAKABLE PUNISHMENT...!
FORGIVE ME, BELLDANDY! I COULD ENDURE ANY DEBASEMENT... BUT NOT... NOT THAT!
THEY LOOK DELICIOUS!
COME ON ...!
...
NO! NO!
mmm...
do it! do it!

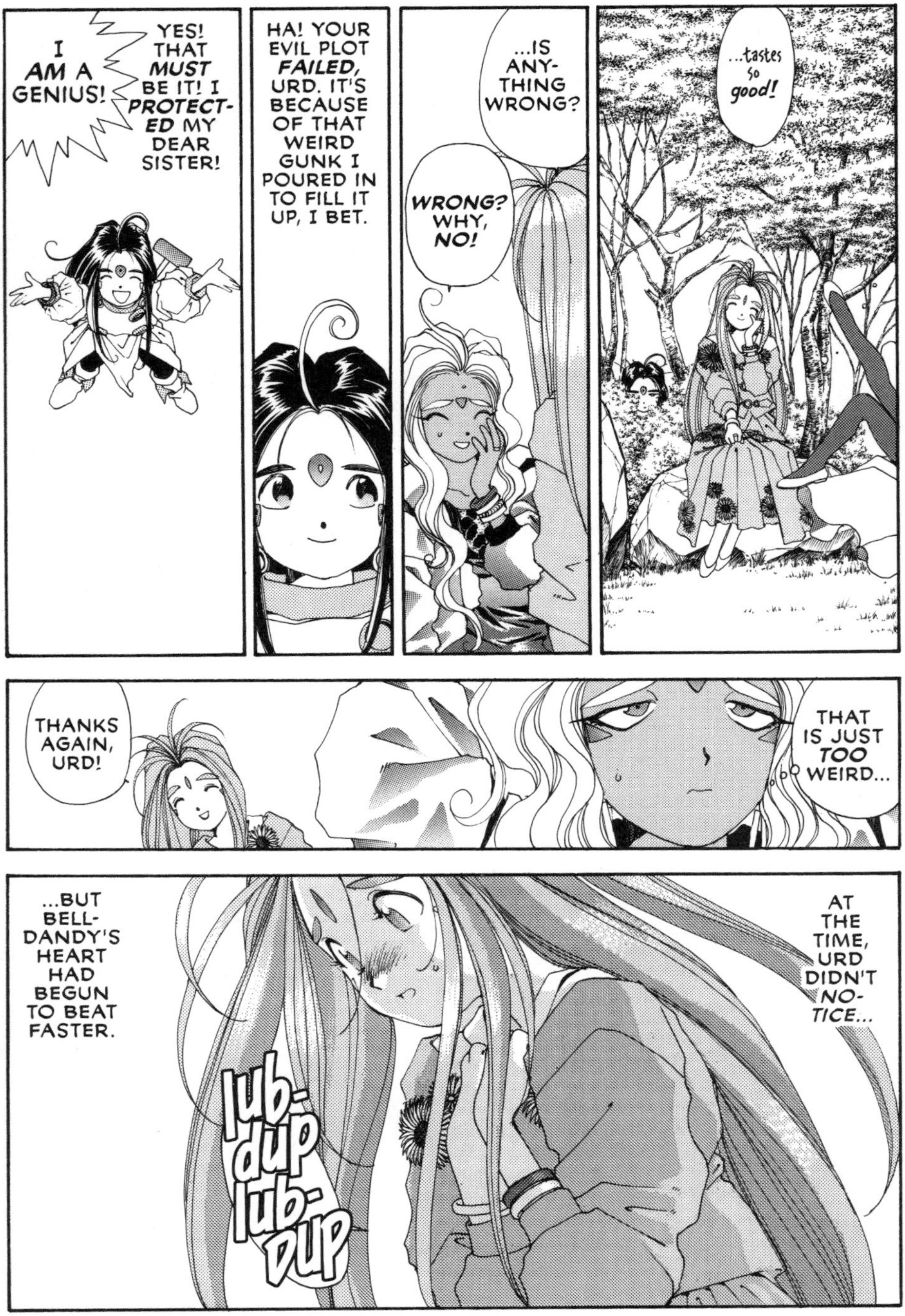
...tastes so good!
...IS ANYTHING WRONG?
WRONG? WHY, NO!
HA! YOUR EVIL PLOT FAILED, URD. IT'S BECAUSE OF THAT WEIRD GUNK I POURED IN TO FILL IT UP, I BET.
YES! THAT MUST BE IT! I PROTECTED MY DEAR SISTER!
I AM A GENIUS!
THAT IS JUST TOO WEIRD...
THANKS AGAIN, URD!
AT THE TIME, URD DIDN'T NOTICE...
...BUT BELLDANDY'S HEART HAD BEGUN TO BEAT FASTER.
lub-dup lub-DUP

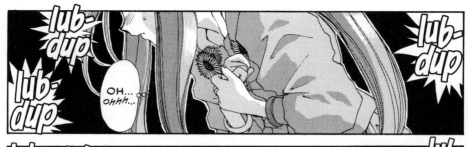

lub-dup
lub-dup
OH... ohhh...
lub-dup
lub-dup
lub-dup
lub-dup
lub-dup
DANG, THOUGHT SO...
...THE PROB-LEM'S WITH CYLINDER ONE. THE PLUG'S ALL WHITE.
leeean
chink
ke
i
i
chi--

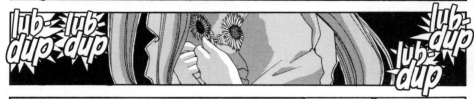

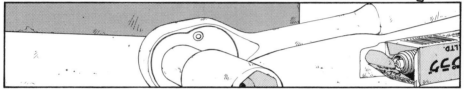

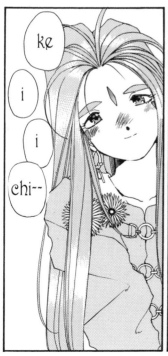

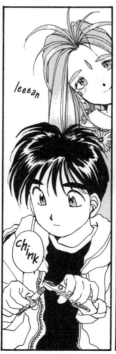

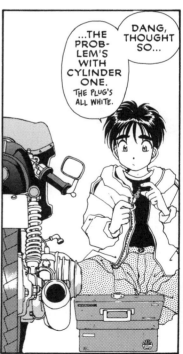

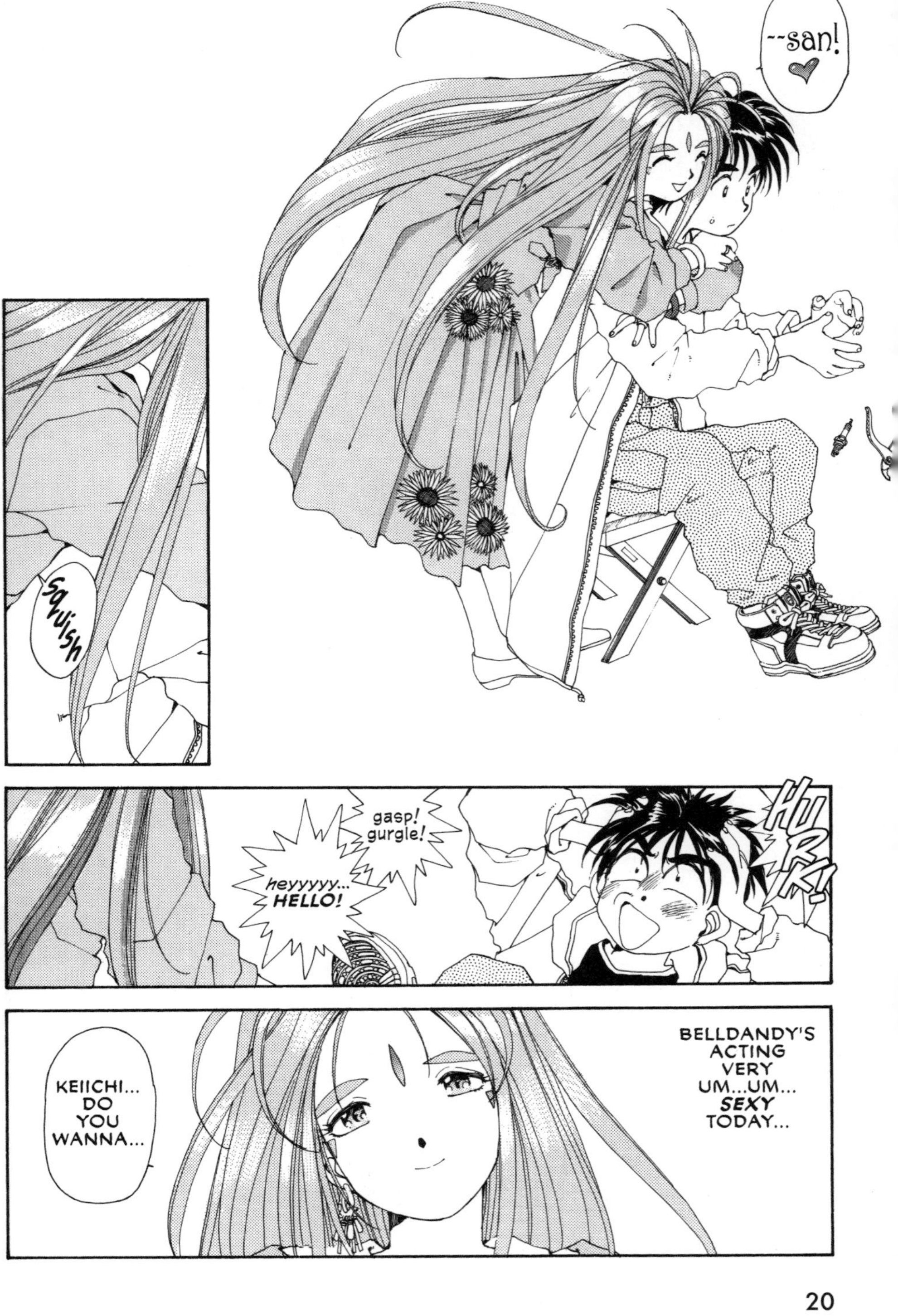
--san! ♥
squish
HURK!
gasp! gurgle!
heyyyyy... HELLO!
BELLDANDY'S ACTING VERY UM...UM... *SEXY* TODAY...
KEIICHI... DO YOU WANNA...

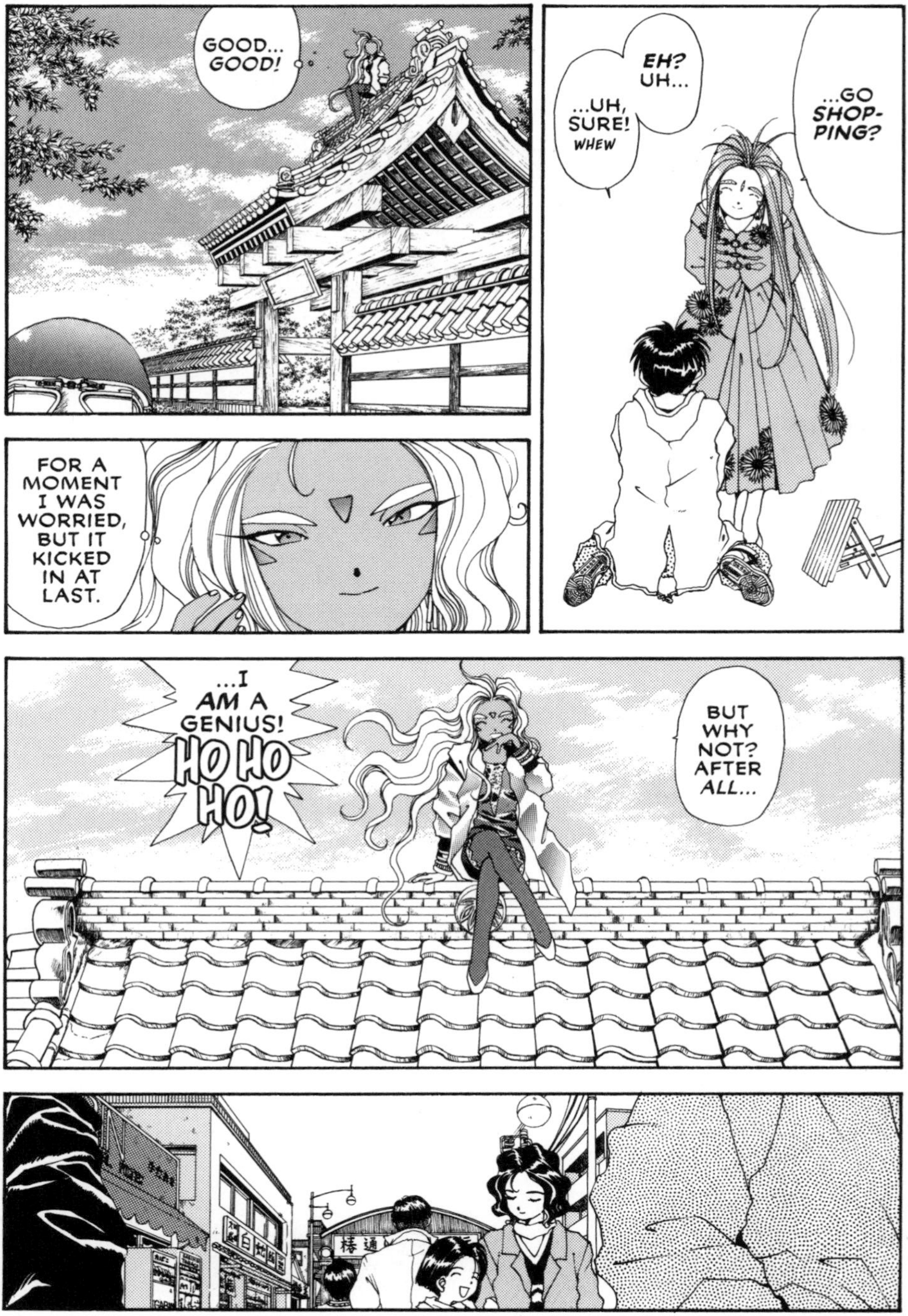
...GO SHOP-PING?
EH? UH...
...UH, SURE! WHEW
GOOD... GOOD!
FOR A MOMENT I WAS WORRIED, BUT IT KICKED IN AT LAST.
BUT WHY NOT? AFTER ALL...
...I AM A GENIUS! HO HO HO!

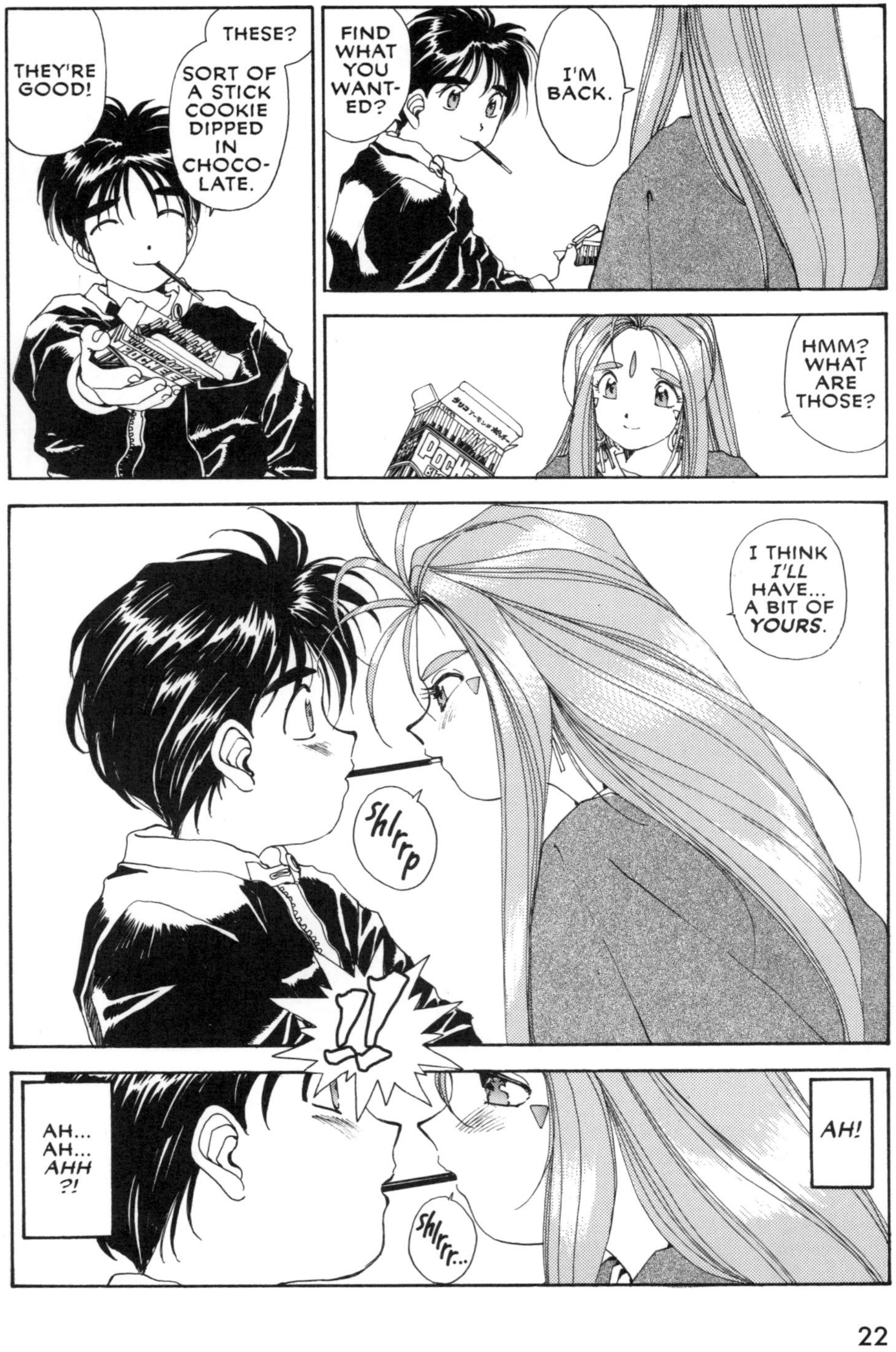
I'M BACK.
FIND WHAT YOU WANT-ED?
HMM? WHAT ARE THOSE?
THESE?
SORT OF A STICK COOKIE DIPPED IN CHOCO-LATE.
THEY'RE GOOD!
POCHEE
I THINK I'LL HAVE... A BIT OF YOURS.
Shlrrp
!!
AH!
shlrrr...
AH... AH... AHH ?!

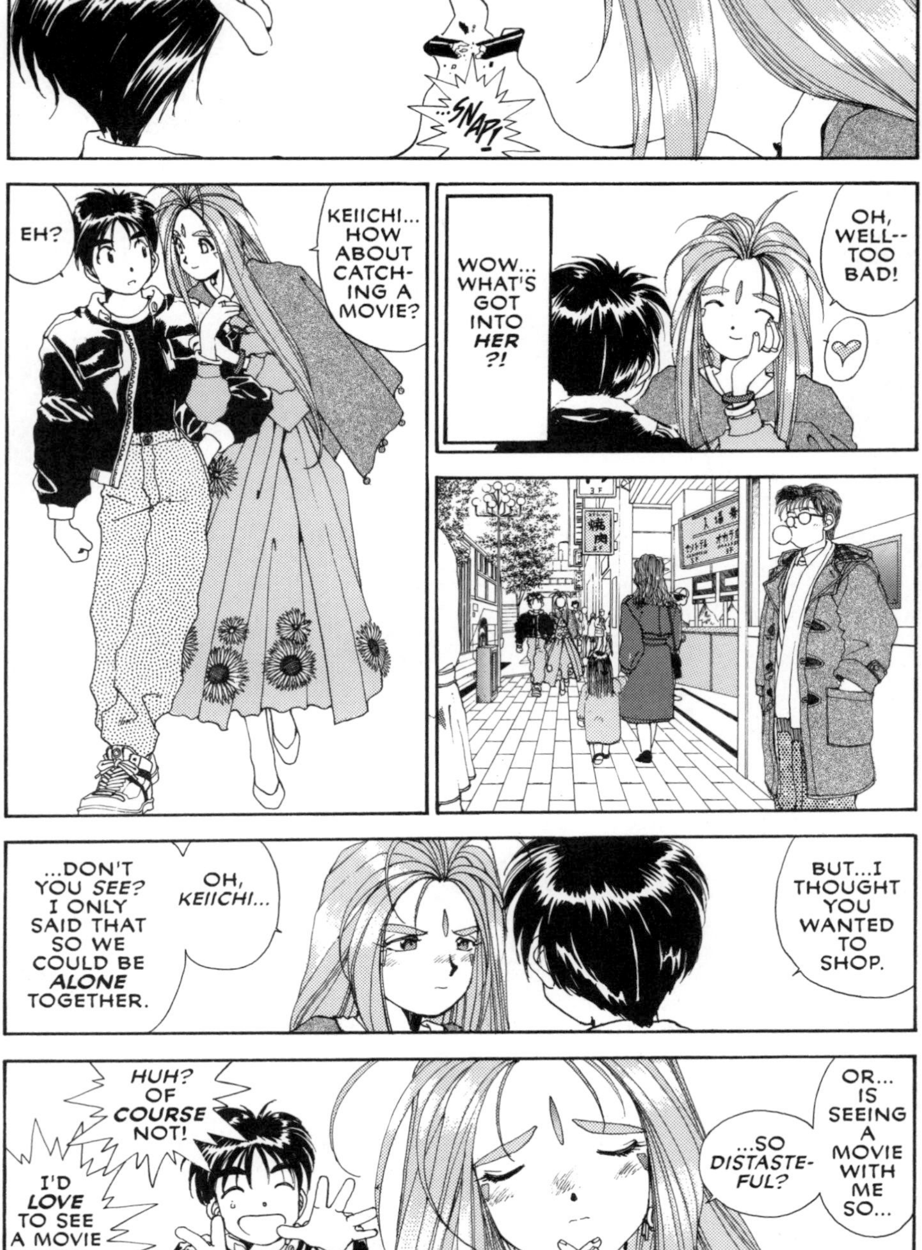
...SNAP!
OH, WELL--TOO BAD!
WOW... WHAT'S GOT INTO HER?!
KEIICHI... HOW ABOUT CATCHING A MOVIE?
EH?
BUT...I THOUGHT YOU WANTED TO SHOP.
OH, KEIICHI...
...DON'T YOU SEE? I ONLY SAID THAT SO WE COULD BE ALONE TOGETHER.
OR... IS SEEING A MOVIE WITH ME SO...
...SO DISTASTEFUL?
HUH? OF COURSE NOT!
I'D LOVE TO SEE A MOVIE WITH YOU!

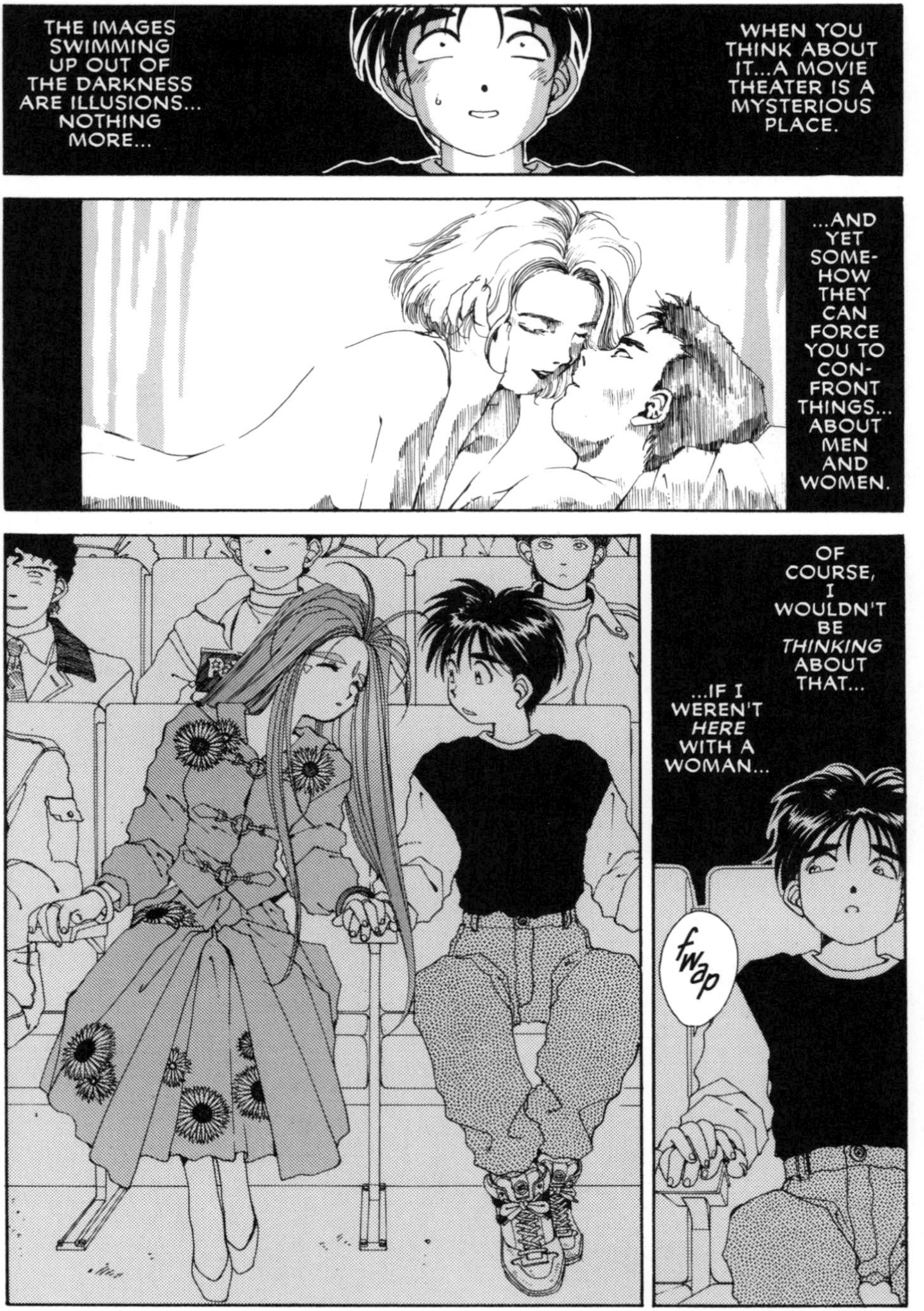
WHEN YOU THINK ABOUT IT...A MOVIE THEATER IS A MYSTERIOUS PLACE.
THE IMAGES SWIMMING UP OUT OF THE DARKNESS ARE ILLUSIONS... NOTHING MORE...
...AND YET SOME-HOW THEY CAN FORCE YOU TO CON-FRONT THINGS... ABOUT MEN AND WOMEN.
OF COURSE, I WOULDN'T BE *THINKING* ABOUT THAT...
...IF I WEREN'T *HERE* WITH A WOMAN...
fwap

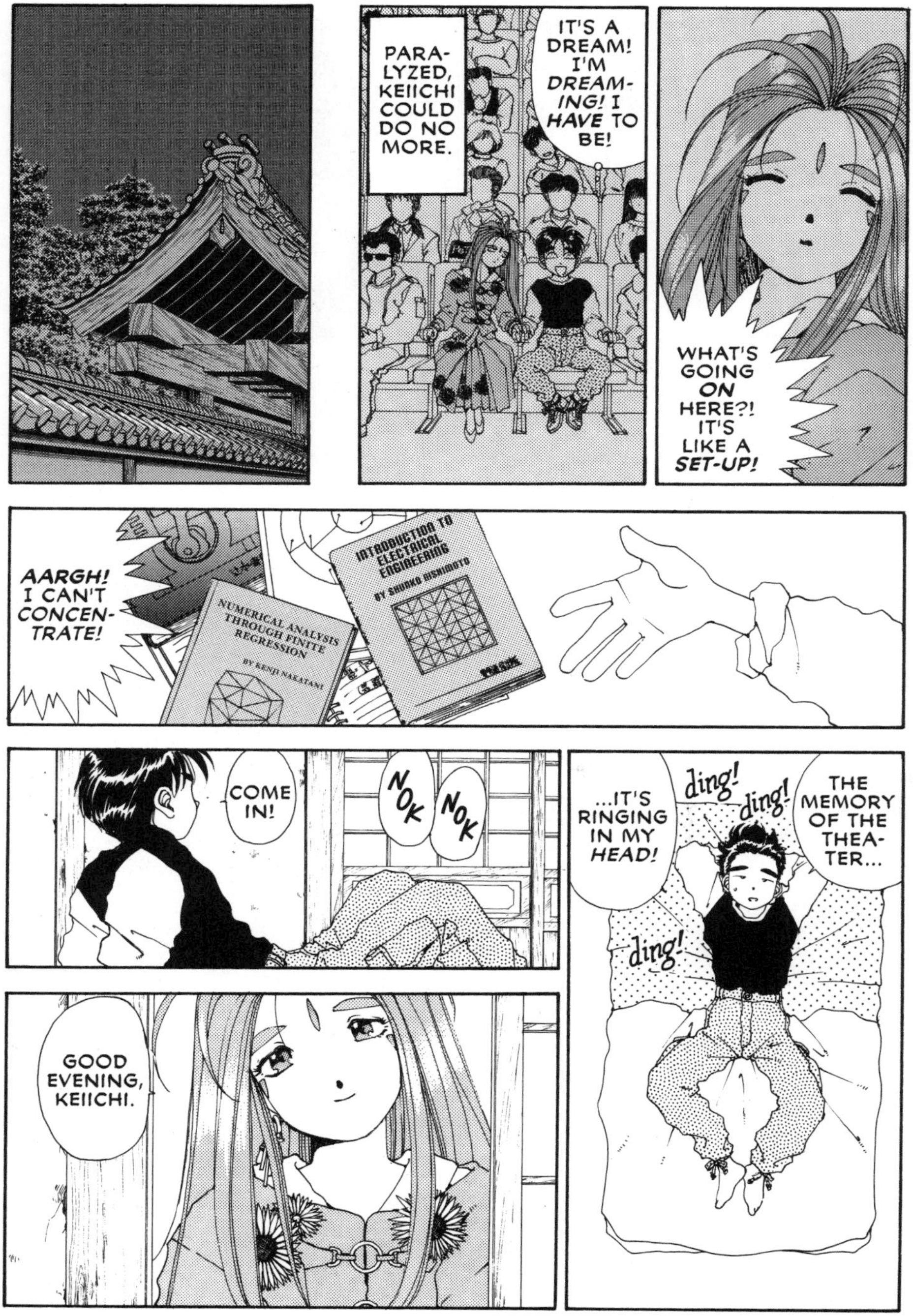
WHAT'S GOING ON HERE?! IT'S LIKE A SET-UP!
IT'S A DREAM! I'M DREAMING! I HAVE TO BE!
PARALYZED, KEIICHI COULD DO NO MORE.
INTRODUCTION TO ELECTRICAL ENGINEERING
BY SHOKO OSHIMOTO
NUMERICAL ANALYSIS THROUGH FINITE REGRESSION
BY KENJI NAKATANI
AARGH! I CAN'T CONCENTRATE!
THE MEMORY OF THE THEATER...
...IT'S RINGING IN MY HEAD!
ding! ding!
ding!
NOK NOK
COME IN!
GOOD EVENING, KEIICHI.

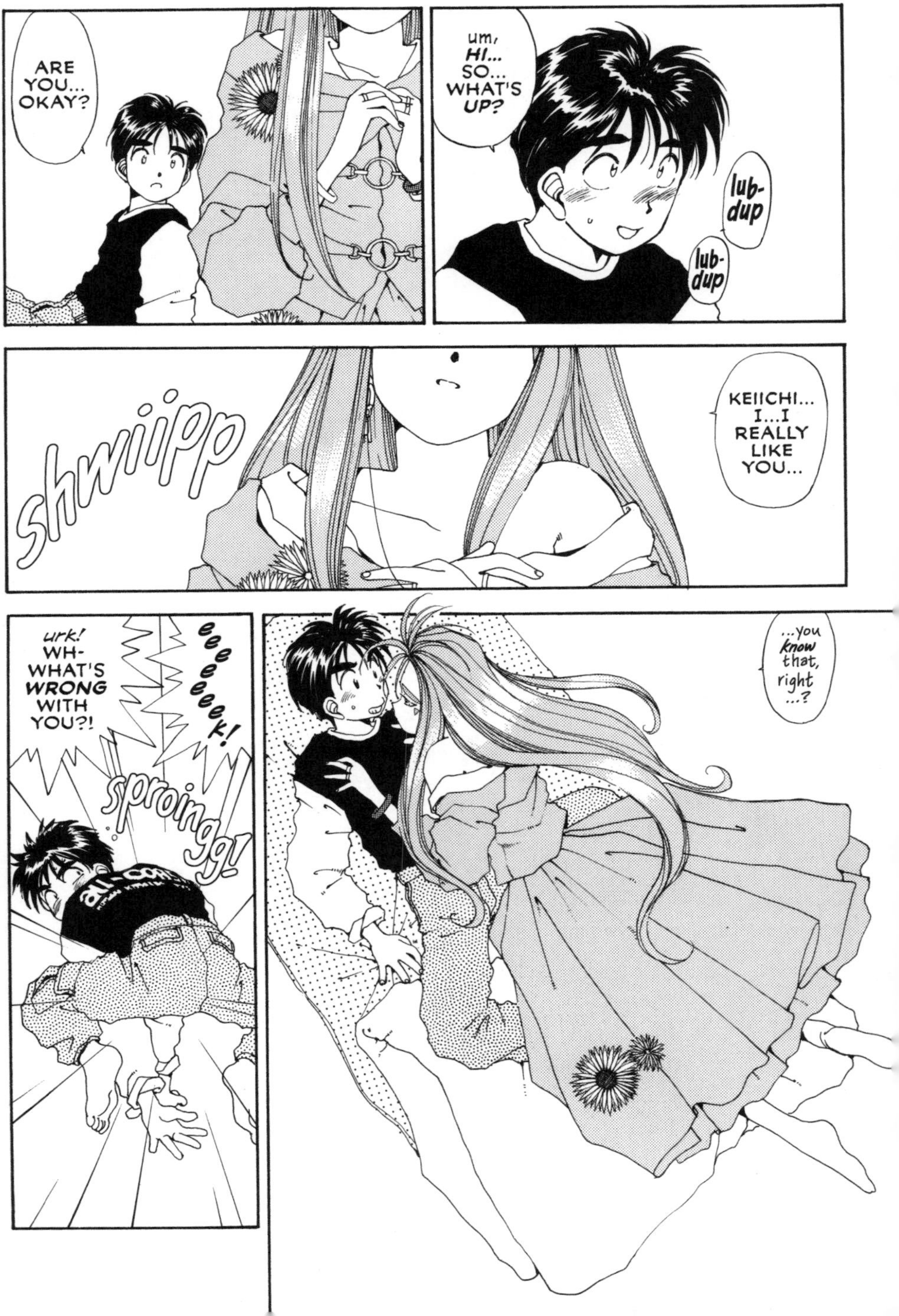
um, HI... SO... WHAT'S UP?
lub-dup
lub-dup
ARE YOU... OKAY?
KEIICHI... I...I REALLY LIKE YOU...
shwiipp
...you know that, right...?
urk! WH-WHAT'S WRONG WITH YOU?!
eeeeeeek!
sproingg!

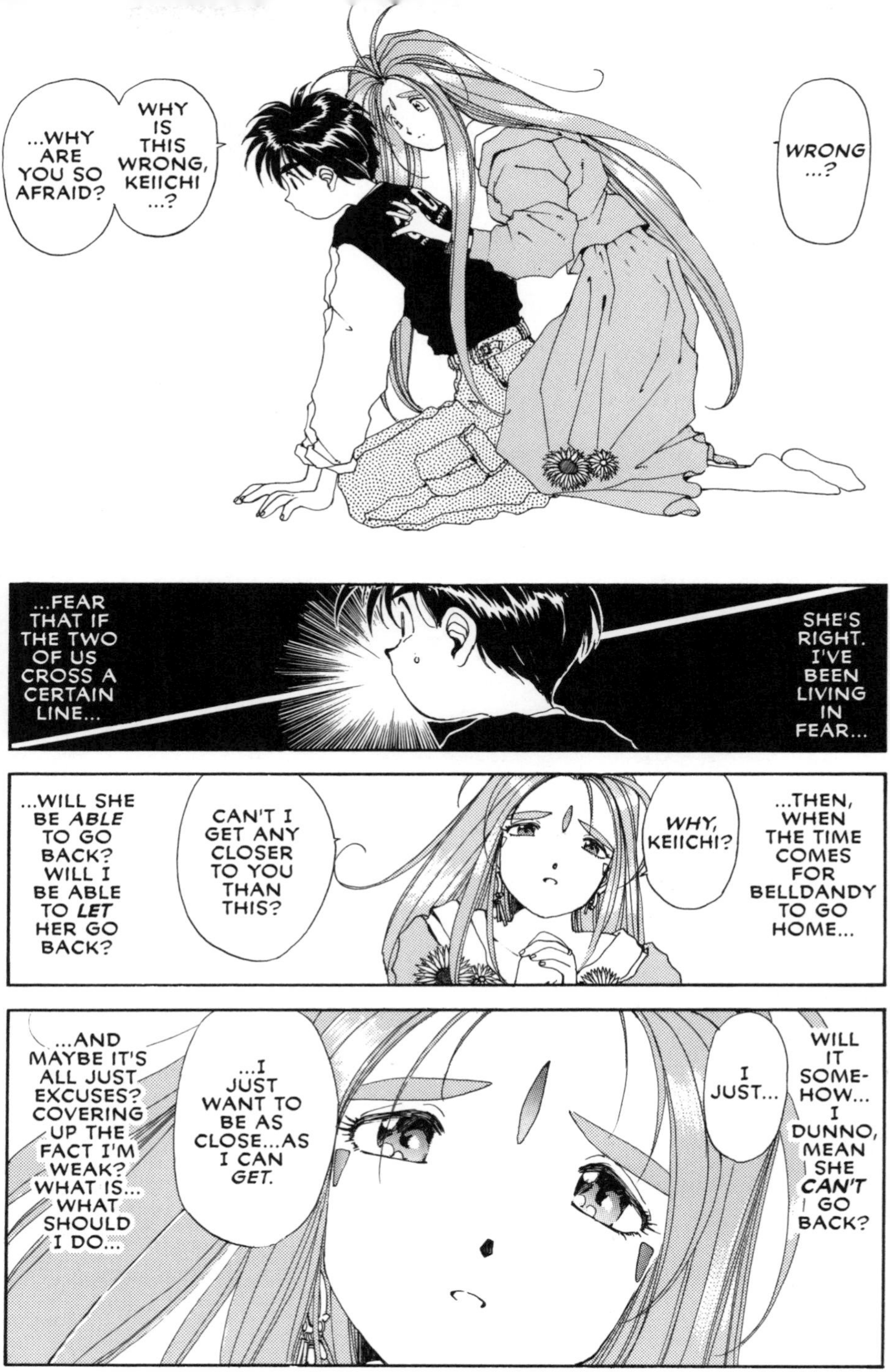
WRONG ...?
WHY IS THIS WRONG, KEIICHI ...?
...WHY ARE YOU SO AFRAID?
SHE'S RIGHT. I'VE BEEN LIVING IN FEAR...
...FEAR THAT IF THE TWO OF US CROSS A CERTAIN LINE...
...THEN, WHEN THE TIME COMES FOR BELLDANDY TO GO HOME...
WHY, KEIICHI?
CAN'T I GET ANY CLOSER TO YOU THAN THIS?
...WILL SHE BE *ABLE* TO GO BACK? WILL I BE ABLE TO *LET* HER GO BACK?
WILL IT SOME-HOW... I DUNNO, MEAN SHE *CAN'T* GO BACK?
I JUST...
...I JUST WANT TO BE AS CLOSE...AS I CAN *GET.*
...AND MAYBE IT'S ALL JUST EXCUSES? COVERING UP THE FACT I'M WEAK? WHAT IS... WHAT SHOULD I DO...

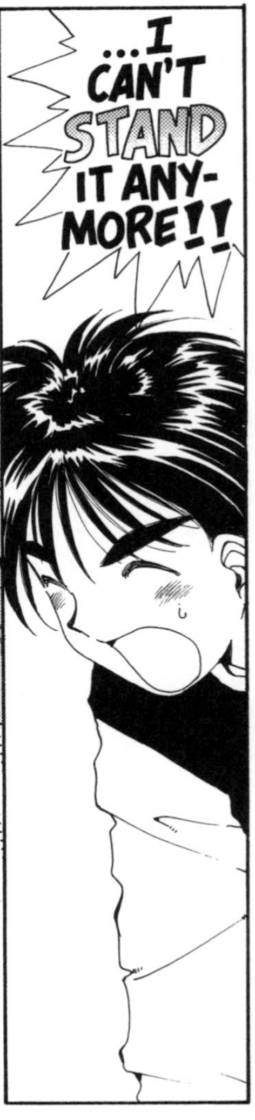
...I CAN'T STAND IT ANY-MORE!!
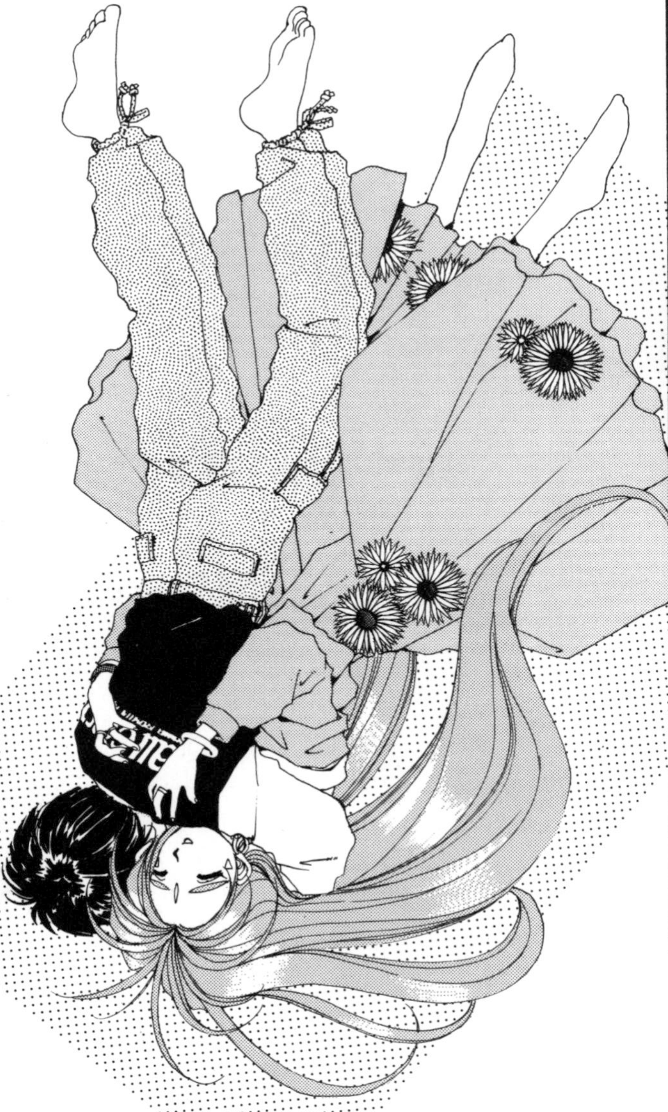

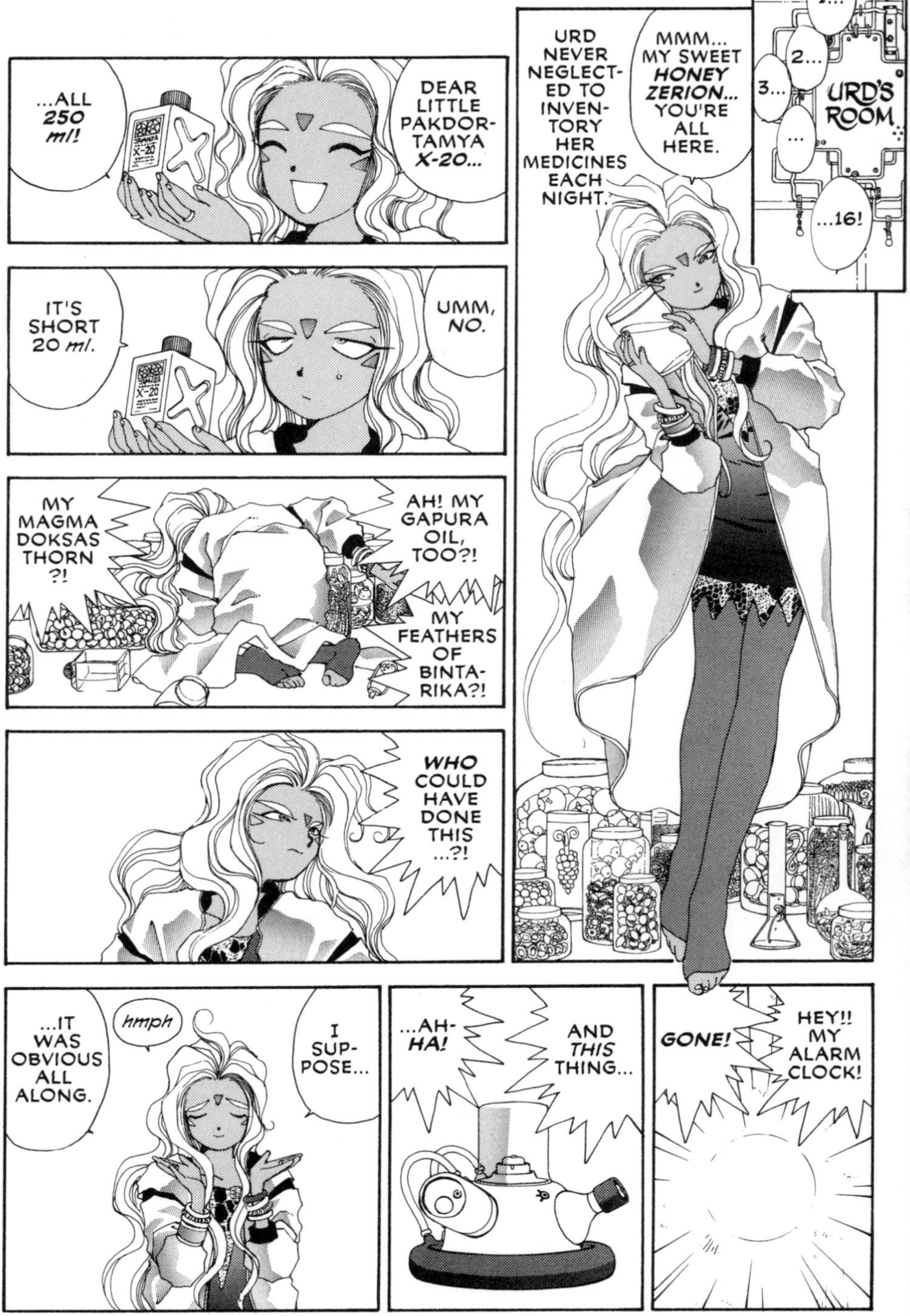
URD'S ROOM
1...
2...
3...
...
...16!
MMM... MY SWEET HONEY ZERION... YOU'RE ALL HERE.
URD NEVER NEGLECTED TO INVENTORY HER MEDICINES EACH NIGHT.
DEAR LITTLE PAKDOR-TAMYA X-20...
...ALL 250 ml!
UMM, NO.
IT'S SHORT 20 ml.
AH! MY GAPURA OIL, TOO?!
MY FEATHERS OF BINTA-RIKA?!
MY MAGMA DOKSAS THORN?!
WHO COULD HAVE DONE THIS ...?!
HEY!! MY ALARM CLOCK!
GONE!
AND THIS THING...
...AH-HA!
I SUPPOSE...
hmph
...IT WAS OBVIOUS ALL ALONG.

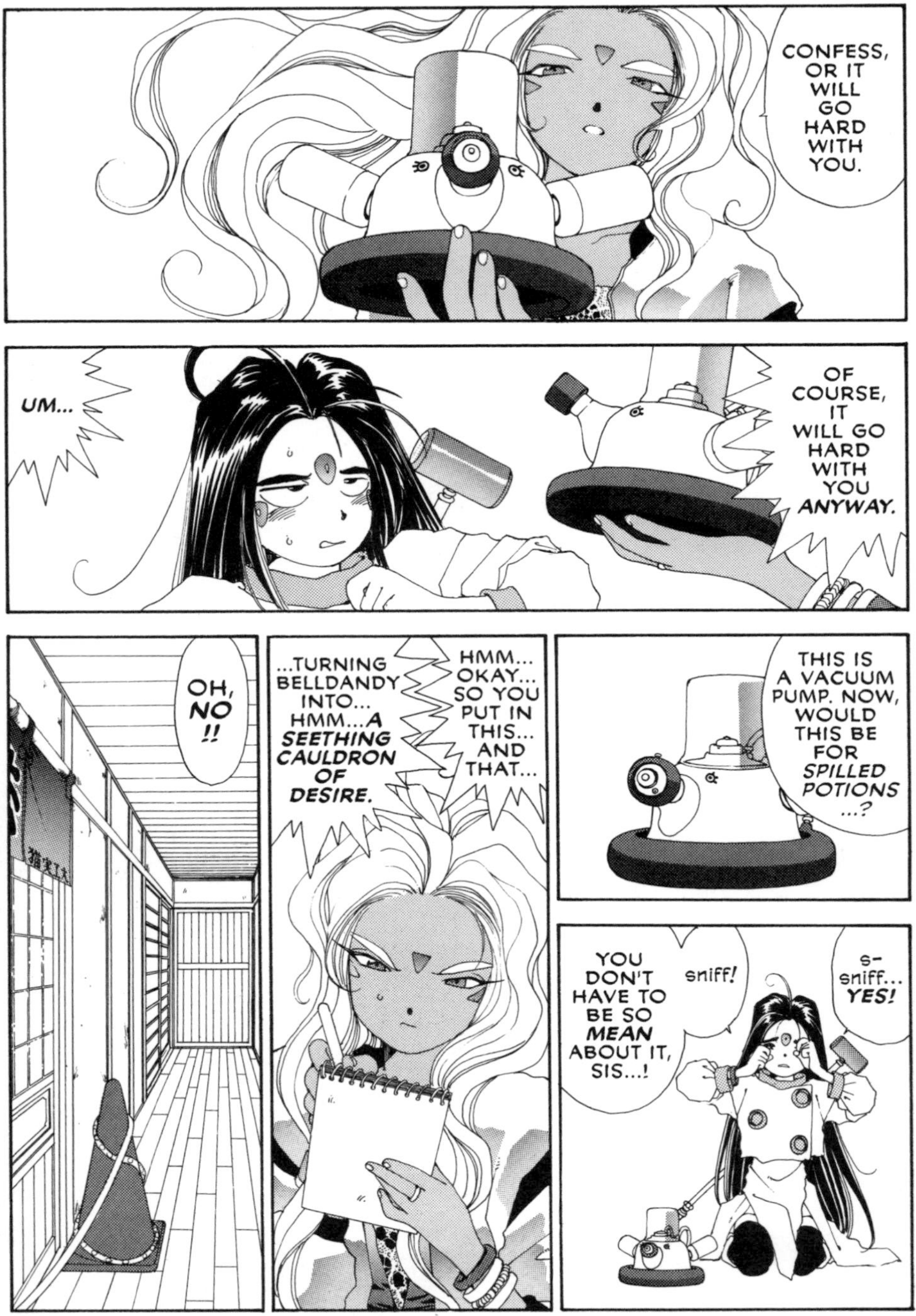
CONFESS, OR IT WILL GO HARD WITH YOU.
OF COURSE, IT WILL GO HARD WITH YOU *ANYWAY.*
UM...
THIS IS A VACUUM PUMP. NOW, WOULD THIS BE FOR *SPILLED POTIONS* ...?
s-sniff... *YES!*
sniff!
YOU DON'T HAVE TO BE SO *MEAN* ABOUT IT, SIS...!
HMM... OKAY... SO YOU PUT IN THIS... AND THAT...
...TURNING BELLDANDY INTO... HMM...*A SEETHING CAULDRON OF DESIRE.*
OH, *NO !!*

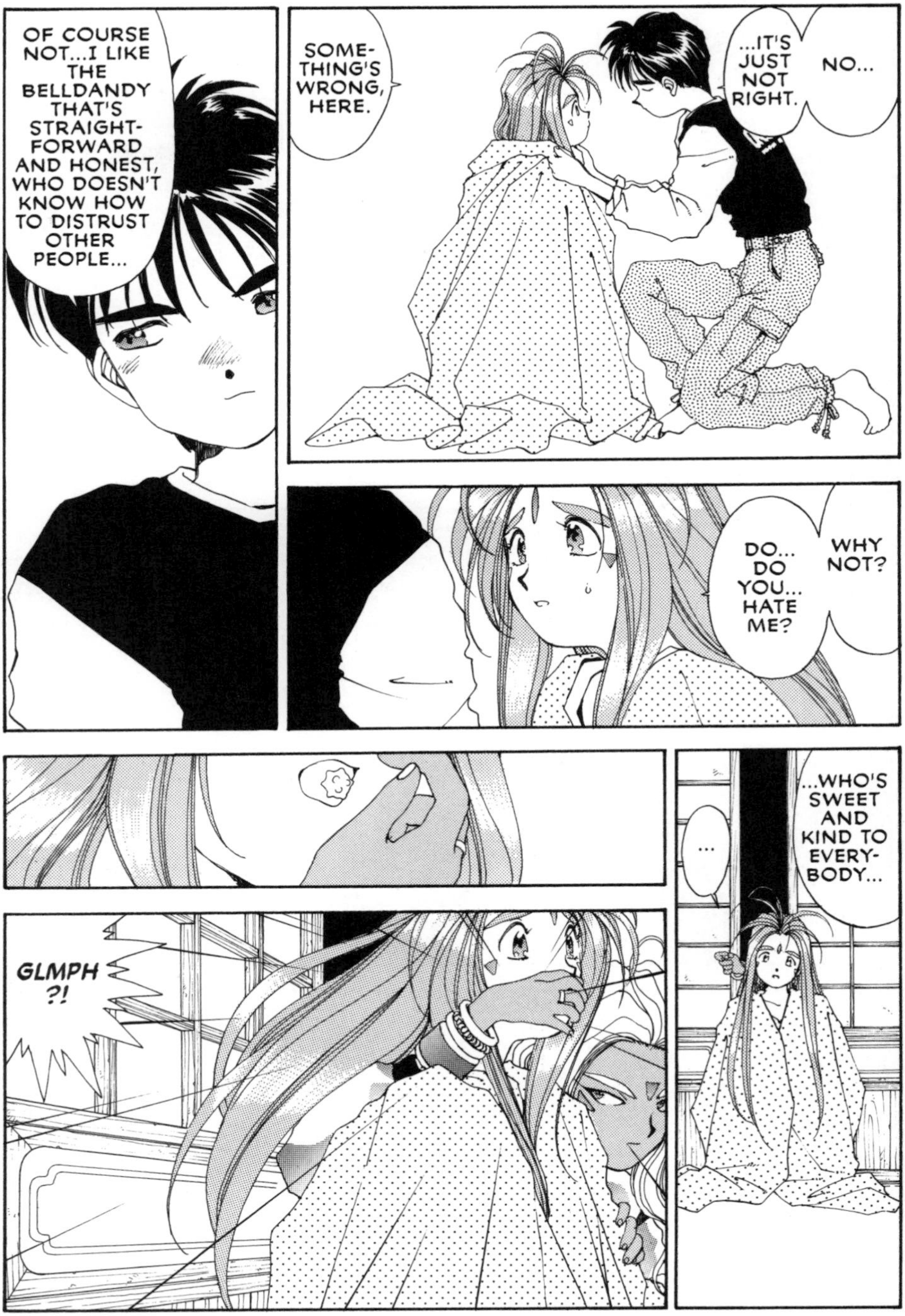
NO...
...IT'S JUST NOT RIGHT.
SOME-THING'S WRONG, HERE.
WHY NOT?
DO... DO YOU... HATE ME?
OF COURSE NOT...I LIKE THE BELLDANDY THAT'S STRAIGHT-FORWARD AND HONEST, WHO DOESN'T KNOW HOW TO DISTRUST OTHER PEOPLE...
...WHO'S SWEET AND KIND TO EVERY-BODY...
...
GLMPH ?!

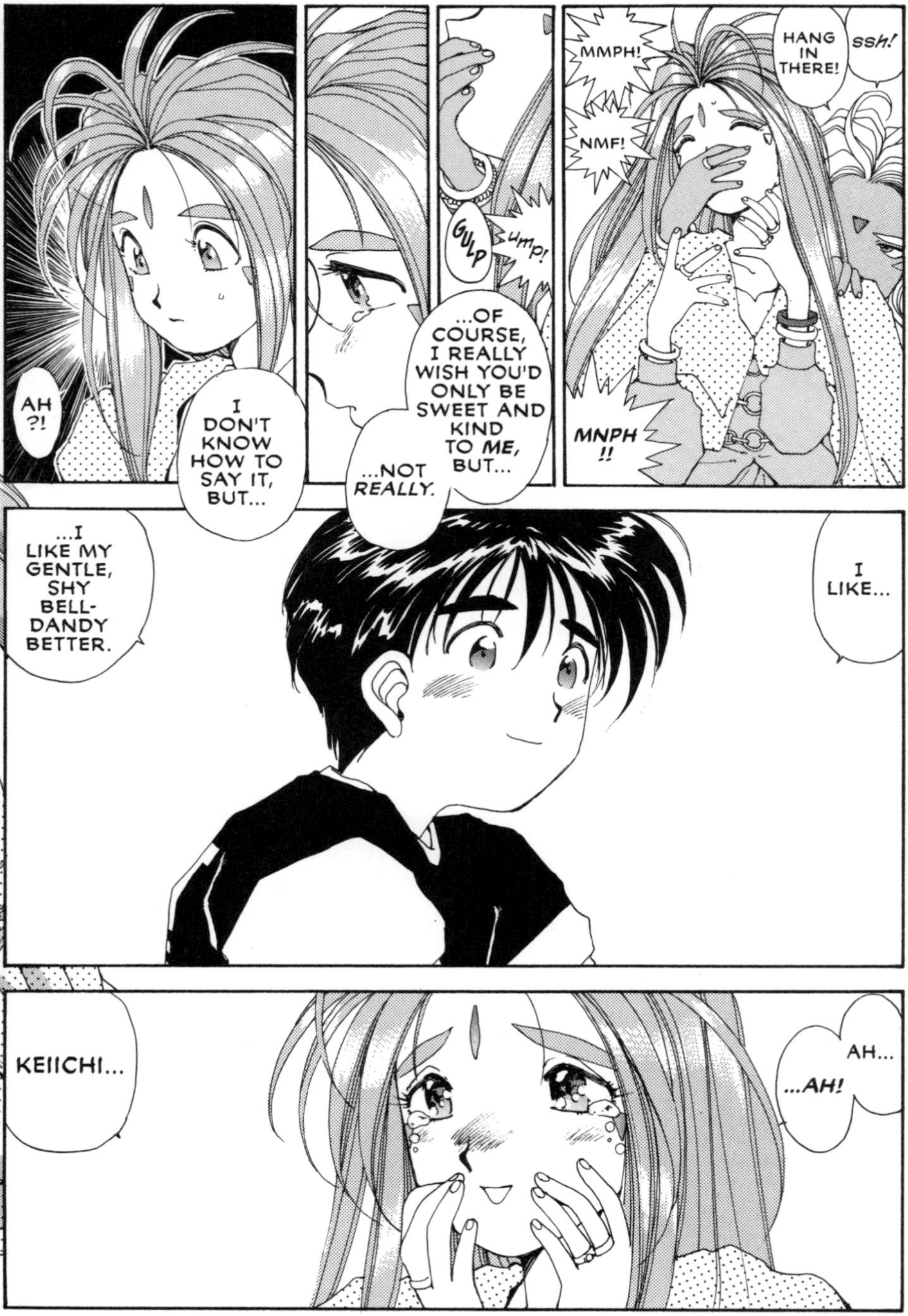

ssh!
HANG IN THERE!
MMPH!
NMF!
MNPH !!
GULP
ump!
...OF COURSE, I REALLY WISH YOU'D ONLY BE SWEET AND KIND TO *ME*, BUT...
...NOT *REALLY*.
I DON'T KNOW HOW TO SAY IT, BUT...
AH ?!
I LIKE...
...I LIKE MY GENTLE, SHY BELL-DANDY BETTER.
AH... ...*AH!*
KEIICHI...

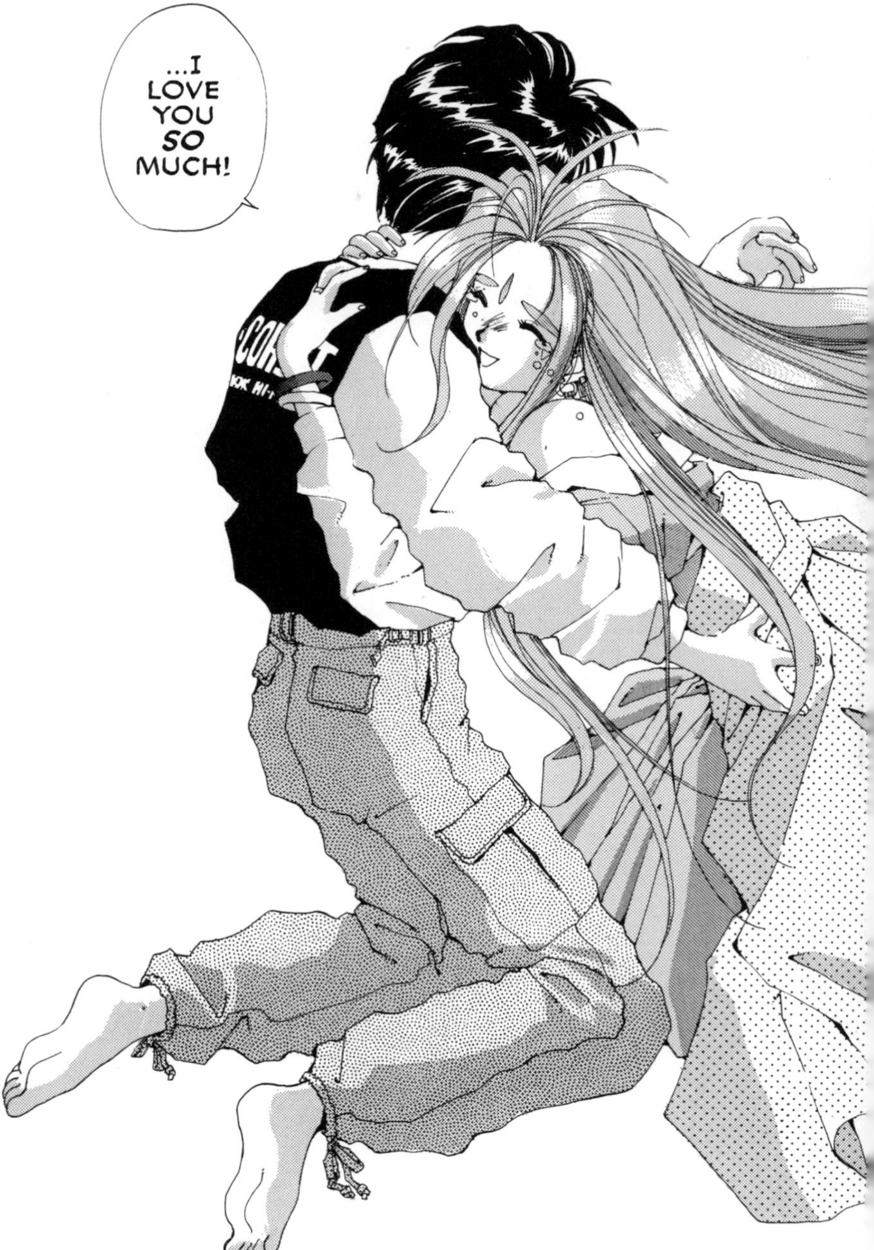
...I LOVE YOU SO MUCH!

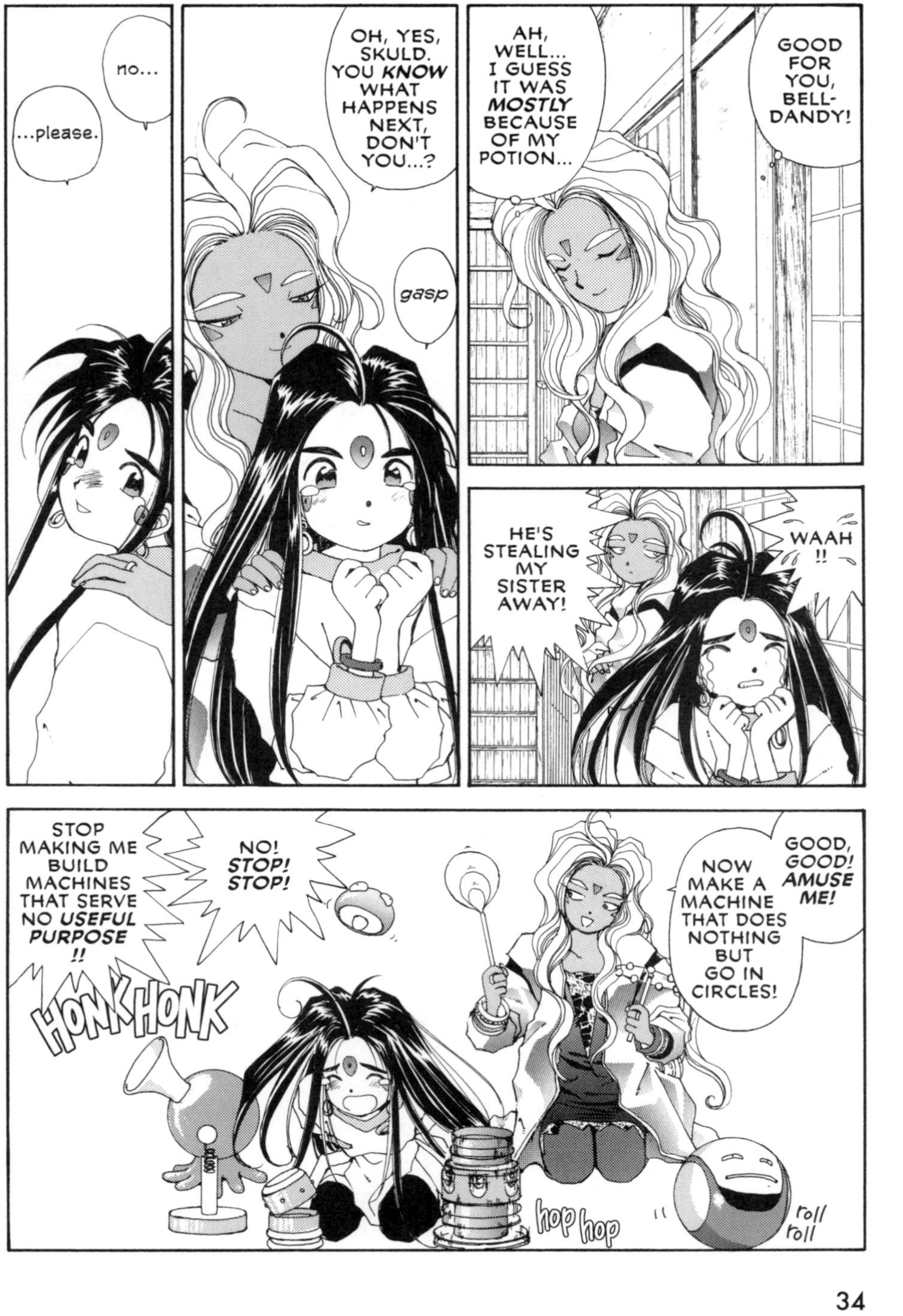
GOOD FOR YOU, BELL-DANDY!
AH, WELL... I GUESS IT WAS MOSTLY BECAUSE OF MY POTION...
WAAH !!
HE'S STEALING MY SISTER AWAY!
OH, YES, SKULD. YOU KNOW WHAT HAPPENS NEXT, DON'T YOU...?
gasp
no...
...please.
GOOD, GOOD! AMUSE ME!
NOW MAKE A MACHINE THAT DOES NOTHING BUT GO IN CIRCLES!
NO! STOP! STOP!
STOP MAKING ME BUILD MACHINES THAT SERVE NO USEFUL PURPOSE !!
HONK HONK
roll roll
hop hop

THE ADVENTURES OF MINI-URD

In the handy PETITE SIZE!

◆CATCHING RAYS◆

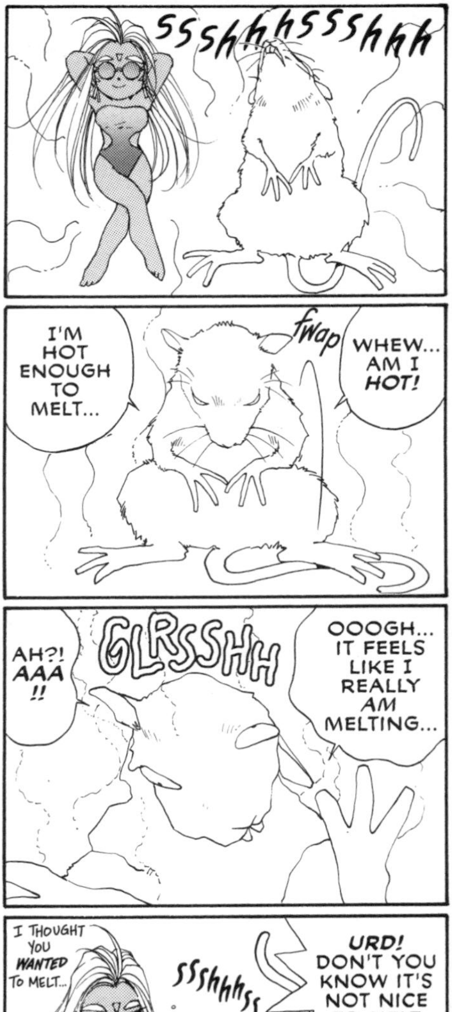
SSShhhSSSShhh
WHEW... AM I HOT!
fwap
I'M HOT ENOUGH TO MELT...
OOOGH... IT FEELS LIKE I REALLY AM MELTING...
GLRSSHH
AH?! AAA !!
URD! DON'T YOU KNOW IT'S NOT NICE TO MELT PEOPLE?!
SSShhhss
I THOUGHT YOU WANTED TO MELT...

◆A COOL BREEZE IN SUMMER◆

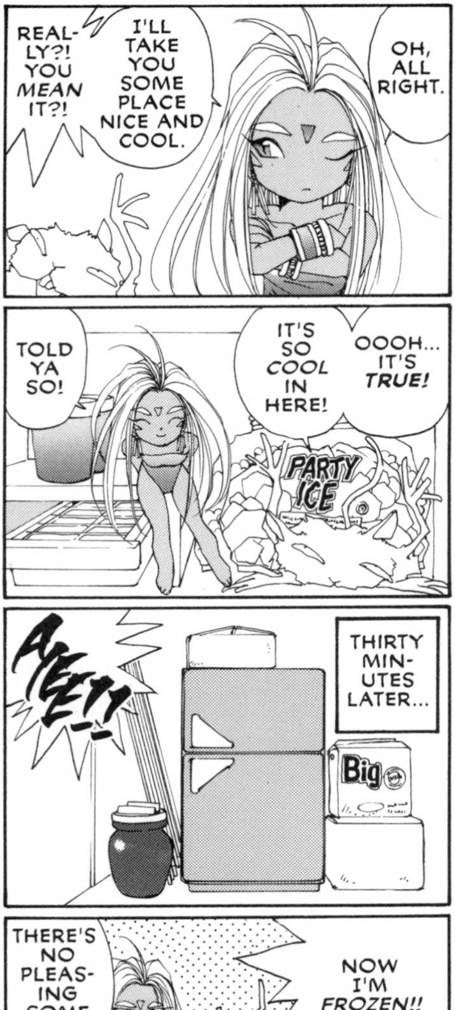
OH, ALL RIGHT.
I'LL TAKE YOU SOME PLACE NICE AND COOL.
REAL-LY?! YOU MEAN IT?!
OOOH... IT'S TRUE!
IT'S SO COOL IN HERE!
TOLD YA SO!
PARTY ICE
THIRTY MIN-UTES LATER...
Big
NOW I'M FROZEN!!
THERE'S NO PLEAS-ING SOME PEOPLE.

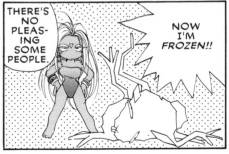

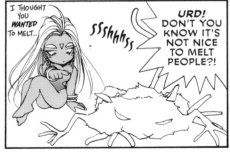

◆ GOLDEN GOURMAND ◆

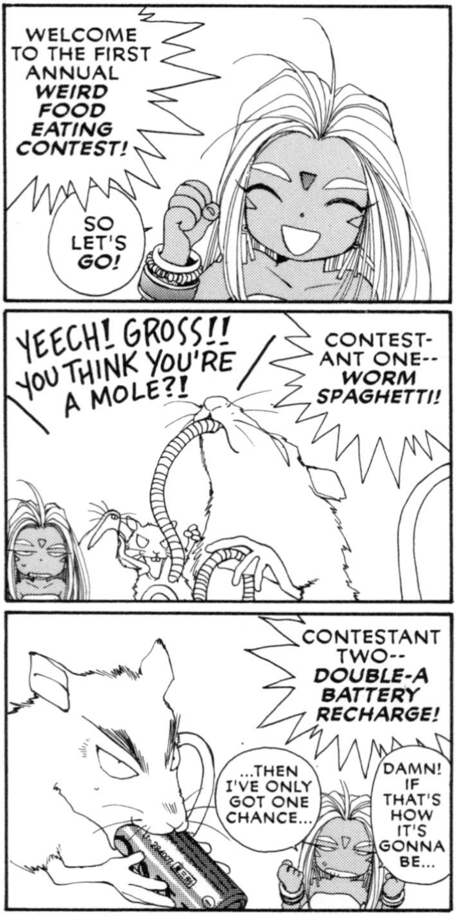
WELCOME TO THE FIRST ANNUAL WEIRD FOOD EATING CONTEST!
SO LET'S GO!
CONTESTANT ONE-- WORM SPAGHETTI!
YEECH! GROSS!! YOU THINK YOU'RE A MOLE?!
CONTESTANT TWO-- DOUBLE-A BATTERY RECHARGE!
DAMN! IF THAT'S HOW IT'S GONNA BE...
...THEN I'VE ONLY GOT ONE CHANCE...
CONTESTANT THREE-- BBQ RAT ON A STICK!
W-WHAT DID YOU SAY...?!

AMAZING! THE ALL-YOU-CAN-EAT CONTEST! ◆

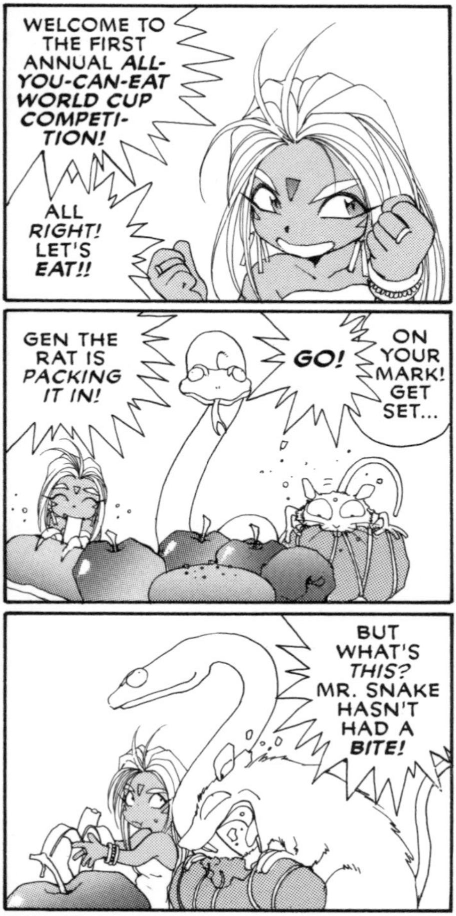
WELCOME TO THE FIRST ANNUAL ALL-YOU-CAN-EAT WORLD CUP COMPETITION!
ALL RIGHT! LET'S EAT!!
ON YOUR MARK! GET SET...
GO!
GEN THE RAT IS PACKING IT IN!
BUT WHAT'S THIS? MR. SNAKE HASN'T HAD A BITE!
WAIT! MR. SNAKE JUST ATE GEN THE RAT!!
AND IT'S MR. SNAKE BY A MILE!!
GEEZ, IT WAS JUST ANOTHER "WEIRD FOOD EATING CONTEST" AFTER ALL...

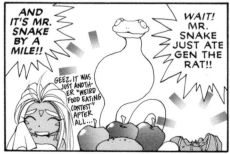

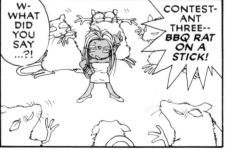

CHAPTER 44

The Queen of Vengeance

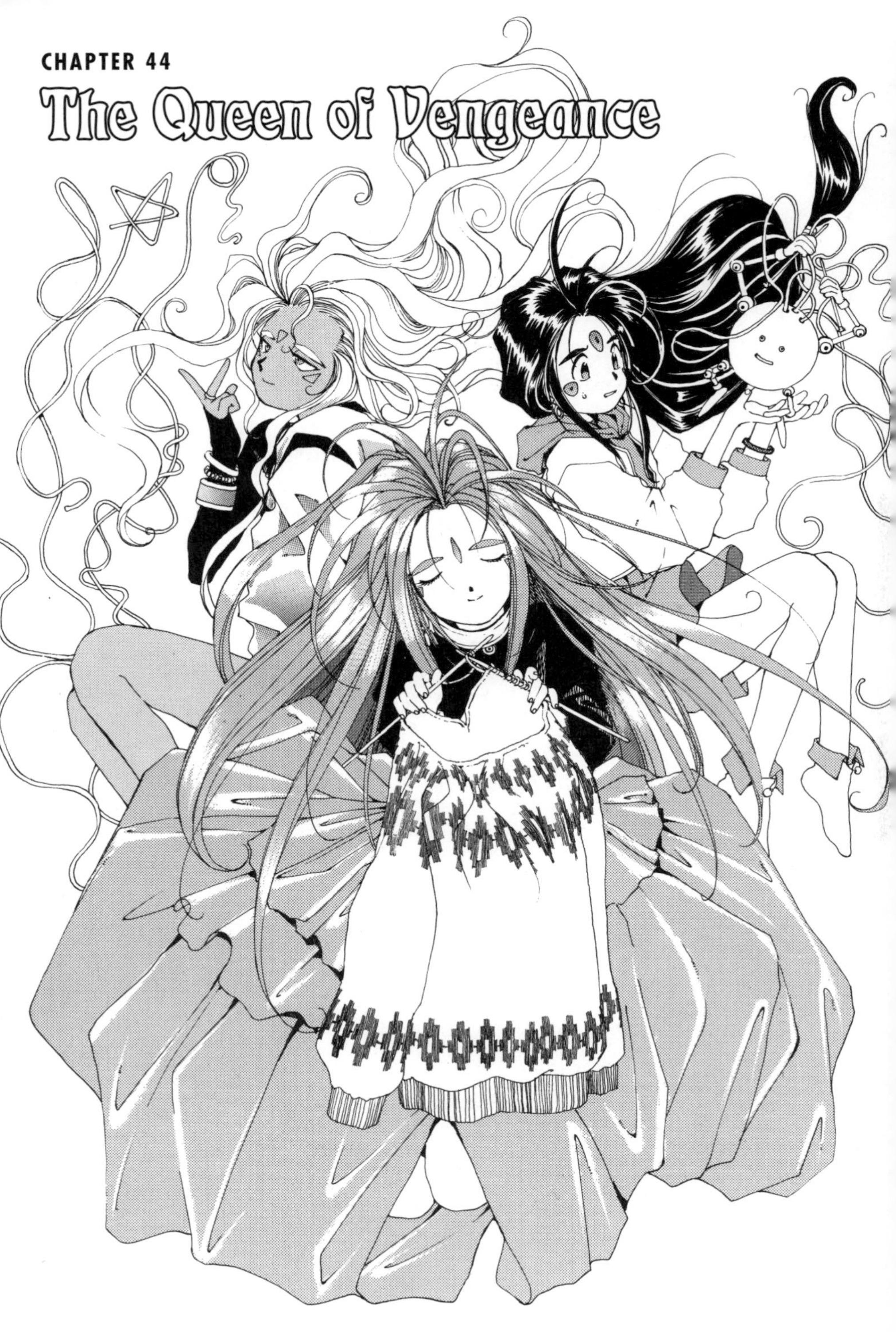

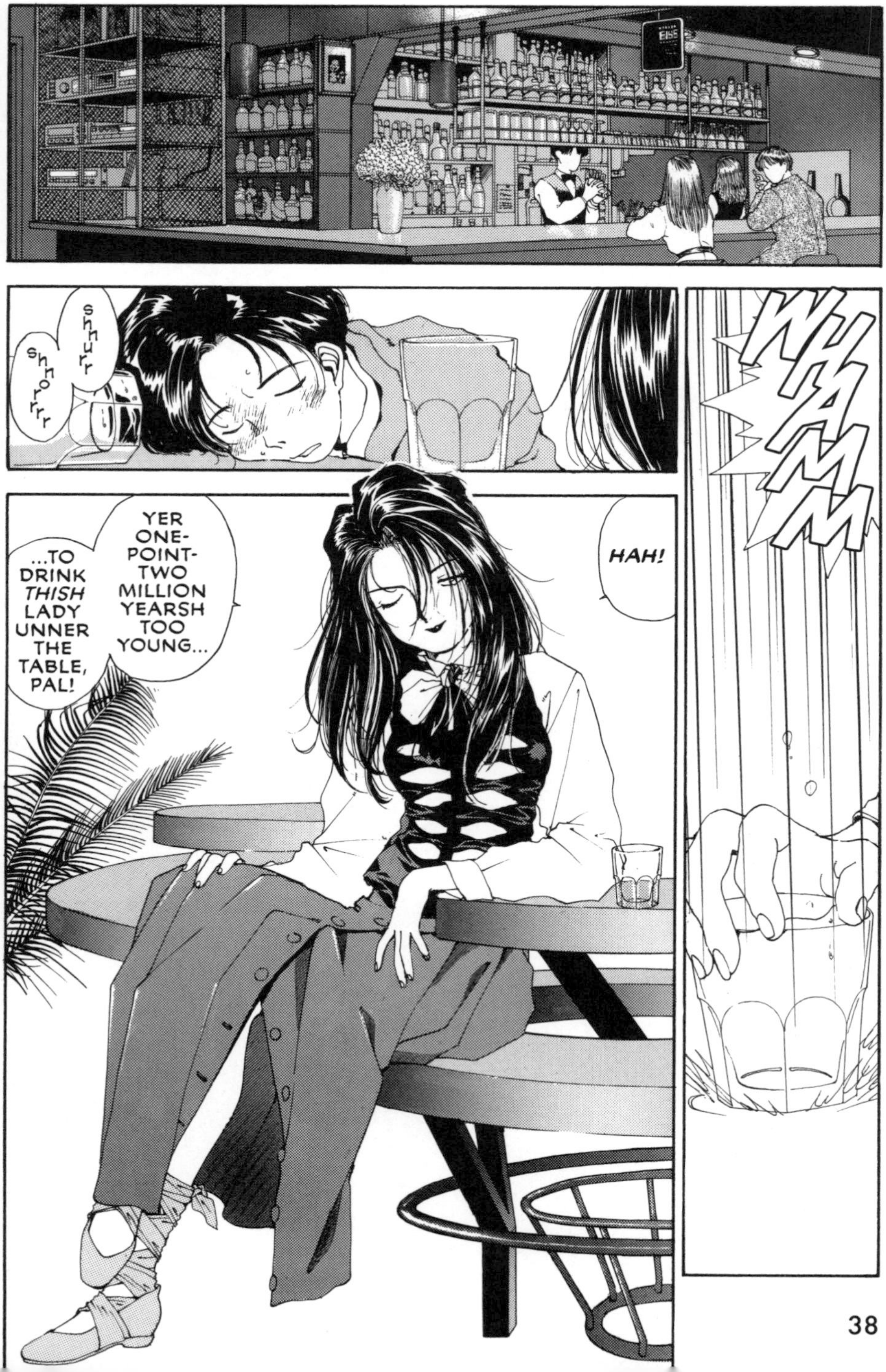
WHAMM
shnurr
shnorrrr
HAH!
YER ONE-POINT-TWO MILLION YEARSH TOO YOUNG...
...TO DRINK *THISH* LADY UNNER THE TABLE, PAL!

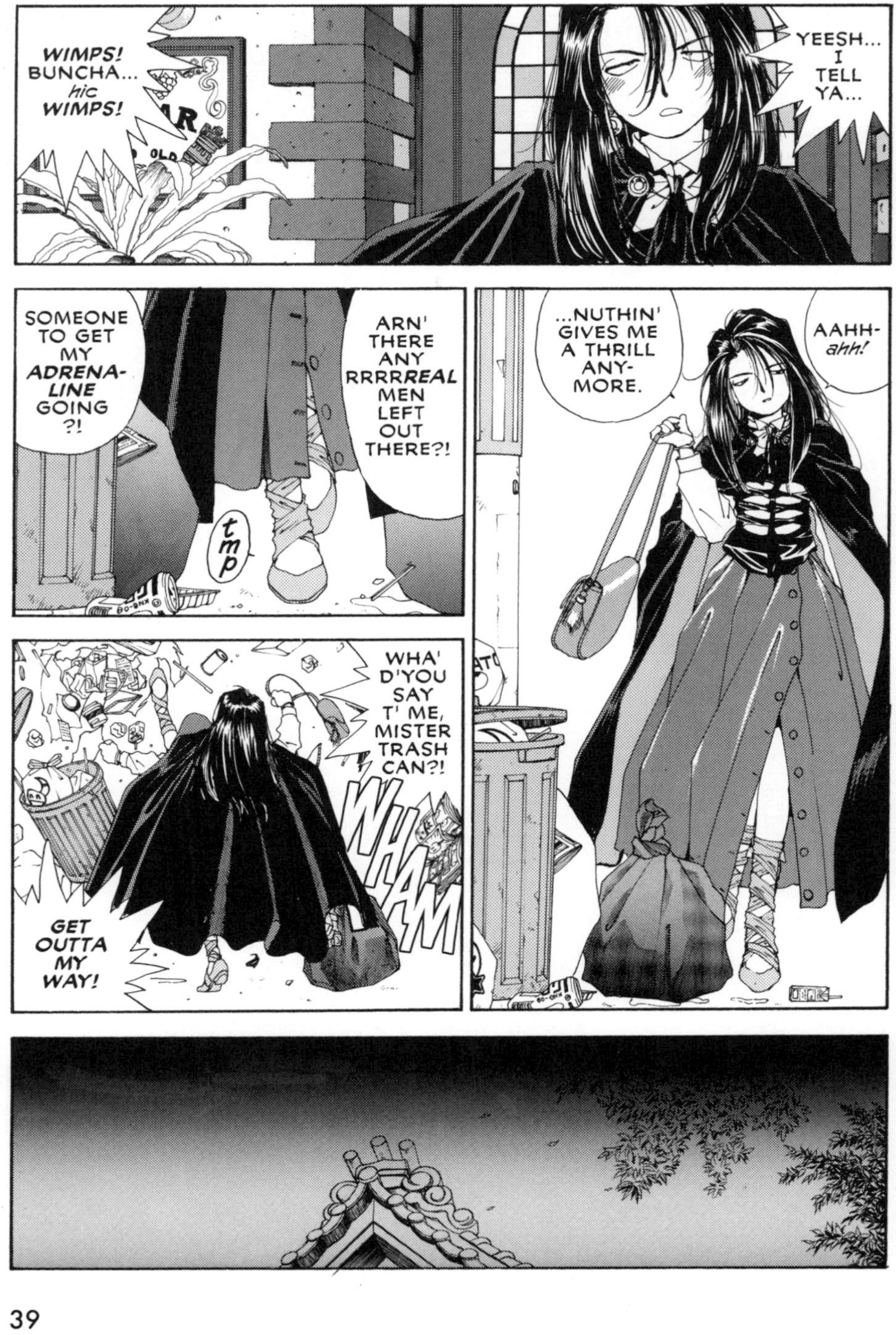
YEESH... I TELL YA...
WIMPS! BUNCHA... *hic* WIMPS!
AAHH-*ahh!*
...NUTHIN' GIVES ME A THRILL ANYMORE.
ARN' THERE ANY RRRR*REAL* MEN LEFT OUT THERE?!
SOMEONE TO GET MY *ADRENALINE* GOING ?!
tmp
WHA' D'YOU SAY T' ME, MISTER TRASH CAN?!
WHAM
GET OUTTA MY WAY!

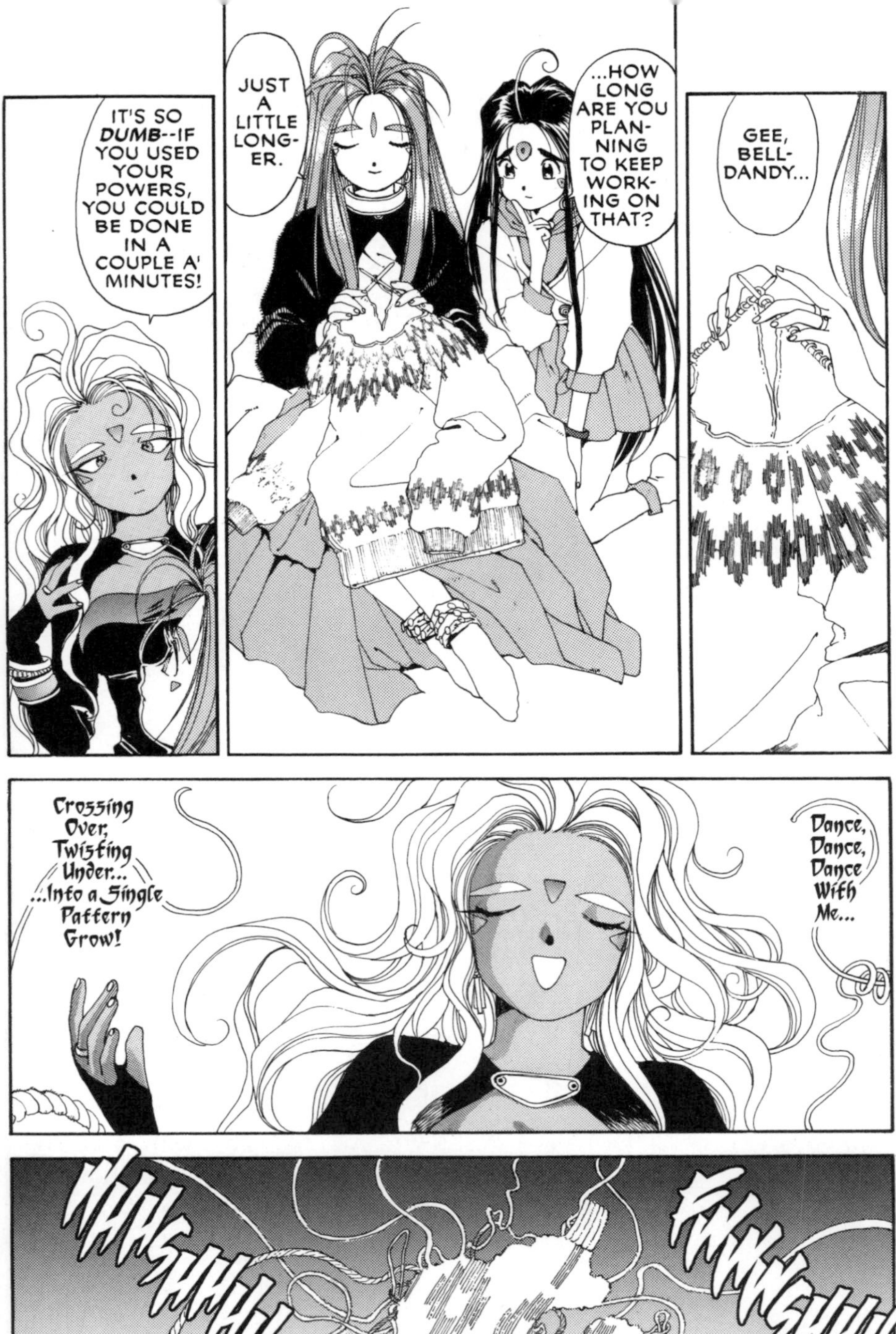
GEE, BELL-DANDY...
...HOW LONG ARE YOU PLAN-NING TO KEEP WORK-ING ON THAT?
JUST A LITTLE LONG-ER.
IT'S SO *DUMB*--IF YOU USED YOUR POWERS, YOU COULD BE DONE IN A COUPLE A' MINUTES!
Dance, Dance, Dance With Me...
Crossing Over, Twisting Under... ...Into a Single Pattern Grow!
FWWWSHHH
WHHSHHHH

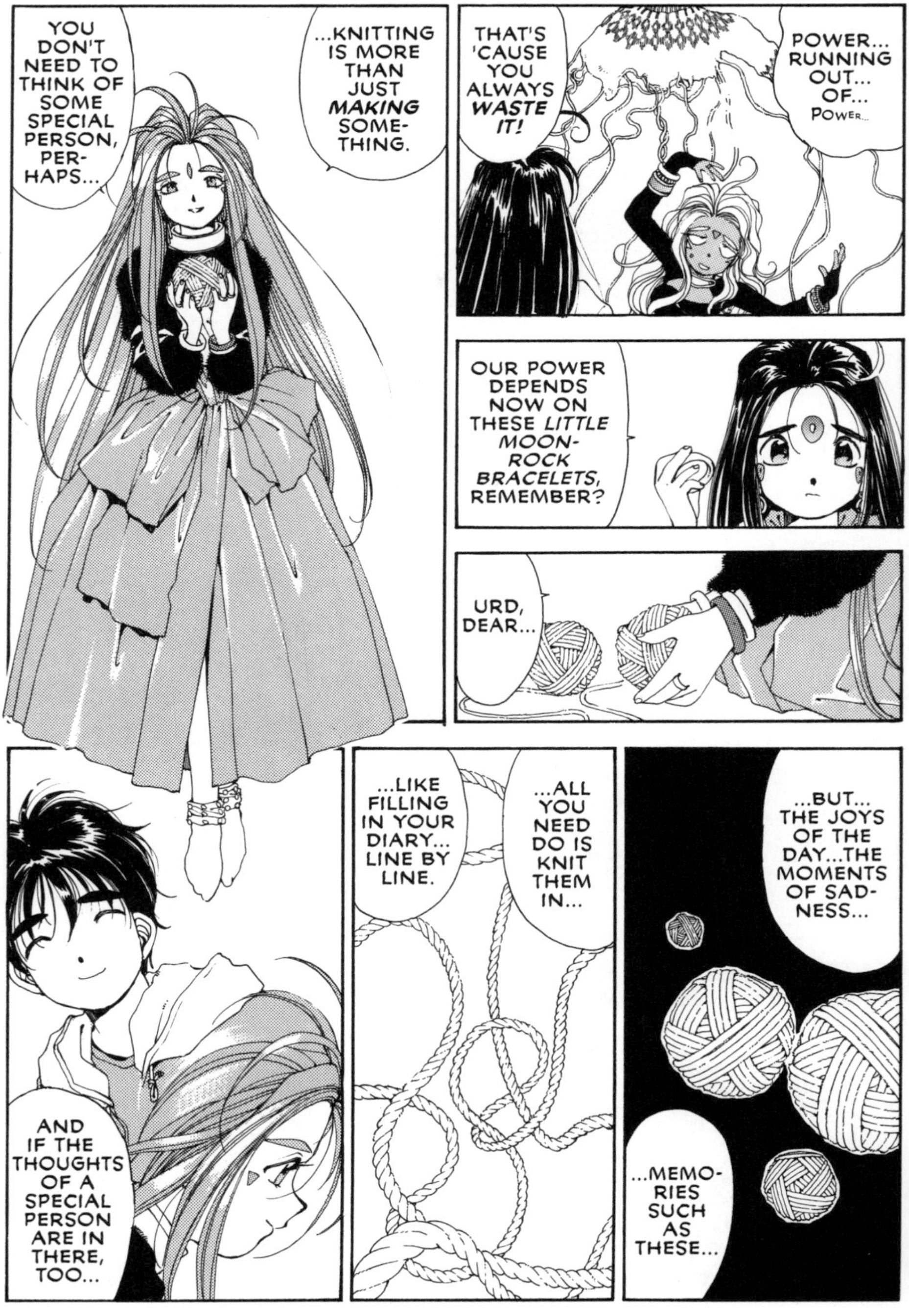
POWER... RUNNING OUT... OF... POWER...
THAT'S 'CAUSE YOU ALWAYS *WASTE IT!*
OUR POWER DEPENDS NOW ON THESE *LITTLE MOON-ROCK BRACELETS*, REMEMBER?
URD, DEAR...
...KNITTING IS MORE THAN JUST *MAKING* SOME-THING.
YOU DON'T NEED TO THINK OF SOME SPECIAL PERSON, PER-HAPS...
...BUT... THE JOYS OF THE DAY...THE MOMENTS OF SAD-NESS...
...MEMO-RIES SUCH AS THESE...
...ALL YOU NEED DO IS KNIT THEM IN...
...LIKE FILLING IN YOUR DIARY... LINE BY LINE.
AND IF THE THOUGHTS OF A SPECIAL PERSON ARE IN THERE, TOO...

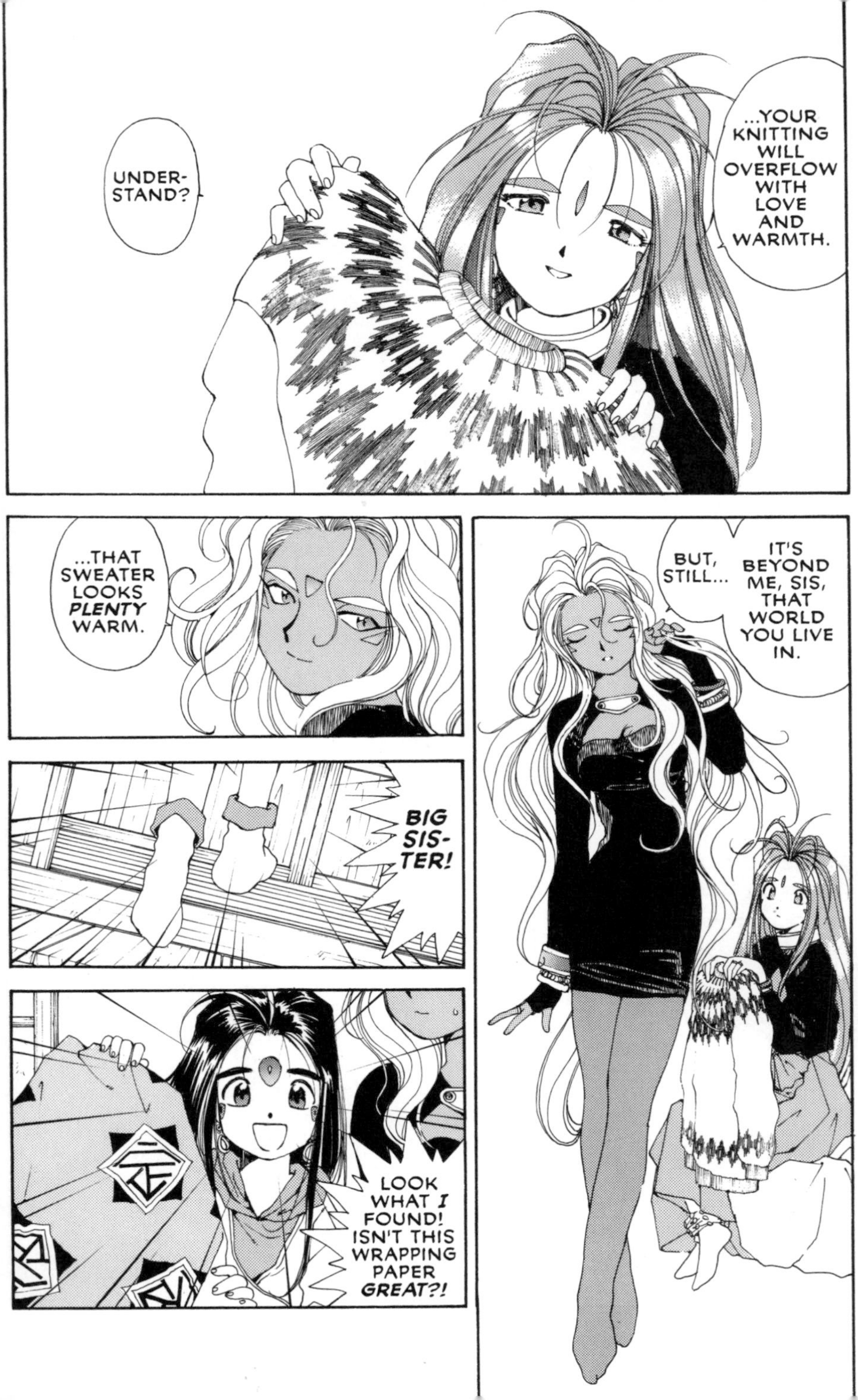
...YOUR KNITTING WILL OVERFLOW WITH LOVE AND WARMTH.
UNDER-STAND?
IT'S BEYOND ME, SIS, THAT WORLD YOU LIVE IN.
BUT, STILL...
...THAT SWEATER LOOKS *PLENTY* WARM.
BIG SIS-TER!
LOOK WHAT *I* FOUND! ISN'T THIS WRAPPING PAPER *GREAT?!*

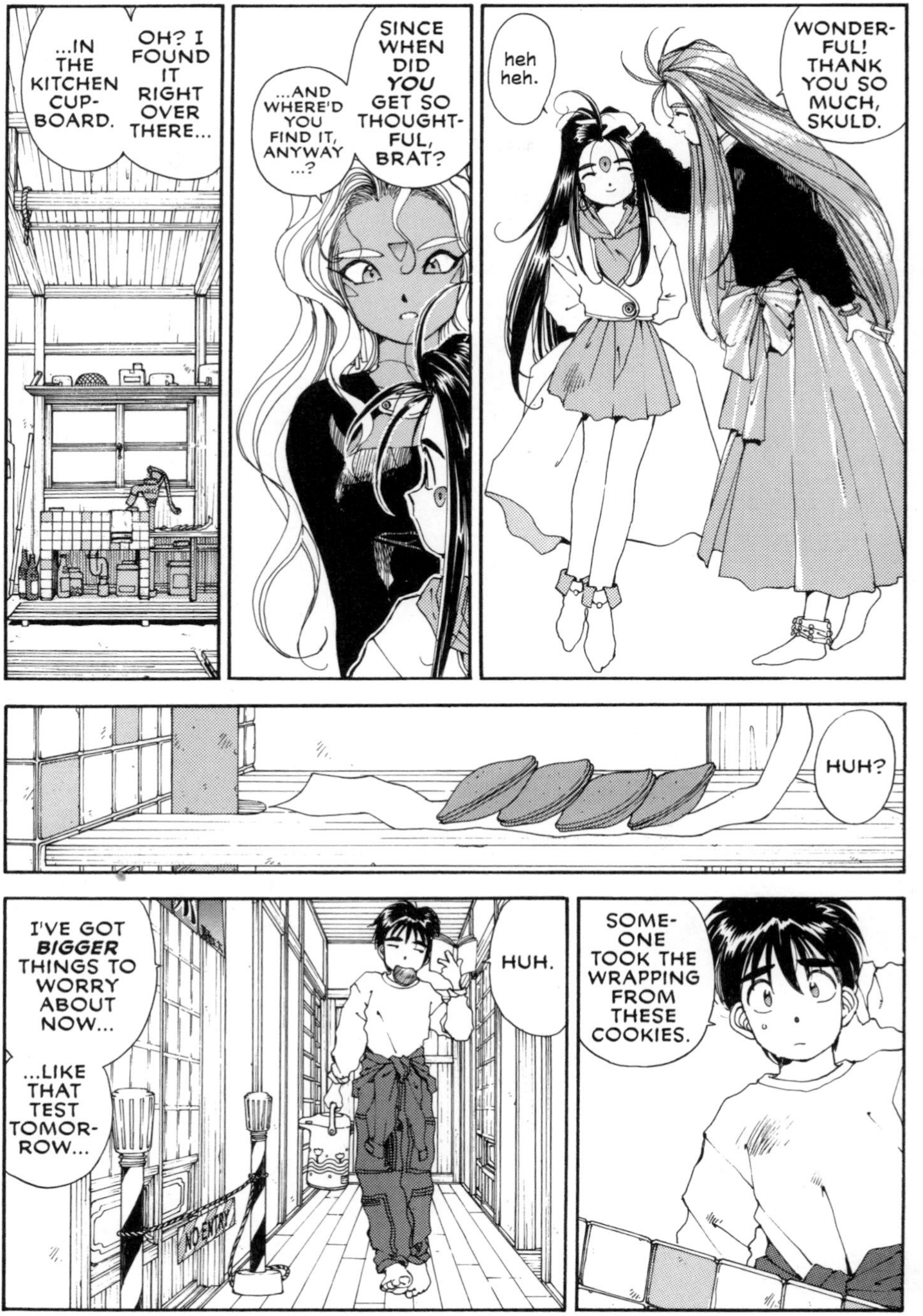
WONDER-FUL! THANK YOU SO MUCH, SKULD.
heh heh.
SINCE WHEN DID YOU GET SO THOUGHT-FUL, BRAT?
...AND WHERE'D YOU FIND IT, ANYWAY ...?
OH? I FOUND IT RIGHT OVER THERE...
...IN THE KITCHEN CUP-BOARD.
HUH?
SOME-ONE TOOK THE WRAPPING FROM THESE COOKIES.
HUH.
I'VE GOT BIGGER THINGS TO WORRY ABOUT NOW...
...LIKE THAT TEST TOMOR-ROW...
NO ENTRY

BONGGG
THIS ISN'T GOING TO HELP ME STUDY.
BONGG
WIMPS! WIMPS !!
HA HA HA (HIC) HA!!
BONNGGG

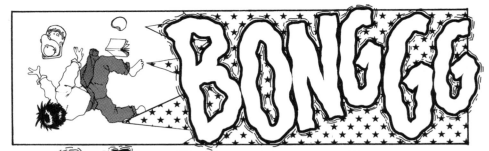

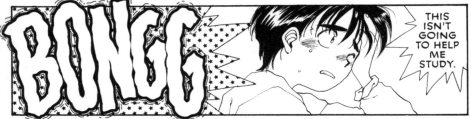

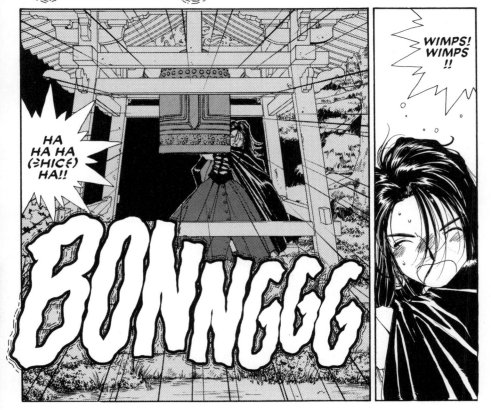

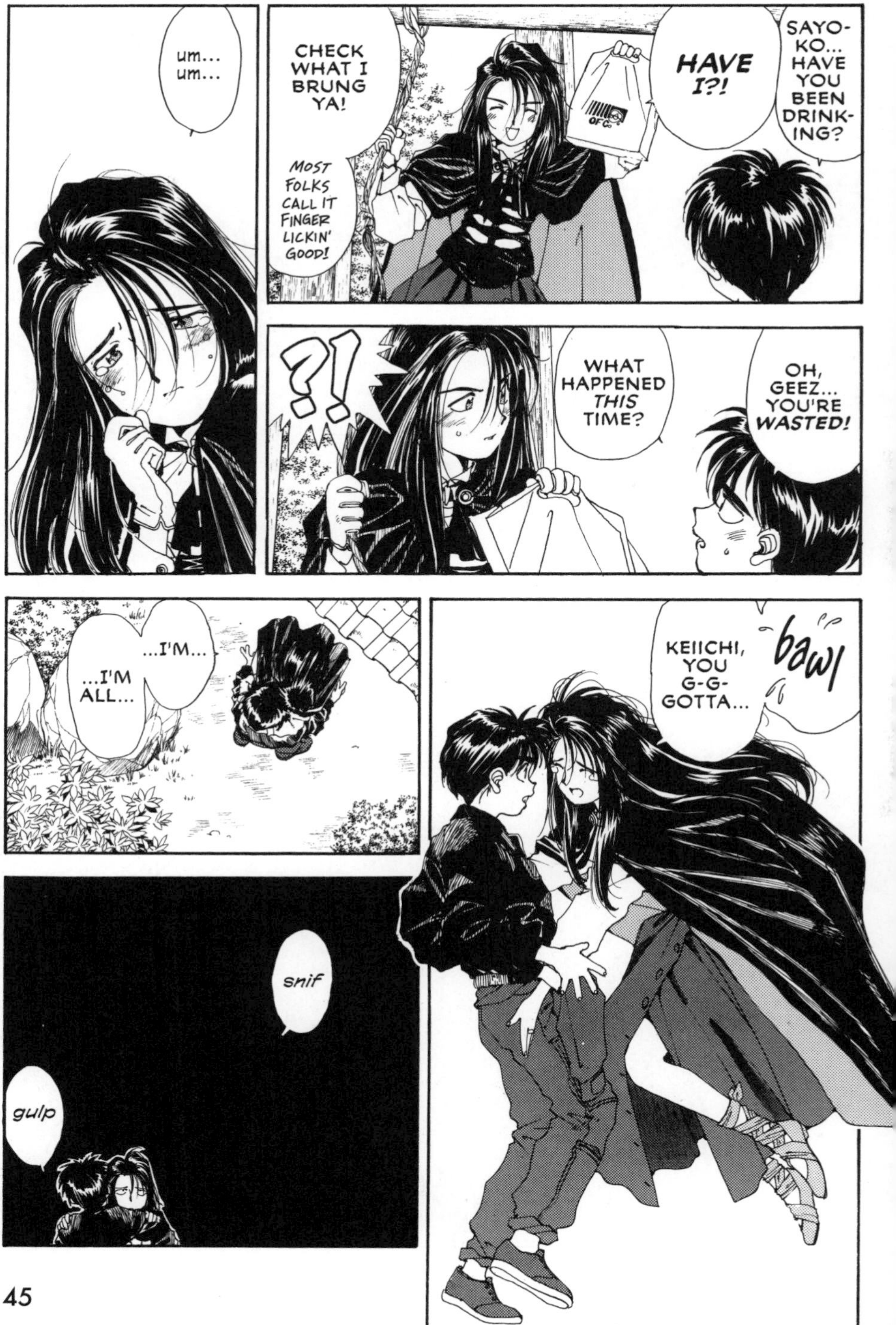
SAYO-KO... HAVE YOU BEEN DRINKING?
HAVE I?!
CHECK WHAT I BRUNG YA!
MOST FOLKS CALL IT FINGER LICKIN' GOOD!
OFC
OH, GEEZ... YOU'RE WASTED!
WHAT HAPPENED THIS TIME?
?!
um... um...
bawl
KEIICHI, YOU G-G-GOTTA...
...I'M...
...I'M ALL...
snif
gulp

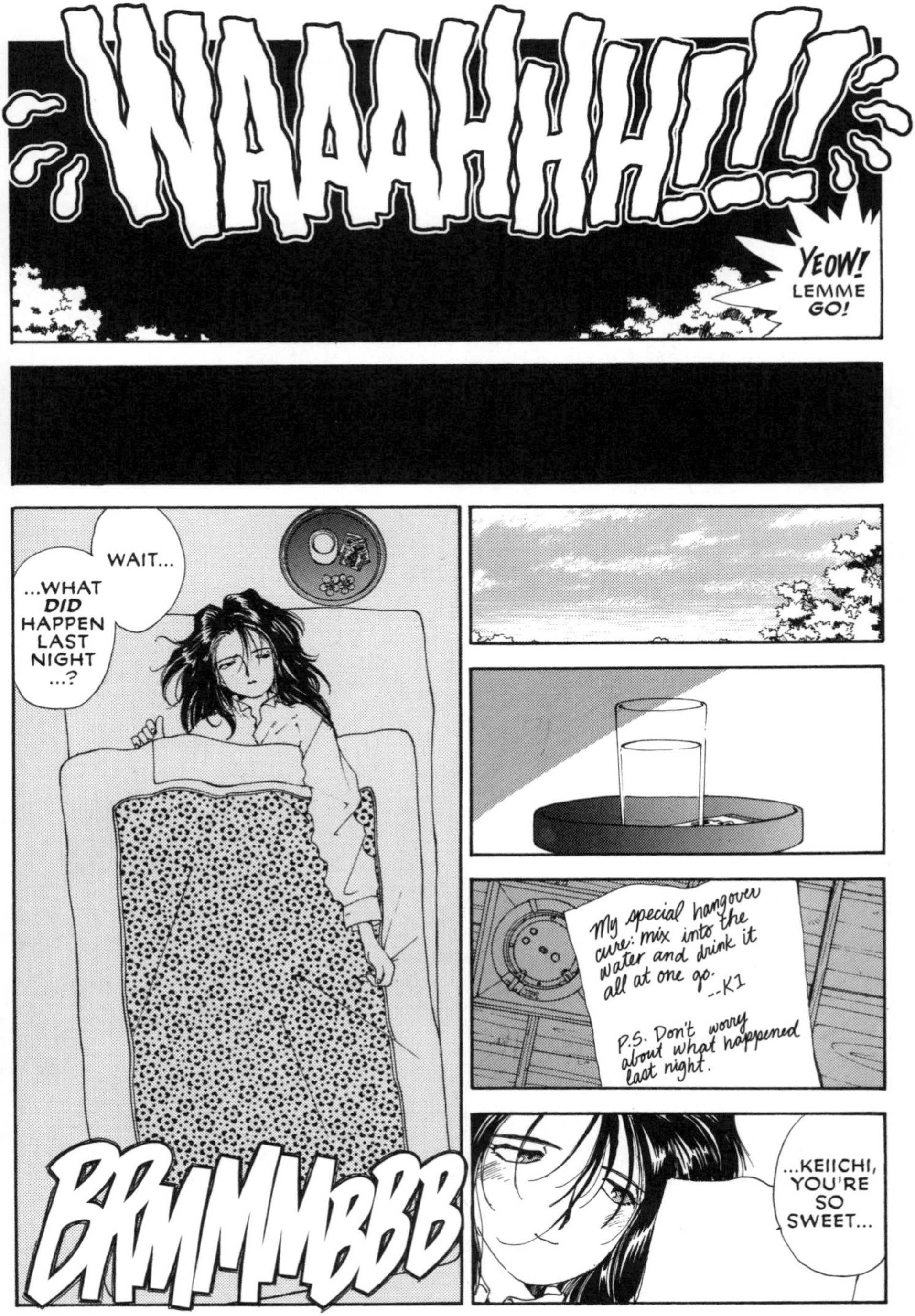
WAAAHHH!!!
YEOW! LEMME GO!
My special hangover cure: mix into the water and drink it all at one go. --K1
P.S. Don't worry about what happened last night.
...KEIICHI, YOU'RE SO SWEET...
WAIT...
...WHAT DID HAPPEN LAST NIGHT ...?
BRMMMBBB

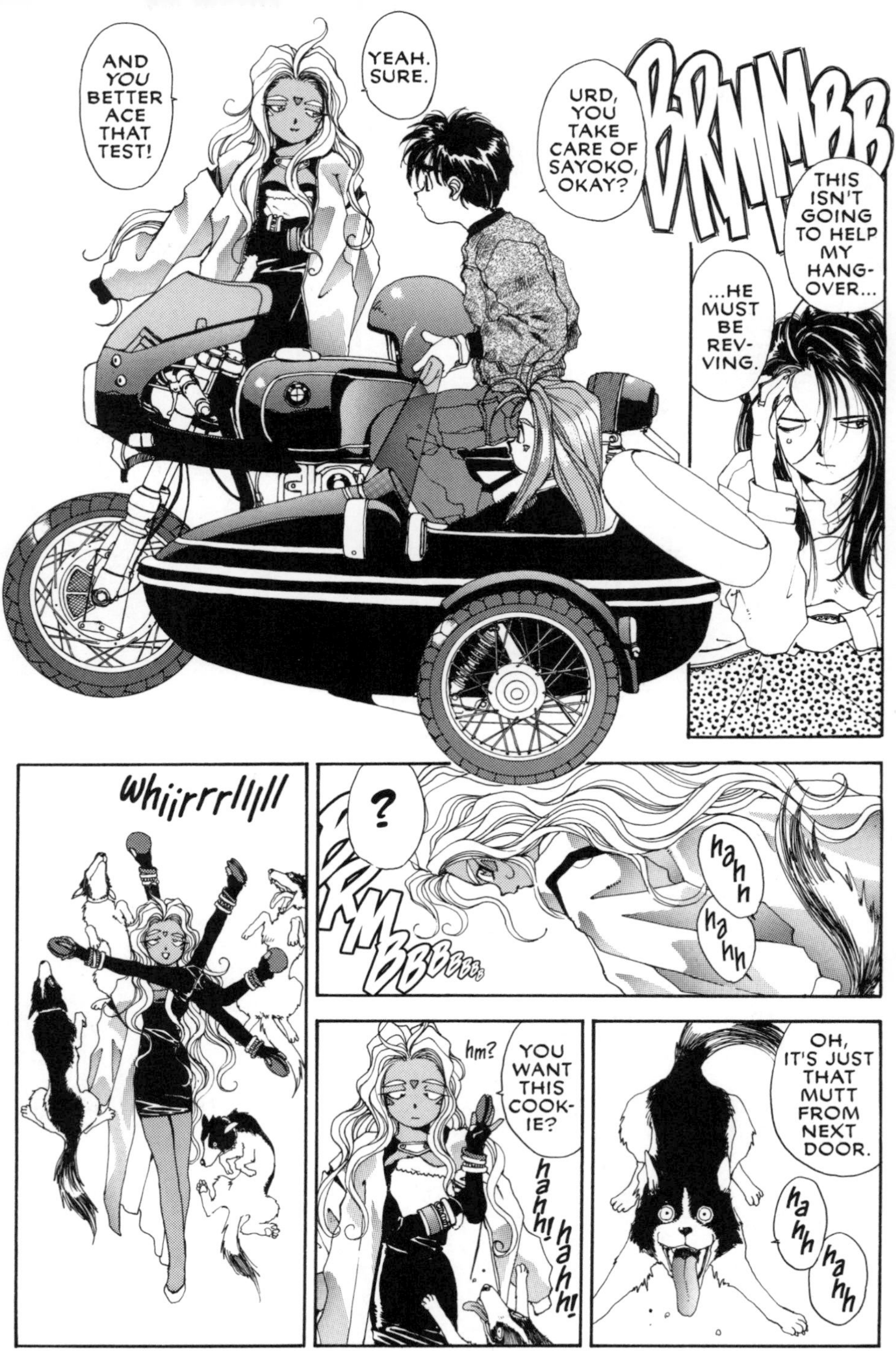
URD, YOU TAKE CARE OF SAYOKO, OKAY?
YEAH. SURE.
AND YOU BETTER ACE THAT TEST!
BRMMBB
THIS ISN'T GOING TO HELP MY HANG-OVER...
...HE MUST BE REV-VING.
?
RMBBBbbb
hanh
hanh
OH, IT'S JUST THAT MUTT FROM NEXT DOOR.
hanh
hanh
hm?
YOU WANT THIS COOK-IE?
hanh!
hanh!
whiirrrlllll

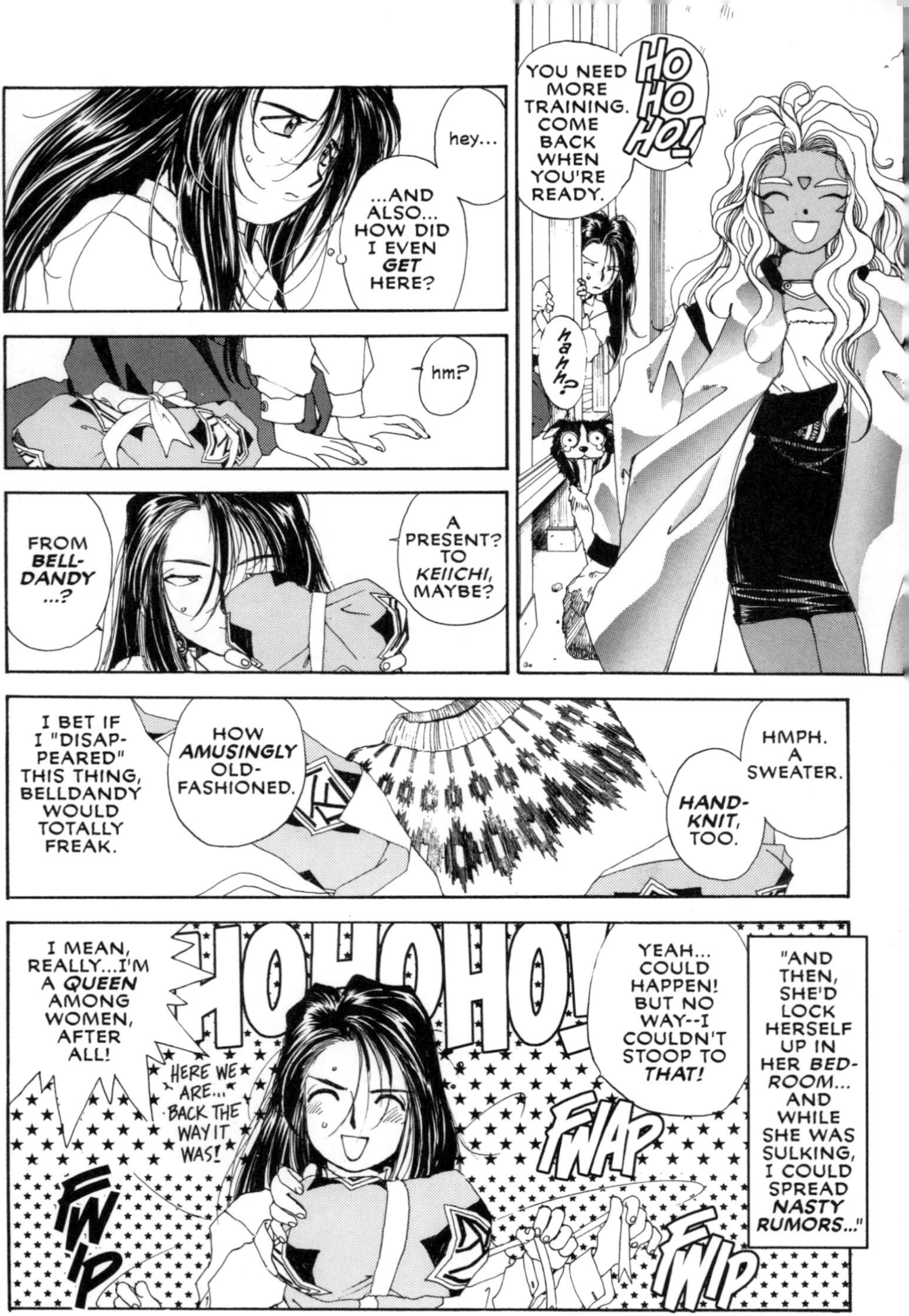

HO HO HO!
YOU NEED MORE TRAINING. COME BACK WHEN YOU'RE READY.
hahh?
hey...
...AND ALSO... HOW DID I EVEN GET HERE?
hm?
A PRESENT? TO KEIICHI, MAYBE?
FROM BELLDANDY ...?
HMPH. A SWEATER.
HAND-KNIT, TOO.
HOW AMUSINGLY OLD-FASHIONED.
I BET IF I "DISAPPEARED" THIS THING, BELLDANDY WOULD TOTALLY FREAK.
"AND THEN, SHE'D LOCK HERSELF UP IN HER BEDROOM... AND WHILE SHE WAS SULKING, I COULD SPREAD NASTY RUMORS..."
YEAH... COULD HAPPEN! BUT NO WAY--I COULDN'T STOOP TO THAT!
HOHOHO!
I MEAN, REALLY...I'M A QUEEN AMONG WOMEN, AFTER ALL!
HERE WE ARE... BACK THE WAY IT WAS!
FWAP
FWIP
FWIP

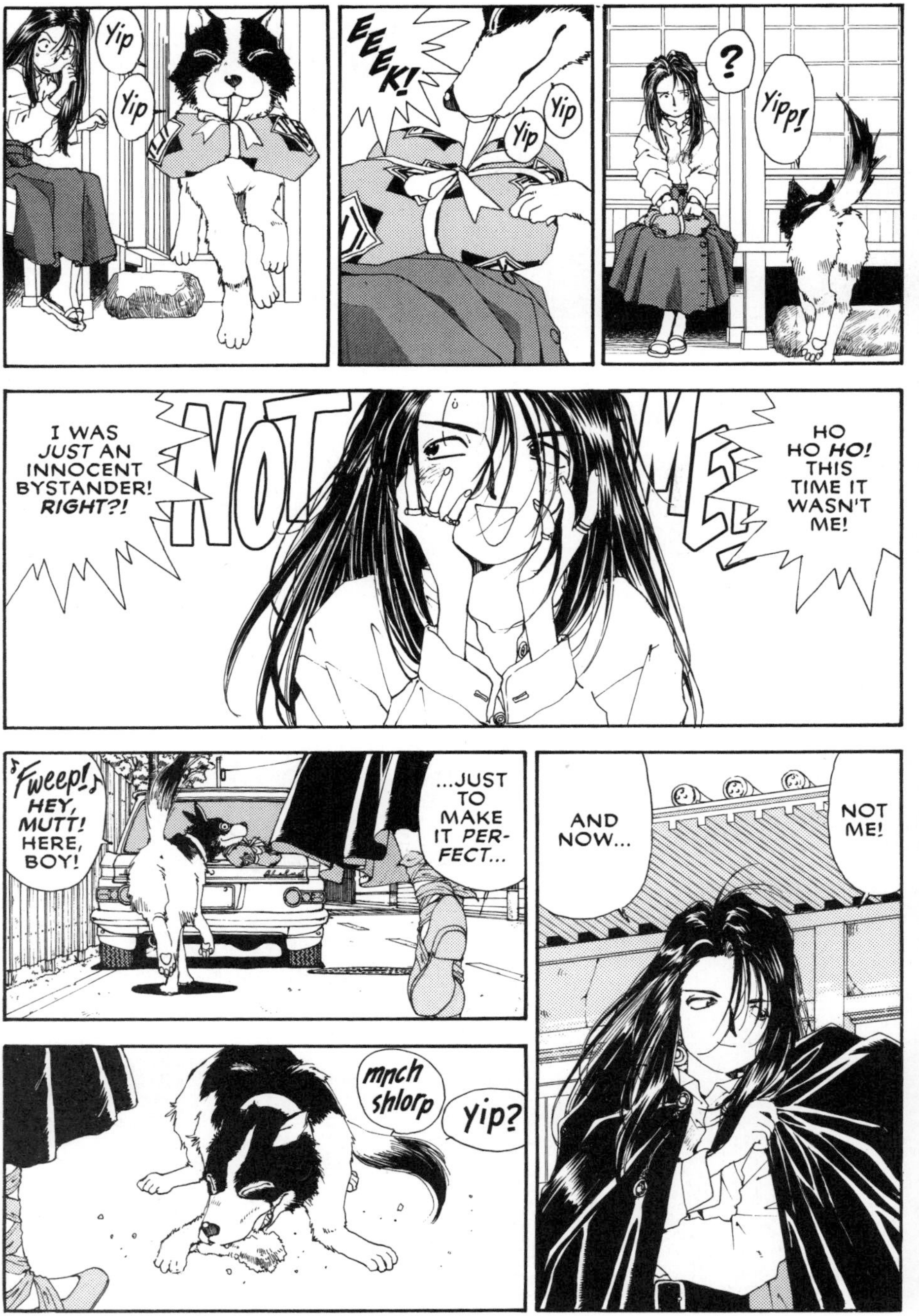
?
Yipp!
EEEK!
Yip
Yip
Yip
Yip
HO HO HO! THIS TIME IT WASN'T ME!
NOT ME
I WAS JUST AN INNOCENT BYSTANDER! RIGHT?!
NOT ME!
AND NOW...
...JUST TO MAKE IT PERFECT...
Fweep! HEY, MUTT! HERE, BOY!
mnch shlorp
yip?

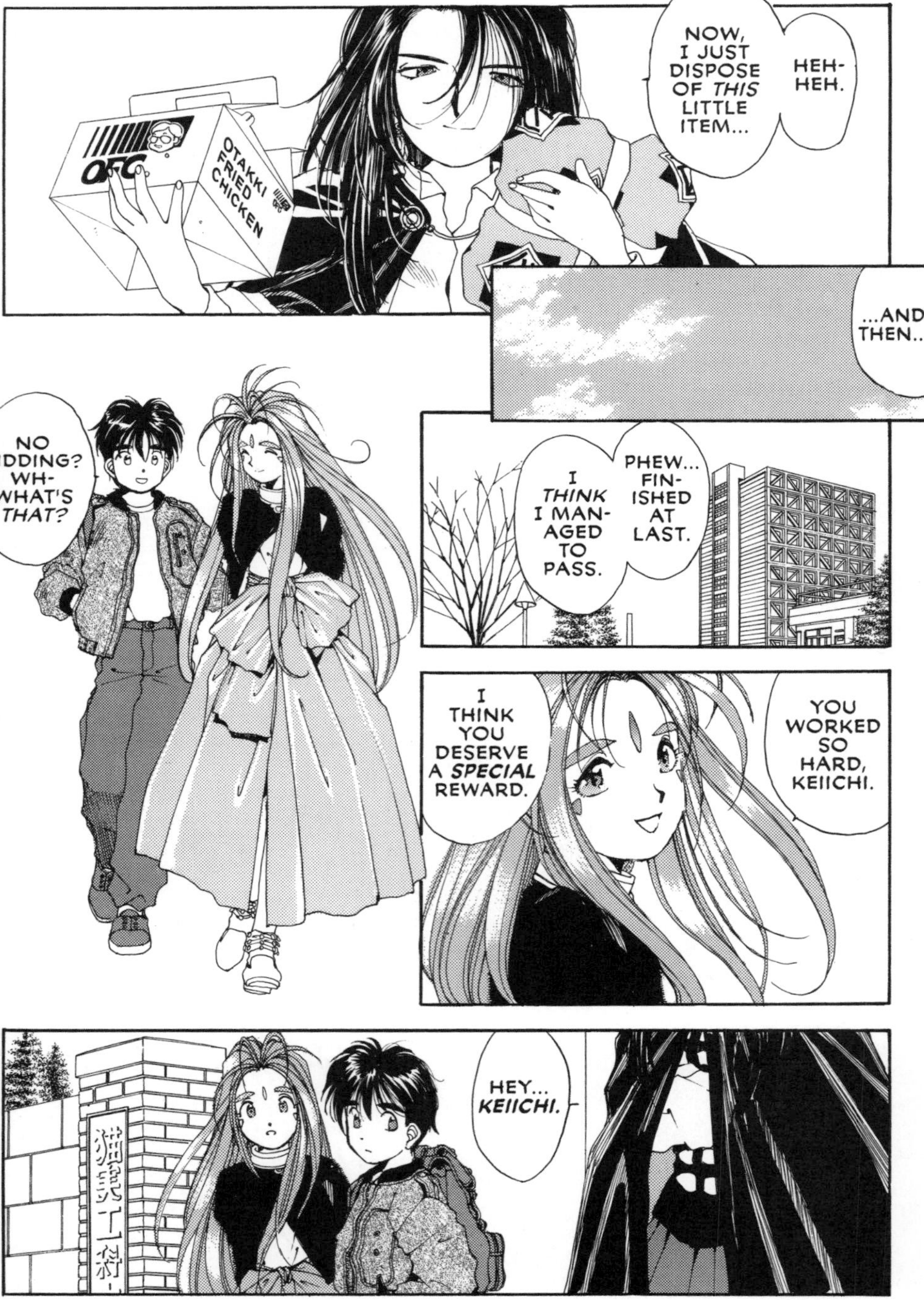
HEH-HEH.
NOW, I JUST DISPOSE OF *THIS* LITTLE ITEM...
OFC
OTAKKI FRIED CHICKEN
...AND THEN...
PHEW... FIN-ISHED AT LAST.
I *THINK* I MAN-AGED TO PASS.
YOU WORKED SO HARD, KEIICHI.
I THINK YOU DESERVE A *SPECIAL* REWARD.
NO KIDDING? WH-WHAT'S *THAT?*
HEY... *KEIICHI.*
猫実工科

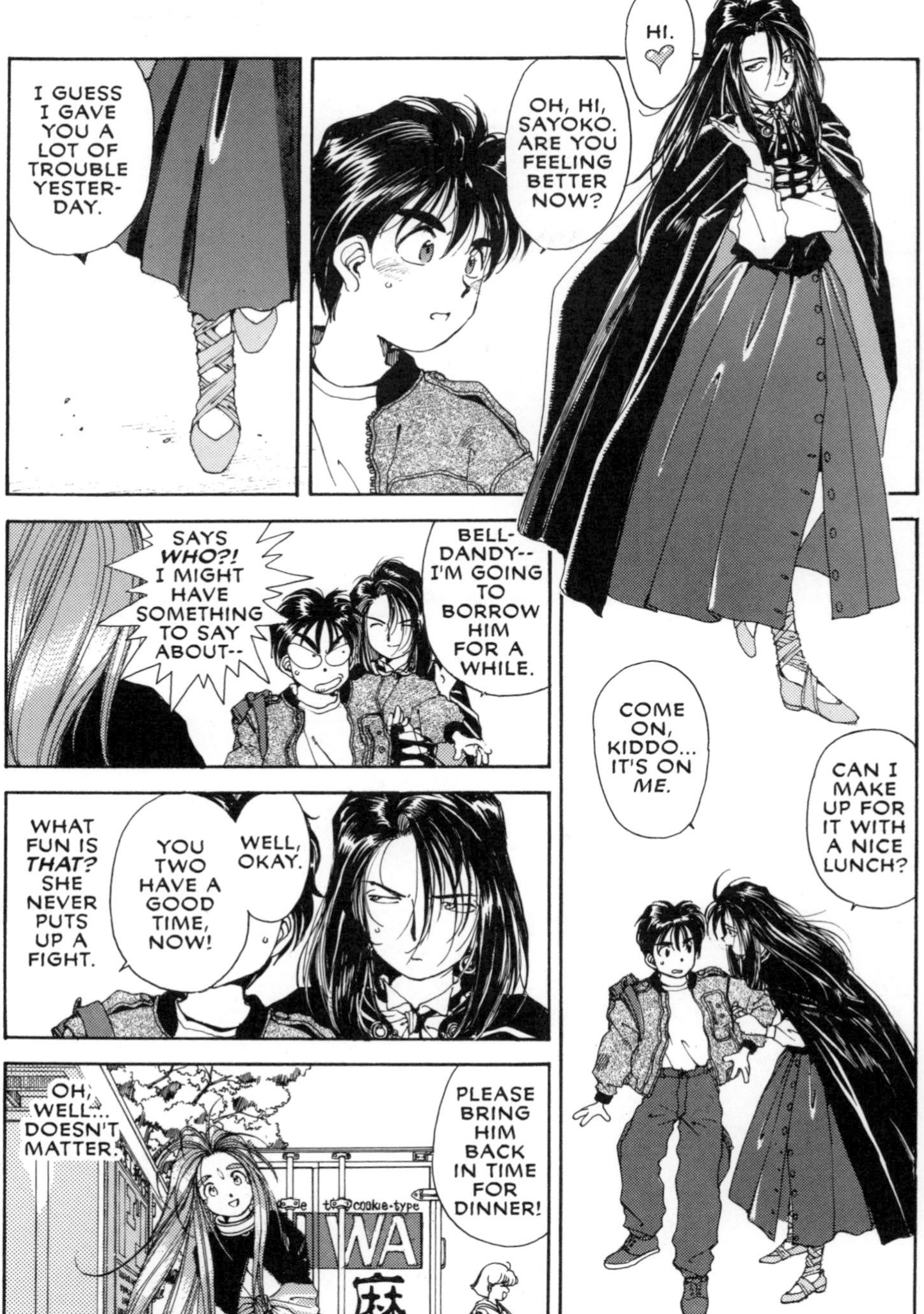

HI.
OH, HI, SAYOKO. ARE YOU FEELING BETTER NOW?
I GUESS I GAVE YOU A LOT OF TROUBLE YESTER-DAY.
CAN I MAKE UP FOR IT WITH A NICE LUNCH?
COME ON, KIDDO... IT'S ON *ME.*
BELL-DANDY-- I'M GOING TO BORROW HIM FOR A WHILE.
SAYS ***WHO?!*** I MIGHT HAVE SOMETHING TO SAY ABOUT--
WELL, OKAY.
YOU TWO HAVE A GOOD TIME, NOW!
WHAT FUN IS ***THAT?*** SHE NEVER PUTS UP A FIGHT.
PLEASE BRING HIM BACK IN TIME FOR DINNER!
OH, WELL... DOESN'T MATTER.

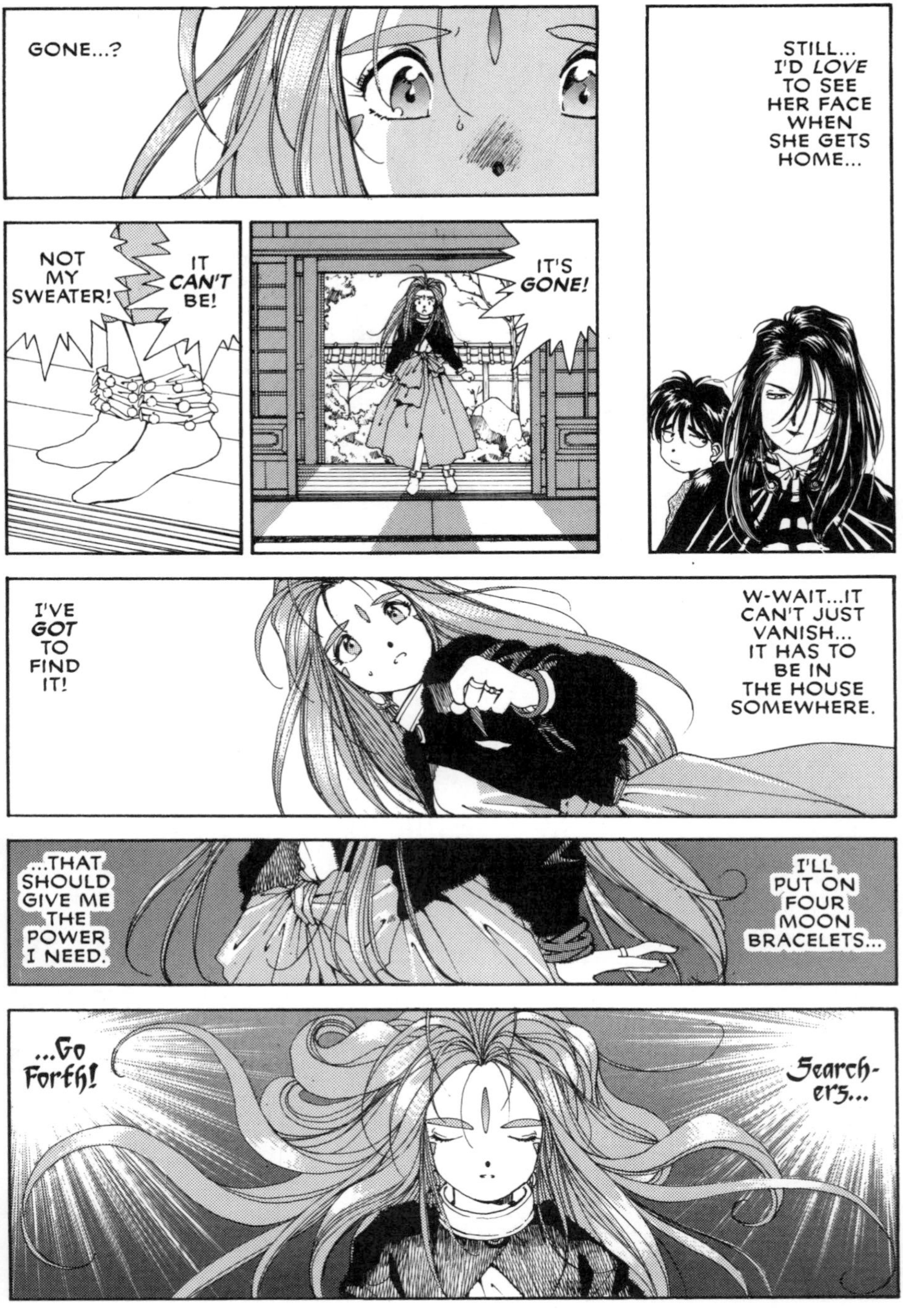
STILL... I'D LOVE TO SEE HER FACE WHEN SHE GETS HOME...
GONE...?
IT'S GONE!
IT CAN'T BE!
NOT MY SWEATER!
W-WAIT...IT CAN'T JUST VANISH... IT HAS TO BE IN THE HOUSE SOMEWHERE.
I'VE GOT TO FIND IT!
I'LL PUT ON FOUR MOON BRACELETS...
...THAT SHOULD GIVE ME THE POWER I NEED.
Searchers...
...Go Forth!

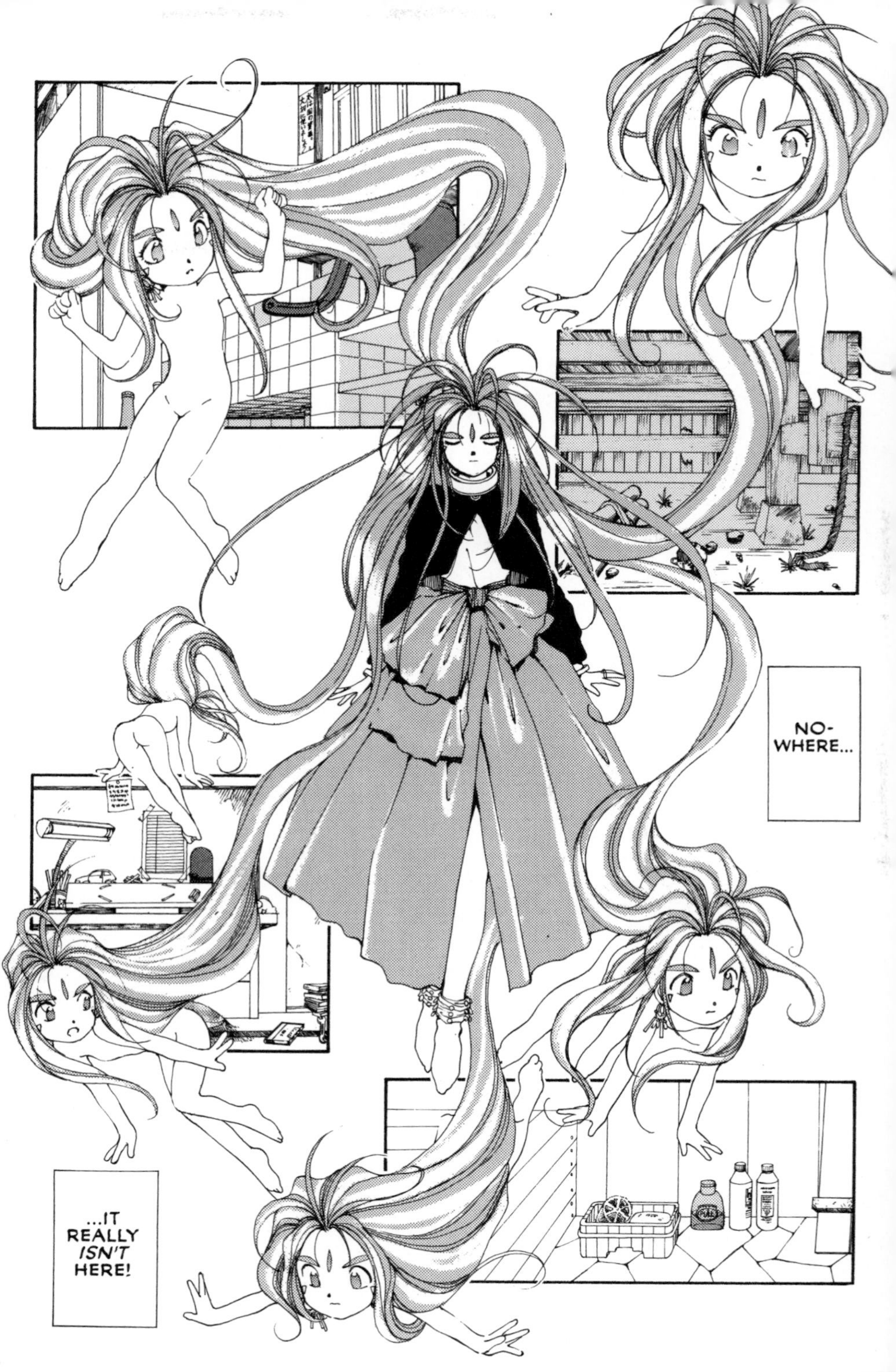
NO-WHERE...
...IT REALLY ISN'T HERE!

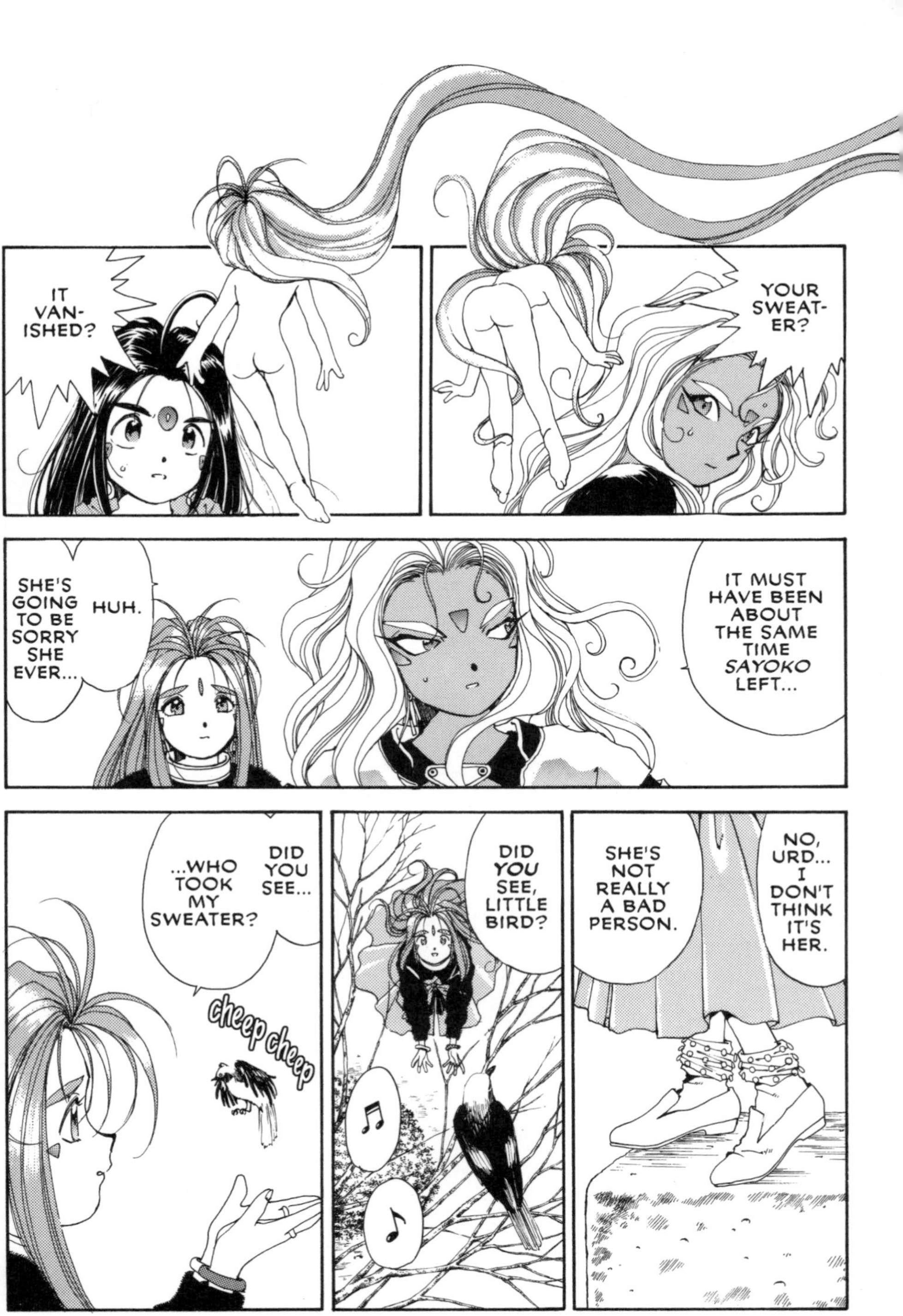
YOUR SWEATER?
IT VANISHED?
IT MUST HAVE BEEN ABOUT THE SAME TIME *SAYOKO* LEFT...
HUH.
SHE'S GOING TO BE SORRY SHE EVER...
NO, URD... I DON'T THINK IT'S HER.
SHE'S NOT REALLY A BAD PERSON.
DID *YOU* SEE, LITTLE BIRD?
DID YOU SEE...
...WHO TOOK MY SWEATER?
cheep cheep

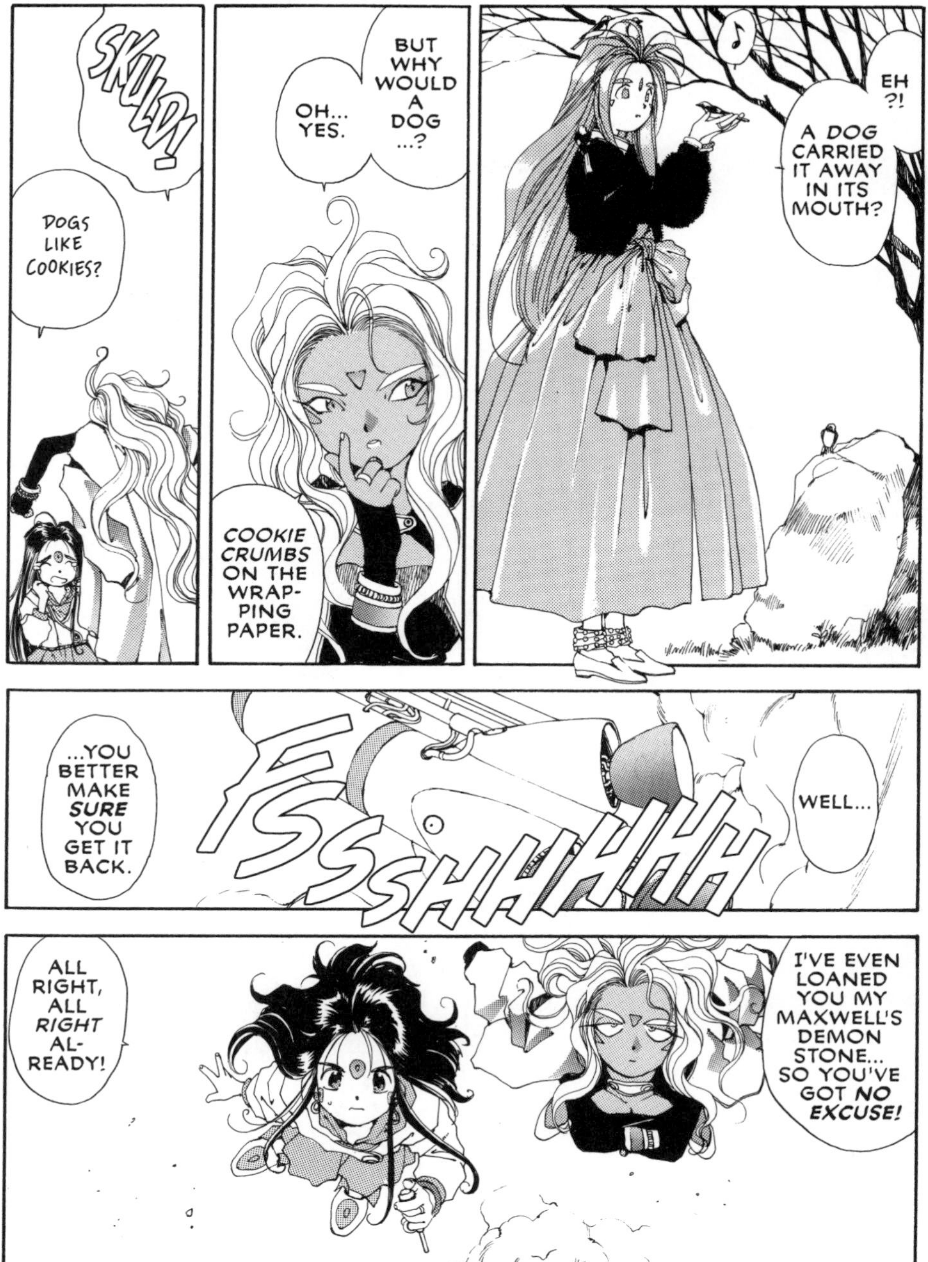
EH ?!
A *DOG* CARRIED IT AWAY IN ITS MOUTH?
BUT WHY WOULD A DOG ...?
OH... YES.
COOKIE CRUMBS ON THE WRAP-PING PAPER.
SKULD!
DOGS LIKE COOKIES?
WELL...
FSSSHHHHHH
...YOU BETTER MAKE ***SURE*** YOU GET IT BACK.
I'VE EVEN LOANED YOU MY MAXWELL'S DEMON STONE... SO YOU'VE GOT ***NO EXCUSE!***
ALL RIGHT, ALL *RIGHT* AL-READY!

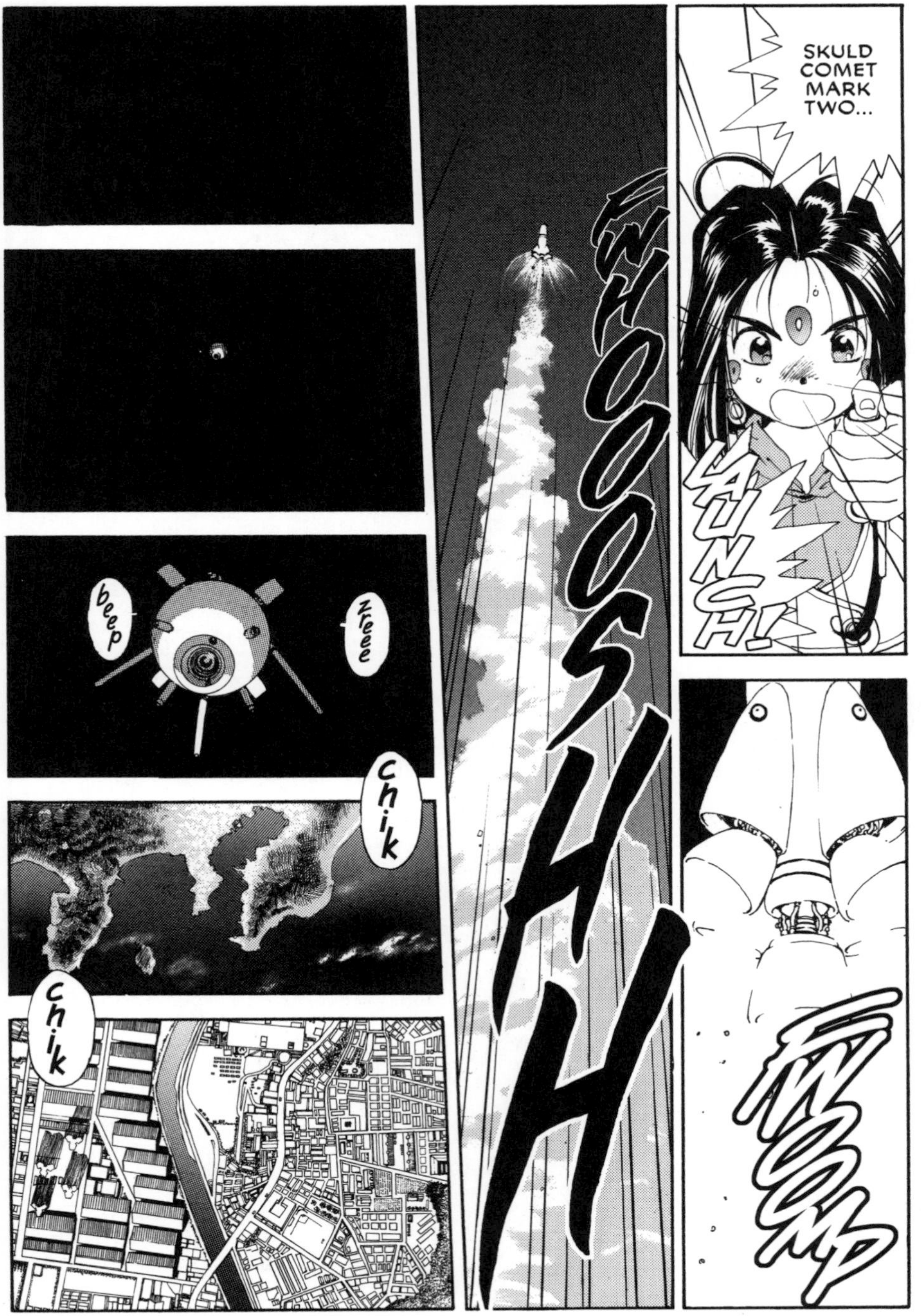
SKULD COMET MARK TWO...
LAUNCH!
FWOOMP
FWHOOOOSHHH
zreee
beep
chnik
chnik

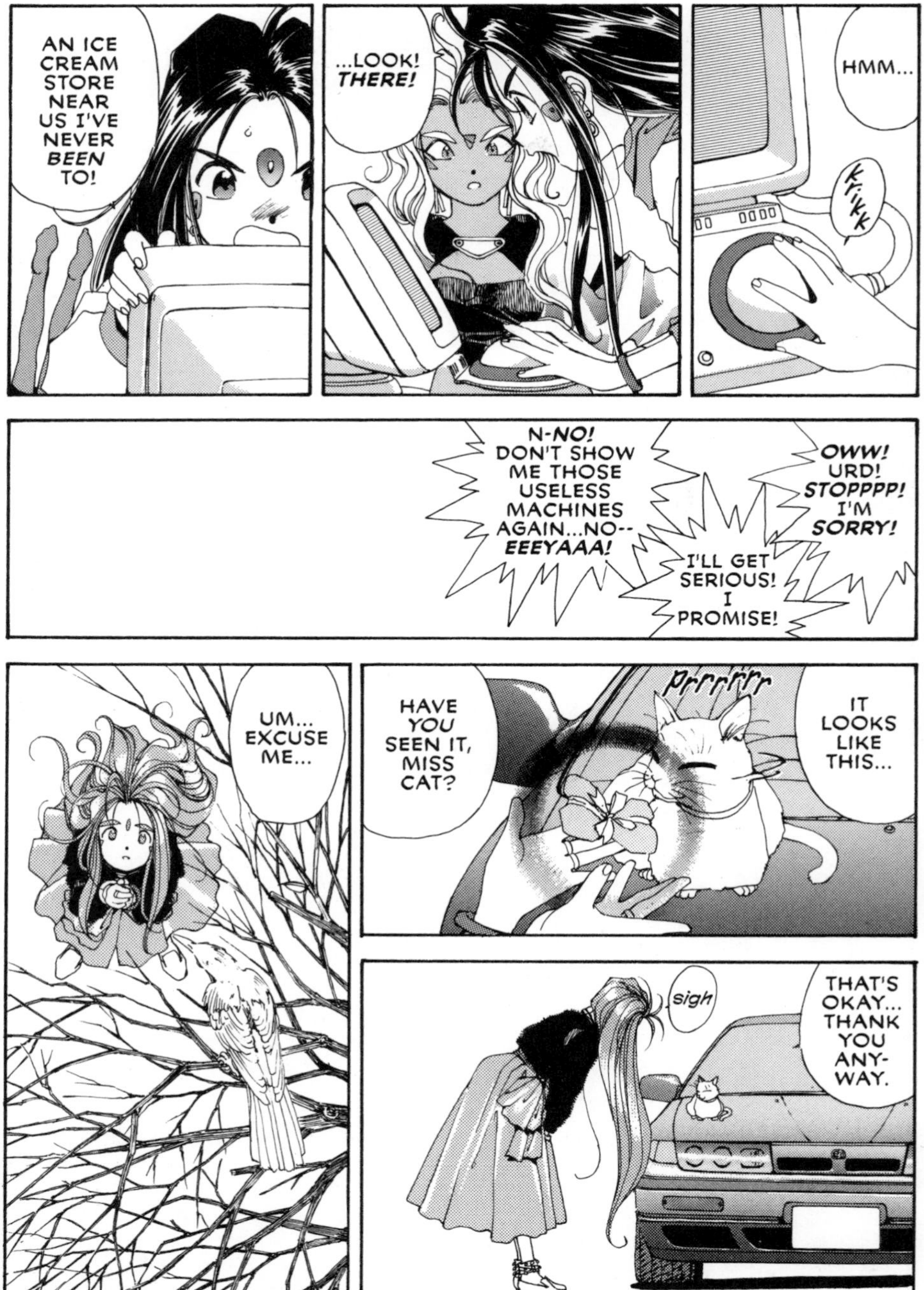

AN ICE CREAM STORE NEAR US I'VE NEVER *BEEN* TO!
...LOOK! *THERE!*
HMM...
krikk
N-*NO!* DON'T SHOW ME THOSE USELESS MACHINES AGAIN...NO-- *EEEYAAA!*
OWW! URD! *STOPPPP!* I'M *SORRY!*
I'LL GET SERIOUS! I PROMISE!
UM... EXCUSE ME...
HAVE *YOU* SEEN IT, MISS CAT?
Prrrrrr
IT LOOKS LIKE THIS...
sigh
THAT'S OKAY... THANK YOU ANY-WAY.

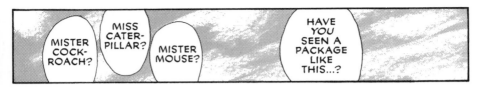

HAVE YOU SEEN A PACKAGE LIKE THIS...?
MISTER MOUSE?
MISS CATER-PILLAR?
MISTER COCK-ROACH?
I...I JUST CAN'T GIVE UP...
...
AS
300
91 4
FACE IT...
...IT'S **GONE.**
I CAN'T GIVE UP ON THAT SWEATER.
IT'S THE SUM OF ALL THE LOVE IN MY HEART.

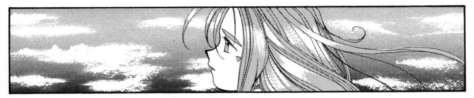

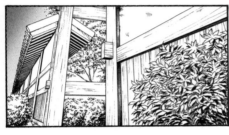

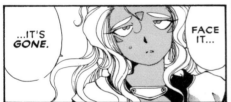

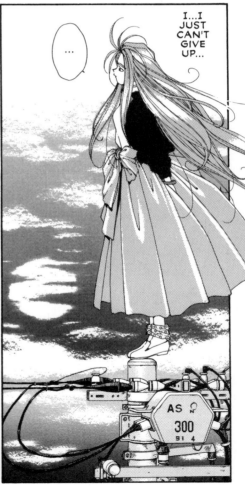

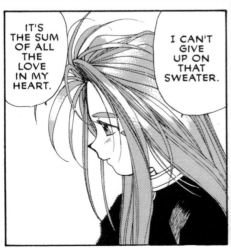

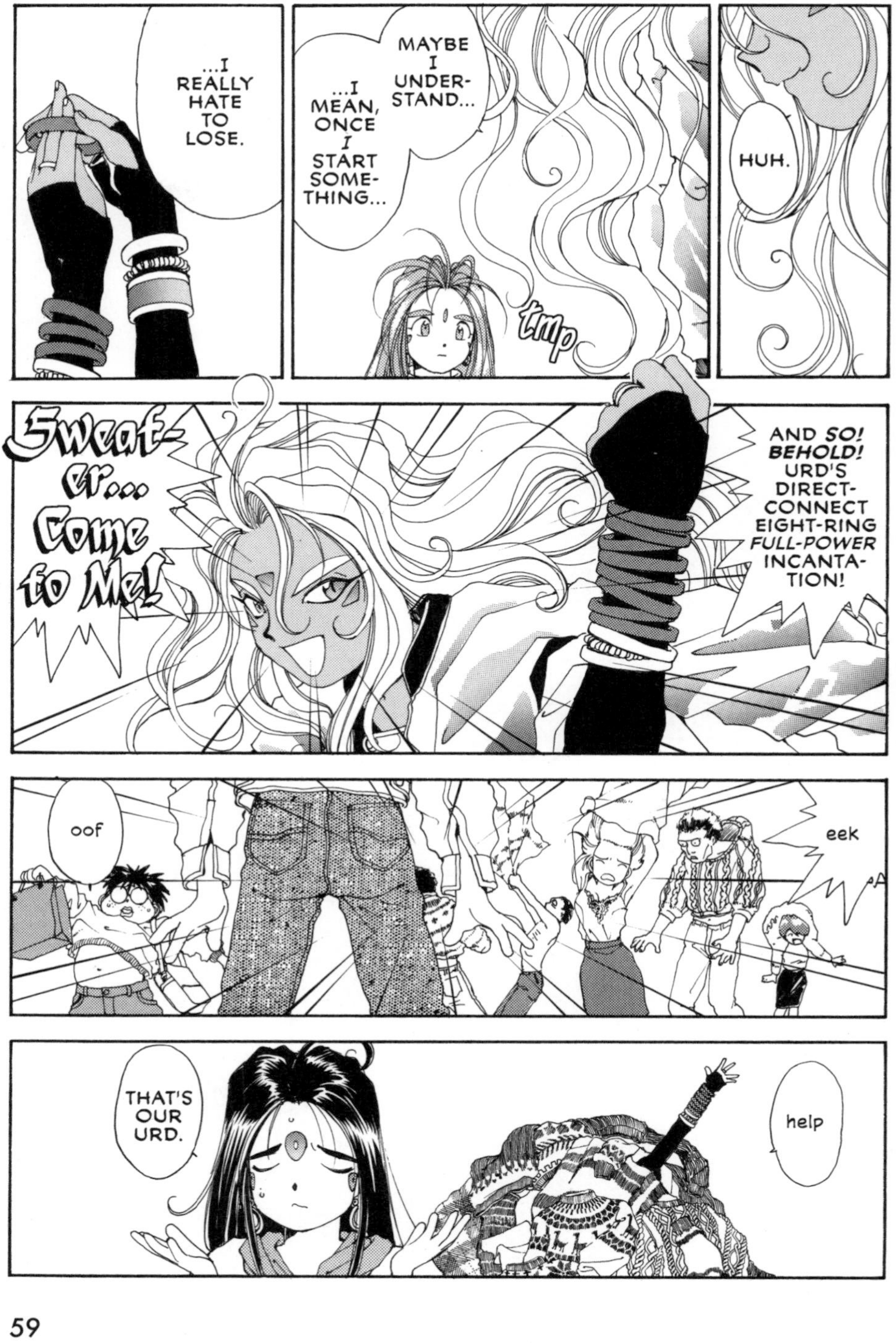
HUH.
MAYBE I UNDER-STAND...
...I MEAN, ONCE I START SOME-THING...
tmp
...I REALLY HATE TO LOSE.
AND SO! BEHOLD! URD'S DIRECT-CONNECT EIGHT-RING FULL-POWER INCANTA-TION!
Sweat-er... Come to Me!
eek
oof
help
THAT'S OUR URD.

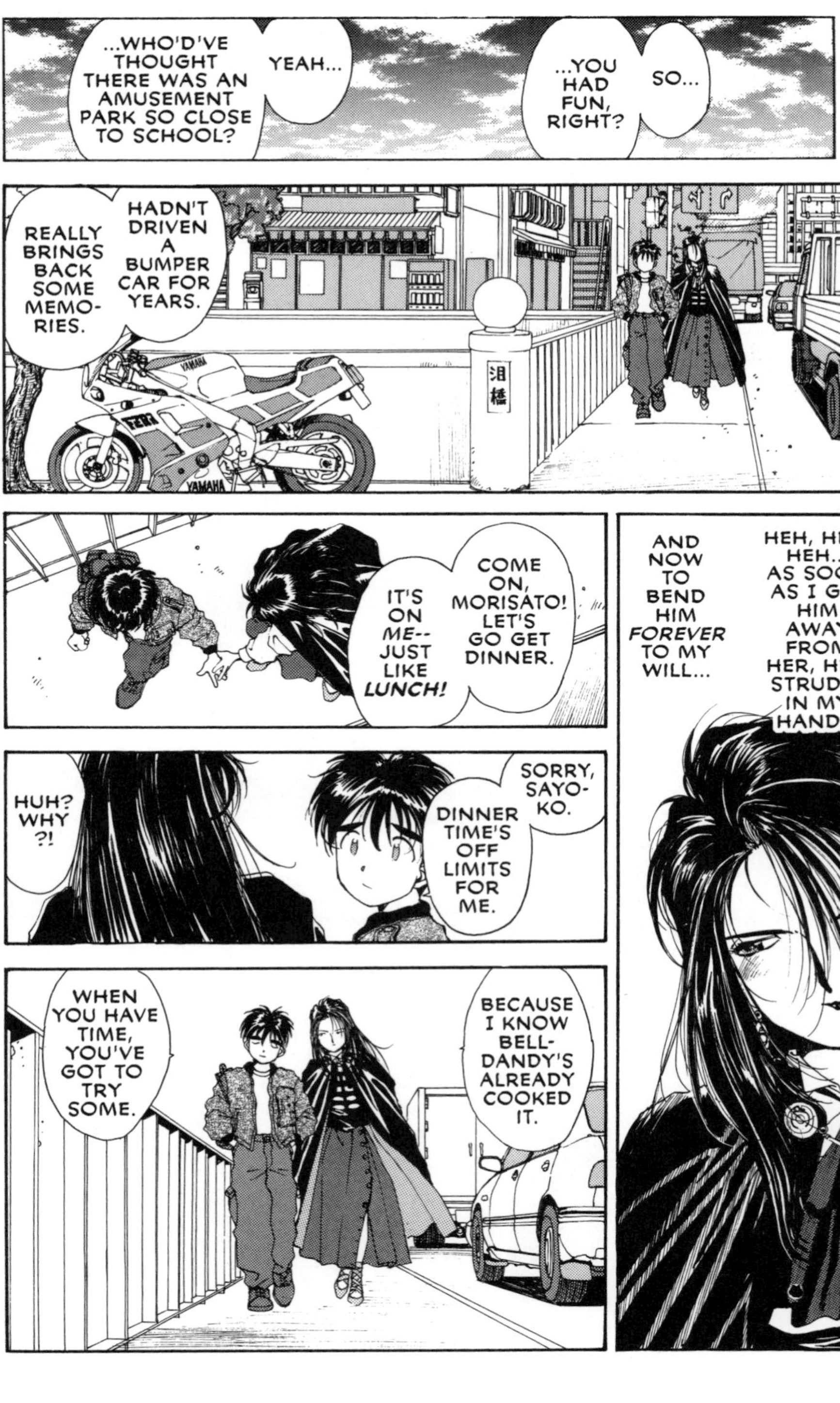

SO...
...YOU HAD FUN, RIGHT?
YEAH...
...WHO'D'VE THOUGHT THERE WAS AN AMUSEMENT PARK SO CLOSE TO SCHOOL?
HADN'T DRIVEN A BUMPER CAR FOR YEARS.
REALLY BRINGS BACK SOME MEMORIES.
泪橋
HEH, HEH, HEH... AS SOON AS I GET HIM AWAY FROM HER, HE'S STRUDEL IN MY HANDS.
AND NOW TO BEND HIM *FOREVER* TO MY WILL...
COME ON, MORISATO! LET'S GO GET DINNER.
IT'S ON *ME*--JUST LIKE *LUNCH!*
SORRY, SAYOKO.
DINNER TIME'S OFF LIMITS FOR ME.
HUH? WHY?!
BECAUSE I KNOW BELLDANDY'S ALREADY COOKED IT.
WHEN YOU HAVE TIME, YOU'VE GOT TO TRY SOME.

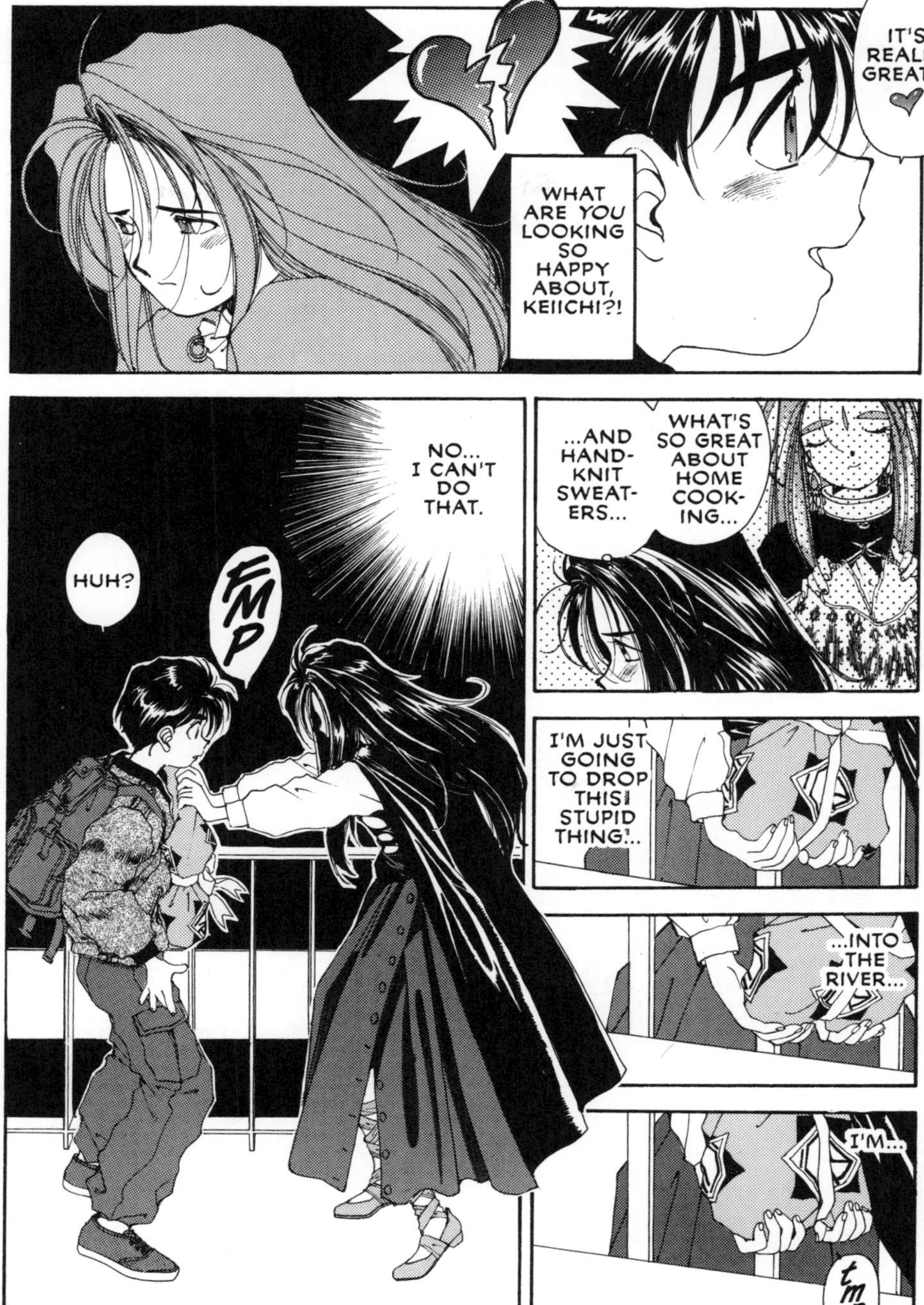
IT'S REALLY GREAT--!
WHAT ARE YOU LOOKING SO HAPPY ABOUT, KEIICHI?!
WHAT'S SO GREAT ABOUT HOME COOKING...
...AND HAND-KNIT SWEATERS...
I'M JUST GOING TO DROP THIS STUPID THING...
...INTO THE RIVER...
I'M...
tmp
NO... I CAN'T DO THAT.
FMP
HUH?

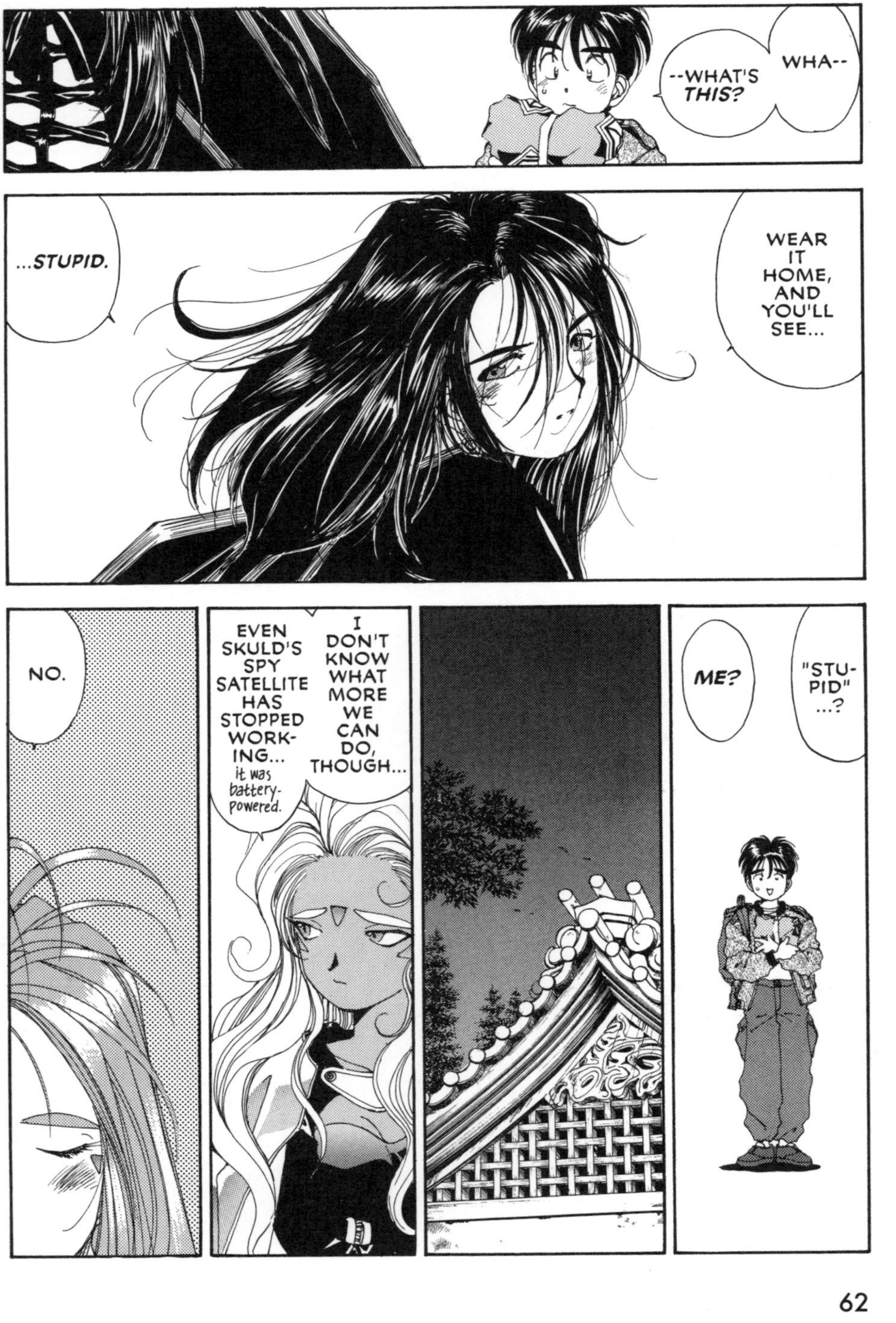
WHA--
--WHAT'S THIS?
WEAR IT HOME, AND YOU'LL SEE...
...STUPID.
"STU-PID"...?
ME?
I DON'T KNOW WHAT MORE WE CAN DO, THOUGH...
EVEN SKULD'S SPY SATELLITE HAS STOPPED WORKING... it was battery-powered.
NO.

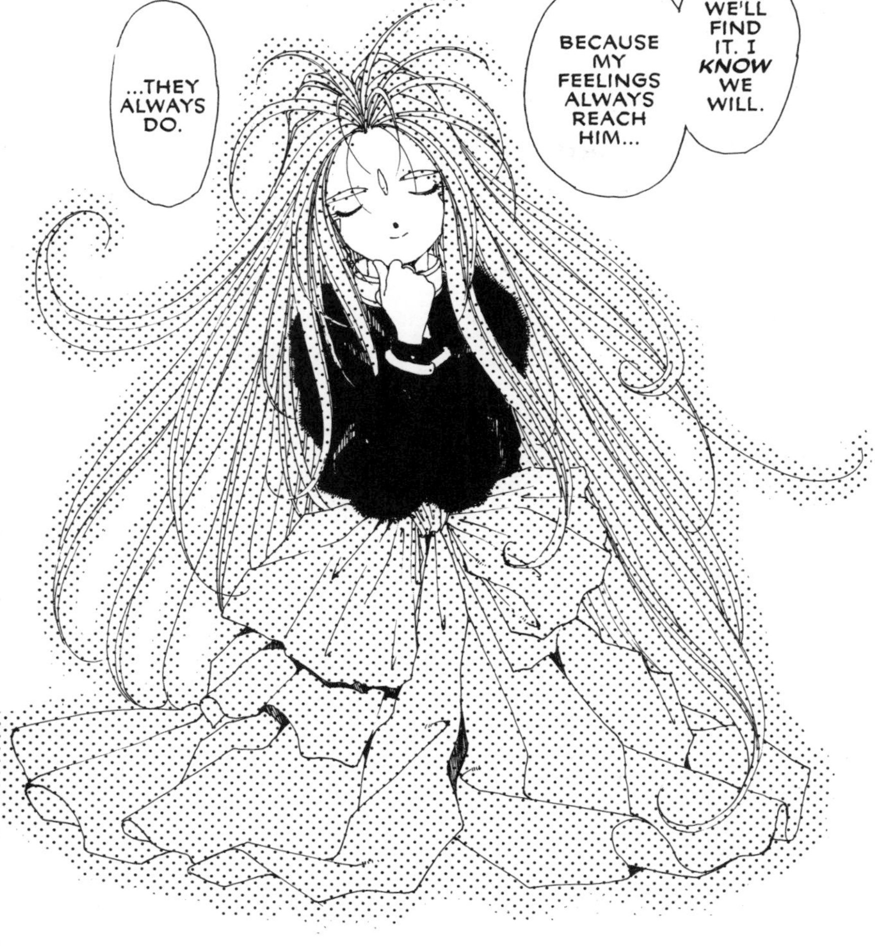
WE'LL FIND IT. I *KNOW* WE WILL.
BECAUSE MY FEELINGS ALWAYS REACH HIM...
...THEY ALWAYS DO.

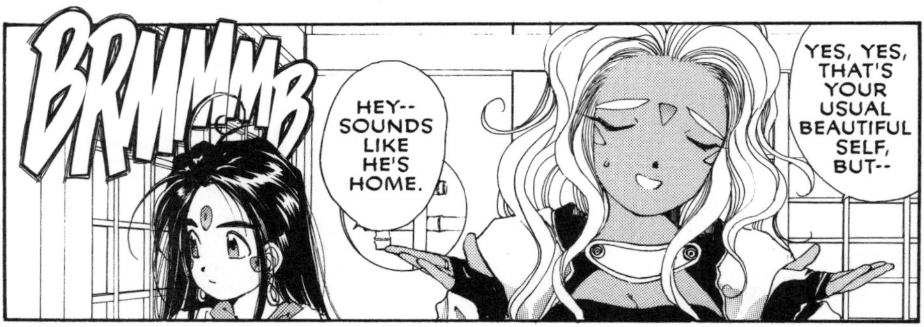
YES, YES, THAT'S YOUR USUAL BEAUTIFUL SELF, BUT--
HEY--SOUNDS LIKE HE'S HOME.
BRMMMB

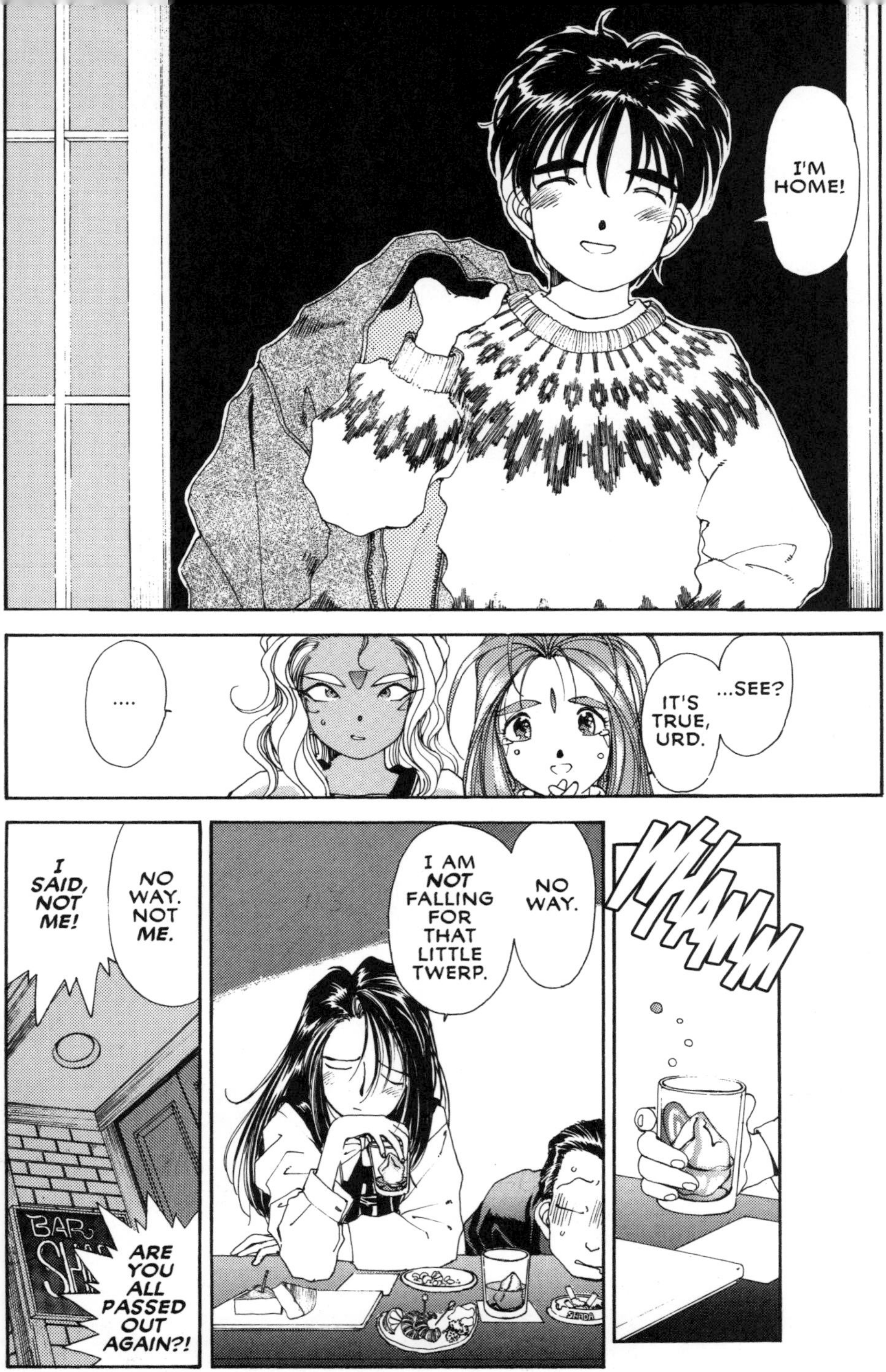
I'M HOME!
...SEE?
IT'S TRUE, URD.
....
WHAMM
NO WAY.
I AM NOT FALLING FOR THAT LITTLE TWERP.
NO WAY. NOT ME.
I SAID, NOT ME!
BAR
ARE YOU ALL PASSED OUT AGAIN?!

THE ADVENTURES OF MINI-URD

Now with added MINI-SKULD!

◆ STORMWRACK--A TALE OF BASEBALL ◆

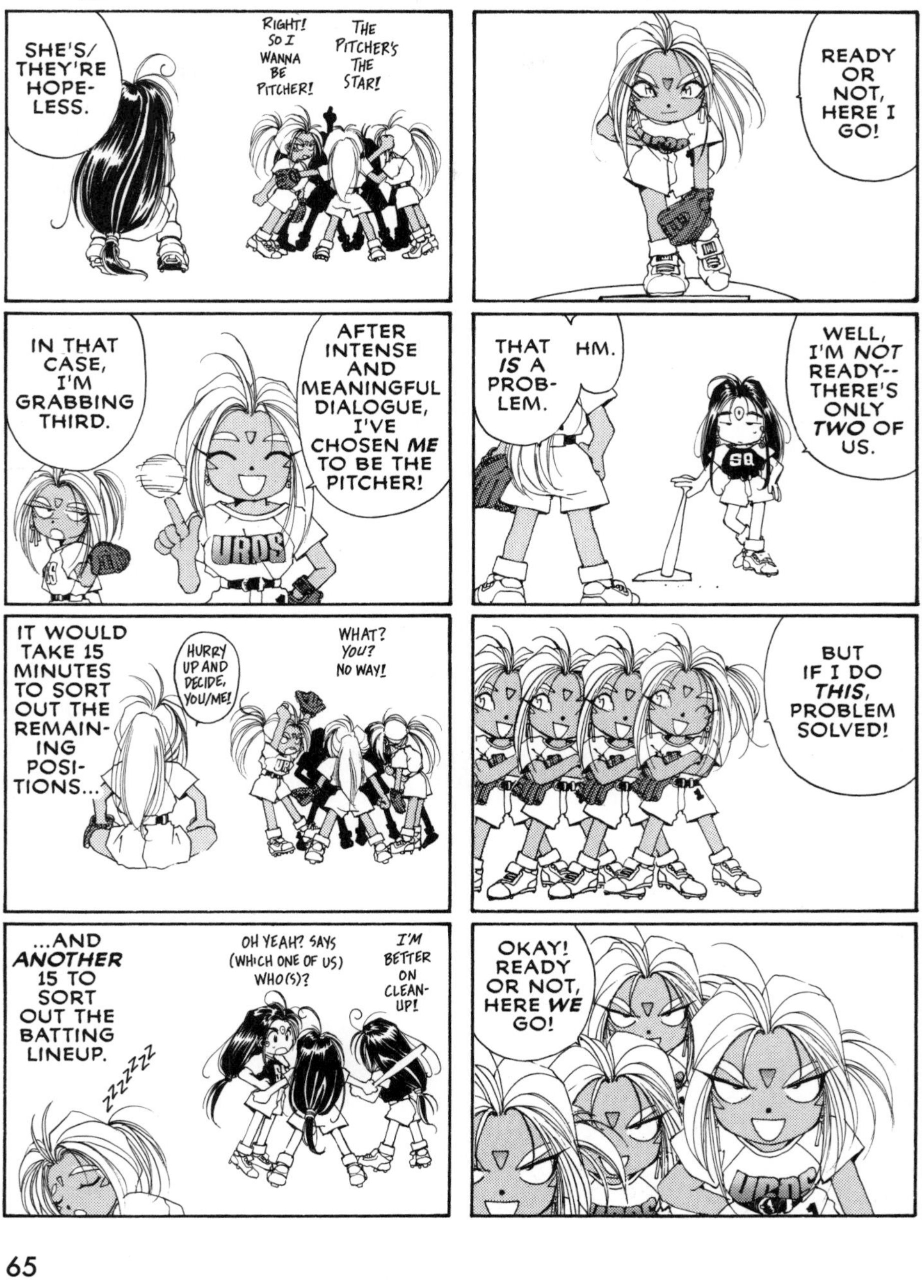

READY OR NOT, HERE I GO!
WELL, I'M *NOT* READY--THERE'S ONLY *TWO* OF US.
HM.
THAT *IS* A PROBLEM.
BUT IF I DO *THIS*, PROBLEM SOLVED!
OKAY! READY OR NOT, HERE *WE* GO!
THE PITCHER'S THE STAR!
RIGHT! SO I WANNA BE PITCHER!
SHE'S/THEY'RE HOPELESS.
AFTER INTENSE AND MEANINGFUL DIALOGUE, I'VE CHOSEN *ME* TO BE THE PITCHER!
IN THAT CASE, I'M GRABBING THIRD.
WHAT? *YOU?* NO WAY!
HURRY UP AND DECIDE, YOU/ME!
IT WOULD TAKE 15 MINUTES TO SORT OUT THE REMAINING POSITIONS...
I'M BETTER ON CLEAN-UP!
OH YEAH? SAYS (WHICH ONE OF US) WHO(S)?
...AND ***ANOTHER*** 15 TO SORT OUT THE BATTING LINEUP.
ZZZZZZZ

◆ STORMWRACK--A TALE OF BASEBALL (PART DEUX) ◆

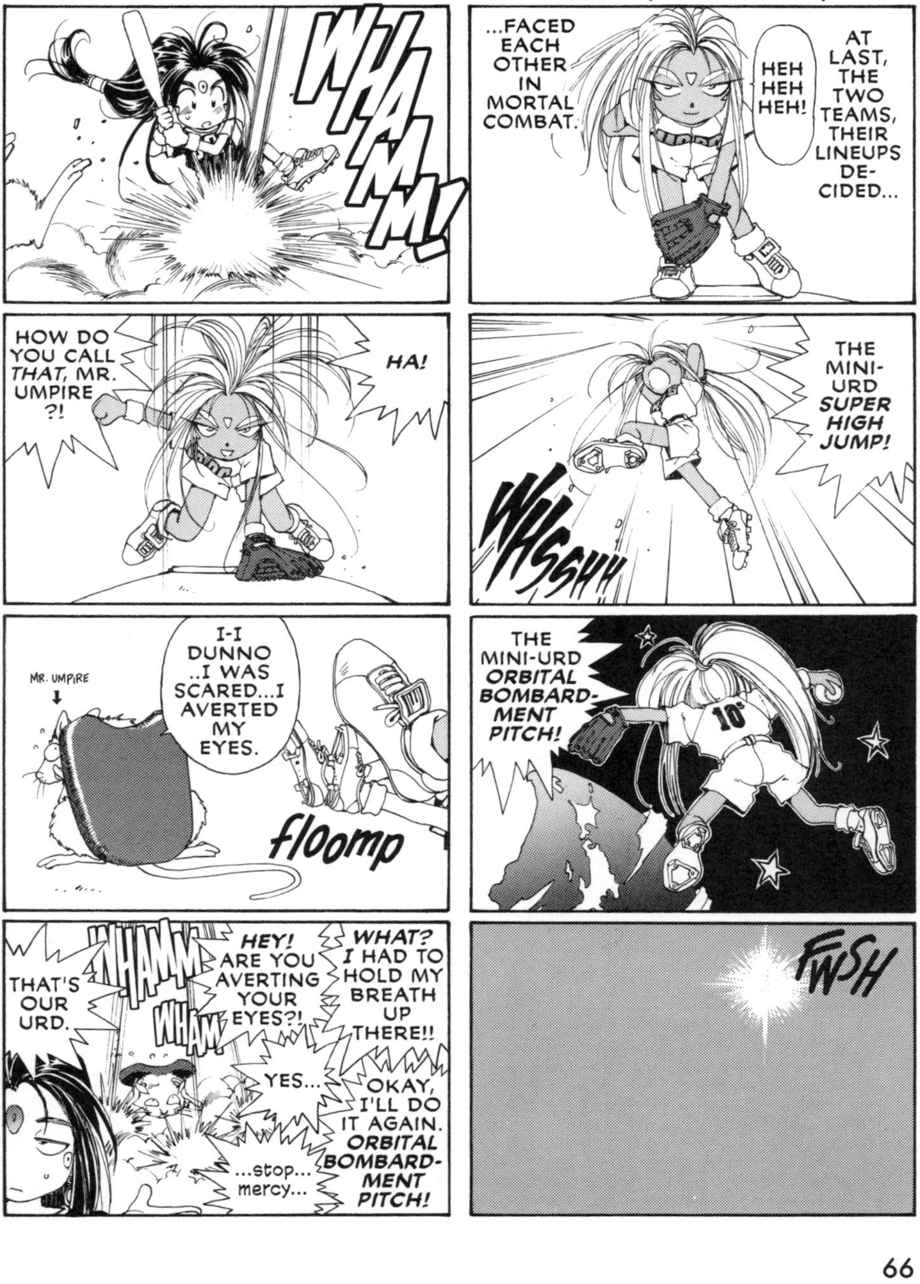
AT LAST, THE TWO TEAMS, THEIR LINEUPS DECIDED...
HEH HEH HEH!
...FACED EACH OTHER IN MORTAL COMBAT.
WHAMM!
THE MINI-URD SUPER HIGH JUMP!
WHSSHH
HA!
HOW DO YOU CALL THAT, MR. UMPIRE?!
THE MINI-URD ORBITAL BOMBARDMENT PITCH!
I-I DUNNO ..I WAS SCARED...I AVERTED MY EYES.
MR. UMPIRE
floomp
FWSH
WHAT? I HAD TO HOLD MY BREATH UP THERE!!
HEY! ARE YOU AVERTING YOUR EYES?!
WHAMM
THAT'S OUR URD.
WHAM
OKAY, I'LL DO IT AGAIN. ORBITAL BOMBARDMENT PITCH!
YES...
...stop... mercy...

◆STORMWRACK--A TALE OF BASEBALL (PART DER DRITTE)◆

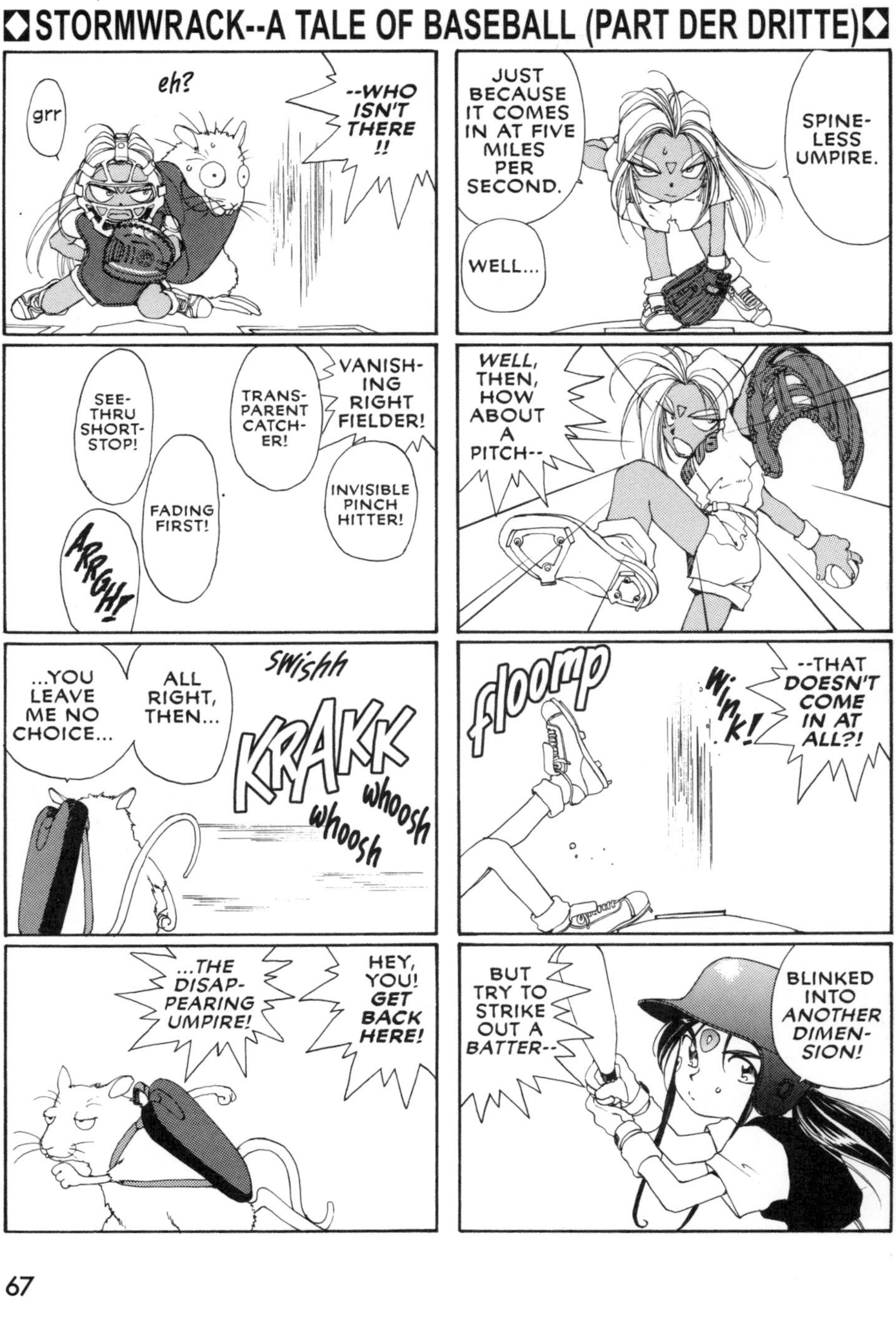
SPINE-LESS UMPIRE.
JUST BECAUSE IT COMES IN AT FIVE MILES PER SECOND.
WELL...
--WHO ISN'T THERE !!
eh?
grr
WELL, THEN, HOW ABOUT A PITCH--
VANISH-ING RIGHT FIELDER!
TRANS-PARENT CATCH-ER!
SEE-THRU SHORT-STOP!
INVISIBLE PINCH HITTER!
FADING FIRST!
ARRGH!
--THAT DOESN'T COME IN AT ALL?!
wink!
floomp
ALL RIGHT, THEN...
...YOU LEAVE ME NO CHOICE...
swishh
KRAKK
whoosh
whoosh
BLINKED INTO ANOTHER DIMEN-SION!
BUT TRY TO STRIKE OUT A BATTER--
HEY, YOU! GET BACK HERE!
...THE DISAP-PEARING UMPIRE!

STORMWRACK--A TALE OF BASEBALL
◆ (WHATEVER COMES AFTER THAT) ◆

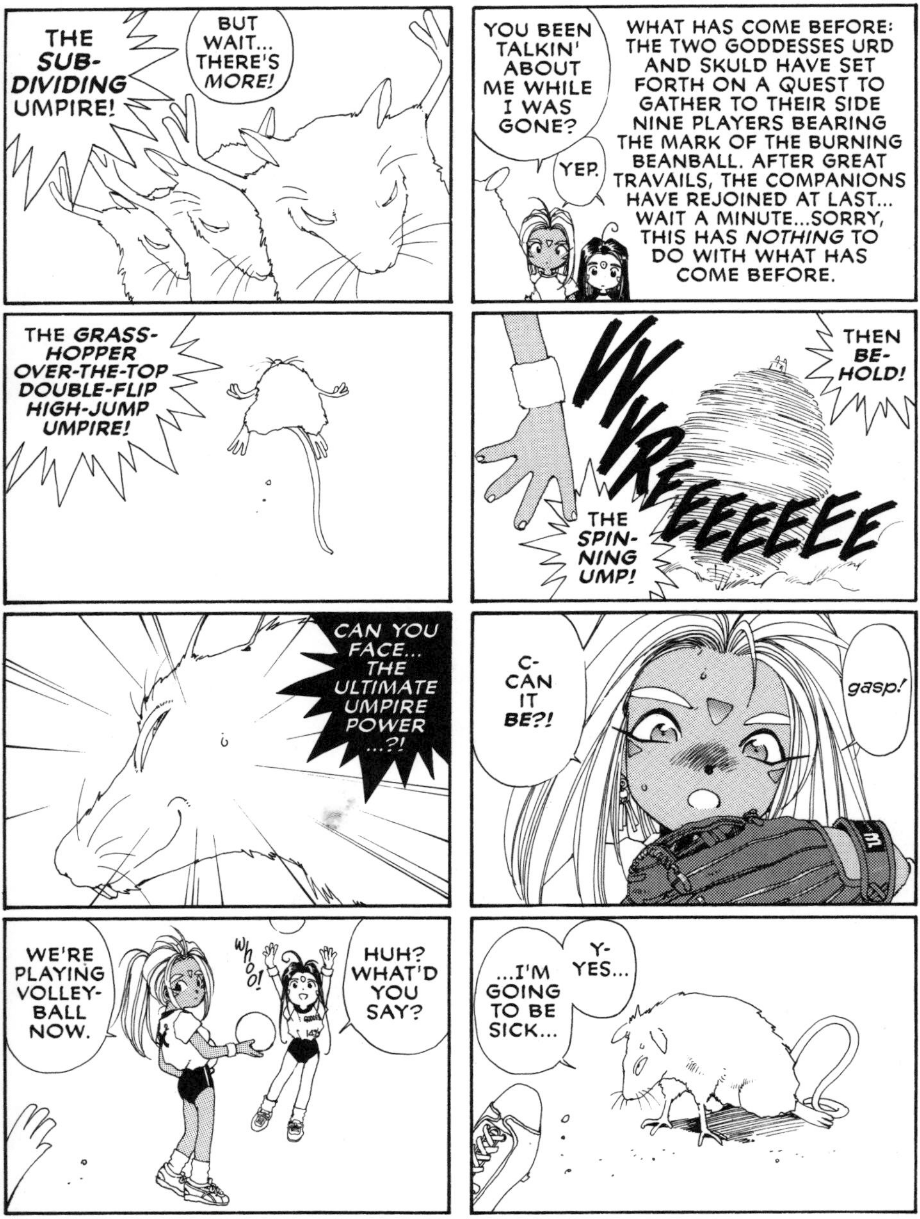

WHAT HAS COME BEFORE: THE TWO GODDESSES URD AND SKULD HAVE SET FORTH ON A QUEST TO GATHER TO THEIR SIDE NINE PLAYERS BEARING THE MARK OF THE BURNING BEANBALL. AFTER GREAT TRAVAILS, THE COMPANIONS HAVE REJOINED AT LAST... WAIT A MINUTE...SORRY, THIS HAS *NOTHING* TO DO WITH WHAT HAS COME BEFORE.
YOU BEEN TALKIN' ABOUT ME WHILE I WAS GONE?
YEP.
BUT WAIT... THERE'S *MORE!*
THE *SUB-DIVIDING* UMPIRE!
THEN *BE-HOLD!*
VVYREEEEEEE
THE *SPIN-NING UMP!*
THE *GRASS-HOPPER OVER-THE-TOP DOUBLE-FLIP HIGH-JUMP UMPIRE!*
gasp!
C-CAN IT *BE?!*
CAN YOU FACE... THE ULTIMATE UMPIRE POWER ...?!
Y-YES...
...I'M GOING TO BE SICK...
HUH? WHAT'D YOU SAY?
whoo!
WE'RE PLAYING VOLLEY-BALL NOW.

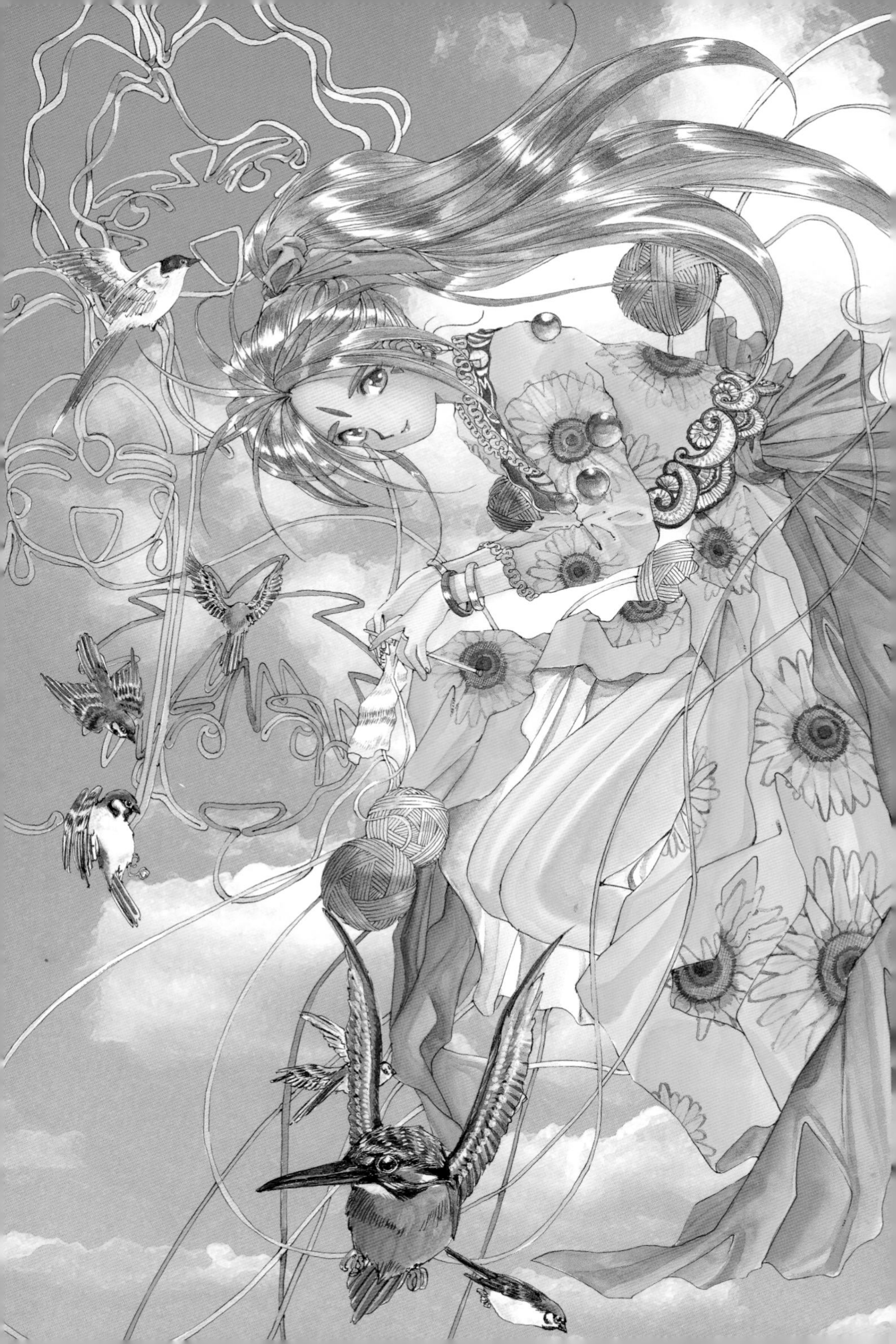

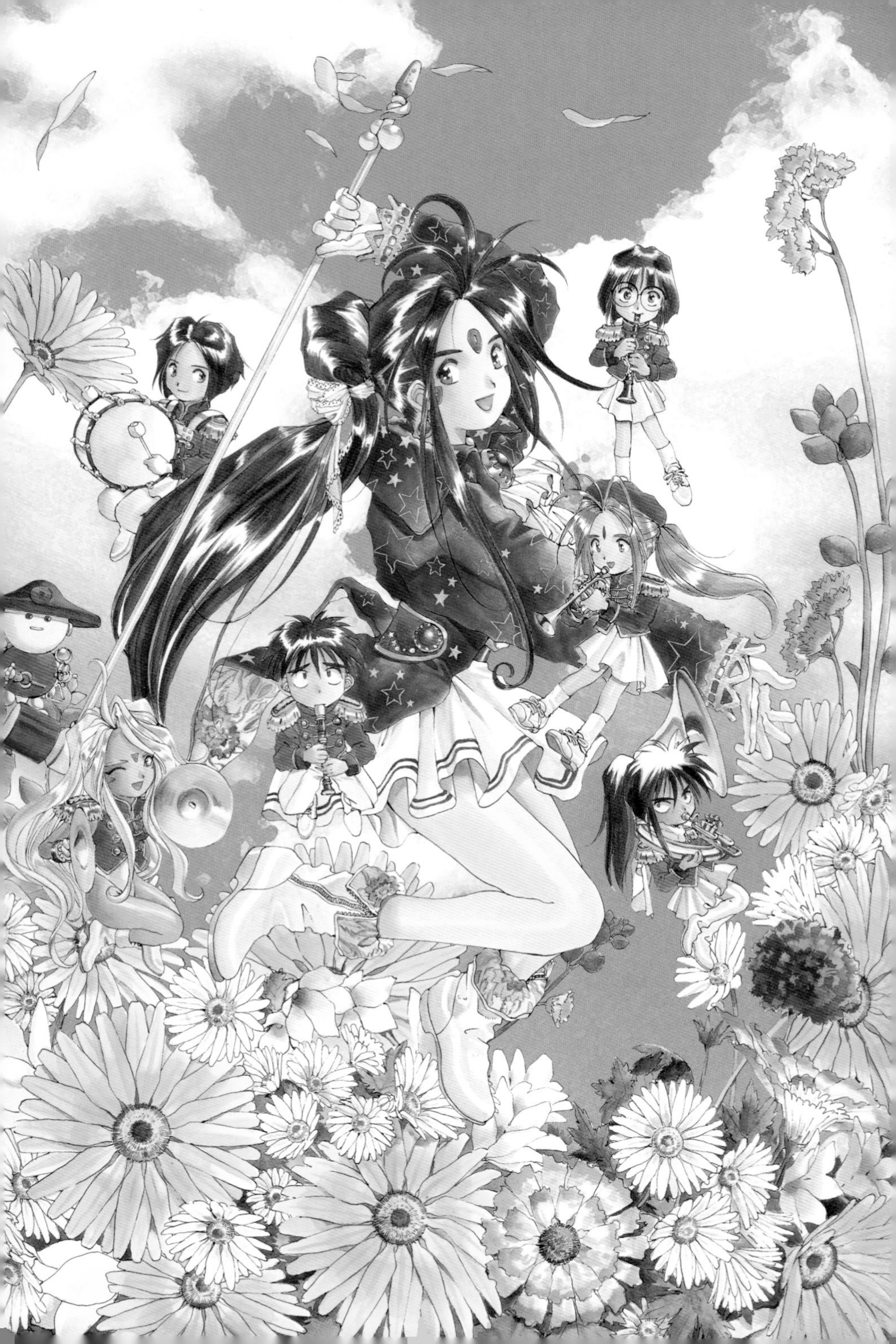

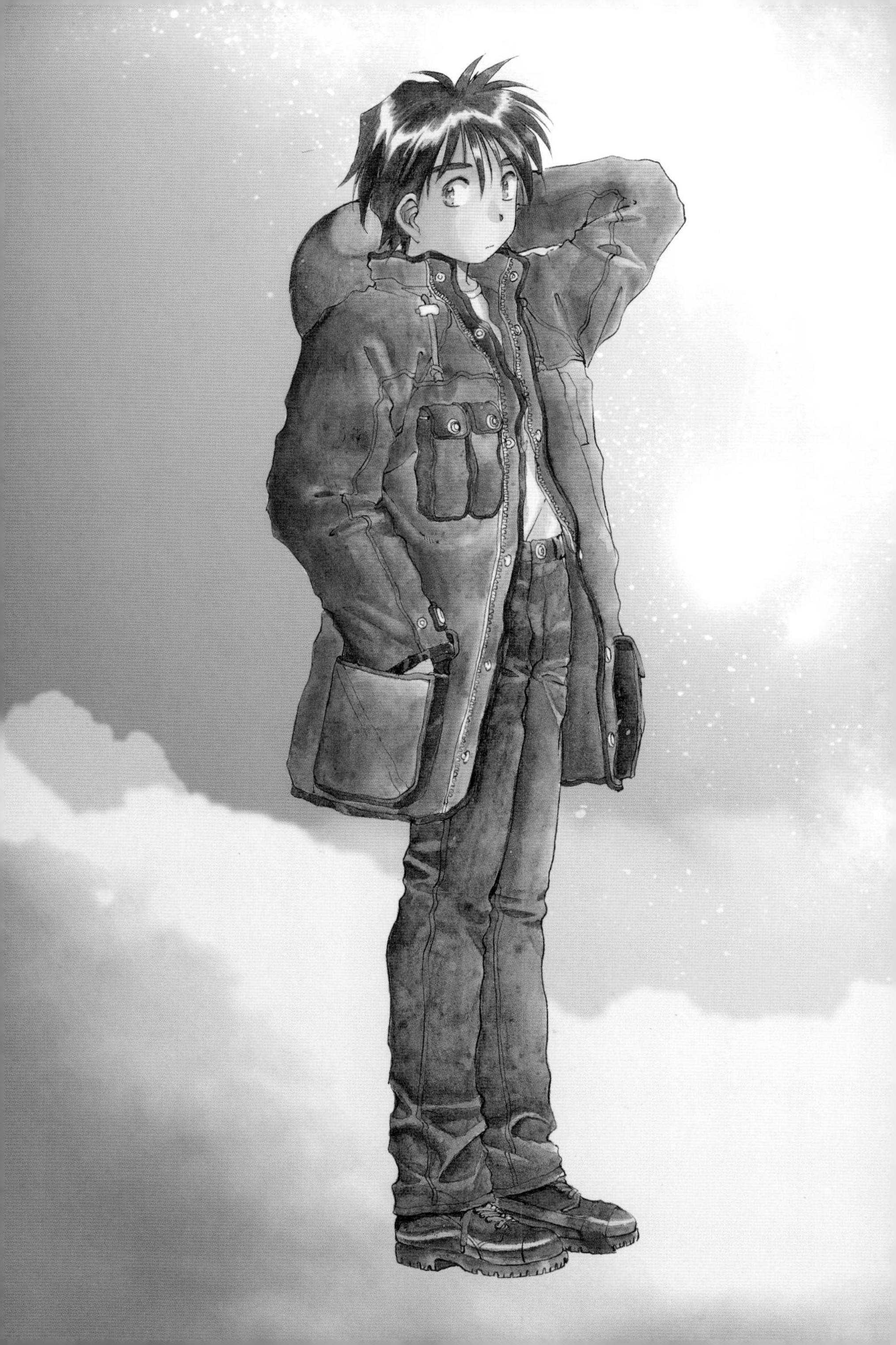

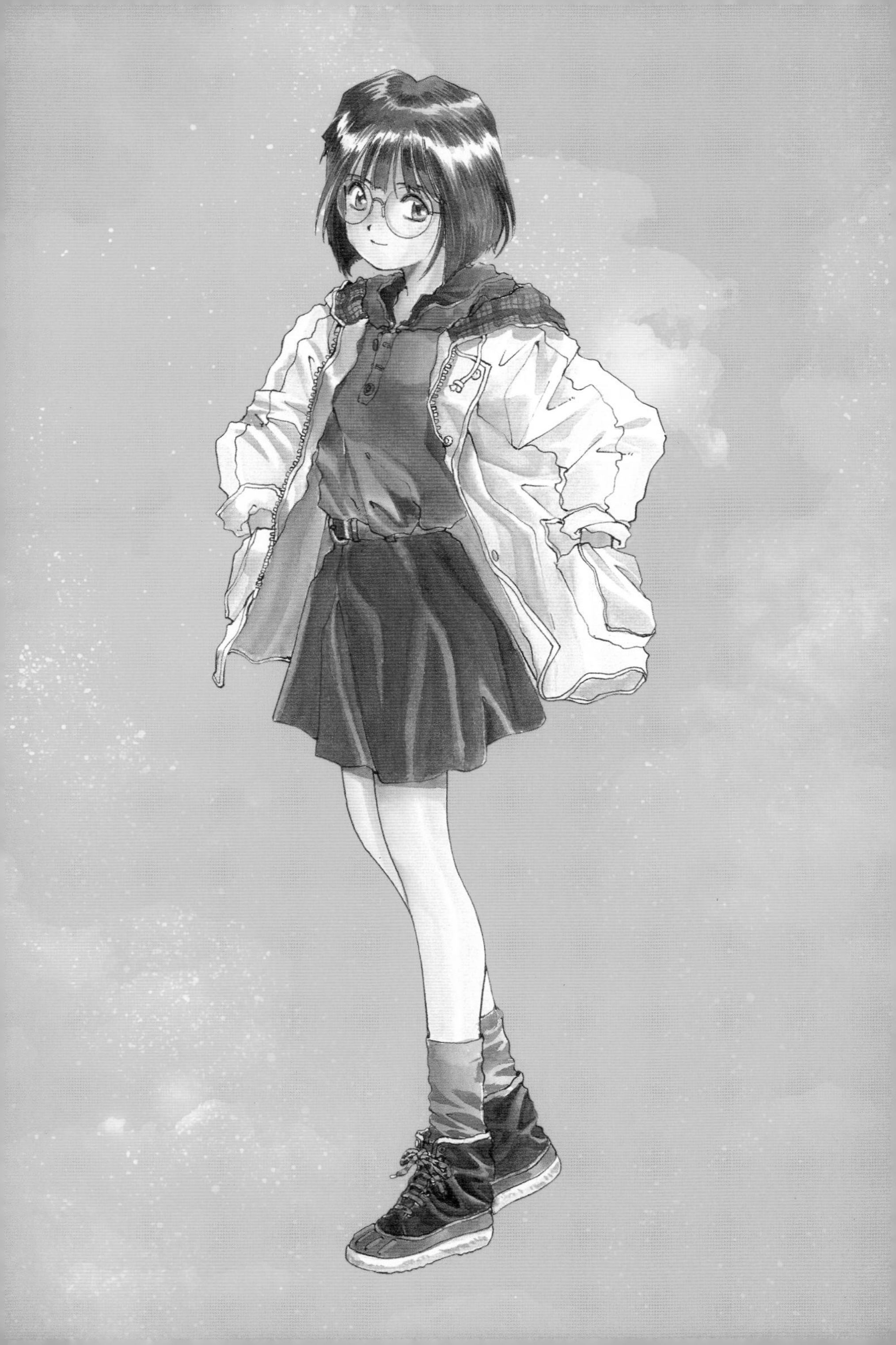

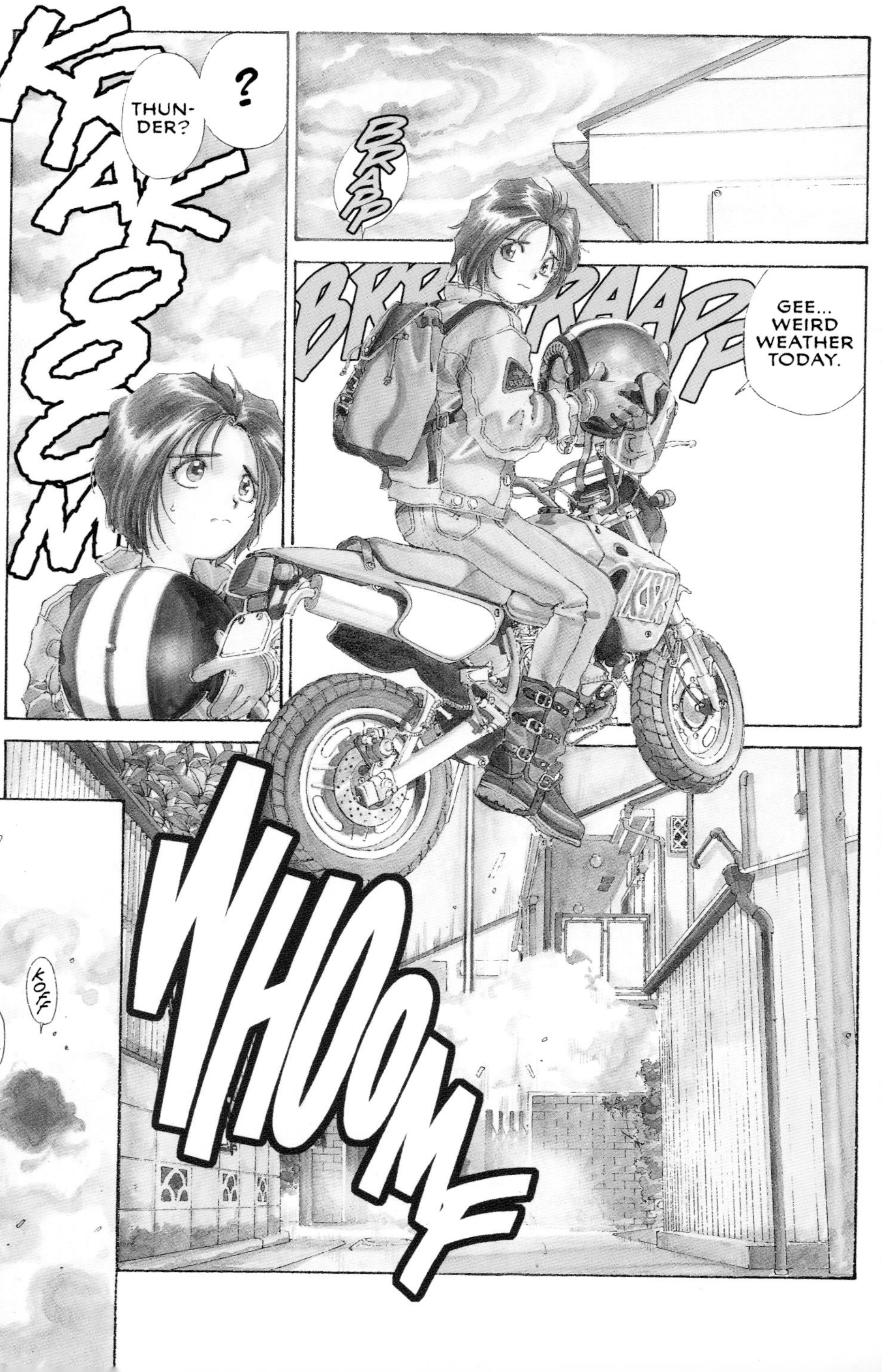
BRAP
BRRRRAAPP
GEE... WEIRD WEATHER TODAY.
KRAKOOOM
?
THUN-DER?
WHOOMF
KOFF
KOFF

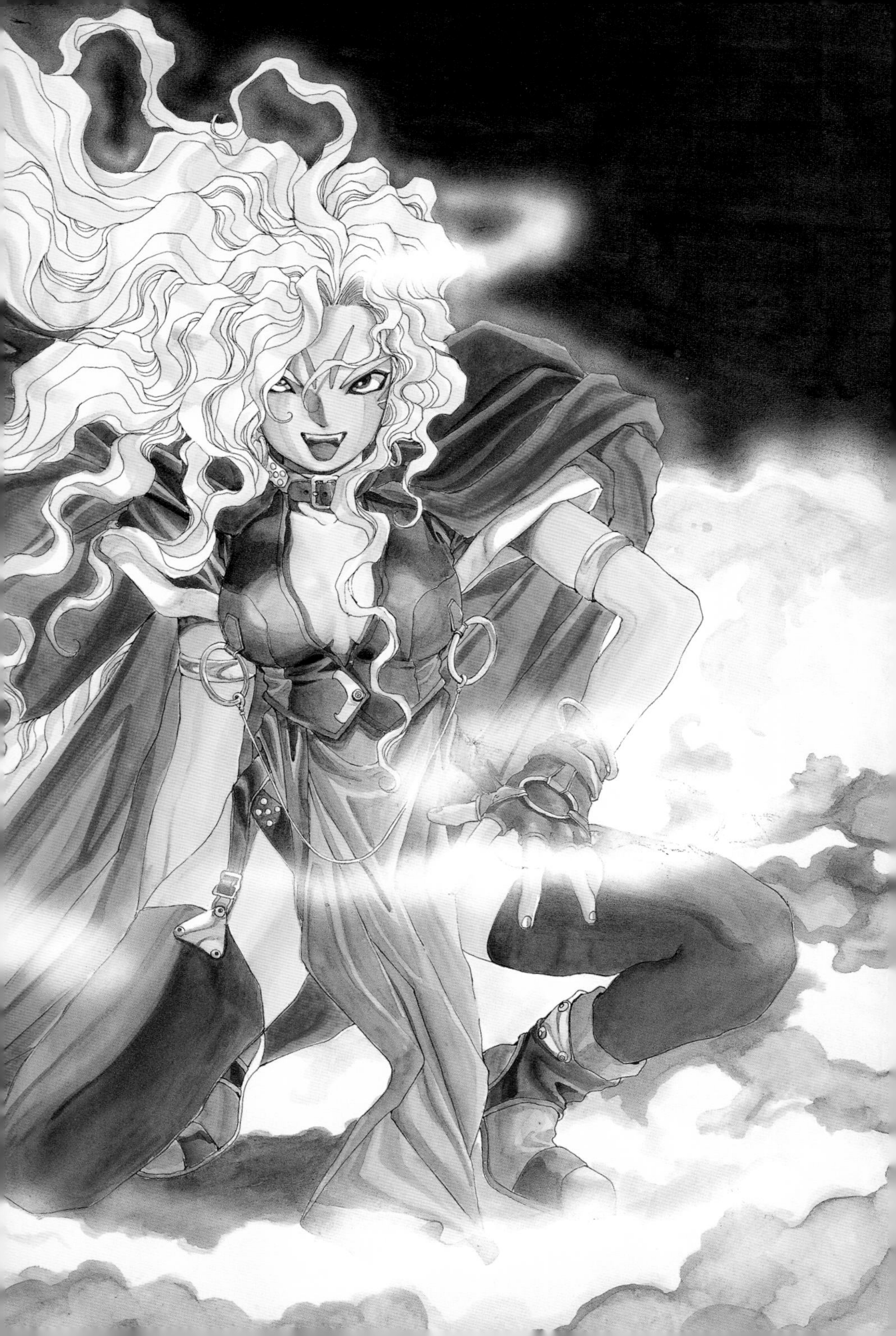

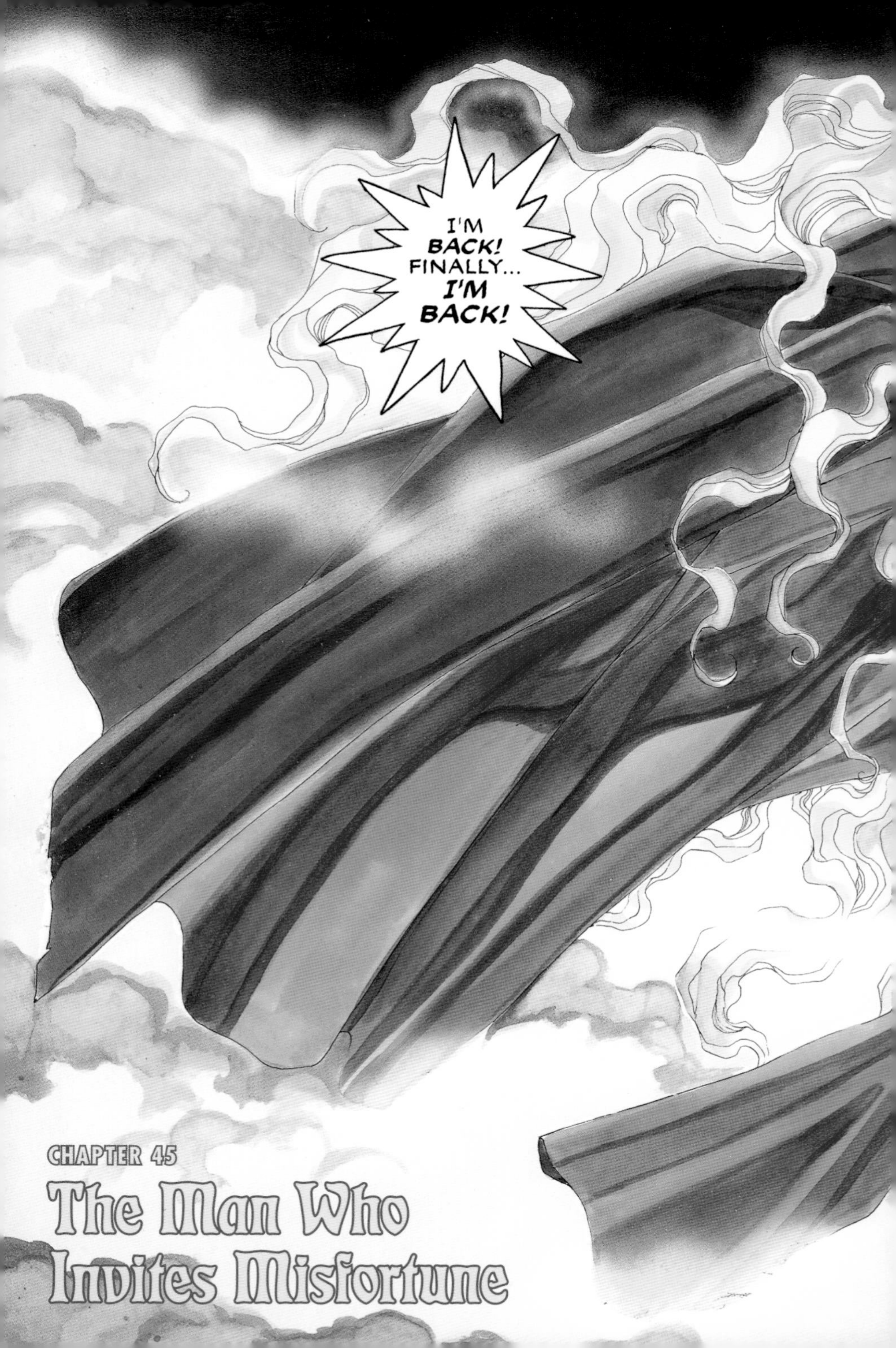
I'M BACK! FINALLY... I'M BACK!

CHAPTER 45

The Man Who Invites Misfortune

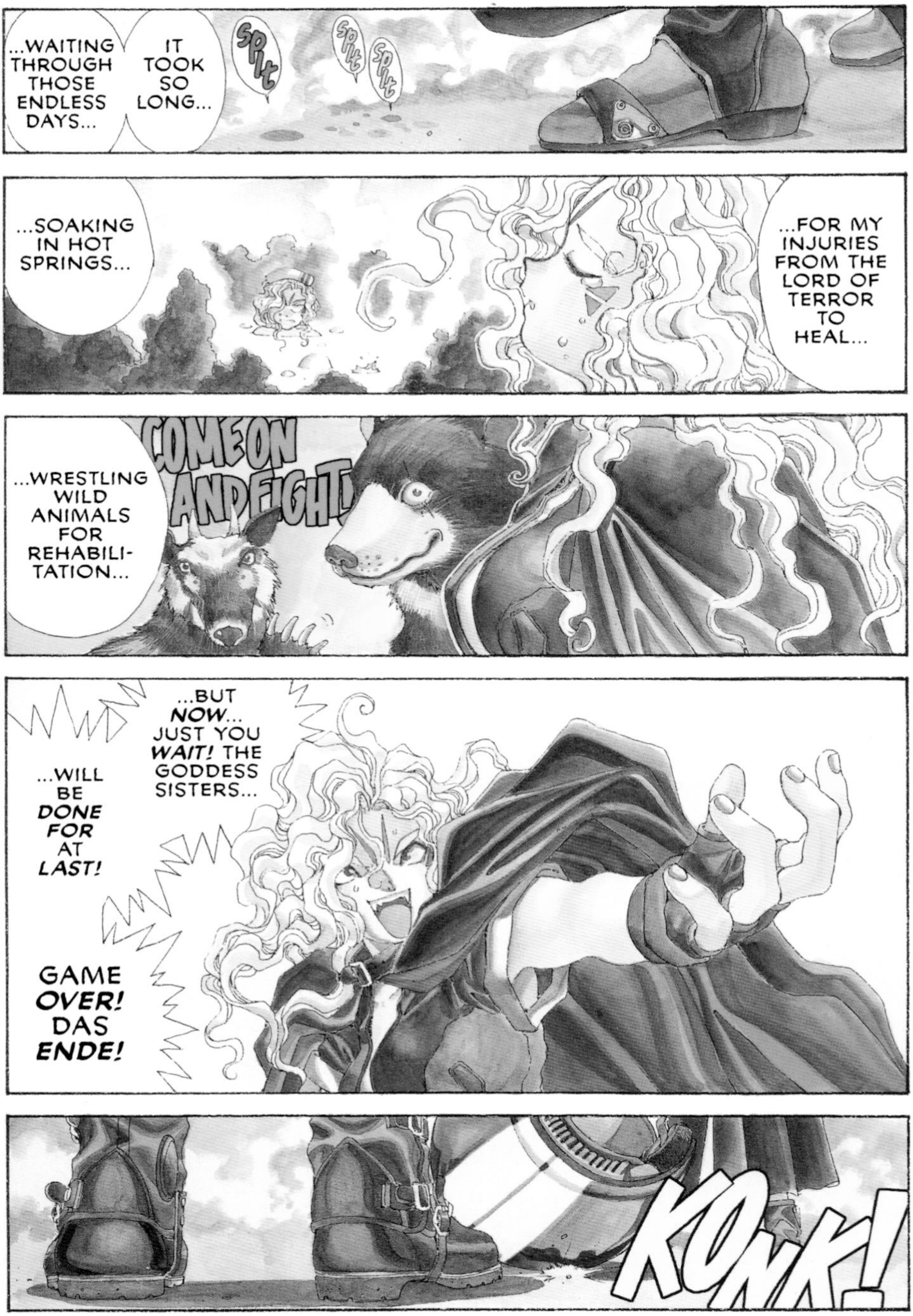
Spit
Spit
Spit
IT TOOK SO LONG...
...WAITING THROUGH THOSE ENDLESS DAYS...
...FOR MY INJURIES FROM THE LORD OF TERROR TO HEAL...
...SOAKING IN HOT SPRINGS...
COME ON AND FIGHT!
...WRESTLING WILD ANIMALS FOR REHABILITATION...
...BUT *NOW*... JUST YOU *WAIT!* THE GODDESS SISTERS...
...WILL BE *DONE FOR* AT *LAST!*
GAME *OVER!* DAS *ENDE!*
KONK!

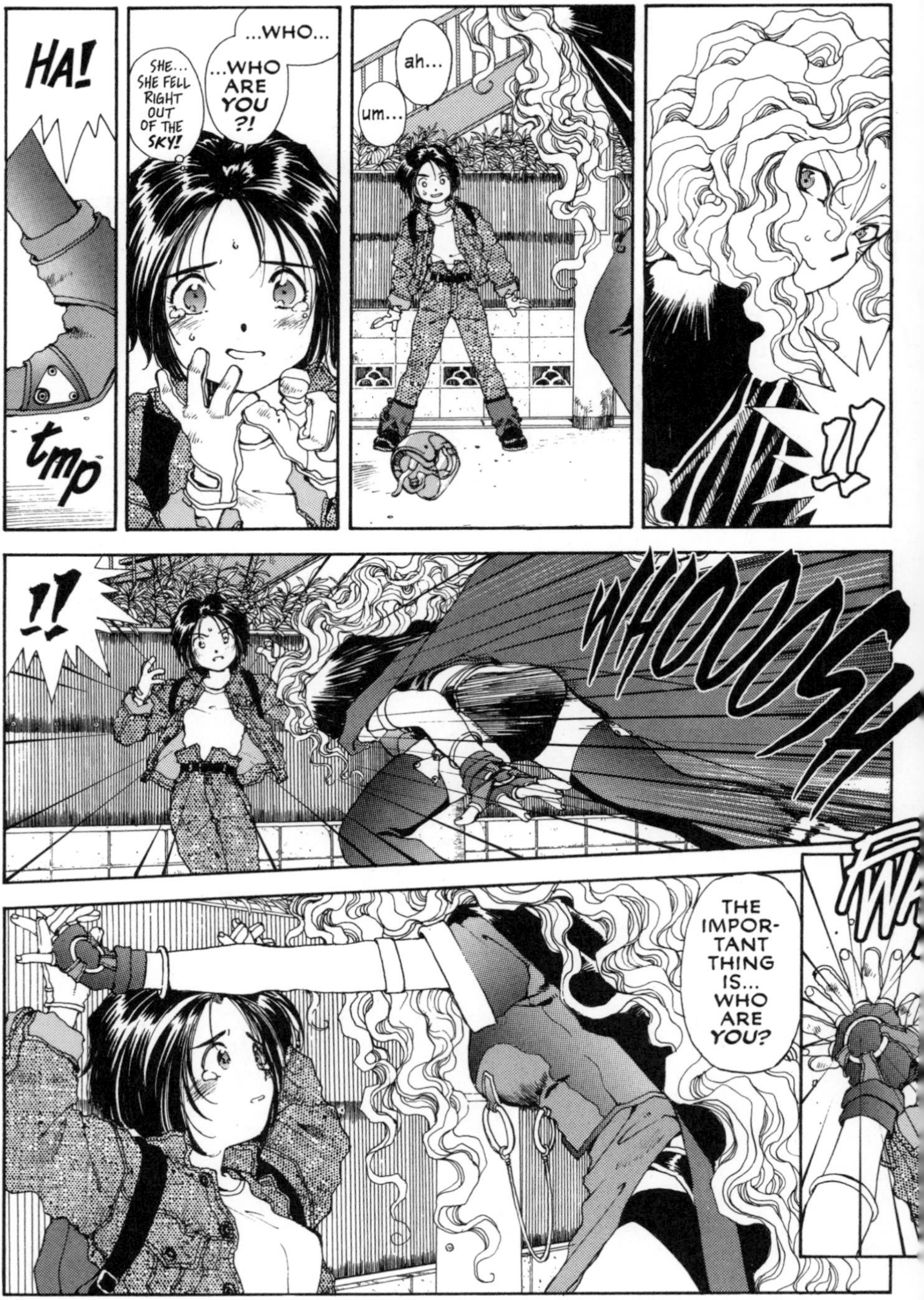
!!
ah...
um...
...WHO...
...WHO ARE YOU?!
SHE... SHE FELL RIGHT OUT OF THE SKY!
HA!
tmp
WHOOOSH
!!
THE IMPORTANT THING IS... WHO ARE YOU?

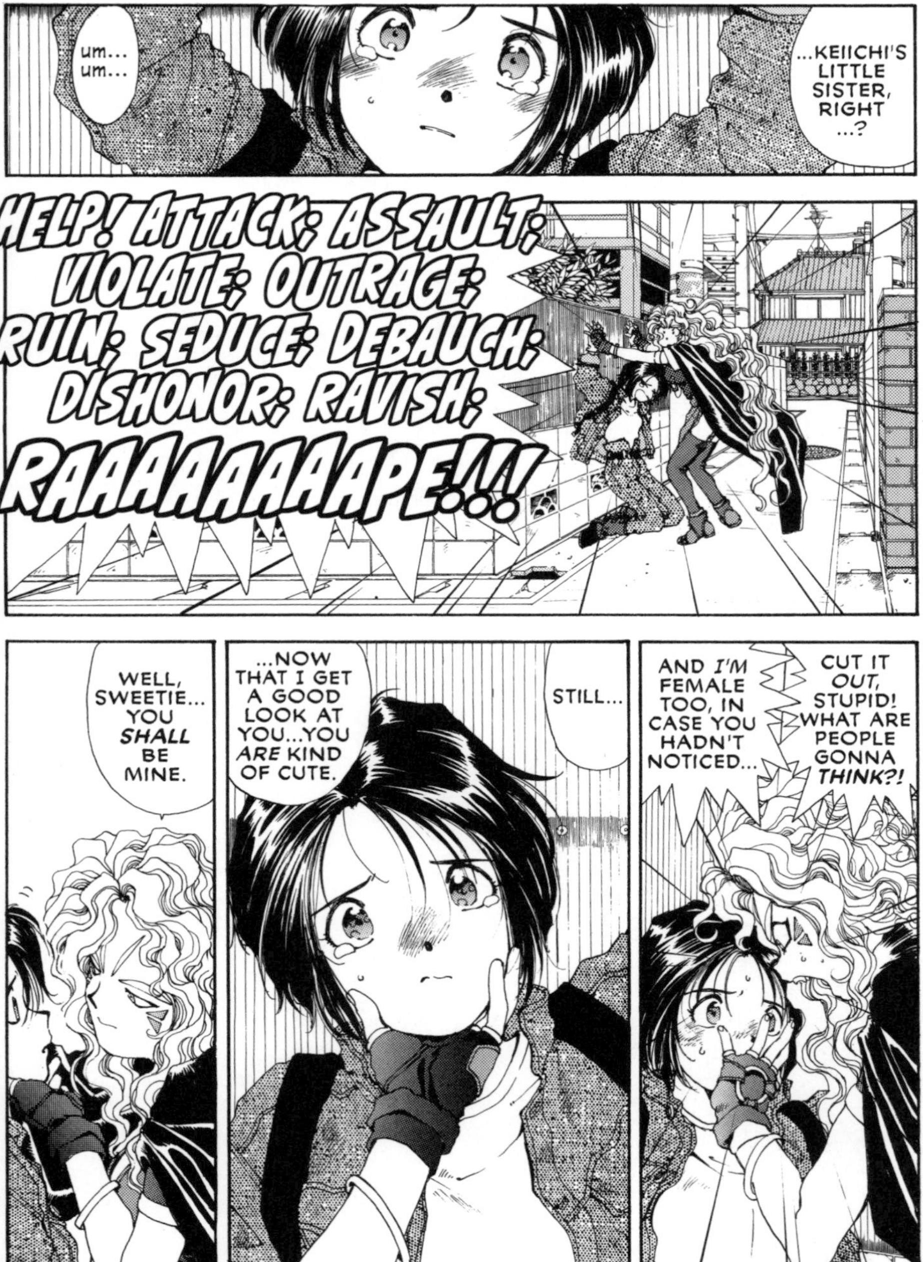
...KEIICHI'S LITTLE SISTER, RIGHT ...?
um... um...
HELP! ATTACK; ASSAULT; VIOLATE; OUTRAGE; RUIN; SEDUCE; DEBAUCH; DISHONOR; RAVISH; RAAAAAAAAAPE!!!
CUT IT *OUT*, STUPID! WHAT ARE PEOPLE GONNA *THINK?!*
AND *I'M* FEMALE TOO, IN CASE YOU HADN'T NOTICED...
STILL...
...NOW THAT I GET A GOOD LOOK AT YOU...YOU *ARE* KIND OF CUTE.
WELL, SWEETIE... YOU *SHALL* BE MINE.

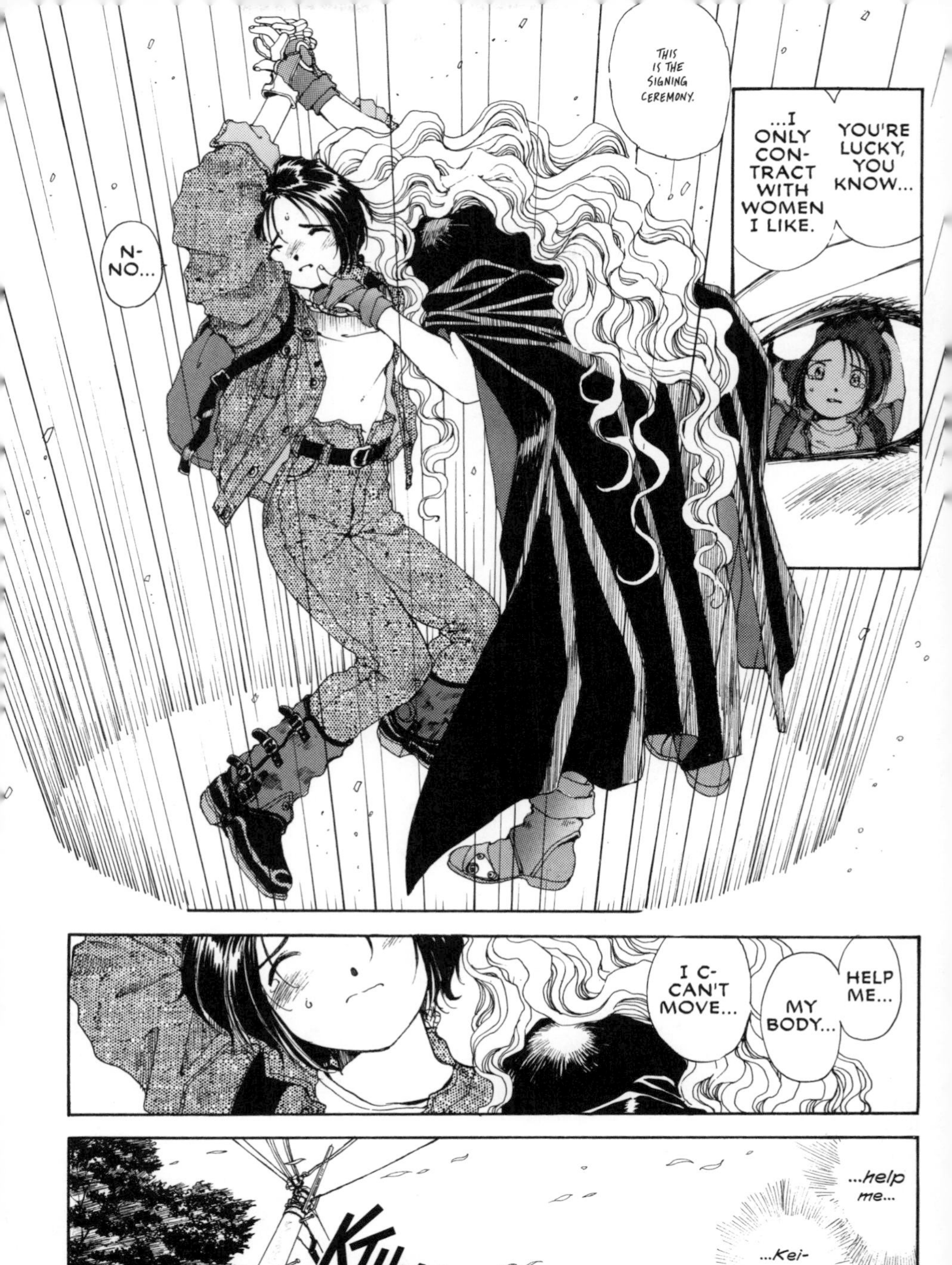
YOU'RE LUCKY, YOU KNOW...
...I ONLY CONTRACT WITH WOMEN I LIKE.
THIS IS THE SIGNING CEREMONY.
N-NO...
HELP ME...
MY BODY...
I C-CAN'T MOVE...
...help me...
...Kei-chan...
KTHMP

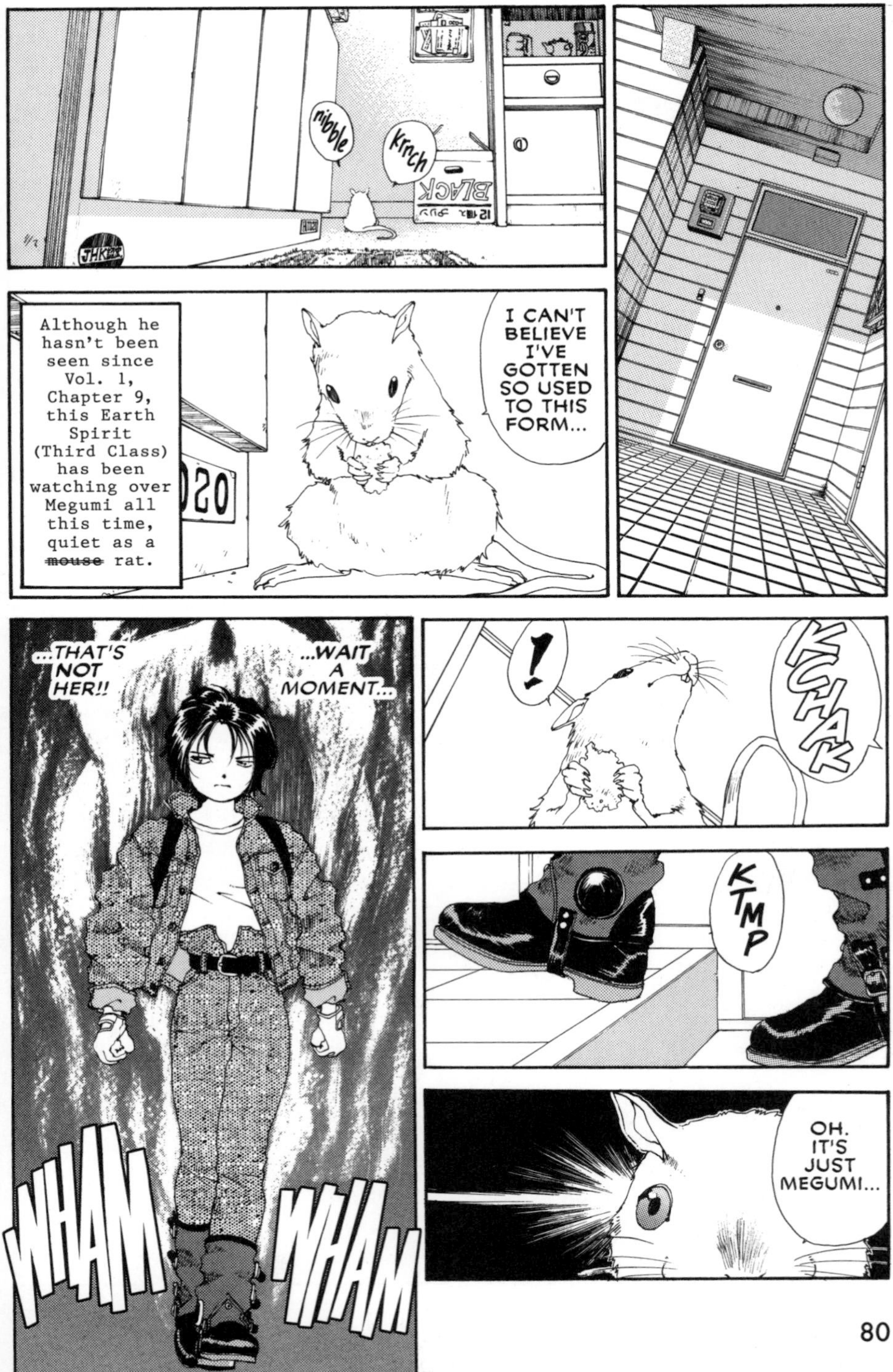
ribble
krrch
I CAN'T BELIEVE I'VE GOTTEN SO USED TO THIS FORM...
Although he hasn't been seen since Vol. 1, Chapter 9, this Earth Spirit (Third Class) has been watching over Megumi all this time, quiet as a ~~mouse~~ rat.
KCHAK
!
KTMP
OH. IT'S JUST MEGUMI...
...WAIT A MOMENT...
...THAT'S NOT HER!!
WHAM
WHAM

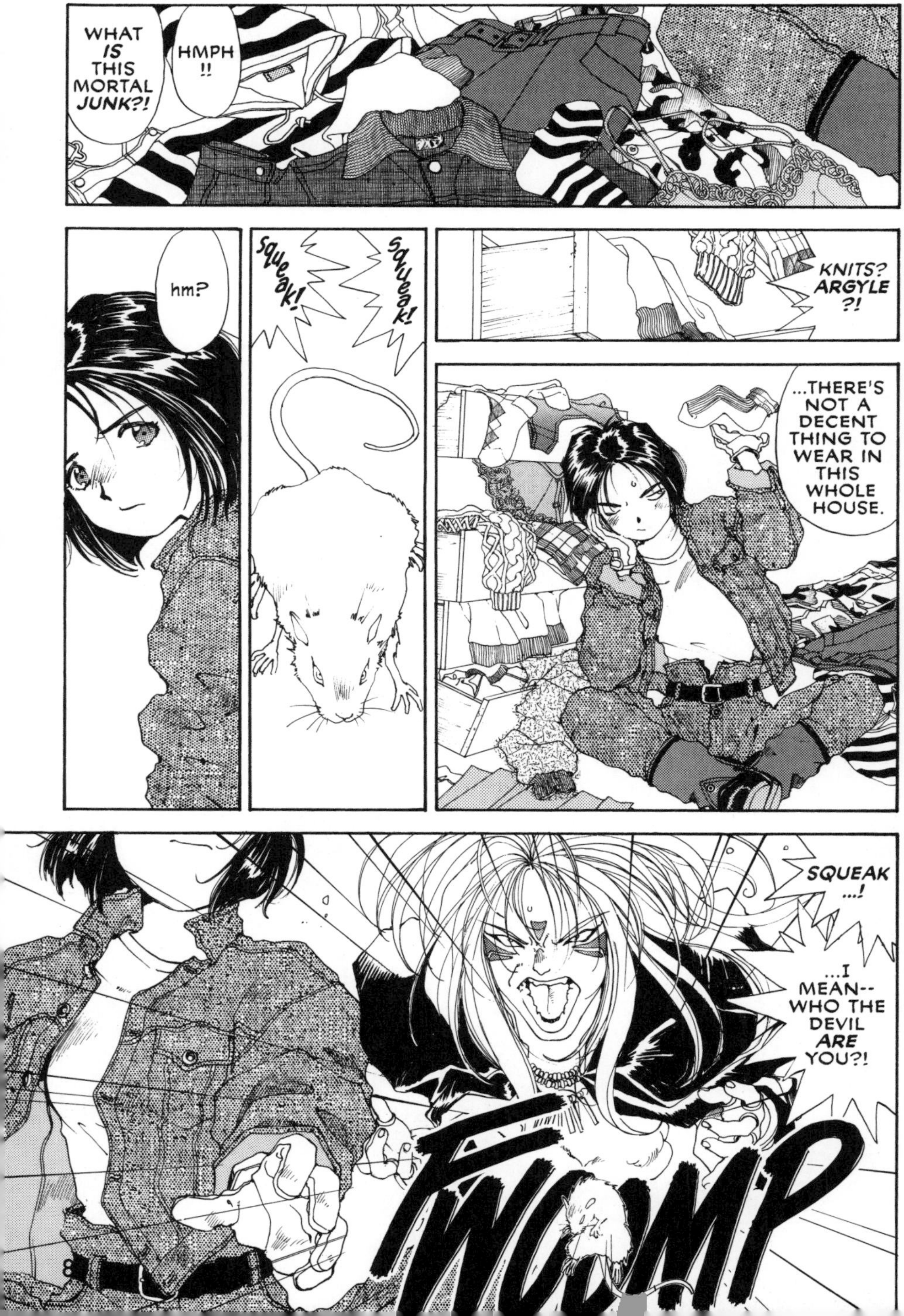
HMPH !!
WHAT IS THIS MORTAL JUNK?!
KNITS? ARGYLE ?!
...THERE'S NOT A DECENT THING TO WEAR IN THIS WHOLE HOUSE.
squeak!
squeak!
hm?
SQUEAK ...!
...I MEAN-- WHO THE DEVIL ARE YOU?!
THOMP

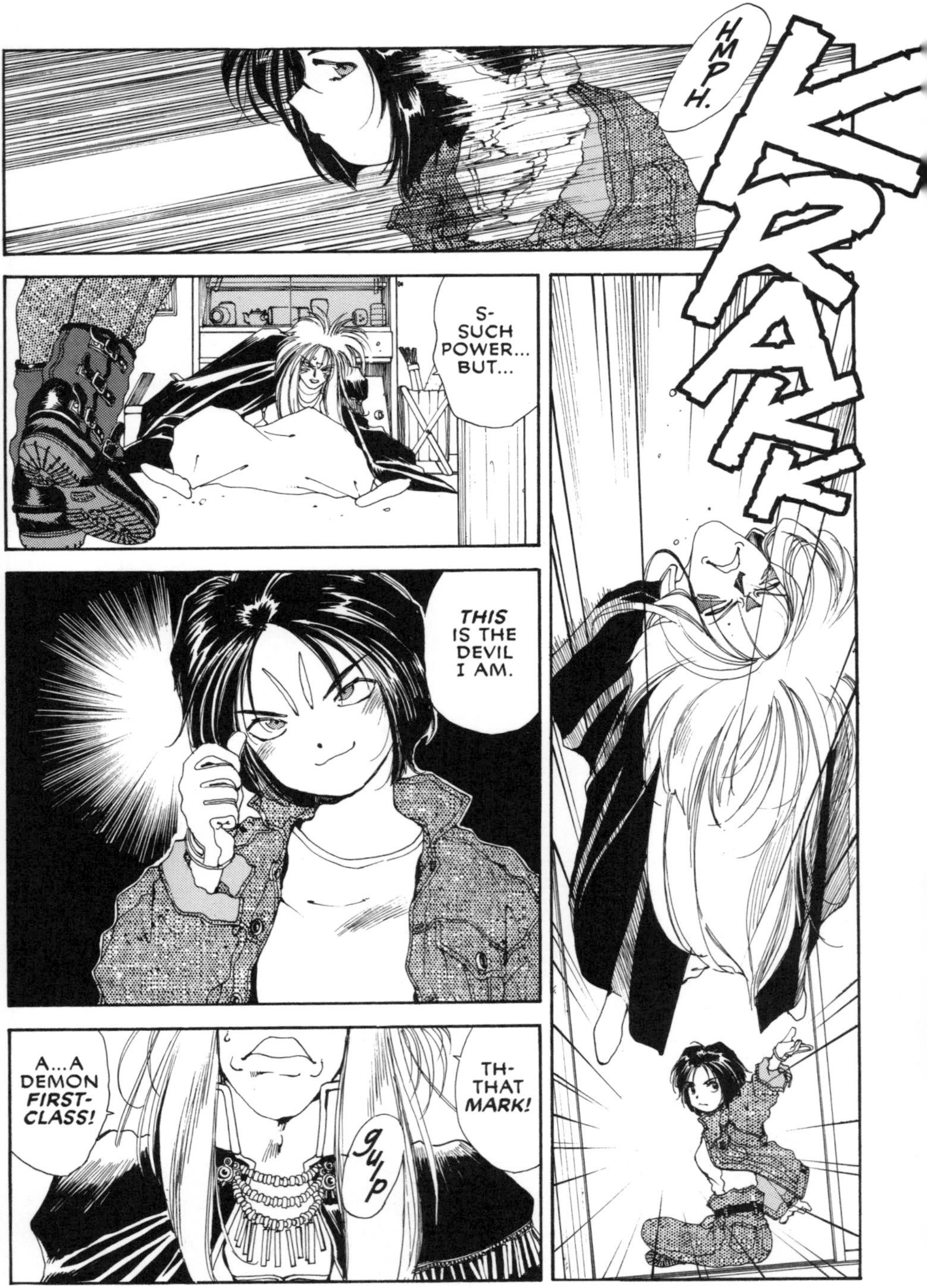
HMPH.
KRAKK
S-SUCH POWER... BUT...
THIS IS THE DEVIL I AM.
TH-THAT MARK!
gulp
A...A DEMON FIRST-CLASS!

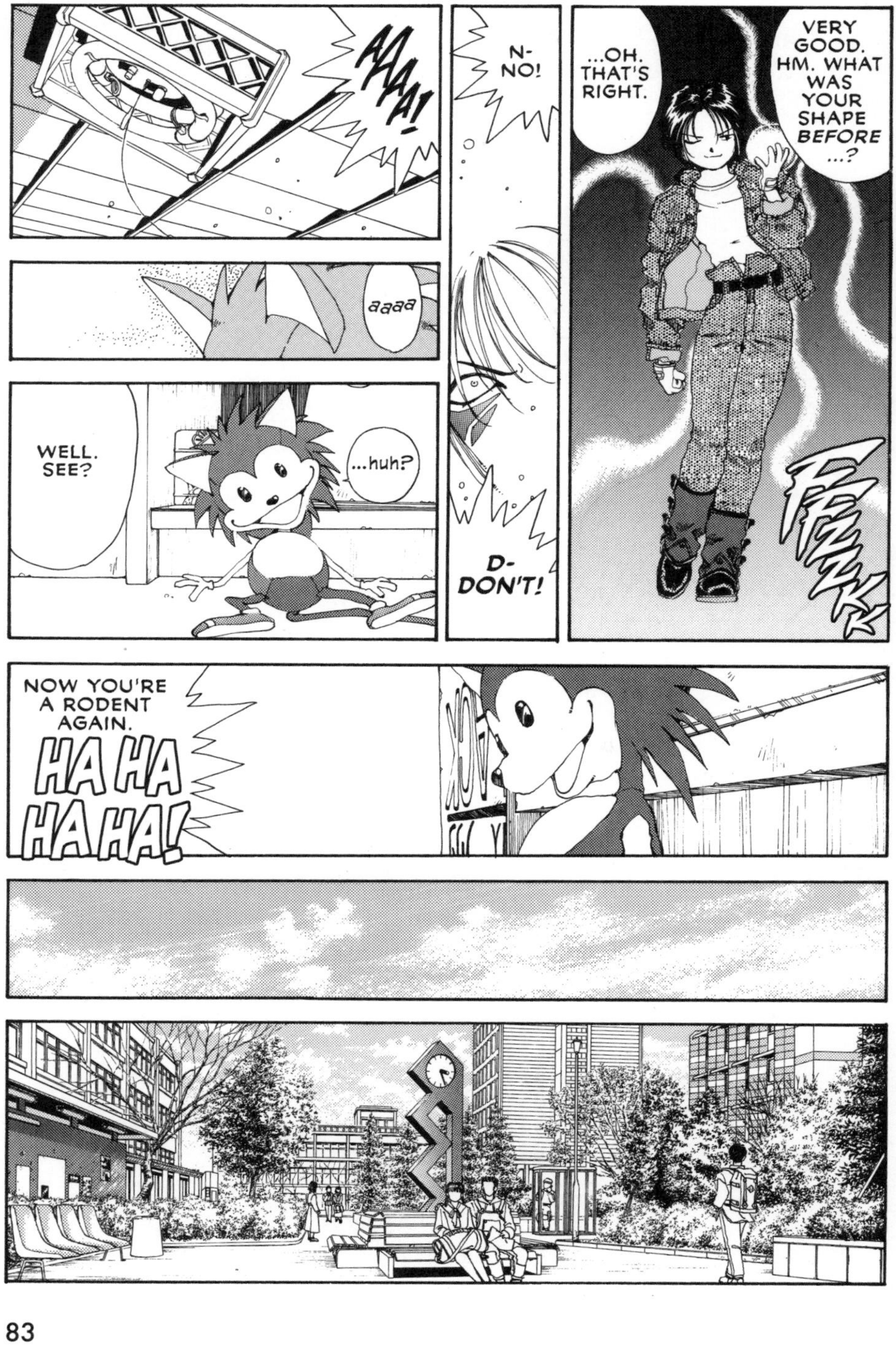
VERY GOOD. HM. WHAT WAS YOUR SHAPE BEFORE ...?
...OH. THAT'S RIGHT.
N- NO!
D- DON'T!
AAAAA!
aaaa
...huh?
WELL. SEE?
NOW YOU'RE A RODENT AGAIN.
HA HA HA HA!

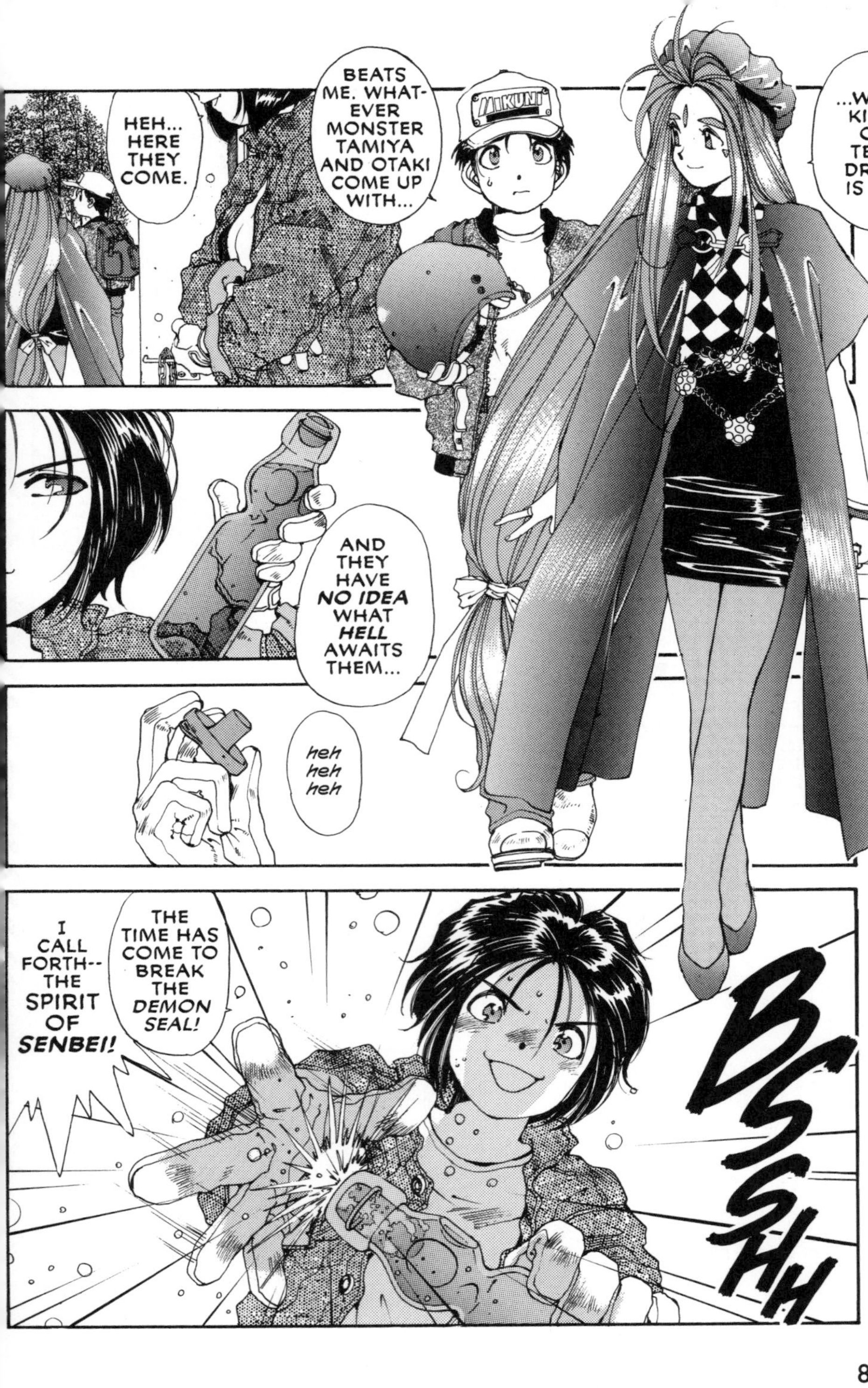
...WHAT KIND OF TEST DRIVE IS IT?
BEATS ME. WHAT-EVER MONSTER TAMIYA AND OTAKI COME UP WITH...
HEH... HERE THEY COME.
AND THEY HAVE *NO IDEA* WHAT *HELL* AWAITS THEM...
heh heh heh
THE TIME HAS COME TO BREAK THE *DEMON SEAL!*
I CALL FORTH-- THE SPIRIT OF *SENBEI!*
BSSHH

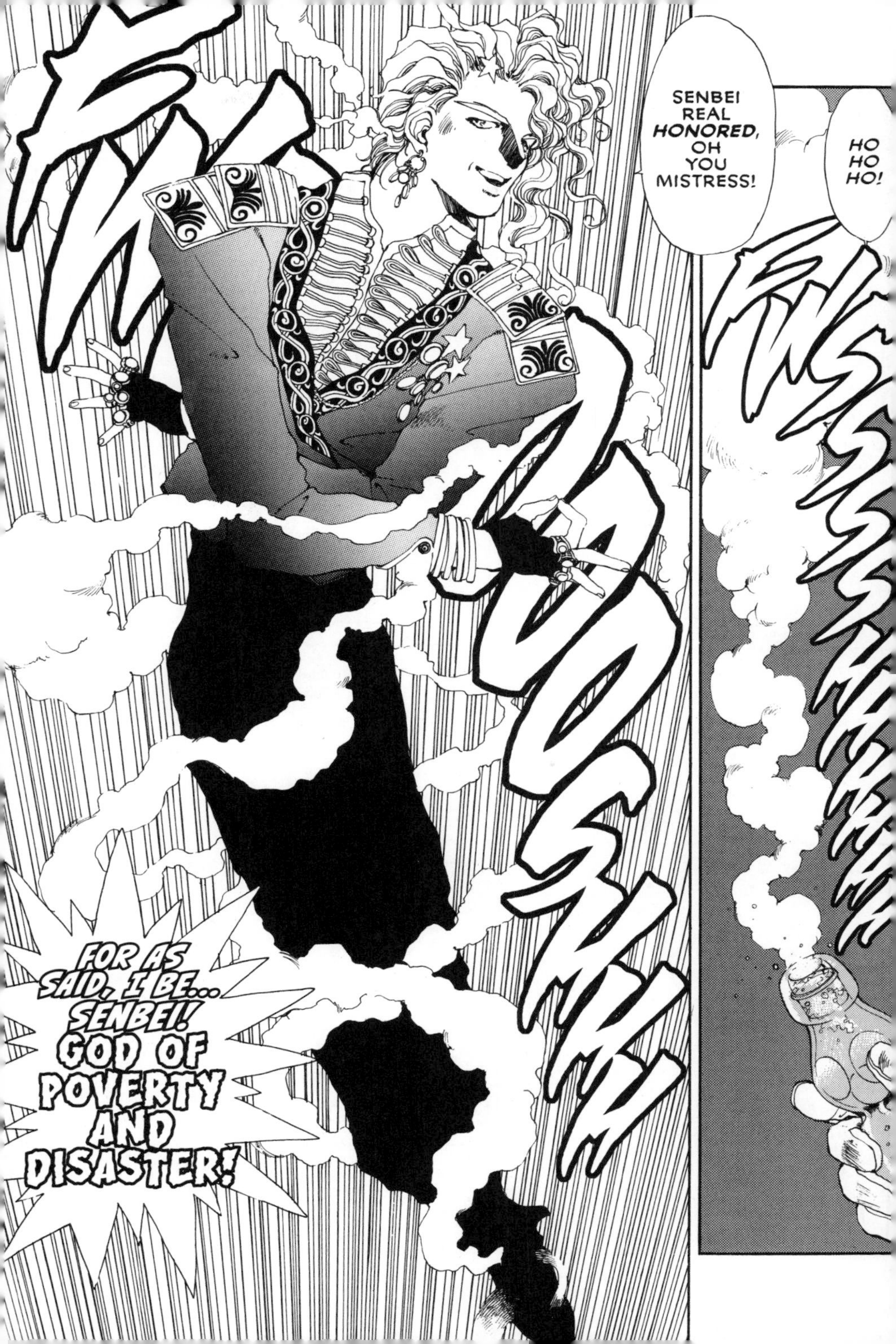
HO HO HO!
SENBEI REAL HONORED, OH YOU MISTRESS!
FOR AS SAID, I BE... SENBEI! GOD OF POVERTY AND DISASTER!

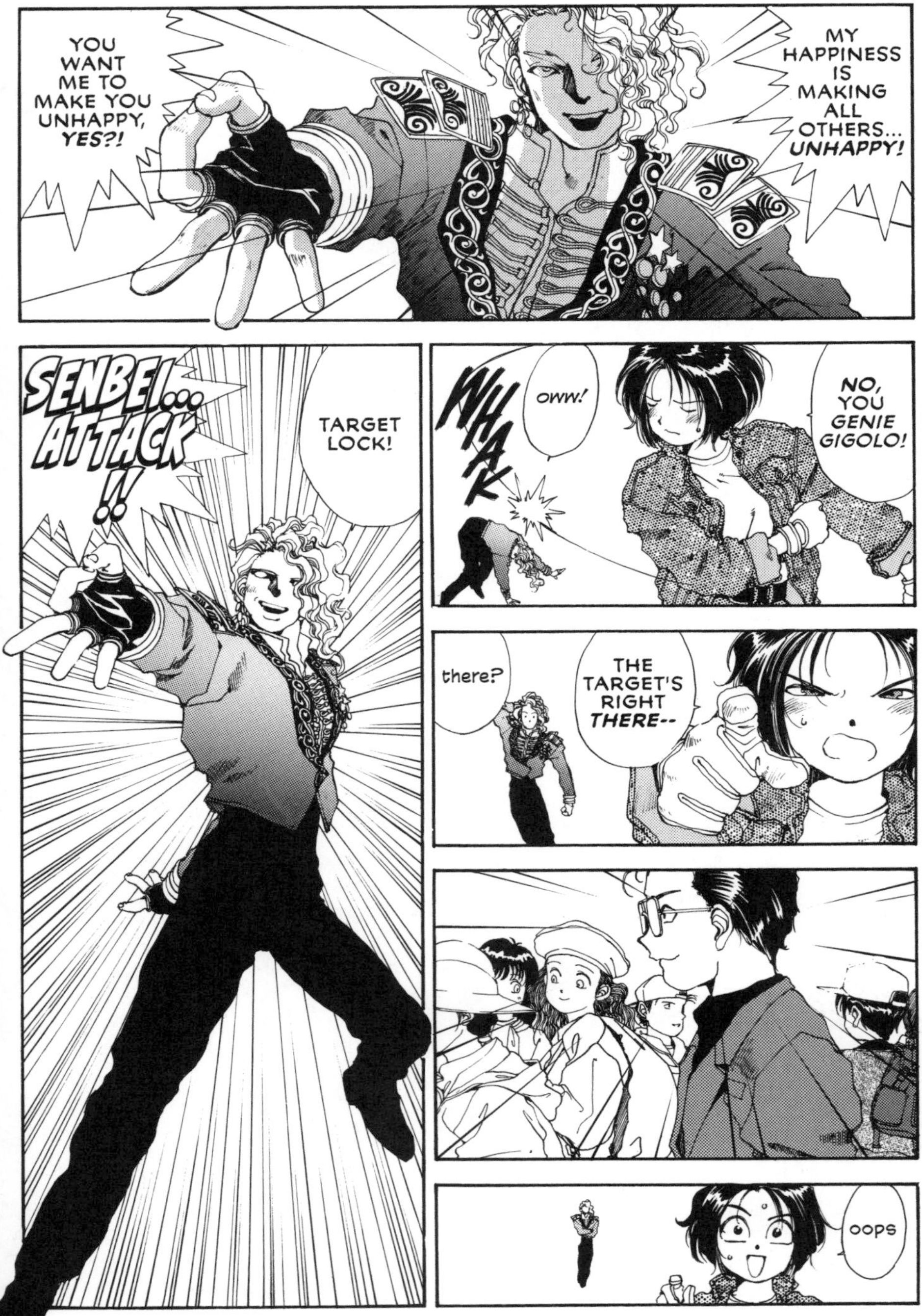
MY HAPPINESS IS MAKING ALL OTHERS... *UNHAPPY!*
YOU WANT ME TO MAKE YOU UNHAPPY, *YES?!*
NO, YOU GENIE GIGOLO!
OWW!
WHAK
THE TARGET'S RIGHT *THERE--*
there?
oops
TARGET LOCK!
SENBEI... ATTACK!!

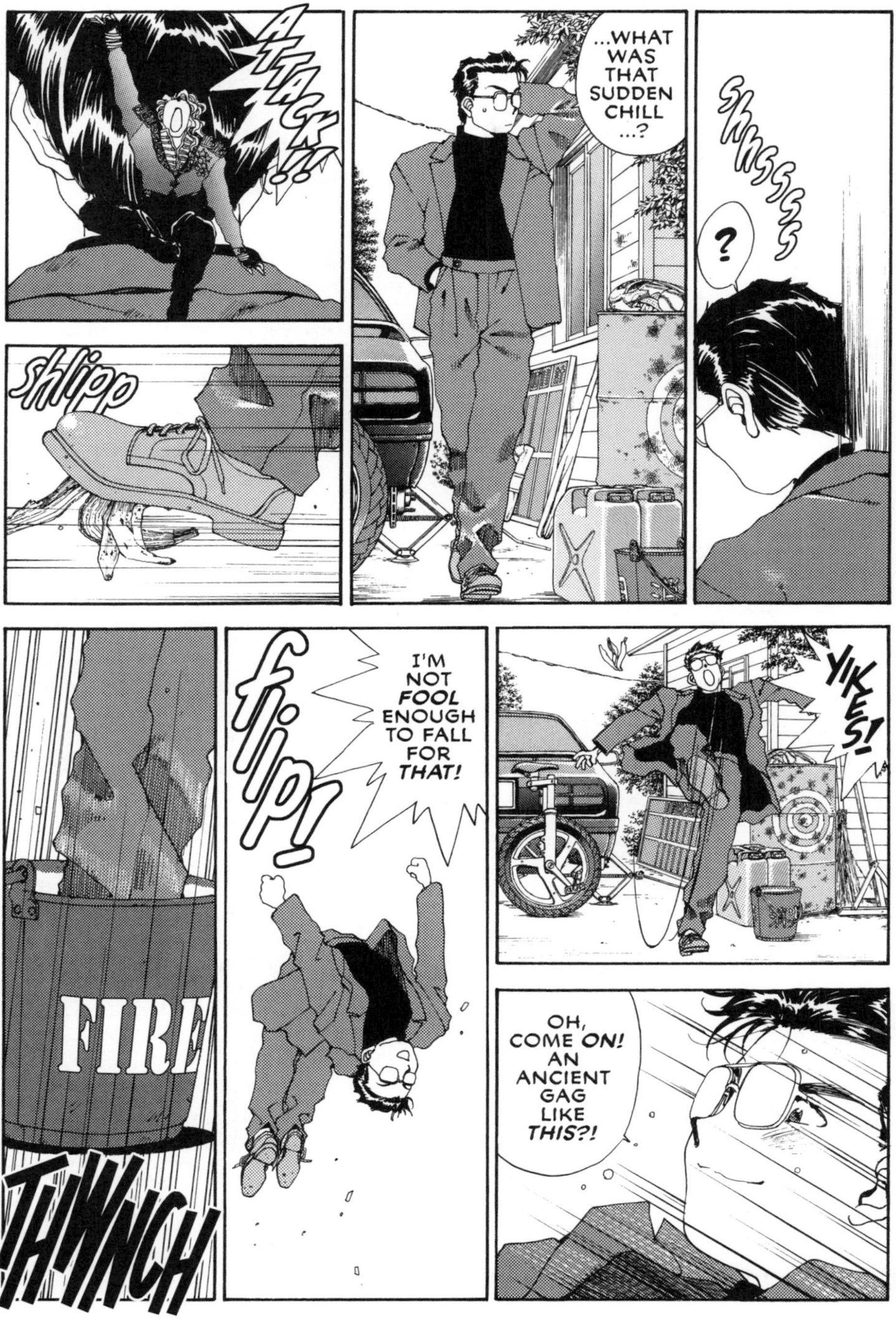

SHHSSSSS
?
...WHAT WAS THAT SUDDEN CHILL ...?
ATTACK!!
shlipp
YIKES!
OH, COME *ON!* AN ANCIENT GAG LIKE *THIS?!*
flip!
I'M NOT *FOOL* ENOUGH TO FALL FOR *THAT!*
FIRE
THWNCH

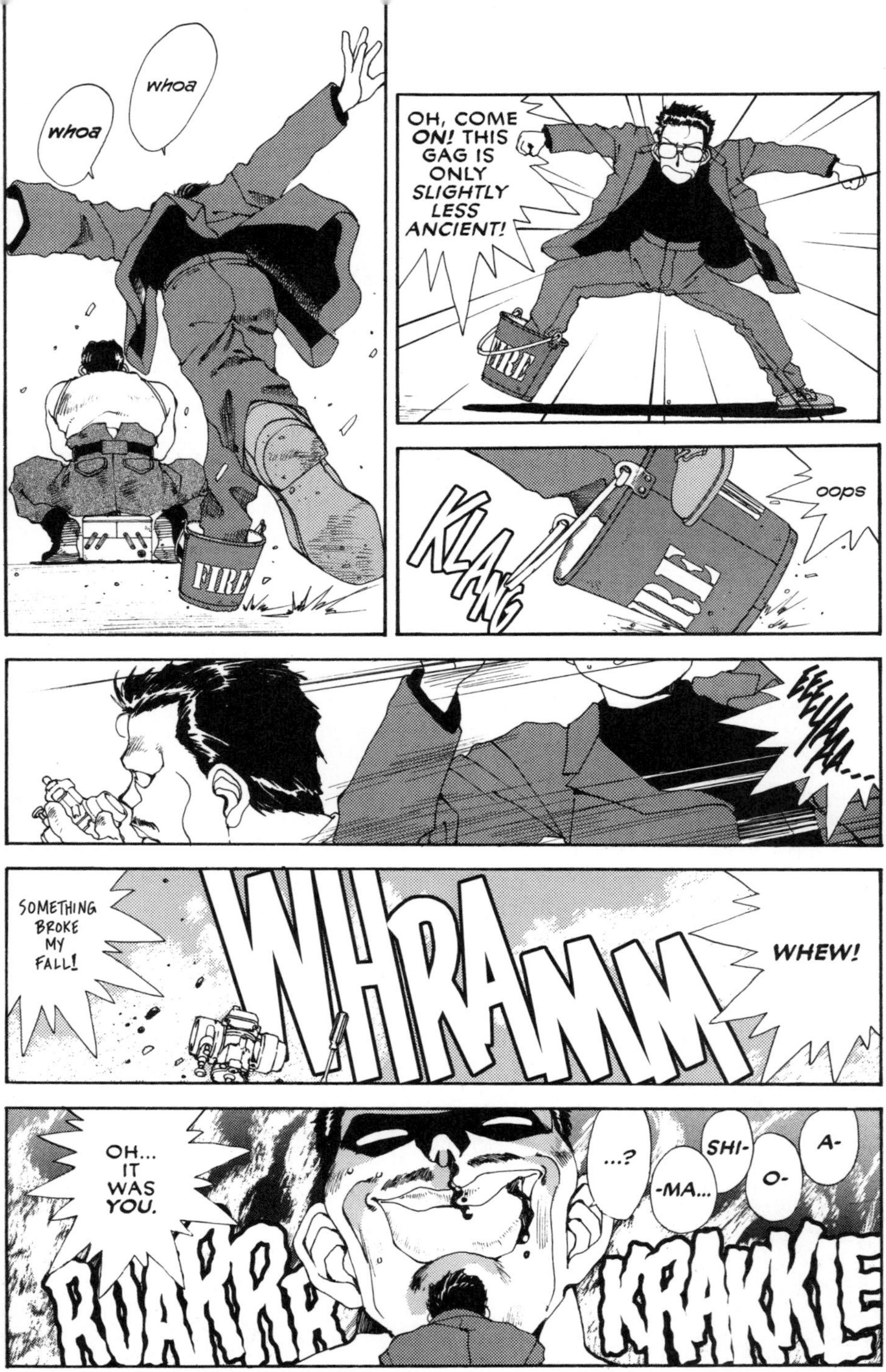
OH, COME ON! THIS GAG IS ONLY SLIGHTLY LESS ANCIENT!
FIRE
oops
KLANG
FIRE
whoa
whoa
FIRE
EEEYAAAA...
WHEW!
WHRAMM
SOMETHING BROKE MY FALL!
A-
O-
SHI-
-MA...
...?
KRAKKLE
OH... IT WAS YOU.

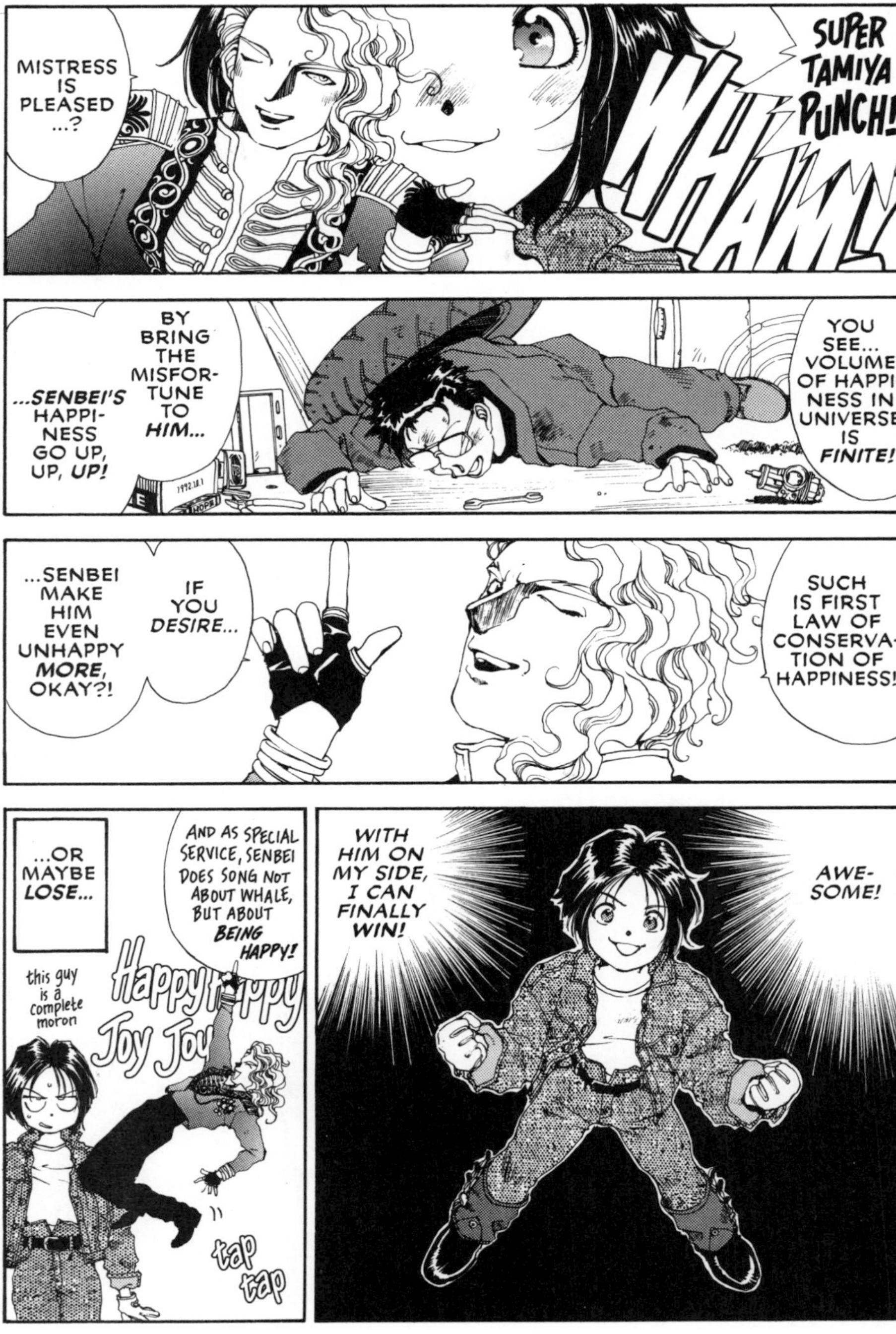
SUPER TAMIYA PUNCH!
WHAM!
MISTRESS IS PLEASED ...?
YOU SEE... VOLUME OF HAPPINESS IN UNIVERSE IS FINITE!
BY BRING THE MISFORTUNE TO HIM...
...SENBEI'S HAPPINESS GO UP, UP, UP!
SUCH IS FIRST LAW OF CONSERVATION OF HAPPINESS!
IF YOU DESIRE...
...SENBEI MAKE HIM EVEN UNHAPPY MORE, OKAY?!
AWESOME!
WITH HIM ON MY SIDE, I CAN FINALLY WIN!
AND AS SPECIAL SERVICE, SENBEI DOES SONG NOT ABOUT WHALE, BUT ABOUT BEING HAPPY!
...OR MAYBE LOSE...
Happy Happy Joy Joy
this guy is a complete moron
tap tap

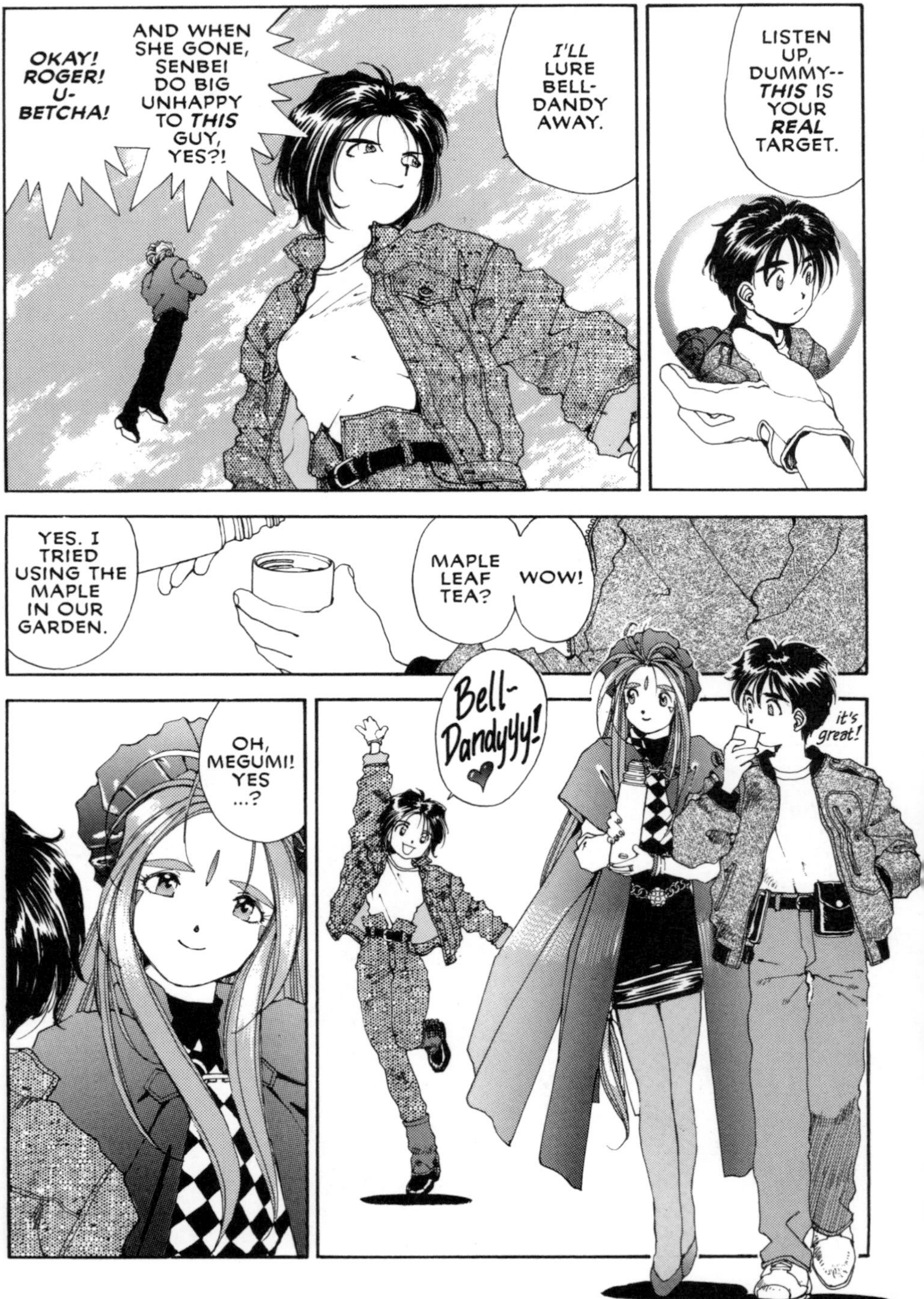
LISTEN UP, DUMMY-- *THIS* IS YOUR *REAL* TARGET.
I'LL LURE BELL-DANDY AWAY.
AND WHEN SHE GONE, SENBEI DO BIG UNHAPPY TO *THIS* GUY, YES?!
OKAY! ROGER! U-BETCHA!
WOW!
MAPLE LEAF TEA?
YES. I TRIED USING THE MAPLE IN OUR GARDEN.
it's great!
Bell-Dandyyy! ♥
OH, MEGUMI! YES ...?

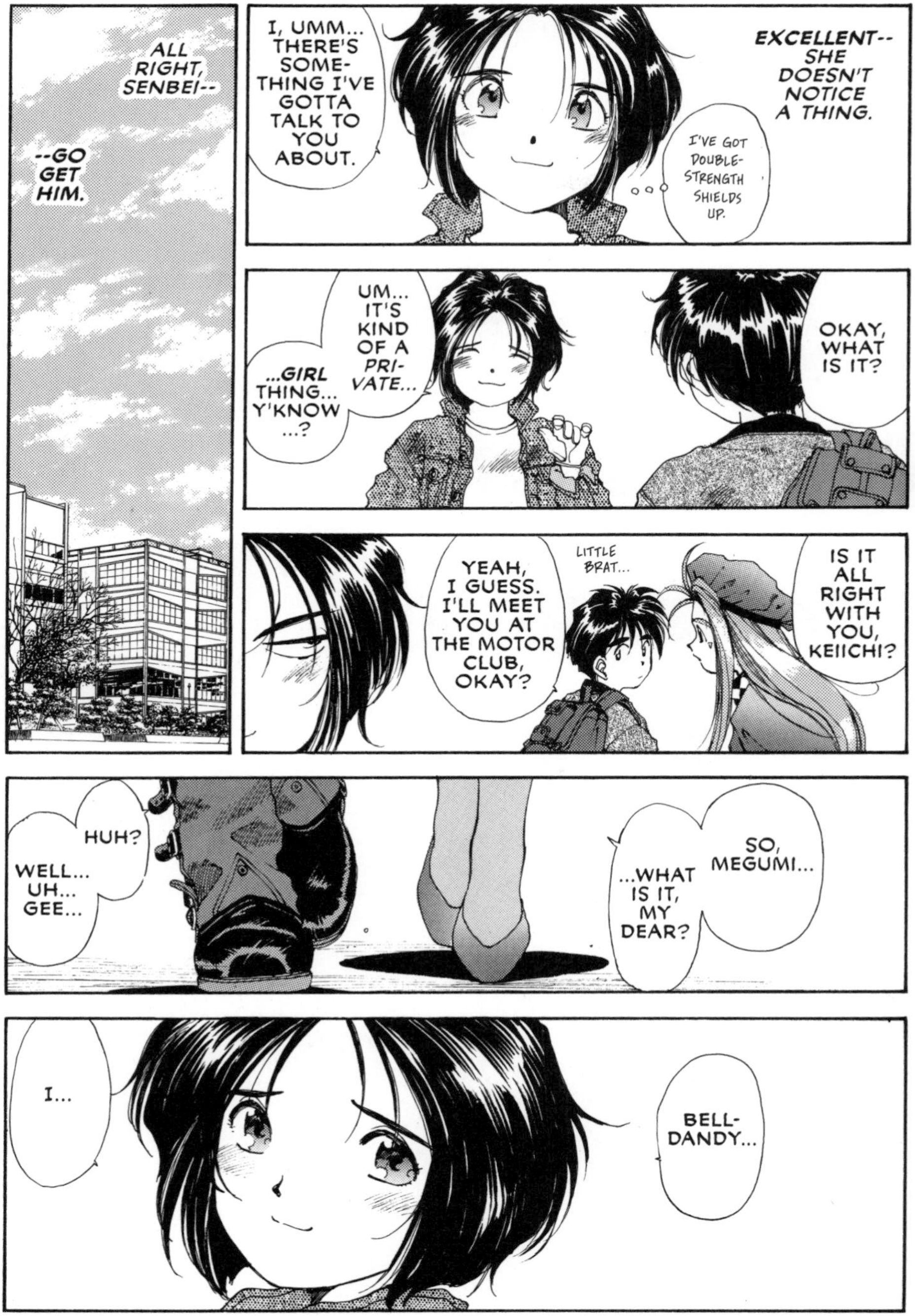
EXCELLENT-- SHE DOESN'T NOTICE A THING.
I'VE GOT DOUBLE-STRENGTH SHIELDS UP.
I, UMM... THERE'S SOME-THING I'VE GOTTA TALK TO YOU ABOUT.
OKAY, WHAT IS IT?
UM... IT'S KIND OF A PRI-VATE...
...GIRL THING... Y'KNOW ...?
IS IT ALL RIGHT WITH YOU, KEIICHI?
LITTLE BRAT...
YEAH, I GUESS. I'LL MEET YOU AT THE MOTOR CLUB, OKAY?
ALL RIGHT, SENBEI--
--GO GET HIM.
SO, MEGUMI...
...WHAT IS IT, MY DEAR?
HUH?
WELL... UH... GEE...
BELL-DANDY...
I...

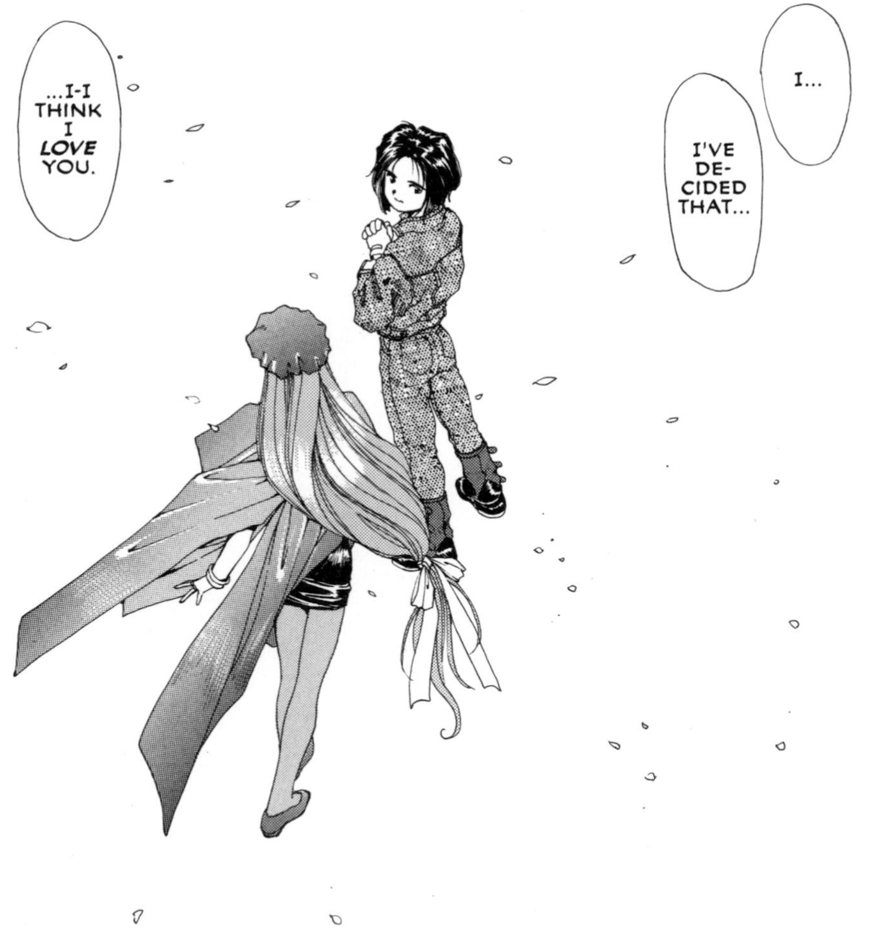
I...
I'VE DE-CIDED THAT...
...I-I THINK I ***LOVE*** YOU.

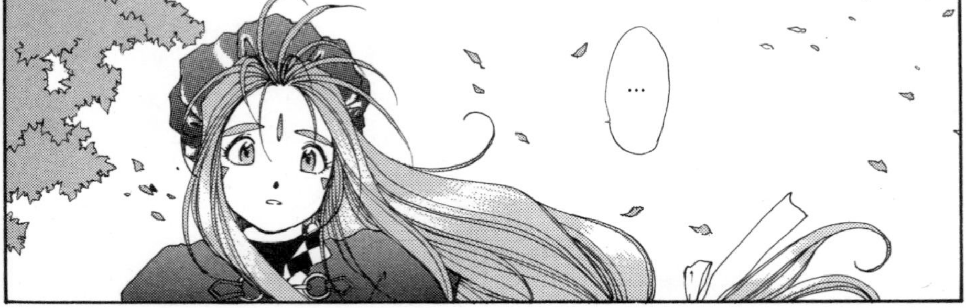
...

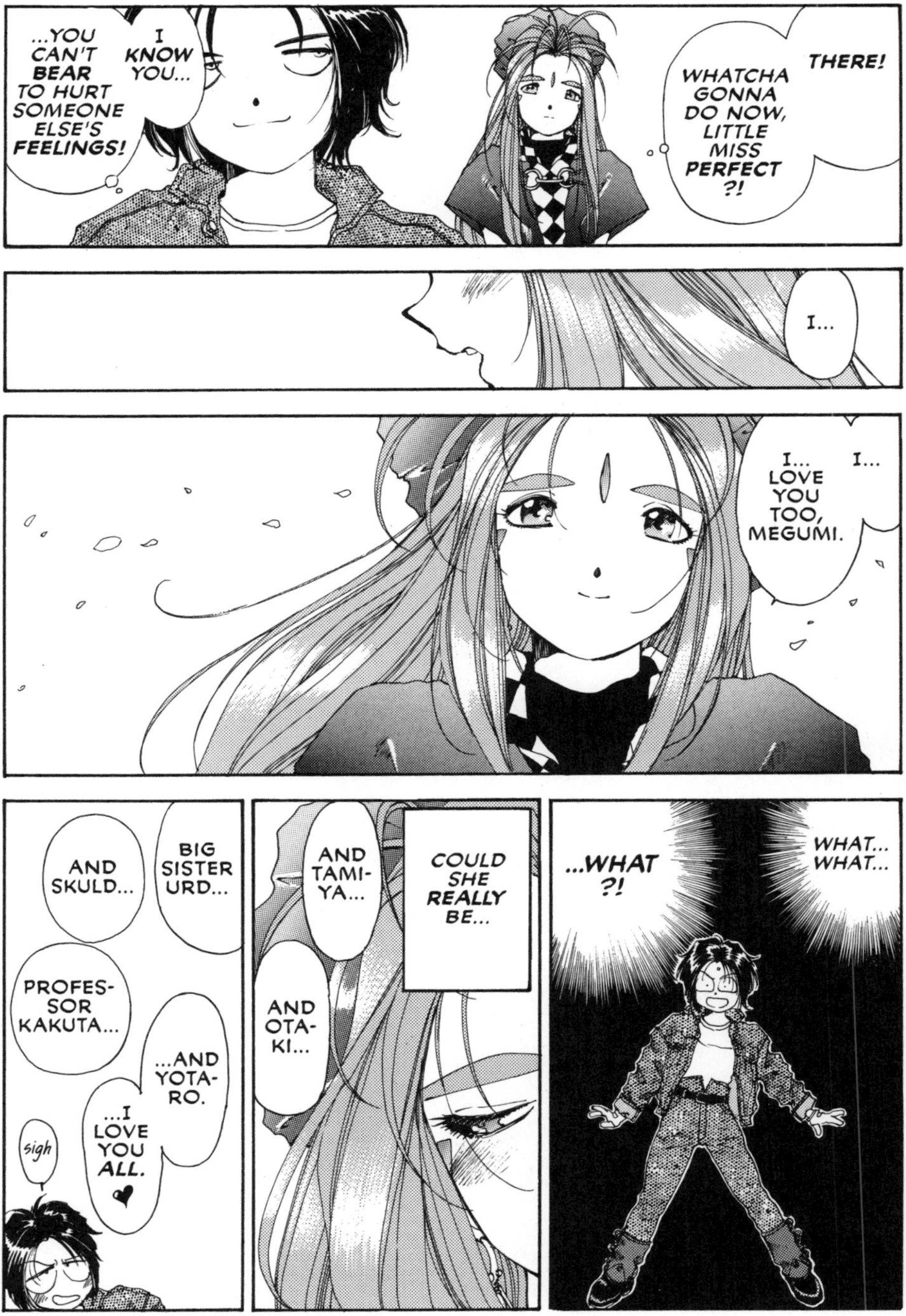
THERE! WHATCHA GONNA DO NOW, LITTLE MISS PERFECT ?!
I KNOW YOU...
...YOU CAN'T BEAR TO HURT SOMEONE ELSE'S FEELINGS!
I...
I... I... LOVE YOU TOO, MEGUMI.
WHAT... WHAT...
...WHAT ?!
COULD SHE REALLY BE...
AND TAMIYA...
AND OTAKI...
BIG SISTER URD...
AND SKULD...
PROFESSOR KAKUTA...
...AND YOTARO.
...I LOVE YOU ALL. ♥
sigh

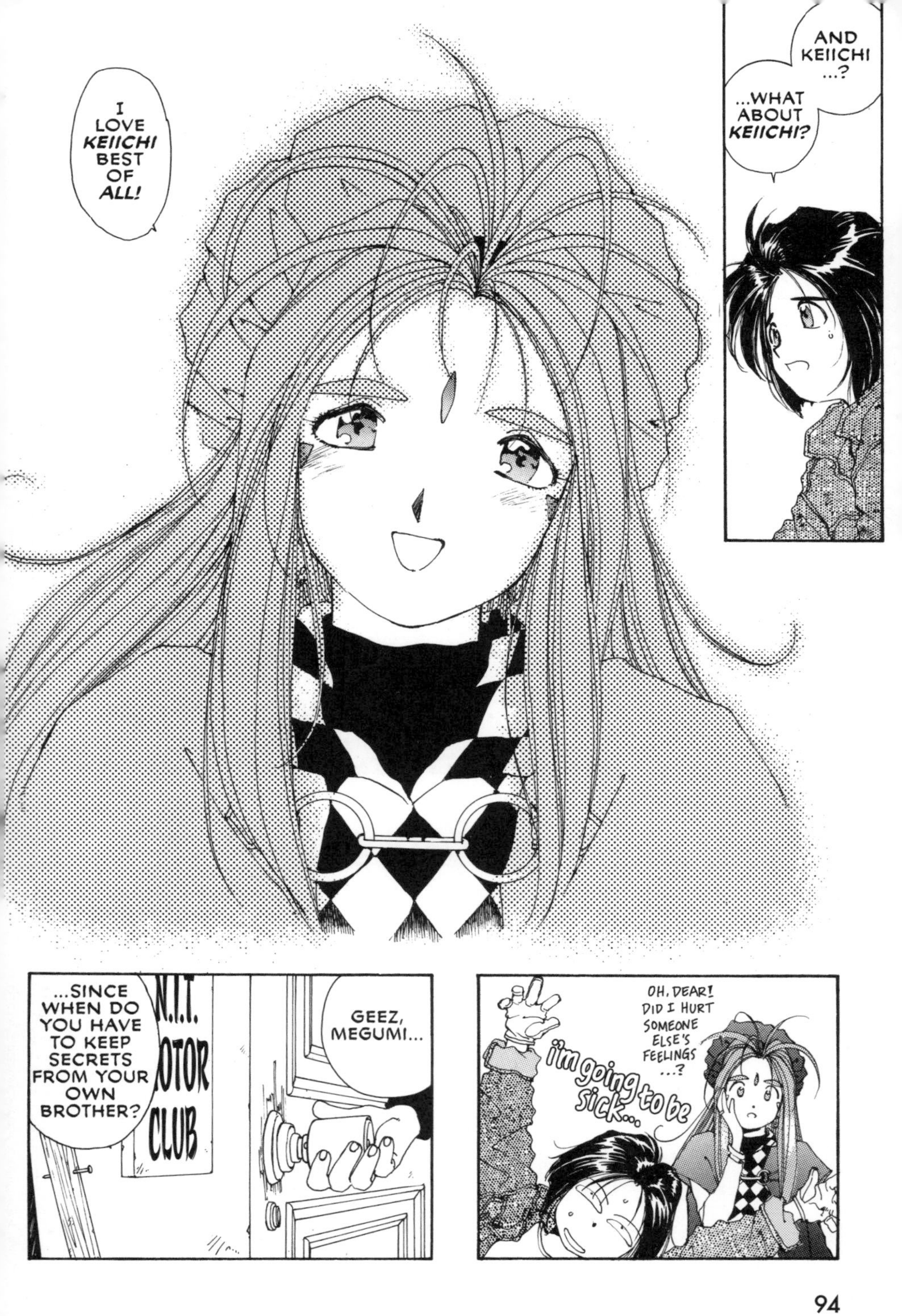
AND KEIICHI ...?
...WHAT ABOUT KEIICHI?
I LOVE KEIICHI BEST OF ALL!
OH, DEAR! DID I HURT SOMEONE ELSE'S FEELINGS ...?
i'm going to be sick...
GEEZ, MEGUMI...
...SINCE WHEN DO YOU HAVE TO KEEP SECRETS FROM YOUR OWN BROTHER?
N.I.T.
CLUB

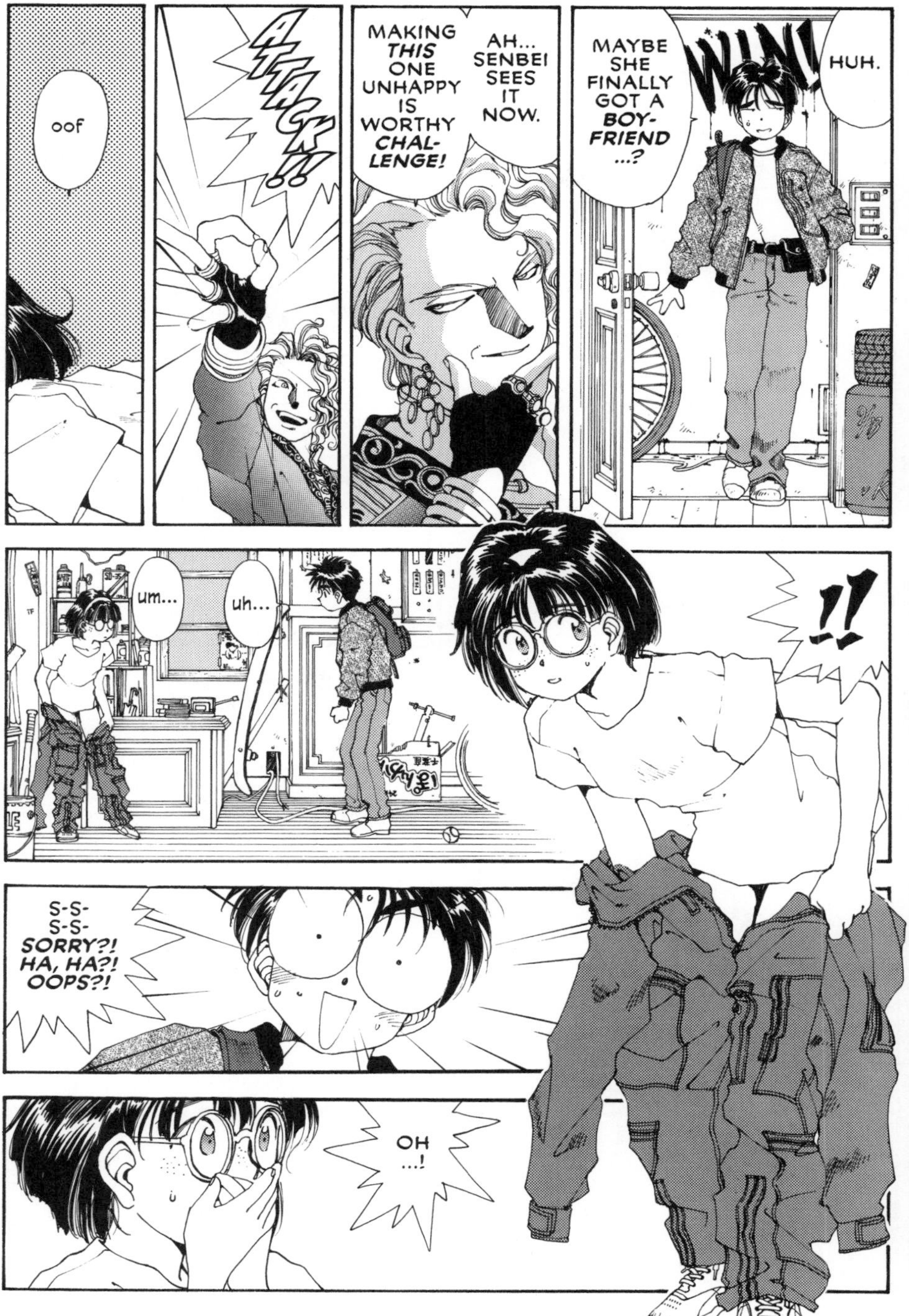
HUH.
WIN!
MAYBE SHE FINALLY GOT A BOY-FRIEND ...?
AH... SENBEI SEES IT NOW.
MAKING THIS ONE UNHAPPY IS WORTHY CHAL-LENGE!
ATTACK!!
oof
!!
uh...
um...
S-S-S-S-SORRY?! HA, HA?! OOPS?!
OH ...!
← CLUB MEMBER SORA HASEGAWA

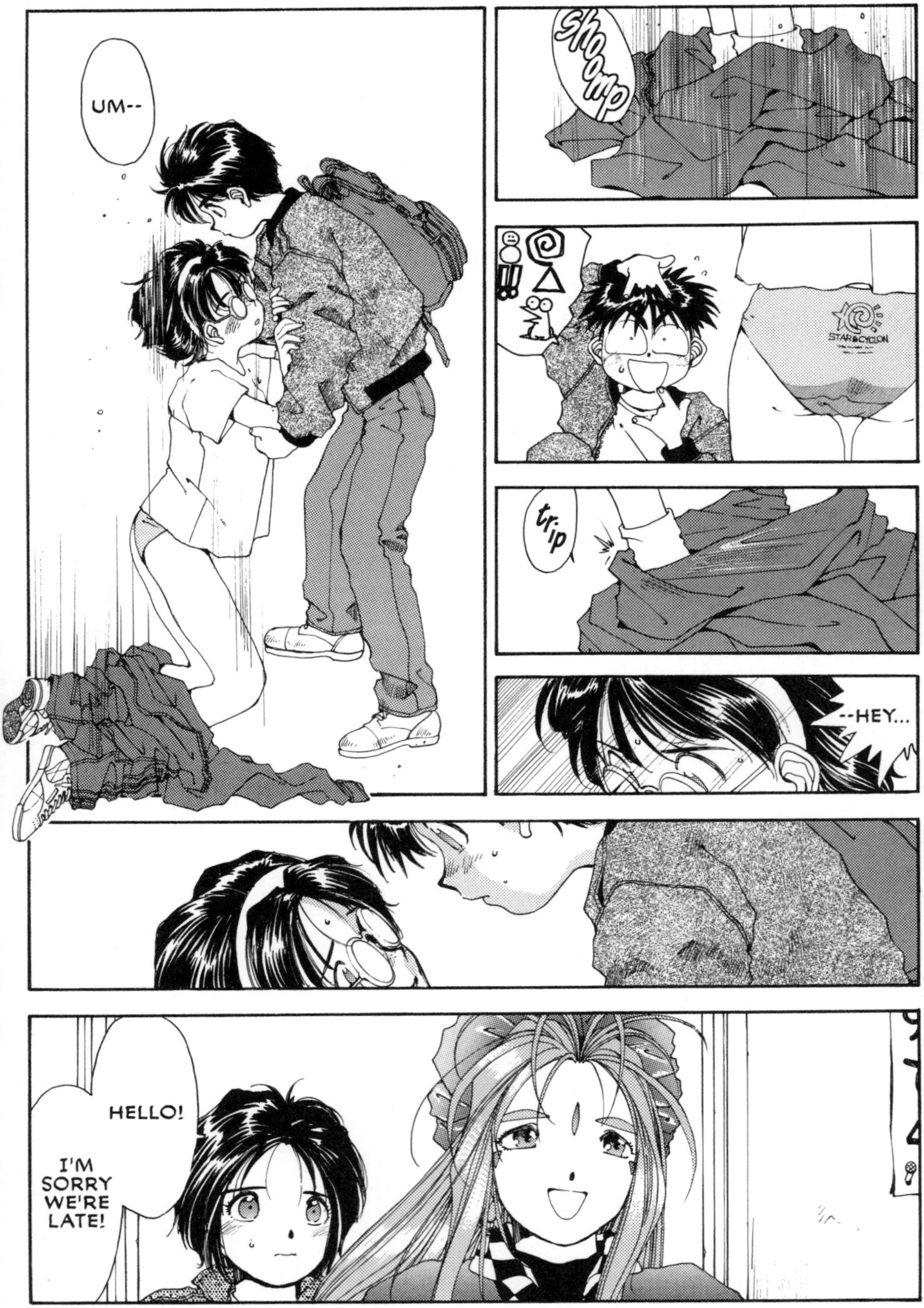
shoomp
STAR CYCLON
trip
--HEY...
UM--
HELLO!
I'M SORRY WE'RE LATE!

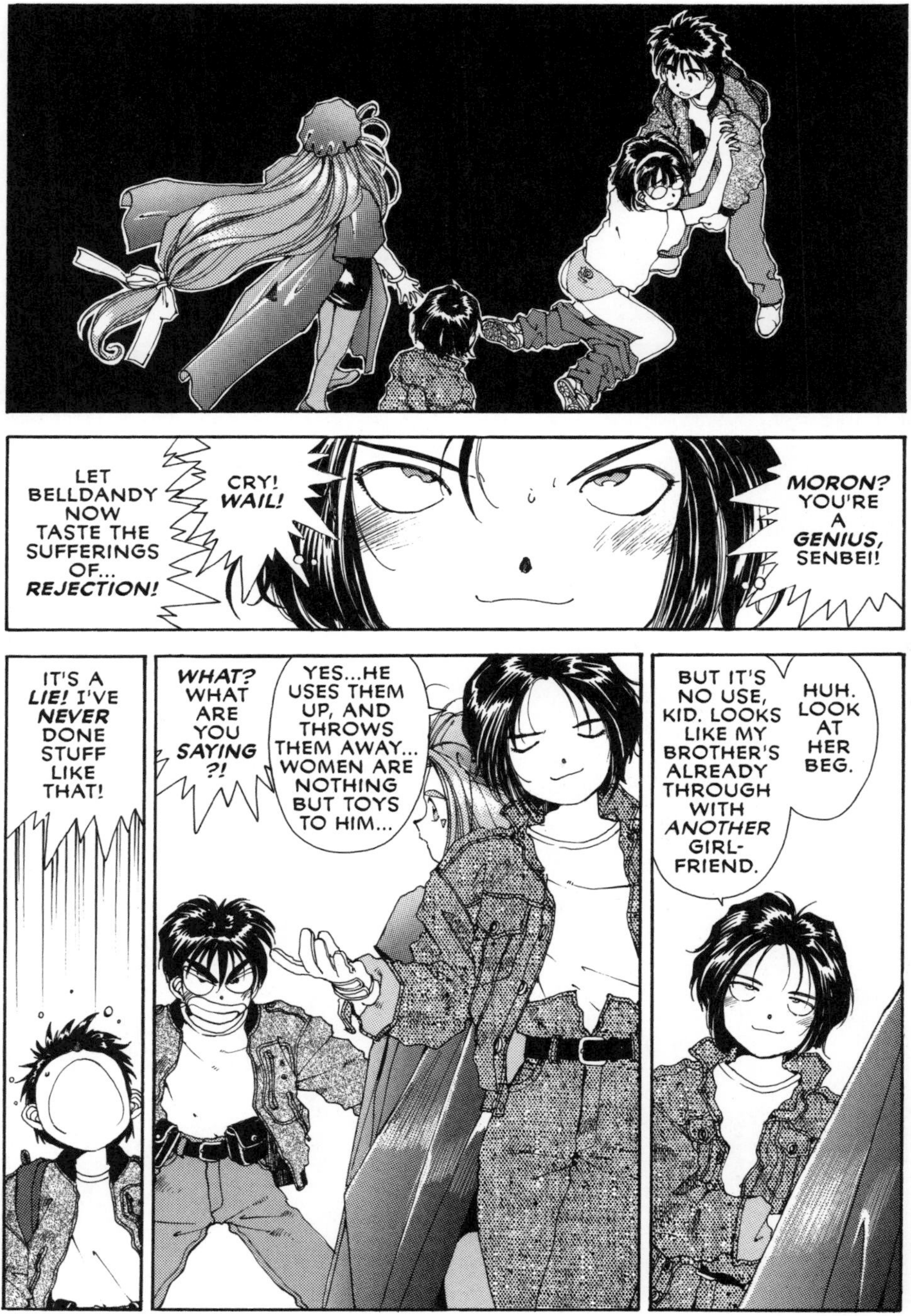
MORON? YOU'RE A GENIUS, SENBEI!
CRY! WAIL!
LET BELLDANDY NOW TASTE THE SUFFERINGS OF... REJECTION!
HUH. LOOK AT HER BEG.
BUT IT'S NO USE, KID. LOOKS LIKE MY BROTHER'S ALREADY THROUGH WITH ANOTHER GIRL-FRIEND.
YES...HE USES THEM UP, AND THROWS THEM AWAY... WOMEN ARE NOTHING BUT TOYS TO HIM...
WHAT? WHAT ARE YOU SAYING?!
IT'S A LIE! I'VE NEVER DONE STUFF LIKE THAT!

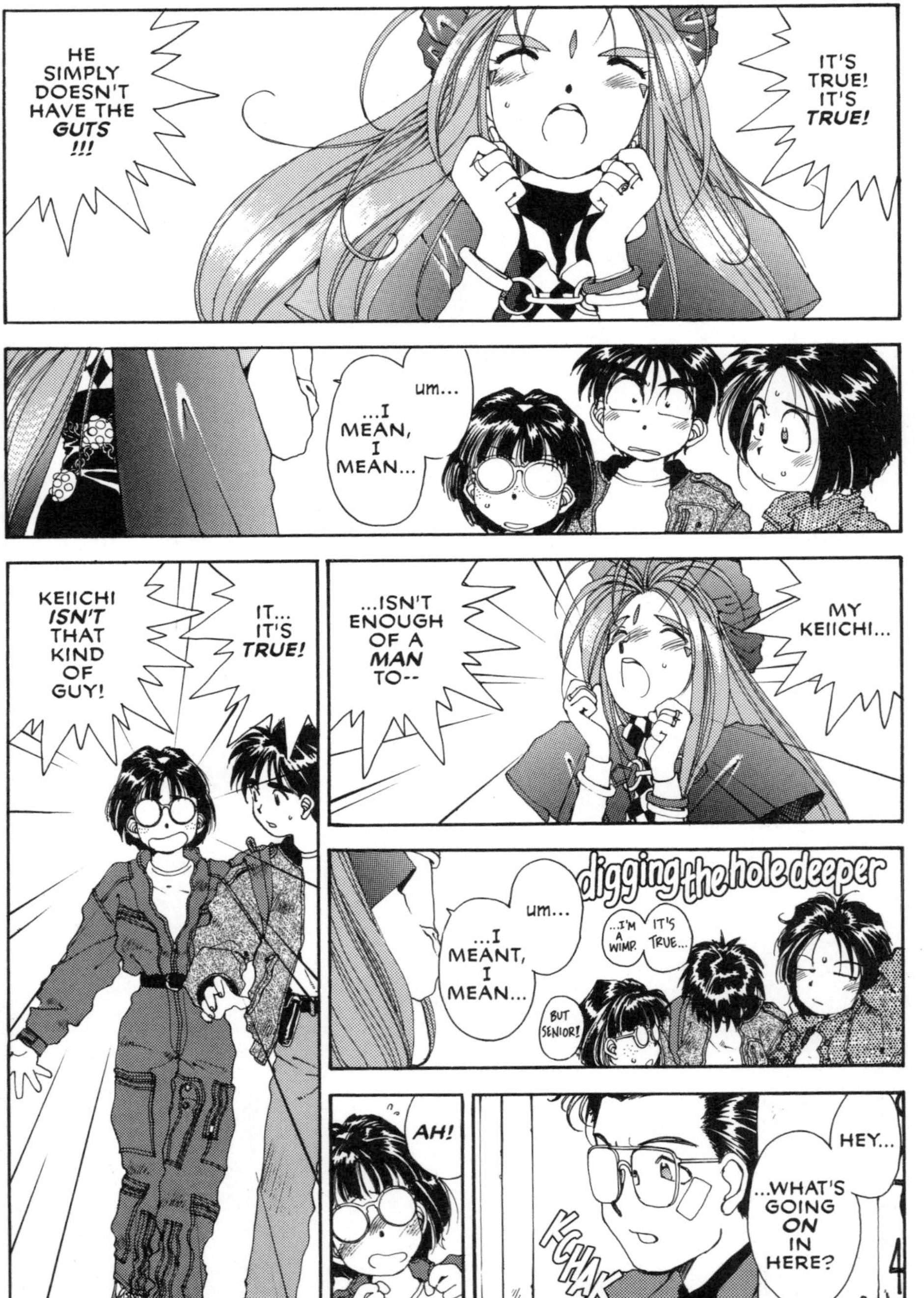
IT'S TRUE! IT'S *TRUE!*
HE SIMPLY DOESN'T HAVE THE *GUTS* !!!
um... ...I MEAN, I MEAN...
MY KEIICHI...
...ISN'T ENOUGH OF A *MAN* TO--
digging the hole deeper
IT'S TRUE...
...I'M A WIMP.
um... ...I MEANT, I MEAN...
BUT SENIOR!
HEY... ...WHAT'S GOING *ON* IN HERE?
KCHAK
AH!
IT... IT'S *TRUE!*
KEIICHI *ISN'T* THAT KIND OF GUY!

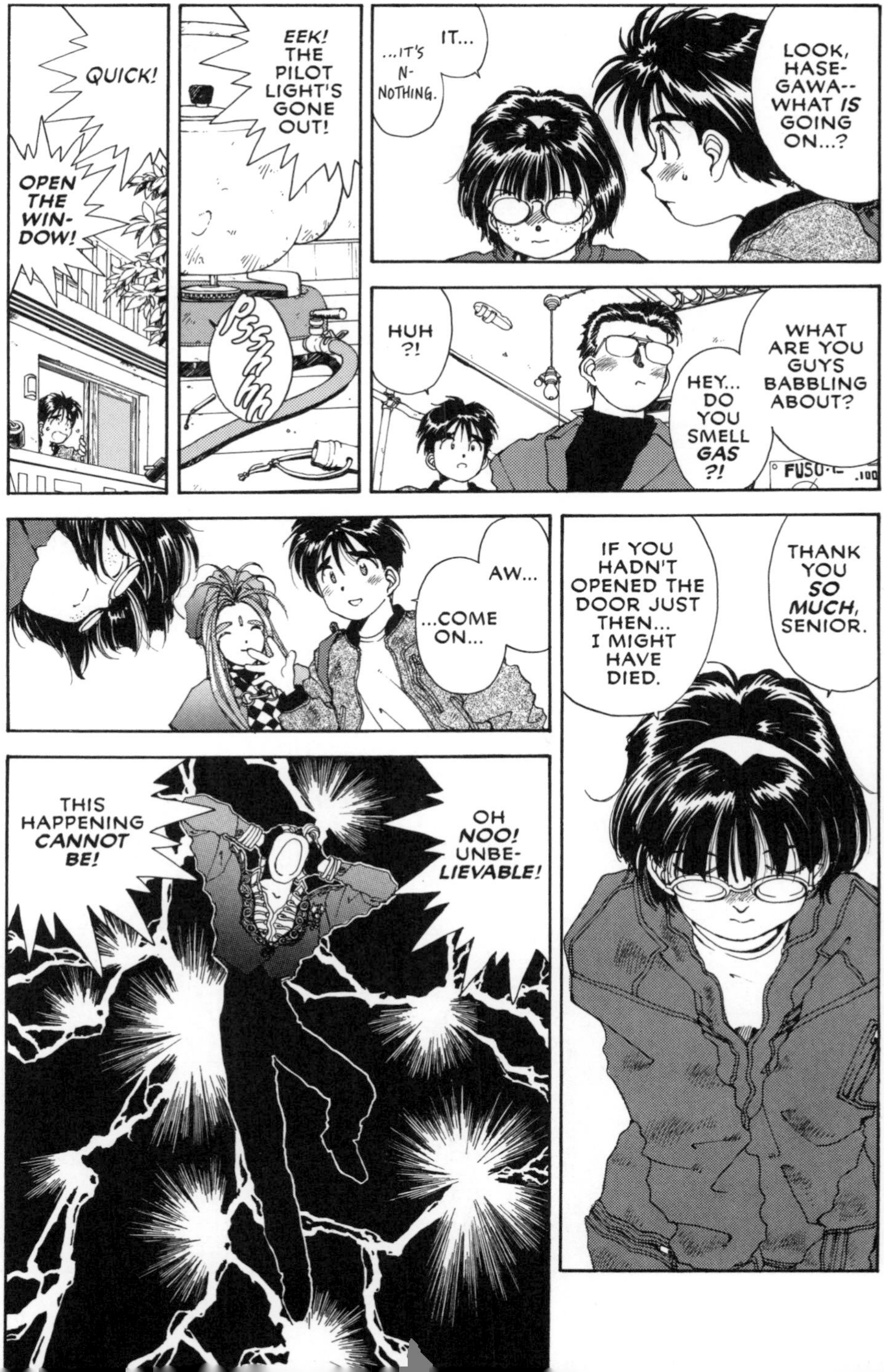
LOOK, HASE-GAWA-- WHAT *IS* GOING ON...?
IT...
...IT'S N-NOTHING.
WHAT ARE YOU GUYS BABBLING ABOUT?
HEY... DO YOU SMELL *GAS*?!
HUH?!
EEK! THE PILOT LIGHT'S GONE OUT!
PSSHHH
QUICK!
OPEN THE WIN-DOW!
THANK YOU *SO MUCH*, SENIOR.
IF YOU HADN'T OPENED THE DOOR JUST THEN... I MIGHT HAVE DIED.
AW...
...COME ON...
OH *NOO!* UNBE-*LIEVABLE!*
THIS HAPPENING *CANNOT* BE!

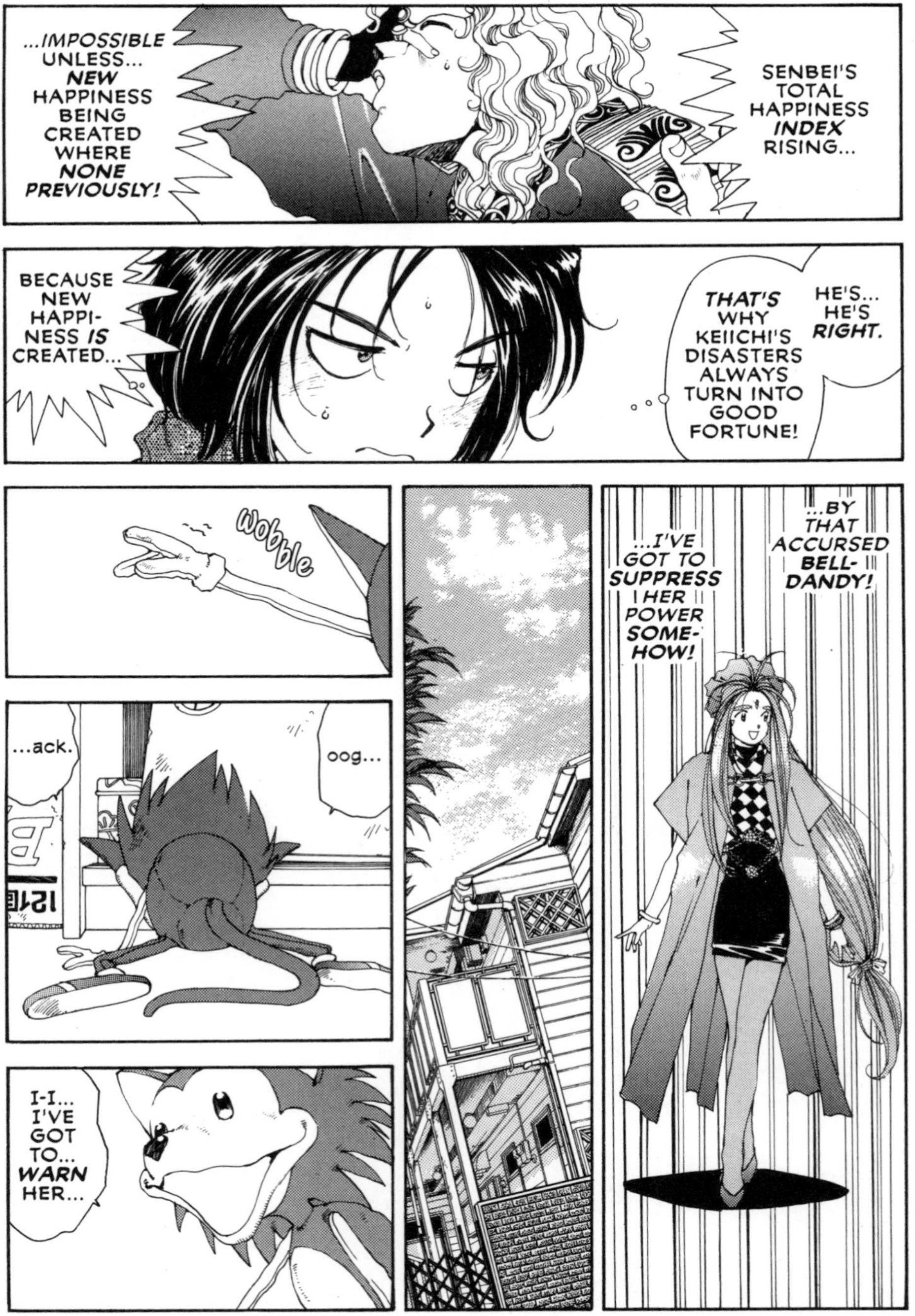

SENBEI'S TOTAL HAPPINESS INDEX RISING...
...IMPOSSIBLE UNLESS... NEW HAPPINESS BEING CREATED WHERE NONE PREVIOUSLY!
HE'S... HE'S RIGHT.
THAT'S WHY KEIICHI'S DISASTERS ALWAYS TURN INTO GOOD FORTUNE!
BECAUSE NEW HAPPINESS IS CREATED...
...BY THAT ACCURSED BELL-DANDY!
...I'VE GOT TO SUPPRESS HER POWER SOME-HOW!
wobble
oog...
...ack.
I-I... I'VE GOT TO... WARN HER...

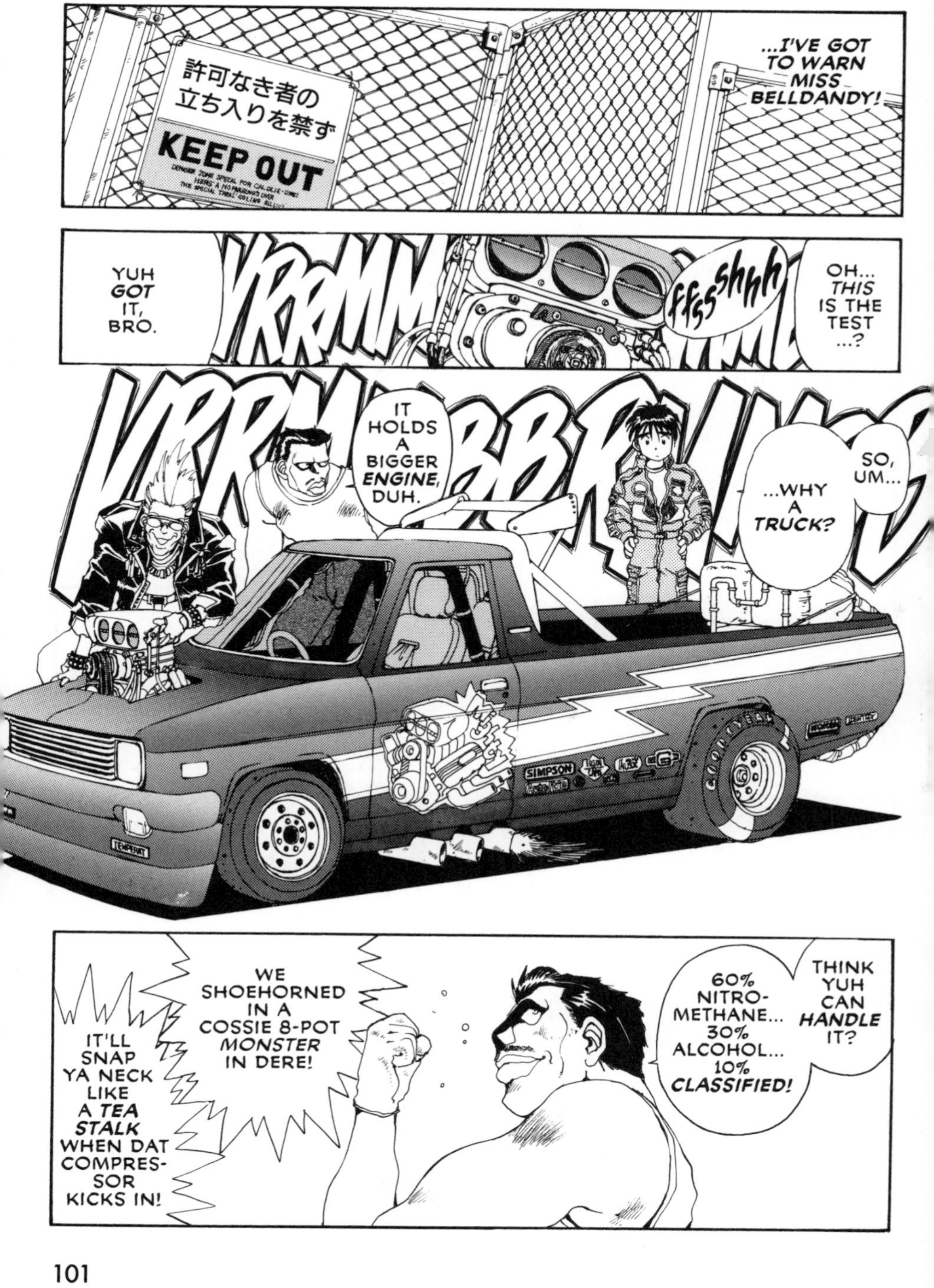
...I'VE GOT TO WARN MISS BELLDANDY!
許可なき者の立ち入りを禁ず
KEEP OUT
OH... *THIS* IS THE TEST ...?
ffssshhh
VRRMM
YUH *GOT* IT, BRO.
SO, UM...
...WHY A *TRUCK?*
IT HOLDS A BIGGER *ENGINE,* DUH.
SIMPSON
THINK YUH CAN *HANDLE* IT?
60% NITRO-METHANE... 30% ALCOHOL... 10% *CLASSIFIED!*
WE SHOEHORNED IN A COSSIE 8-POT *MONSTER* IN DERE!
IT'LL SNAP YA NECK LIKE A *TEA STALK* WHEN DAT COMPRES-SOR KICKS IN!

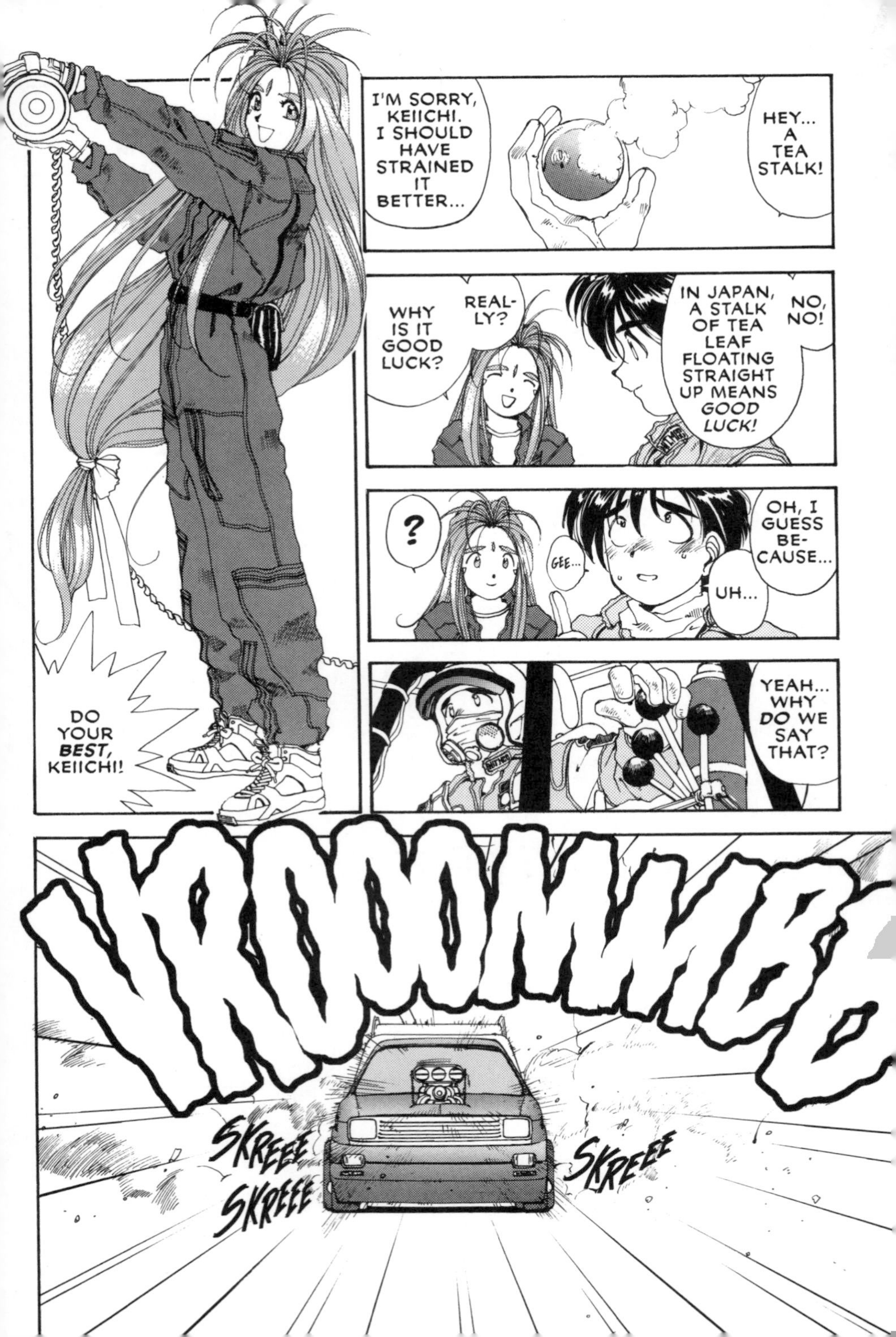
HEY... A TEA STALK!
I'M SORRY, KEIICHI. I SHOULD HAVE STRAINED IT BETTER...
NO, NO!
IN JAPAN, A STALK OF TEA LEAF FLOATING STRAIGHT UP MEANS *GOOD LUCK!*
REAL-LY?
WHY IS IT GOOD LUCK?
OH, I GUESS BE-CAUSE...
UH...
GEE...
?
YEAH... WHY *DO* WE SAY THAT?
DO YOUR *BEST*, KEIICHI!
VROOOMMB
SKREEE
SKREEE
SKREEE

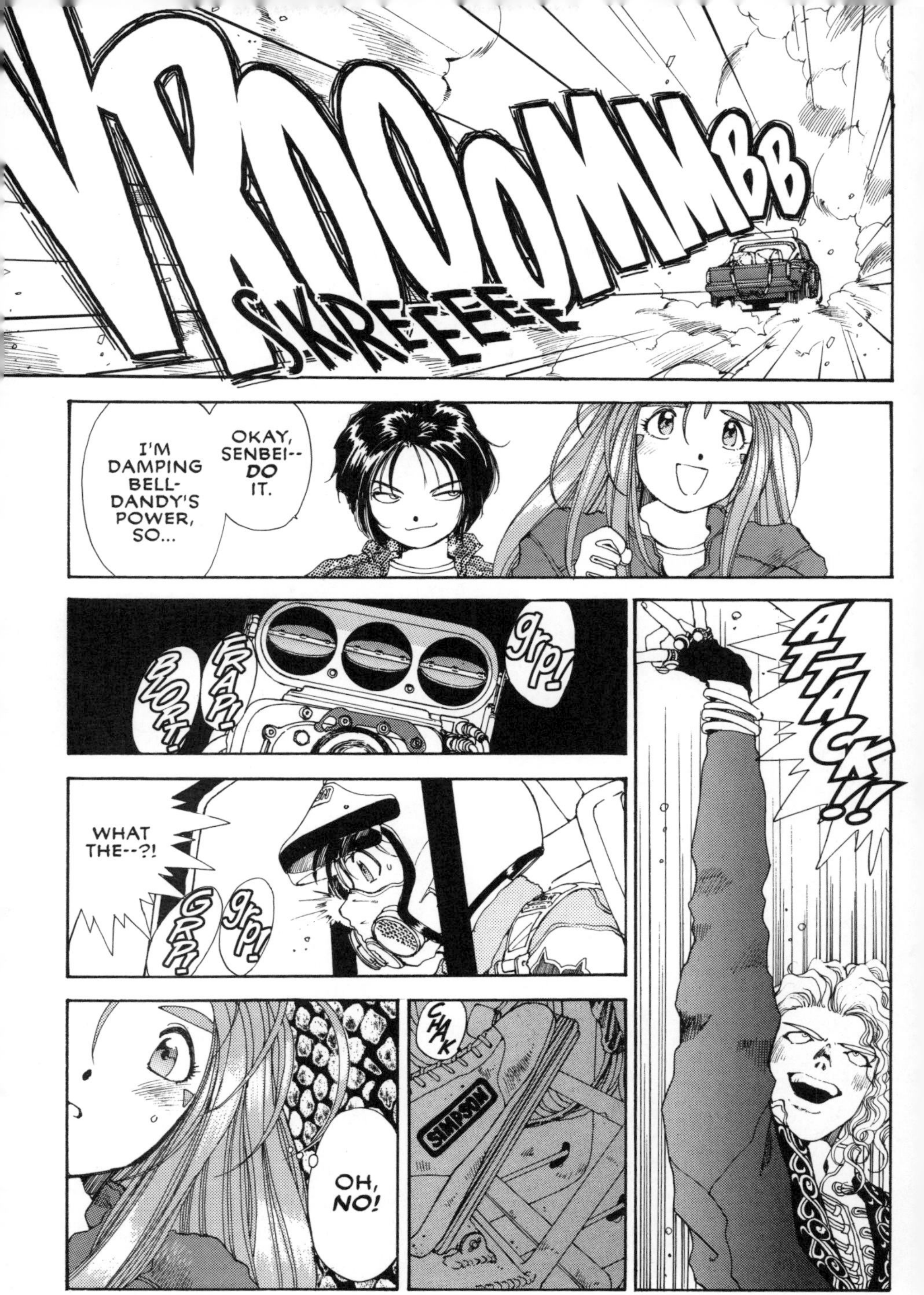
VROOOMMBB
SKREEEEE
OKAY, SENBEI-- DO IT.
I'M DAMPING BELL-DANDY'S POWER, SO...
ATTACK!!
grp!
FRAP!
BLORT!
WHAT THE--?!
grp!
GRP!
CHAK
SIMPSON
OH, NO!

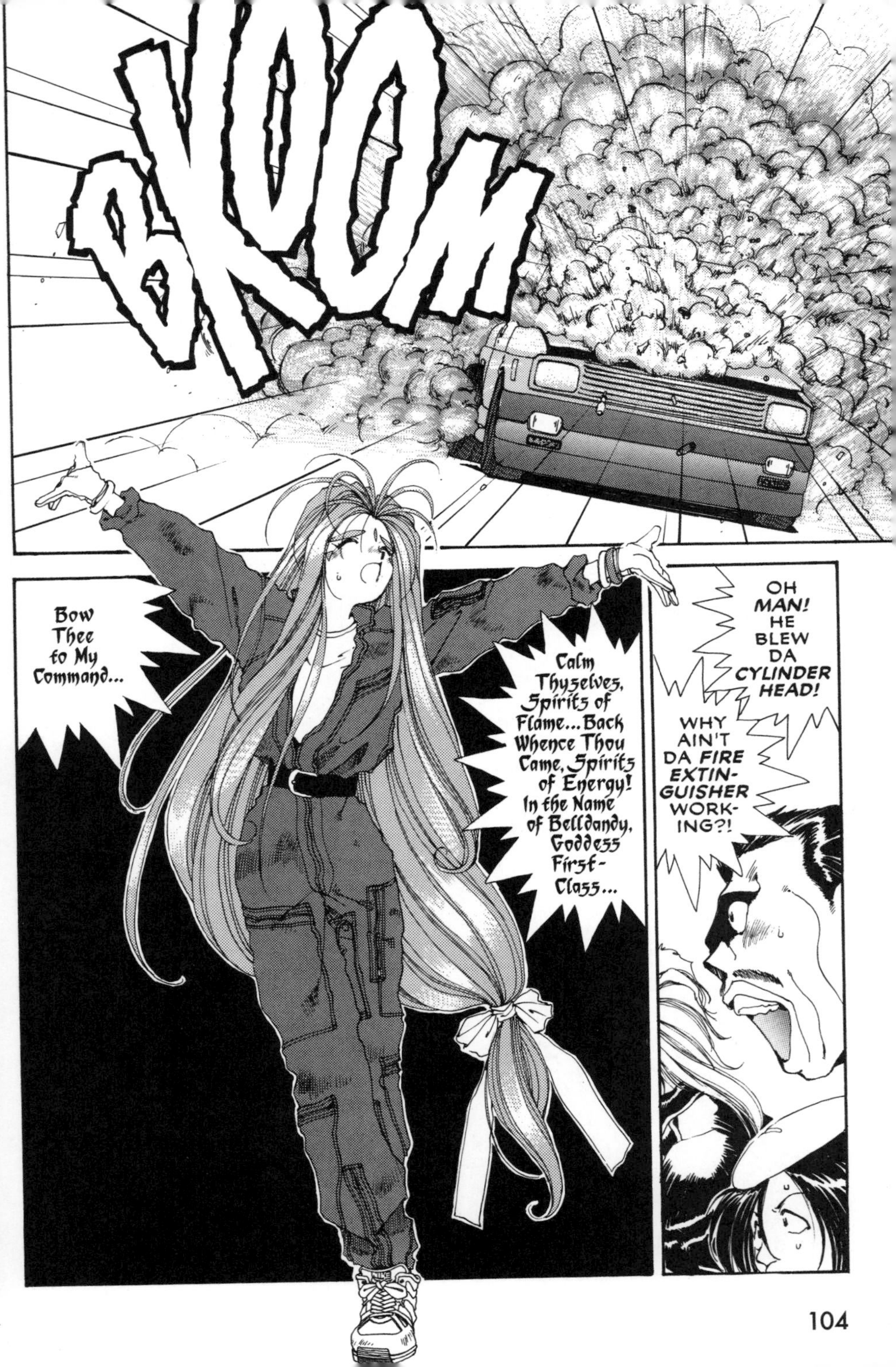
BKOOM
OH MAN! HE BLEW DA CYLINDER HEAD!
WHY AIN'T DA FIRE EXTINGUISHER WORKING?!
Calm Thyselves, Spirits of Flame... Back Whence Thou Came, Spirits of Energy! In the Name of Belldandy, Goddess First-Class...
Bow Thee to My Command...

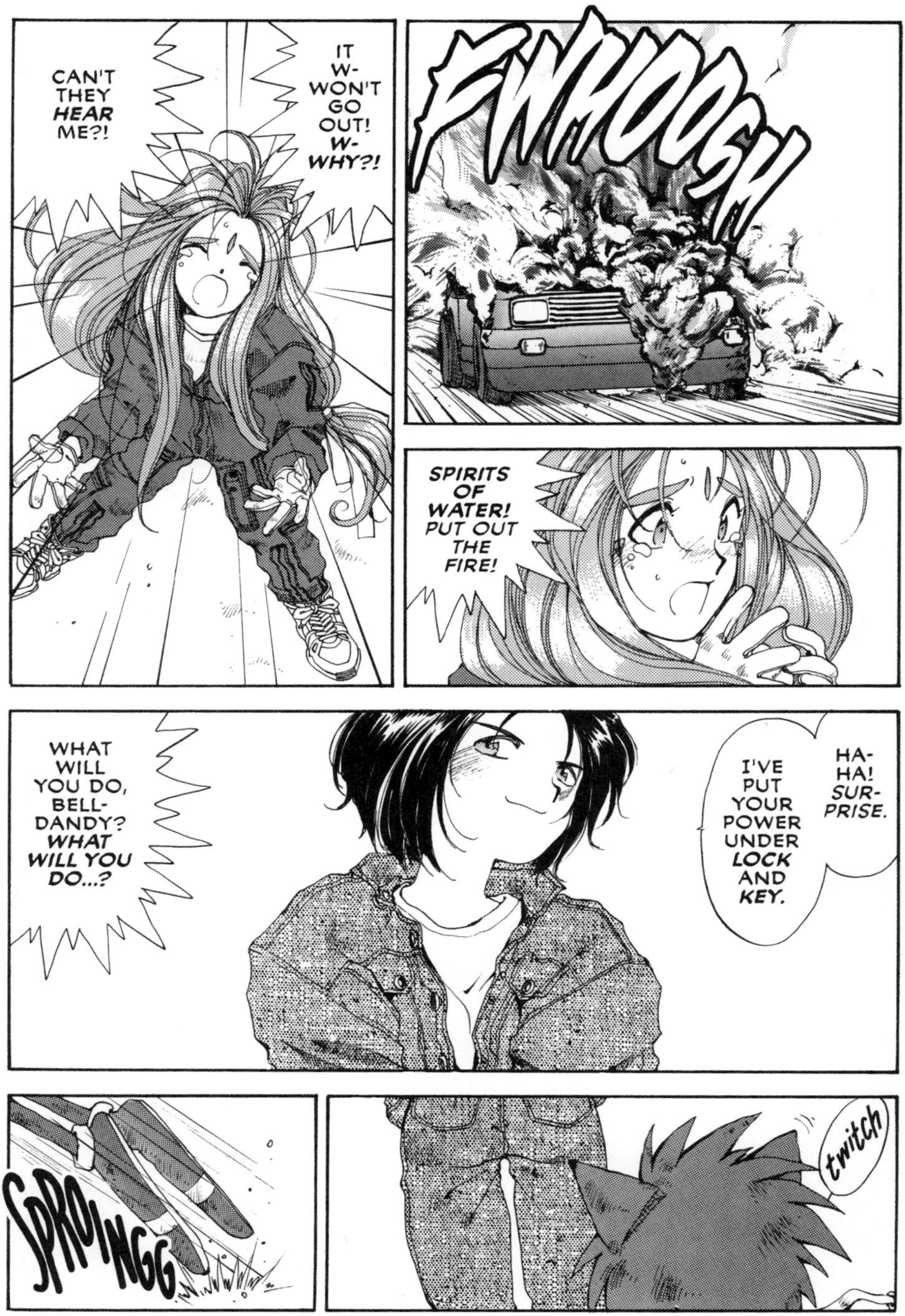
FWHOOSH
SPIRITS OF WATER! PUT OUT THE FIRE!
IT W-WON'T GO OUT! W-WHY?!
CAN'T THEY HEAR ME?!
HA-HA! SURPRISE.
I'VE PUT YOUR POWER UNDER LOCK AND KEY.
WHAT WILL YOU DO, BELL-DANDY? WHAT WILL YOU DO...?
twitch
SPROINGG

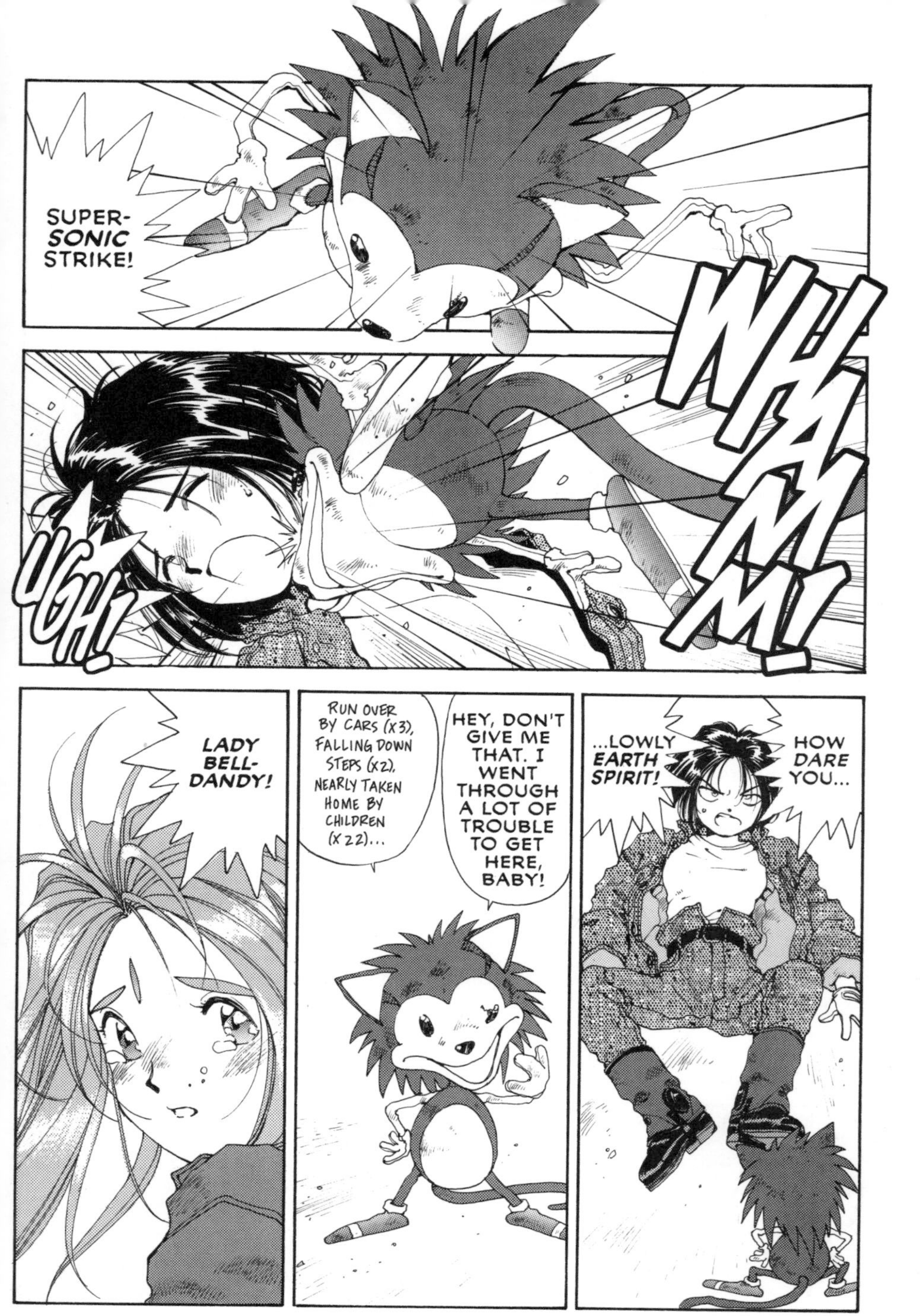
SUPER-SONIC STRIKE!
WHAMMM!
UGH!
HOW DARE YOU...
...LOWLY EARTH SPIRIT!
HEY, DON'T GIVE ME THAT. I WENT THROUGH A LOT OF TROUBLE TO GET HERE, BABY!
RUN OVER BY CARS (x3), FALLING DOWN STEPS (x2), NEARLY TAKEN HOME BY CHILDREN (x22)...
LADY BELL-DANDY!

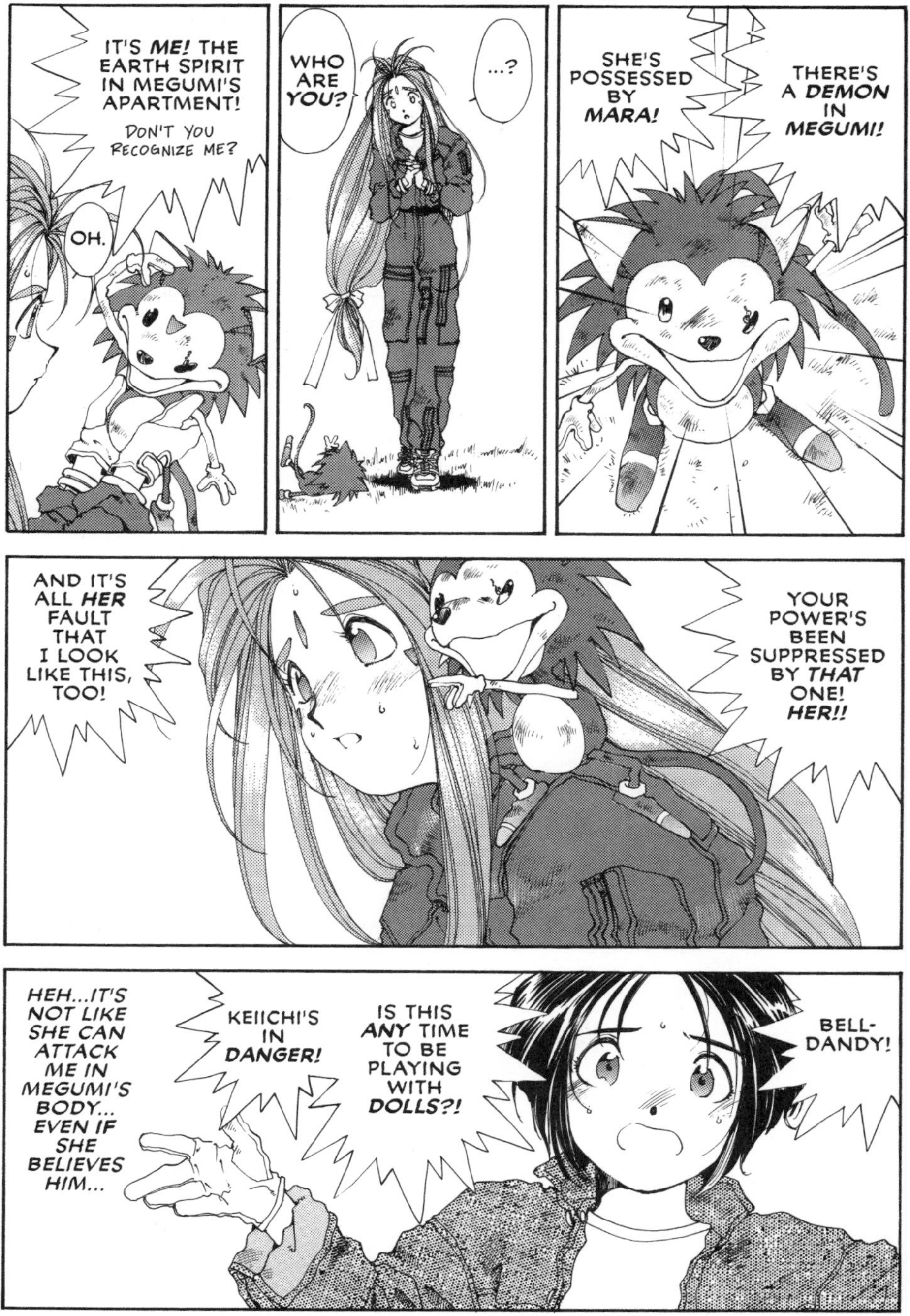
THERE'S A DEMON IN MEGUMI!
SHE'S POSSESSED BY MARA!
...?
WHO ARE YOU?
IT'S ME! THE EARTH SPIRIT IN MEGUMI'S APARTMENT!
DON'T YOU RECOGNIZE ME?
OH.
YOUR POWER'S BEEN SUPPRESSED BY THAT ONE! HER!!
AND IT'S ALL HER FAULT THAT I LOOK LIKE THIS, TOO!
BELL-DANDY!
IS THIS ANY TIME TO BE PLAYING WITH DOLLS?!
KEIICHI'S IN DANGER!
HEH...IT'S NOT LIKE SHE CAN ATTACK ME IN MEGUMI'S BODY... EVEN IF SHE BELIEVES HIM...

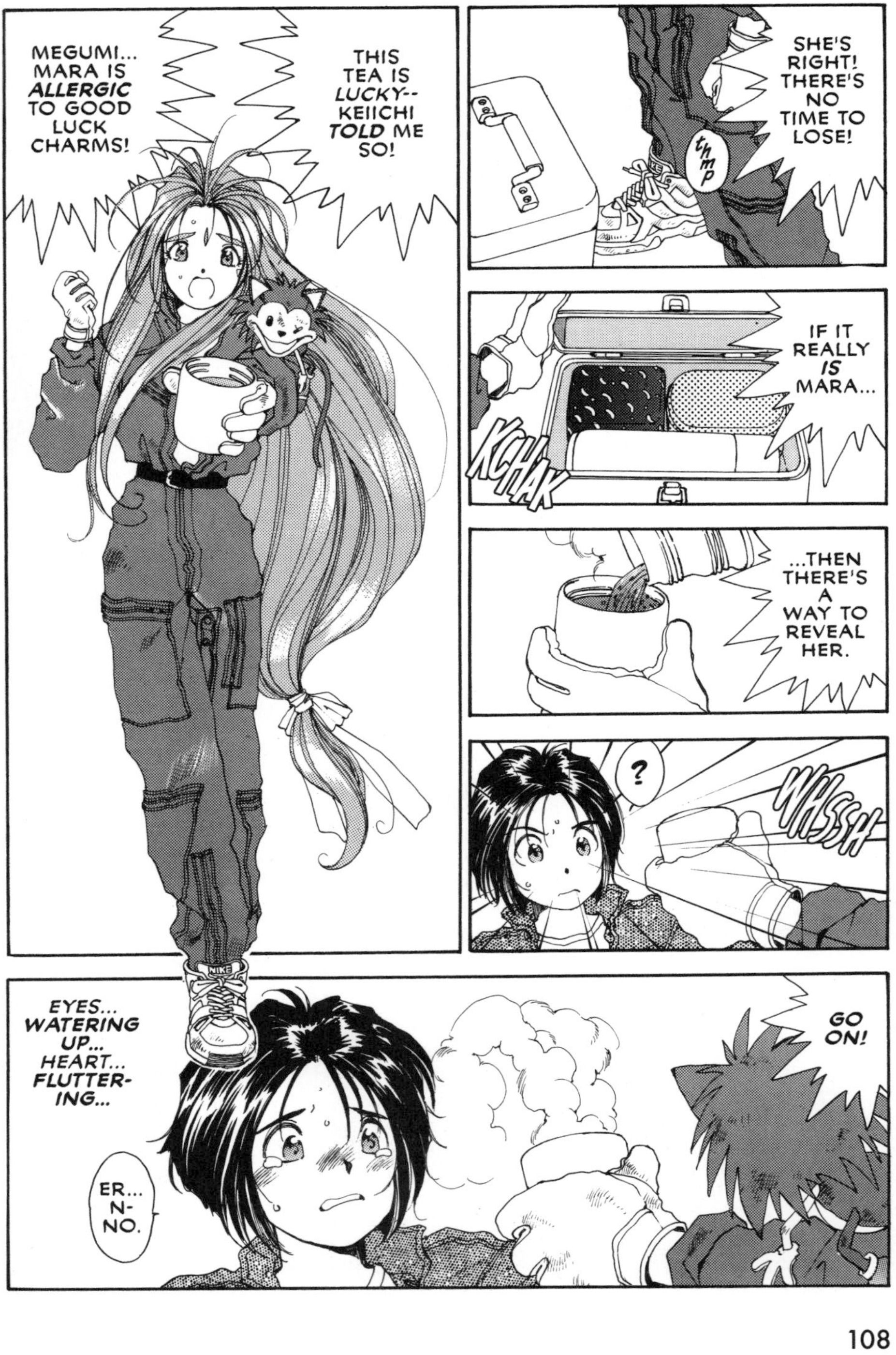
SHE'S RIGHT! THERE'S NO TIME TO LOSE!
thmp
IF IT REALLY IS MARA...
KCHAK
...THEN THERE'S A WAY TO REVEAL HER.
?
WHSSSH
THIS TEA IS LUCKY-- KEIICHI TOLD ME SO!
MEGUMI... MARA IS ALLERGIC TO GOOD LUCK CHARMS!
NIKE
GO ON!
EYES... WATERING UP... HEART... FLUTTERING...
ER... N-NO.

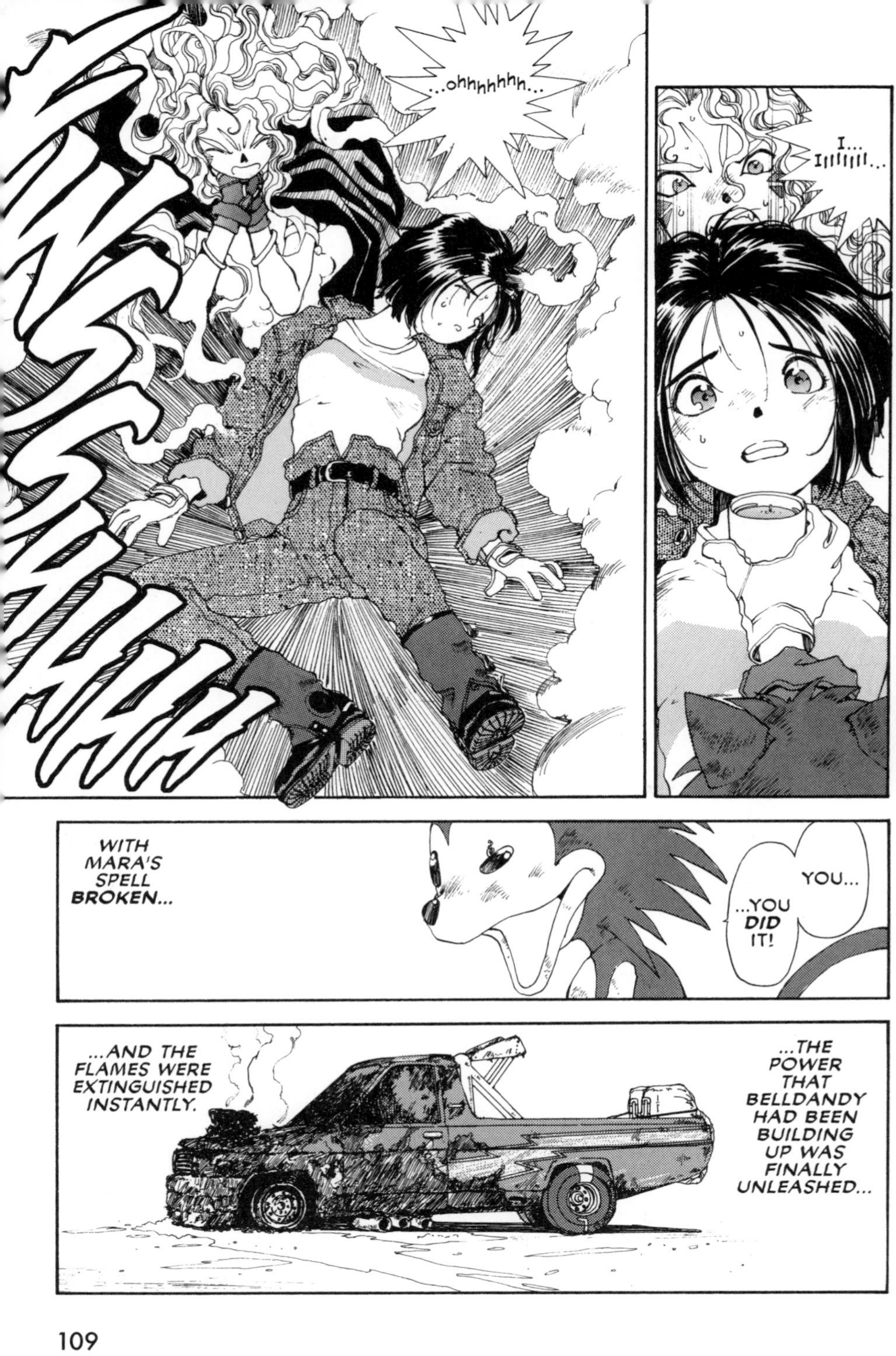
I... Illllll...
...ohhhhhhh...
YOU... ...YOU DID IT!
WITH MARA'S SPELL BROKEN...
...THE POWER THAT BELLDANDY HAD BEEN BUILDING UP WAS FINALLY UNLEASHED...
...AND THE FLAMES WERE EXTINGUISHED INSTANTLY.

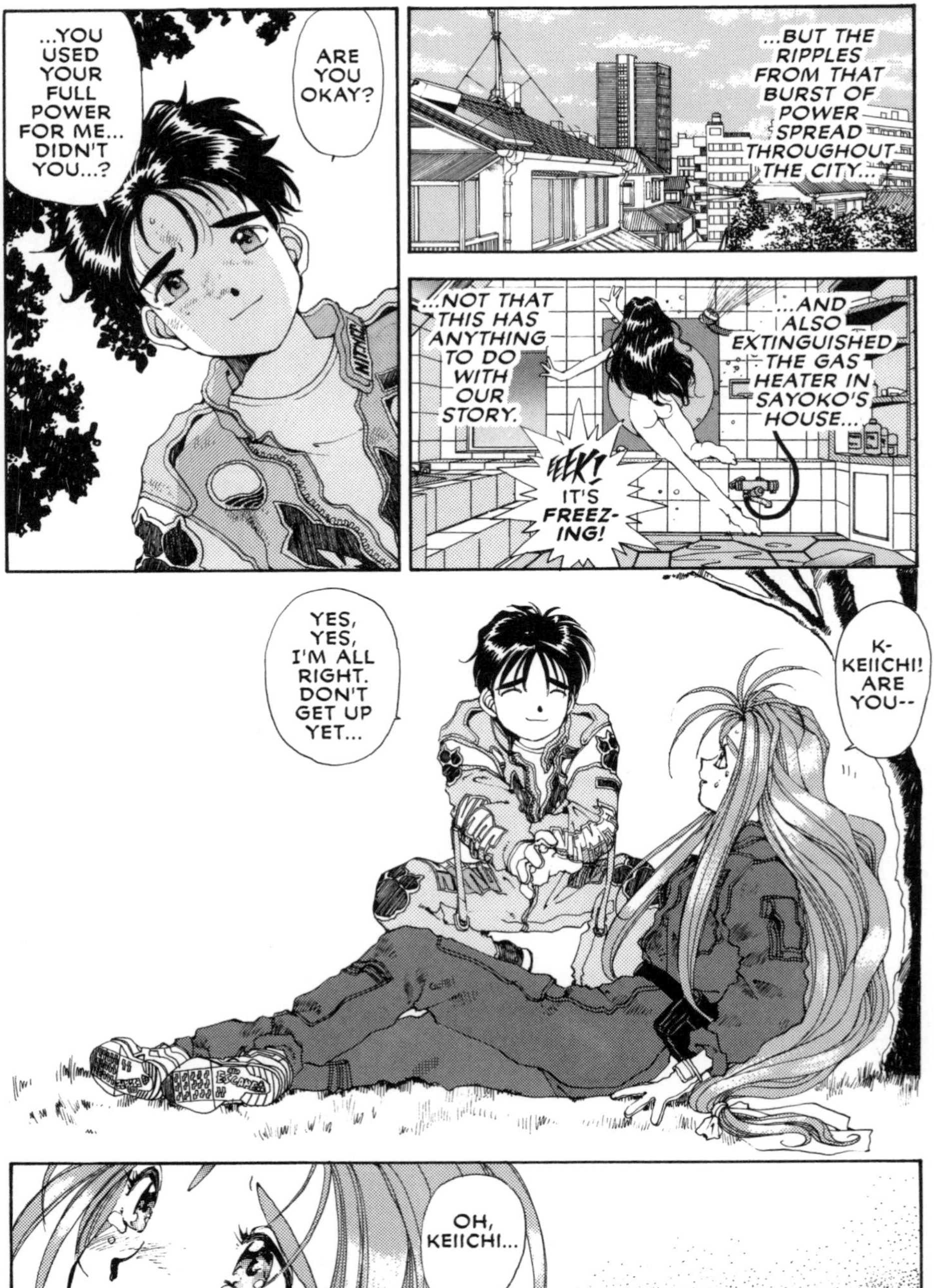
...BUT THE RIPPLES FROM THAT BURST OF POWER SPREAD THROUGHOUT THE CITY...
...AND ALSO EXTINGUISHED THE GAS HEATER IN SAYOKO'S HOUSE...
...NOT THAT THIS HAS ANYTHING TO DO WITH OUR STORY.
EEEK! IT'S FREEZ-ING!
ARE YOU OKAY?
...YOU USED YOUR FULL POWER FOR ME... DIDN'T YOU...?
K-KEIICHI! ARE YOU--
YES, YES, I'M ALL RIGHT. DON'T GET UP YET...
OH, KEIICHI...

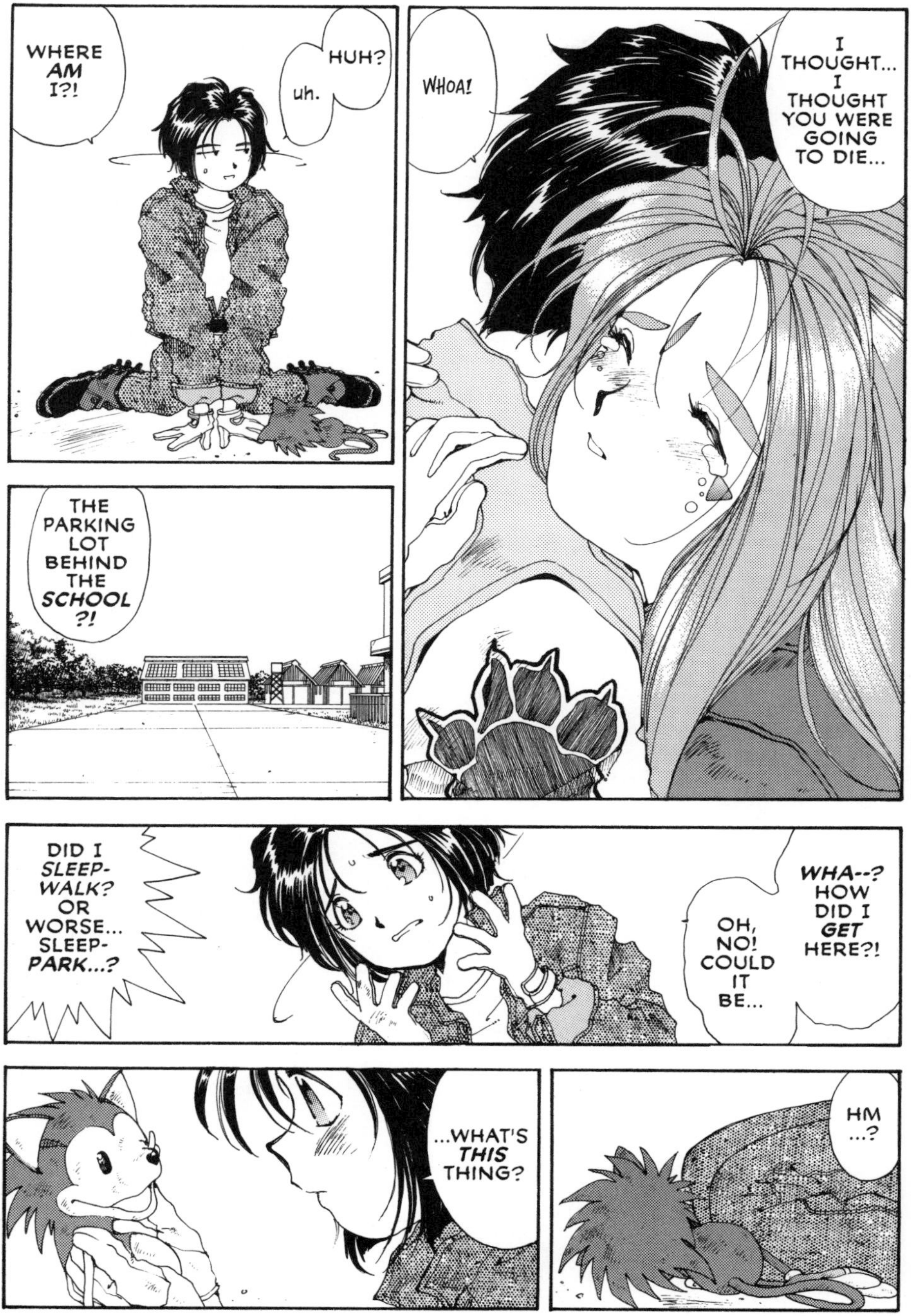
I THOUGHT... I THOUGHT YOU WERE GOING TO DIE...
WHOA!
HUH? uh.
WHERE AM I?!
THE PARKING LOT BEHIND THE SCHOOL ?!
WHA--? HOW DID I GET HERE?!
OH, NO! COULD IT BE...
DID I SLEEP-WALK? OR WORSE... SLEEP-PARK...?
HM ...?
...WHAT'S THIS THING?

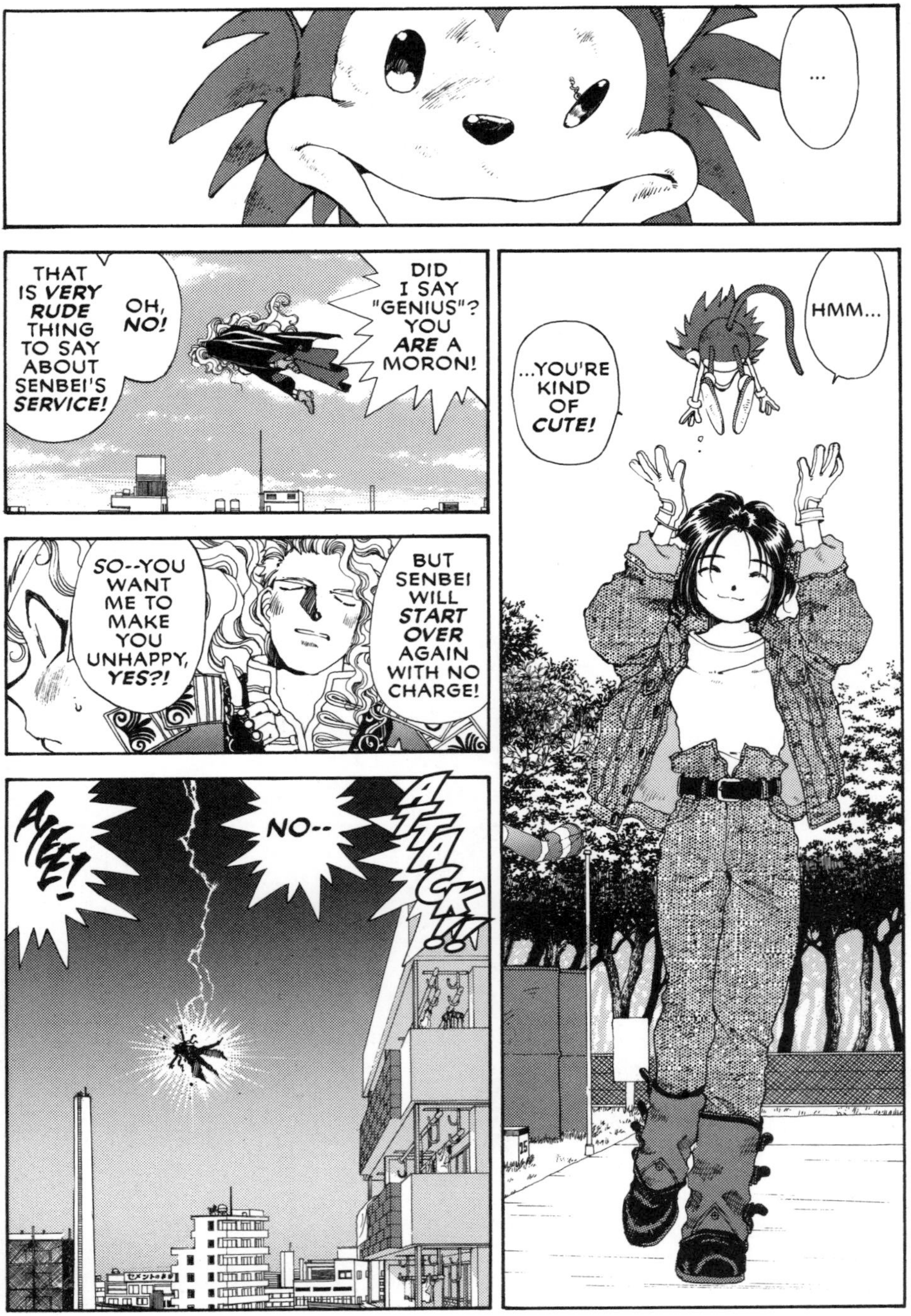
...
HMM...
...YOU'RE KIND OF CUTE!
DID I SAY "GENIUS"? YOU ARE A MORON!
OH, NO!
THAT IS VERY RUDE THING TO SAY ABOUT SENBEI'S SERVICE!
BUT SENBEI WILL START OVER AGAIN WITH NO CHARGE!
SO--YOU WANT ME TO MAKE YOU UNHAPPY, YES?!
ATTACK!!
NO--
AIEE!

CHAPTER 46

Thank You

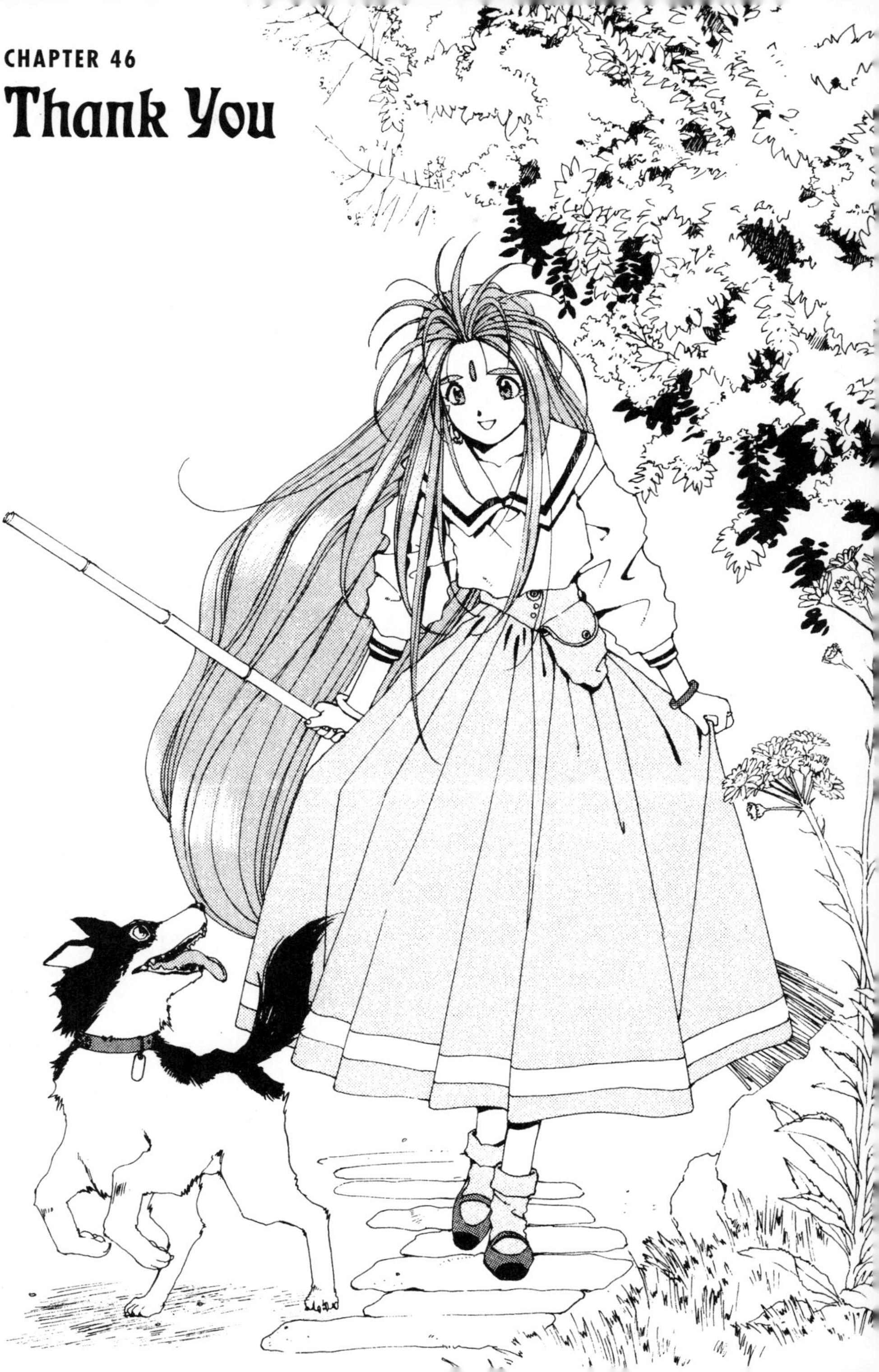

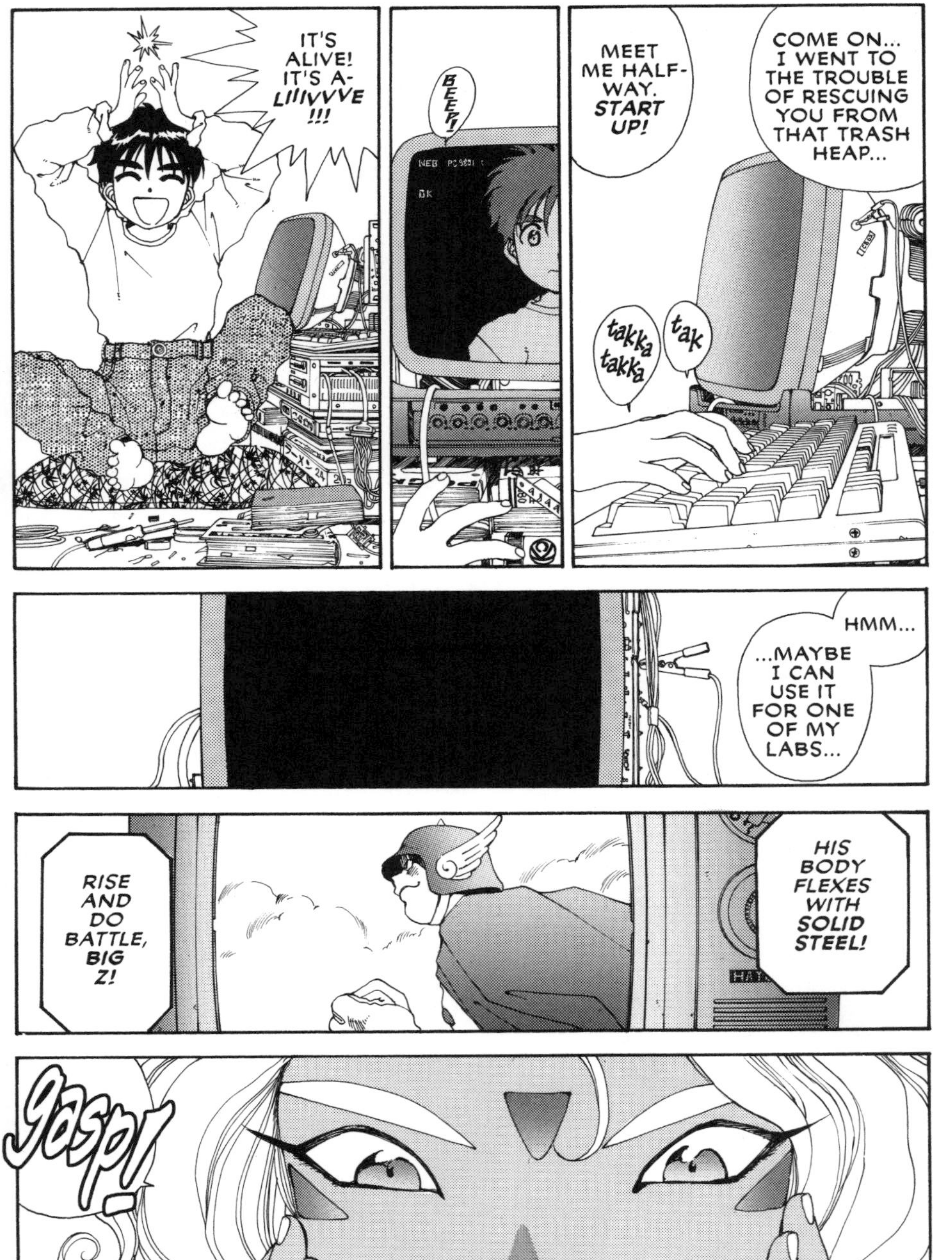
COME ON... I WENT TO THE TROUBLE OF RESCUING YOU FROM THAT TRASH HEAP...
MEET ME HALF-WAY. START UP!
tak
takka takka
BEEP!
IT'S ALIVE! IT'S A-LIIIVVVE!!!
HMM...
...MAYBE I CAN USE IT FOR ONE OF MY LABS...
HIS BODY FLEXES WITH SOLID STEEL!
RISE AND DO BATTLE, BIG Z!
gasp!

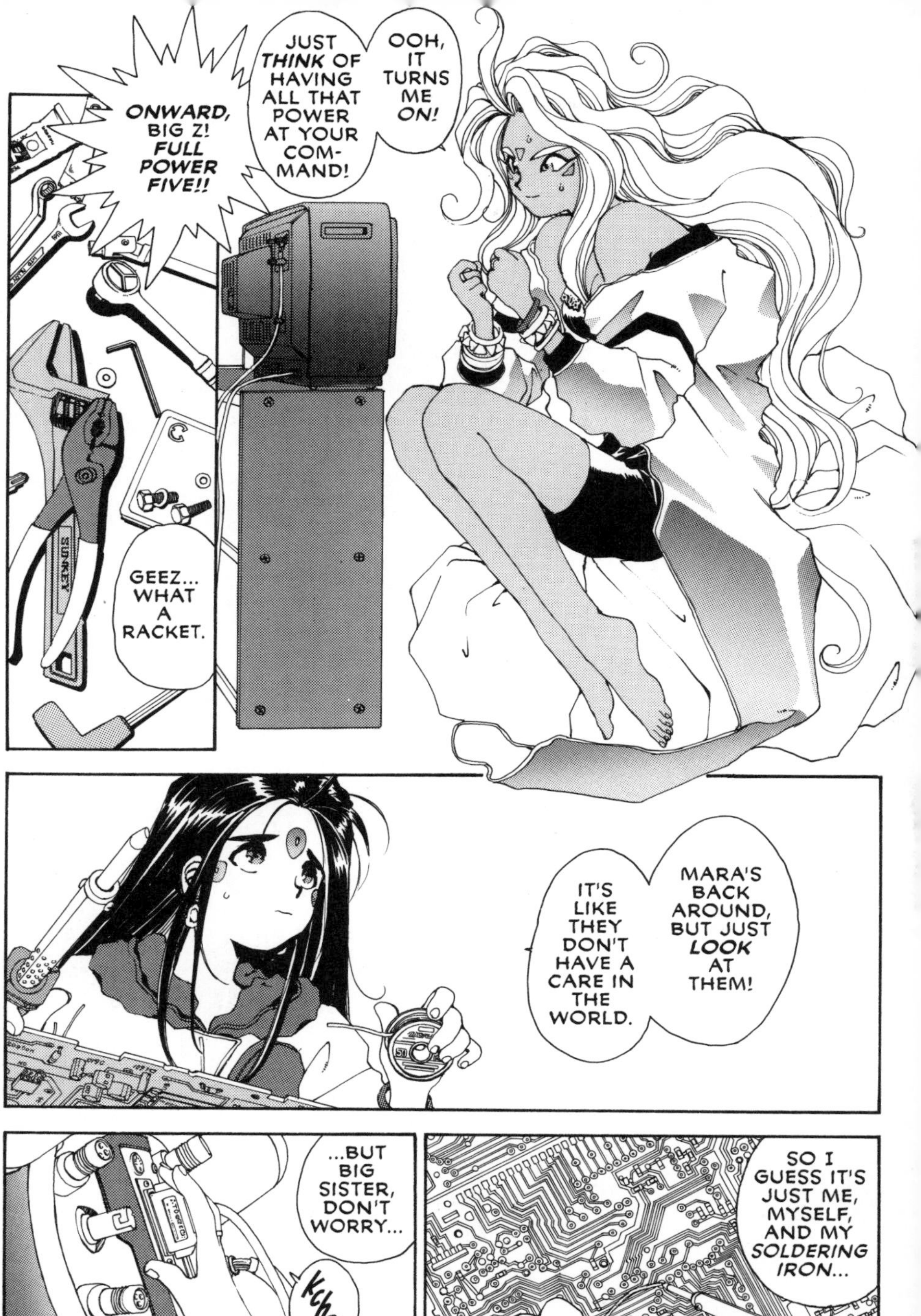
OOH, IT TURNS ME ON!
JUST THINK OF HAVING ALL THAT POWER AT YOUR COMMAND!
ONWARD, BIG Z! FULL POWER FIVE!!
GEEZ... WHAT A RACKET.
MARA'S BACK AROUND, BUT JUST LOOK AT THEM!
IT'S LIKE THEY DON'T HAVE A CARE IN THE WORLD.
SO I GUESS IT'S JUST ME, MYSELF, AND MY SOLDERING IRON...
...BUT BIG SISTER, DON'T WORRY...
Kchak

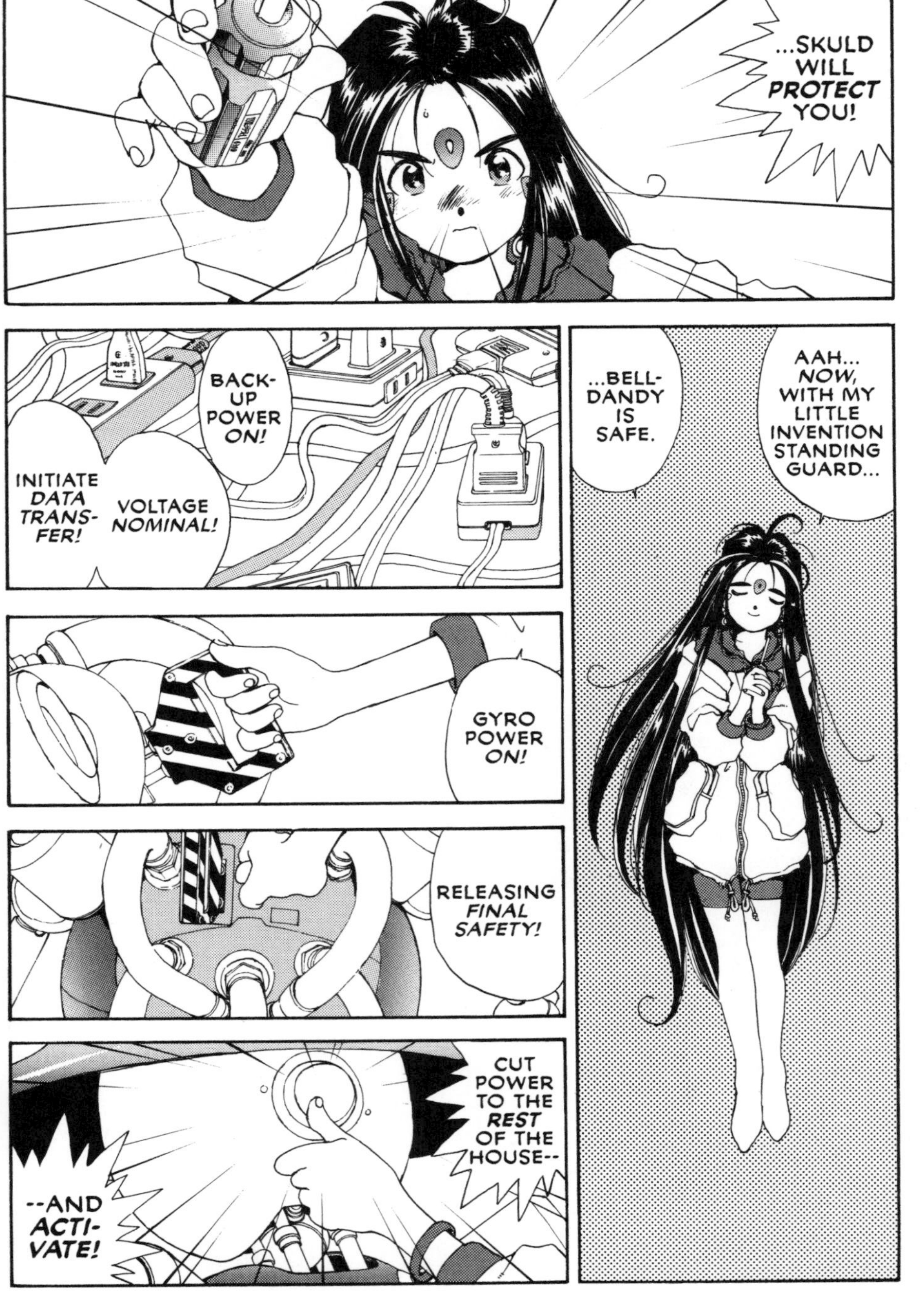
...SKULD WILL PROTECT YOU!
AAH... NOW, WITH MY LITTLE INVENTION STANDING GUARD...
...BELL-DANDY IS SAFE.
BACK-UP POWER ON!
VOLTAGE NOMINAL!
INITIATE DATA TRANS-FER!
GYRO POWER ON!
RELEASING FINAL SAFETY!
CUT POWER TO THE REST OF THE HOUSE--
--AND ACTI-VATE!

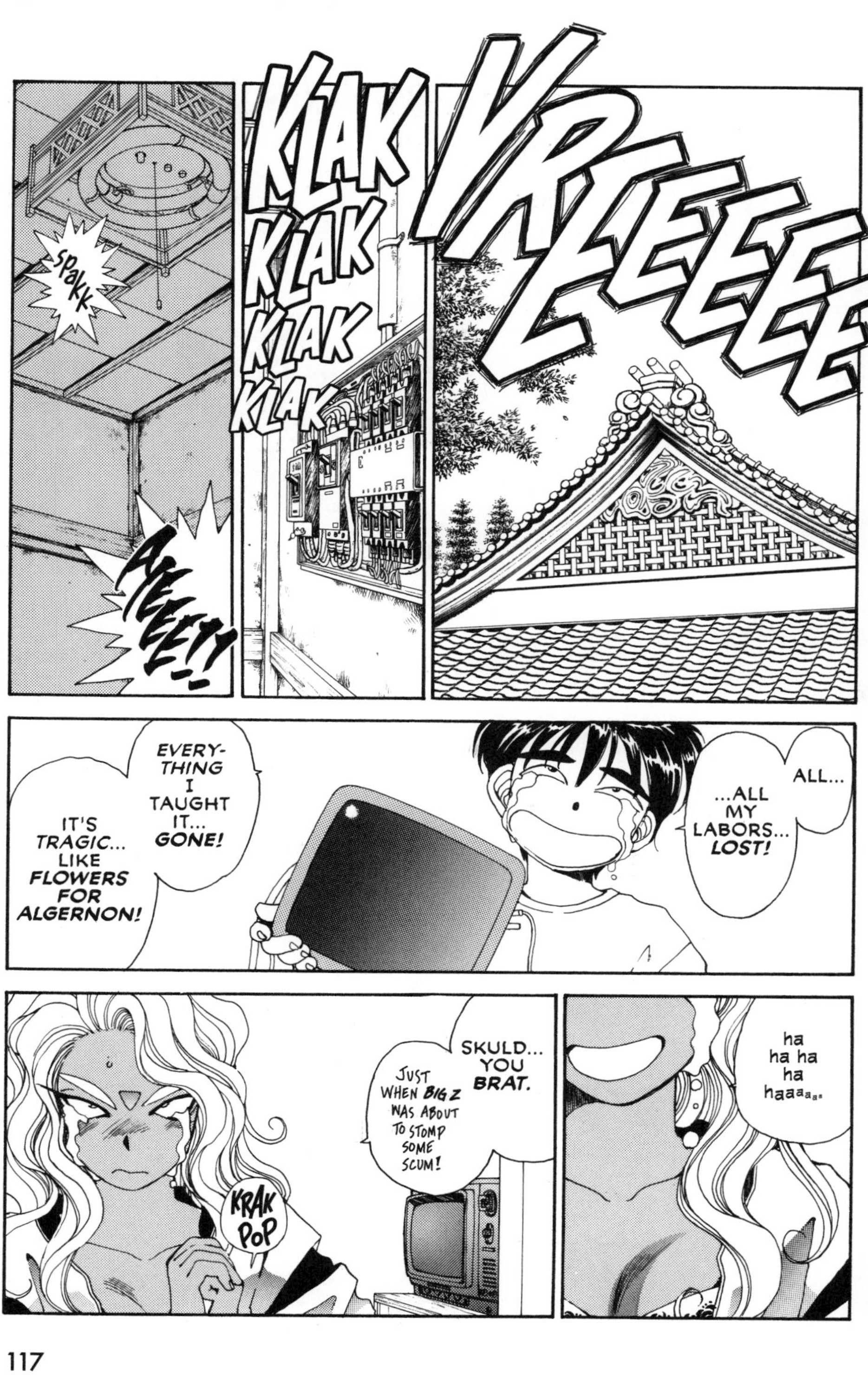

VREEEEEE
KLAK KLAK KLAK KLAK
SPAKK
AIEEEE!!
ALL...
...ALL MY LABORS... LOST!
EVERY-THING I TAUGHT IT... GONE!
IT'S TRAGIC... LIKE FLOWERS FOR ALGERNON!
ha ha ha ha haaaaa
SKULD... YOU BRAT.
JUST WHEN BIG Z WAS ABOUT TO STOMP SOME SCUM!
KRAK POP

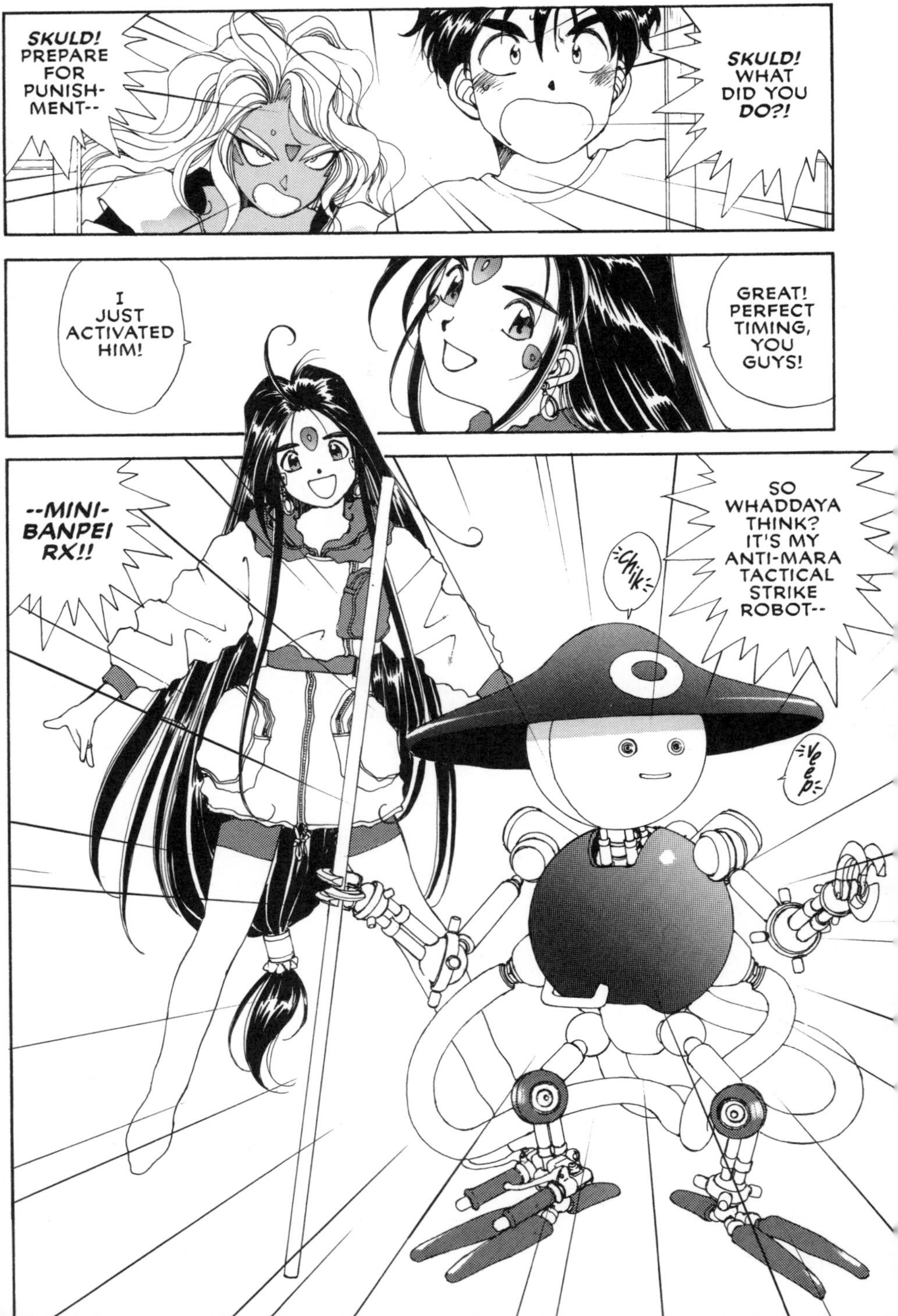
SKULD! WHAT DID YOU DO?!
SKULD! PREPARE FOR PUNISHMENT--
GREAT! PERFECT TIMING, YOU GUYS!
I JUST ACTIVATED HIM!
SO WHADDAYA THINK? IT'S MY ANTI-MARA TACTICAL STRIKE ROBOT--
Chik
Veep
--MINI-BANPEI RX!!

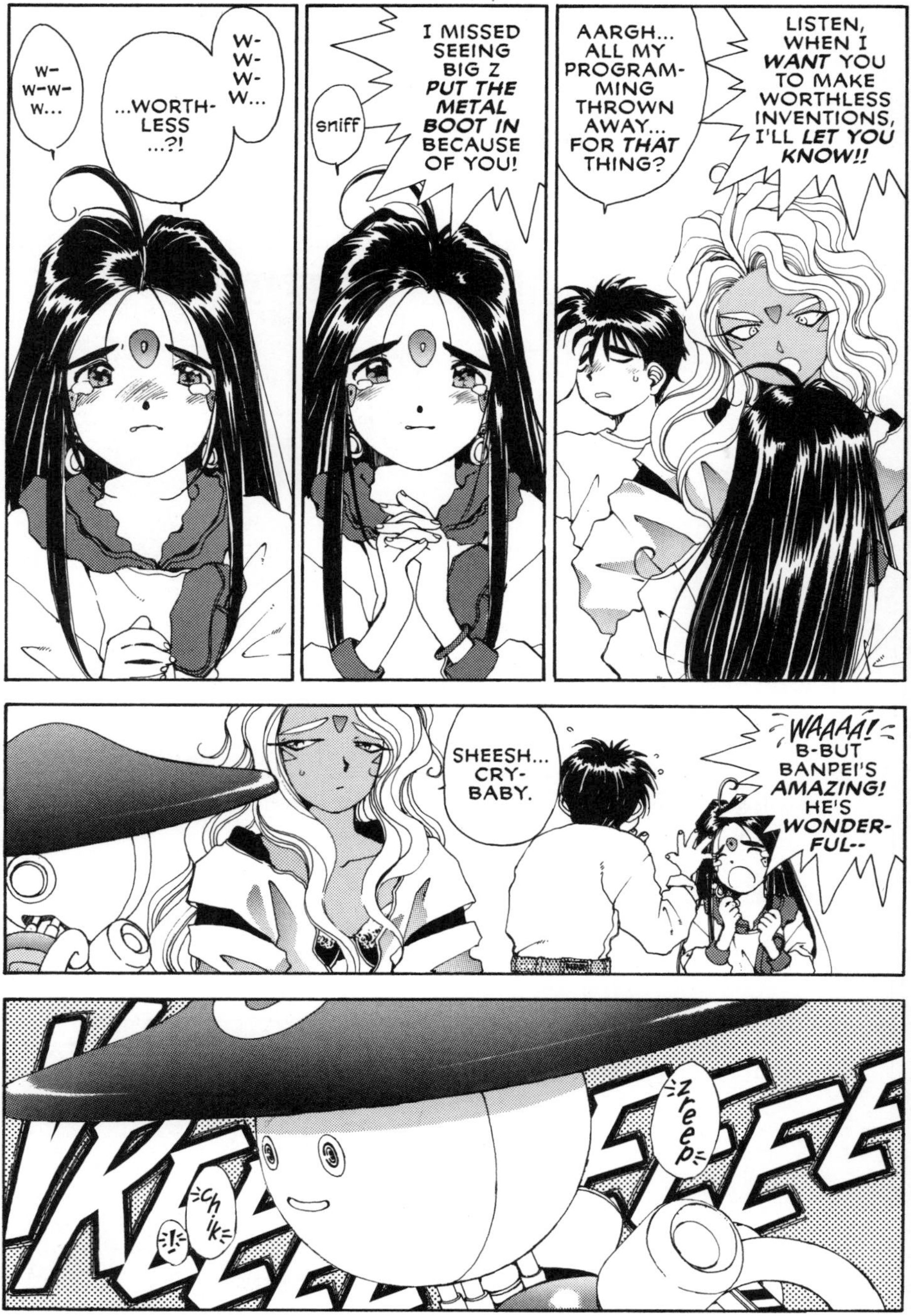
LISTEN, WHEN I *WANT* YOU TO MAKE WORTHLESS INVENTIONS, I'LL *LET YOU KNOW!!*
AARGH... ALL MY PROGRAMMING THROWN AWAY... FOR *THAT* THING?
I MISSED SEEING BIG Z *PUT THE METAL BOOT IN* BECAUSE OF YOU!
sniff
W-W-W-W-W...
...WORTHLESS...?!
W-W-W-W...
WAAAA! B-BUT BANPEI'S *AMAZING!* HE'S *WONDERFUL--*
SHEESH... CRY-BABY.
zreep
chik
!

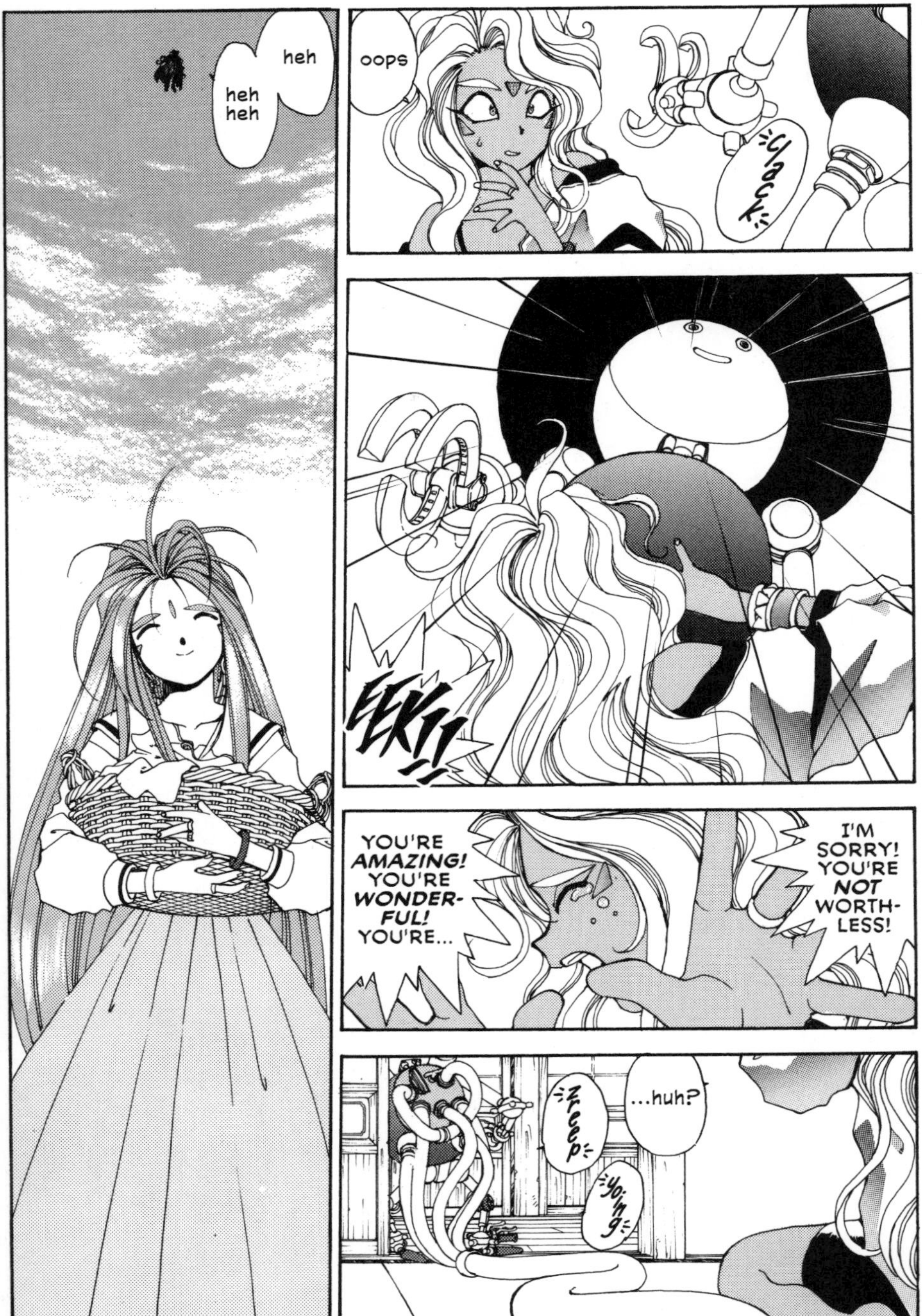
oops
clack
EEK!!
I'M SORRY! YOU'RE *NOT* WORTHLESS!
YOU'RE *AMAZING!* YOU'RE *WONDERFUL!* YOU'RE...
...huh?
zreep
yoing
heh
heh heh

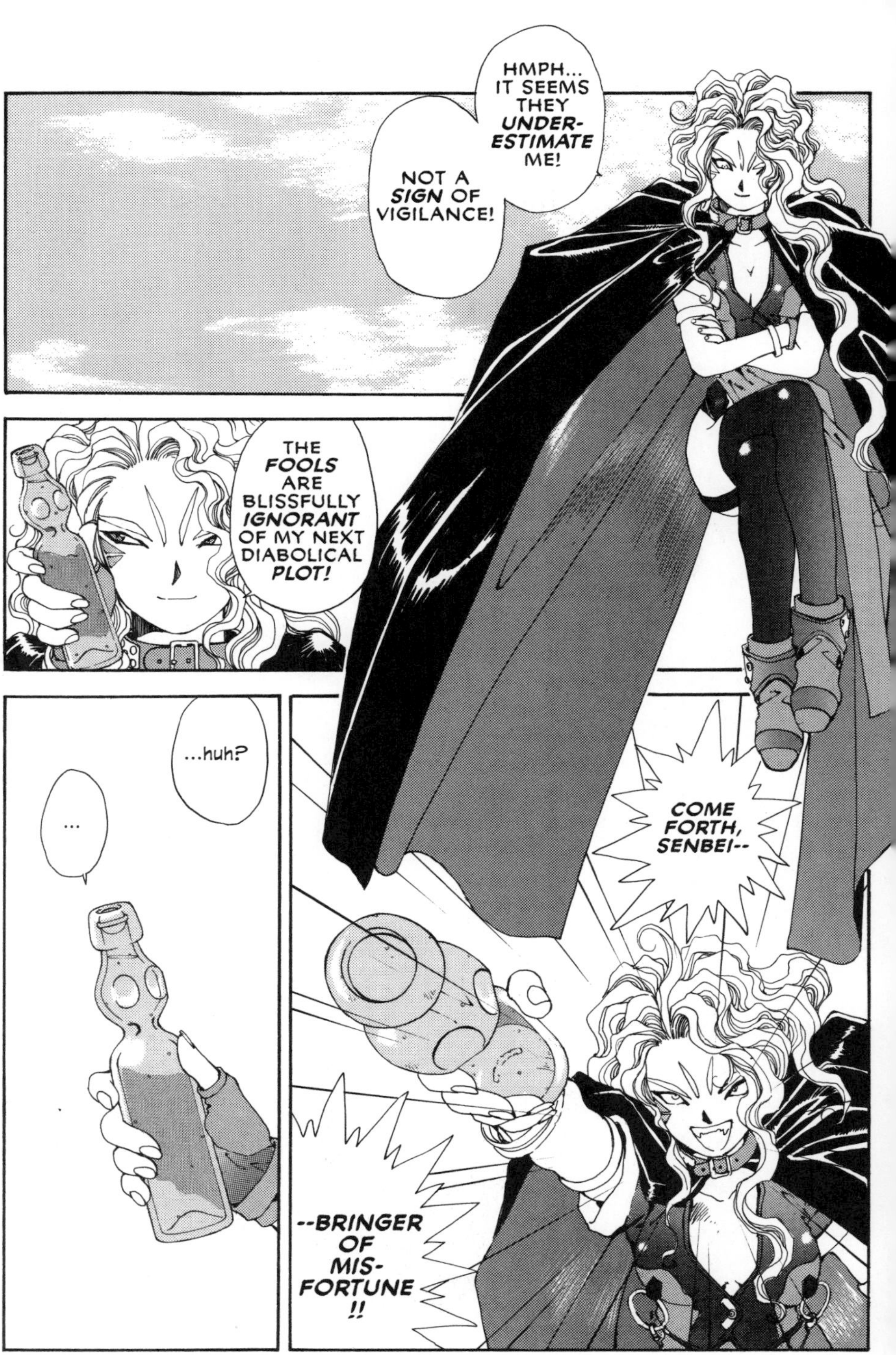
HMPH... IT SEEMS THEY UNDER-ESTIMATE ME!
NOT A SIGN OF VIGILANCE!
THE FOOLS ARE BLISSFULLY IGNORANT OF MY NEXT DIABOLICAL PLOT!
COME FORTH, SENBEI--
--BRINGER OF MIS-FORTUNE !!
...huh?
...

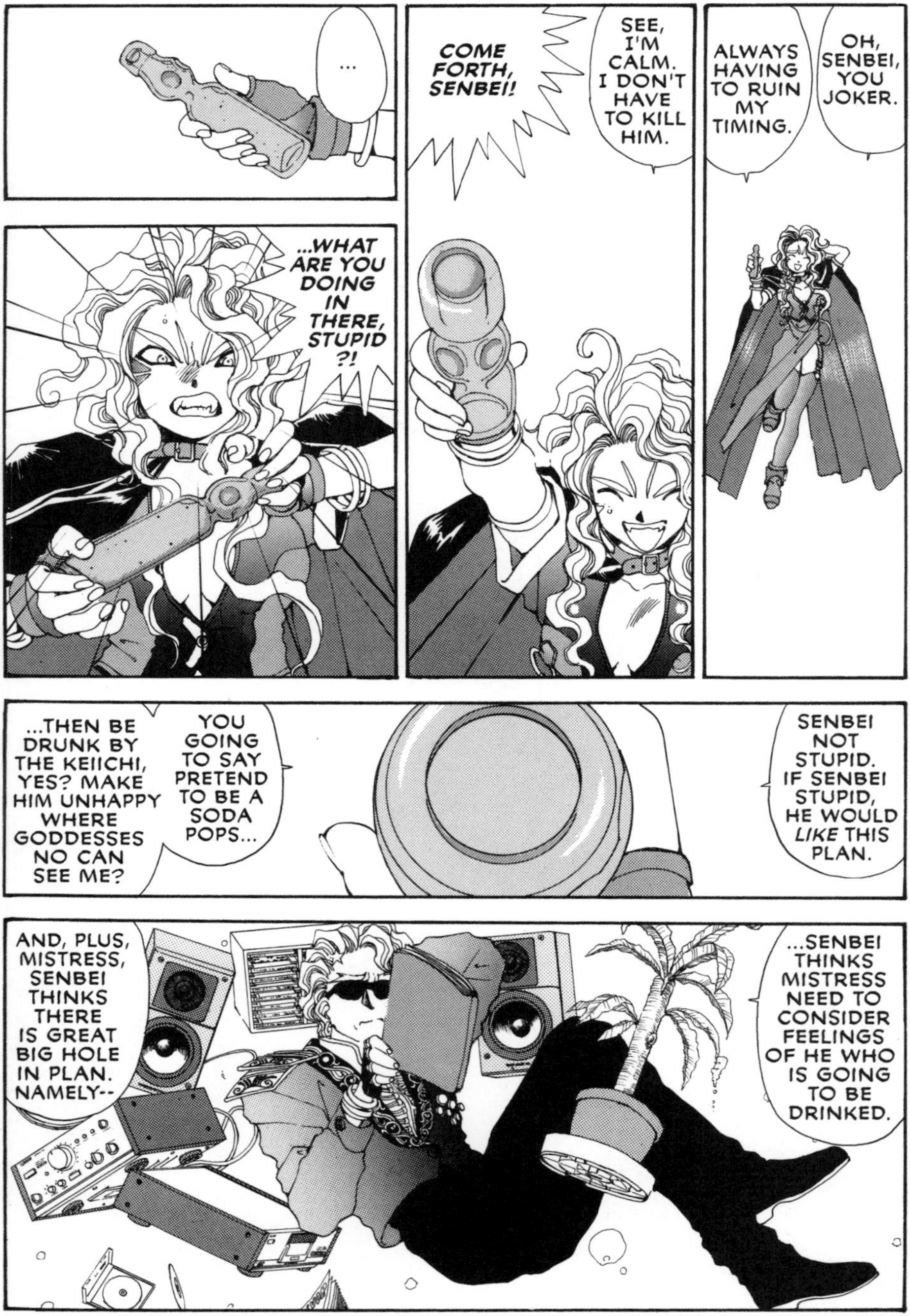
OH, SENBEI, YOU JOKER.
ALWAYS HAVING TO RUIN MY TIMING.
SEE, I'M CALM. I DON'T HAVE TO KILL HIM.
COME FORTH, SENBEI!
...
...WHAT ARE YOU DOING IN THERE, STUPID?!
SENBEI NOT STUPID. IF SENBEI STUPID, HE WOULD *LIKE* THIS PLAN.
YOU GOING TO SAY PRETEND TO BE A SODA POPS...
...THEN BE DRUNK BY THE KEIICHI, YES? MAKE HIM UNHAPPY WHERE GODDESSES NO CAN SEE ME?
...SENBEI THINKS MISTRESS NEED TO CONSIDER FEELINGS OF HE WHO IS GOING TO BE DRINKED.
AND, PLUS, MISTRESS, SENBEI THINKS THERE IS GREAT BIG HOLE IN PLAN. NAMELY--

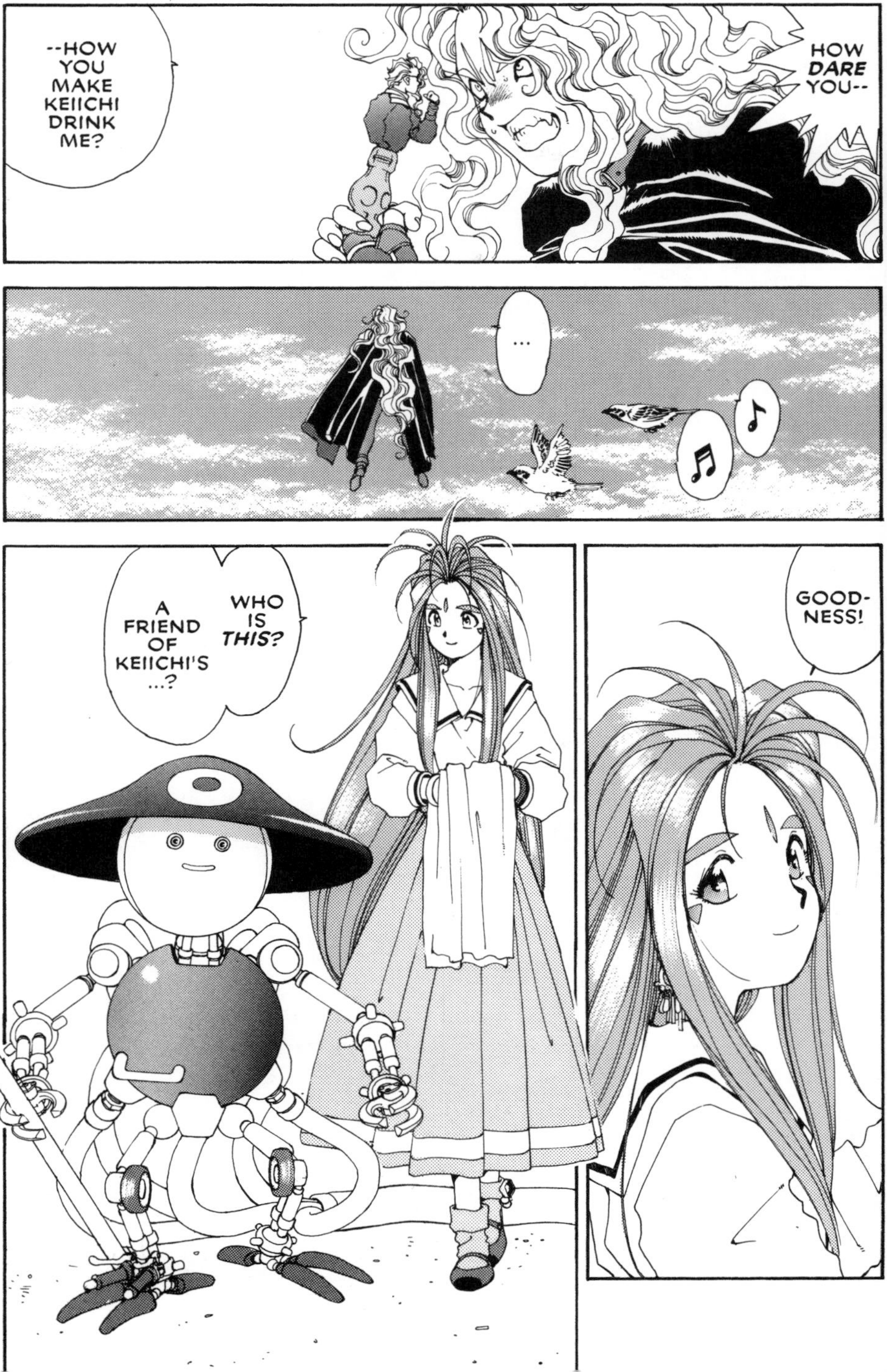
HOW *DARE* YOU--
--HOW YOU MAKE KEIICHI DRINK ME?
...
♪
♫
GOOD-NESS!
WHO IS *THIS?*
A FRIEND OF KEIICHI'S ...?

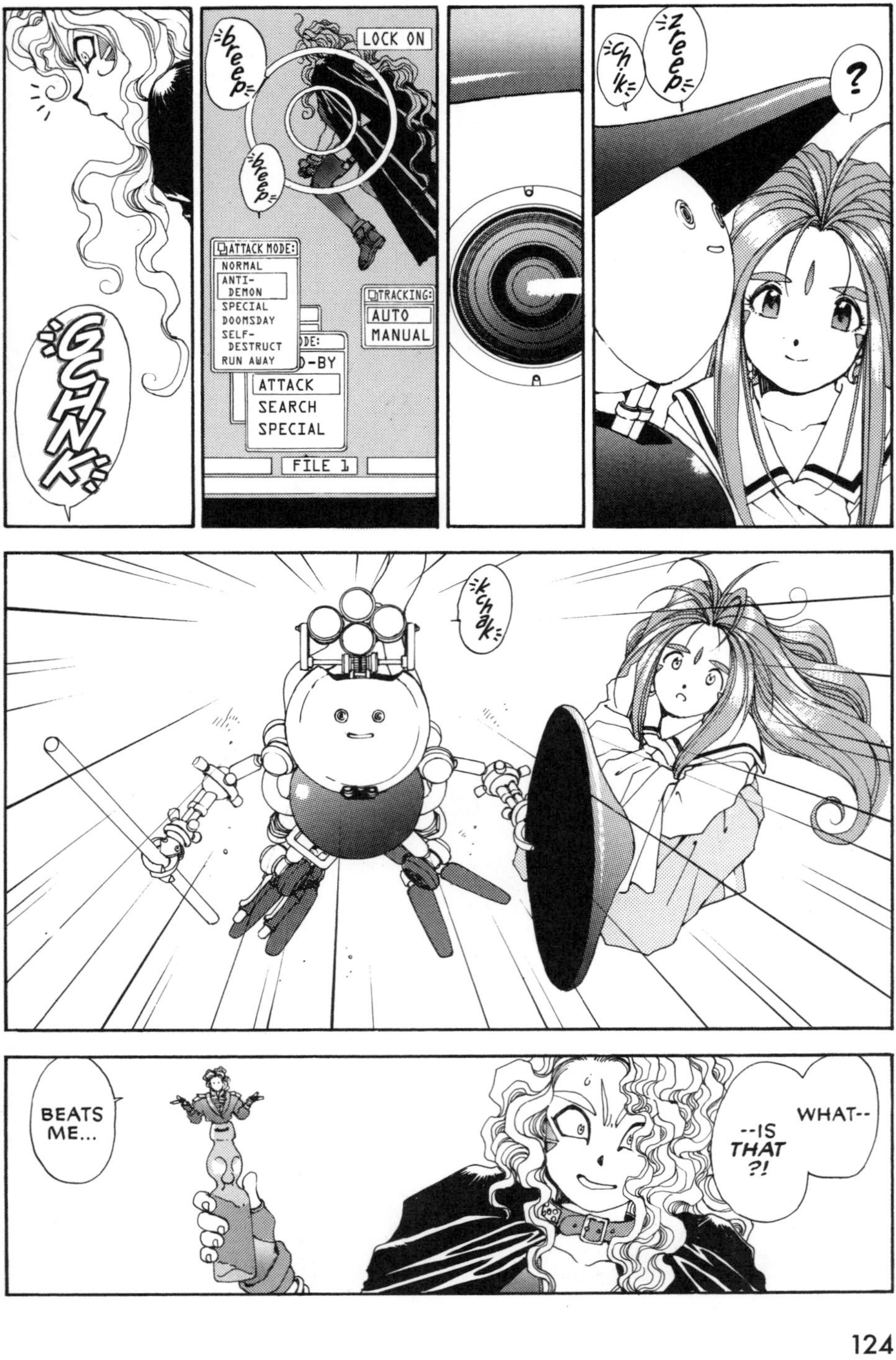
zreep
chik
?
breep
LOCK ON
breep
ATTACK MODE:
NORMAL
ANTI-DEMON
SPECIAL
DOOMSDAY
SELF-DESTRUCT
RUN AWAY
TRACKING:
AUTO
MANUAL
ATTACK
SEARCH
SPECIAL
FILE 1
GCHNK
kchak
WHAT--
--IS *THAT*?!
BEATS ME...

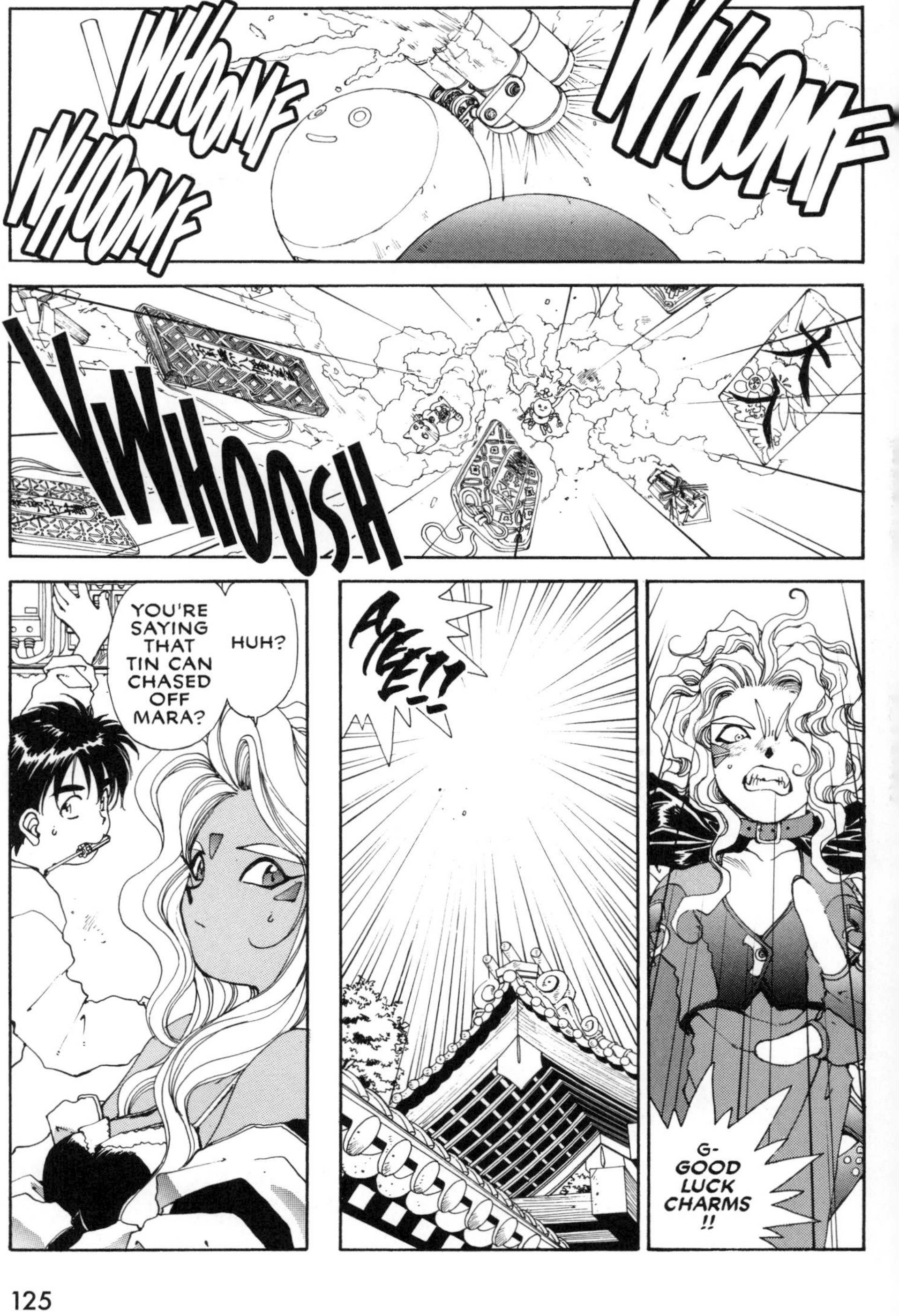
WHOOMF
WHOOMF
WHOOMF
VWHOOSH
G- GOOD LUCK CHARMS !!
AIEE!!
HUH?
YOU'RE SAYING THAT TIN CAN CHASED OFF MARA?

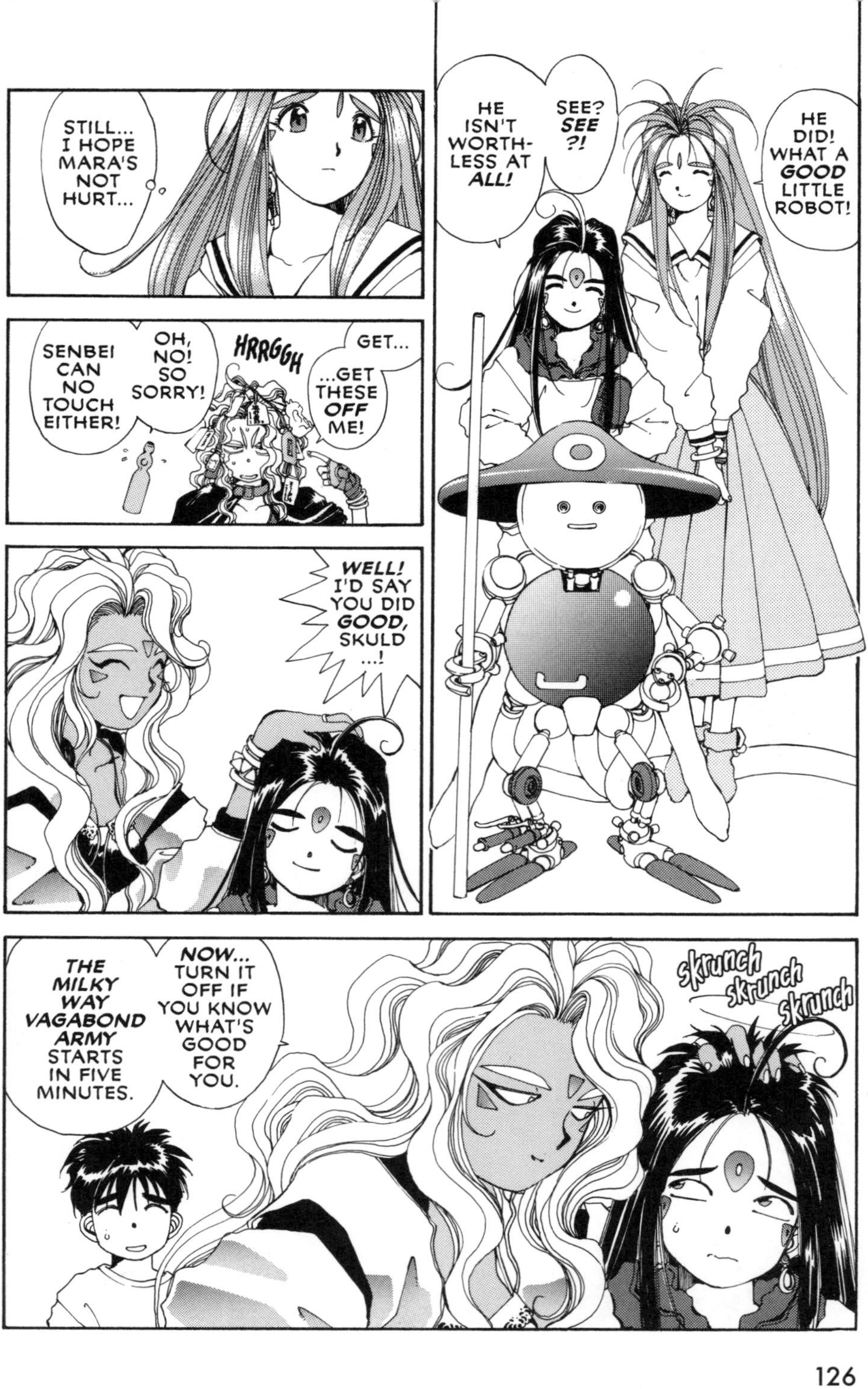
HE DID! WHAT A GOOD LITTLE ROBOT!
SEE? SEE?!
HE ISN'T WORTHLESS AT ALL!
STILL... I HOPE MARA'S NOT HURT...
GET...
...GET THESE OFF ME!
HRRGGH
OH, NO! SO SORRY!
SENBEI CAN NO TOUCH EITHER!
WELL! I'D SAY YOU DID GOOD, SKULD ...!
skrunch skrunch skrunch
NOW... TURN IT OFF IF YOU KNOW WHAT'S GOOD FOR YOU.
THE MILKY WAY VAGABOND ARMY STARTS IN FIVE MINUTES.

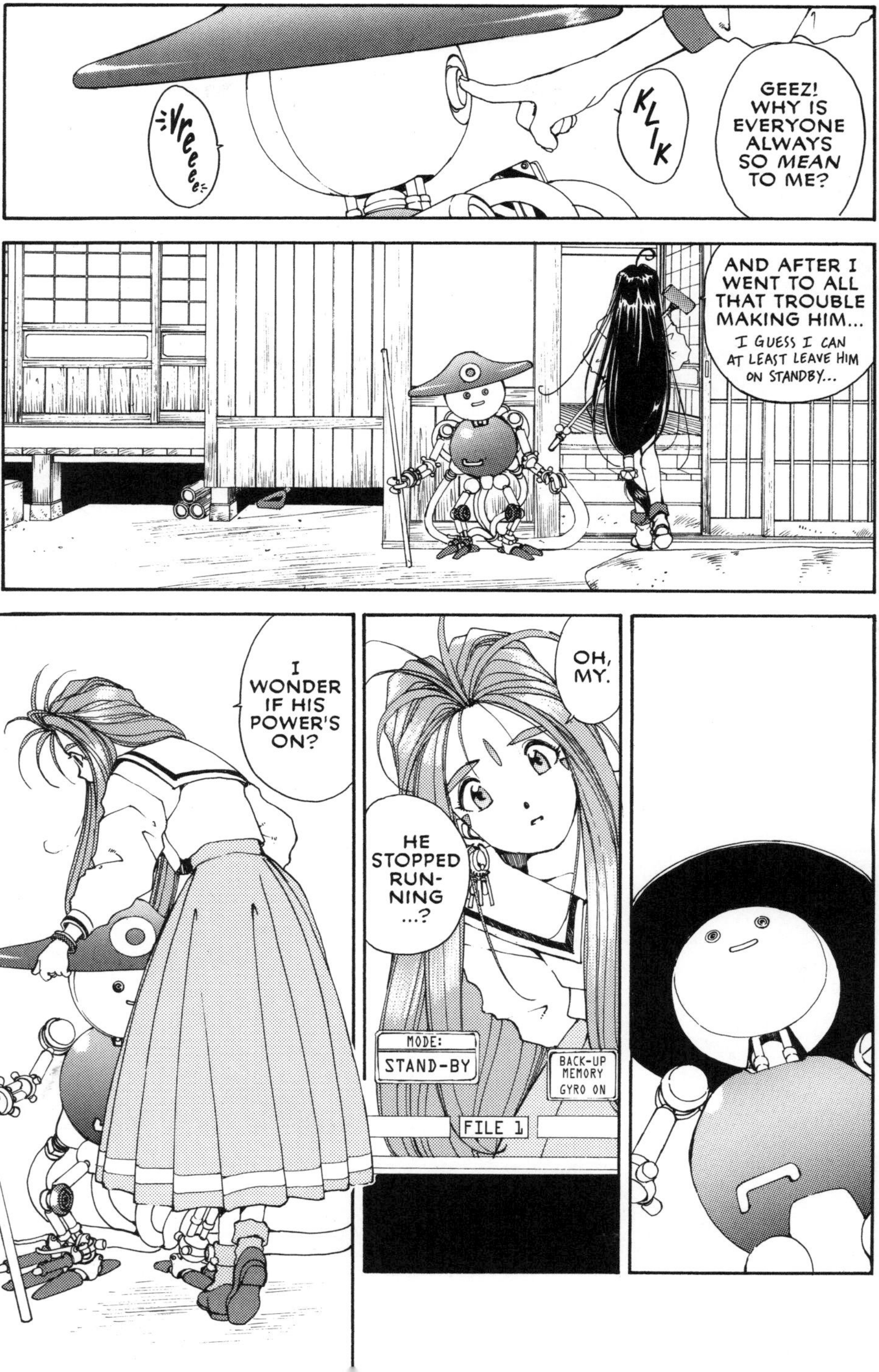
GEEZ! WHY IS EVERYONE ALWAYS SO MEAN TO ME?
KLIK
Vreeeee
AND AFTER I WENT TO ALL THAT TROUBLE MAKING HIM...
I GUESS I CAN AT LEAST LEAVE HIM ON STANDBY...
OH, MY.
HE STOPPED RUN-NING ...?
MODE:
STAND-BY
BACK-UP MEMORY GYRO ON
FILE 1
I WONDER IF HIS POWER'S ON?

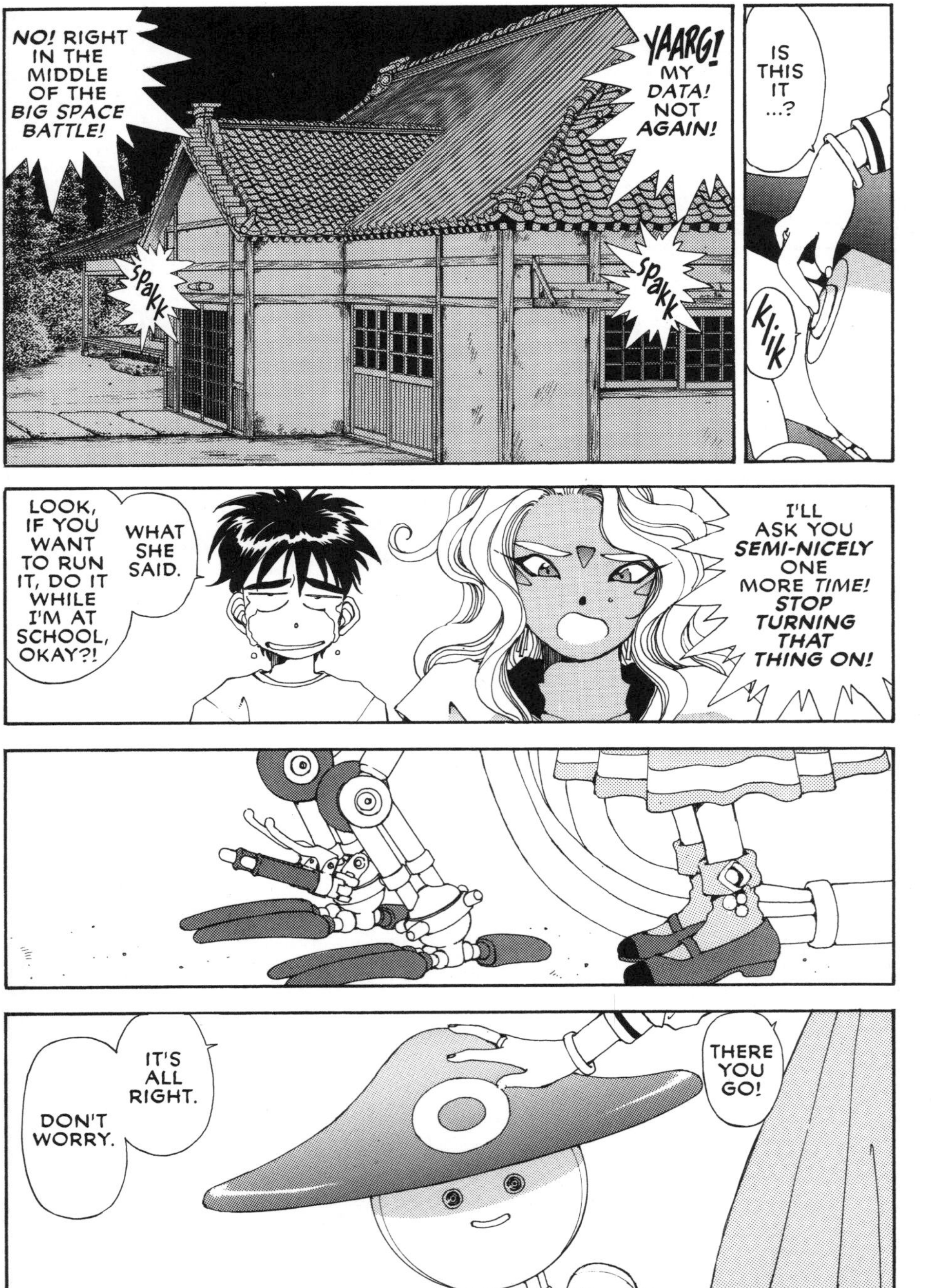
IS THIS IT ...?
klik
YAARG! MY DATA! NOT AGAIN!
spakk
NO! RIGHT IN THE MIDDLE OF THE BIG SPACE BATTLE!
spakk
I'LL ASK YOU SEMI-NICELY ONE MORE TIME! STOP TURNING THAT THING ON!
WHAT SHE SAID.
LOOK, IF YOU WANT TO RUN IT, DO IT WHILE I'M AT SCHOOL, OKAY?!
THERE YOU GO!
IT'S ALL RIGHT.
DON'T WORRY.

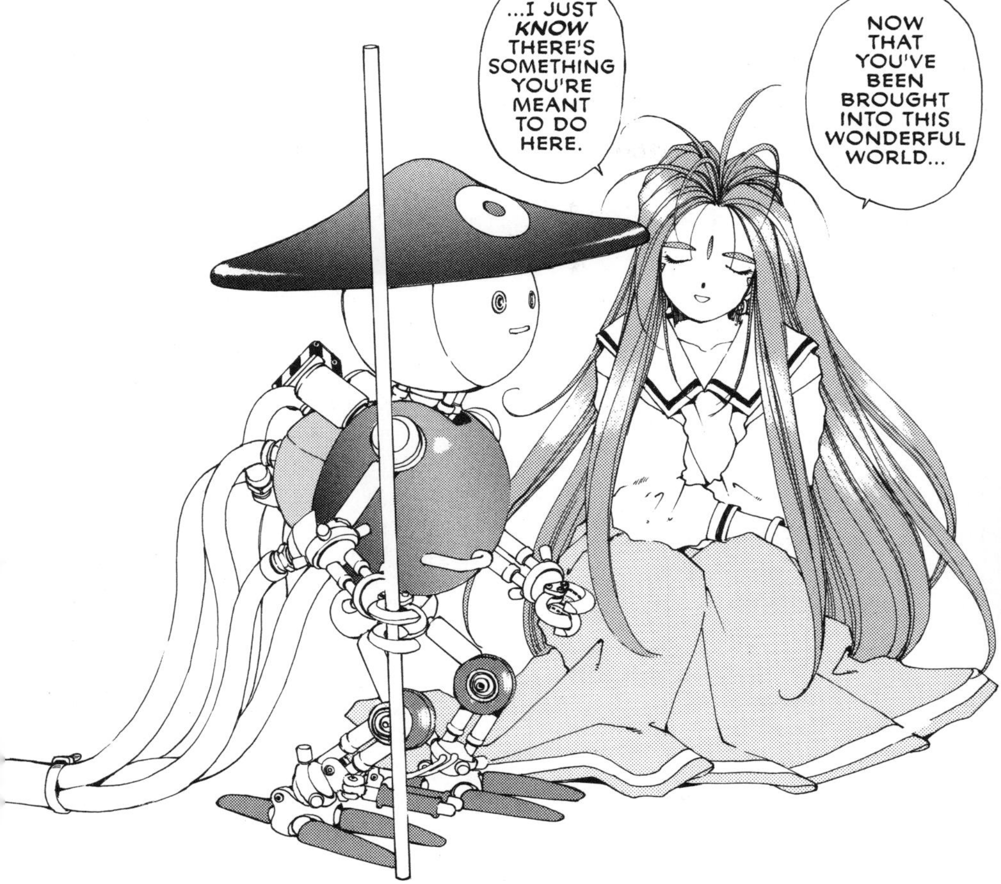
NOW THAT YOU'VE BEEN BROUGHT INTO THIS WONDERFUL WORLD...
...I JUST *KNOW* THERE'S SOMETHING YOU'RE MEANT TO DO HERE.

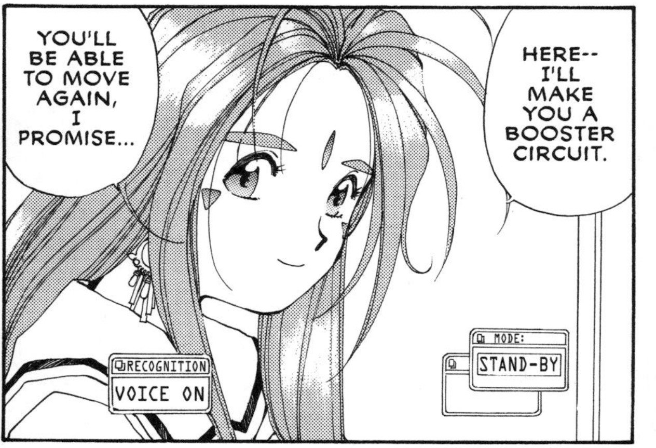
HERE-- I'LL MAKE YOU A BOOSTER CIRCUIT.
YOU'LL BE ABLE TO MOVE AGAIN, I PROMISE...
MODE:
STAND-BY
RECOGNITION
VOICE ON

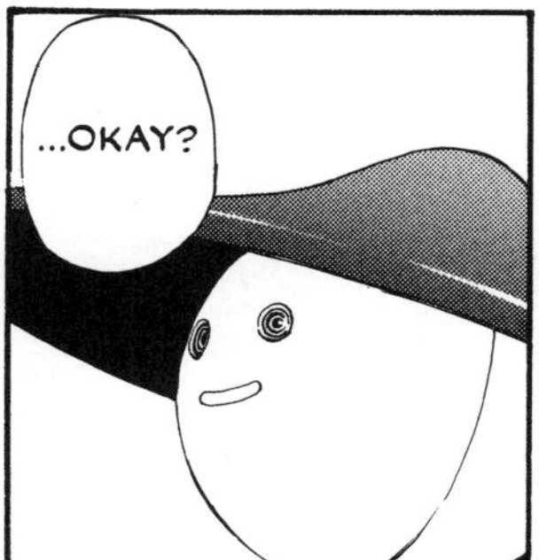
...OKAY?

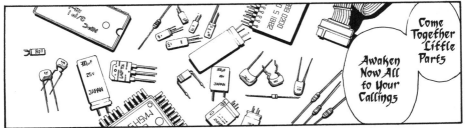

Come Together Little Parts
Awaken Now All to Your Callings
Join Hands... Become as One
...Become the Power... Making Greater Power Still!
NOW...
ALL WE DO IS PLUG THIS IN...
hah
hahh
?

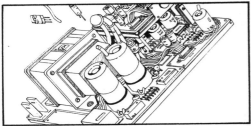

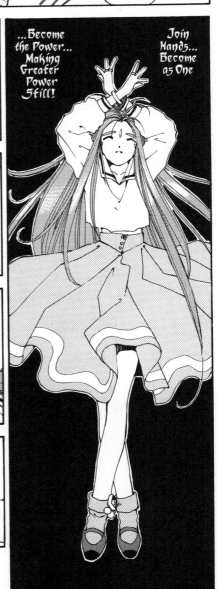

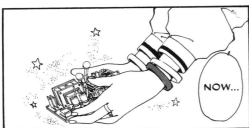

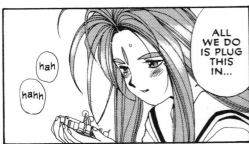

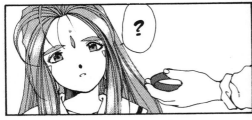

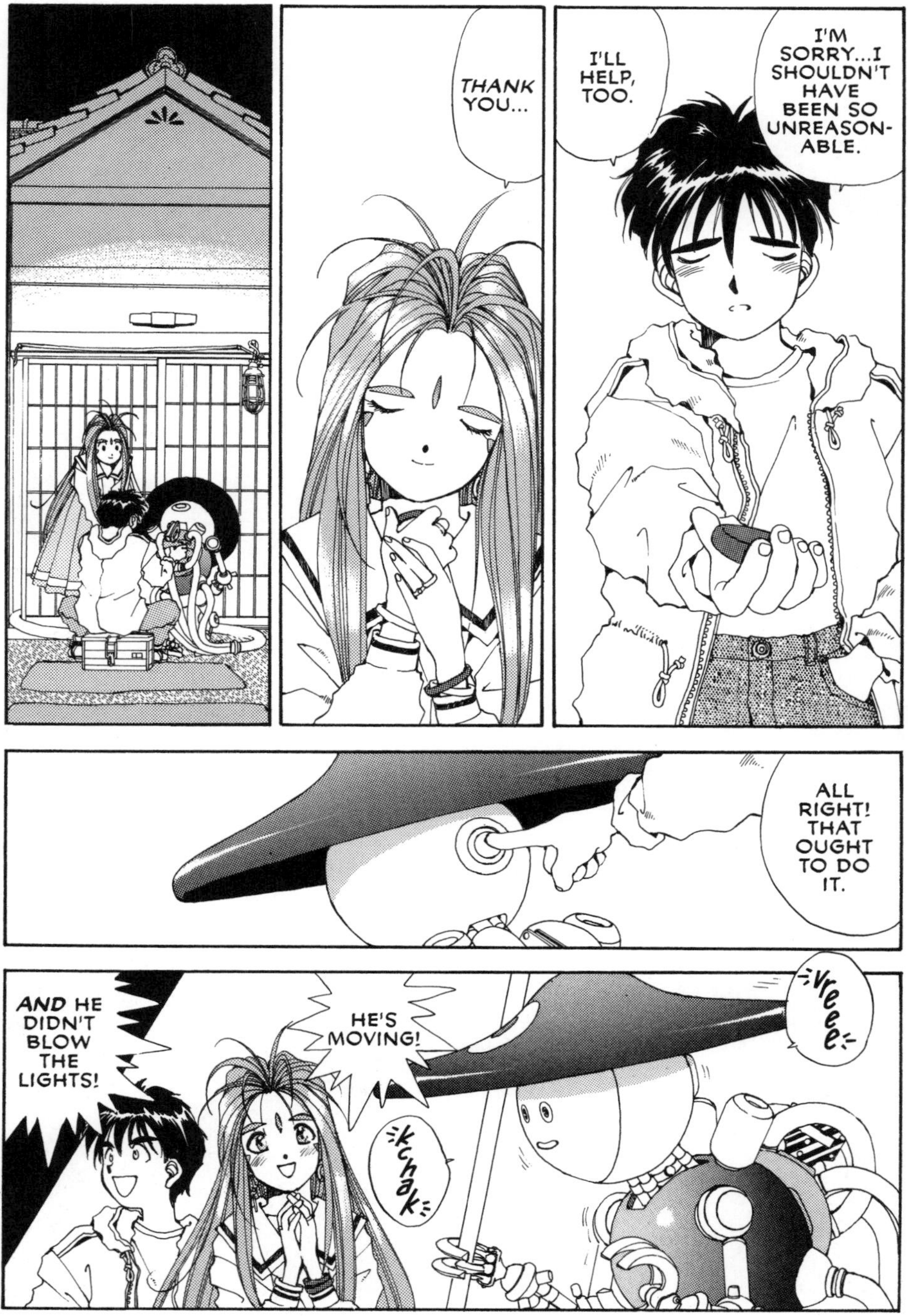
I'M SORRY...I SHOULDN'T HAVE BEEN SO UNREASON-ABLE.
I'LL HELP, TOO.
THANK YOU...
ALL RIGHT! THAT OUGHT TO DO IT.
vreeee
HE'S MOVING!
AND HE DIDN'T BLOW THE LIGHTS!
kchak

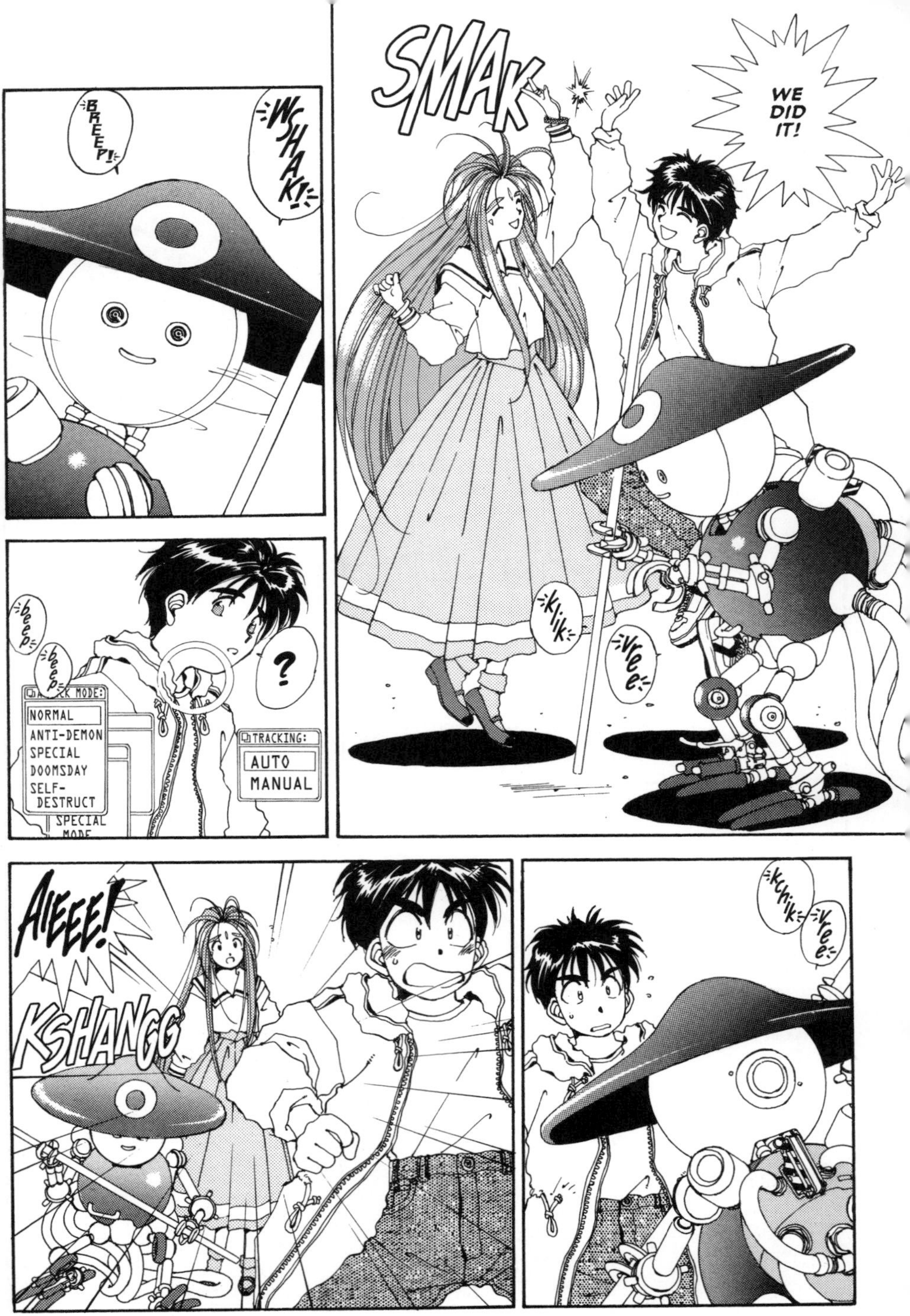

SMAK
WE DID IT!
klik
vree
BREEP!
WSHAK!
beep
beep
?
NORMAL
ANTI-DEMON
SPECIAL
DOOMSDAY
SELF-DESTRUCT
SPECIAL
TRACKING:
AUTO
MANUAL
kchik
vree
AIEEE!
KSHANGG

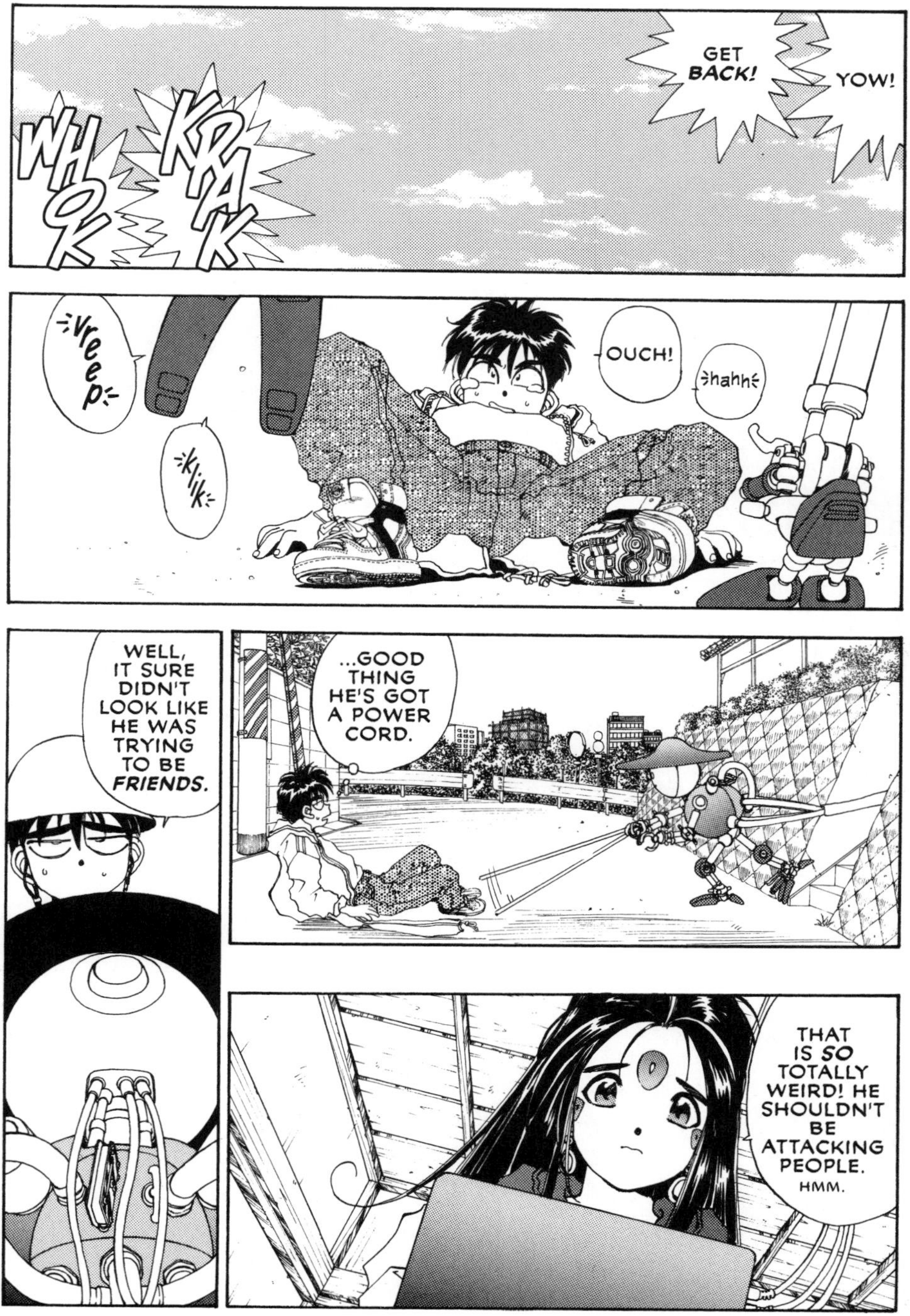
GET BACK!
YOW!
KRAK
WHOK
OUCH!
hahh
vreep
klik
...GOOD THING HE'S GOT A POWER CORD.
THAT IS SO TOTALLY WEIRD! HE SHOULDN'T BE ATTACKING PEOPLE.
HMM.
WELL, IT SURE DIDN'T LOOK LIKE HE WAS TRYING TO BE FRIENDS.

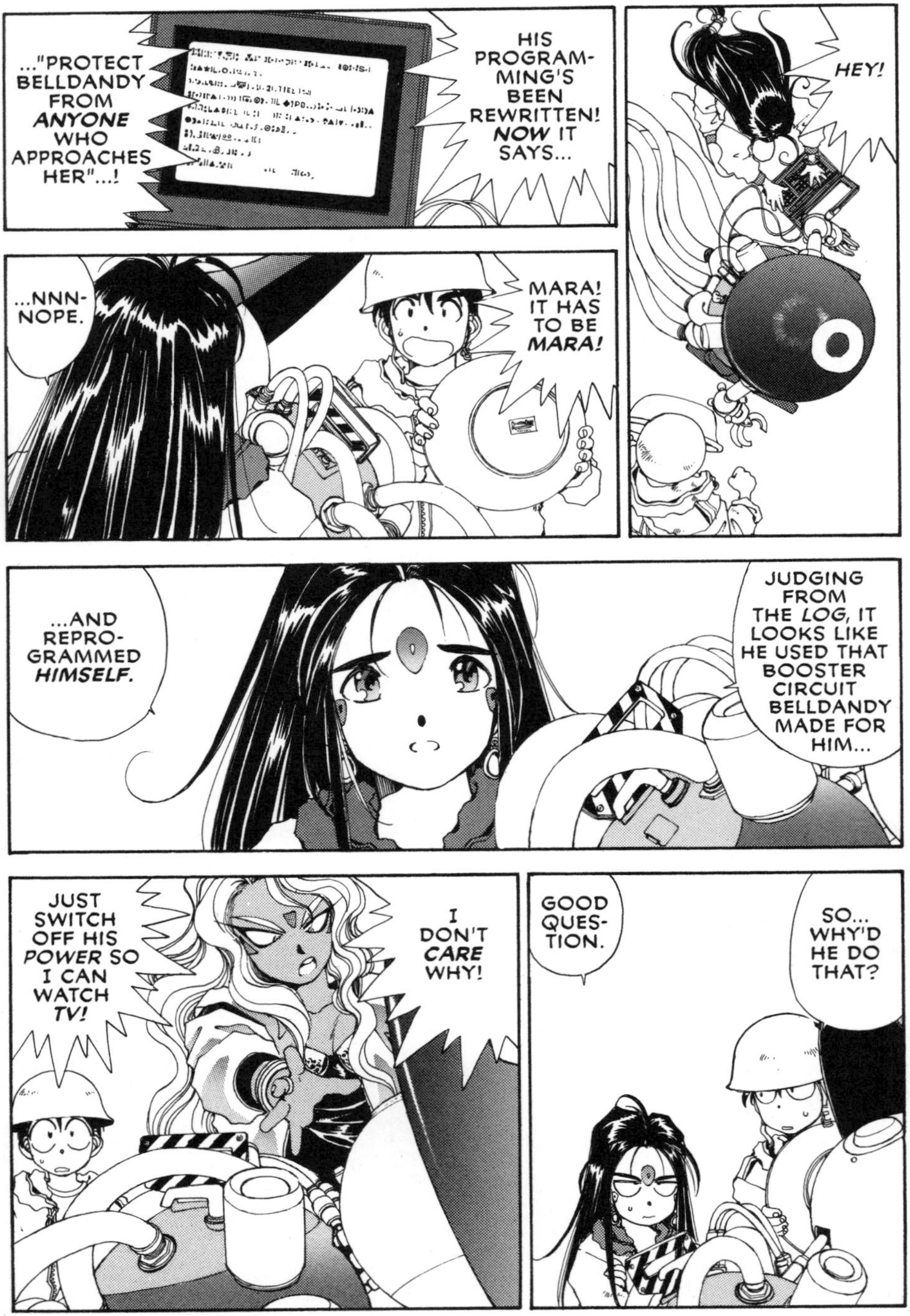
HEY!
HIS PROGRAMMING'S BEEN REWRITTEN! NOW IT SAYS...
..."PROTECT BELLDANDY FROM ANYONE WHO APPROACHES HER"...!
MARA! IT HAS TO BE MARA!
...NNN-NOPE.
JUDGING FROM THE LOG, IT LOOKS LIKE HE USED THAT BOOSTER CIRCUIT BELLDANDY MADE FOR HIM...
...AND REPROGRAMMED HIMSELF.
SO... WHY'D HE DO THAT?
GOOD QUESTION.
I DON'T CARE WHY!
JUST SWITCH OFF HIS POWER SO I CAN WATCH TV!

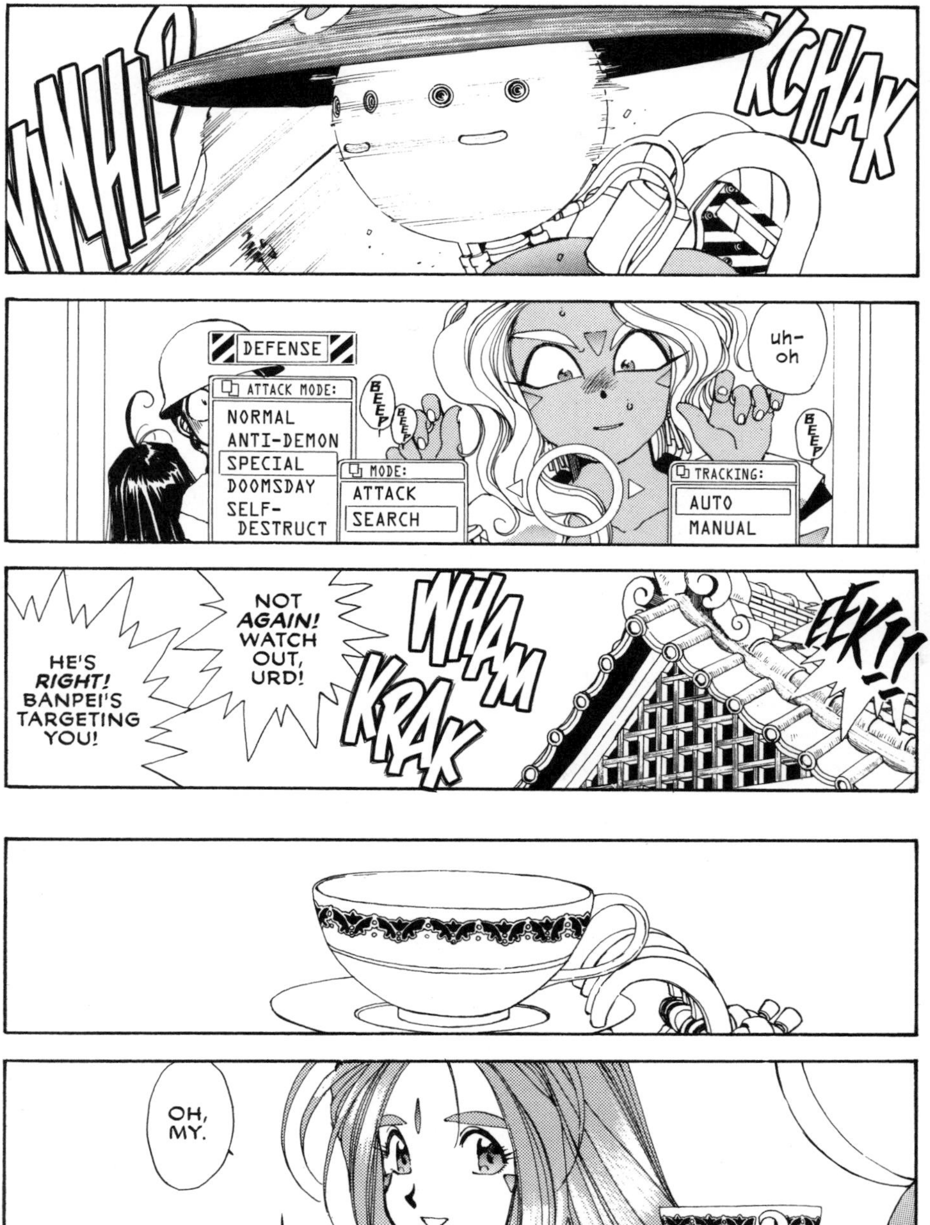
KCHAK
WHIP
uh-oh
BEEP
TRACKING:
AUTO
MANUAL
BEEP
BEEP
MODE:
ATTACK
SEARCH
DEFENSE
ATTACK MODE:
NORMAL
ANTI-DEMON
SPECIAL
DOOMSDAY
SELF-DESTRUCT
EEK!!
WHAM
KRAK
NOT AGAIN! WATCH OUT, URD!
HE'S RIGHT! BANPEI'S TARGETING YOU!
OH, MY.

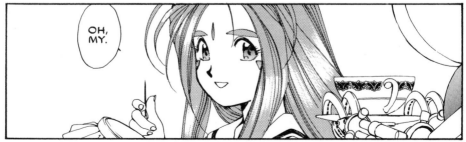

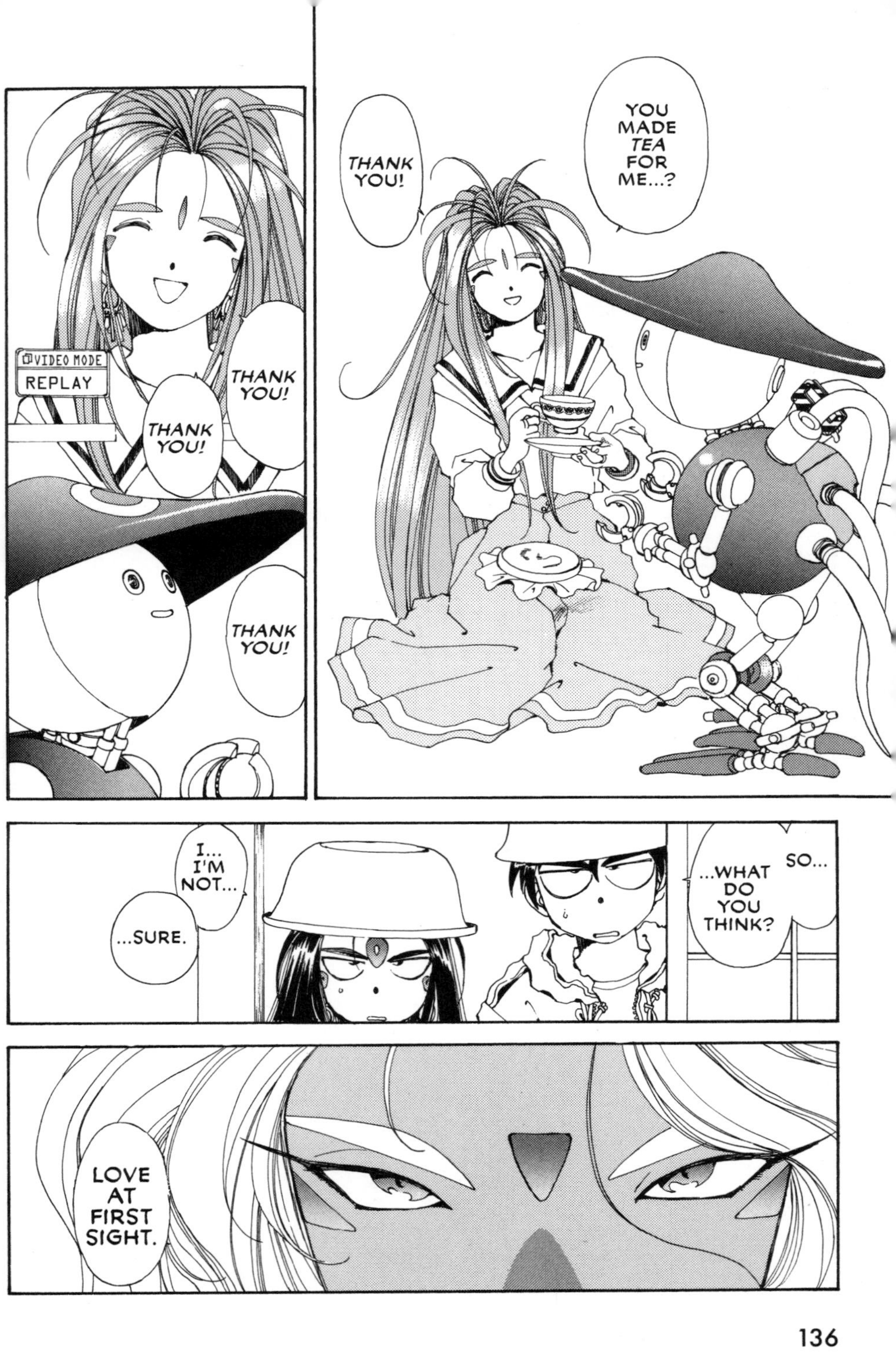
YOU MADE TEA FOR ME...?
THANK YOU!
THANK YOU!
VIDEO MODE
REPLAY
THANK YOU!
THANK YOU!
SO...
...WHAT DO YOU THINK?
I... I'M NOT...
...SURE.
LOVE AT FIRST SIGHT.

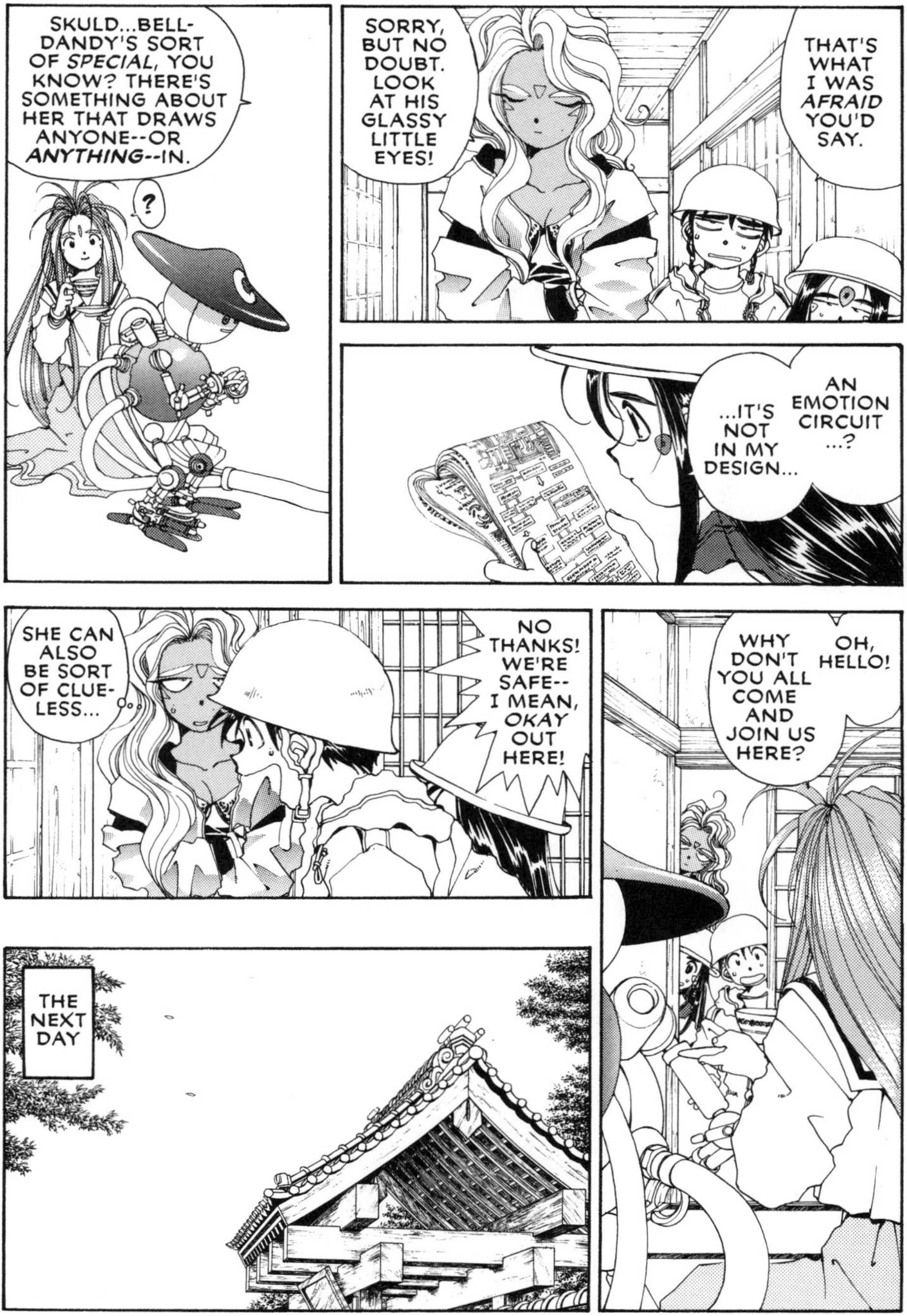
SORRY, BUT NO DOUBT. LOOK AT HIS GLASSY LITTLE EYES!
THAT'S WHAT I WAS *AFRAID* YOU'D SAY.
AN EMOTION CIRCUIT ...?
...IT'S NOT IN MY DESIGN...
SKULD...BELL-DANDY'S SORT OF *SPECIAL*, YOU KNOW? THERE'S SOMETHING ABOUT HER THAT DRAWS ANYONE--OR ***ANYTHING***--IN.
?
OH, HELLO!
WHY DON'T YOU ALL COME AND JOIN US HERE?
NO THANKS! WE'RE SAFE-- I MEAN, *OKAY* OUT HERE!
SHE CAN ALSO BE SORT OF CLUE-LESS...
THE NEXT DAY

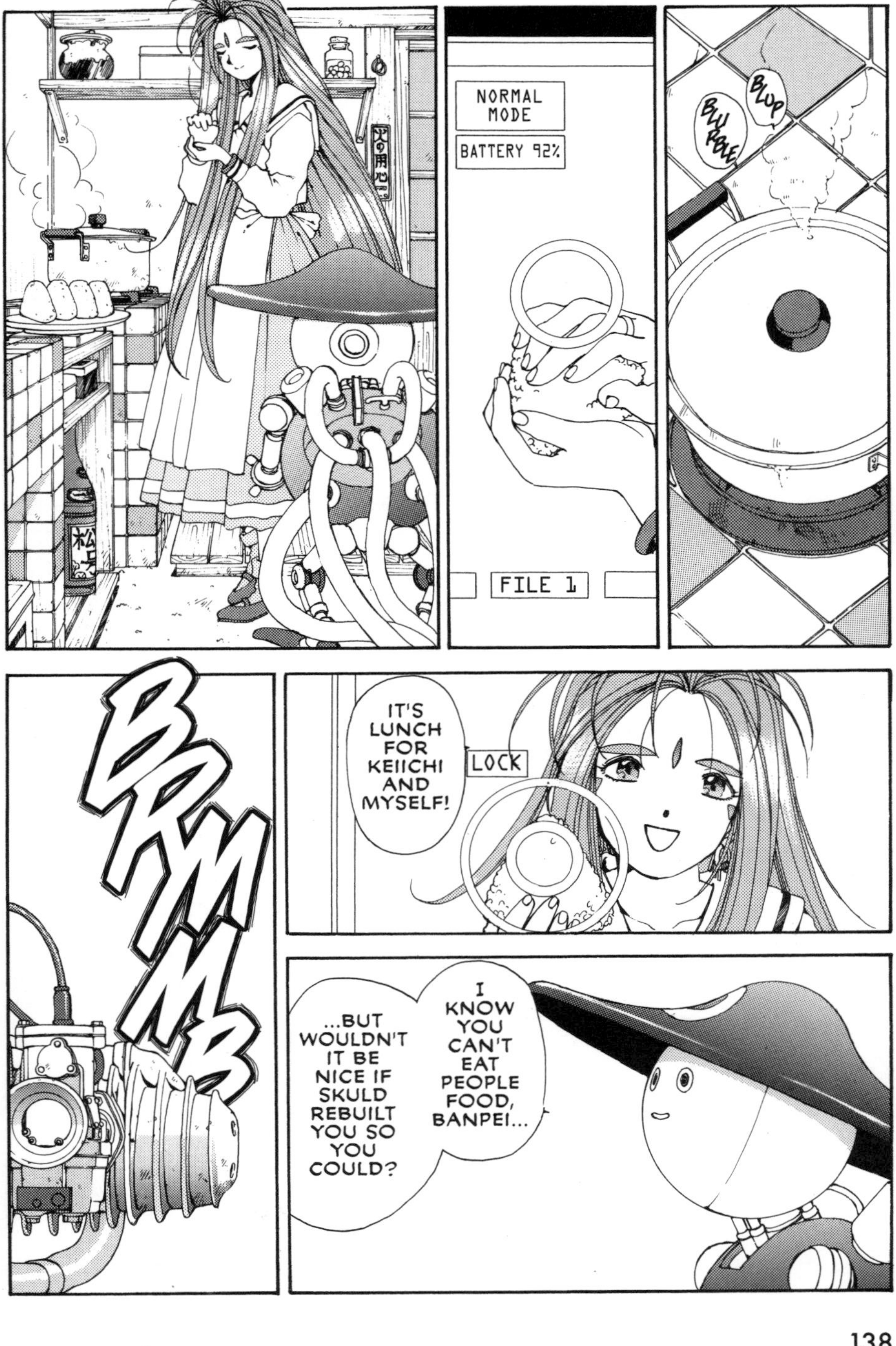
BLUP
BLUBBLE
NORMAL MODE
BATTERY 92%
FILE 1
火の用心
IT'S LUNCH FOR KEIICHI AND MYSELF!
LOCK
I KNOW YOU CAN'T EAT PEOPLE FOOD, BANPEI...
...BUT WOULDN'T IT BE NICE IF SKULD REBUILT YOU SO YOU COULD?
BRMMB

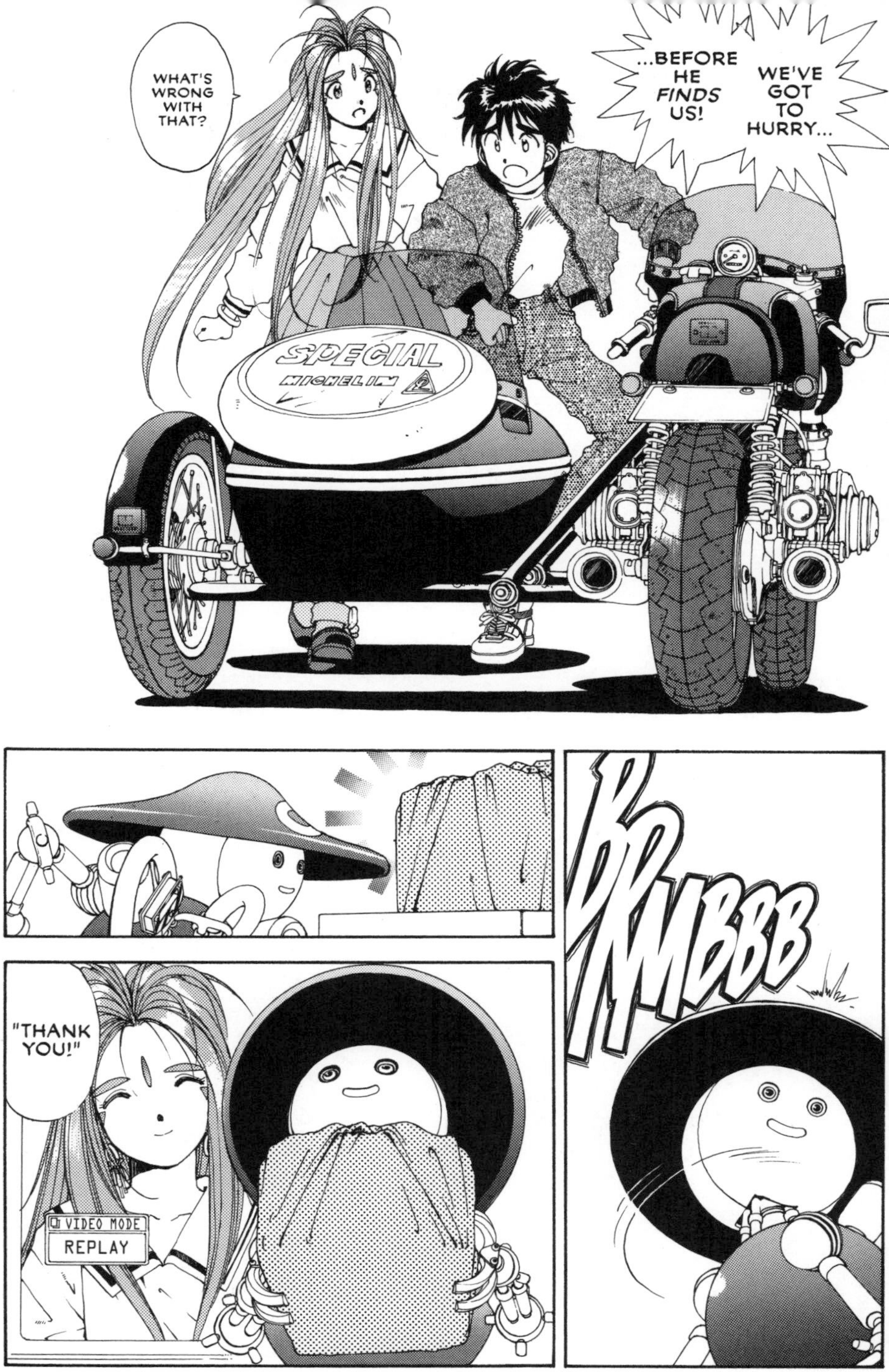
WE'VE GOT TO HURRY...
...BEFORE HE *FINDS* US!
WHAT'S WRONG WITH THAT?
BRRMBBB
"THANK YOU!"
VIDEO MODE
REPLAY

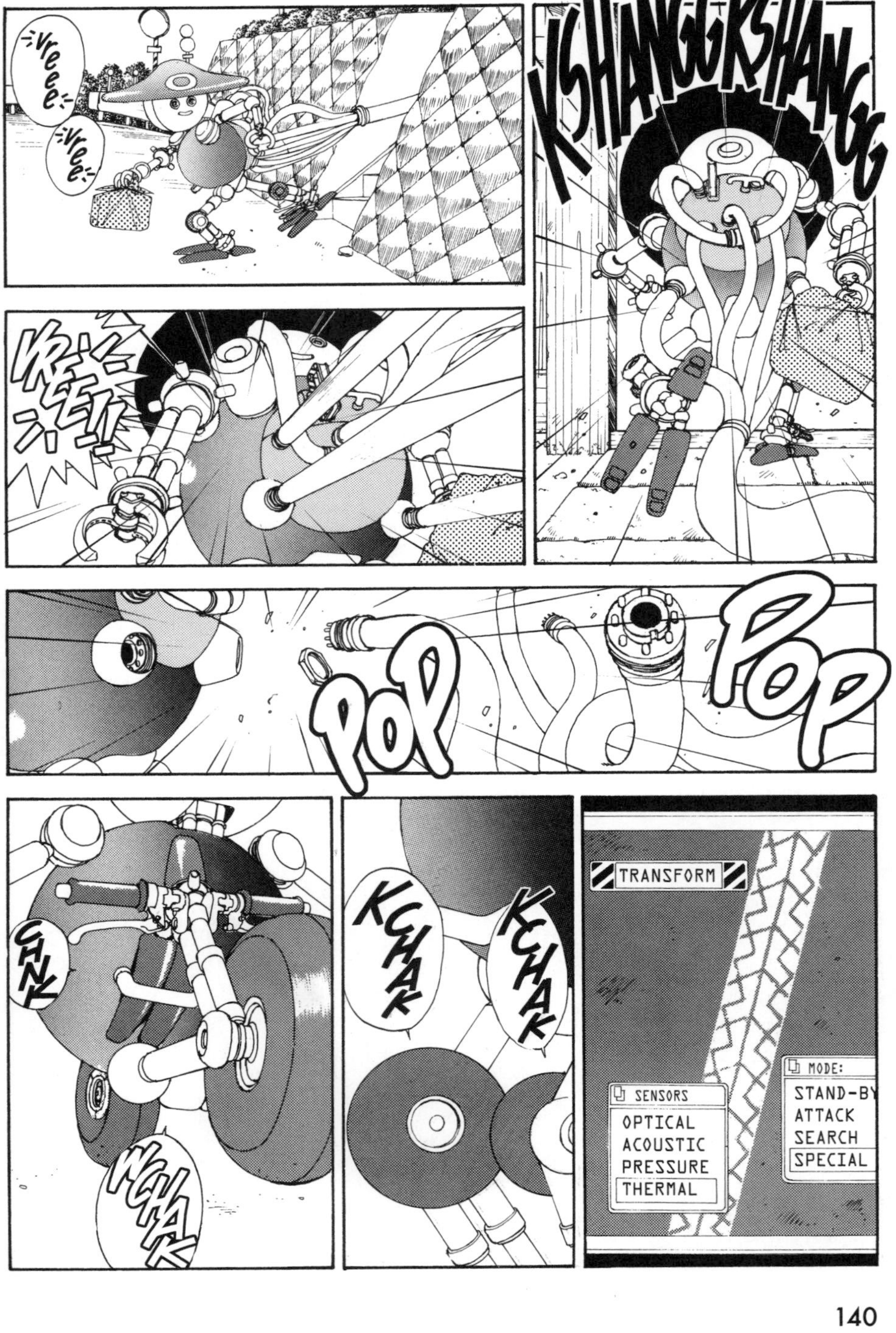
KSHANGG KSHANGG
vreee
vree
VREEE!!
POP
POP
TRANSFORM
MODE:
STAND-BY
ATTACK
SEARCH
SPECIAL
SENSORS
OPTICAL
ACOUSTIC
PRESSURE
THERMAL
KCHAK
KCHAK
CHNK
WCHAK

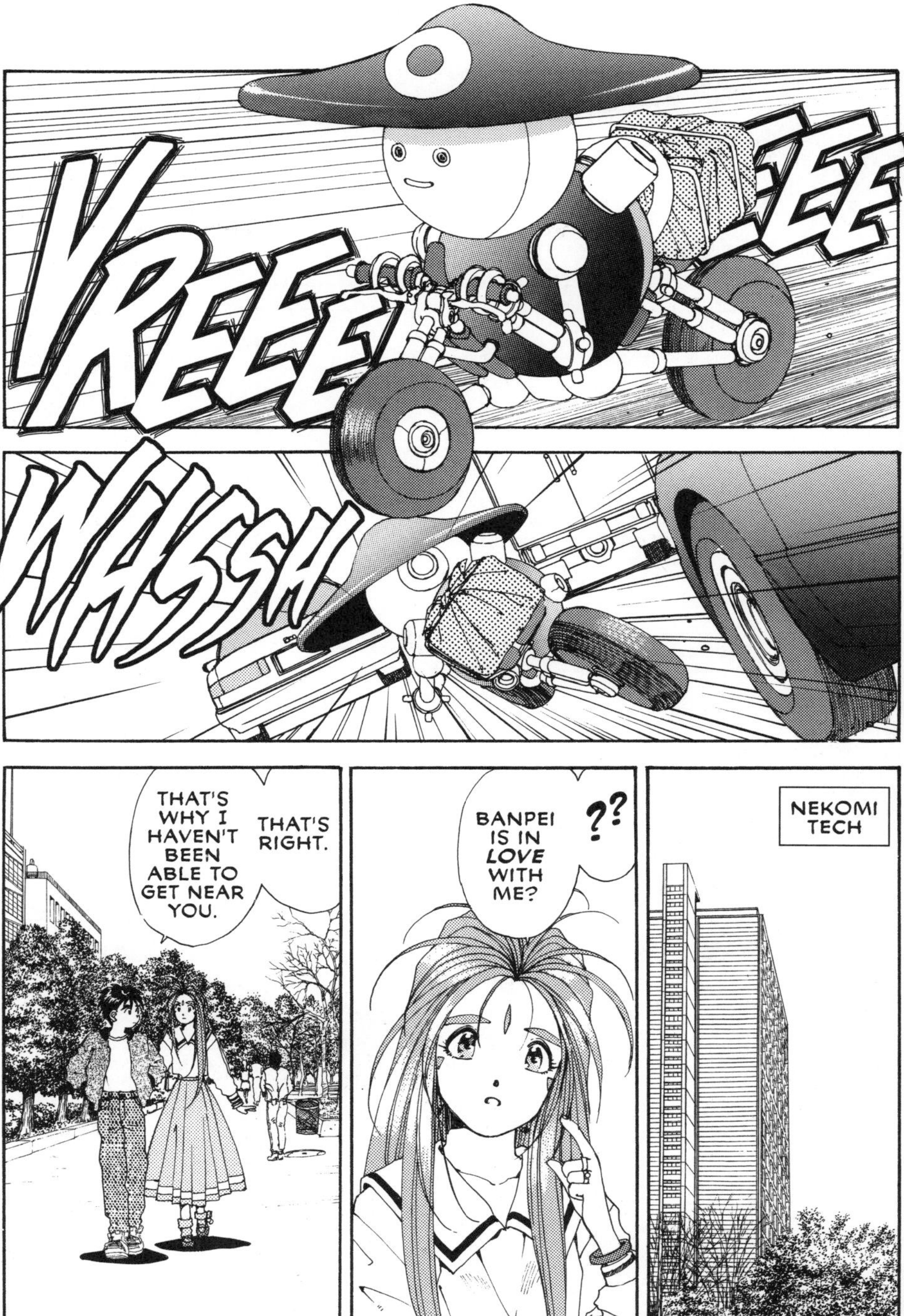
VREEEEEEE
WASSH
NEKOMI TECH
BANPEI IS IN *LOVE* WITH ME?
??
THAT'S RIGHT.
THAT'S WHY I HAVEN'T BEEN ABLE TO GET NEAR YOU.

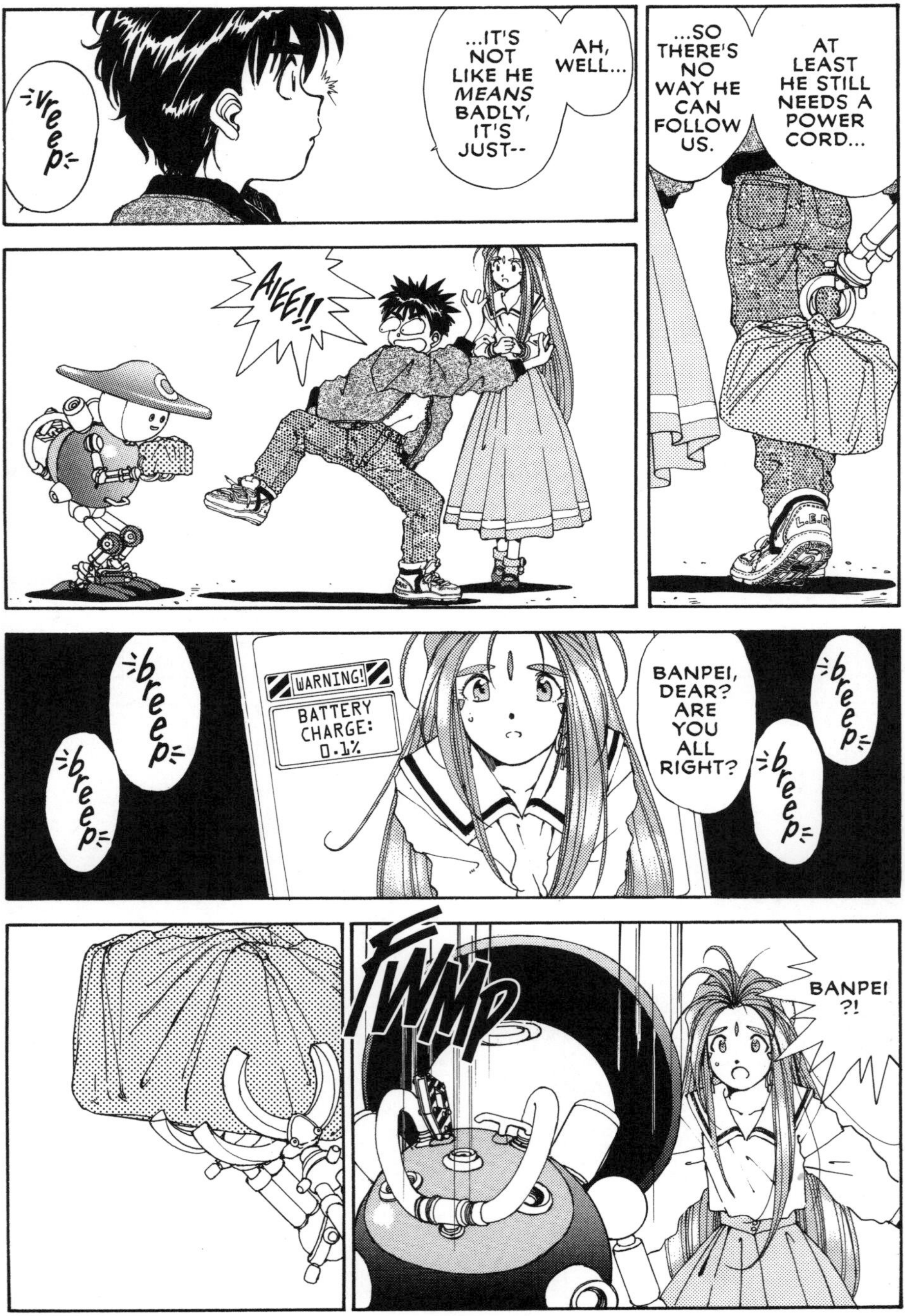
AT LEAST HE STILL NEEDS A POWER CORD...
...SO THERE'S NO WAY HE CAN FOLLOW US.
AH, WELL...
...IT'S NOT LIKE HE *MEANS* BADLY, IT'S JUST--
vreep
AIEEE!!
breep
breep
BANPEI, DEAR? ARE YOU ALL RIGHT?
WARNING!
BATTERY CHARGE: 0.1%
breep
breep
BANPEI ?!
FWMP

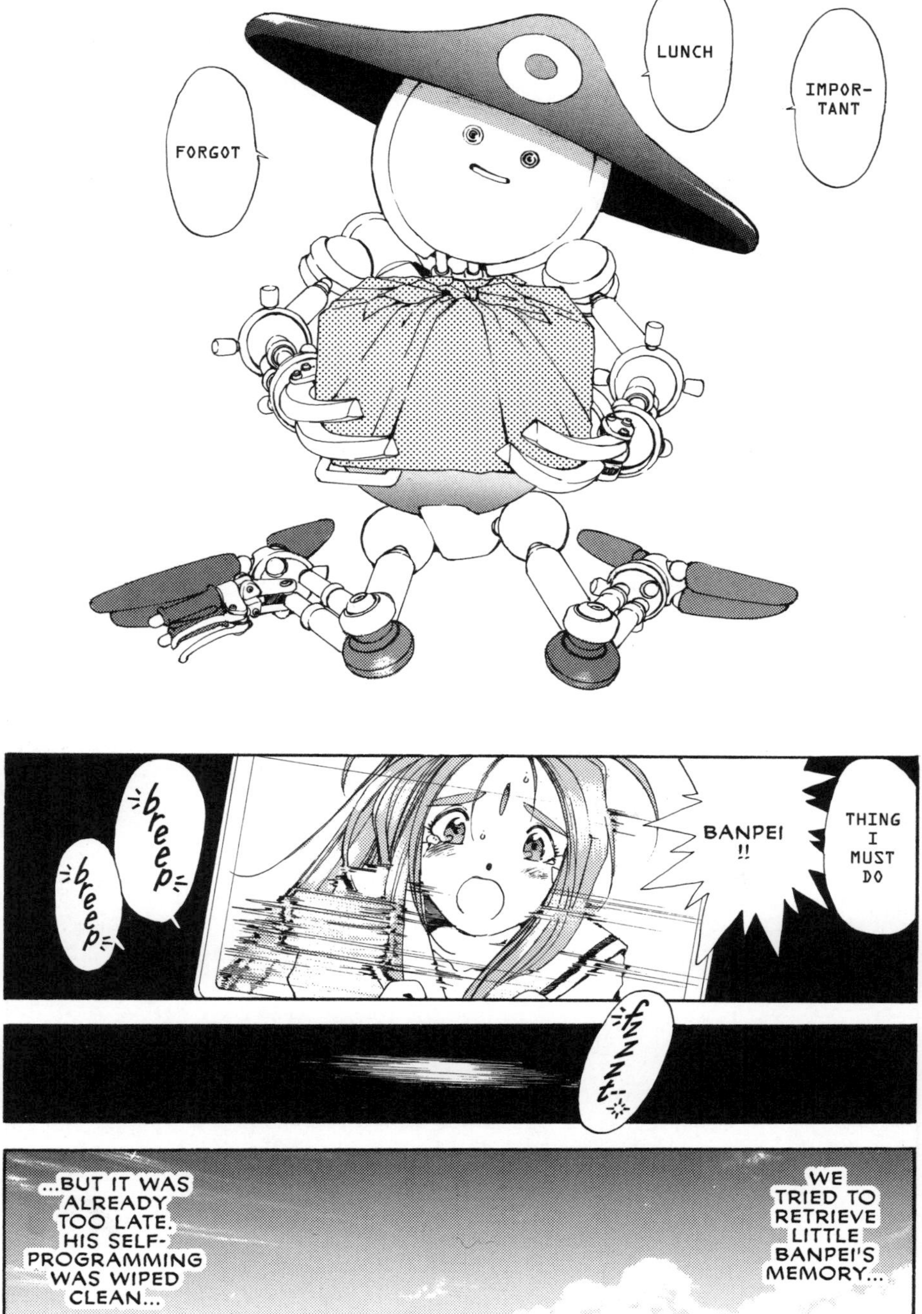
IMPOR-TANT
LUNCH
FORGOT
THING I MUST DO
BANPEI !!
breep
breep
fwzzt
WE TRIED TO RETRIEVE LITTLE BANPEI'S MEMORY...
...BUT IT WAS ALREADY TOO LATE. HIS SELF-PROGRAMMING WAS WIPED CLEAN...

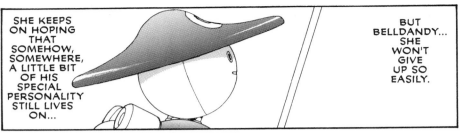

BUT BELLDANDY... SHE WON'T GIVE UP SO EASILY.
SHE KEEPS ON HOPING THAT SOMEHOW, SOMEWHERE, A LITTLE BIT OF HIS SPECIAL PERSONALITY STILL LIVES ON...
SEE YOU LATER, BANPEI!
vreeee
COME BACK SOON.

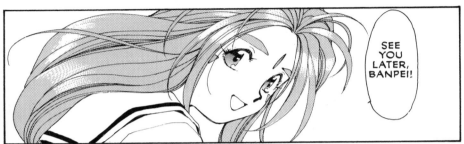

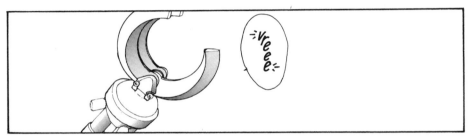

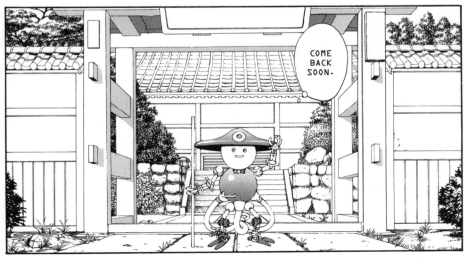

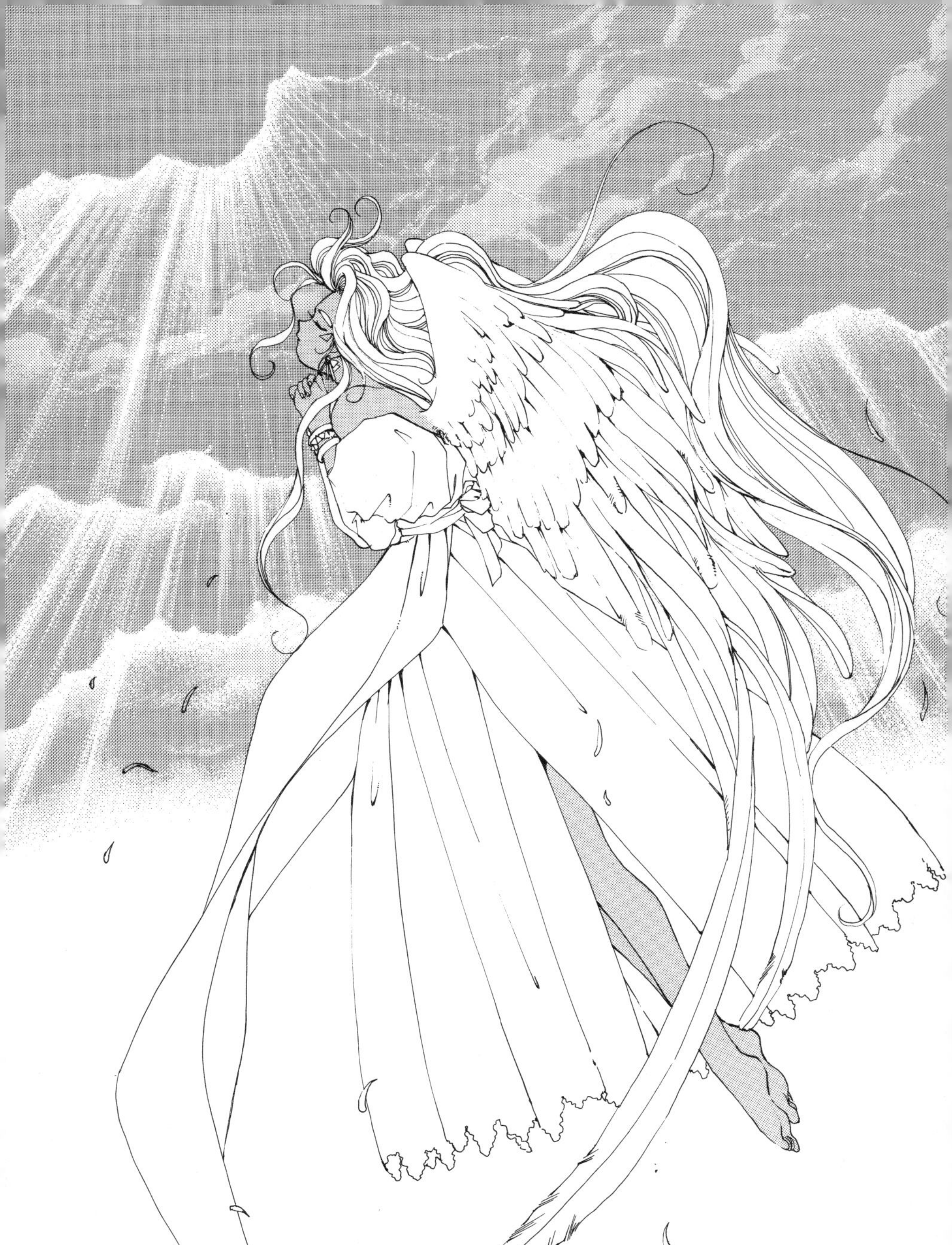

CHAPTER 47

Goodbye and Hello

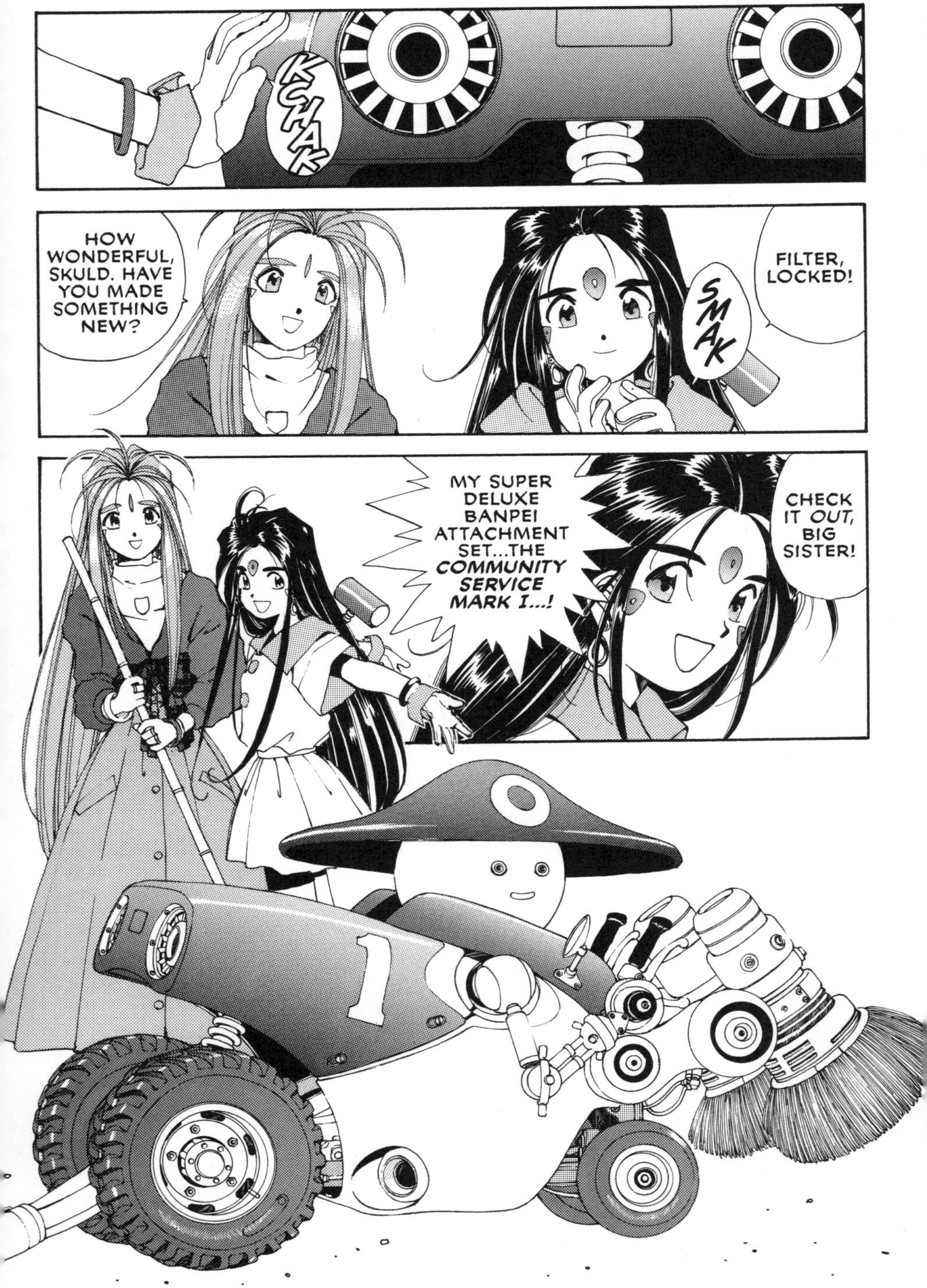
KCHAK
FILTER, LOCKED!
SMAK
HOW WONDERFUL, SKULD. HAVE YOU MADE SOMETHING NEW?
CHECK IT *OUT*, BIG SISTER!
MY SUPER DELUXE BANPEI ATTACHMENT SET...THE *COMMUNITY SERVICE MARK I*...!
1

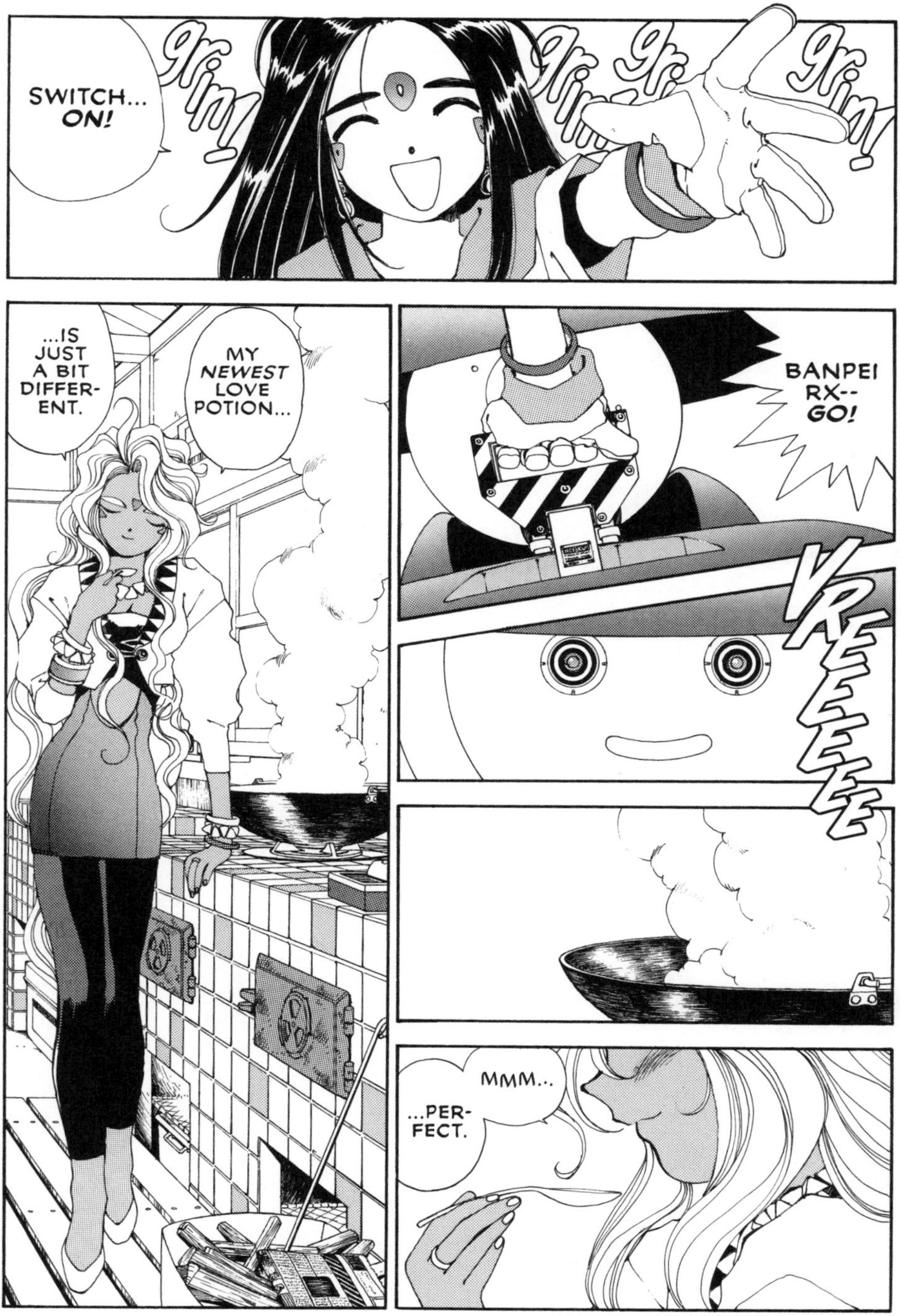
grin!
gri
grin
grin!
SWITCH... ON!
BANPEI RX-- GO!
VREEEEE
MMM...
...PER-FECT.
MY NEWEST LOVE POTION...
...IS JUST A BIT DIFFER-ENT.

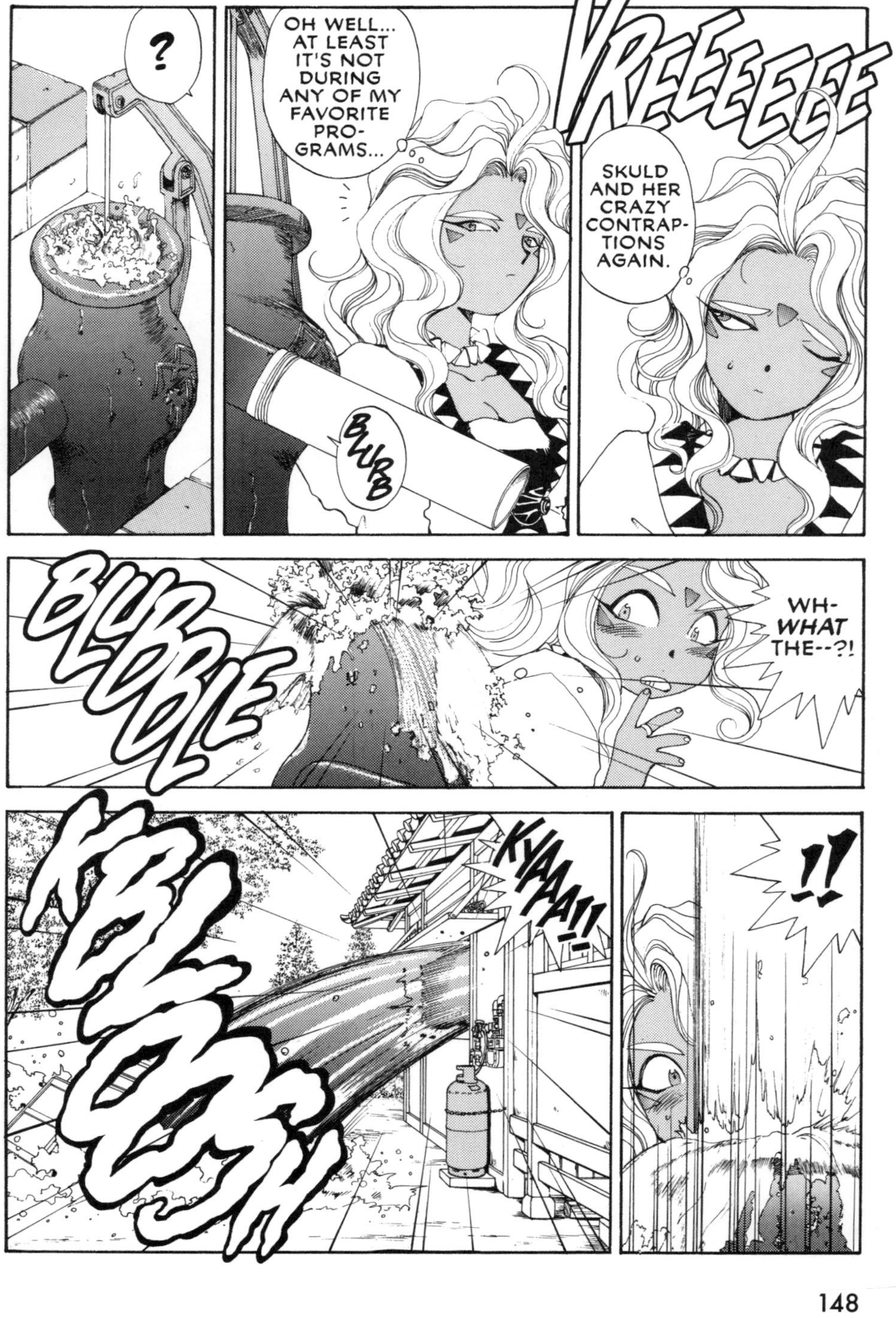
SKULD AND HER CRAZY CONTRAPTIONS AGAIN.
OH WELL... AT LEAST IT'S NOT DURING ANY OF MY FAVORITE PROGRAMS...
BLURB
?
WH-WHAT THE--?!
BLUBBLE
!!
KYAAAA!!

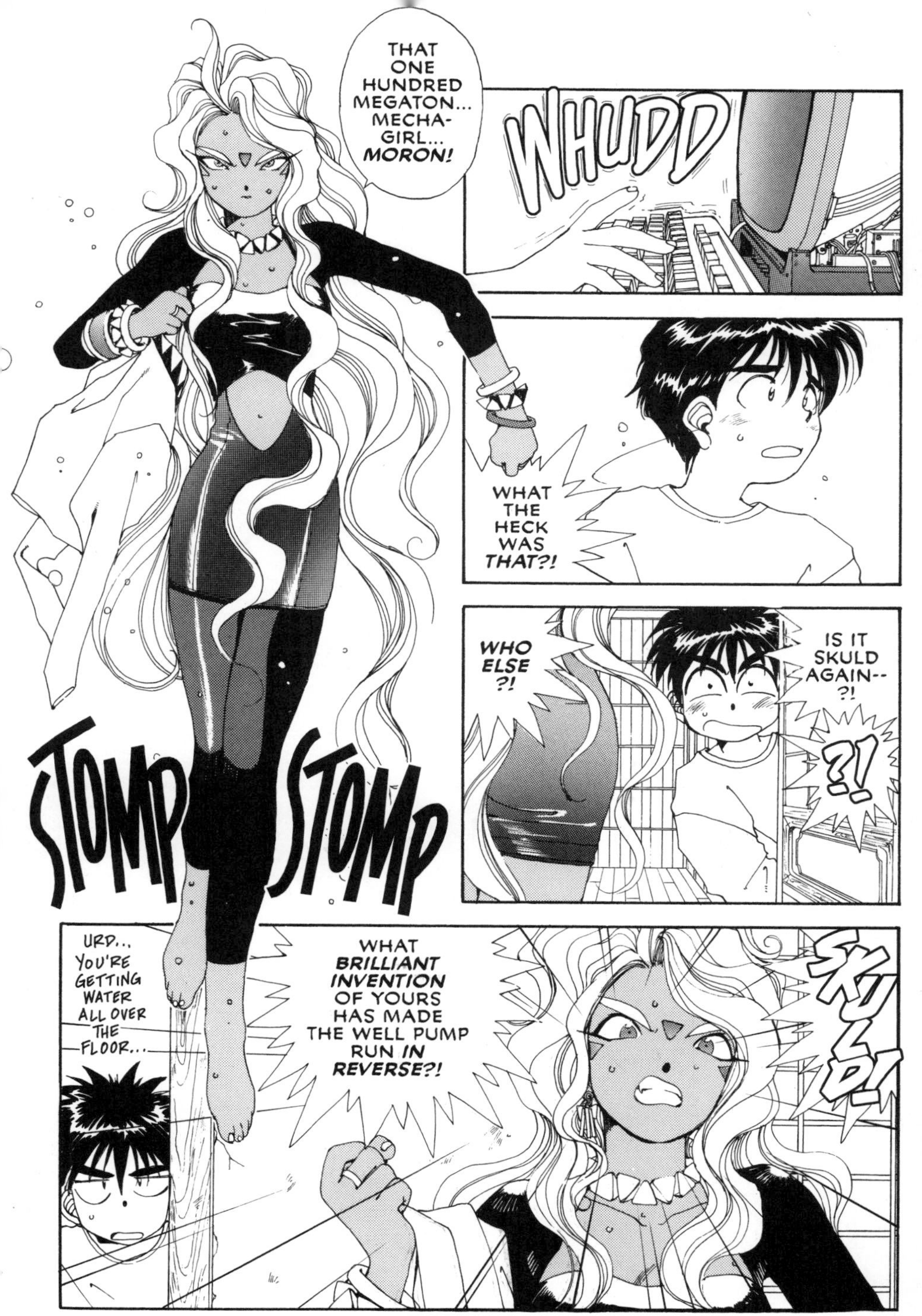
THAT ONE HUNDRED MEGATON... MECHA-GIRL... MORON!
WHUDD
WHAT THE HECK WAS THAT?!
IS IT SKULD AGAIN--?!
WHO ELSE?!
?!
STOMP STOMP
SKULD!
WHAT BRILLIANT INVENTION OF YOURS HAS MADE THE WELL PUMP RUN IN REVERSE?!
URD... YOU'RE GETTING WATER ALL OVER THE FLOOR...

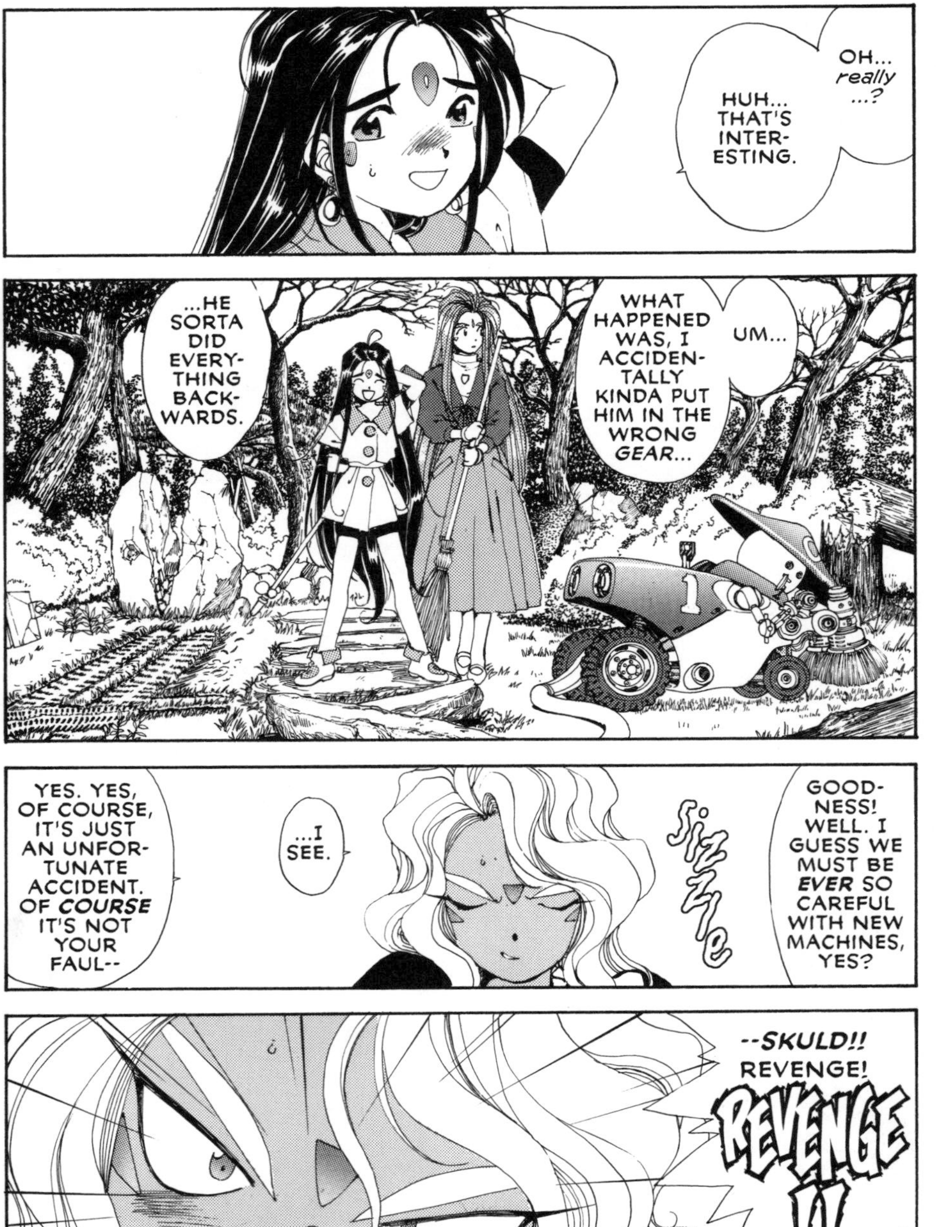

OH... *really* ...?
HUH... THAT'S INTER-ESTING.
UM...
WHAT HAPPENED WAS, I ACCIDEN-TALLY KINDA PUT HIM IN THE WRONG *GEAR*...
...HE SORTA DID EVERY-THING BACK-WARDS.
GOOD-NESS! WELL. I GUESS WE MUST BE ***EVER*** SO CAREFUL WITH NEW MACHINES, YES?
sizzle
...I SEE.
YES. YES, OF COURSE, IT'S JUST AN UNFOR-TUNATE ACCIDENT. OF ***COURSE*** IT'S NOT YOUR FAUL--
--SKULD!! REVENGE!
REVENGE !!

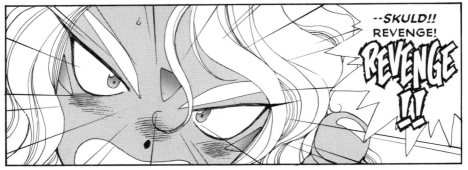

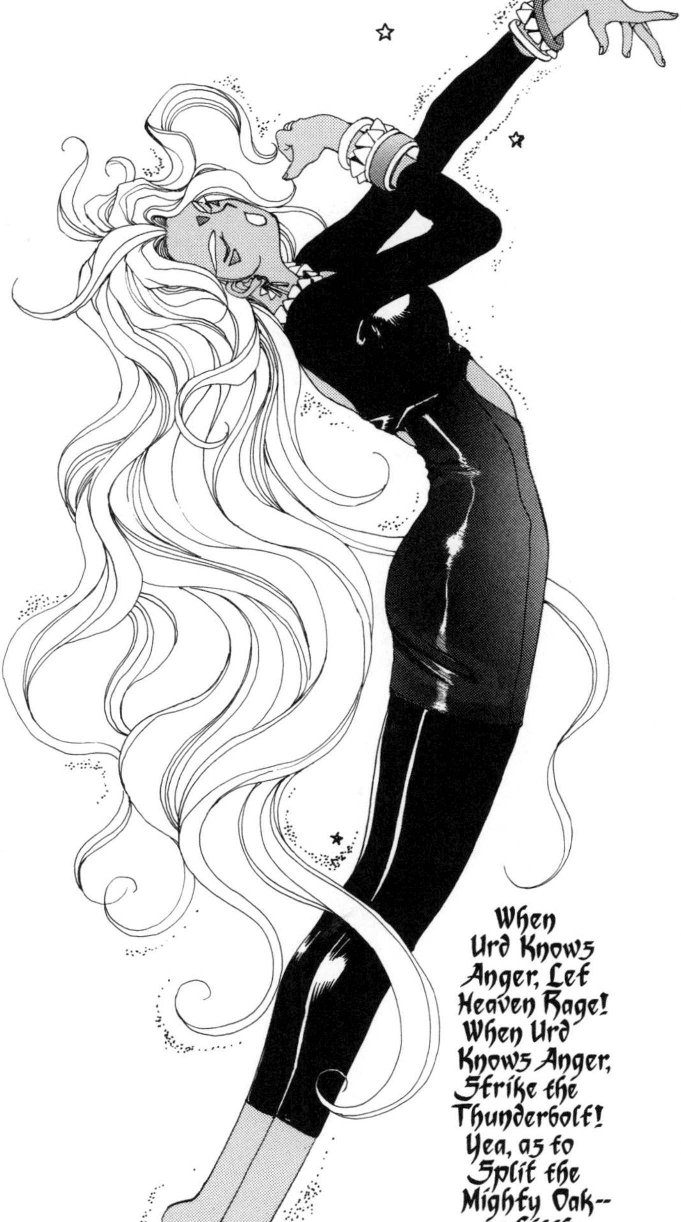
When Urd Knows Anger, Let Heaven Rage! When Urd Knows Anger, Strike the Thunderbolt! Yea, as to Split the Mighty Oak-- or Little Shrimp!

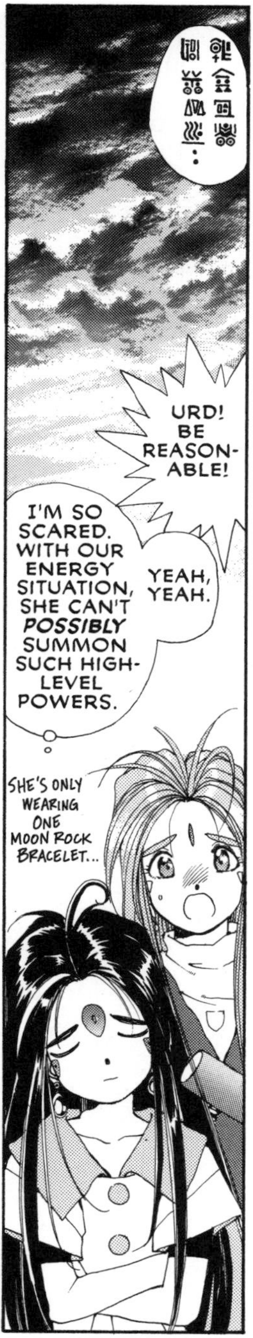
URD! BE REASON-ABLE!
YEAH, YEAH.
I'M SO SCARED. WITH OUR ENERGY SITUATION, SHE CAN'T *POSSIBLY* SUMMON SUCH HIGH-LEVEL POWERS.
SHE'S ONLY WEARING ONE MOON ROCK BRACELET...

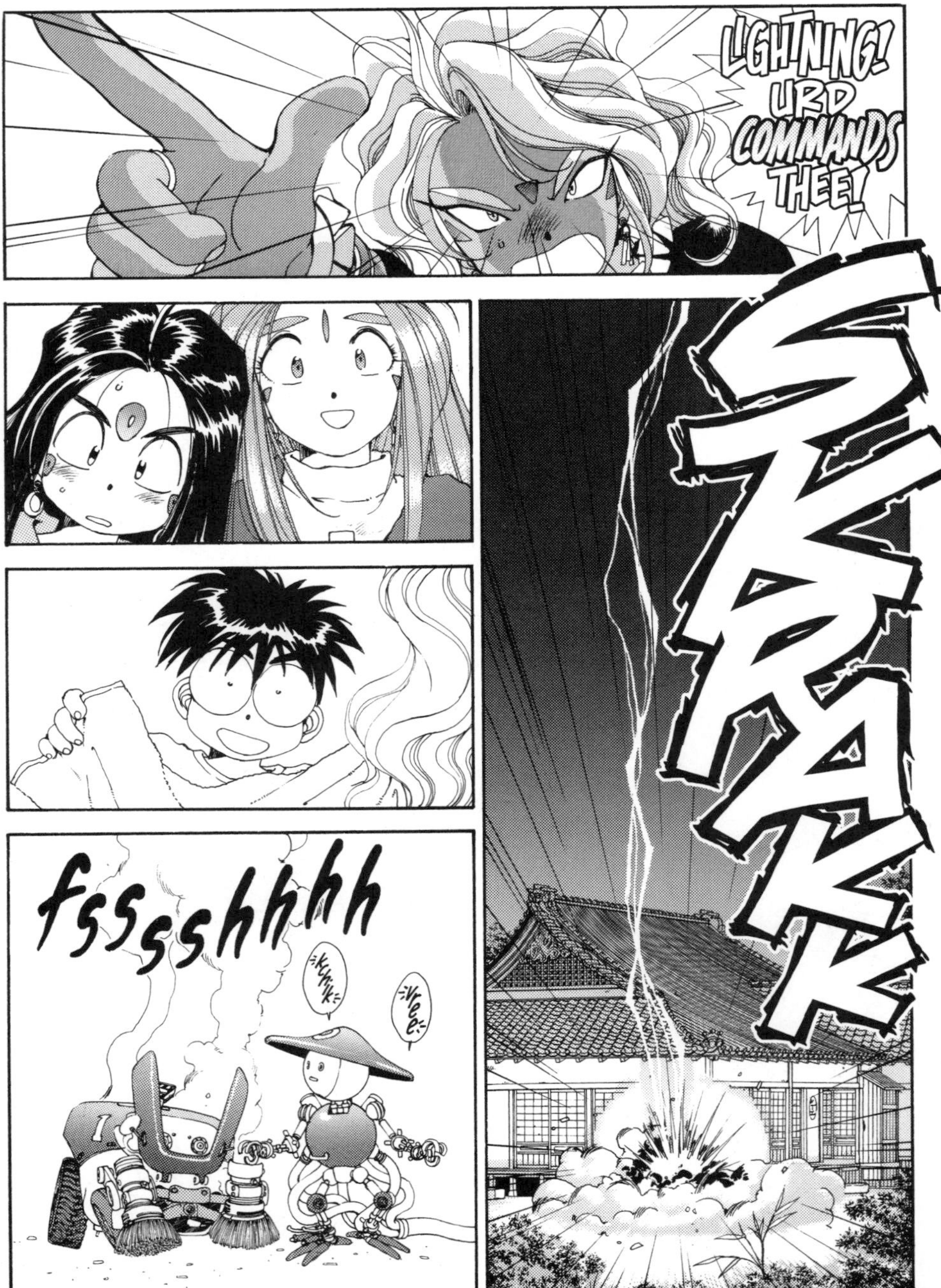
LIGHTNING! URD COMMANDS THEE!
SKRAKK
fsssshhhh
vree
kchik

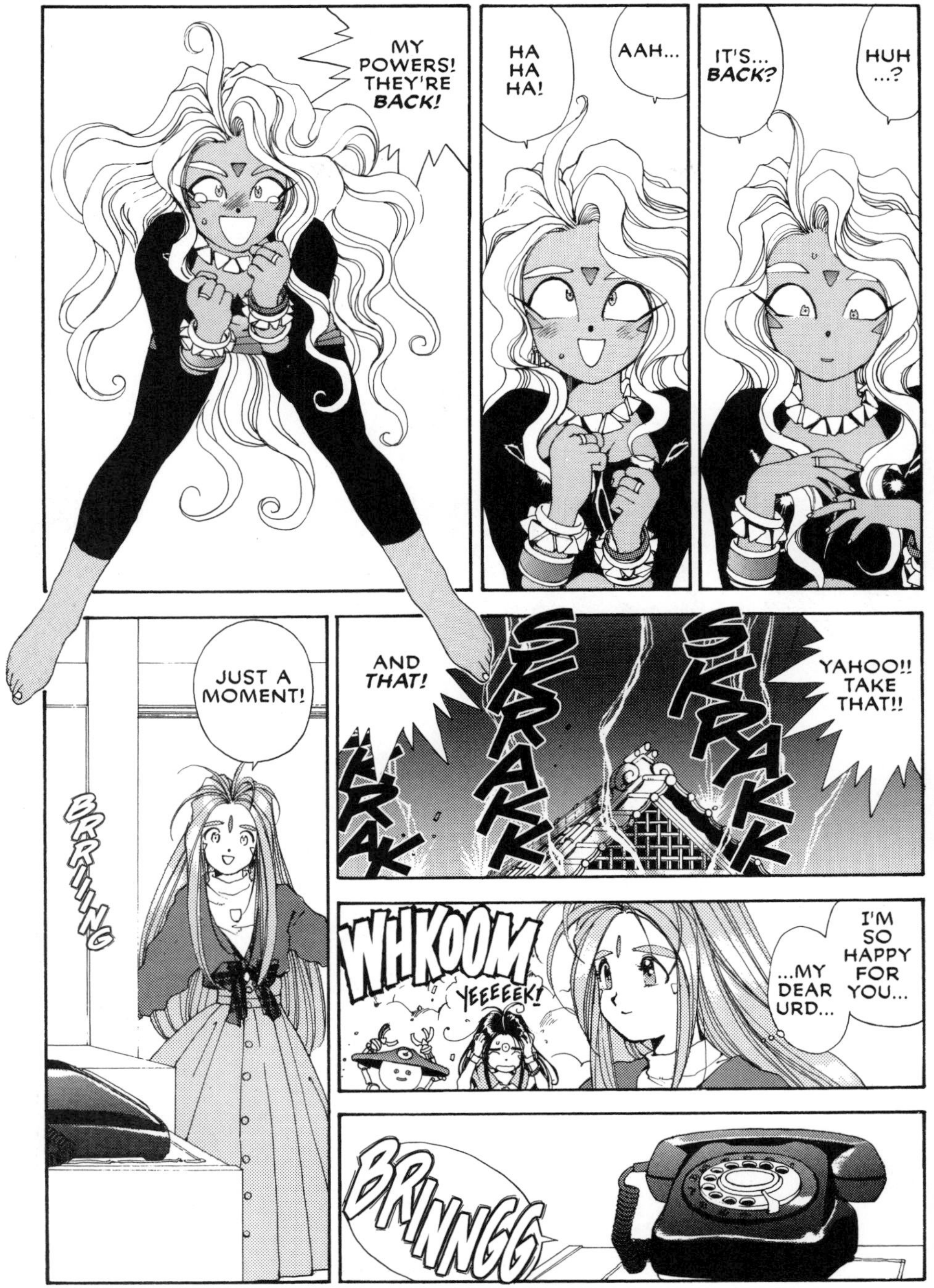
HUH ...?
IT'S... *BACK?*
AAH...
HA HA HA!
MY POWERS! THEY'RE *BACK!*
YAHOO!! TAKE THAT!!
SKRAKK
SKRAKK
AND *THAT!*
KRAK
I'M SO HAPPY FOR YOU...
...MY DEAR URD...
YEEEEEK!
WHKOOM
BRINNGG
JUST A MOMENT!
BRRIIING

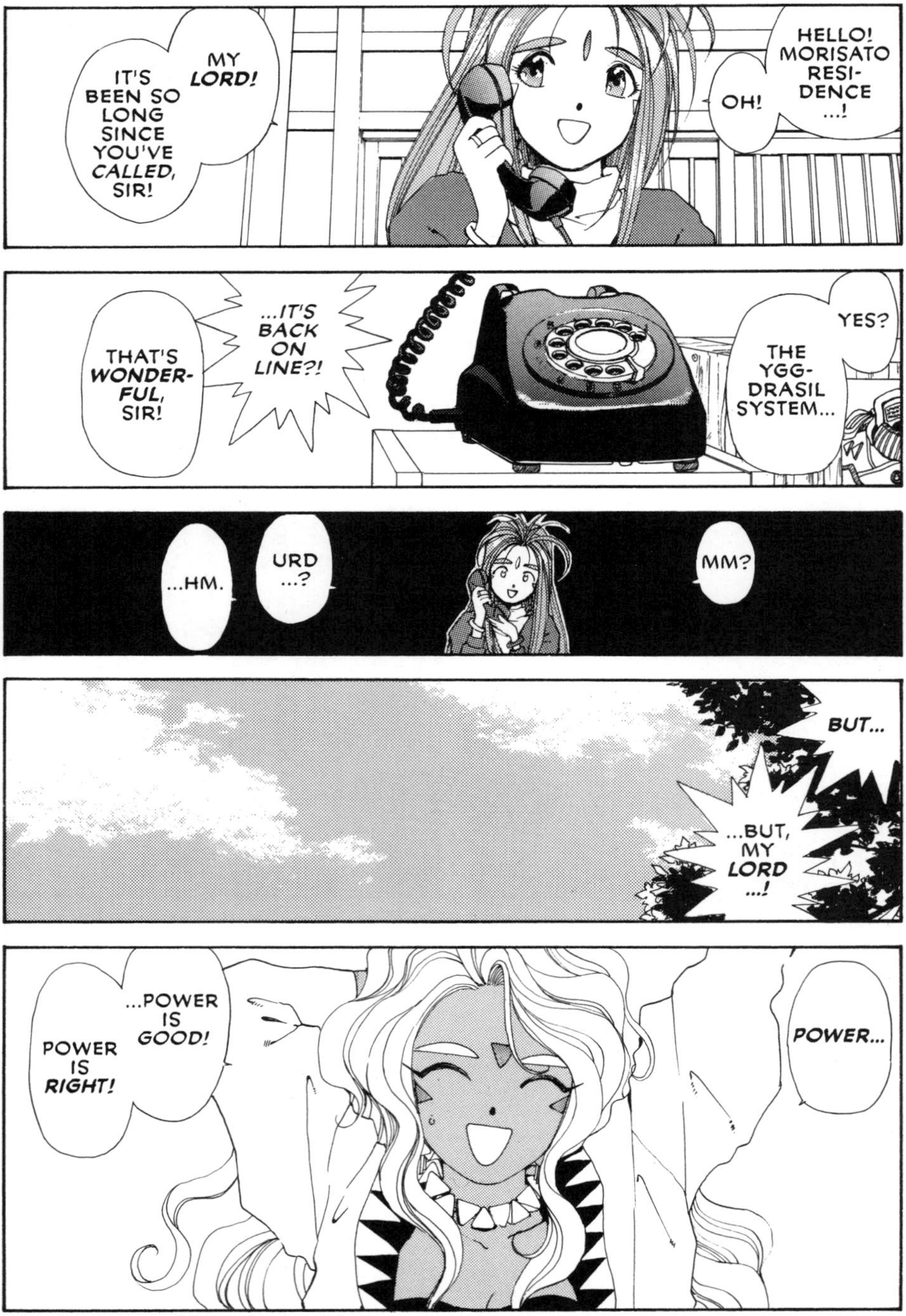
HELLO! MORISATO RESIDENCE ...!
OH!
MY LORD!
IT'S BEEN SO LONG SINCE YOU'VE CALLED, SIR!
YES?
THE YGGDRASIL SYSTEM...
...IT'S BACK ON LINE?!
THAT'S WONDERFUL, SIR!
MM?
URD ...?
...HM.
BUT...
...BUT, MY LORD ...!
POWER...
...POWER IS GOOD!
POWER IS RIGHT!

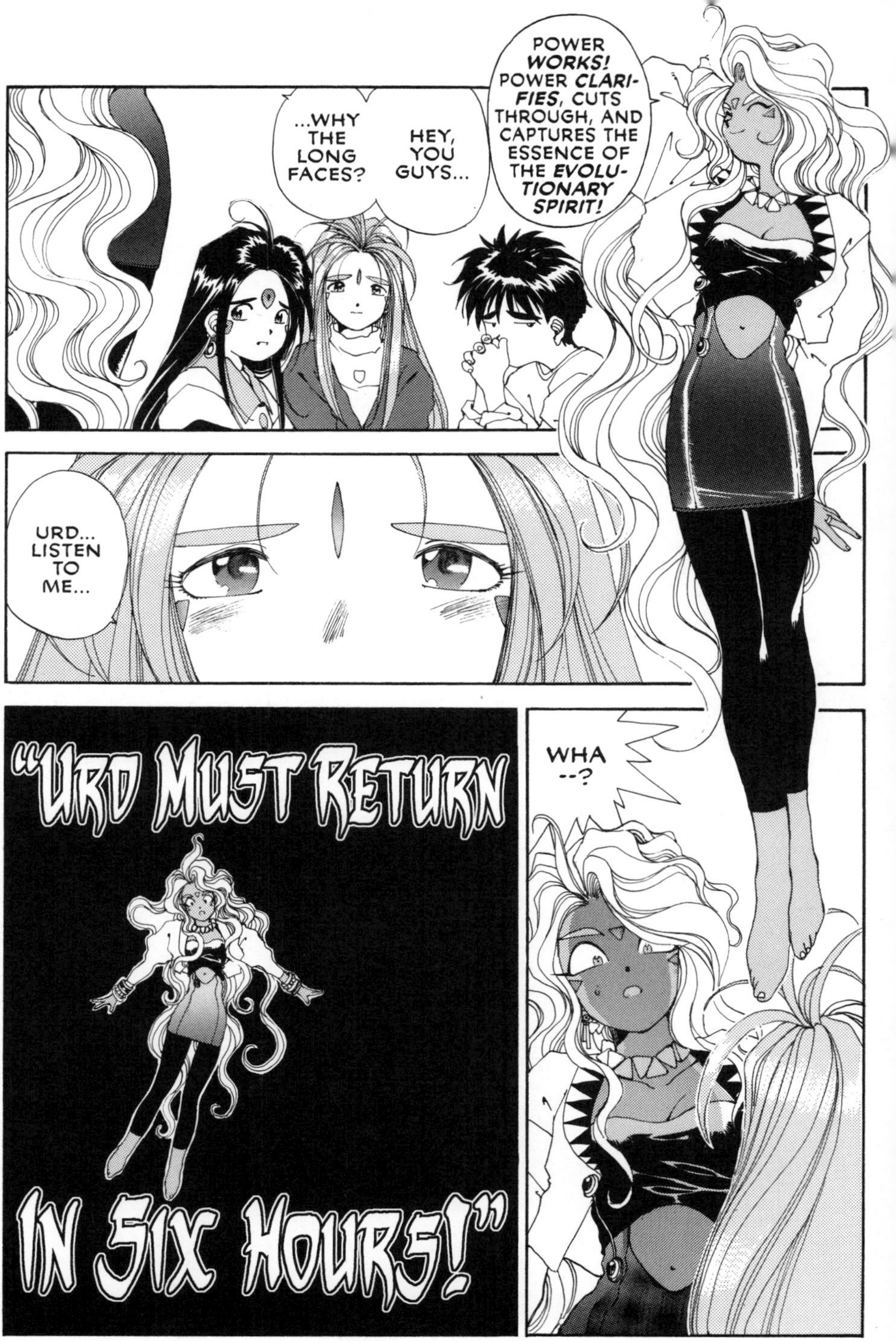
POWER *WORKS!* POWER *CLARIFIES*, CUTS THROUGH, AND CAPTURES THE ESSENCE OF THE *EVOLUTIONARY SPIRIT!*
HEY, YOU GUYS...
...WHY THE LONG FACES?
URD... LISTEN TO ME...
WHA--?
"URD MUST RETURN IN SIX HOURS!"

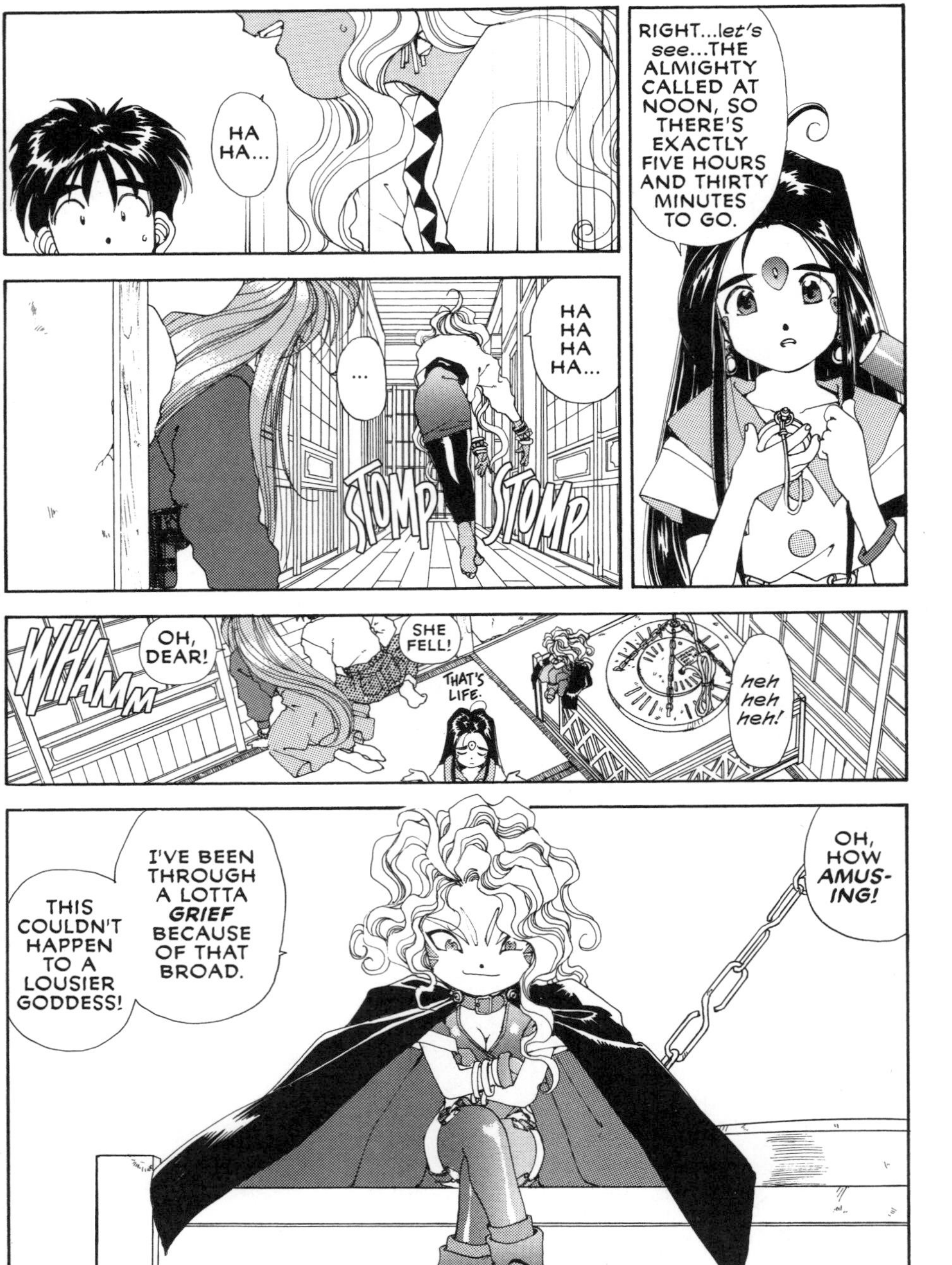
RIGHT...*let's see*...THE ALMIGHTY CALLED AT NOON, SO THERE'S EXACTLY FIVE HOURS AND THIRTY MINUTES TO GO.
HA HA...
HA HA HA HA...
...
STOMP STOMP
heh heh heh!
SHE FELL!
THAT'S LIFE.
OH, DEAR!
WHAMM
OH, HOW *AMUSING!*
I'VE BEEN THROUGH A LOTTA *GRIEF* BECAUSE OF THAT BROAD.
THIS COULDN'T HAPPEN TO A LOUSIER GODDESS!

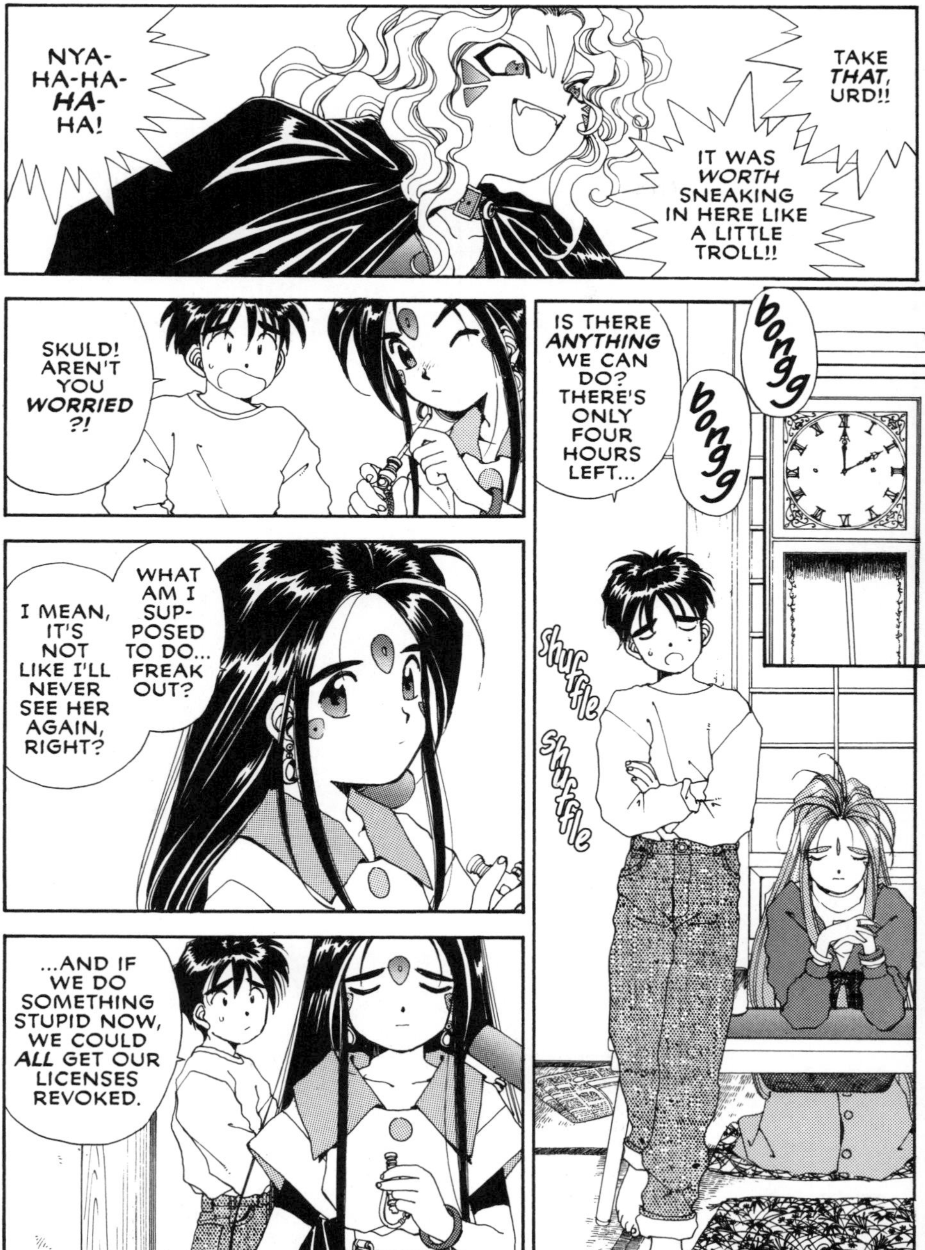
TAKE *THAT*, URD!!
IT WAS *WORTH* SNEAKING IN HERE LIKE A LITTLE TROLL!!
NYA-HA-HA-*HA*-HA!
bongg
bongg
IS THERE *ANYTHING* WE CAN DO? THERE'S ONLY FOUR HOURS LEFT...
shuffle
shuffle
SKULD! AREN'T YOU *WORRIED* ?!
WHAT AM I SUP-POSED TO DO... FREAK OUT?
I MEAN, IT'S NOT LIKE I'LL NEVER SEE HER AGAIN, RIGHT?
...AND IF WE DO SOMETHING STUPID NOW, WE COULD *ALL* GET OUR LICENSES REVOKED.

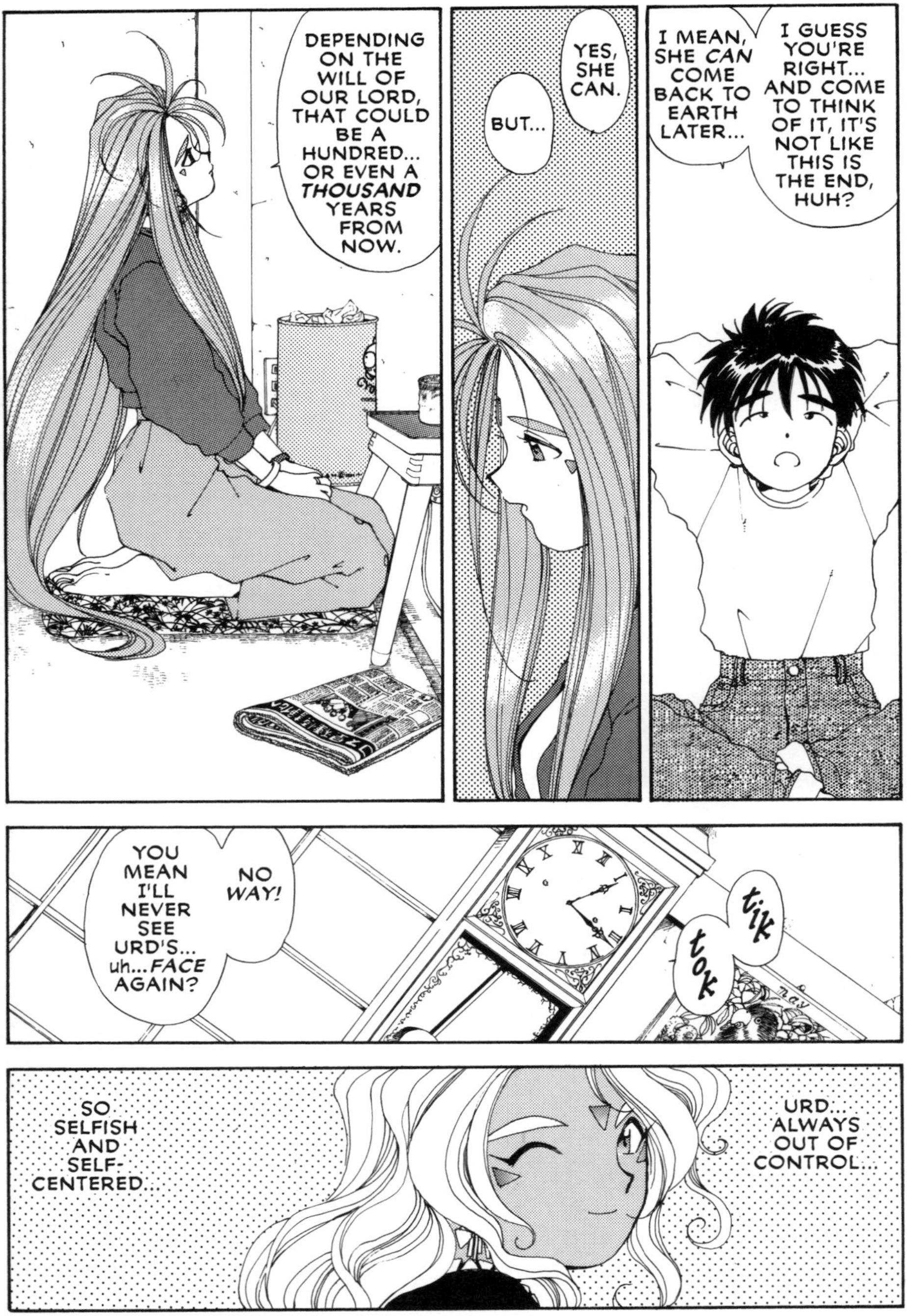
I GUESS YOU'RE RIGHT... AND COME TO THINK OF IT, IT'S NOT LIKE THIS IS THE END, HUH?
I MEAN, SHE *CAN* COME BACK TO EARTH LATER...
YES, SHE CAN.
BUT...
DEPENDING ON THE WILL OF OUR LORD, THAT COULD BE A HUNDRED... OR EVEN A *THOUSAND* YEARS FROM NOW.
tik tok
NO *WAY!*
YOU MEAN I'LL NEVER SEE URD'S... uh...*FACE* AGAIN?
URD... ALWAYS OUT OF CONTROL...
SO SELFISH AND SELF-CENTERED...

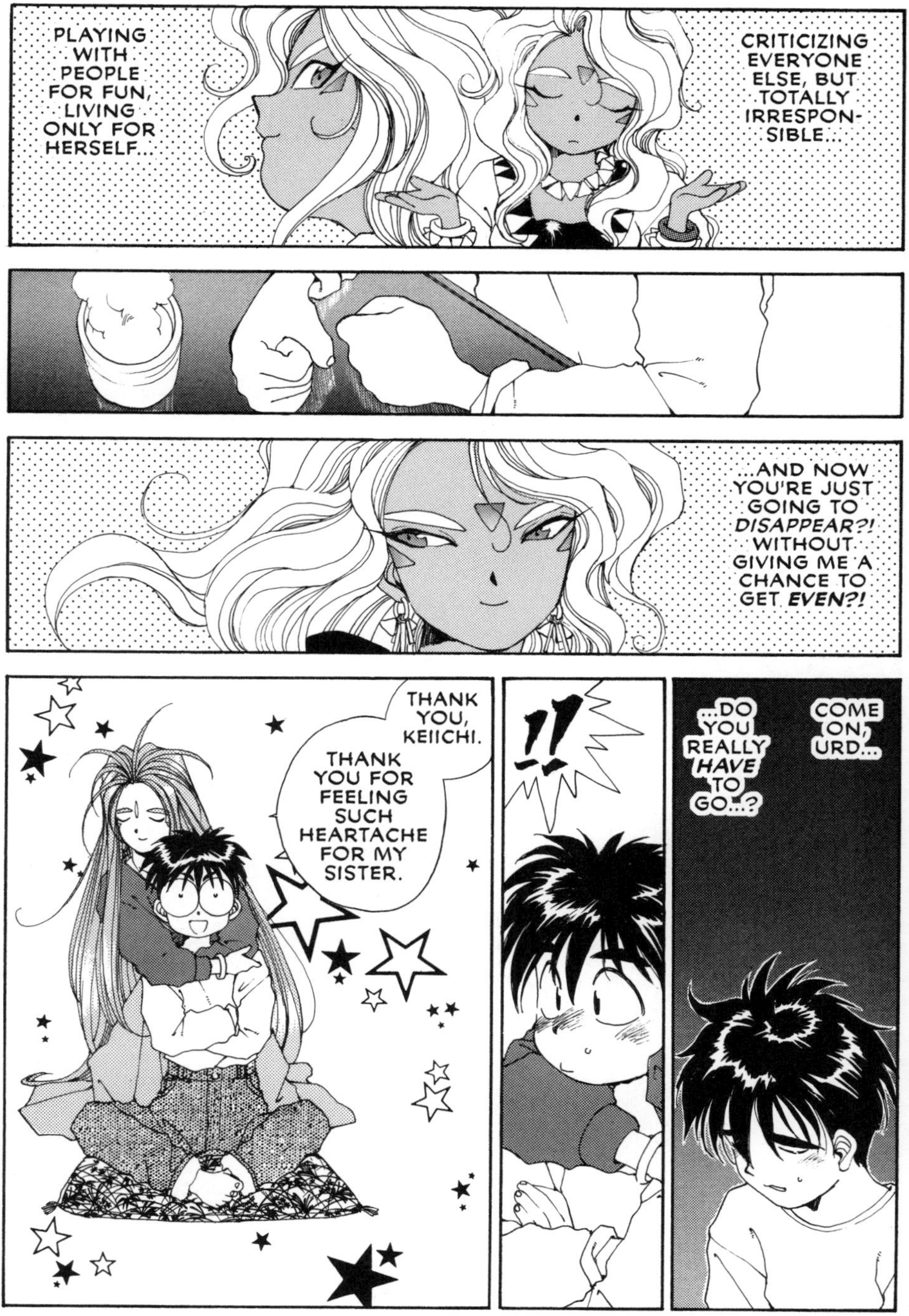
CRITICIZING EVERYONE ELSE, BUT TOTALLY IRRESPON-SIBLE...
PLAYING WITH PEOPLE FOR FUN, LIVING ONLY FOR HERSELF...
...AND NOW YOU'RE JUST GOING TO *DISAPPEAR?!* WITHOUT GIVING ME A CHANCE TO GET *EVEN?!*
COME ON, URD...
...DO YOU REALLY *HAVE* TO GO...?
!!
THANK YOU, KEIICHI.
THANK YOU FOR FEELING SUCH HEARTACHE FOR MY SISTER.

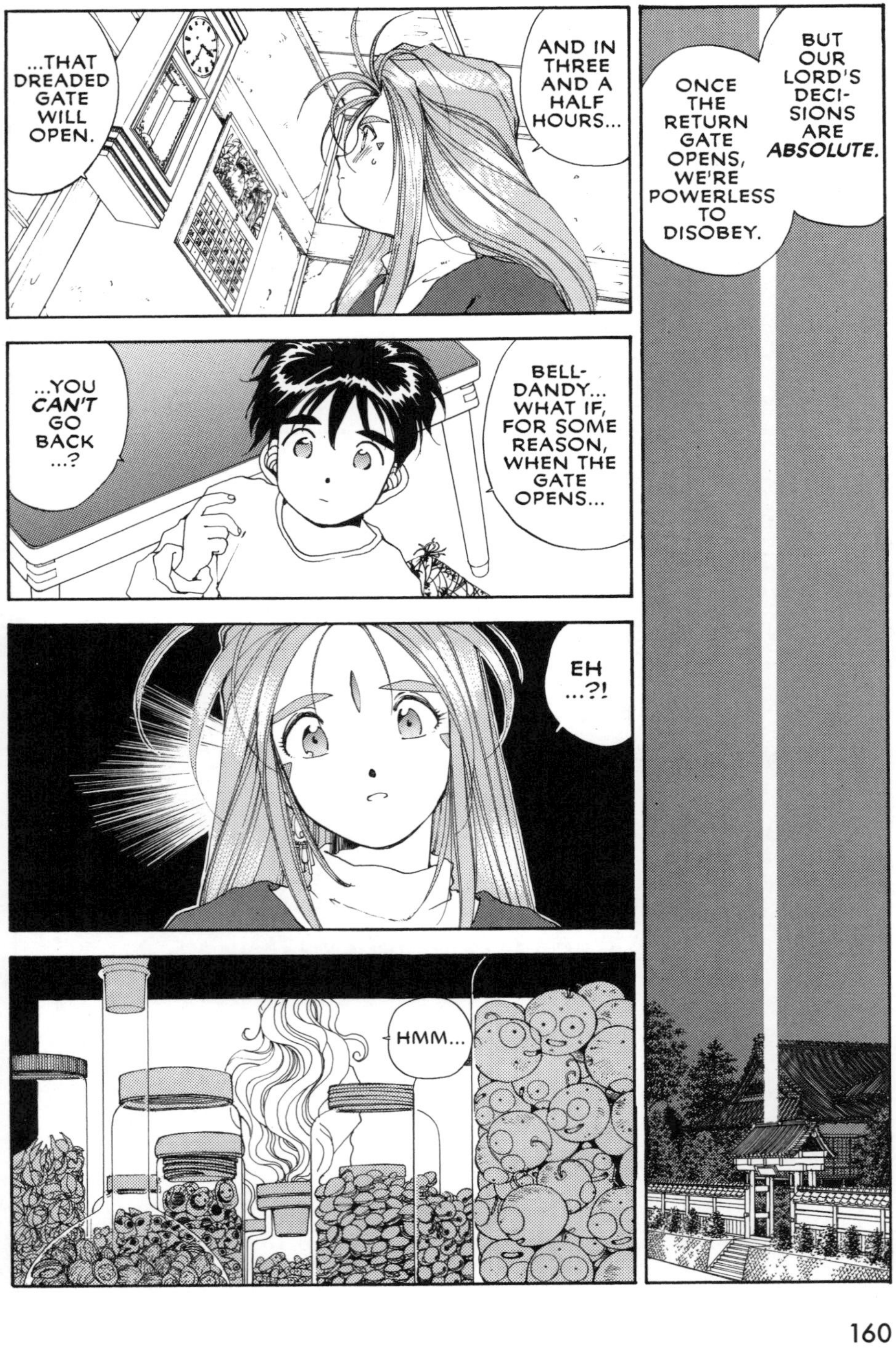
BUT OUR LORD'S DECI-SIONS ARE *ABSOLUTE.*
ONCE THE RETURN GATE OPENS, WE'RE POWERLESS TO DISOBEY.
AND IN THREE AND A HALF HOURS...
...THAT DREADED GATE WILL OPEN.
BELL-DANDY... WHAT IF, FOR SOME REASON, WHEN THE GATE OPENS...
...YOU *CAN'T* GO BACK ...?
EH ...?!
HMM...

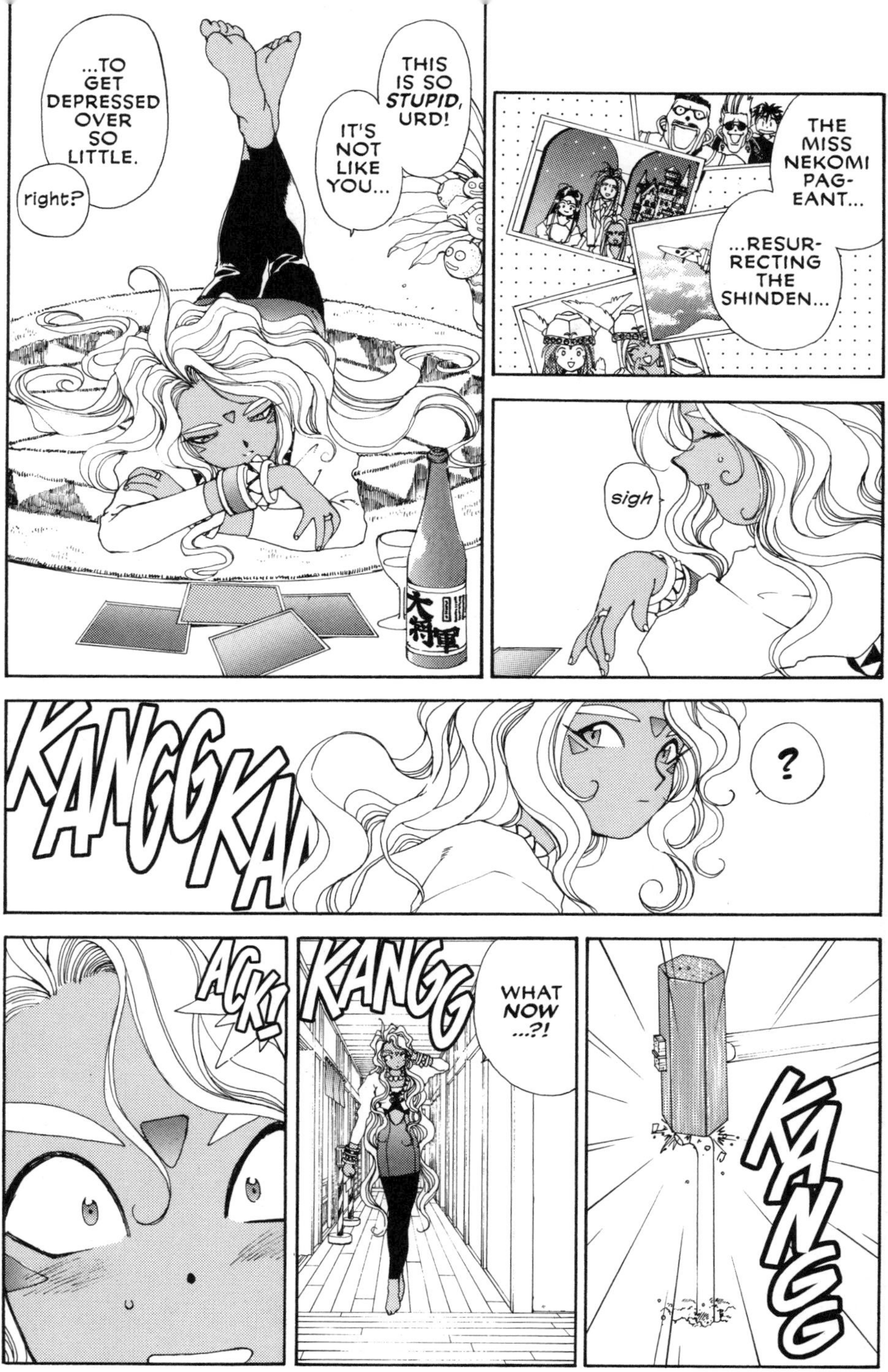
THE MISS NEKOMI PAGEANT...
...RESURRECTING THE SHINDEN...
sigh
THIS IS SO *STUPID*, URD!
IT'S NOT LIKE YOU...
...TO GET DEPRESSED OVER SO LITTLE.
right?
?
KANGG KAN
KANG
WHAT NOW ...?!
KANGG
ACK!

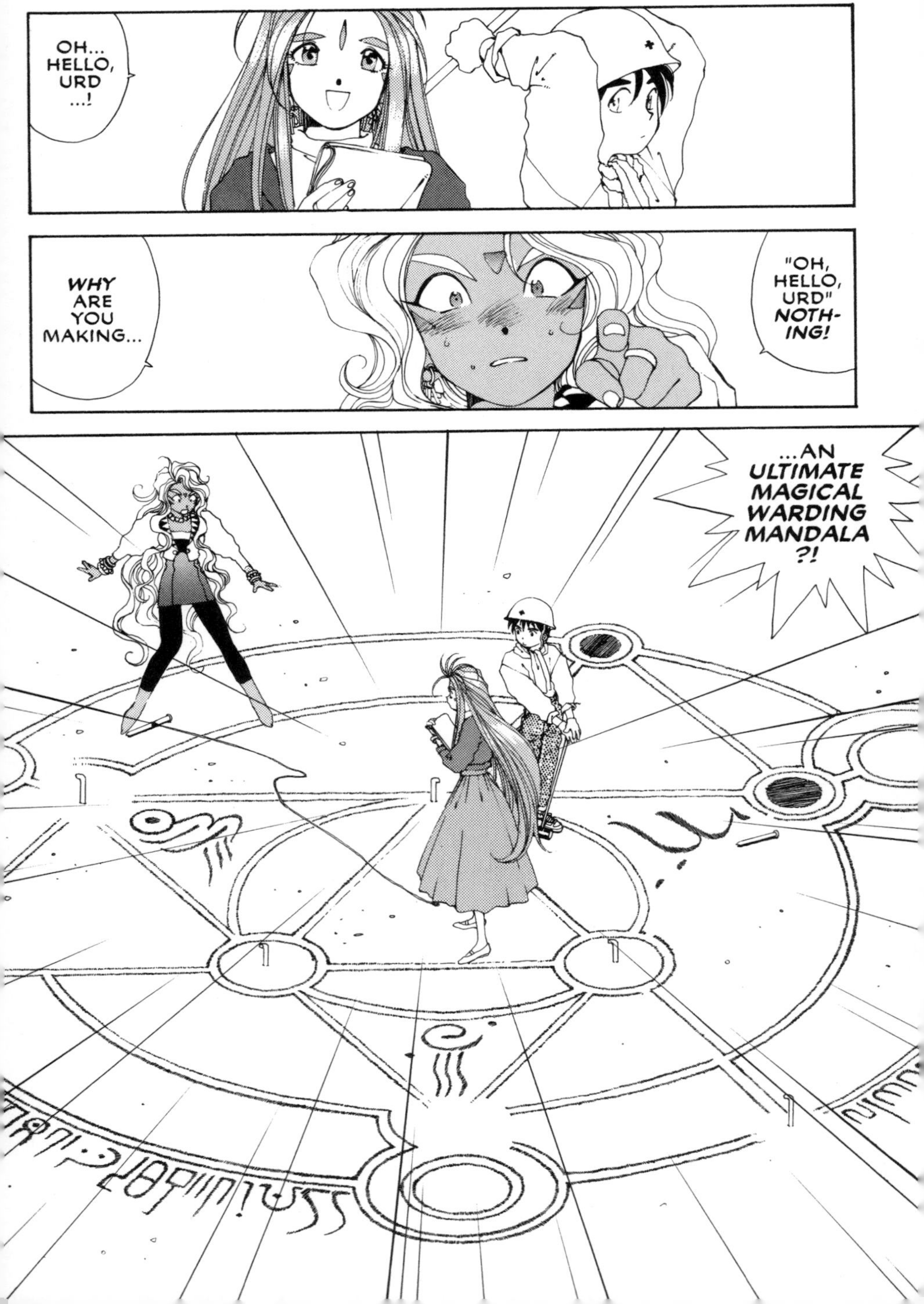
OH... HELLO, URD ...!
"OH, HELLO, URD" NOTHING!
WHY ARE YOU MAKING...
...AN ULTIMATE MAGICAL WARDING MANDALA ?!

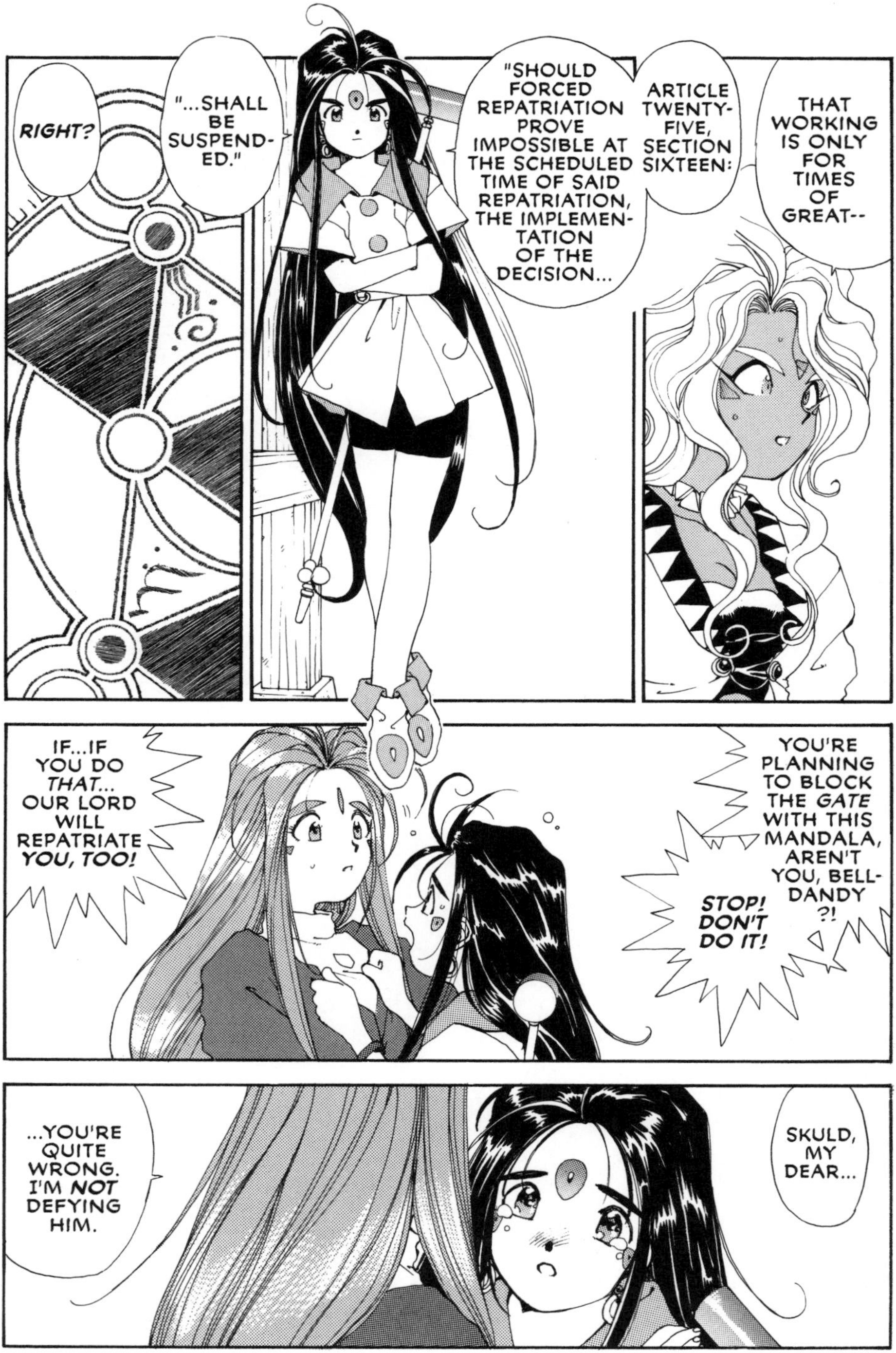
THAT WORKING IS ONLY FOR TIMES OF GREAT--
ARTICLE TWENTY-FIVE, SECTION SIXTEEN:
"SHOULD FORCED REPATRIATION PROVE IMPOSSIBLE AT THE SCHEDULED TIME OF SAID REPATRIATION, THE IMPLEMENTATION OF THE DECISION...
"...SHALL BE SUSPENDED."
RIGHT?
YOU'RE PLANNING TO BLOCK THE GATE WITH THIS MANDALA, AREN'T YOU, BELLDANDY?!
STOP! DON'T DO IT!
IF...IF YOU DO THAT... OUR LORD WILL REPATRIATE YOU, TOO!
SKULD, MY DEAR...
...YOU'RE QUITE WRONG. I'M NOT DEFYING HIM.

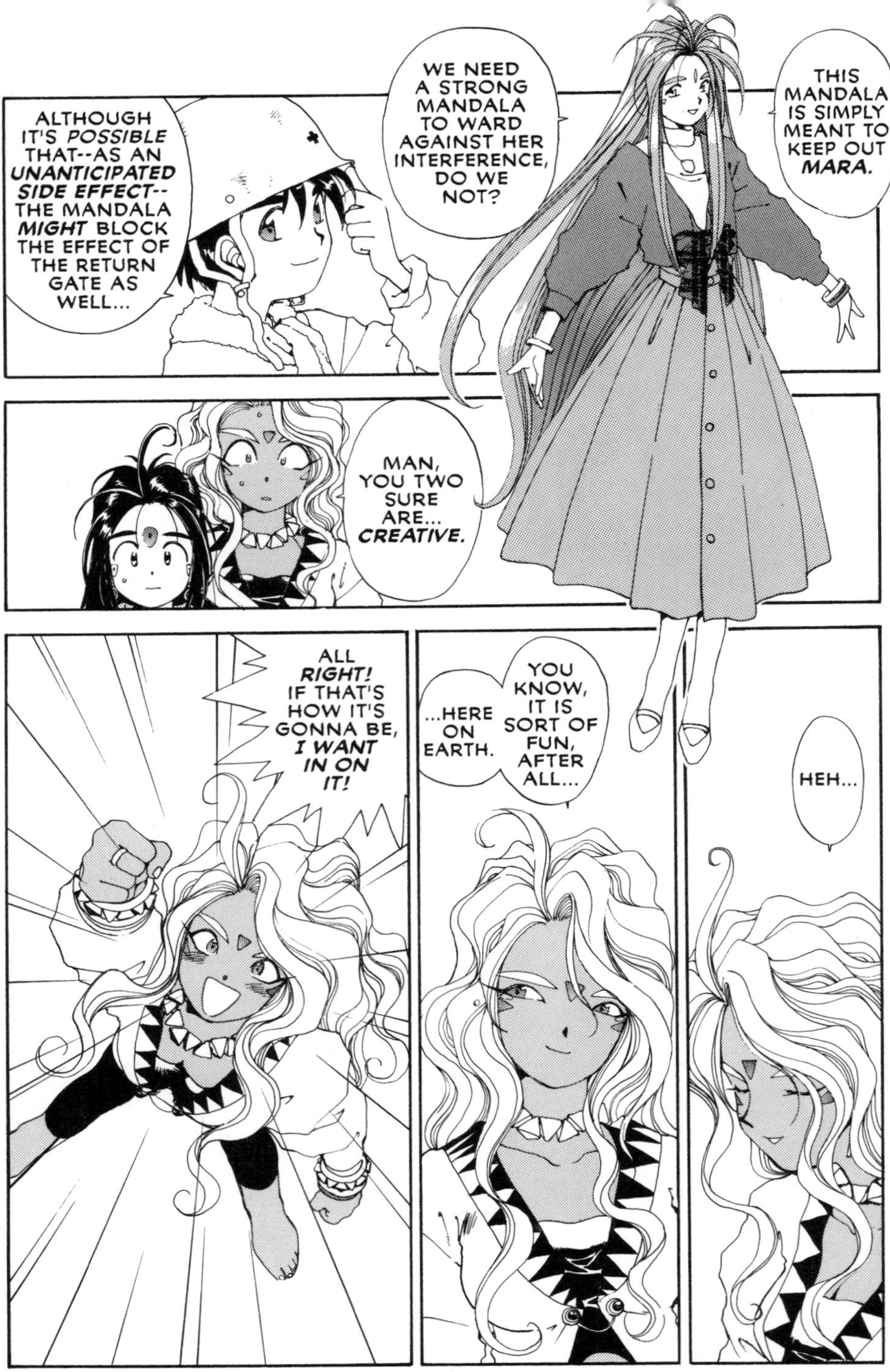
THIS MANDALA IS SIMPLY MEANT TO KEEP OUT *MARA.*
WE NEED A STRONG MANDALA TO WARD AGAINST HER INTERFERENCE, DO WE NOT?
ALTHOUGH IT'S *POSSIBLE* THAT--AS AN *UNANTICIPATED SIDE EFFECT*--THE MANDALA *MIGHT* BLOCK THE EFFECT OF THE RETURN GATE AS WELL...
MAN, YOU TWO SURE ARE... *CREATIVE.*
HEH...
YOU KNOW, IT IS SORT OF FUN, AFTER ALL...
...HERE ON EARTH.
ALL *RIGHT!* IF THAT'S HOW IT'S GONNA BE, *I WANT IN ON IT!*

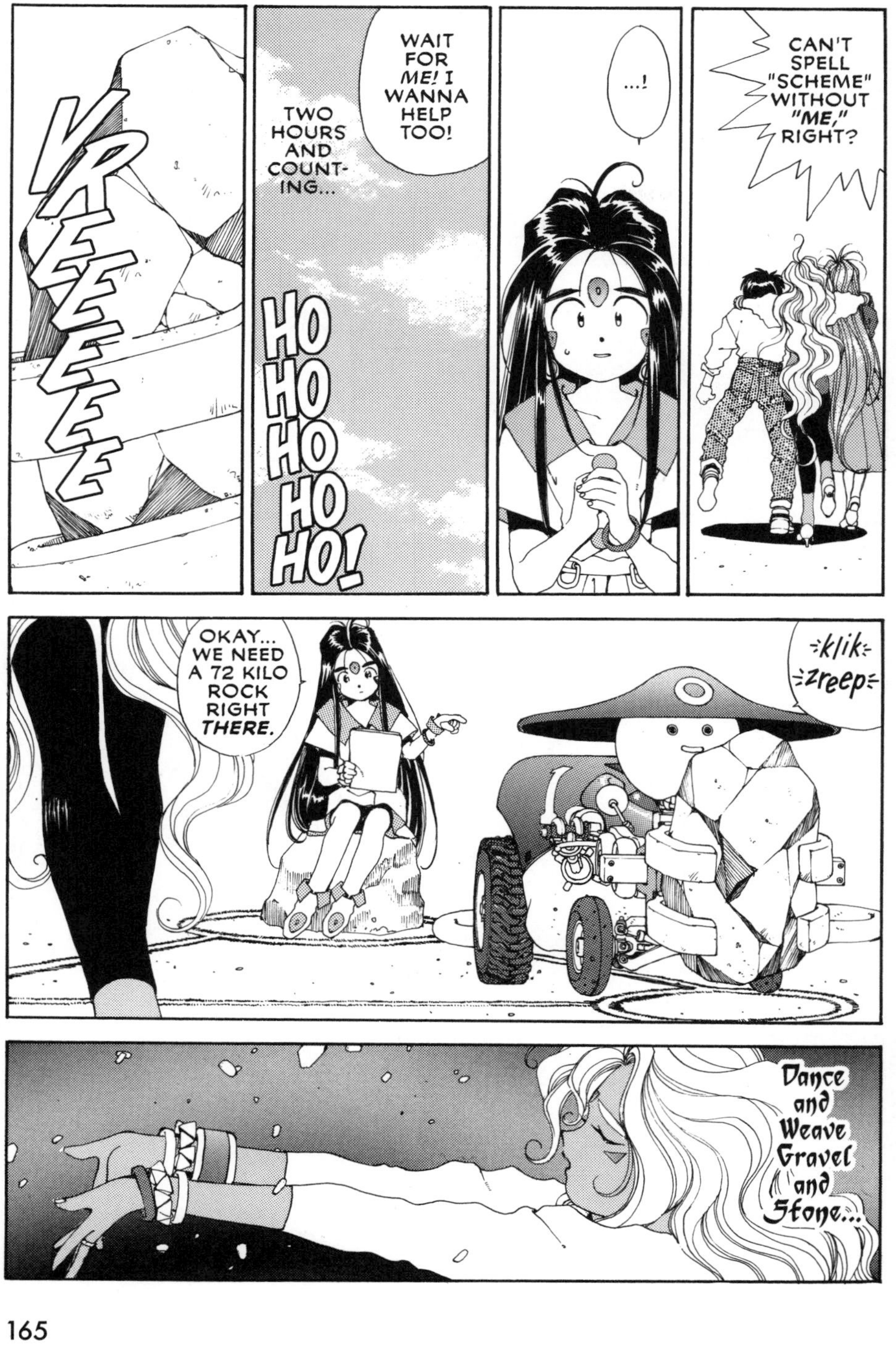
CAN'T SPELL "SCHEME" WITHOUT "ME," RIGHT?
...!
WAIT FOR ME! I WANNA HELP TOO!
TWO HOURS AND COUNTING...
HO HO HO HO HO HO!
VREEEEEE
-klik- -zreep-
OKAY... WE NEED A 72 KILO ROCK RIGHT THERE.
Dance and Weave Gravel and Stone...

Obey We Goddesses Three Past, Present, and Future...

...Hark to the Covenant of Urd, Belldandy, and Skuld...

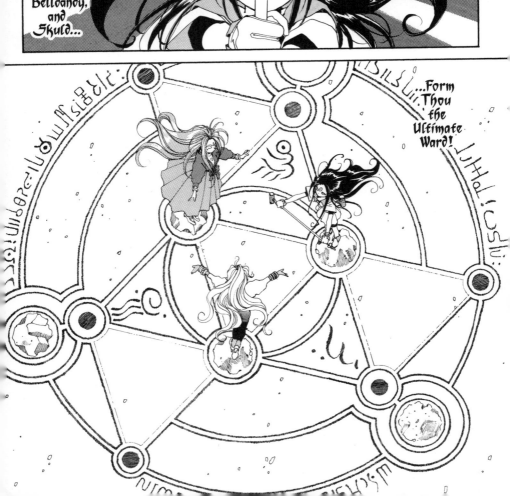

...Form Thou the Ultimate Ward!

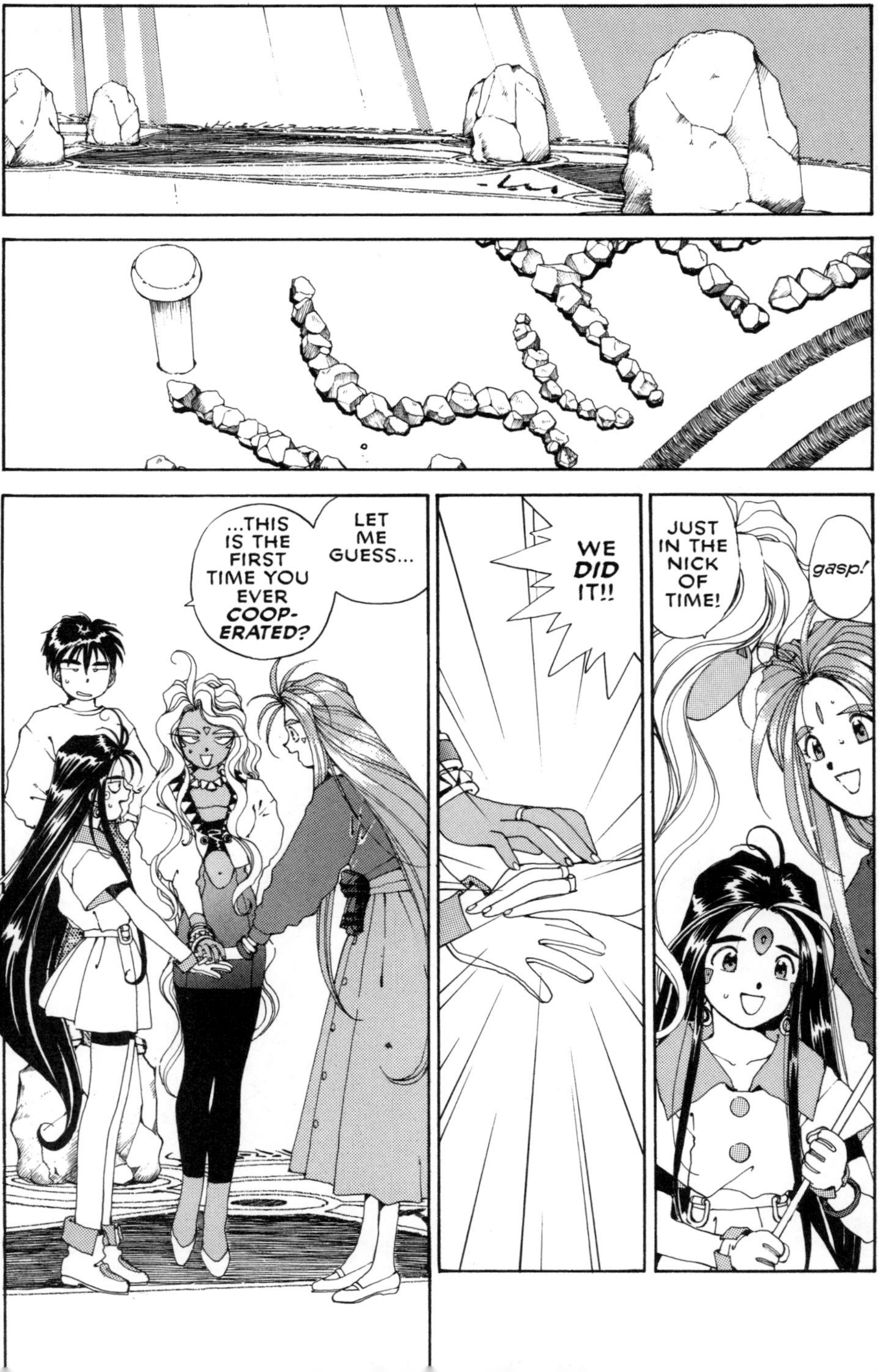
gasp!
JUST IN THE NICK OF TIME!
WE *DID* IT!!
LET ME GUESS...
...THIS IS THE FIRST TIME YOU EVER *COOP-ERATED?*

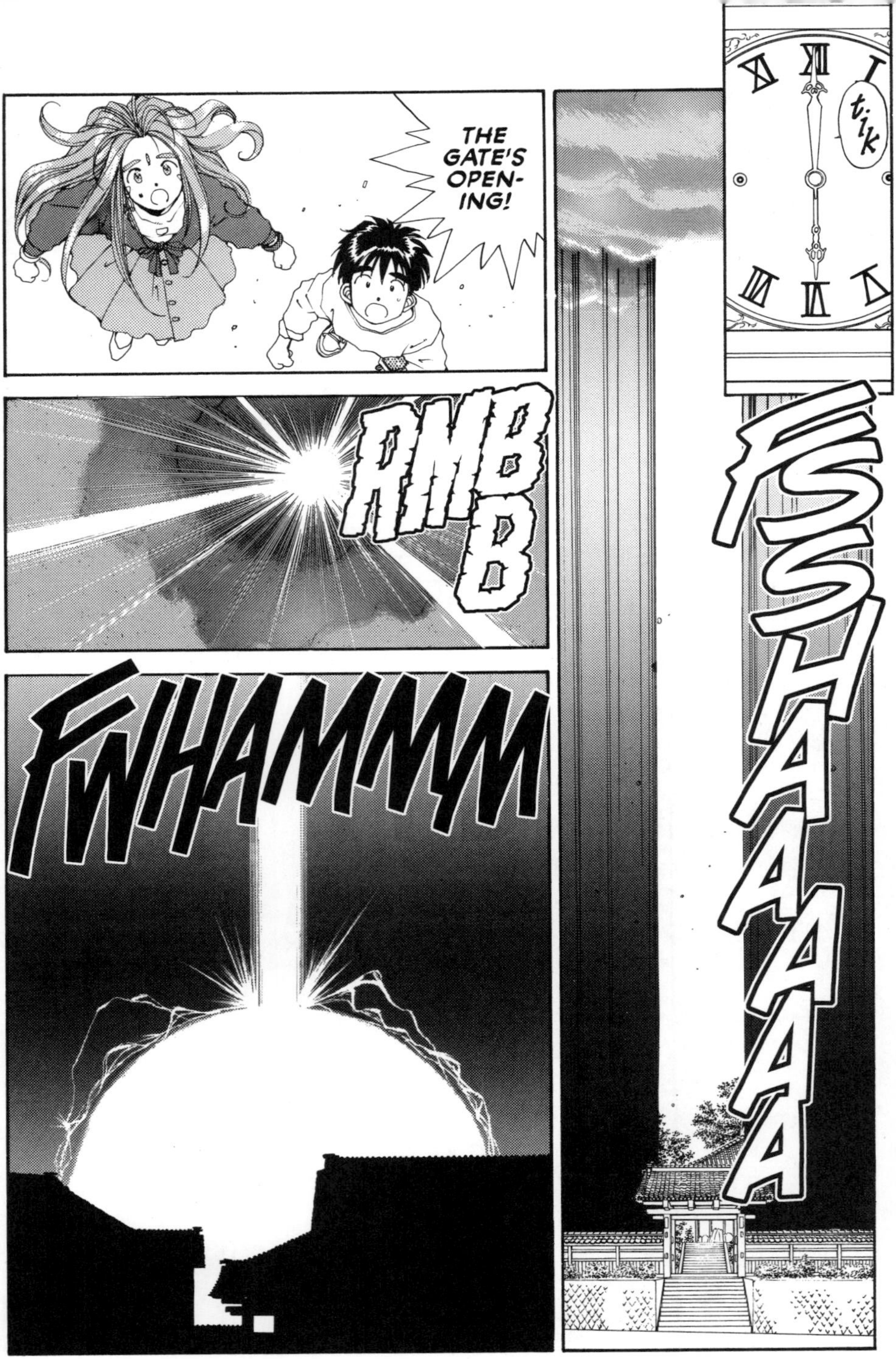

tik
FSHAAAAAA
THE GATE'S OPENING!
RMBB
FWHAMMMM

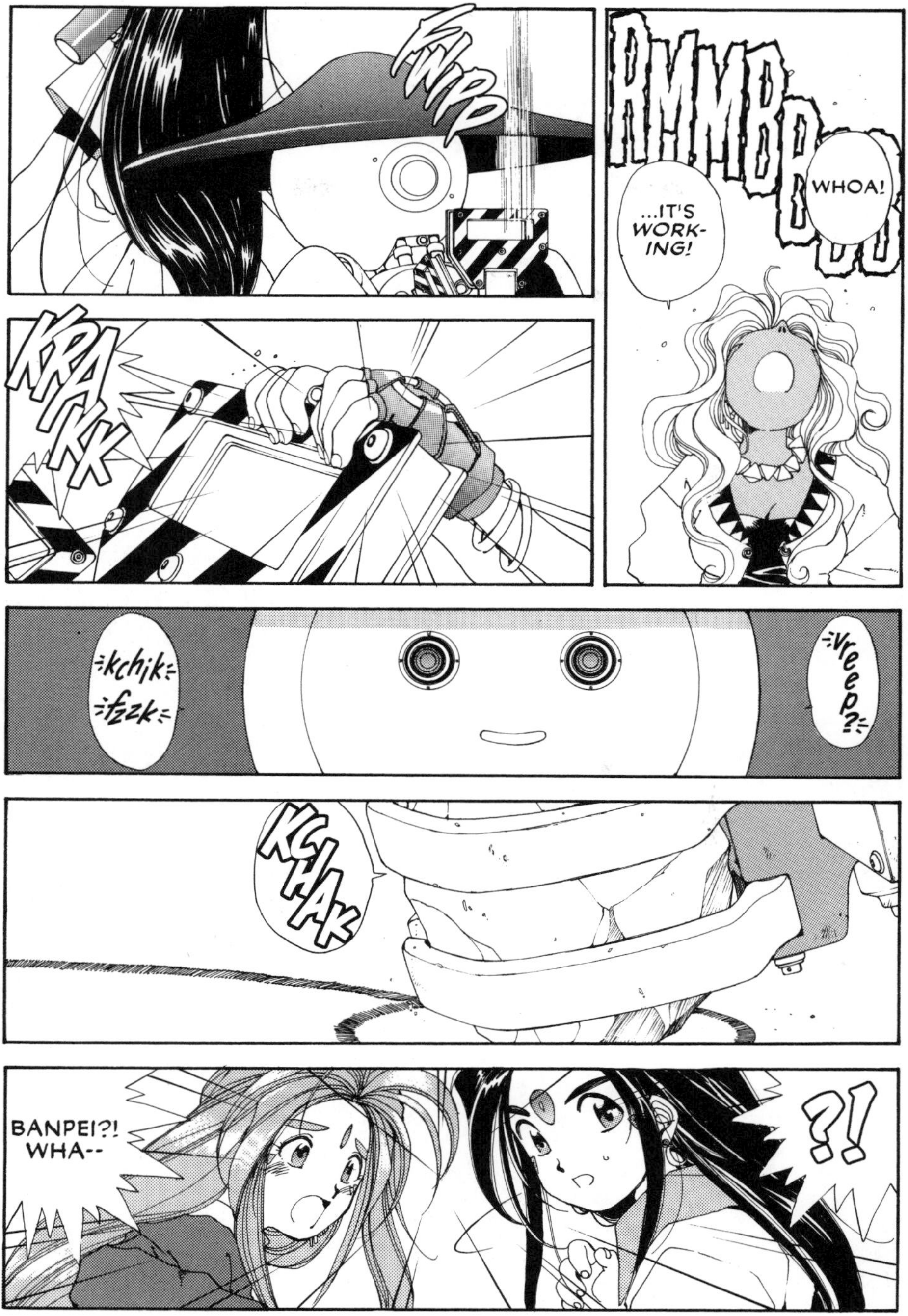
RMMBDDD
WHOA!
...IT'S WORKING!
KWIPP
KRAKKK
vreep?
kchik
fzzk
KCHAK
?!
BANPEI?! WHA--

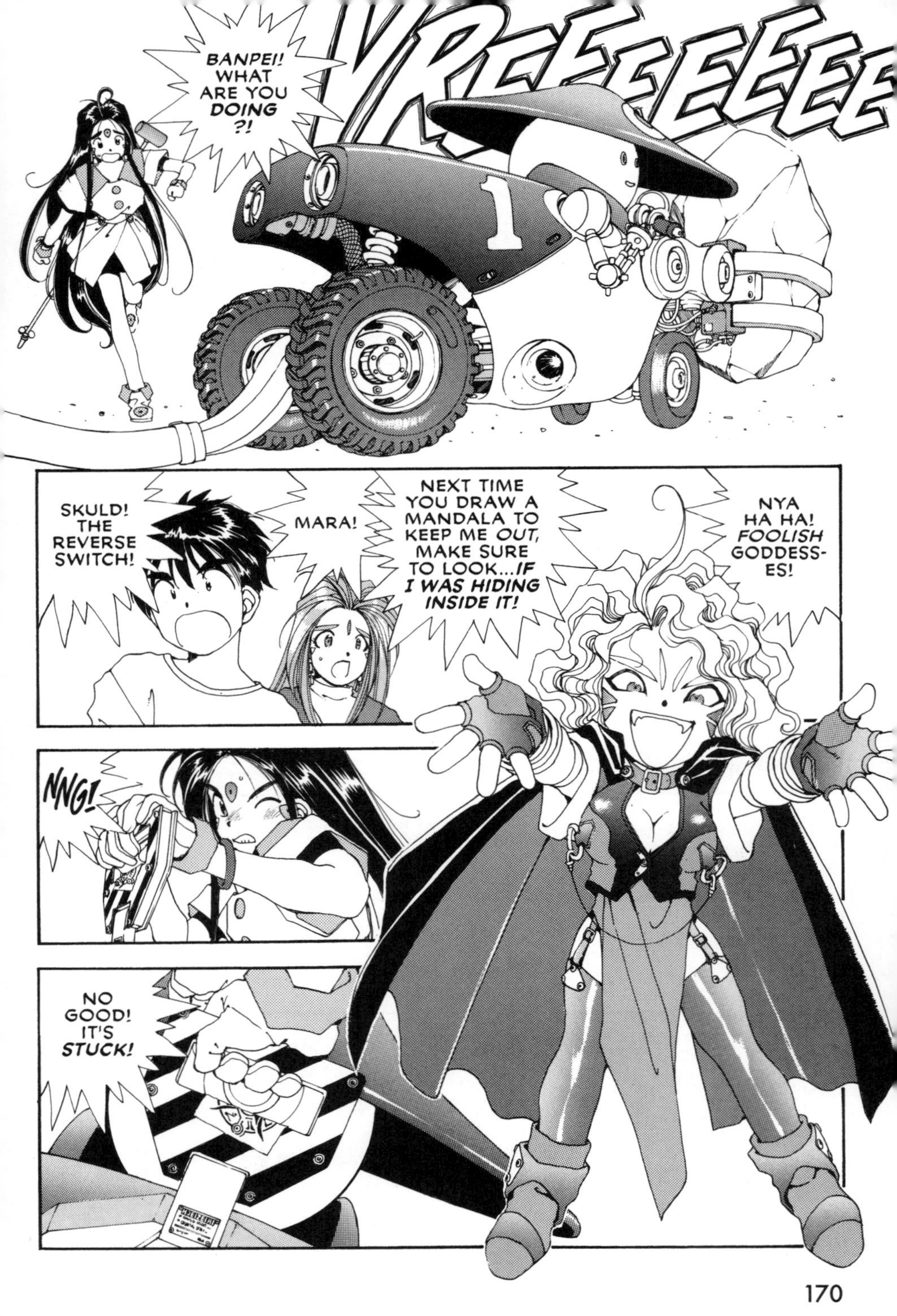
VREEEEEEE
BANPEI! WHAT ARE YOU *DOING* ?!
NYA HA HA! *FOOLISH* GODDESSES!
NEXT TIME YOU DRAW A MANDALA TO KEEP ME *OUT*, MAKE SURE TO LOOK...*IF I WAS HIDING INSIDE IT!*
MARA!
SKULD! THE REVERSE SWITCH!
NNG!
NO GOOD! IT'S *STUCK!*

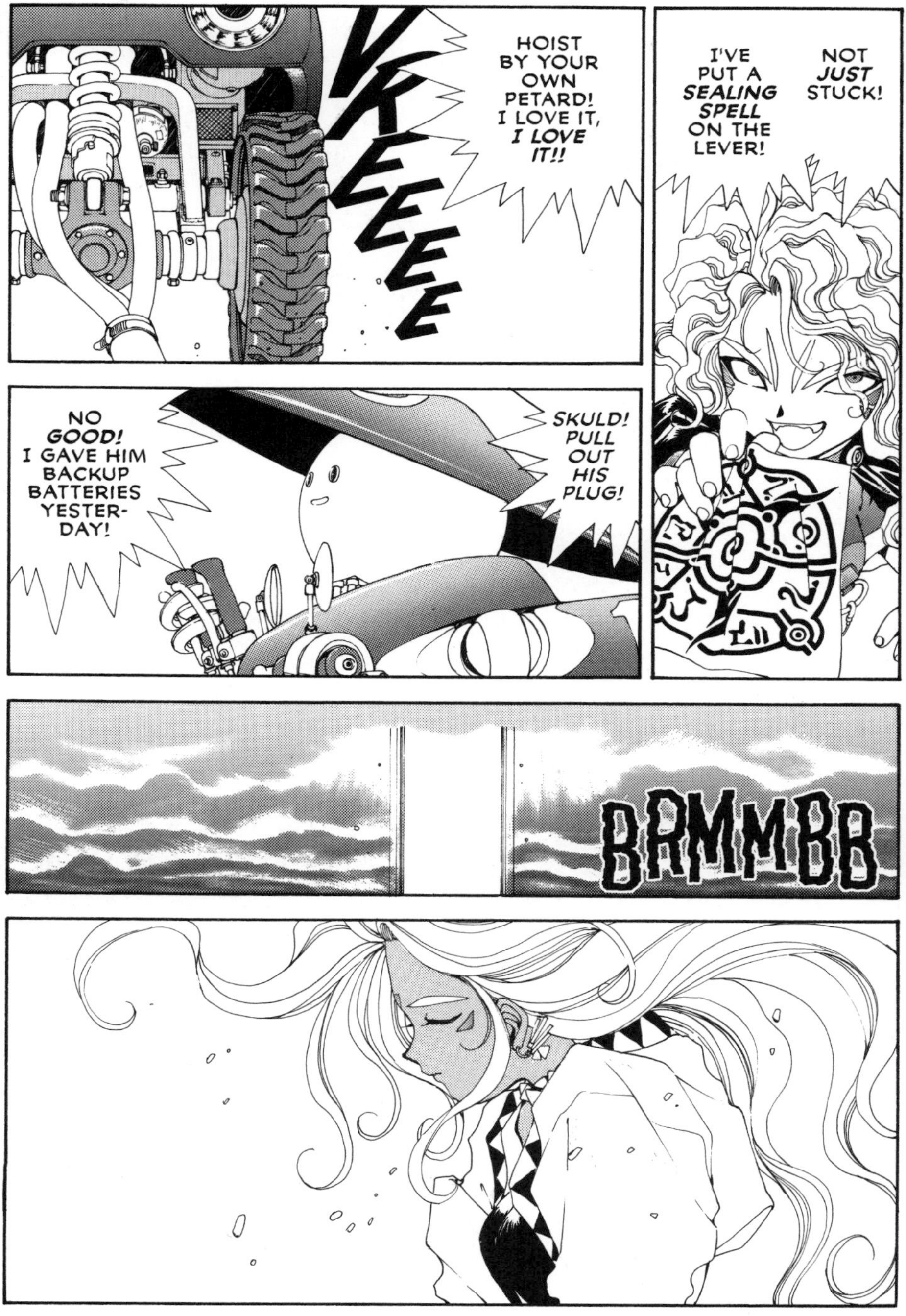
NOT JUST STUCK!
I'VE PUT A SEALING SPELL ON THE LEVER!
HOIST BY YOUR OWN PETARD! I LOVE IT, I LOVE IT!!
VKEEEEE
SKULD! PULL OUT HIS PLUG!
NO GOOD! I GAVE HIM BACKUP BATTERIES YESTER-DAY!
BRMMBB

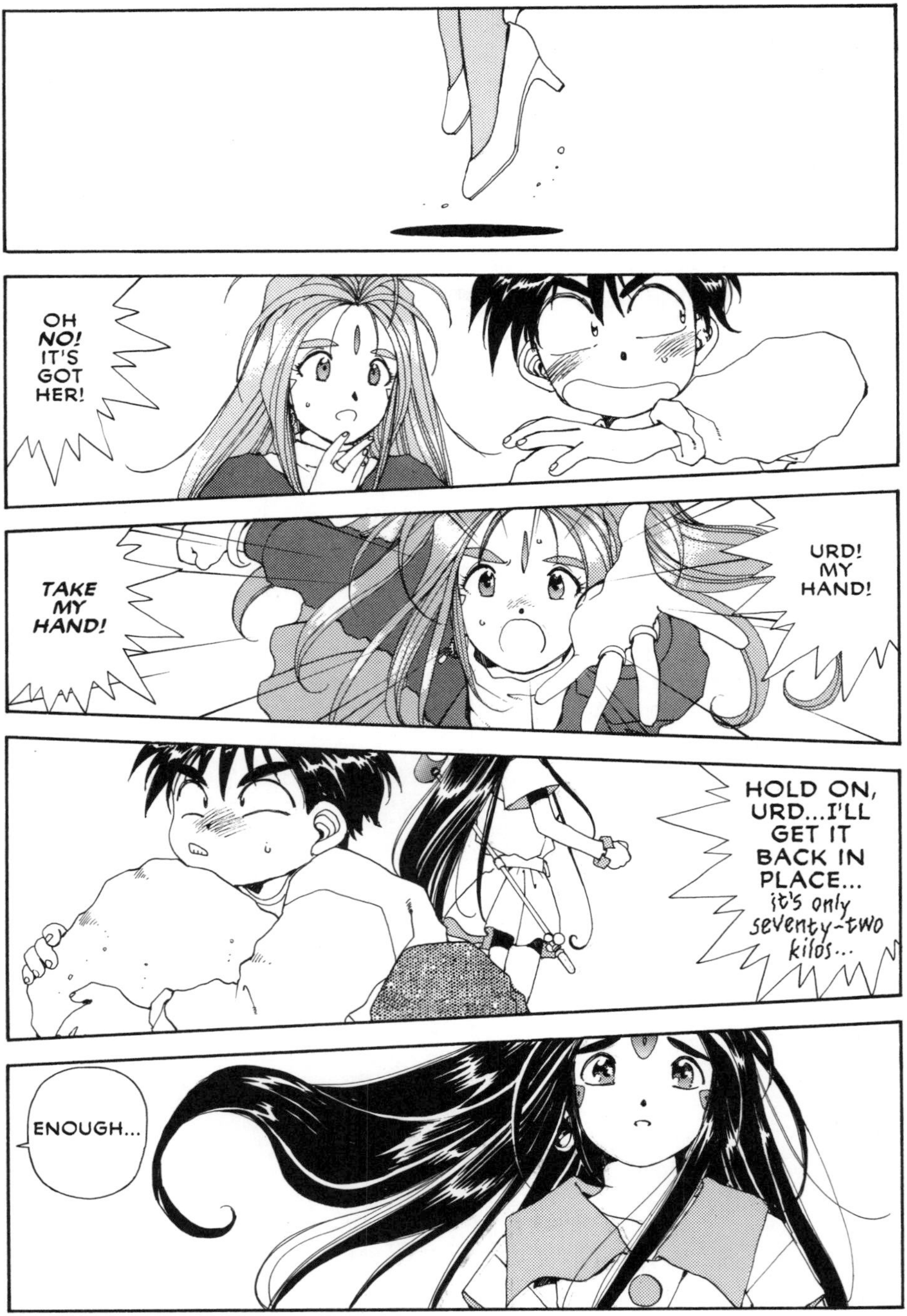
OH NO! IT'S GOT HER!
URD! MY HAND!
TAKE MY HAND!
HOLD ON, URD...I'LL GET IT BACK IN PLACE... it's only seventy-two kilos...
ENOUGH...

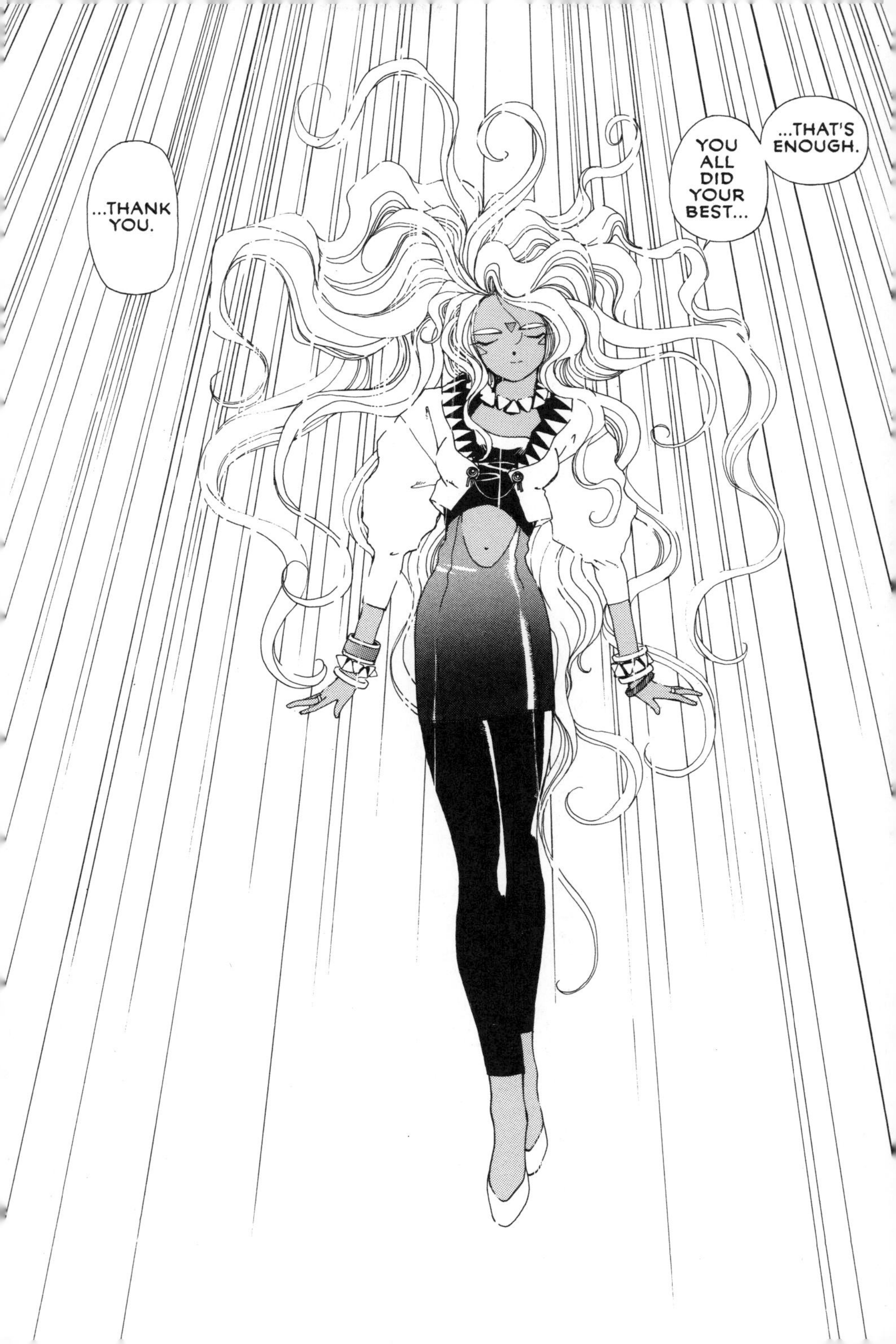
...THAT'S ENOUGH.
YOU ALL DID YOUR BEST...
...THANK YOU.

URD!!
YOU CAN'T GIVE UP!
WHUDD
!!

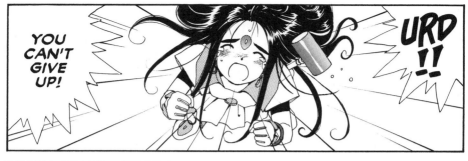

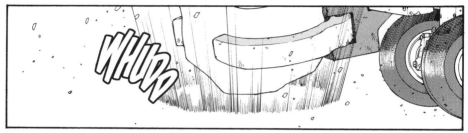

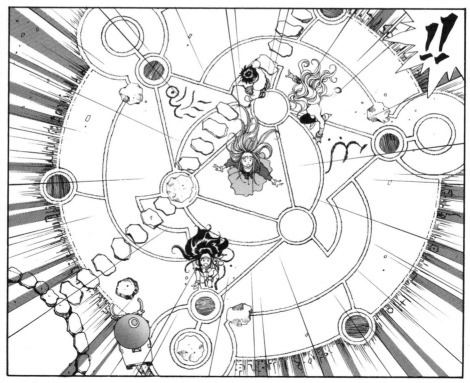

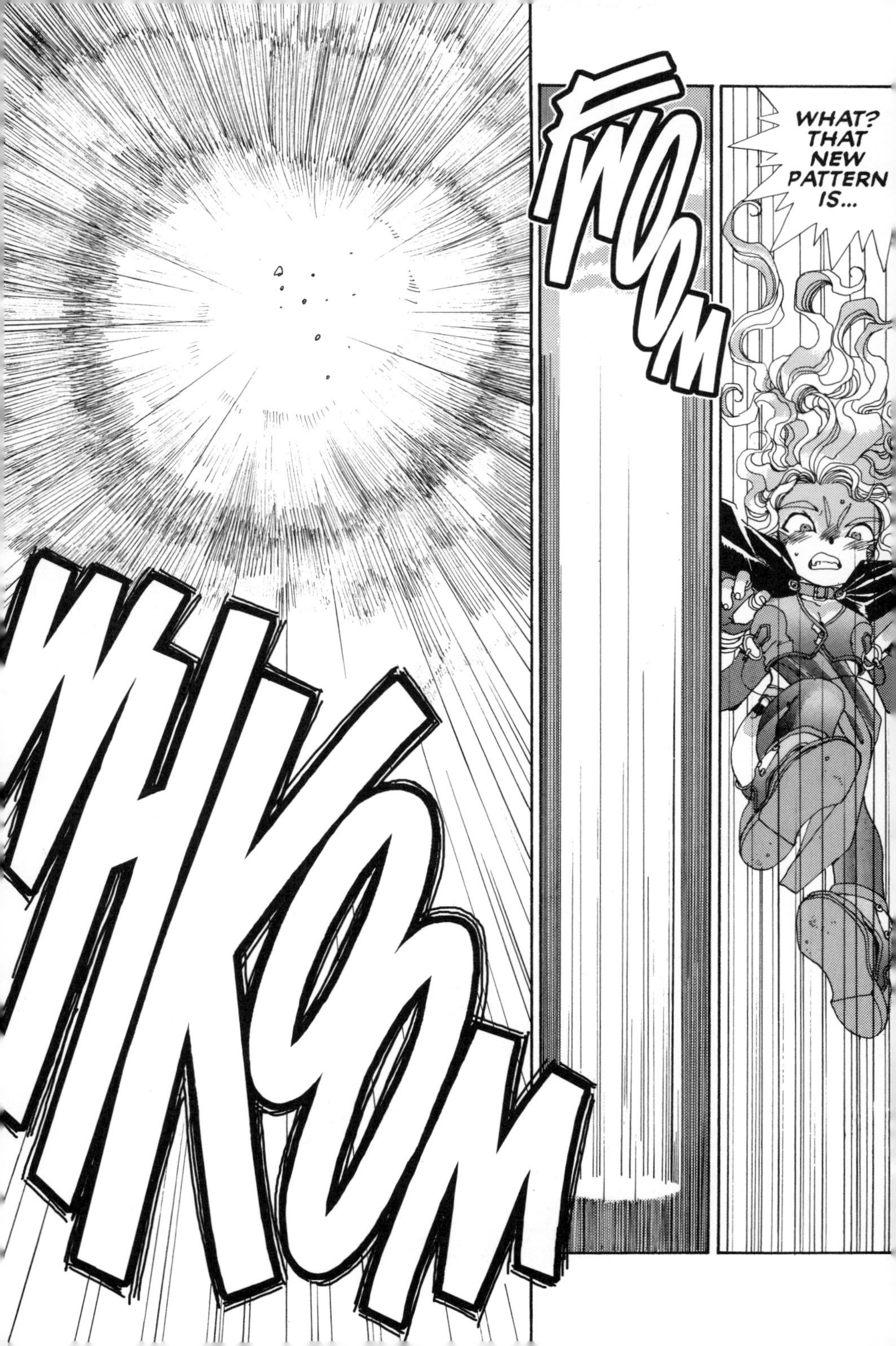
WHAT? THAT NEW PATTERN IS...

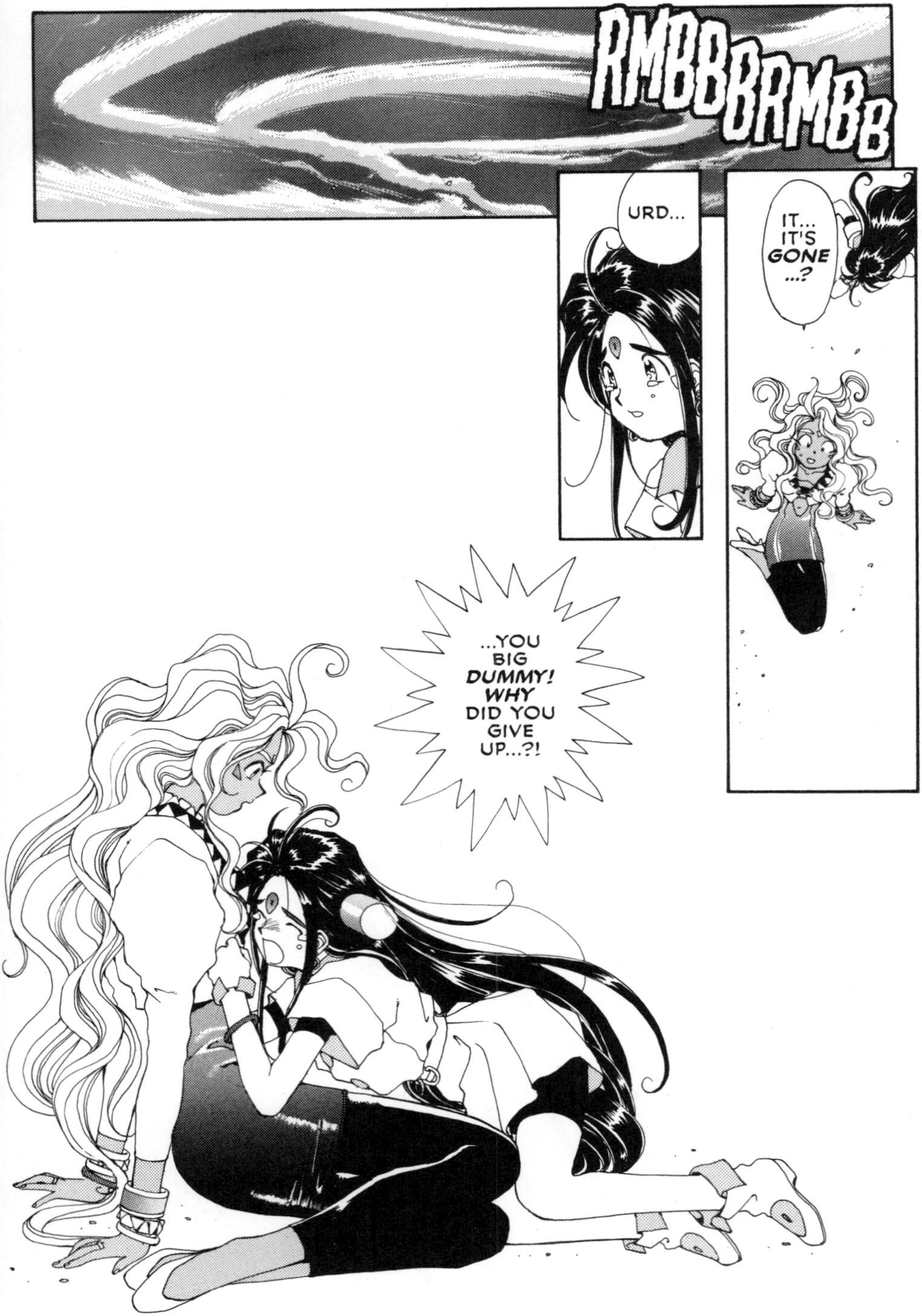
RMBBBRMBB
IT... IT'S GONE ...?
URD...
...YOU BIG DUMMY! WHY DID YOU GIVE UP...?!

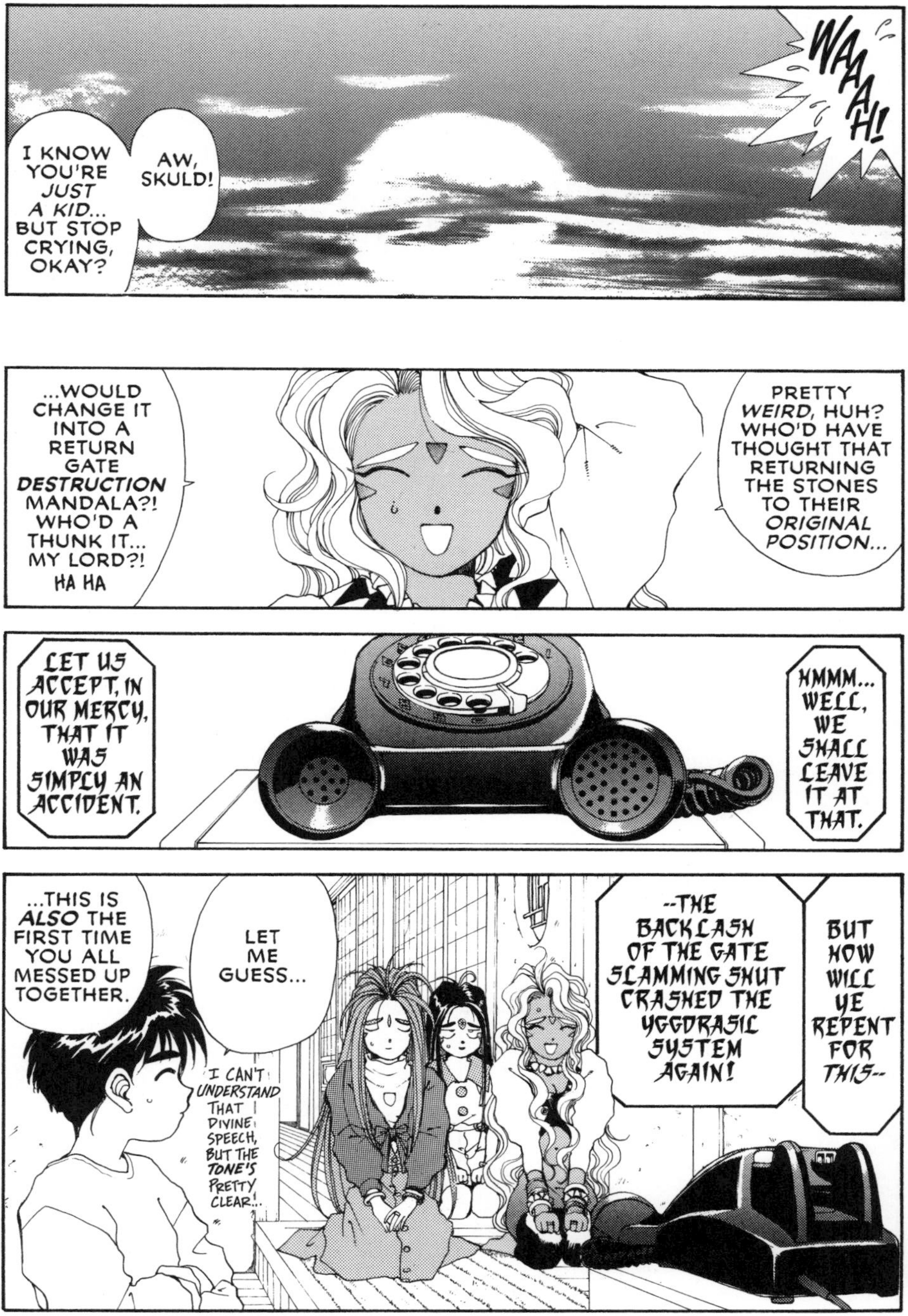
WAAAH!
AW, SKULD!
I KNOW YOU'RE JUST A KID... BUT STOP CRYING, OKAY?
PRETTY WEIRD, HUH? WHO'D HAVE THOUGHT THAT RETURNING THE STONES TO THEIR ORIGINAL POSITION...
...WOULD CHANGE IT INTO A RETURN GATE DESTRUCTION MANDALA?! WHO'D A THUNK IT... MY LORD?!
HA HA
HMMM... WELL, WE SHALL LEAVE IT AT THAT.
LET US ACCEPT, IN OUR MERCY, THAT IT WAS SIMPLY AN ACCIDENT.
BUT HOW WILL YE REPENT FOR THIS--
--THE BACKLASH OF THE GATE SLAMMING SHUT CRASHED THE YGGDRASIL SYSTEM AGAIN!
LET ME GUESS...
...THIS IS ALSO THE FIRST TIME YOU ALL MESSED UP TOGETHER.
I CAN'T UNDERSTAND THAT DIVINE SPEECH, BUT THE TONE'S PRETTY CLEAR...

THE ADVENTURES OF MINI-URD

With the Miracle Ingredient: MINI-SKULD!

◆ FORWARD TO THE FUTURE! ◆

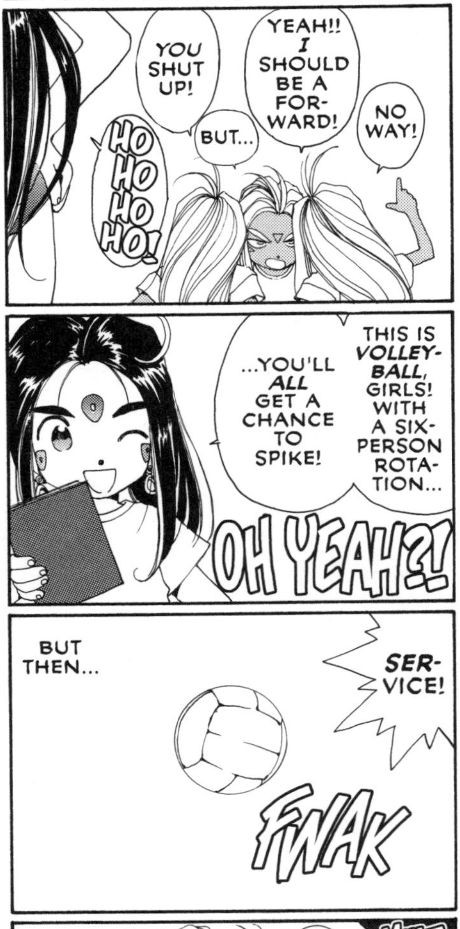
YEAH!! *I* SHOULD BE A FOR-WARD!
NO WAY!
YOU SHUT UP!
BUT...
HO HO HO HO HO!
THIS IS *VOLLEY-BALL*, GIRLS! WITH A SIX-PERSON ROTA-TION...
...YOU'LL *ALL* GET A CHANCE TO SPIKE!
OH YEAH?!
*SER-*VICE!
BUT THEN...
FWAK
MULTI-SPIKE!!
WILL YOU GUYS JUST *LISTEN* FOR ONCE?!

◆ BLOOMERS OF DOOM ◆

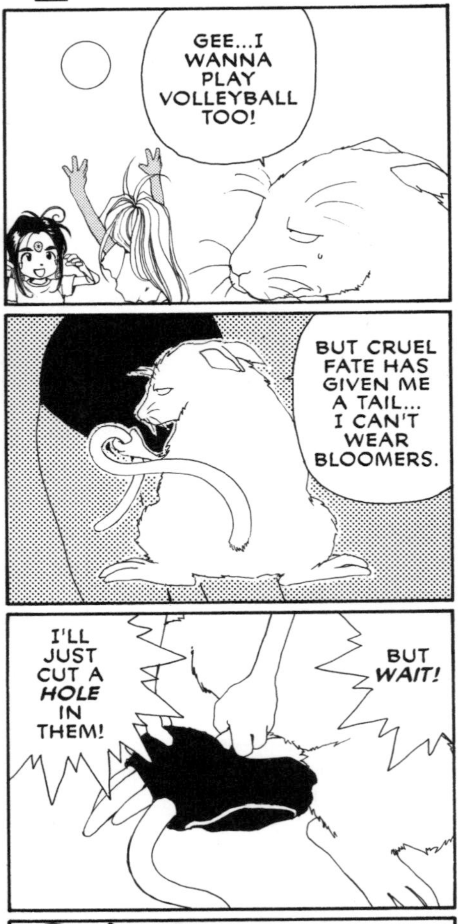
GEE...I WANNA PLAY VOLLEYBALL TOO!
BUT CRUEL FATE HAS GIVEN ME A TAIL... I CAN'T WEAR BLOOMERS.
BUT *WAIT!*
I'LL JUST CUT A *HOLE* IN THEM!
OOPS... PUT 'EM ON BACK-WARDS.
KYAAAAA! DISGUSTING!

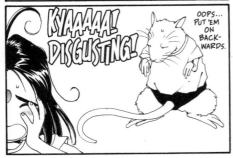

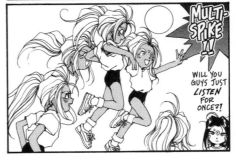

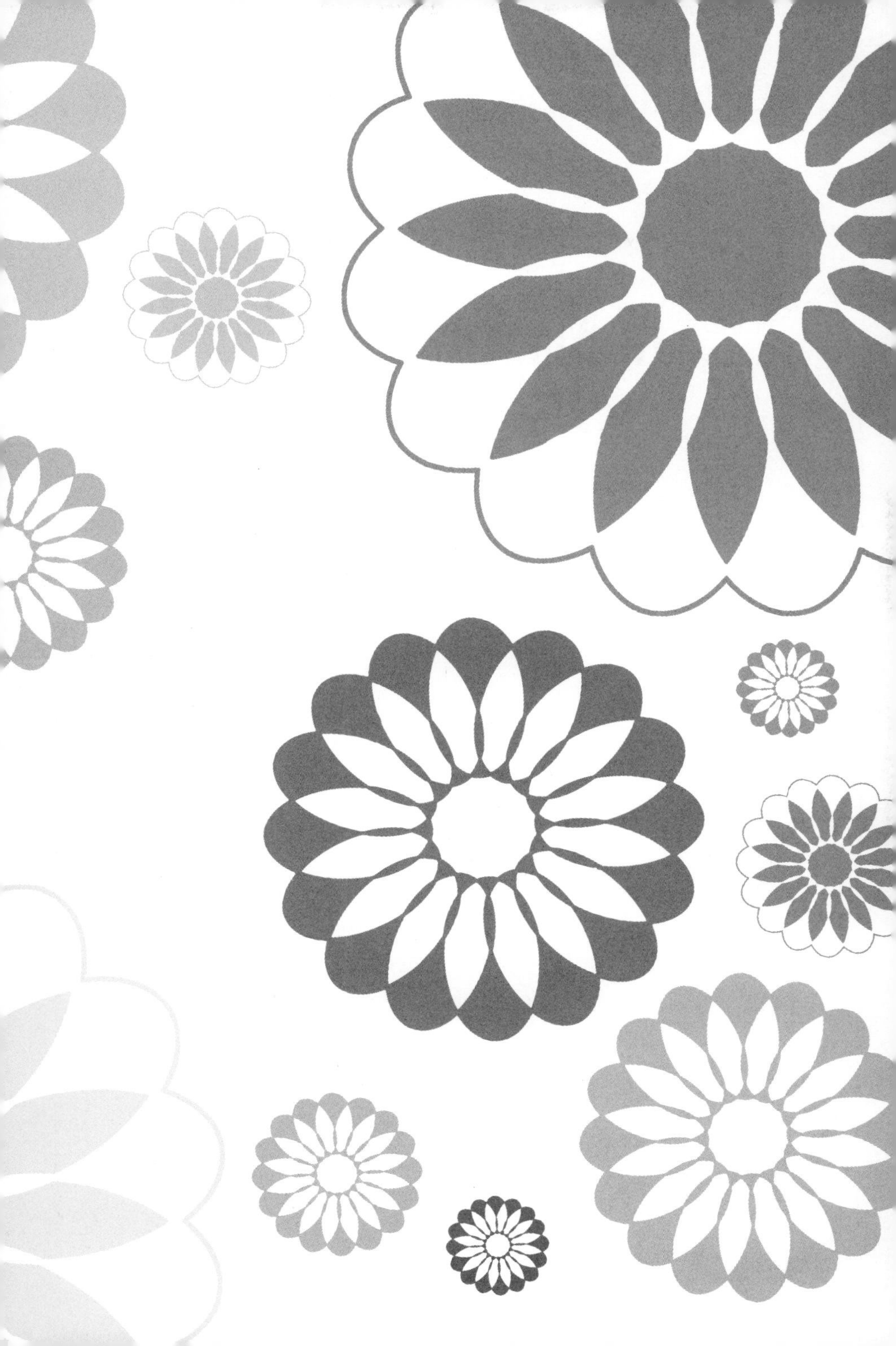

OH MY GODDESS!

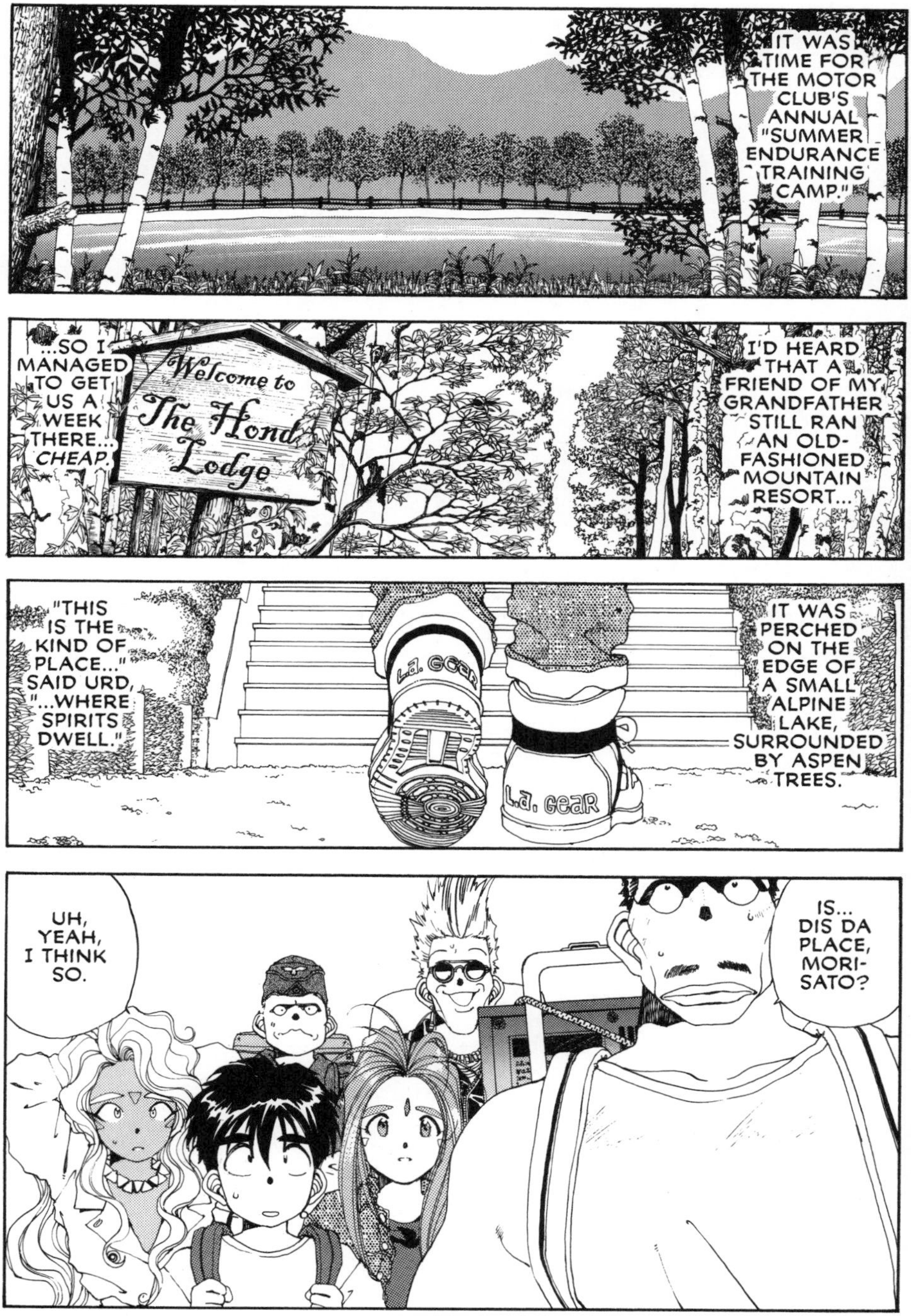
IT WAS TIME FOR THE MOTOR CLUB'S ANNUAL "SUMMER ENDURANCE TRAINING CAMP."
I'D HEARD THAT A FRIEND OF MY GRANDFATHER STILL RAN AN OLD-FASHIONED MOUNTAIN RESORT...
Welcome to The Hond Lodge
...SO I MANAGED TO GET US A WEEK THERE... *CHEAP.*
IT WAS PERCHED ON THE EDGE OF A SMALL ALPINE LAKE, SURROUNDED BY ASPEN TREES.
L.A. GEAR
L.A. GEAR
"THIS IS THE KIND OF PLACE..." SAID URD, "...WHERE SPIRITS DWELL."
IS... DIS DA PLACE, MORI-SATO?
UH, YEAH, I THINK SO.

APTER 48

he Forgotten Promise

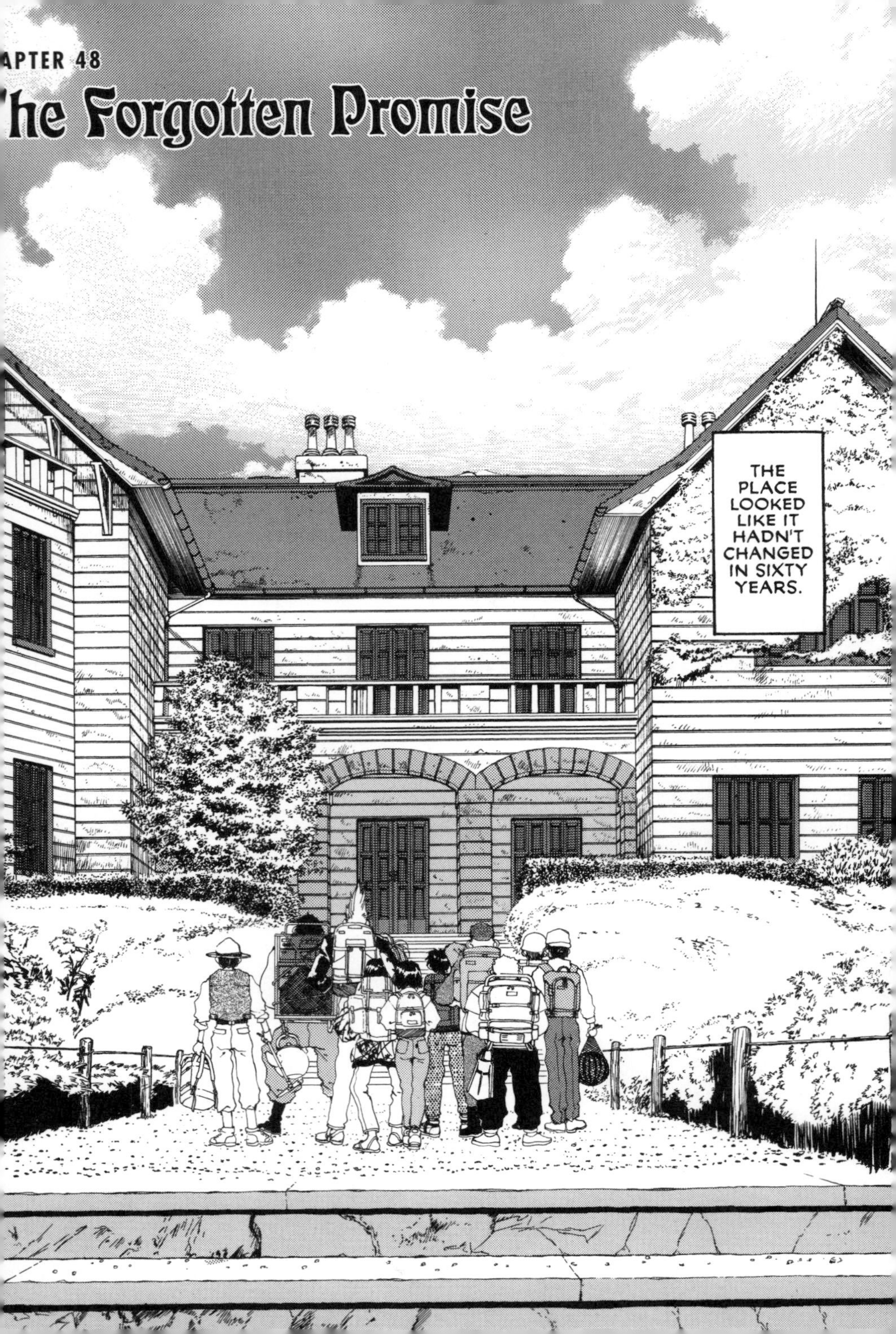
THE PLACE LOOKED LIKE IT HADN'T CHANGED IN SIXTY YEARS.

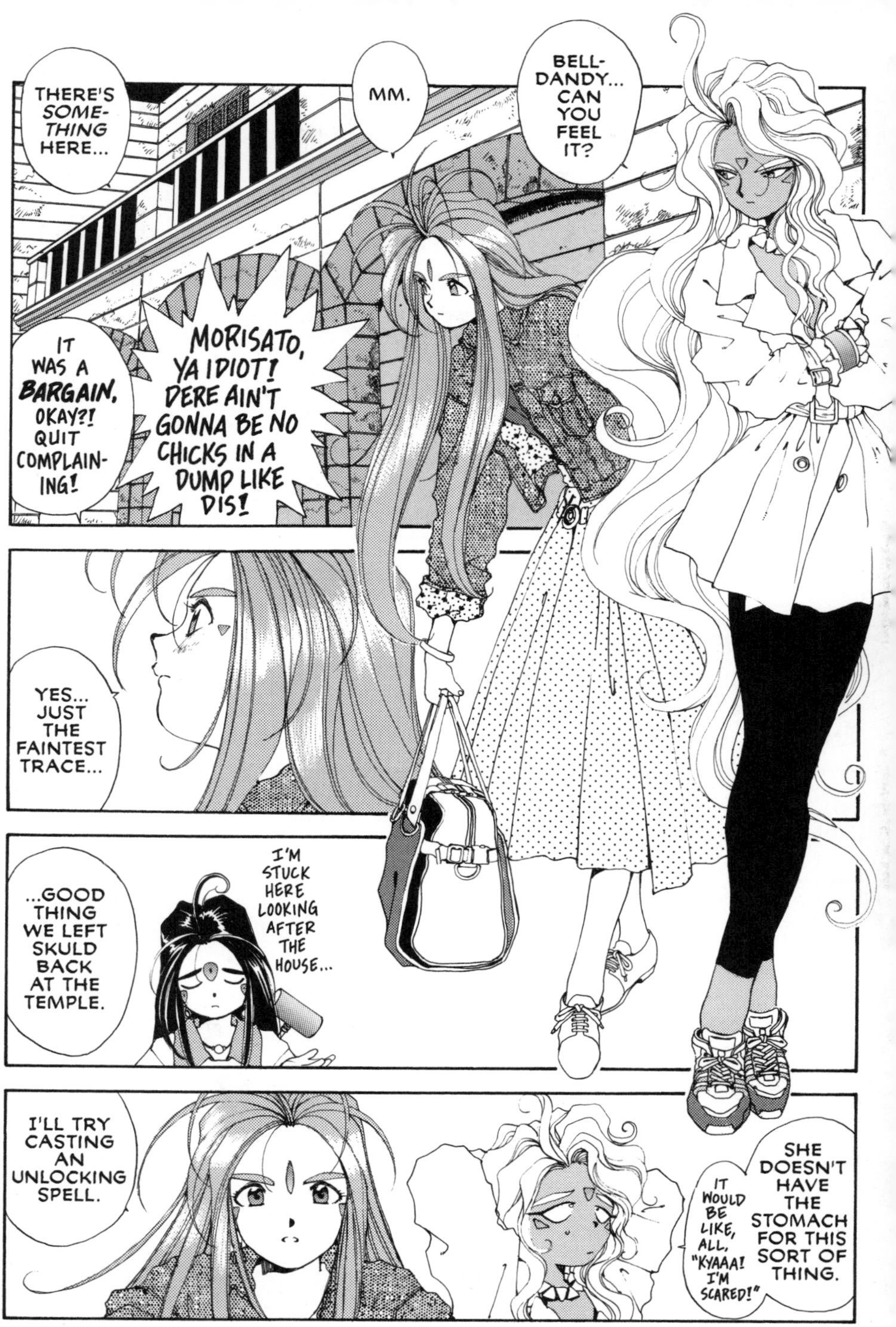
BELL-DANDY... CAN YOU FEEL IT?
MM.
THERE'S SOMETHING HERE...
MORISATO, YA IDIOT! DERE AIN'T GONNA BE NO CHICKS IN A DUMP LIKE DIS!
IT WAS A BARGAIN, OKAY?! QUIT COMPLAINING!
YES... JUST THE FAINTEST TRACE...
I'M STUCK HERE LOOKING AFTER THE HOUSE...
...GOOD THING WE LEFT SKULD BACK AT THE TEMPLE.
SHE DOESN'T HAVE THE STOMACH FOR THIS SORT OF THING.
IT WOULD BE LIKE, ALL, "KYAAA! I'M SCARED!"
I'LL TRY CASTING AN UNLOCKING SPELL.

IT'S ALREADY OPEN...?

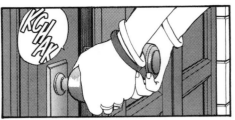

KCHAK

SKREEEEEEEK

HA! IF YOU'RE A DEMON, URD'S SPECIAL EXORCISM PROGRAM WILL--

gasp

FSSST

--UM, DESTROY YOU... YEAH...

184

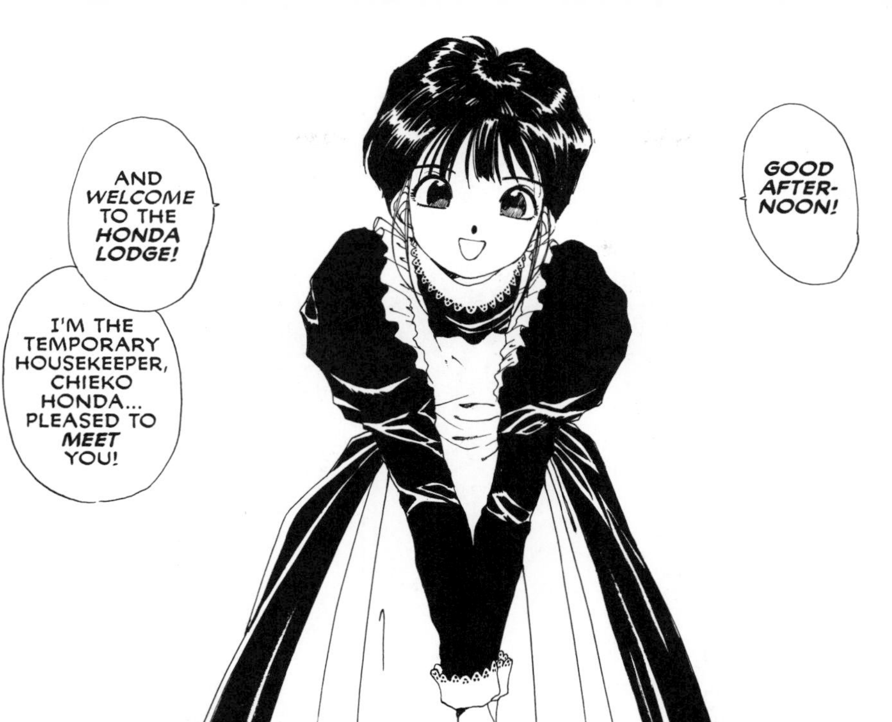
GOOD AFTER-NOON!
AND WELCOME TO THE HONDA LODGE!
I'M THE TEMPORARY HOUSEKEEPER, CHIEKO HONDA... PLEASED TO MEET YOU!

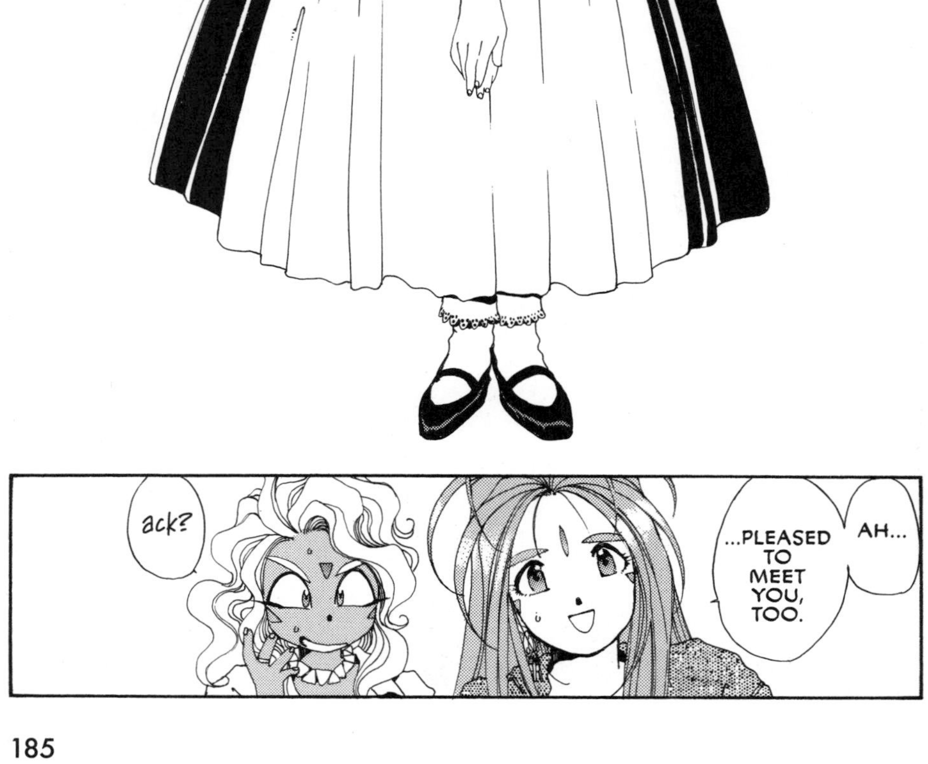
AH...
...PLEASED TO MEET YOU, TOO.
ack?

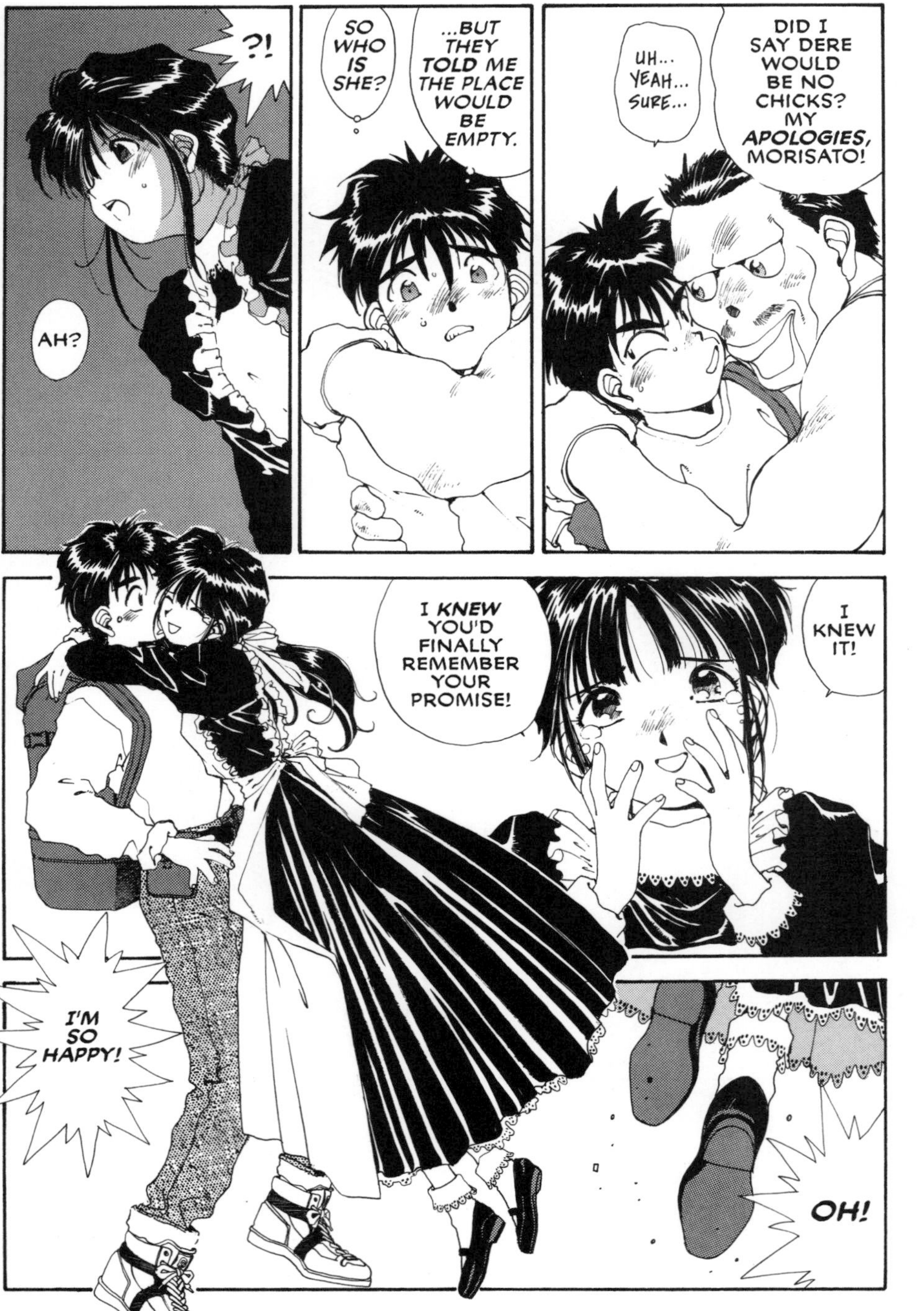
DID I SAY DERE WOULD BE NO CHICKS? MY APOLOGIES, MORISATO!
UH... YEAH... SURE...
...BUT THEY TOLD ME THE PLACE WOULD BE EMPTY.
SO WHO IS SHE?
?!
AH?
I KNEW IT!
I KNEW YOU'D FINALLY REMEMBER YOUR PROMISE!
OH!
I'M SO HAPPY!

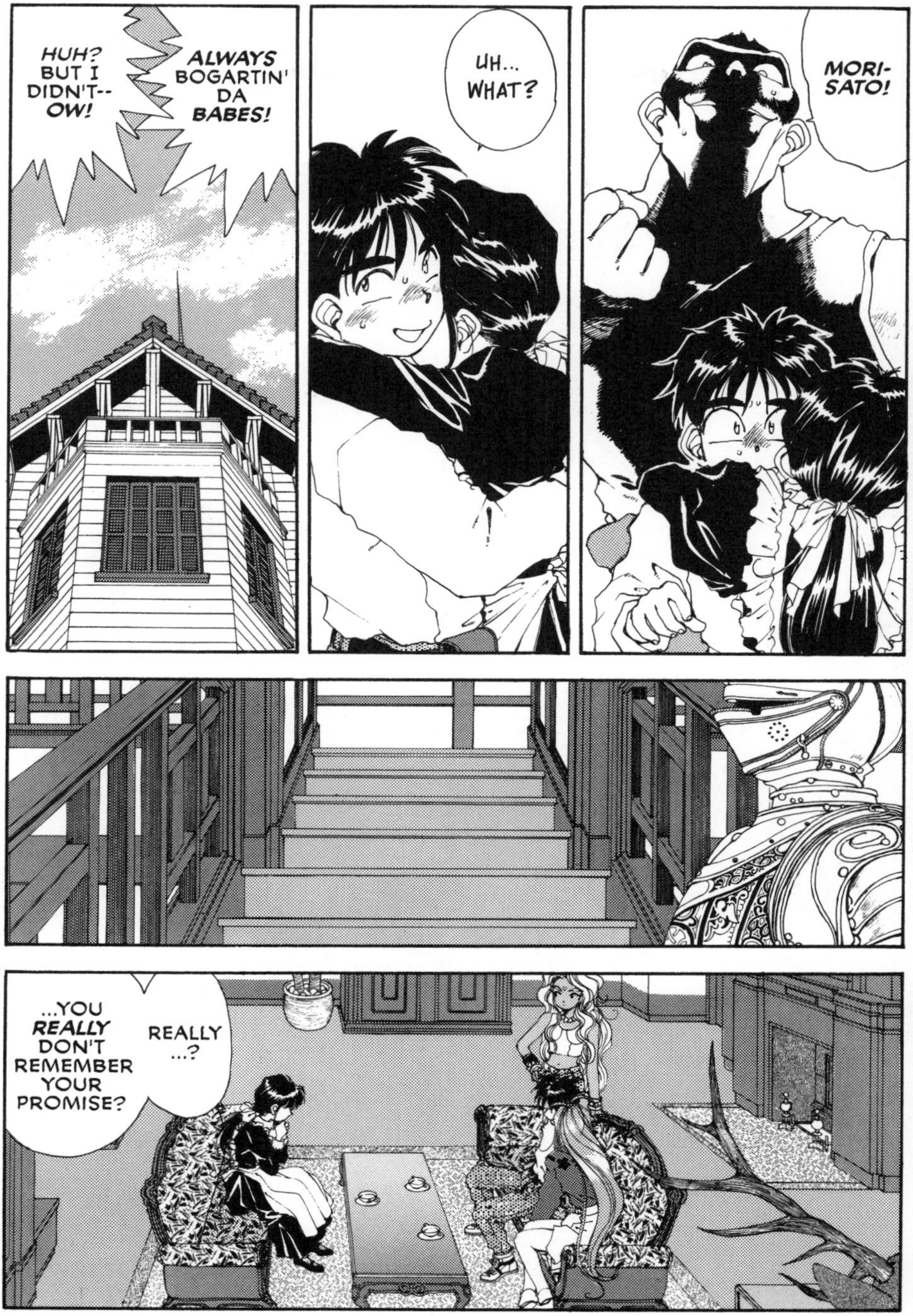
MORI-SATO!
UH... WHAT?
ALWAYS BOGARTIN' DA BABES!
HUH? BUT I DIDN'T-- OW!
REALLY ...?
...YOU REALLY DON'T REMEMBER YOUR PROMISE?

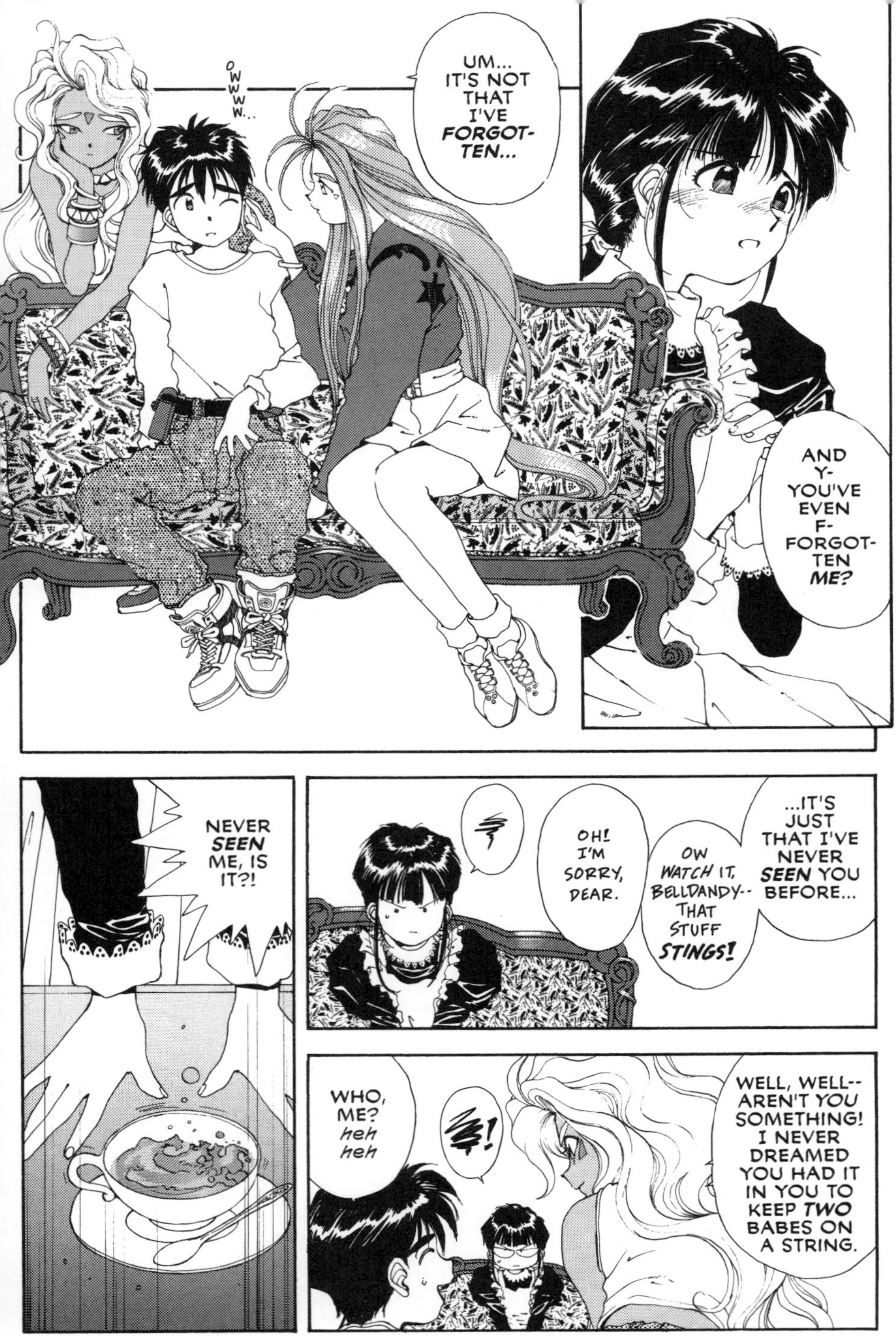
AND Y-YOU'VE EVEN F-FORGOTTEN *ME?*
UM... IT'S NOT THAT I'VE ***FORGOTTEN...***
OWWWW...
...IT'S JUST THAT I'VE NEVER ***SEEN*** YOU BEFORE...
OW *WATCH* IT, BELLDANDY-- THAT STUFF ***STINGS!***
OH! I'M SORRY, DEAR.
WELL, WELL-- AREN'T *YOU* SOMETHING! I NEVER DREAMED YOU HAD IT IN YOU TO KEEP ***TWO*** BABES ON A STRING.
WHO, ME? *heh heh*
NEVER ***SEEN*** ME, IS IT?!

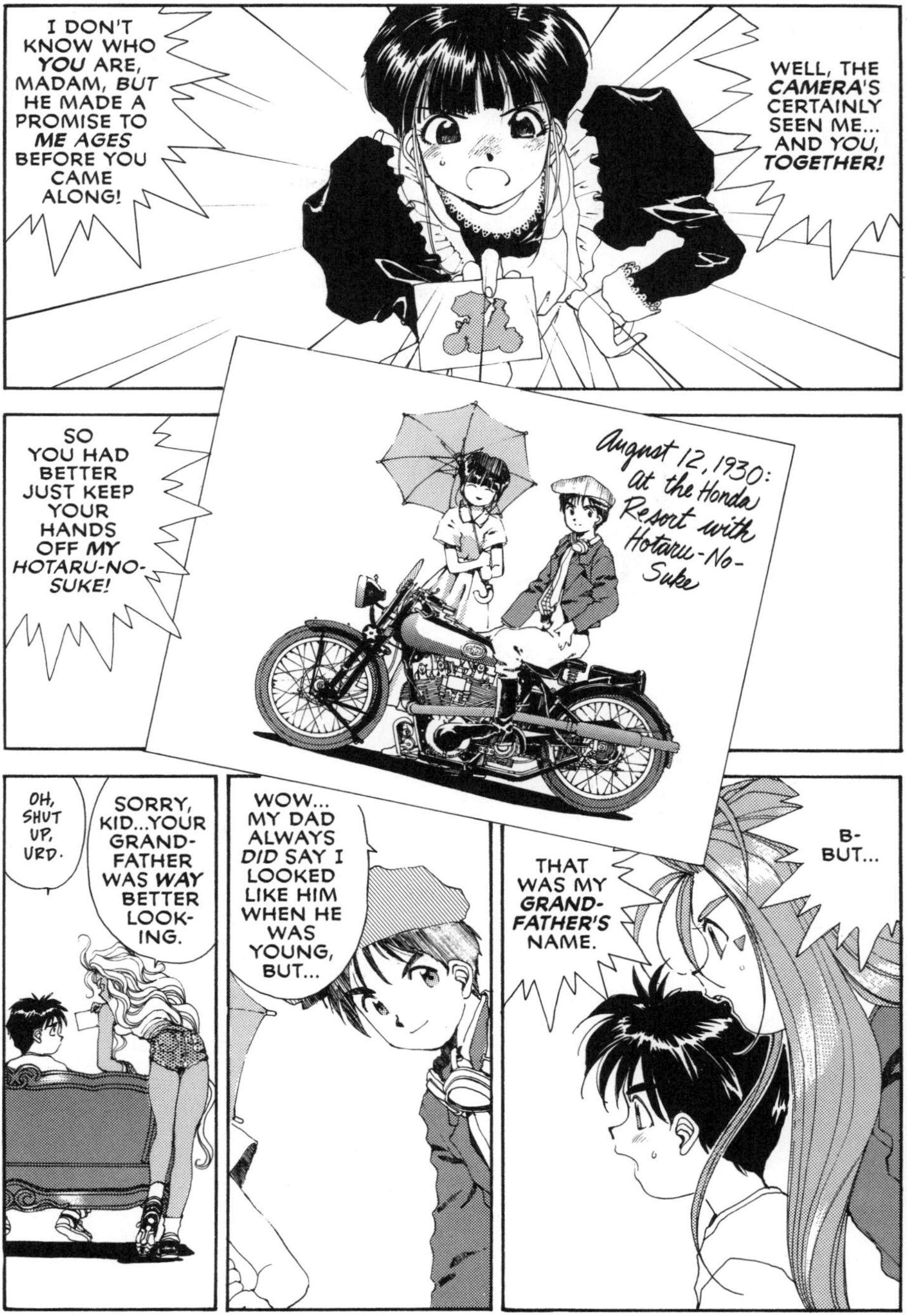
WELL, THE CAMERA'S CERTAINLY SEEN ME... AND YOU, TOGETHER!
I DON'T KNOW WHO YOU ARE, MADAM, BUT HE MADE A PROMISE TO ME AGES BEFORE YOU CAME ALONG!
August 12, 1930: At the Honda Resort with Hotaru-No-Suke
SO YOU HAD BETTER JUST KEEP YOUR HANDS OFF MY HOTARU-NO-SUKE!
B-BUT...
THAT WAS MY GRANDFATHER'S NAME.
WOW... MY DAD ALWAYS DID SAY I LOOKED LIKE HIM WHEN HE WAS YOUNG, BUT...
SORRY, KID...YOUR GRANDFATHER WAS WAY BETTER LOOKING.
OH, SHUT UP, URD.

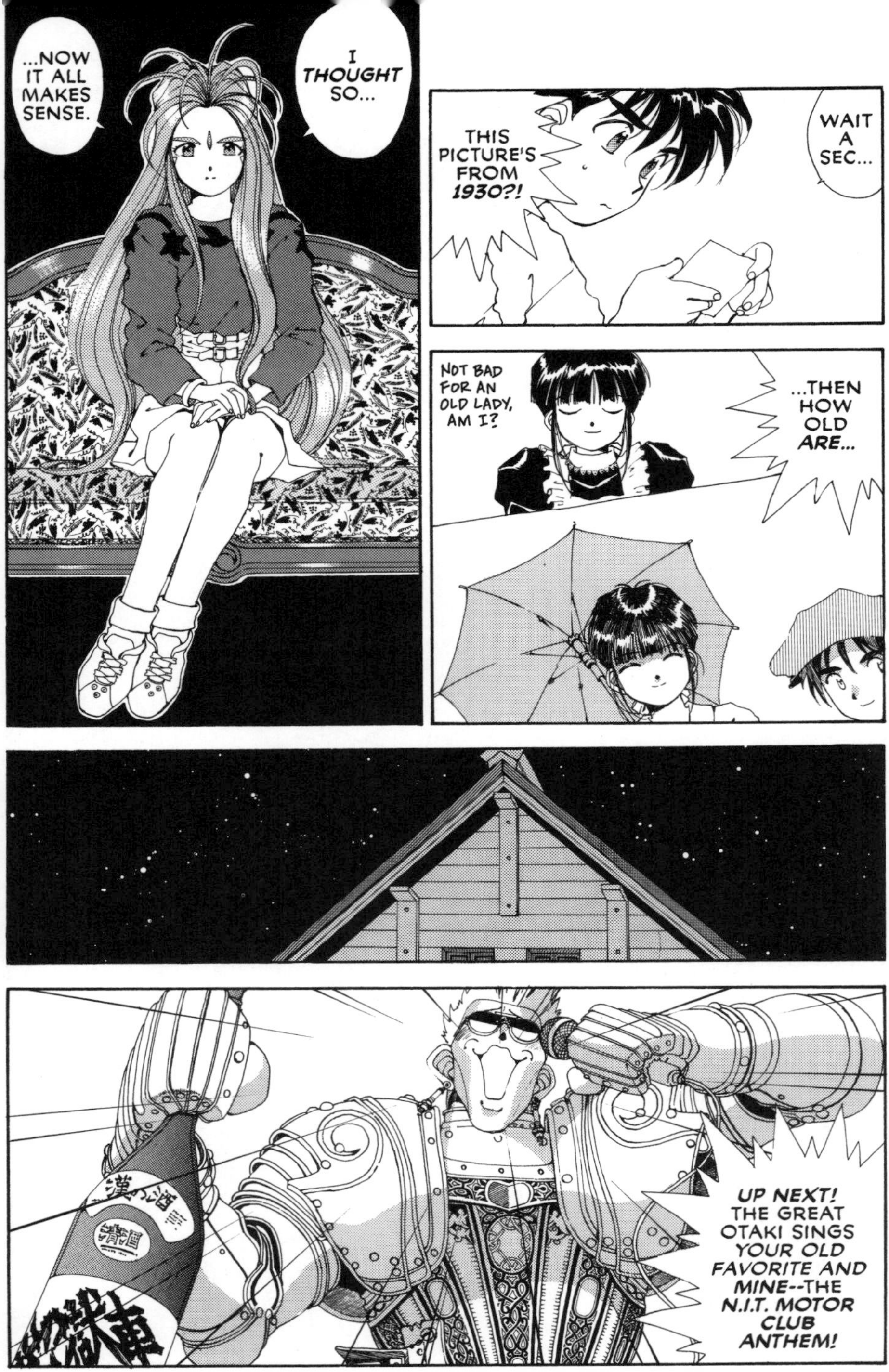
WAIT A SEC...
THIS PICTURE'S FROM *1930?!*
...THEN HOW OLD *ARE*...
NOT BAD FOR AN OLD LADY, AM I?
I *THOUGHT* SO...
...NOW IT ALL MAKES SENSE.
UP NEXT! THE GREAT OTAKI SINGS *YOUR OLD FAVORITE AND MINE--THE N.I.T. MOTOR CLUB ANTHEM!*

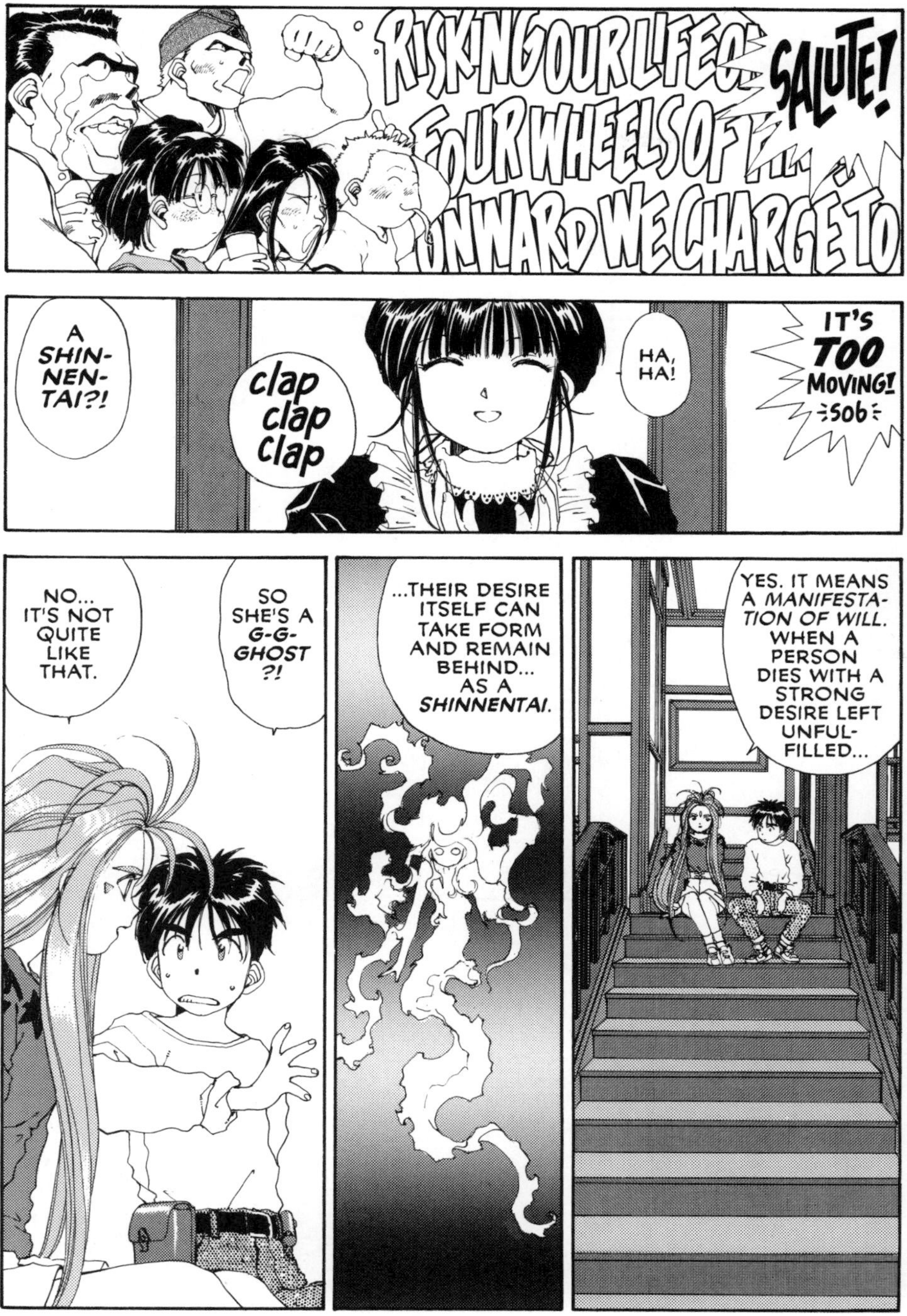
RISKING OUR LIFE O
FOUR WHEELS OF
ONWARD WE CHARGE TO
SALUTE!
IT'S TOO MOVING! sob
HA, HA!
clap clap clap
A SHIN-NEN-TAI?!
YES. IT MEANS A MANIFESTATION OF WILL. WHEN A PERSON DIES WITH A STRONG DESIRE LEFT UNFULFILLED...
...THEIR DESIRE ITSELF CAN TAKE FORM AND REMAIN BEHIND... AS A SHINNENTAI.
SO SHE'S A G-G-GHOST?!
NO... IT'S NOT QUITE LIKE THAT.

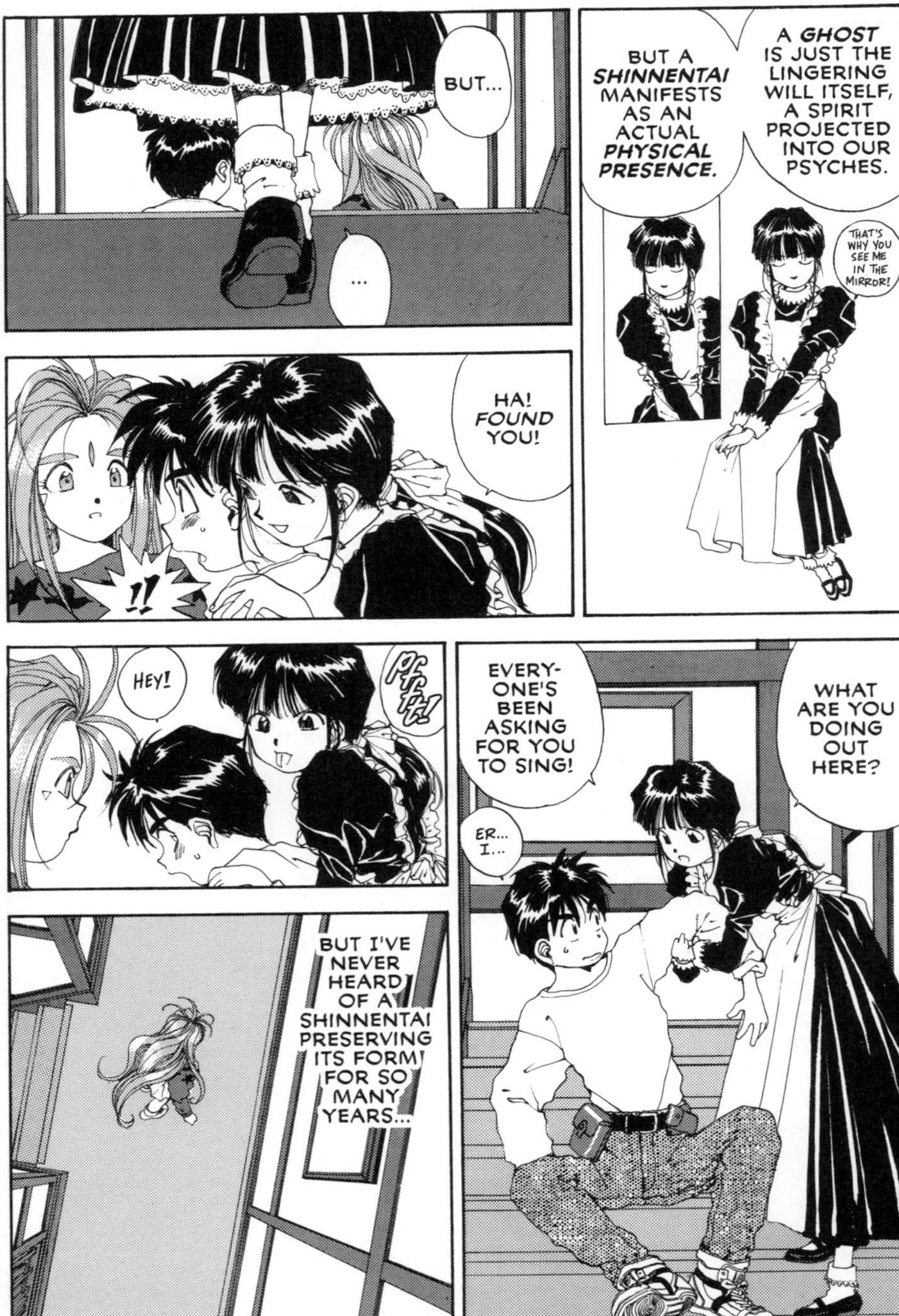
A GHOST IS JUST THE LINGERING WILL ITSELF, A SPIRIT PROJECTED INTO OUR PSYCHES.
BUT A SHINNENTAI MANIFESTS AS AN ACTUAL PHYSICAL PRESENCE.
THAT'S WHY YOU SEE ME IN THE MIRROR!
BUT...
...
HA! FOUND YOU!
!!
WHAT ARE YOU DOING OUT HERE?
EVERY-ONE'S BEEN ASKING FOR YOU TO SING!
ER... I...
Pffft!
HEY!
BUT I'VE NEVER HEARD OF A SHINNENTAI PRESERVING ITS FORM FOR SO MANY YEARS...

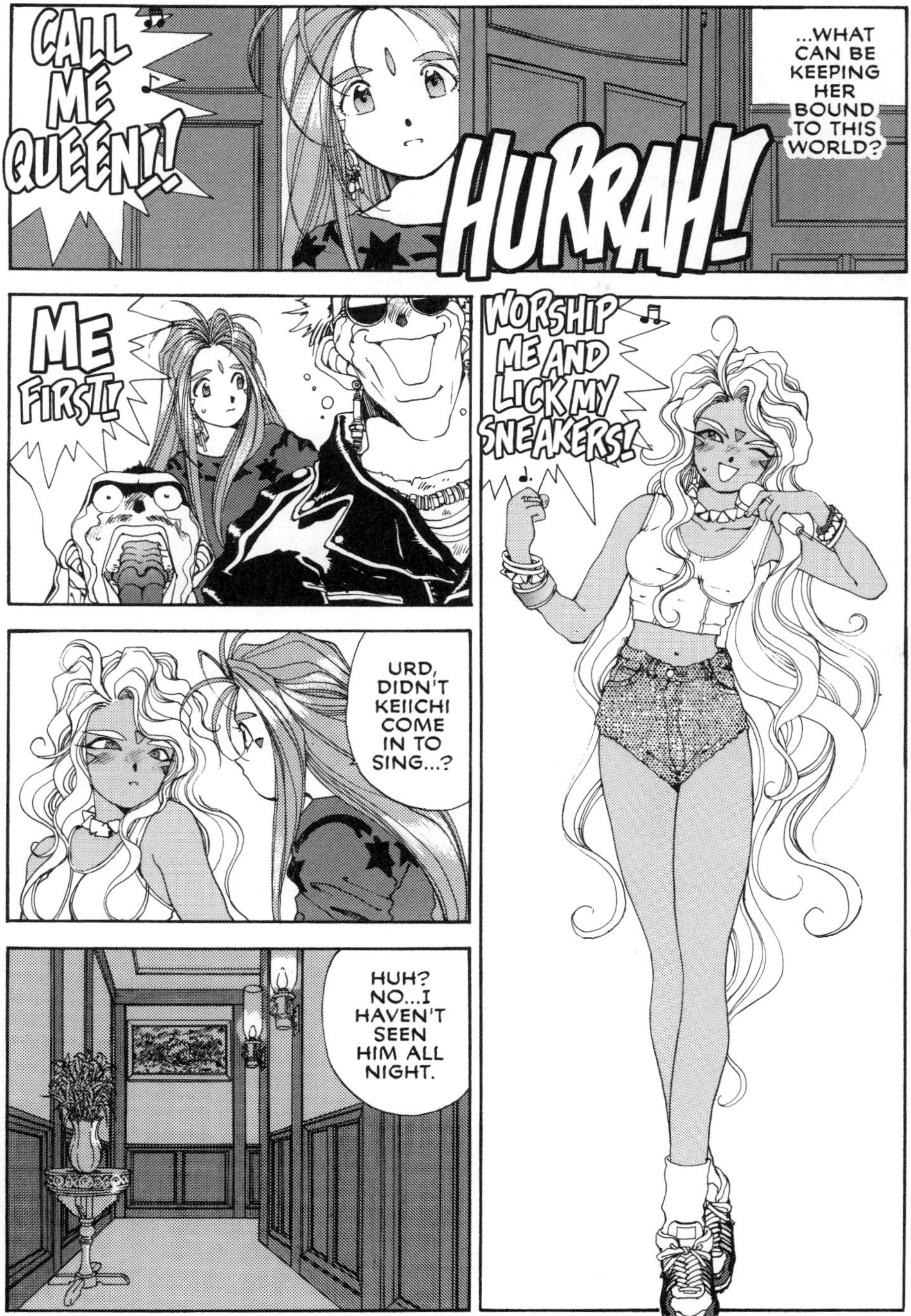
...WHAT CAN BE KEEPING HER BOUND TO THIS WORLD?
HURRAH!
CALL ME QUEEN!!
WORSHIP ME AND LICK MY SNEAKERS!
ME FIRST!!
URD, DIDN'T KEIICHI COME IN TO SING...?
HUH? NO...I HAVEN'T SEEN HIM ALL NIGHT.

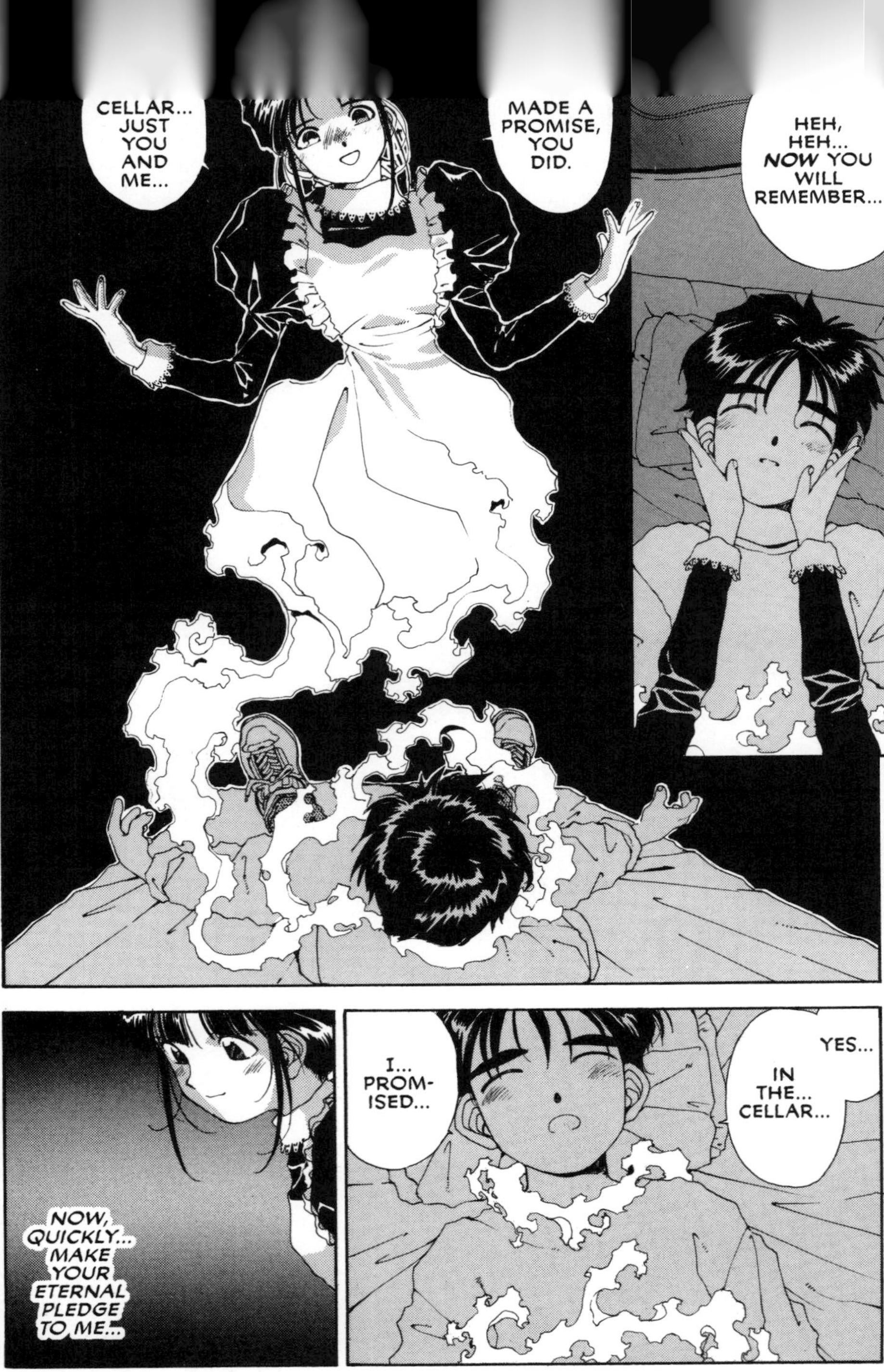
HEH, HEH... NOW YOU WILL REMEMBER...
MADE A PROMISE, YOU DID.
CELLAR... JUST YOU AND ME...
YES... IN THE... CELLAR...
I... PROMISED...
NOW, QUICKLY... MAKE YOUR ETERNAL PLEDGE TO ME...

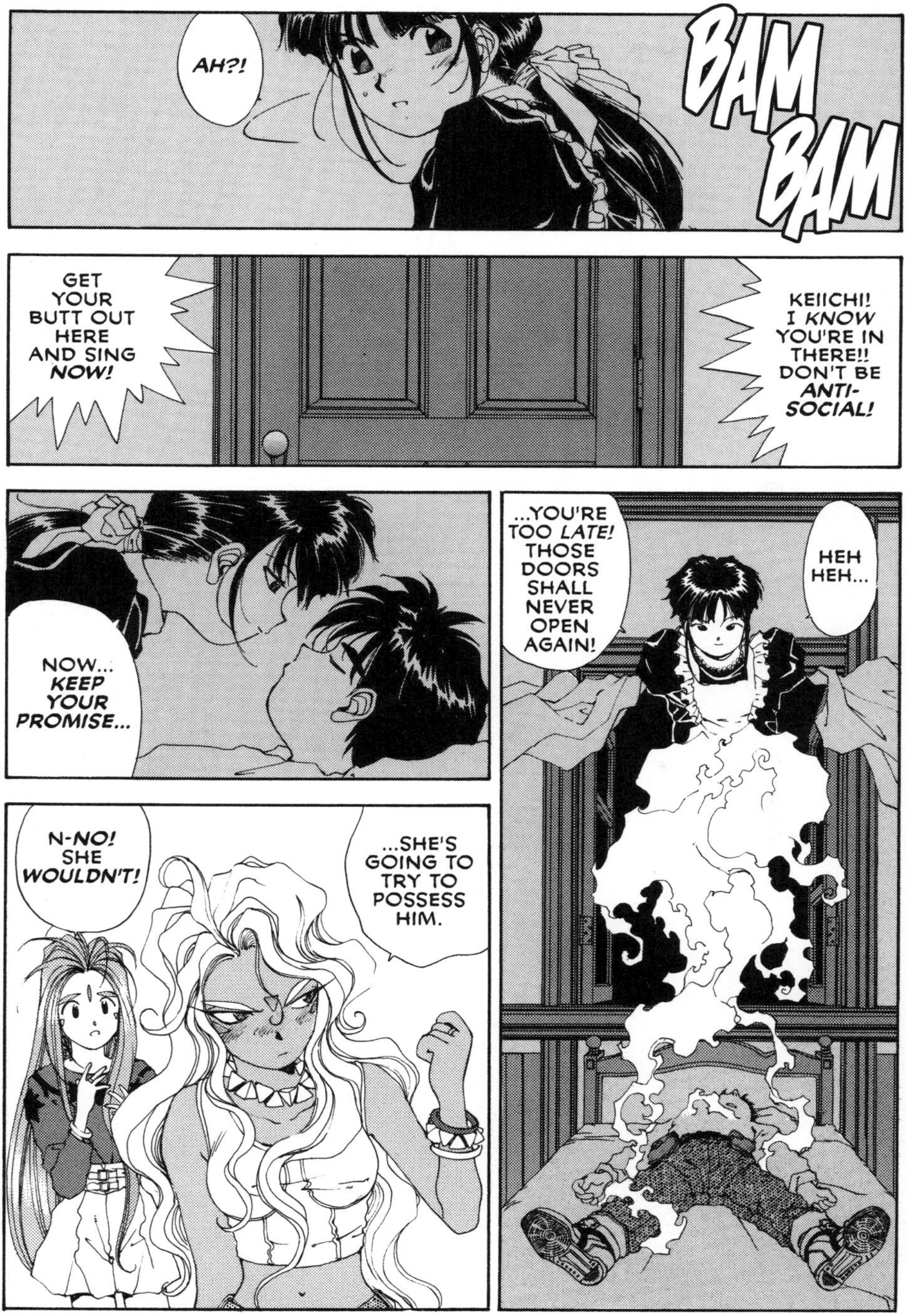
BAM BAM
AH?!
KEIICHI! I KNOW YOU'RE IN THERE!! DON'T BE ANTI-SOCIAL!
GET YOUR BUTT OUT HERE AND SING NOW!
HEH HEH...
...YOU'RE TOO LATE! THOSE DOORS SHALL NEVER OPEN AGAIN!
NOW... KEEP YOUR PROMISE...
...SHE'S GOING TO TRY TO POSSESS HIM.
N-NO! SHE WOULDN'T!

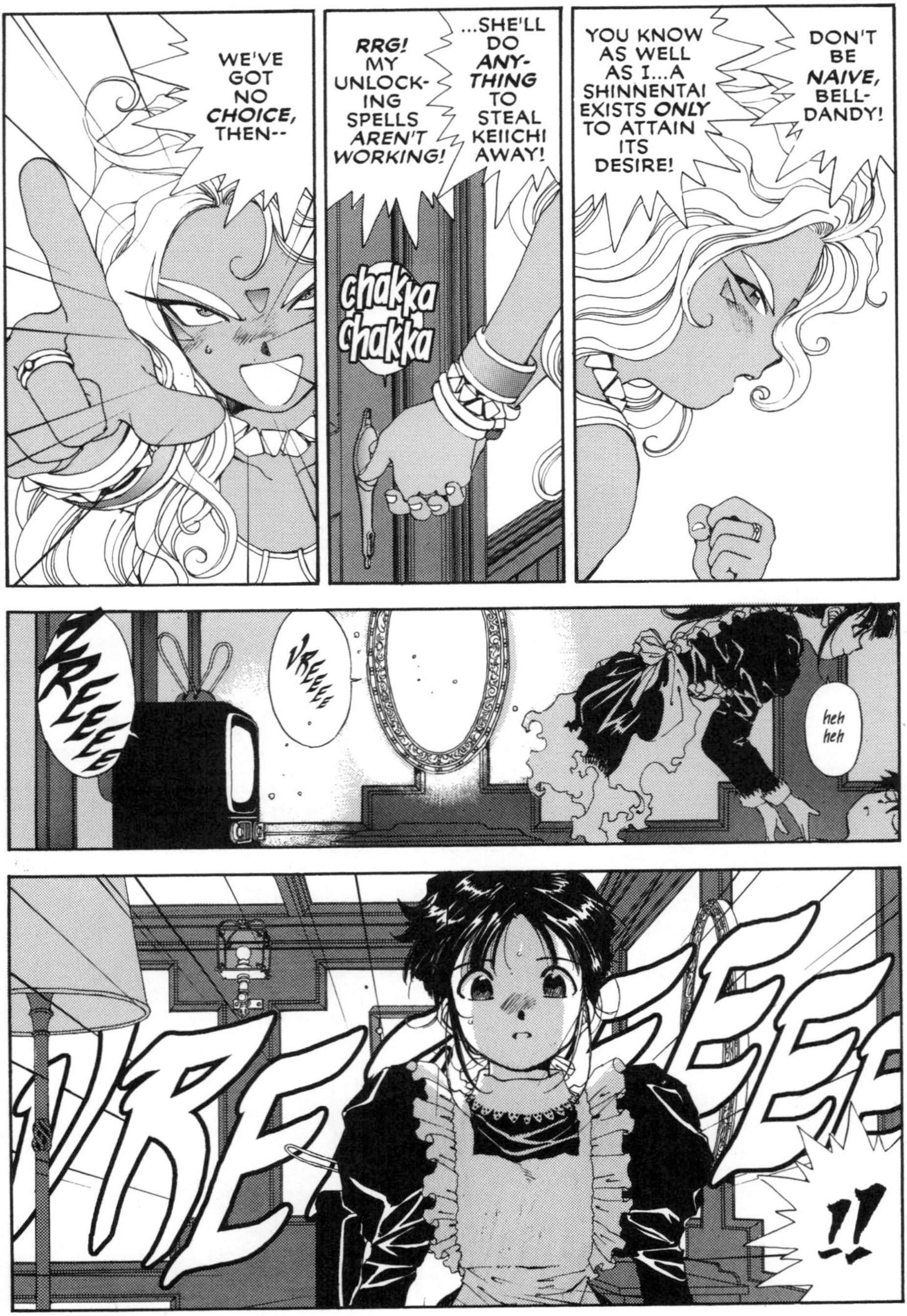
DON'T BE NAIVE, BELL-DANDY!
YOU KNOW AS WELL AS I...A SHINNENTAI EXISTS ONLY TO ATTAIN ITS DESIRE!
...SHE'LL DO ANYTHING TO STEAL KEIICHI AWAY!
RRG! MY UNLOCKING SPELLS AREN'T WORKING!
chakka chakka
WE'VE GOT NO CHOICE, THEN--
heh heh
VREEEE
VREEEE
VREEEEEE
!!

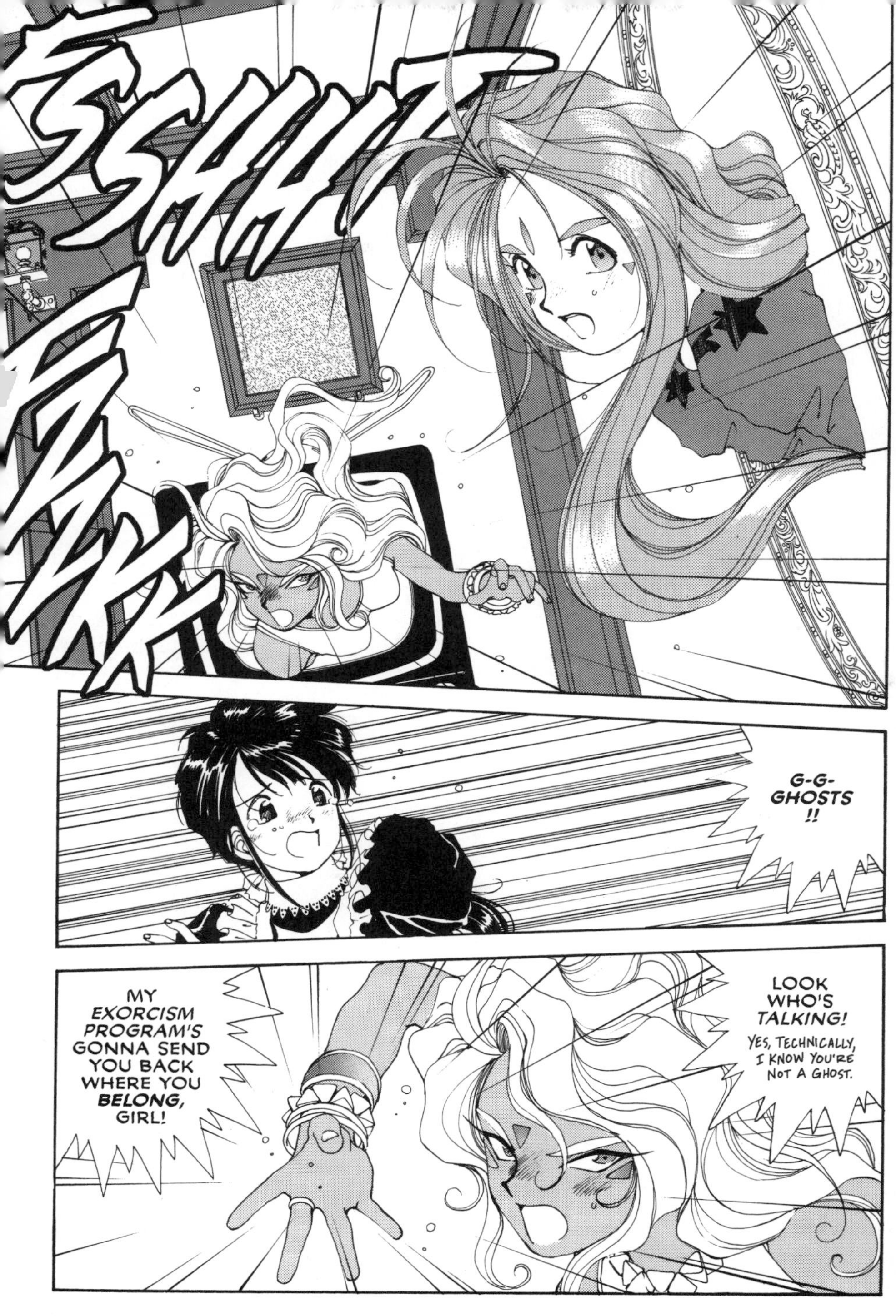
SSHHHZZZAAAKKK
G-G-GHOSTS!!
LOOK WHO'S TALKING!
YES, TECHNICALLY, I KNOW YOU'RE NOT A GHOST.
MY EXORCISM PROGRAM'S GONNA SEND YOU BACK WHERE YOU BELONG, GIRL!

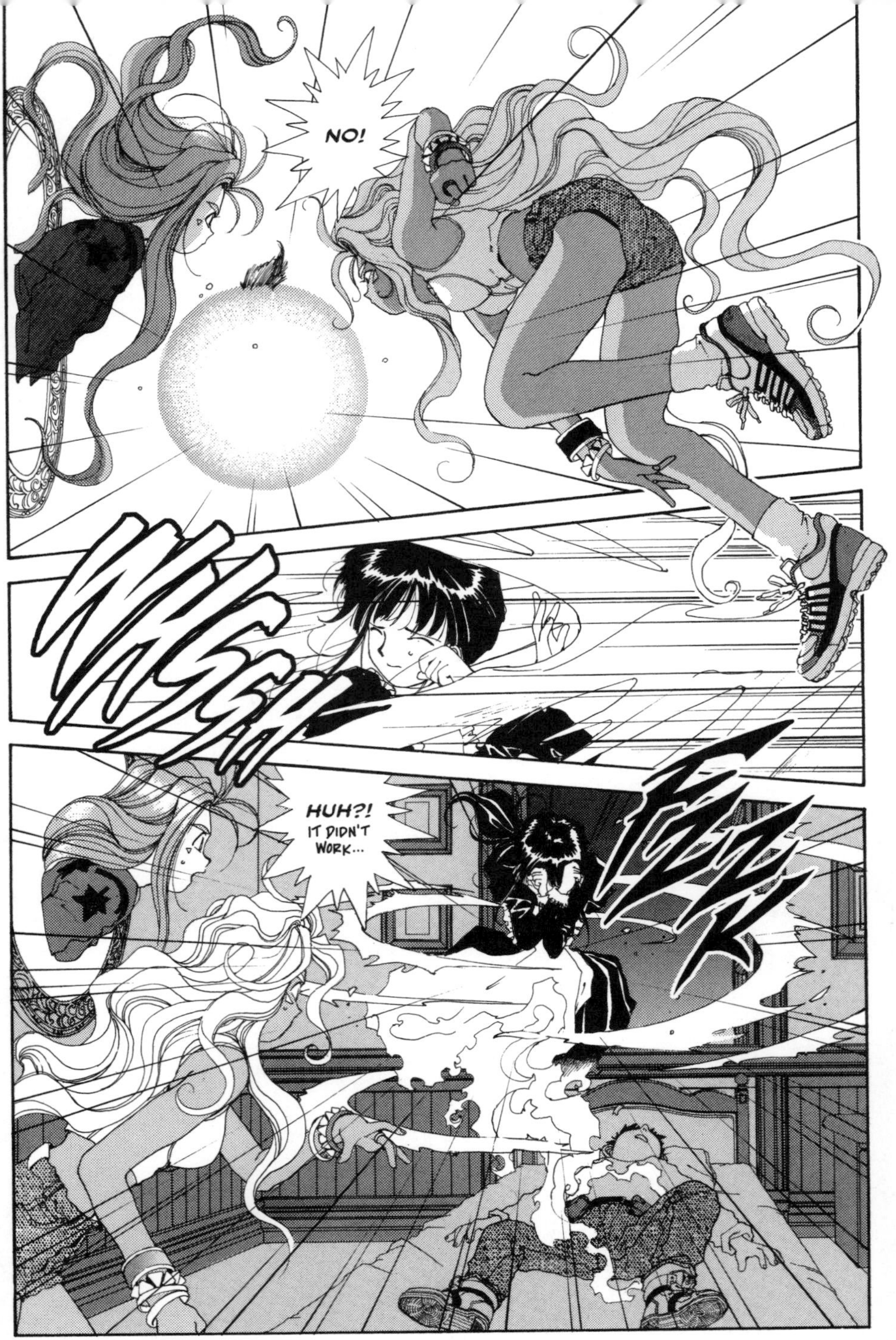
NO!
WHSSH
HUH?! IT DIDN'T WORK...
FZZZK

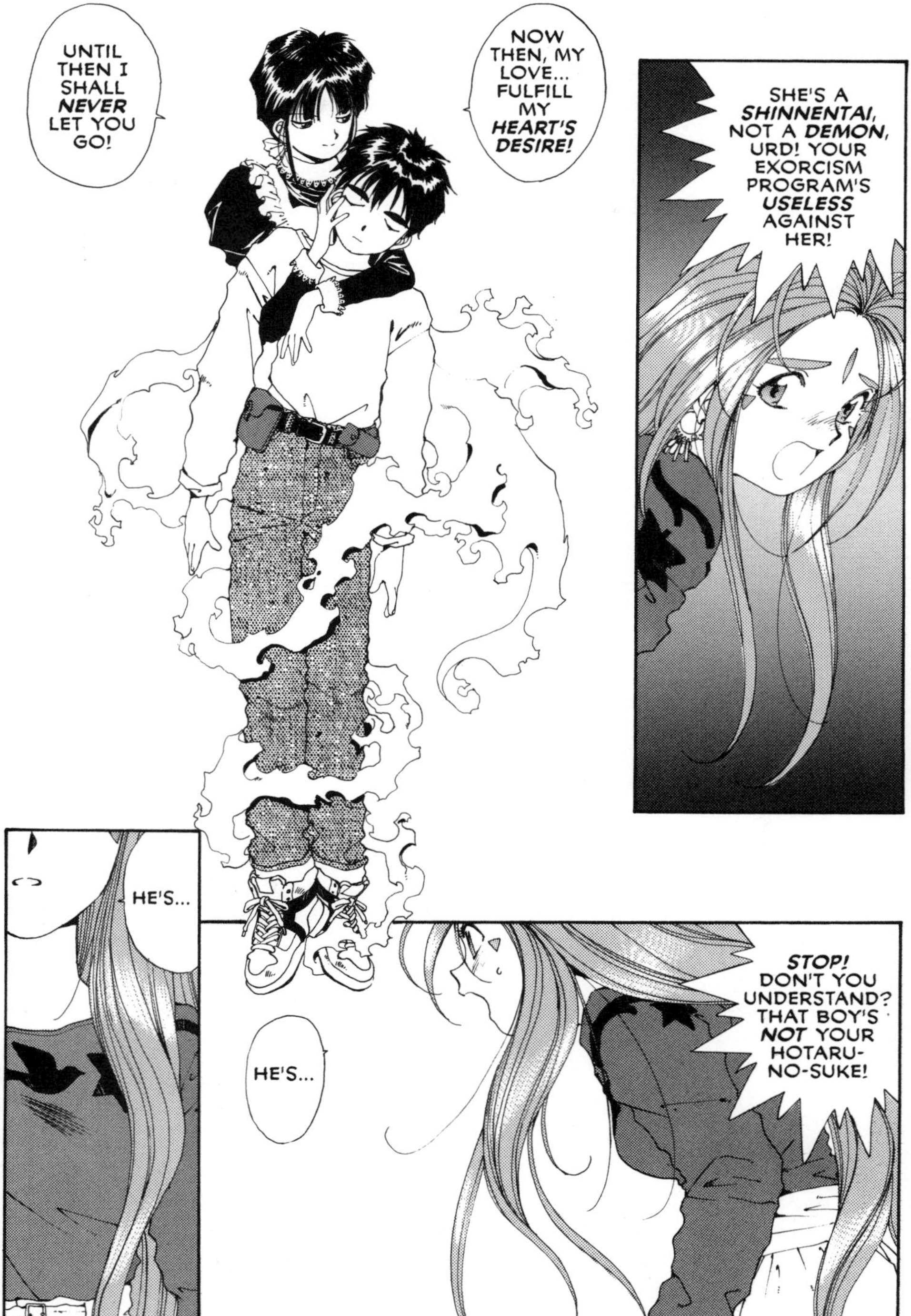
SHE'S A SHINNENTAI, NOT A DEMON, URD! YOUR EXORCISM PROGRAM'S USELESS AGAINST HER!
NOW THEN, MY LOVE... FULFILL MY HEART'S DESIRE!
UNTIL THEN I SHALL NEVER LET YOU GO!
STOP! DON'T YOU UNDERSTAND? THAT BOY'S NOT YOUR HOTARU-NO-SUKE!
HE'S...
HE'S...

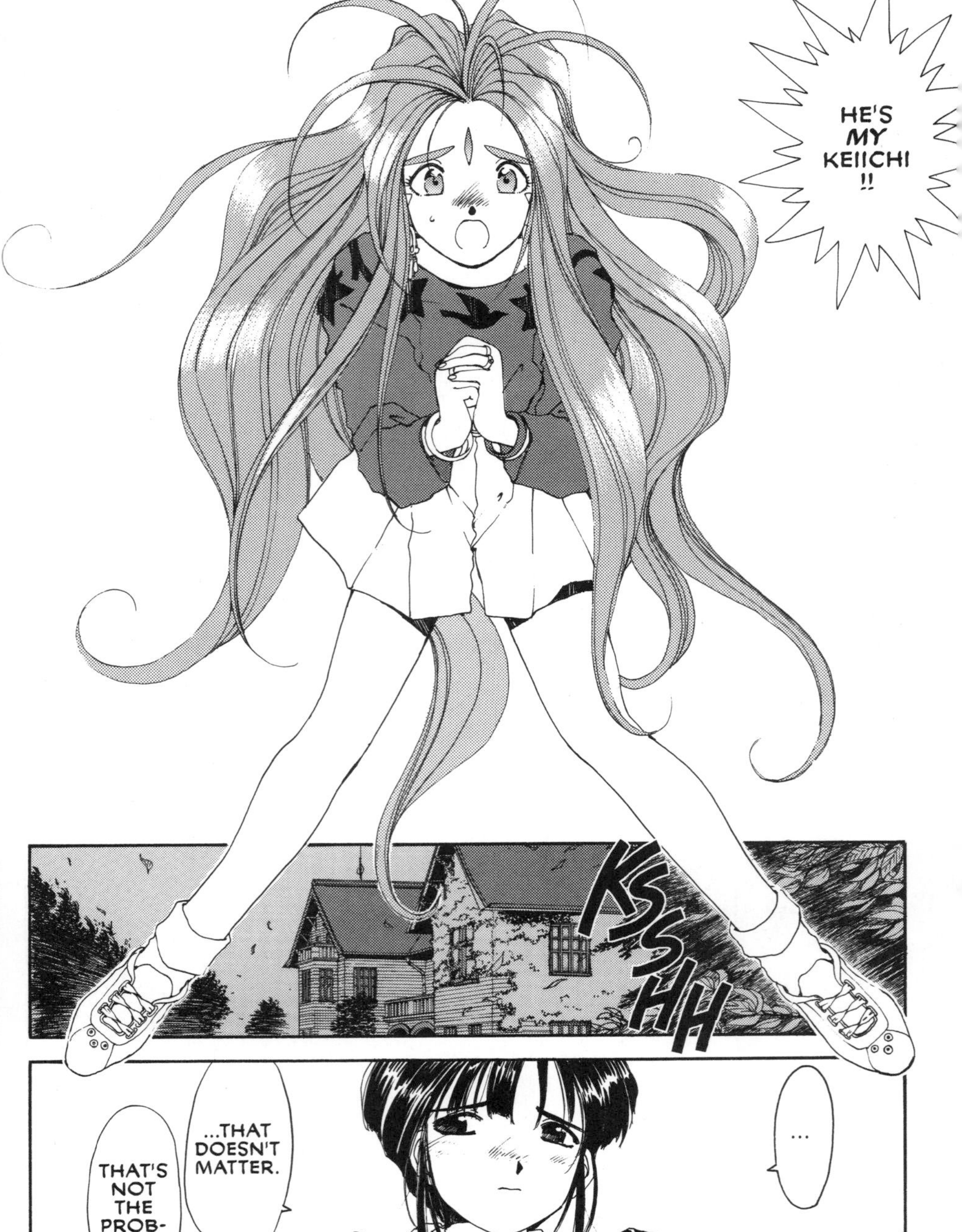
HE'S MY KEIICHI !!
KSSHH
...
...THAT DOESN'T MATTER.
THAT'S NOT THE PROB-LEM.

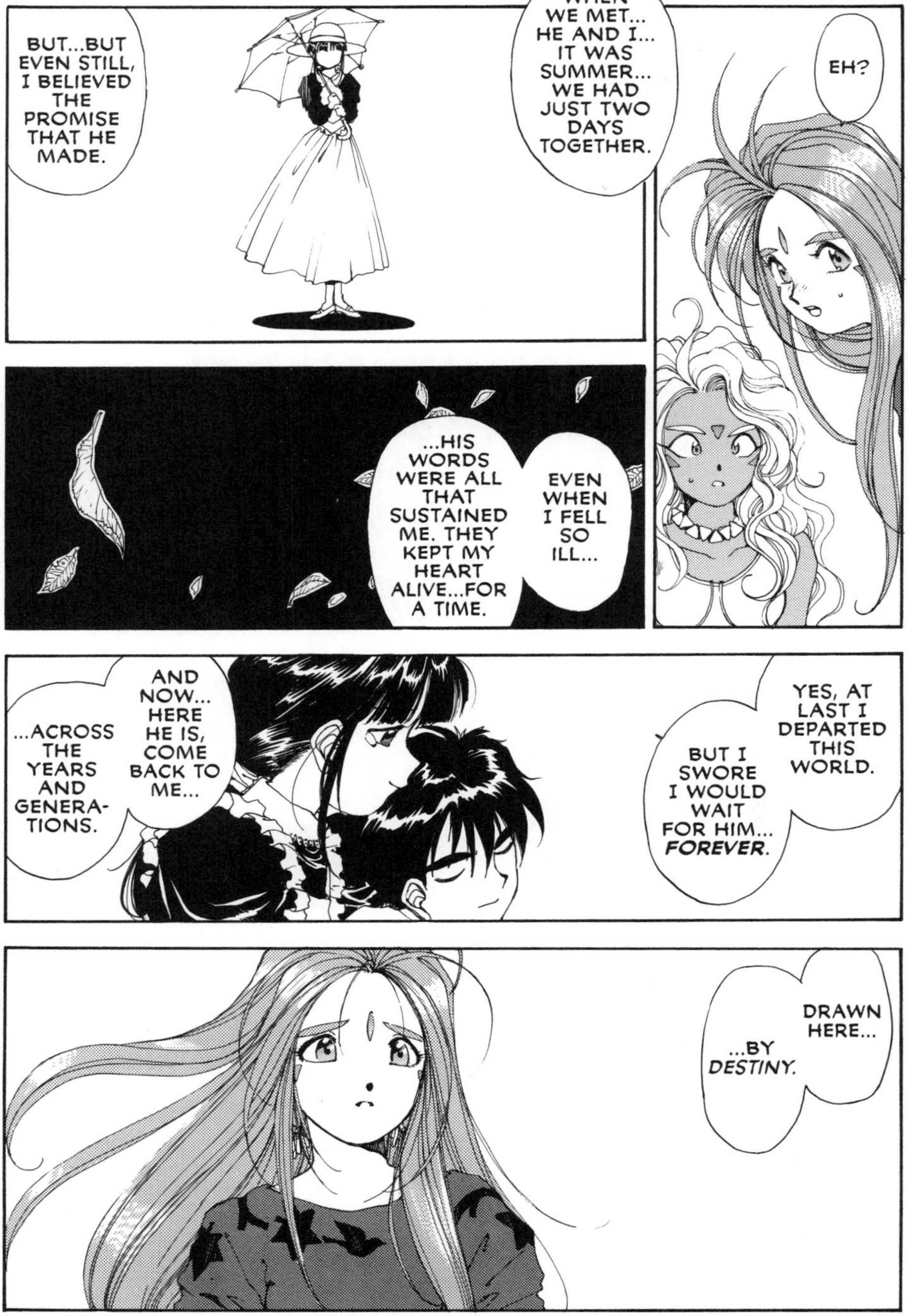
EH?
WHEN WE MET... HE AND I... IT WAS SUMMER... WE HAD JUST TWO DAYS TOGETHER.
BUT...BUT EVEN STILL, I BELIEVED THE PROMISE THAT HE MADE.
EVEN WHEN I FELL SO ILL...
...HIS WORDS WERE ALL THAT SUSTAINED ME. THEY KEPT MY HEART ALIVE...FOR A TIME.
YES, AT LAST I DEPARTED THIS WORLD.
BUT I SWORE I WOULD WAIT FOR HIM... *FOREVER*.
AND NOW... HERE HE IS, COME BACK TO ME...
...ACROSS THE YEARS AND GENERATIONS.
DRAWN HERE...
...BY *DESTINY*.

JUST TELL US ONE THING, DEAR...

WHAT EXACT-LY...

...*WAS* THE PROMISE...?

GOOD *MORNING,* KEIICHI!

WHY AM I IN BED?

WHAT TH--?

?

?

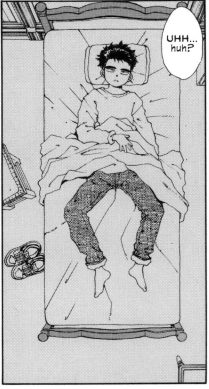

UHH... huh?

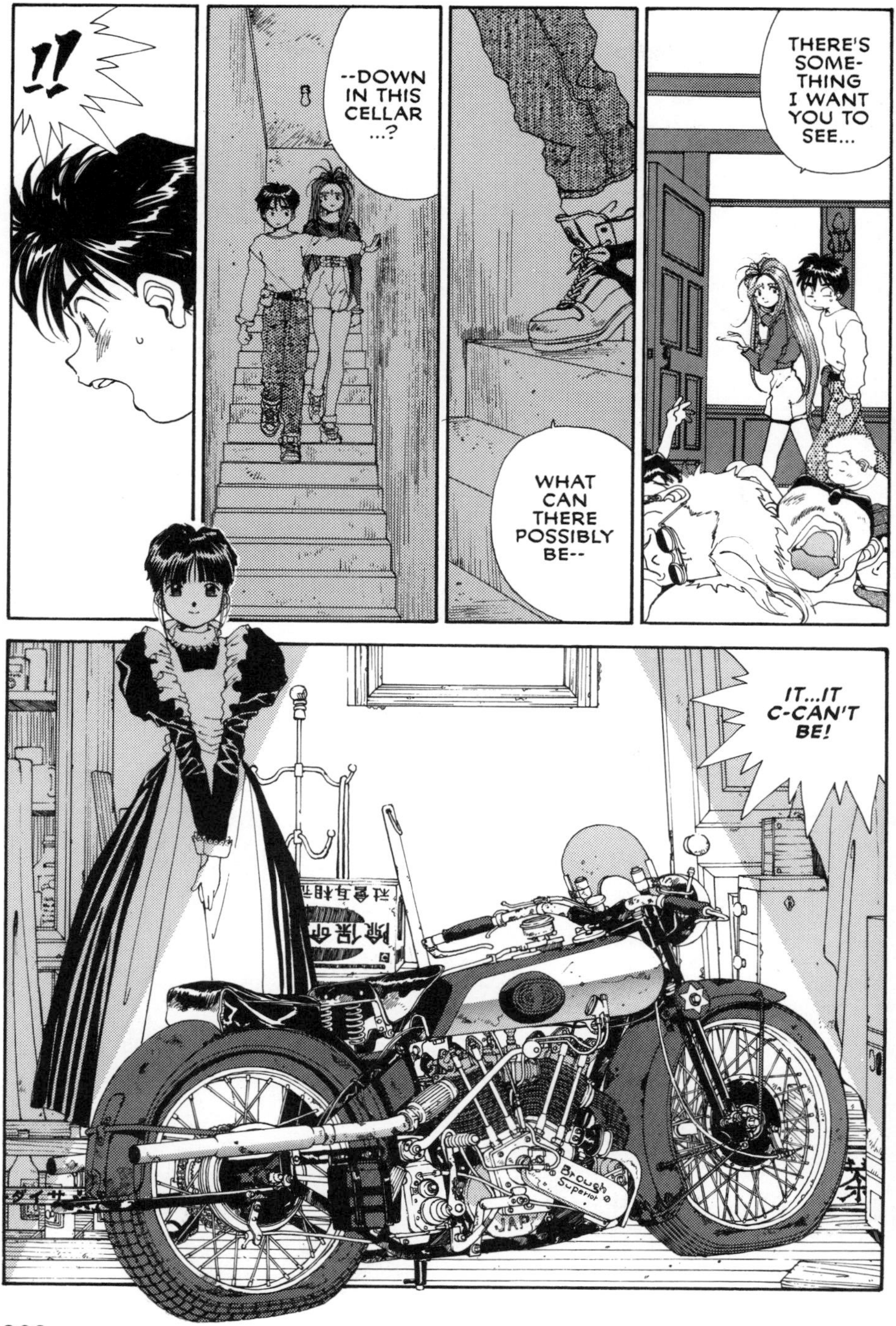

THERE'S SOMETHING I WANT YOU TO SEE...
WHAT CAN THERE POSSIBLY BE--
--DOWN IN THIS CELLAR ...?
!!
IT...IT C-CAN'T BE!
Brough Superior
JAP

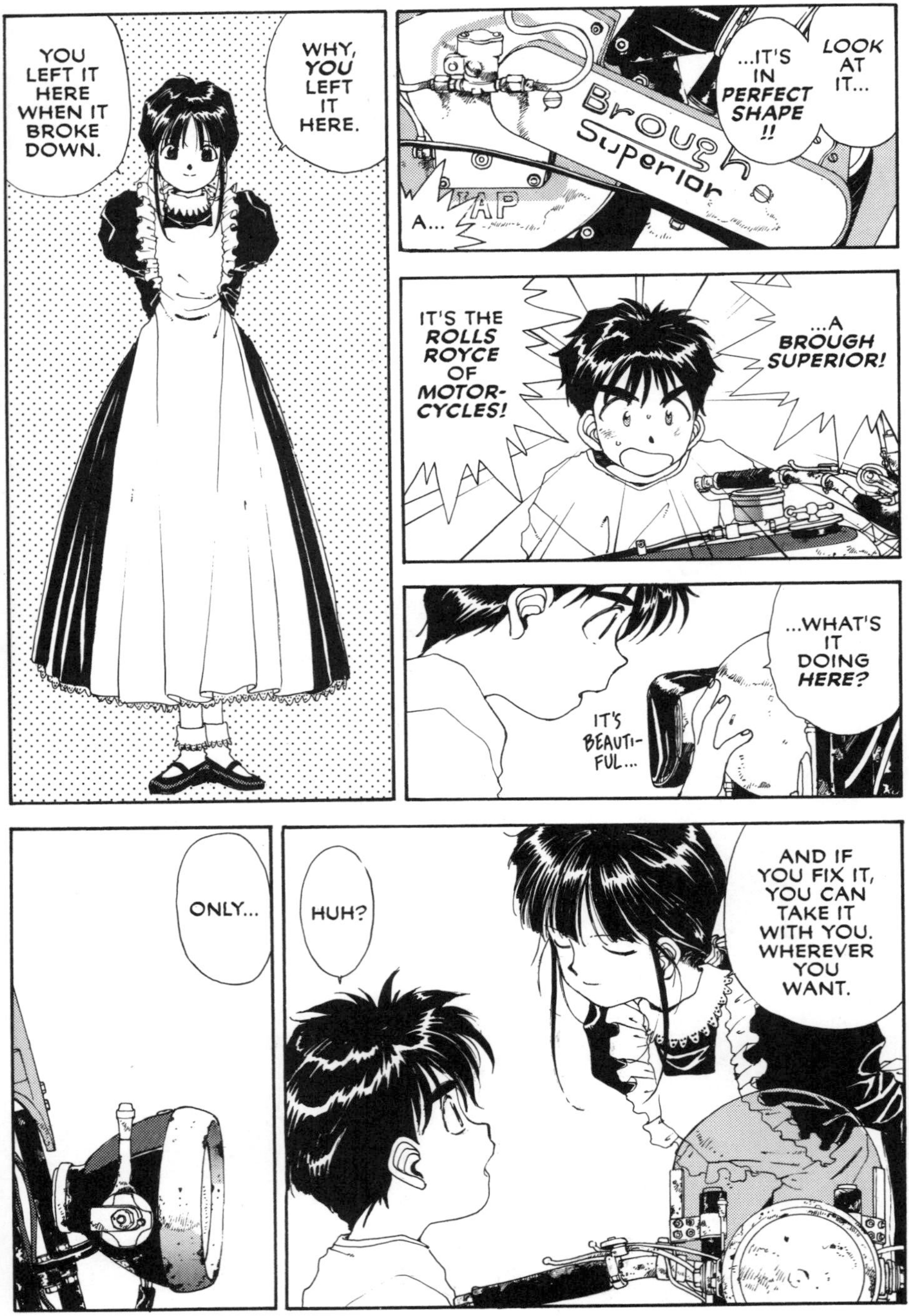
LOOK AT IT...
...IT'S IN PERFECT SHAPE !!
Brough Superior
A...
...A BROUGH SUPERIOR!
IT'S THE ROLLS ROYCE OF MOTORCYCLES!
...WHAT'S IT DOING HERE?
IT'S BEAUTIFUL...
WHY, YOU LEFT IT HERE.
YOU LEFT IT HERE WHEN IT BROKE DOWN.
AND IF YOU FIX IT, YOU CAN TAKE IT WITH YOU. WHEREVER YOU WANT.
HUH?
ONLY...

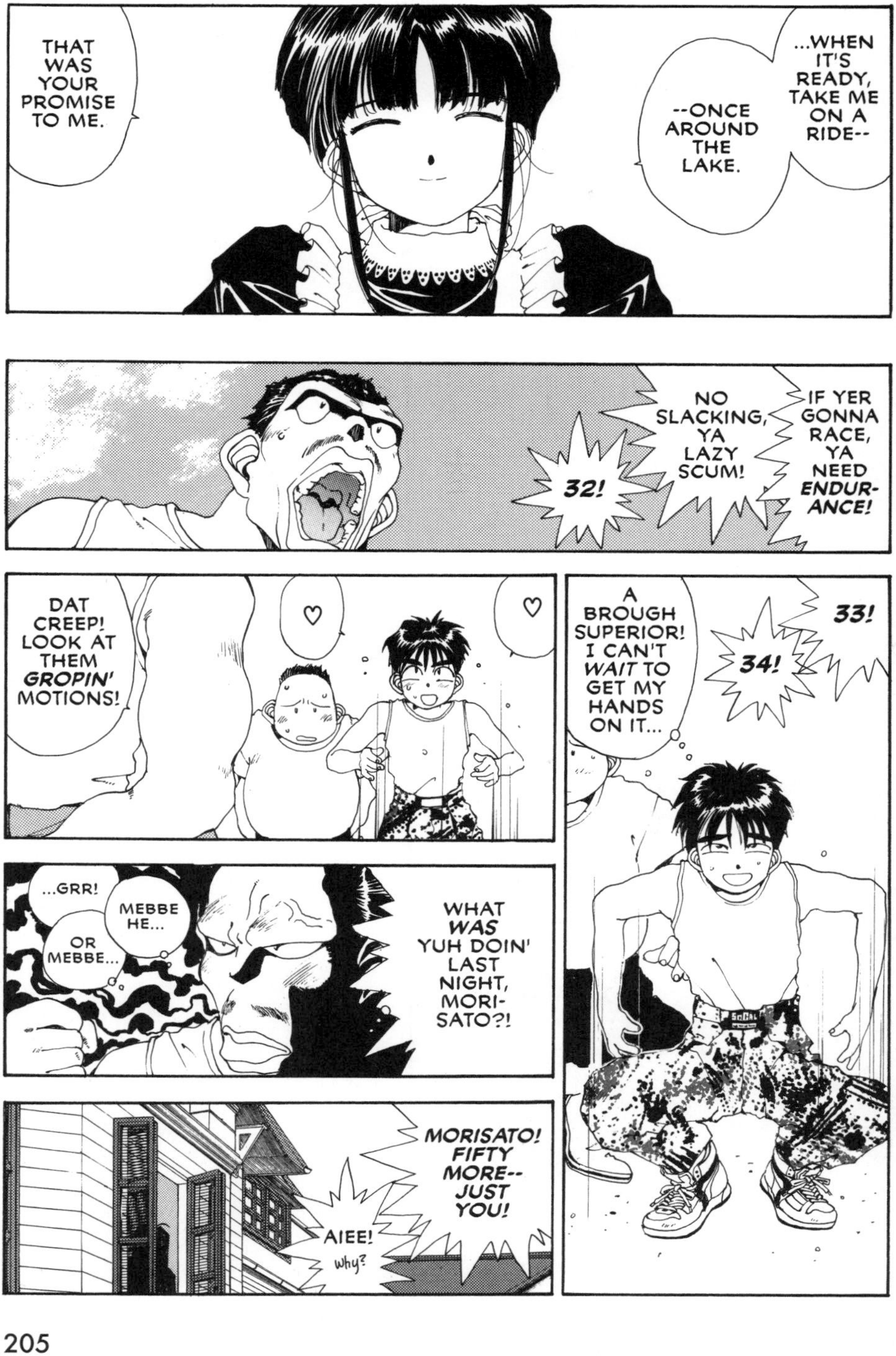

...WHEN IT'S READY, TAKE ME ON A RIDE--
--ONCE AROUND THE LAKE.
THAT WAS YOUR PROMISE TO ME.
IF YER GONNA RACE, YA NEED *ENDURANCE!*
NO SLACKING, YA LAZY SCUM!
32!
33!
34!
A BROUGH SUPERIOR! I CAN'T *WAIT* TO GET MY HANDS ON IT...
♡
♡
DAT CREEP! LOOK AT THEM *GROPIN'* MOTIONS!
WHAT *WAS* YUH DOIN' LAST NIGHT, MORI-SATO?!
MEBBE HE...
...GRR!
OR MEBBE...
MORISATO! FIFTY MORE-- JUST YOU!
AIEE! why?

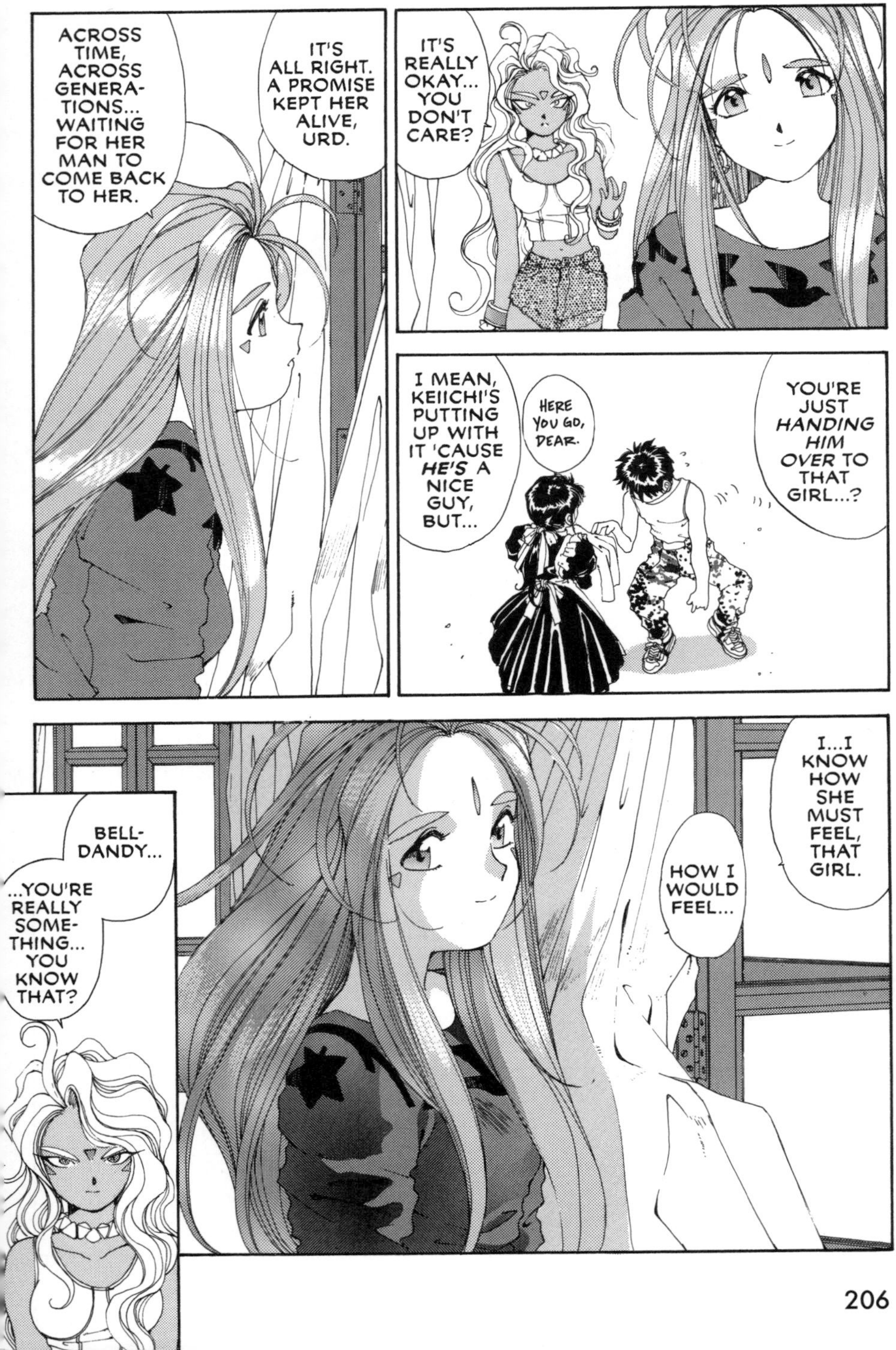
IT'S REALLY OKAY... YOU DON'T CARE?
YOU'RE JUST *HANDING HIM OVER* TO THAT GIRL...?
HERE YOU GO, DEAR.
I MEAN, KEIICHI'S PUTTING UP WITH IT 'CAUSE *HE'S* A NICE GUY, BUT...
IT'S ALL RIGHT. A PROMISE KEPT HER ALIVE, URD.
ACROSS TIME, ACROSS GENERATIONS... WAITING FOR HER MAN TO COME BACK TO HER.
I...I KNOW HOW SHE MUST FEEL, THAT GIRL.
HOW I WOULD FEEL...
BELL-DANDY...
...YOU'RE REALLY SOMETHING... YOU KNOW THAT?

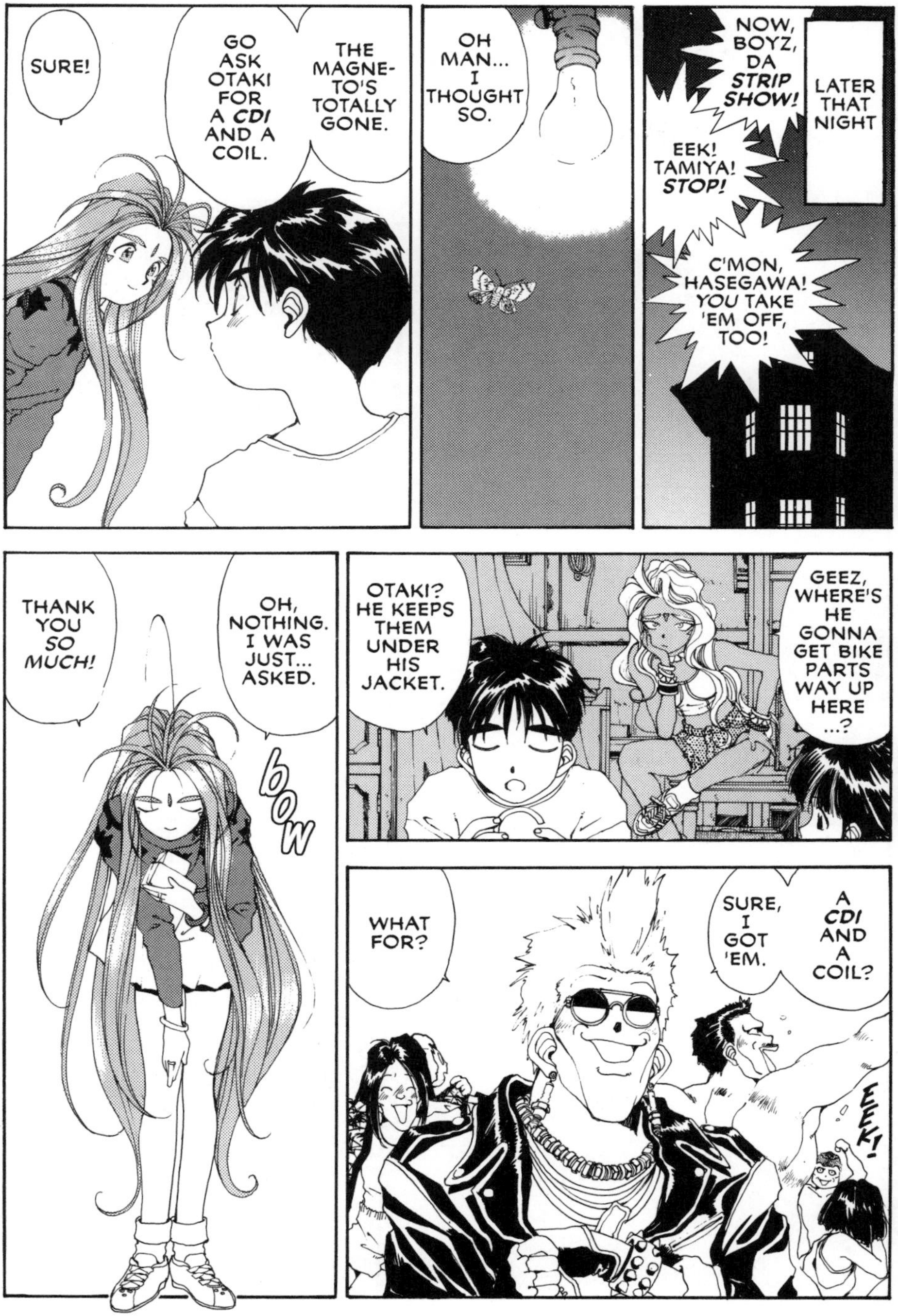
LATER THAT NIGHT
NOW, BOYZ, DA STRIP SHOW!
EEK! TAMIYA! STOP!
C'MON, HASEGAWA! YOU TAKE 'EM OFF, TOO!
OH MAN... I THOUGHT SO.
THE MAGNETO'S TOTALLY GONE.
GO ASK OTAKI FOR A CDI AND A COIL.
SURE!
GEEZ, WHERE'S HE GONNA GET BIKE PARTS WAY UP HERE ...?
OTAKI? HE KEEPS THEM UNDER HIS JACKET.
A CDI AND A COIL?
SURE, I GOT 'EM.
WHAT FOR?
EEEK!
OH, NOTHING. I WAS JUST... ASKED.
THANK YOU SO MUCH!
BOW

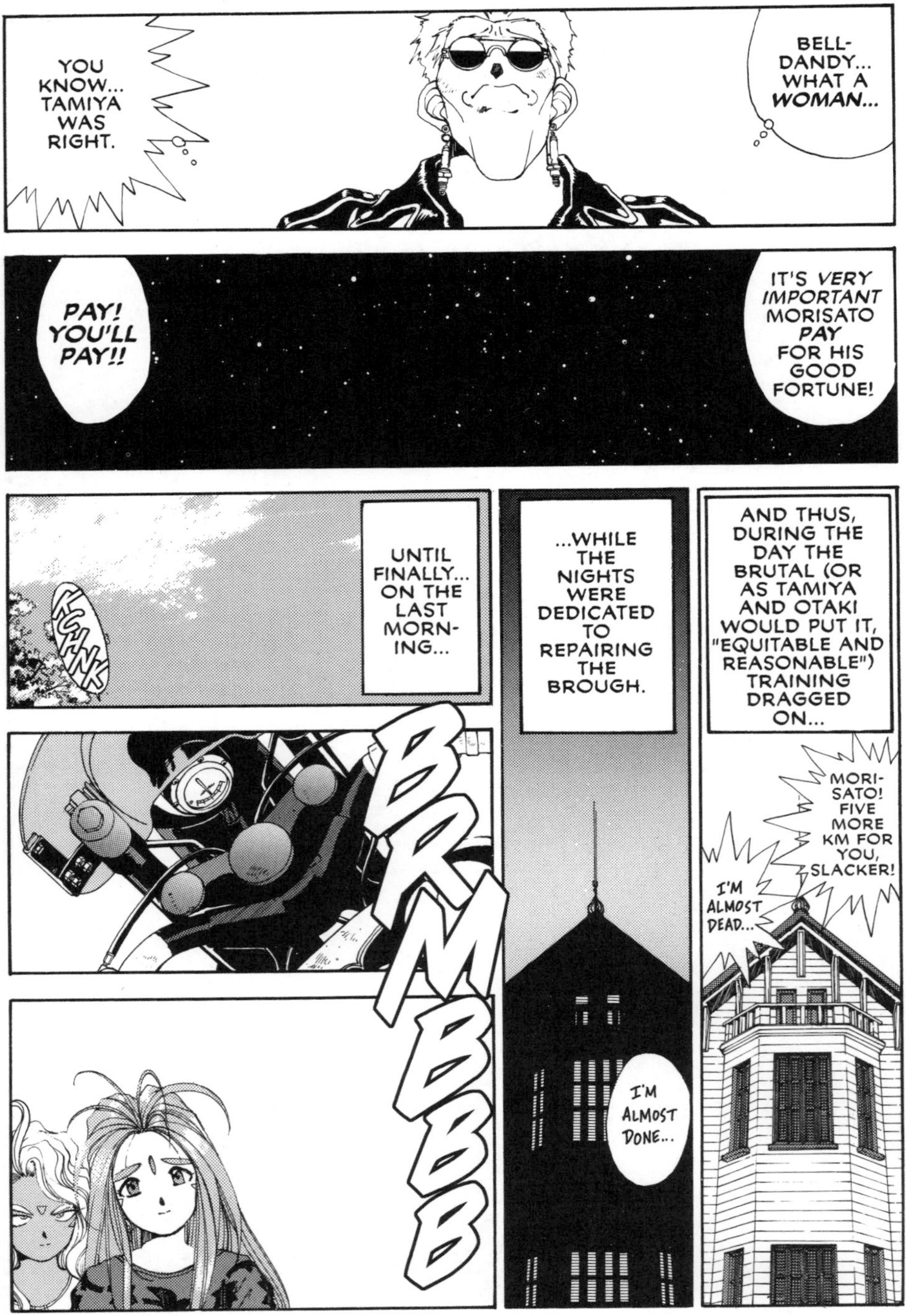
BELL-DANDY... WHAT A WOMAN...
YOU KNOW... TAMIYA WAS RIGHT.
IT'S VERY IMPORTANT MORISATO PAY FOR HIS GOOD FORTUNE!
PAY! YOU'LL PAY!!
AND THUS, DURING THE DAY THE BRUTAL (OR AS TAMIYA AND OTAKI WOULD PUT IT, "EQUITABLE AND REASONABLE") TRAINING DRAGGED ON...
MORI-SATO! FIVE MORE KM FOR YOU, SLACKER!
I'M ALMOST DEAD...
...WHILE THE NIGHTS WERE DEDICATED TO REPAIRING THE BROUGH.
I'M ALMOST DONE...
UNTIL FINALLY... ON THE LAST MORN-ING...
KCHNK
BRMMBBB

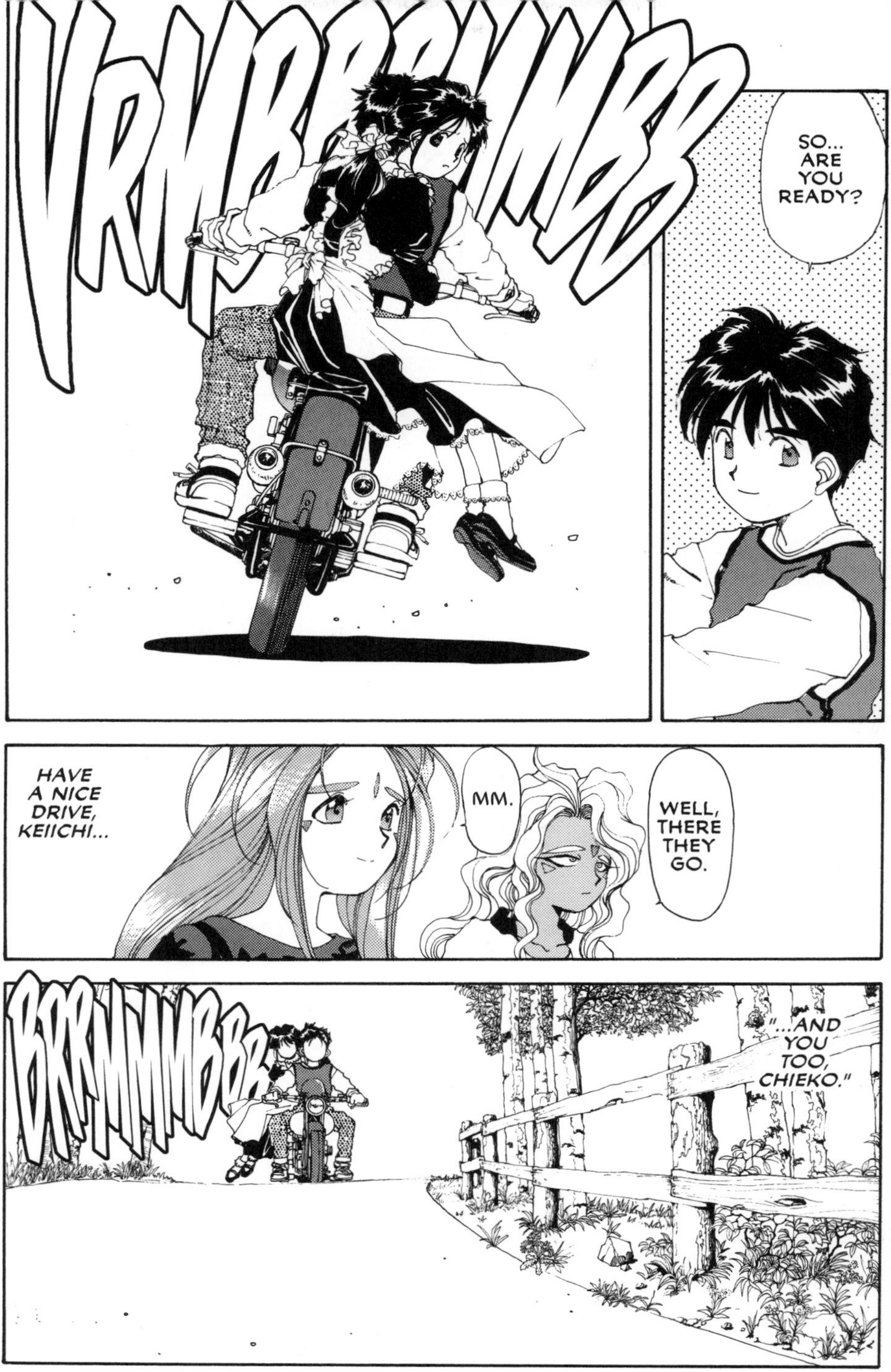
SO... ARE YOU READY?
VRMBRRMBB
WELL, THERE THEY GO.
MM.
HAVE A NICE DRIVE, KEIICHI...
"...AND YOU TOO, CHIEKO."
BRRMMMBBR

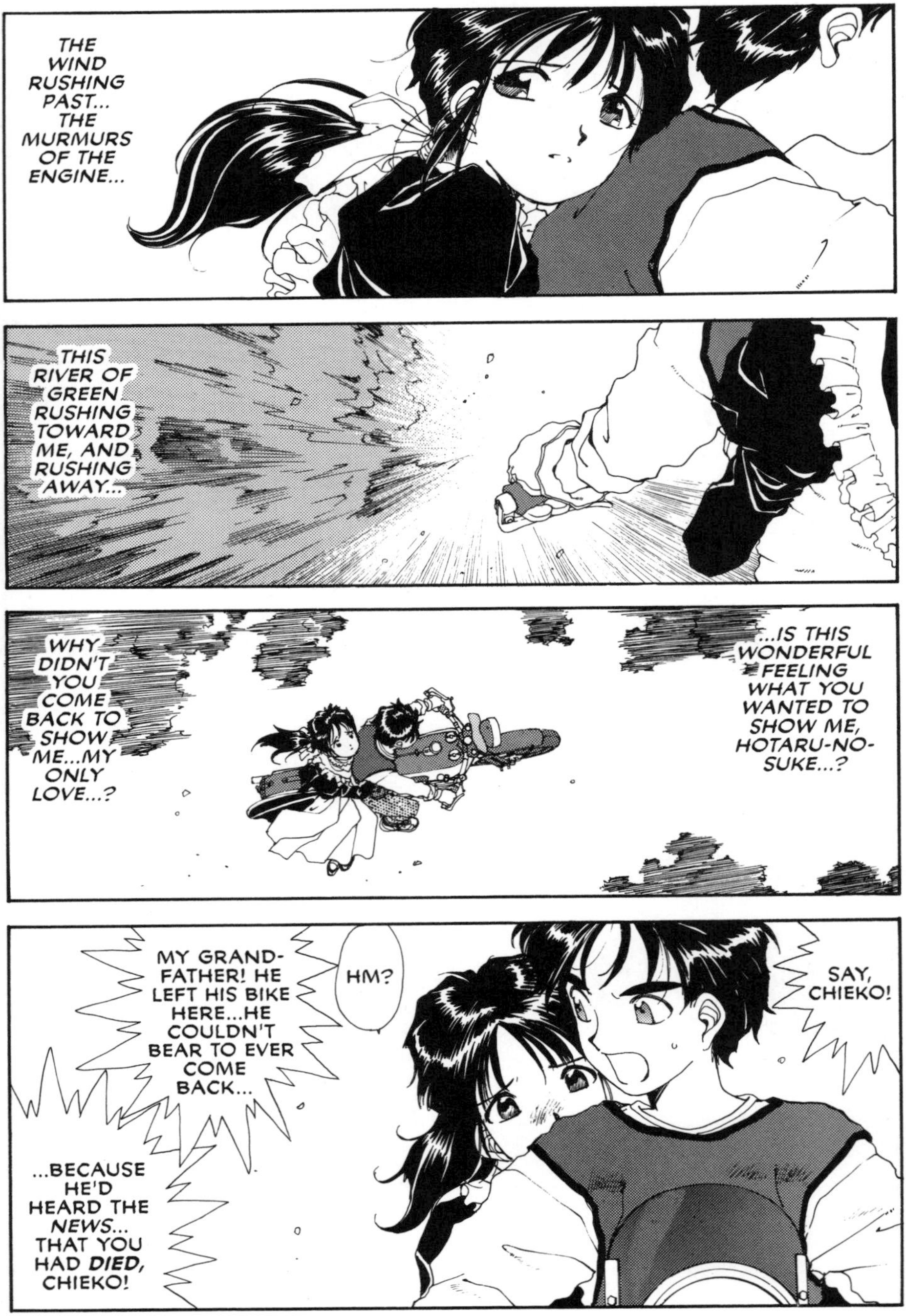

THE WIND RUSHING PAST... THE MURMURS OF THE ENGINE...
THIS RIVER OF GREEN RUSHING TOWARD ME, AND RUSHING AWAY...
...IS THIS WONDERFUL FEELING WHAT YOU WANTED TO SHOW ME, HOTARU-NO-SUKE...?
WHY DIDN'T YOU COME BACK TO SHOW ME...MY ONLY LOVE...?
SAY, CHIEKO!
HM?
MY GRAND-FATHER! HE LEFT HIS BIKE HERE...HE COULDN'T BEAR TO EVER COME BACK...
...BECAUSE HE'D HEARD THE *NEWS*... THAT YOU HAD *DIED*, CHIEKO!

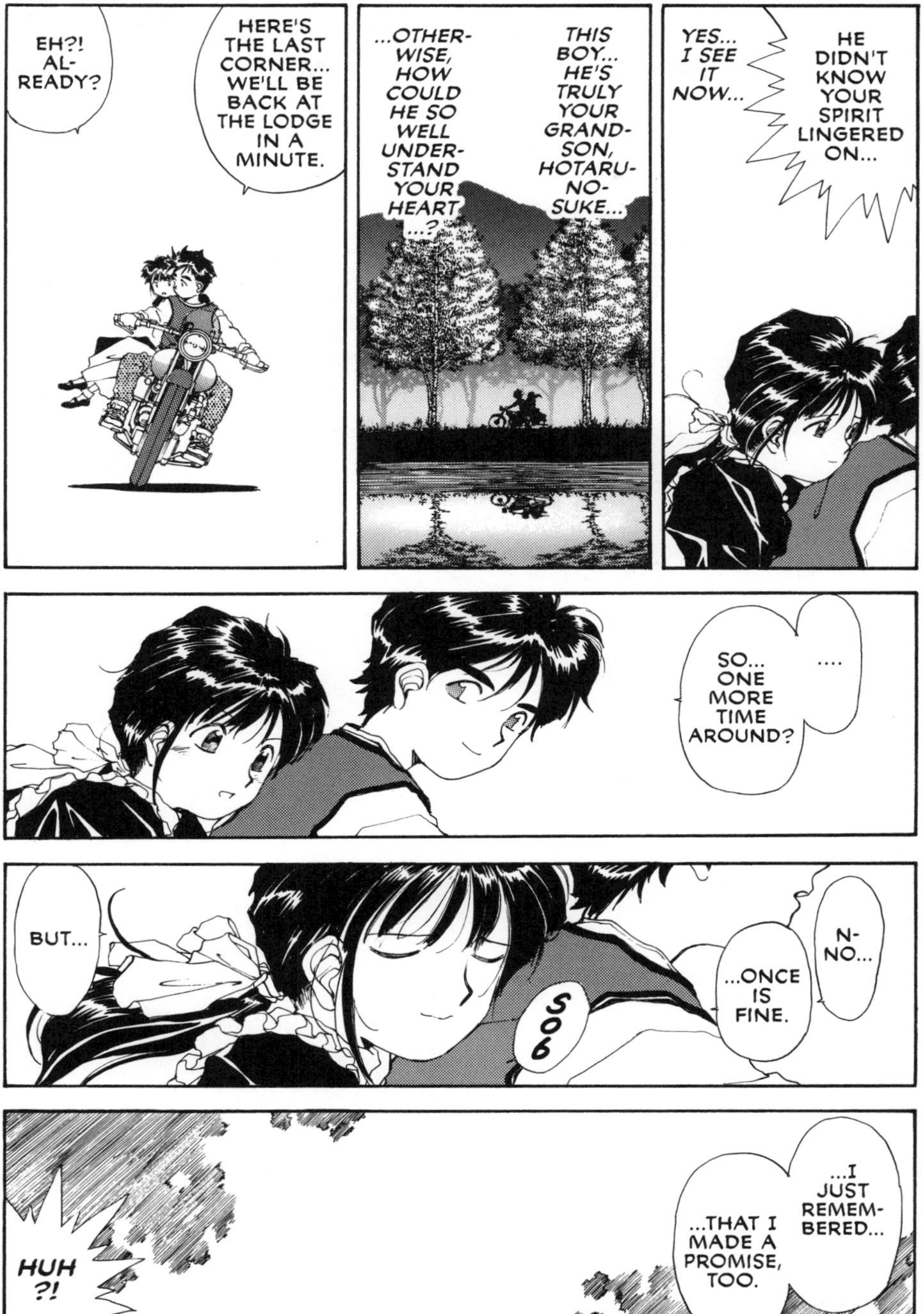
HE DIDN'T KNOW YOUR SPIRIT LINGERED ON...
YES... I SEE IT NOW...
THIS BOY... HE'S TRULY YOUR GRANDSON, HOTARU-NO-SUKE...
...OTHERWISE, HOW COULD HE SO WELL UNDERSTAND YOUR HEART...?
HERE'S THE LAST CORNER... WE'LL BE BACK AT THE LODGE IN A MINUTE.
EH?! ALREADY?
....
SO... ONE MORE TIME AROUND?
N-NO...
...ONCE IS FINE.
BUT...
...I JUST REMEMBERED...
...THAT I MADE A PROMISE, TOO.
HUH?!

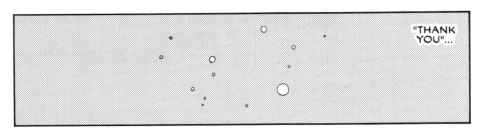

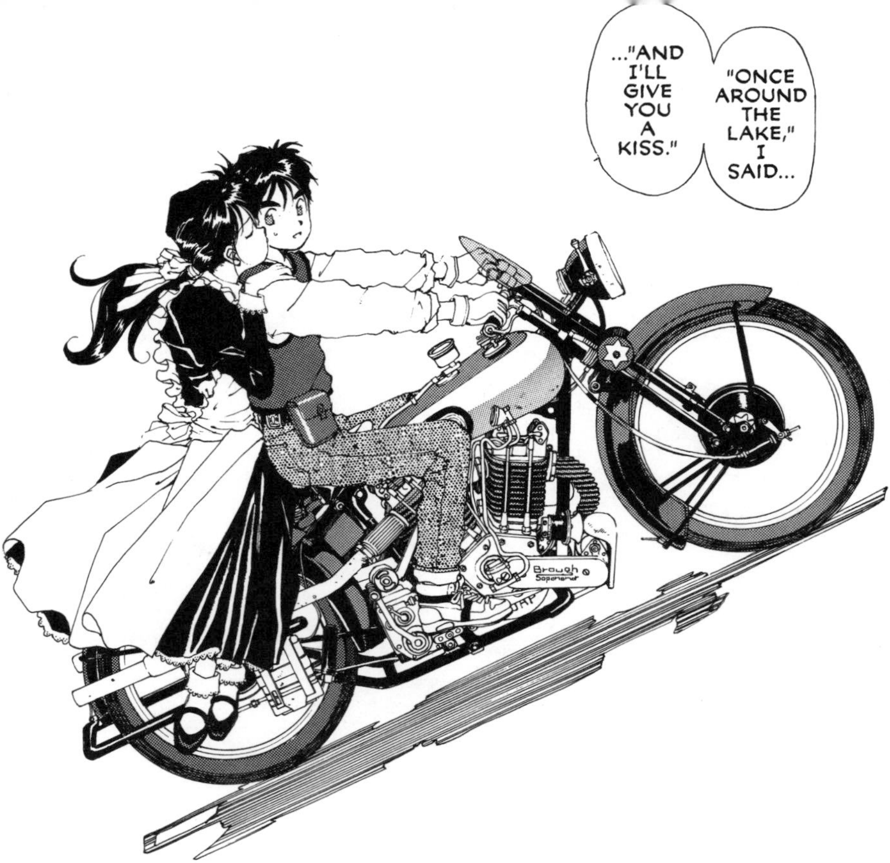
"ONCE AROUND THE LAKE," I SAID...
..."AND I'LL GIVE YOU A KISS."

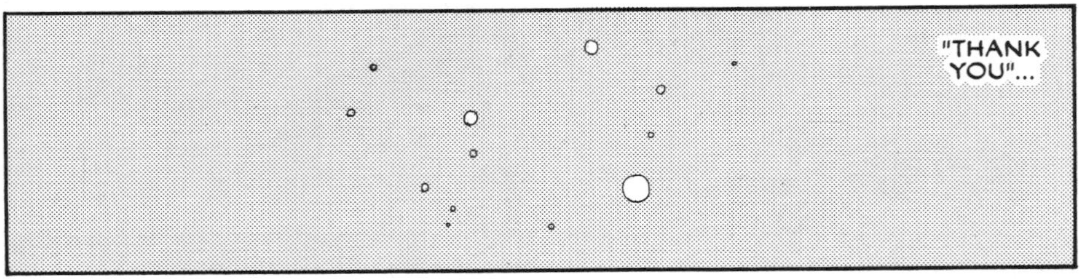
"THANK YOU"...

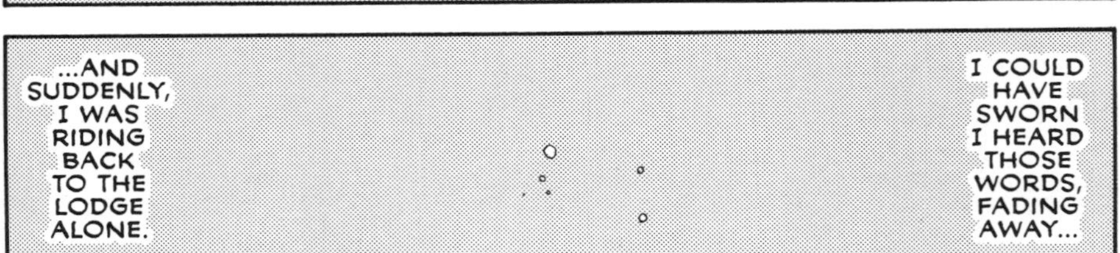
I COULD HAVE SWORN I HEARD THOSE WORDS, FADING AWAY...
...AND SUDDENLY, I WAS RIDING BACK TO THE LODGE ALONE.

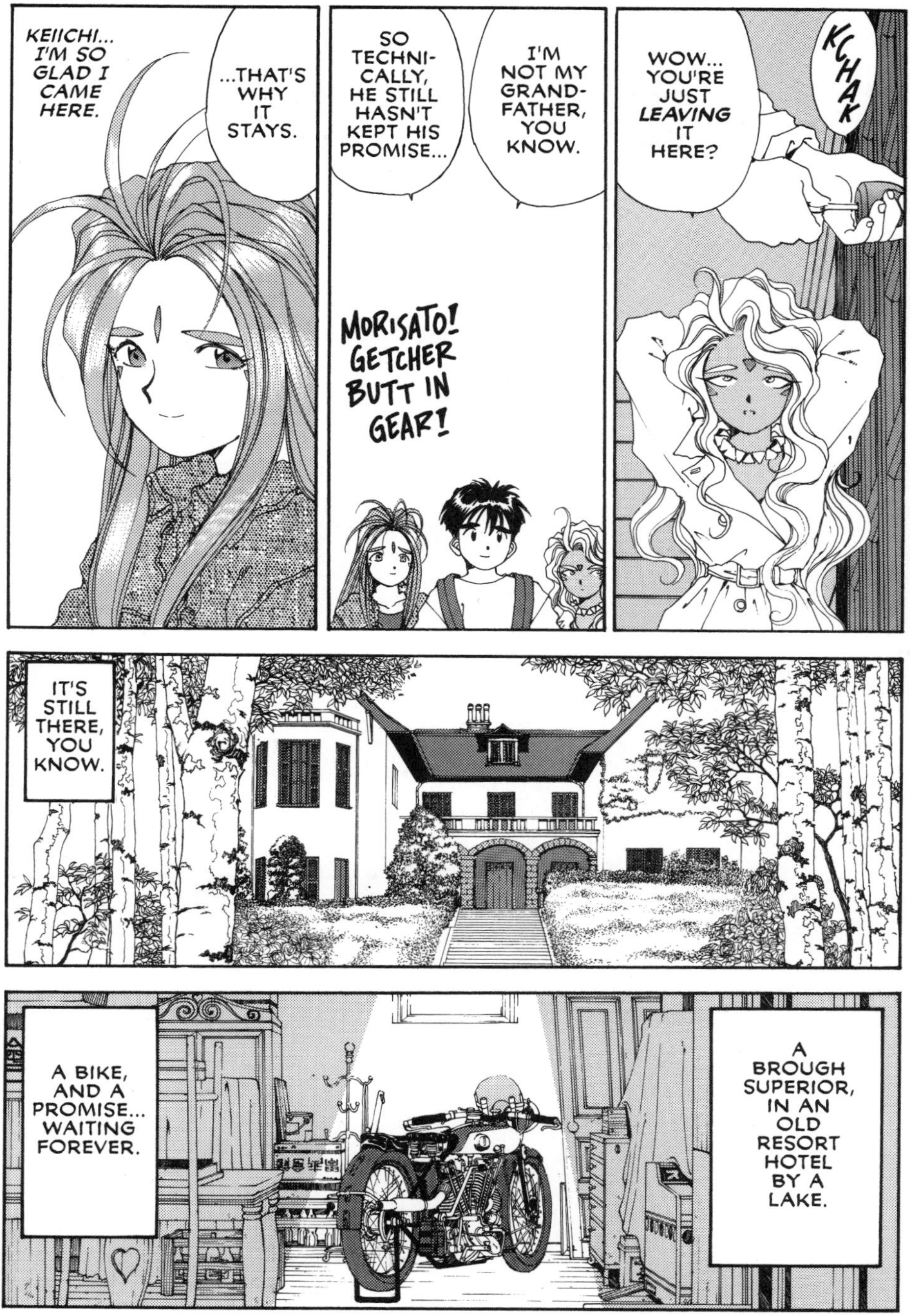
KCHAK
WOW... YOU'RE JUST *LEAVING* IT HERE?
I'M NOT MY GRANDFATHER, YOU KNOW.
SO TECHNICALLY, HE STILL HASN'T KEPT HIS PROMISE...
MORISATO! GETCHER BUTT IN GEAR!
...THAT'S WHY IT STAYS.
KEIICHI... I'M SO GLAD I CAME HERE.
IT'S STILL THERE, YOU KNOW.
A BROUGH SUPERIOR, IN AN OLD RESORT HOTEL BY A LAKE.
A BIKE, AND A PROMISE... WAITING FOREVER.

THE ADVENTURES OF MINI-URD

Now with added MINI-SKULD!

SUPER SPIKE!

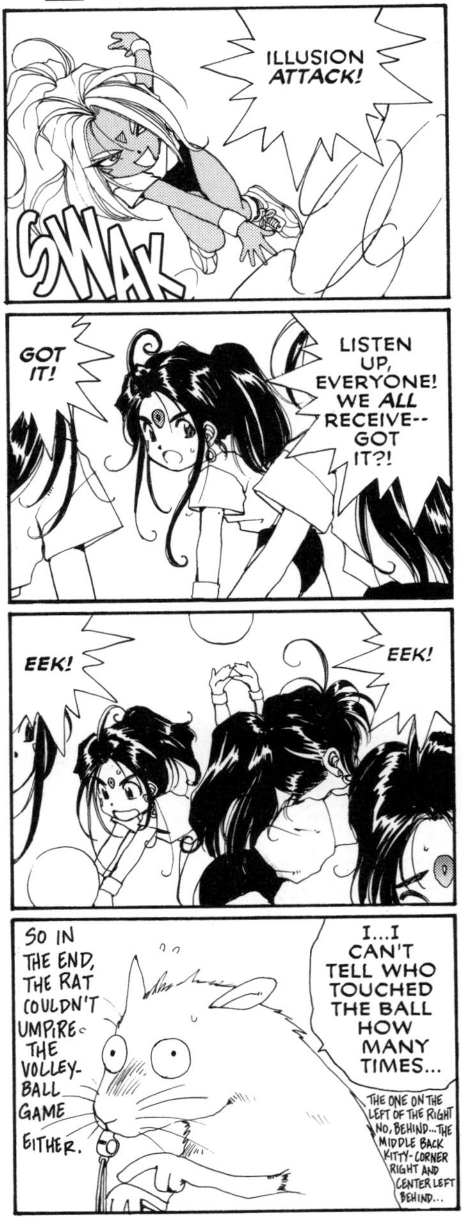
ILLUSION ATTACK!
SWAK
LISTEN UP, EVERYONE! WE ALL RECEIVE--GOT IT?!
GOT IT!
EEK!
EEK!
I...I CAN'T TELL WHO TOUCHED THE BALL HOW MANY TIMES...
THE ONE ON THE LEFT OF THE RIGHT NO, BEHIND...THE MIDDLE BACK KITTY-CORNER RIGHT AND CENTER LEFT BEHIND...
SO IN THE END, THE RAT COULDN'T UMPIRE THE VOLLEY-BALL GAME EITHER.

ATTACKING FURIES

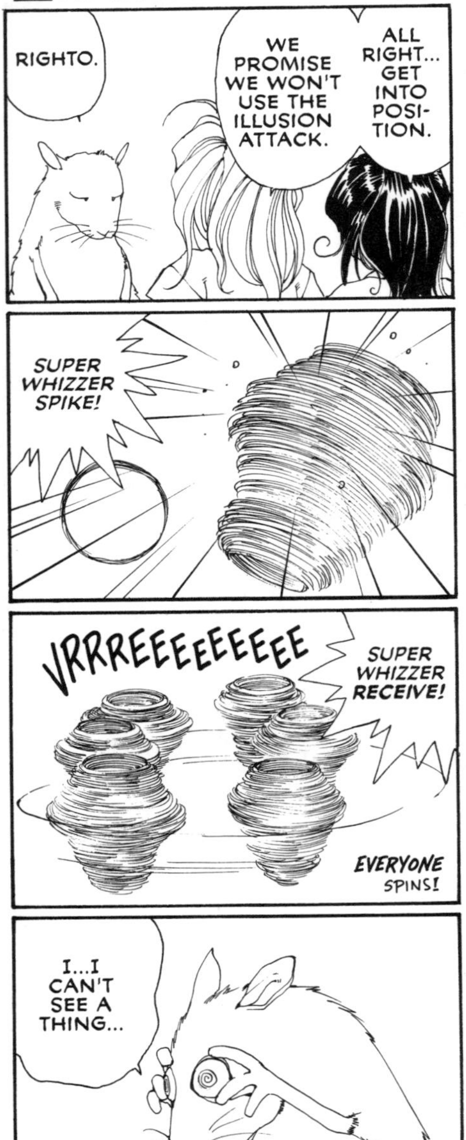
ALL RIGHT... GET INTO POSITION.
WE PROMISE WE WON'T USE THE ILLUSION ATTACK.
RIGHTO.
SUPER WHIZZER SPIKE!
SUPER WHIZZER RECEIVE!
VRRREEEEEEEEE
EVERYONE SPINS!
I...I CAN'T SEE A THING...

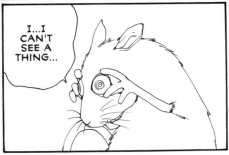

IT HAS ITS ADVANTAGES

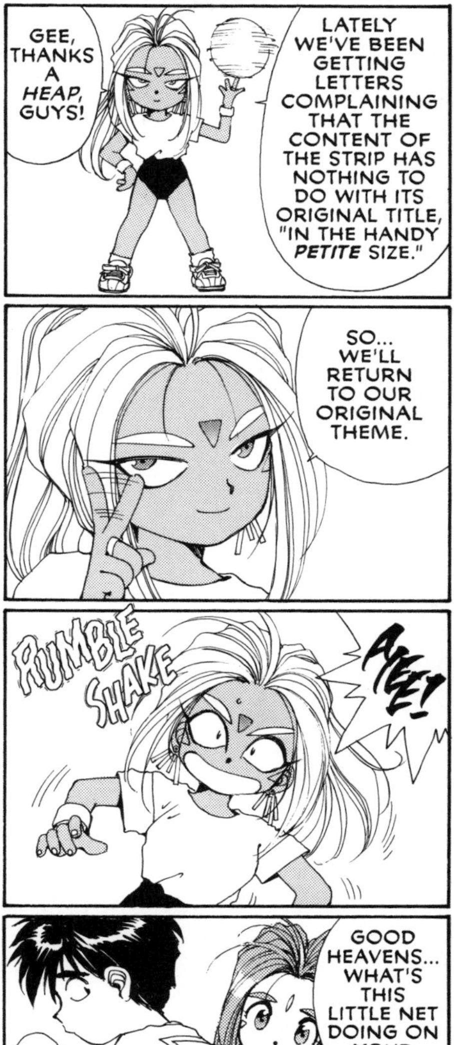
LATELY WE'VE BEEN GETTING LETTERS COMPLAINING THAT THE CONTENT OF THE STRIP HAS NOTHING TO DO WITH ITS ORIGINAL TITLE, "IN THE HANDY *PETITE* SIZE."
GEE, THANKS A *HEAP*, GUYS!
SO... WE'LL RETURN TO OUR ORIGINAL THEME.
AYEE!
RUMBLE
SHAKE
GOOD HEAVENS... WHAT'S THIS LITTLE NET DOING ON YOUR BACK?
huh?

AN IDOL APPEARS— INTRODUCING THE NEW URD!

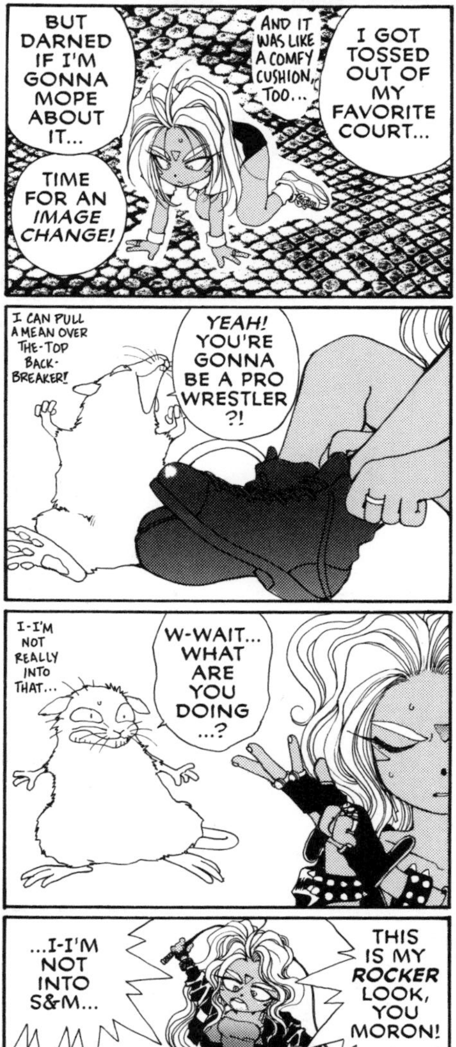
I GOT TOSSED OUT OF MY FAVORITE COURT...
AND IT WAS LIKE A COMFY CUSHION, TOO...
BUT DARNED IF I'M GONNA MOPE ABOUT IT...
TIME FOR AN *IMAGE CHANGE!*
YEAH! YOU'RE GONNA BE A PRO WRESTLER?!
I CAN PULL A MEAN OVER-THE-TOP BACK-BREAKER!
W-WAIT... WHAT ARE YOU DOING...?
I-I'M NOT REALLY INTO THAT...
THIS IS MY *ROCKER* LOOK, YOU MORON!
KRAK! KRAK!
...I-I'M NOT INTO S&M...

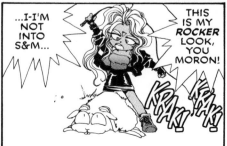

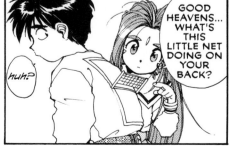

IT'S THE NON-STOP ROCK SHOW!

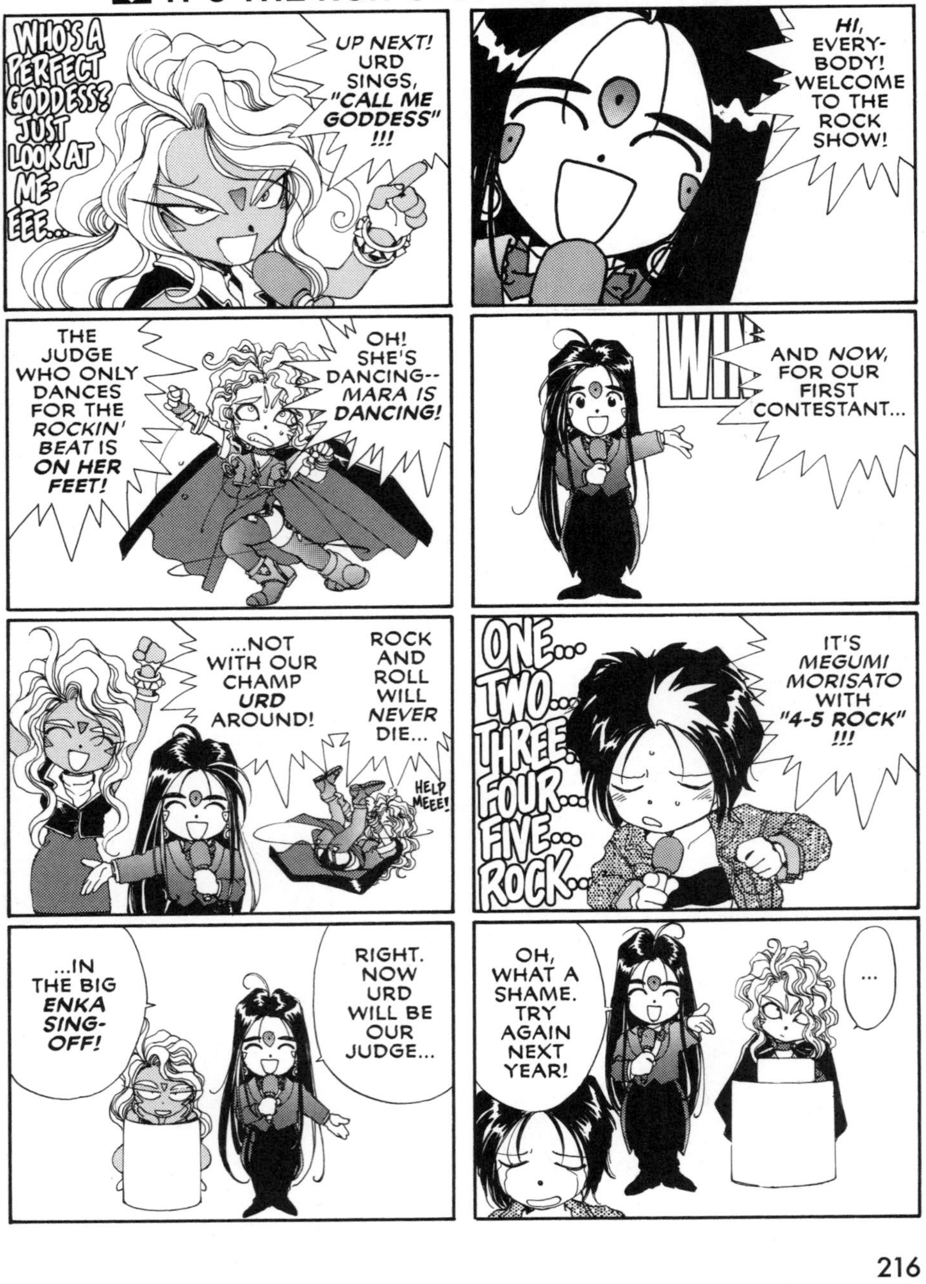
HI, EVERY-BODY! WELCOME TO THE ROCK SHOW!
AND NOW, FOR OUR FIRST CONTESTANT...
WII
IT'S MEGUMI MORISATO WITH "4-5 ROCK" !!!
ONE... TWO... THREE. FOUR... FIVE... ROCK...
...
OH, WHAT A SHAME. TRY AGAIN NEXT YEAR!
UP NEXT! URD SINGS, "CALL ME GODDESS" !!!
WHO'S A PERFECT GODDESS? JUST LOOK AT ME-EEE...
OH! SHE'S DANCING-- MARA IS DANCING!
THE JUDGE WHO ONLY DANCES FOR THE ROCKIN' BEAT IS ON HER FEET!
ROCK AND ROLL WILL NEVER DIE...
...NOT WITH OUR CHAMP URD AROUND!
HELP MEEE!
RIGHT. NOW URD WILL BE OUR JUDGE...
...IN THE BIG ENKA SING-OFF!

CHAPTER 49

Lunchbox with Love

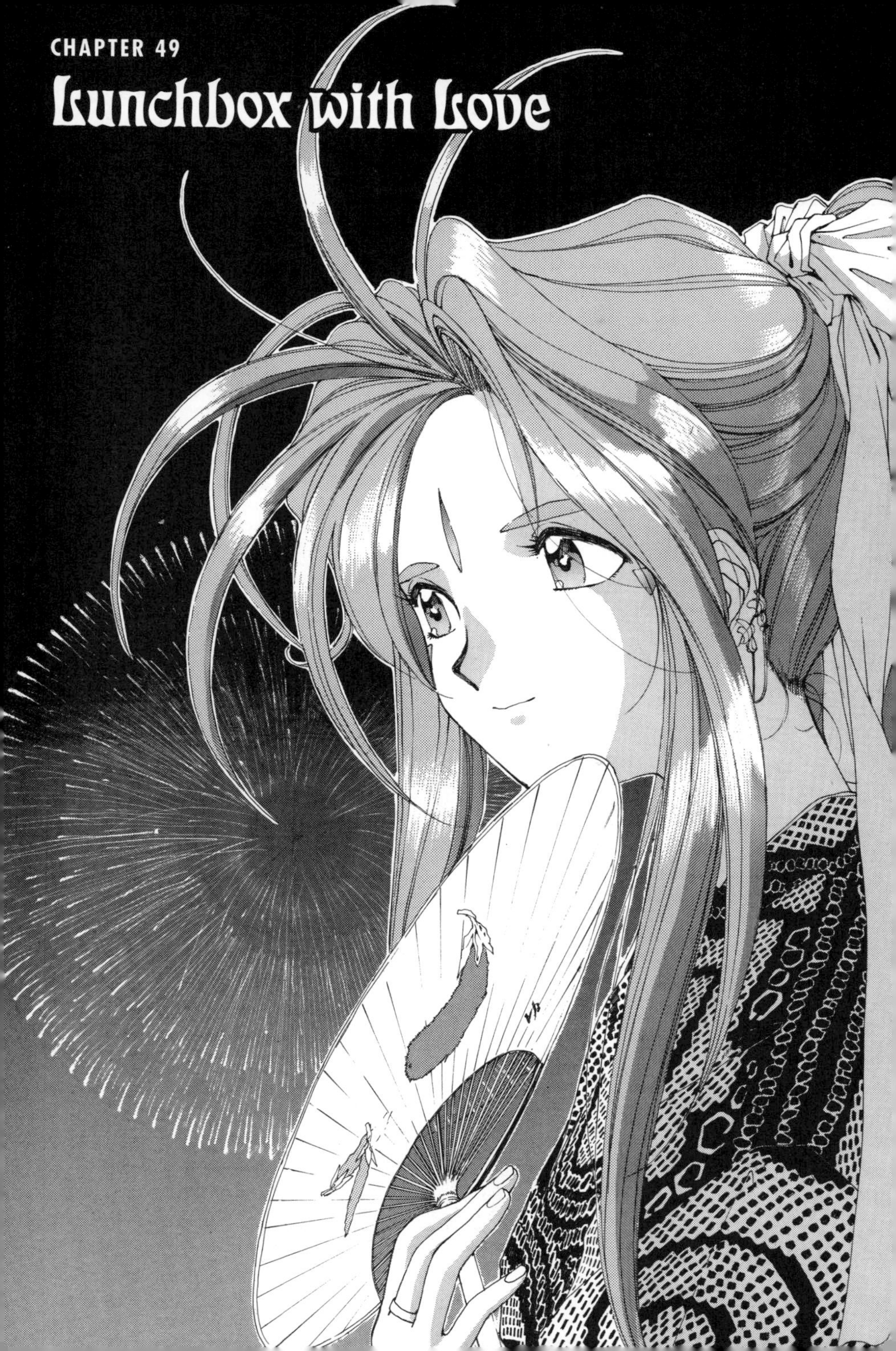

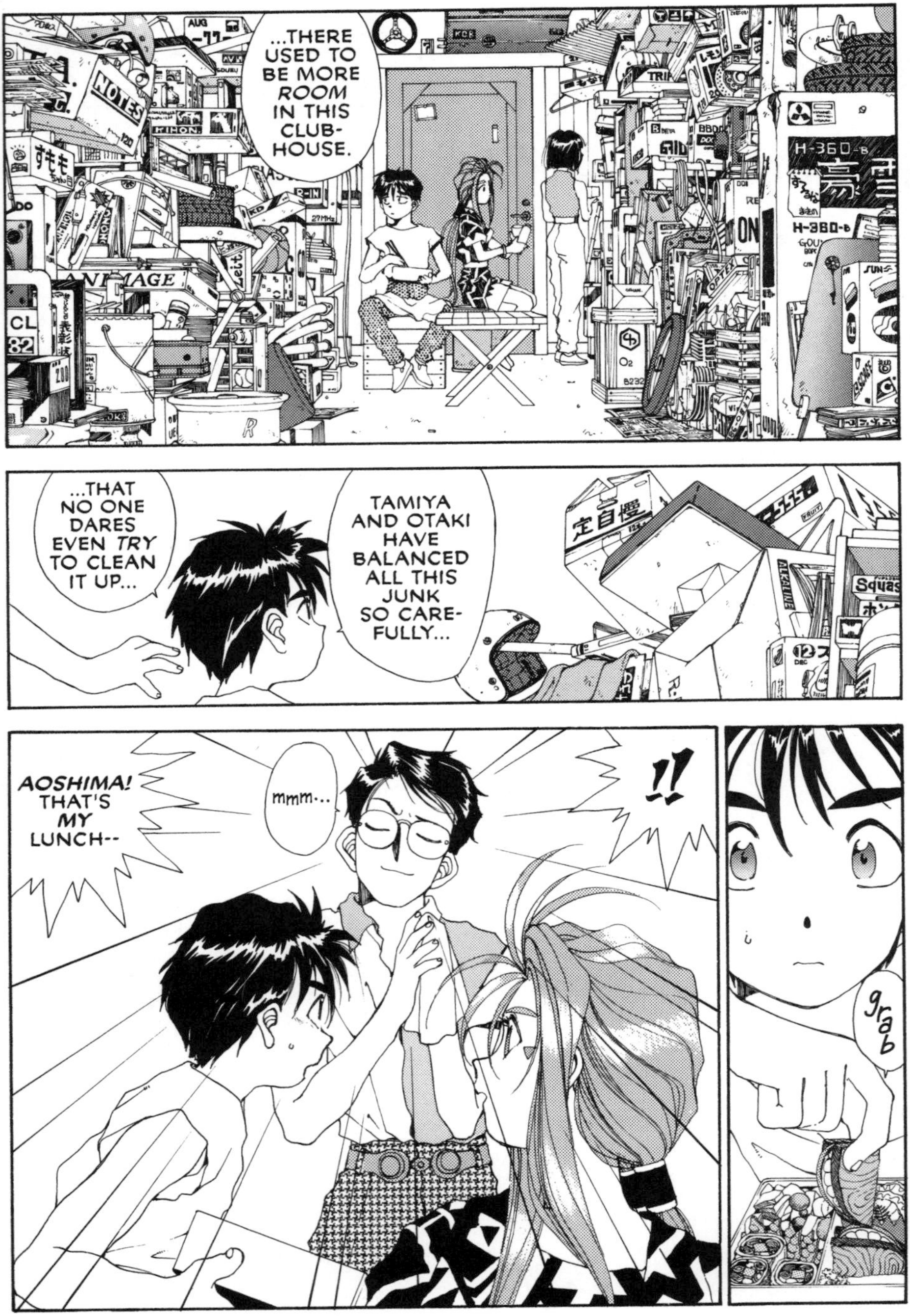
...THERE USED TO BE MORE ROOM IN THIS CLUB-HOUSE.
TAMIYA AND OTAKI HAVE BALANCED ALL THIS JUNK SO CARE-FULLY...
...THAT NO ONE DARES EVEN TRY TO CLEAN IT UP...
grab
!!
mmm...
AOSHIMA! THAT'S MY LUNCH--

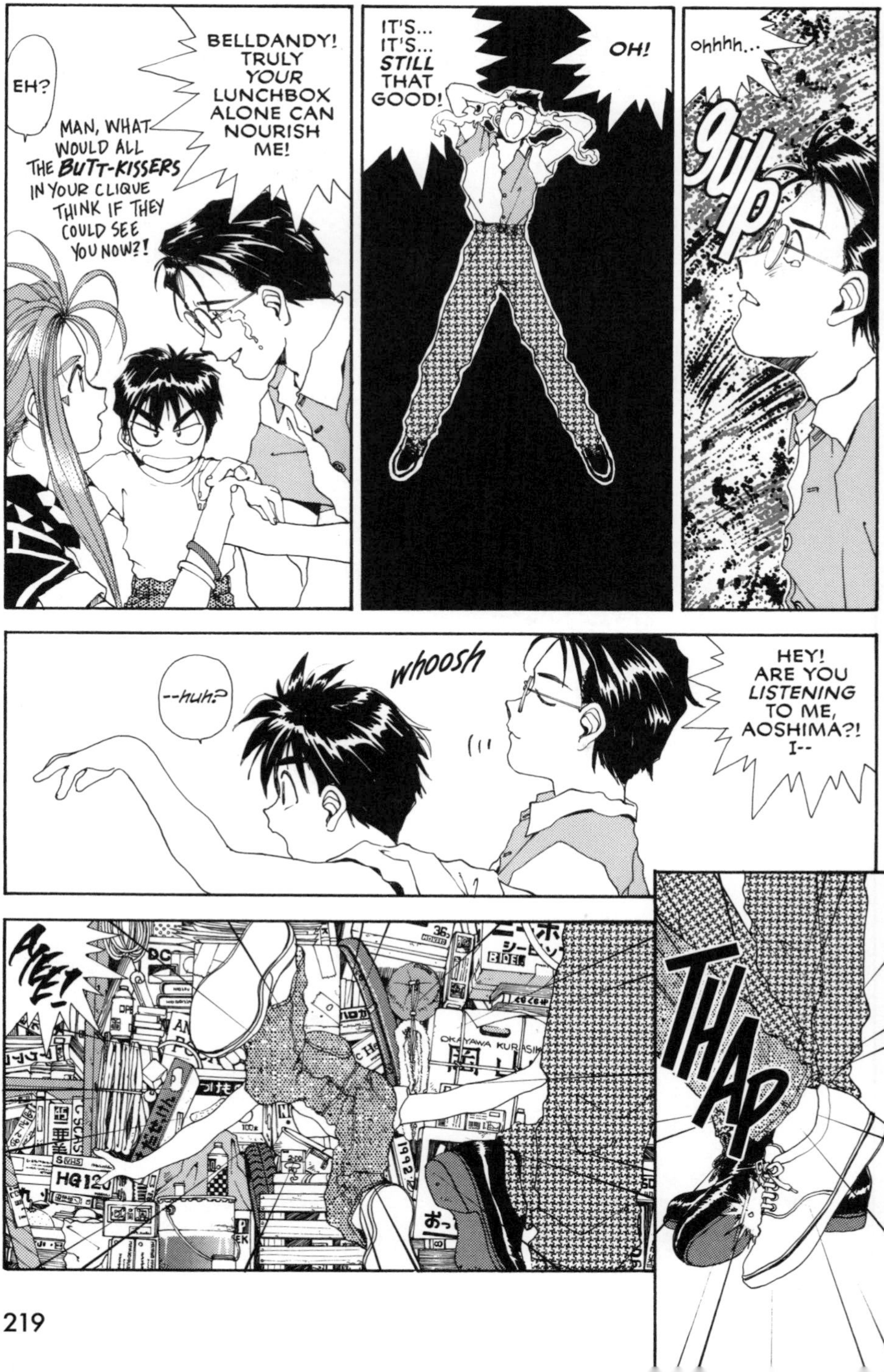
ohhhh...
gulp
IT'S... IT'S... STILL THAT GOOD!
OH!
BELLDANDY! TRULY YOUR LUNCHBOX ALONE CAN NOURISH ME!
EH?
MAN, WHAT WOULD ALL THE BUTT-KISSERS IN YOUR CLIQUE THINK IF THEY COULD SEE YOU NOW?!
HEY! ARE YOU LISTENING TO ME, AOSHIMA?! I--
whoosh
--huh?
THAP
AEEE!

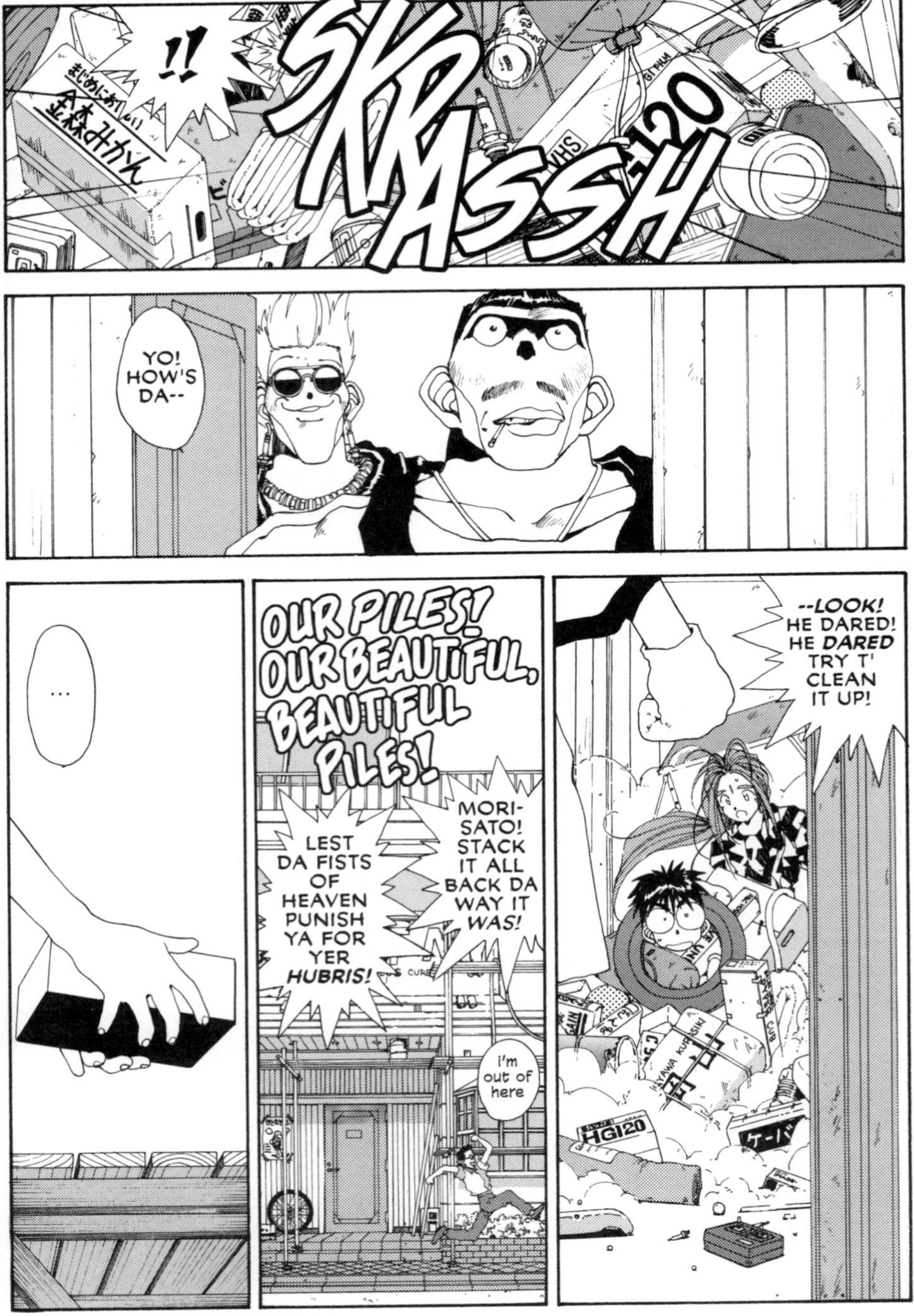
!!
SKRASSH
YO! HOW'S DA--
--LOOK! HE DARED! HE DARED TRY T' CLEAN IT UP!
OUR PILES! OUR BEAUTIFUL, BEAUTIFUL PILES!
MORI-SATO! STACK IT ALL BACK DA WAY IT WAS!
LEST DA FISTS OF HEAVEN PUNISH YA FOR YER HUBRIS!
i'm out of here
...

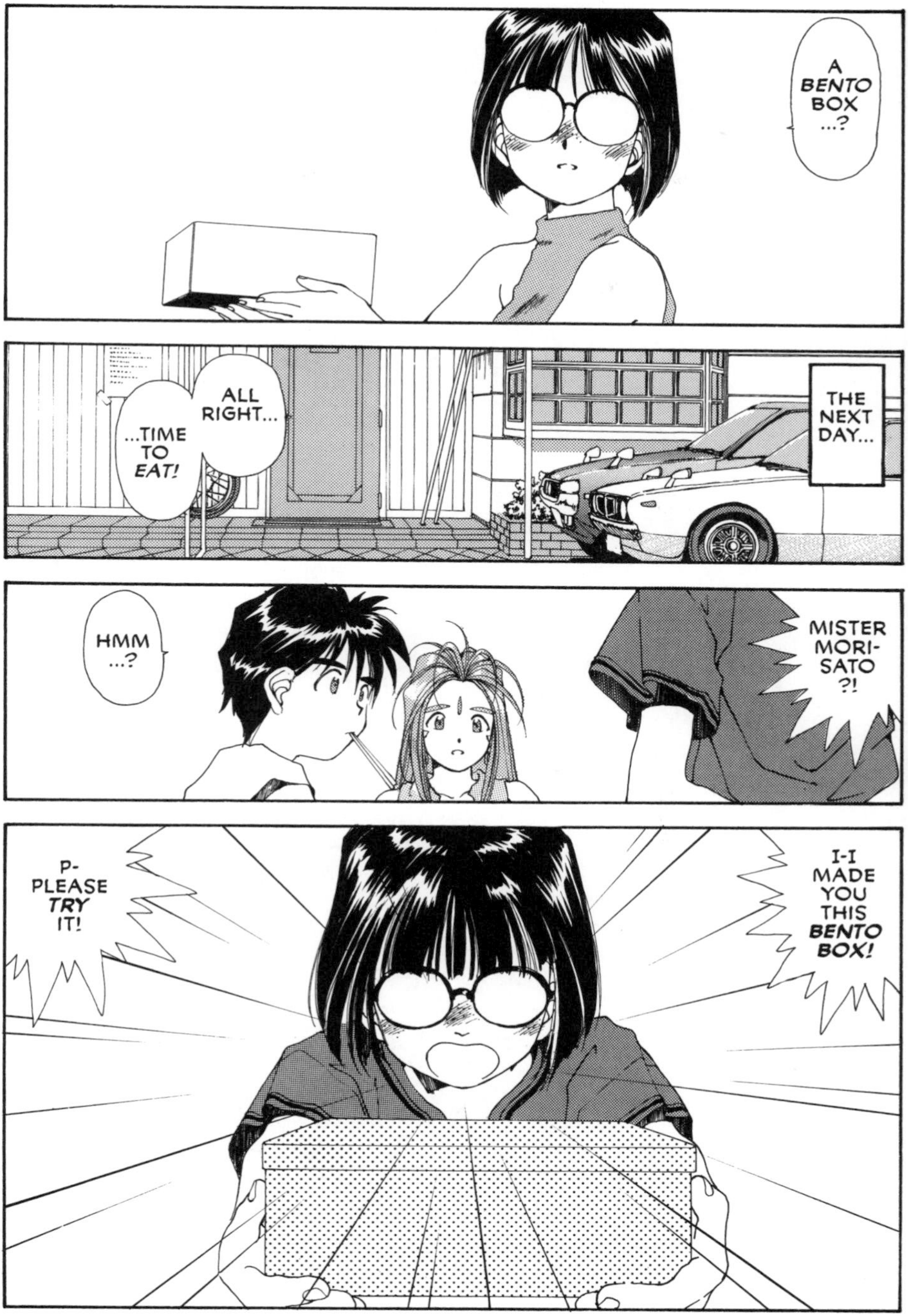
A BENTO BOX ...?
THE NEXT DAY...
ALL RIGHT...
...TIME TO EAT!
MISTER MORI-SATO ?!
HMM ...?
I-I MADE YOU THIS BENTO BOX!
P-PLEASE TRY IT!

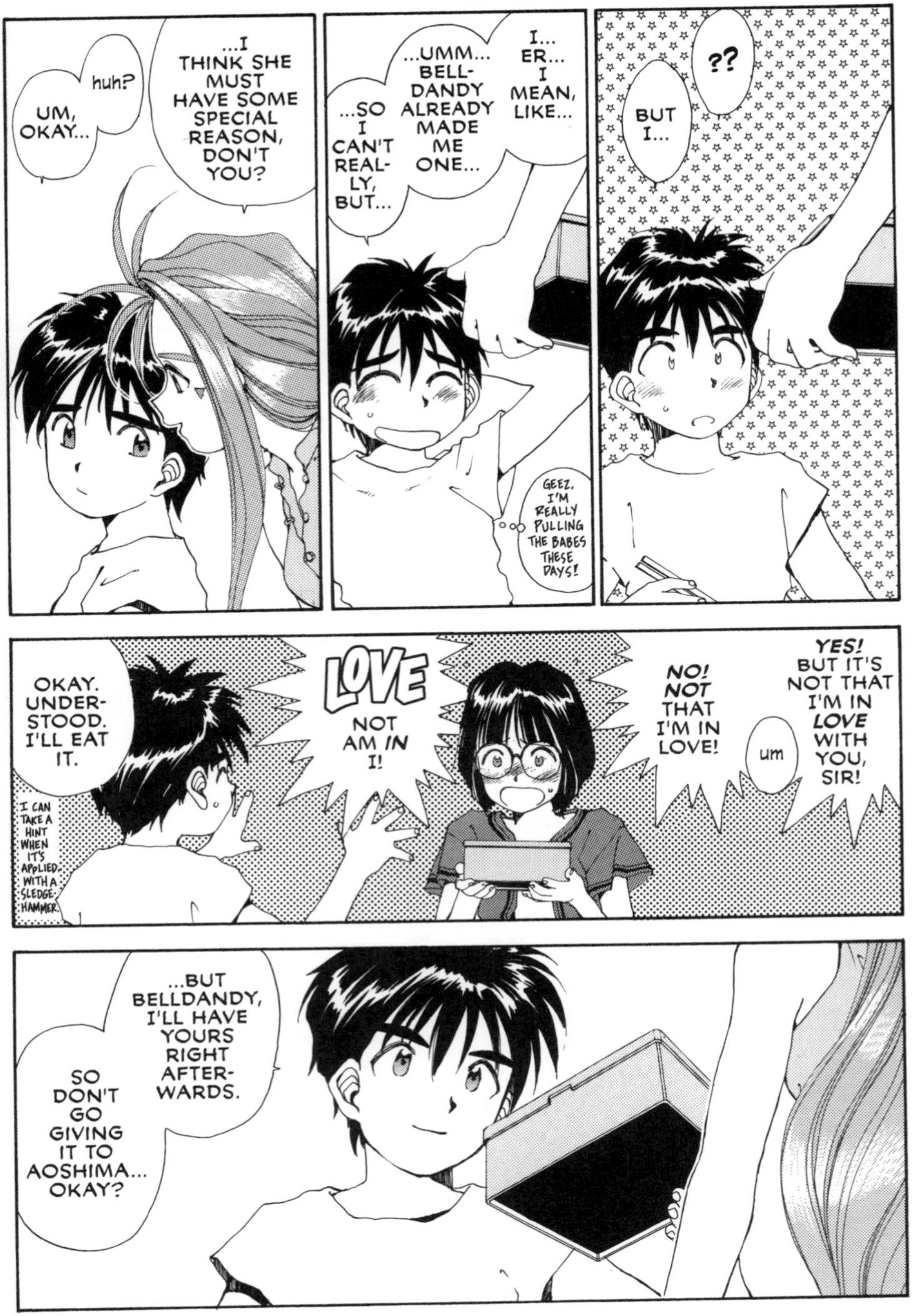
??
BUT I...
I... ER... I MEAN, LIKE...
...UMM... BELLDANDY ALREADY MADE ME ONE...
...SO I CAN'T REALLY, BUT...
GEEZ, I'M REALLY PULLING THE BABES THESE DAYS!
...I THINK SHE MUST HAVE SOME SPECIAL REASON, DON'T YOU?
huh?
UM, OKAY...
YES! BUT IT'S NOT THAT I'M IN LOVE WITH YOU, SIR!
um
NO! NOT THAT I'M IN LOVE!
LOVE
NOT AM IN I!
OKAY. UNDERSTOOD. I'LL EAT IT.
I CAN TAKE A HINT WHEN IT'S APPLIED WITH A SLEDGEHAMMER.
...BUT BELLDANDY, I'LL HAVE YOURS RIGHT AFTERWARDS.
SO DON'T GO GIVING IT TO AOSHIMA... OKAY?

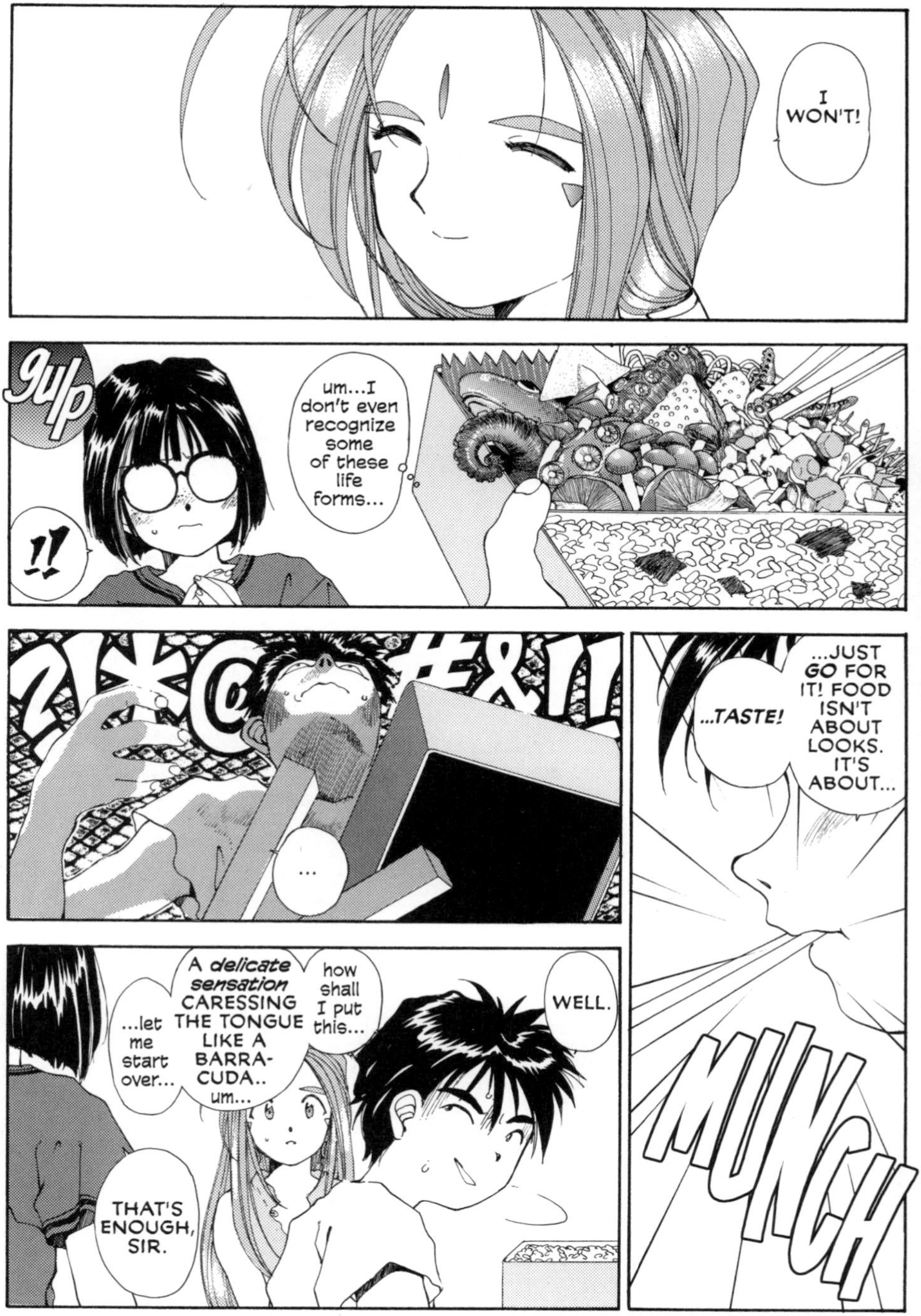
I WON'T!
um...I don't even recognize some of these life forms...
gulp
!!
...JUST GO FOR IT! FOOD ISN'T ABOUT LOOKS. IT'S ABOUT...
...TASTE!
MUNCH
...
WELL.
how shall I put this...
A delicate sensation CARESSING THE TONGUE LIKE A BARRA-CUDA.. um...
...let me start over...
THAT'S ENOUGH, SIR.

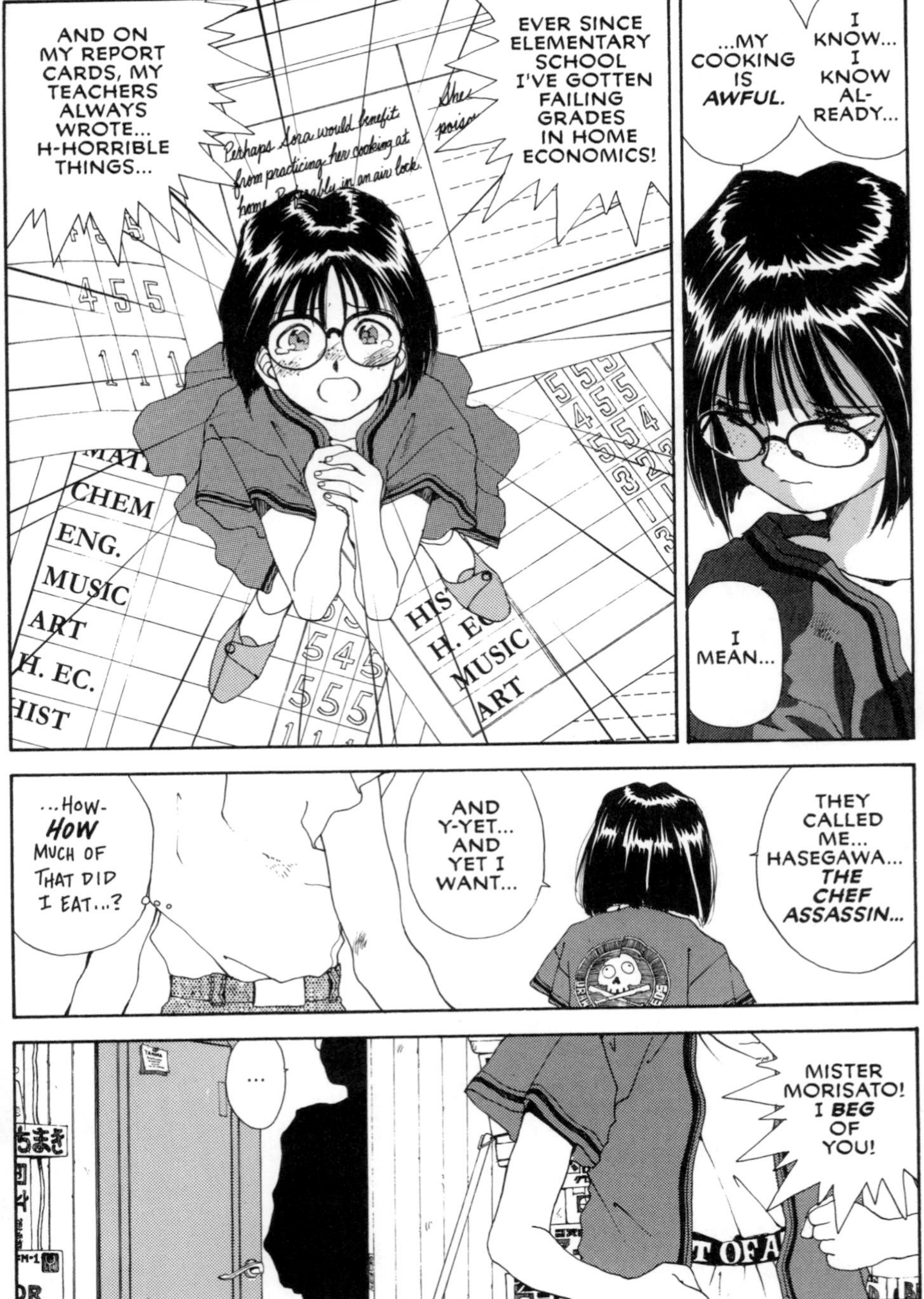

I KNOW... I KNOW AL-READY...
...MY COOKING IS *AWFUL.*
I MEAN...
EVER SINCE ELEMENTARY SCHOOL I'VE GOTTEN FAILING GRADES IN HOME ECONOMICS!
AND ON MY REPORT CARDS, MY TEACHERS ALWAYS WROTE... H-HORRIBLE THINGS...
Perhaps Sora would benefit from practicing her cooking at
CHEM
ENG.
MUSIC
ART
H. EC.
HIST
MUSIC
ART
THEY CALLED ME... HASEGAWA... *THE CHEF ASSASSIN...*
AND Y-YET... AND YET I WANT...
...HOW- *HOW* MUCH OF THAT DID I EAT...?
MISTER MORISATO! I *BEG* OF YOU!
...

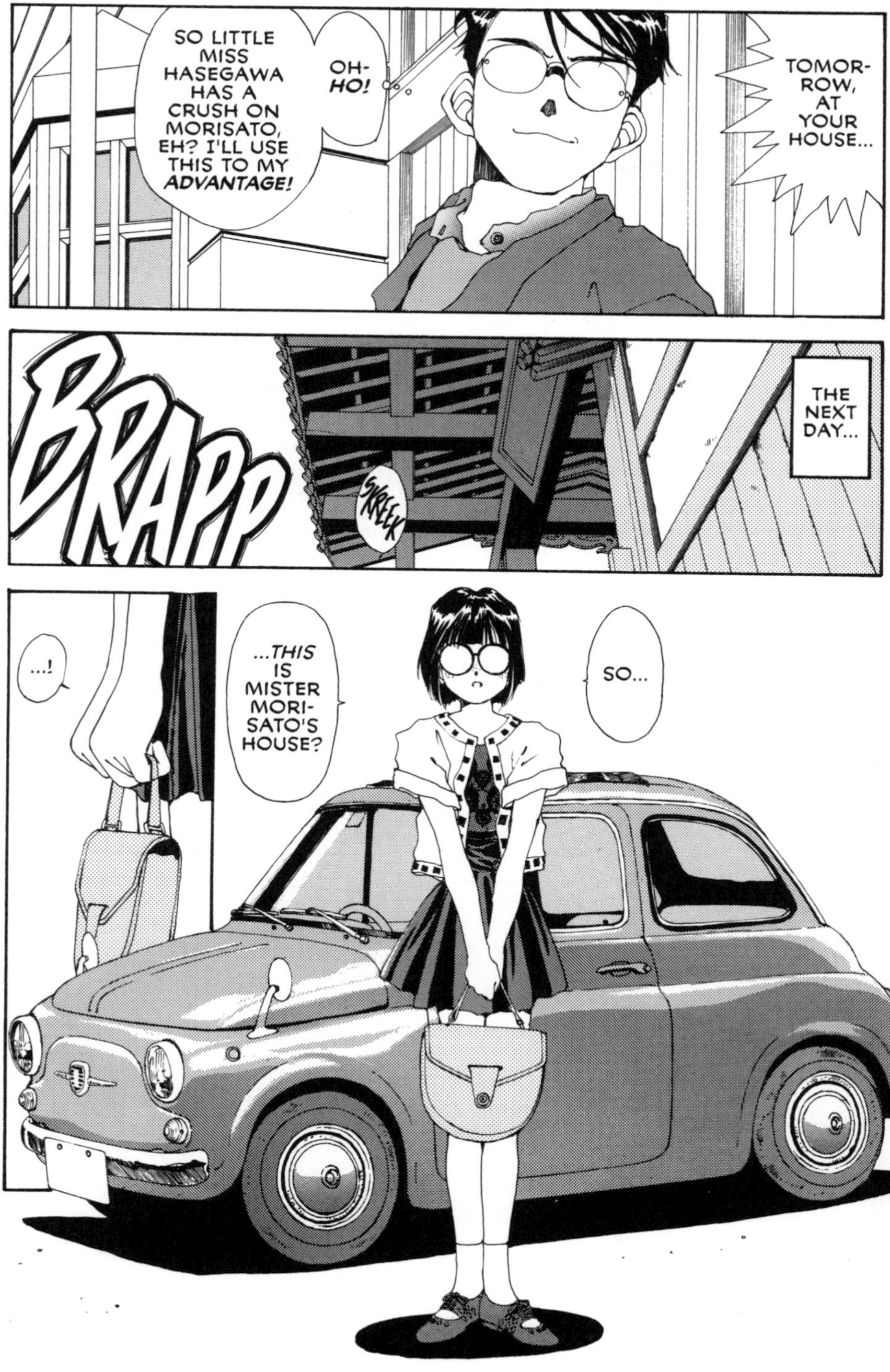
TOMORROW, AT YOUR HOUSE...
OH-HO!
SO LITTLE MISS HASEGAWA HAS A CRUSH ON MORISATO, EH? I'LL USE THIS TO MY ADVANTAGE!
THE NEXT DAY...
SKREEK
BRAPP
SO...
...THIS IS MISTER MORISATO'S HOUSE?
...!

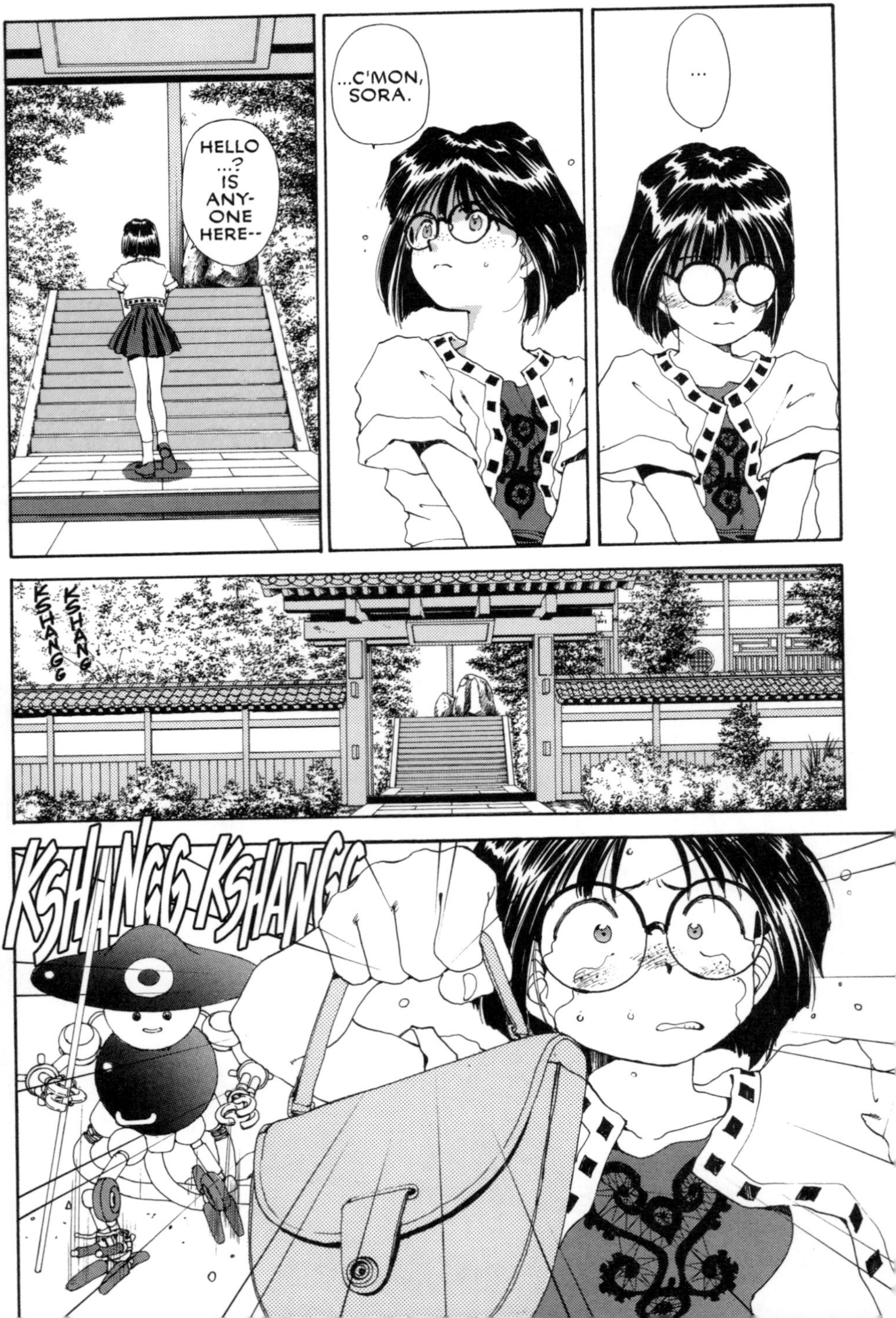
...
...C'MON, SORA.
HELLO ...? IS ANYONE HERE--
KSHANG
KSHANGG
KSHANGG KSHANGG

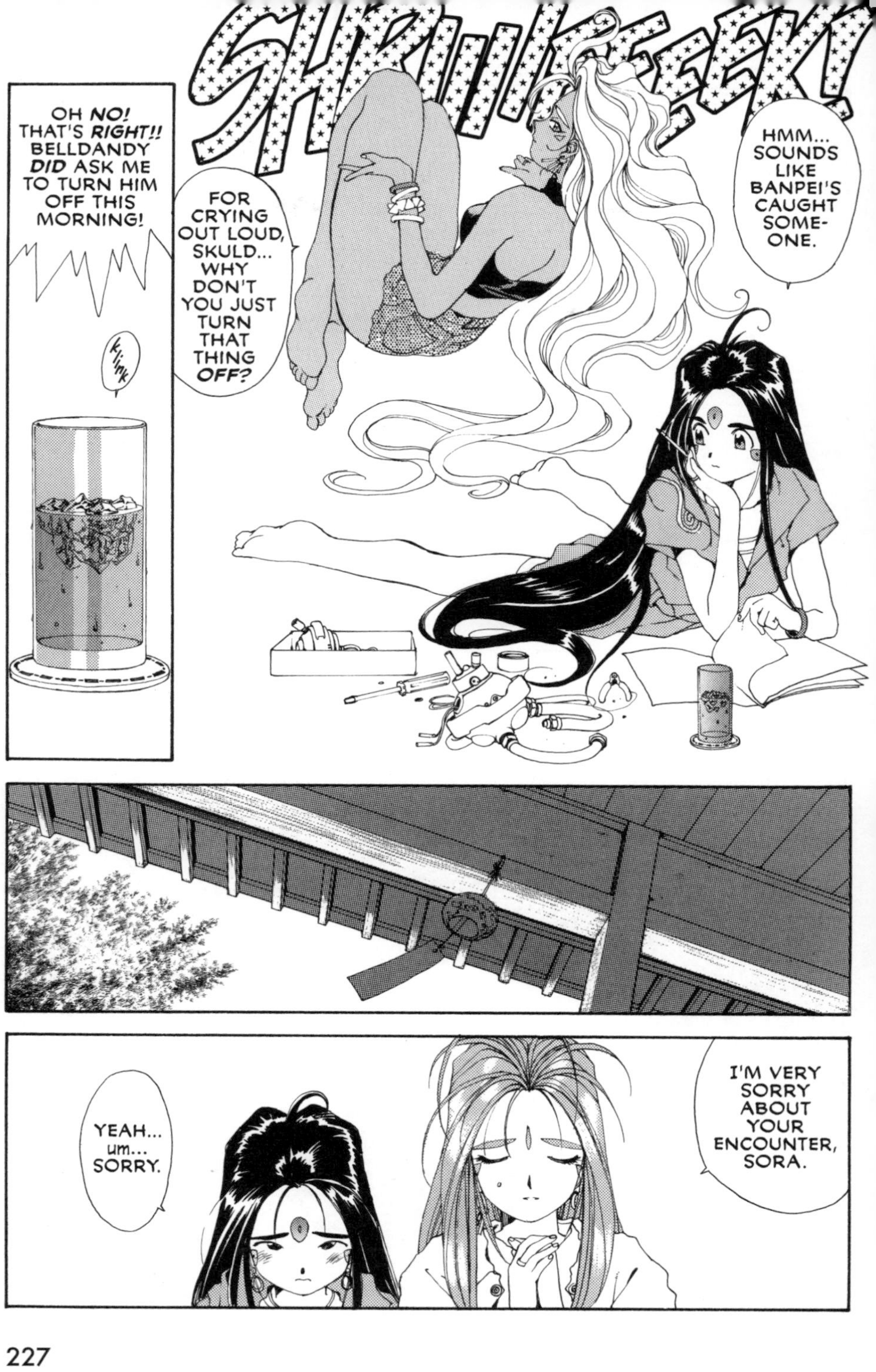
SHRIIIEEEK!
HMM... SOUNDS LIKE BANPEI'S CAUGHT SOME-ONE.
FOR CRYING OUT LOUD, SKULD... WHY DON'T YOU JUST TURN THAT THING *OFF?*
OH *NO!* THAT'S *RIGHT!!* BELLDANDY *DID* ASK ME TO TURN HIM OFF THIS MORNING!
klink
I'M VERY SORRY ABOUT YOUR ENCOUNTER, SORA.
YEAH... um... SORRY.

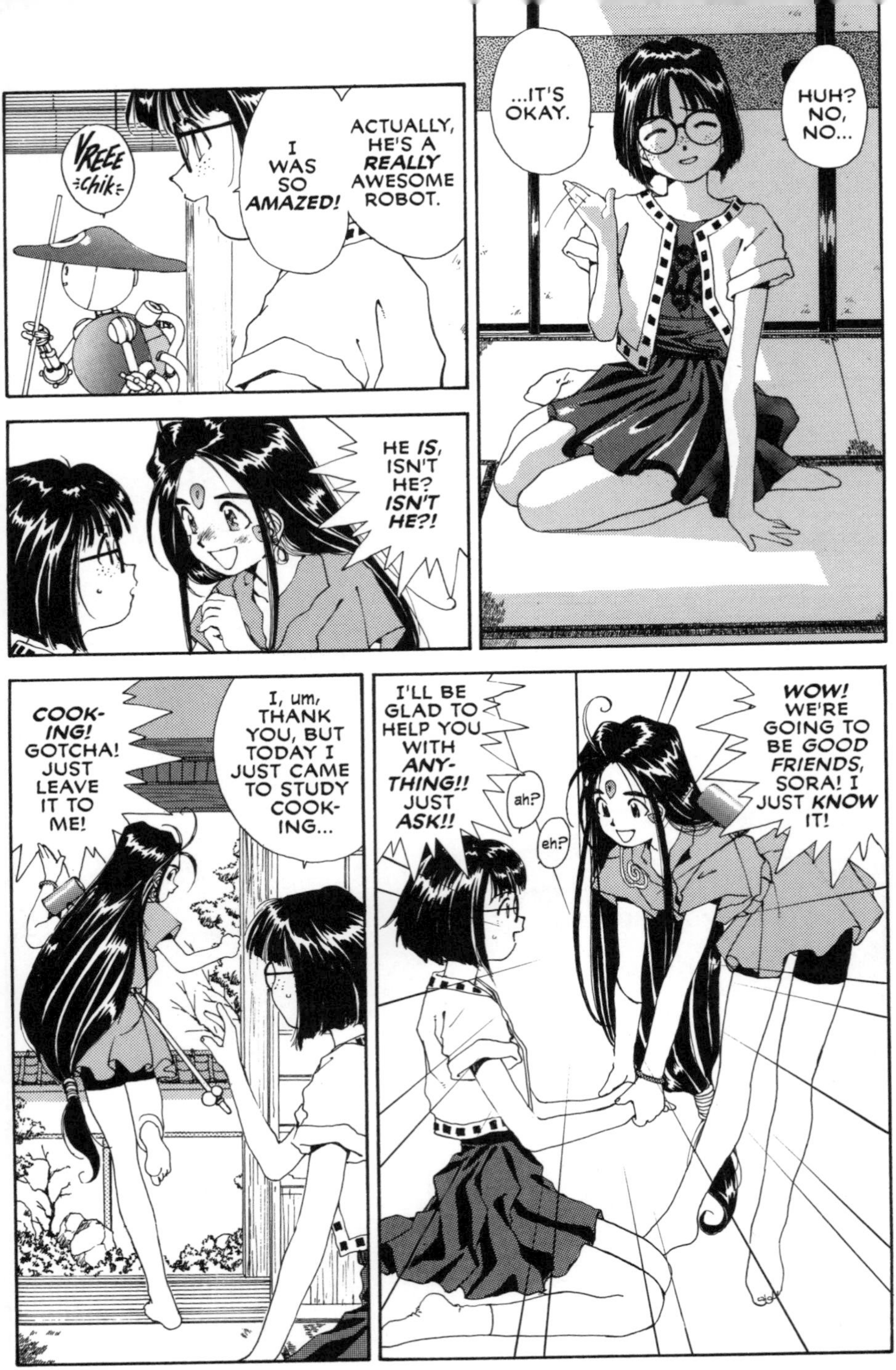
HUH? NO, NO...
...IT'S OKAY.
ACTUALLY, HE'S A *REALLY* AWESOME ROBOT.
I WAS SO *AMAZED!*
VREEE chik
HE *IS*, ISN'T HE? *ISN'T HE?!*
WOW! WE'RE GOING TO BE *GOOD FRIENDS*, SORA! I JUST *KNOW* IT!
I'LL BE GLAD TO HELP YOU WITH *ANY-THING!!* JUST *ASK!!*
ah?
eh?
I, um, THANK YOU, BUT TODAY I JUST CAME TO STUDY COOK-ING...
COOK-ING! GOTCHA! JUST LEAVE IT TO ME!

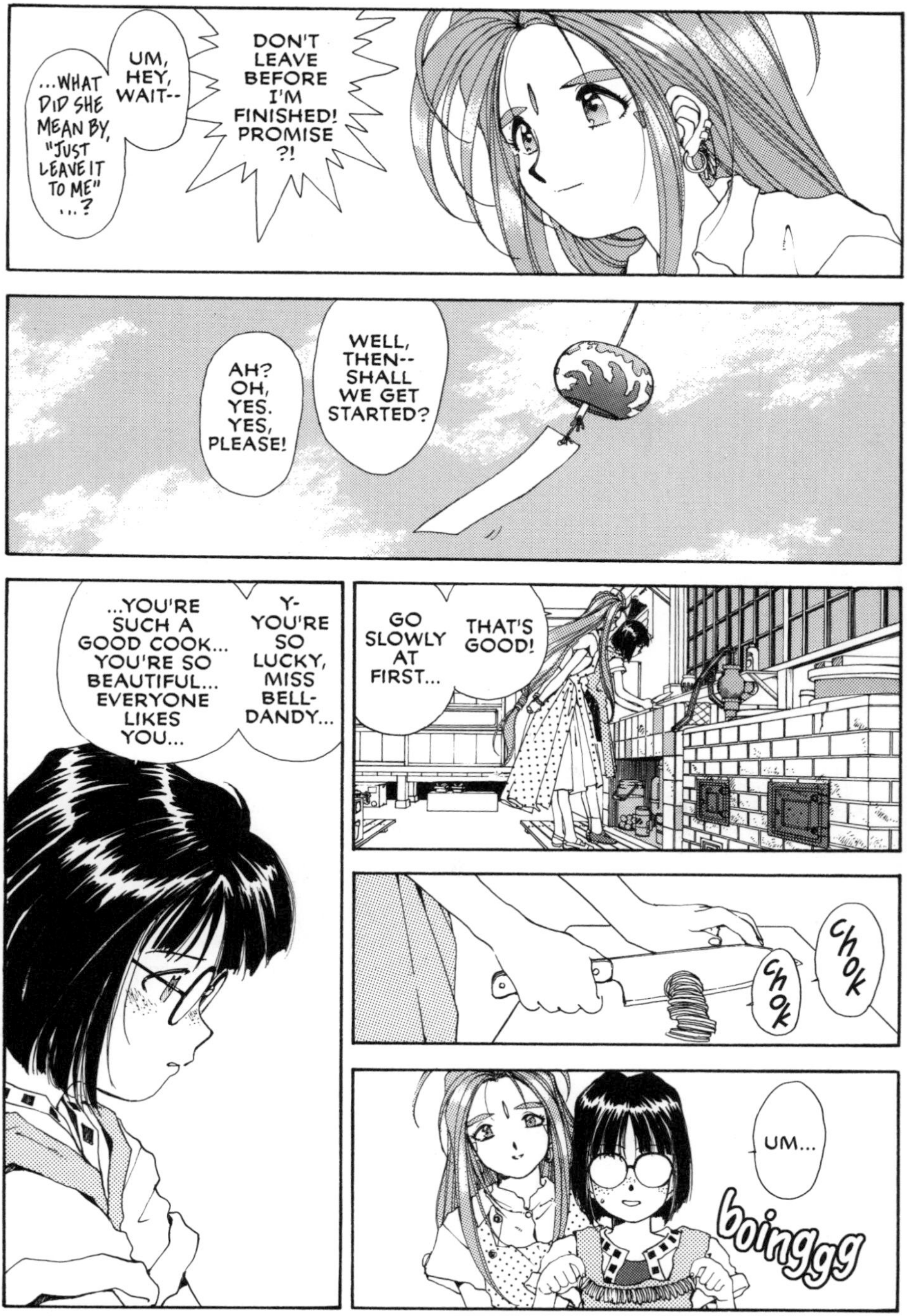
DON'T LEAVE BEFORE I'M FINISHED! PROMISE?!
UM, HEY, WAIT--
...WHAT DID SHE MEAN BY, "JUST LEAVE IT TO ME"...?
WELL, THEN--SHALL WE GET STARTED?
AH? OH, YES. YES, PLEASE!
THAT'S GOOD!
GO SLOWLY AT FIRST...
chok
chok
UM...
boinggg
Y-YOU'RE SO LUCKY, MISS BELL-DANDY...
...YOU'RE SUCH A GOOD COOK... YOU'RE SO BEAUTIFUL... EVERYONE LIKES YOU...

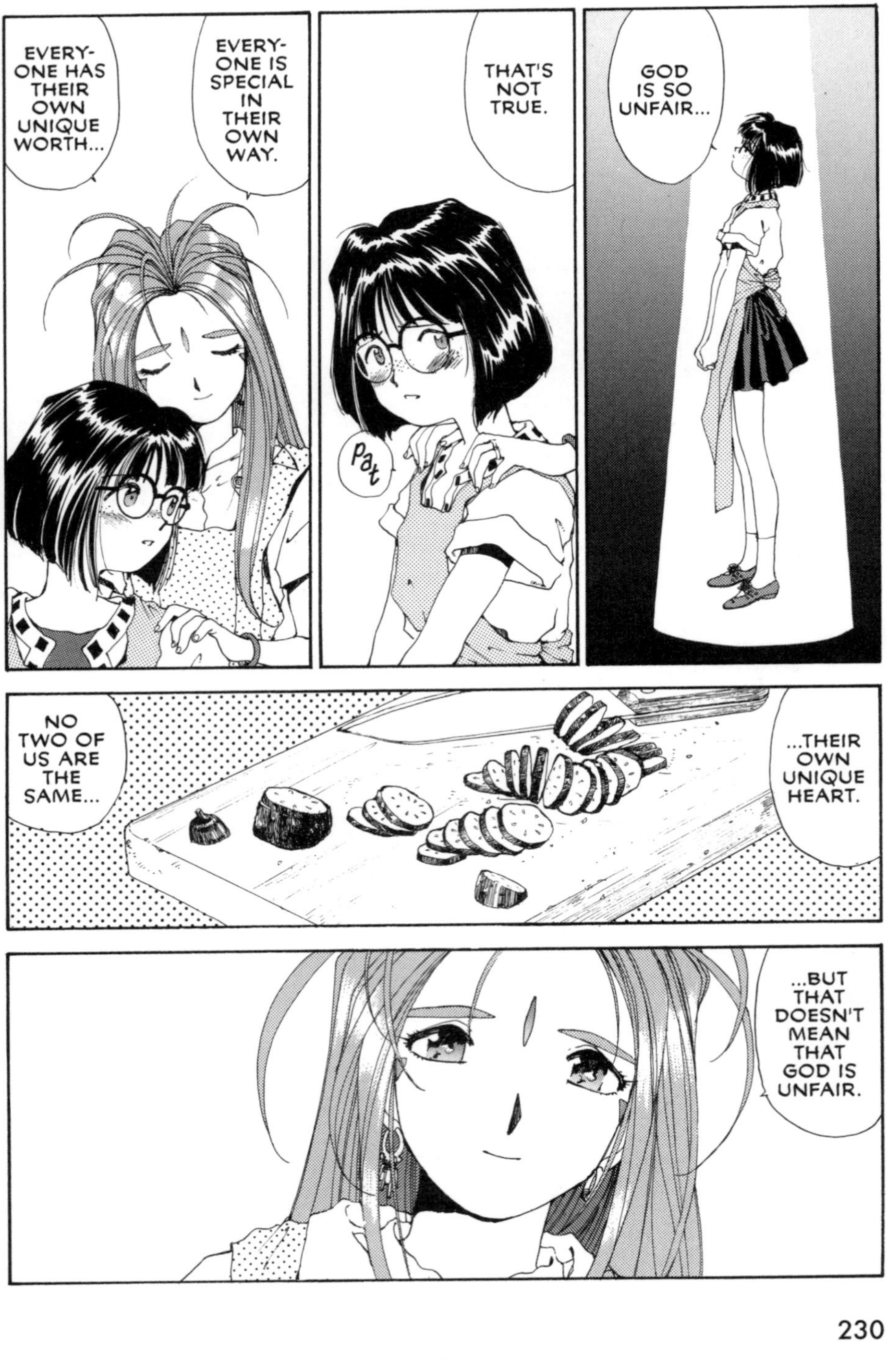
GOD IS SO UNFAIR...
THAT'S NOT TRUE.
Pat
EVERY-ONE IS SPECIAL IN THEIR OWN WAY.
EVERY-ONE HAS THEIR OWN UNIQUE WORTH...
...THEIR OWN UNIQUE HEART.
NO TWO OF US ARE THE SAME...
...BUT THAT DOESN'T MEAN THAT GOD IS UNFAIR.

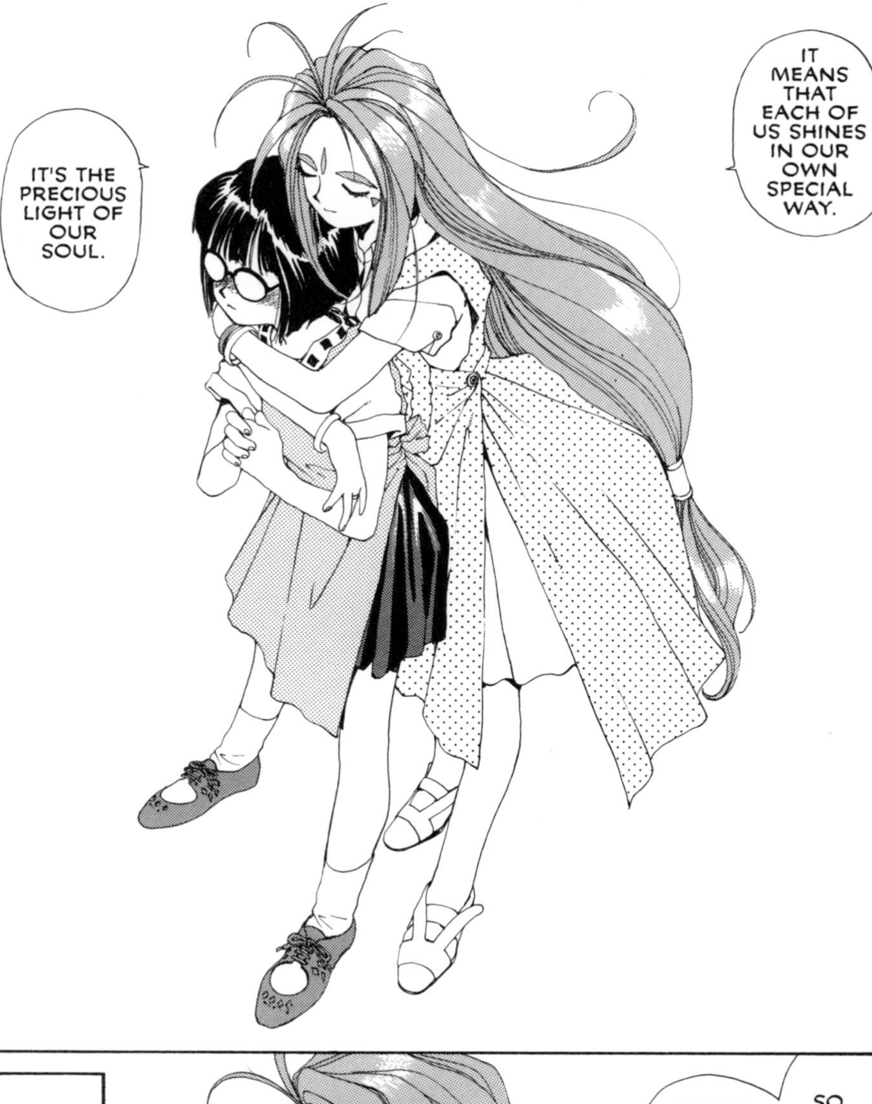
IT'S THE PRECIOUS LIGHT OF OUR SOUL.
IT MEANS THAT EACH OF US SHINES IN OUR OWN SPECIAL WAY.

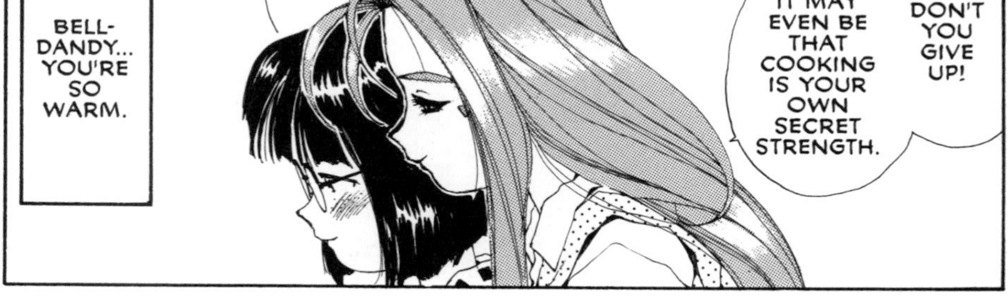
BELL-DANDY... YOU'RE SO WARM.
IT MAY EVEN BE THAT COOKING IS YOUR OWN SECRET STRENGTH.
SO DON'T YOU GIVE UP!

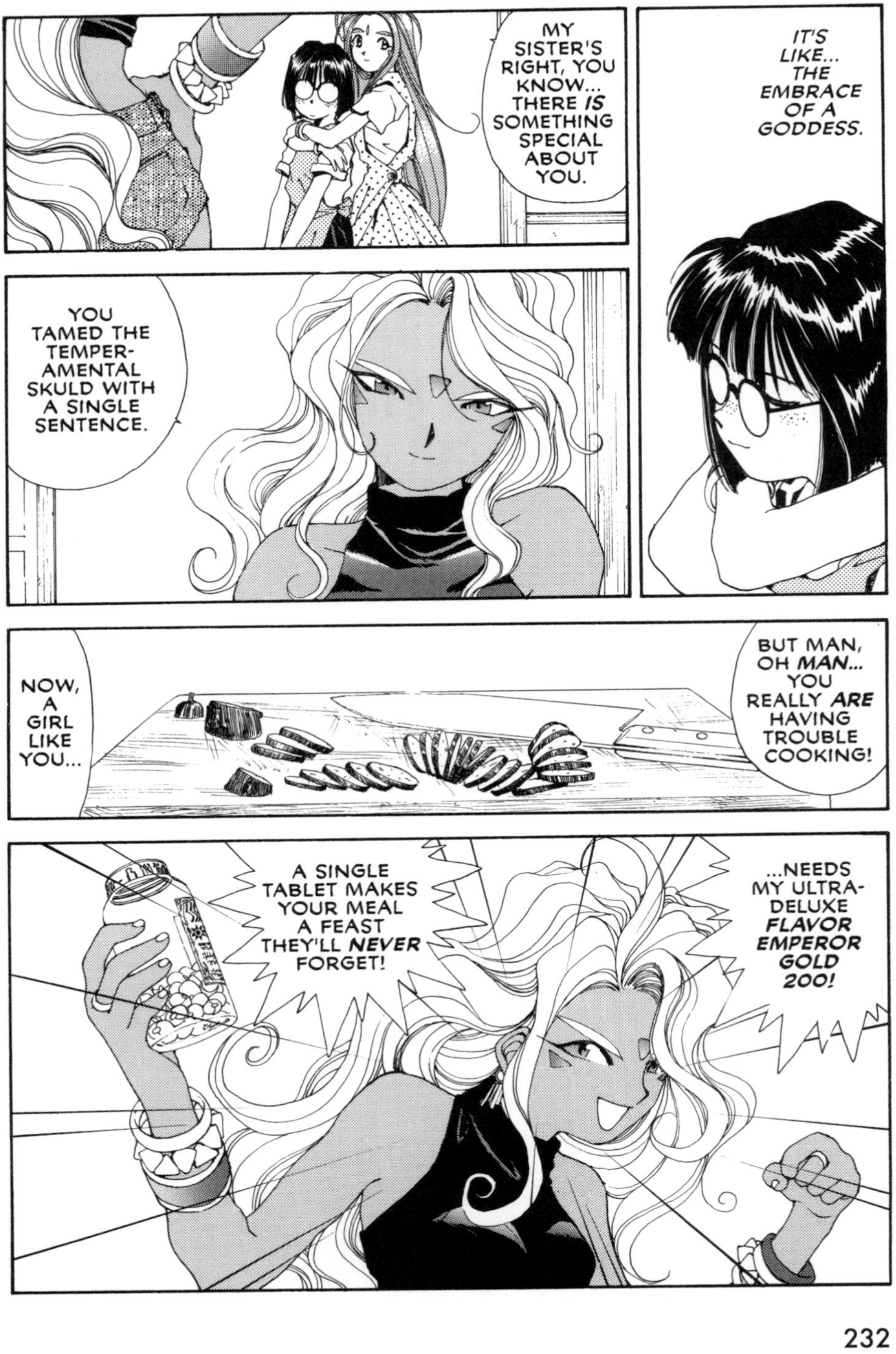
IT'S LIKE... THE EMBRACE OF A GODDESS.
MY SISTER'S RIGHT, YOU KNOW... THERE *IS* SOMETHING SPECIAL ABOUT YOU.
YOU TAMED THE TEMPER-AMENTAL SKULD WITH A SINGLE SENTENCE.
BUT MAN, OH *MAN*... YOU REALLY *ARE* HAVING TROUBLE COOKING!
NOW, A GIRL LIKE YOU...
...NEEDS MY ULTRA-DELUXE *FLAVOR EMPEROR GOLD 200!*
A SINGLE TABLET MAKES YOUR MEAL A FEAST THEY'LL *NEVER* FORGET!

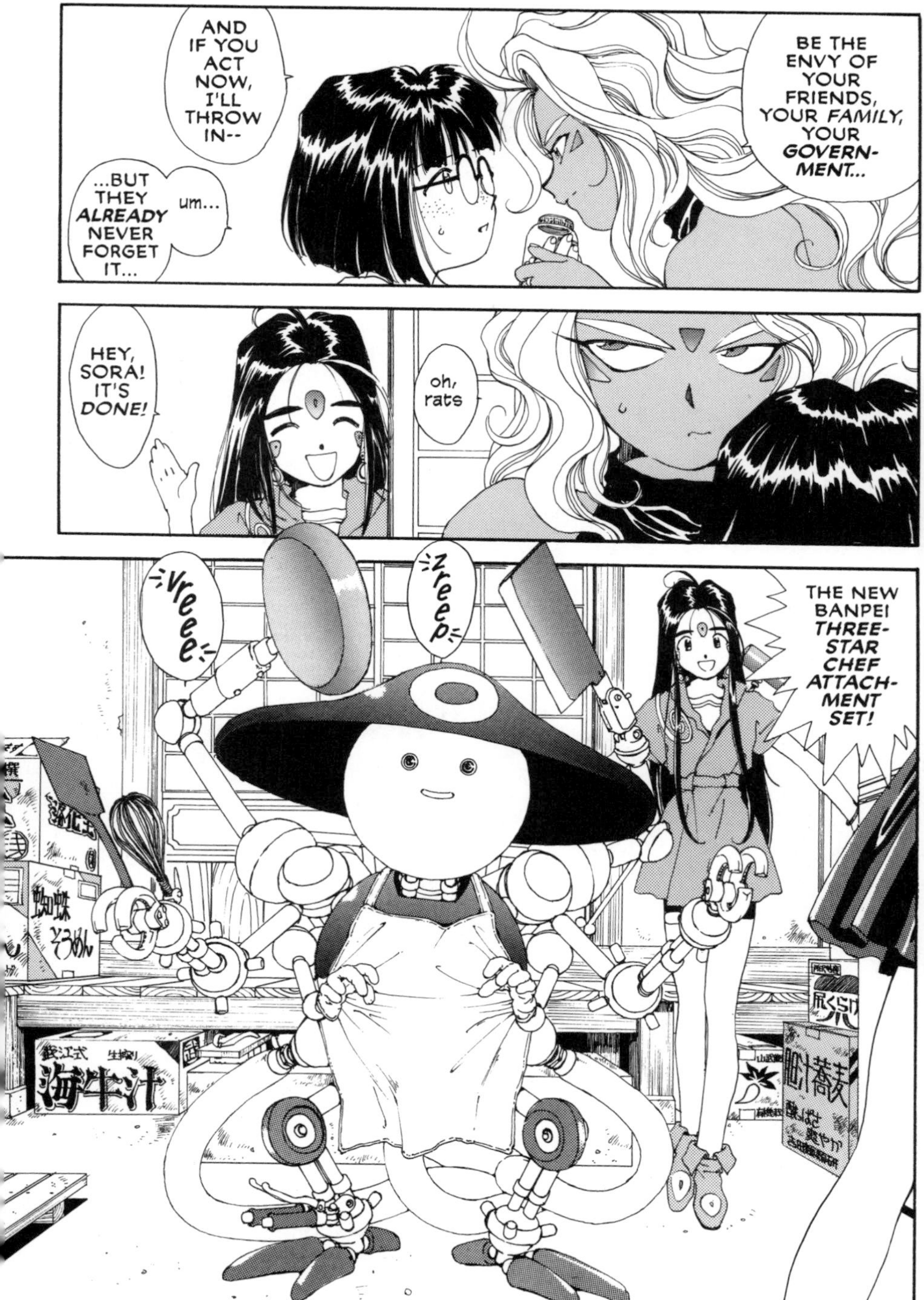
BE THE ENVY OF YOUR FRIENDS, YOUR *FAMILY*, YOUR ***GOVERNMENT***...
AND IF YOU ACT NOW, I'LL THROW IN--
um...
...BUT THEY ***ALREADY*** NEVER FORGET IT...
oh, rats
HEY, SORA! IT'S *DONE!*
THE NEW BANPEI ***THREE-STAR CHEF*** ***ATTACHMENT SET!***
zreeep
vreeee

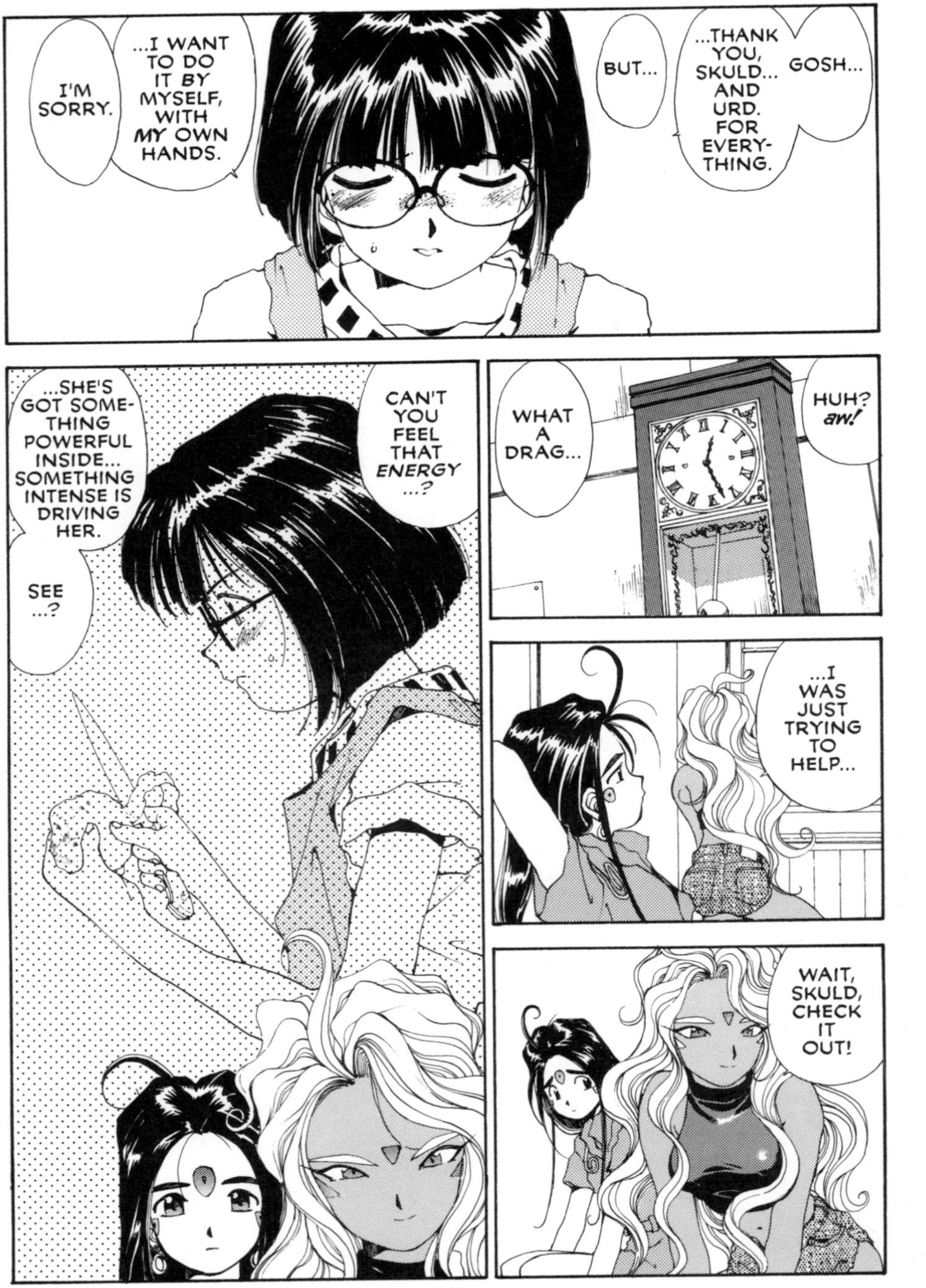
GOSH...
...THANK YOU, SKULD... AND URD. FOR EVERYTHING.
BUT...
...I WANT TO DO IT BY MYSELF, WITH MY OWN HANDS.
I'M SORRY.
HUH? aw!
WHAT A DRAG...
...I WAS JUST TRYING TO HELP...
WAIT, SKULD, CHECK IT OUT!
CAN'T YOU FEEL THAT ENERGY ...?
...SHE'S GOT SOMETHING POWERFUL INSIDE... SOMETHING INTENSE IS DRIVING HER.
SEE ...?

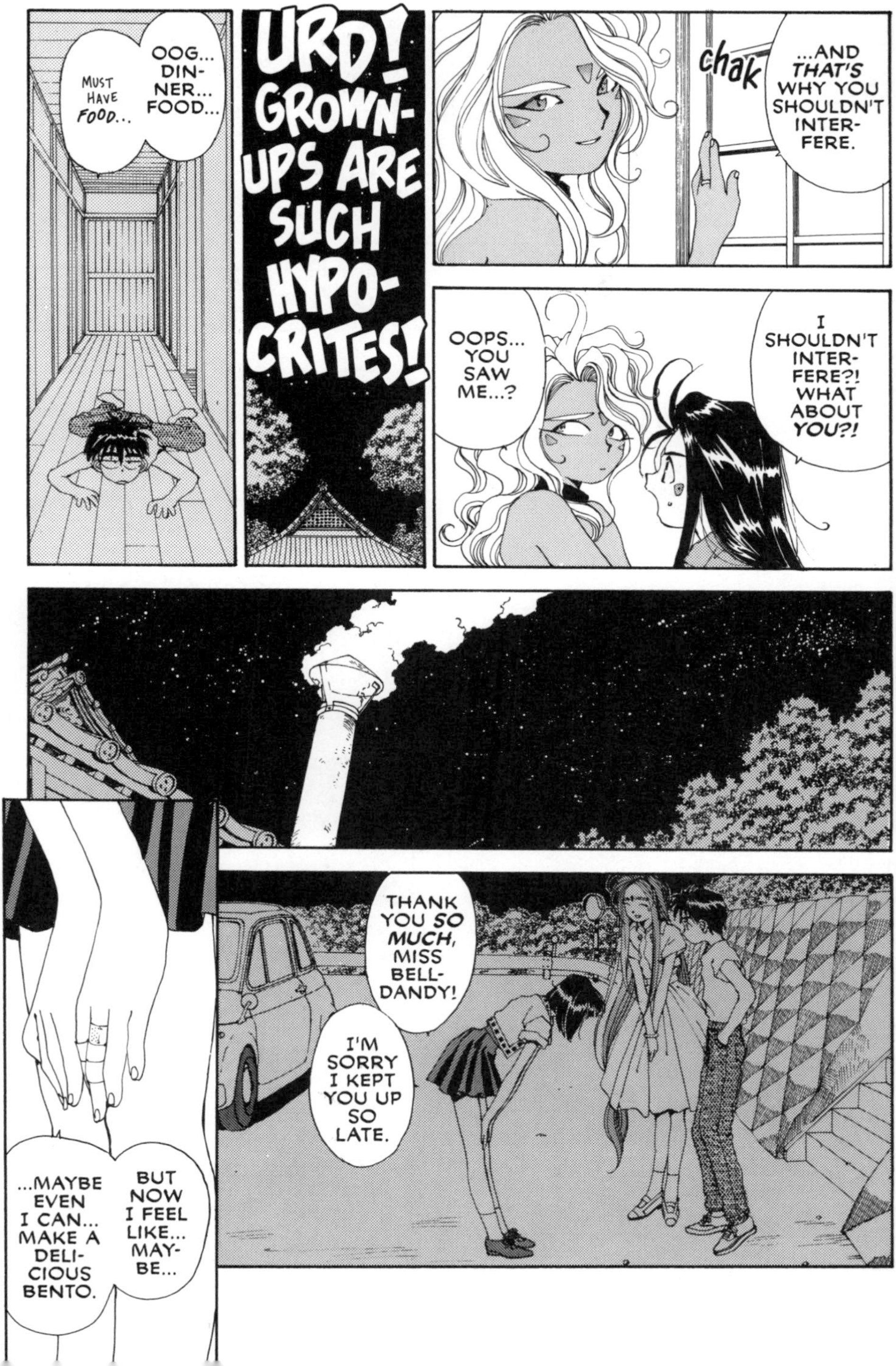
chak
...AND THAT'S WHY YOU SHOULDN'T INTERFERE.
I SHOULDN'T INTERFERE?! WHAT ABOUT YOU?!
OOPS... YOU SAW ME...?
URD! GROWN-UPS ARE SUCH HYPOCRITES!
OOG... DINNER... FOOD...
MUST HAVE FOOD...
THANK YOU SO MUCH, MISS BELLDANDY!
I'M SORRY I KEPT YOU UP SO LATE.
BUT NOW I FEEL LIKE... MAYBE...
...MAYBE EVEN I CAN... MAKE A DELICIOUS BENTO.

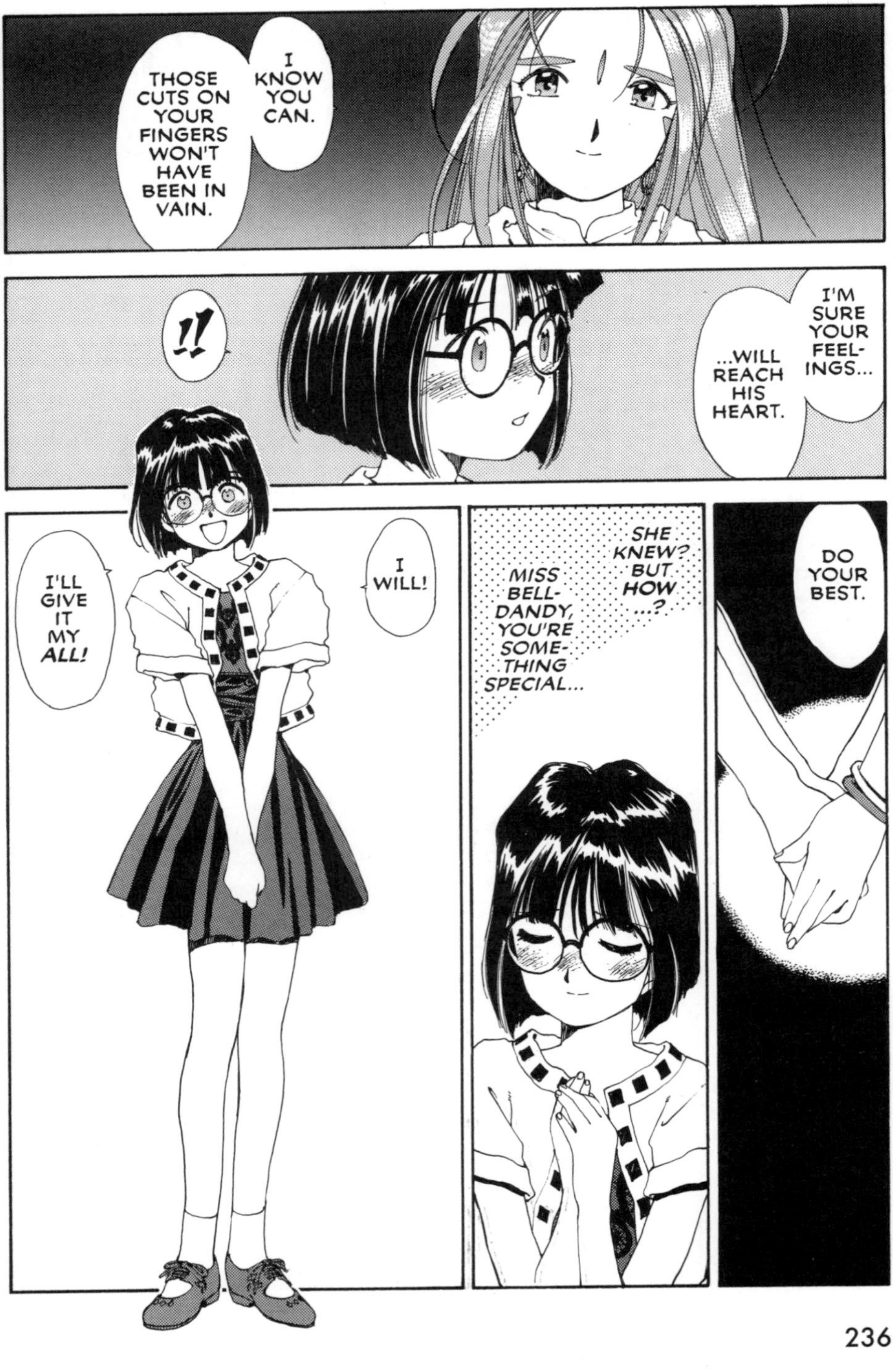
I KNOW YOU CAN.
THOSE CUTS ON YOUR FINGERS WON'T HAVE BEEN IN VAIN.
I'M SURE YOUR FEELINGS...
...WILL REACH HIS HEART.
!!
DO YOUR BEST.
SHE KNEW? BUT HOW...?
MISS BELLDANDY, YOU'RE SOMETHING SPECIAL...
I WILL!
I'LL GIVE IT MY ALL!

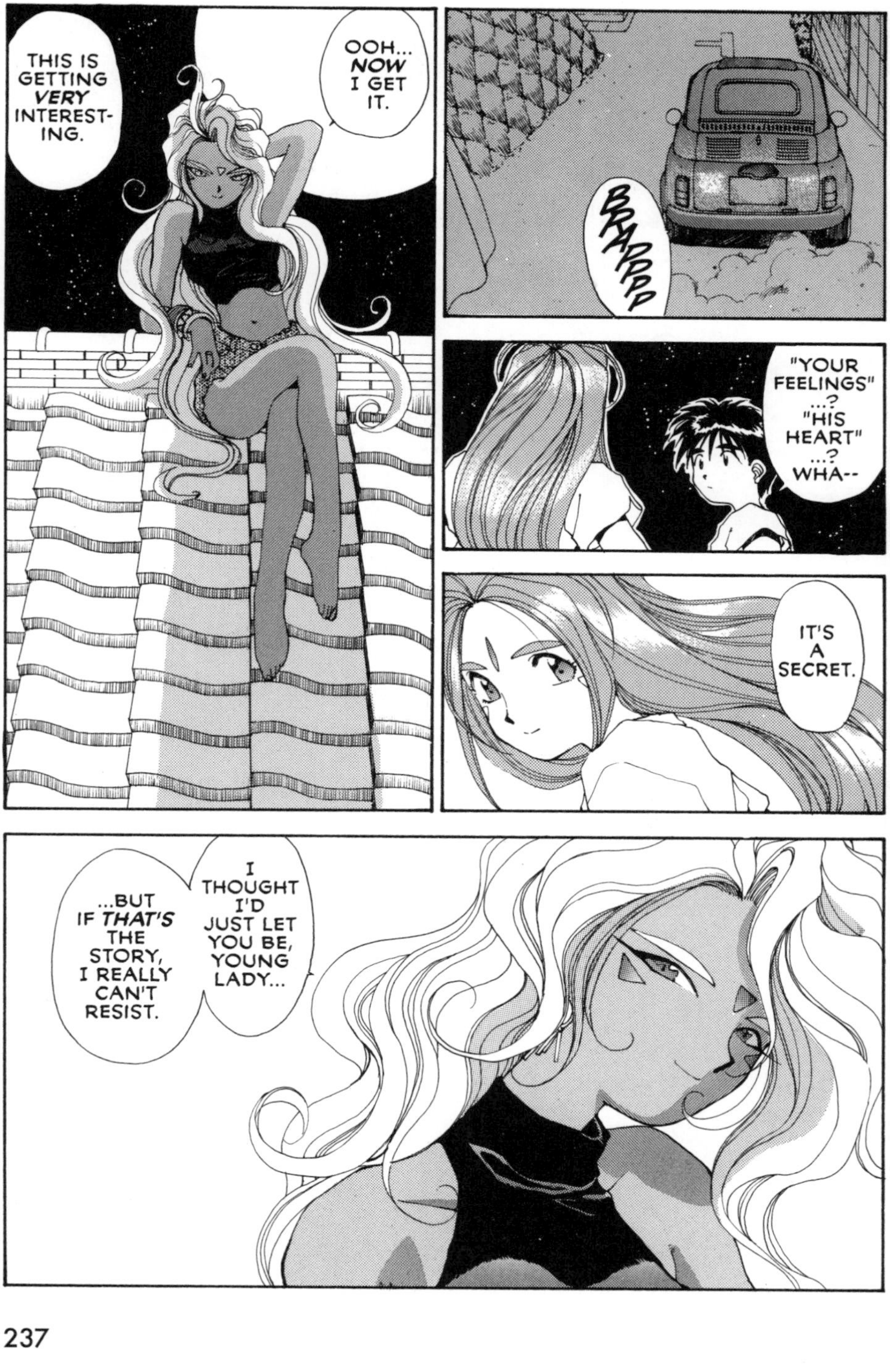
BRAPPPP
"YOUR FEELINGS" ...? "HIS HEART" ...? WHA--
IT'S A SECRET.
OOH... *NOW* I GET IT.
THIS IS GETTING *VERY* INTERESTING.
I THOUGHT I'D JUST LET YOU BE, YOUNG LADY...
...BUT IF *THAT'S* THE STORY, I REALLY CAN'T RESIST.

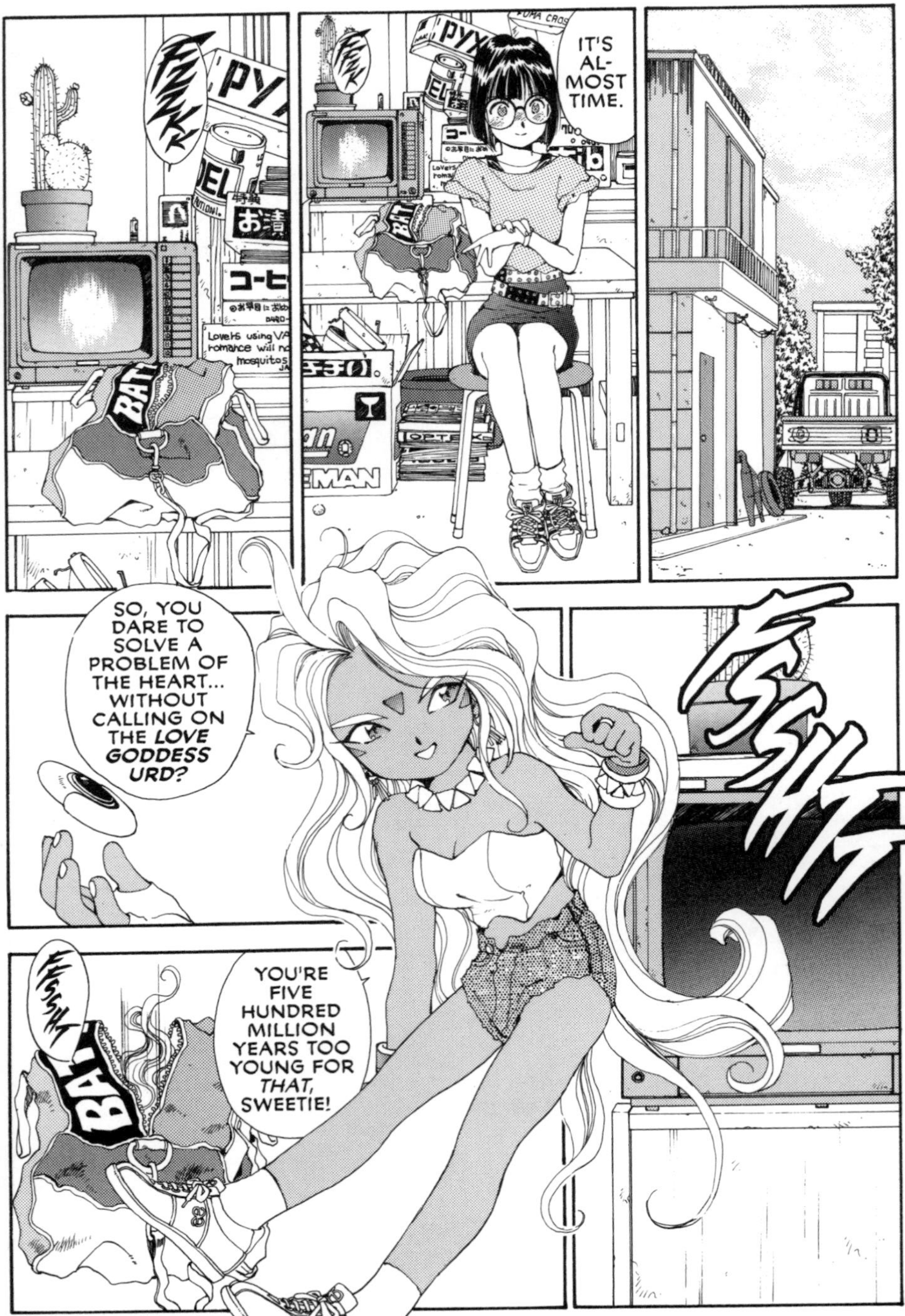
IT'S AL-MOST TIME.
SO, YOU DARE TO SOLVE A PROBLEM OF THE HEART... WITHOUT CALLING ON THE *LOVE GODDESS URD?*
YOU'RE FIVE HUNDRED MILLION YEARS TOO YOUNG FOR *THAT,* SWEETIE!

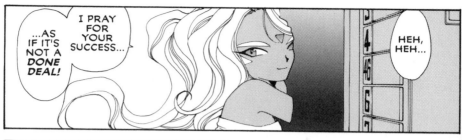

HEH, HEH...
I PRAY FOR YOUR SUCCESS...
...AS IF IT'S NOT A *DONE DEAL!*
...SORRY WE'RE SO LATE!
OH, HI!
FWK
ALL MY PRACTICE WENT INTO THIS...
...SO HERE-- PLEASE TRY A BITE.
...WHAT IS IT, BELL-DANDY?
I THOUGHT I REMEMBERED SEEING SOME TEA HERE BEFORE...
TEA? I DON'T REMEMBER SEEING ANY. ARE YOU SURE?

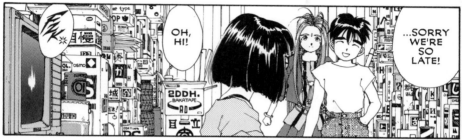

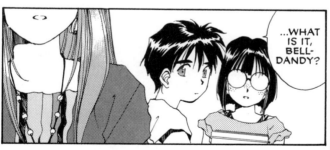

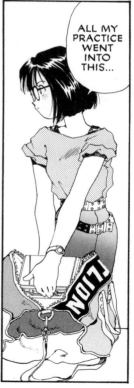

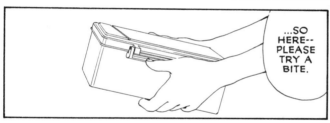

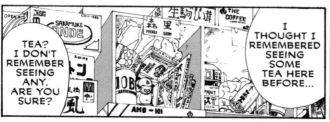

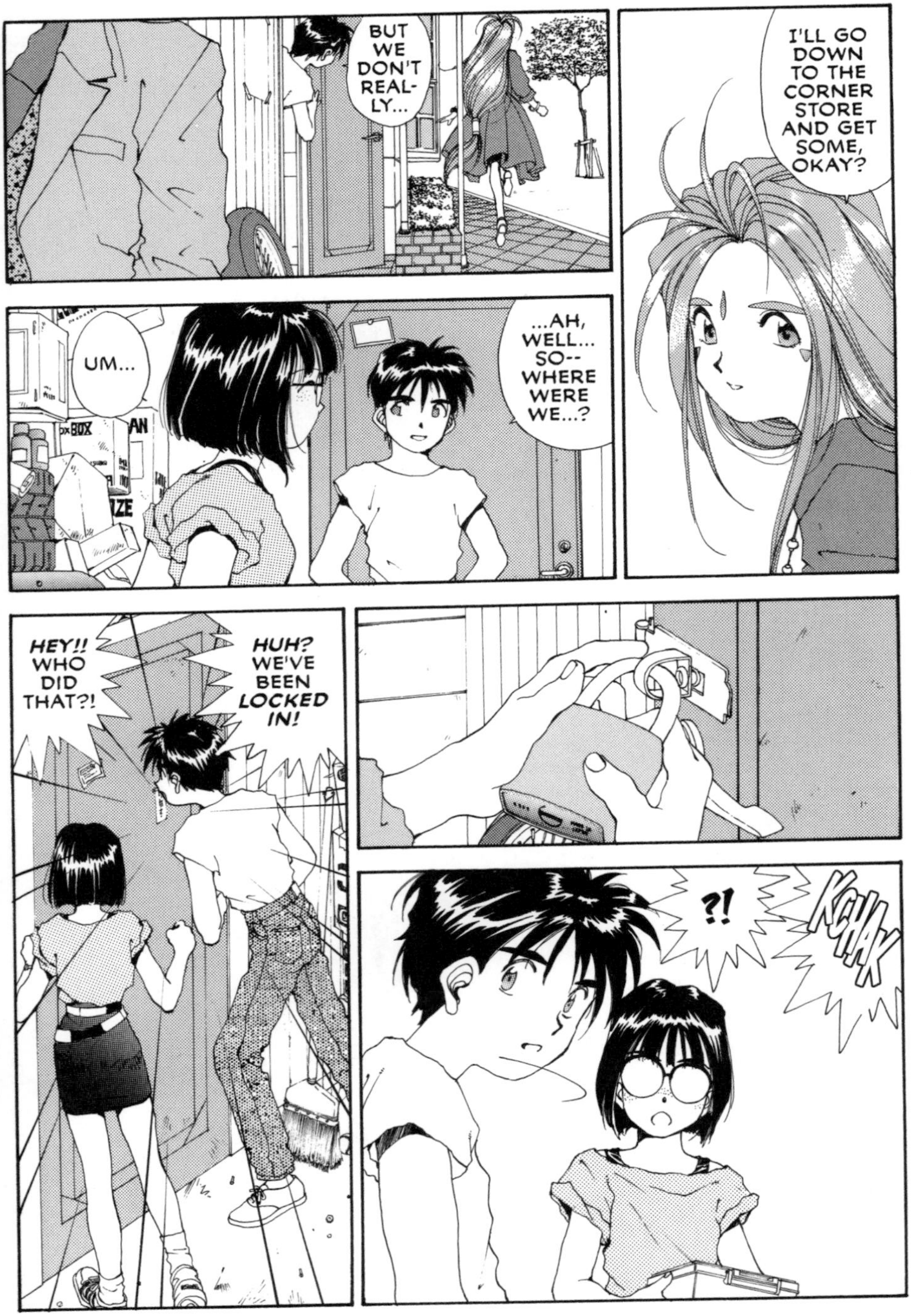
I'LL GO DOWN TO THE CORNER STORE AND GET SOME, OKAY?
BUT WE DON'T REALLY...
...AH, WELL... SO-- WHERE WERE WE...?
UM...
KCHAK
?!
HUH? WE'VE BEEN *LOCKED* IN!
HEY!! WHO DID THAT?!

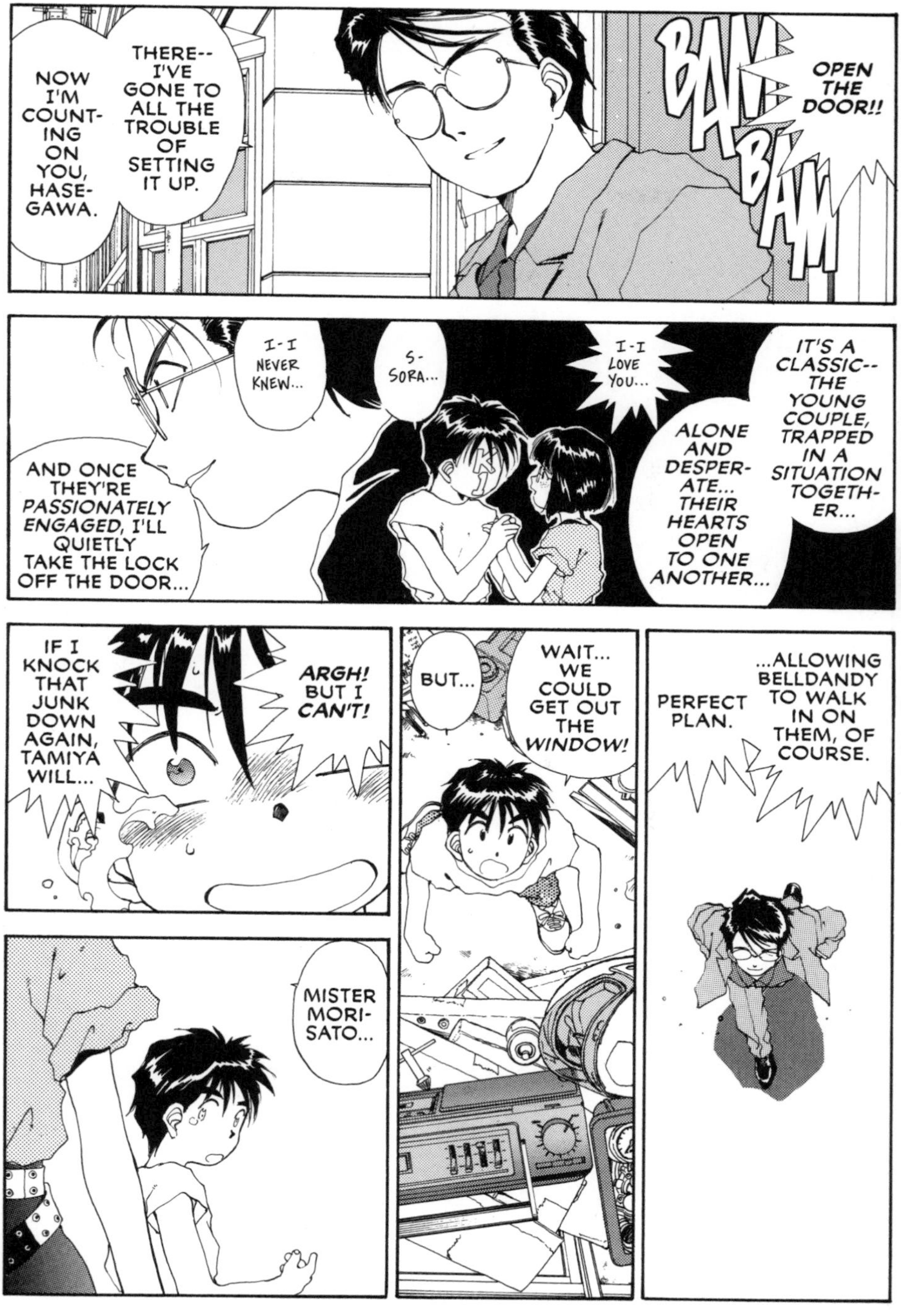
OPEN THE DOOR!!
BAM BAM BAM
THERE-- I'VE GONE TO ALL THE TROUBLE OF SETTING IT UP.
NOW I'M COUNTING ON YOU, HASEGAWA.
IT'S A CLASSIC-- THE YOUNG COUPLE, TRAPPED IN A SITUATION TOGETHER...
ALONE AND DESPERATE... THEIR HEARTS OPEN TO ONE ANOTHER...
I-I LOVE YOU...
S-SORA...
I-I NEVER KNEW...
AND ONCE THEY'RE *PASSIONATELY ENGAGED*, I'LL QUIETLY TAKE THE LOCK OFF THE DOOR...
...ALLOWING BELLDANDY TO WALK IN ON THEM, OF COURSE.
PERFECT PLAN.
WAIT... WE COULD GET OUT THE *WINDOW!*
BUT...
ARGH! BUT I *CAN'T!*
IF I KNOCK THAT JUNK DOWN AGAIN, TAMIYA WILL...
MISTER MORISATO...

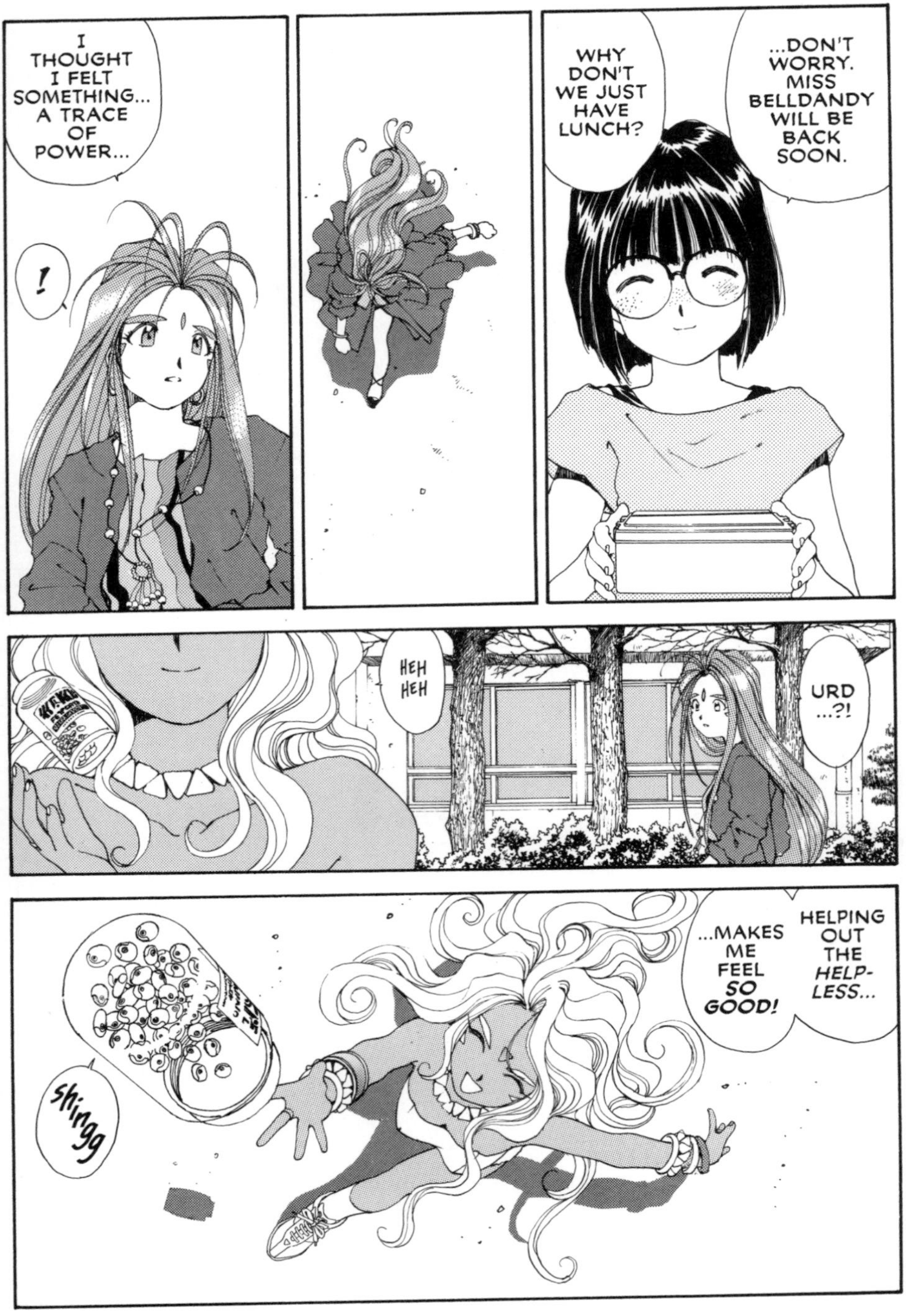
...DON'T WORRY. MISS BELLDANDY WILL BE BACK SOON.
WHY DON'T WE JUST HAVE LUNCH?
I THOUGHT I FELT SOMETHING... A TRACE OF POWER...
!
URD ...?!
HEH HEH
HELPING OUT THE *HELPLESS...*
...MAKES ME FEEL ***SO GOOD!***
shringg

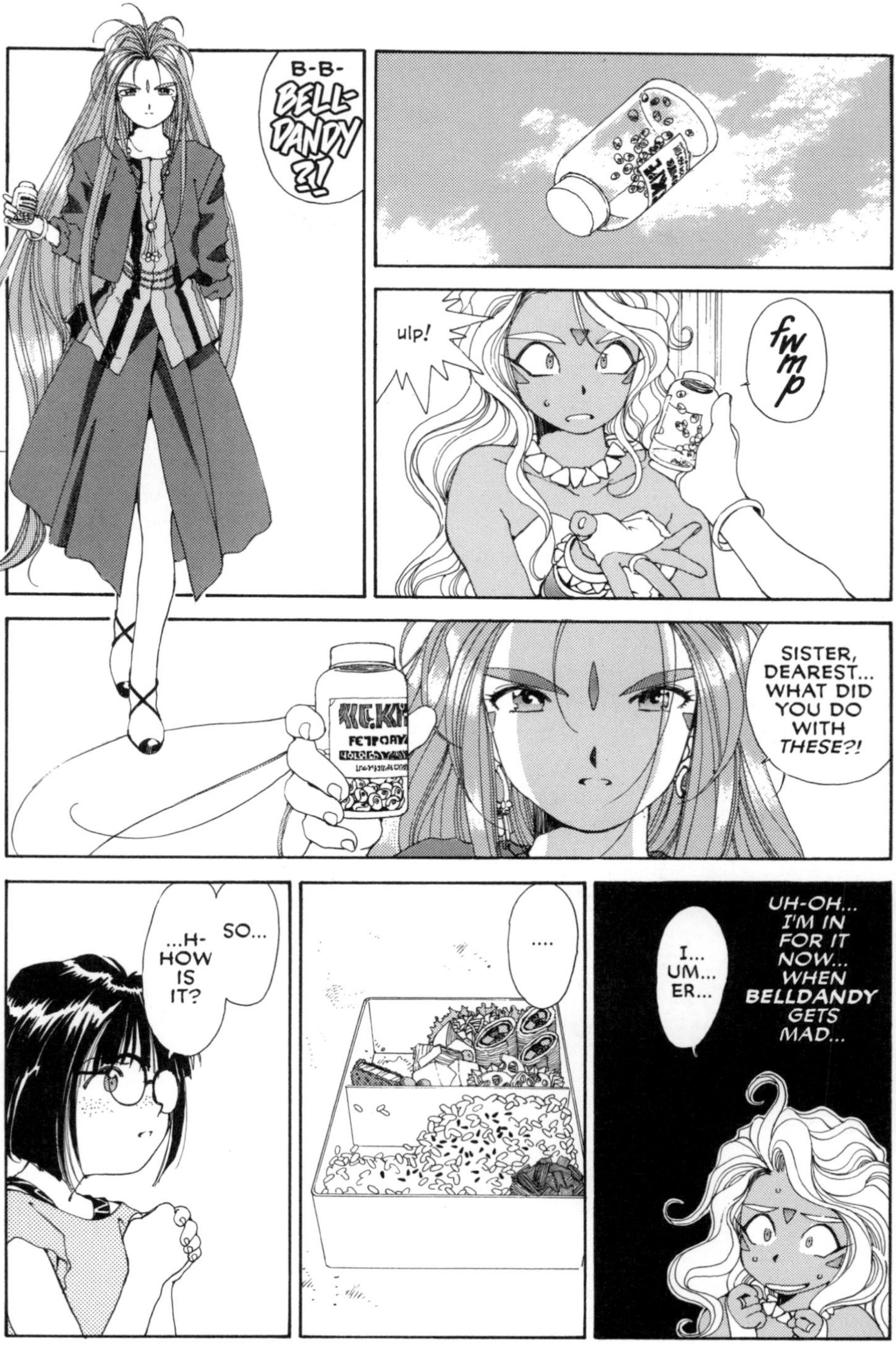
ulp!
fwmp
B-B-BELL-DANDY?!
SISTER, DEAREST... WHAT DID YOU DO WITH THESE?!
UH-OH... I'M IN FOR IT NOW... WHEN BELLDANDY GETS MAD...
I... UM... ER...
....
SO...
...H-HOW IS IT?

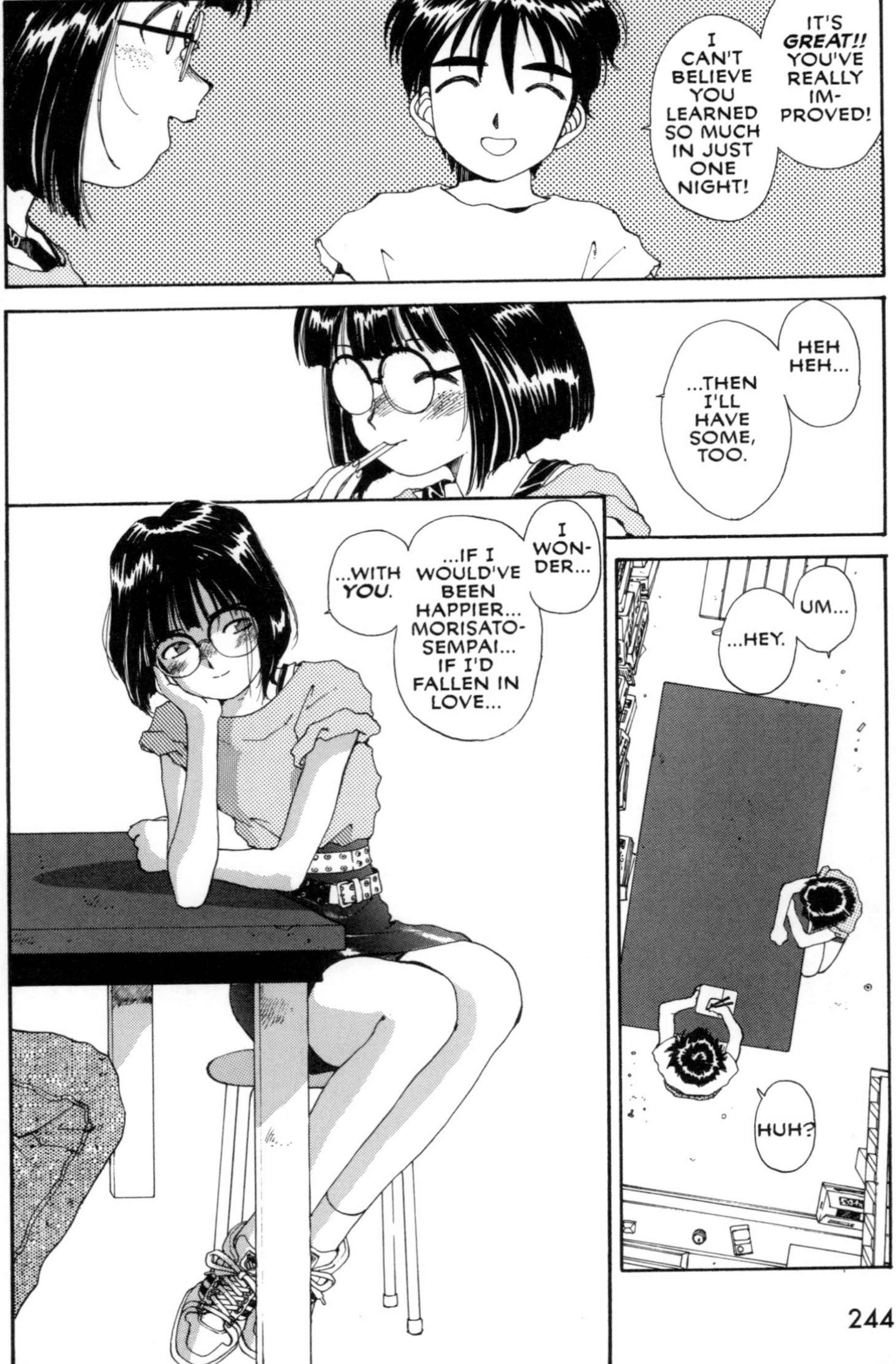
IT'S GREAT!! YOU'VE REALLY IM-PROVED!
I CAN'T BELIEVE YOU LEARNED SO MUCH IN JUST ONE NIGHT!
HEH HEH...
...THEN I'LL HAVE SOME, TOO.
UM...
...HEY.
HUH?
I WONDER...
...IF I WOULD'VE BEEN HAPPIER... MORISATO-SEMPAI... IF I'D FALLEN IN LOVE...
...WITH YOU.

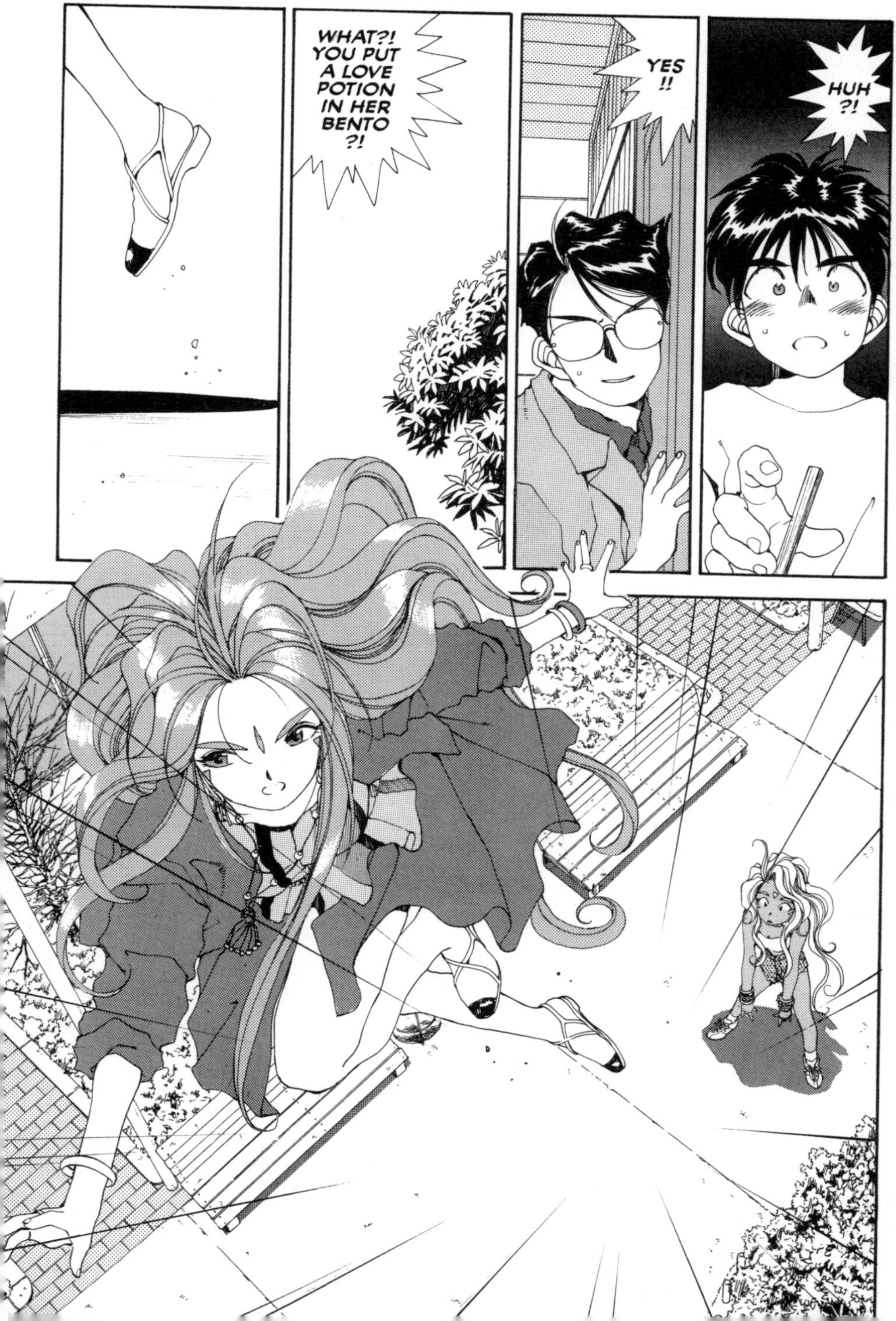
HUH ?!
YES !!
WHAT?! YOU PUT A LOVE POTION IN HER BENTO ?!

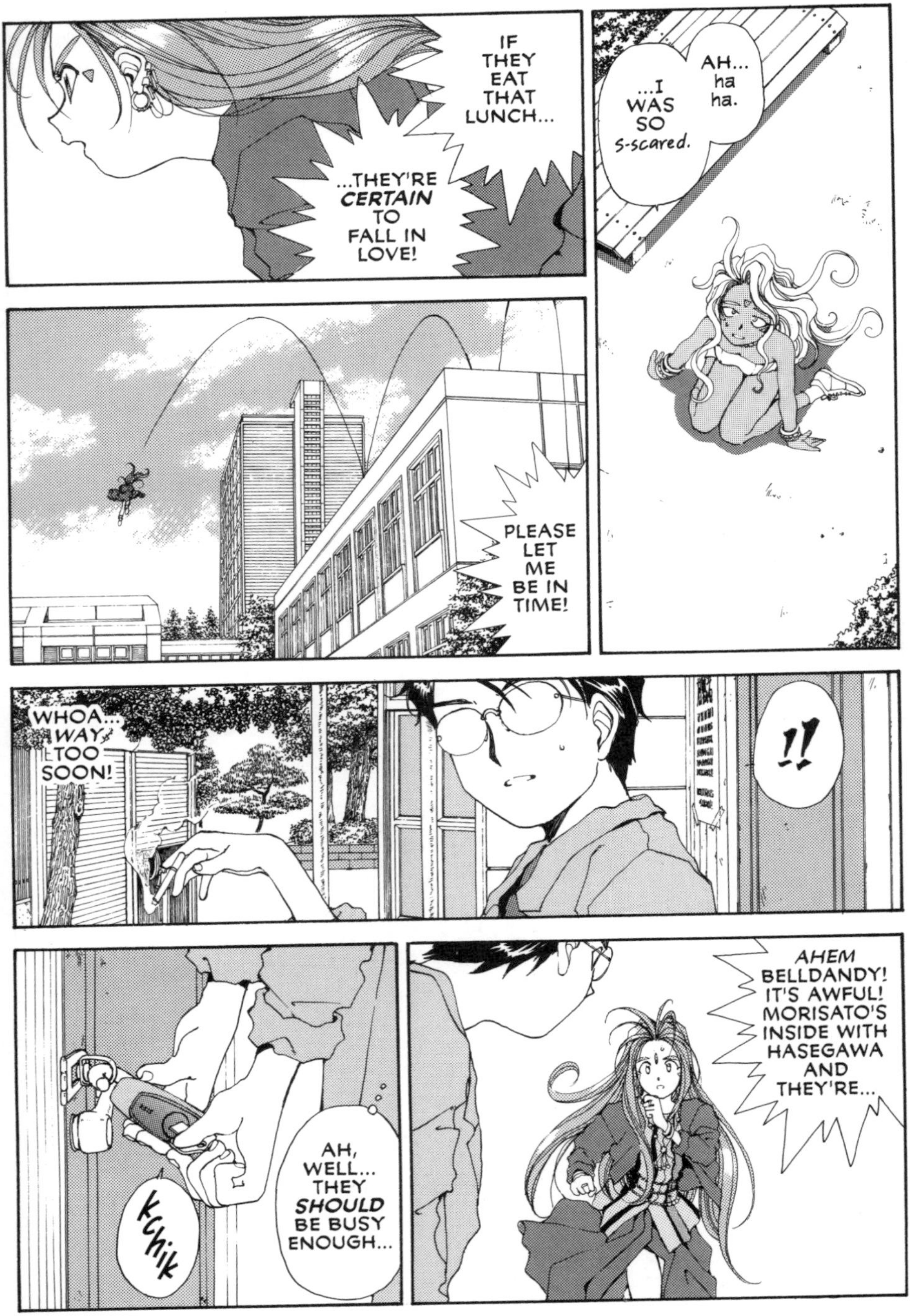
AH... ha ha.
...I WAS SO s-scared.
IF THEY EAT THAT LUNCH...
...THEY'RE CERTAIN TO FALL IN LOVE!
PLEASE LET ME BE IN TIME!
!!
WHOA... WAY TOO SOON!
AHEM BELLDANDY! IT'S AWFUL! MORISATO'S INSIDE WITH HASEGAWA AND THEY'RE...
AH, WELL... THEY SHOULD BE BUSY ENOUGH...
kchik

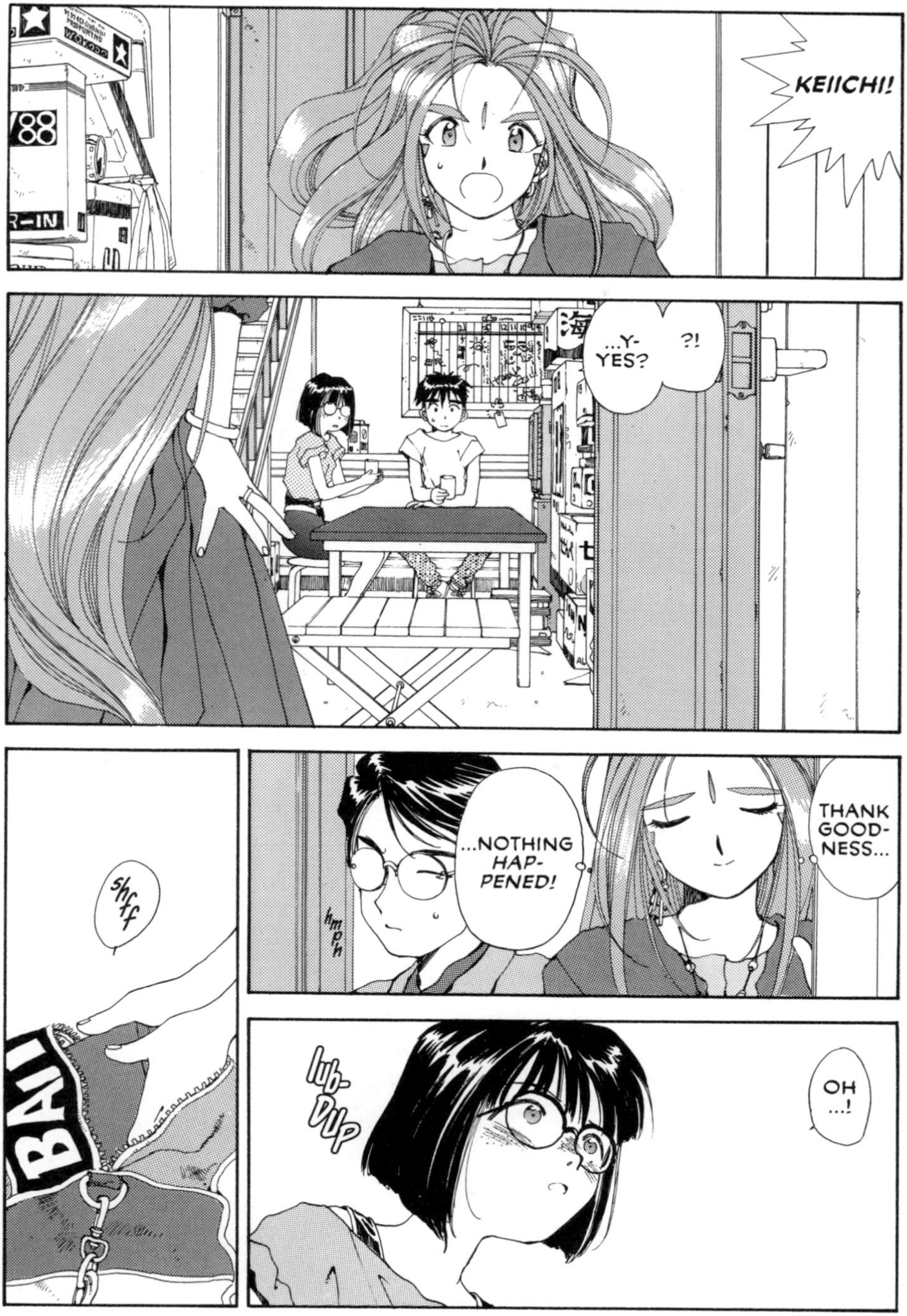
KEIICHI!
?!
...Y-YES?
THANK GOODNESS...
...NOTHING HAPPENED!
hmph
OH ...!
lub-DUP
shfff

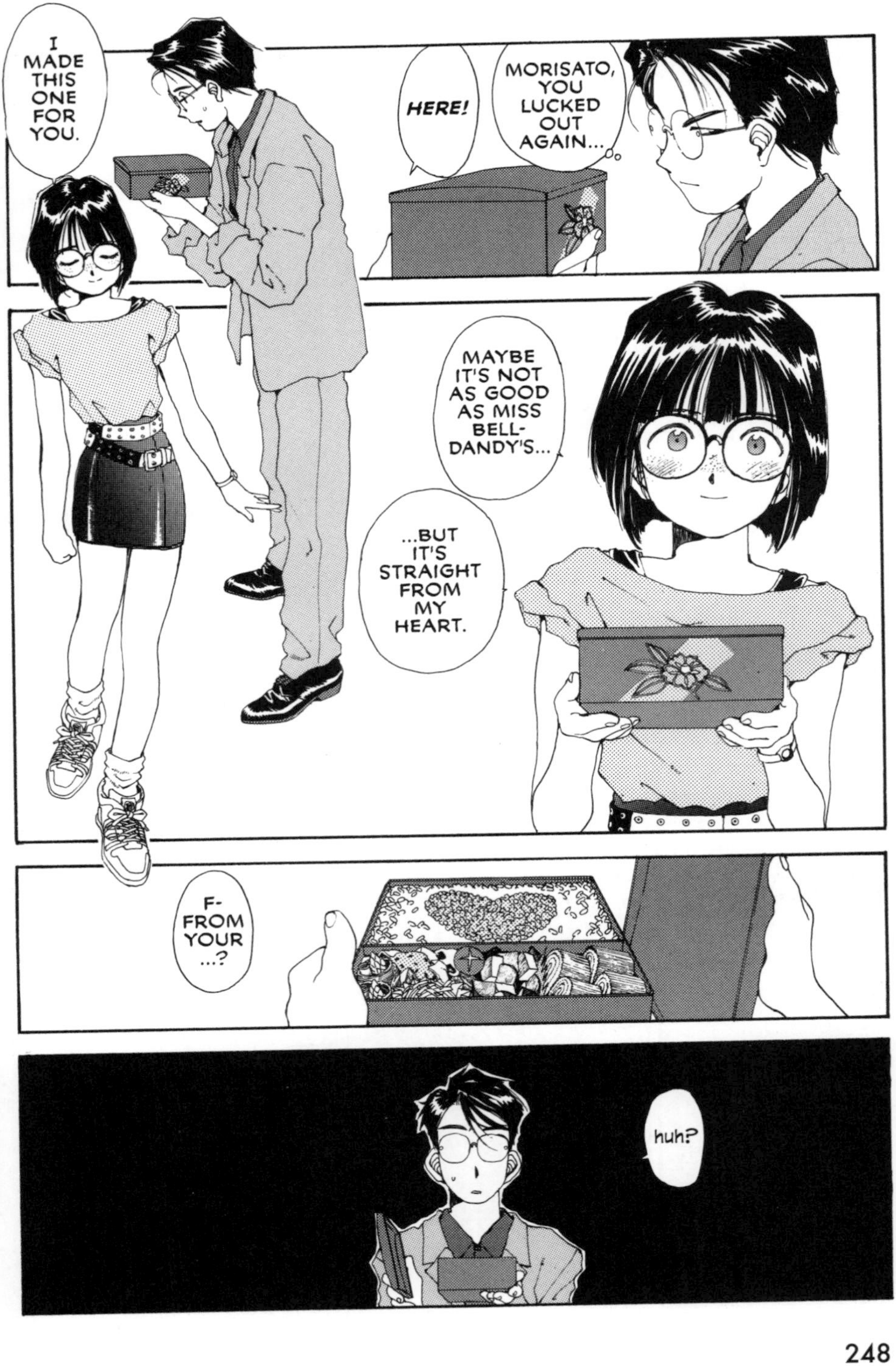
MORISATO, YOU LUCKED OUT AGAIN...
HERE!
I MADE THIS ONE FOR YOU.
MAYBE IT'S NOT AS GOOD AS MISS BELL-DANDY'S...
...BUT IT'S STRAIGHT FROM MY HEART.
F-FROM YOUR ...?
huh?

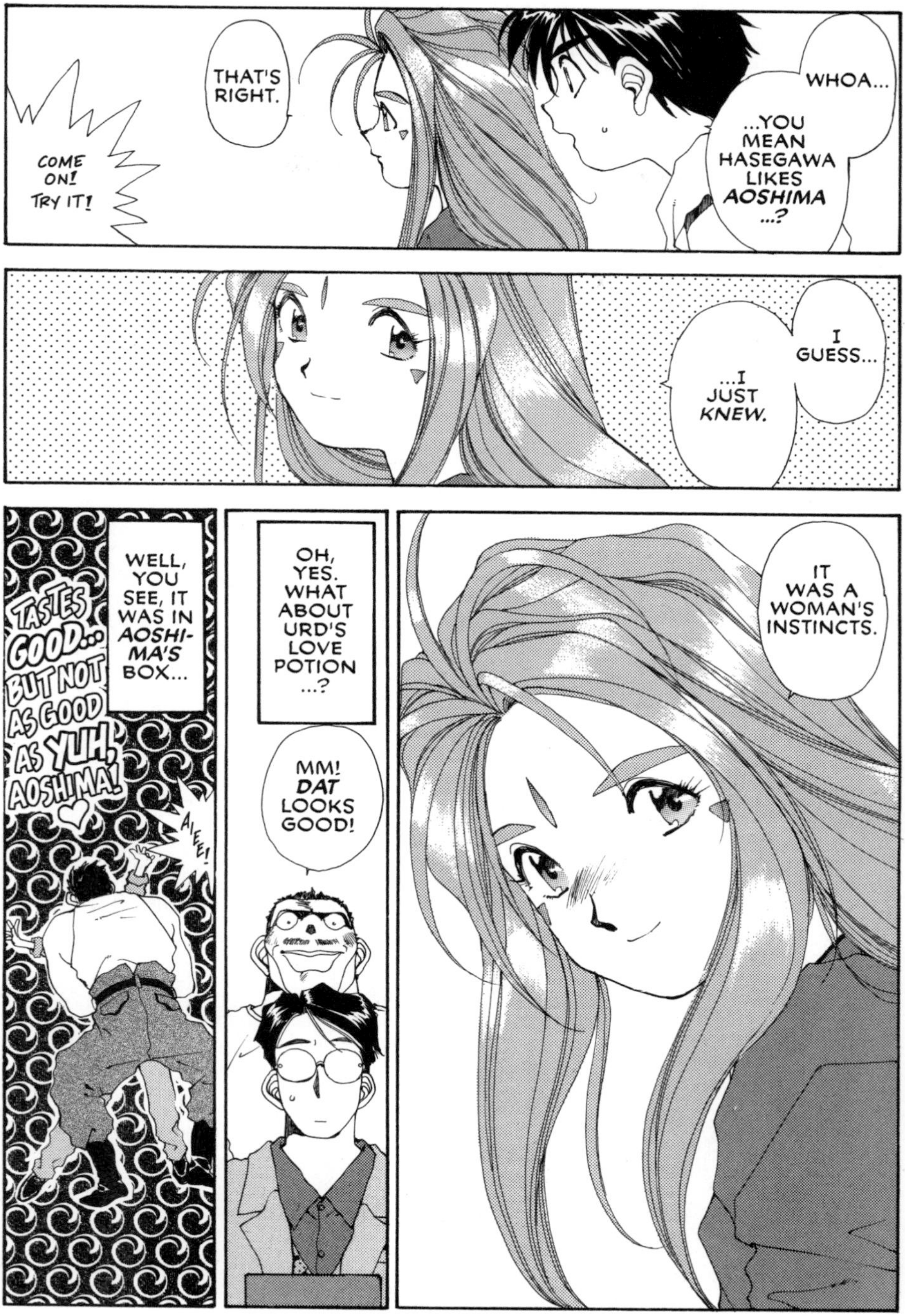
WHOA...
...YOU MEAN HASEGAWA LIKES AOSHIMA ...?
THAT'S RIGHT.
COME ON! TRY IT!
I GUESS...
...I JUST KNEW.
IT WAS A WOMAN'S INSTINCTS.
OH, YES. WHAT ABOUT URD'S LOVE POTION ...?
MM! DAT LOOKS GOOD!
WELL, YOU SEE, IT WAS IN AOSHIMA'S BOX...
TASTES GOOD... BUT NOT AS GOOD AS YUH, AOSHIMA! ♥
AIEEE!

THE ADVENTURES OF MINI-URD

Now with added MINI-SKULD!

LET'S START A BAND!

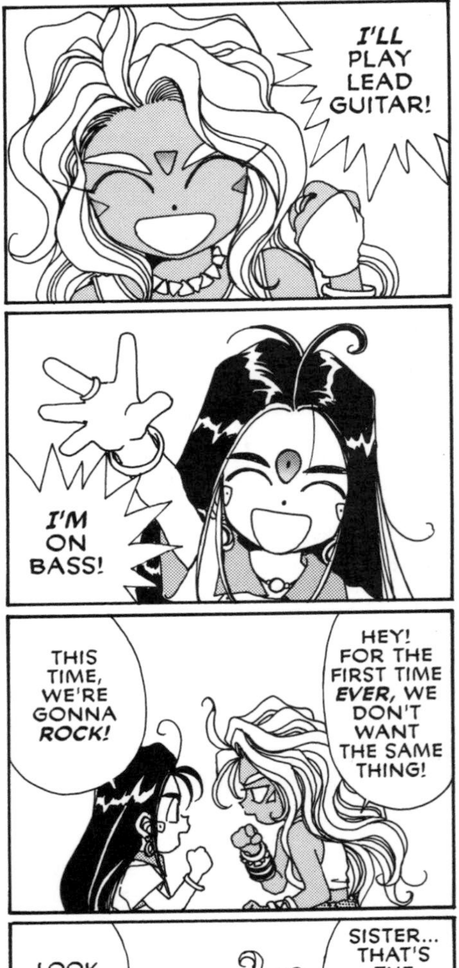
I'LL PLAY LEAD GUITAR!
I'M ON BASS!
HEY! FOR THE FIRST TIME EVER, WE DON'T WANT THE SAME THING!
THIS TIME, WE'RE GONNA ROCK!
SISTER... THAT'S THE WRONG KIND OF BASS.
LOOK WHO'S TALKING!

(INSERT DRUMMER JOKE HERE)

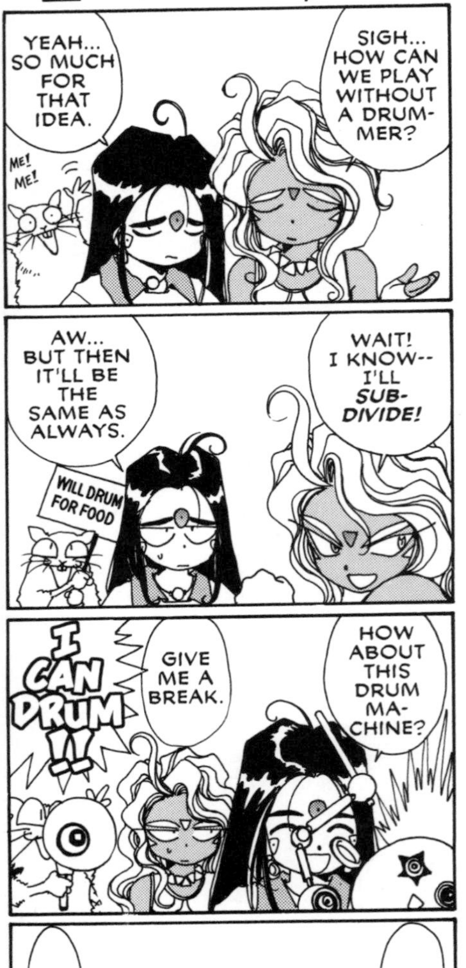
SIGH... HOW CAN WE PLAY WITHOUT A DRUMMER?
YEAH... SO MUCH FOR THAT IDEA.
ME! ME!
WAIT! I KNOW-- I'LL SUB-DIVIDE!
AW... BUT THEN IT'LL BE THE SAME AS ALWAYS.
WILL DRUM FOR FOOD
HOW ABOUT THIS DRUM MACHINE?
GIVE ME A BREAK.
I CAN DRUM!!
...
...

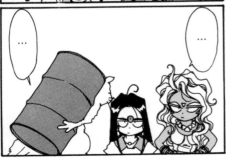

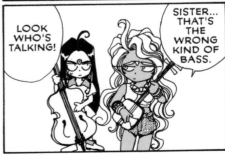

◆ YOU TOO CAN PLAY DRUMS! ◆

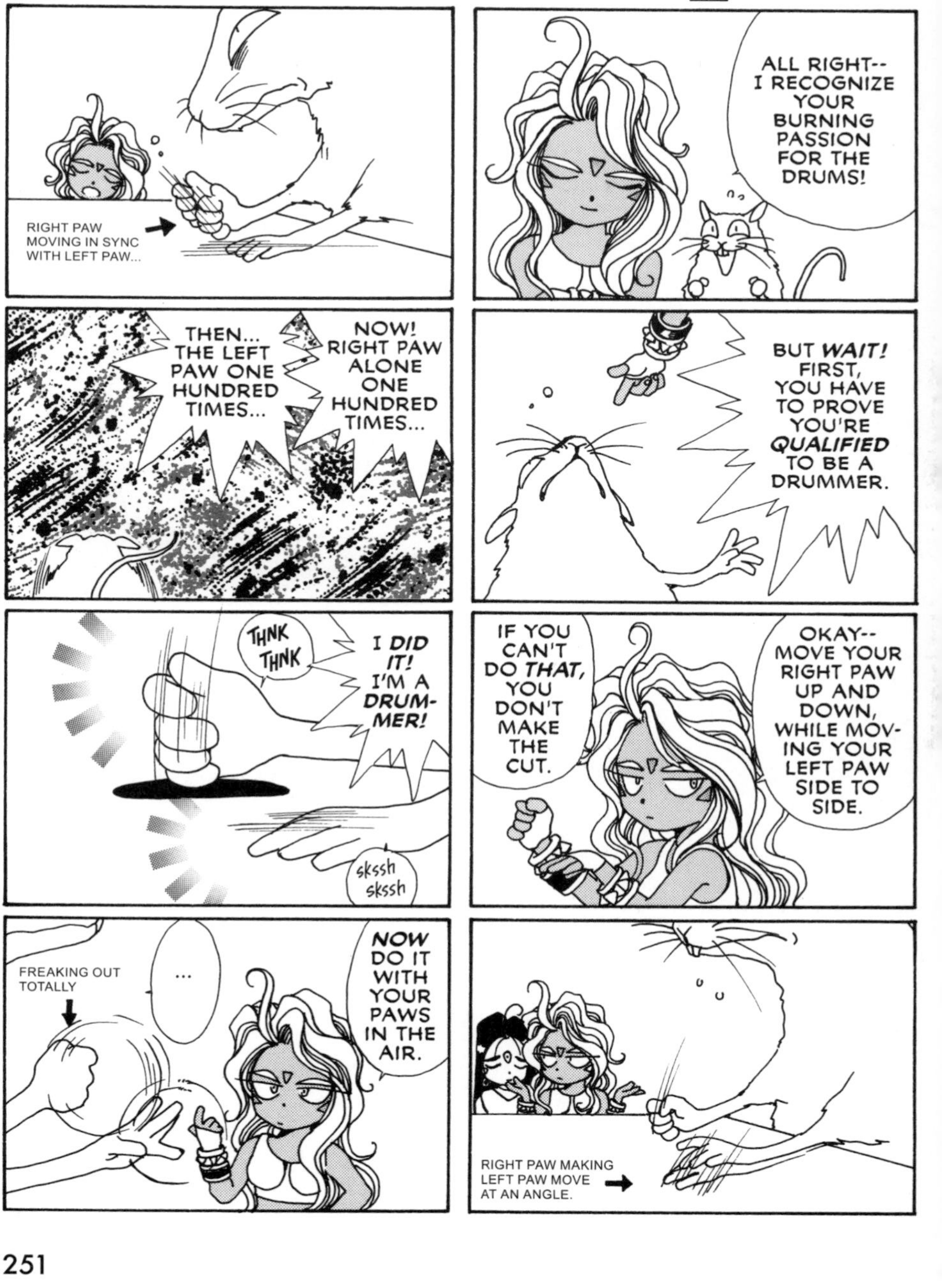

ALL RIGHT-- I RECOGNIZE YOUR BURNING PASSION FOR THE DRUMS!
RIGHT PAW MOVING IN SYNC WITH LEFT PAW...
BUT *WAIT!* FIRST, YOU HAVE TO PROVE YOU'RE ***QUALIFIED*** TO BE A DRUMMER.
NOW! RIGHT PAW ALONE ONE HUNDRED TIMES...
THEN... THE LEFT PAW ONE HUNDRED TIMES...
OKAY-- MOVE YOUR RIGHT PAW UP AND DOWN, WHILE MOVING YOUR LEFT PAW SIDE TO SIDE.
IF YOU CAN'T DO ***THAT,*** YOU DON'T MAKE THE CUT.
I ***DID IT!*** I'M A ***DRUMMER!***
THNK THNK
skssh skssh
RIGHT PAW MAKING LEFT PAW MOVE AT AN ANGLE.
NOW DO IT WITH YOUR PAWS IN THE AIR.
...
FREAKING OUT TOTALLY

SPECIAL TRAINING: OBSERVATIONS ON PRACTICAL TECHNIQUE

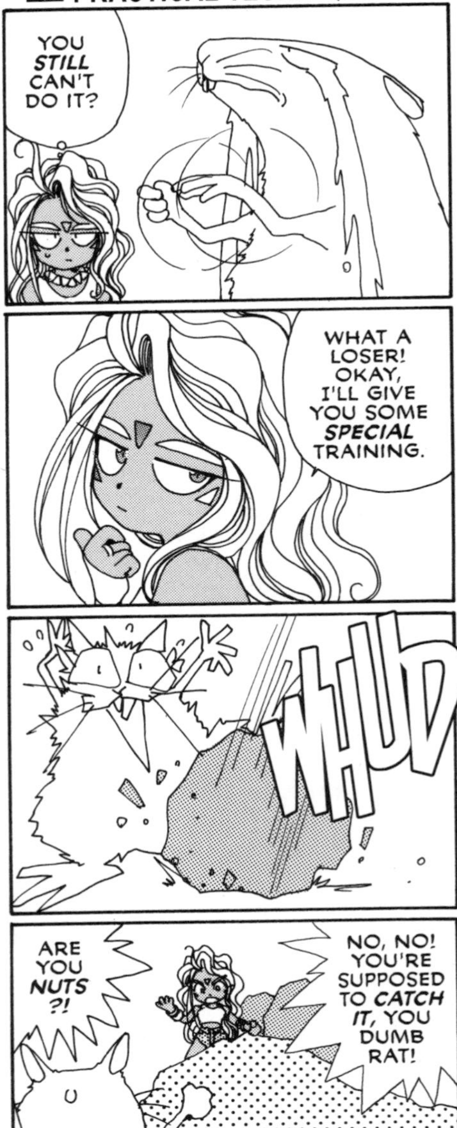
YOU *STILL* CAN'T DO IT?
WHAT A LOSER! OKAY, I'LL GIVE YOU SOME *SPECIAL* TRAINING.
WHUD
ARE YOU *NUTS* ?!
NO, NO! YOU'RE SUPPOSED TO *CATCH IT,* YOU DUMB RAT!

SPECIAL TRAINING VERSUS RESULTS: A STUDY IN NON-CAUSALITY

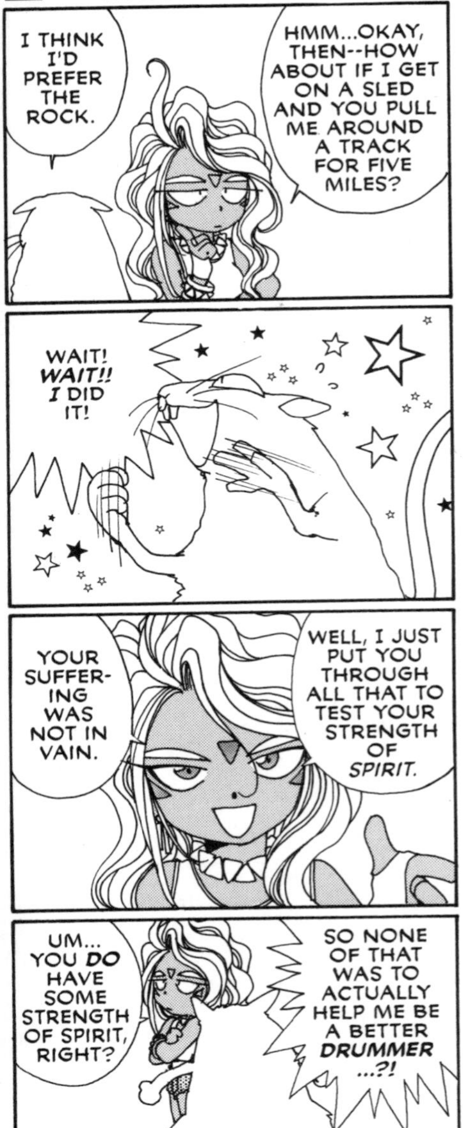
HMM...OKAY, THEN--HOW ABOUT IF I GET ON A SLED AND YOU PULL ME AROUND A TRACK FOR FIVE MILES?
I THINK I'D PREFER THE ROCK.
WAIT! *WAIT!! I* DID IT!
WELL, I JUST PUT YOU THROUGH ALL THAT TO TEST YOUR STRENGTH OF *SPIRIT.*
YOUR SUFFERING WAS NOT IN VAIN.
SO NONE OF THAT WAS TO ACTUALLY HELP ME BE A BETTER *DRUMMER* ...?!
UM... YOU *DO* HAVE SOME STRENGTH OF SPIRIT, RIGHT?

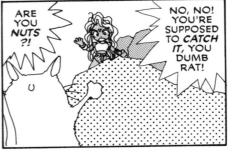

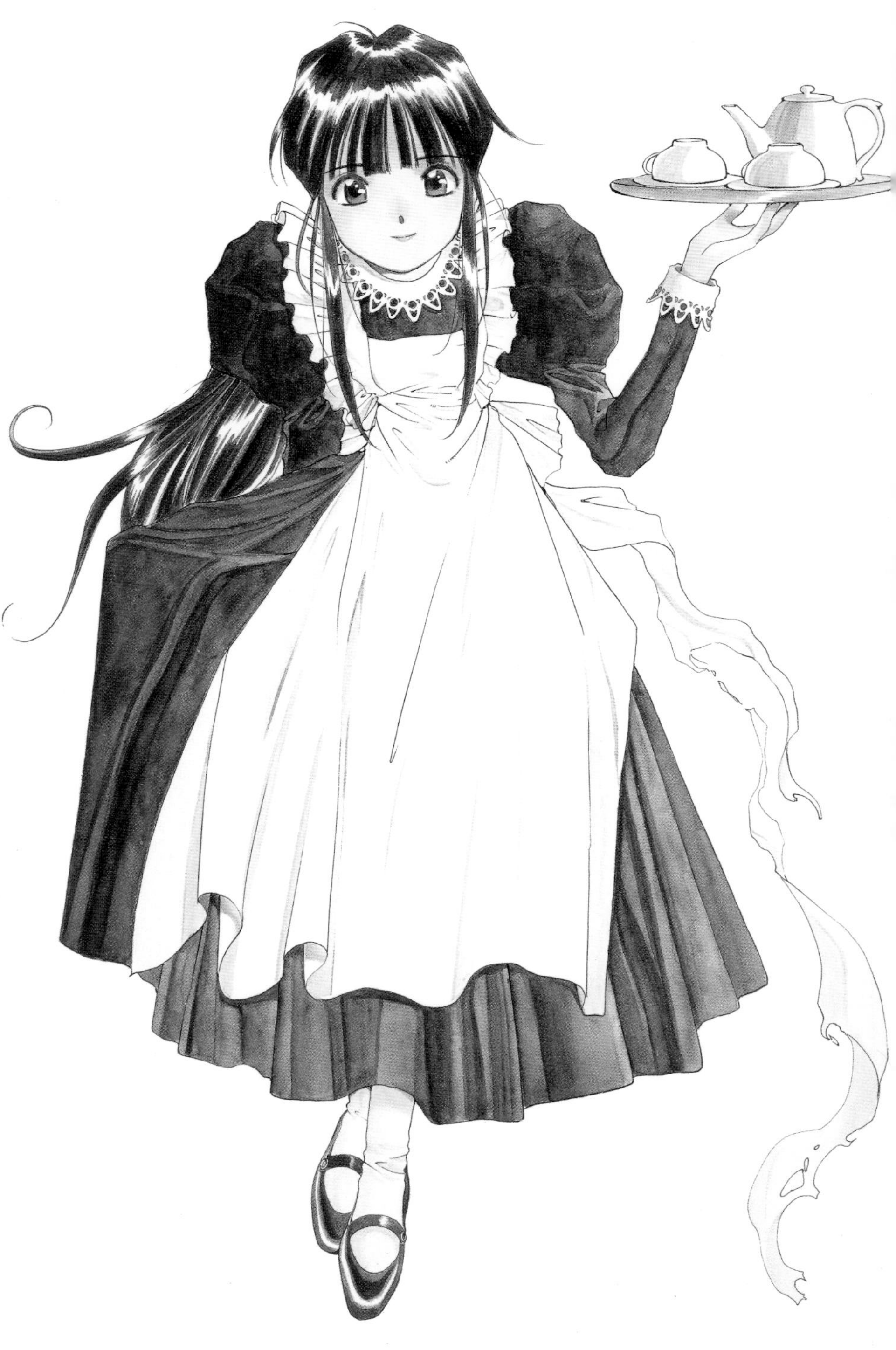

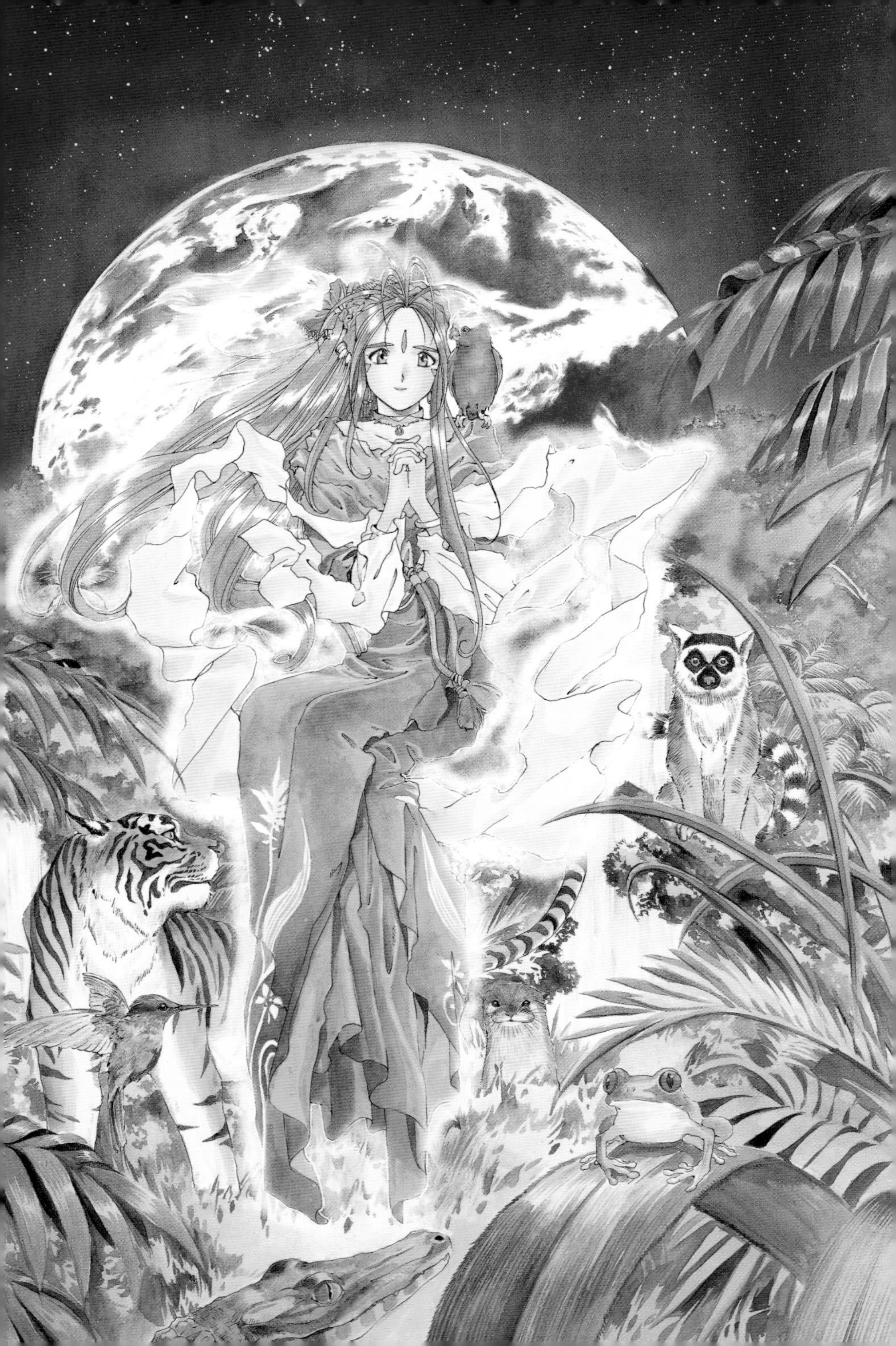

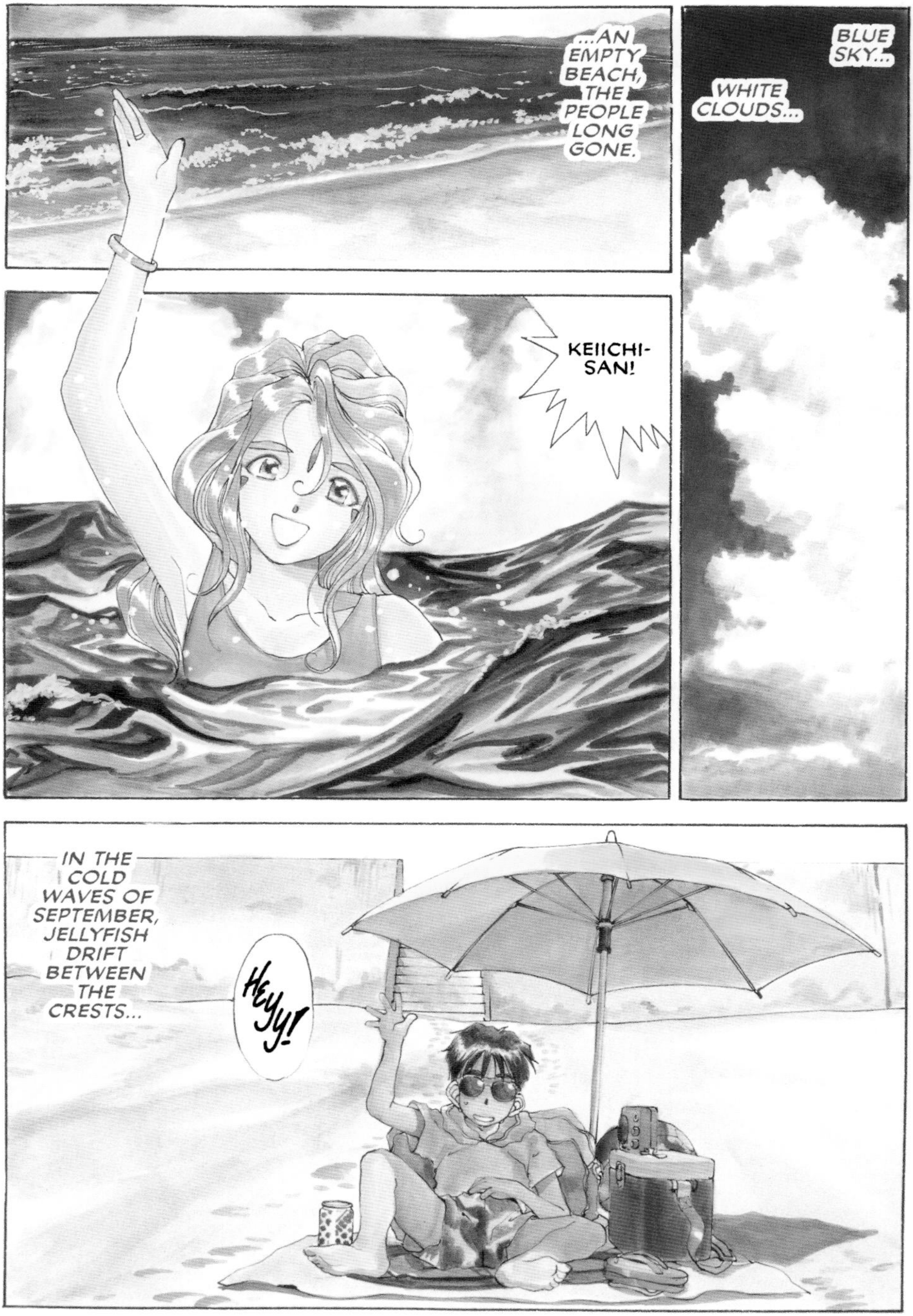
BLUE SKY...
WHITE CLOUDS...
...AN EMPTY BEACH, THE PEOPLE LONG GONE.
KEIICHI-SAN!
HEYY!
IN THE COLD WAVES OF SEPTEMBER, JELLYFISH DRIFT BETWEEN THE CRESTS...

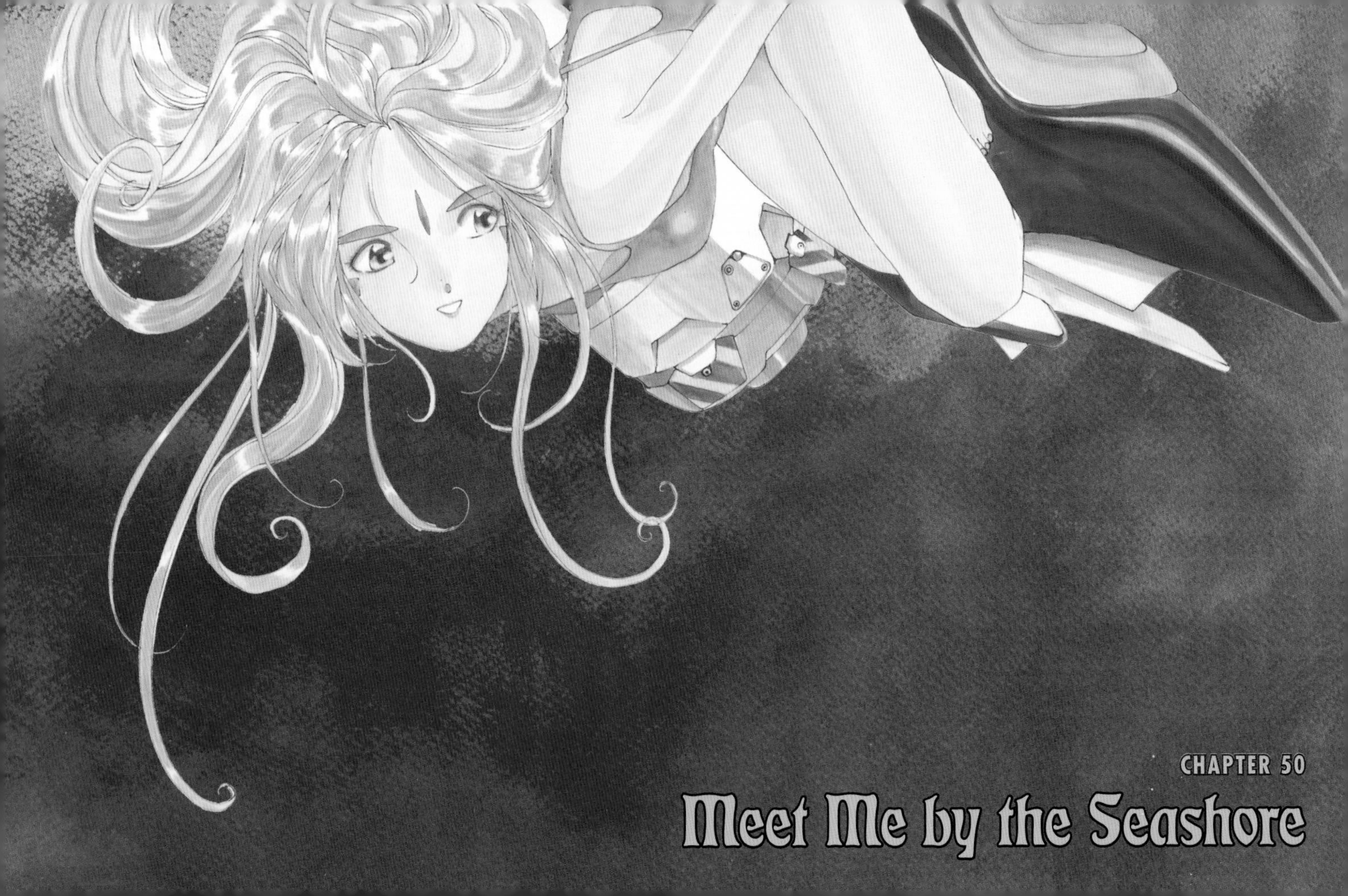
CHAPTER 50
Meet Me by the Seashore

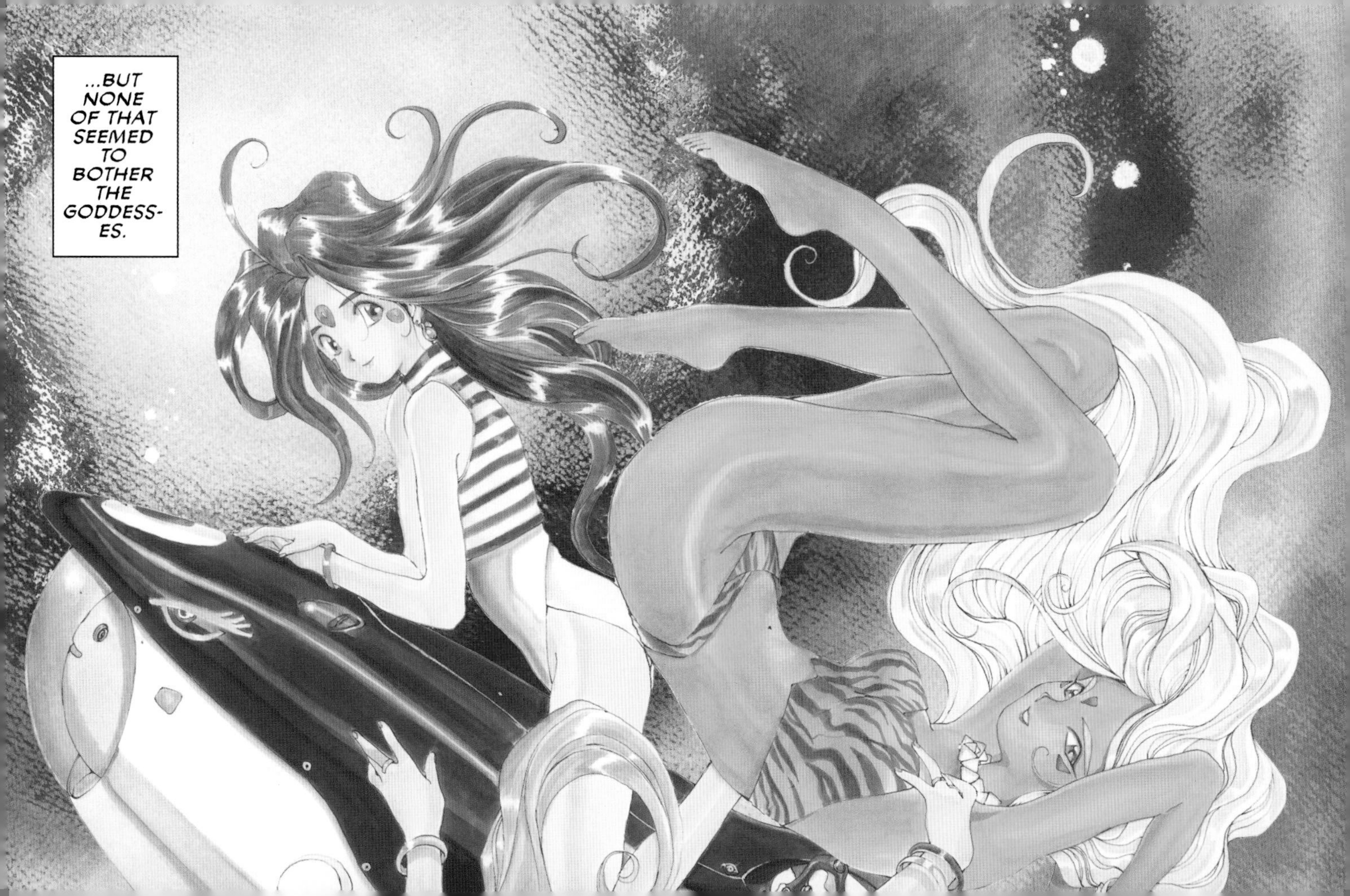
...BUT NONE OF THAT SEEMED TO BOTHER THE GODDESS-ES.

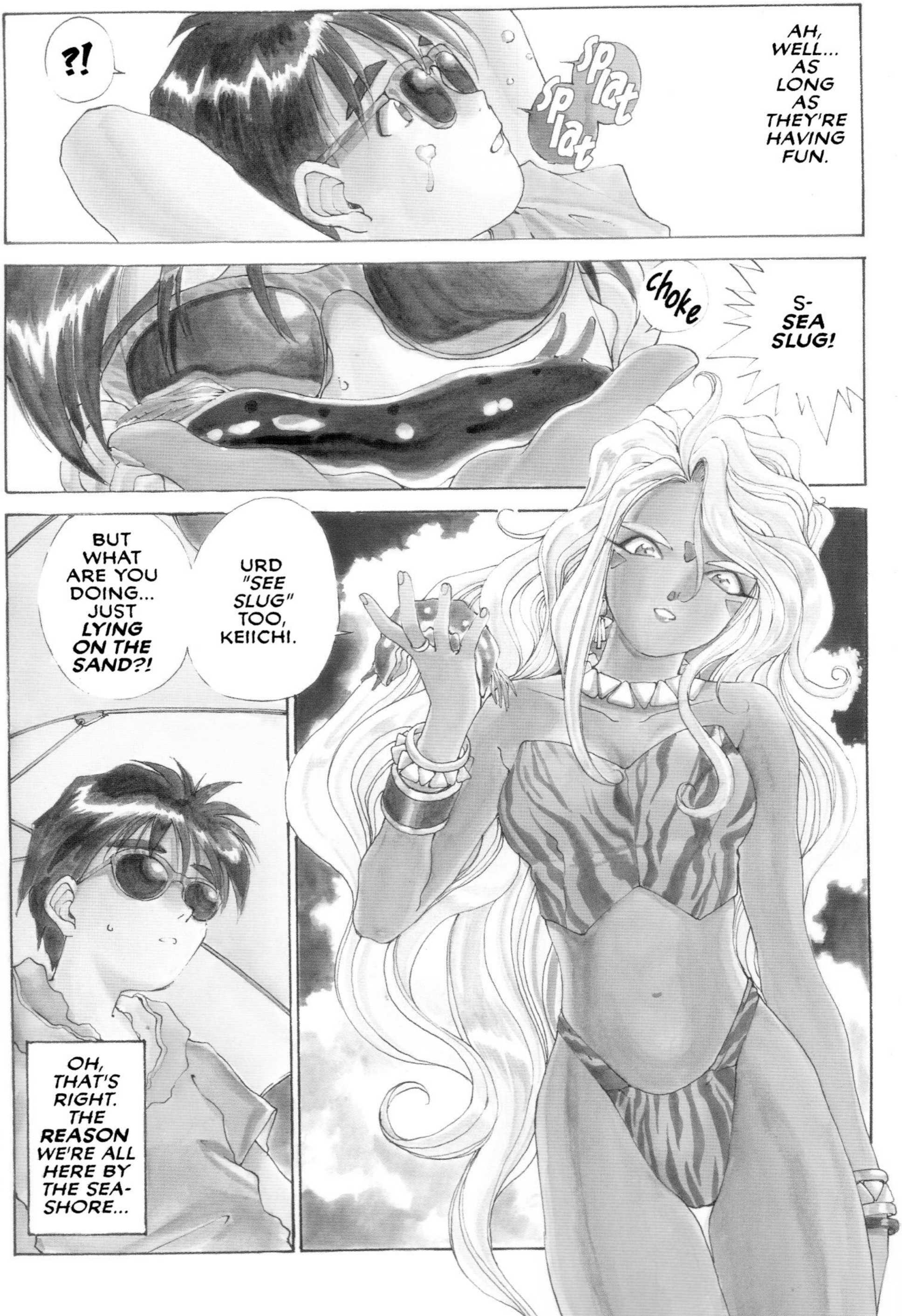
AH, WELL... AS LONG AS THEY'RE HAVING FUN.
splat splat
?!
S-SEA SLUG!
choke
URD "SEE SLUG" TOO, KEIICHI.
BUT WHAT ARE YOU DOING... JUST LYING ON THE SAND?!
OH, THAT'S RIGHT. THE REASON WE'RE ALL HERE BY THE SEA-SHORE...

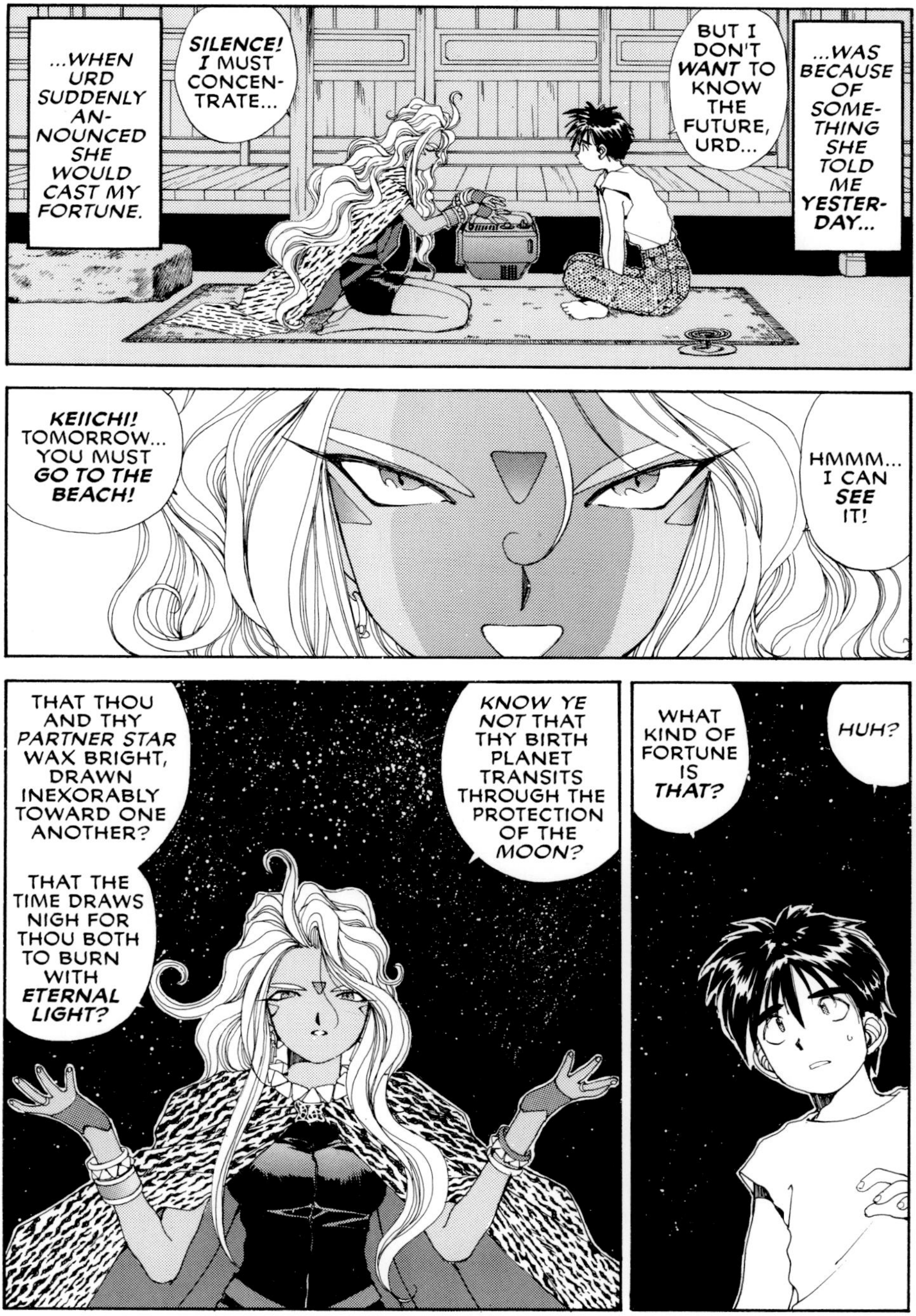
...WAS BECAUSE OF SOMETHING SHE TOLD ME YESTERDAY...
BUT I DON'T WANT TO KNOW THE FUTURE, URD...
SILENCE! I MUST CONCENTRATE...
...WHEN URD SUDDENLY ANNOUNCED SHE WOULD CAST MY FORTUNE.
HMMM... I CAN SEE IT!
KEIICHI! TOMORROW... YOU MUST GO TO THE BEACH!
HUH?
WHAT KIND OF FORTUNE IS THAT?
KNOW YE NOT THAT THY BIRTH PLANET TRANSITS THROUGH THE PROTECTION OF THE MOON?
THAT THOU AND THY PARTNER STAR WAX BRIGHT, DRAWN INEXORABLY TOWARD ONE ANOTHER?
THAT THE TIME DRAWS NIGH FOR THOU BOTH TO BURN WITH ETERNAL LIGHT?

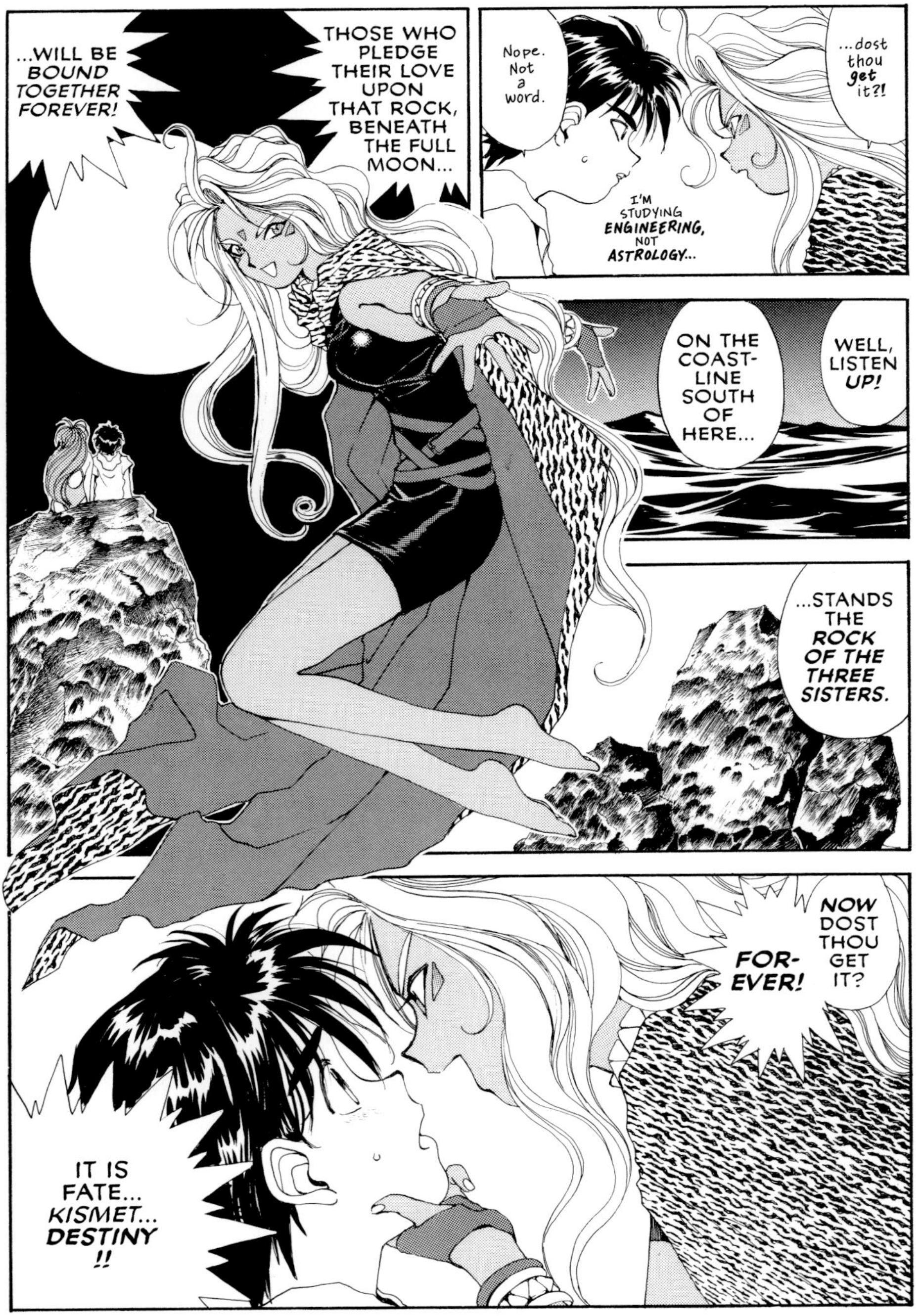
...dost thou get it?!
Nope. Not a word.
I'M STUDYING ENGINEERING, NOT ASTROLOGY...
WELL, LISTEN UP!
ON THE COAST-LINE SOUTH OF HERE...
...STANDS THE ROCK OF THE THREE SISTERS.
THOSE WHO PLEDGE THEIR LOVE UPON THAT ROCK, BENEATH THE FULL MOON...
...WILL BE BOUND TOGETHER FOREVER!
NOW DOST THOU GET IT?
FOR-EVER!
IT IS FATE... KISMET... DESTINY !!

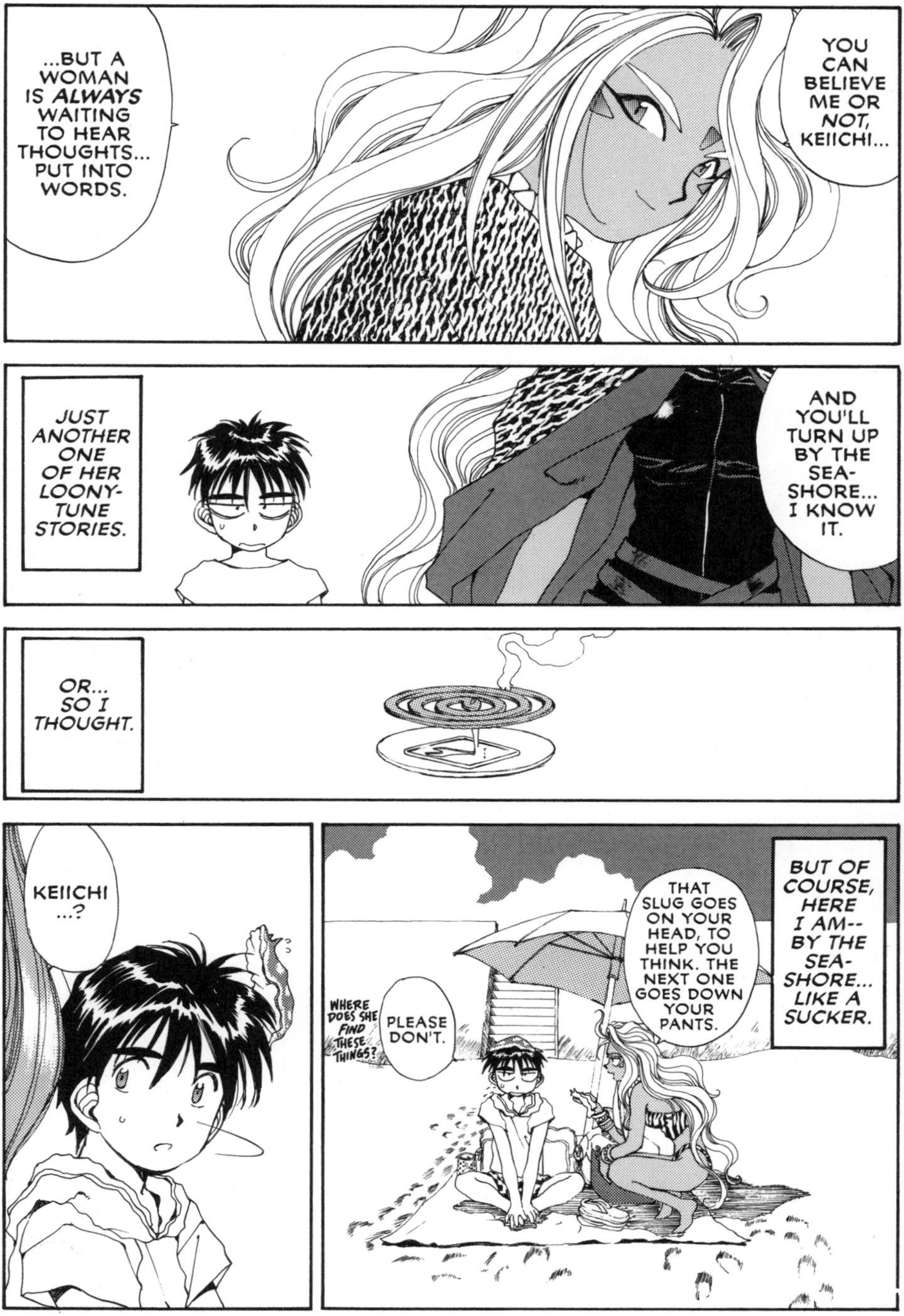
YOU CAN BELIEVE ME OR *NOT,* KEIICHI...
...BUT A WOMAN IS ***ALWAYS*** WAITING TO HEAR THOUGHTS... PUT INTO WORDS.
AND YOU'LL TURN UP BY THE SEA-SHORE... I KNOW IT.
JUST ANOTHER ONE OF HER LOONY-TUNE STORIES.
OR... SO I THOUGHT.
BUT OF COURSE, HERE I AM-- BY THE SEA-SHORE... LIKE A SUCKER.
THAT SLUG GOES ON YOUR HEAD, TO HELP YOU THINK. THE NEXT ONE GOES DOWN YOUR PANTS.
PLEASE DON'T.
WHERE DOES SHE *FIND* THESE THINGS?
KEIICHI ...?

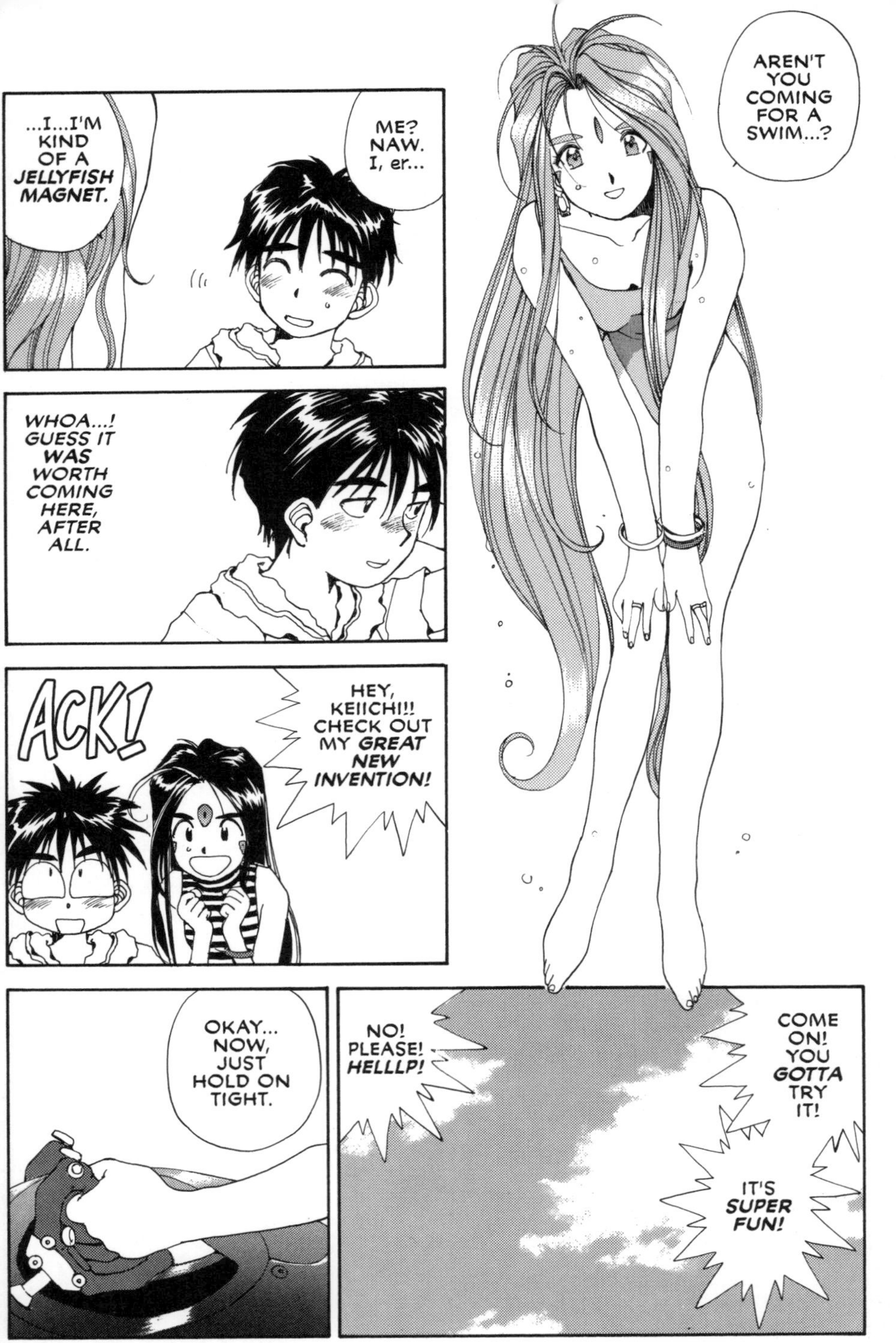
AREN'T YOU COMING FOR A SWIM...?
ME? NAW. I, er...
...I...I'M KIND OF A JELLYFISH MAGNET.
WHOA...! GUESS IT WAS WORTH COMING HERE, AFTER ALL.
HEY, KEIICHI!! CHECK OUT MY GREAT NEW INVENTION!
ACK!
COME ON! YOU GOTTA TRY IT!
NO! PLEASE! HELLLP!
IT'S SUPER FUN!
OKAY... NOW, JUST HOLD ON TIGHT.

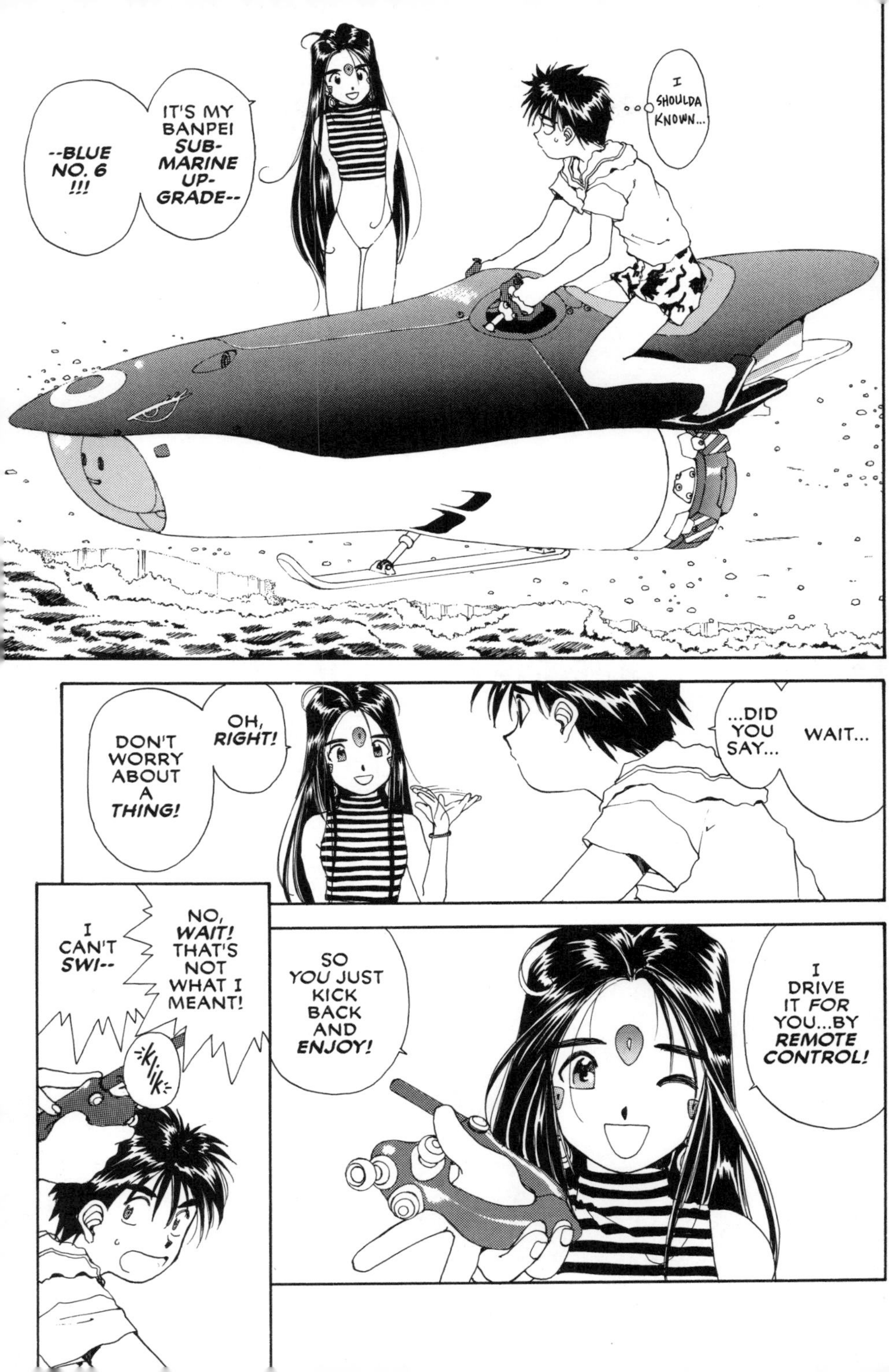
I SHOULDA KNOWN...
IT'S MY BANPEI SUB-MARINE UP-GRADE--
--BLUE NO. 6 !!!
WAIT...
...DID YOU SAY...
OH, RIGHT!
DON'T WORRY ABOUT A THING!
I DRIVE IT FOR YOU...BY REMOTE CONTROL!
SO YOU JUST KICK BACK AND ENJOY!
NO, WAIT! THAT'S NOT WHAT I MEANT!
I CAN'T SWI--
KLIK

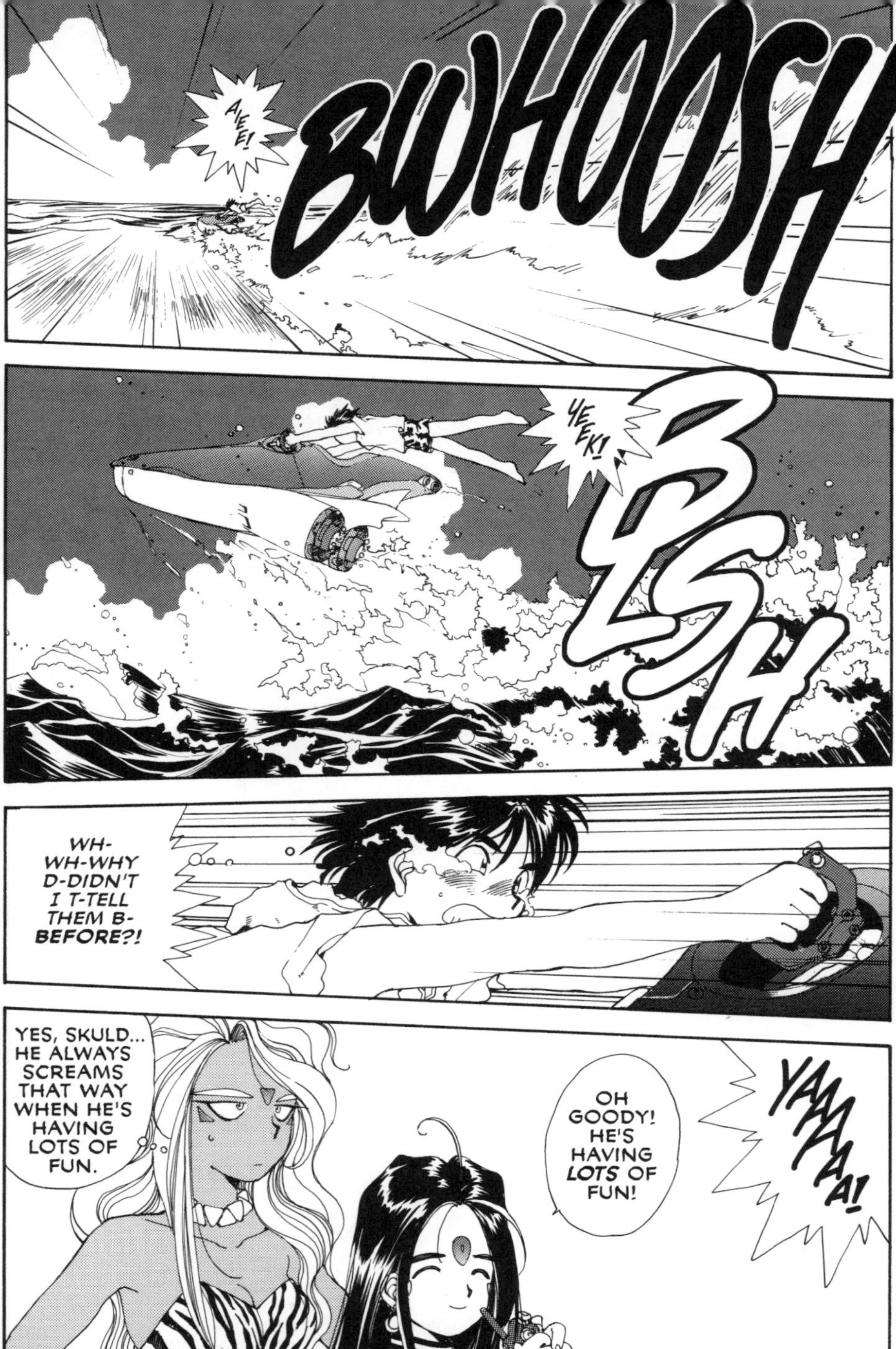
AIEE!
BWHOOSH
YEEK!
BLSH
WH- WH-WHY D-DIDN'T I T-TELL THEM B- BEFORE?!
YAAAAA!
OH GOODY! HE'S HAVING LOTS OF FUN!
YES, SKULD... HE ALWAYS SCREAMS THAT WAY WHEN HE'S HAVING LOTS OF FUN.

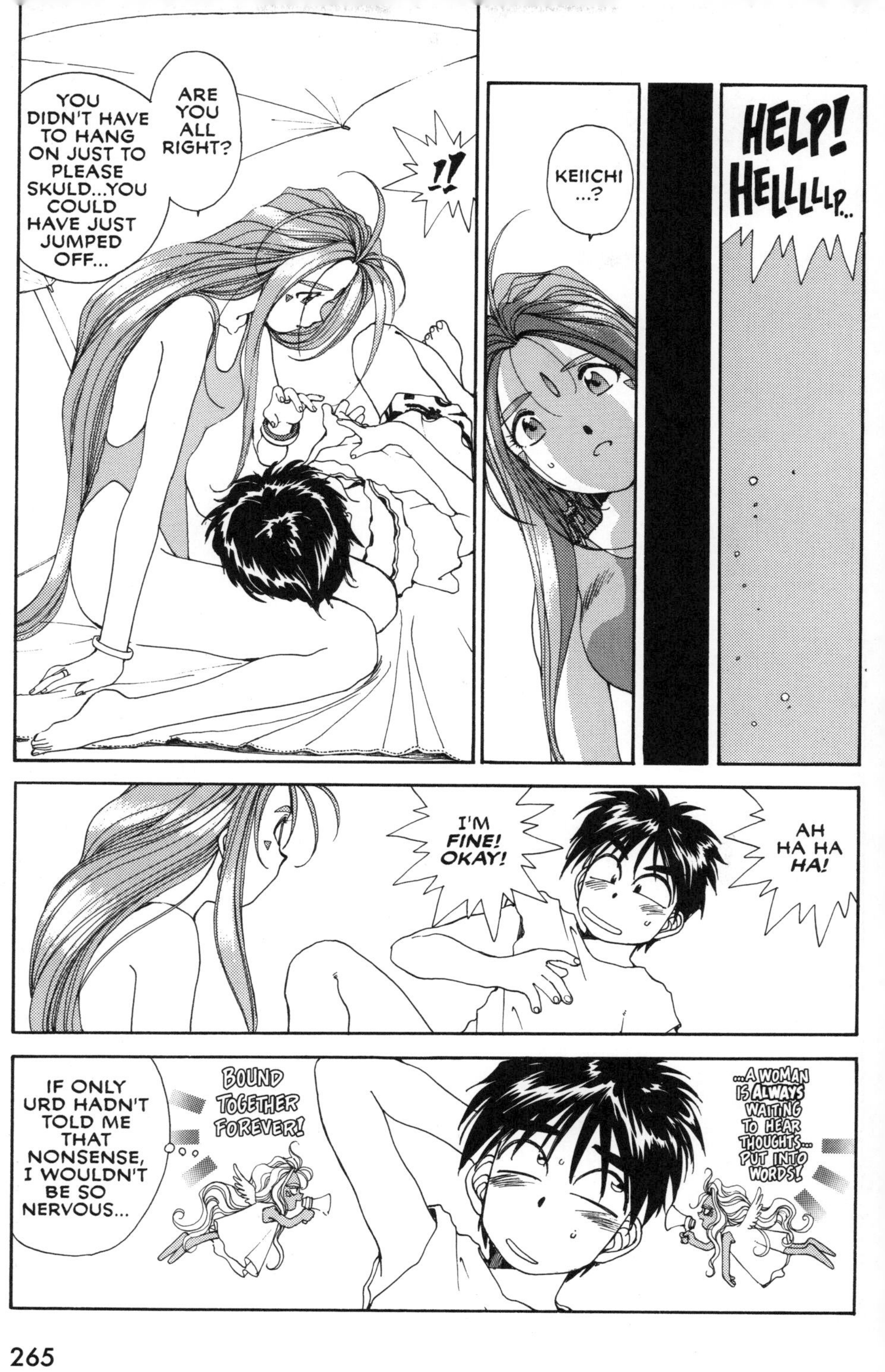
HELP! HELLLLLP...
KEIICHI ...?
!!
ARE YOU ALL RIGHT?
YOU DIDN'T HAVE TO HANG ON JUST TO PLEASE SKULD...YOU COULD HAVE JUST JUMPED OFF...
AH HA HA *HA!*
I'M *FINE! OKAY!*
...A WOMAN IS **ALWAYS** WAITING TO HEAR THOUGHTS... PUT INTO WORDS!
BOUND TOGETHER FOREVER!
IF ONLY URD HADN'T TOLD ME THAT NONSENSE, I WOULDN'T BE SO NERVOUS...

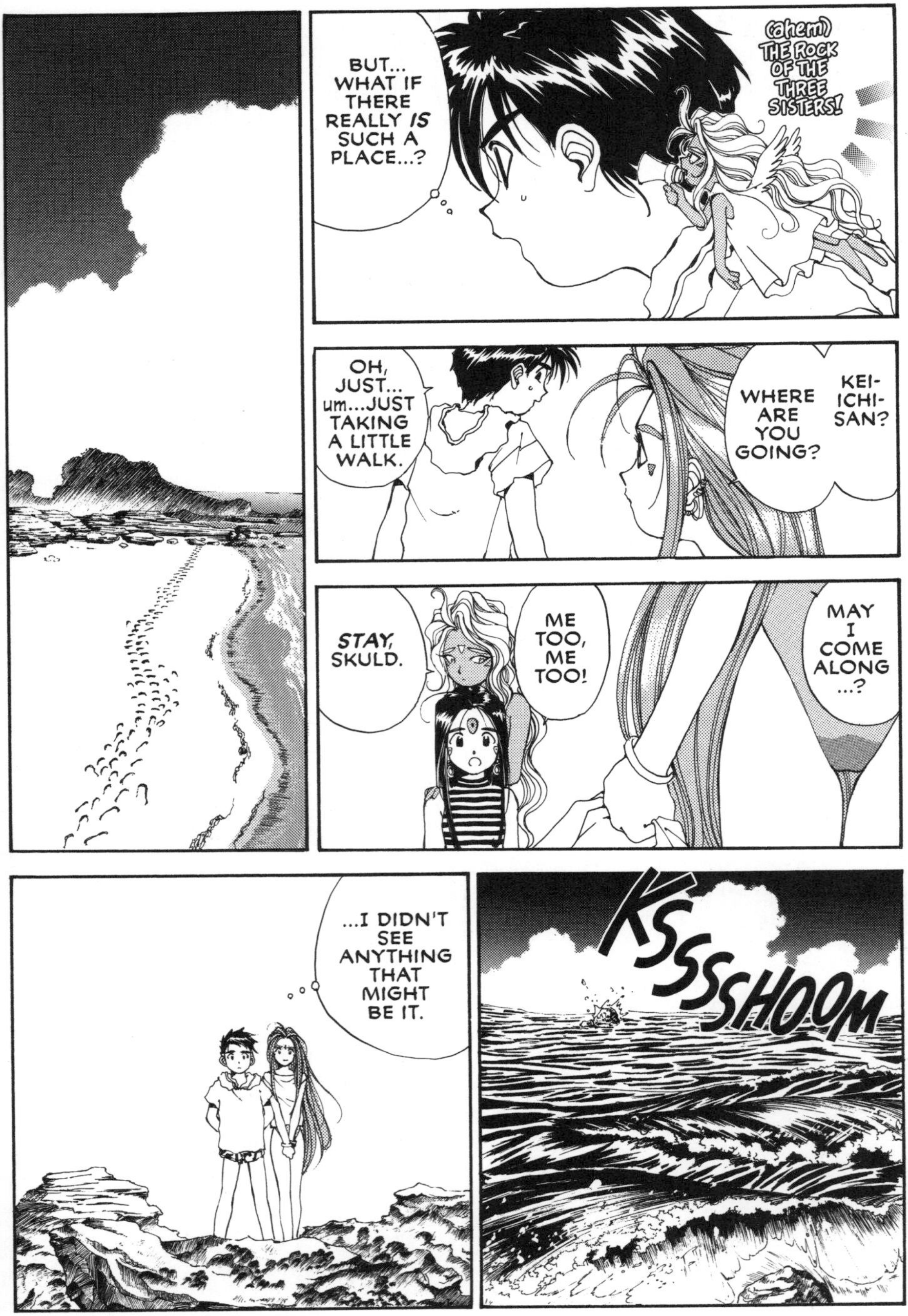

(ahem) THE ROCK OF THE THREE SISTERS!
BUT... WHAT IF THERE REALLY *IS* SUCH A PLACE...?
KEI-ICHI-SAN?
WHERE ARE YOU GOING?
OH, JUST... um...JUST TAKING A LITTLE WALK.
MAY I COME ALONG ...?
ME TOO, ME TOO!
STAY, SKULD.
KSSSSHOOM
...I DIDN'T SEE ANYTHING THAT MIGHT BE IT.

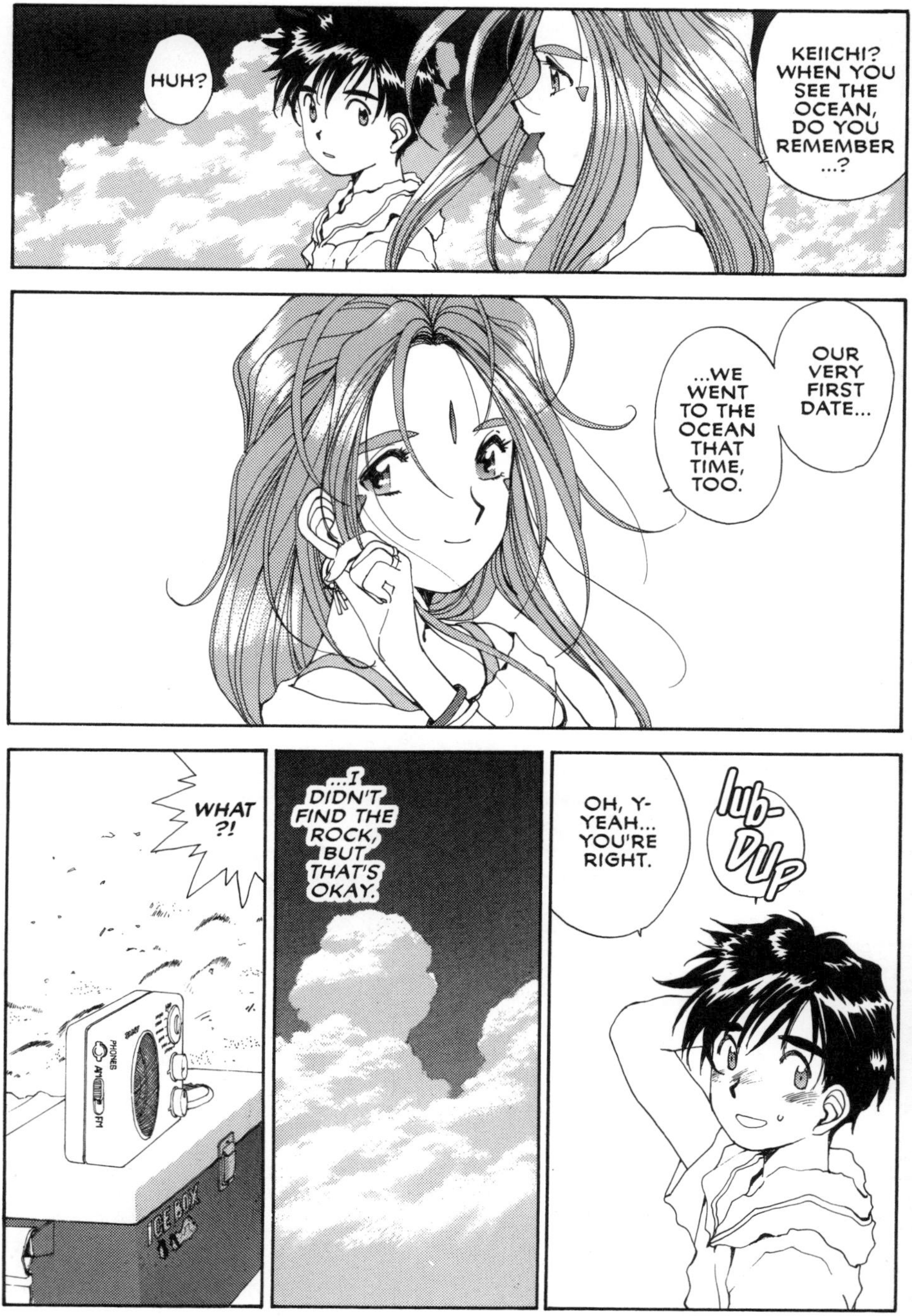
KEIICHI? WHEN YOU SEE THE OCEAN, DO YOU REMEMBER ...?
HUH?
OUR VERY FIRST DATE...
...WE WENT TO THE OCEAN THAT TIME, TOO.
lub-DUP
OH, Y-YEAH... YOU'RE RIGHT.
...I DIDN'T FIND THE ROCK, BUT THAT'S OKAY.
WHAT?!
ICE BOX

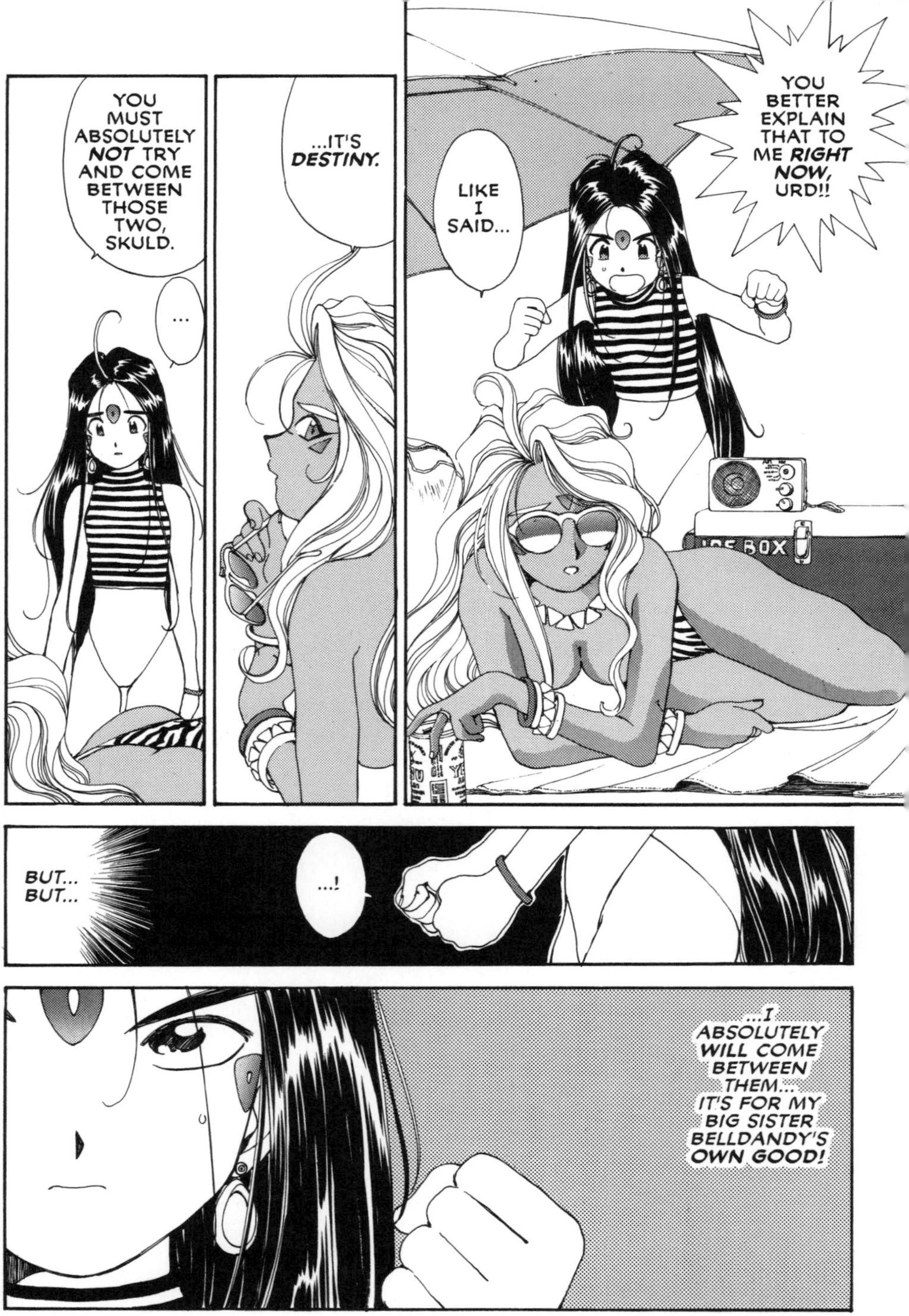
YOU BETTER EXPLAIN THAT TO ME RIGHT NOW, URD!!
LIKE I SAID...
...IT'S DESTINY.
YOU MUST ABSOLUTELY NOT TRY AND COME BETWEEN THOSE TWO, SKULD.
...
...!
BUT... BUT...
...I ABSOLUTELY WILL COME BETWEEN THEM... IT'S FOR MY BIG SISTER BELLDANDY'S OWN GOOD!

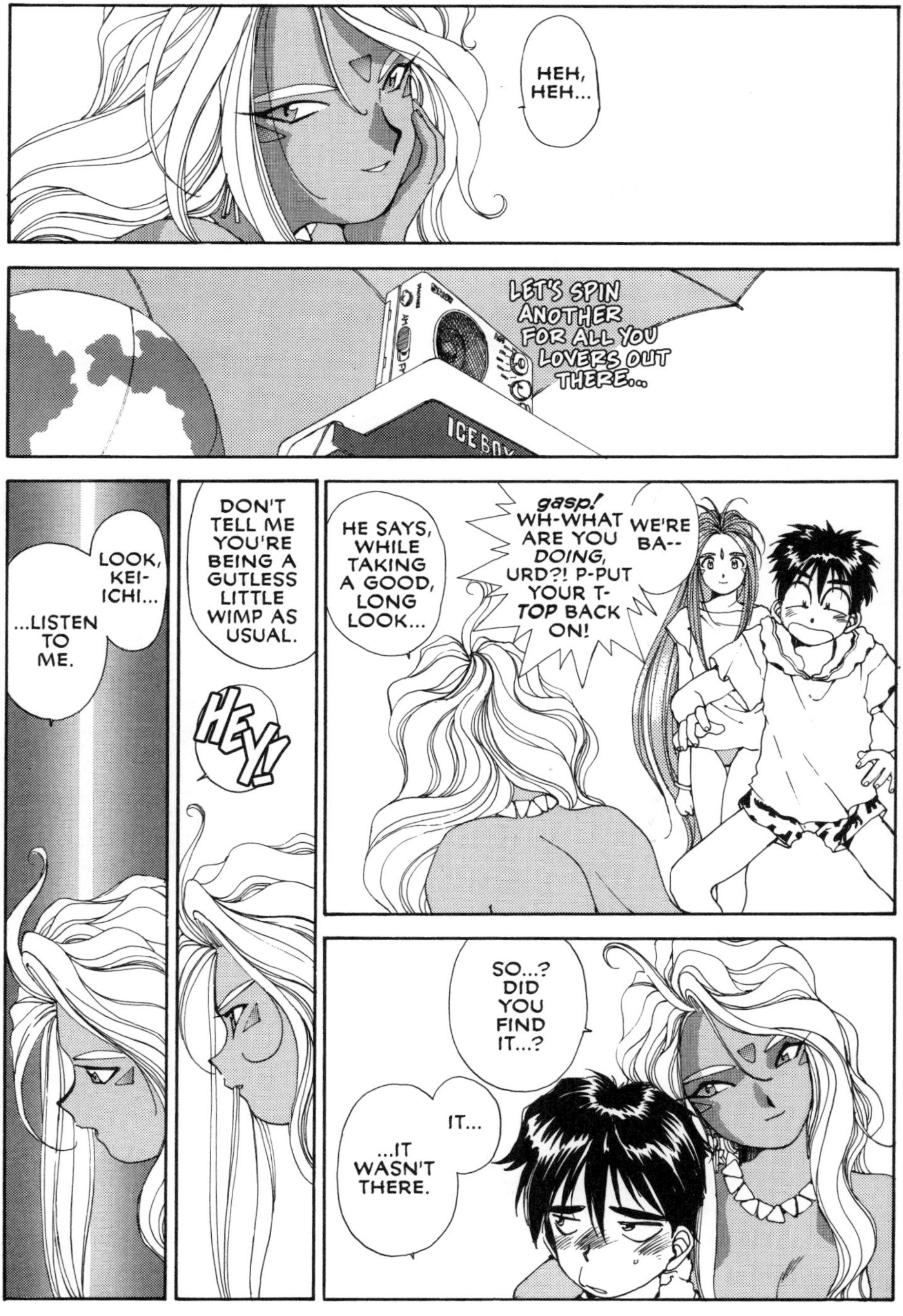
HEH, HEH...
LET'S SPIN ANOTHER FOR ALL YOU LOVERS OUT THERE...
ICE BOX
WE'RE BA--
gasp! WH-WHAT ARE YOU DOING, URD?! P-PUT YOUR T-TOP BACK ON!
HE SAYS, WHILE TAKING A GOOD, LONG LOOK...
SO...? DID YOU FIND IT...?
IT...
...IT WASN'T THERE.
DON'T TELL ME YOU'RE BEING A GUTLESS LITTLE WIMP AS USUAL.
HEY!
LOOK, KEI-ICHI...
...LISTEN TO ME.

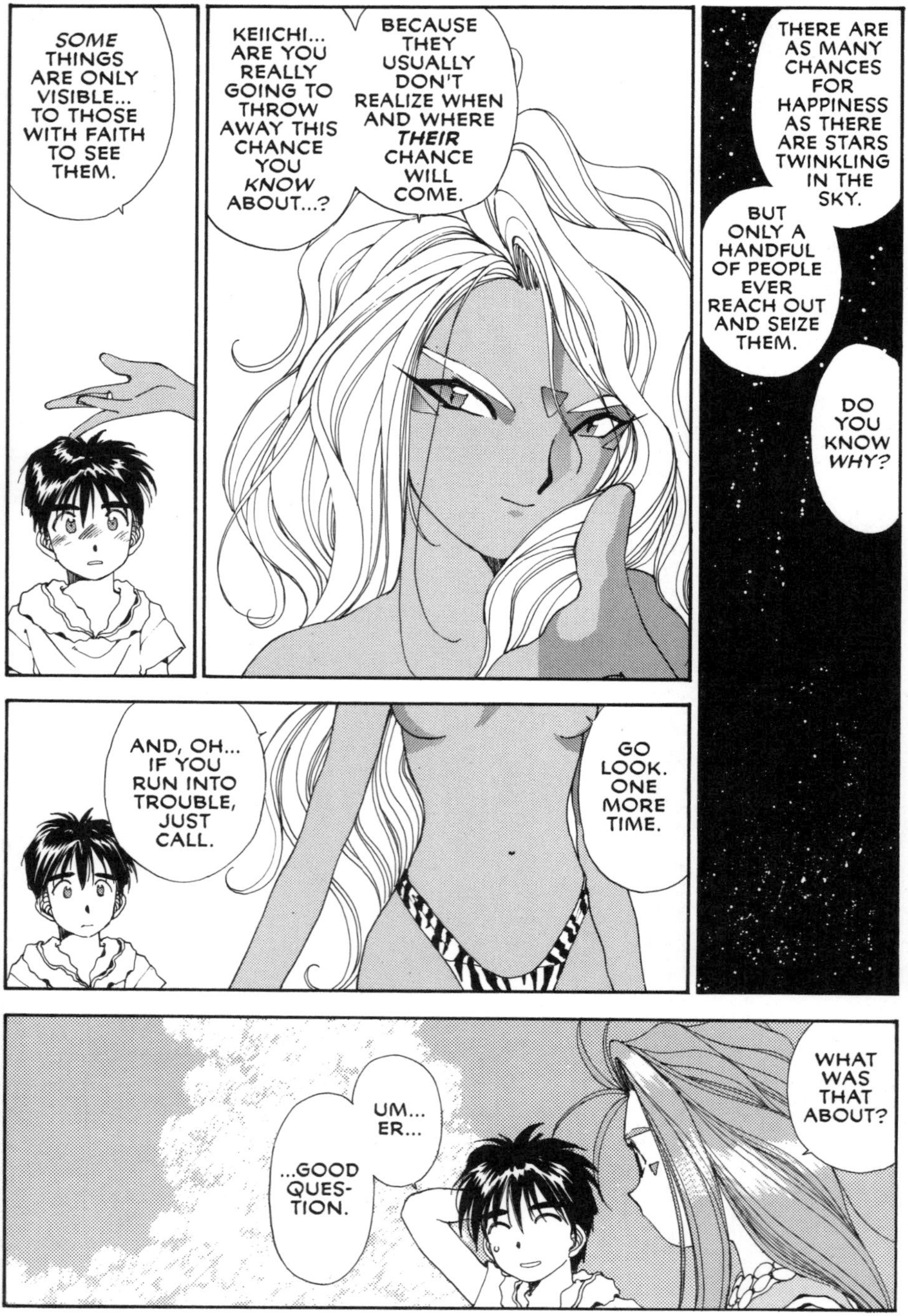

THERE ARE AS MANY CHANCES FOR HAPPINESS AS THERE ARE STARS TWINKLING IN THE SKY.
BUT ONLY A HANDFUL OF PEOPLE EVER REACH OUT AND SEIZE THEM.
DO YOU KNOW *WHY?*
BECAUSE THEY USUALLY DON'T REALIZE WHEN AND WHERE *THEIR* CHANCE WILL COME.
KEIICHI... ARE YOU REALLY GOING TO THROW AWAY THIS CHANCE YOU *KNOW* ABOUT...?
SOME THINGS ARE ONLY VISIBLE... TO THOSE WITH FAITH TO SEE THEM.
GO LOOK. ONE MORE TIME.
AND, OH... IF YOU RUN INTO TROUBLE, JUST CALL.
WHAT WAS THAT ABOUT?
UM... ER...
...GOOD QUES-TION.

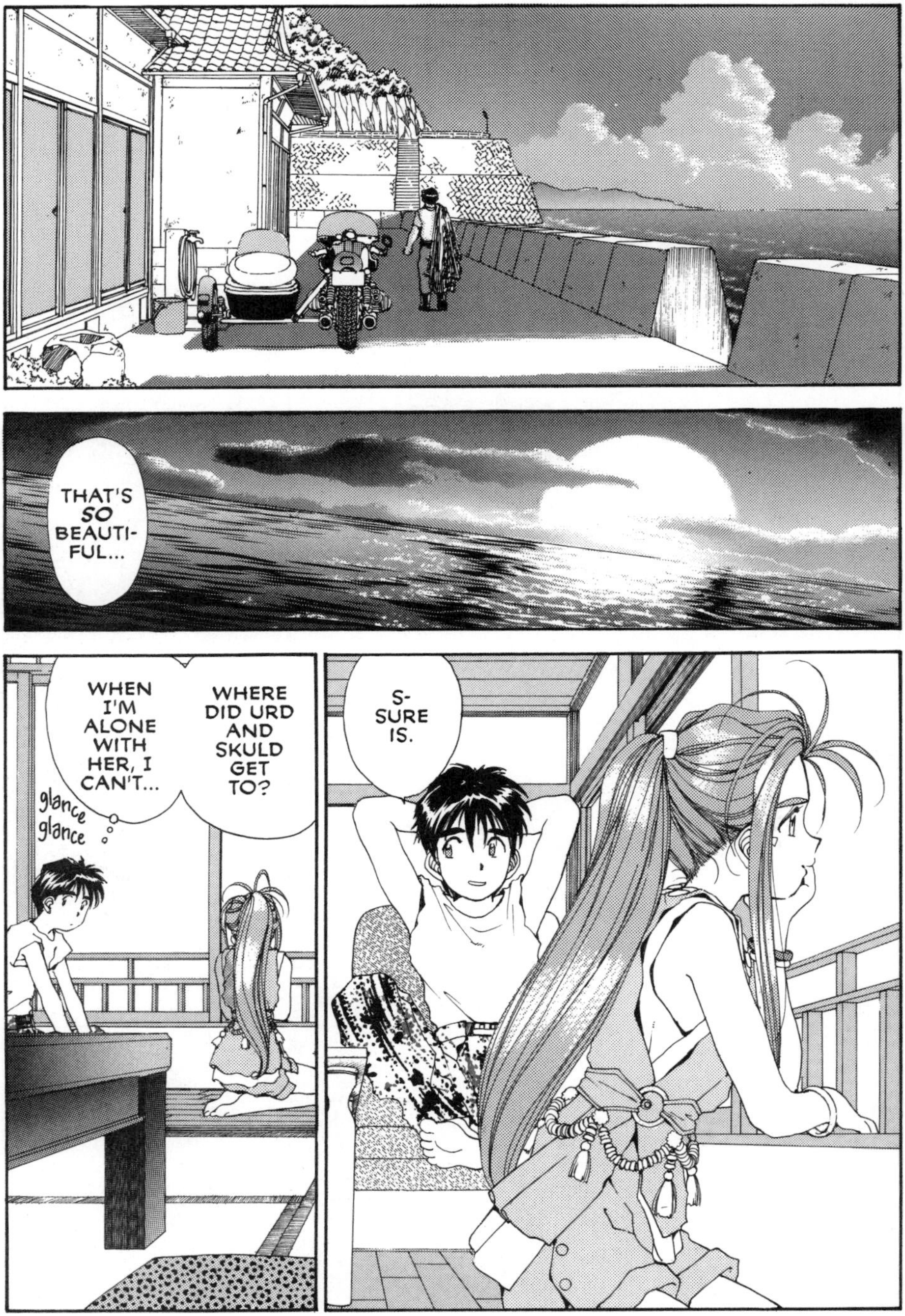
THAT'S *SO* BEAUTIFUL...
S-SURE IS.
WHERE DID URD AND SKULD GET TO?
WHEN I'M ALONE WITH HER, I CAN'T...
glance glance

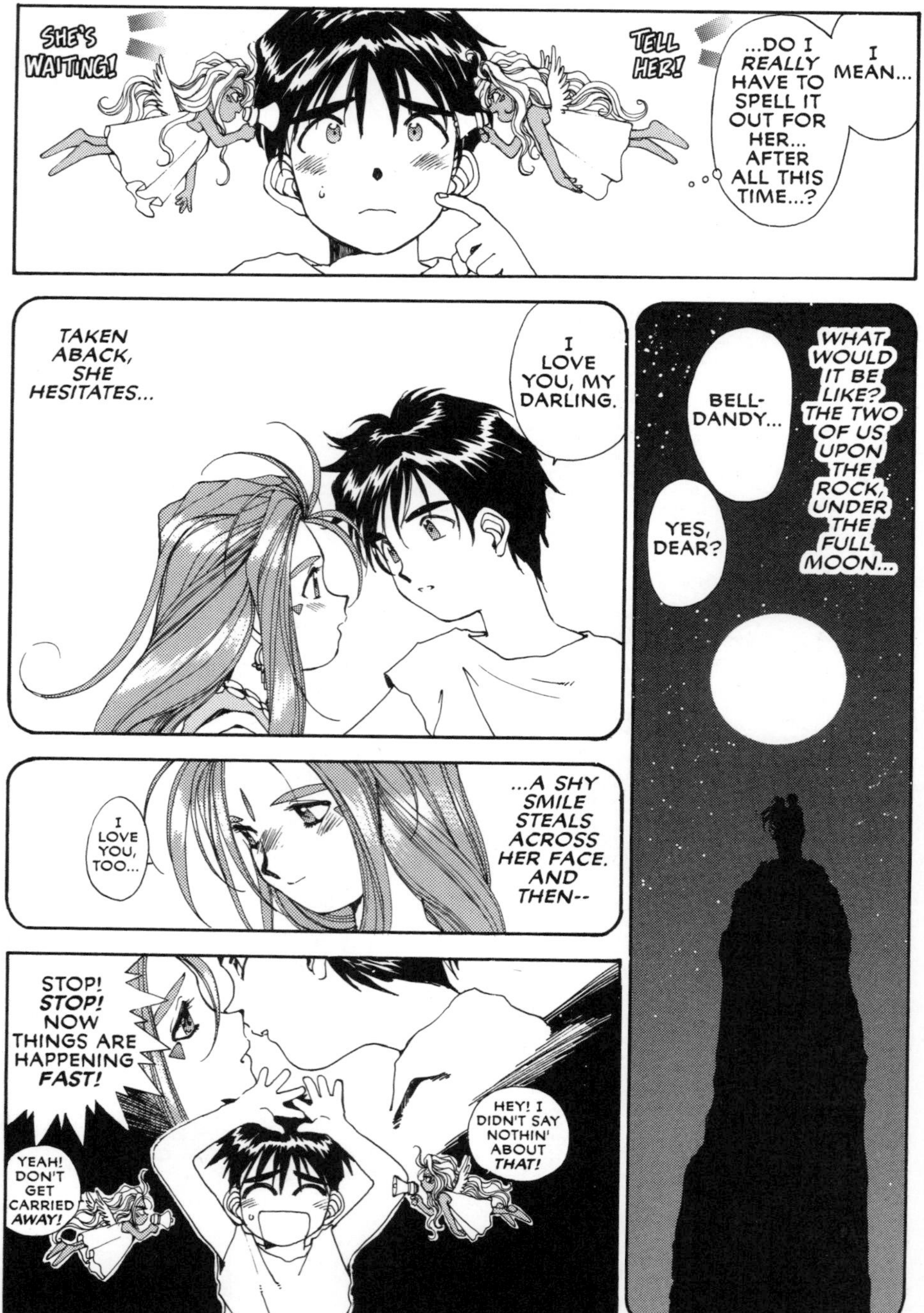
I MEAN...
...DO I *REALLY* HAVE TO SPELL IT OUT FOR HER... AFTER ALL THIS TIME...?
TELL HER!
SHE'S WAITING!
WHAT WOULD IT BE LIKE? THE TWO OF US UPON THE ROCK, UNDER THE FULL MOON...
BELL-DANDY...
YES, DEAR?
I LOVE YOU, MY DARLING.
TAKEN ABACK, SHE HESITATES...
...A SHY SMILE STEALS ACROSS HER FACE. AND THEN--
I LOVE YOU, TOO...
STOP! *STOP!* NOW THINGS ARE HAPPENING *FAST!*
HEY! I DIDN'T SAY NOTHIN' ABOUT *THAT!*
YEAH! DON'T GET CARRIED *AWAY!*

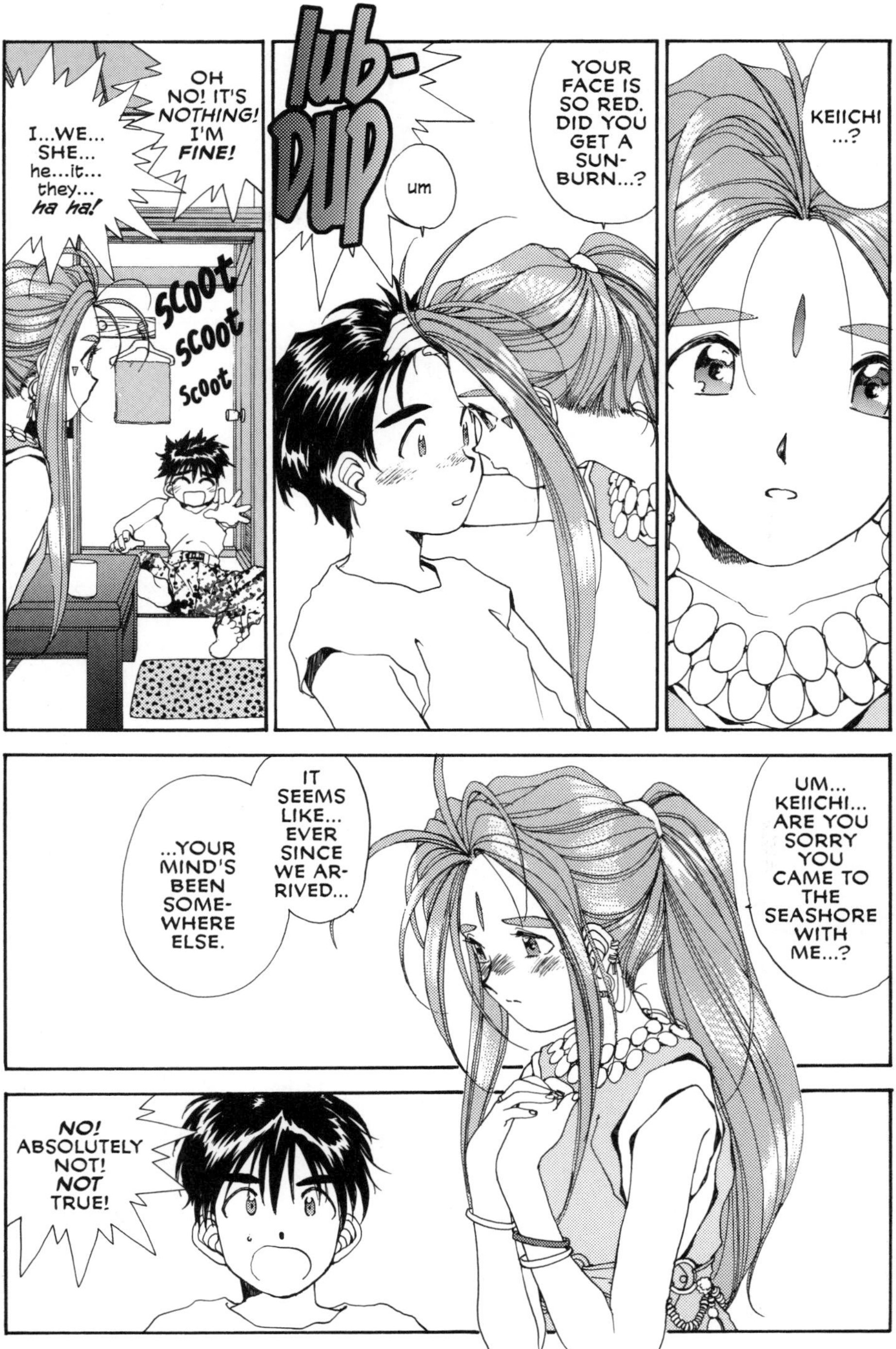
KEIICHI ...?
YOUR FACE IS SO RED. DID YOU GET A SUN-BURN...?
lub-DUP
um
OH NO! IT'S *NOTHING!* I'M *FINE!*
I...WE... SHE... he...it... they... *ha ha!*
scoot scoot scoot
UM... KEIICHI... ARE YOU SORRY YOU CAME TO THE SEASHORE WITH ME...?
IT SEEMS LIKE... EVER SINCE WE AR-RIVED...
...YOUR MIND'S BEEN SOME-WHERE ELSE.
NO! ABSOLUTELY NOT! *NOT* TRUE!

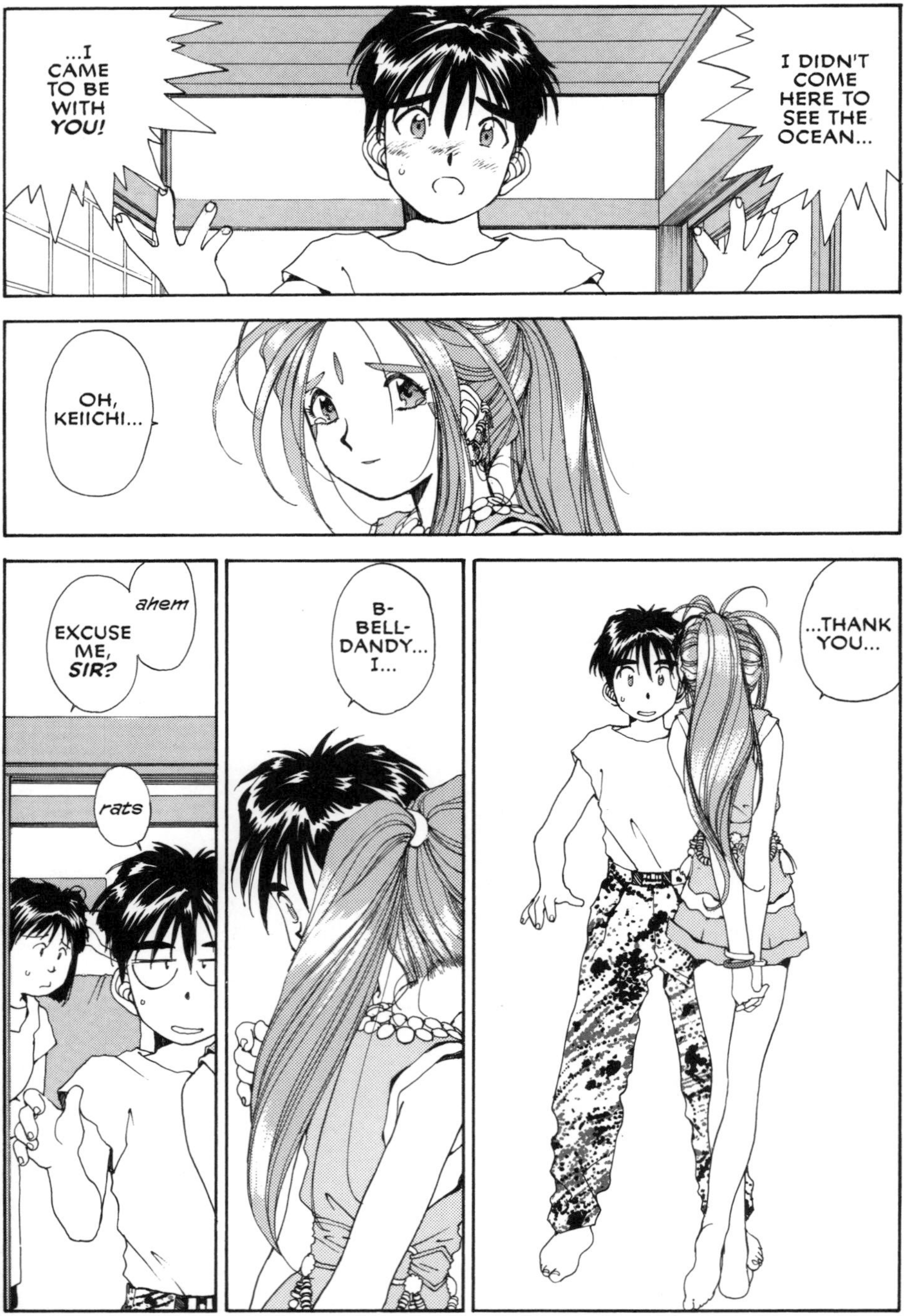
I DIDN'T COME HERE TO SEE THE OCEAN...
...I CAME TO BE WITH *YOU!*
OH, KEIICHI...
...THANK YOU...
B-BELL-DANDY... I...
ahem
EXCUSE ME, *SIR?*
rats

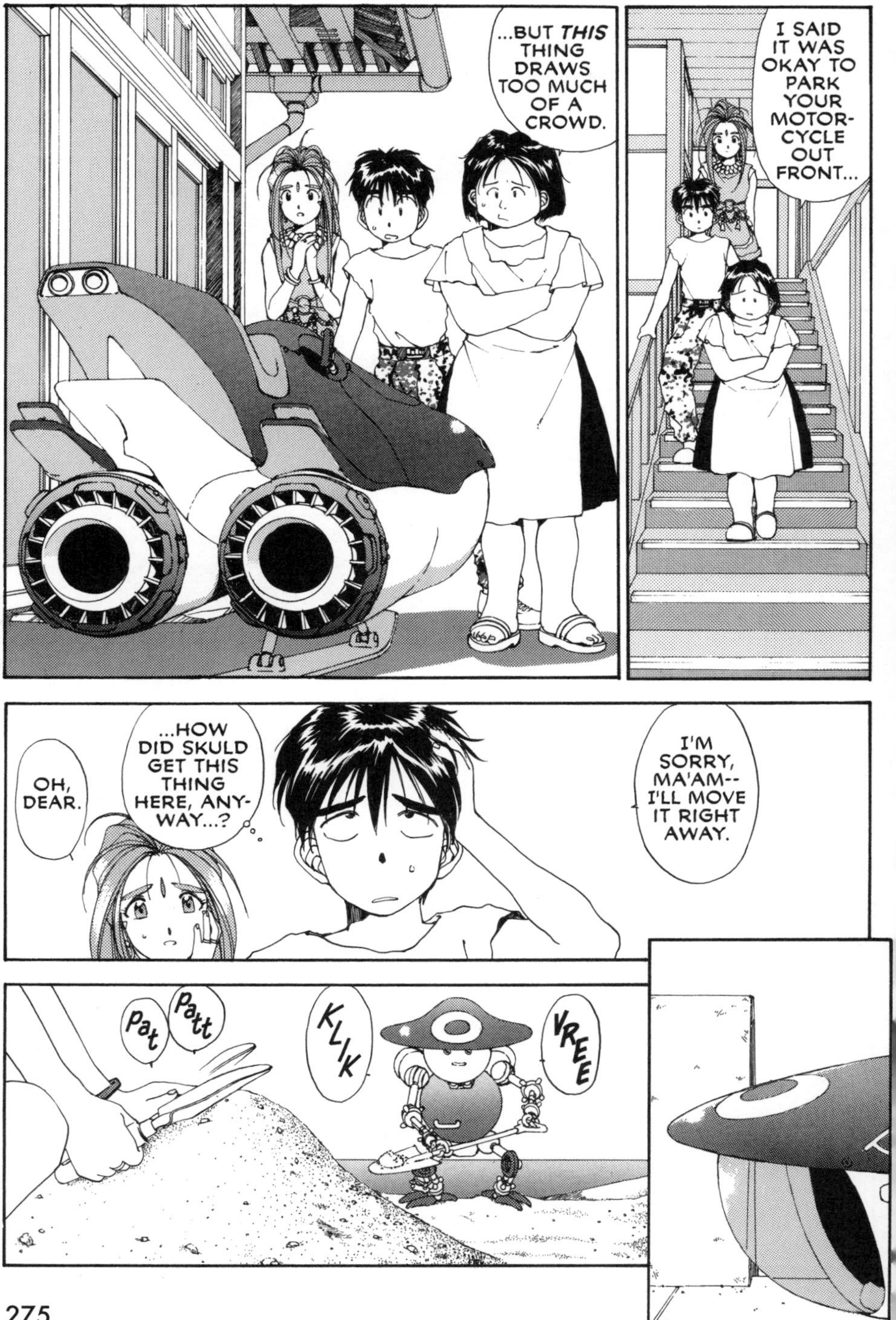
I SAID IT WAS OKAY TO PARK YOUR MOTOR-CYCLE OUT FRONT...
...BUT *THIS* THING DRAWS TOO MUCH OF A CROWD.
I'M SORRY, MA'AM-- I'LL MOVE IT RIGHT AWAY.
...HOW DID SKULD GET THIS THING HERE, ANY-WAY...?
OH, DEAR.
VREE
KLIK
Patt
Pat

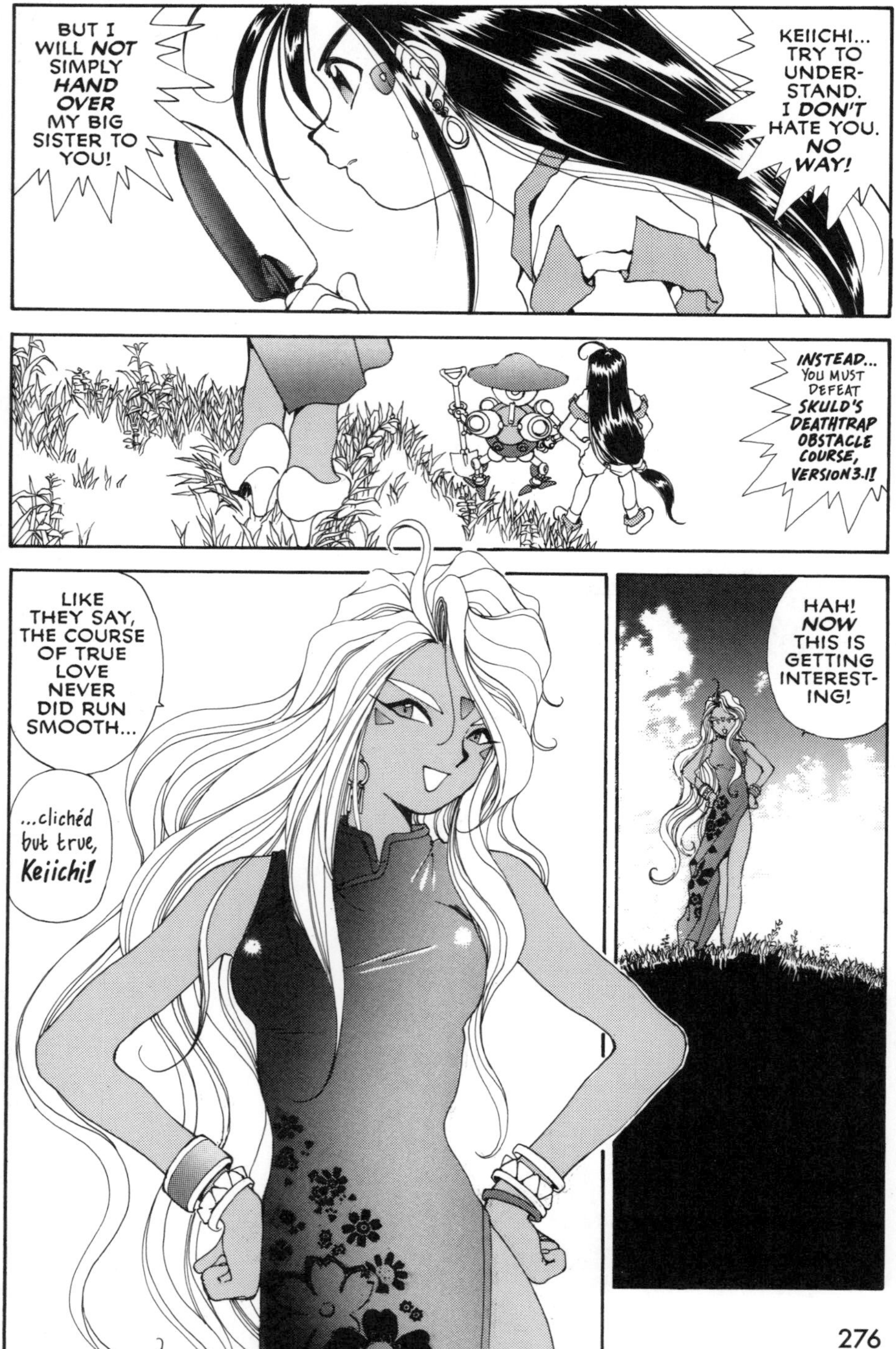
KEIICHI... TRY TO UNDER-STAND. I DON'T HATE YOU. NO WAY!
BUT I WILL NOT SIMPLY HAND OVER MY BIG SISTER TO YOU!
INSTEAD... YOU MUST DEFEAT SKULD'S DEATHTRAP OBSTACLE COURSE, VERSION 3.1!
HAH! NOW THIS IS GETTING INTEREST-ING!
LIKE THEY SAY, THE COURSE OF TRUE LOVE NEVER DID RUN SMOOTH...
...clichéd but true, Keiichi!

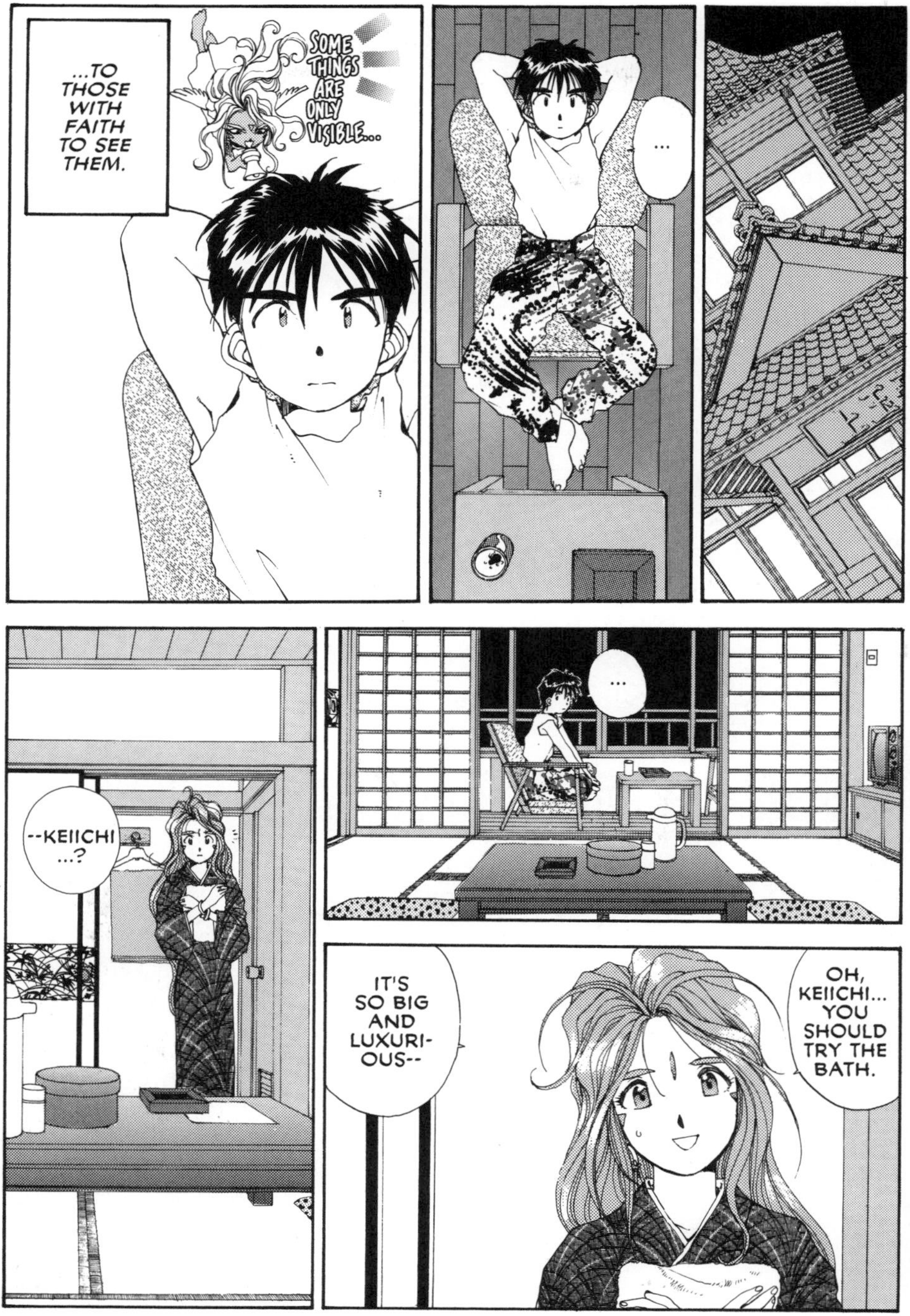
...
SOME THINGS ARE ONLY VISIBLE...
...TO THOSE WITH FAITH TO SEE THEM.
...
OH, KEIICHI... YOU SHOULD TRY THE BATH.
IT'S SO BIG AND LUXURIOUS--
--KEIICHI ...?

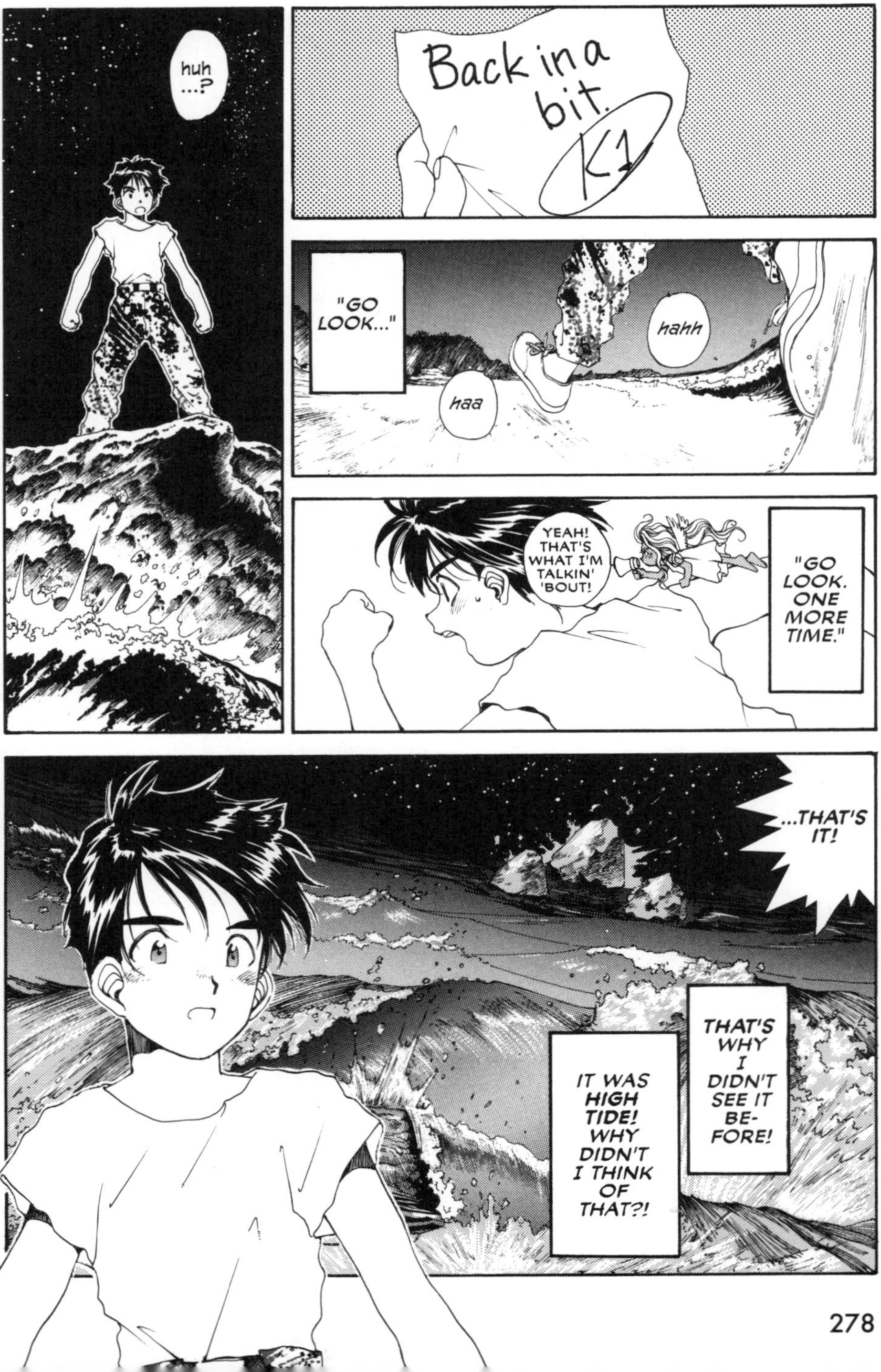
Back in a bit.
K1
"GO LOOK..."
hahh
haa
"GO LOOK. ONE MORE TIME."
YEAH! THAT'S WHAT I'M TALKIN' 'BOUT!
huh ...?
...THAT'S IT!
THAT'S WHY I DIDN'T SEE IT BE-FORE!
IT WAS HIGH TIDE! WHY DIDN'T I THINK OF THAT?!

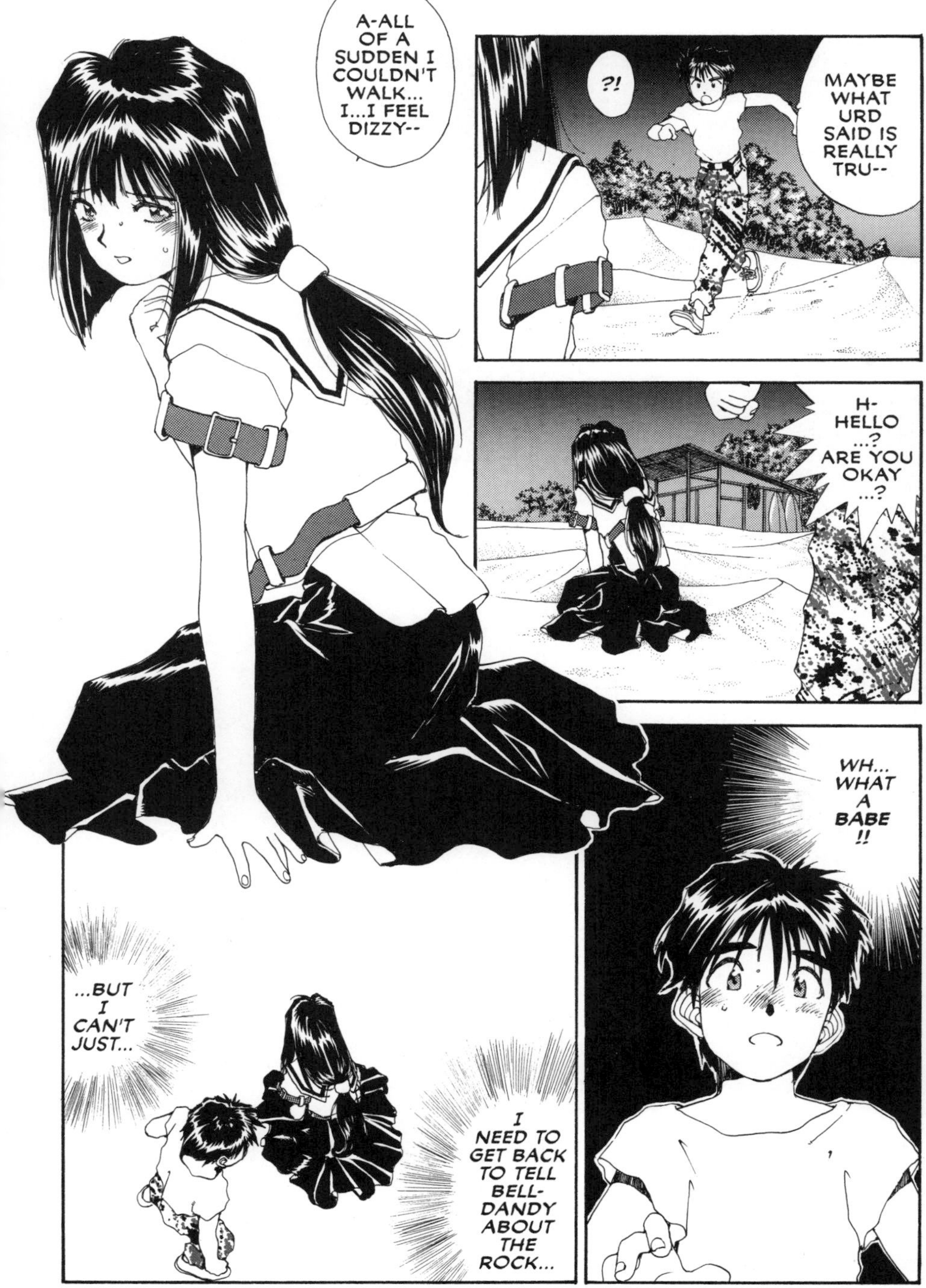
MAYBE WHAT URD SAID IS REALLY TRU--
?!
H-HELLO ...? ARE YOU OKAY ...?
A-ALL OF A SUDDEN I COULDN'T WALK... I...I FEEL DIZZY--
WH... WHAT A BABE !!
...BUT I CAN'T JUST...
I NEED TO GET BACK TO TELL BELL-DANDY ABOUT THE ROCK...

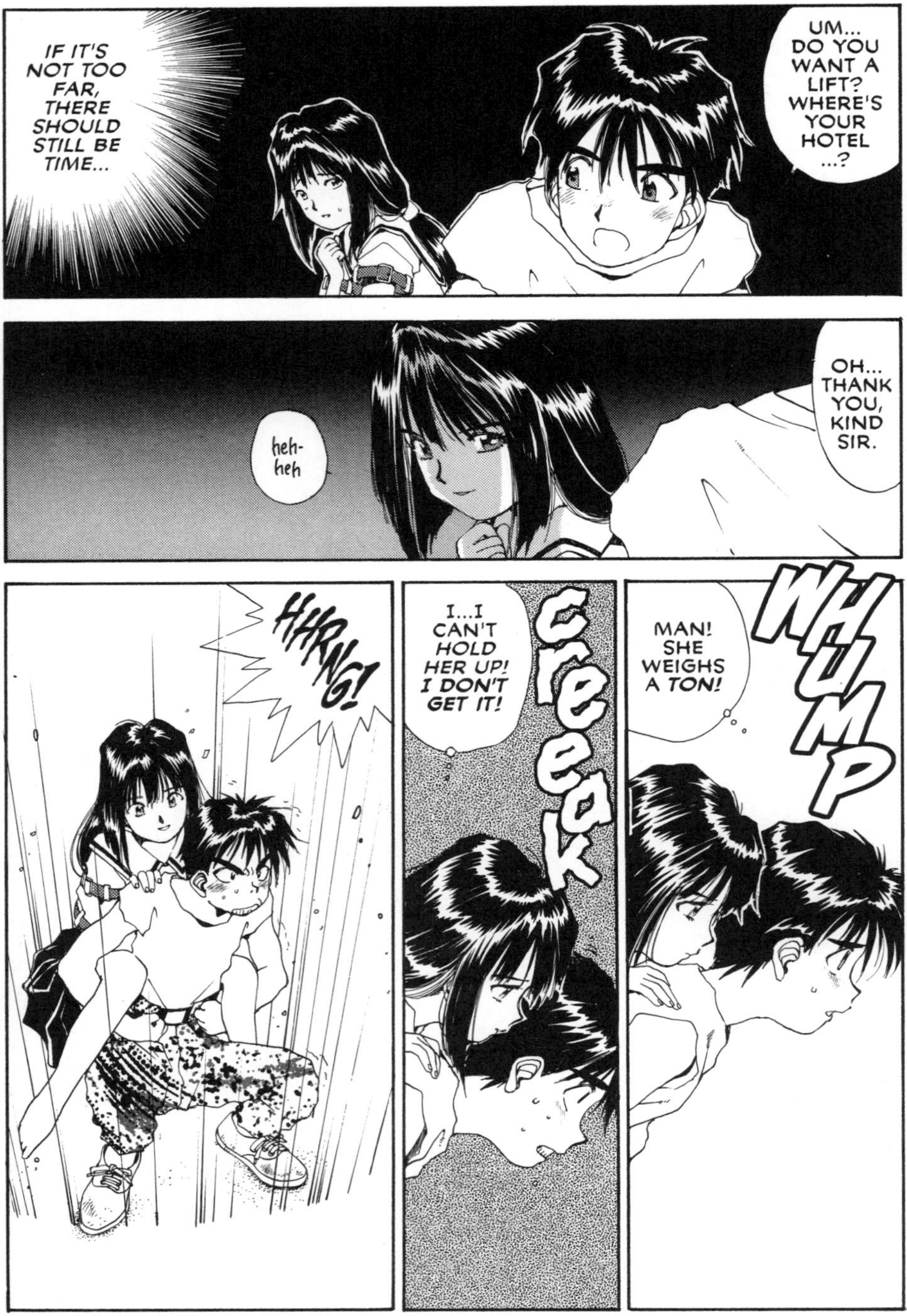
UM... DO YOU WANT A LIFT? WHERE'S YOUR HOTEL ...?
IF IT'S NOT TOO FAR, THERE SHOULD STILL BE TIME...
OH... THANK YOU, KIND SIR.
heh-heh
WHUMP
MAN! SHE WEIGHS A TON!
creak
I...I CAN'T HOLD HER UP! I DON'T GET IT!
HHRNG!

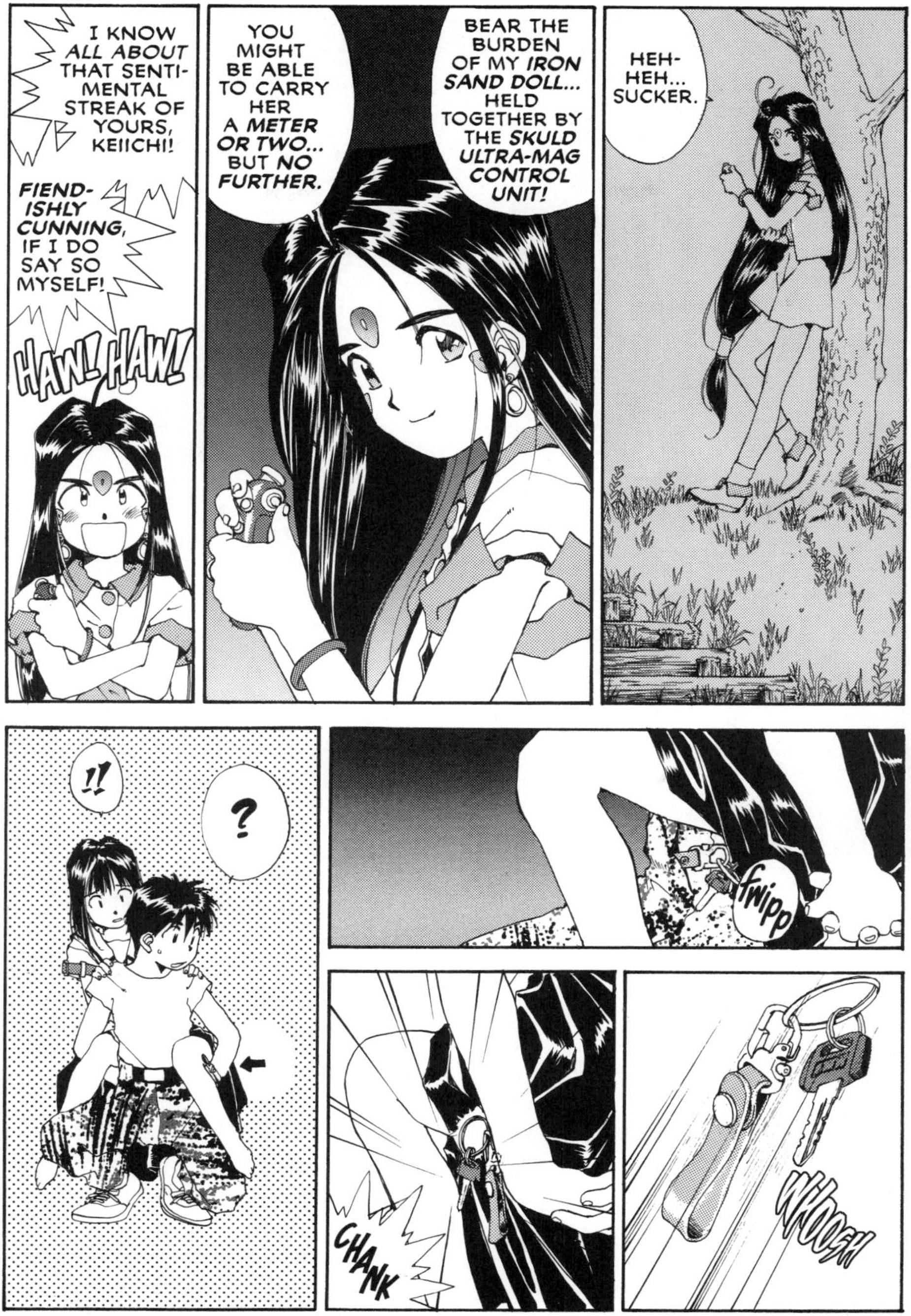
HEH-HEH... SUCKER.
BEAR THE BURDEN OF MY IRON SAND DOLL... HELD TOGETHER BY THE SKULD ULTRA-MAG CONTROL UNIT!
YOU MIGHT BE ABLE TO CARRY HER A METER OR TWO... BUT NO FURTHER.
I KNOW ALL ABOUT THAT SENTI-MENTAL STREAK OF YOURS, KEIICHI!
FIEND-ISHLY CUNNING, IF I DO SAY SO MYSELF!
HAW! HAW!
fwipp
WHOOSH
CHANK
!!
?

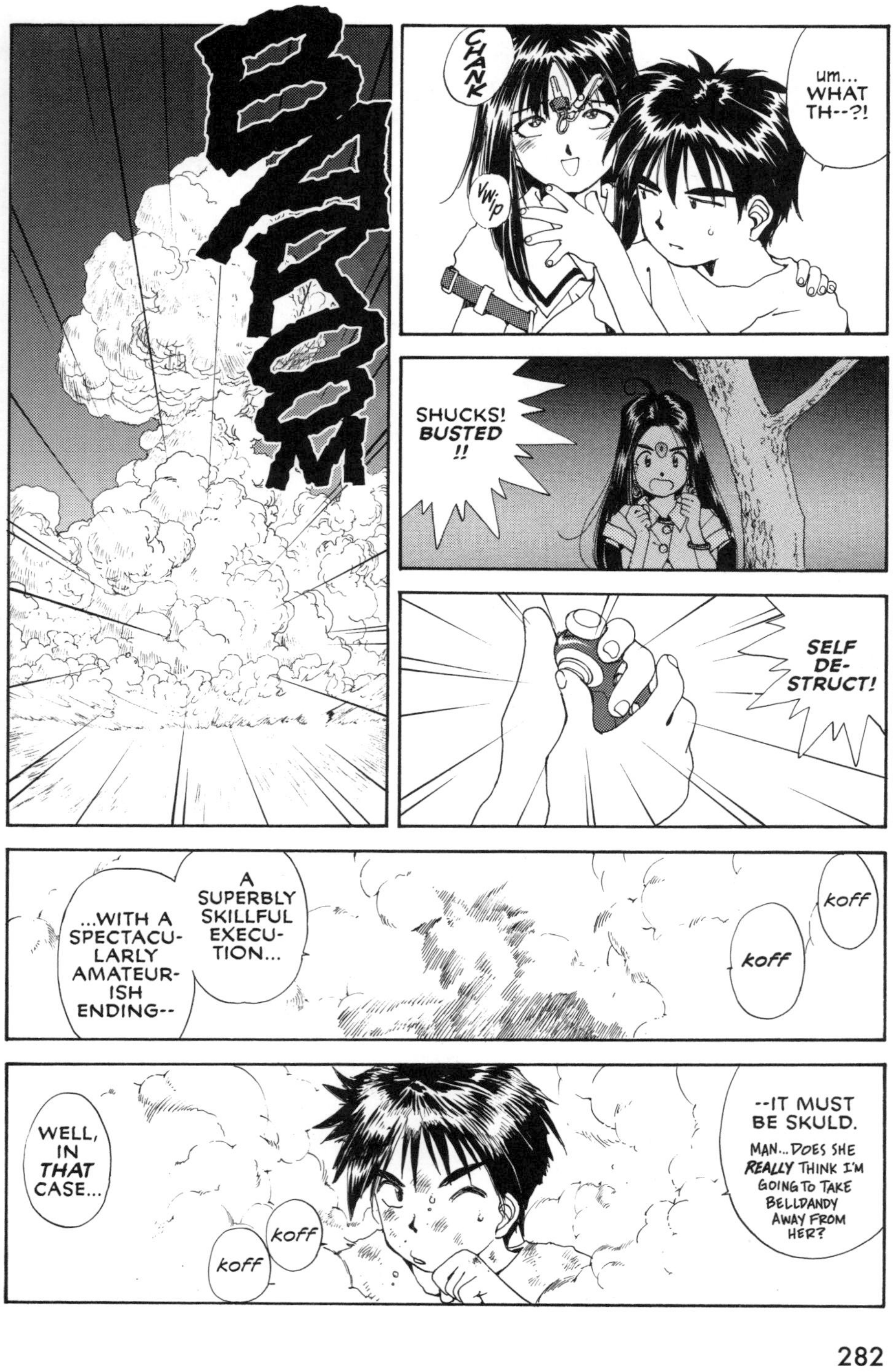
CHANK
um... WHAT TH--?!
vwip
SHUCKS! BUSTED !!
SELF DE-STRUCT!
koff
koff
A SUPERBLY SKILLFUL EXECU-TION...
...WITH A SPECTACU-LARLY AMATEUR-ISH ENDING--
--IT MUST BE SKULD.
MAN... DOES SHE *REALLY* THINK I'M GOING TO TAKE BELLDANDY AWAY FROM HER?
WELL, IN *THAT* CASE...
koff
koff

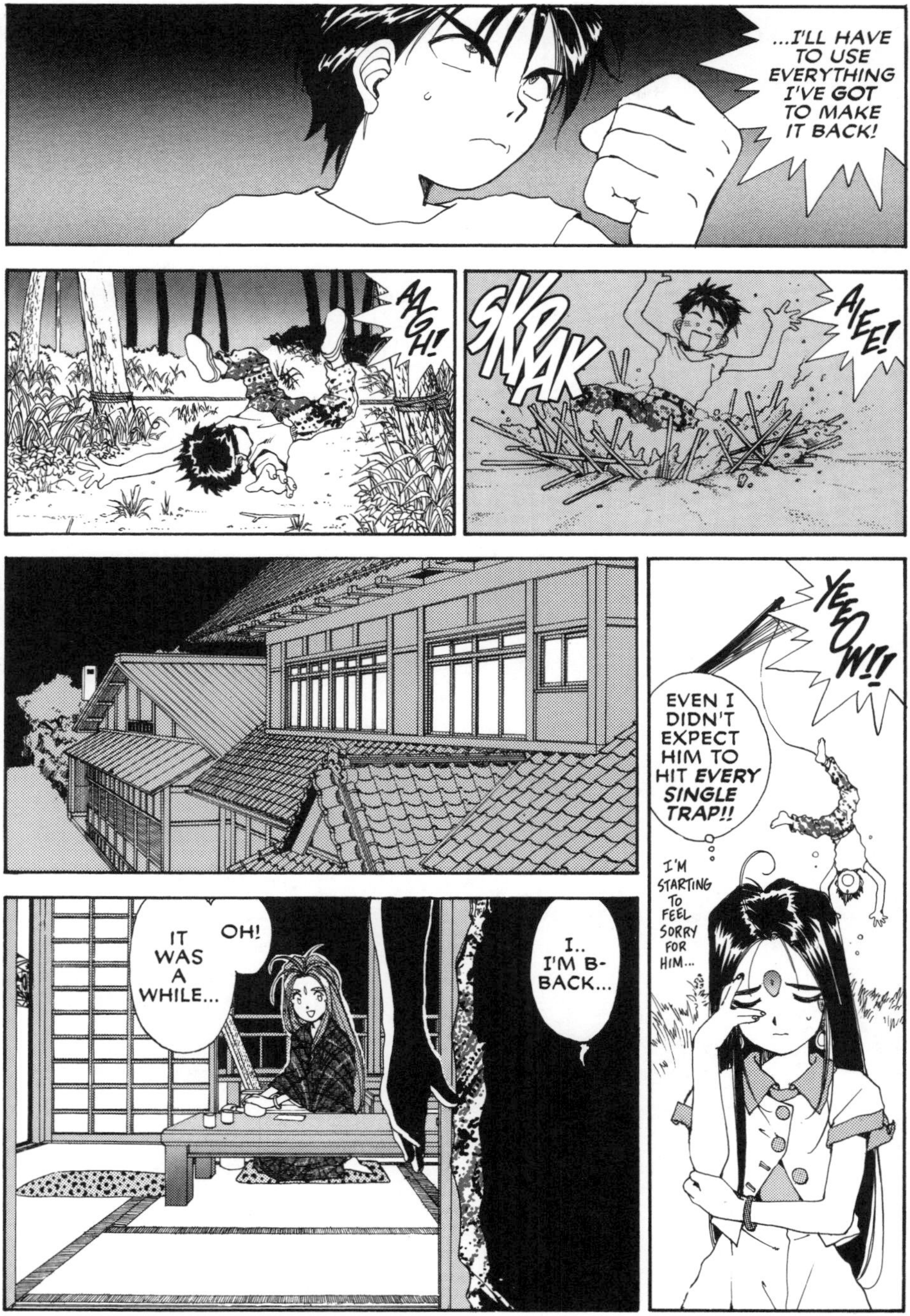
...I'LL HAVE TO USE EVERYTHING I'VE GOT TO MAKE IT BACK!
SKRAK
AIEEE!
AAGH!
YEEOW!!
EVEN I DIDN'T EXPECT HIM TO HIT EVERY SINGLE TRAP!!
I'M STARTING TO FEEL SORRY FOR HIM...
I.. I'M B-BACK...
OH!
IT WAS A WHILE...

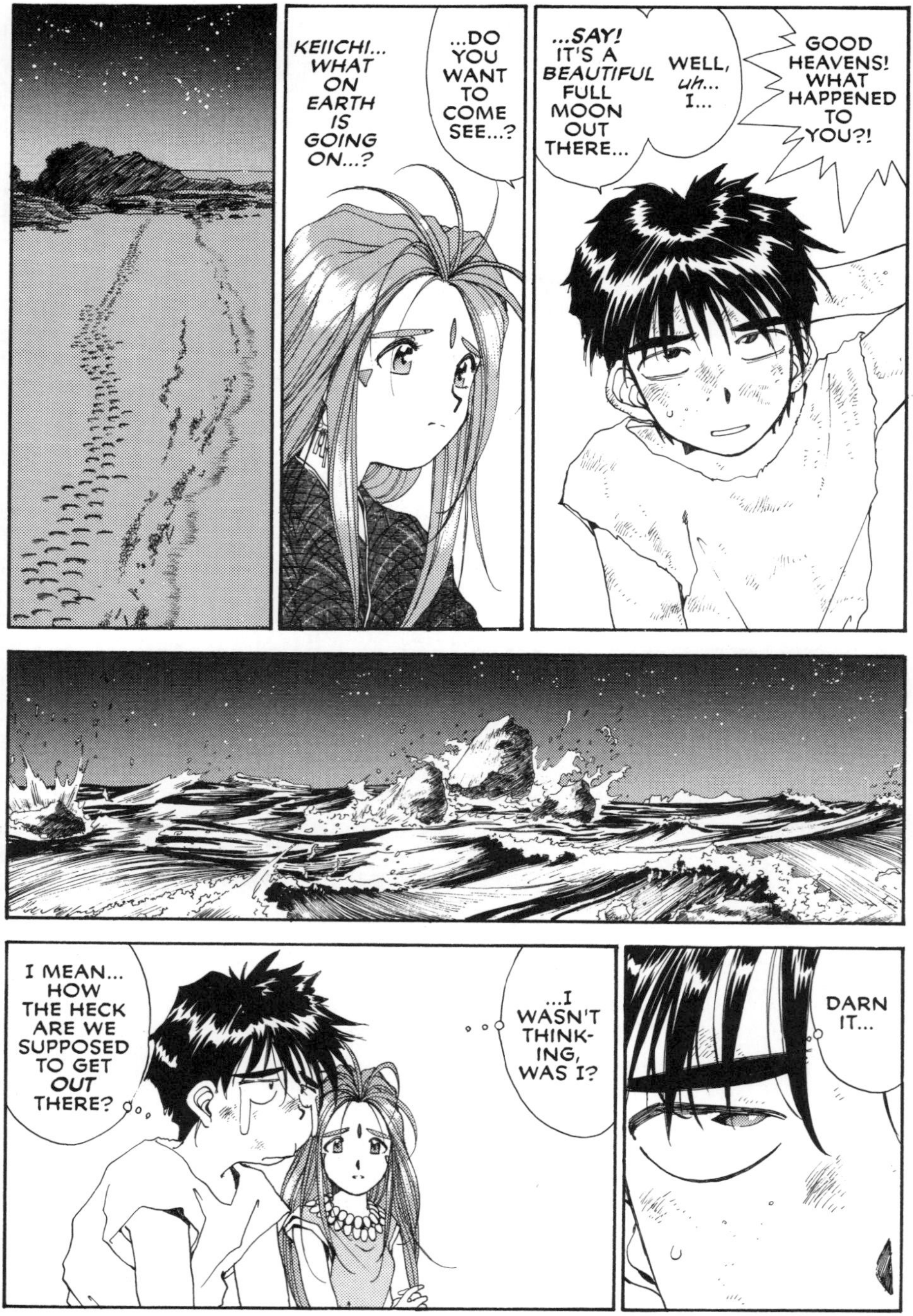
GOOD HEAVENS! WHAT HAPPENED TO YOU?!
WELL, *uh*... I...
...**SAY!** IT'S A *BEAUTIFUL* FULL MOON OUT THERE...
...DO YOU WANT TO COME SEE...?
KEIICHI... WHAT ON EARTH IS GOING ON...?
DARN IT...
...I WASN'T THINKING, WAS I?
I MEAN... HOW THE HECK ARE WE SUPPOSED TO GET ***OUT*** THERE?

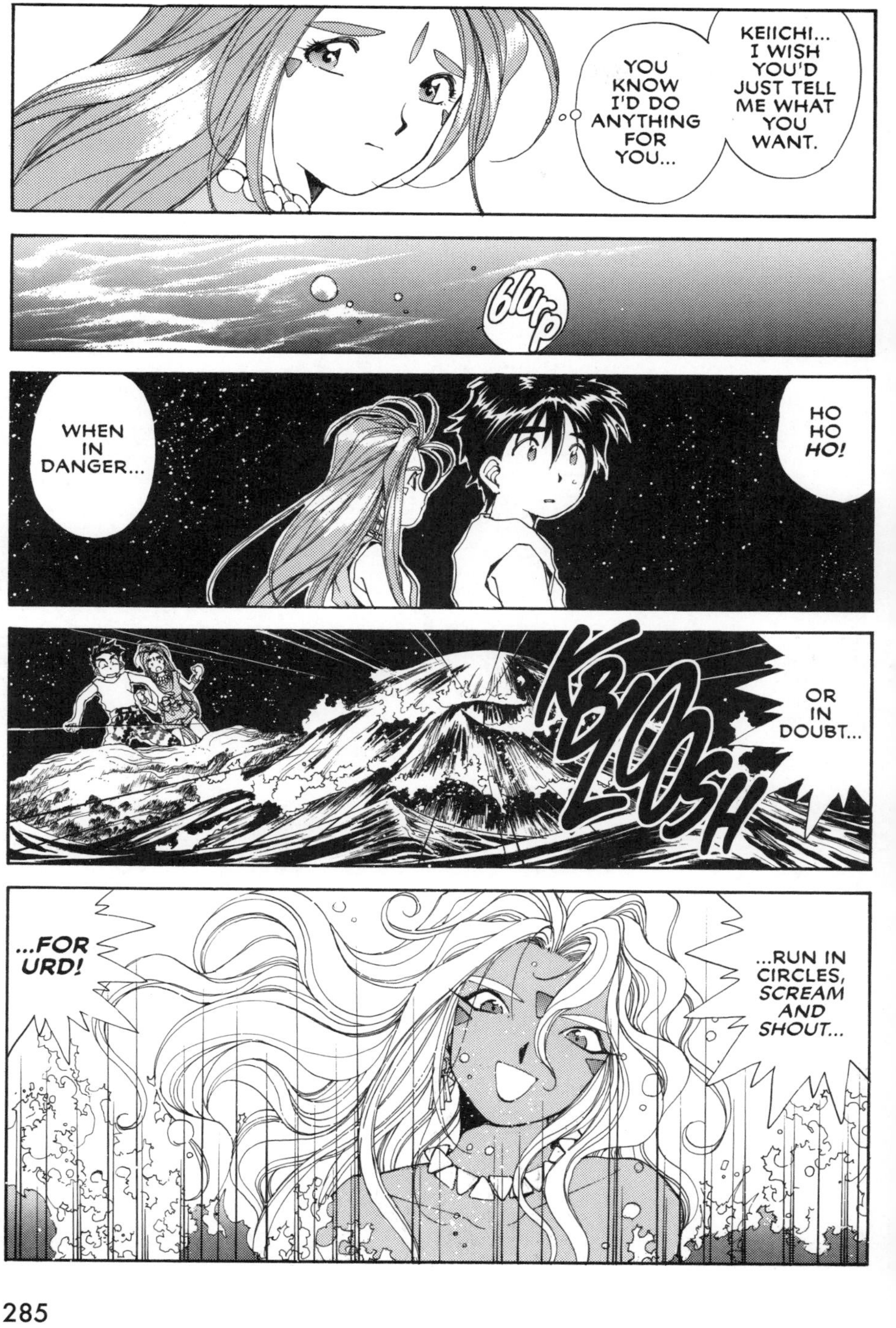
KEIICHI... I WISH YOU'D JUST TELL ME WHAT YOU WANT.
YOU KNOW I'D DO ANYTHING FOR YOU...
blurp
HO HO HO!
WHEN IN DANGER...
KBLOOSH
OR IN DOUBT...
...RUN IN CIRCLES, SCREAM AND SHOUT...
...FOR URD!

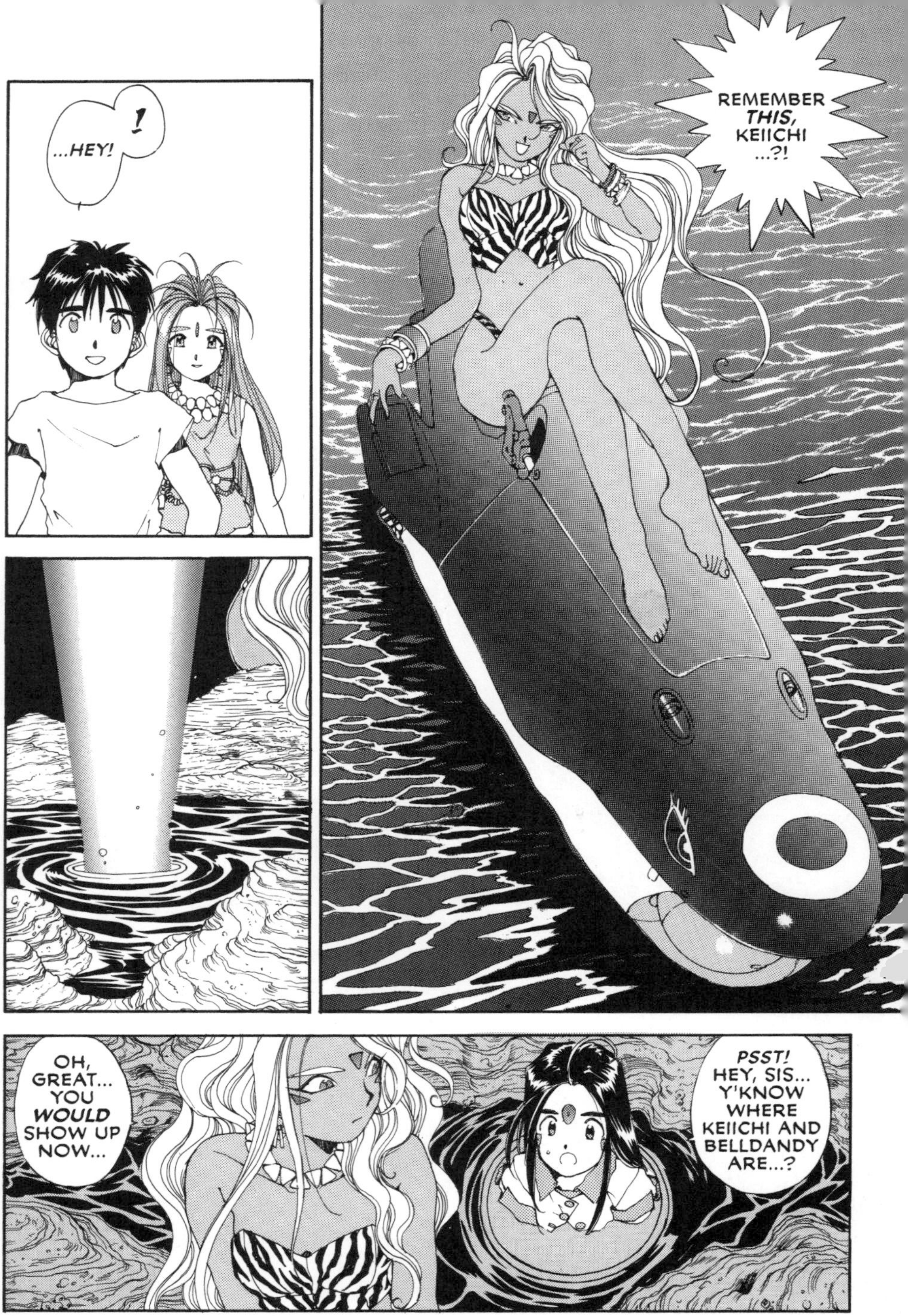
REMEMBER THIS, KEIICHI ...?!
!
...HEY!
PSST! HEY, SIS... Y'KNOW WHERE KEIICHI AND BELLDANDY ARE...?
OH, GREAT... YOU WOULD SHOW UP NOW...

...THAT'S THEM!

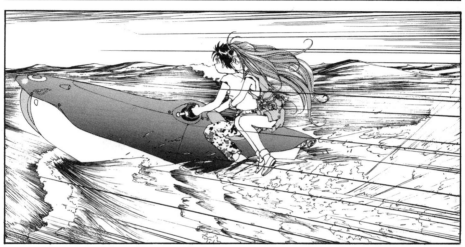

BLUE NO. 6... DIVE!!

klick

OH NO, YOU DON'T!

...ALMOST THERE...

ALMOST THERE...

287

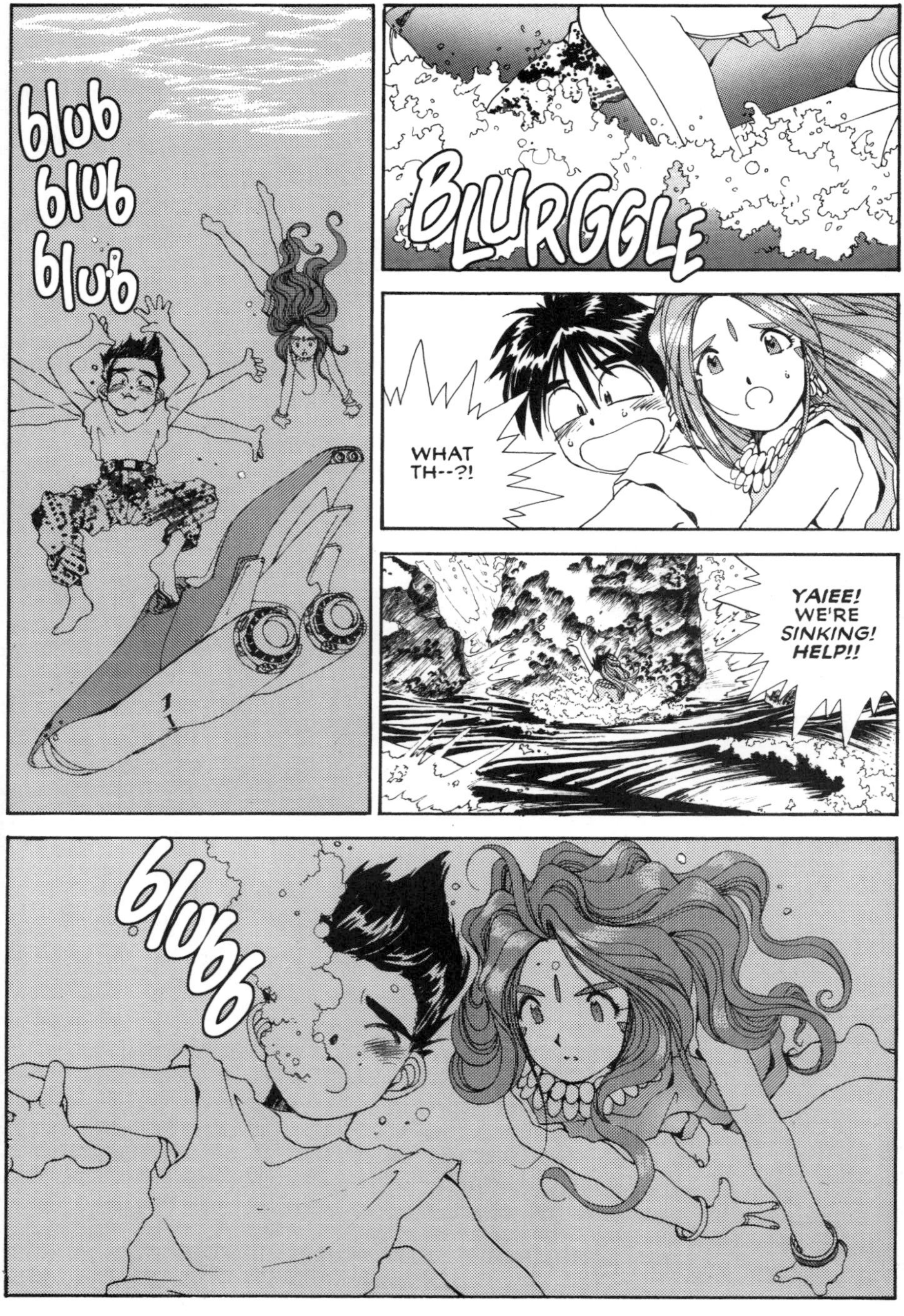
BLURGGLE
WHAT TH--?!
YAIEE! WE'RE SINKING! HELP!!
blub blub blub
blubb

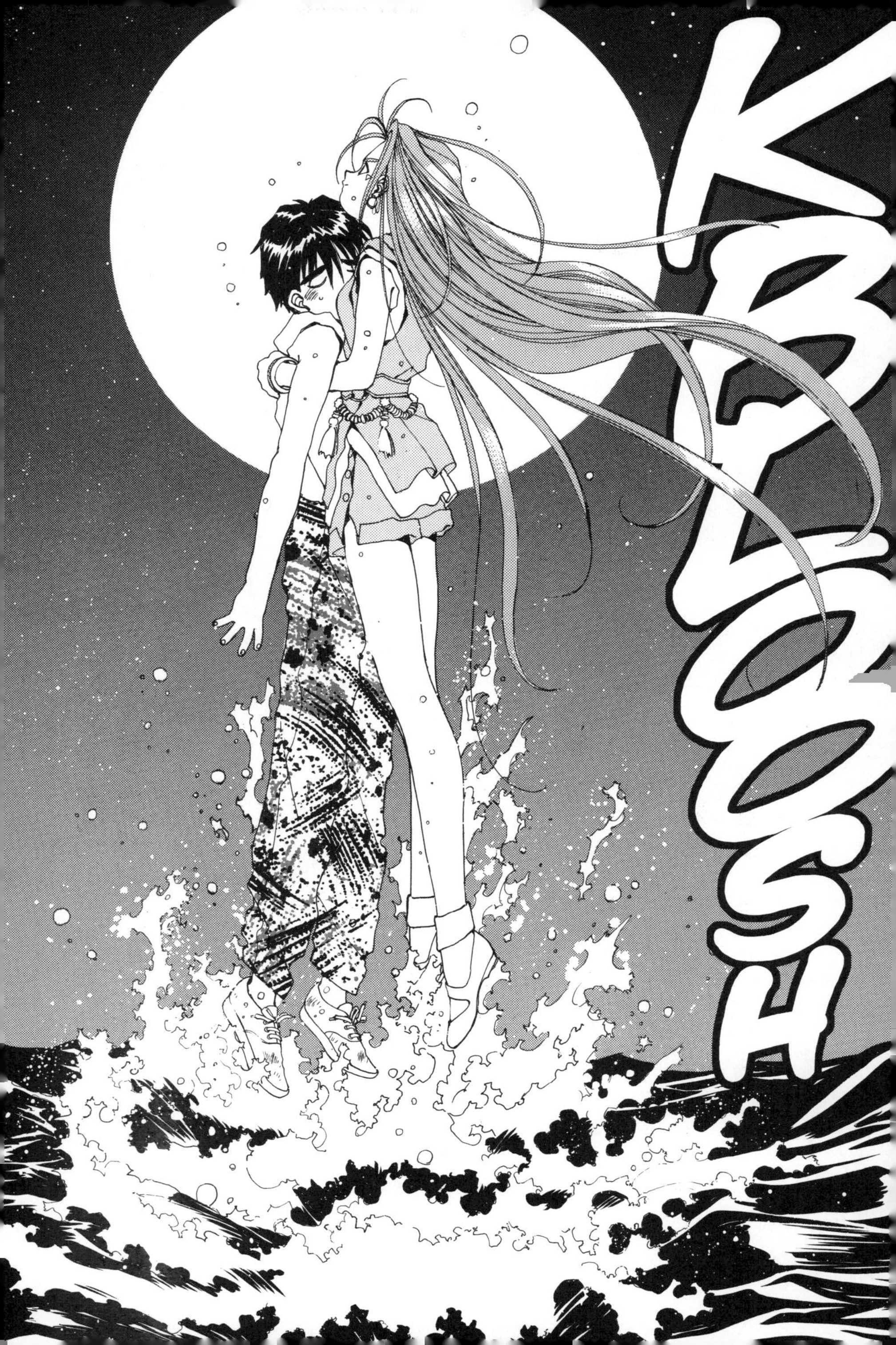
KRASHOOSH

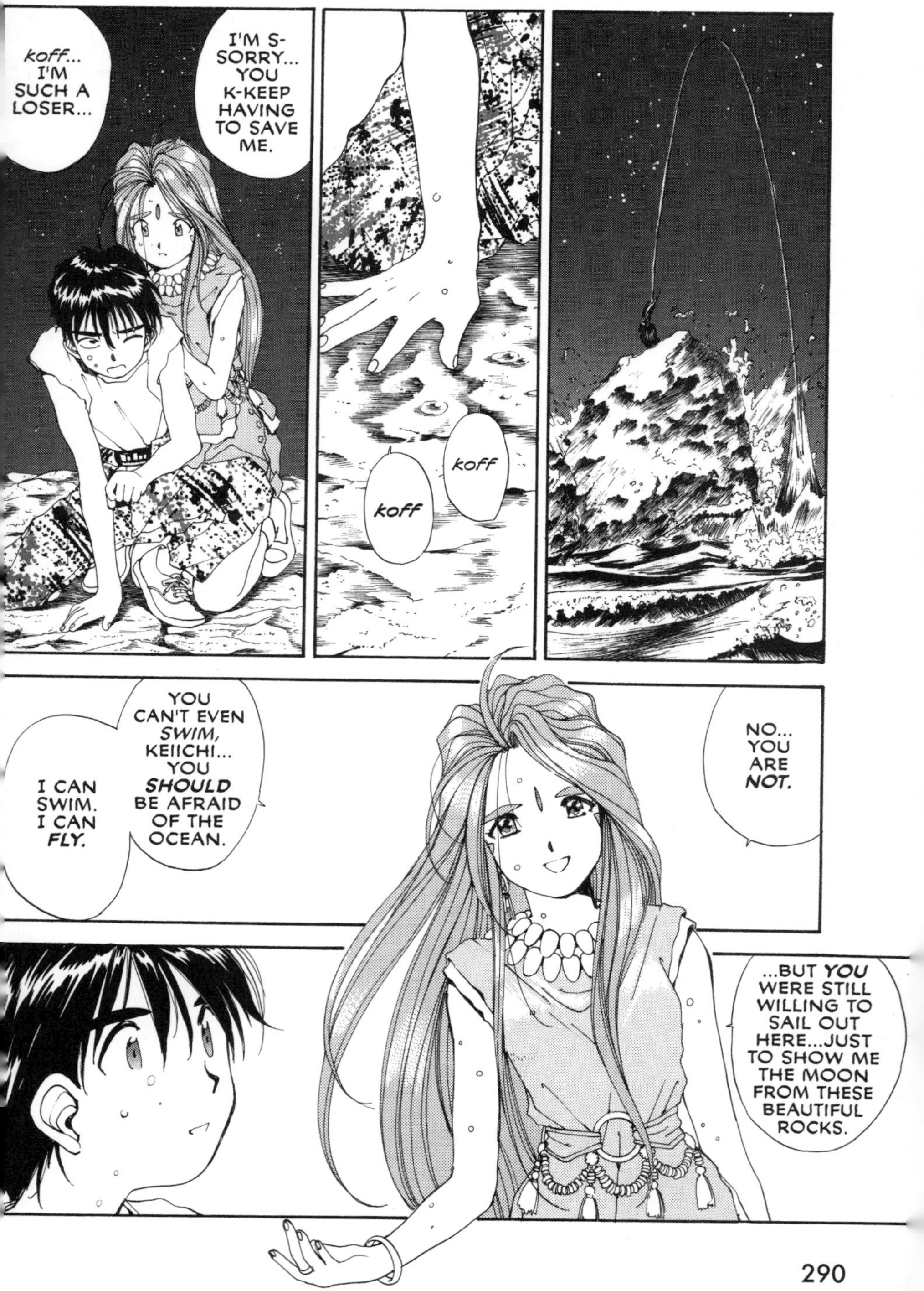
koff
koff
I'M S-SORRY... YOU K-KEEP HAVING TO SAVE ME.
koff... I'M SUCH A LOSER...
NO... YOU ARE NOT.
YOU CAN'T EVEN SWIM, KEIICHI... YOU SHOULD BE AFRAID OF THE OCEAN.
I CAN SWIM. I CAN FLY.
...BUT YOU WERE STILL WILLING TO SAIL OUT HERE...JUST TO SHOW ME THE MOON FROM THESE BEAUTIFUL ROCKS.

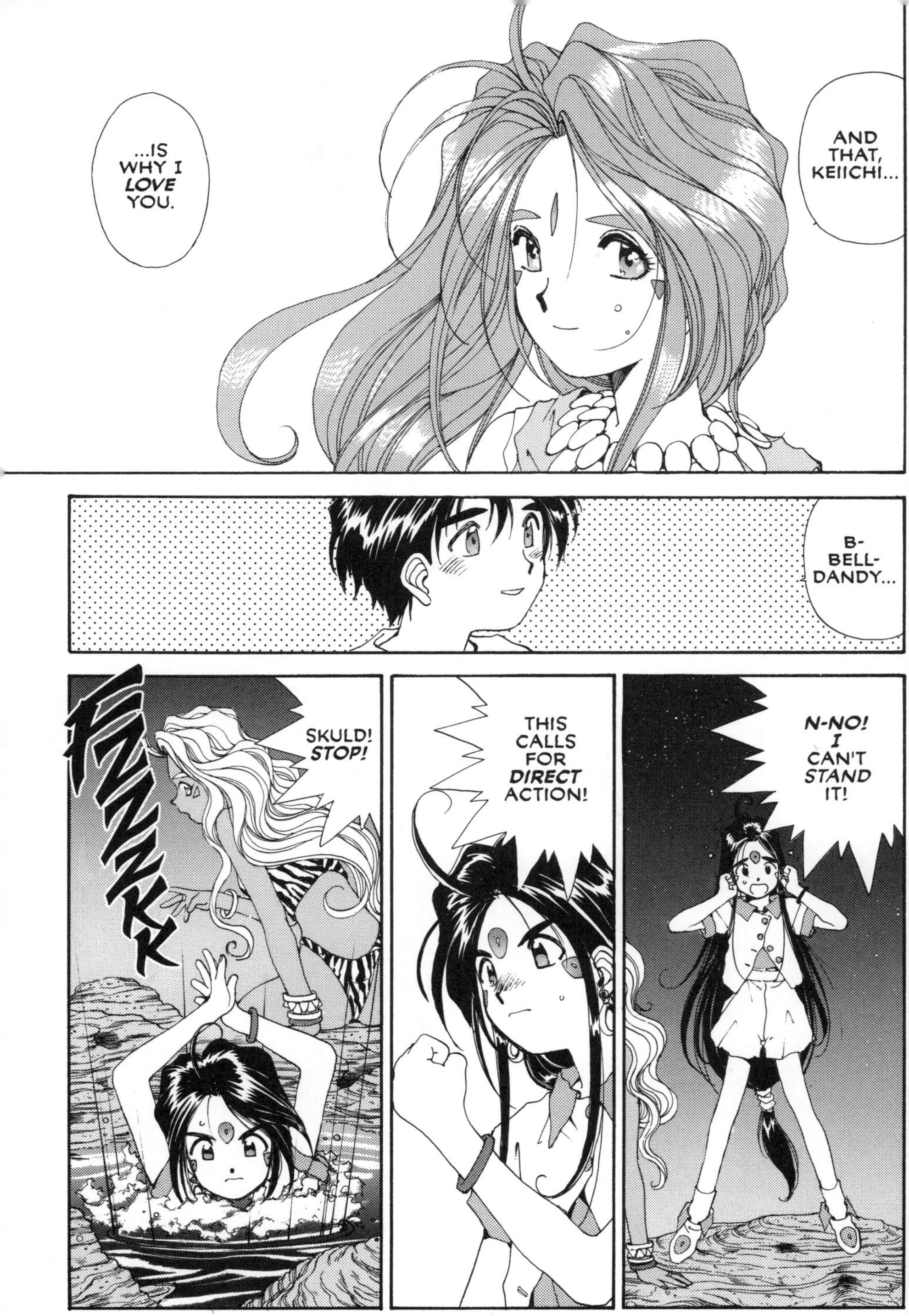
AND THAT, KEIICHI...
...IS WHY I LOVE YOU.
B-BELL-DANDY...
N-NO! I CAN'T STAND IT!
THIS CALLS FOR DIRECT ACTION!
SKULD! STOP!

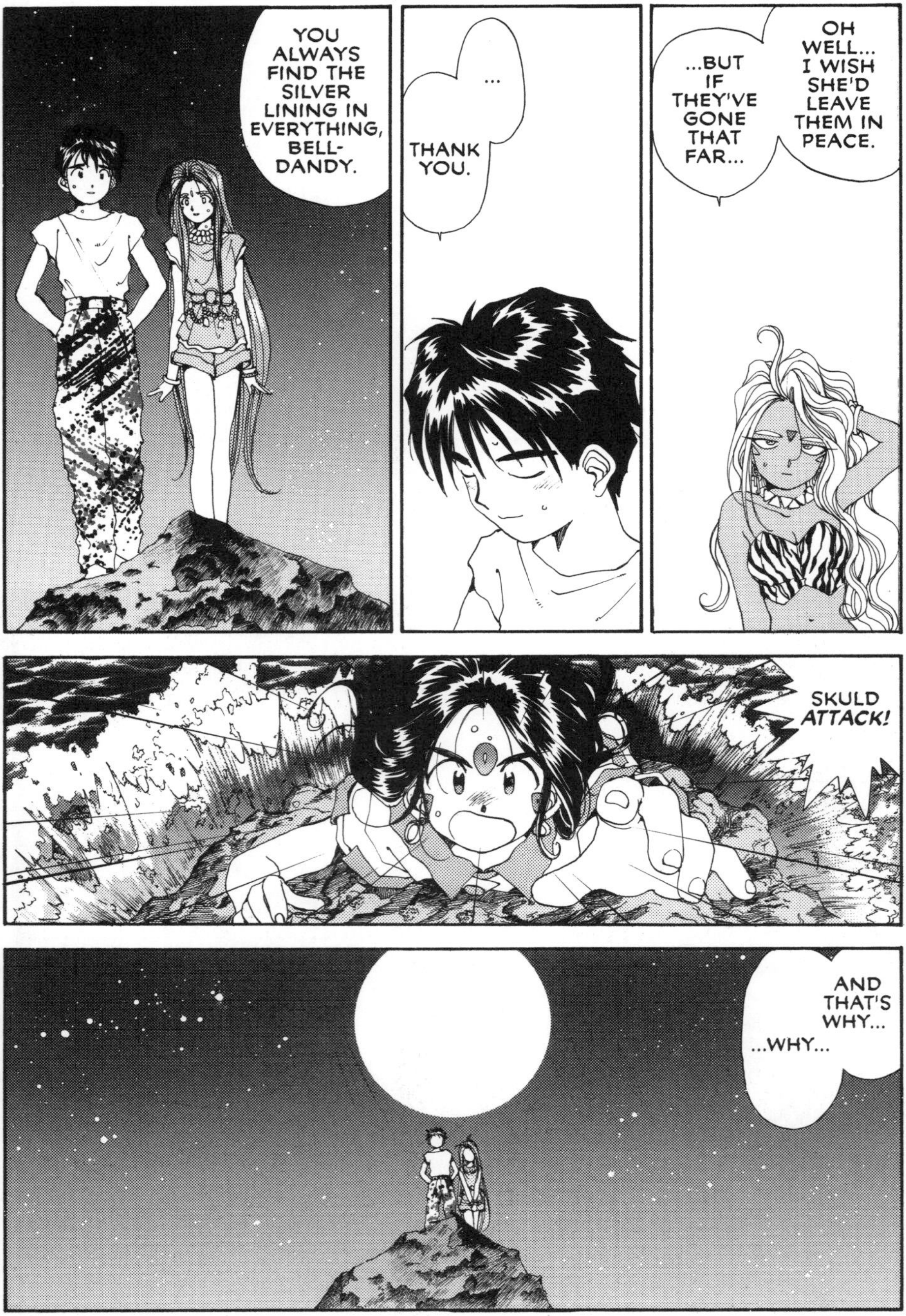
OH WELL... I WISH SHE'D LEAVE THEM IN PEACE.
...BUT IF THEY'VE GONE THAT FAR...
...
THANK YOU.
YOU ALWAYS FIND THE SILVER LINING IN EVERYTHING, BELL-DANDY.
SKULD *ATTACK!*
AND THAT'S WHY...
...WHY...

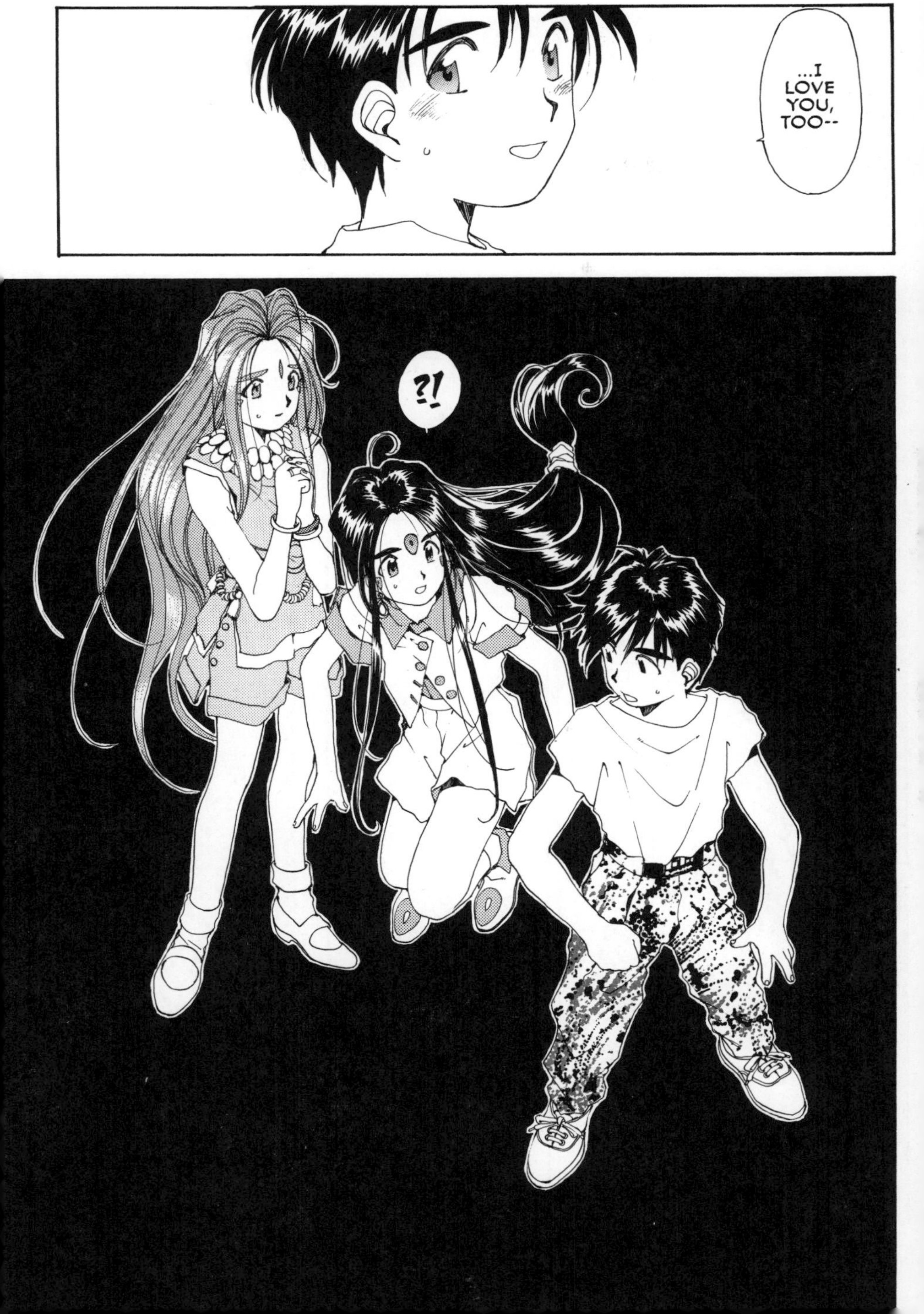
...I LOVE YOU, TOO--
?!

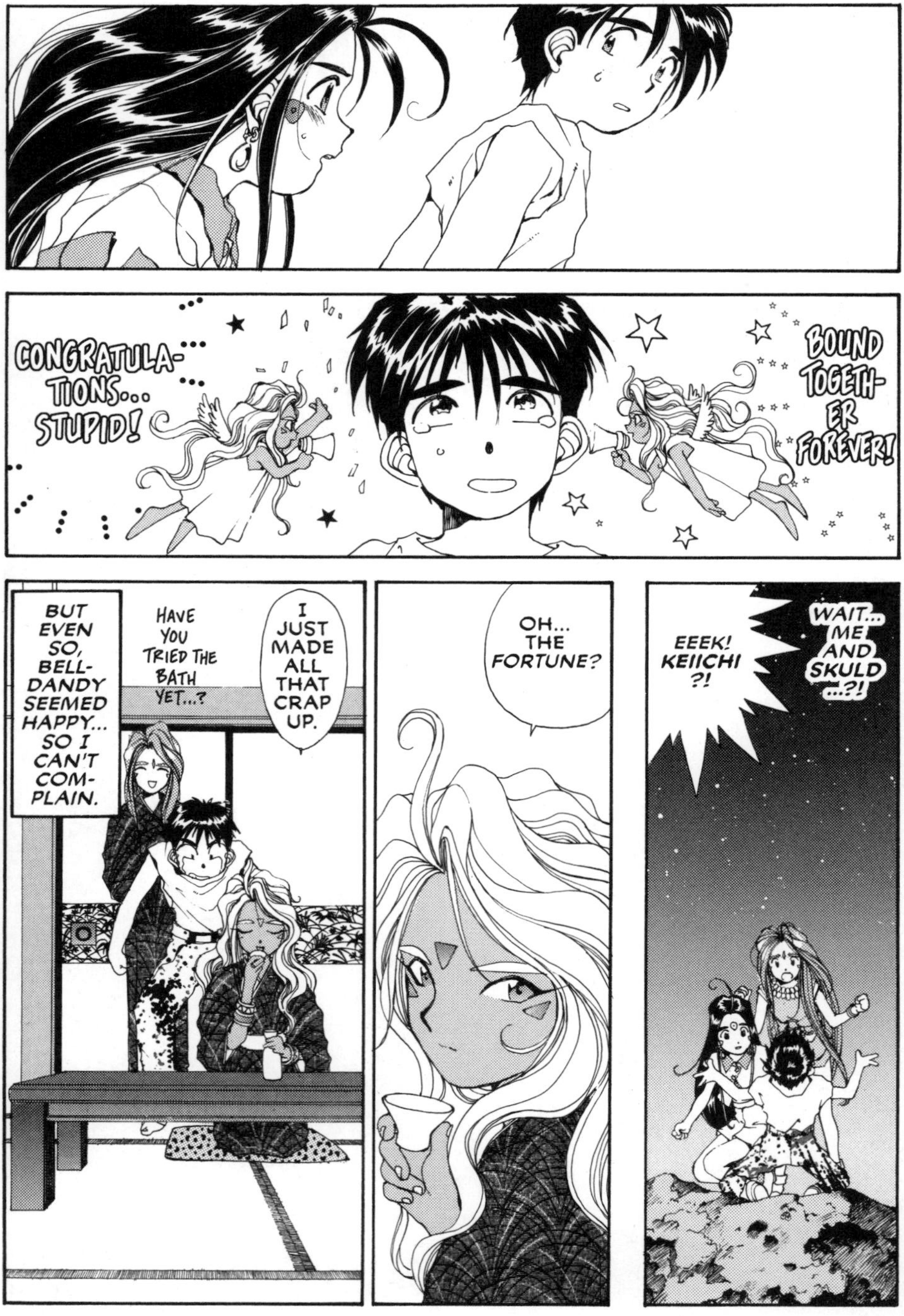
BOUND TOGETHER FOREVER!
CONGRATULATIONS... STUPID!
WAIT... ME AND SKULD ...?!
EEEK! KEIICHI ?!
OH... THE FORTUNE?
I JUST MADE ALL THAT CRAP UP.
HAVE YOU TRIED THE BATH YET...?
BUT EVEN SO, BELLDANDY SEEMED HAPPY... SO I CAN'T COMPLAIN.

CHAPTER 51

No, Sweetie

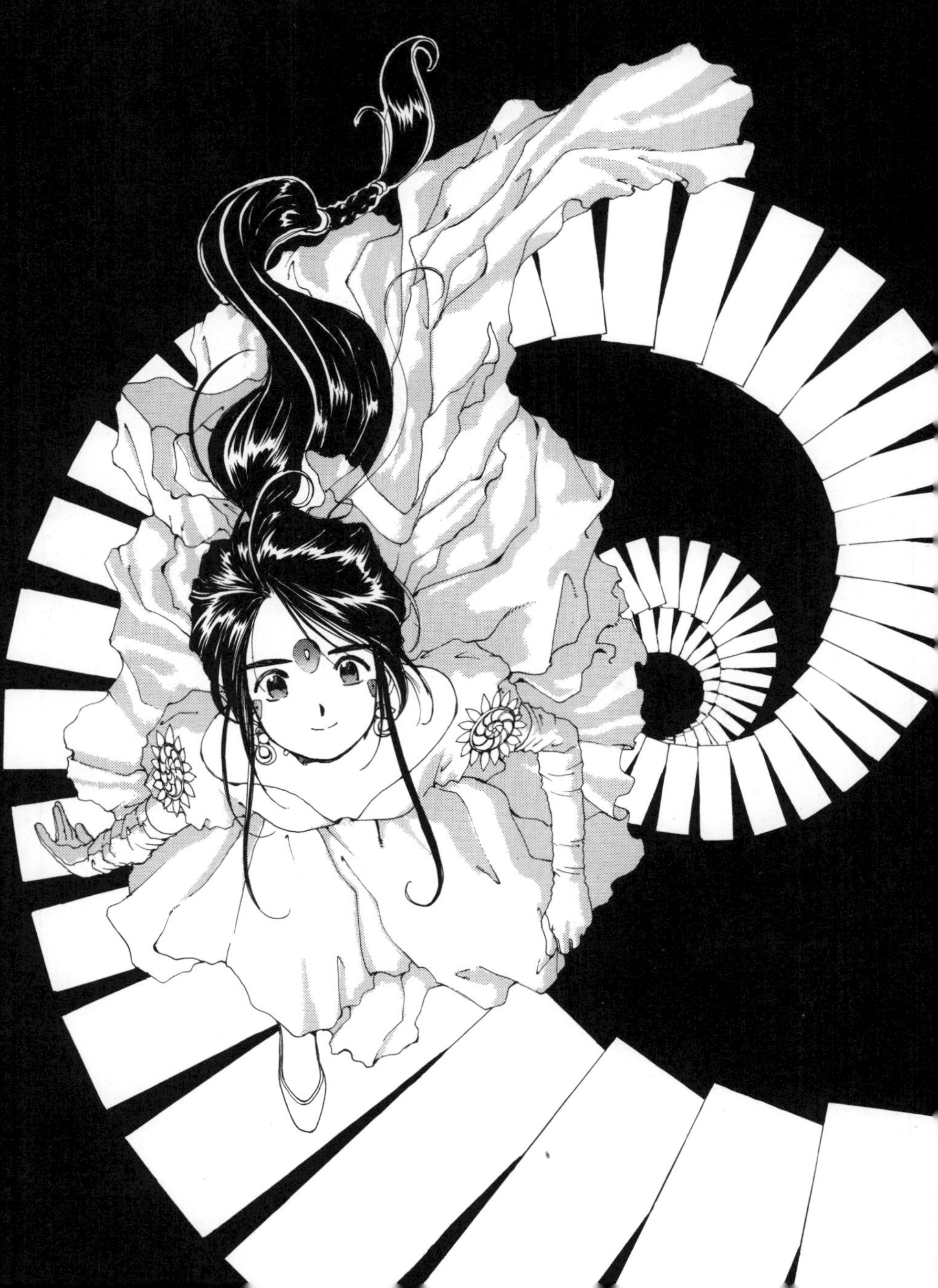

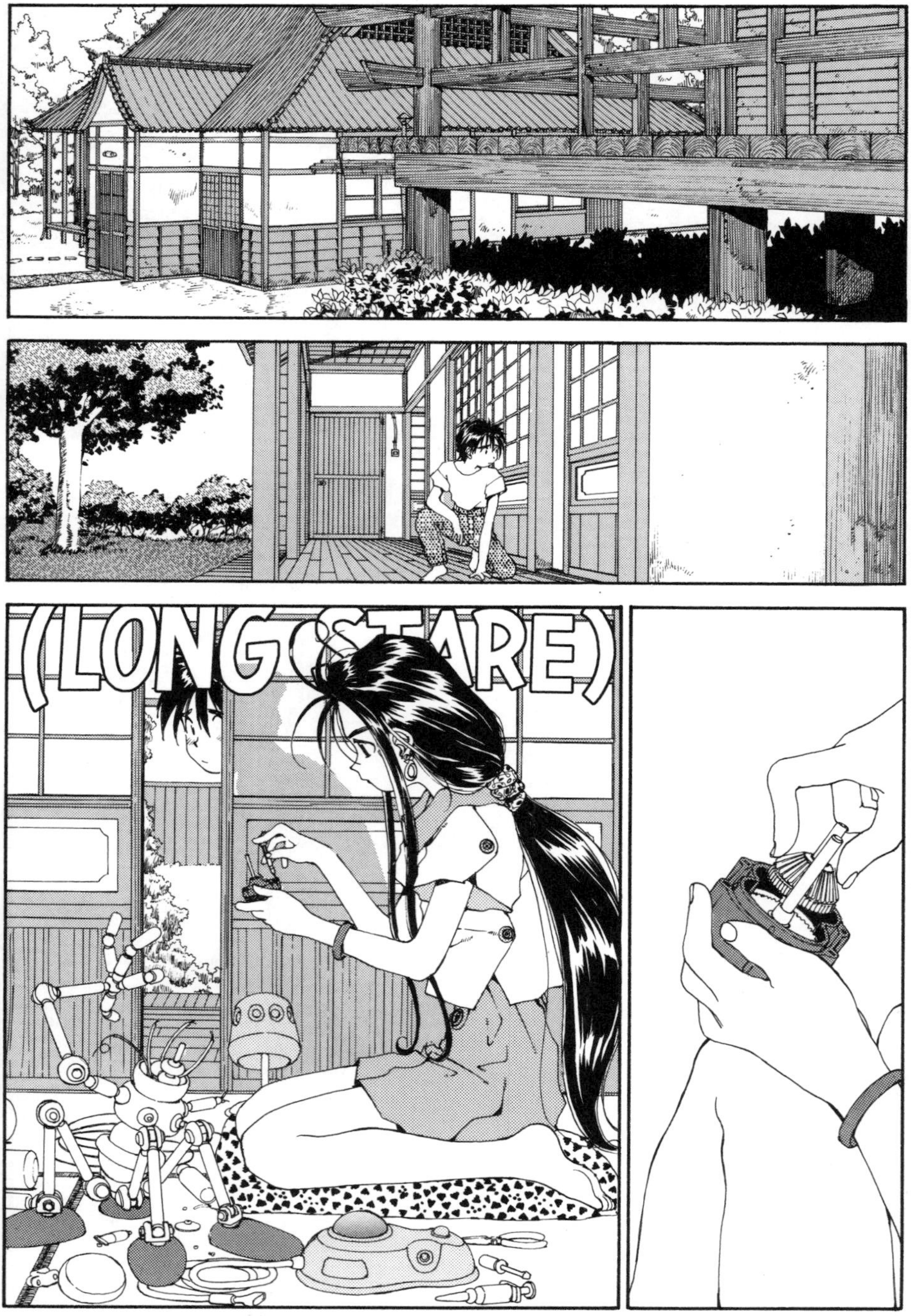
(LONG STARE)

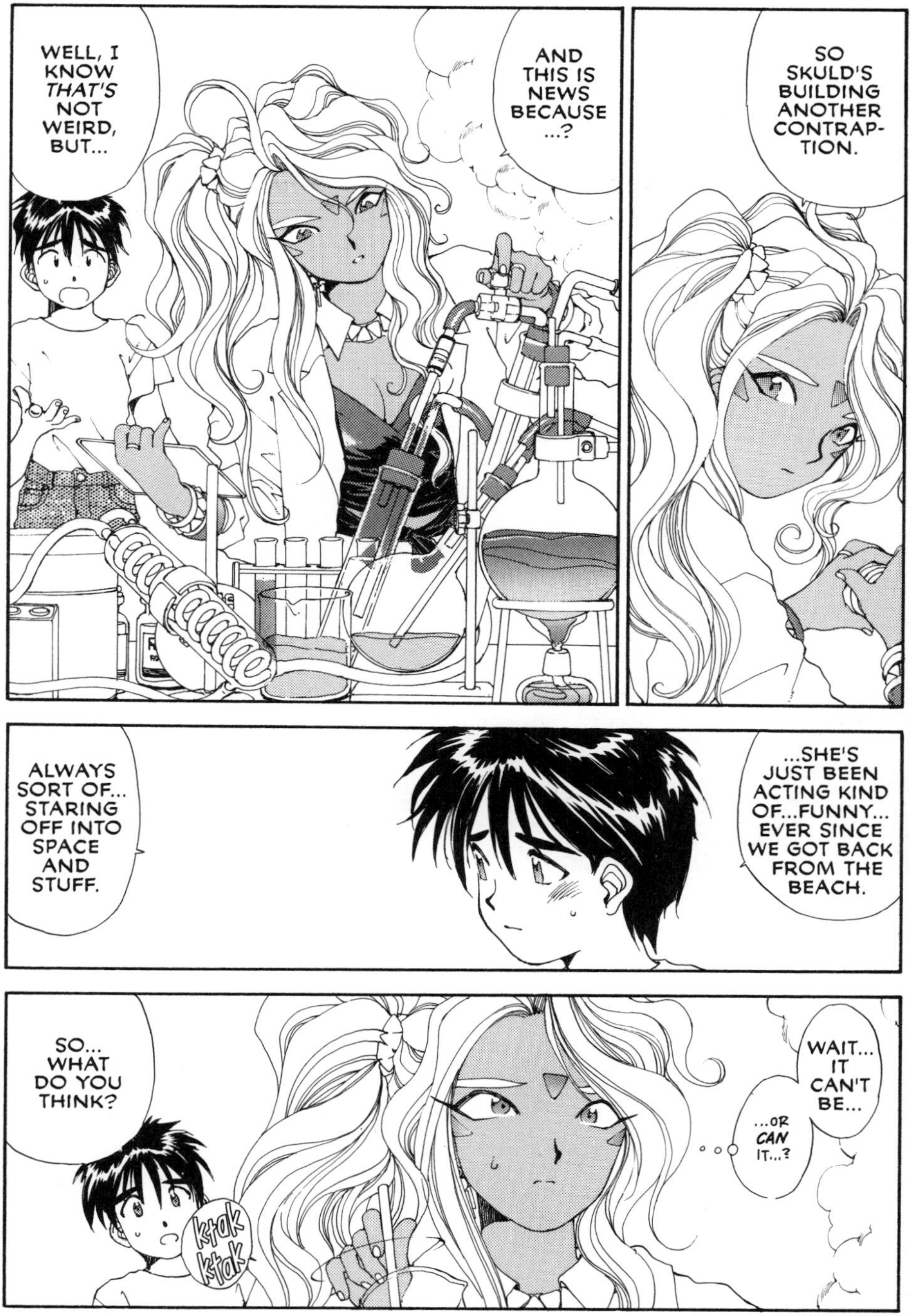
SO SKULD'S BUILDING ANOTHER CONTRAPTION.
AND THIS IS NEWS BECAUSE ...?
WELL, I KNOW *THAT'S* NOT WEIRD, BUT...
...SHE'S JUST BEEN ACTING KIND OF...FUNNY... EVER SINCE WE GOT BACK FROM THE BEACH.
ALWAYS SORT OF... STARING OFF INTO SPACE AND STUFF.
WAIT... IT CAN'T BE...
...OR **CAN** IT...?
SO... WHAT DO YOU THINK?
ktak ktak

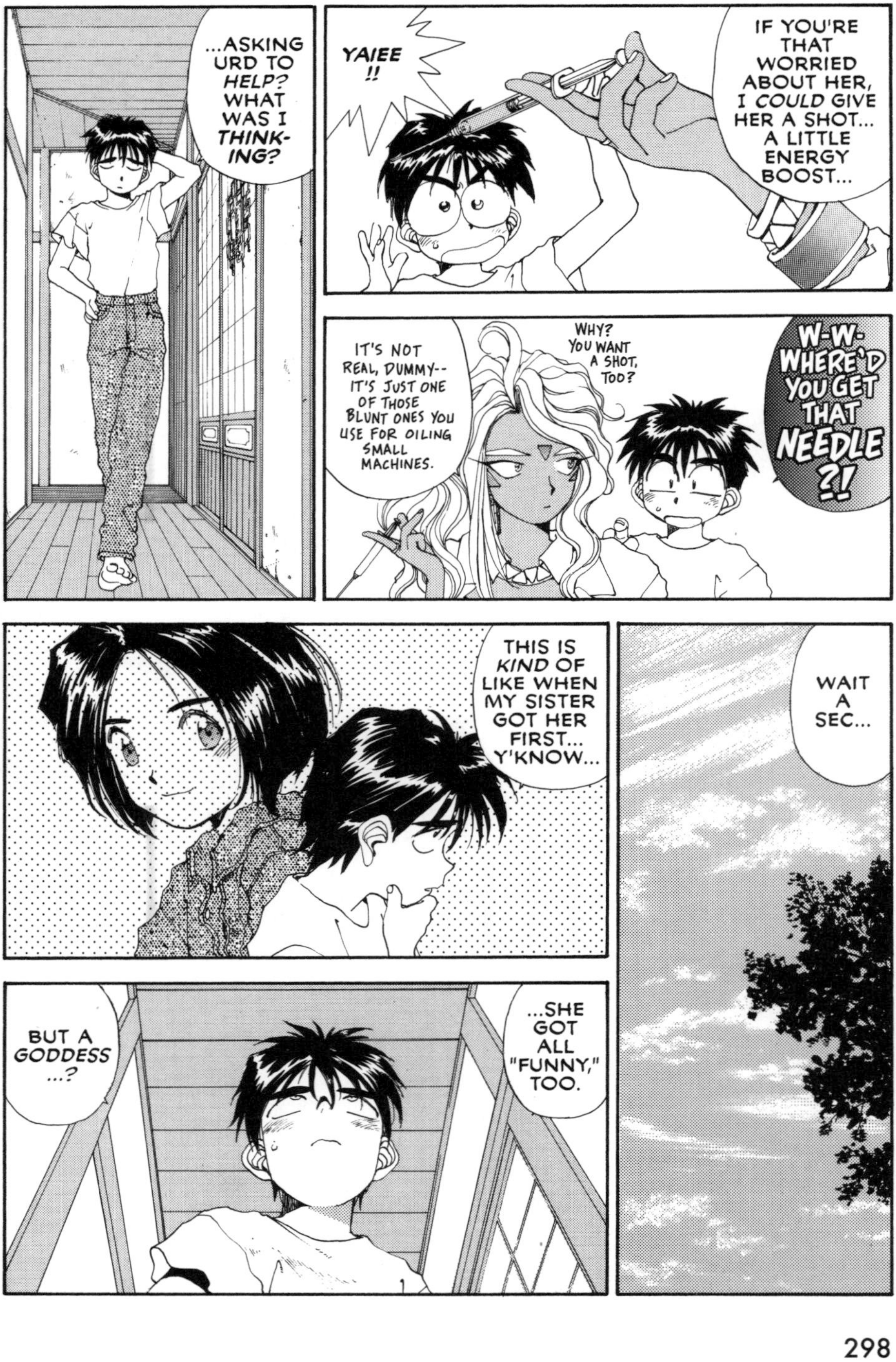
IF YOU'RE THAT WORRIED ABOUT HER, I COULD GIVE HER A SHOT... A LITTLE ENERGY BOOST...
YAIEE!!
W-W-WHERE'D YOU GET THAT NEEDLE?!
WHY? YOU WANT A SHOT, TOO?
IT'S NOT REAL, DUMMY-- IT'S JUST ONE OF THOSE BLUNT ONES YOU USE FOR OILING SMALL MACHINES.
...ASKING URD TO HELP? WHAT WAS I THINKING?
WAIT A SEC...
THIS IS KIND OF LIKE WHEN MY SISTER GOT HER FIRST... Y'KNOW...
...SHE GOT ALL "FUNNY," TOO.
BUT A GODDESS...?

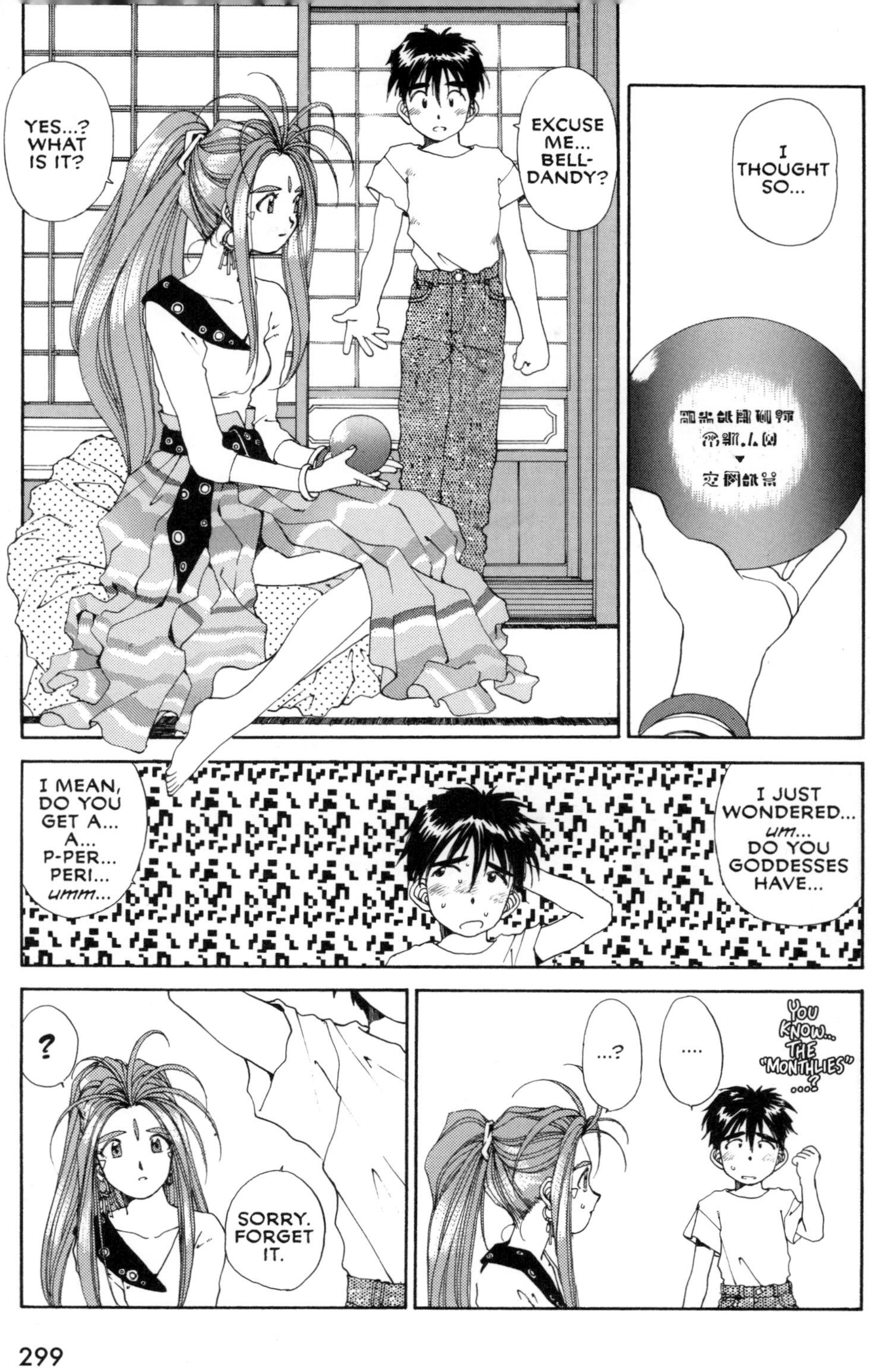
I THOUGHT SO...
EXCUSE ME... BELL-DANDY?
YES...? WHAT IS IT?
I JUST WONDERED... *um*... DO YOU GODDESSES HAVE...
I MEAN, DO YOU GET A... A... P-PER... PERI... *umm*...
YOU KNOW... THE "MONTHLIES"...?
....
...?
?
SORRY. FORGET IT.

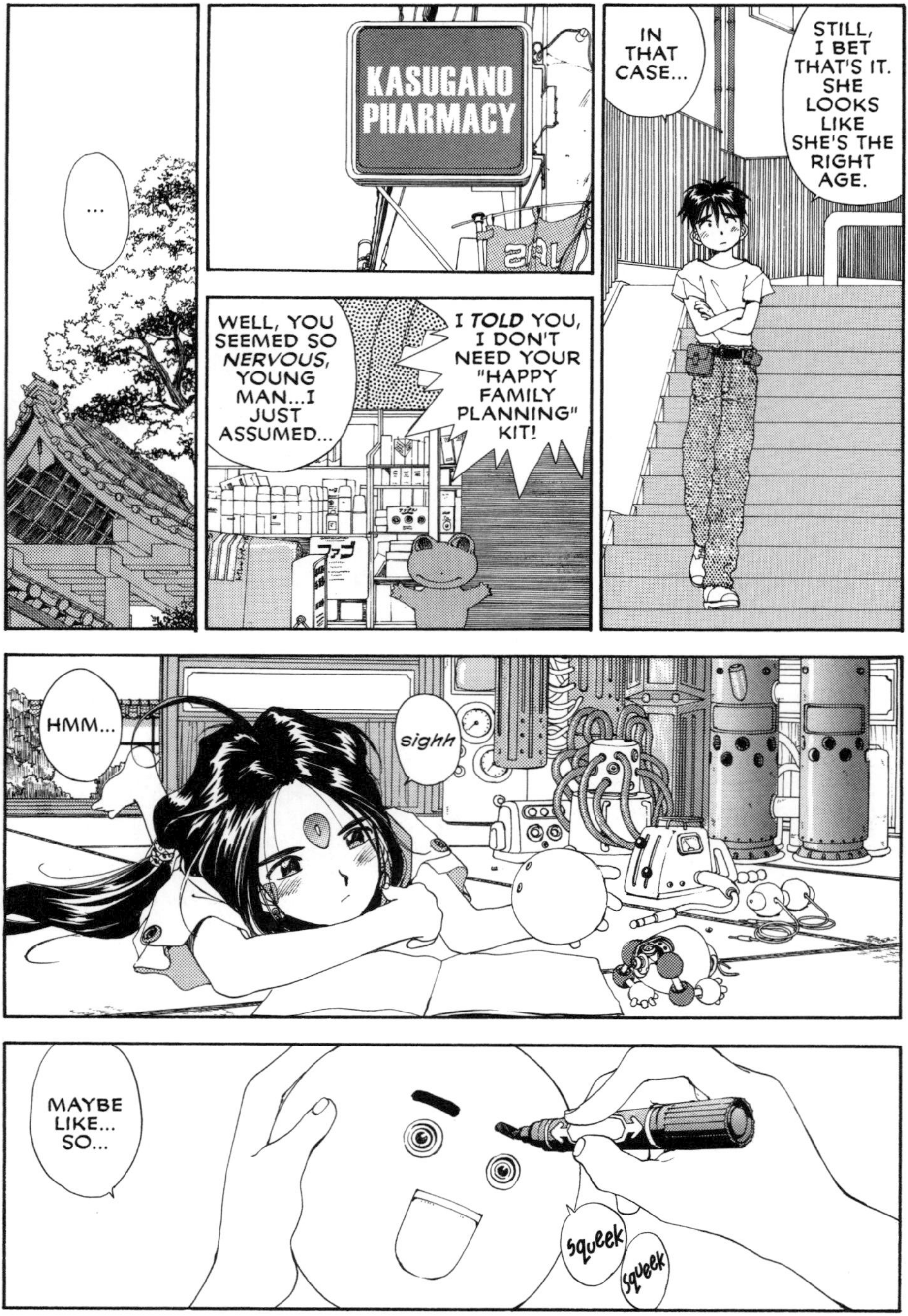
STILL, I BET THAT'S IT. SHE LOOKS LIKE SHE'S THE RIGHT AGE.
IN THAT CASE...
KASUGANO PHARMACY
I *TOLD* YOU, I DON'T NEED YOUR "HAPPY FAMILY PLANNING" KIT!
WELL, YOU SEEMED SO *NERVOUS*, YOUNG MAN...I JUST ASSUMED...
...
sighh
HMM...
squeek
squeek
MAYBE LIKE... SO...

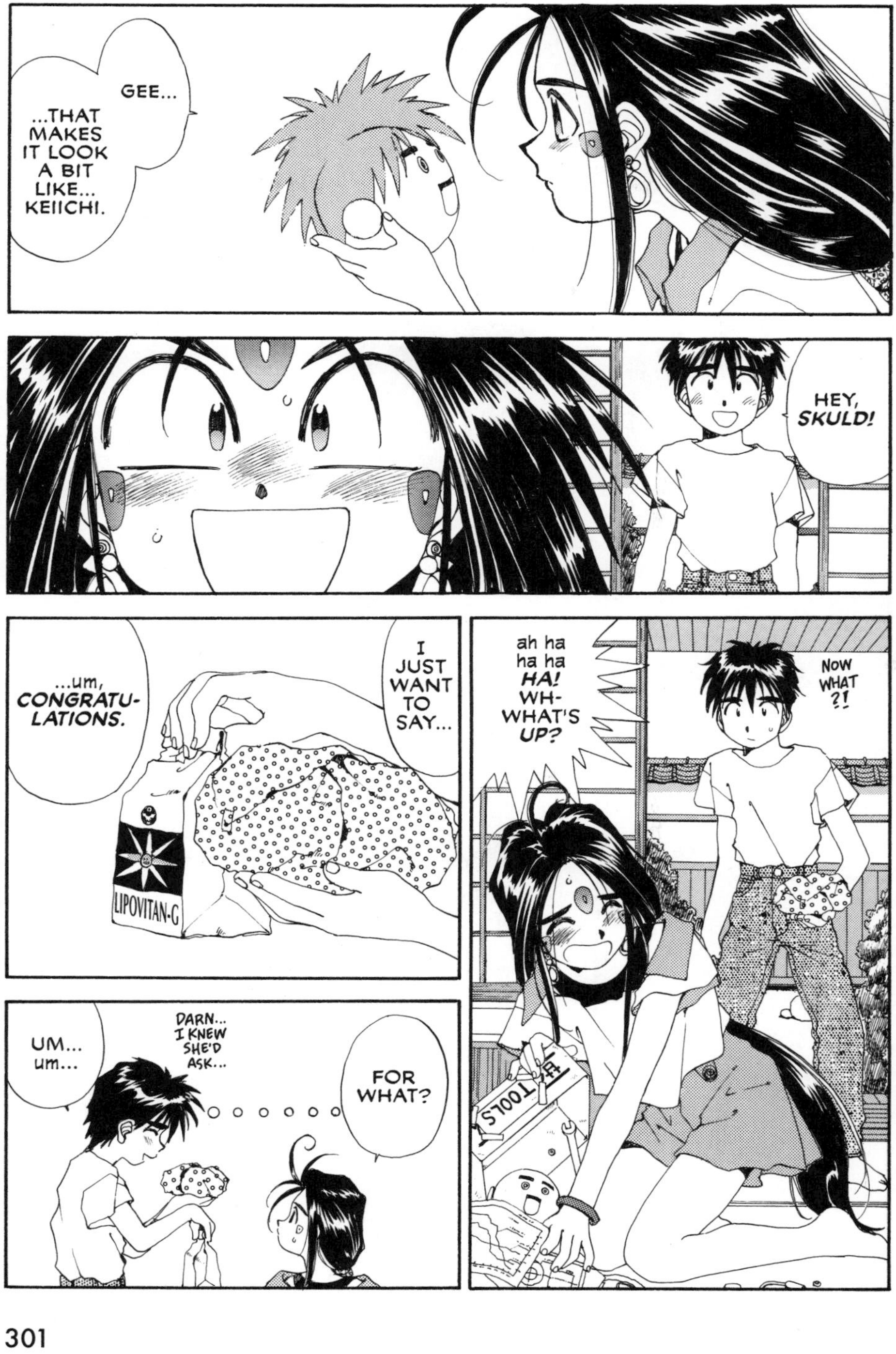
GEE...
...THAT MAKES IT LOOK A BIT LIKE... KEIICHI.
HEY, SKULD!
ah ha ha ha HA! WH-WHAT'S UP?
NOW WHAT?!
TOOLS
I JUST WANT TO SAY...
...um, CONGRATULATIONS.
LIPOVITAN-G
FOR WHAT?
DARN... I KNEW SHE'D ASK...
UM... um...

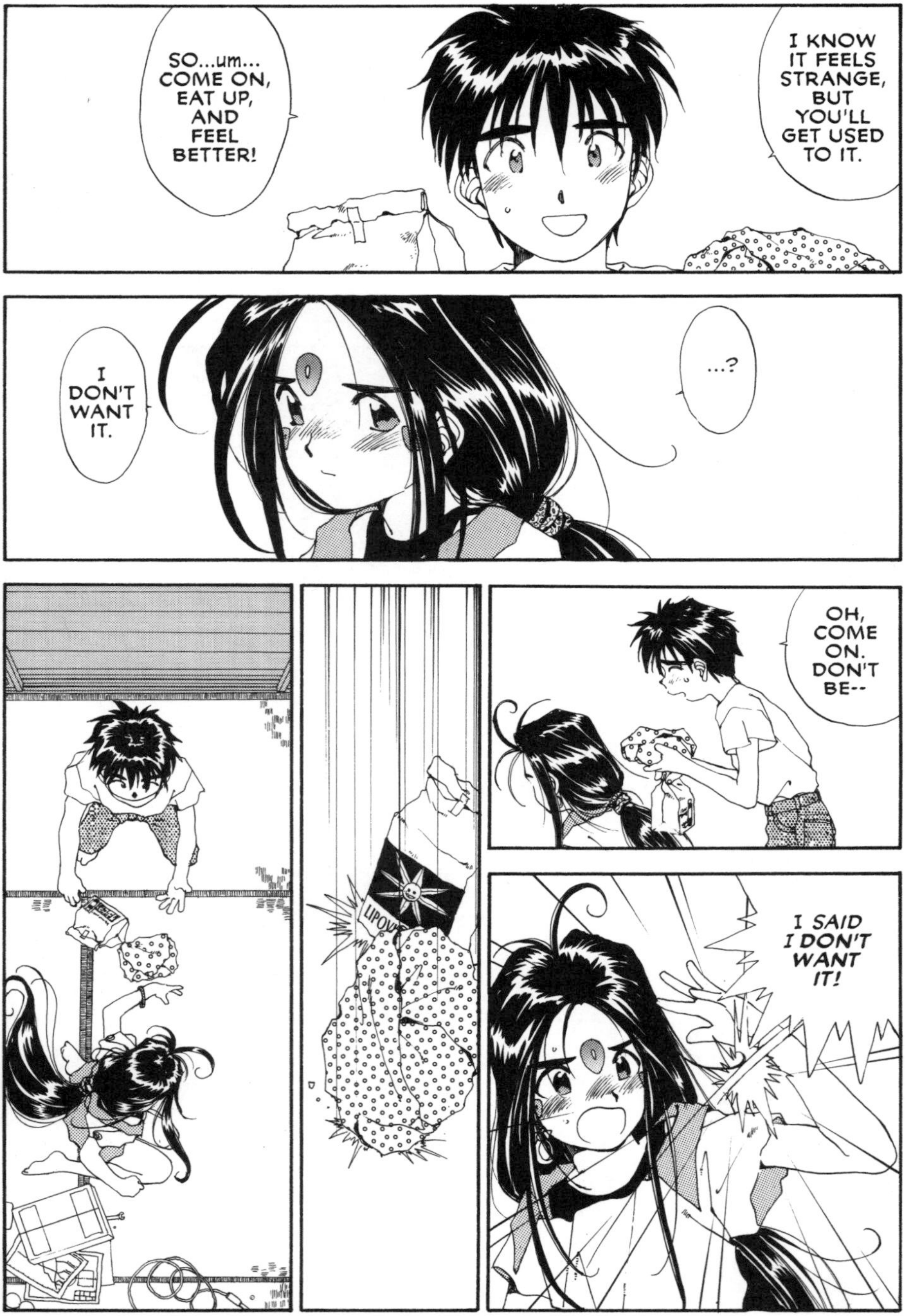
I KNOW IT FEELS STRANGE, BUT YOU'LL GET USED TO IT.
SO...um... COME ON, EAT UP, AND FEEL BETTER!
...?
I DON'T WANT IT.
OH, COME ON. DON'T BE--
I SAID I DON'T WANT IT!

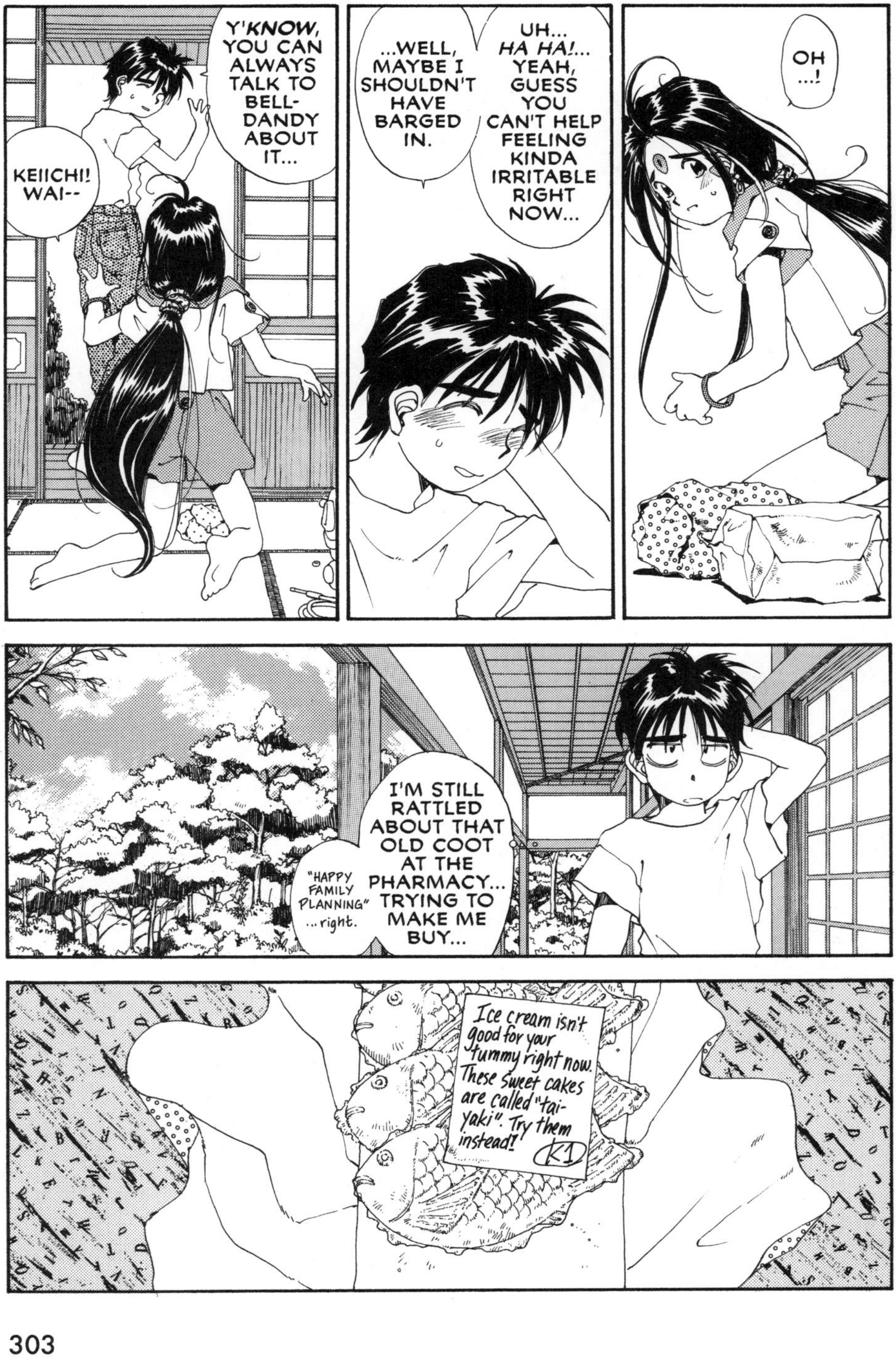
OH ...!
UH... HA HA!... YEAH, GUESS YOU CAN'T HELP FEELING KINDA IRRITABLE RIGHT NOW...
...WELL, MAYBE I SHOULDN'T HAVE BARGED IN.
Y'KNOW, YOU CAN ALWAYS TALK TO BELL-DANDY ABOUT IT...
KEIICHI! WAI--
I'M STILL RATTLED ABOUT THAT OLD COOT AT THE PHARMACY... TRYING TO MAKE ME BUY...
"HAPPY FAMILY PLANNING" ...right.
Ice cream isn't good for your tummy right now. These sweet cakes are called "tai-yaki". Try them instead! K1

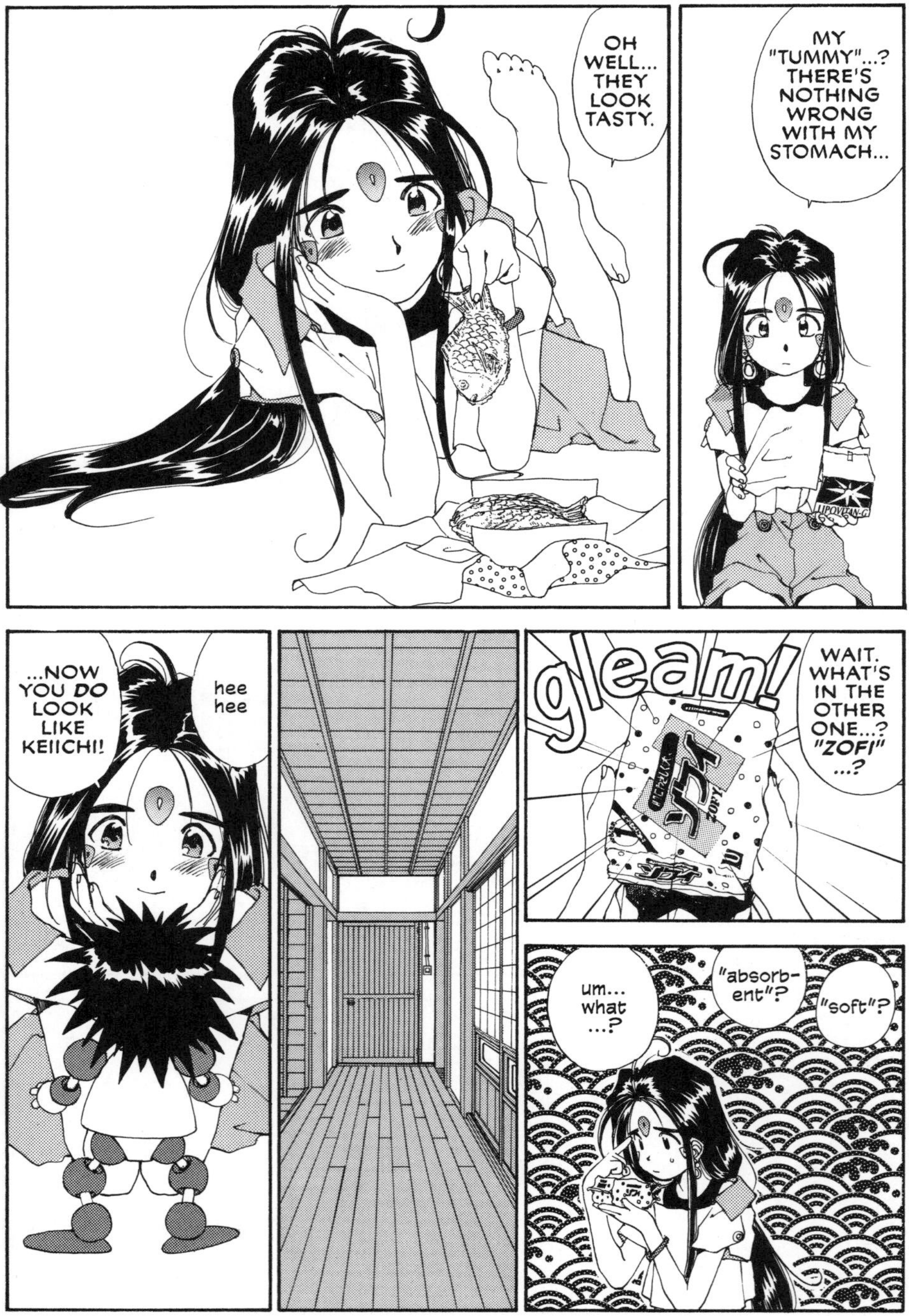
MY "TUMMY"...? THERE'S NOTHING WRONG WITH MY STOMACH...
LIPOVITAN-G
OH WELL... THEY LOOK TASTY.
WAIT. WHAT'S IN THE OTHER ONE...? "*ZOFI*" ...?
gleam!
"soft"?
"absorb-ent"?
um... what ...?
hee hee
...NOW YOU *DO* LOOK LIKE KEIICHI!

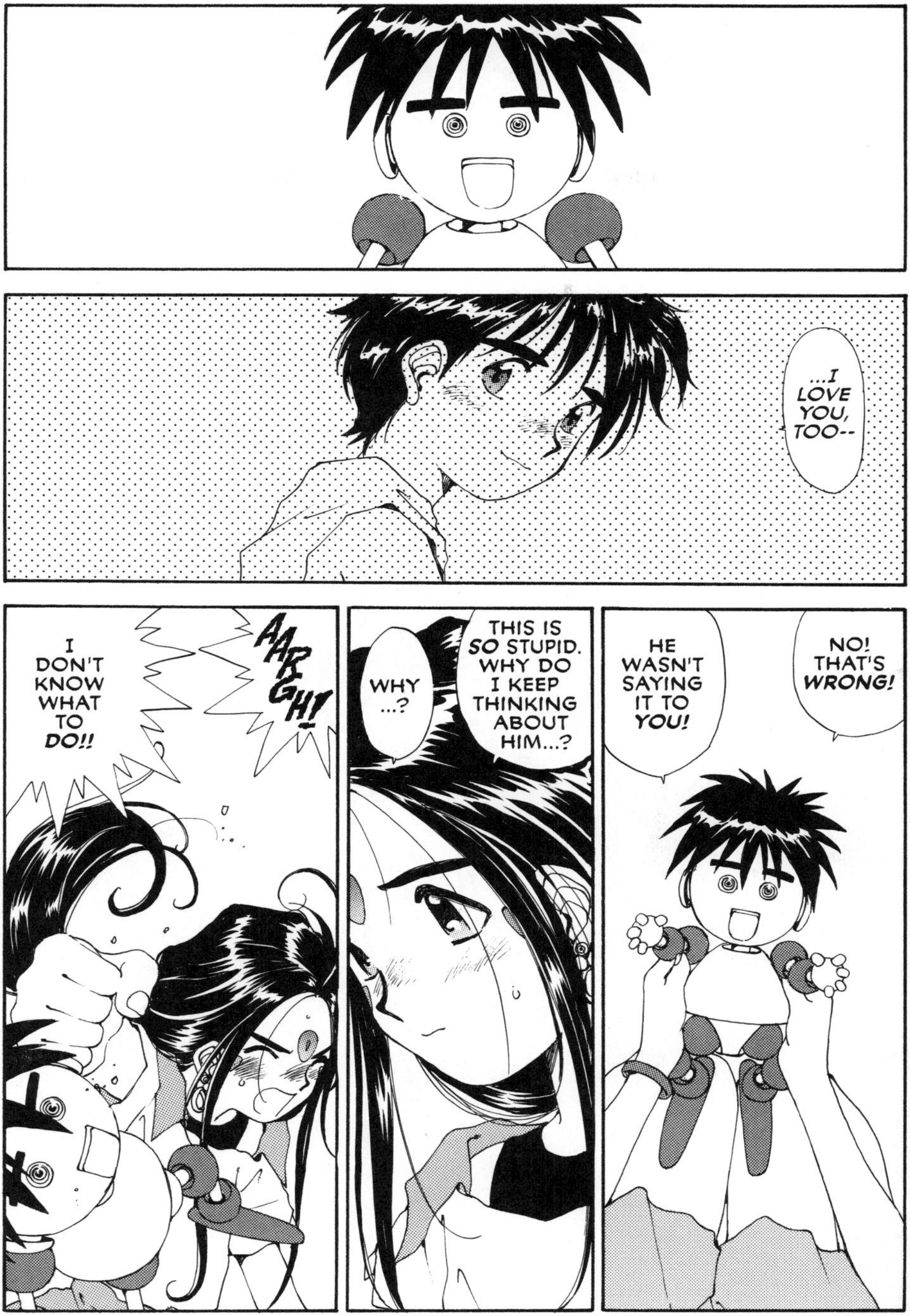
...I LOVE YOU, TOO--
NO! THAT'S *WRONG!*
HE WASN'T SAYING IT TO *YOU!*
THIS IS *SO* STUPID. WHY DO I KEEP THINKING ABOUT HIM...?
WHY ...?
AARGH!
I DON'T KNOW WHAT TO *DO!!*

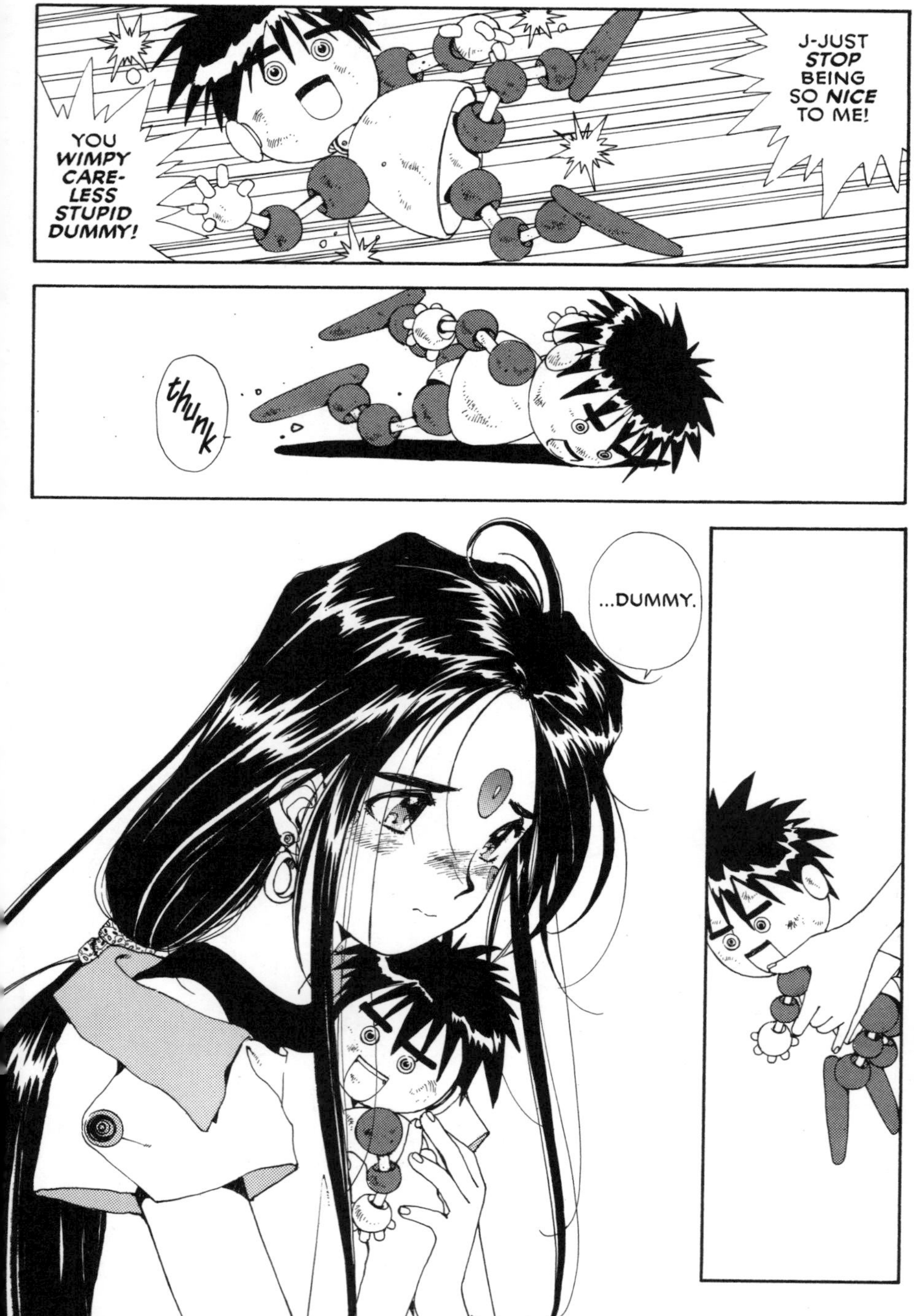
J-JUST STOP BEING SO NICE TO ME!
YOU WIMPY CARE-LESS STUPID DUMMY!
thunk
...DUMMY.

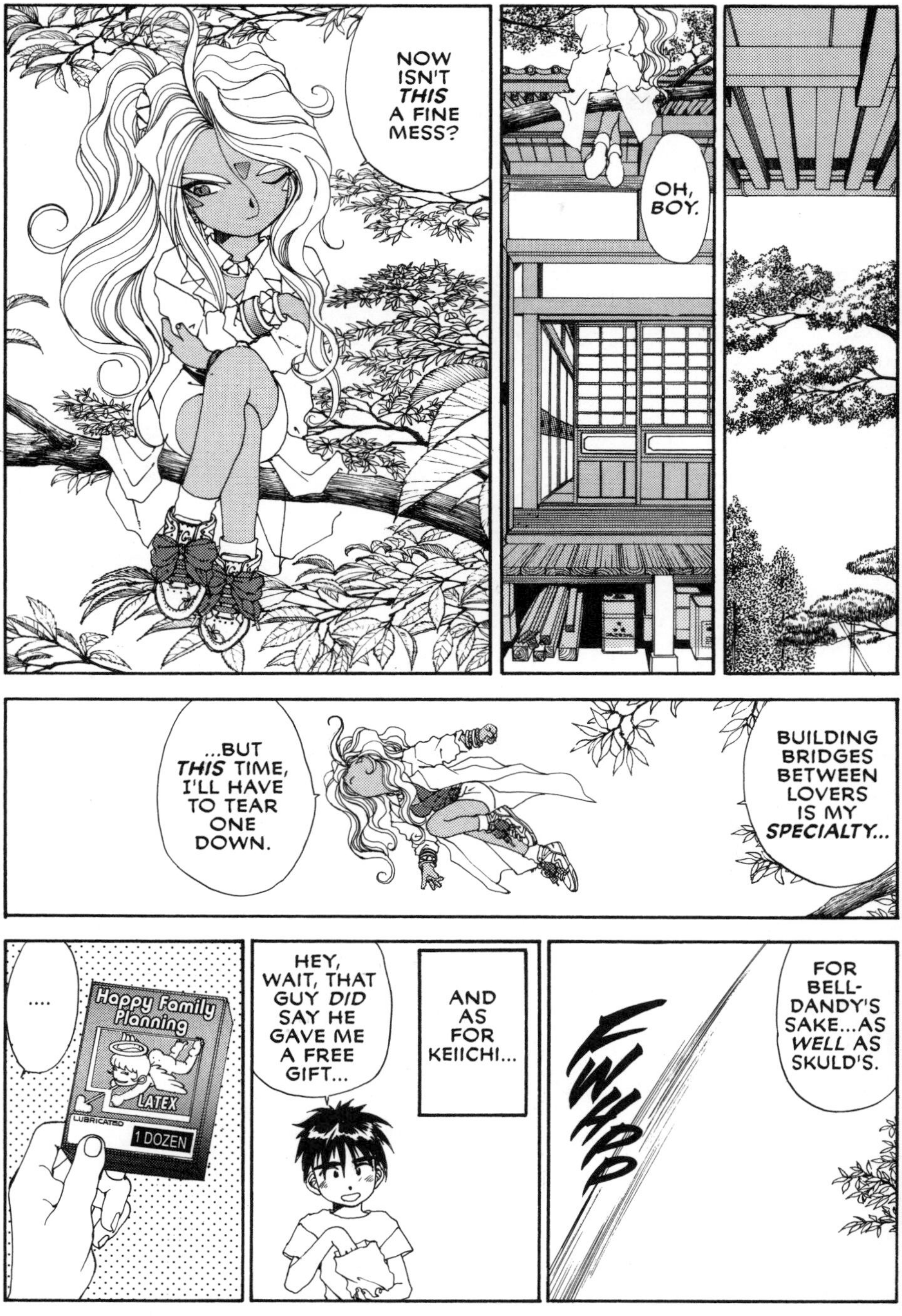
OH, BOY.
NOW ISN'T THIS A FINE MESS?
BUILDING BRIDGES BETWEEN LOVERS IS MY SPECIALTY...
...BUT THIS TIME, I'LL HAVE TO TEAR ONE DOWN.
FOR BELL-DANDY'S SAKE...AS WELL AS SKULD'S.
AND AS FOR KEIICHI...
HEY, WAIT, THAT GUY DID SAY HE GAVE ME A FREE GIFT...
....
Happy Family Planning
LATEX
LUBRICATED
1 DOZEN

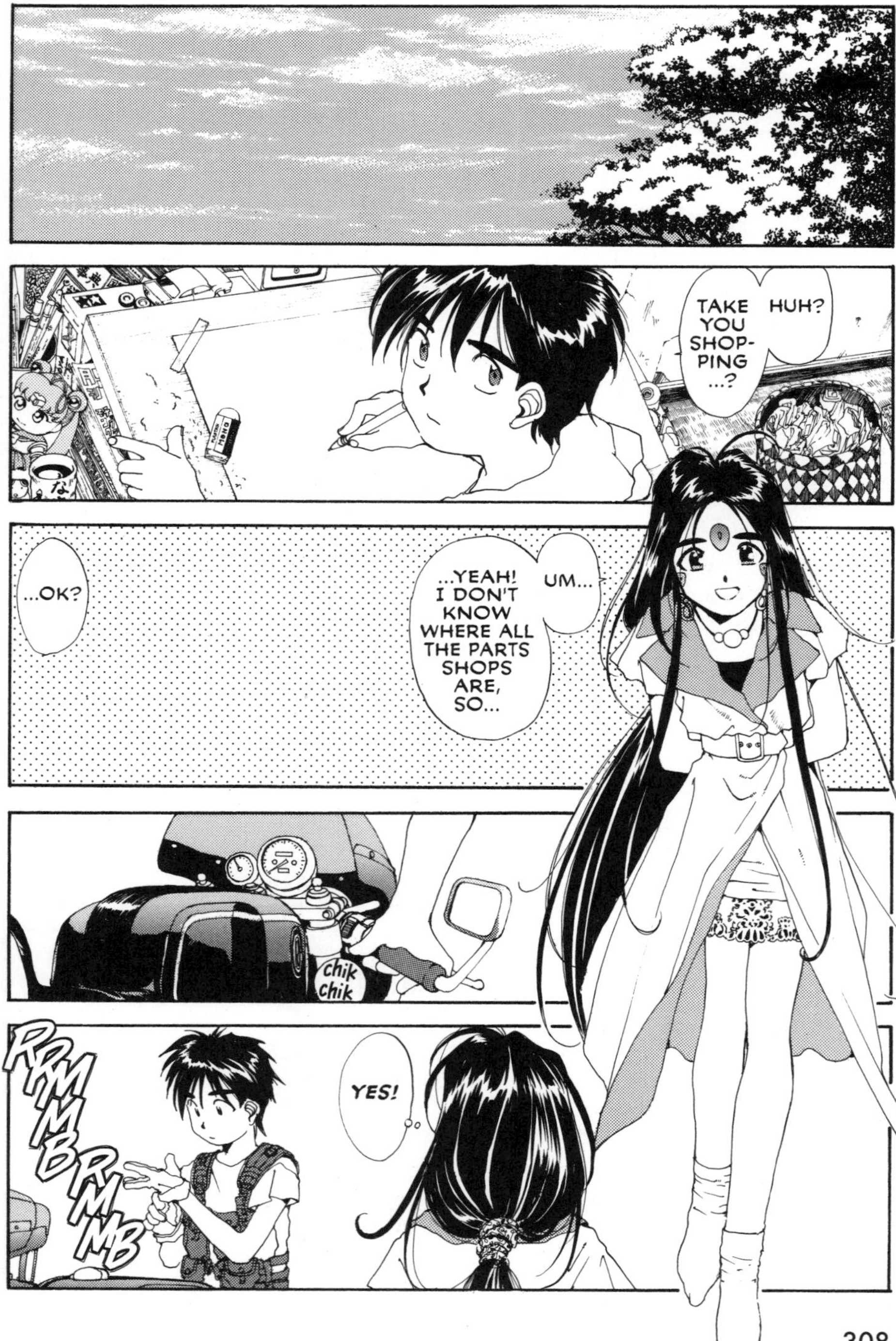
HUH?
TAKE YOU SHOPPING...?
UM...
...YEAH! I DON'T KNOW WHERE ALL THE PARTS SHOPS ARE, SO...
...OK?
chik chik
YES!
RRMMB RMMB

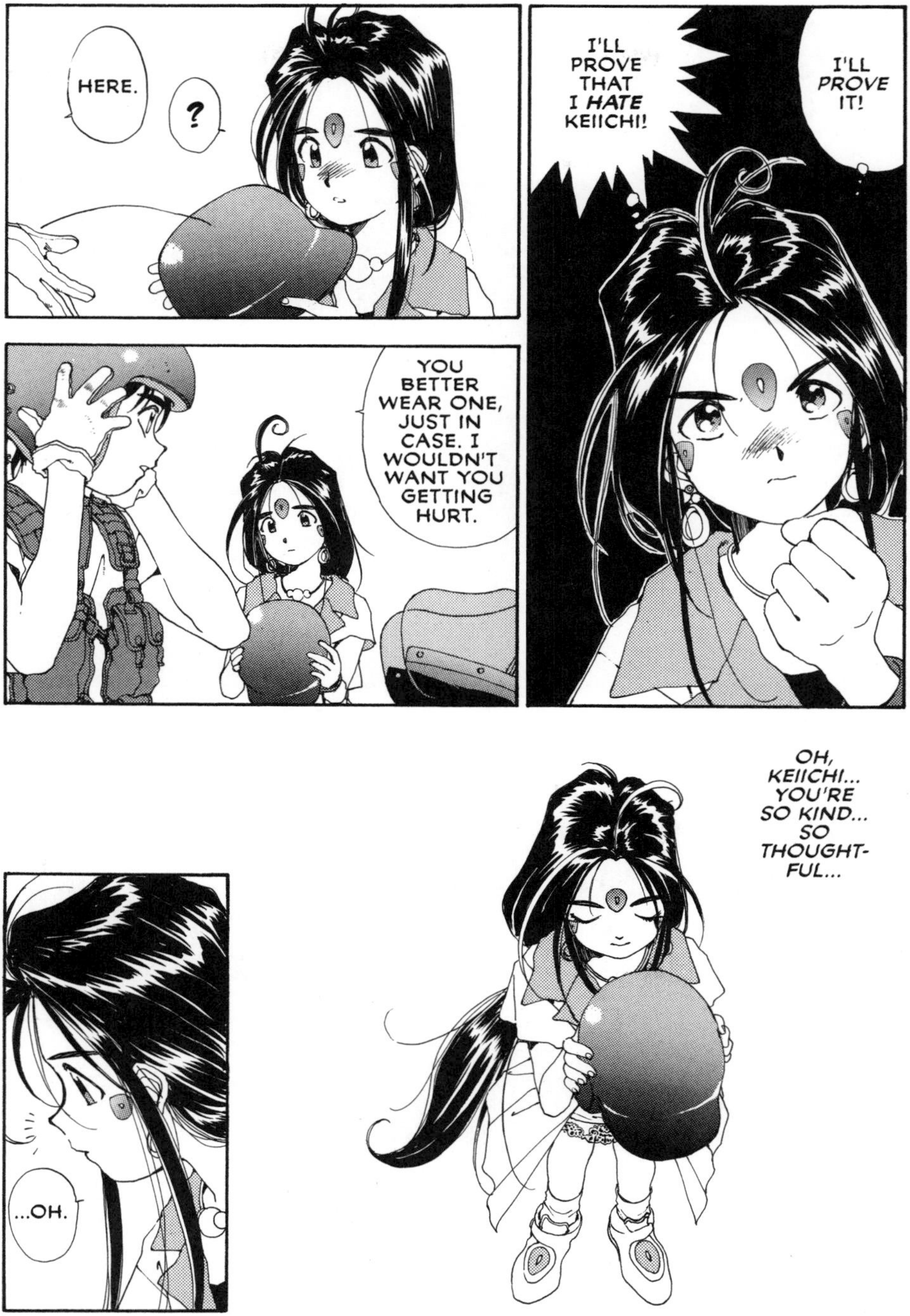
I'LL PROVE IT!
I'LL PROVE THAT I *HATE* KEIICHI!
HERE.
?
YOU BETTER WEAR ONE, JUST IN CASE. I WOULDN'T WANT YOU GETTING HURT.
OH, KEIICHI... YOU'RE SO KIND... SO THOUGHT-FUL...
...OH.

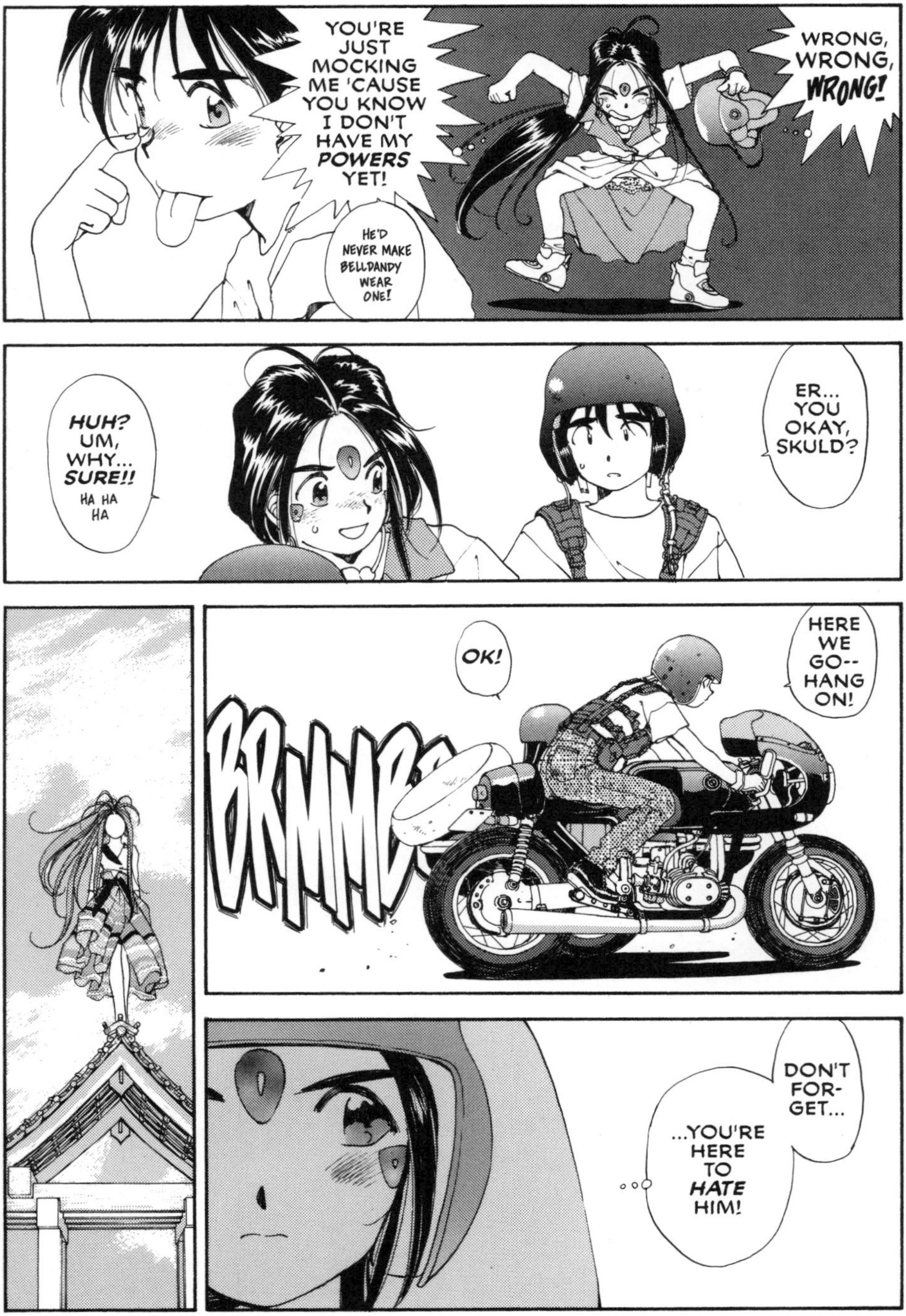
WRONG, WRONG, WRONG!
YOU'RE JUST MOCKING ME 'CAUSE YOU KNOW I DON'T HAVE MY POWERS YET!
HE'D NEVER MAKE BELLDANDY WEAR ONE!
ER... YOU OKAY, SKULD?
HUH? UM, WHY... SURE!! HA HA HA
HERE WE GO-- HANG ON!
OK!
BRMMB
DON'T FOR- GET...
...YOU'RE HERE TO HATE HIM!

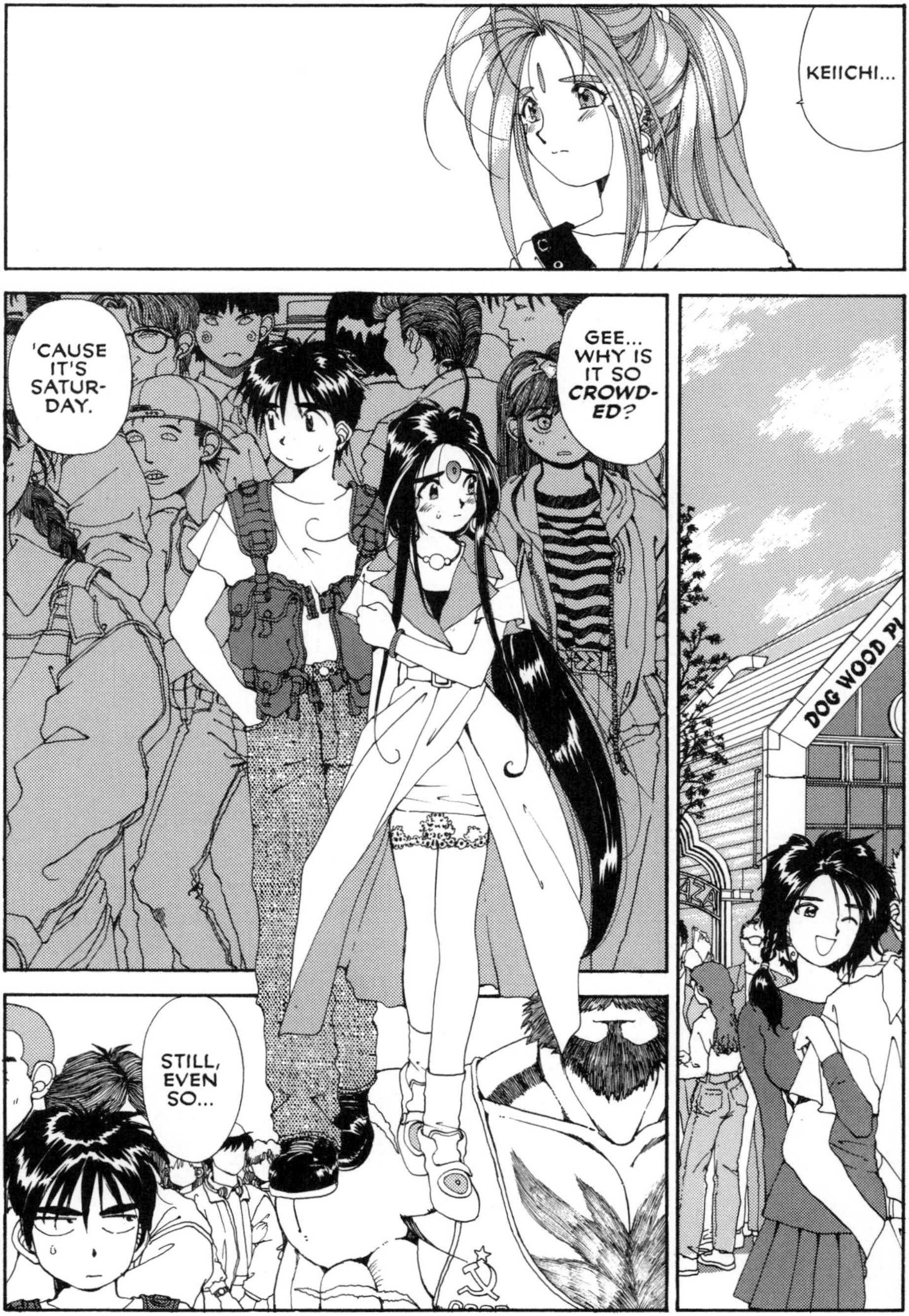
KEIICHI...
GEE... WHY IS IT SO *CROWDED?*
'CAUSE IT'S SATURDAY.
STILL, EVEN SO...

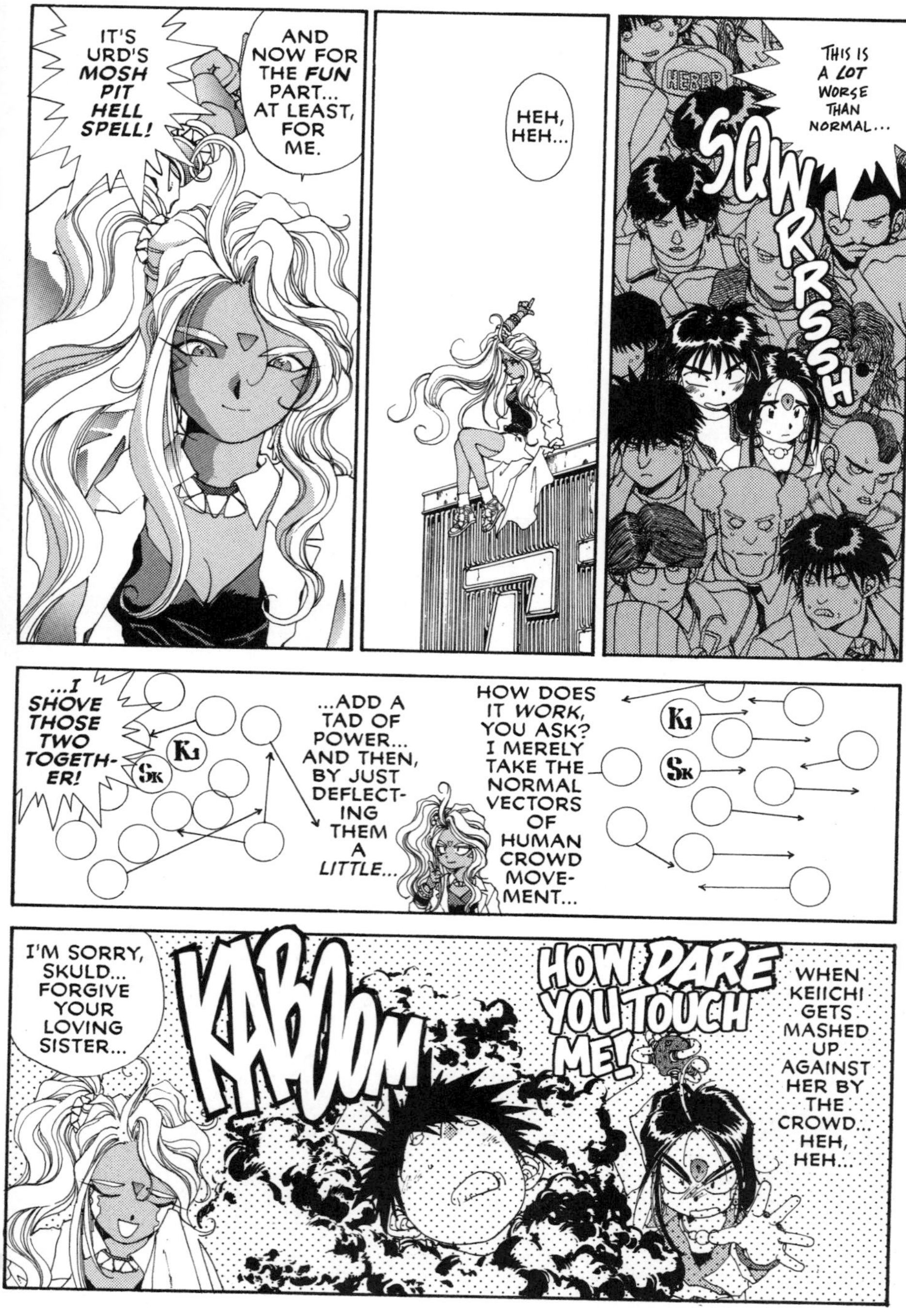
THIS IS A LOT WORSE THAN NORMAL...
SQWRRSSH
HEH, HEH...
AND NOW FOR THE FUN PART... AT LEAST, FOR ME.
IT'S URD'S MOSH PIT HELL SPELL!
HOW DOES IT WORK, YOU ASK? I MERELY TAKE THE NORMAL VECTORS OF HUMAN CROWD MOVEMENT...
K1
SK
...ADD A TAD OF POWER... AND THEN, BY JUST DEFLECTING THEM A LITTLE...
...I SHOVE THOSE TWO TOGETHER!
WHEN KEIICHI GETS MASHED UP AGAINST HER BY THE CROWD... HEH, HEH...
HOW DARE YOU TOUCH ME!
KABOOM
I'M SORRY, SKULD... FORGIVE YOUR LOVING SISTER...

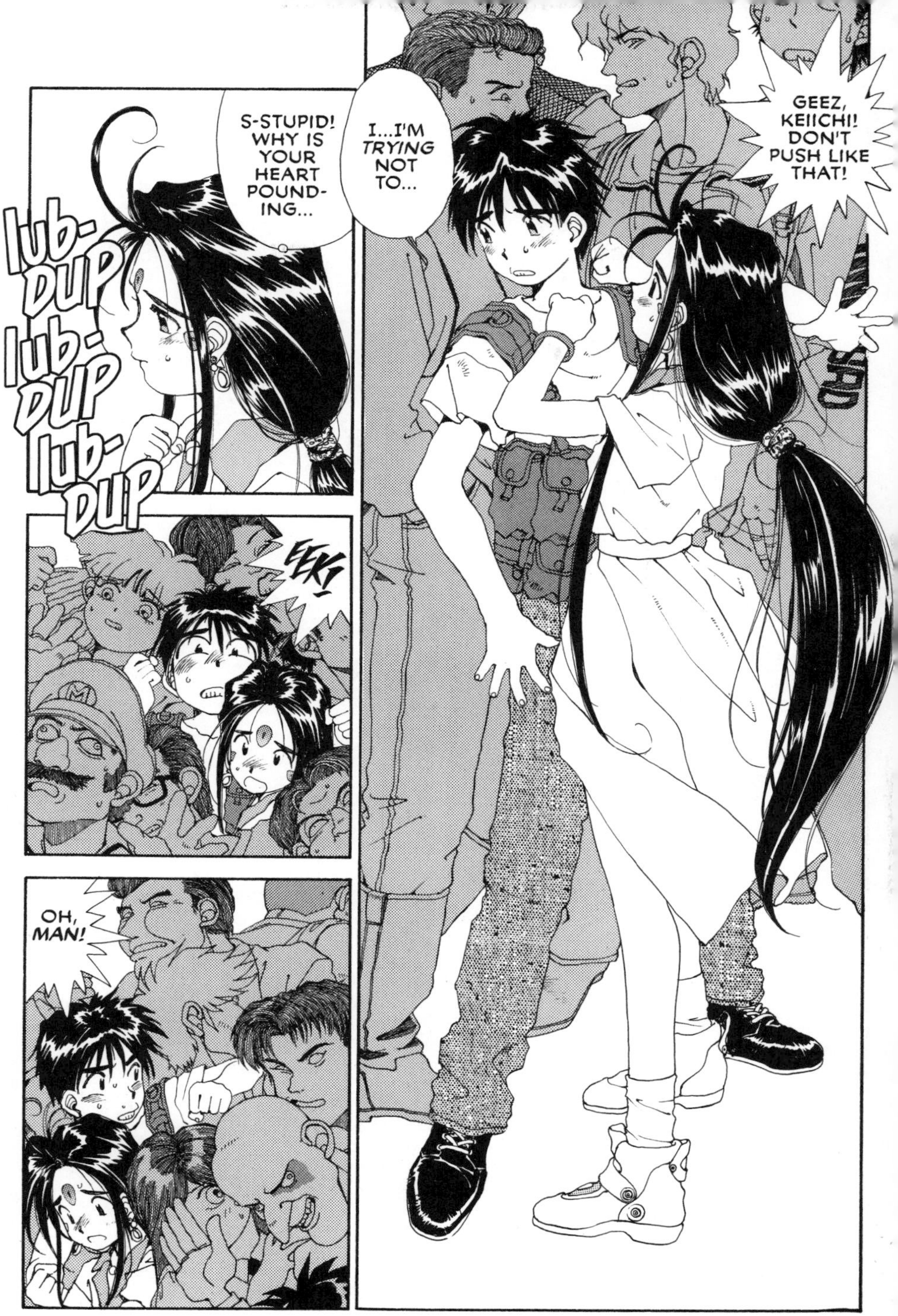
GEEZ, KEIICHI! DON'T PUSH LIKE THAT!
I...I'M *TRYING* NOT TO...
S-STUPID! WHY IS YOUR HEART POUNDING...
lub-DUP lub-DUP lub-DUP
EEK!
OH, *MAN*!

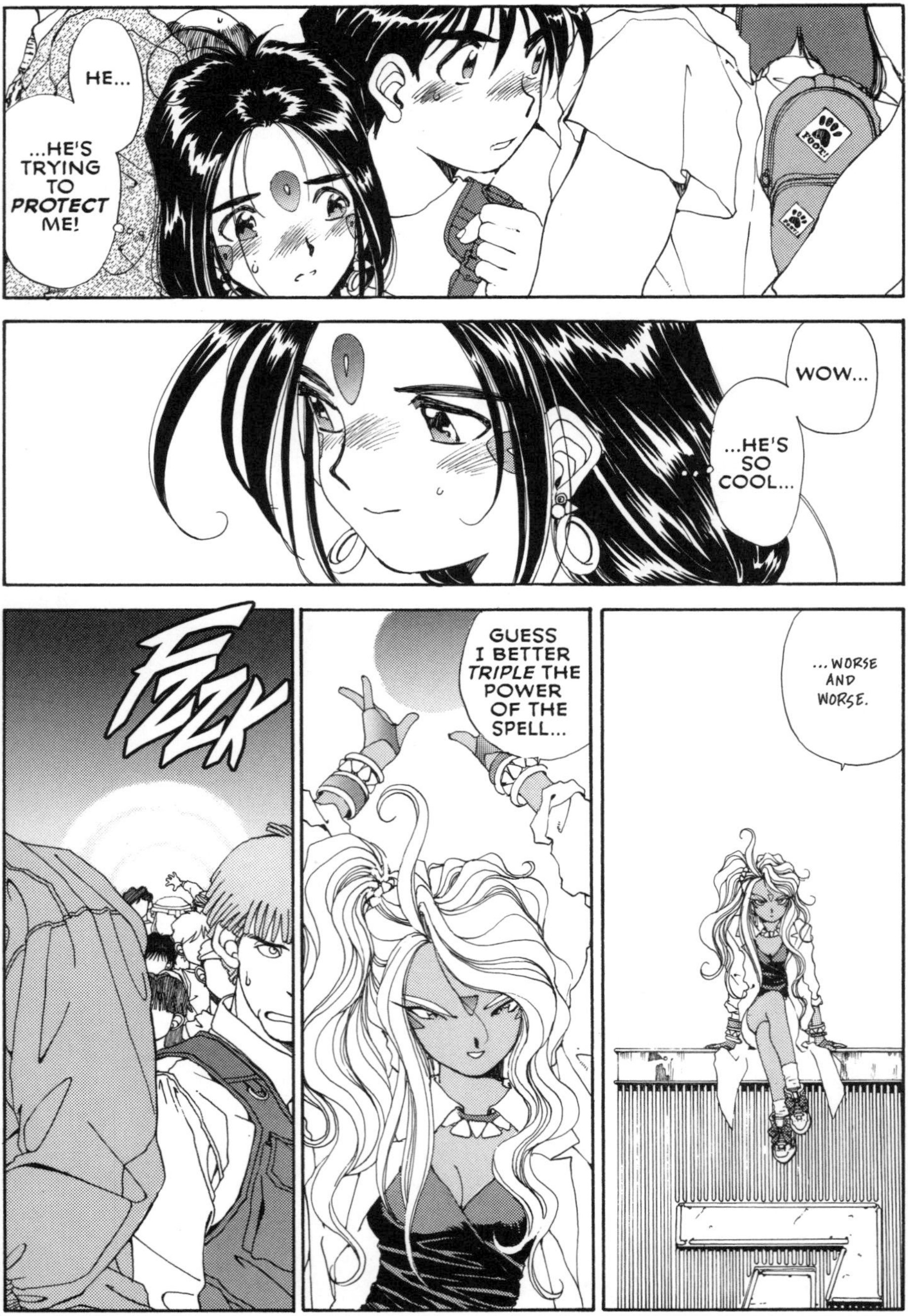
HE...
...HE'S TRYING TO PROTECT ME!
WOW...
...HE'S SO COOL...
...WORSE AND WORSE.
GUESS I BETTER TRIPLE THE POWER OF THE SPELL...
FZZK

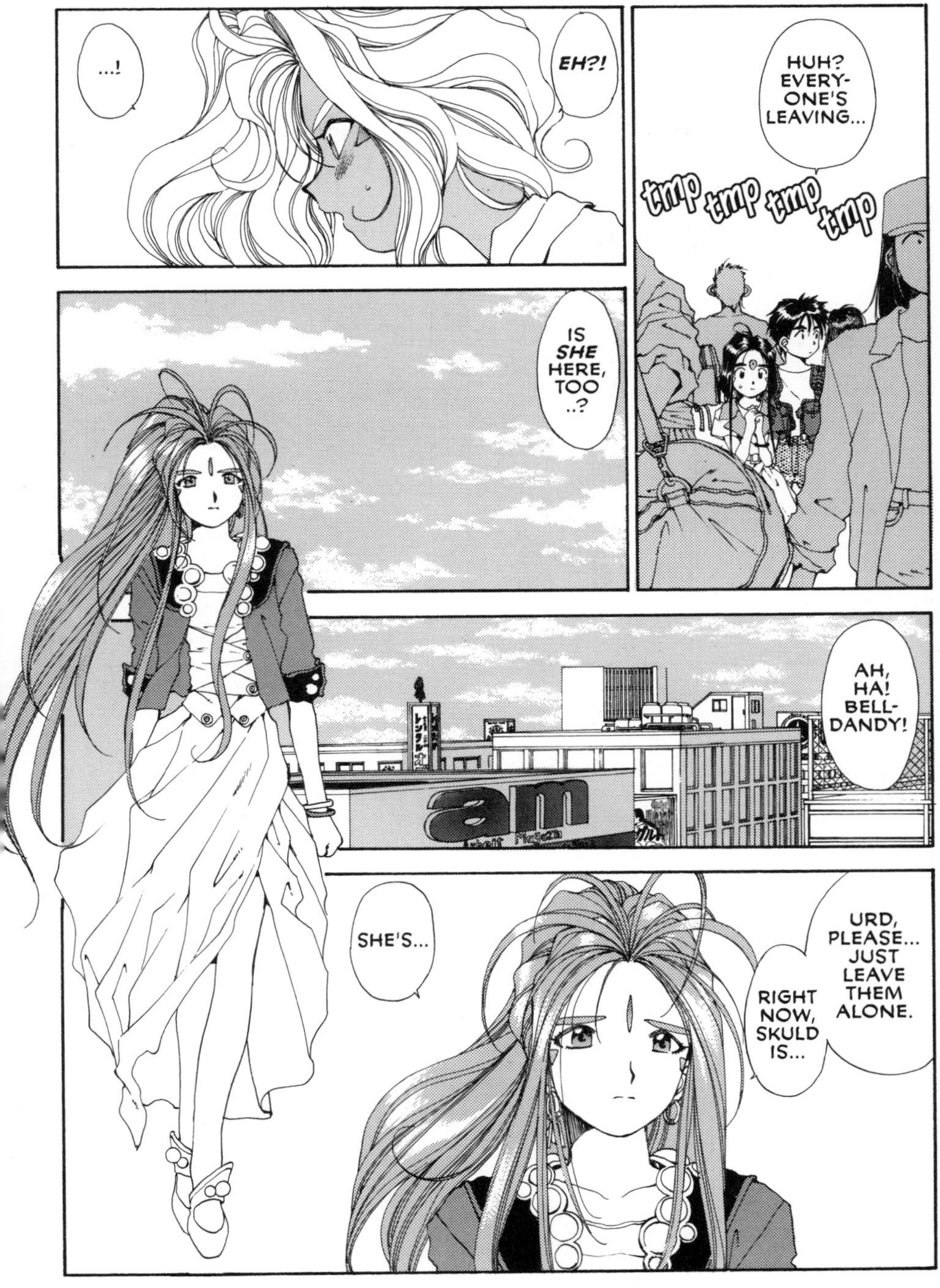
HUH? EVERY-ONE'S LEAVING...
tmp tmp tmp tmp
EH?!
...!
IS SHE HERE, TOO ..?
AH, HA! BELL-DANDY!
URD, PLEASE... JUST LEAVE THEM ALONE.
RIGHT NOW, SKULD IS...
SHE'S...

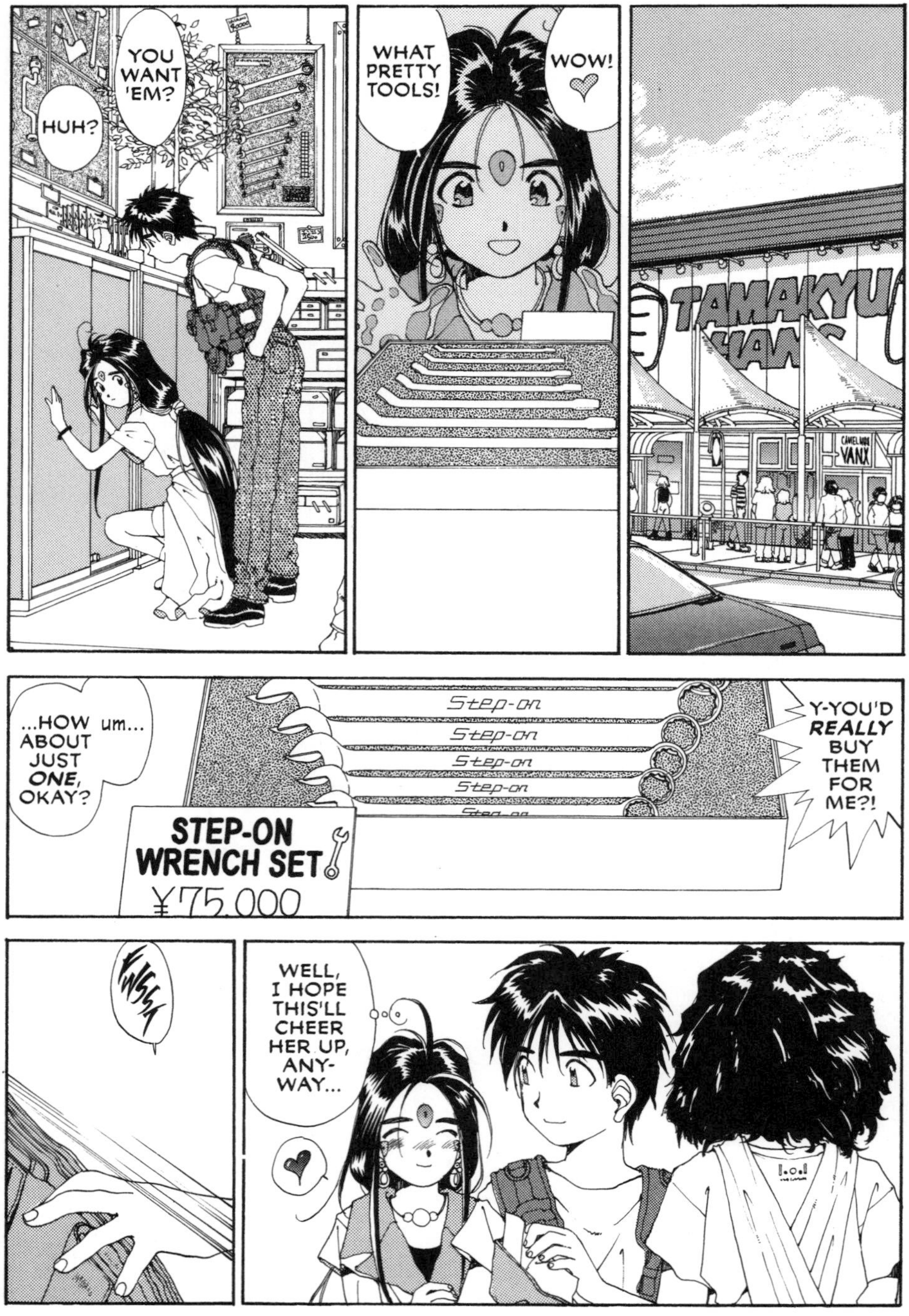
TAMAKYU
VANX
WOW!
WHAT PRETTY TOOLS!
YOU WANT 'EM?
HUH?
Y-YOU'D REALLY BUY THEM FOR ME?!
...HOW um... ABOUT JUST ONE, OKAY?
Step-on
Step-on
Step-on
Step-on
STEP-ON WRENCH SET
¥75,000
WELL, I HOPE THIS'LL CHEER HER UP, ANYWAY...

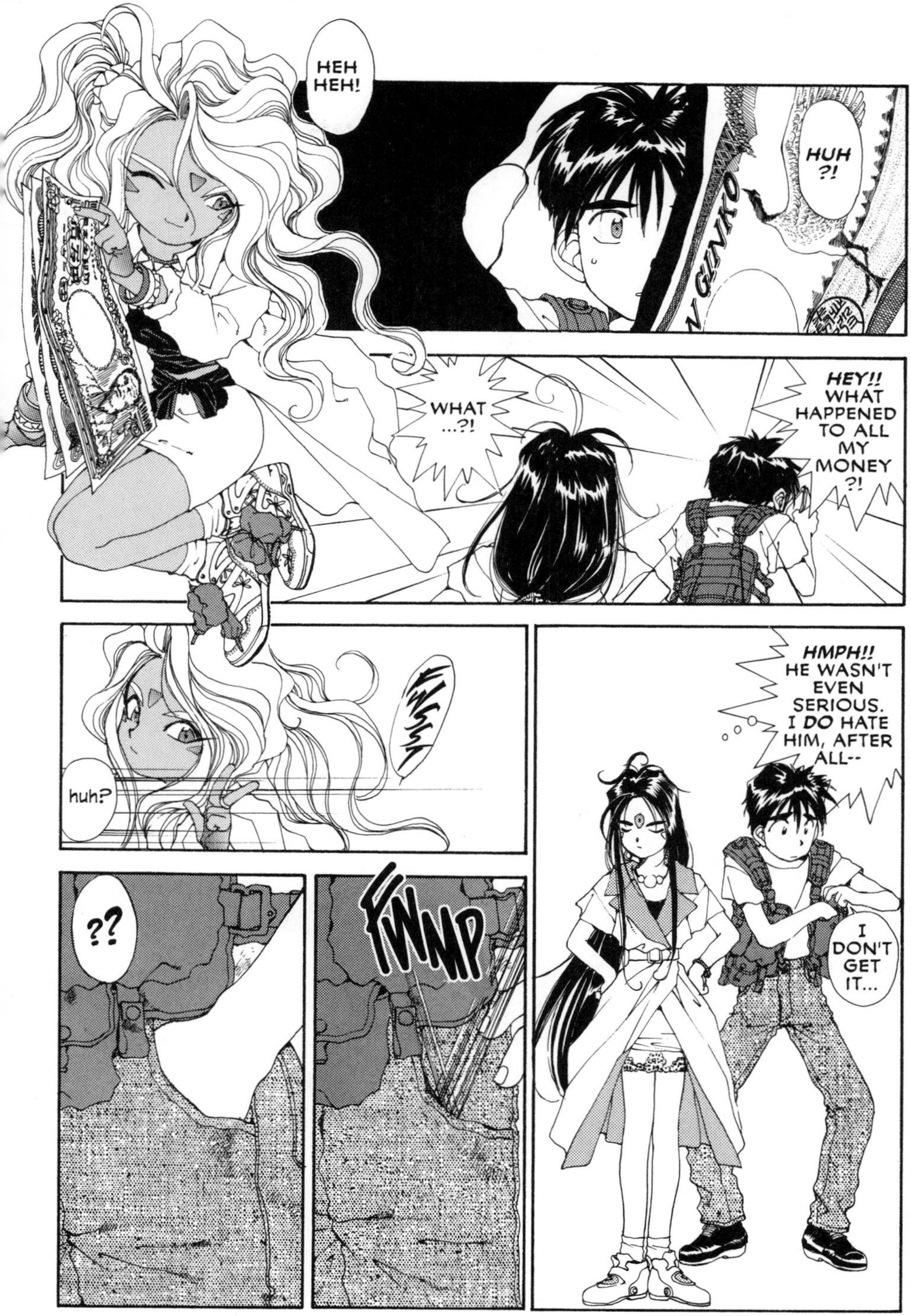
HUH ?!
HEH HEH!
HEY!! WHAT HAPPENED TO ALL MY MONEY ?!
WHAT ...?!
HMPH!! HE WASN'T EVEN SERIOUS. I DO HATE HIM, AFTER ALL--
I DON'T GET IT...
FWSSH
huh?
FWMP
??

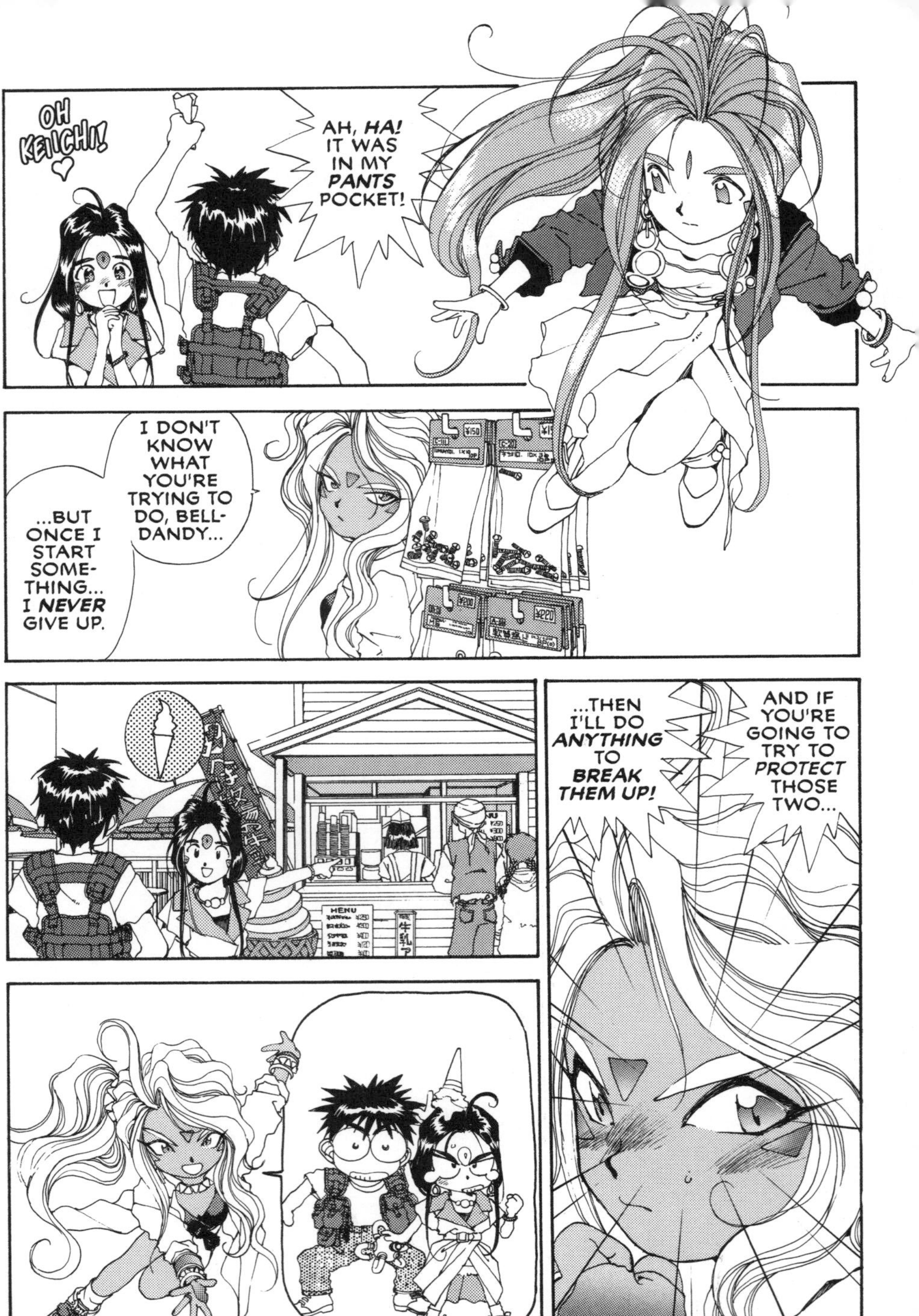
AH, *HA!* IT WAS IN MY *PANTS* POCKET!
OH KEIICHI! ♡
I DON'T KNOW WHAT YOU'RE TRYING TO DO, BELL-DANDY...
...BUT ONCE I START SOME-THING... I *NEVER* GIVE UP.
AND IF YOU'RE GOING TO TRY TO *PROTECT* THOSE TWO...
...THEN I'LL DO *ANYTHING* TO *BREAK THEM UP!*

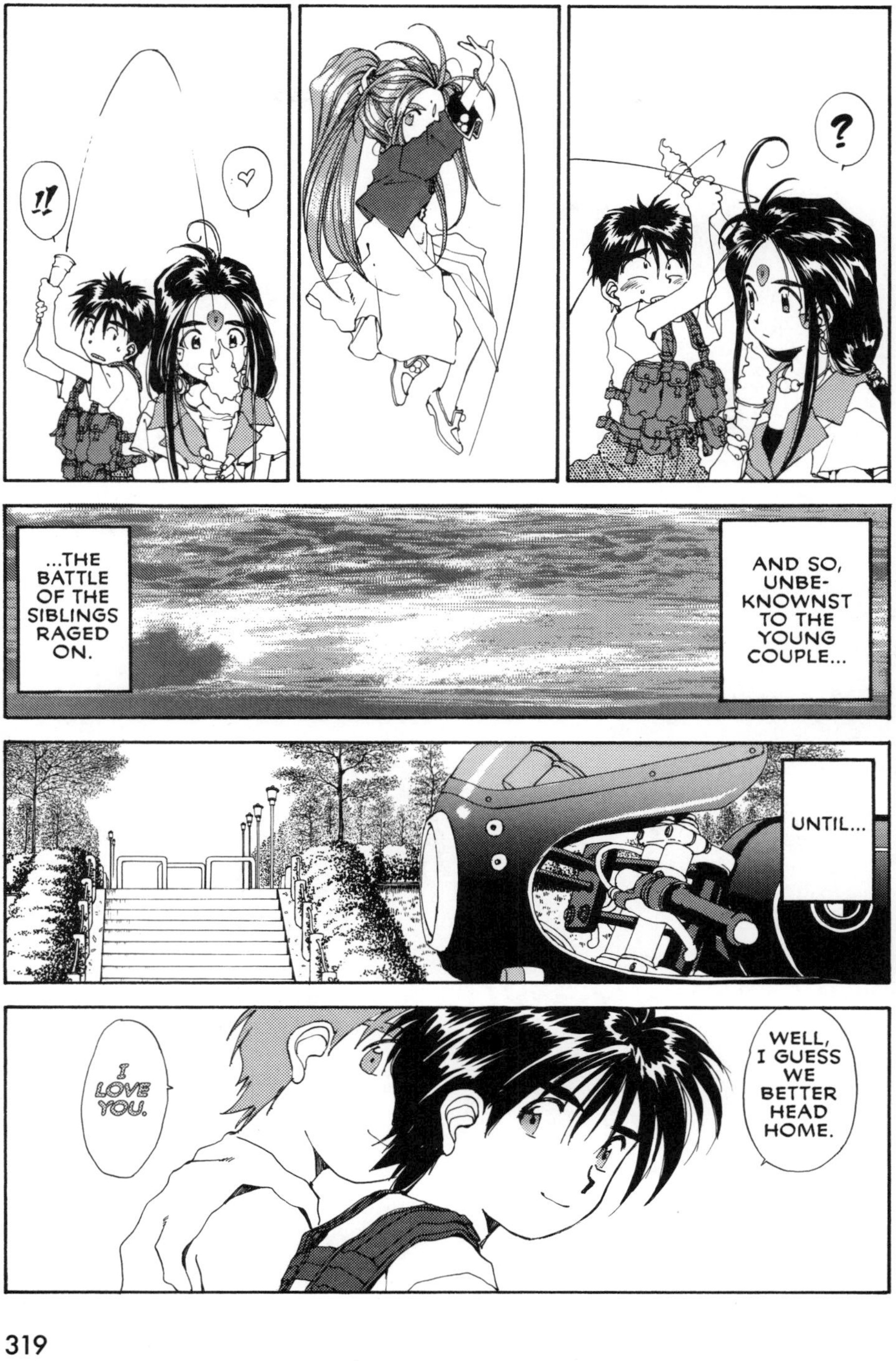
?
♡
!!
AND SO, UNBE-KNOWNST TO THE YOUNG COUPLE...
...THE BATTLE OF THE SIBLINGS RAGED ON.
UNTIL...
WELL, I GUESS WE BETTER HEAD HOME.
I LOVE YOU.

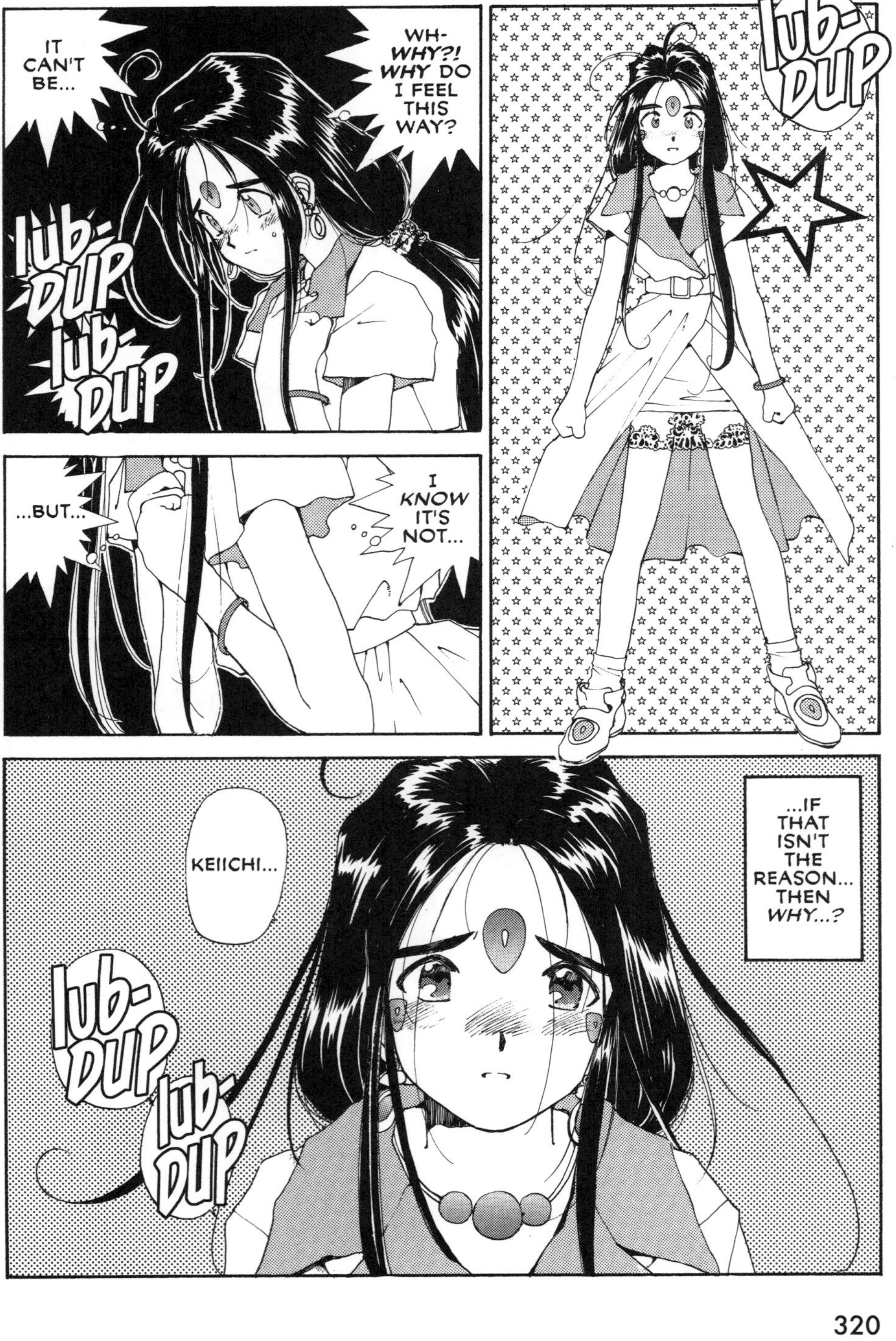
lub-DUP
WH- WHY?! WHY DO I FEEL THIS WAY?
IT CAN'T BE...
lub-DUP lub-DUP
I KNOW IT'S NOT...
...BUT...
...IF THAT ISN'T THE REASON... THEN WHY...?
KEIICHI...
lub-DUP lub-DUP

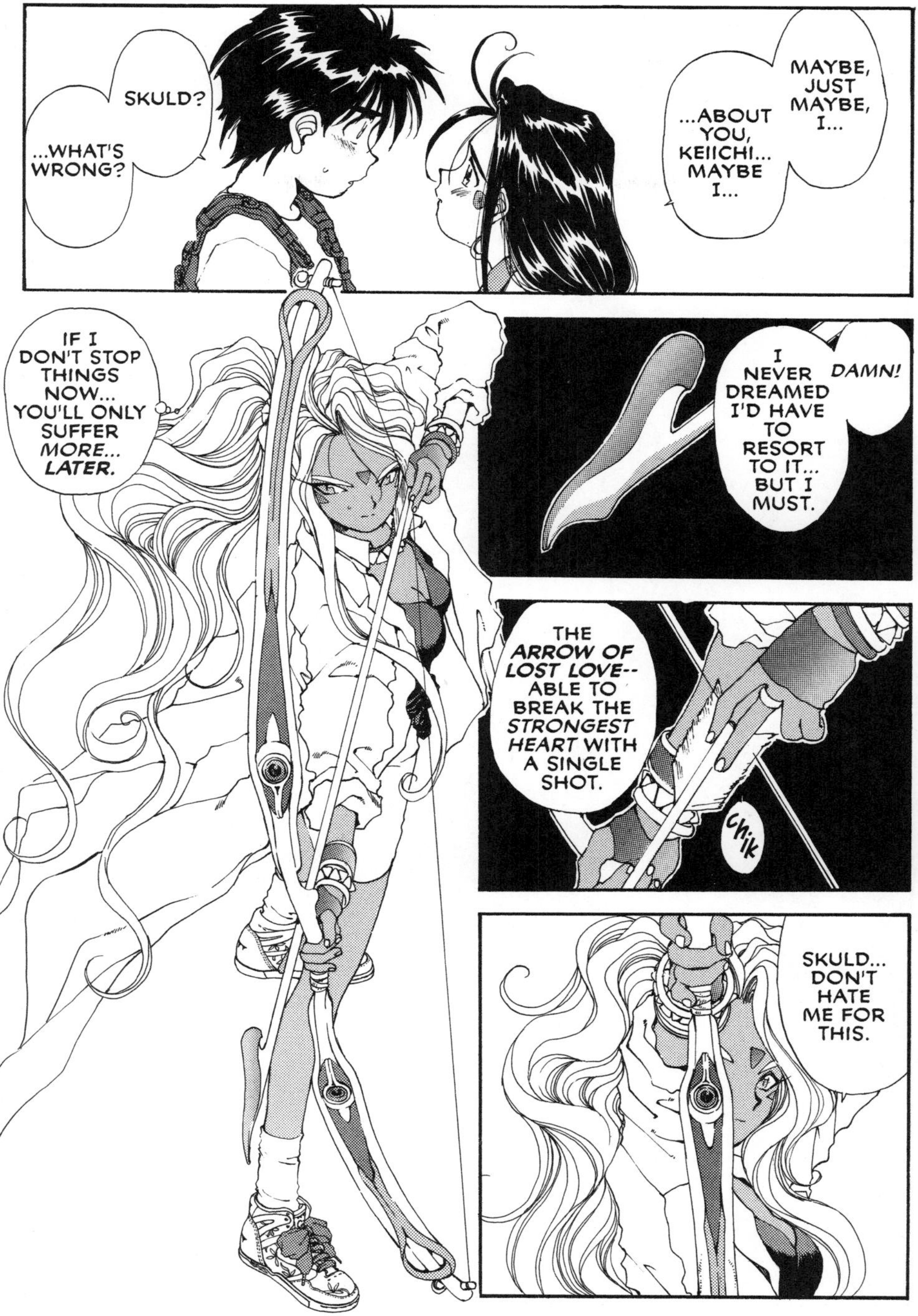
MAYBE, JUST MAYBE, I...
...ABOUT YOU, KEIICHI... MAYBE I...
SKULD?
...WHAT'S WRONG?
DAMN!
I NEVER DREAMED I'D HAVE TO RESORT TO IT... BUT I MUST.
THE *ARROW OF LOST LOVE*-- ABLE TO BREAK THE *STRONGEST HEART* WITH A SINGLE SHOT.
CHIK
SKULD... DON'T HATE ME FOR THIS.
IF I DON'T STOP THINGS NOW... YOU'LL ONLY SUFFER *MORE*... ***LATER.***

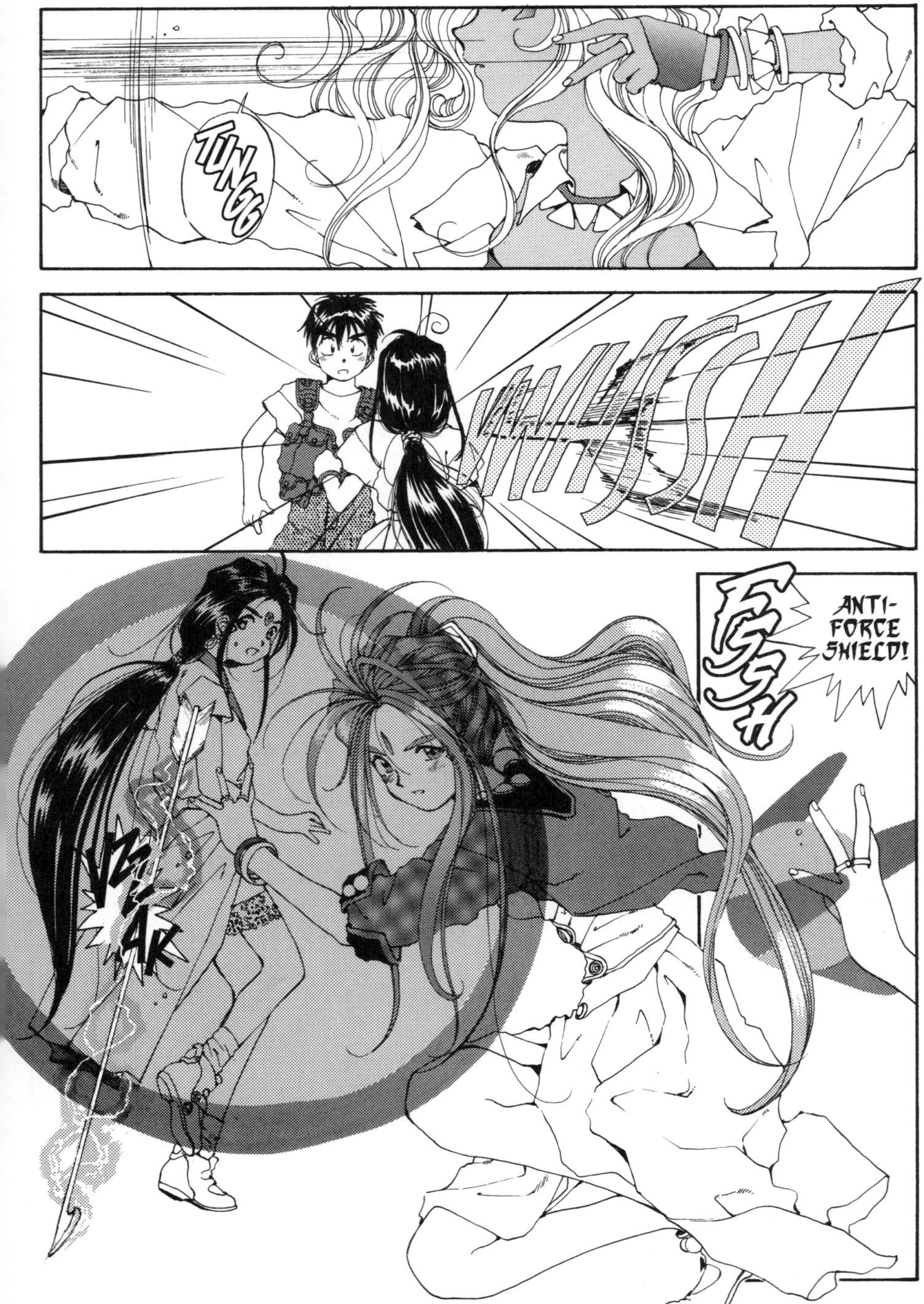
TUNGG
WHSSH
FSSH
ANTI-FORCE SHIELD!
VZZAK

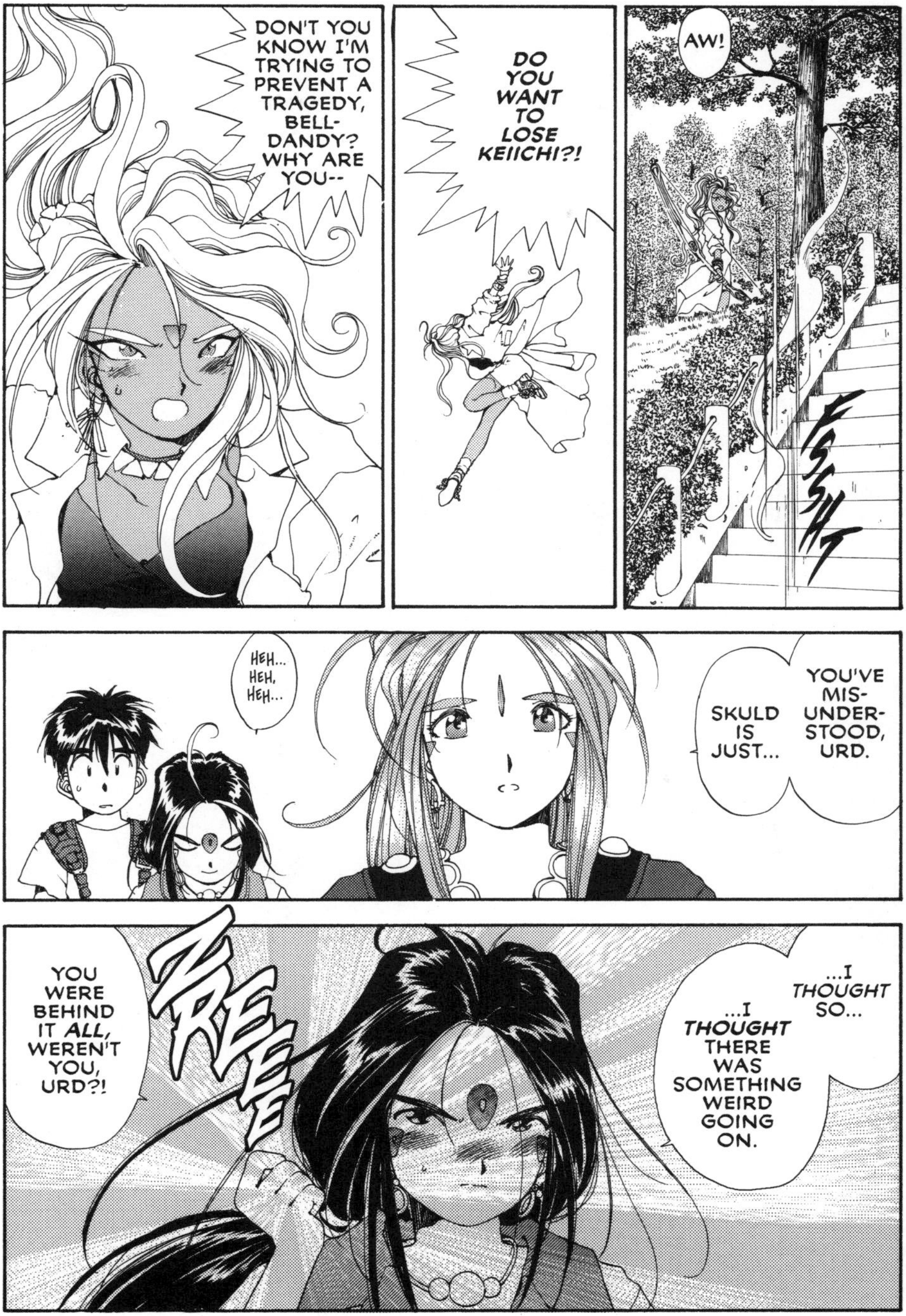
AW!
FSSHT
DO YOU WANT TO LOSE KEIICHI?!
DON'T YOU KNOW I'M TRYING TO PREVENT A TRAGEDY, BELL-DANDY? WHY ARE YOU--
YOU'VE MIS-UNDER-STOOD, URD.
SKULD IS JUST...
HEH... HEH, HEH...
...I THOUGHT SO...
...I THOUGHT THERE WAS SOMETHING WEIRD GOING ON.
ZREEE
YOU WERE BEHIND IT ALL, WEREN'T YOU, URD?!

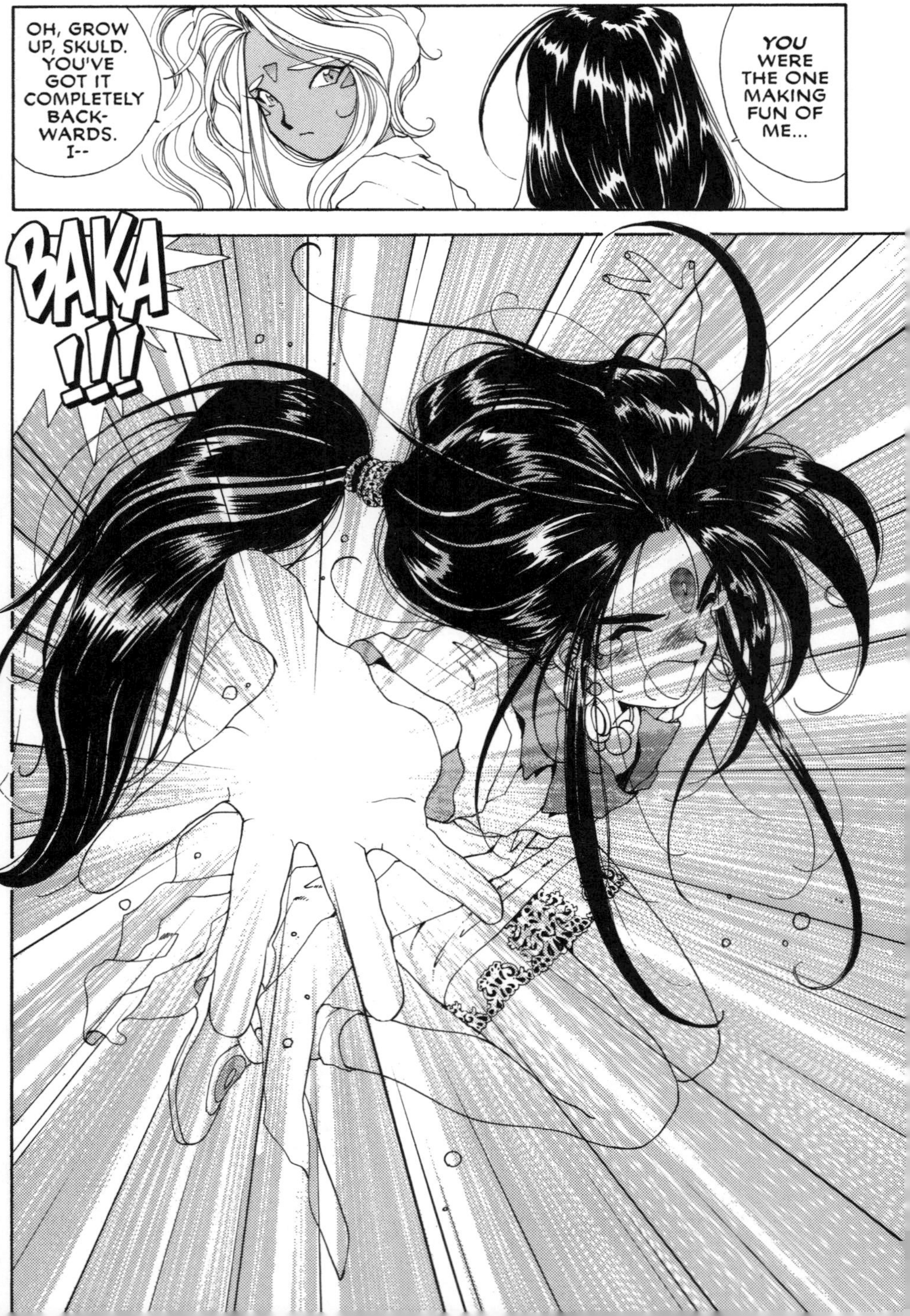
YOU WERE THE ONE MAKING FUN OF ME...
OH, GROW UP, SKULD. YOU'VE GOT IT COMPLETELY BACK-WARDS. I--
BAKA !!!

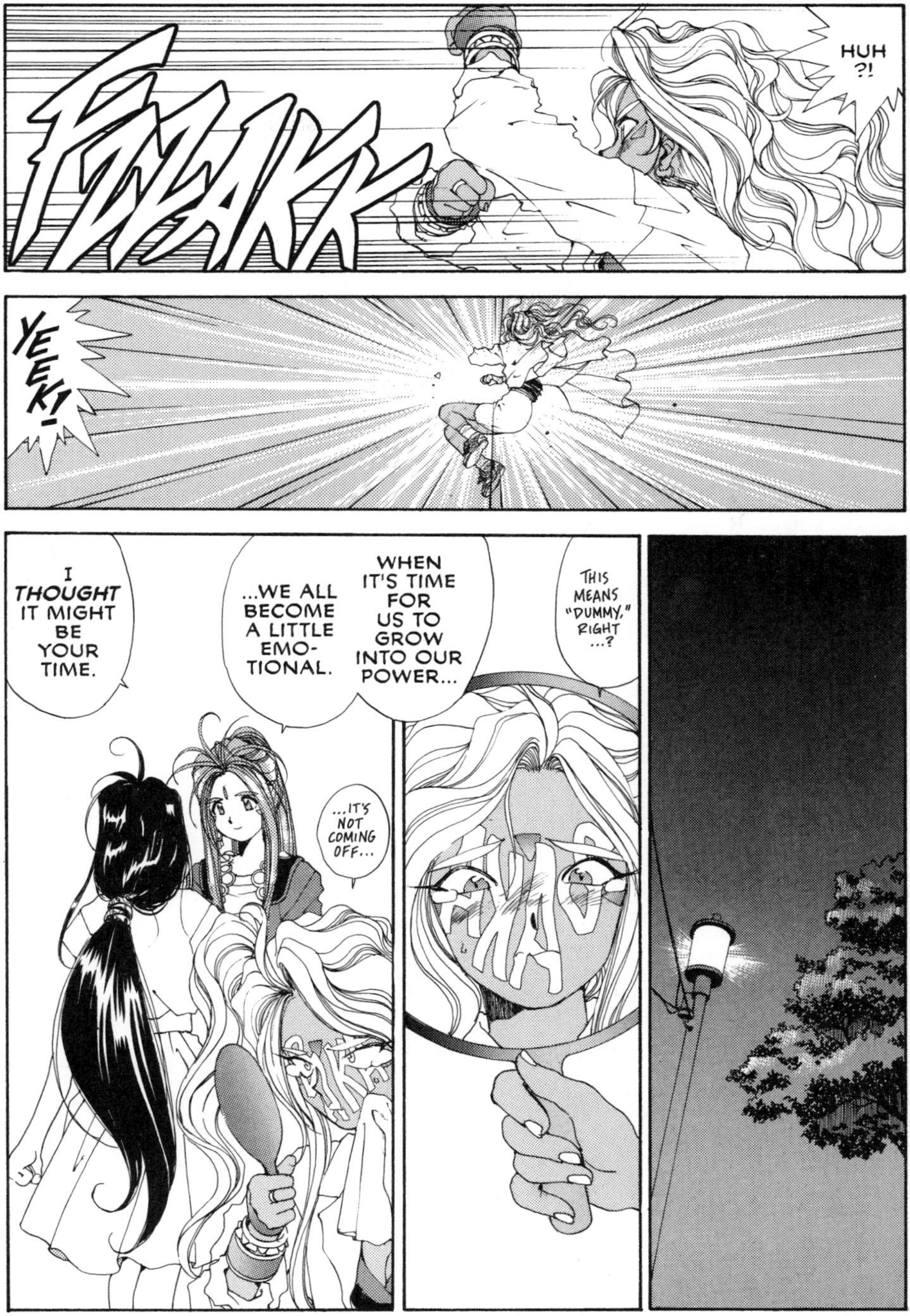
HUH ?!
FIZZAKK
YEEK!
THIS MEANS "DUMMY," RIGHT ...?
WHEN IT'S TIME FOR US TO GROW INTO OUR POWER...
...WE ALL BECOME A LITTLE EMO- TIONAL.
I *THOUGHT* IT MIGHT BE YOUR TIME.
...IT'S NOT COMING OFF...

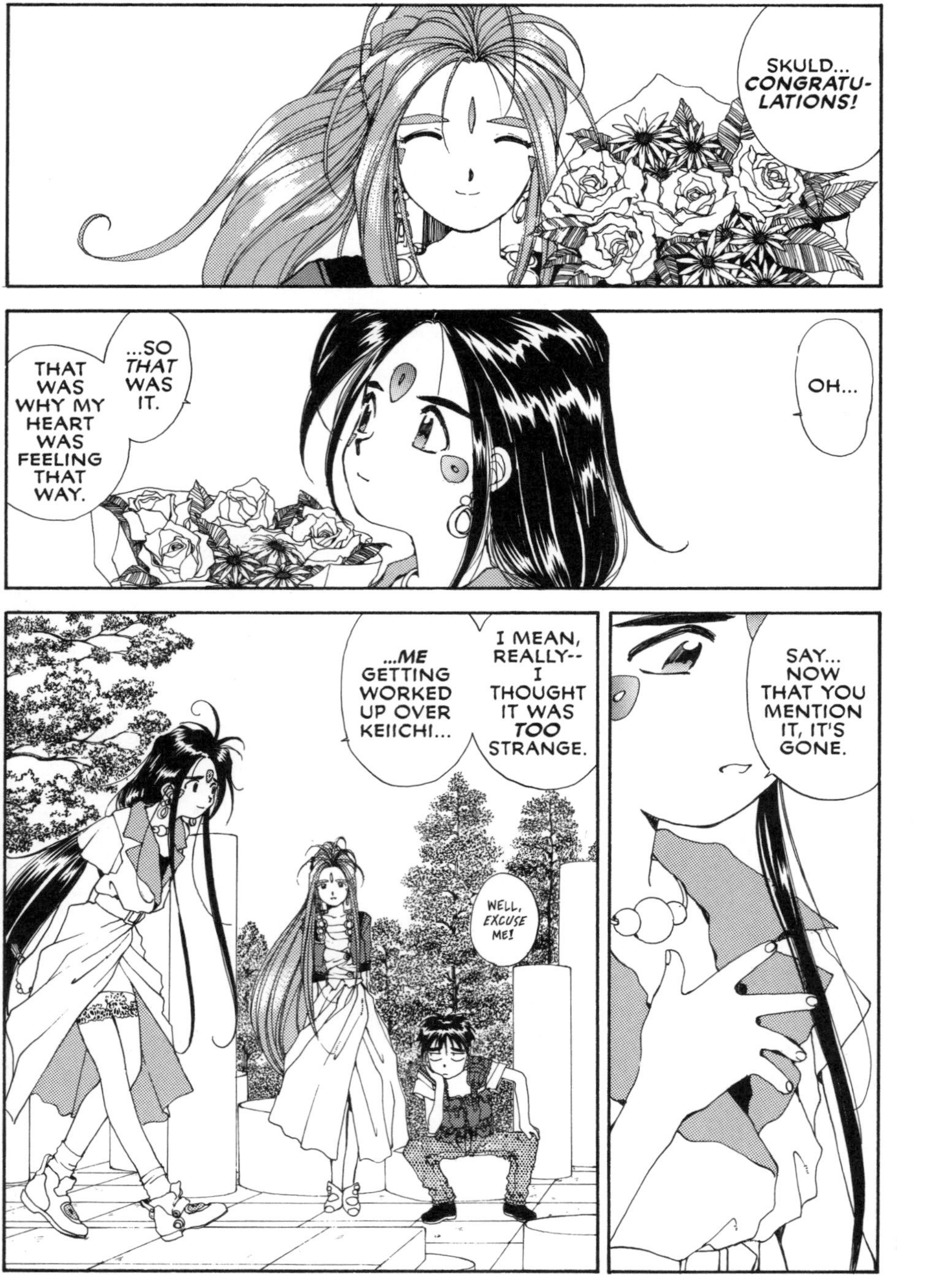
SKULD... CONGRATULATIONS!
OH...
...SO THAT WAS IT.
THAT WAS WHY MY HEART WAS FEELING THAT WAY.
SAY... NOW THAT YOU MENTION IT, IT'S GONE.
I MEAN, REALLY-- I THOUGHT IT WAS TOO STRANGE.
...ME GETTING WORKED UP OVER KEIICHI...
WELL, EXCUSE ME!

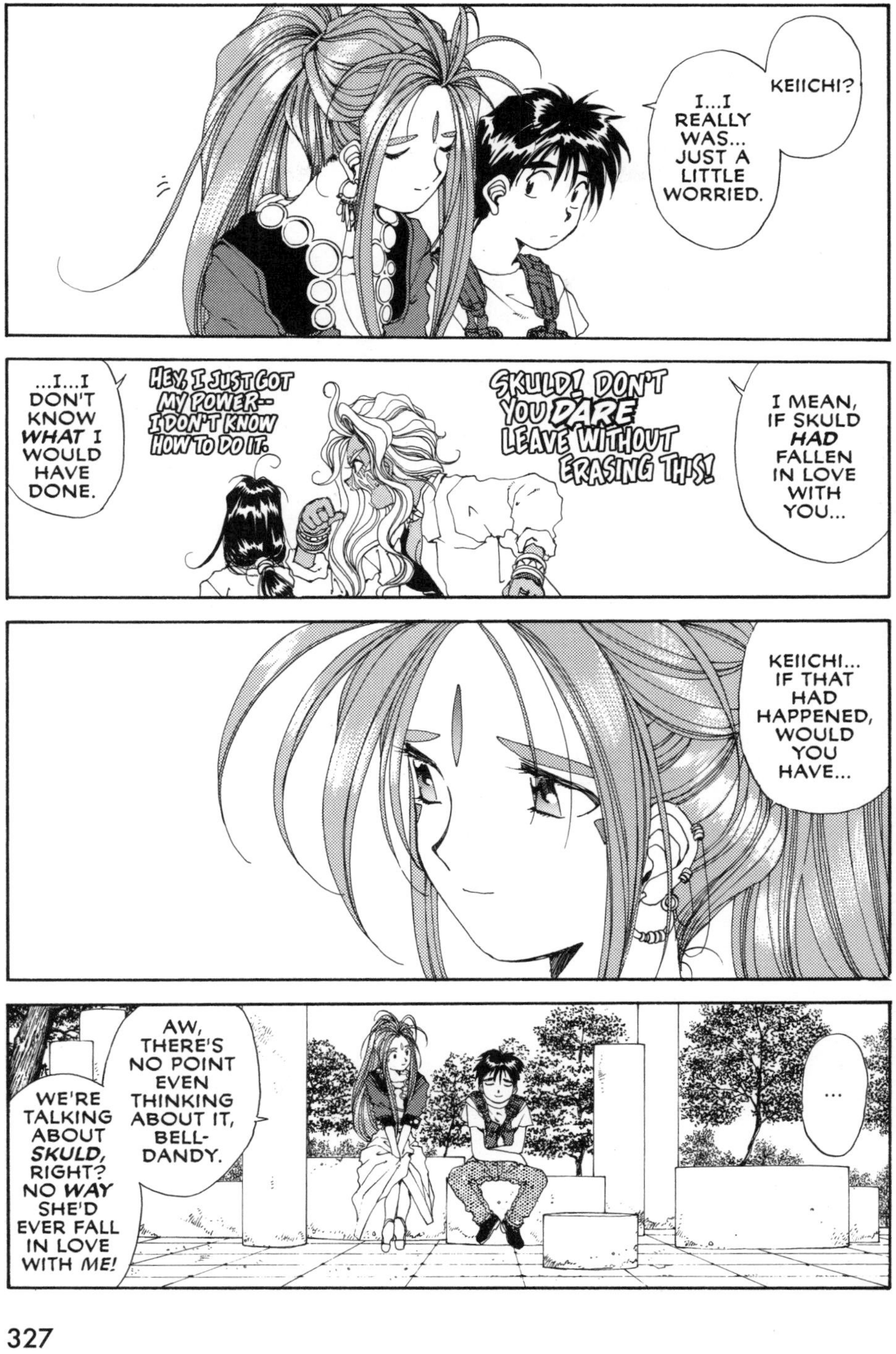
KEIICHI?
I...I REALLY WAS... JUST A LITTLE WORRIED.
I MEAN, IF SKULD *HAD* FALLEN IN LOVE WITH YOU...
SKULD! DON'T YOU *DARE* LEAVE WITHOUT ERASING THIS!
HEY, I JUST GOT MY POWER-- I DON'T KNOW HOW TO DO IT.
...I...I DON'T KNOW *WHAT* I WOULD HAVE DONE.
KEIICHI... IF THAT HAD HAPPENED, WOULD YOU HAVE...
...
AW, THERE'S NO POINT EVEN THINKING ABOUT IT, BELL-DANDY.
WE'RE TALKING ABOUT *SKULD,* RIGHT? NO *WAY* SHE'D EVER FALL IN LOVE WITH *ME!*

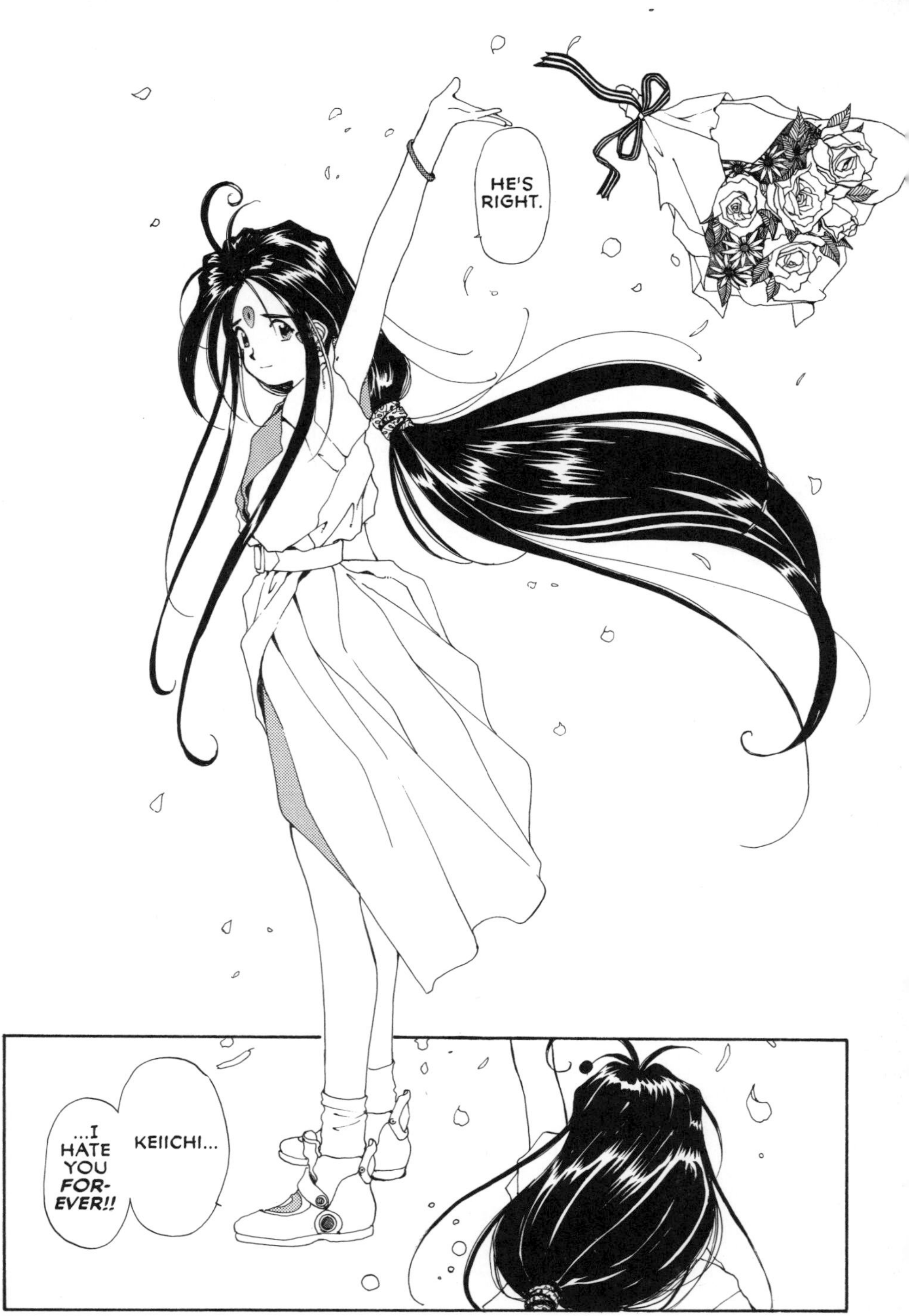
HE'S RIGHT.
KEIICHI...
...I HATE YOU FOR-EVER!!

CHAPTER 52

Ninja Master

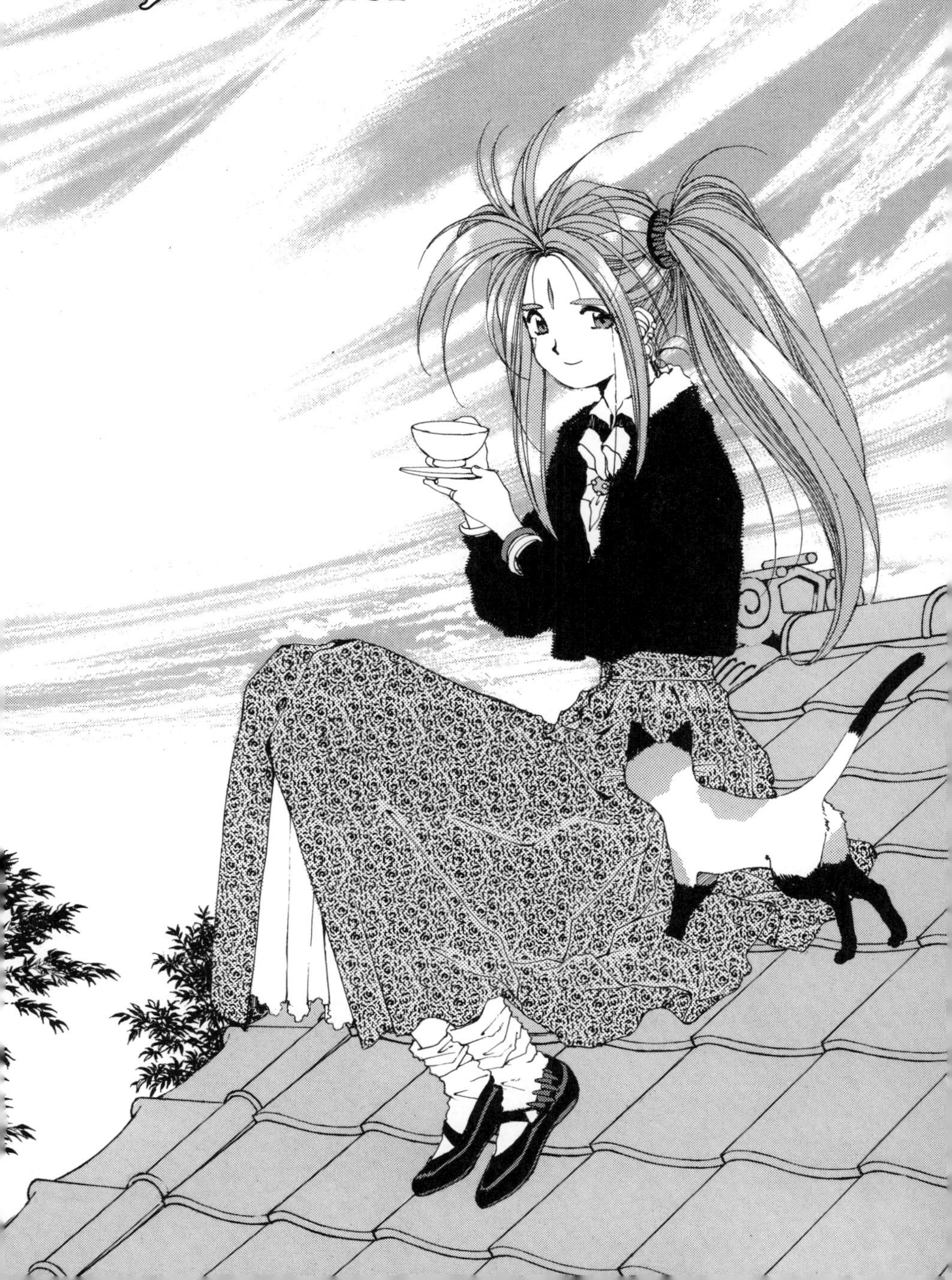

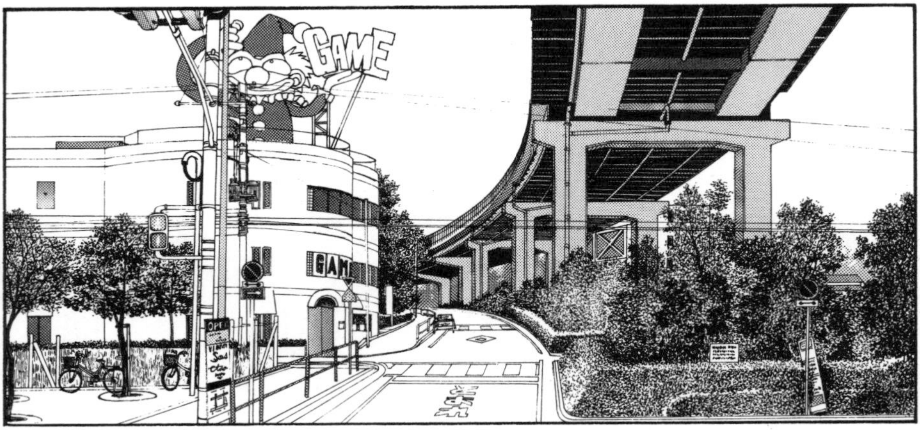
GAME
GAME
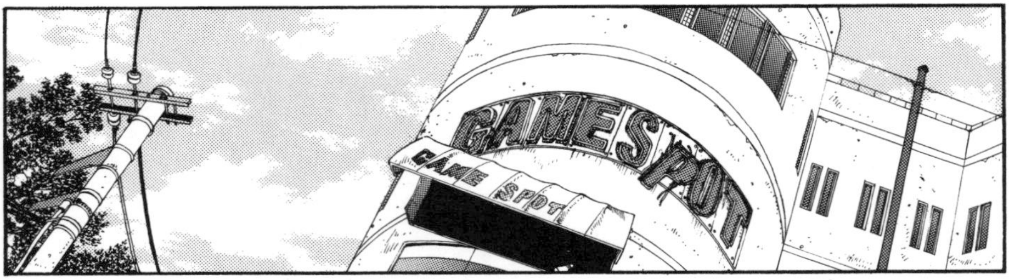
GAMESPOT
GAME SPOT
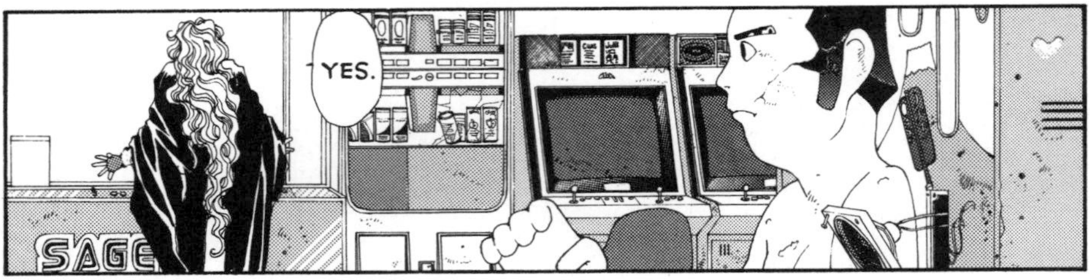
YES.
SAGE
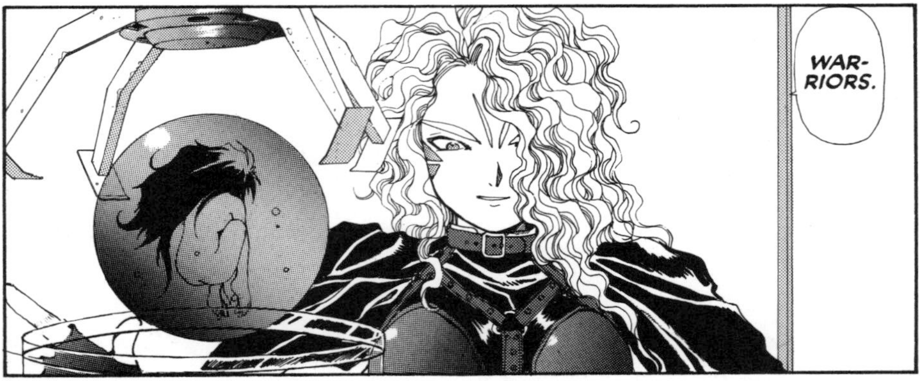
WAR-RIORS.

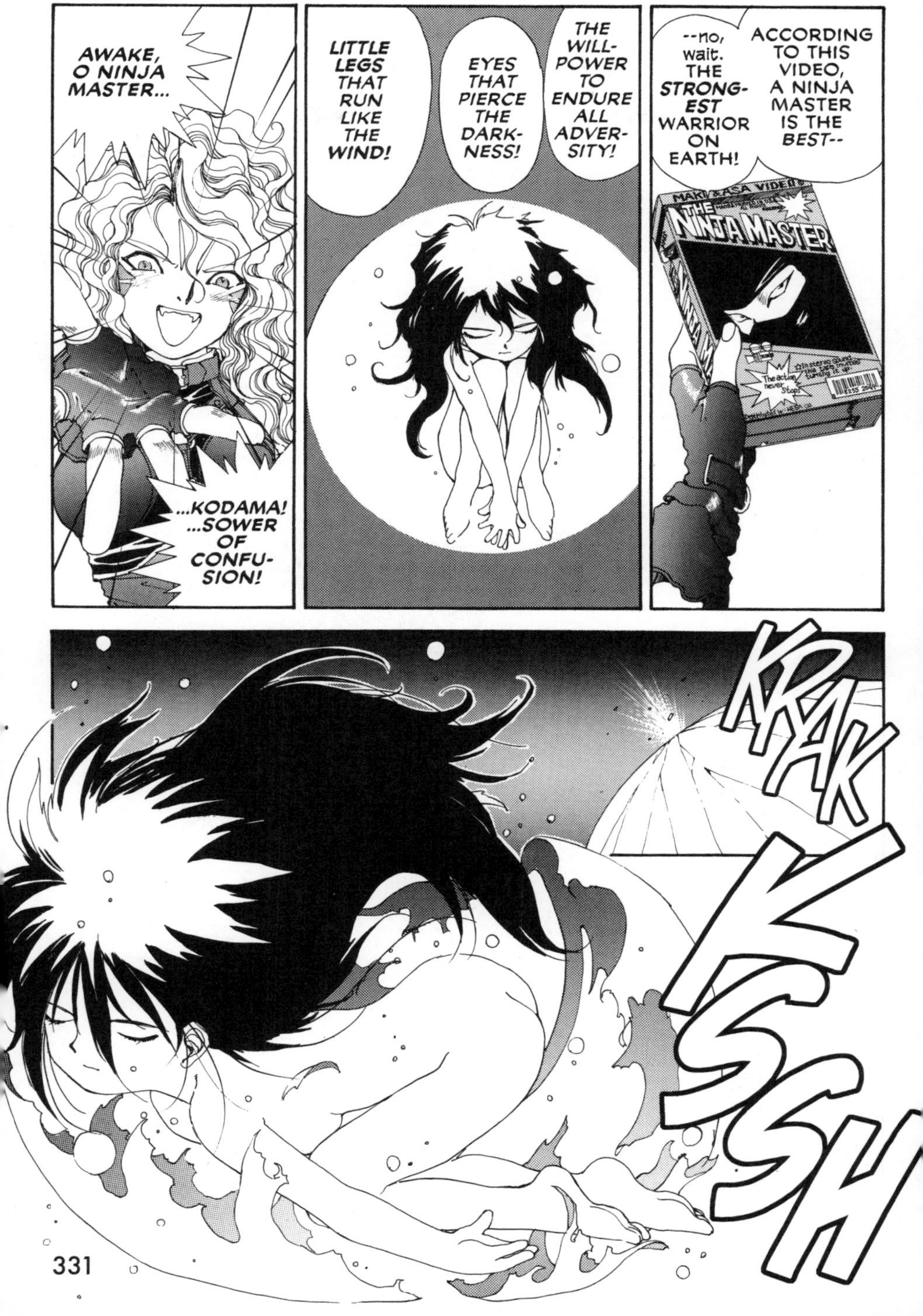
ACCORDING TO THIS VIDEO, A NINJA MASTER IS THE BEST--
--no, wait. THE STRONGEST WARRIOR ON EARTH!
MAKI & ASA VIDEO
THE NINJA MASTER
The action never stops
THE WILL-POWER TO ENDURE ALL ADVERSITY!
EYES THAT PIERCE THE DARKNESS!
LITTLE LEGS THAT RUN LIKE THE WIND!
AWAKE, O NINJA MASTER...
...KODAMA! ...SOWER OF CONFUSION!
KRAKAK
KSSSH

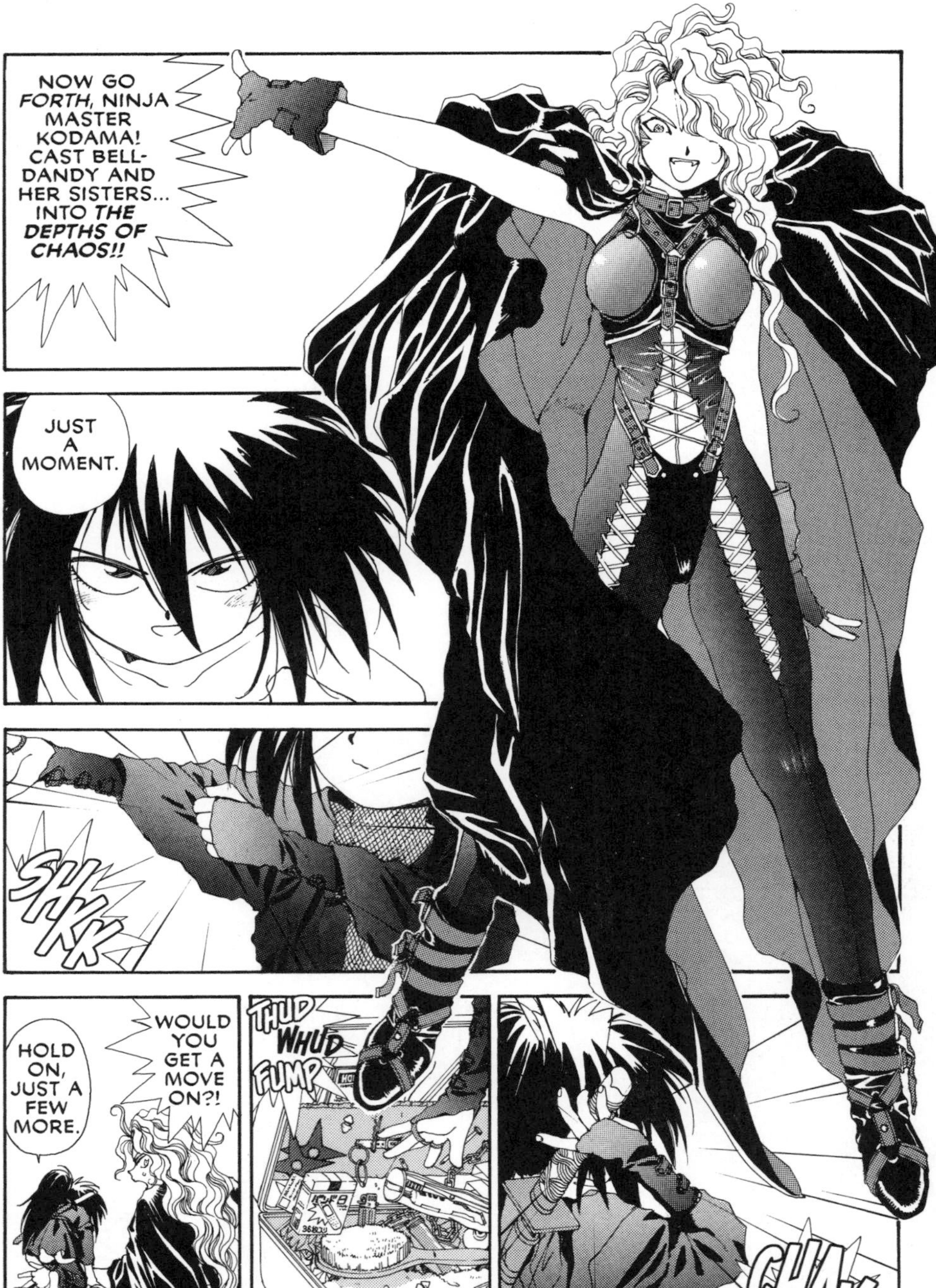
NOW GO FORTH, NINJA MASTER KODAMA! CAST BELL-DANDY AND HER SISTERS... INTO THE DEPTHS OF CHAOS!!
JUST A MOMENT.
SHKK
CHAK
THUD
WHUD
FUMP
WOULD YOU GET A MOVE ON?!
HOLD ON, JUST A FEW MORE.

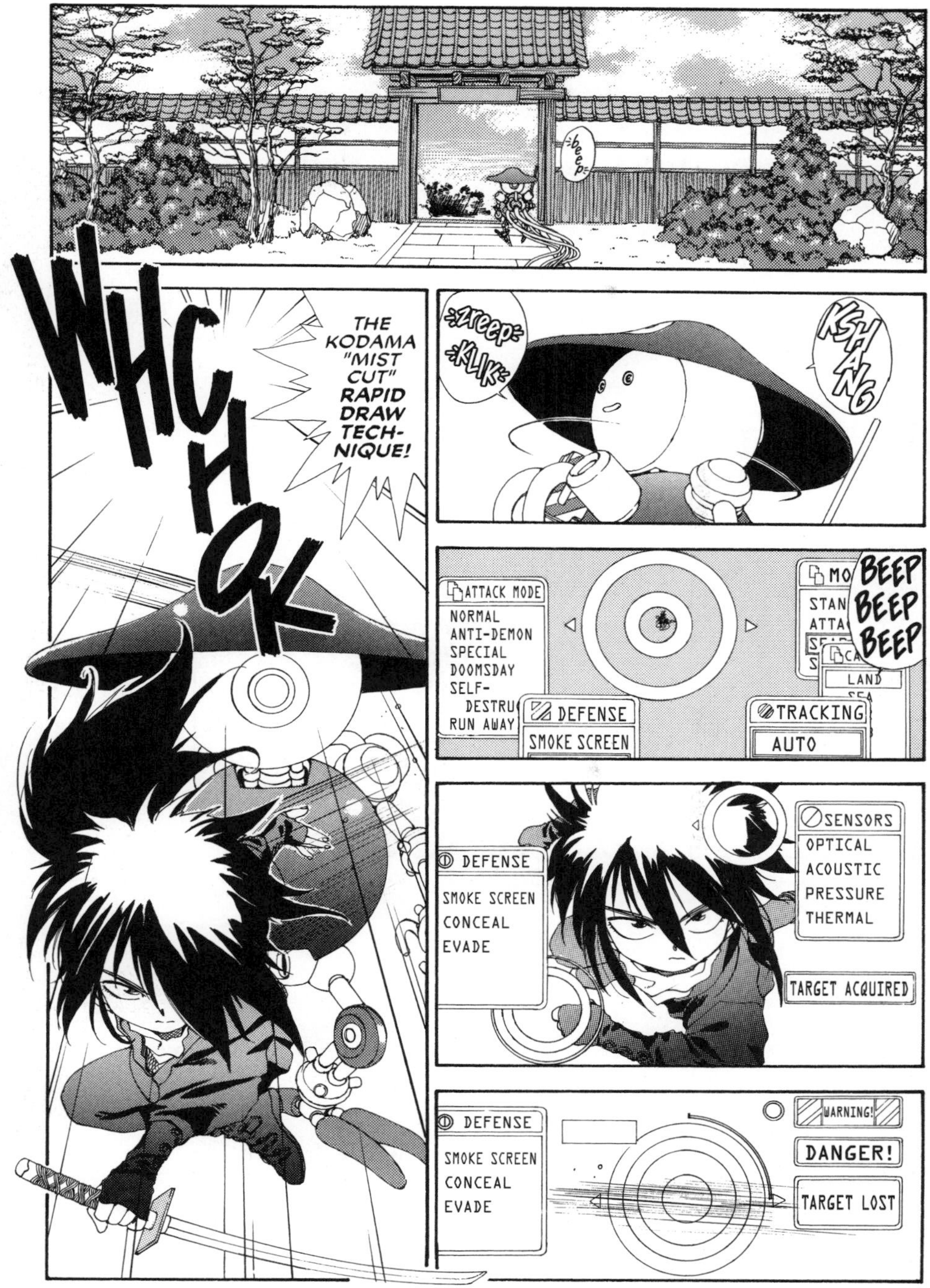
beep
KSHANG
zreep
KLIK
BEEP BEEP BEEP
ATTACK MODE
NORMAL
ANTI-DEMON
SPECIAL
DOOMSDAY
SELF-DESTRU
RUN AWAY
DEFENSE
SMOKE SCREEN
TRACKING
AUTO
LAND
SENSORS
OPTICAL
ACOUSTIC
PRESSURE
THERMAL
TARGET ACQUIRED
DEFENSE
SMOKE SCREEN
CONCEAL
EVADE
WARNING!
DANGER!
TARGET LOST
DEFENSE
SMOKE SCREEN
CONCEAL
EVADE
THE KODAMA "MIST CUT" RAPID DRAW TECH-NIQUE!
WHCHOK

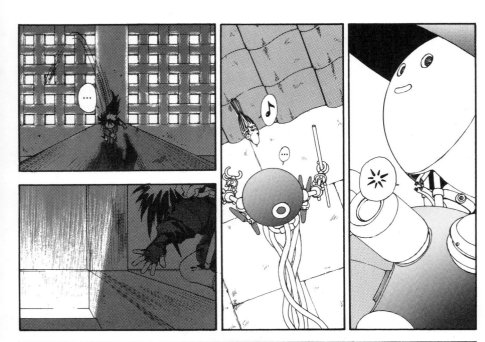

♪
...
...
BORN FROM DARKNESS, DYING IN DARKNESS...
...THAT IS THE FATE OF ALL NINJA!
HYAAAA!!
....

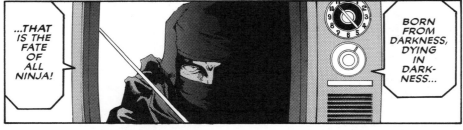

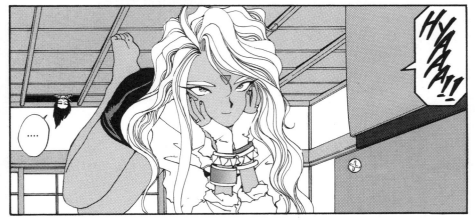

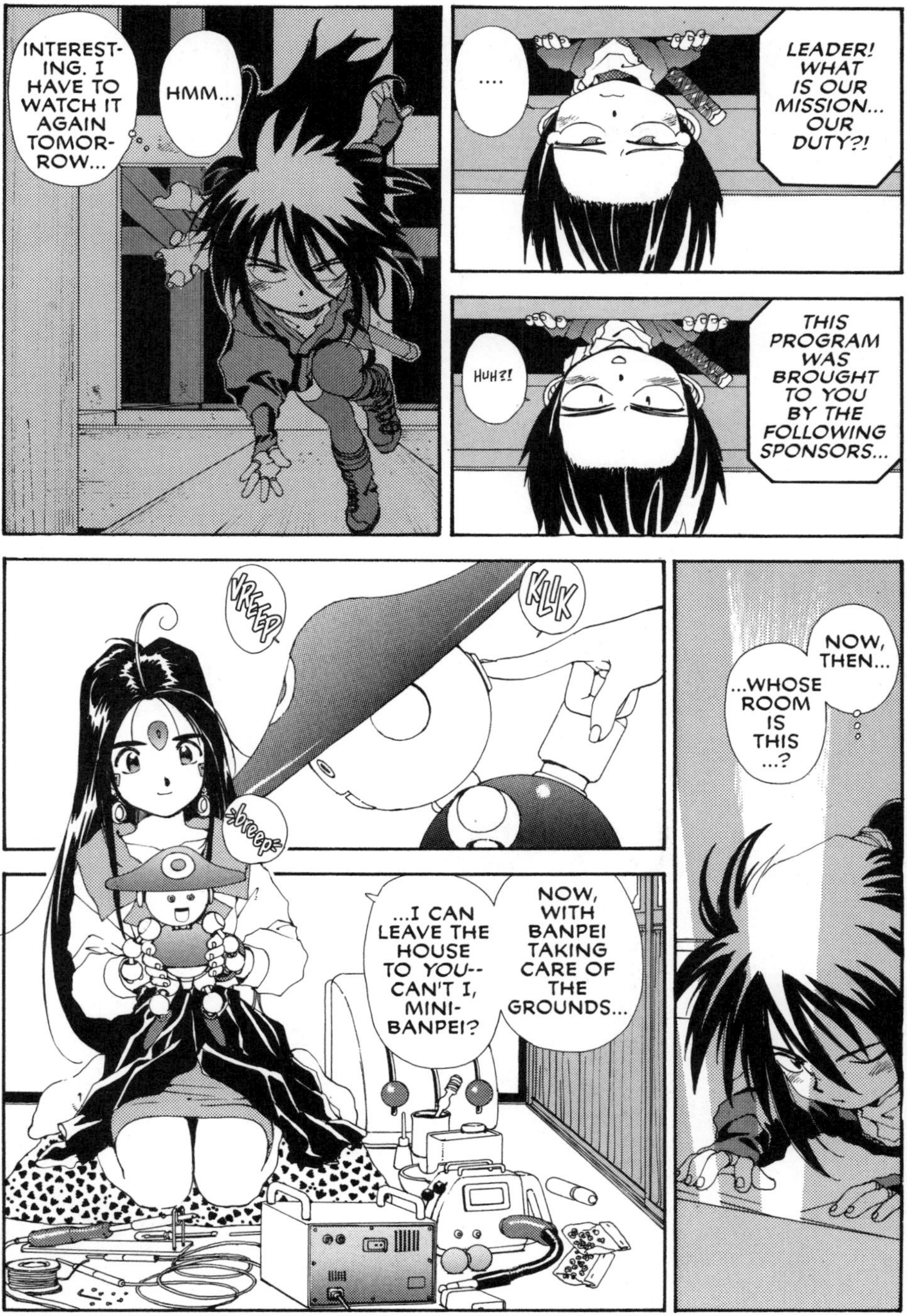
LEADER! WHAT IS OUR MISSION... OUR DUTY?!
....
THIS PROGRAM WAS BROUGHT TO YOU BY THE FOLLOWING SPONSORS...
HUH?!
HMM...
INTERESTING. I HAVE TO WATCH IT AGAIN TOMORROW...
NOW, THEN...
...WHOSE ROOM IS THIS ...?
KLIK
VREEP
breep
NOW, WITH BANPEI TAKING CARE OF THE GROUNDS...
...I CAN LEAVE THE HOUSE TO YOU-- CAN'T I, MINI-BANPEI?

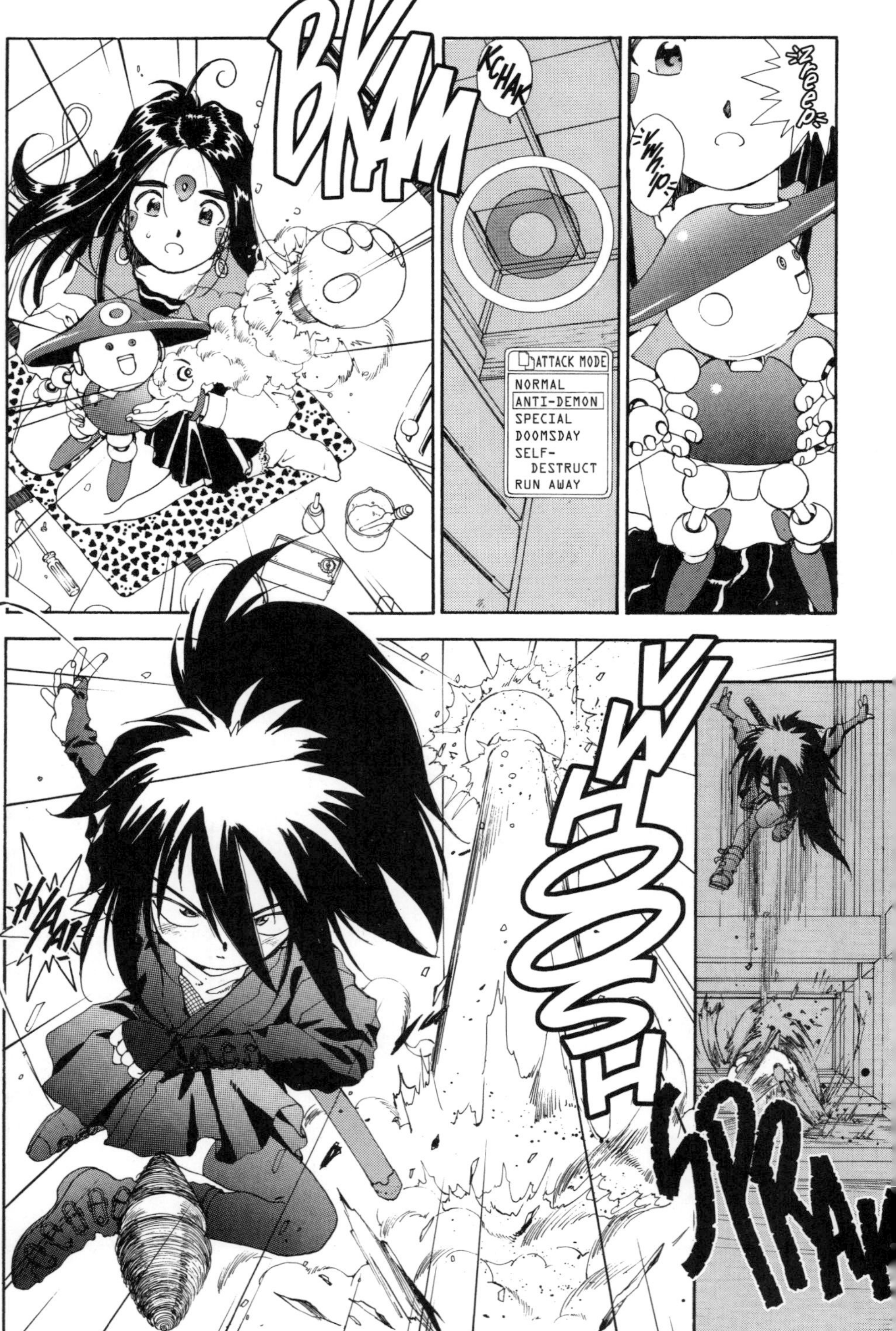
zreep
whip
KCHAK
ATTACK MODE
NORMAL
ANTI-DEMON
SPECIAL
DOOMSDAY
SELF-DESTRUCT
RUN AWAY
BKAM
SPRAK
VWHOOSH
HYAA!

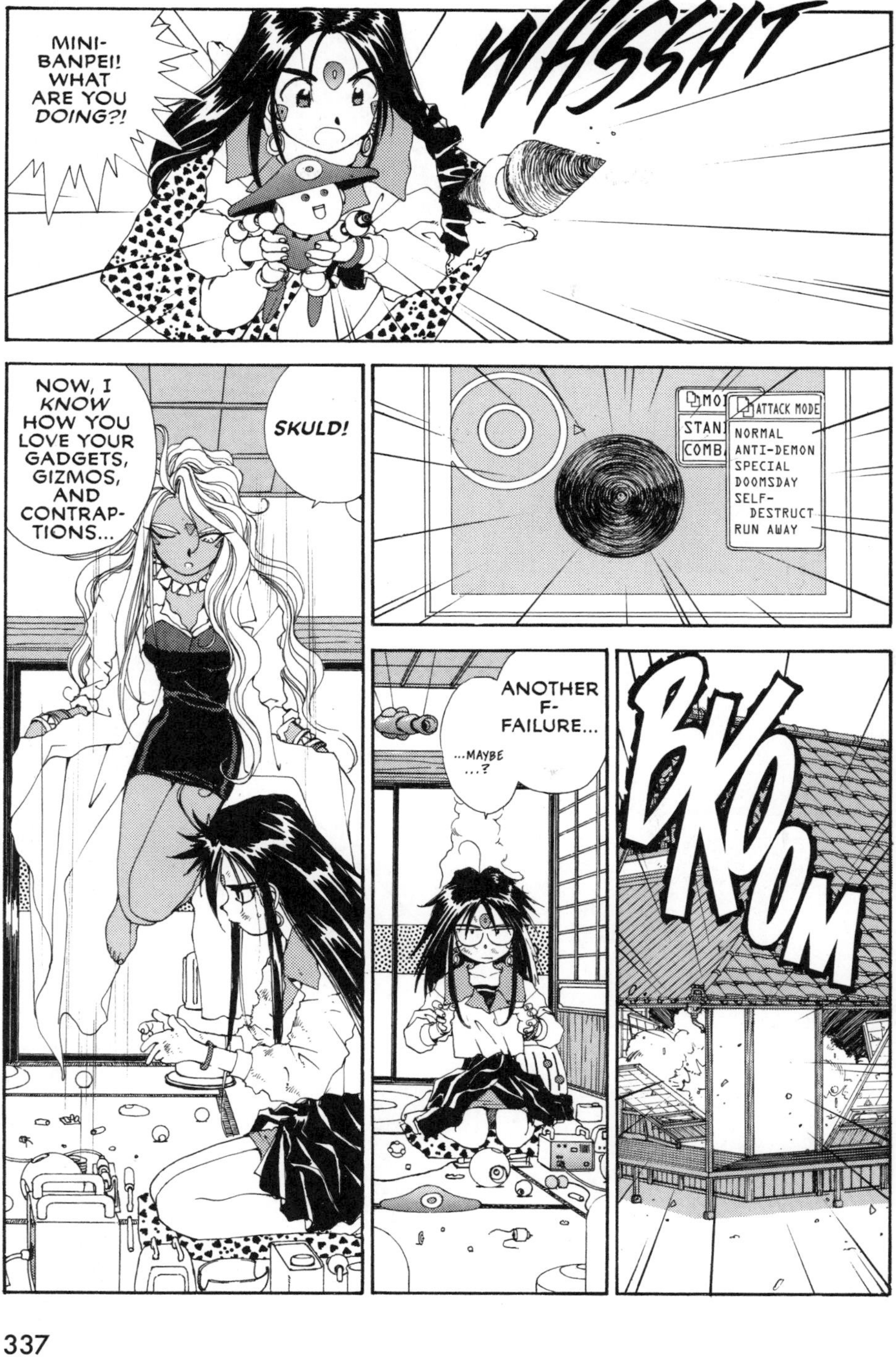
WHSSHT
MINI-BANPEI! WHAT ARE YOU *DOING*?!
ATTACK MODE
NORMAL
ANTI-DEMON
SPECIAL
DOOMSDAY
SELF-DESTRUCT
RUN AWAY
BKOOM
ANOTHER F-FAILURE...
...MAYBE ...?
SKULD!
NOW, I *KNOW* HOW YOU LOVE YOUR GADGETS, GIZMOS, AND CONTRAPTIONS...

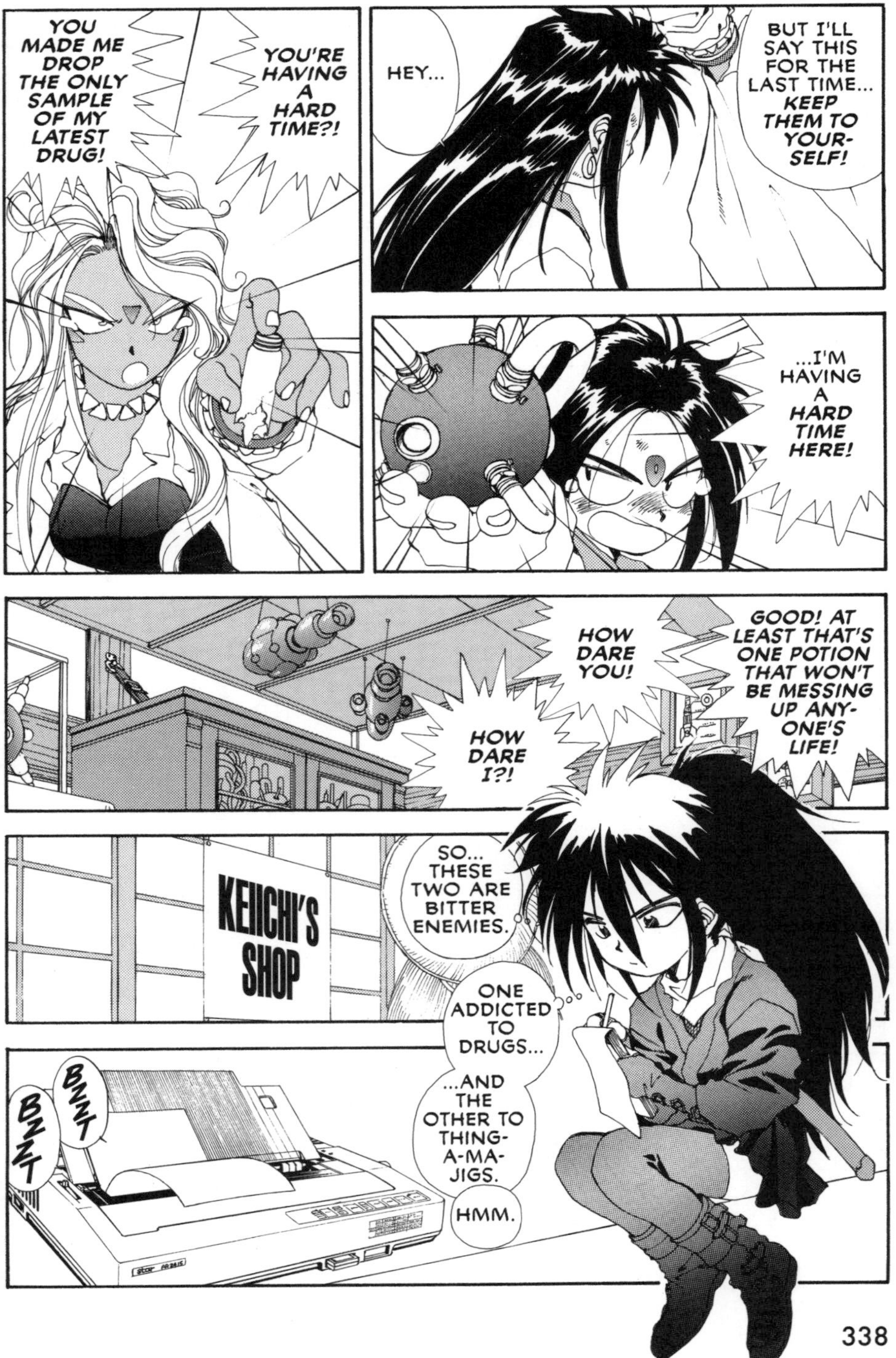
BUT I'LL SAY THIS FOR THE LAST TIME... KEEP THEM TO YOUR-SELF!
HEY...
...I'M HAVING A HARD TIME HERE!
YOU'RE HAVING A HARD TIME?!
YOU MADE ME DROP THE ONLY SAMPLE OF MY LATEST DRUG!
GOOD! AT LEAST THAT'S ONE POTION THAT WON'T BE MESSING UP ANY-ONE'S LIFE!
HOW DARE YOU!
HOW DARE I?!
SO... THESE TWO ARE BITTER ENEMIES.
KEIICHI'S SHOP
ONE ADDICTED TO DRUGS...
...AND THE OTHER TO THING-A-MA-JIGS.
HMM.
BZZT
BZZT

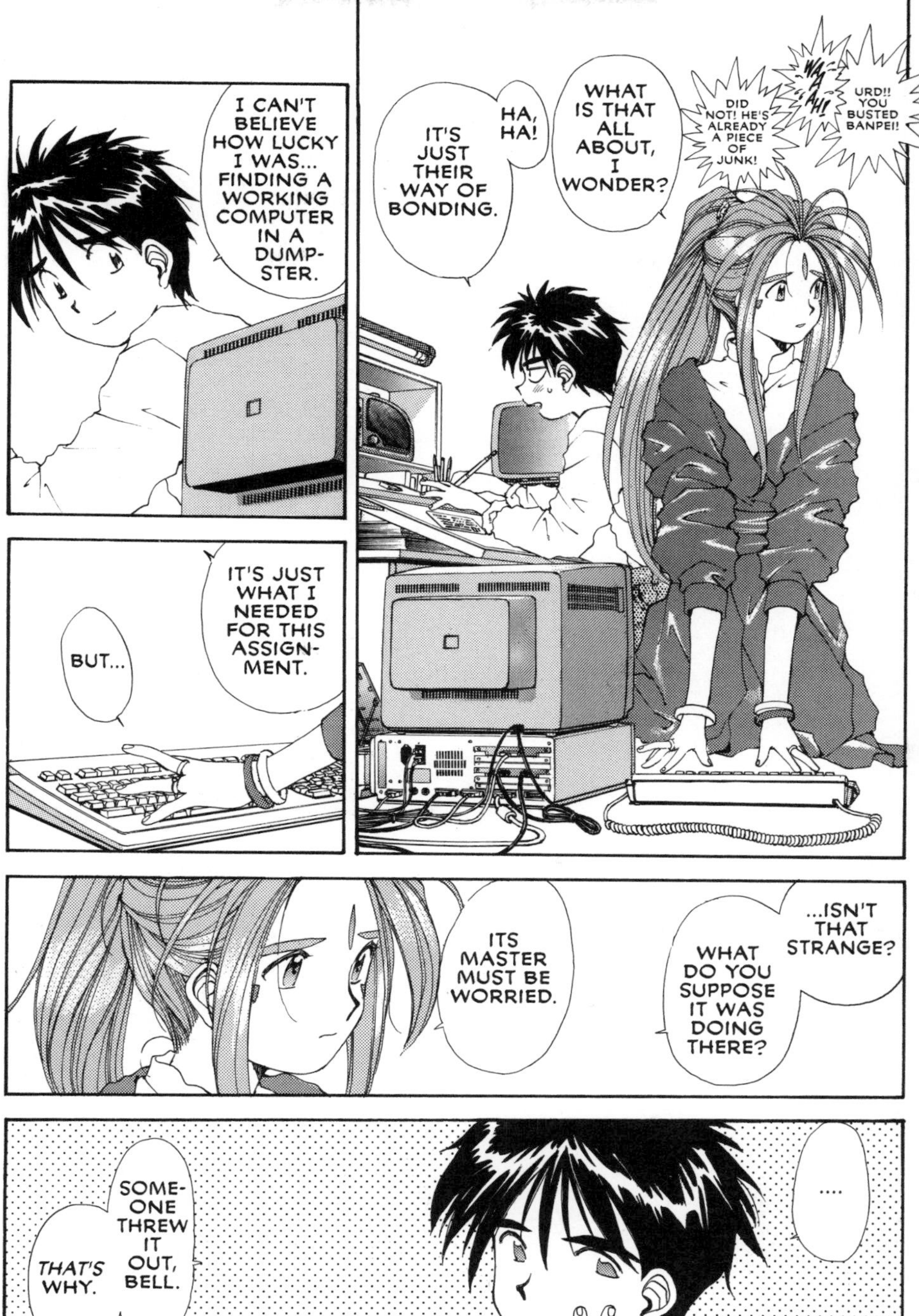
URD!! YOU BUSTED BANPEI!!
WAAAH!!
DID NOT! HE'S ALREADY A PIECE OF JUNK!
WHAT IS THAT ALL ABOUT, I WONDER?
HA, HA!
IT'S JUST THEIR WAY OF BONDING.
I CAN'T BELIEVE HOW LUCKY I WAS... FINDING A WORKING COMPUTER IN A DUMP-STER.
IT'S JUST WHAT I NEEDED FOR THIS ASSIGN-MENT.
BUT...
...ISN'T THAT STRANGE?
WHAT DO YOU SUPPOSE IT WAS DOING THERE?
ITS MASTER MUST BE WORRIED.
....
SOME-ONE THREW IT OUT, BELL.
THAT'S WHY.

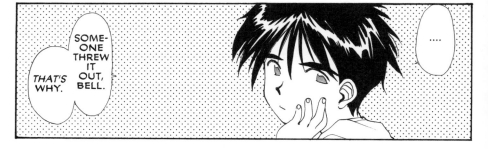

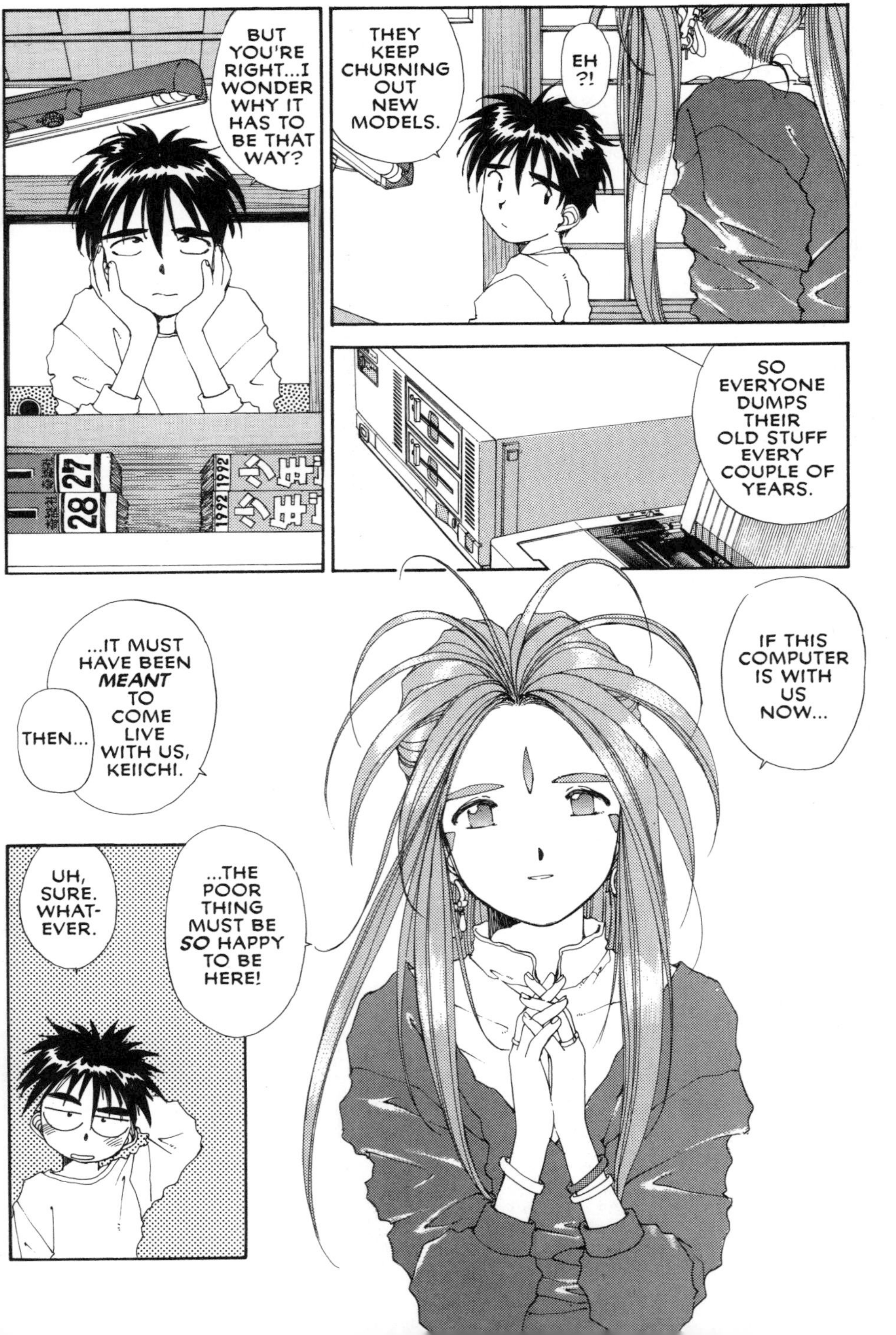
EH ?!
THEY KEEP CHURNING OUT NEW MODELS.
BUT YOU'RE RIGHT...I WONDER WHY IT HAS TO BE THAT WAY?
SO EVERYONE DUMPS THEIR OLD STUFF EVERY COUPLE OF YEARS.
IF THIS COMPUTER IS WITH US NOW...
...IT MUST HAVE BEEN *MEANT* TO COME LIVE WITH US, KEIICHI.
THEN...
...THE POOR THING MUST BE *SO* HAPPY TO BE HERE!
UH, SURE. WHAT-EVER.

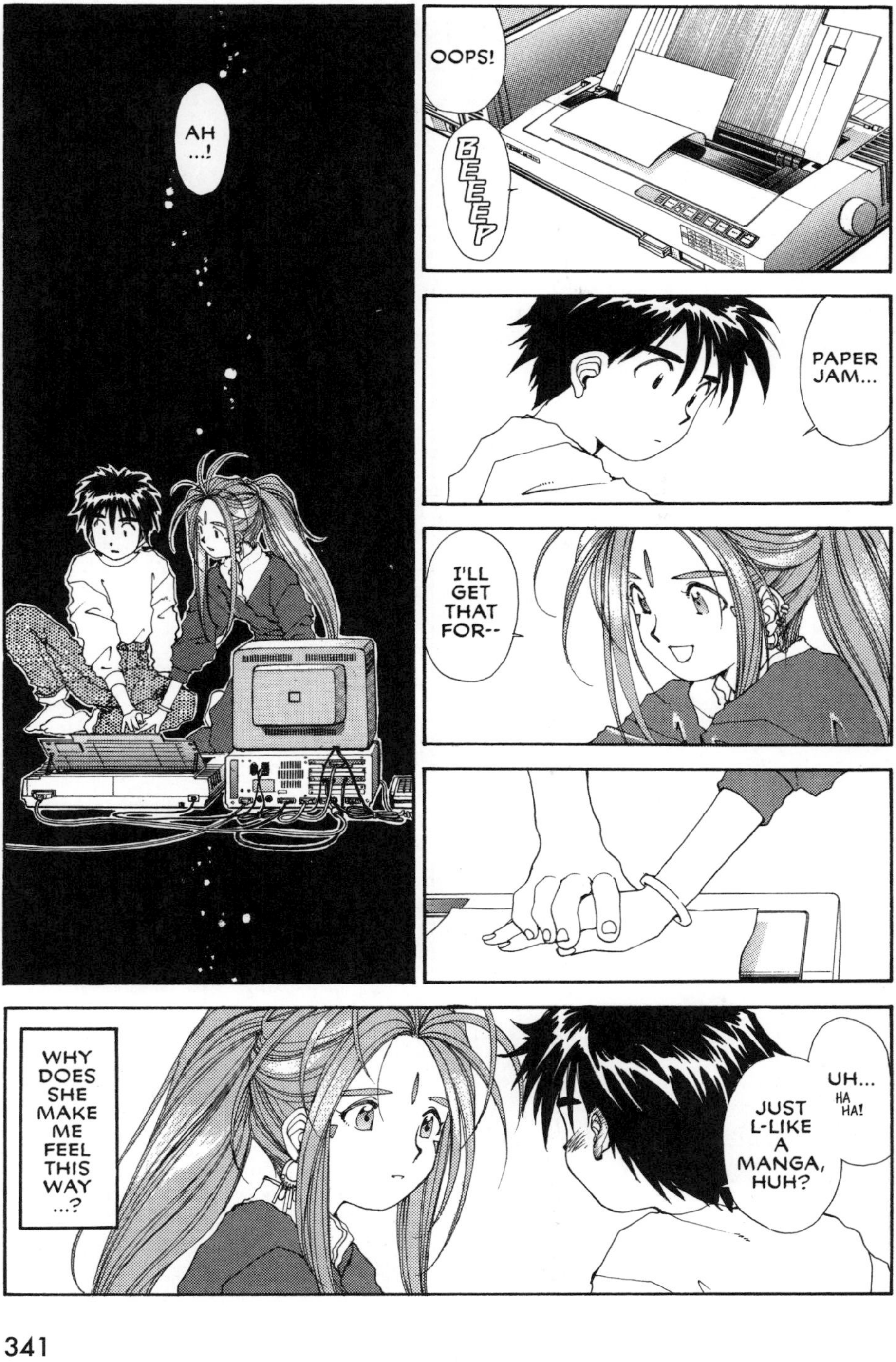
OOPS!
BEEEP
PAPER JAM...
I'LL GET THAT FOR--
AH ...!
UH... JUST L-LIKE A MANGA, HUH?
HA HA!
WHY DOES SHE MAKE ME FEEL THIS WAY ...?

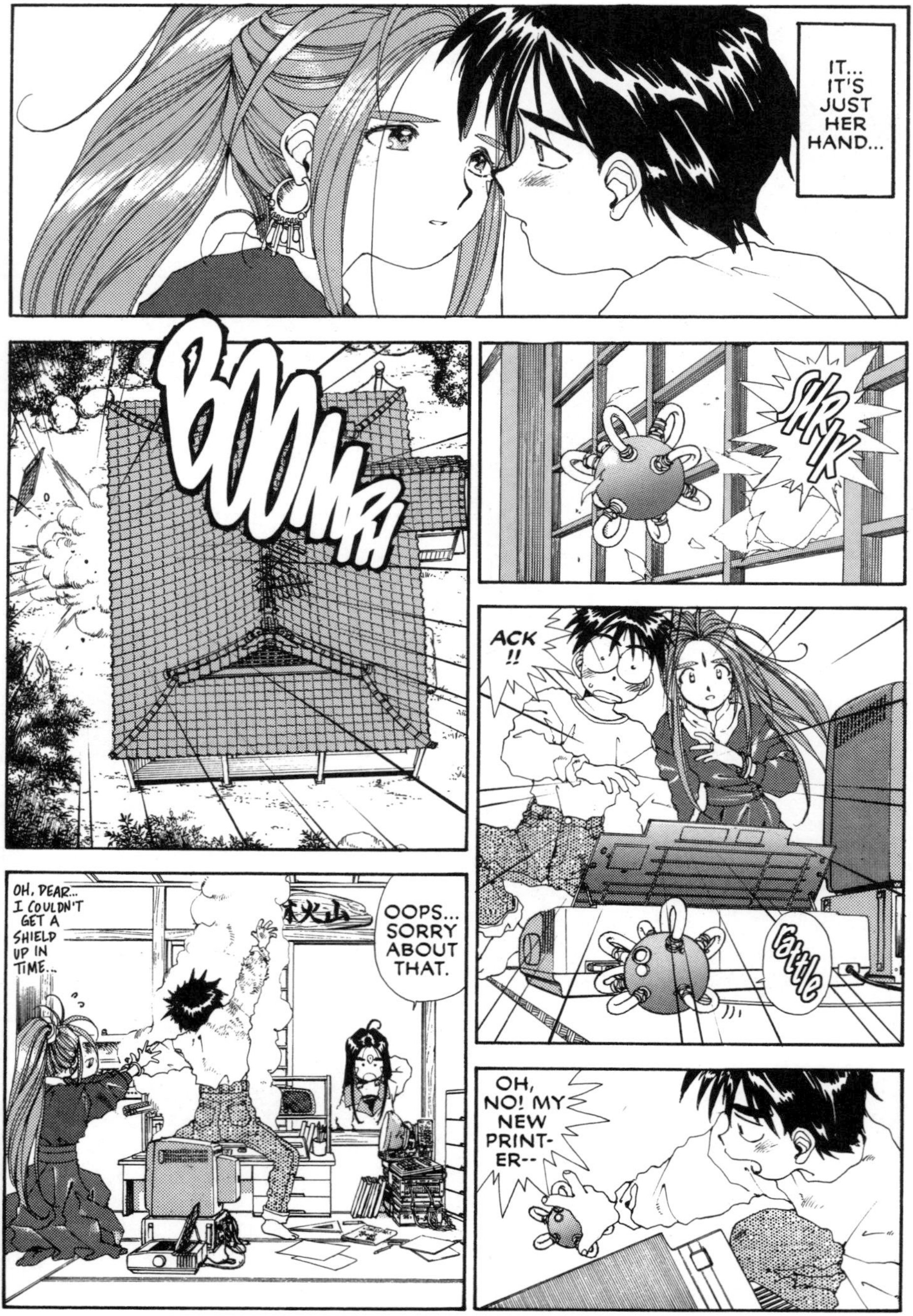
IT... IT'S JUST HER HAND...
SHRIK
BOOMPH
ACK !!
rattle
OOPS... SORRY ABOUT THAT.
OH, DEAR... I COULDN'T GET A SHIELD UP IN TIME...
OH, NO! MY NEW PRINTER--

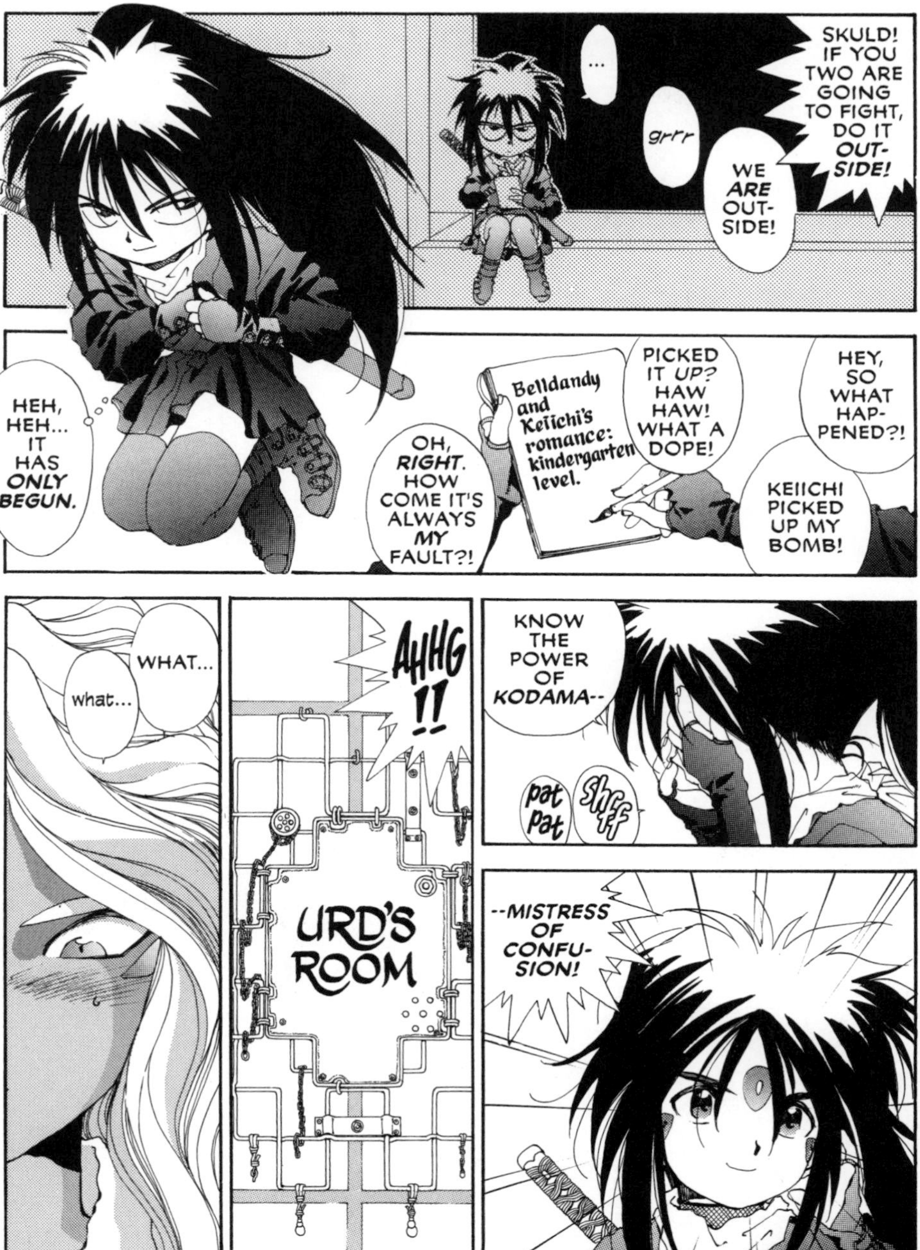
SKULD! IF YOU TWO ARE GOING TO FIGHT, DO IT OUTSIDE!
WE ARE OUTSIDE!
grrr
...
HEY, SO WHAT HAPPENED?!
KEIICHI PICKED UP MY BOMB!
PICKED IT UP? HAW HAW! WHAT A DOPE!
Belldandy and Keiichi's romance: kindergarten level.
OH, RIGHT. HOW COME IT'S ALWAYS MY FAULT?!
HEH, HEH... IT HAS ONLY BEGUN.
KNOW THE POWER OF KODAMA--
pat pat
shff
--MISTRESS OF CONFUSION!
AHHG !!
URD'S ROOM
WHAT...
what...

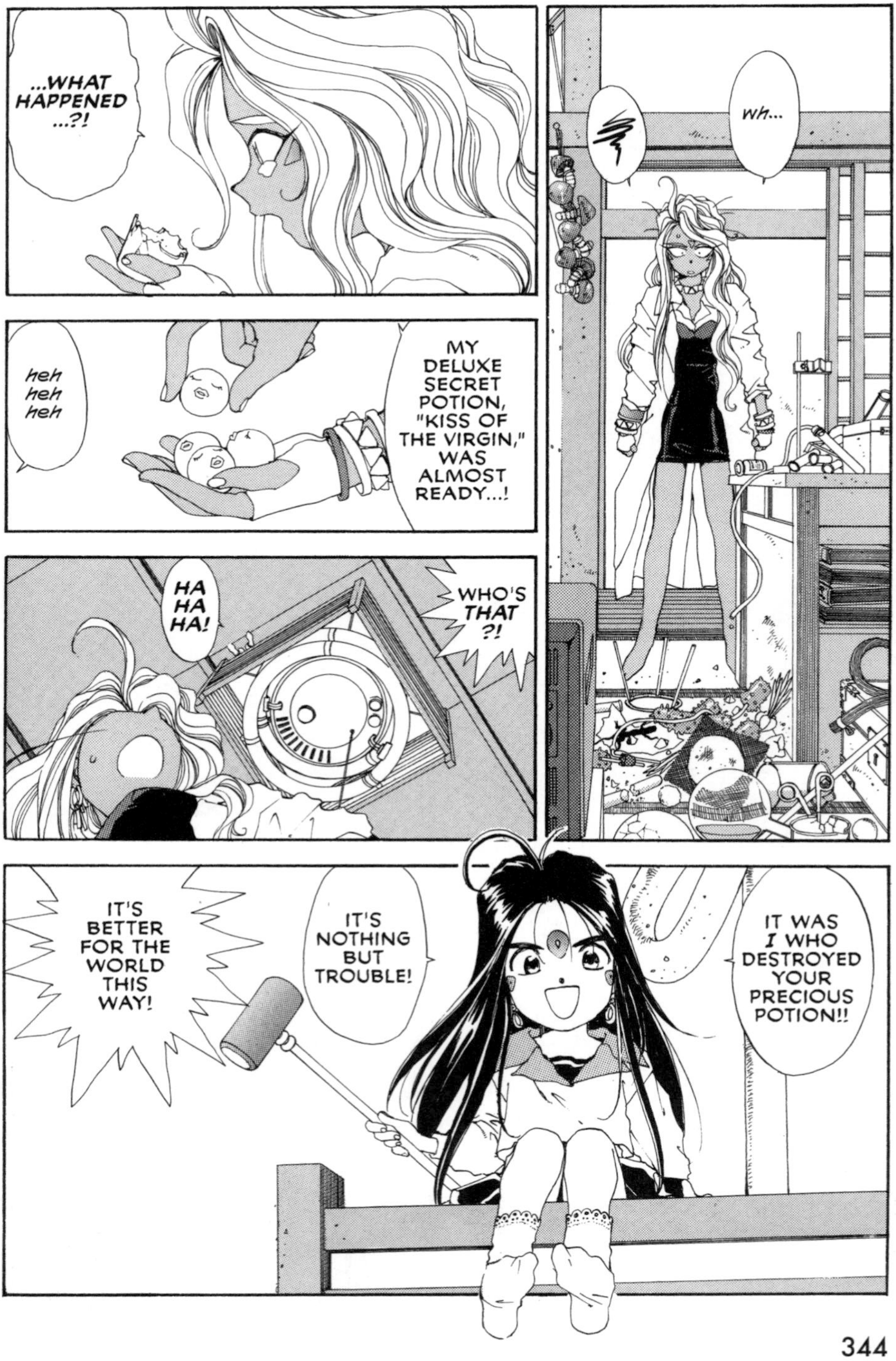
wh...
...WHAT HAPPENED ...?!
MY DELUXE SECRET POTION, "KISS OF THE VIRGIN," WAS ALMOST READY...!
heh heh heh
WHO'S THAT ?!
HA HA HA!
IT WAS I WHO DESTROYED YOUR PRECIOUS POTION!!
IT'S NOTHING BUT TROUBLE!
IT'S BETTER FOR THE WORLD THIS WAY!

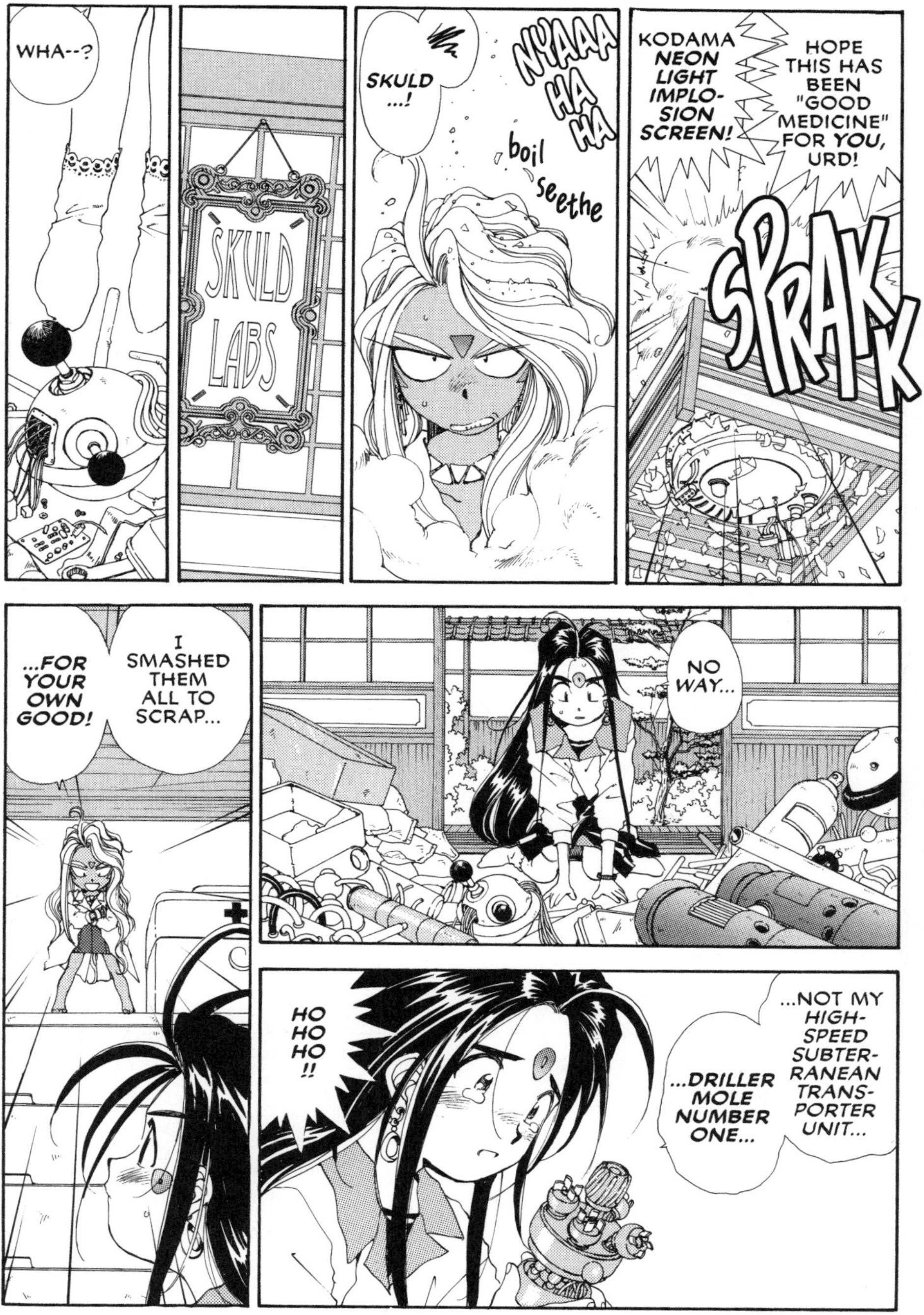
HOPE THIS HAS BEEN "GOOD MEDICINE" FOR YOU, URD!
KODAMA NEON LIGHT IMPLOSION SCREEN!
SPRAKK
NYAAA HA HA
SKULD ...!
boil
seethe
SKULD LABS
WHA--?
NO WAY...
...NOT MY HIGH-SPEED SUBTERRANEAN TRANSPORTER UNIT...
...DRILLER MOLE NUMBER ONE...
HO HO HO!!
I SMASHED THEM ALL TO SCRAP...
...FOR YOUR OWN GOOD!

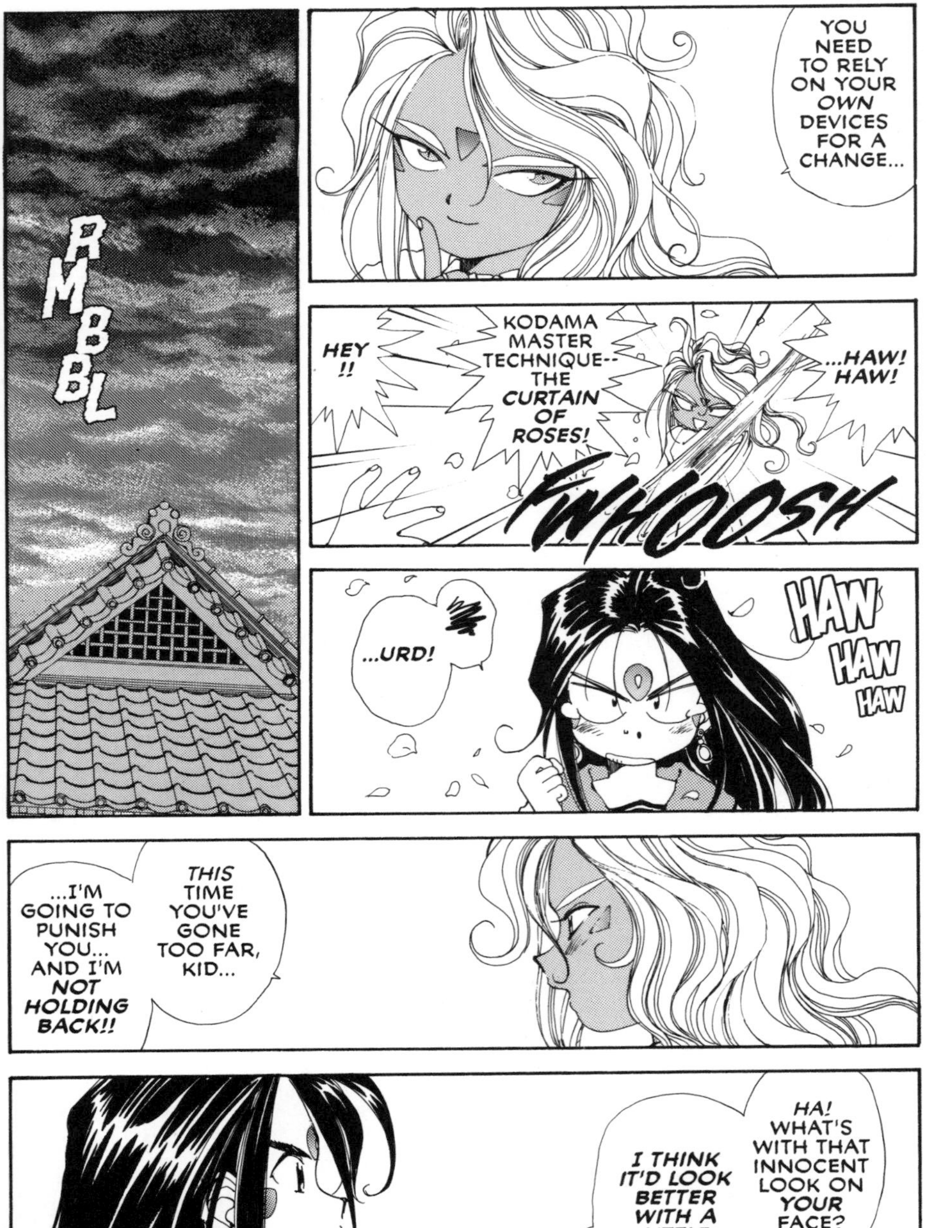
YOU NEED TO RELY ON YOUR *OWN* DEVICES FOR A CHANGE...
...HAW! HAW!
KODAMA MASTER TECHNIQUE-- THE *CURTAIN OF ROSES!*
HEY !!
FWHOOSH
HAW HAW HAW
...URD!
RMBBL
THIS TIME YOU'VE GONE TOO FAR, KID...
...I'M GOING TO PUNISH YOU... AND I'M *NOT HOLDING BACK!!*
HA! WHAT'S WITH THAT INNOCENT LOOK ON *YOUR* FACE?
I THINK IT'D LOOK BETTER WITH A LITTLE "BAKA"!

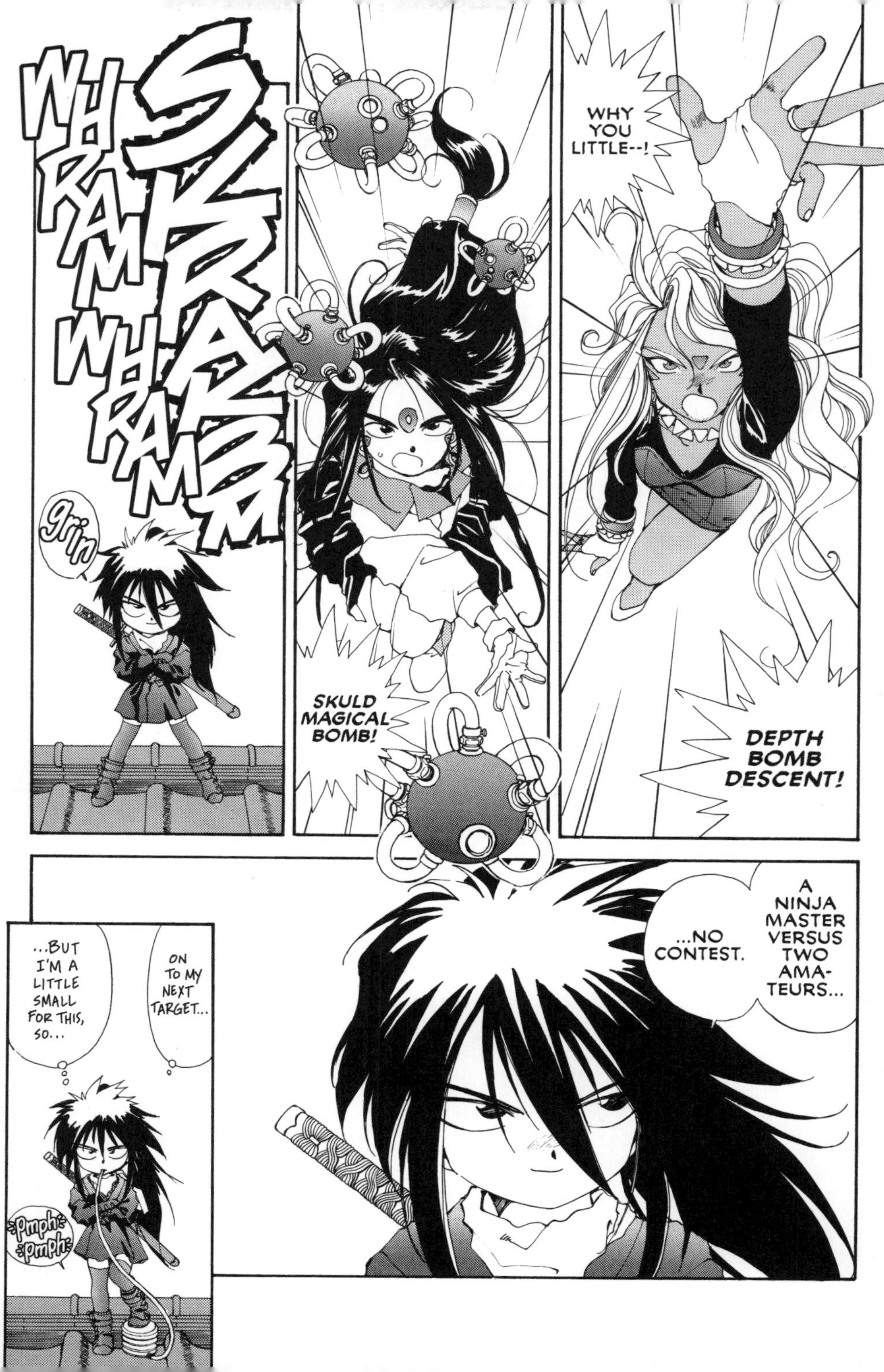
WHY YOU LITTLE--!
DEPTH BOMB DESCENT!
SKULD MAGICAL BOMB!
WHRAM WHRAM
grin
A NINJA MASTER VERSUS TWO AMA-TEURS...
...NO CONTEST.
ON TO MY NEXT TARGET...
...BUT I'M A LITTLE SMALL FOR THIS, SO...
pmph pmph

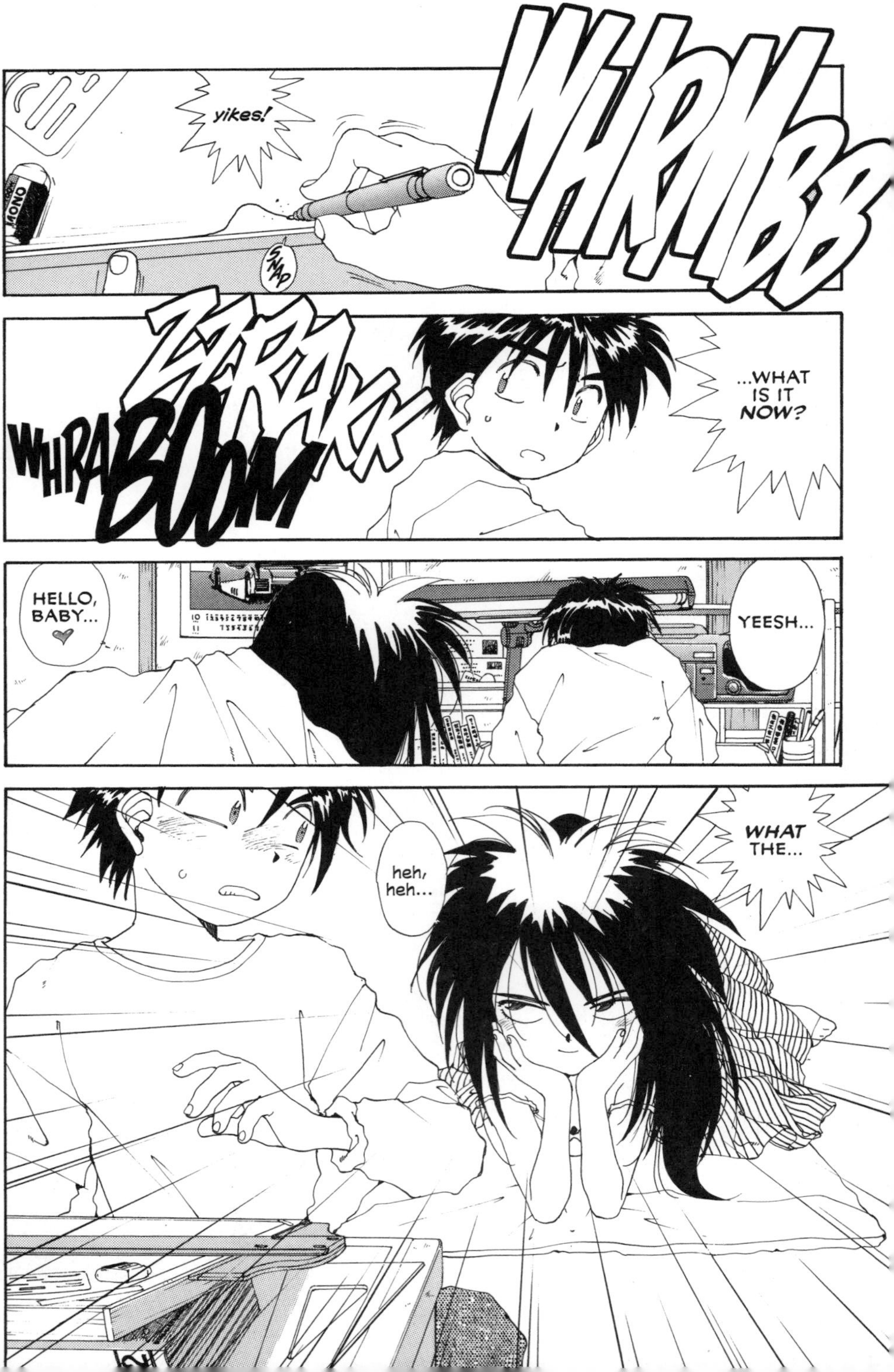
yikes!
SNAP
...WHAT IS IT NOW?
WHRABOOM
YEESH...
HELLO, BABY...
WHAT THE...
heh, heh...

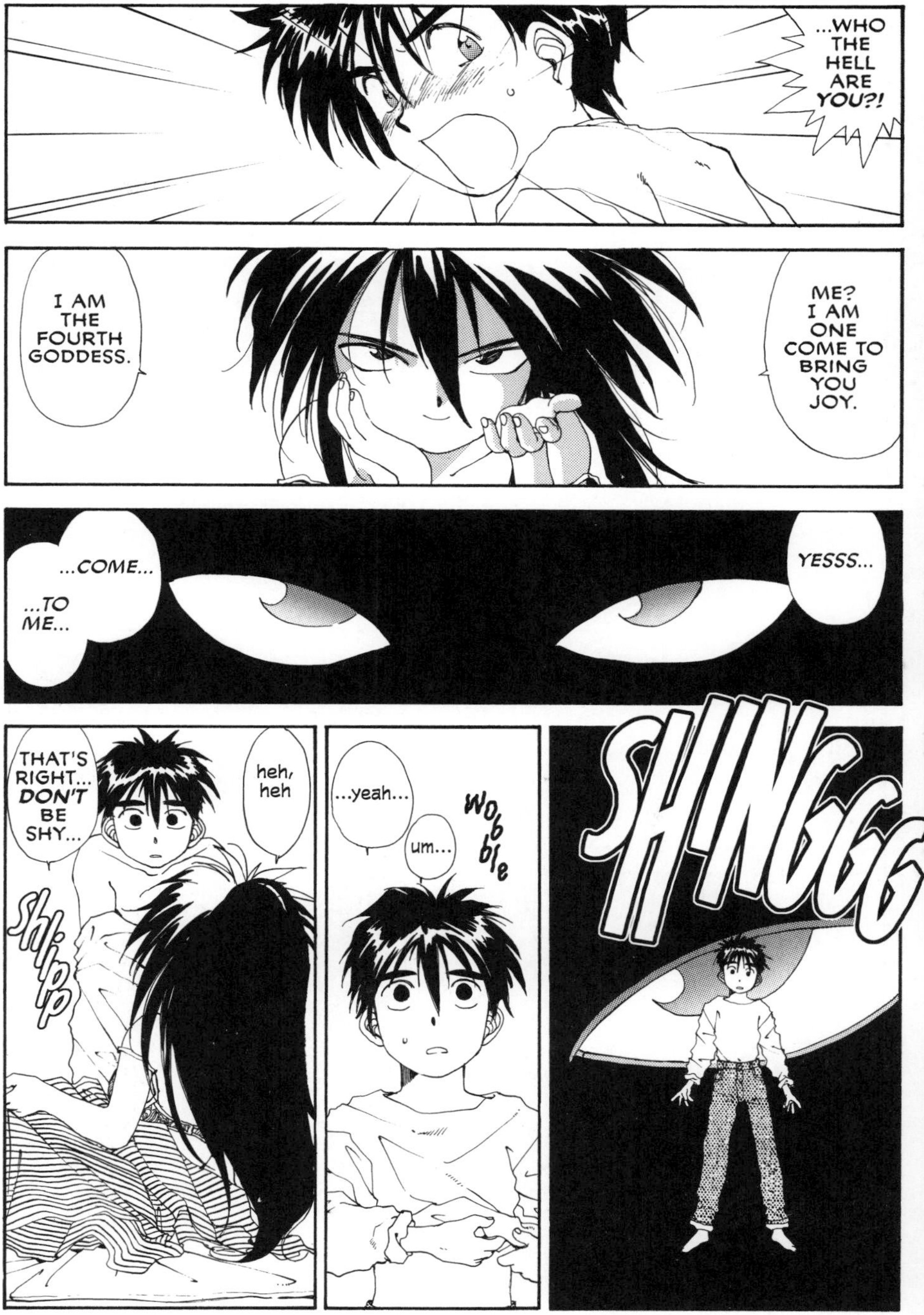
...WHO THE HELL ARE YOU?!
ME? I AM ONE COME TO BRING YOU JOY.
I AM THE FOURTH GODDESS.
YESSS...
...COME...
...TO ME...
SHINGGG
...yeah...
um...
wobble
heh, heh
THAT'S RIGHT... DON'T BE SHY...
shipp

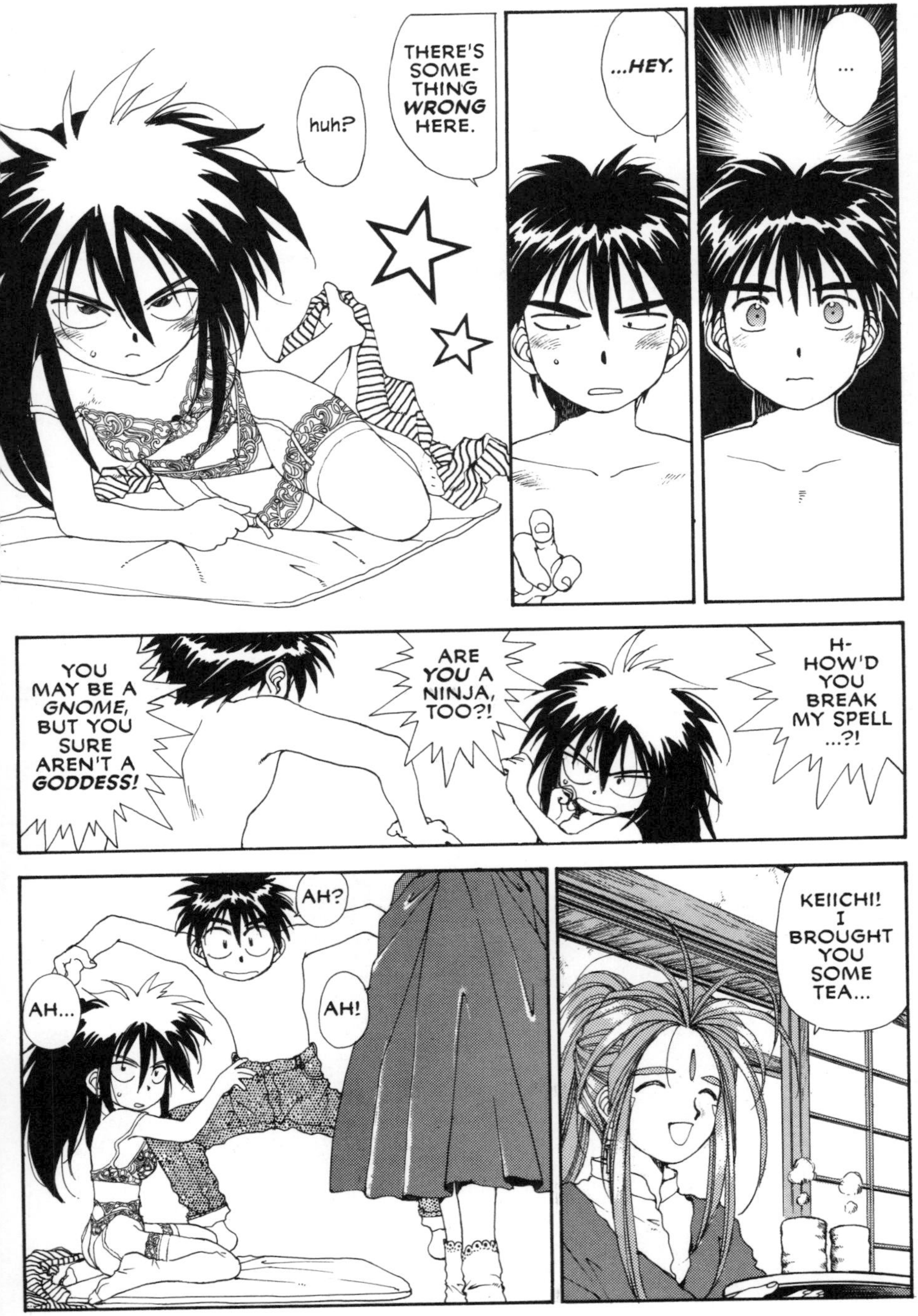
...
...HEY.
THERE'S SOMETHING WRONG HERE.
huh?
H-HOW'D YOU BREAK MY SPELL ...?!
ARE YOU A NINJA, TOO?!
YOU MAY BE A GNOME, BUT YOU SURE AREN'T A GODDESS!
KEIICHI! I BROUGHT YOU SOME TEA...
AH?
AH!
AH...

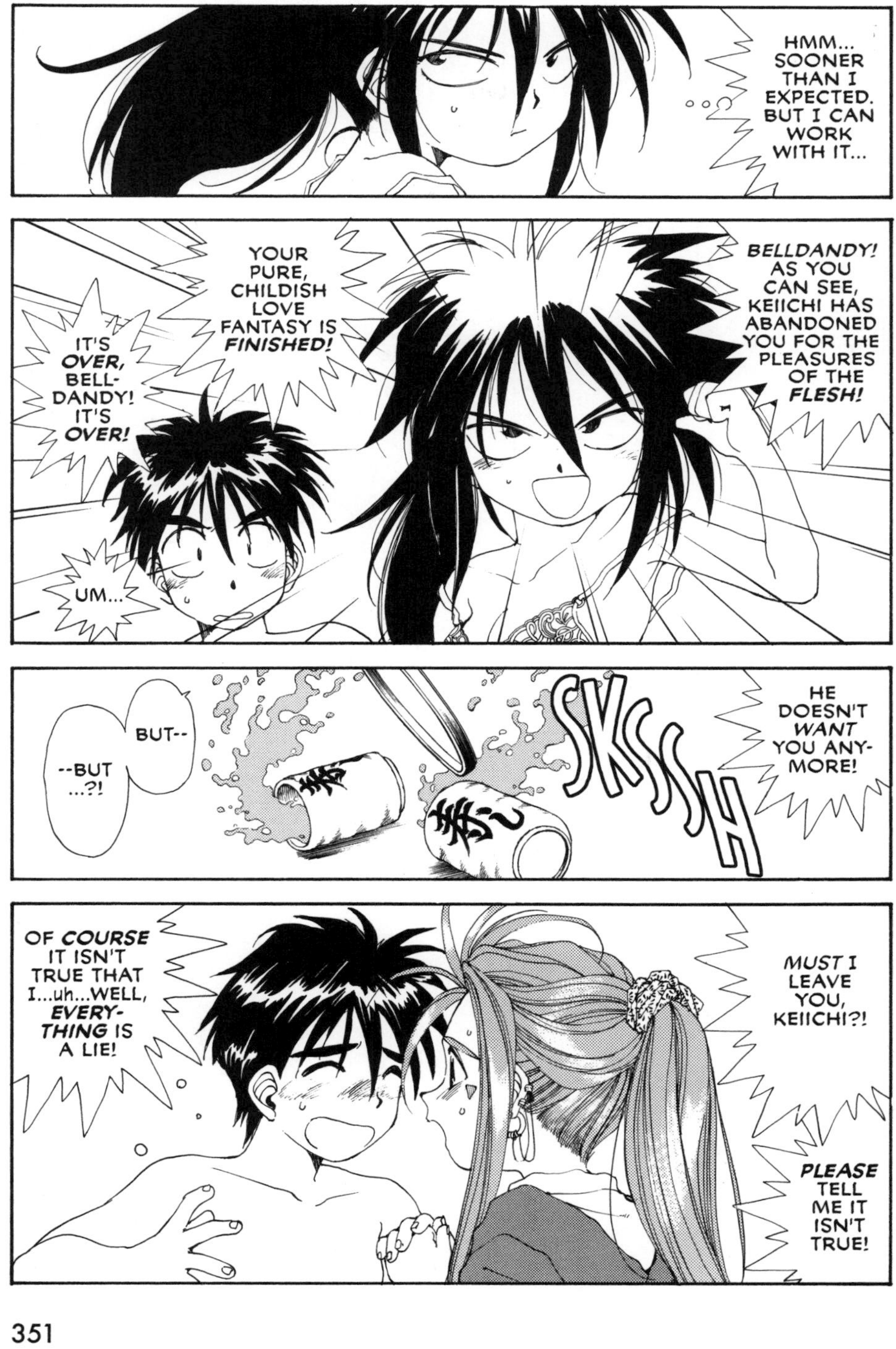
HMM... SOONER THAN I EXPECTED. BUT I CAN WORK WITH IT...
BELLDANDY! AS YOU CAN SEE, KEIICHI HAS ABANDONED YOU FOR THE PLEASURES OF THE FLESH!
YOUR PURE, CHILDISH LOVE FANTASY IS FINISHED!
IT'S OVER, BELL-DANDY! IT'S OVER!
UM...
HE DOESN'T WANT YOU ANY-MORE!
SKSSSH
BUT--
--BUT ...?!
MUST I LEAVE YOU, KEIICHI?!
PLEASE TELL ME IT ISN'T TRUE!
OF COURSE IT ISN'T TRUE THAT I...uh...WELL, EVERY-THING IS A LIE!

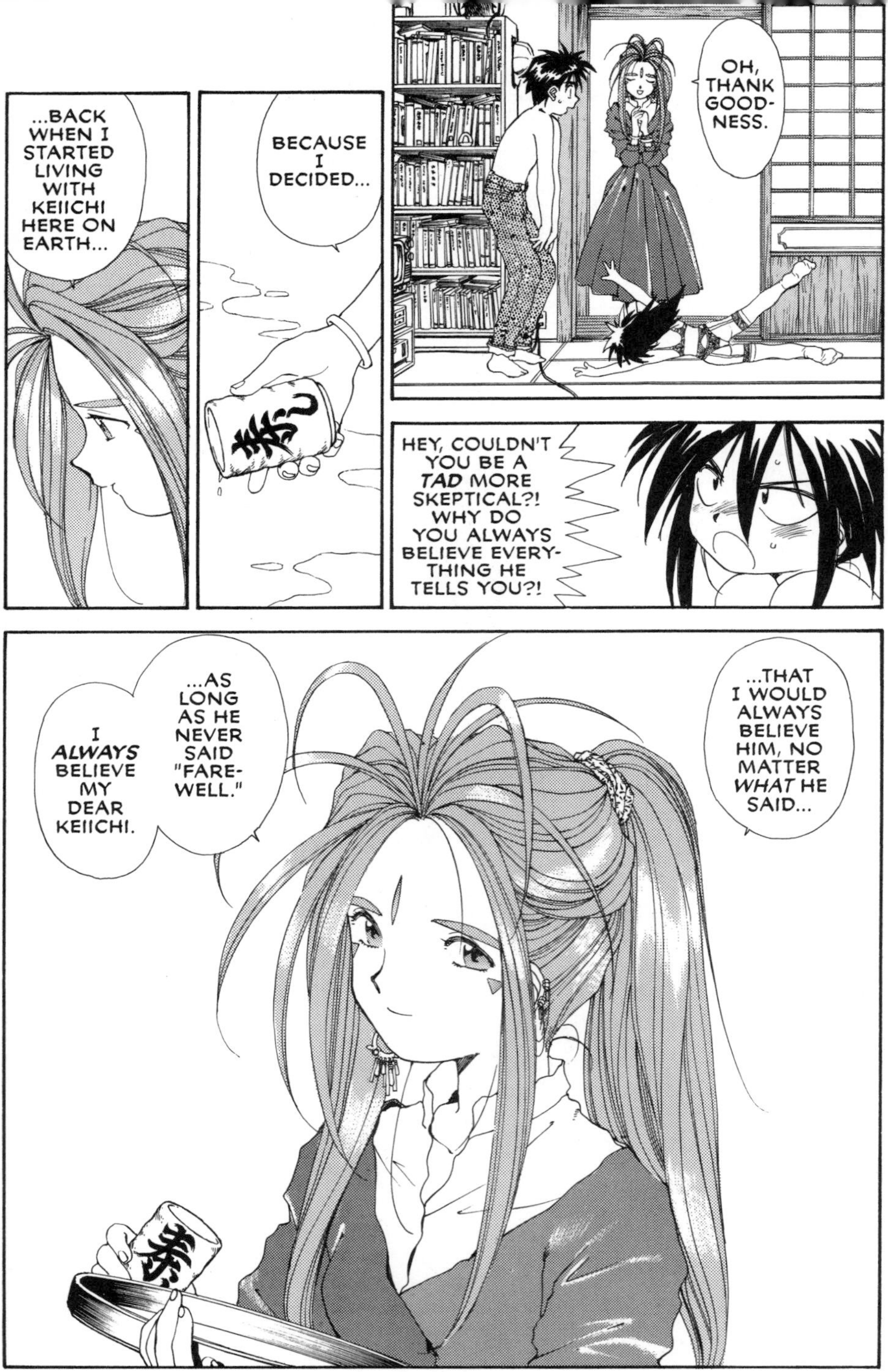
OH, THANK GOODNESS.
HEY, COULDN'T YOU BE A *TAD* MORE SKEPTICAL?! WHY DO YOU ALWAYS BELIEVE EVERYTHING HE TELLS YOU?!
BECAUSE I DECIDED...
...BACK WHEN I STARTED LIVING WITH KEIICHI HERE ON EARTH...
...THAT I WOULD ALWAYS BELIEVE HIM, NO MATTER *WHAT* HE SAID...
...AS LONG AS HE NEVER SAID "FAREWELL."
I *ALWAYS* BELIEVE MY DEAR KEIICHI.

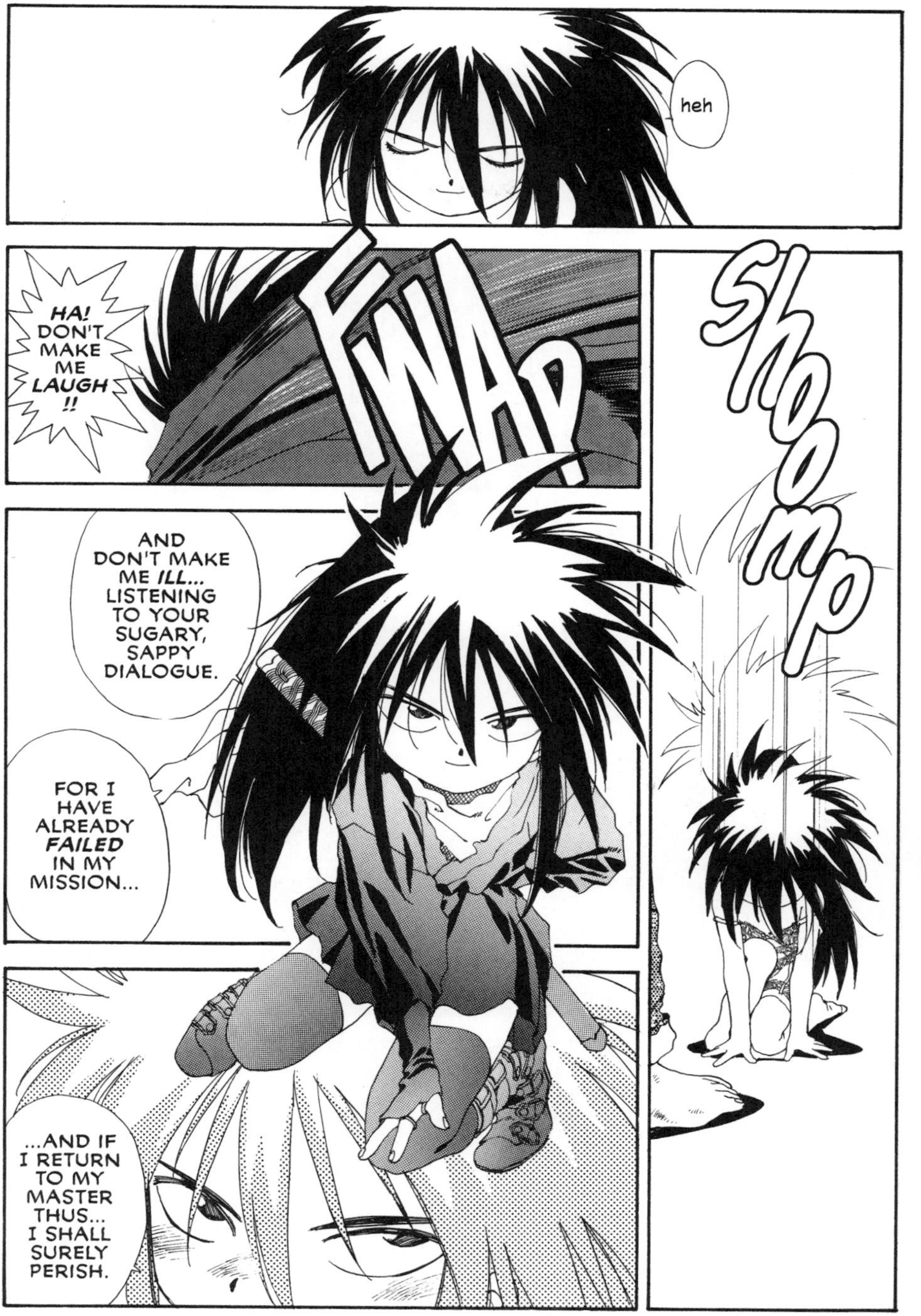
heh
SHOOOMP
HA! DON'T MAKE ME LAUGH!!
FWAP
AND DON'T MAKE ME ILL... LISTENING TO YOUR SUGARY, SAPPY DIALOGUE.
FOR I HAVE ALREADY FAILED IN MY MISSION...
...AND IF I RETURN TO MY MASTER THUS... I SHALL SURELY PERISH.

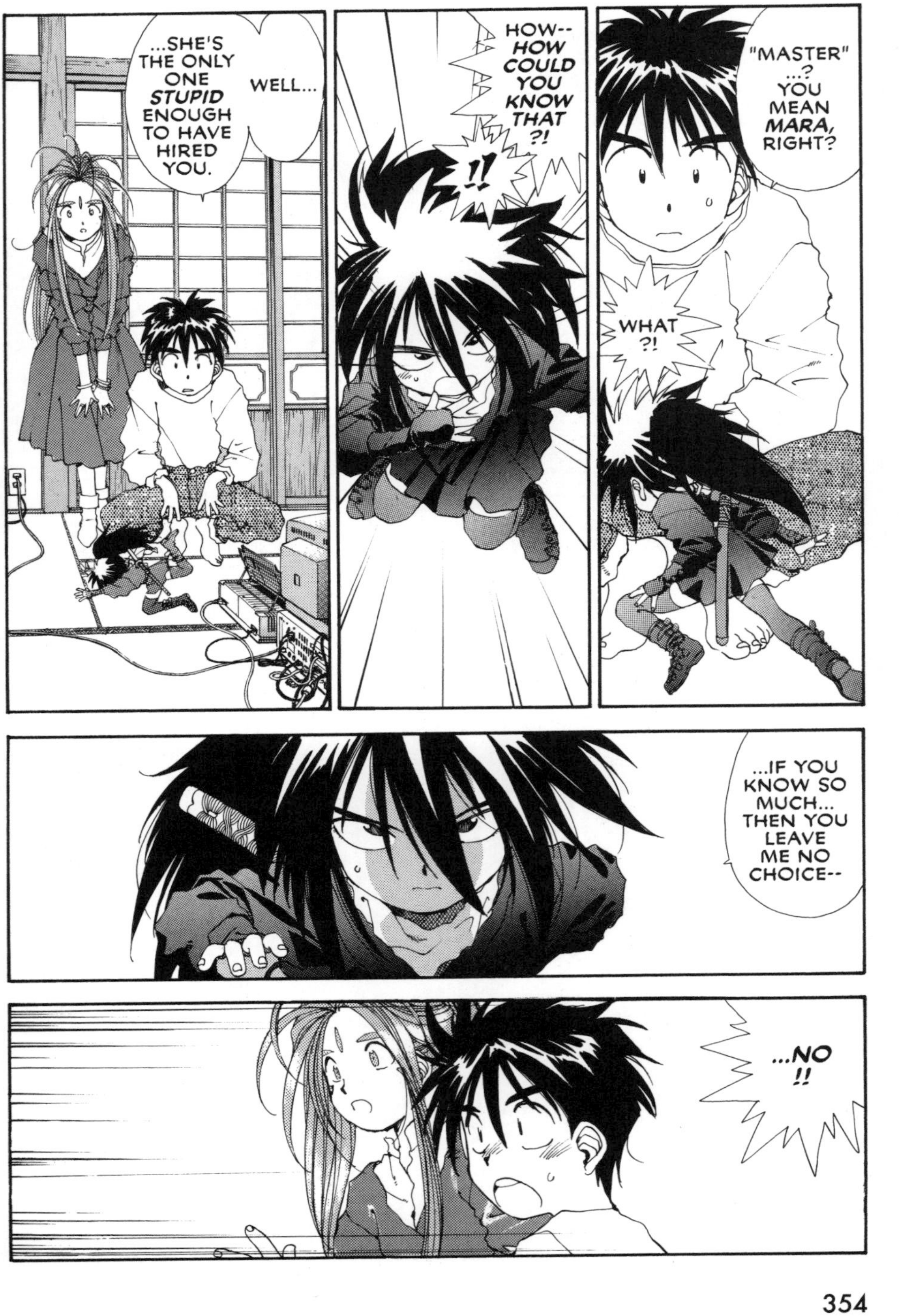
"MASTER" ...? YOU MEAN MARA, RIGHT?
WHAT ?!
HOW-- HOW COULD YOU KNOW THAT ?!
!!
WELL...
...SHE'S THE ONLY ONE STUPID ENOUGH TO HAVE HIRED YOU.
...IF YOU KNOW SO MUCH... THEN YOU LEAVE ME NO CHOICE--
...NO !!

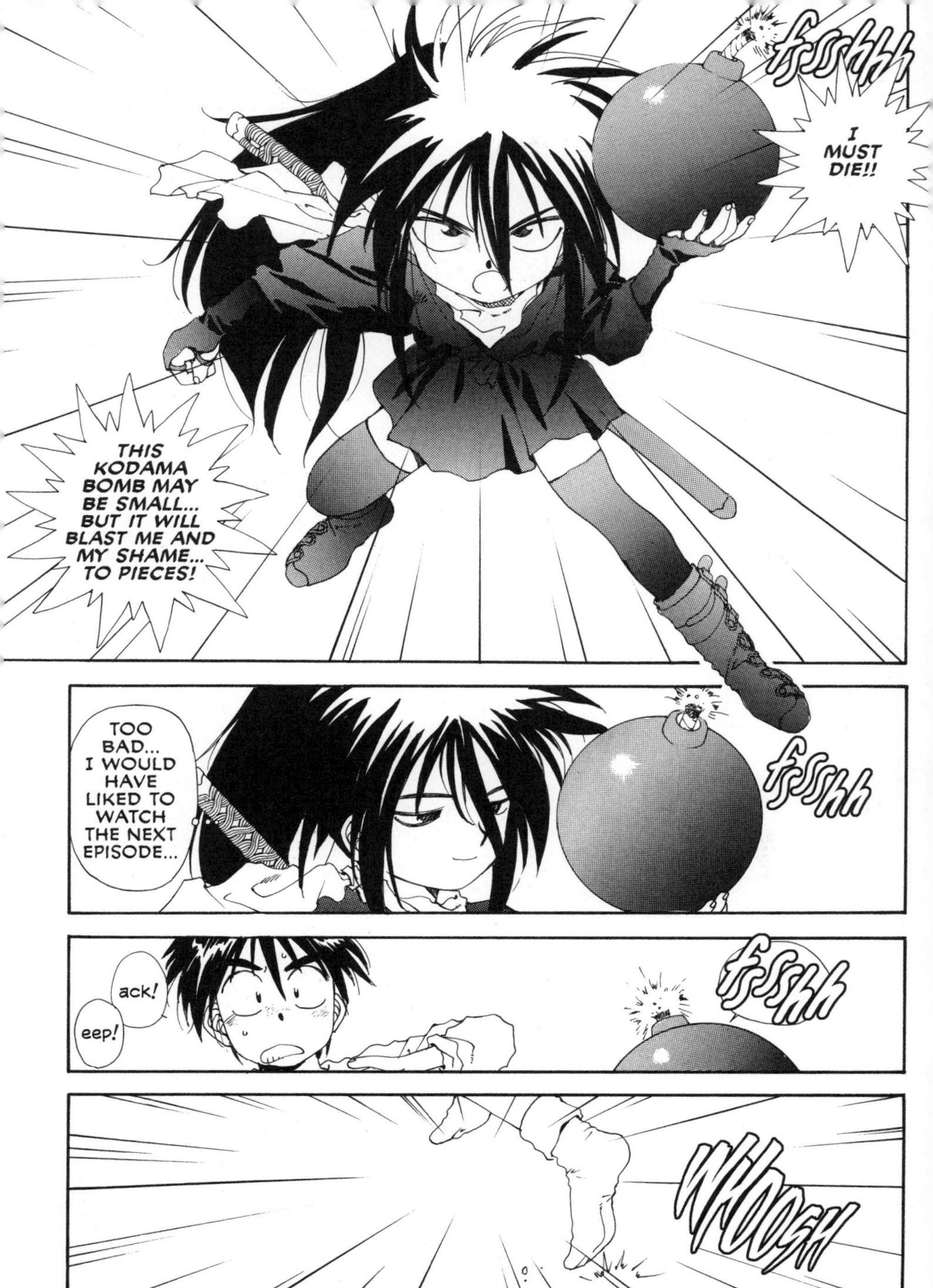
fsshhh
I MUST DIE!!
THIS KODAMA BOMB MAY BE SMALL... BUT IT WILL BLAST ME AND MY SHAME... TO PIECES!
fsshh
TOO BAD... I WOULD HAVE LIKED TO WATCH THE NEXT EPISODE...
fsshh
ack!
eep!
WHOOSH

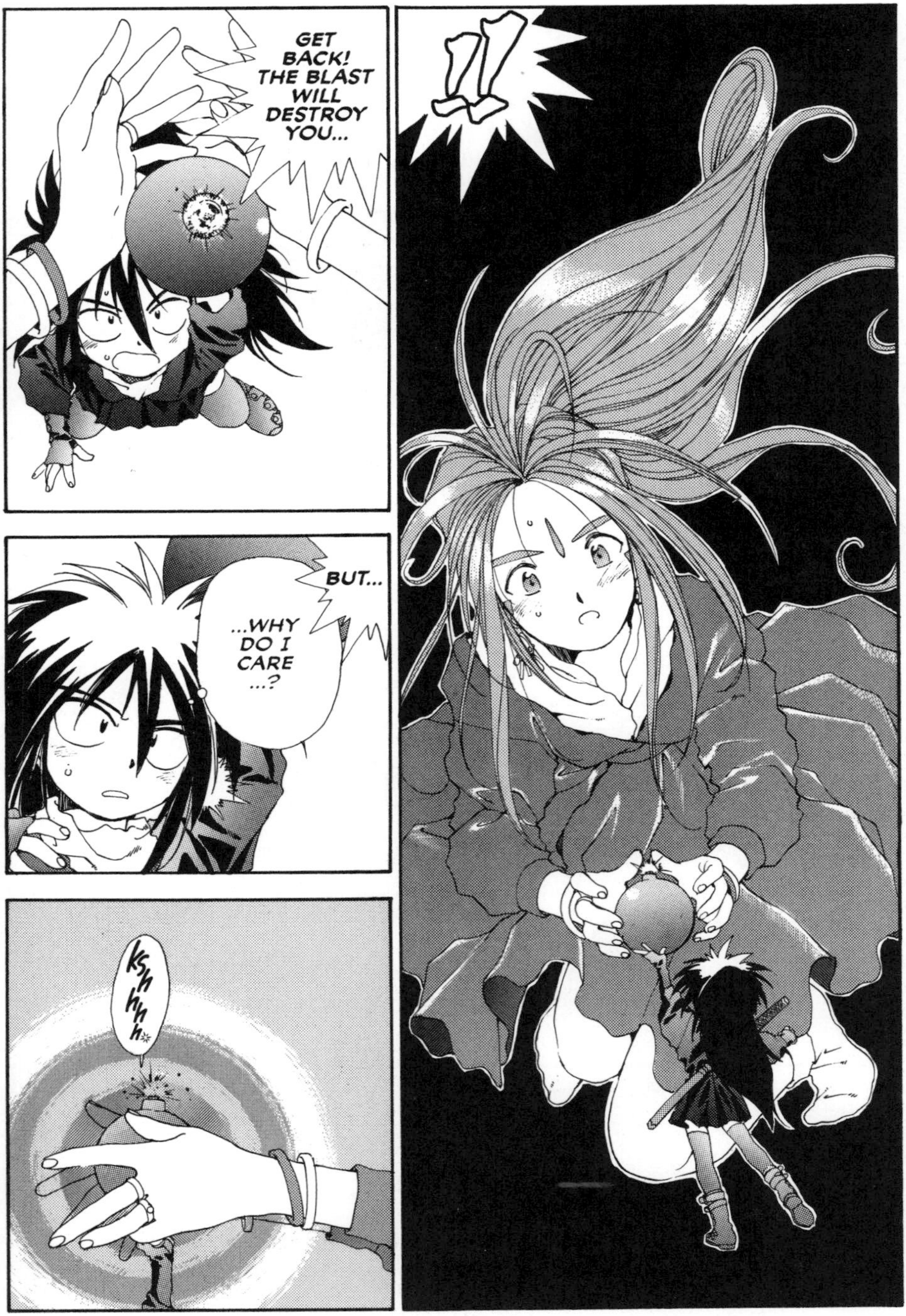
!!
GET BACK! THE BLAST WILL DESTROY YOU...
BUT...
...WHY DO I CARE ...?
kshhhh

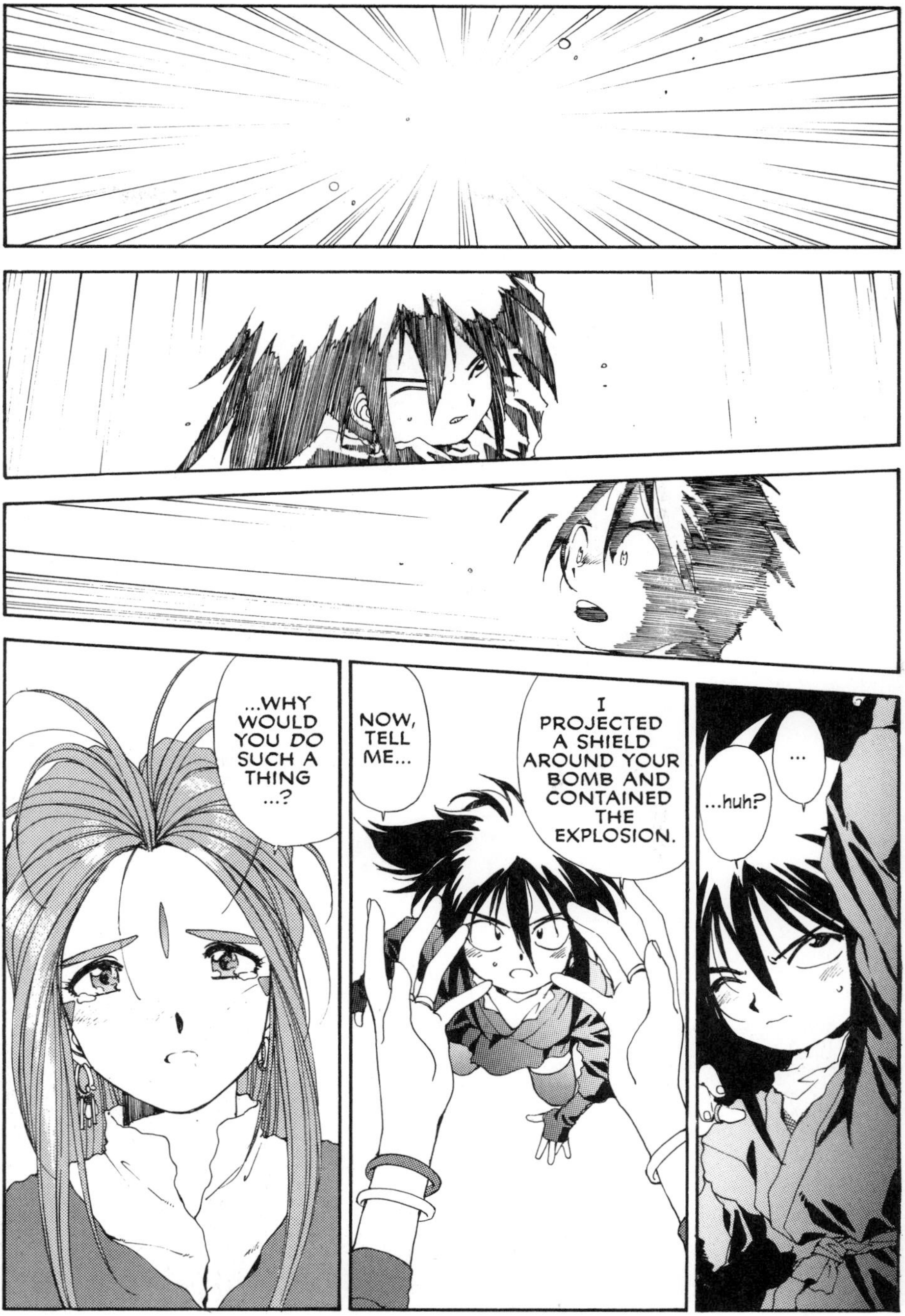
...
...huh?
I PROJECTED A SHIELD AROUND YOUR BOMB AND CONTAINED THE EXPLOSION.
NOW, TELL ME...
...WHY WOULD YOU *DO* SUCH A THING ...?

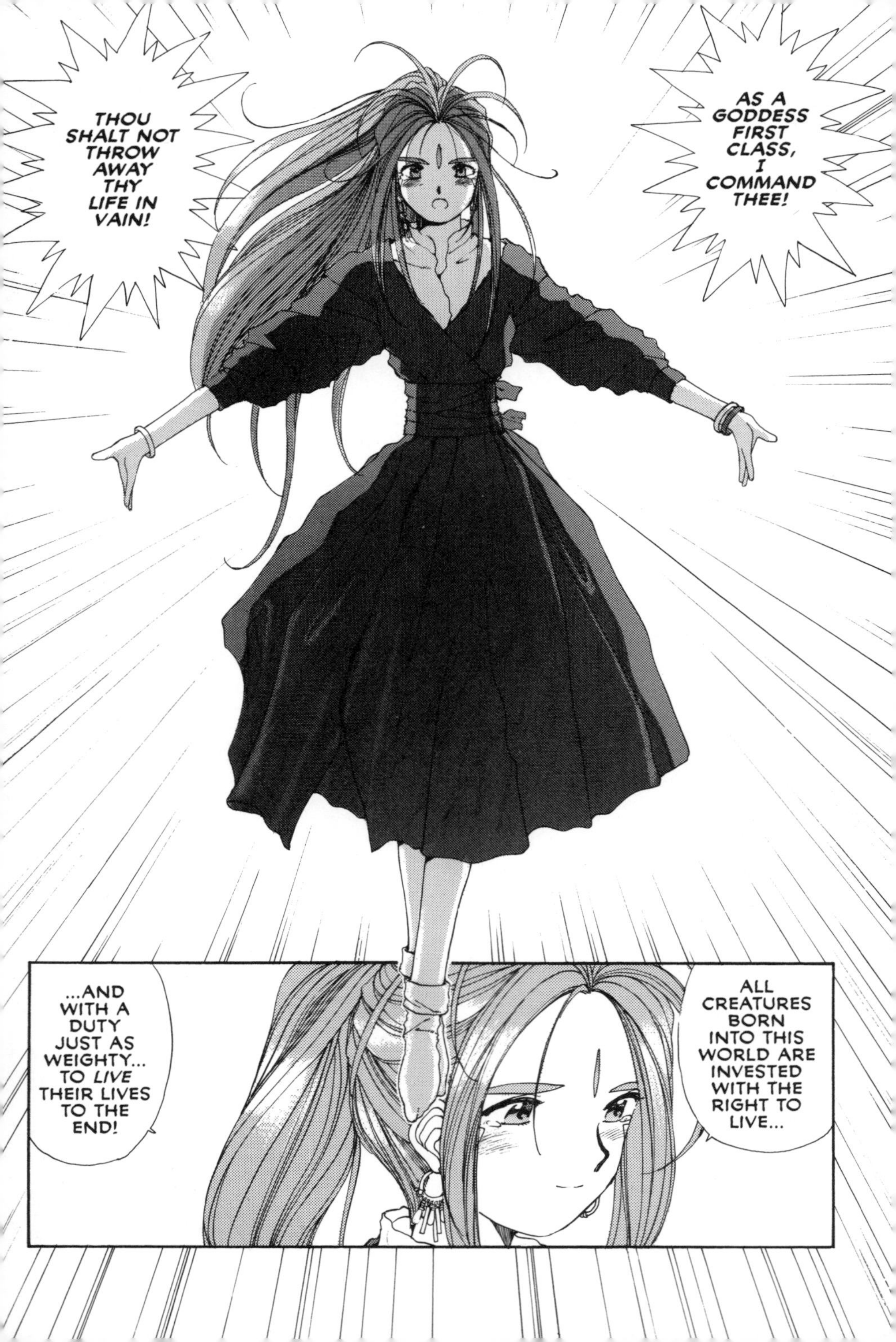
AS A GODDESS FIRST CLASS, I COMMAND THEE!
THOU SHALT NOT THROW AWAY THY LIFE IN VAIN!
ALL CREATURES BORN INTO THIS WORLD ARE INVESTED WITH THE RIGHT TO LIVE...
...AND WITH A DUTY JUST AS WEIGHTY... TO *LIVE* THEIR LIVES TO THE END!

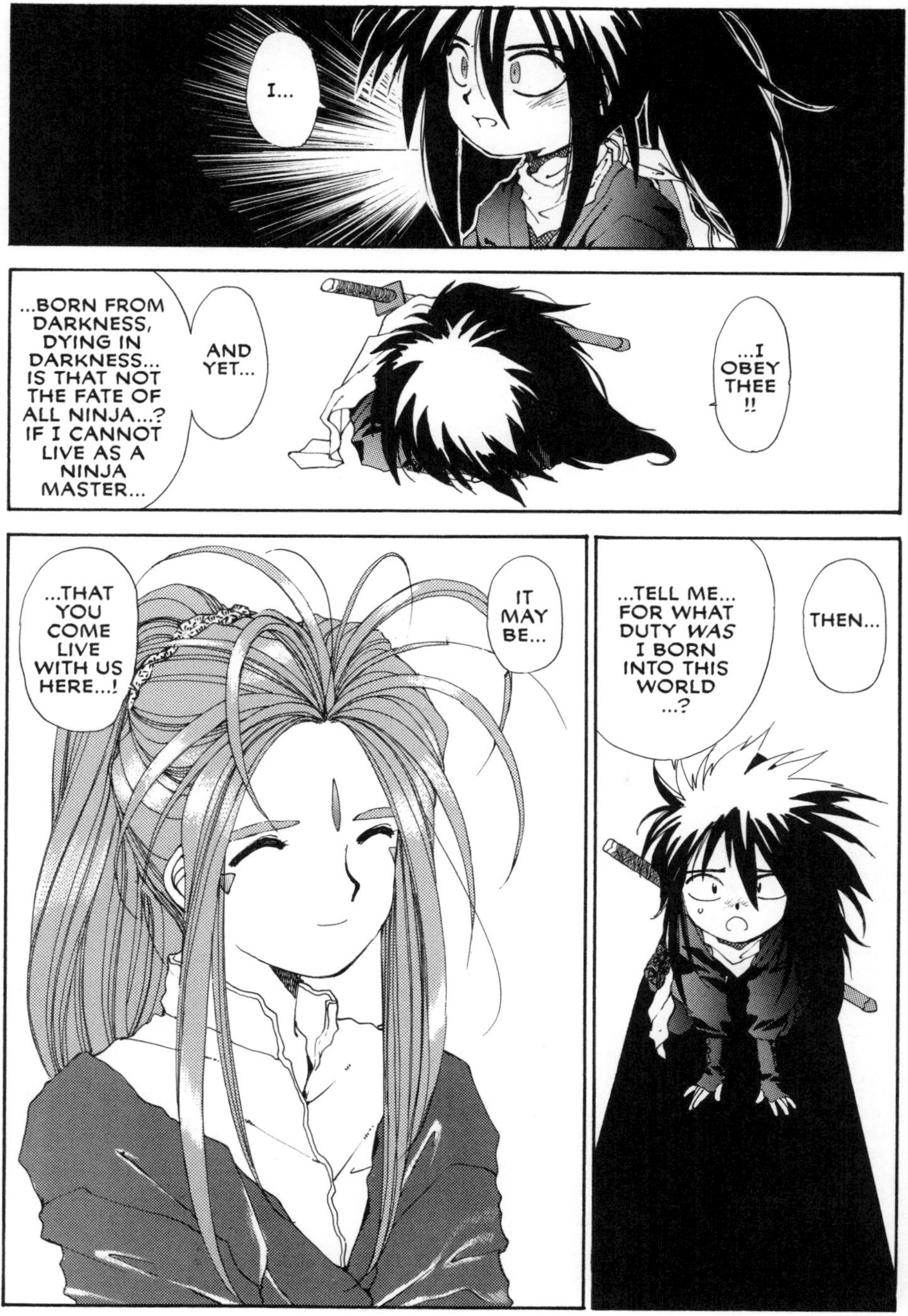
I...
...I OBEY THEE !!
AND YET...
...BORN FROM DARKNESS, DYING IN DARKNESS... IS THAT NOT THE FATE OF ALL NINJA...? IF I CANNOT LIVE AS A NINJA MASTER...
THEN...
...TELL ME... FOR WHAT DUTY *WAS* I BORN INTO THIS WORLD ...?
IT MAY BE...
...THAT YOU COME LIVE WITH US HERE...!

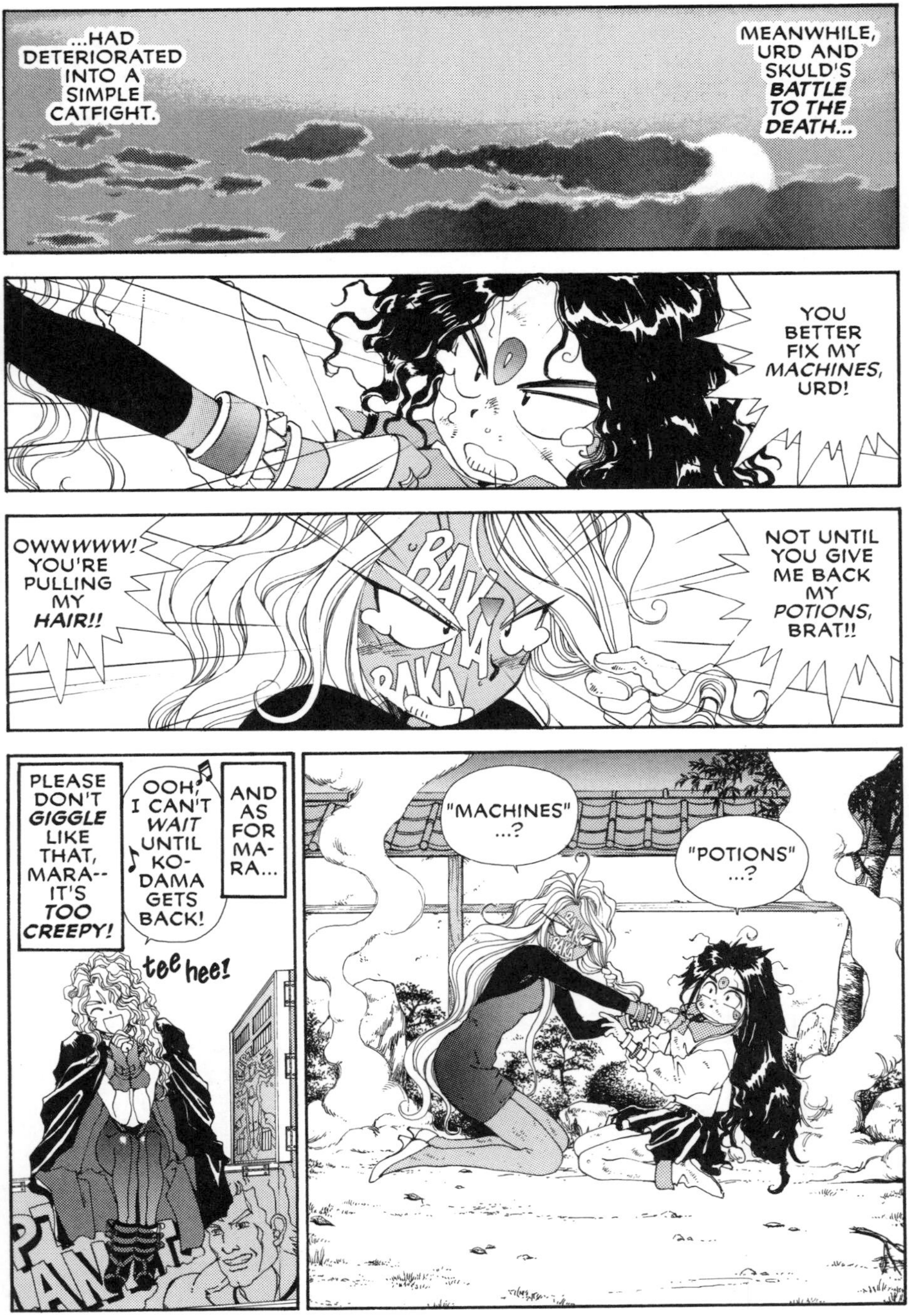
MEANWHILE, URD AND SKULD'S *BATTLE TO THE DEATH...*
...HAD DETERIORATED INTO A SIMPLE CATFIGHT.
YOU BETTER FIX MY *MACHINES,* URD!
NOT UNTIL YOU GIVE ME BACK MY *POTIONS,* BRAT!!
BAKA BAKA BAKA
OWWWWWW! YOU'RE PULLING MY *HAIR!!*
"POTIONS" ...?
"MACHINES" ...?
AND AS FOR MARA...
OOH, I CAN'T *WAIT* UNTIL KODAMA GETS BACK!
tee hee!
PLEASE DON'T *GIGGLE* LIKE THAT, MARA-- IT'S *TOO CREEPY!*

OH MY GODDESS!

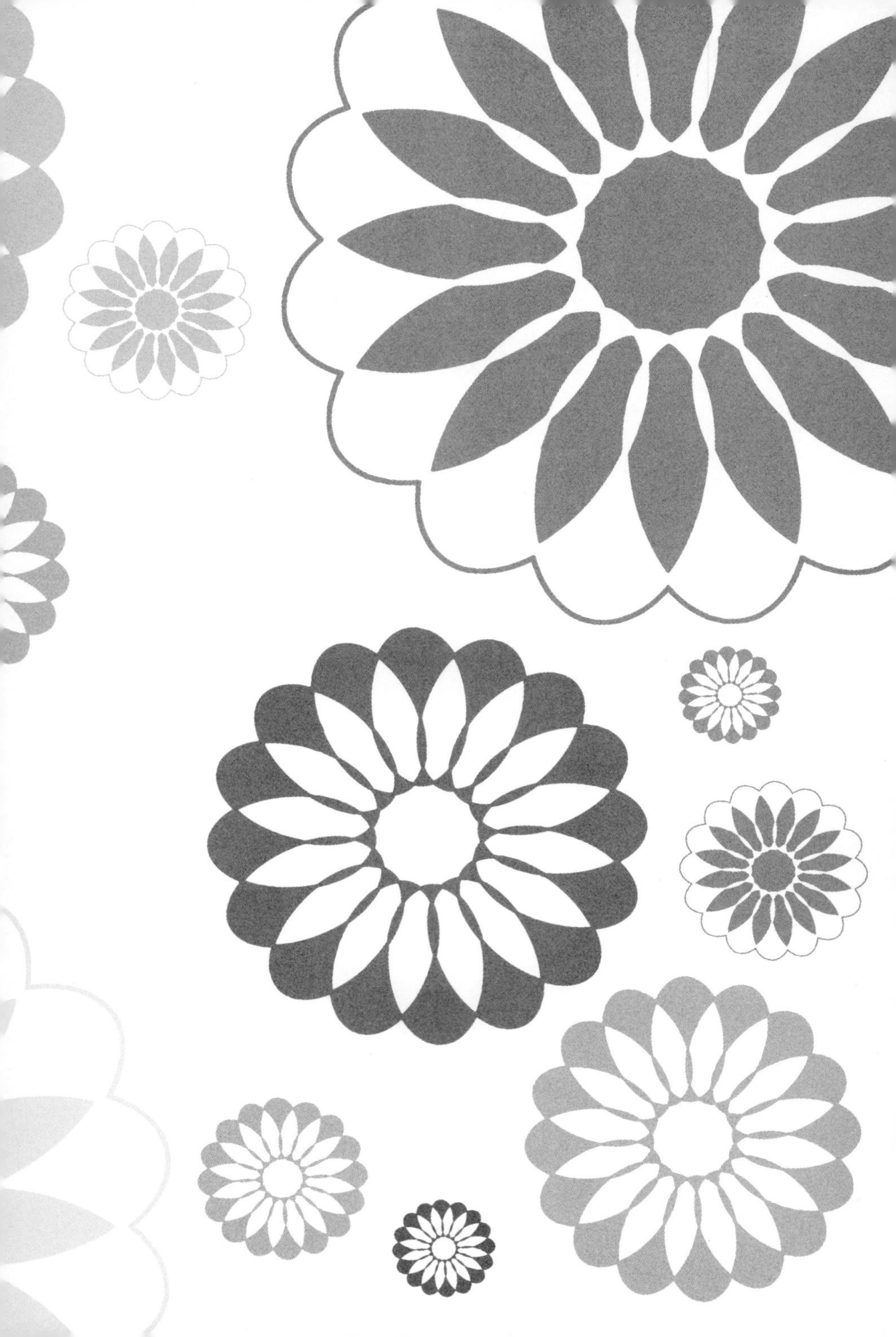

CHAPTER 53

Law of the Ninja

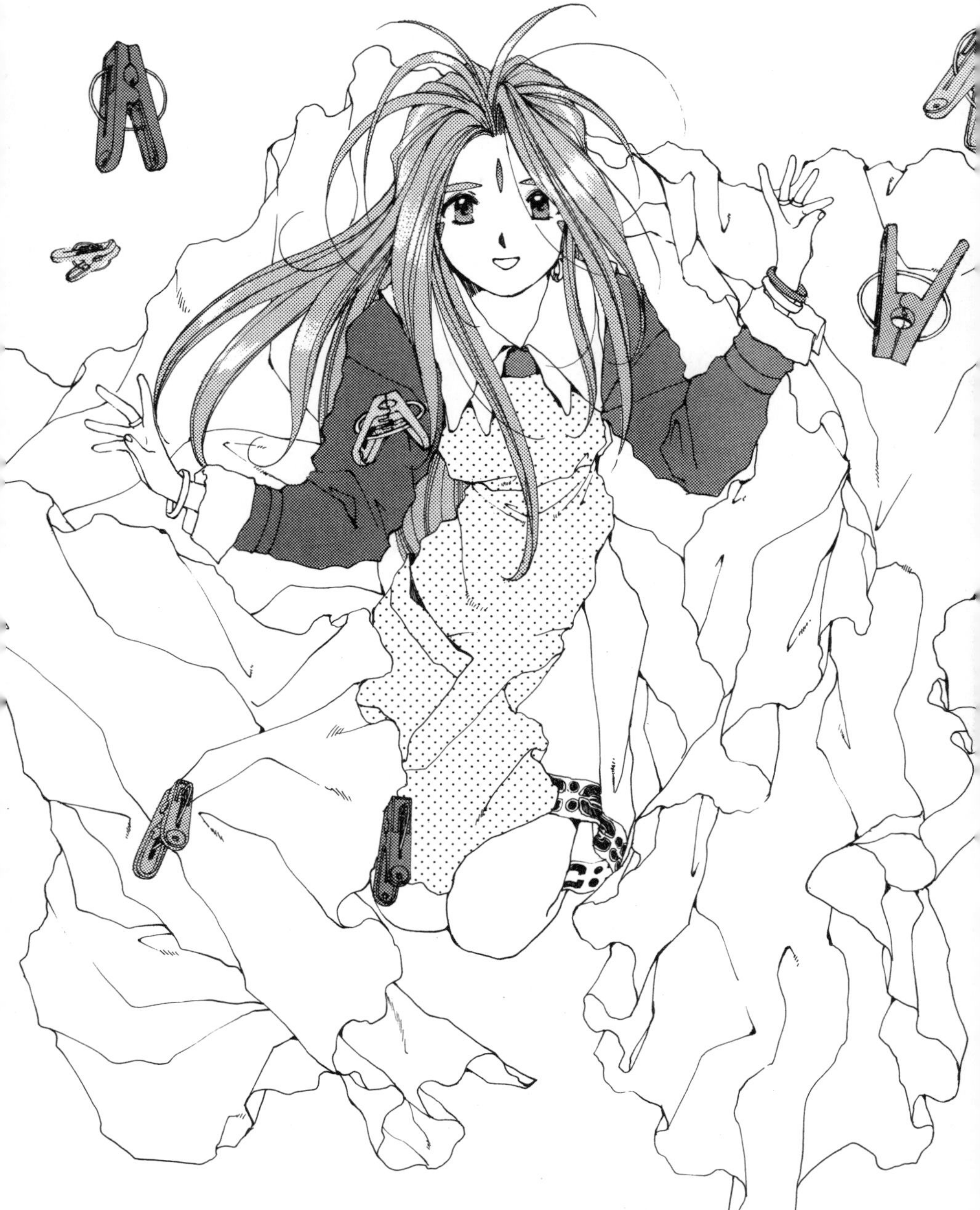

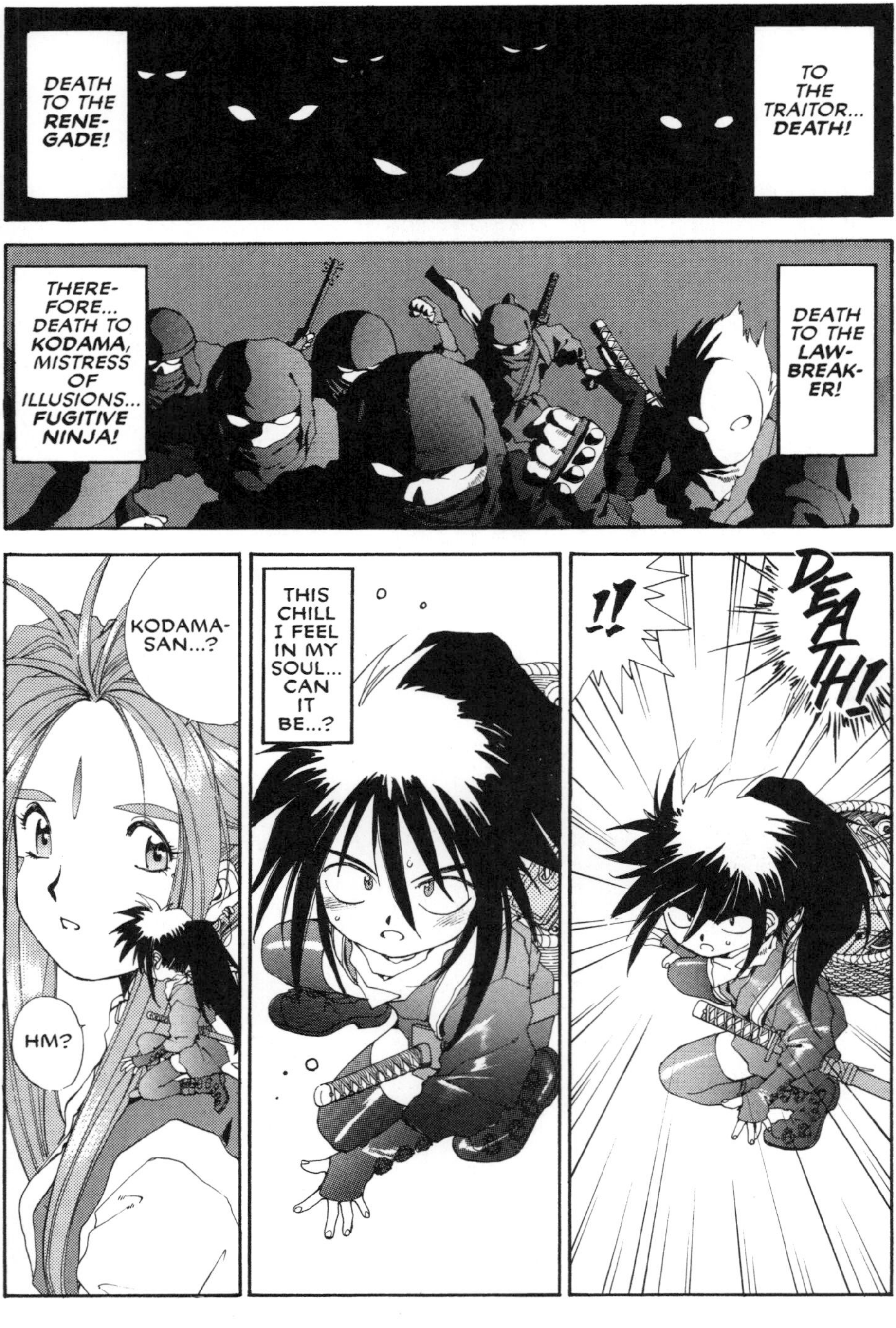

TO THE TRAITOR... DEATH!
DEATH TO THE RENE-GADE!
DEATH TO THE LAW-BREAK-ER!
THERE-FORE... DEATH TO KODAMA, MISTRESS OF ILLUSIONS... FUGITIVE NINJA!
DEATH!
!!
THIS CHILL I FEEL IN MY SOUL... CAN IT BE...?
KODAMA-SAN...?
HM?

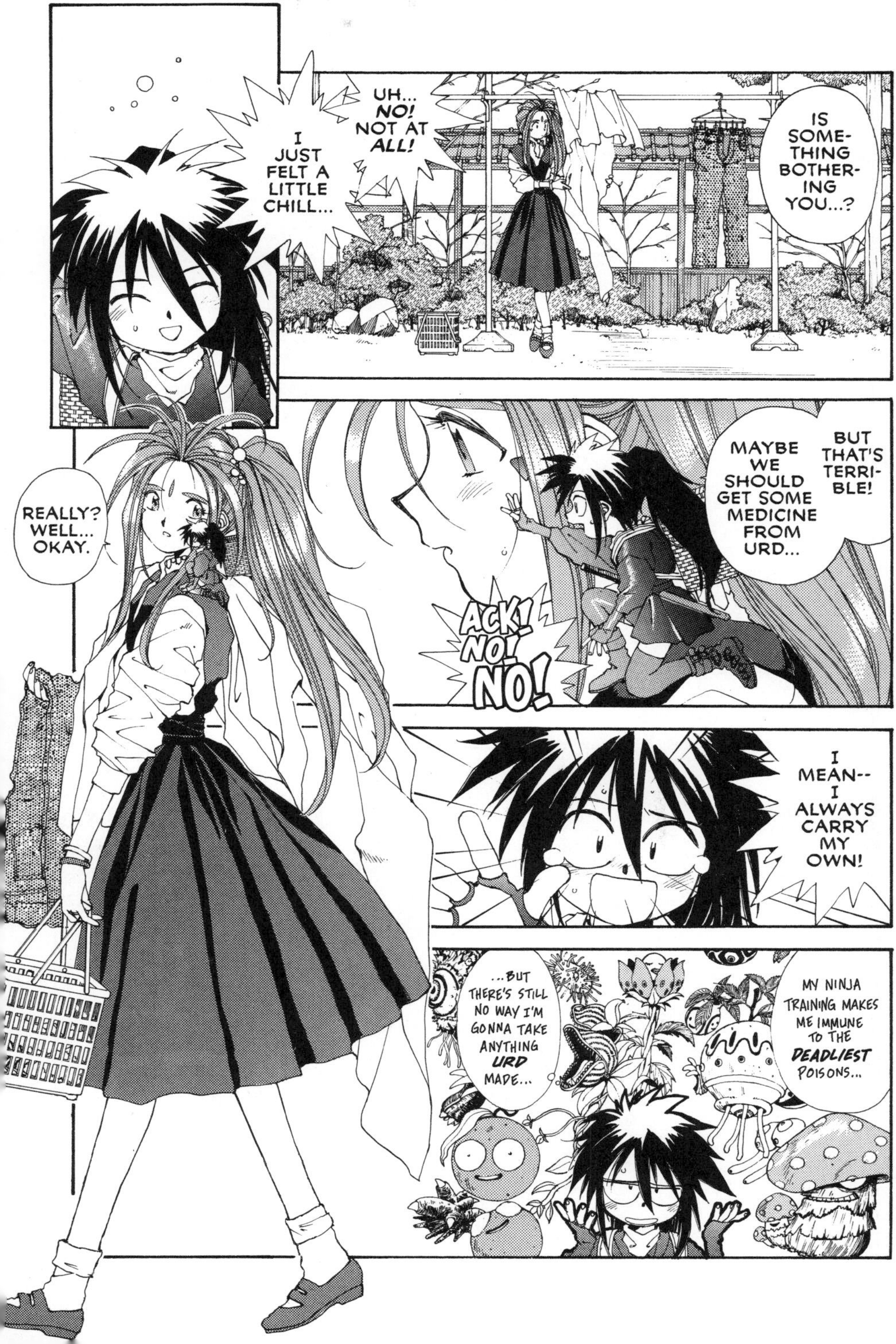
IS SOME-THING BOTHER-ING YOU...?
UH... NO! NOT AT ALL!
I JUST FELT A LITTLE CHILL...
BUT THAT'S TERRI-BLE!
MAYBE WE SHOULD GET SOME MEDICINE FROM URD...
ACK! NO! NO!
I MEAN-- I ALWAYS CARRY MY OWN!
MY NINJA TRAINING MAKES ME IMMUNE TO THE DEADLIEST POISONS...
...BUT THERE'S STILL NO WAY I'M GONNA TAKE ANYTHING URD MADE...
REALLY? WELL... OKAY.

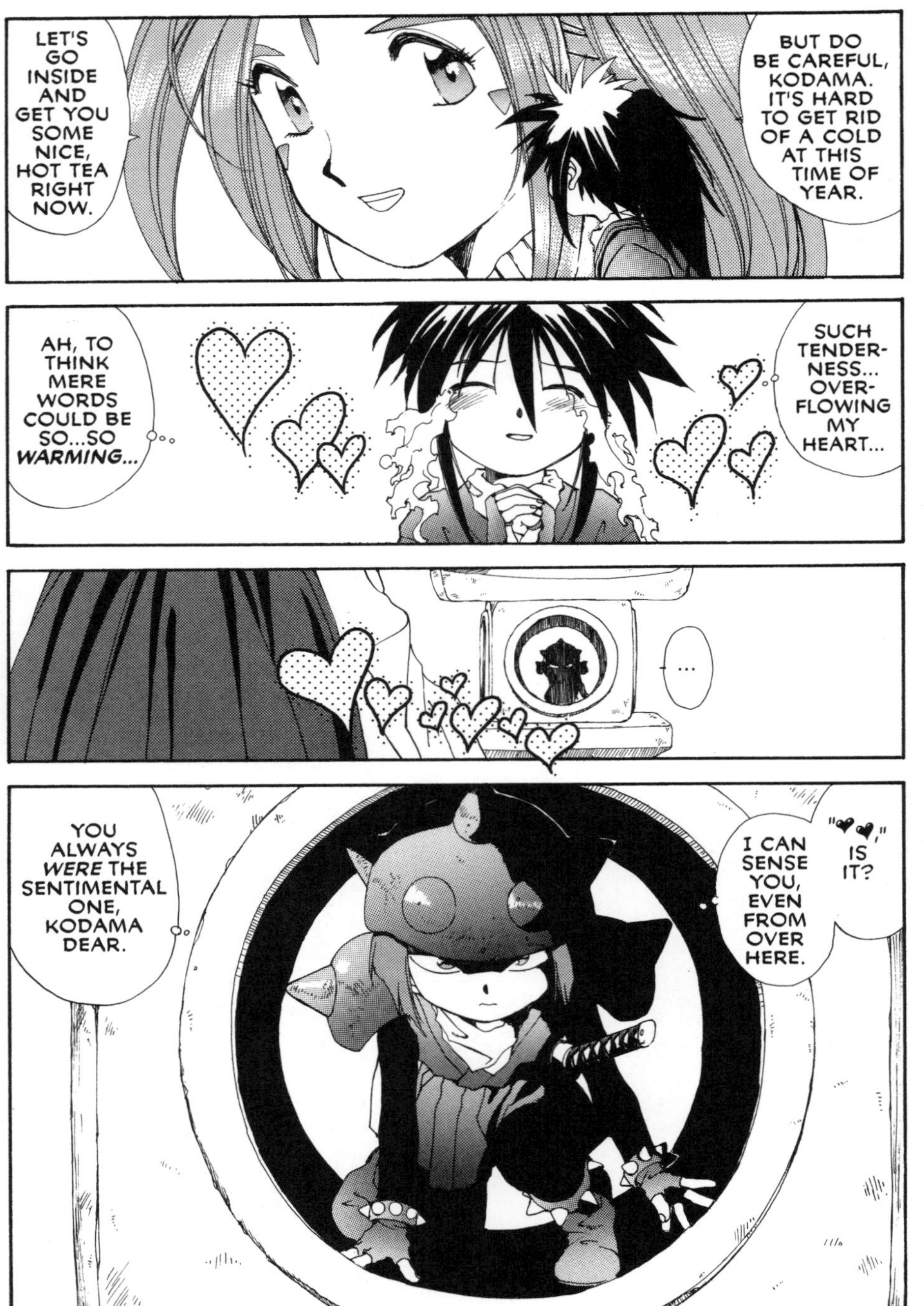
BUT DO BE CAREFUL, KODAMA. IT'S HARD TO GET RID OF A COLD AT THIS TIME OF YEAR.
LET'S GO INSIDE AND GET YOU SOME NICE, HOT TEA RIGHT NOW.
SUCH TENDERNESS... OVERFLOWING MY HEART...
AH, TO THINK MERE WORDS COULD BE SO...SO *WARMING*...
...
"♥♥," IS IT?
I CAN SENSE YOU, EVEN FROM OVER HERE.
YOU ALWAYS *WERE* THE SENTIMENTAL ONE, KODAMA DEAR.

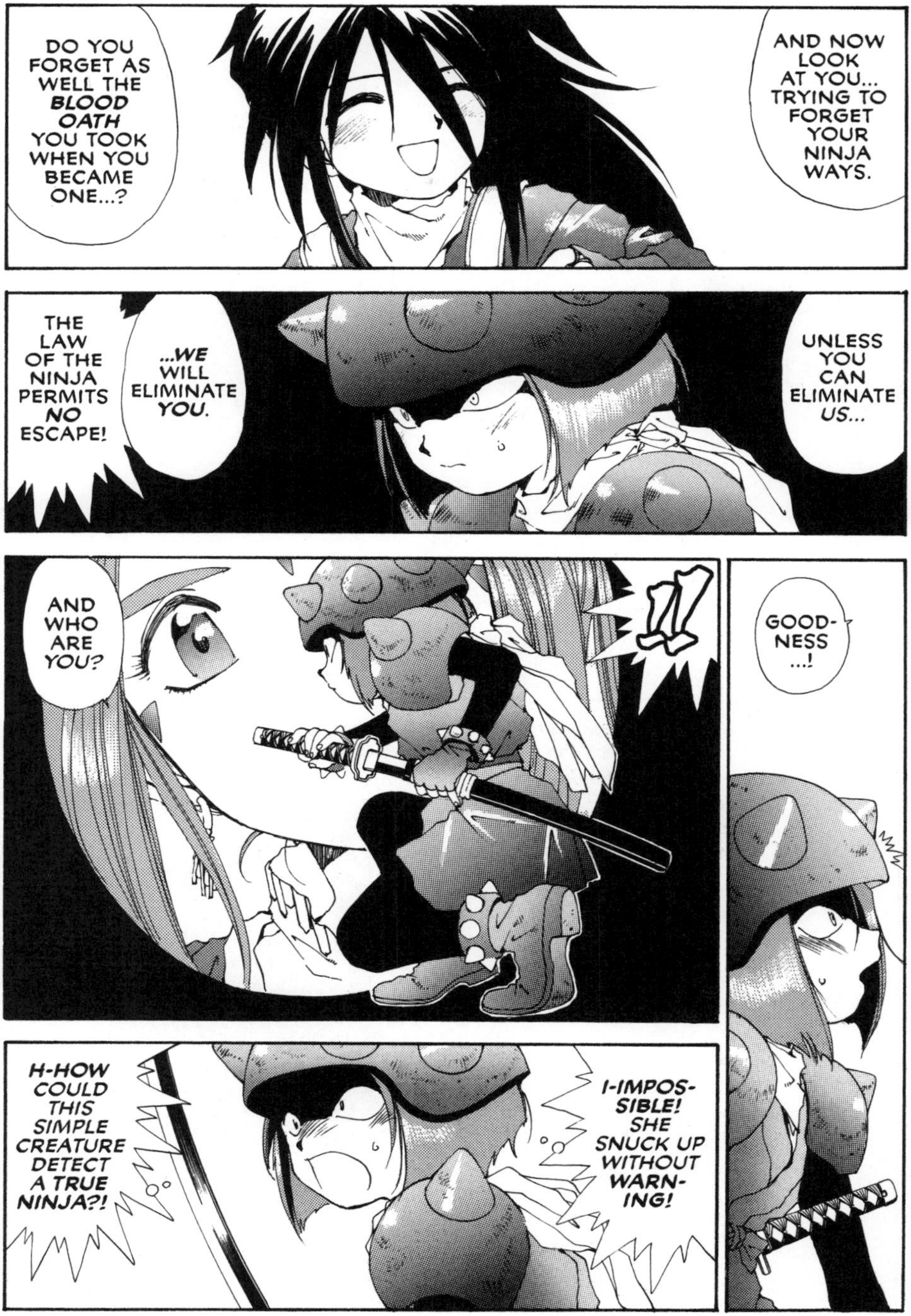
AND NOW LOOK AT YOU... TRYING TO FORGET YOUR NINJA WAYS.
DO YOU FORGET AS WELL THE *BLOOD OATH* YOU TOOK WHEN YOU BECAME ONE...?
UNLESS YOU CAN ELIMINATE *US*...
...WE WILL ELIMINATE *YOU*.
THE LAW OF THE NINJA PERMITS *NO* ESCAPE!
GOOD-NESS ...!
!!
AND WHO ARE *YOU*?
I-IMPOS-SIBLE! SHE SNUCK UP WITHOUT WARN-ING!
H-HOW COULD THIS SIMPLE CREATURE DETECT A TRUE NINJA?!

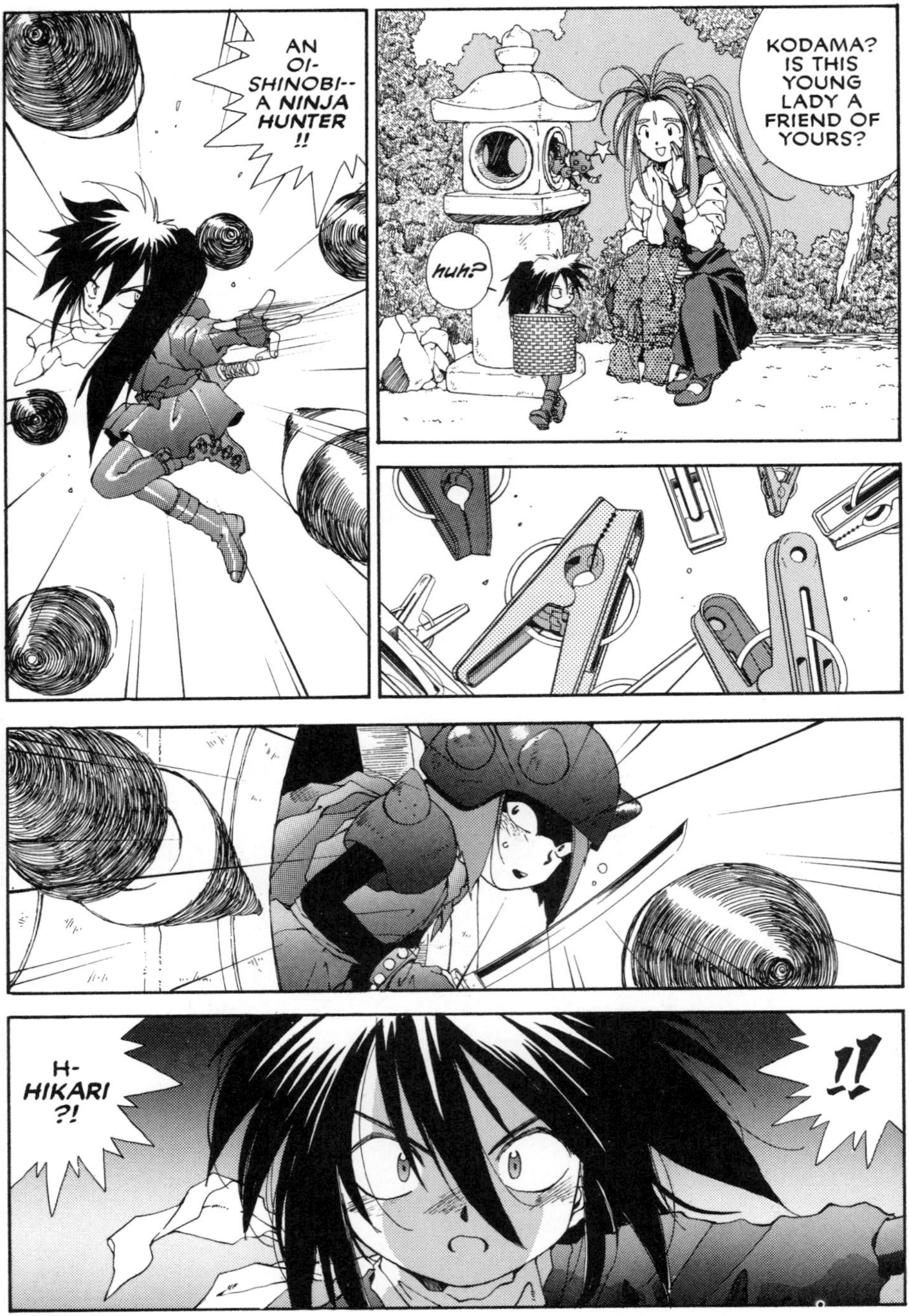
KODAMA? IS THIS YOUNG LADY A FRIEND OF YOURS?
huh?
AN OI-SHINOBI-- A NINJA HUNTER !!
!!
H-HIKARI ?!

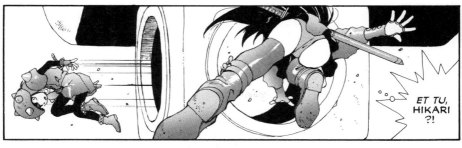

ET TU, HIKARI ?!

...PERHAPS THEY WEREN'T FRIENDS, AFTER ALL.

THE ONE THEY CALL *LIGHTNING HIKARI...*

SHE TOO IS A NINJA MASTER-- CREATED AT THE SAME TIME AS I...

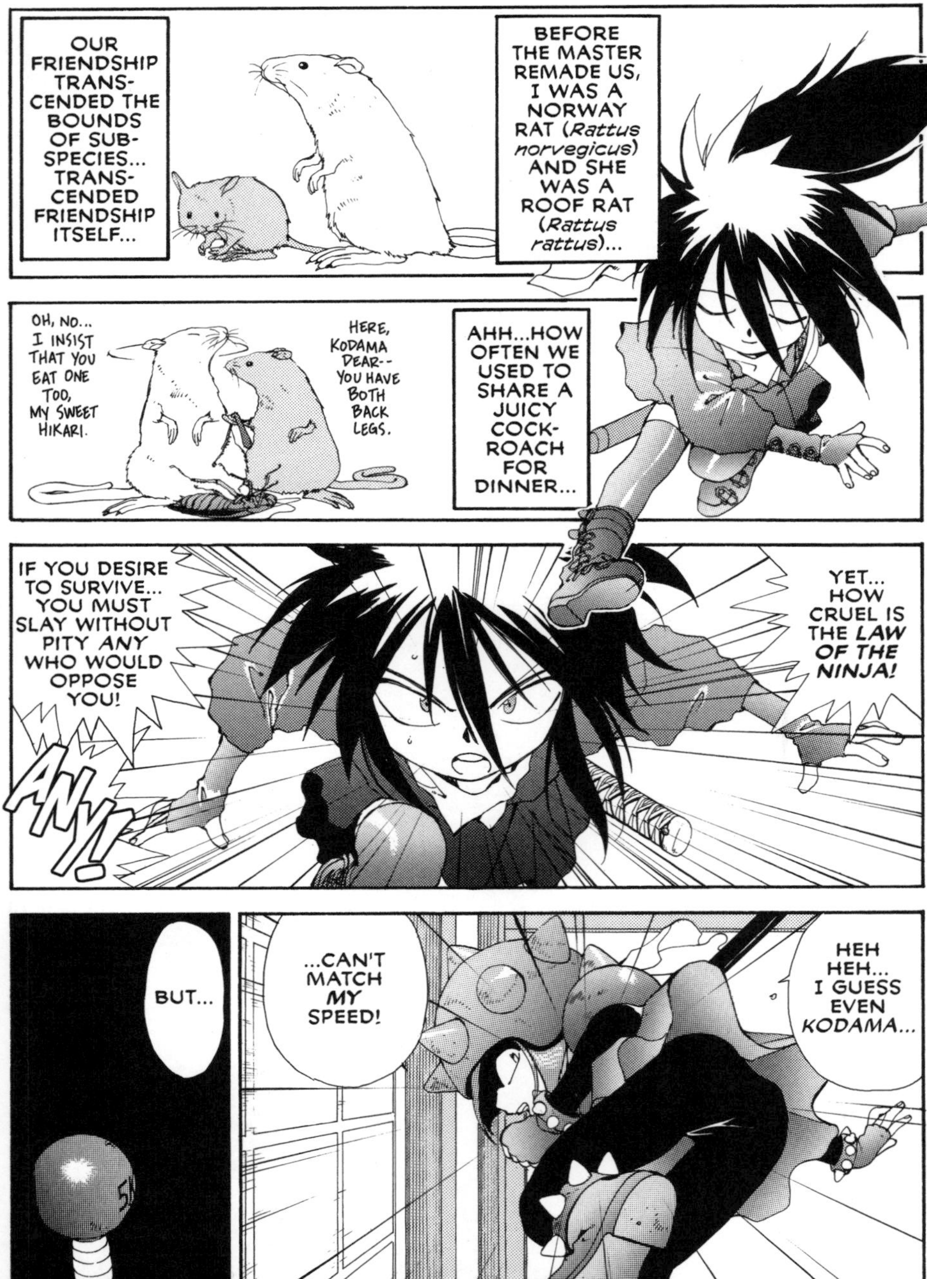
BEFORE THE MASTER REMADE US, I WAS A NORWAY RAT (*Rattus norvegicus*) AND SHE WAS A ROOF RAT (*Rattus rattus*)...
OUR FRIENDSHIP TRANSCENDED THE BOUNDS OF SUBSPECIES... TRANSCENDED FRIENDSHIP ITSELF...
AHH...HOW OFTEN WE USED TO SHARE A JUICY COCKROACH FOR DINNER...
HERE, KODAMA DEAR-- YOU HAVE BOTH BACK LEGS.
OH, NO... I INSIST THAT YOU EAT ONE TOO, MY SWEET HIKARI.
YET... HOW CRUEL IS THE *LAW OF THE NINJA!*
IF YOU DESIRE TO SURVIVE... YOU MUST SLAY WITHOUT PITY *ANY* WHO WOULD OPPOSE YOU!
ANY!
HEH HEH... I GUESS EVEN KODAMA...
...CAN'T MATCH *MY* SPEED!
BUT...

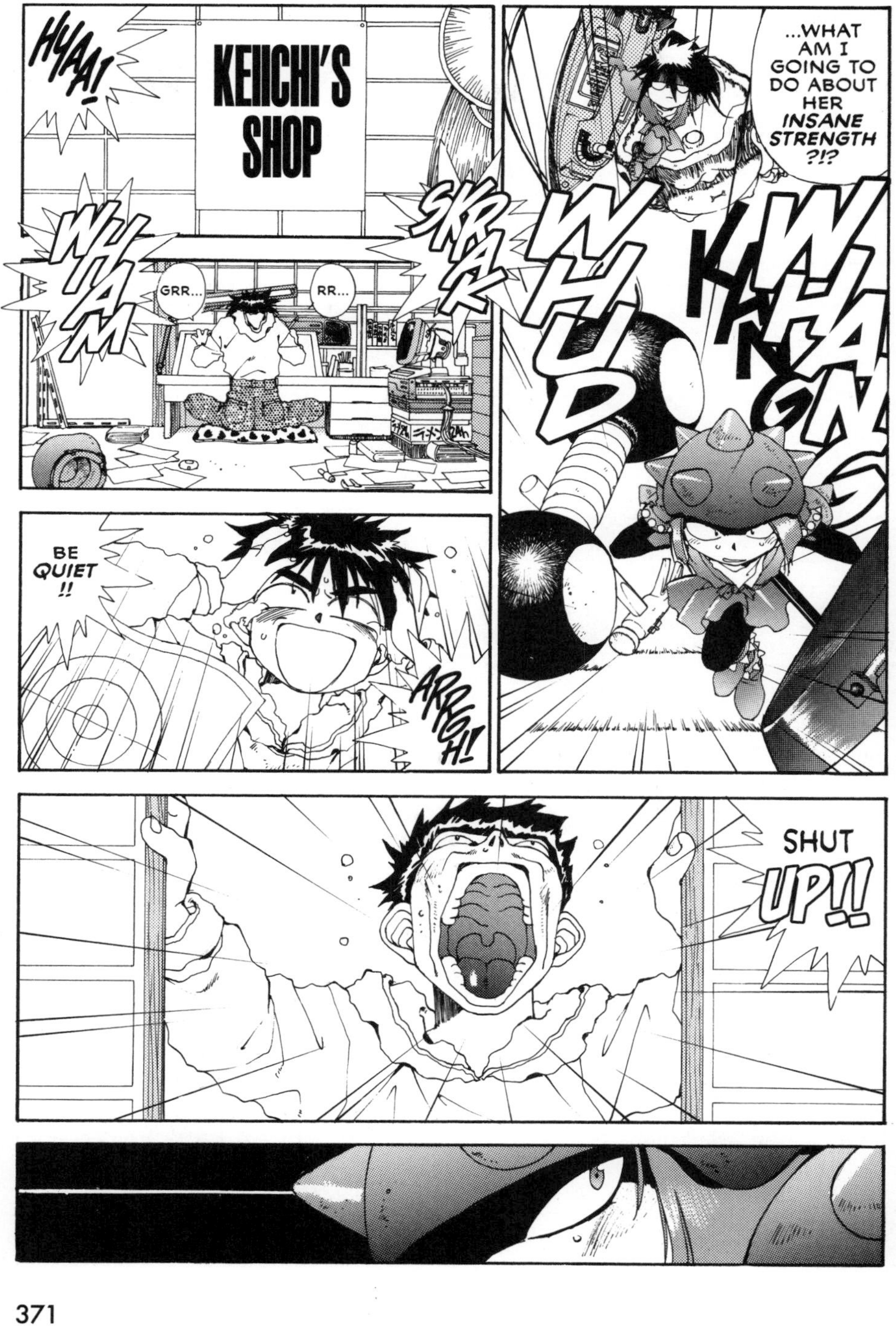
...WHAT AM I GOING TO DO ABOUT HER INSANE STRENGTH ?!?
WHANGS
WHUD
SKRAK
HYAAA!
KEIICHI'S SHOP
WHAM
RR...
GRR...
BE QUIET !!
ARRGH!
SHUT UP!!

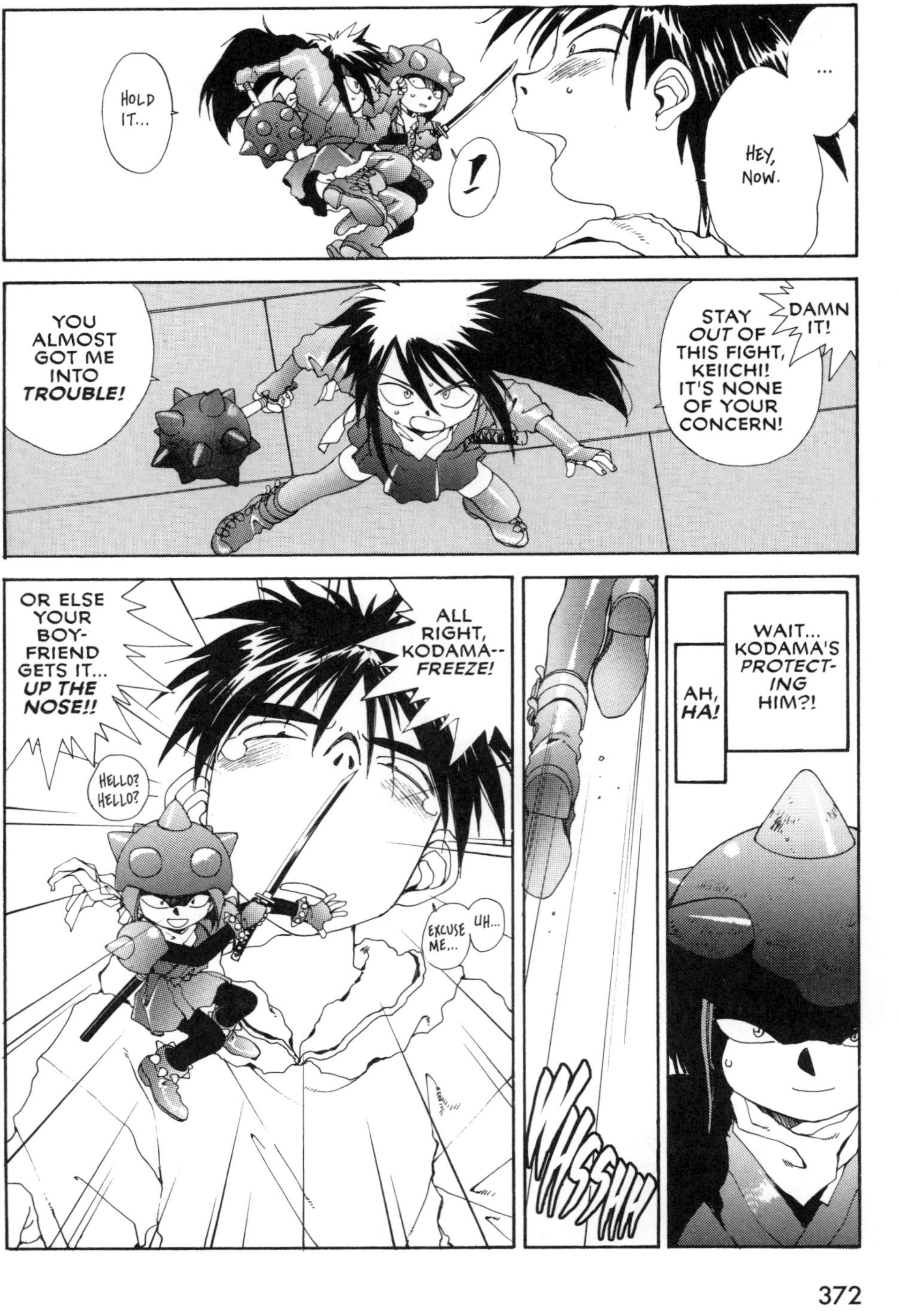
...
HEY, NOW.
!
HOLD IT...
DAMN IT!
STAY *OUT* OF THIS FIGHT, KEIICHI! IT'S NONE OF YOUR CONCERN!
YOU ALMOST GOT ME INTO *TROUBLE!*
WAIT... KODAMA'S *PROTECTING* HIM?!
AH, *HA!*
WHSSHH
ALL RIGHT, KODAMA-- *FREEZE!*
OR ELSE YOUR BOY-FRIEND GETS IT... *UP THE NOSE!!*
HELLO? HELLO?
UH...
EXCUSE ME...

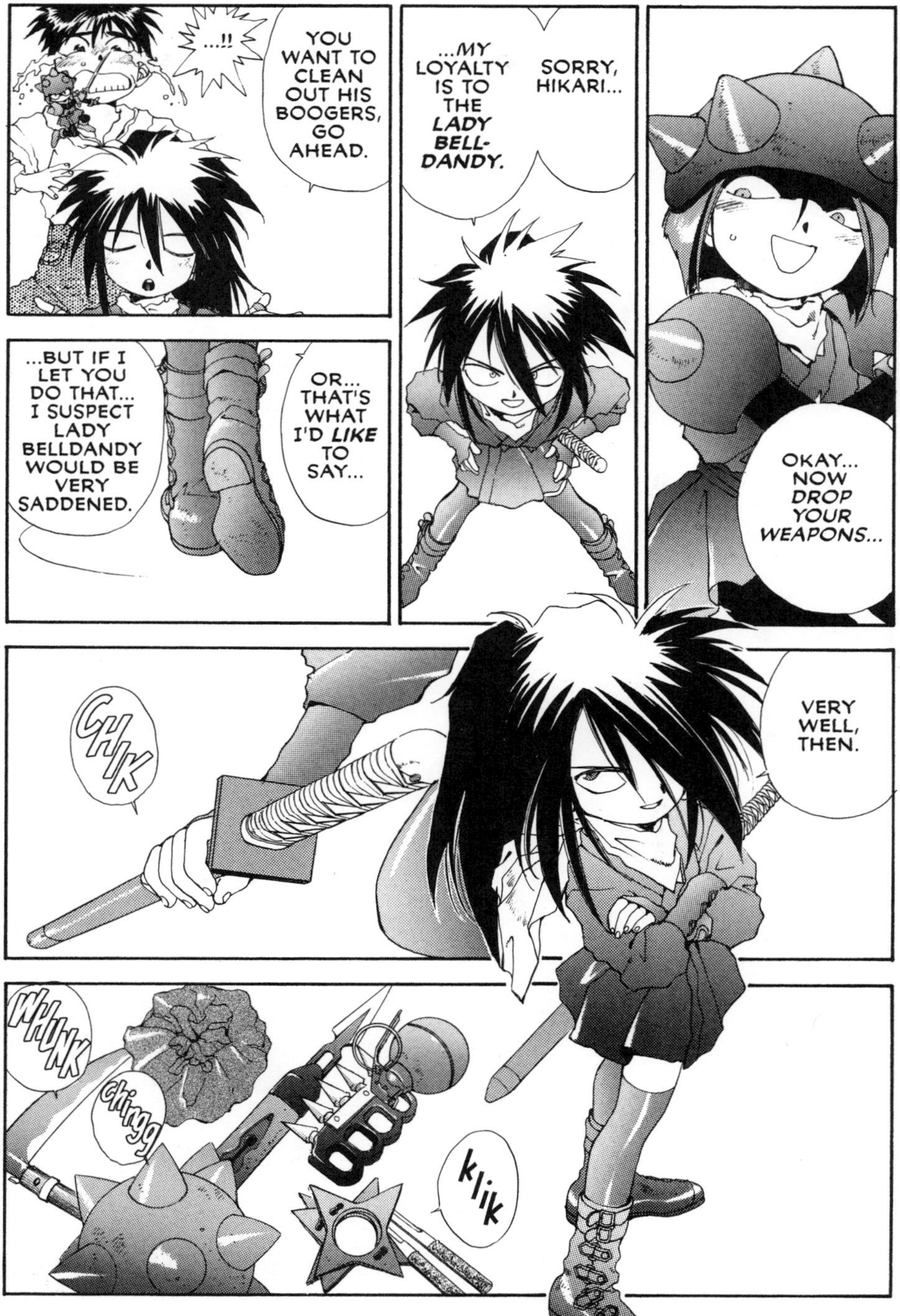
OKAY... NOW *DROP* YOUR *WEAPONS*...
SORRY, HIKARI...
...MY LOYALTY IS TO THE *LADY BELL-DANDY.*
YOU WANT TO CLEAN OUT HIS BOOGERS, GO AHEAD.
...!!
OR... THAT'S WHAT I'D *LIKE* TO SAY...
...BUT IF I LET YOU DO THAT... I SUSPECT LADY BELLDANDY WOULD BE VERY SADDENED.
VERY WELL, THEN.
CHIK
klik
chingg
WHUNK

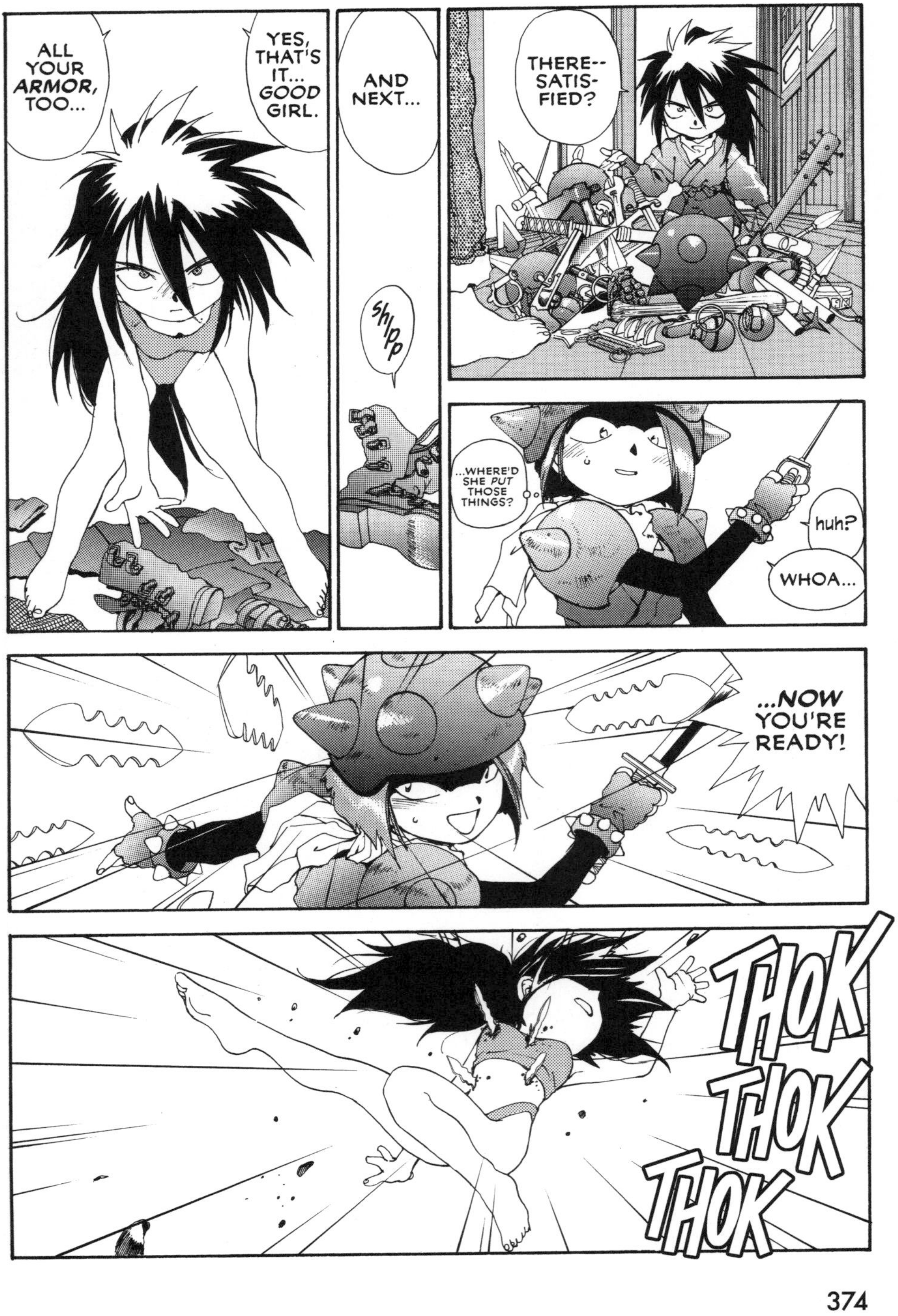
THERE--SATISFIED?
...WHERE'D SHE PUT THOSE THINGS?
huh?
WHOA...
AND NEXT...
shlpp
YES, THAT'S IT... GOOD GIRL.
ALL YOUR ARMOR, TOO...
...NOW YOU'RE READY!
THOK THOK THOK

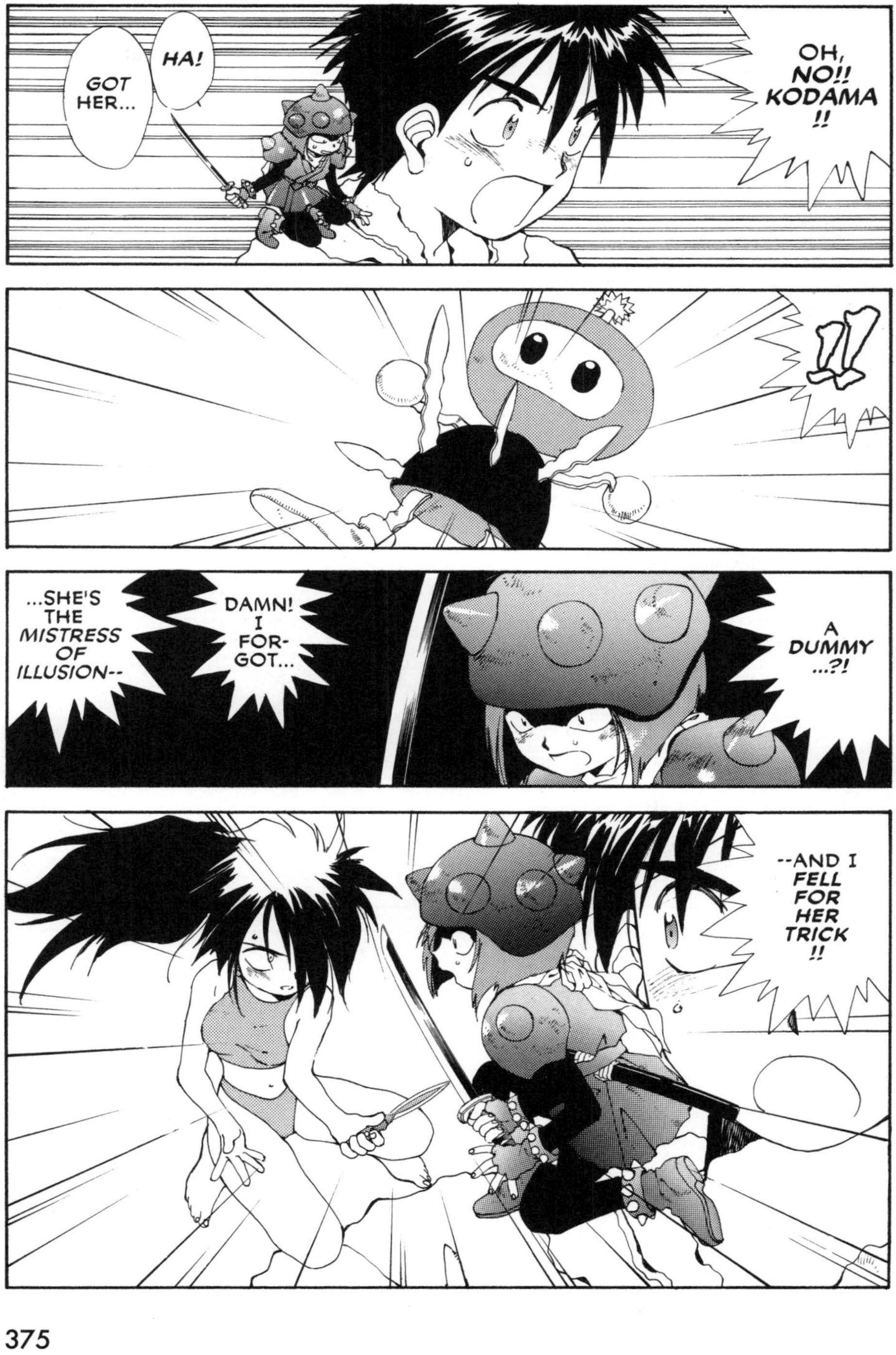
OH, NO!! KODAMA !!
HA!
GOT HER...
!!
A DUMMY ...?!
DAMN! I FORGOT...
...SHE'S THE MISTRESS OF ILLUSION--
--AND I FELL FOR HER TRICK !!

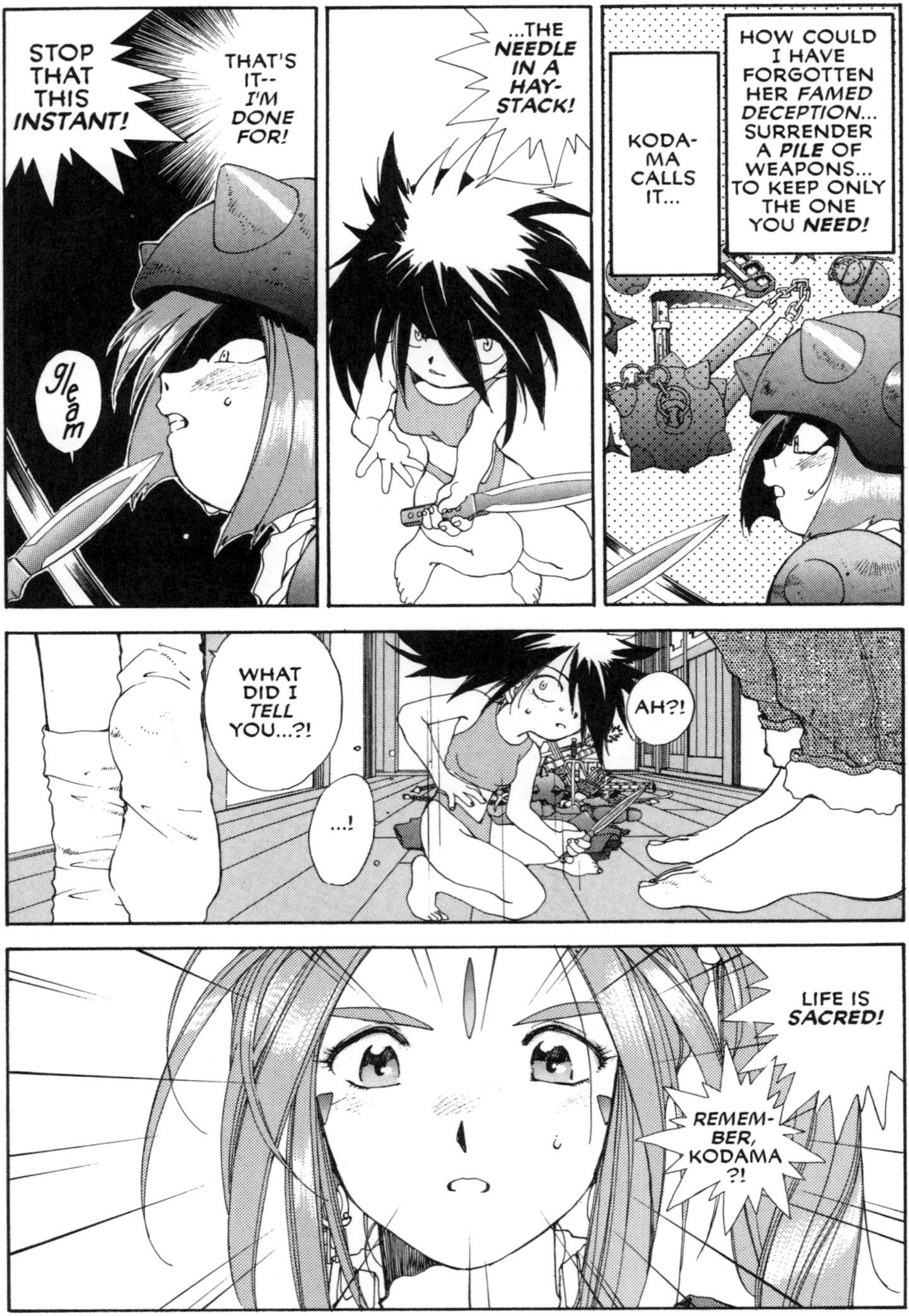
HOW COULD I HAVE FORGOTTEN HER FAMED DECEPTION... SURRENDER A PILE OF WEAPONS... TO KEEP ONLY THE ONE YOU NEED!
KODA-MA CALLS IT...
...THE NEEDLE IN A HAY-STACK!
THAT'S IT-- I'M DONE FOR!
STOP THAT THIS INSTANT!
gleam
AH?!
WHAT DID I TELL YOU...?!
...!
LIFE IS SACRED!
REMEM-BER, KODAMA ?!

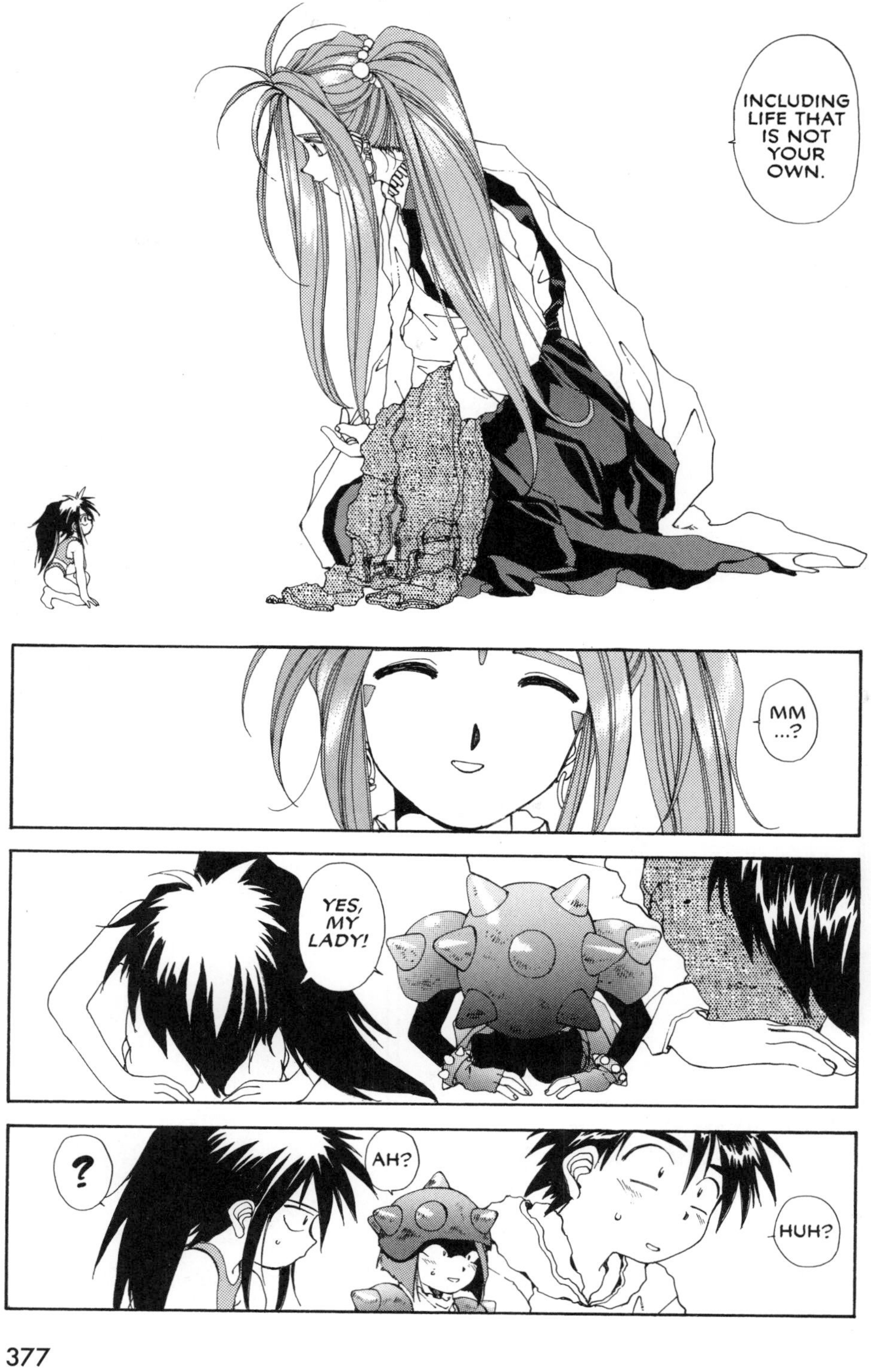

INCLUDING LIFE THAT IS NOT YOUR OWN.
MM ...?
YES, MY LADY!
HUH?
AH?
?

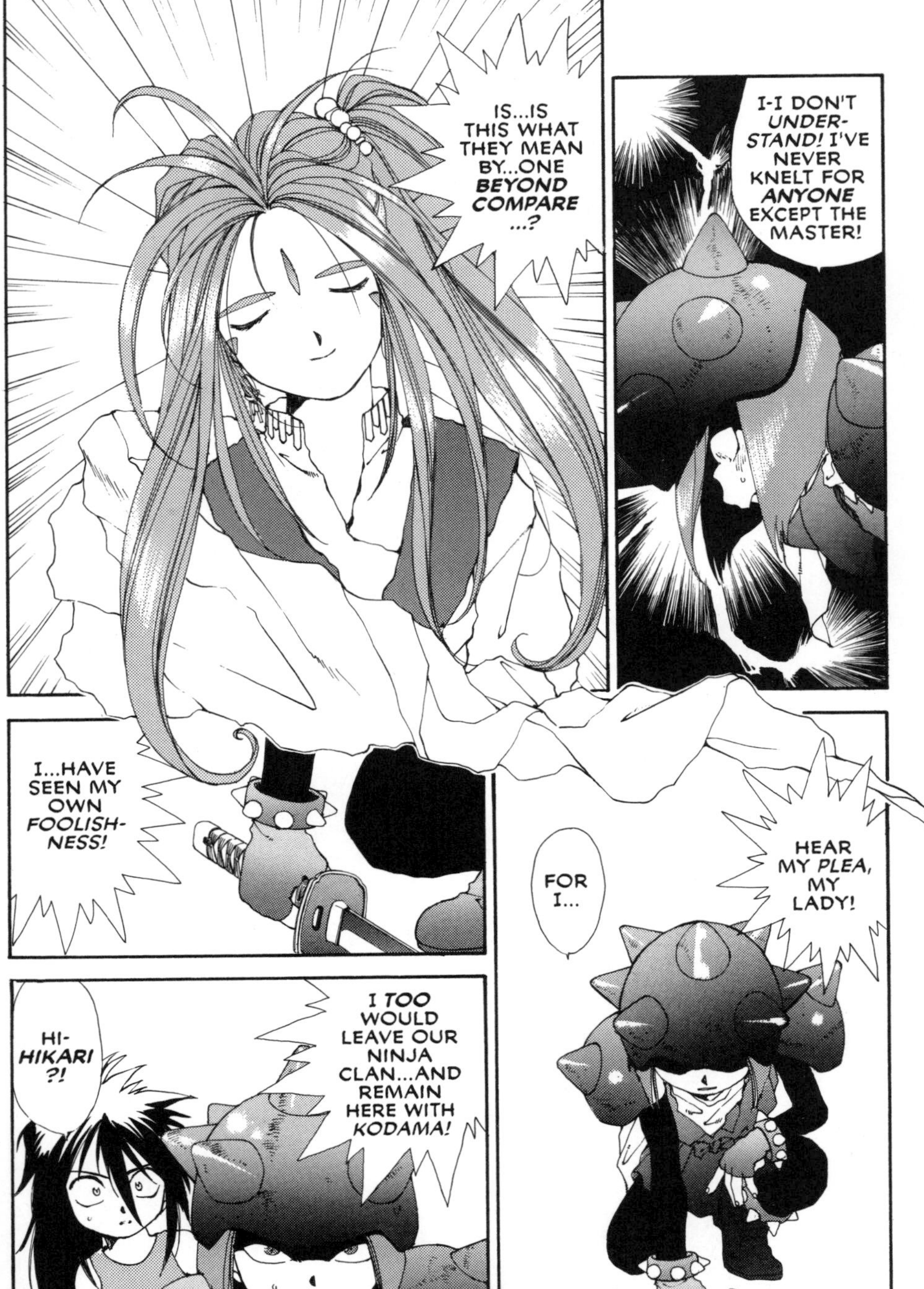
I-I DON'T UNDERSTAND! I'VE NEVER KNELT FOR ANYONE EXCEPT THE MASTER!
IS...IS THIS WHAT THEY MEAN BY...ONE BEYOND COMPARE ...?
HEAR MY PLEA, MY LADY!
FOR I...
I...HAVE SEEN MY OWN FOOLISHNESS!
I TOO WOULD LEAVE OUR NINJA CLAN...AND REMAIN HERE WITH KODAMA!
HI-HIKARI ?!

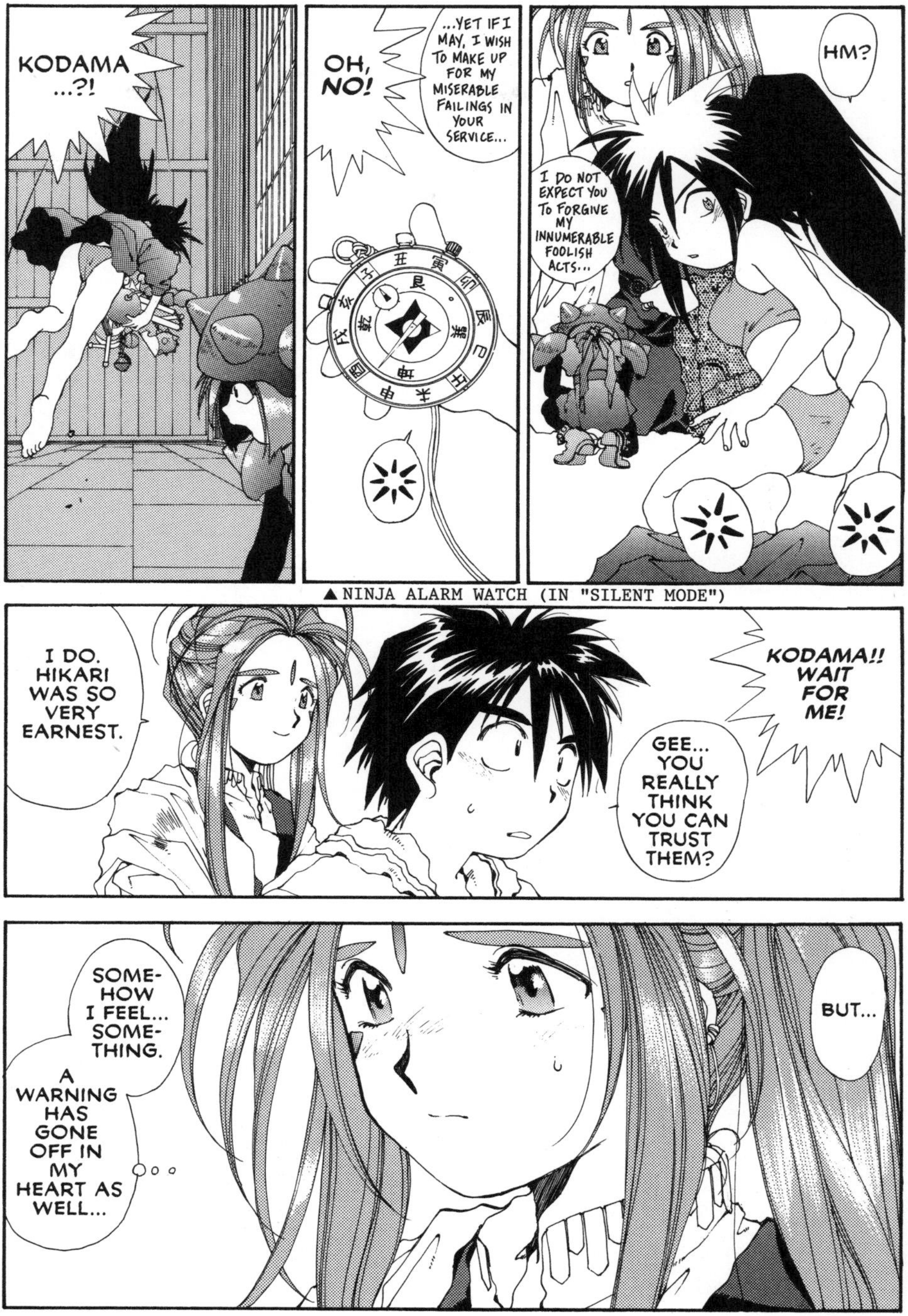
HM?
I DO NOT EXPECT YOU TO FORGIVE MY INNUMERABLE FOOLISH ACTS...
...YET IF I MAY, I WISH TO MAKE UP FOR MY MISERABLE FAILINGS IN YOUR SERVICE...
OH, NO!
KODAMA ...?!
▲NINJA ALARM WATCH (IN "SILENT MODE")
KODAMA!! WAIT FOR ME!
GEE... YOU REALLY THINK YOU CAN TRUST THEM?
I DO. HIKARI WAS SO VERY EARNEST.
BUT...
SOME-HOW I FEEL... SOME-THING.
A WARNING HAS GONE OFF IN MY HEART AS WELL...

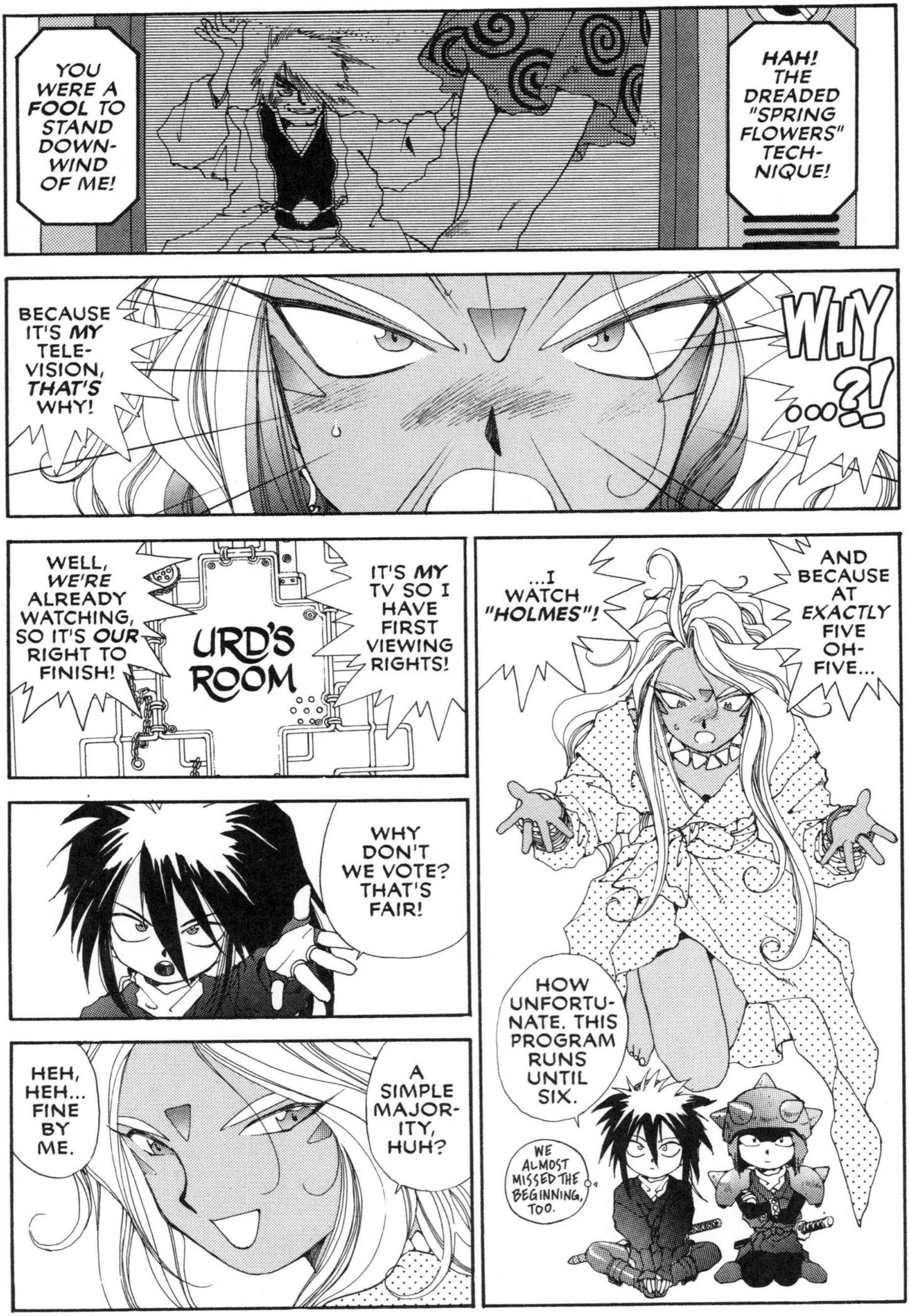

HAH! THE DREADED "SPRING FLOWERS" TECHNIQUE!
YOU WERE A FOOL TO STAND DOWNWIND OF ME!
WHY ooo?!
BECAUSE IT'S MY TELEVISION, THAT'S WHY!
AND BECAUSE AT EXACTLY FIVE OH-FIVE...
...I WATCH "HOLMES"!
HOW UNFORTUNATE. THIS PROGRAM RUNS UNTIL SIX.
WE ALMOST MISSED THE BEGINNING, TOO.
IT'S MY TV SO I HAVE FIRST VIEWING RIGHTS!
URD'S ROOM
WELL, WE'RE ALREADY WATCHING, SO IT'S OUR RIGHT TO FINISH!
WHY DON'T WE VOTE? THAT'S FAIR!
A SIMPLE MAJORITY, HUH?
HEH, HEH... FINE BY ME.

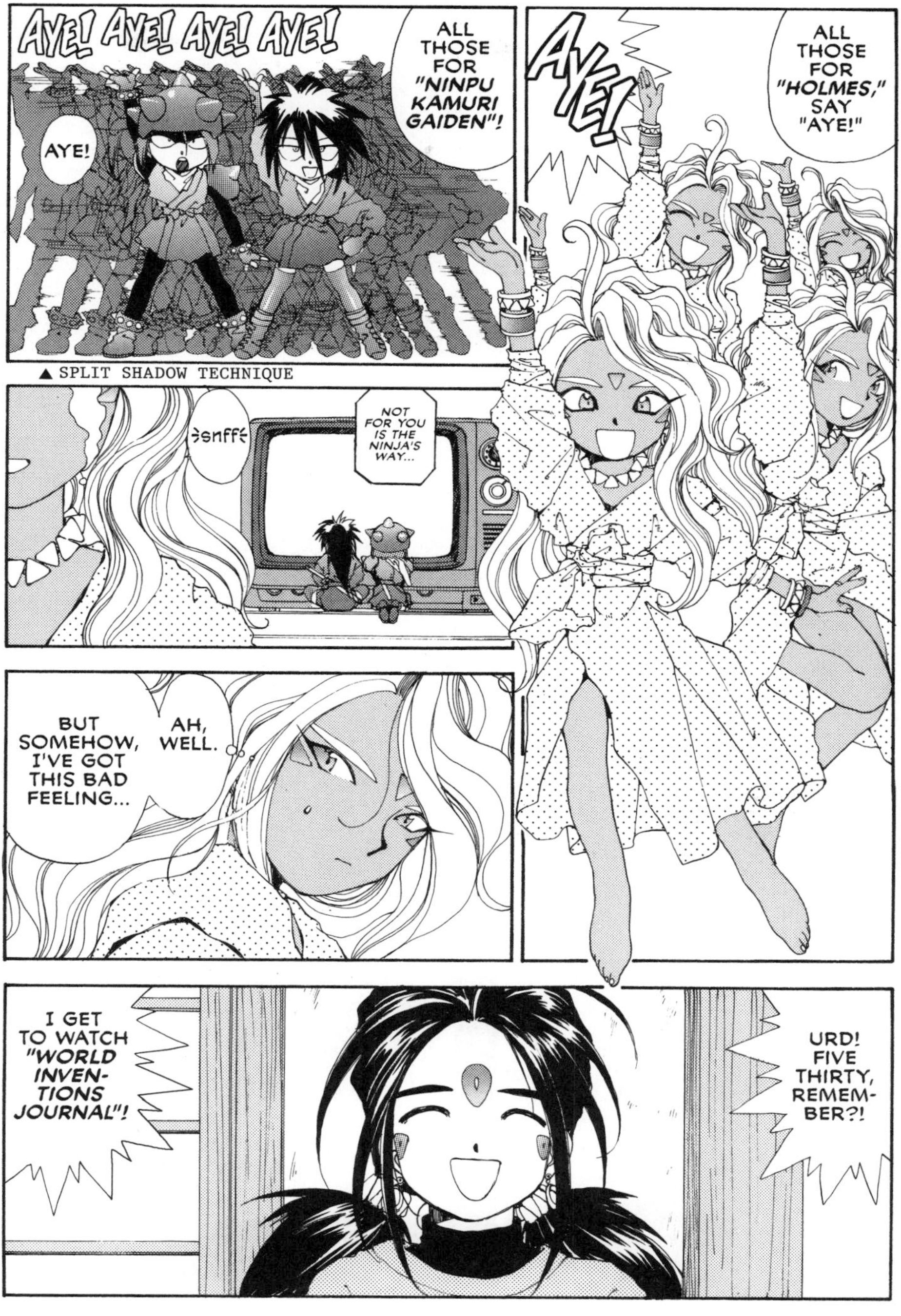
ALL THOSE FOR "HOLMES," SAY "AYE!"
AYE!
ALL THOSE FOR "NINPU KAMURI GAIDEN"!
AYE! AYE! AYE! AYE!
AYE!
▲ SPLIT SHADOW TECHNIQUE
NOT FOR YOU IS THE NINJA'S WAY...
snff
AH, WELL.
BUT SOMEHOW, I'VE GOT THIS BAD FEELING...
URD! FIVE THIRTY, REMEMBER?!
I GET TO WATCH "WORLD INVENTIONS JOURNAL"!

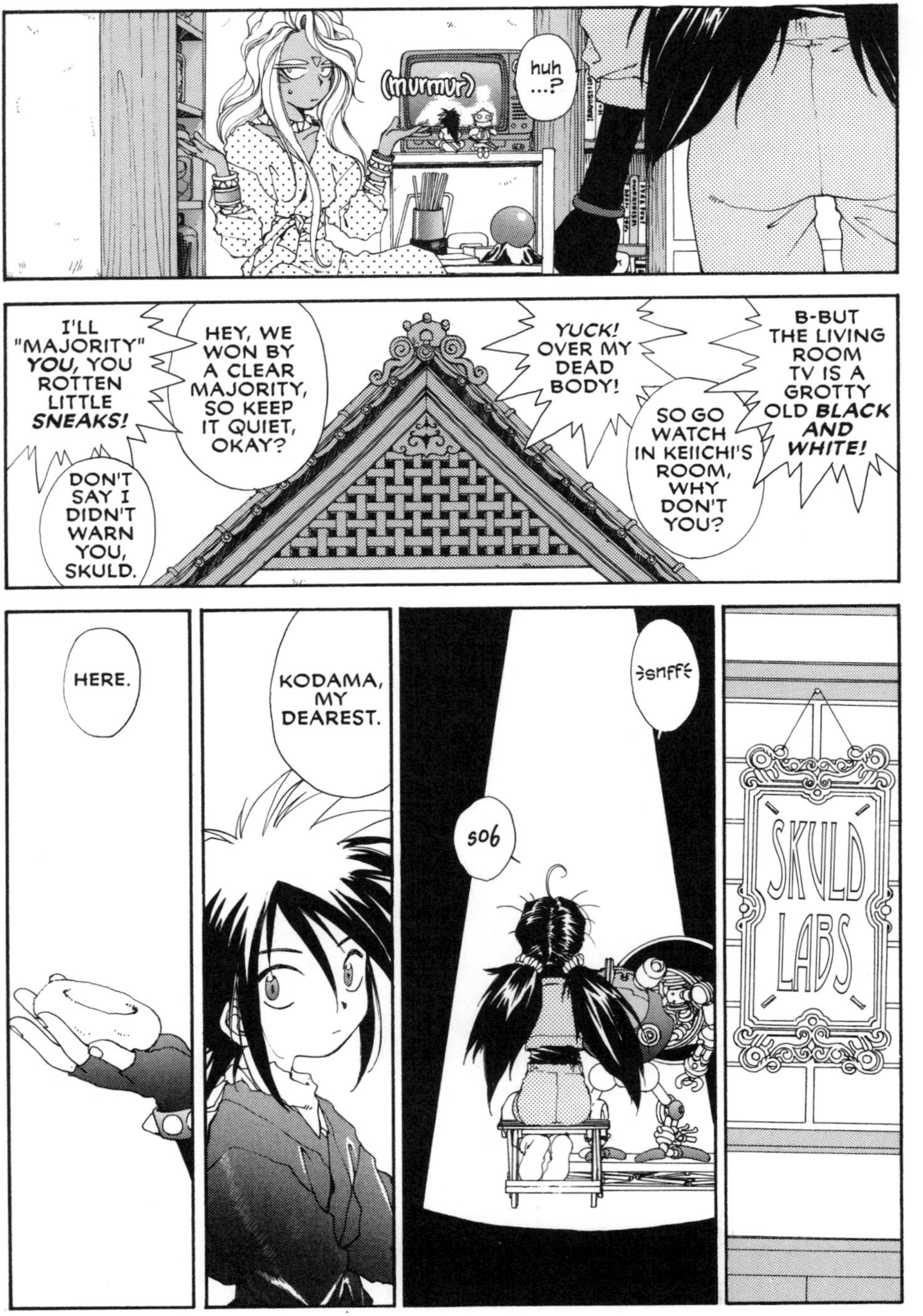
huh ...?
(murmur)
B-BUT THE LIVING ROOM TV IS A GROTTY OLD BLACK AND WHITE!
YUCK! OVER MY DEAD BODY!
SO GO WATCH IN KEIICHI'S ROOM, WHY DON'T YOU?
HEY, WE WON BY A CLEAR MAJORITY, SO KEEP IT QUIET, OKAY?
I'LL "MAJORITY" YOU, YOU ROTTEN LITTLE SNEAKS!
DON'T SAY I DIDN'T WARN YOU, SKULD.
SKULD LABS
snff
sob
KODAMA, MY DEAREST.
HERE.

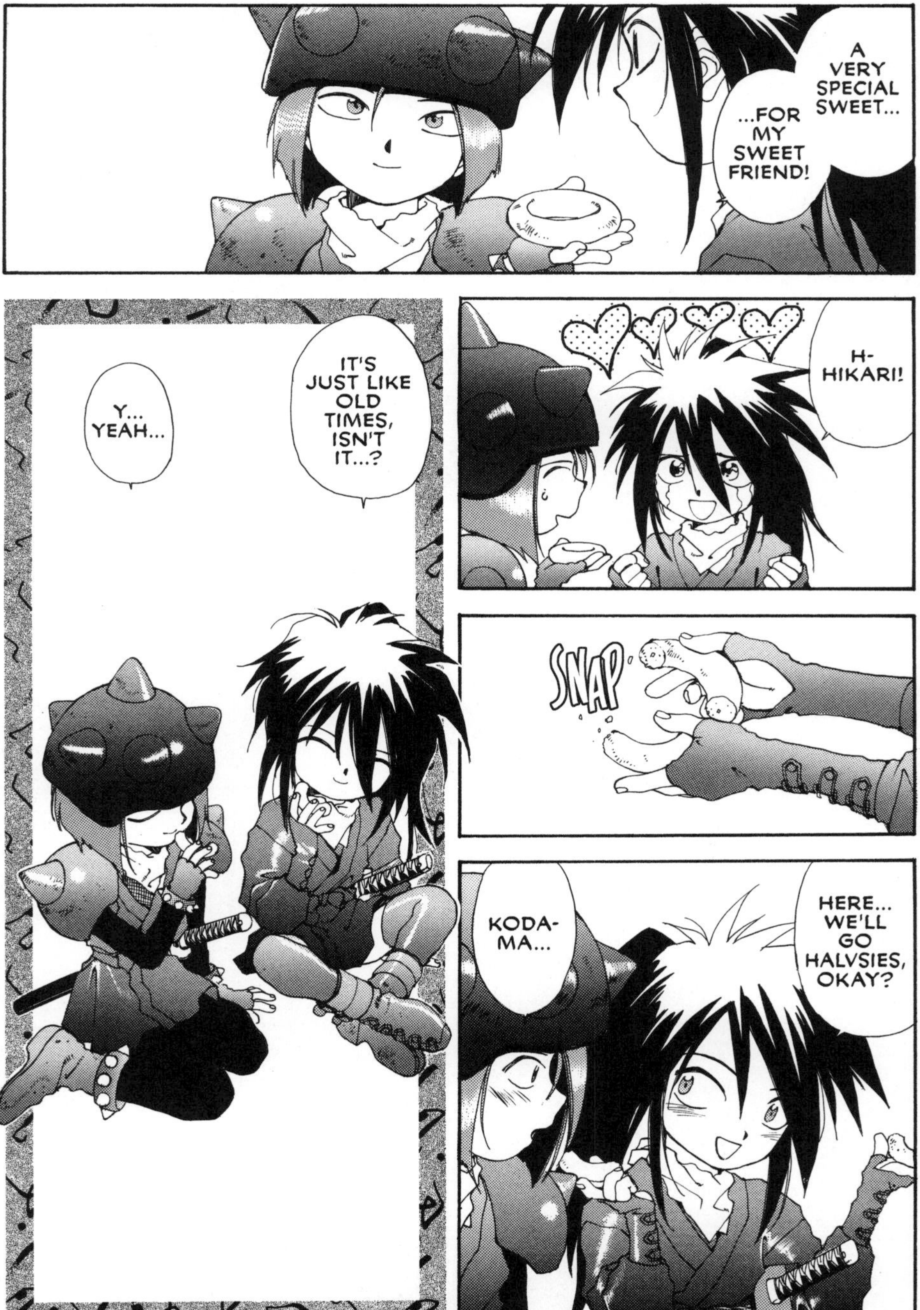
A VERY SPECIAL SWEET...
...FOR MY SWEET FRIEND!
H-HIKARI!
SNAP
HERE... WE'LL GO HALVSIES, OKAY?
KODA-MA...
IT'S JUST LIKE OLD TIMES, ISN'T IT...?
Y... YEAH...

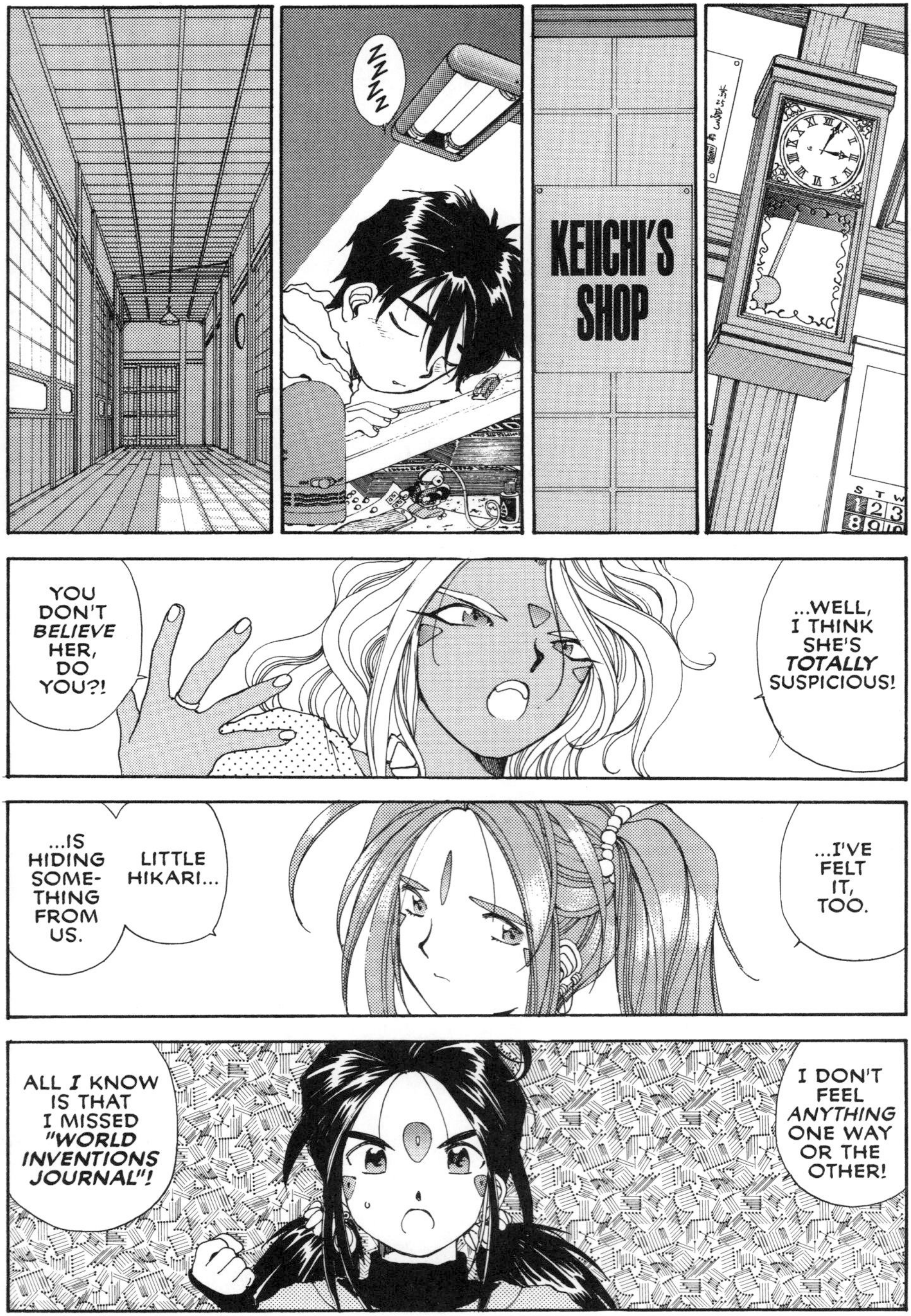
KEIICHI'S SHOP
ZZZZ
...WELL, I THINK SHE'S *TOTALLY* SUSPICIOUS!
YOU DON'T *BELIEVE* HER, DO YOU?!
...I'VE FELT IT, TOO.
LITTLE HIKARI...
...IS HIDING SOMETHING FROM US.
I DON'T FEEL *ANYTHING* ONE WAY OR THE OTHER!
ALL *I* KNOW IS THAT I MISSED *"WORLD INVENTIONS JOURNAL"*!

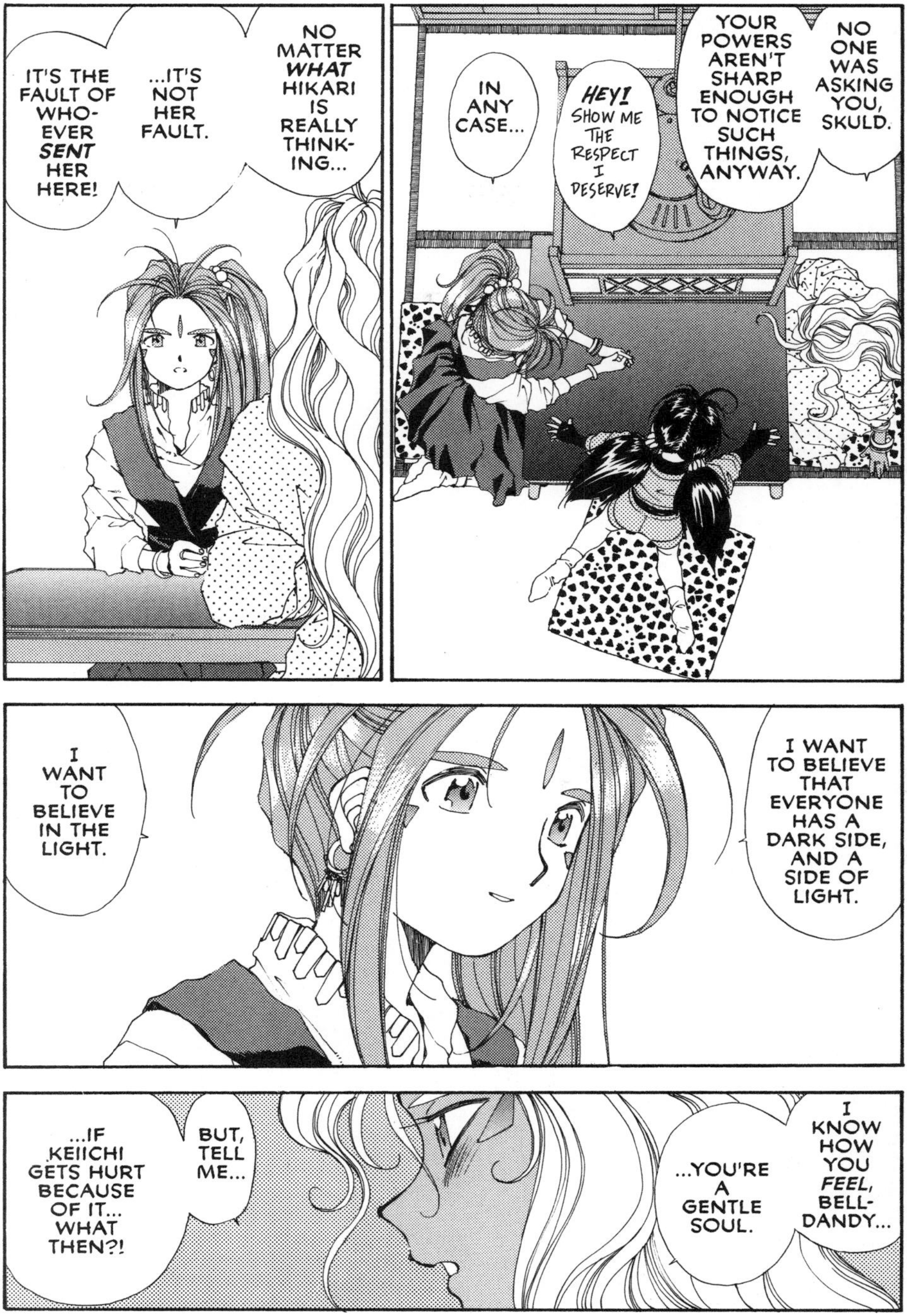
NO ONE WAS ASKING YOU, SKULD.
YOUR POWERS AREN'T SHARP ENOUGH TO NOTICE SUCH THINGS, ANYWAY.
HEY! SHOW ME THE RESPECT I DESERVE!
IN ANY CASE...
NO MATTER WHAT HIKARI IS REALLY THINKING...
...IT'S NOT HER FAULT.
IT'S THE FAULT OF WHO-EVER SENT HER HERE!
I WANT TO BELIEVE THAT EVERYONE HAS A DARK SIDE, AND A SIDE OF LIGHT.
I WANT TO BELIEVE IN THE LIGHT.
I KNOW HOW YOU FEEL, BELL-DANDY...
...YOU'RE A GENTLE SOUL.
BUT, TELL ME...
...IF KEIICHI GETS HURT BECAUSE OF IT... WHAT THEN?!

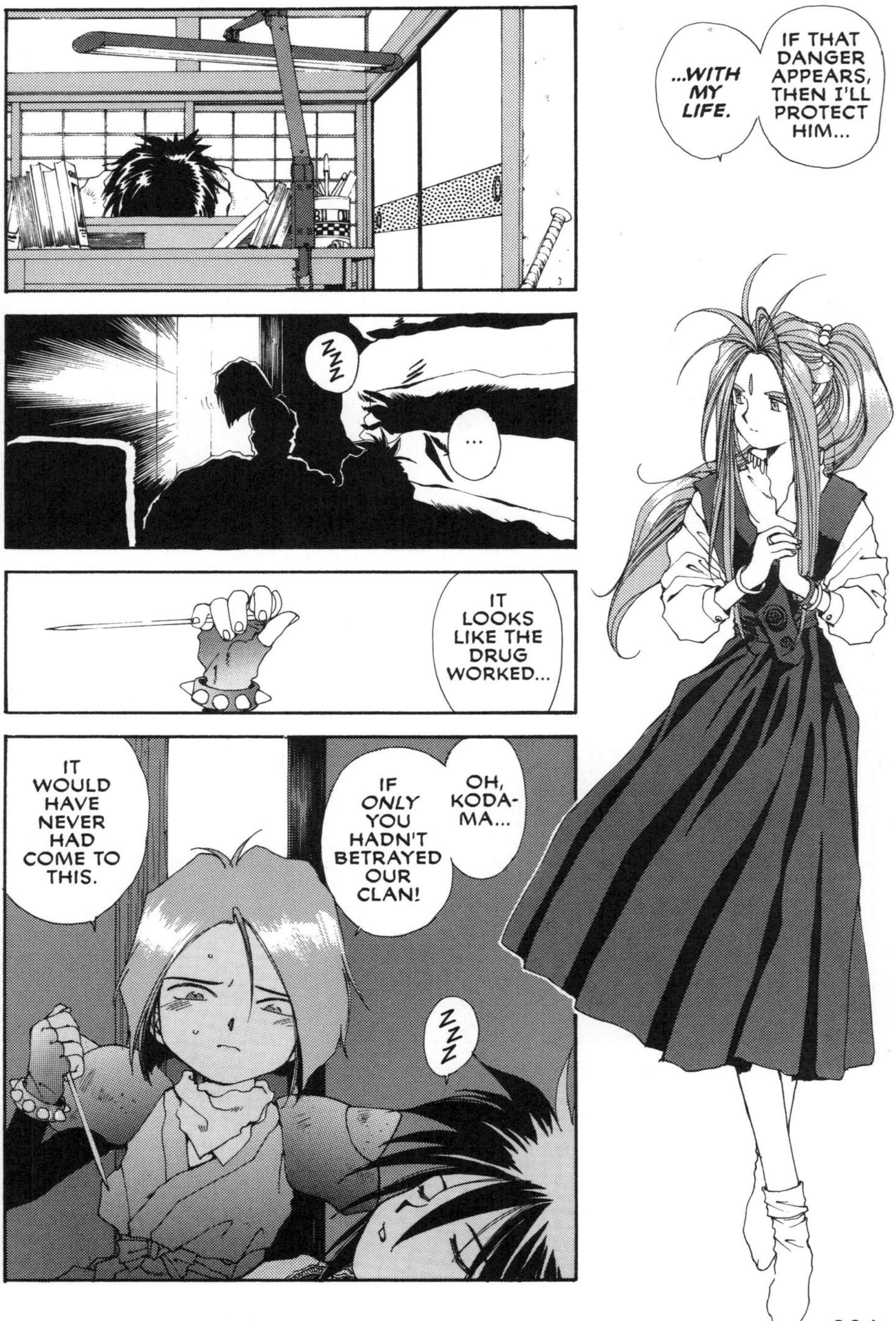
IF THAT DANGER APPEARS, THEN I'LL PROTECT HIM...
...WITH MY LIFE.
ZZZ
...
IT LOOKS LIKE THE DRUG WORKED...
OH, KODAMA...
IF ONLY YOU HADN'T BETRAYED OUR CLAN!
IT WOULD HAVE NEVER HAD COME TO THIS.
ZZZ

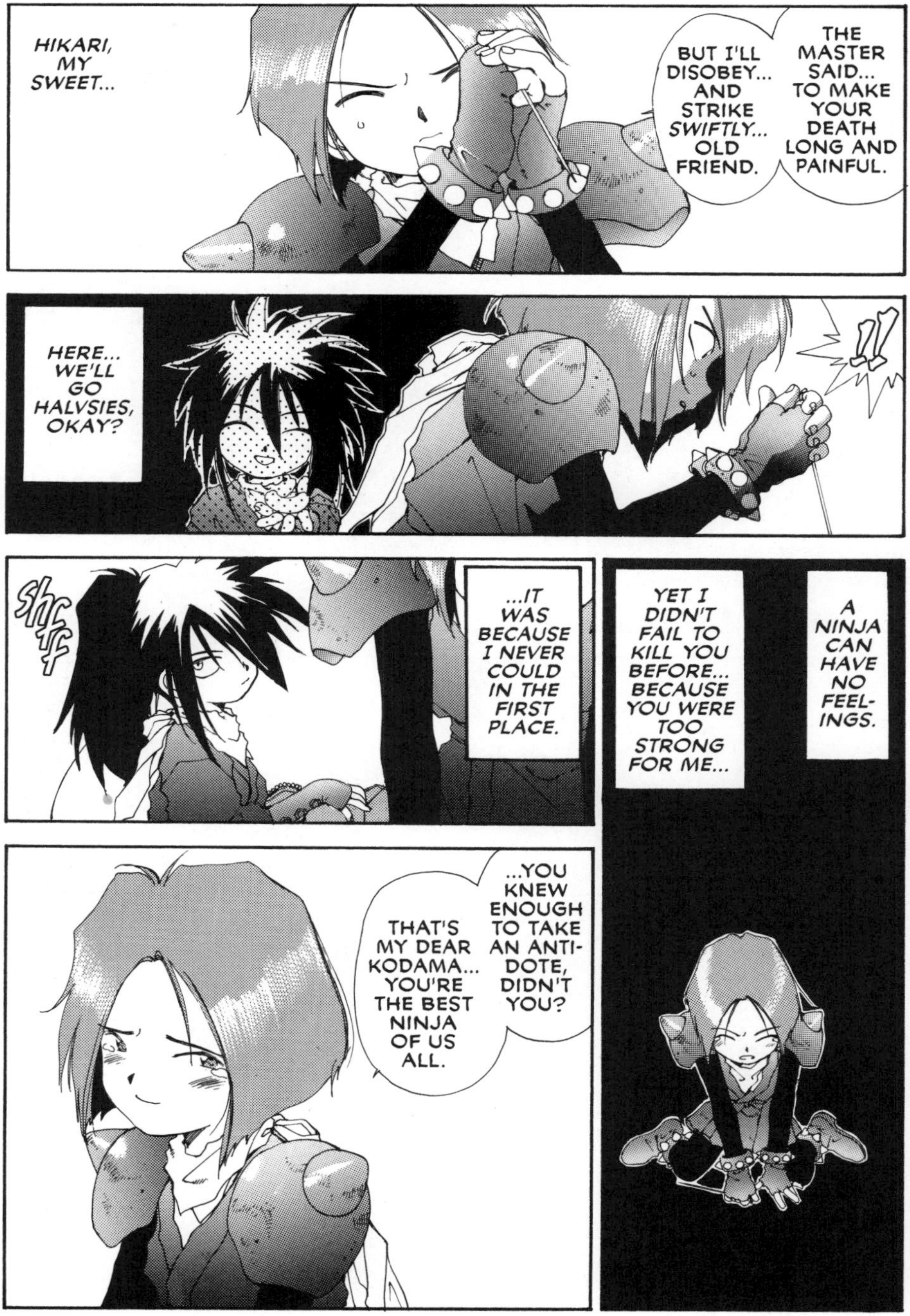
THE MASTER SAID... TO MAKE YOUR DEATH LONG AND PAINFUL.
BUT I'LL DISOBEY... AND STRIKE *SWIFTLY*... OLD FRIEND.
HIKARI, MY SWEET...
!!
HERE... WE'LL GO HALVSIES, OKAY?
A NINJA CAN HAVE NO FEEL-INGS.
YET I DIDN'T FAIL TO KILL YOU BEFORE... BECAUSE YOU WERE TOO STRONG FOR ME...
...IT WAS BECAUSE I NEVER COULD IN THE FIRST PLACE.
shff
...YOU KNEW ENOUGH TO TAKE AN ANTI-DOTE, DIDN'T YOU?
THAT'S MY DEAR KODAMA... YOU'RE THE BEST NINJA OF US ALL.

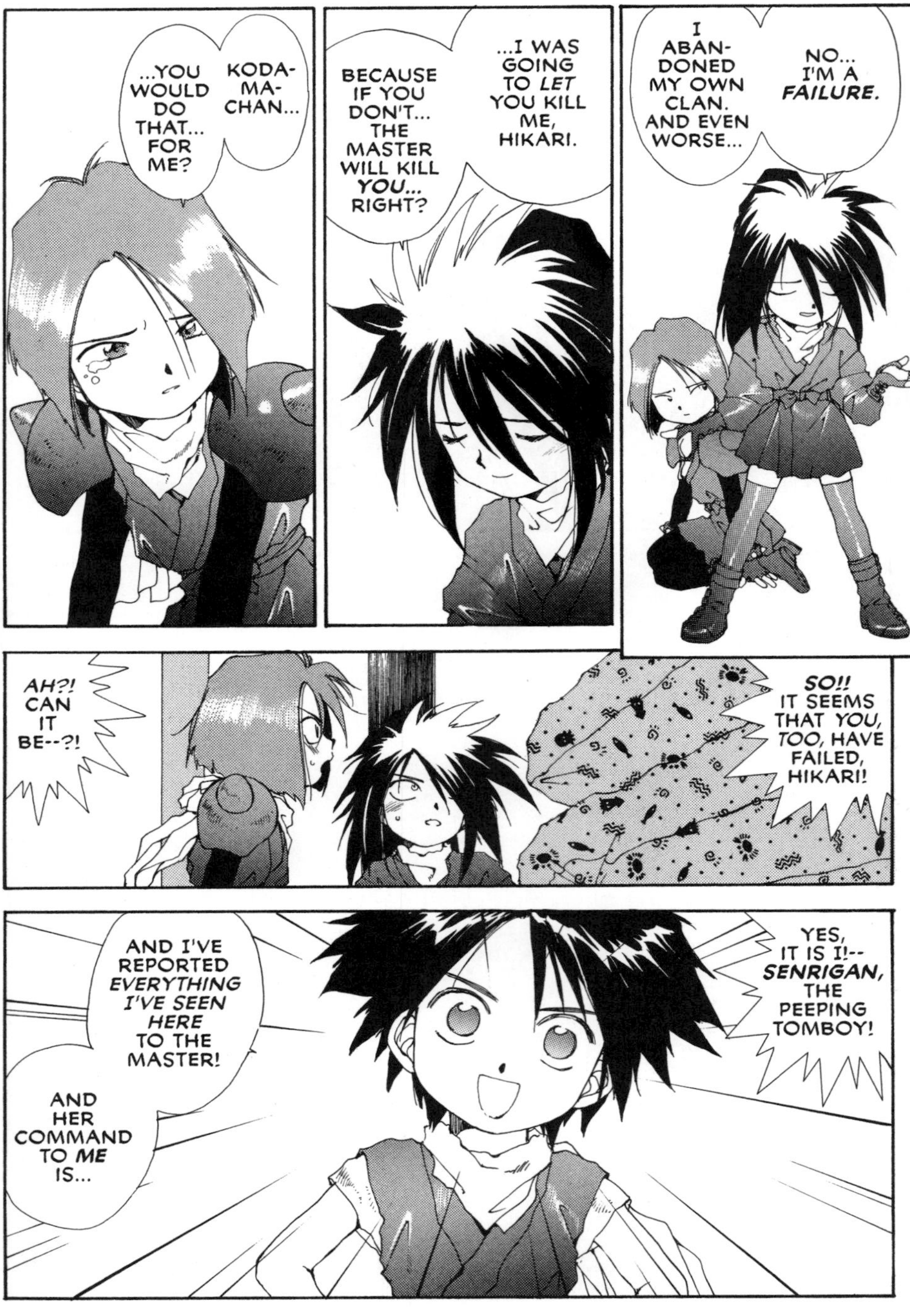
NO... I'M A FAILURE.
I ABANDONED MY OWN CLAN. AND EVEN WORSE...
...I WAS GOING TO LET YOU KILL ME, HIKARI.
BECAUSE IF YOU DON'T... THE MASTER WILL KILL YOU... RIGHT?
KODA-MA-CHAN...
...YOU WOULD DO THAT... FOR ME?
SO!! IT SEEMS THAT YOU, TOO, HAVE FAILED, HIKARI!
AH?! CAN IT BE--?!
YES, IT IS I!-- SENRIGAN, THE PEEPING TOMBOY!
AND I'VE REPORTED EVERYTHING I'VE SEEN HERE TO THE MASTER!
AND HER COMMAND TO ME IS...

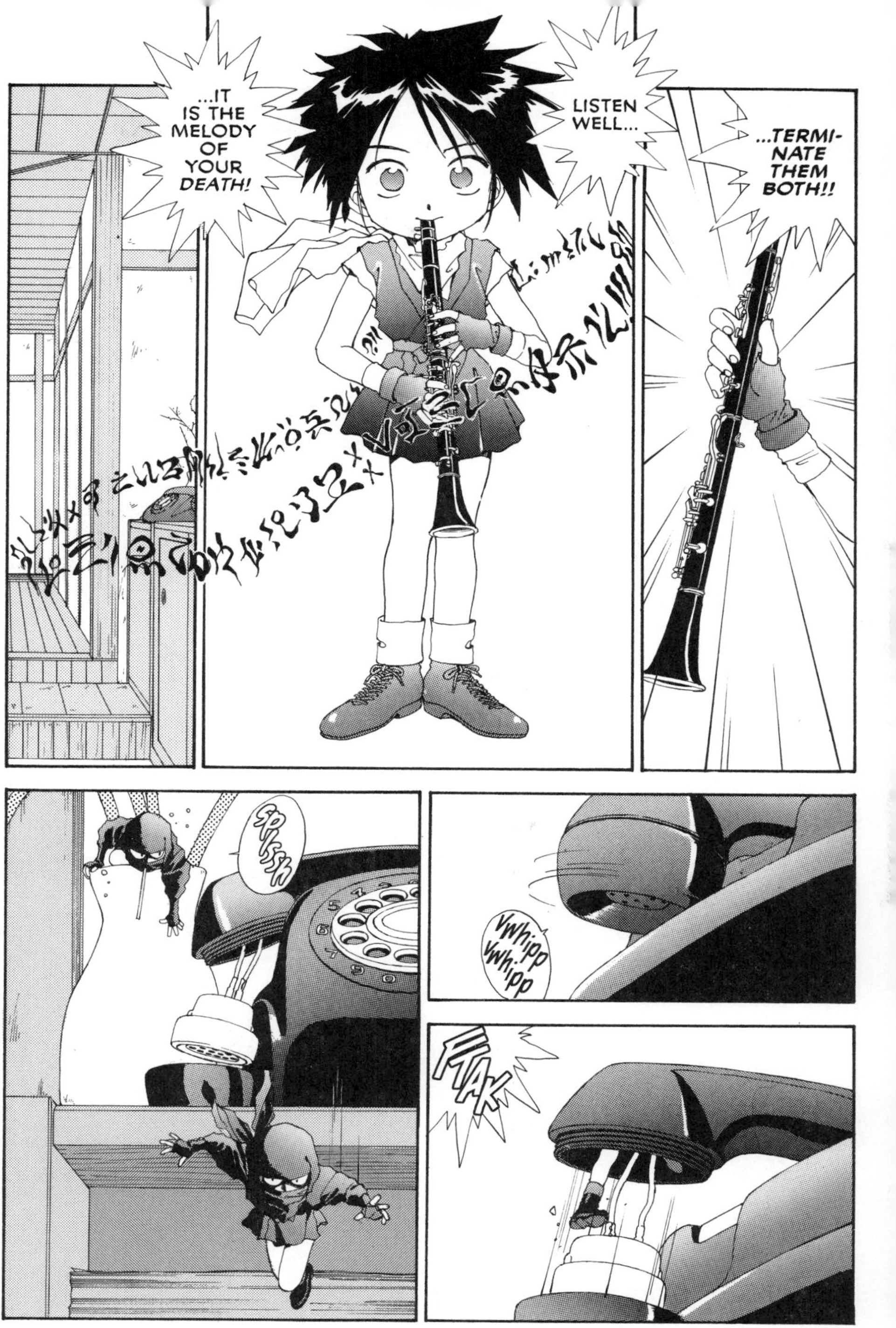
...TERMINATE THEM BOTH!!
LISTEN WELL...
...IT IS THE MELODY OF YOUR DEATH!
VWHIPP VWHIPP
FTAK
SPLSSH

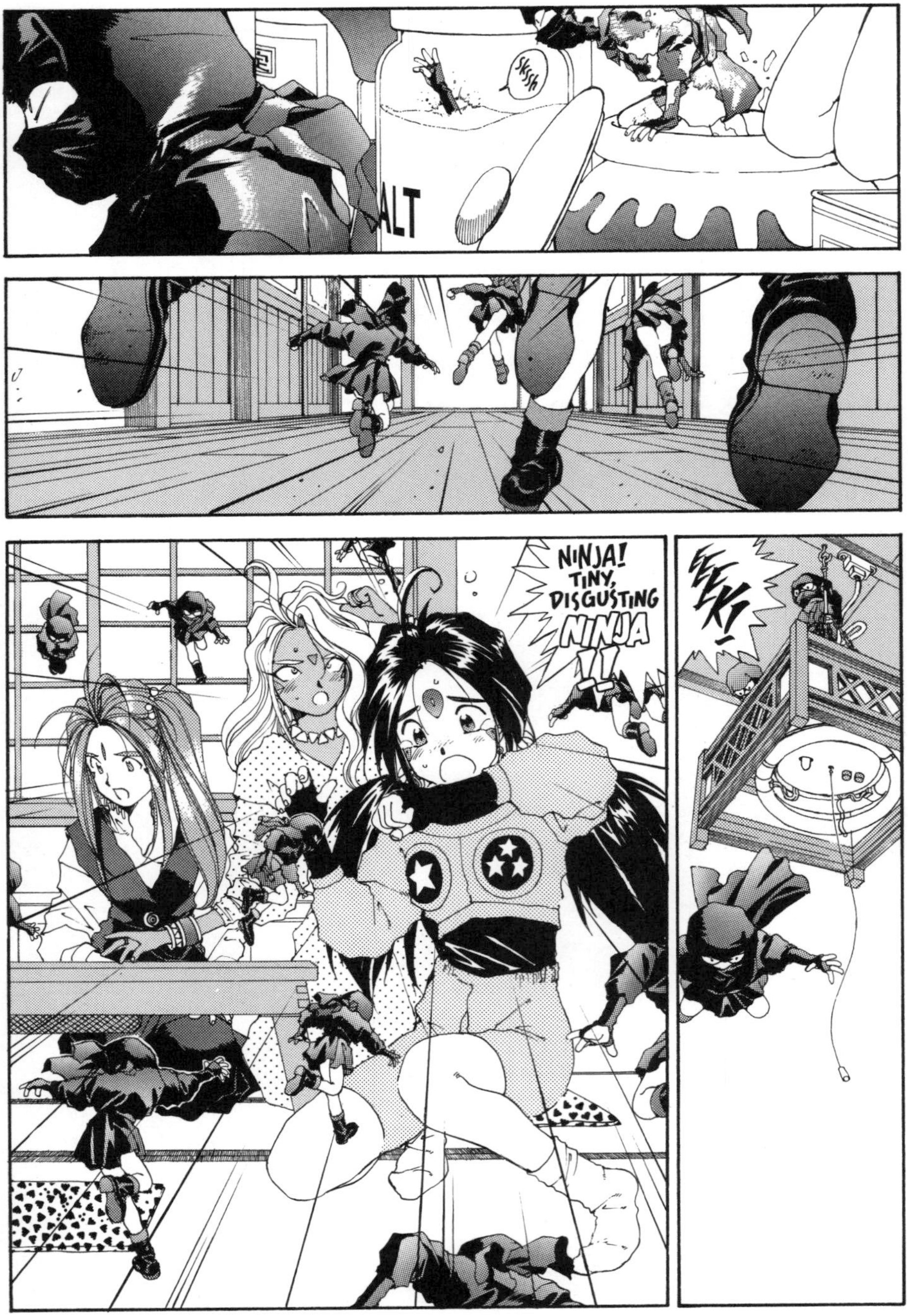
Skssh
ALT
EEEK!
NINJA! TINY, DISGUSTING NINJA!!

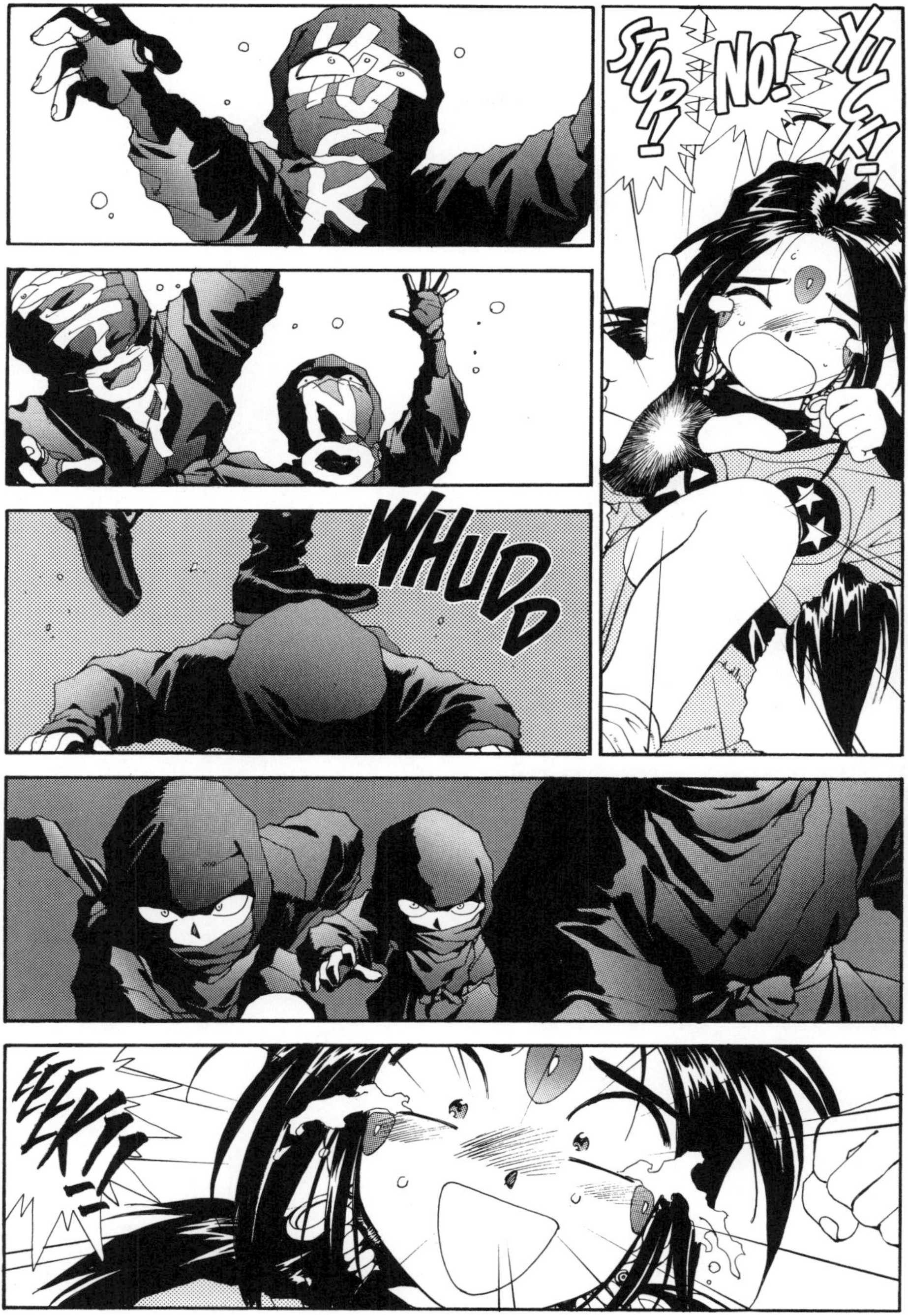
YUCK!
NO!
STOP!
WHUDD
EEEK!!

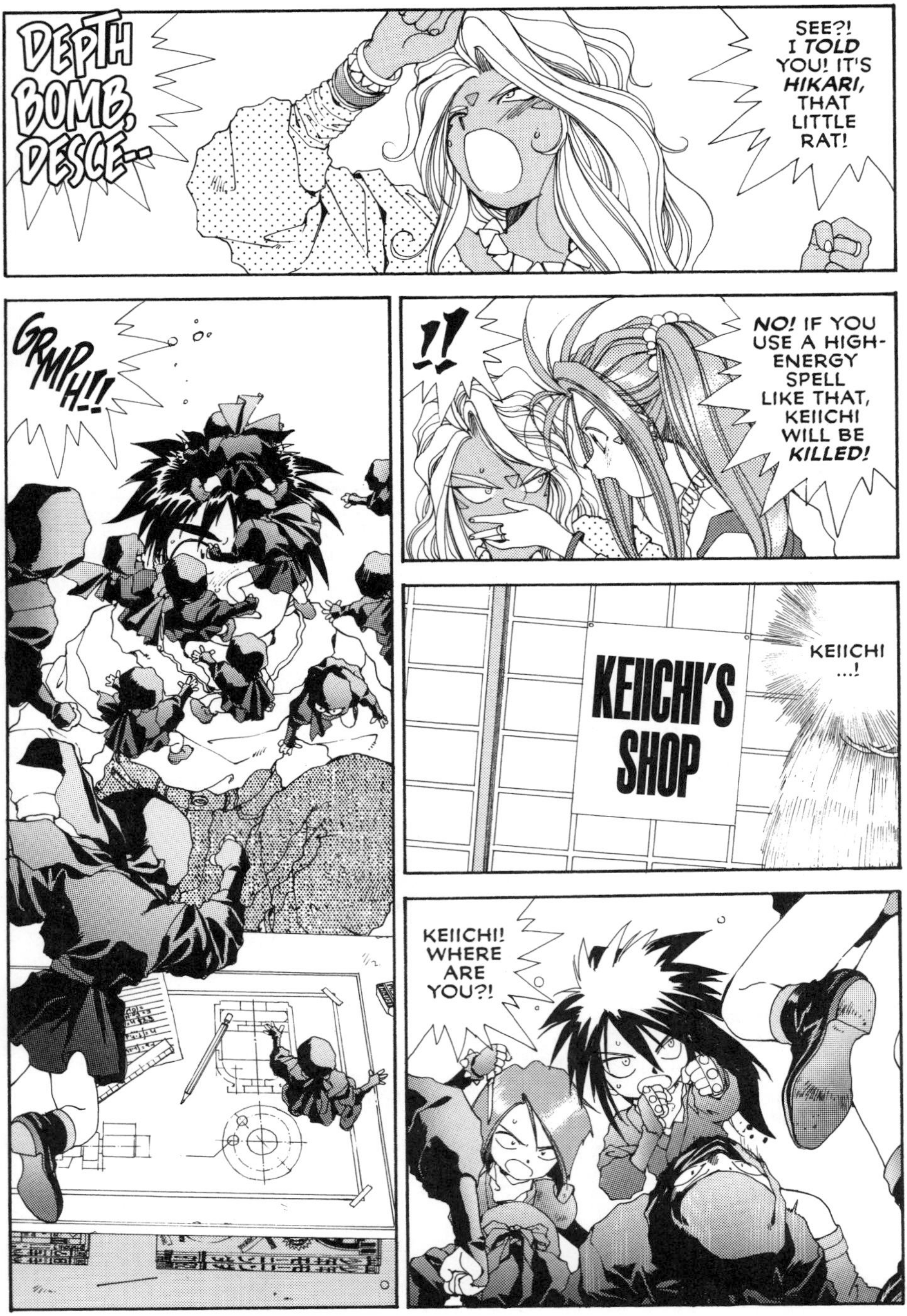
SEE?! I TOLD YOU! IT'S HIKARI, THAT LITTLE RAT!
DEPTH BOMB, DESCE--
NO! IF YOU USE A HIGH-ENERGY SPELL LIKE THAT, KEIICHI WILL BE KILLED!
!!
KEIICHI'S SHOP
KEIICHI ...!
KEIICHI! WHERE ARE YOU?!
GRMPH!!

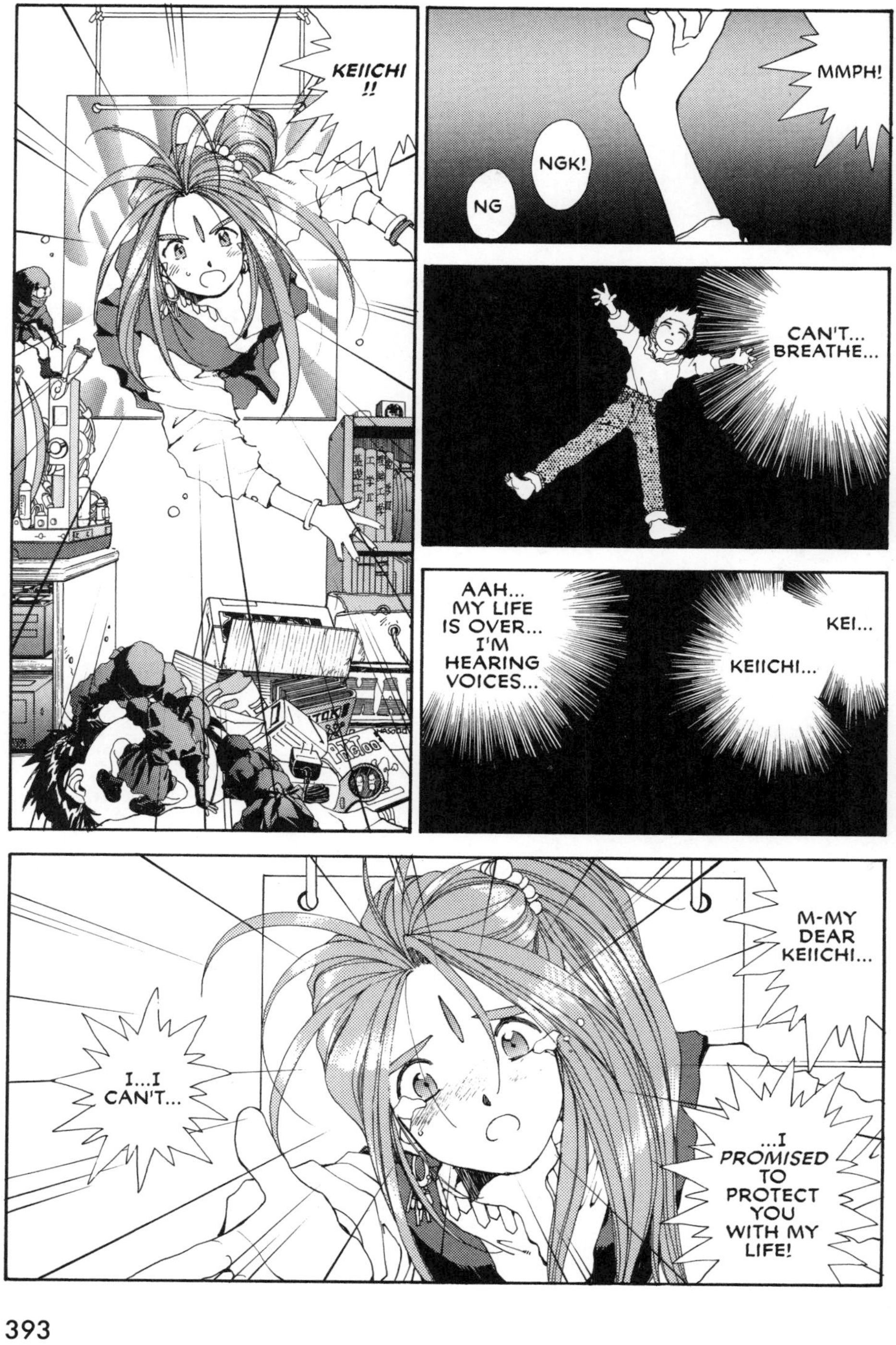
MMPH!
NGK!
NG
CAN'T... BREATHE...
KEI...
KEIICHI...
AAH... MY LIFE IS OVER... I'M HEARING VOICES...
KEIICHI !!
M-MY DEAR KEIICHI...
I...I CAN'T...
...I *PROMISED* TO PROTECT YOU WITH MY LIFE!

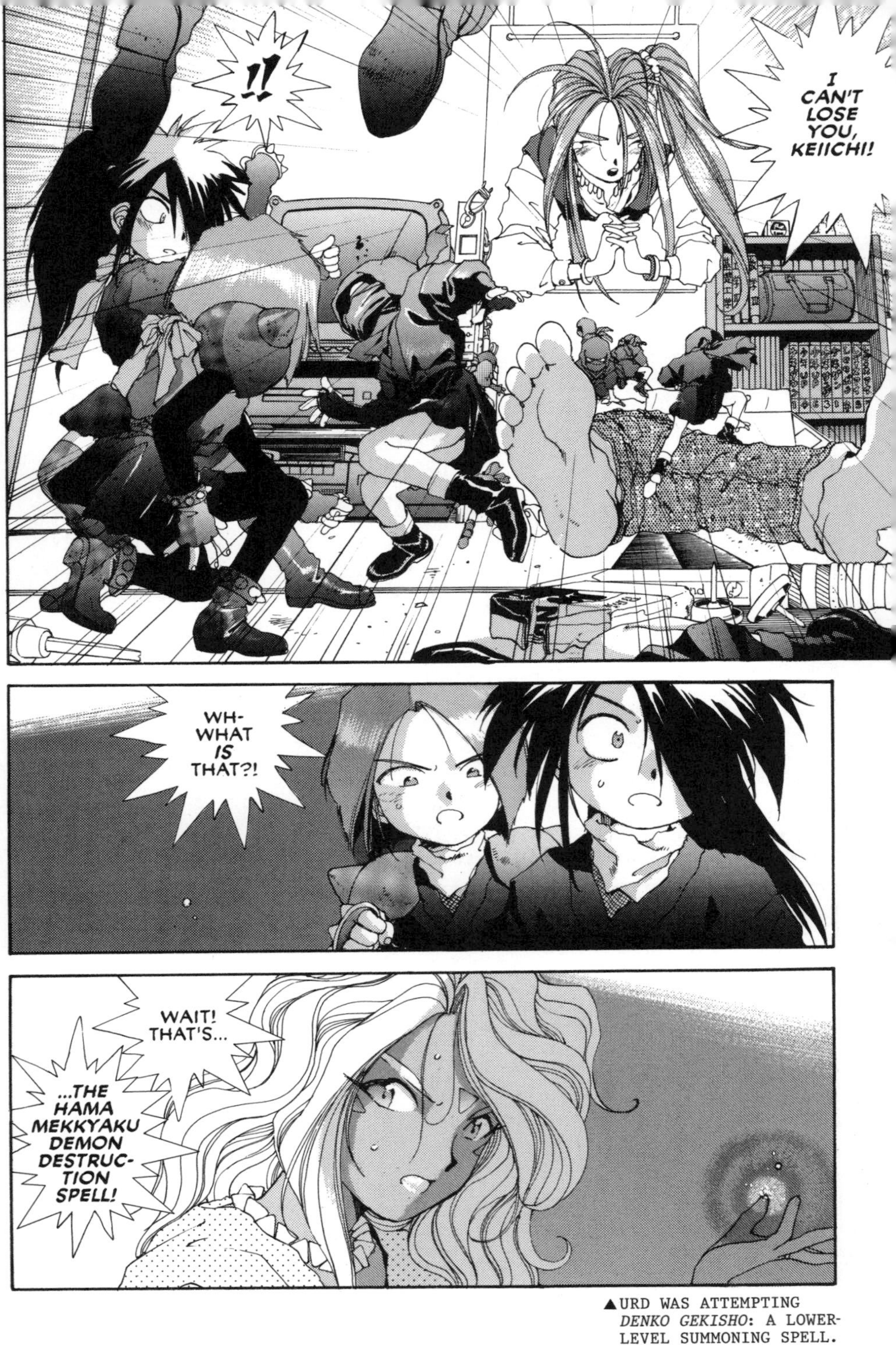
I CAN'T LOSE YOU, KEIICHI!
!!
WH-WHAT *IS* THAT?!
WAIT! THAT'S...
...THE HAMA MEKKYAKU DEMON DESTRUCTION SPELL!

▲URD WAS ATTEMPTING *DENKO GEKISHO*: A LOWER-LEVEL SUMMONING SPELL.

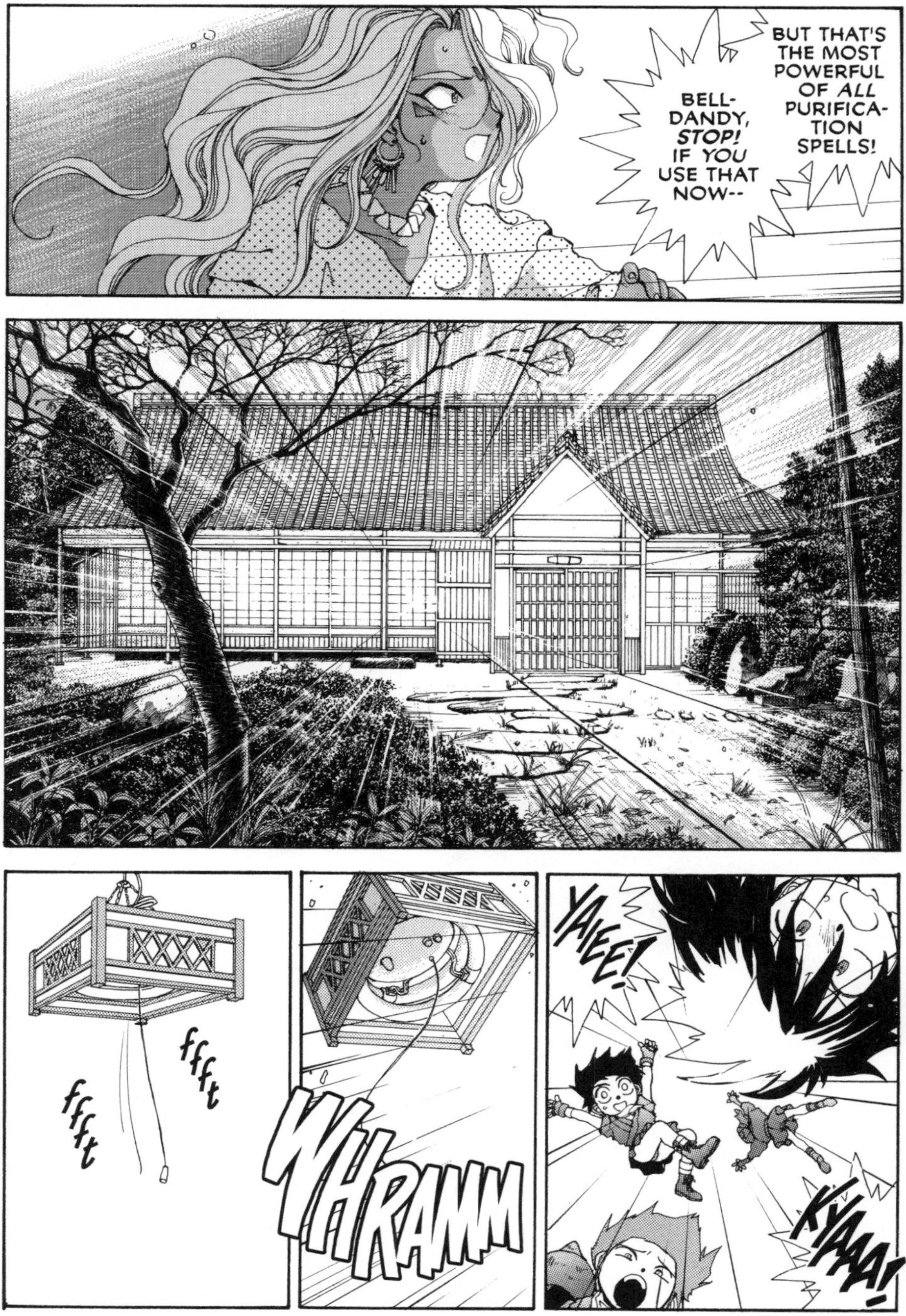
BUT THAT'S THE MOST POWERFUL OF *ALL* PURIFICATION SPELLS!
BELL-DANDY, *STOP!* IF *YOU* USE THAT NOW--
YAIEE!
KYAAA!
WHRAMM
ffft
ffft

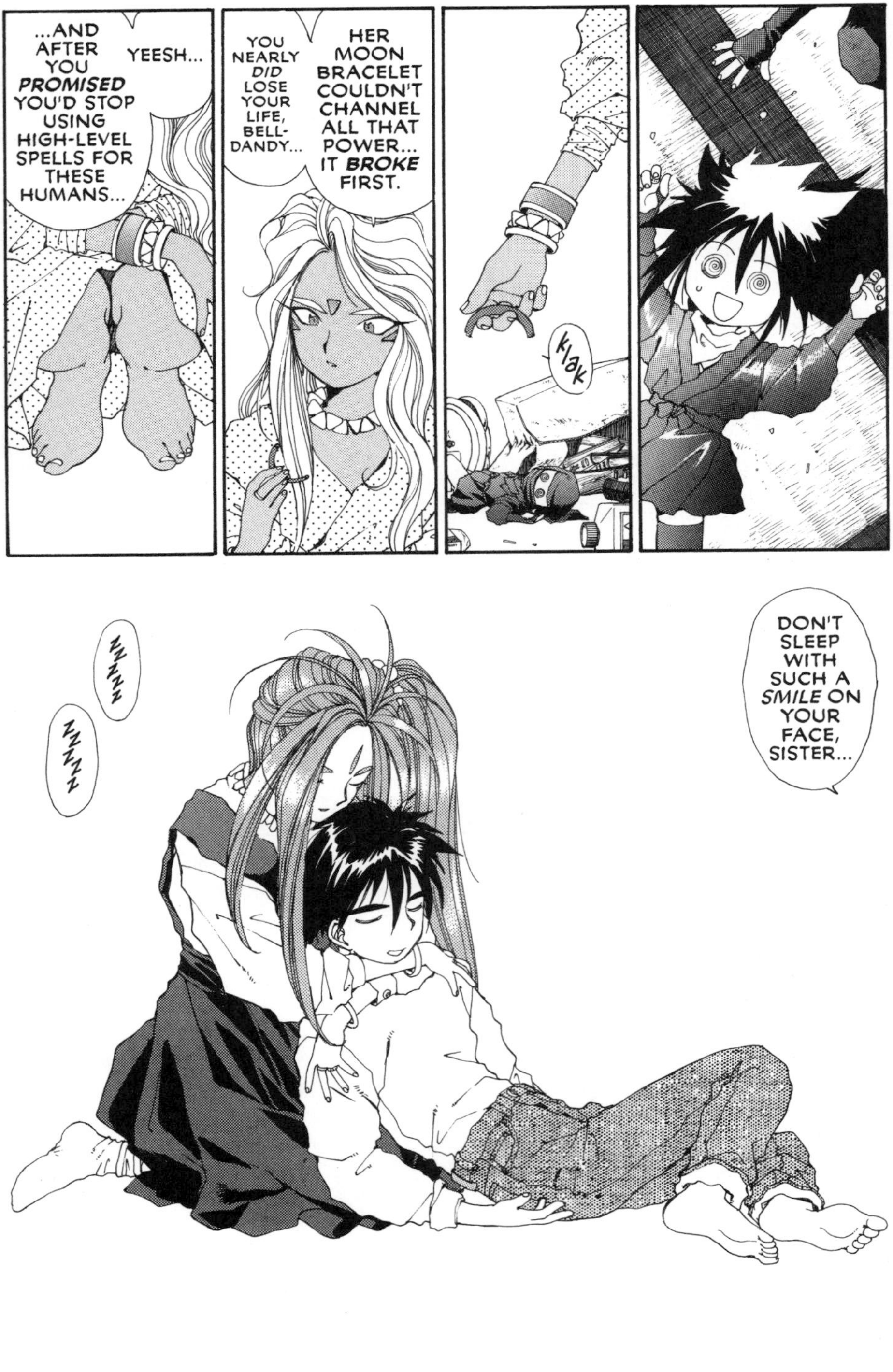
klak
HER MOON BRACELET COULDN'T CHANNEL ALL THAT POWER... IT BROKE FIRST.
YOU NEARLY DID LOSE YOUR LIFE, BELL-DANDY...
YEESH...
...AND AFTER YOU PROMISED YOU'D STOP USING HIGH-LEVEL SPELLS FOR THESE HUMANS...
DON'T SLEEP WITH SUCH A SMILE ON YOUR FACE, SISTER...
ZZZZ
ZZZZ

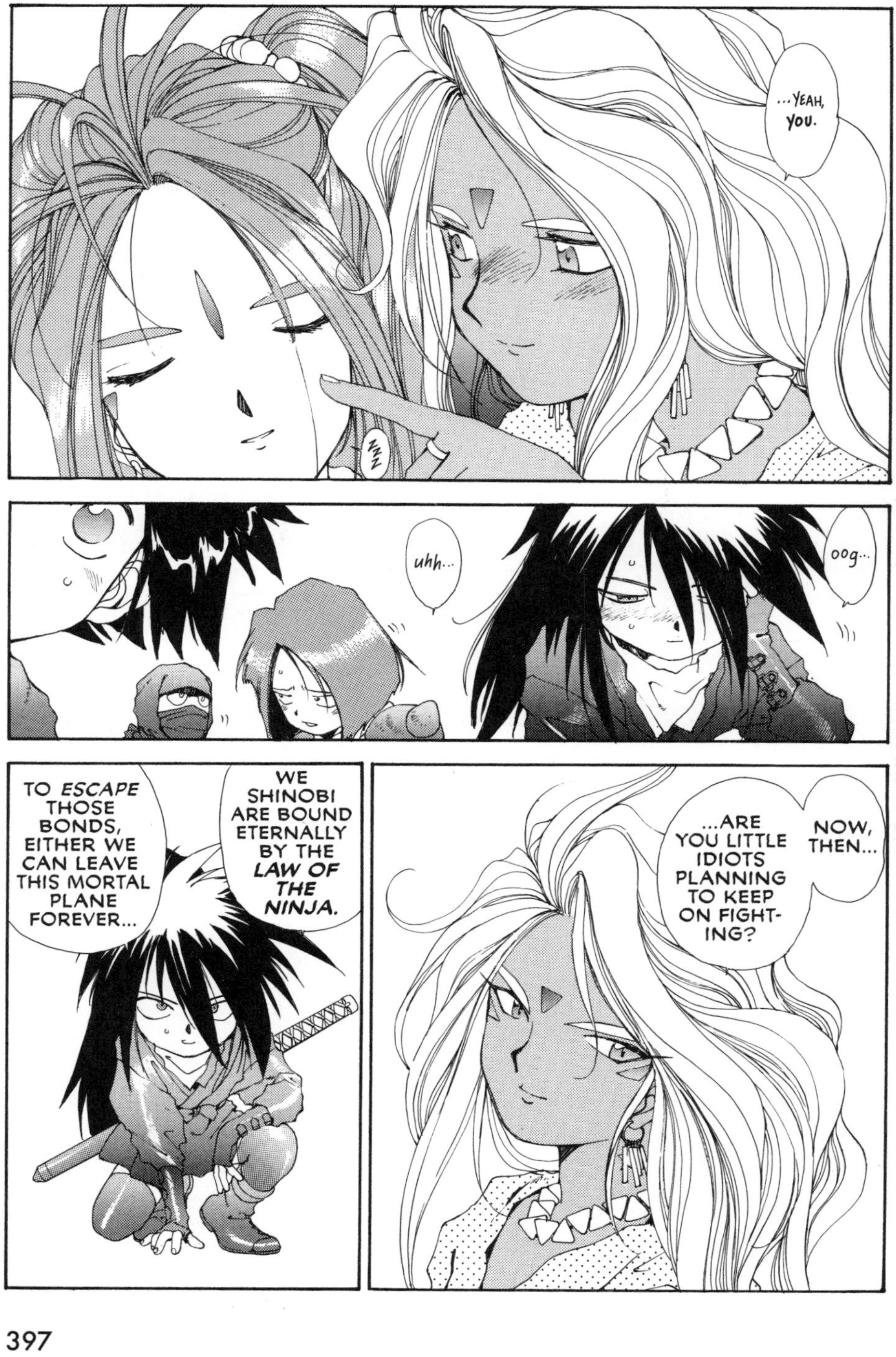
...YEAH, YOU.
NNN
oog...
uhh...
NOW, THEN...
...ARE YOU LITTLE IDIOTS PLANNING TO KEEP ON FIGHTING?
WE SHINOBI ARE BOUND ETERNALLY BY THE *LAW OF THE NINJA.*
TO *ESCAPE* THOSE BONDS, EITHER WE CAN LEAVE THIS MORTAL PLANE FOREVER...

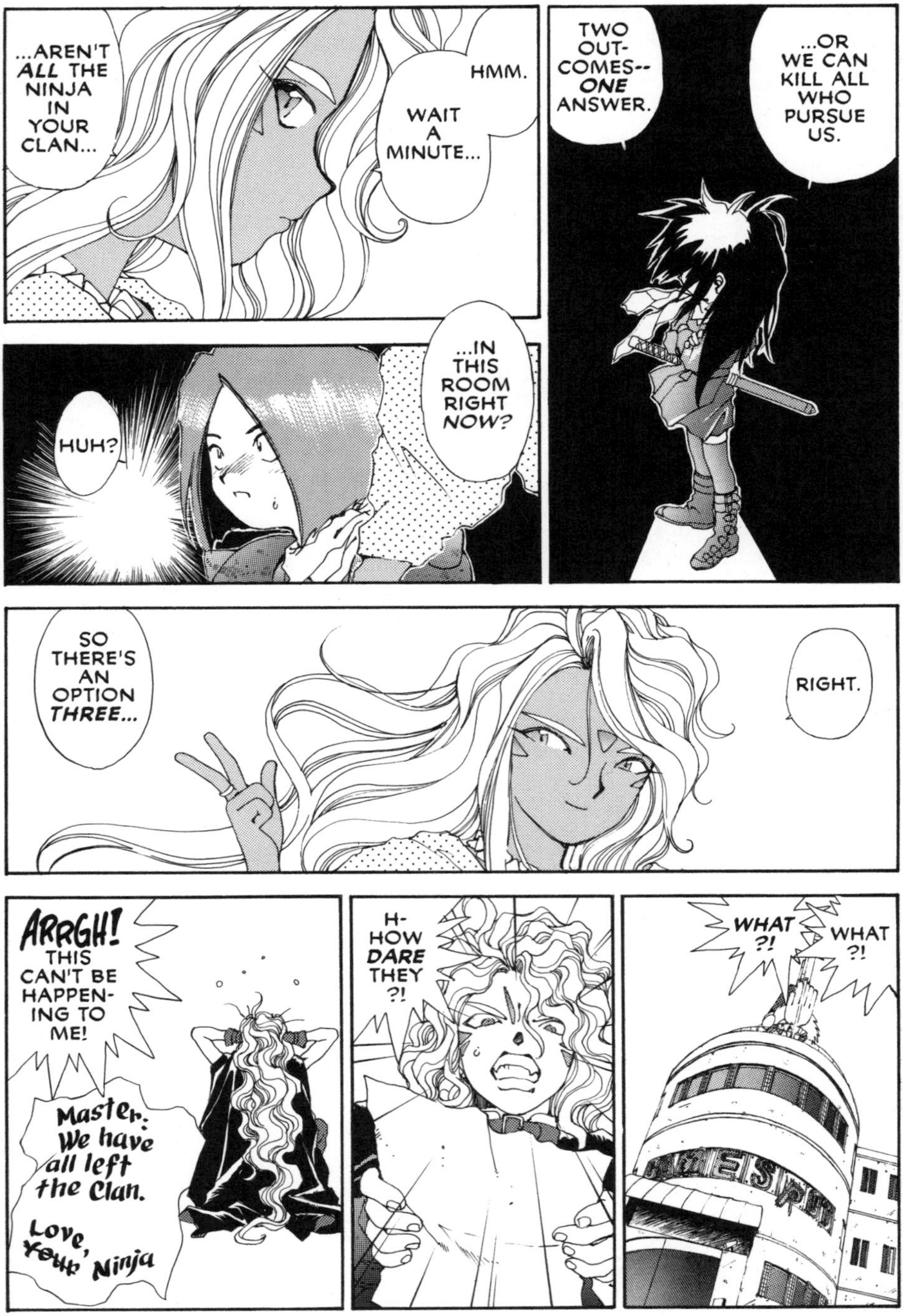
...OR WE CAN KILL ALL WHO PURSUE US.
TWO OUT-COMES-- *ONE* ANSWER.
HMM.
WAIT A MINUTE...
...AREN'T *ALL* THE NINJA IN YOUR CLAN...
...IN THIS ROOM RIGHT *NOW?*
HUH?
SO THERE'S AN OPTION *THREE...*
RIGHT.
WHAT ?!
WHAT ?!
H-HOW *DARE* THEY ?!
ARRGH!
THIS CAN'T BE HAPPEN-ING TO ME!
Master: We have all left the Clan.
Love, Your Ninja

CHAPTER 54

Together for Never

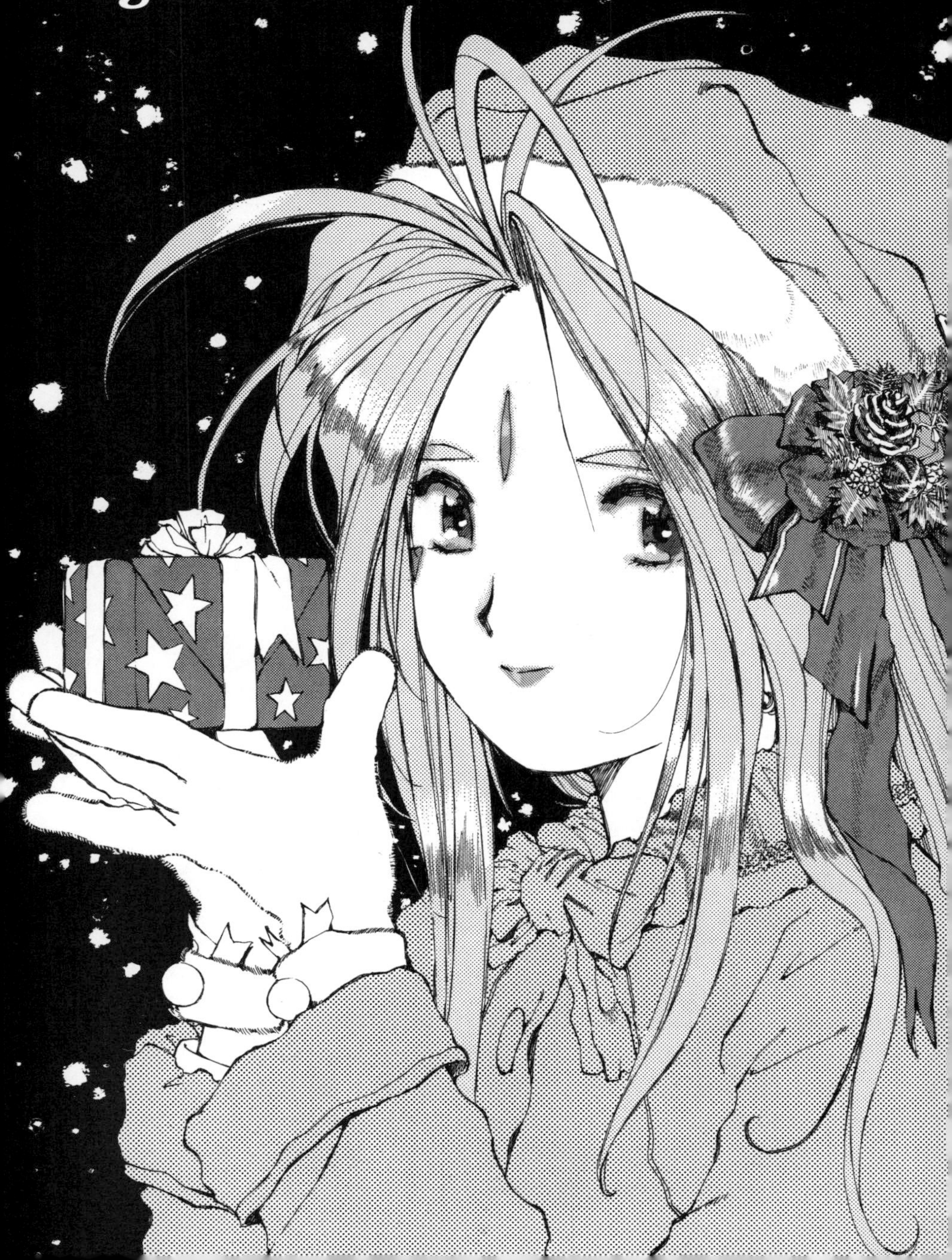

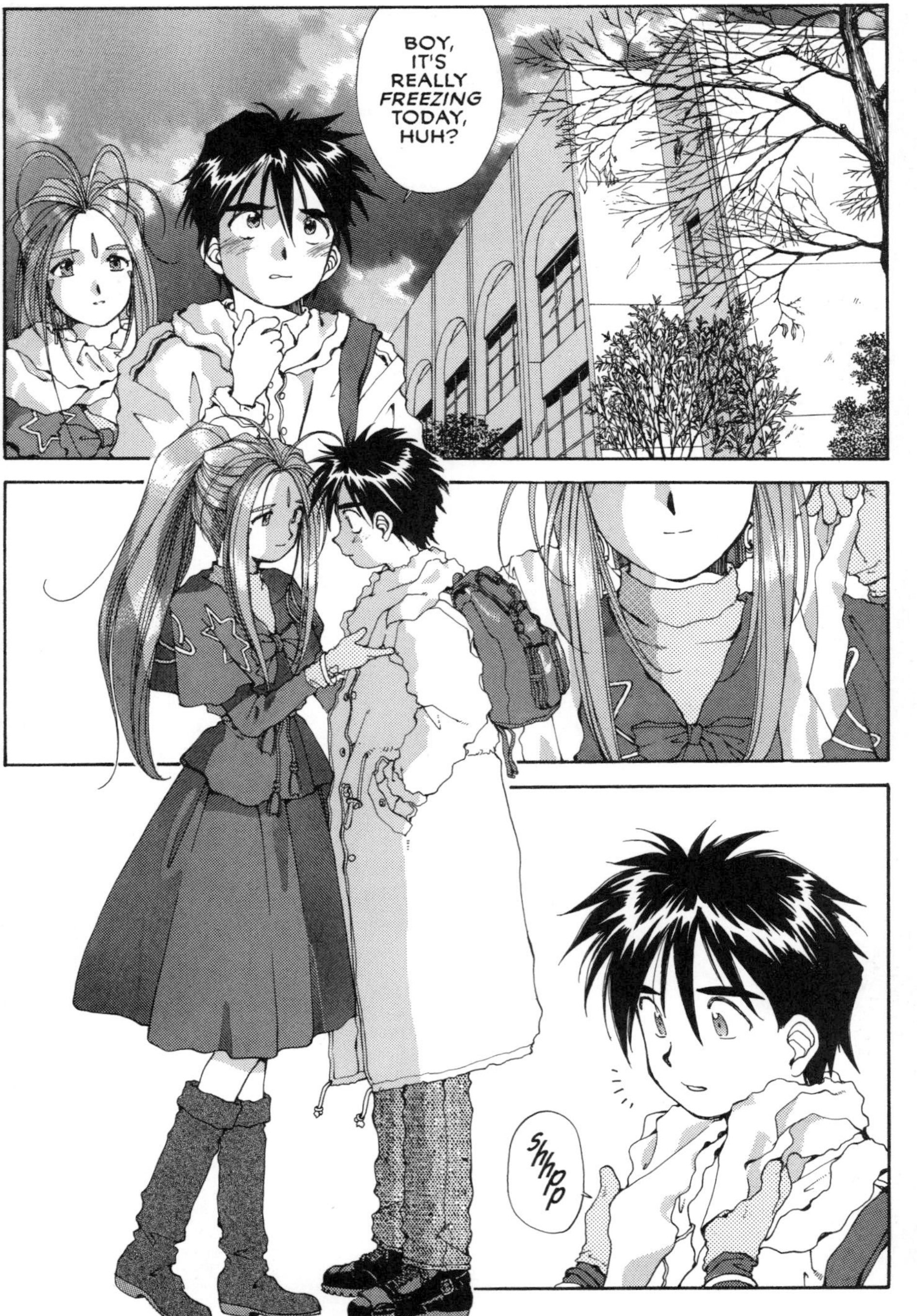
BOY, IT'S REALLY *FREEZING* TODAY, HUH?
SHPP

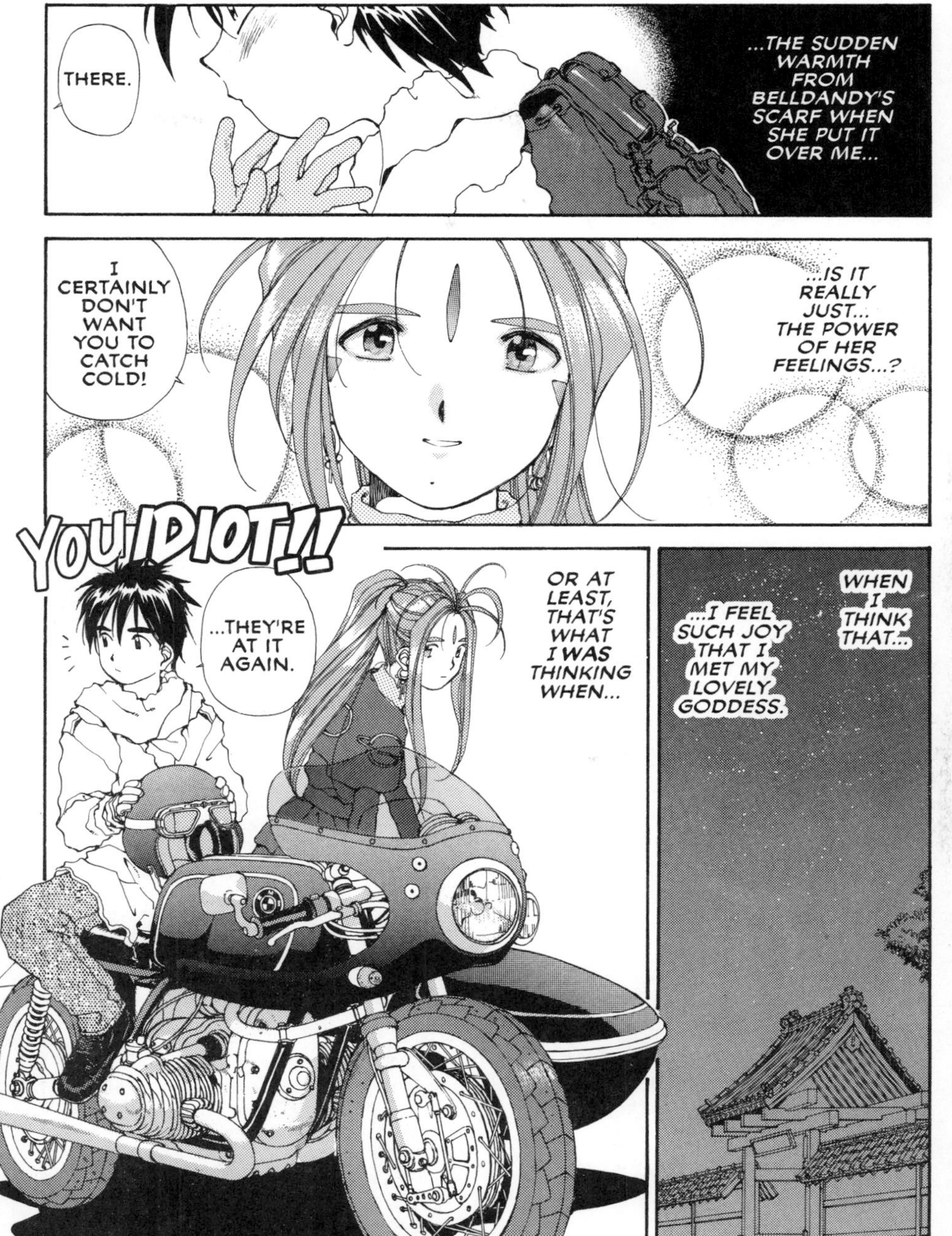
...THE SUDDEN WARMTH FROM BELLDANDY'S SCARF WHEN SHE PUT IT OVER ME...
THERE.
...IS IT REALLY JUST... THE POWER OF HER FEELINGS...?
I CERTAINLY DON'T WANT YOU TO CATCH COLD!
WHEN I THINK THAT...
...I FEEL SUCH JOY THAT I MET MY LOVELY GODDESS.
OR AT LEAST, THAT'S WHAT I WAS THINKING WHEN...
YOU IDIOT!!
...THEY'RE AT IT AGAIN.

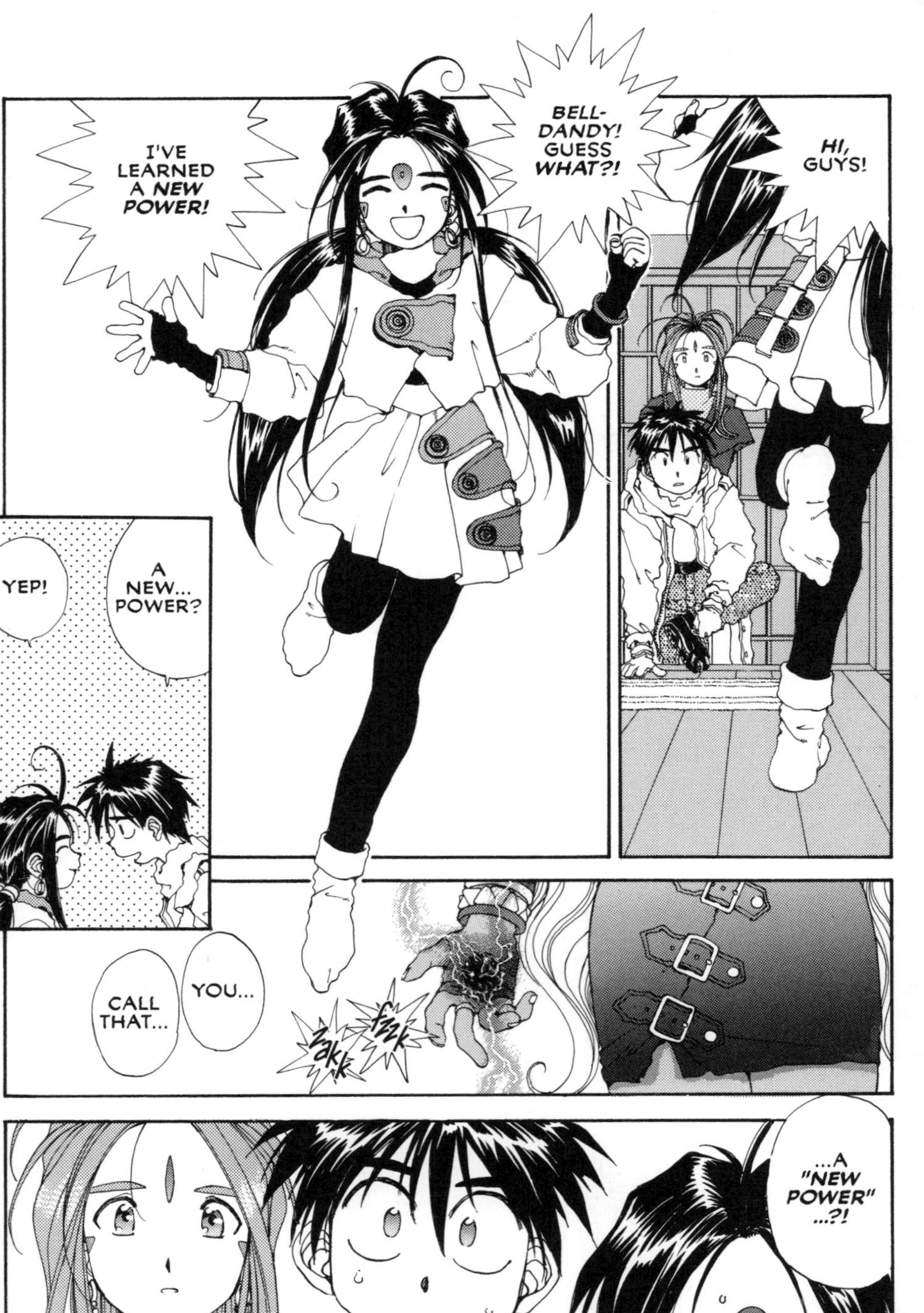
HI, GUYS!
BELL-DANDY! GUESS WHAT?!
I'VE LEARNED A NEW POWER!
A NEW... POWER?
YEP!
YOU...
CALL THAT...
fzzk
zakk
...A "NEW POWER" ...?!

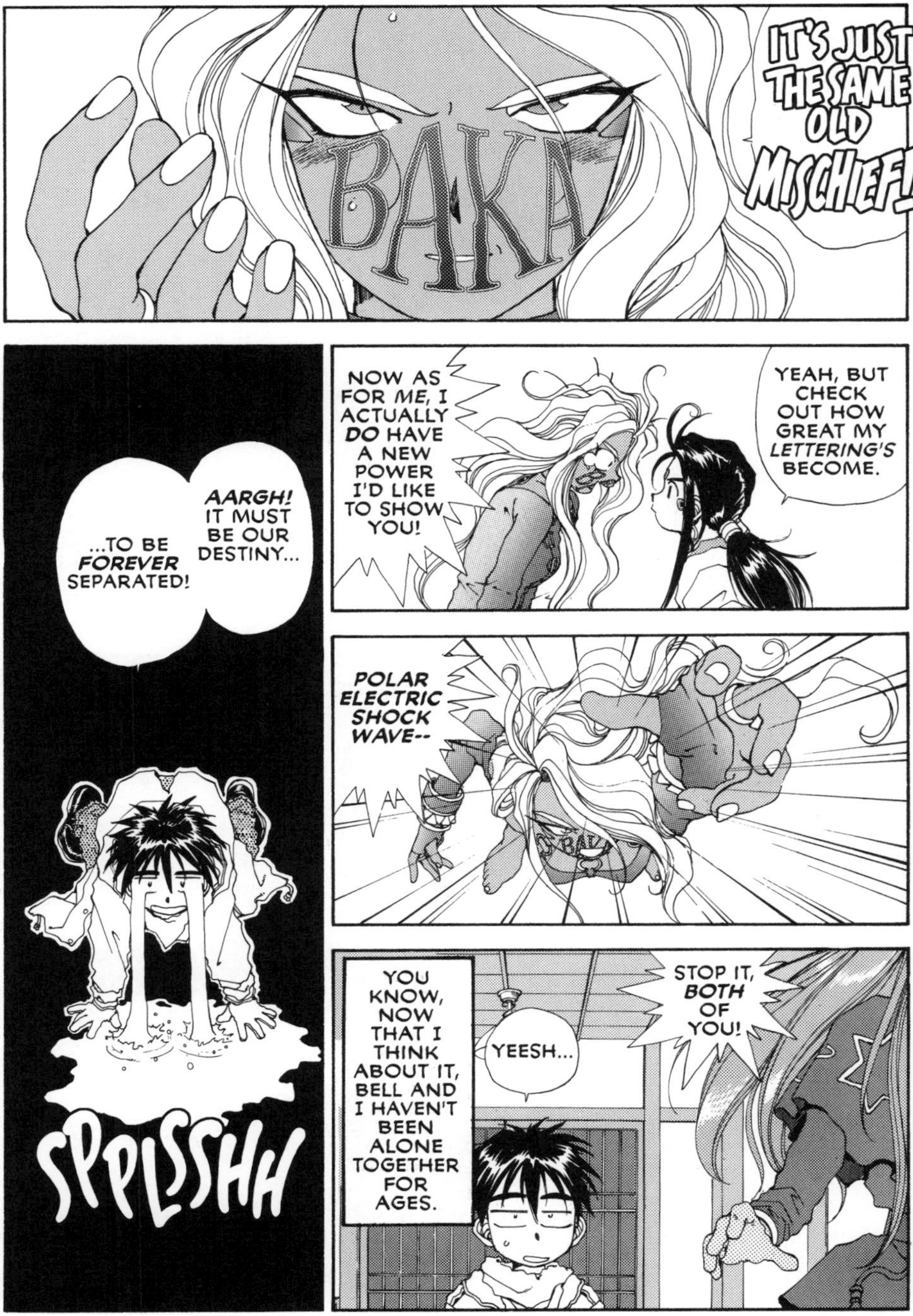
BAKA
IT'S JUST THE SAME OLD MISCHIEF!
YEAH, BUT CHECK OUT HOW GREAT MY *LETTERING'S* BECOME.
NOW AS FOR *ME*, I ACTUALLY ***DO*** HAVE A NEW POWER I'D LIKE TO SHOW YOU!
POLAR ELECTRIC SHOCK WAVE--
STOP IT, ***BOTH*** OF YOU!
YEESH...
YOU KNOW, NOW THAT I THINK ABOUT IT, BELL AND I HAVEN'T BEEN ALONE TOGETHER FOR AGES.
AARGH! IT MUST BE OUR DESTINY...
...TO BE ***FOREVER*** SEPARATED!
SPPLSSHH

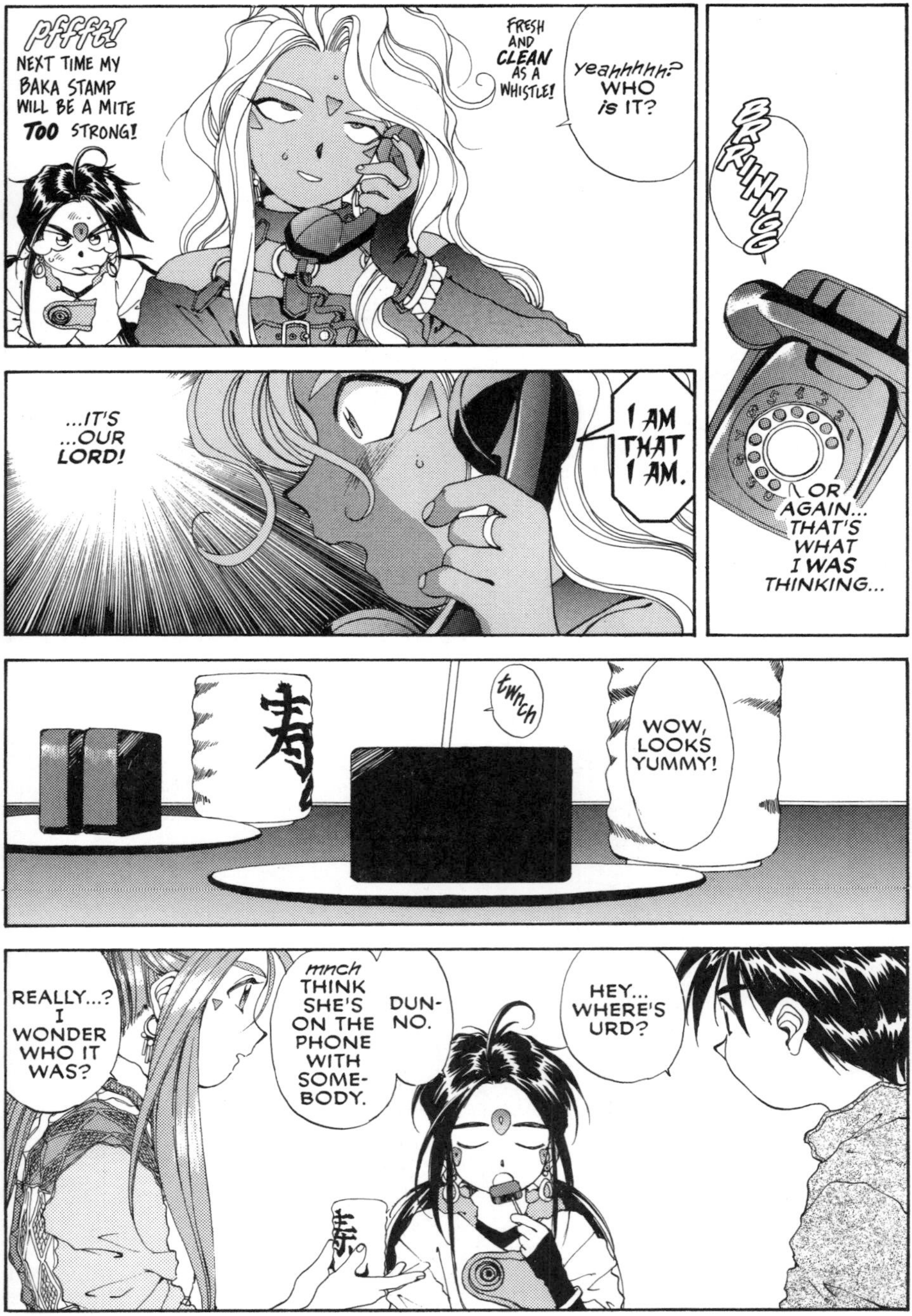
BRRINNGG
OR AGAIN... THAT'S WHAT I WAS THINKING...
yeahhhhh? WHO is IT?
FRESH AND CLEAN AS A WHISTLE!
pfffft!
NEXT TIME MY BAKA STAMP WILL BE A MITE TOO STRONG!
I AM THAT I AM.
...IT'S ...OUR LORD!
WOW, LOOKS YUMMY!
twnch
HEY... WHERE'S URD?
DUN-NO.
mnch THINK SHE'S ON THE PHONE WITH SOME-BODY.
REALLY...? I WONDER WHO IT WAS?

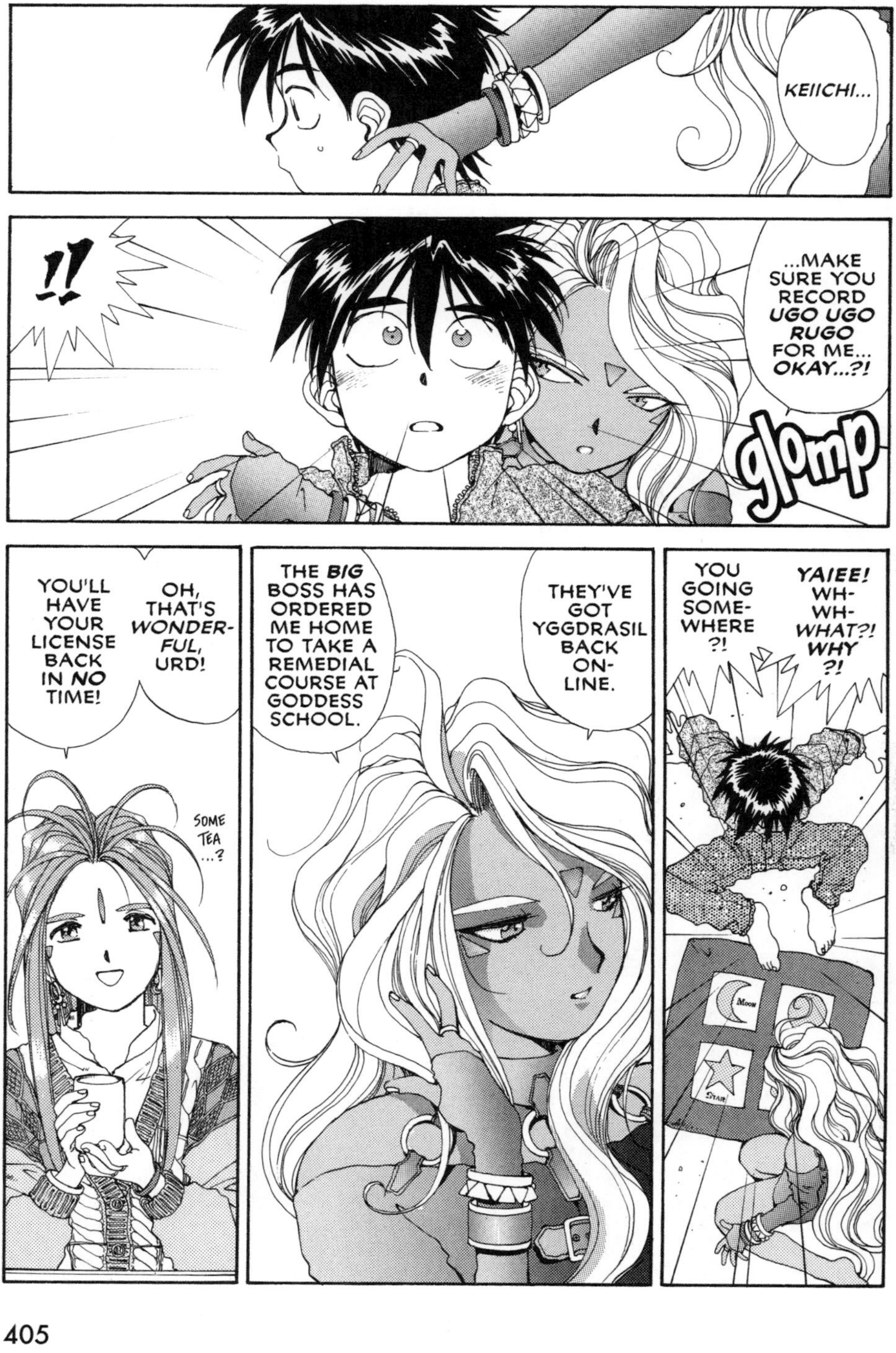
KEIICHI...
...MAKE SURE YOU RECORD UGO UGO RUGO FOR ME... OKAY...?!
glomp
!!
YAIEE! WH-WH-WHAT?! WHY?!
YOU GOING SOME-WHERE?!
THEY'VE GOT YGGDRASIL BACK ON-LINE.
THE BIG BOSS HAS ORDERED ME HOME TO TAKE A REMEDIAL COURSE AT GODDESS SCHOOL.
OH, THAT'S WONDERFUL, URD!
YOU'LL HAVE YOUR LICENSE BACK IN NO TIME!
SOME TEA...?

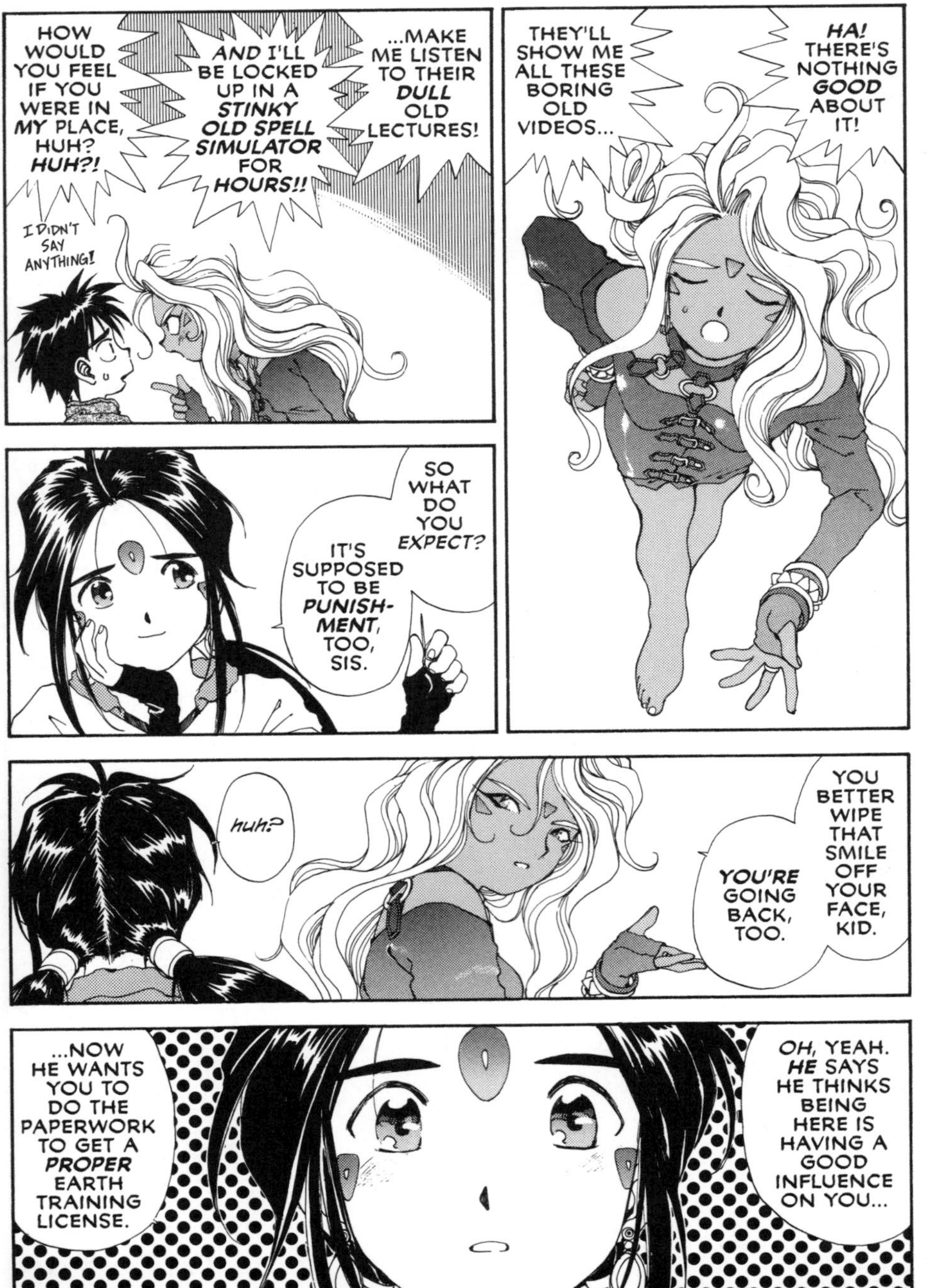
HA! THERE'S NOTHING GOOD ABOUT IT!
THEY'LL SHOW ME ALL THESE BORING OLD VIDEOS...
...MAKE ME LISTEN TO THEIR DULL OLD LECTURES!
AND I'LL BE LOCKED UP IN A STINKY OLD SPELL SIMULATOR FOR HOURS!!
HOW WOULD YOU FEEL IF YOU WERE IN MY PLACE, HUH? HUH?!
I DIDN'T SAY ANYTHING!
SO WHAT DO YOU EXPECT?
IT'S SUPPOSED TO BE PUNISHMENT, TOO, SIS.
YOU BETTER WIPE THAT SMILE OFF YOUR FACE, KID.
YOU'RE GOING BACK, TOO.
huh?
OH, YEAH. HE SAYS HE THINKS BEING HERE IS HAVING A GOOD INFLUENCE ON YOU...
...NOW HE WANTS YOU TO DO THE PAPERWORK TO GET A PROPER EARTH TRAINING LICENSE.

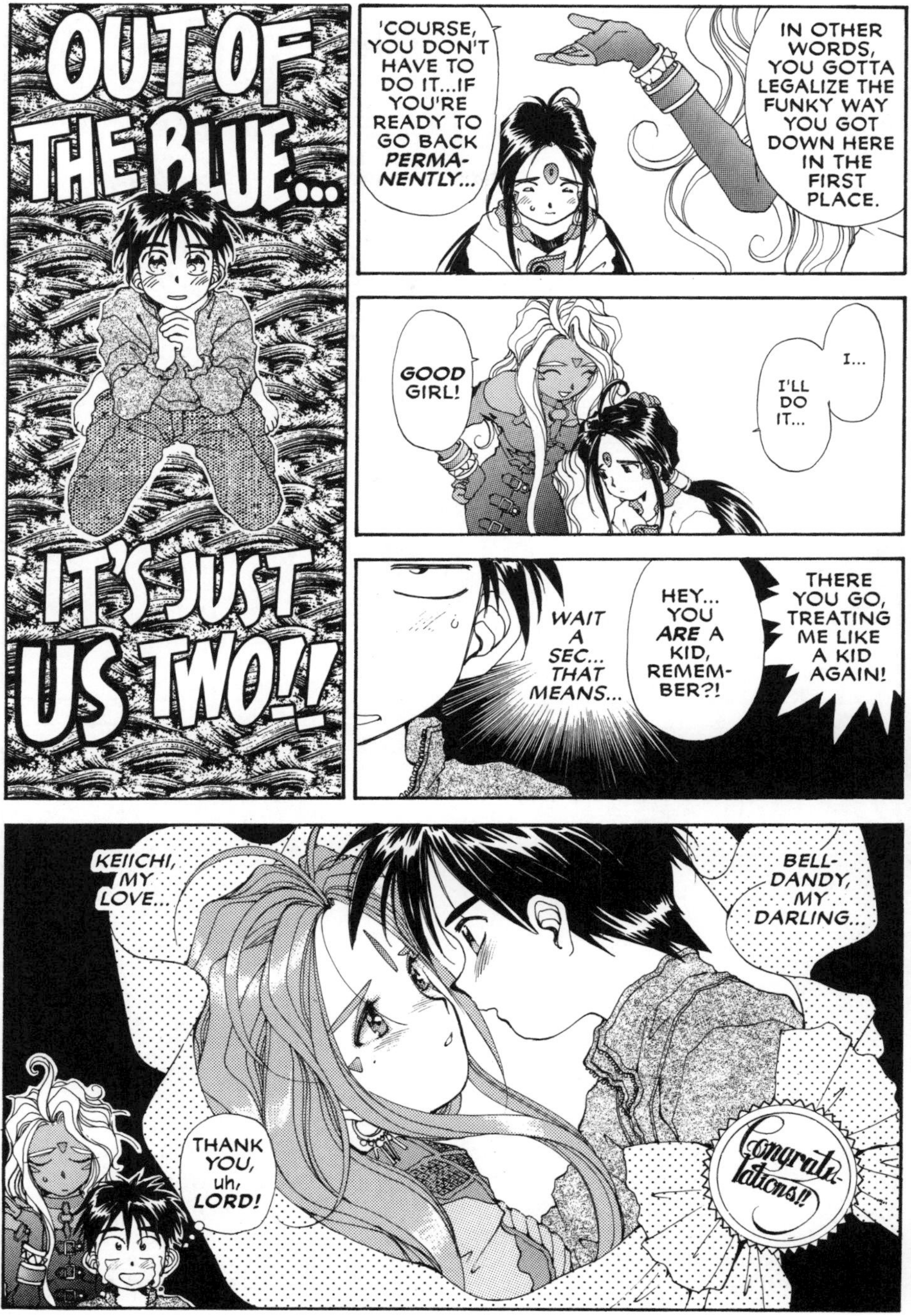
IN OTHER WORDS, YOU GOTTA LEGALIZE THE FUNKY WAY YOU GOT DOWN HERE IN THE FIRST PLACE.
'COURSE, YOU DON'T HAVE TO DO IT...IF YOU'RE READY TO GO BACK *PERMANENTLY*...
I... I'LL DO IT...
GOOD GIRL!
THERE YOU GO, TREATING ME LIKE A KID AGAIN!
HEY... YOU *ARE* A KID, REMEMBER?!
WAIT A SEC... THAT MEANS...
OUT OF THE BLUE...
IT'S JUST US TWO!!
BELL-DANDY, MY DARLING...
KEIICHI, MY LOVE...
Congratulations!!
THANK YOU, uh, *LORD!*

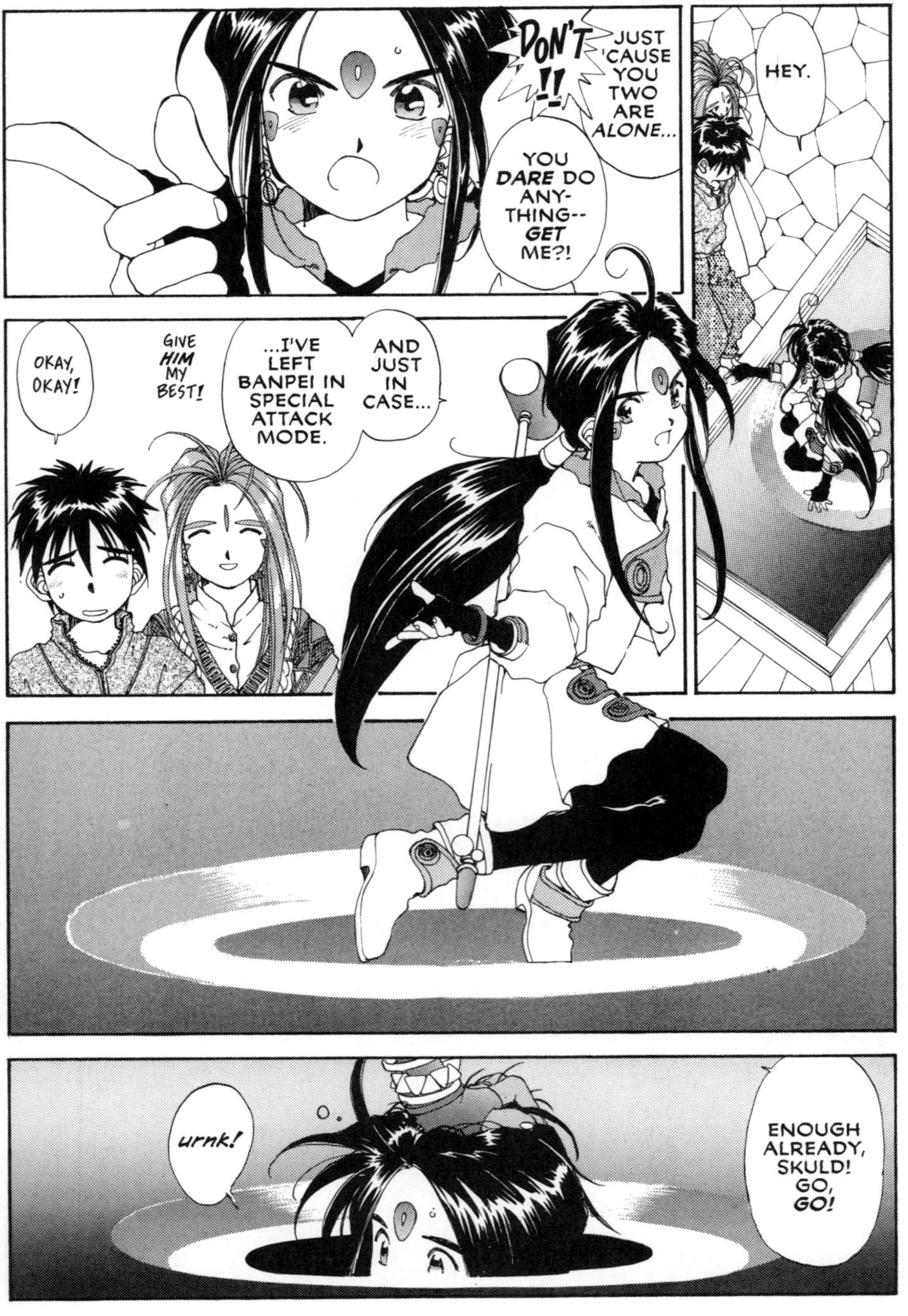
HEY.
DON'T!!
JUST 'CAUSE YOU TWO ARE ALONE...
YOU DARE DO ANYTHING-- GET ME?!
AND JUST IN CASE...
...I'VE LEFT BANPEI IN SPECIAL ATTACK MODE.
GIVE HIM MY BEST!
OKAY, OKAY!
ENOUGH ALREADY, SKULD! GO, GO!
urnk!

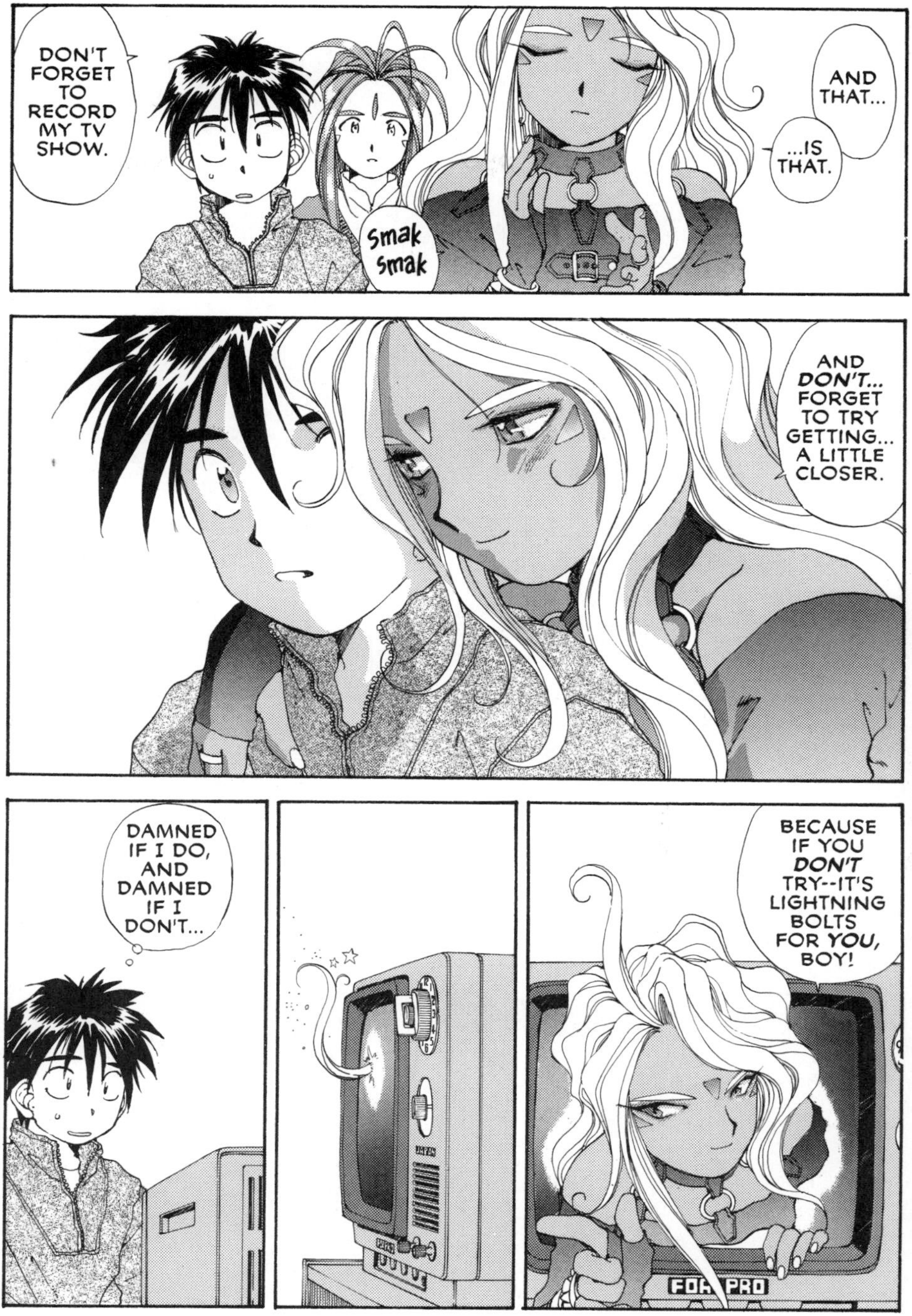
AND THAT...
...IS THAT.
DON'T FORGET TO RECORD MY TV SHOW.
Smak smak
AND DON'T... FORGET TO TRY GETTING... A LITTLE CLOSER.
BECAUSE IF YOU DON'T TRY--IT'S LIGHTNING BOLTS FOR YOU, BOY!
DAMNED IF I DO, AND DAMNED IF I DON'T...

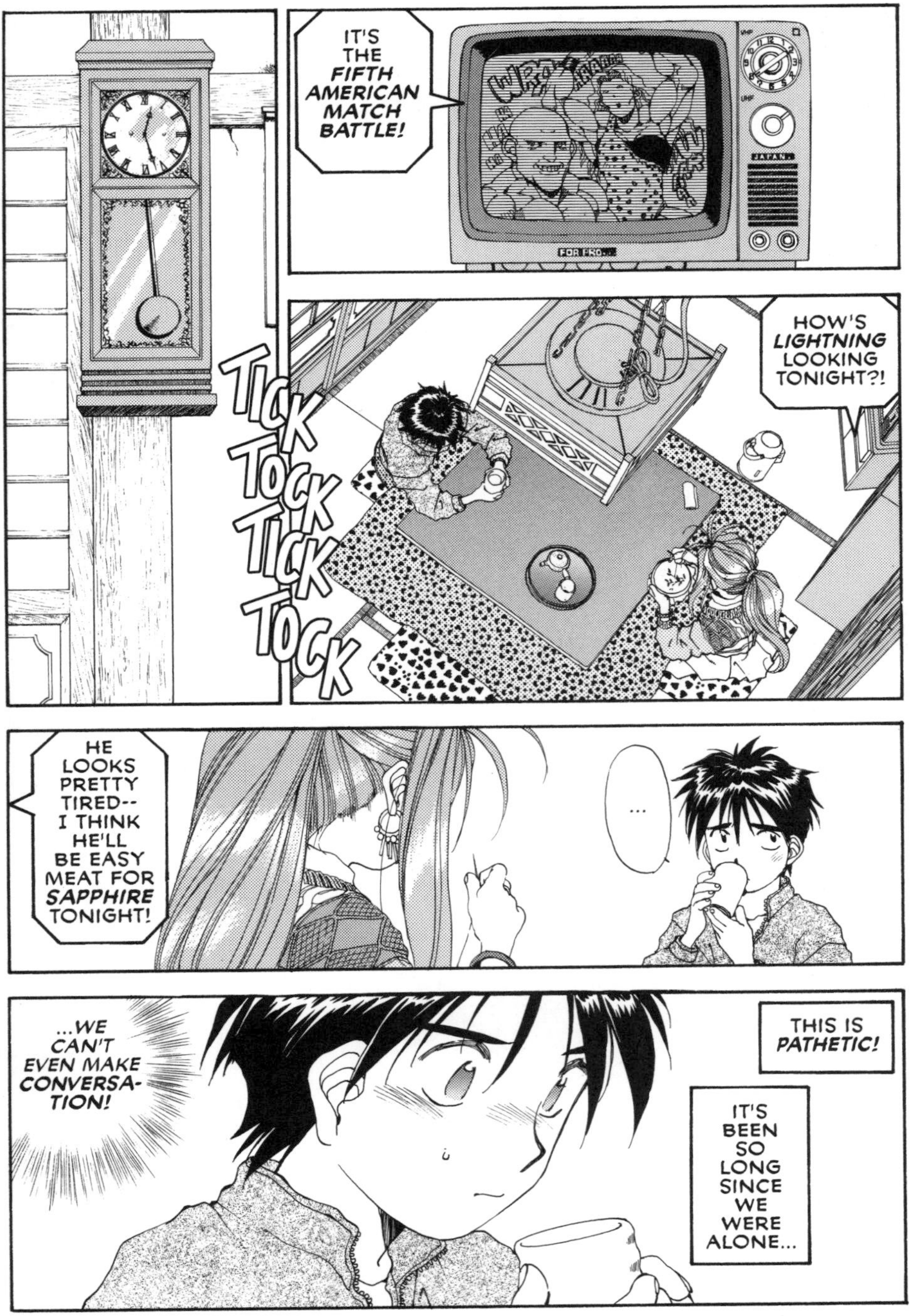
IT'S THE *FIFTH AMERICAN MATCH BATTLE!*
FOR FRO...
HOW'S *LIGHTNING* LOOKING TONIGHT?!
TICK TOCK TICK TOCK
...
HE LOOKS PRETTY TIRED-- I THINK HE'LL BE EASY MEAT FOR *SAPPHIRE* TONIGHT!
THIS IS *PATHETIC!*
IT'S BEEN SO LONG SINCE WE WERE ALONE...
...WE CAN'T EVEN MAKE CONVERSA-TION!

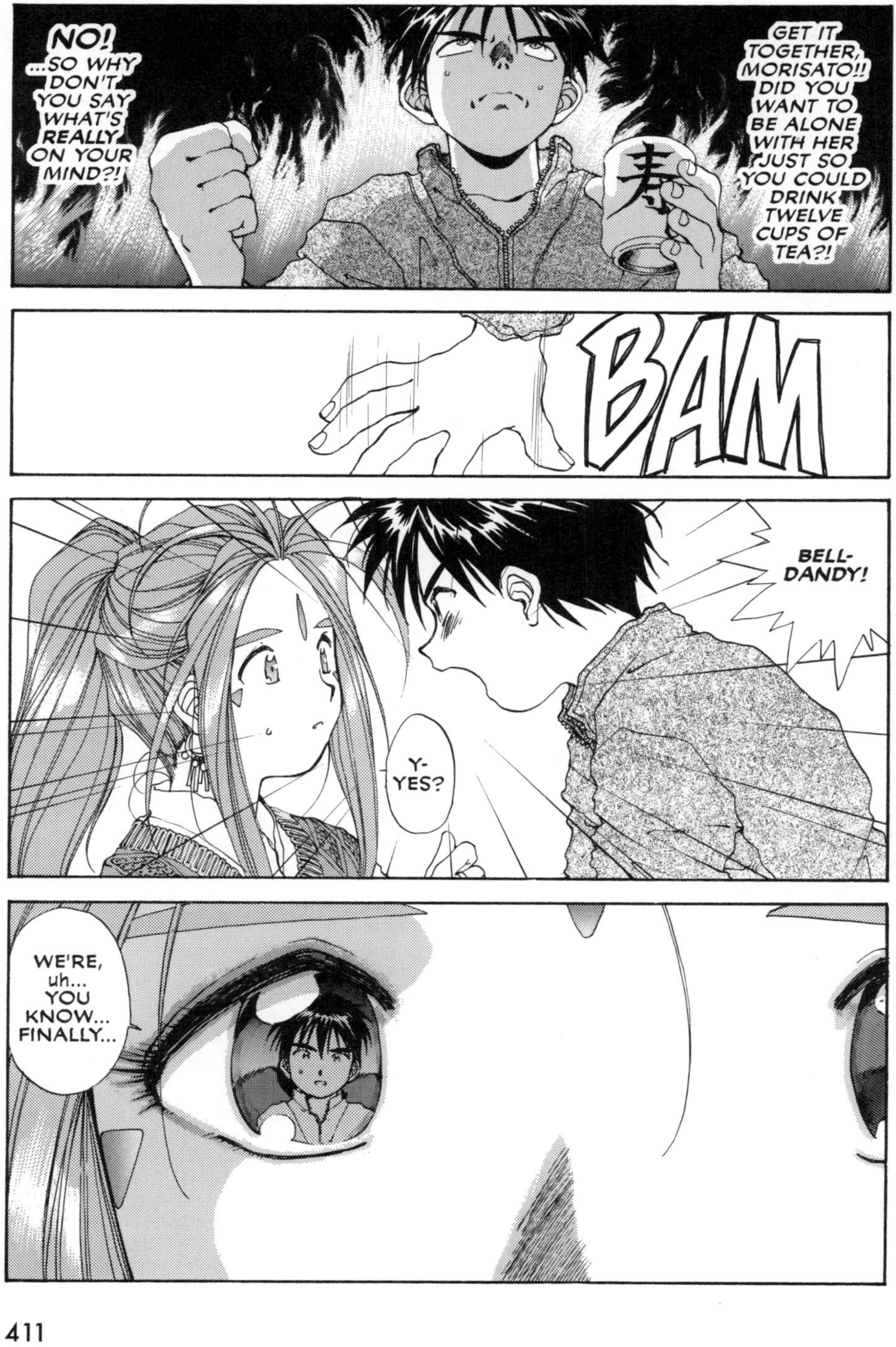
GET IT TOGETHER, MORISATO!! DID YOU WANT TO BE ALONE WITH HER JUST SO YOU COULD DRINK TWELVE CUPS OF TEA?!
NO! ...SO WHY DON'T YOU SAY WHAT'S REALLY ON YOUR MIND?!
BAM
BELL-DANDY!
Y-YES?
WE'RE, uh... YOU KNOW... FINALLY...

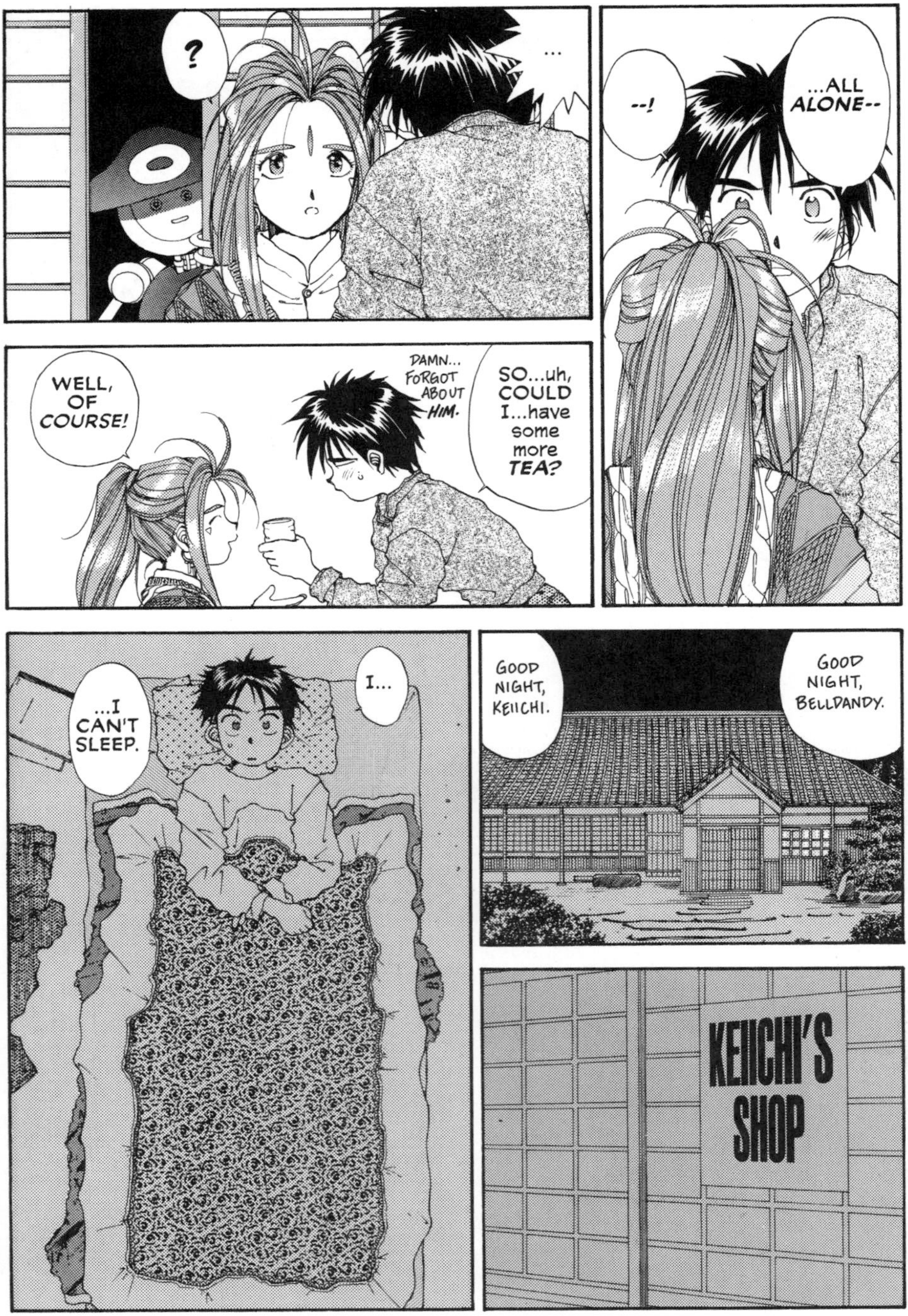
...ALL ALONE--
--!
...
?
SO...uh, COULD I...have some more TEA?
DAMN... FORGOT ABOUT HIM.
WELL, OF COURSE!
GOOD NIGHT, BELLDANDY.
GOOD NIGHT, KEIICHI.
KEIICHI'S SHOP
I...
...I CAN'T SLEEP.

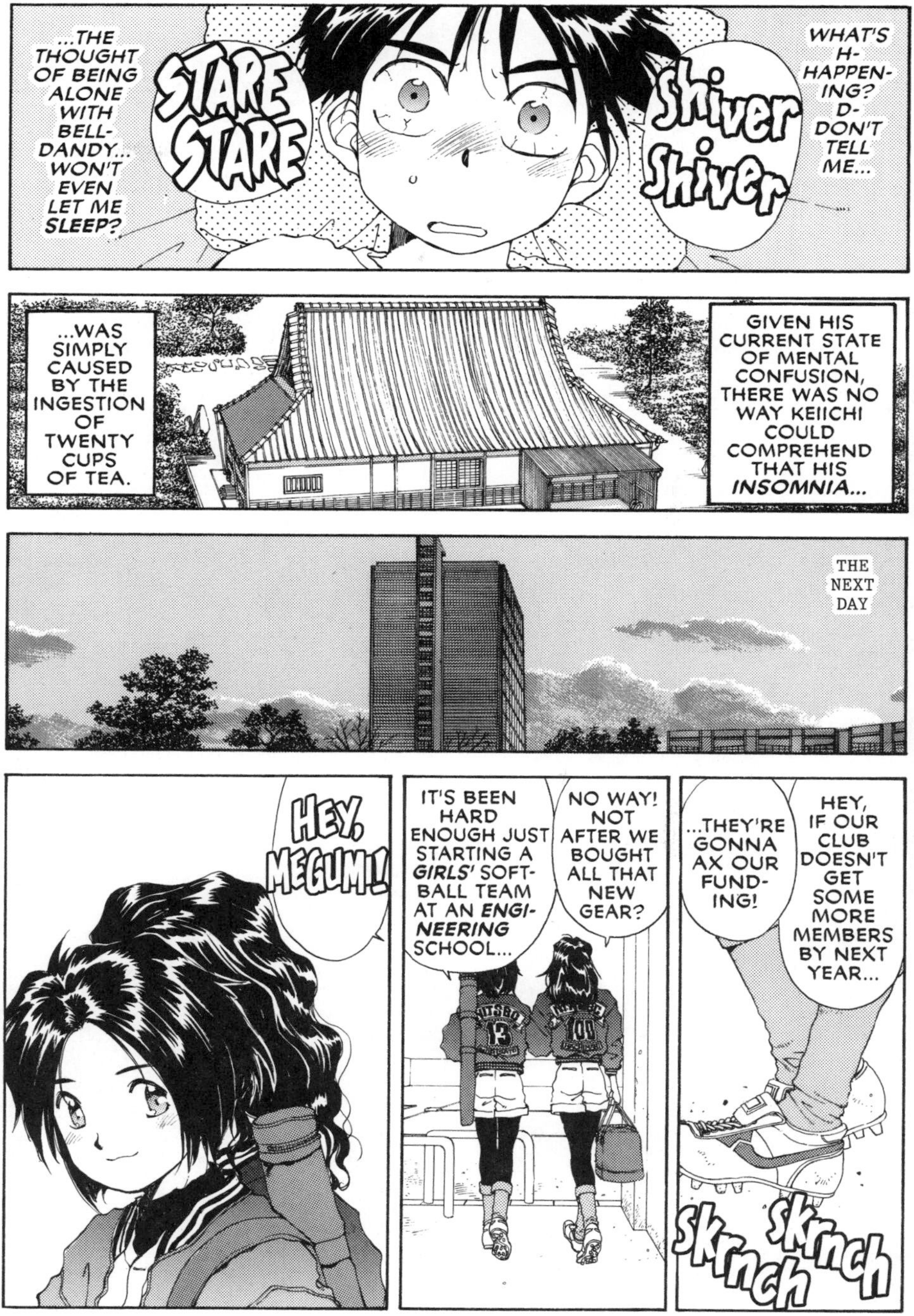
WHAT'S H-HAPPENING? D-DON'T TELL ME...
Shiver Shiver
STARE STARE
...THE THOUGHT OF BEING ALONE WITH BELL-DANDY... WON'T EVEN LET ME SLEEP?
GIVEN HIS CURRENT STATE OF MENTAL CONFUSION, THERE WAS NO WAY KEIICHI COULD COMPREHEND THAT HIS INSOMNIA...
...WAS SIMPLY CAUSED BY THE INGESTION OF TWENTY CUPS OF TEA.
THE NEXT DAY
HEY, IF OUR CLUB DOESN'T GET SOME MORE MEMBERS BY NEXT YEAR...
...THEY'RE GONNA AX OUR FUND-ING!
Skrnch Skrnch
NO WAY! NOT AFTER WE BOUGHT ALL THAT NEW GEAR?
IT'S BEEN HARD ENOUGH JUST STARTING A GIRLS' SOFT-BALL TEAM AT AN ENGI-NEERING SCHOOL...
HEY, MEGUMI!!

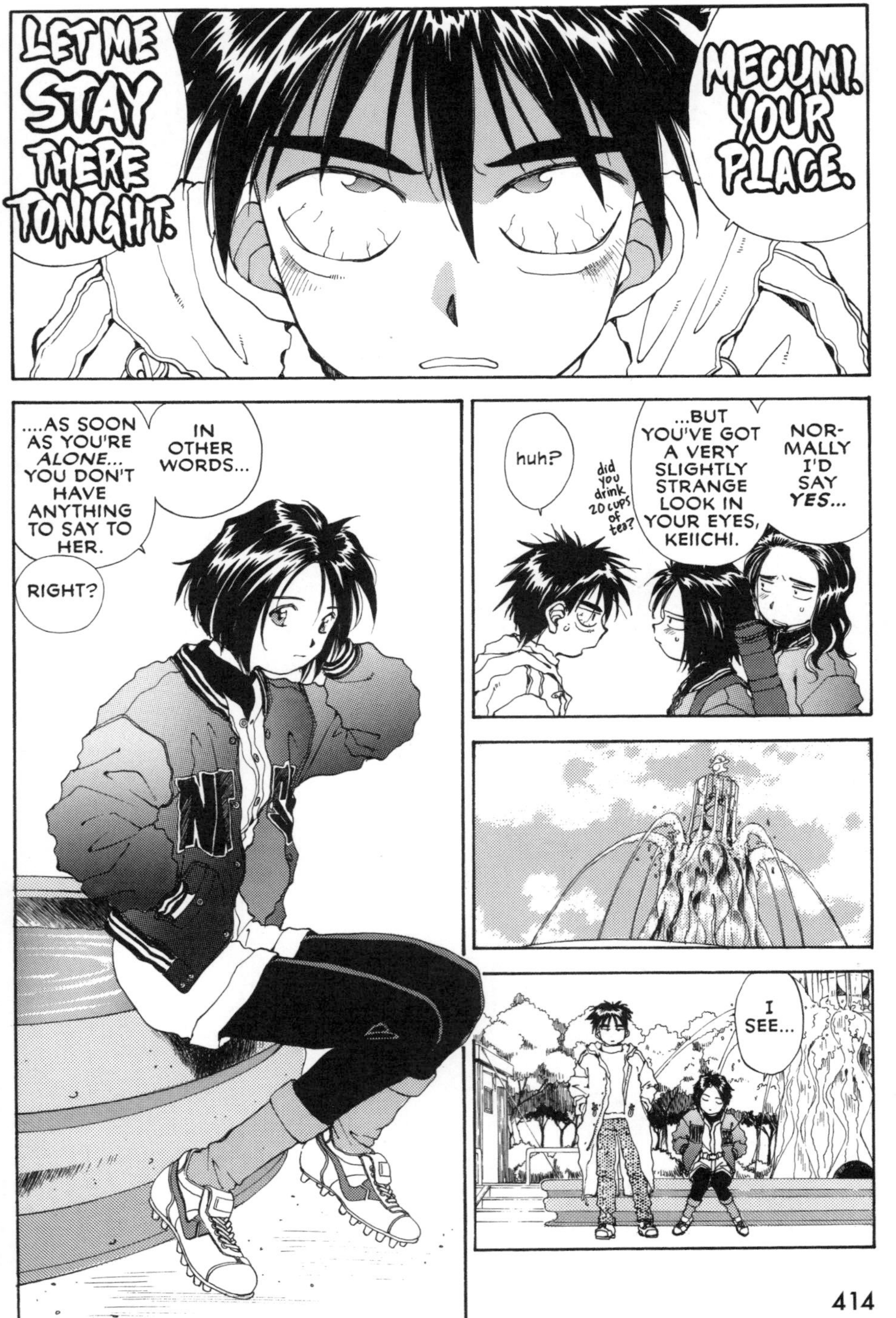
MEGUMI. YOUR PLACE.
LET ME STAY THERE TONIGHT.
NOR-MALLY I'D SAY YES...
...BUT YOU'VE GOT A VERY SLIGHTLY STRANGE LOOK IN YOUR EYES, KEIICHI.
did you drink 20 cups of tea?
huh?
I SEE...
IN OTHER WORDS...
....AS SOON AS YOU'RE ALONE... YOU DON'T HAVE ANYTHING TO SAY TO HER.
RIGHT?

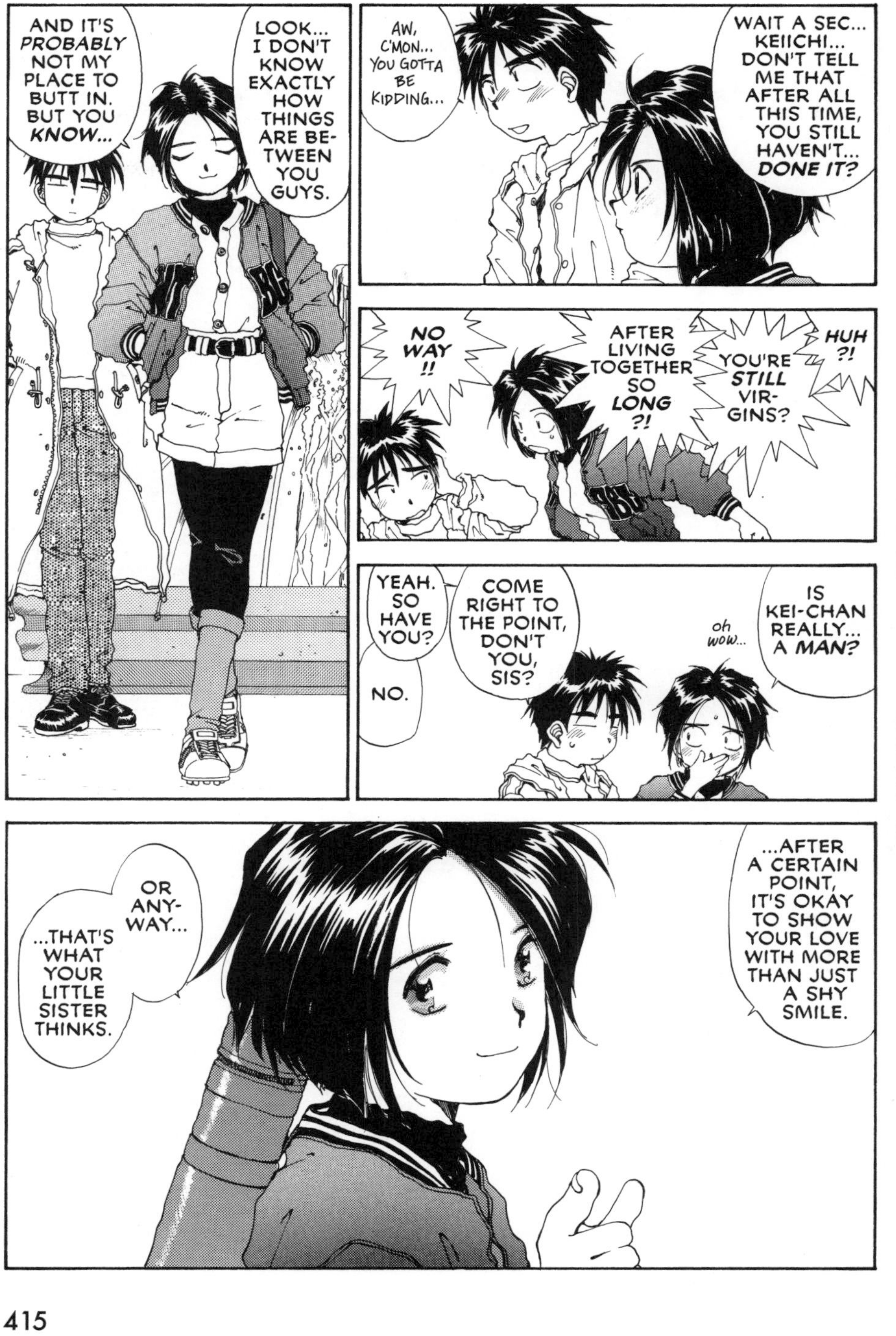
WAIT A SEC... KEIICHI... DON'T TELL ME THAT AFTER ALL THIS TIME, YOU STILL HAVEN'T... DONE IT?
AW, C'MON... YOU GOTTA BE KIDDING...
HUH?!
YOU'RE STILL VIR-GINS?
AFTER LIVING TOGETHER SO LONG?!
NO WAY!!
IS KEI-CHAN REALLY... A MAN?
oh wow...
COME RIGHT TO THE POINT, DON'T YOU, SIS?
YEAH. SO HAVE YOU?
NO.
LOOK... I DON'T KNOW EXACTLY HOW THINGS ARE BE-TWEEN YOU GUYS.
AND IT'S PROBABLY NOT MY PLACE TO BUTT IN. BUT YOU KNOW...
...AFTER A CERTAIN POINT, IT'S OKAY TO SHOW YOUR LOVE WITH MORE THAN JUST A SHY SMILE.
OR ANY-WAY...
...THAT'S WHAT YOUR LITTLE SISTER THINKS.

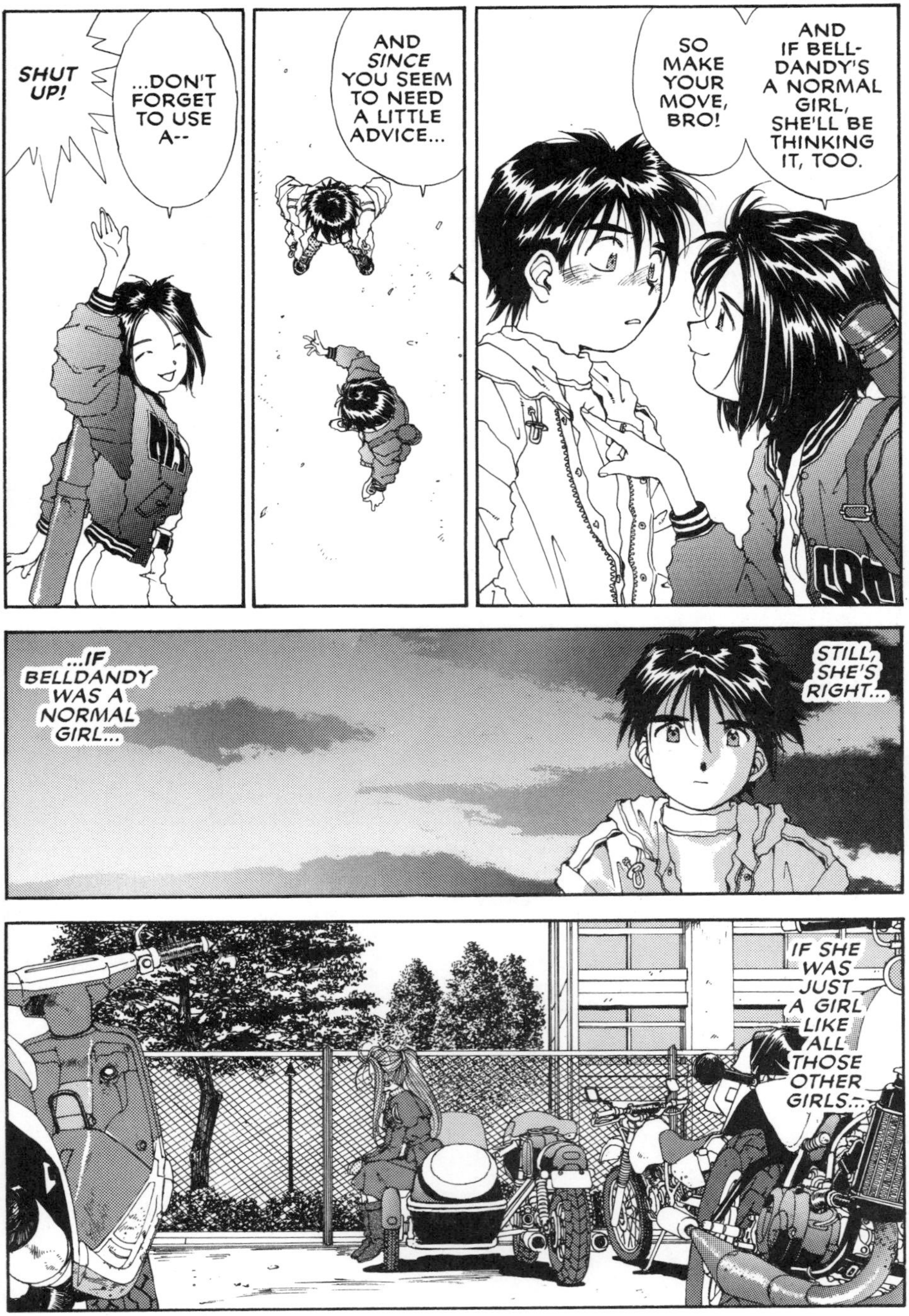
AND IF BELL-DANDY'S A NORMAL GIRL, SHE'LL BE THINKING IT, TOO.
SO MAKE YOUR MOVE, BRO!
AND *SINCE* YOU SEEM TO NEED A LITTLE ADVICE...
...DON'T FORGET TO USE A--
SHUT UP!
STILL, SHE'S RIGHT...
...IF BELLDANDY WAS A NORMAL GIRL...
IF SHE WAS JUST A GIRL LIKE ALL THOSE OTHER GIRLS...

BELL-DANDY...?

NO, BELL-DANDY...

...BE STRONG.

YOU JUST HAVE TO HOLD OUT FOR TWO MORE NIGHTS...

URD WILL BE BACK THE DAY AFTER TOMOR-ROW.

I'M SORRY. I WAS... THINKING.

REALLY? YOUR FACE IS A LITTLE... RED...

OH...

ARE YOU OKAY? YOU DIDN'T SEEM TO HEAR ME...

WHOA!

OH ?!

I'M SORRY. I...I STUMBLED...

THOSE EYES... SO FULL OF LONGING...

THIS FAINTLY BLUSHING FACE...

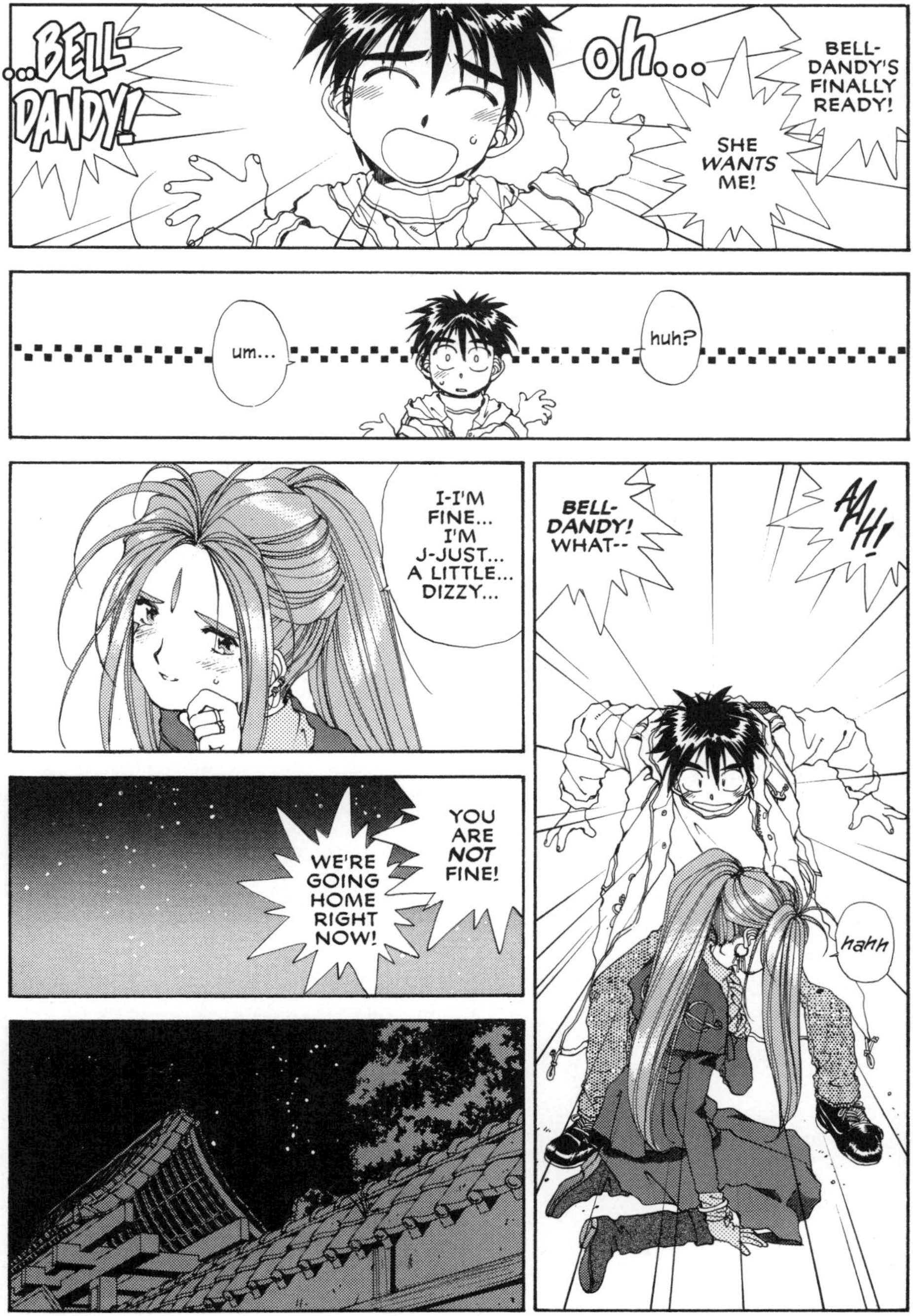
BELL-DANDY'S FINALLY READY!
oh...
SHE *WANTS* ME!
...BELL-DANDY!
huh?
um...
AAH!
BELL-DANDY! WHAT--
hahh
I-I'M FINE... I'M J-JUST... A LITTLE... DIZZY...
YOU ARE *NOT* FINE!
WE'RE GOING HOME RIGHT NOW!

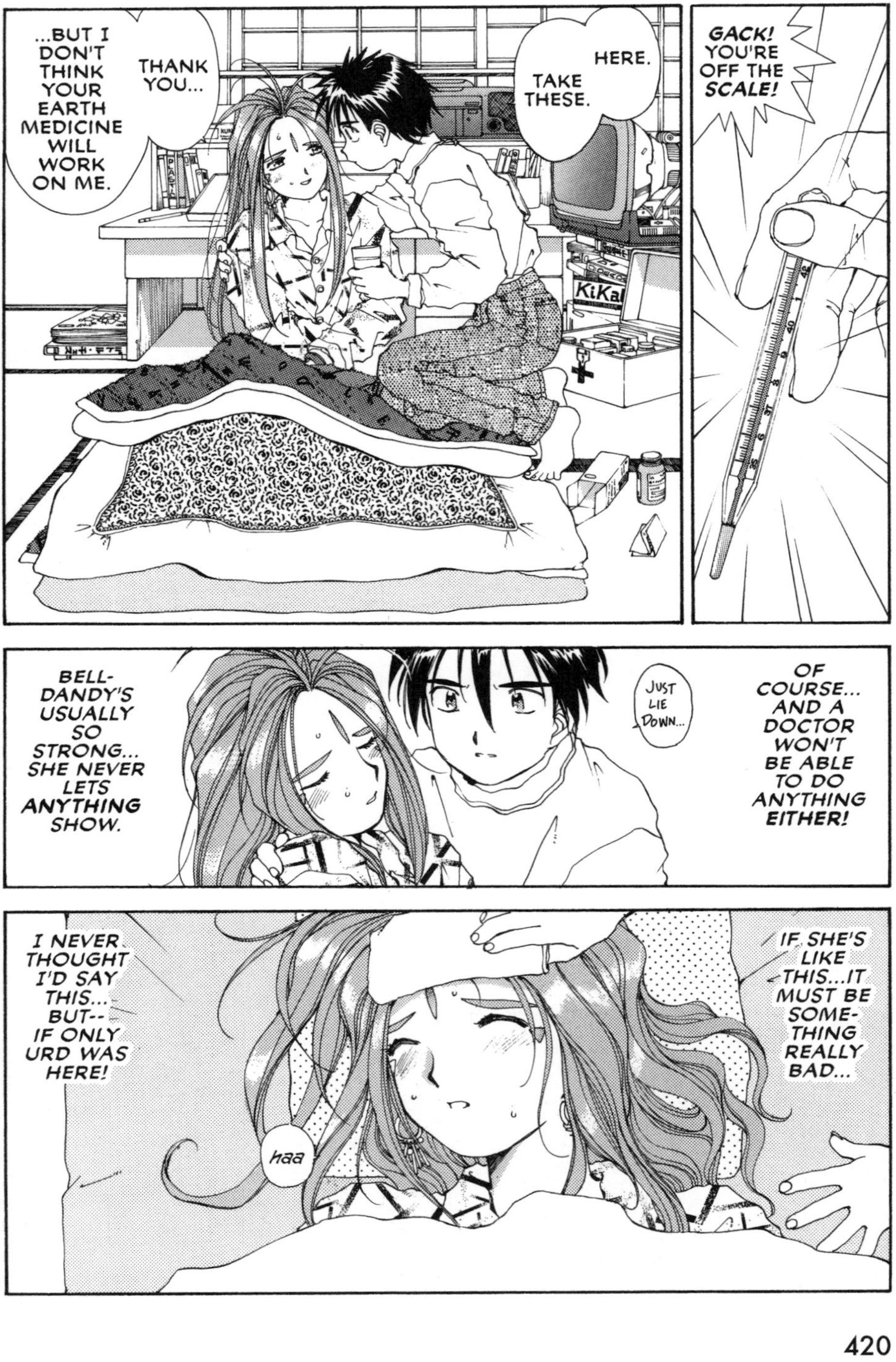
GACK! YOU'RE OFF THE SCALE!
HERE.
TAKE THESE.
THANK YOU...
...BUT I DON'T THINK YOUR EARTH MEDICINE WILL WORK ON ME.
OF COURSE... AND A DOCTOR WON'T BE ABLE TO DO ANYTHING EITHER!
JUST LIE DOWN...
BELL-DANDY'S USUALLY SO STRONG... SHE NEVER LETS ANYTHING SHOW.
IF SHE'S LIKE THIS...IT MUST BE SOME-THING REALLY BAD...
haa
I NEVER THOUGHT I'D SAY THIS... BUT-- IF ONLY URD WAS HERE!

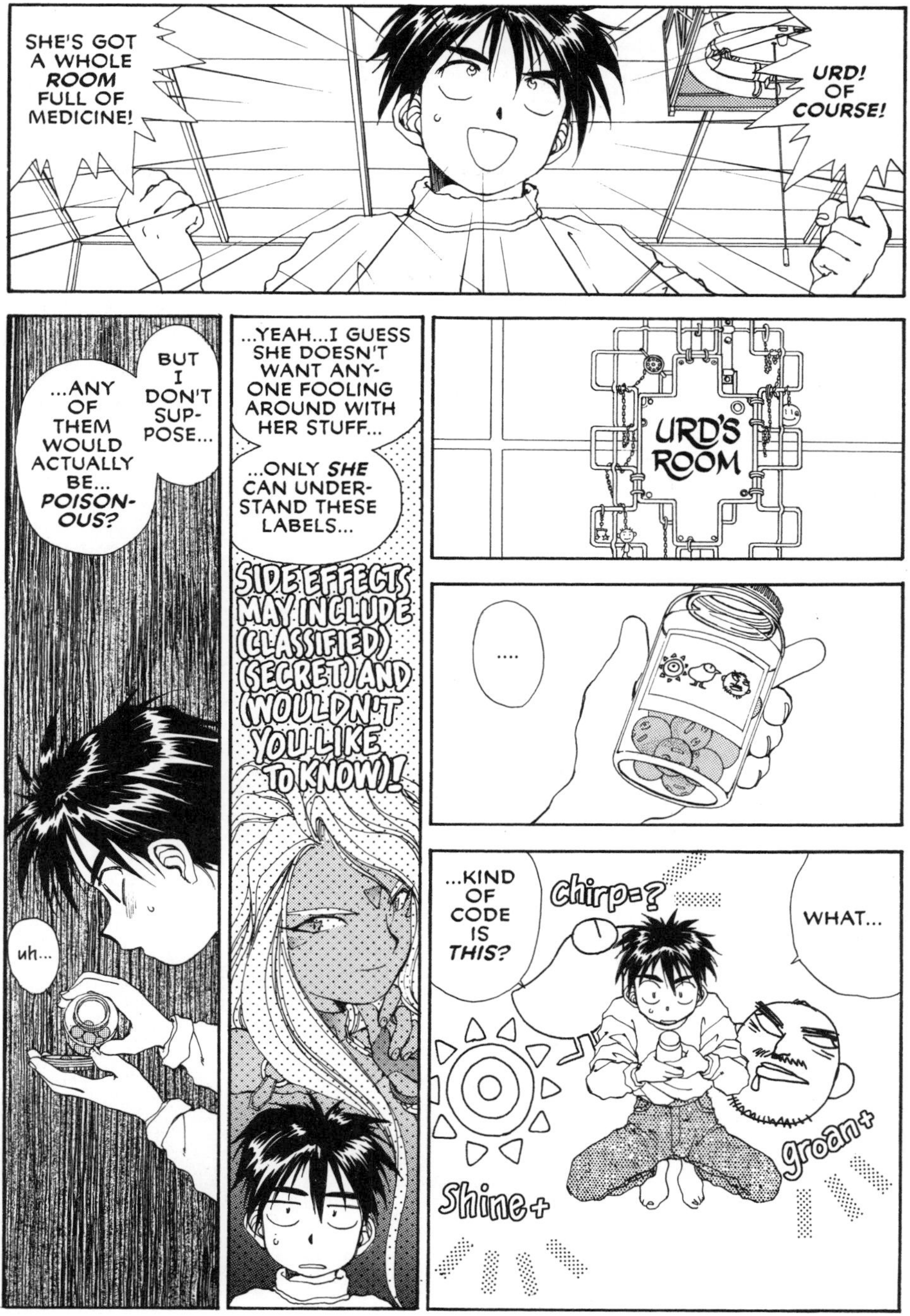
URD! OF COURSE!
SHE'S GOT A WHOLE ROOM FULL OF MEDICINE!
URD'S ROOM
....
WHAT...
...KIND OF CODE IS THIS?
Chirp=?
groan+
Shine+
...YEAH...I GUESS SHE DOESN'T WANT ANY-ONE FOOLING AROUND WITH HER STUFF...
...ONLY SHE CAN UNDER-STAND THESE LABELS...
SIDE EFFECTS MAY INCLUDE (CLASSIFIED) (SECRET) AND (WOULDN'T YOU LIKE TO KNOW)!
BUT I DON'T SUP-POSE...
...ANY OF THEM WOULD ACTUALLY BE... POISON-OUS?
uh...

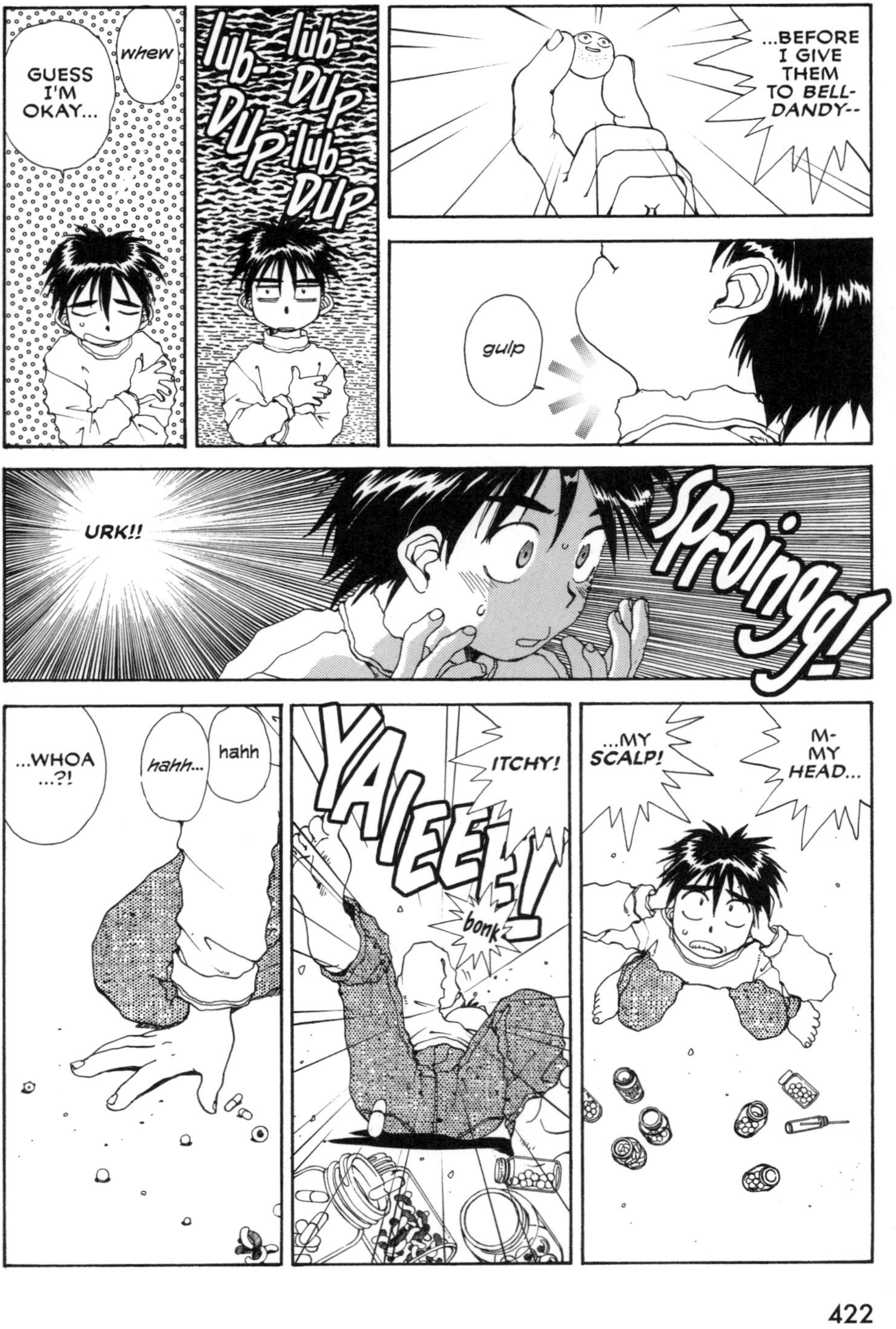
...BEFORE I GIVE THEM TO BELL-DANDY--
gulp
lub-DUP lub-DUP
lub-DUP
whew
GUESS I'M OKAY...
Sproingg!
URK!!
M-MY HEAD...
...MY SCALP!
ITCHY!
YAIEEE!!
bonk
hahh
hahh...
...WHOA ...?!

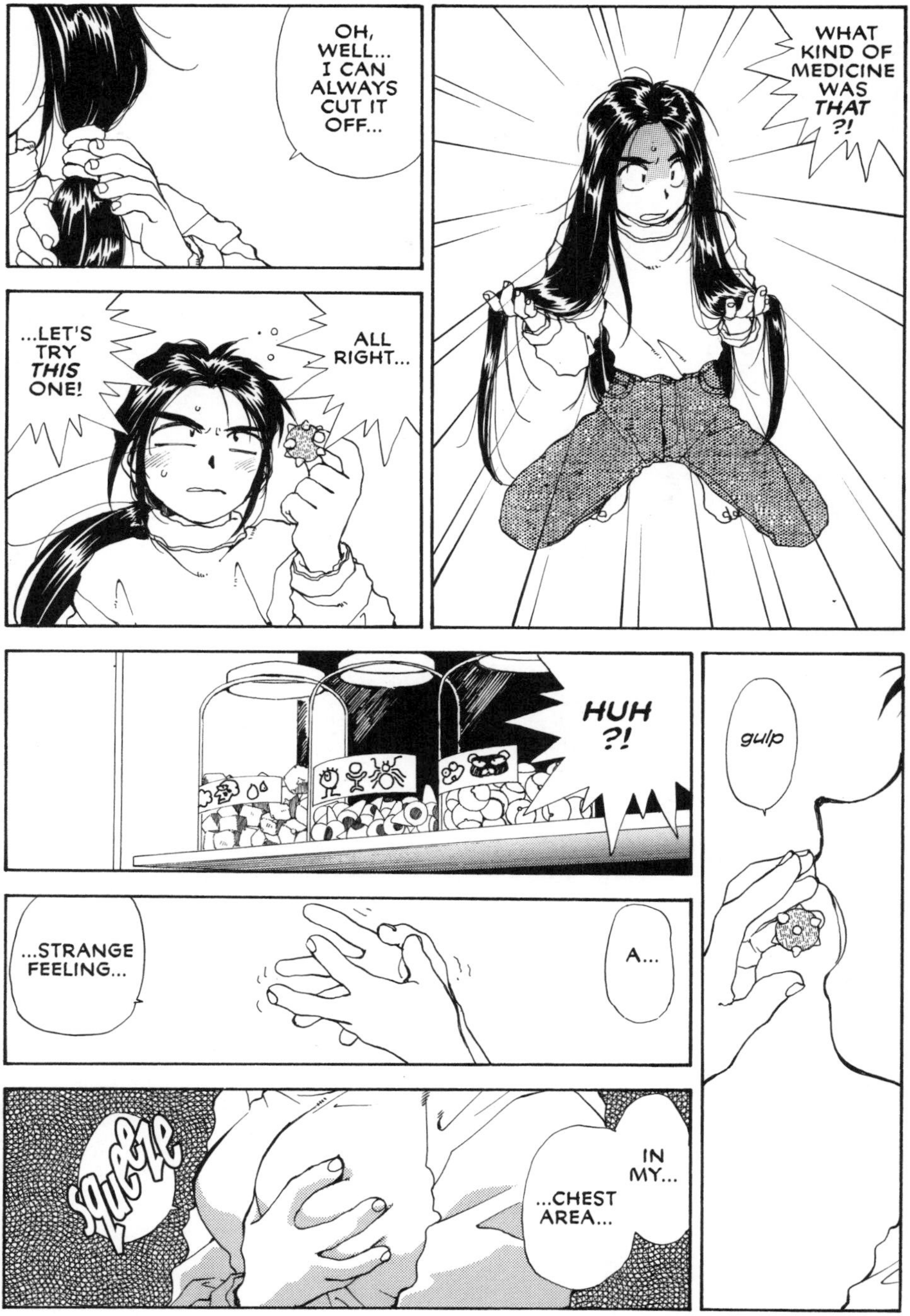
WHAT KIND OF MEDICINE WAS THAT?!
OH, WELL... I CAN ALWAYS CUT IT OFF...
ALL RIGHT...
...LET'S TRY THIS ONE!
gulp
HUH?!
A...
...STRANGE FEELING...
IN MY...
...CHEST AREA...
squeeze

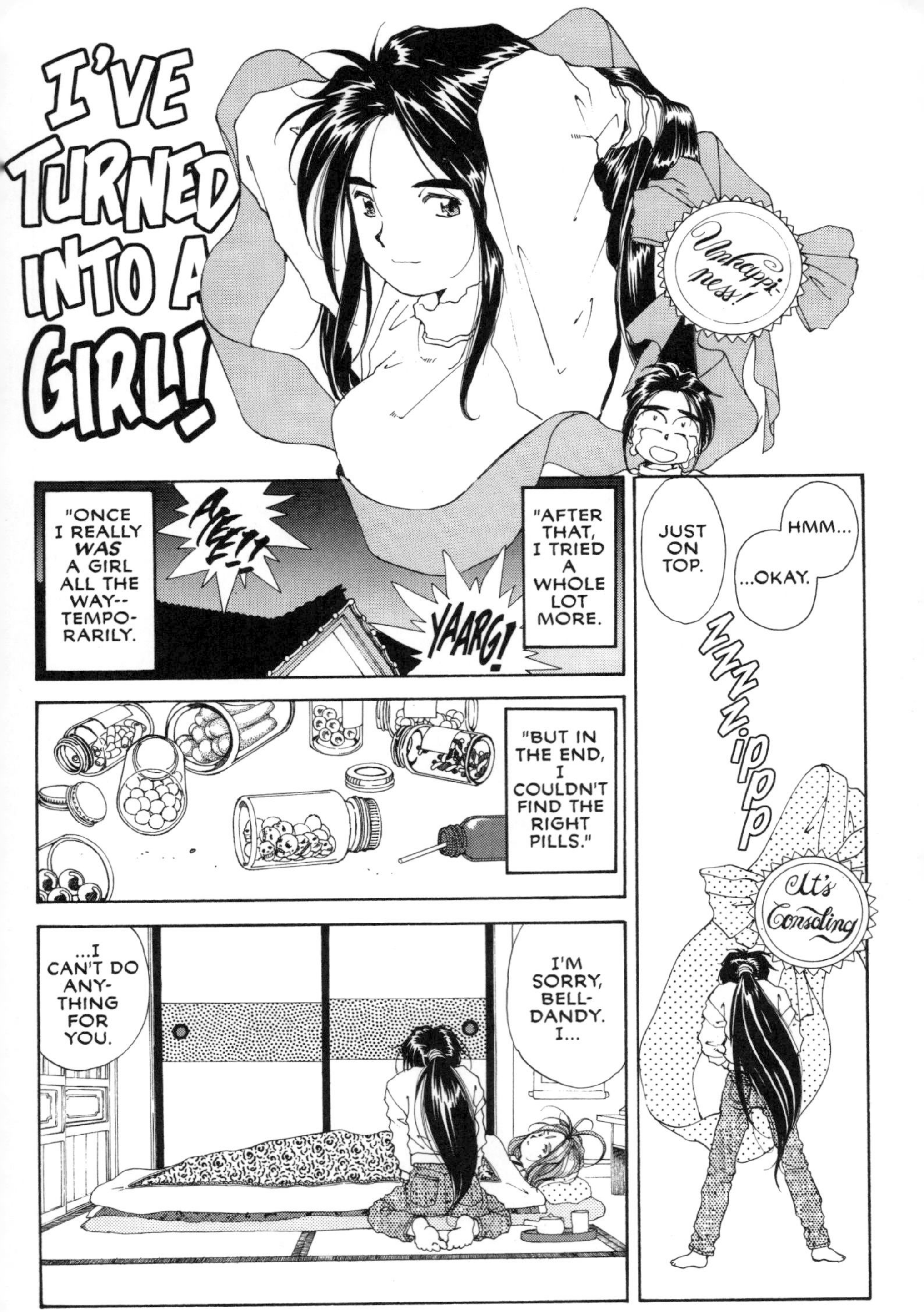

I'VE TURNED INTO A GIRL!
Unhappiness!
"ONCE I REALLY WAS A GIRL ALL THE WAY--TEMPORARILY.
AIEE!!
YAARG!
"AFTER THAT, I TRIED A WHOLE LOT MORE.
"BUT IN THE END, I COULDN'T FIND THE RIGHT PILLS."
I'M SORRY, BELLDANDY. I...
...I CAN'T DO ANYTHING FOR YOU.
HMM...
...OKAY.
JUST ON TOP.
NNNNipp
It's Consoling

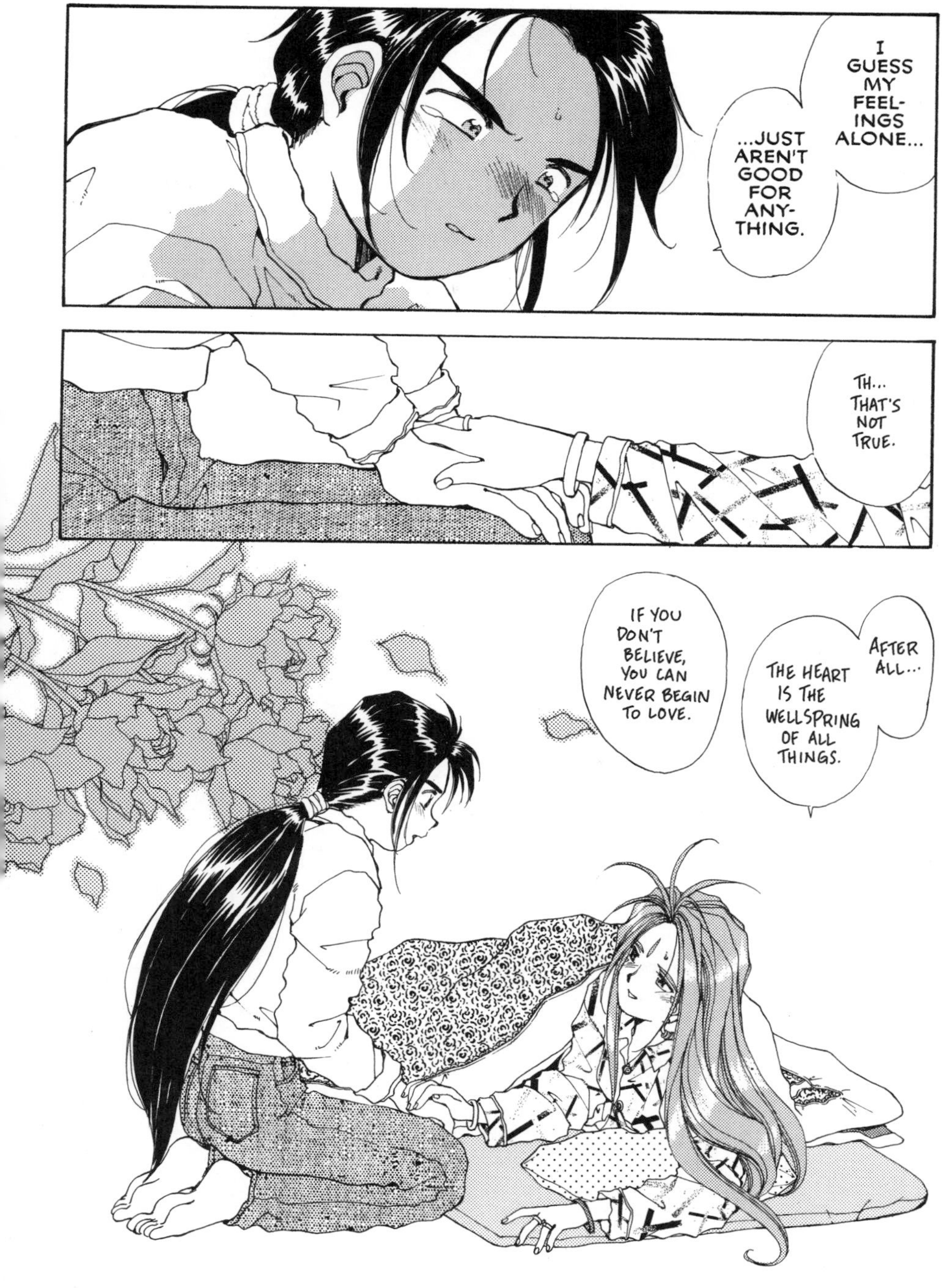
I GUESS MY FEEL-INGS ALONE...
...JUST AREN'T GOOD FOR ANY-THING.
TH... THAT'S NOT TRUE.
AFTER ALL... THE HEART IS THE WELLSPRING OF ALL THINGS.
IF YOU DON'T BELIEVE, YOU CAN NEVER BEGIN TO LOVE.

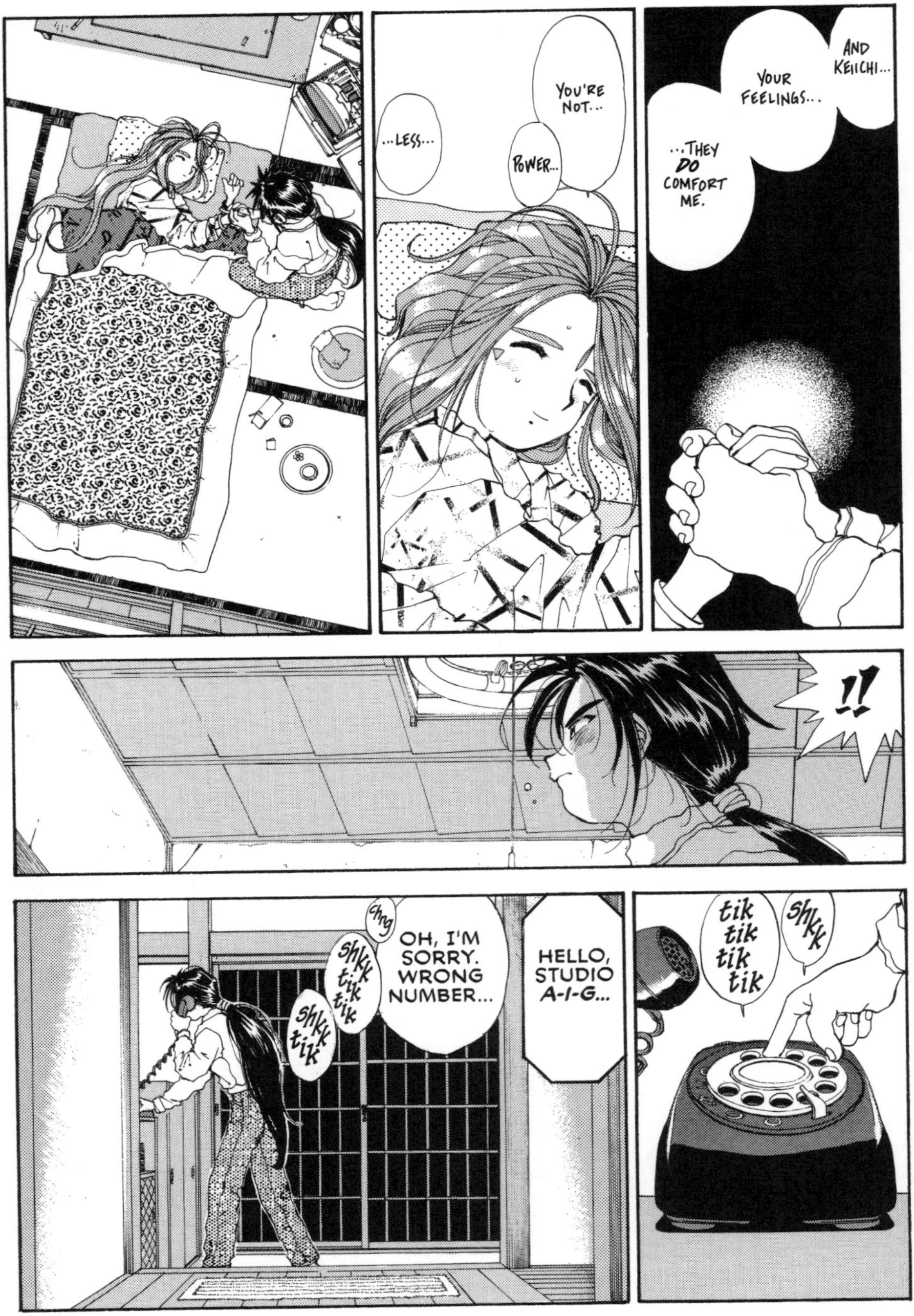
AND KEIICHI...
YOUR FEELINGS...
...THEY DO COMFORT ME.
YOU'RE NOT...
POWER...
...LESS...
!!
SHKK
tik tik tik tik
HELLO, STUDIO A-I-G...
chng
OH, I'M SORRY. WRONG NUMBER...
shkk tik tik
shkk tik

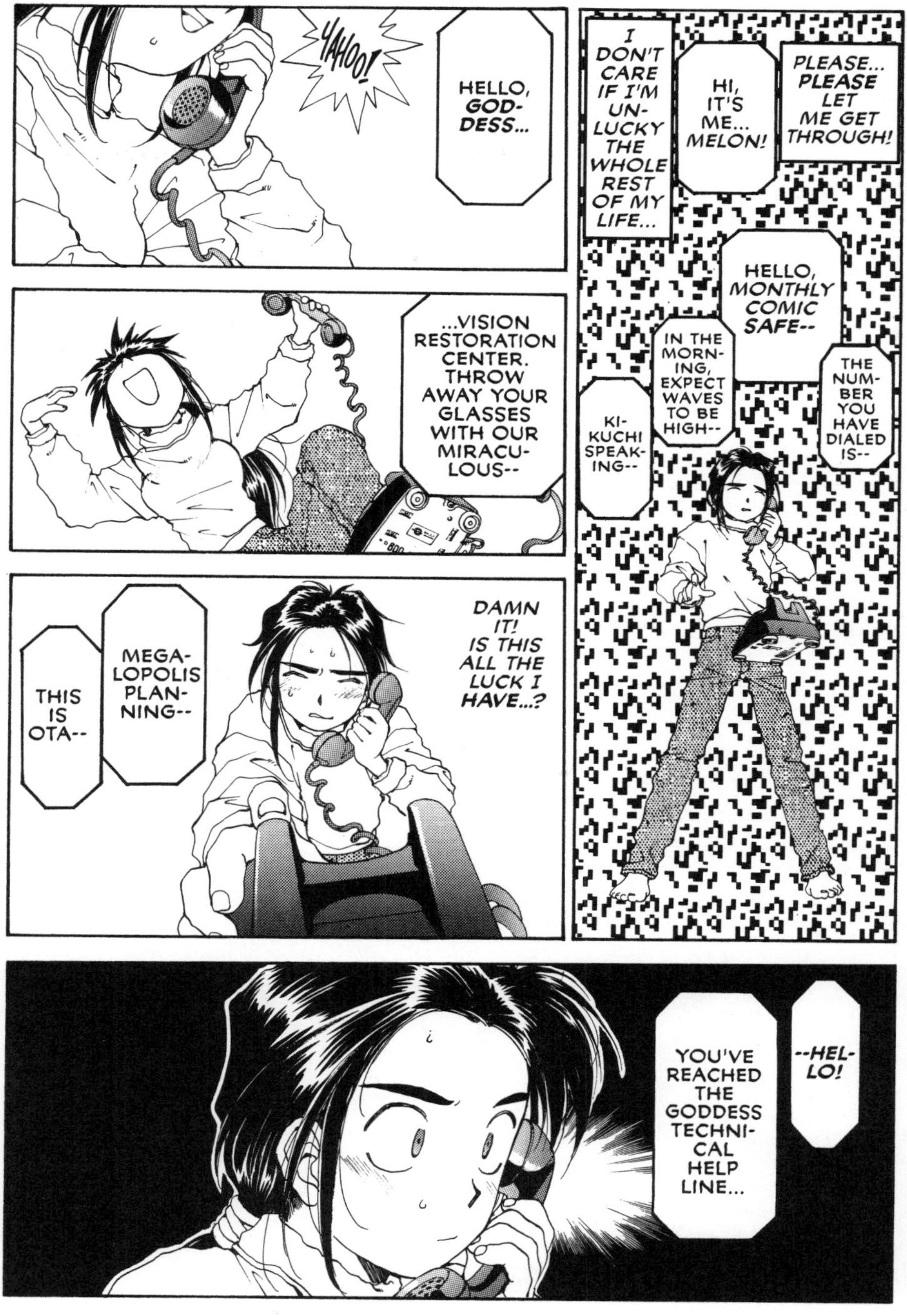
PLEASE... PLEASE LET ME GET THROUGH!
HI, IT'S ME... MELON!
I DON'T CARE IF I'M UNLUCKY THE WHOLE REST OF MY LIFE...
HELLO, MONTHLY COMIC SAFE--
THE NUMBER YOU HAVE DIALED IS--
IN THE MORNING, EXPECT WAVES TO BE HIGH--
KIKUCHI SPEAKING--
HELLO, GODDESS...
YAHOO!
...VISION RESTORATION CENTER. THROW AWAY YOUR GLASSES WITH OUR MIRACULOUS--
DAMN IT! IS THIS ALL THE LUCK I HAVE...?
MEGALOPOLIS PLANNING--
THIS IS OTA--
--HELLO!
YOU'VE REACHED THE GODDESS TECHNICAL HELP LINE...

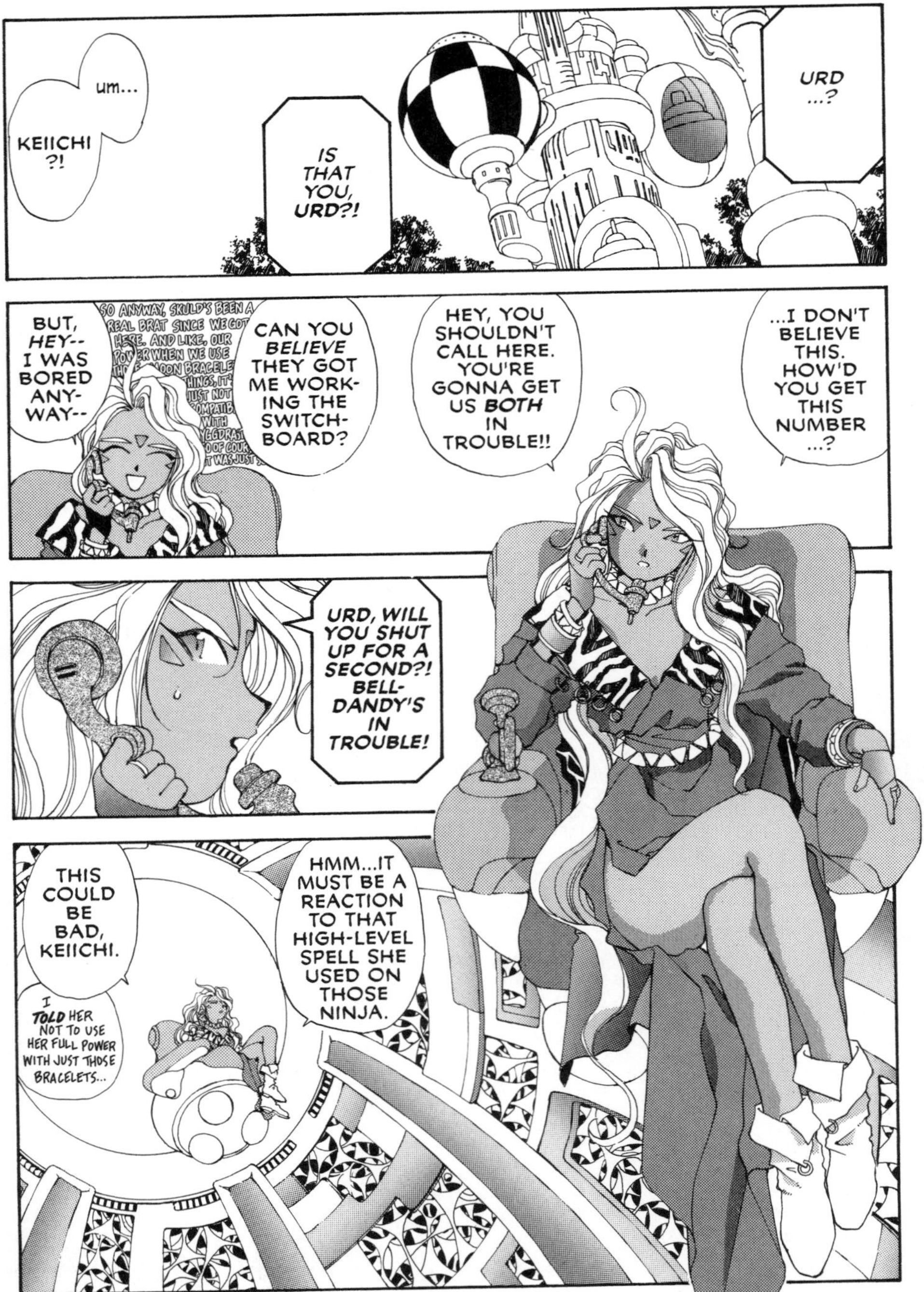
URD ...?
IS THAT YOU, URD?!
um... KEIICHI ?!
...I DON'T BELIEVE THIS. HOW'D YOU GET THIS NUMBER ...?
HEY, YOU SHOULDN'T CALL HERE. YOU'RE GONNA GET US *BOTH* IN TROUBLE!!
CAN YOU *BELIEVE* THEY GOT ME WORKING THE SWITCHBOARD?
SO ANYWAY, SKULD'S BEEN A REAL BRAT SINCE WE GOT HERE. AND LIKE, OUR POWER WHEN WE USE
BUT, *HEY*-- I WAS BORED ANYWAY--
URD, WILL YOU SHUT UP FOR A SECOND?! BELLDANDY'S IN TROUBLE!
HMM...IT MUST BE A REACTION TO THAT HIGH-LEVEL SPELL SHE USED ON THOSE NINJA.
THIS COULD BE BAD, KEIICHI.
I *TOLD* HER NOT TO USE HER FULL POWER WITH JUST THOSE BRACELETS...

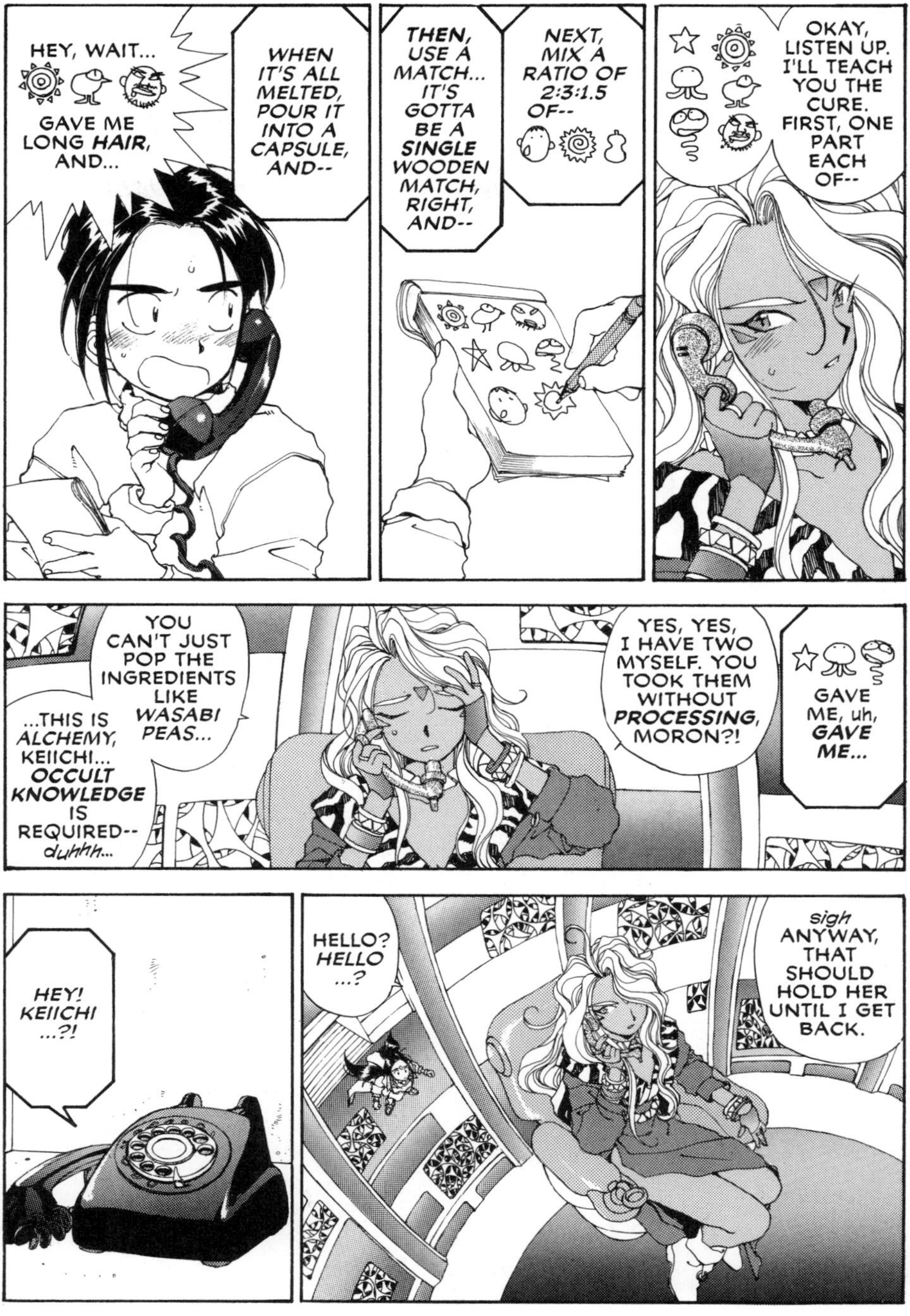
OKAY, LISTEN UP. I'LL TEACH YOU THE CURE. FIRST, ONE PART EACH OF--
NEXT, MIX A RATIO OF 2:3:1.5 OF--
THEN, USE A MATCH... IT'S GOTTA BE A SINGLE WOODEN MATCH, RIGHT, AND--
WHEN IT'S ALL MELTED, POUR IT INTO A CAPSULE, AND--
HEY, WAIT...
GAVE ME LONG HAIR, AND...
GAVE ME, uh, GAVE ME...
YES, YES, I HAVE TWO MYSELF. YOU TOOK THEM WITHOUT PROCESSING, MORON?!
YOU CAN'T JUST POP THE INGREDIENTS LIKE WASABI PEAS...
...THIS IS ALCHEMY, KEIICHI... OCCULT KNOWLEDGE IS REQUIRED-- duhhh...
sigh ANYWAY, THAT SHOULD HOLD HER UNTIL I GET BACK.
HELLO? HELLO ...?
HEY! KEIICHI ...?!

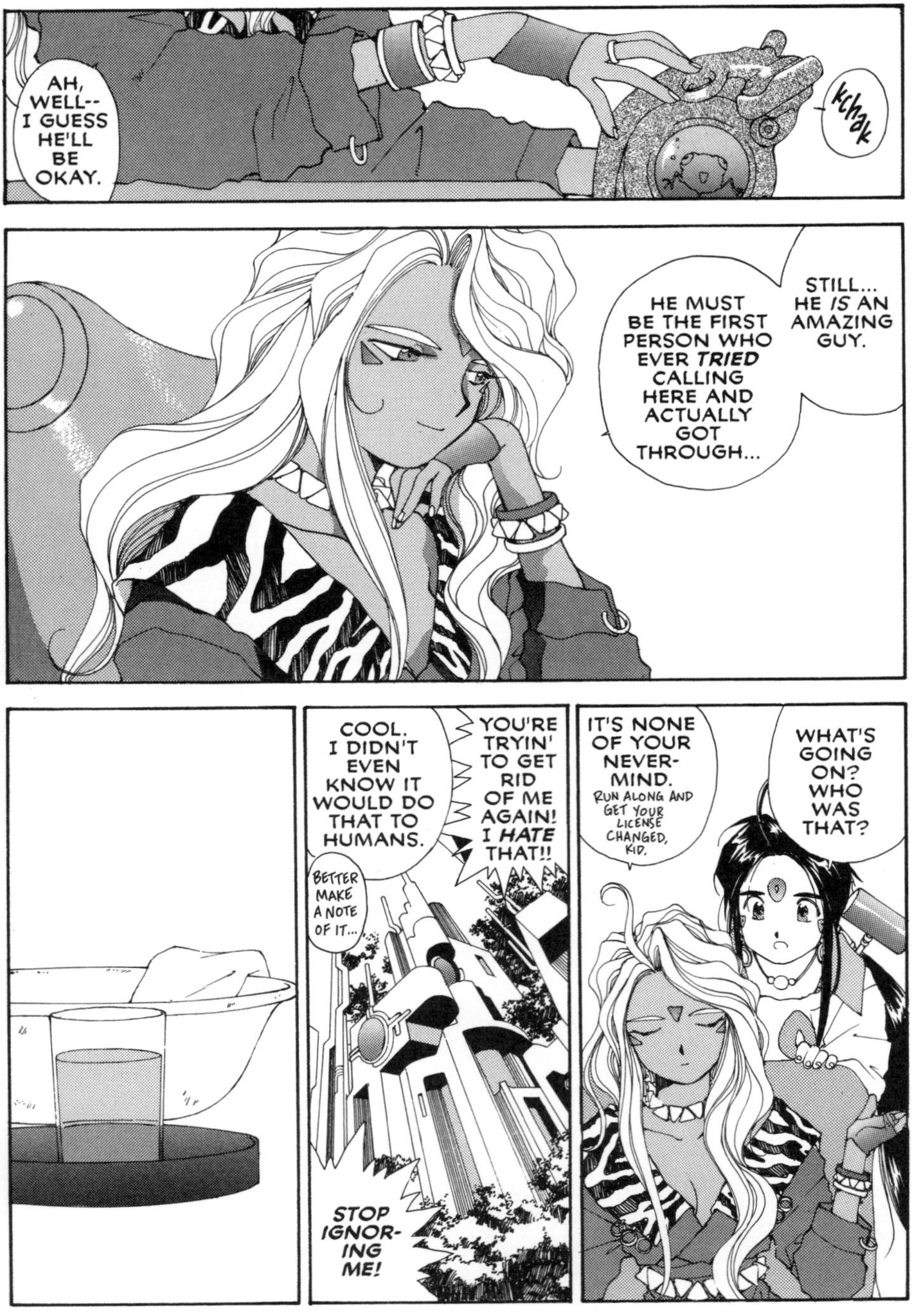
kchak
AH, WELL-- I GUESS HE'LL BE OKAY.
STILL... HE *IS* AN AMAZING GUY.
HE MUST BE THE FIRST PERSON WHO EVER ***TRIED*** CALLING HERE AND ACTUALLY GOT THROUGH...
WHAT'S GOING ON? WHO WAS THAT?
IT'S NONE OF YOUR NEVER-MIND.
RUN ALONG AND GET YOUR LICENSE CHANGED, KID.
YOU'RE TRYIN' TO GET RID OF ME AGAIN! I ***HATE*** THAT!!
COOL. I DIDN'T EVEN KNOW IT WOULD DO THAT TO HUMANS.
BETTER MAKE A NOTE OF IT...
STOP IGNORING ME!

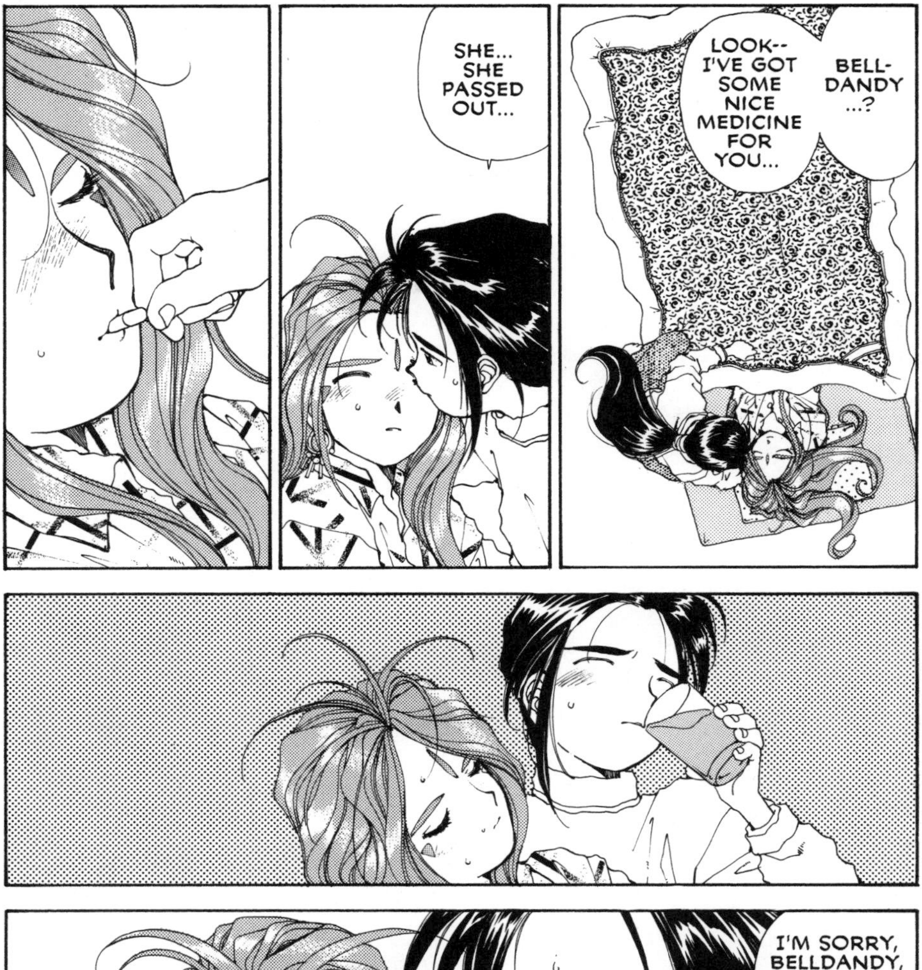
BELL-DANDY ...?
LOOK-- I'VE GOT SOME NICE MEDICINE FOR YOU...
SHE... SHE PASSED OUT...
I'M SORRY, BELLDANDY, BUT I'VE GOT TO GIVE IT TO YOU SOME-HOW...
...PLEASE FORGIVE ME!

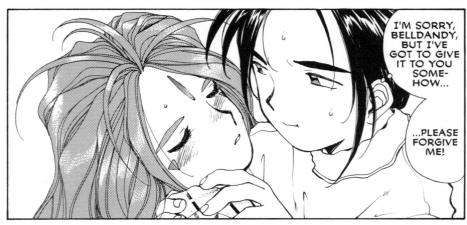

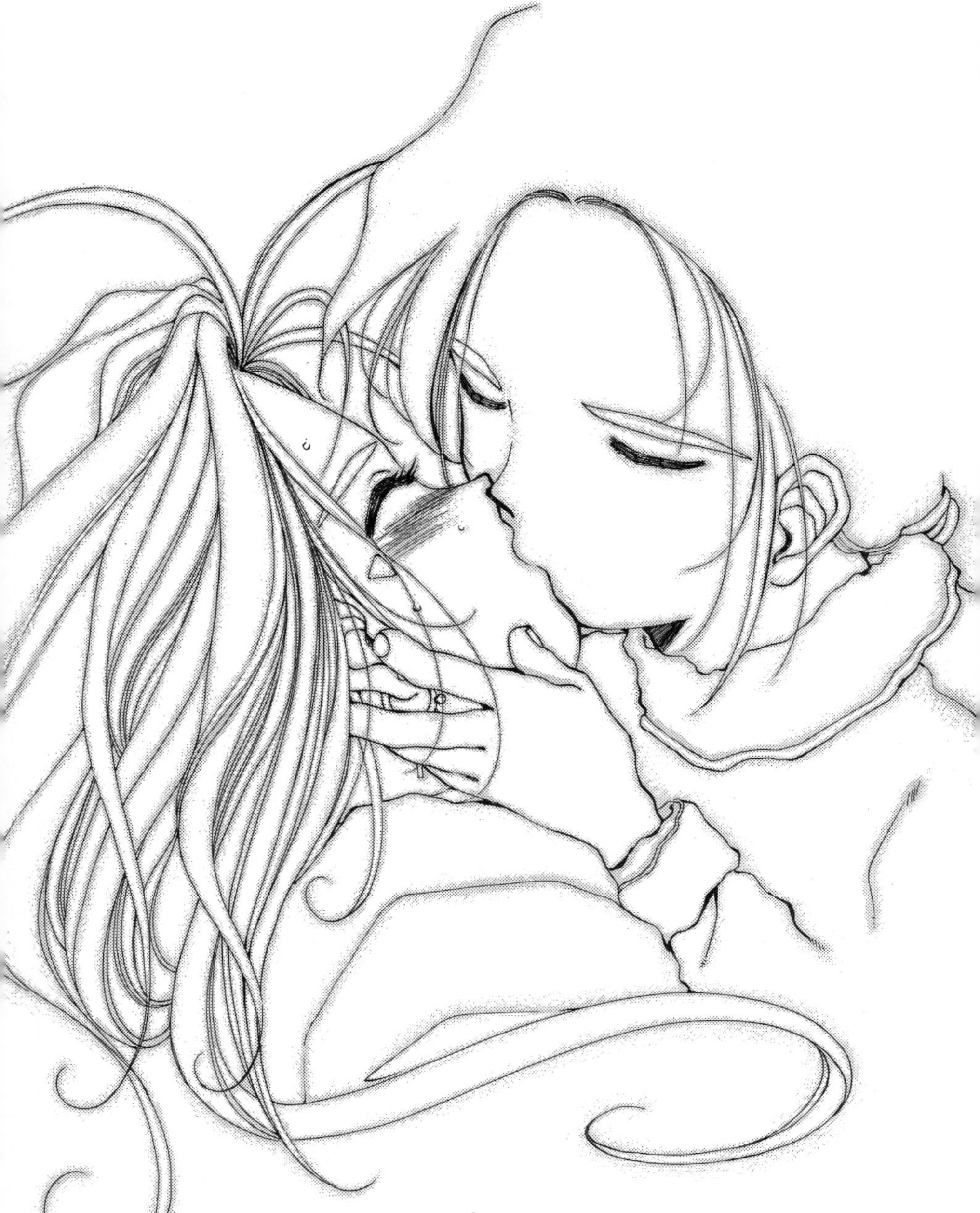

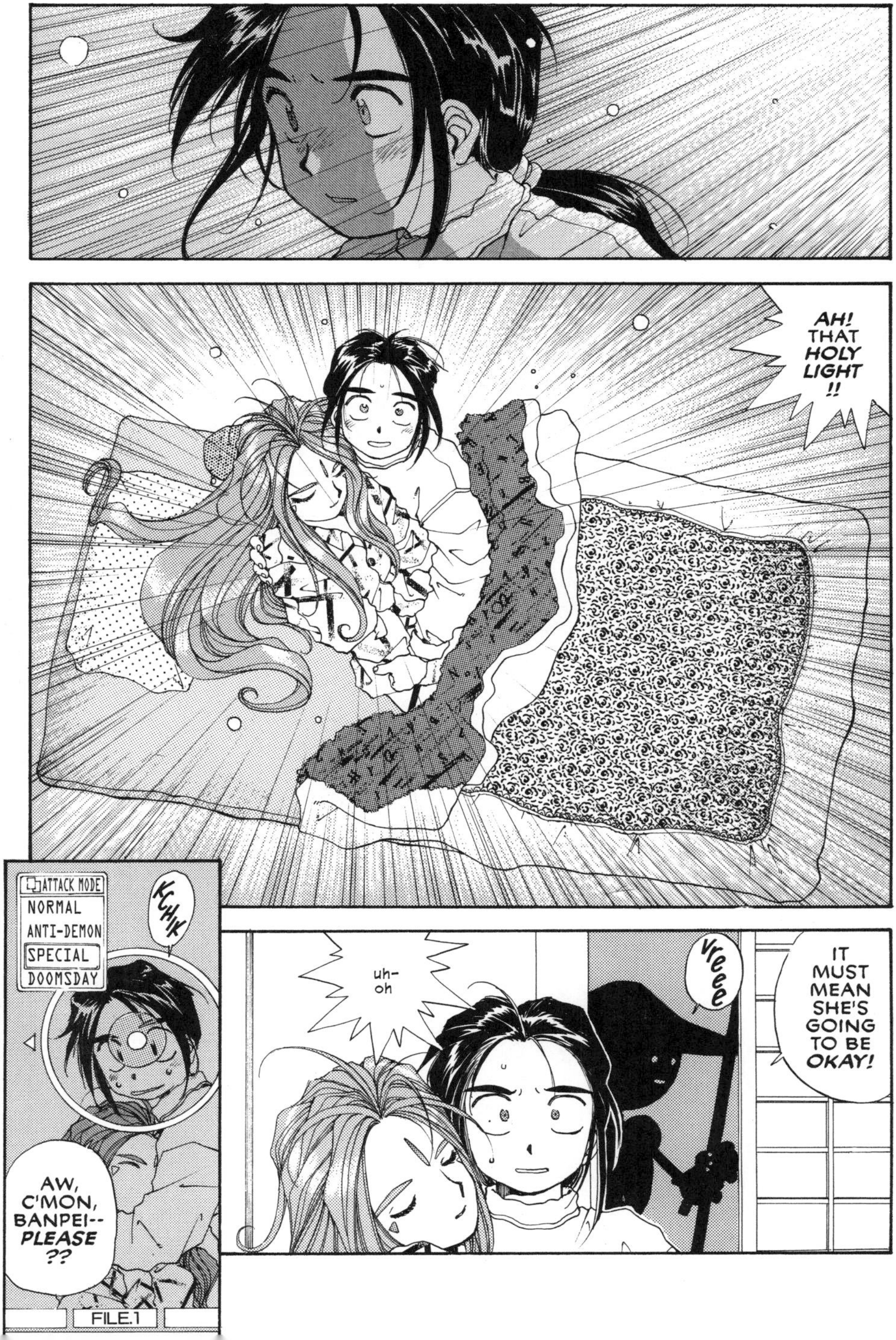

AH! THAT HOLY LIGHT!!
IT MUST MEAN SHE'S GOING TO BE OKAY!
vreee
uh-oh
ATTACK MODE
NORMAL
ANTI-DEMON
SPECIAL
DOOMSDAY
KCHIK
AW, C'MON, BANPEI-- PLEASE??
FILE.1

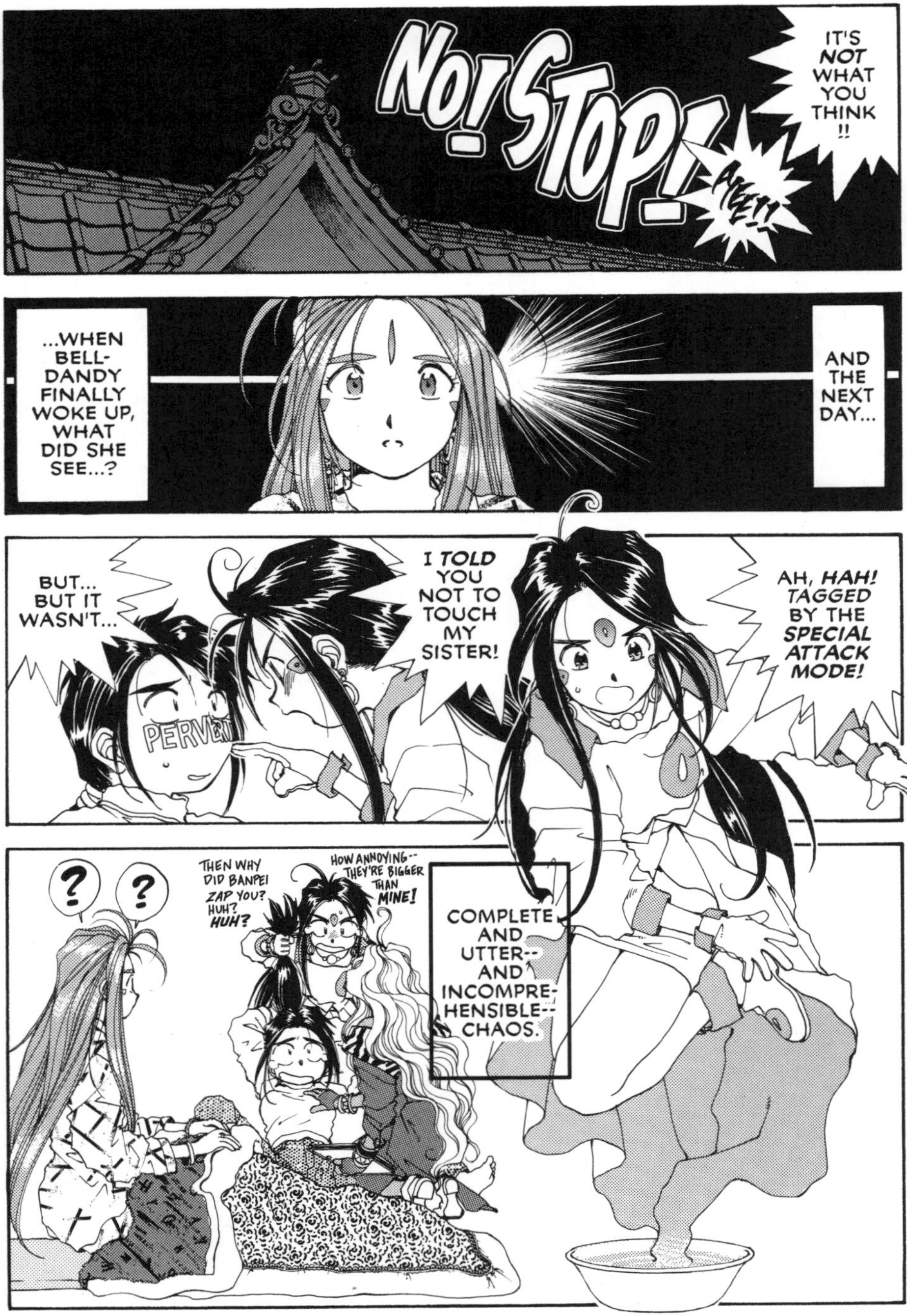
IT'S NOT WHAT YOU THINK!!
NO! STOP!
AEEE!!
AND THE NEXT DAY...
...WHEN BELL-DANDY FINALLY WOKE UP, WHAT DID SHE SEE...?
AH, HAH! TAGGED BY THE SPECIAL ATTACK MODE!
I TOLD YOU NOT TO TOUCH MY SISTER!
BUT... BUT IT WASN'T...
PERVERT
COMPLETE AND UTTER-- AND INCOMPREHENSIBLE-- CHAOS.
HOW ANNOYING-- THEY'RE BIGGER THAN MINE!
THEN WHY DID BANPEI ZAP YOU? HUH? HUH?
?
?

OH MY GODDESS!

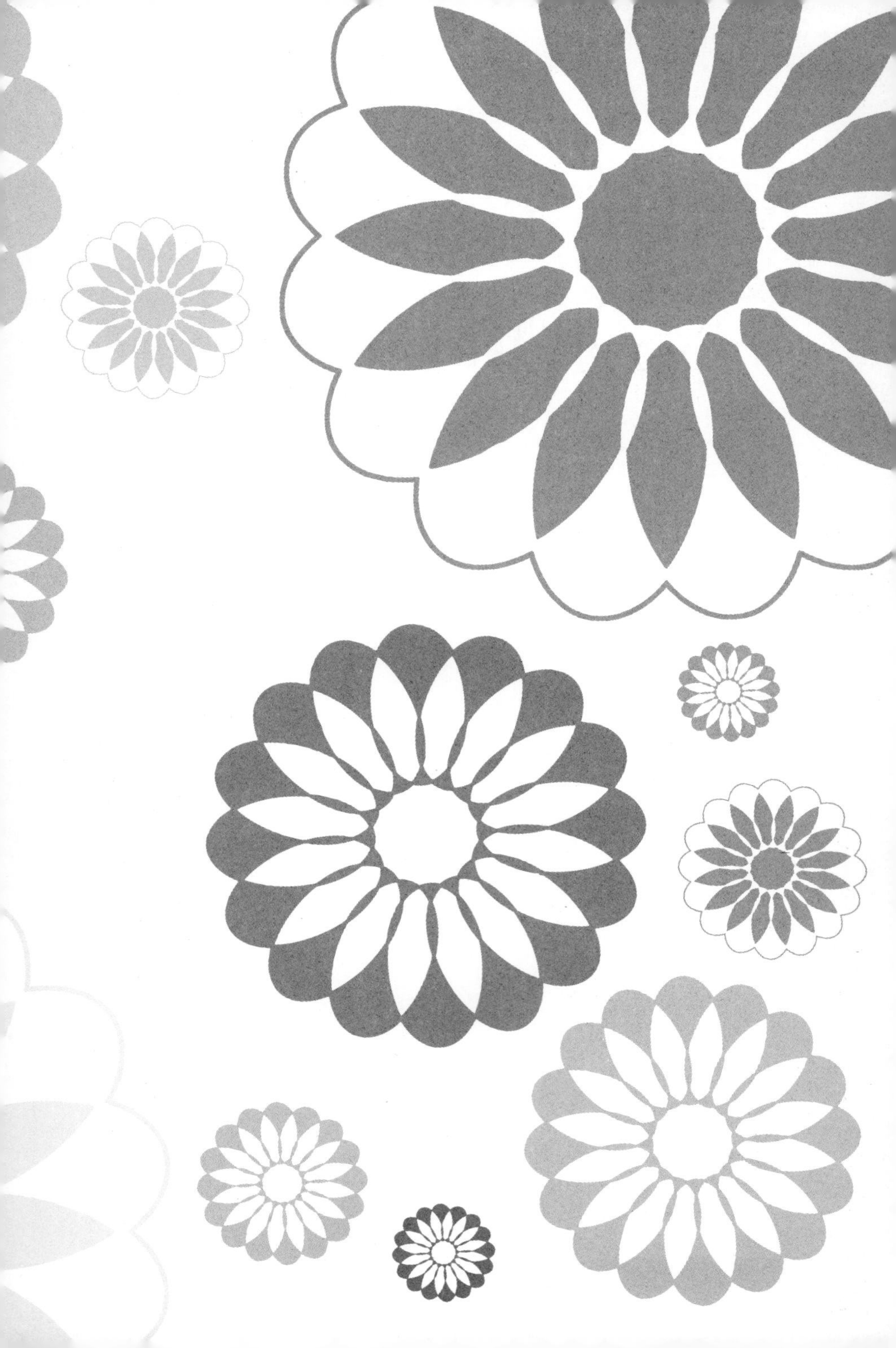

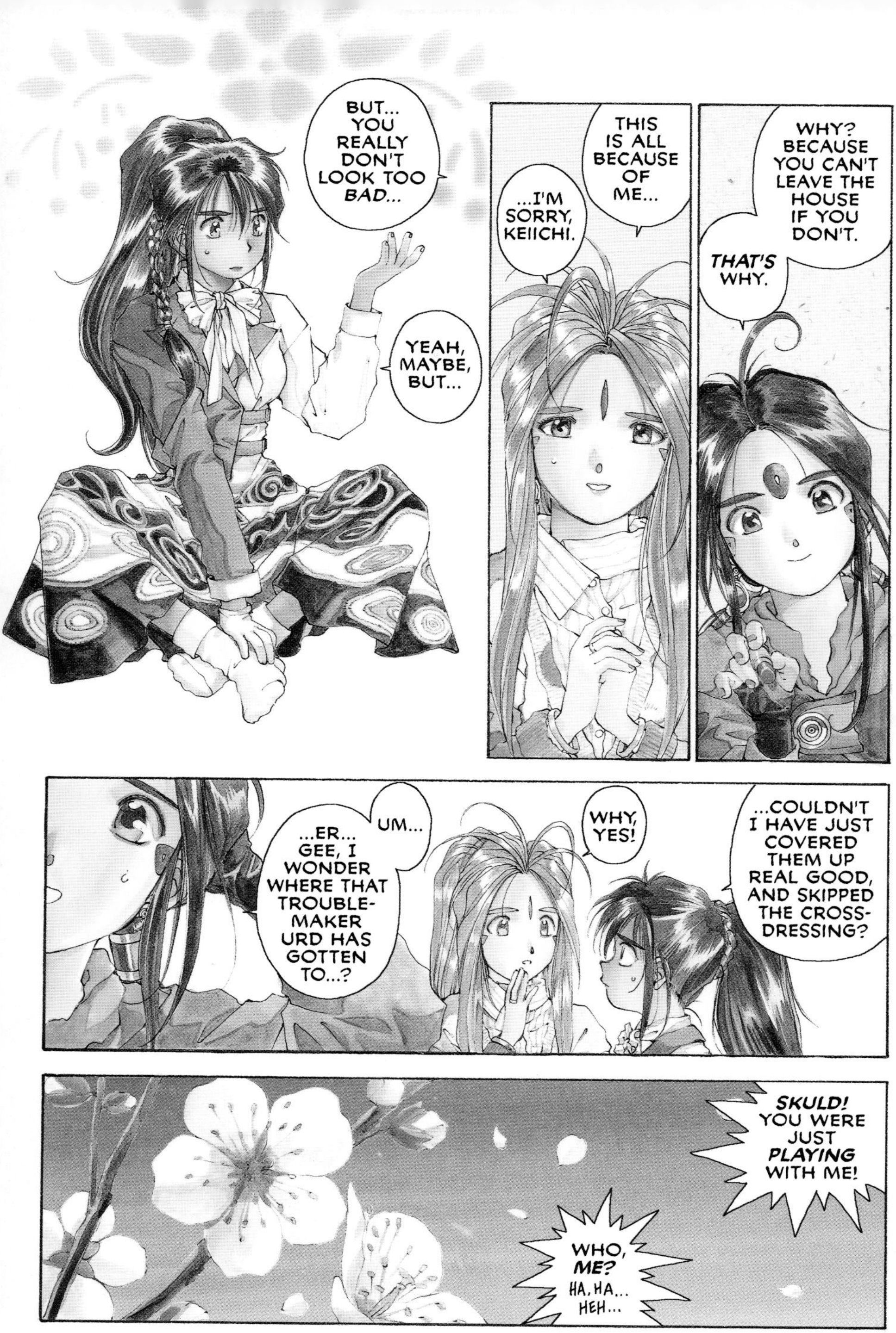
WHY? BECAUSE YOU CAN'T LEAVE THE HOUSE IF YOU DON'T.
THAT'S WHY.
THIS IS ALL BECAUSE OF ME...
...I'M SORRY, KEIICHI.
BUT... YOU REALLY DON'T LOOK TOO BAD...
YEAH, MAYBE, BUT...
...COULDN'T I HAVE JUST COVERED THEM UP REAL GOOD, AND SKIPPED THE CROSS-DRESSING?
WHY, YES!
UM...
...ER... GEE, I WONDER WHERE THAT TROUBLE-MAKER URD HAS GOTTEN TO...?
SKULD! YOU WERE JUST PLAYING WITH ME!
WHO, ME? HA, HA... HEH...

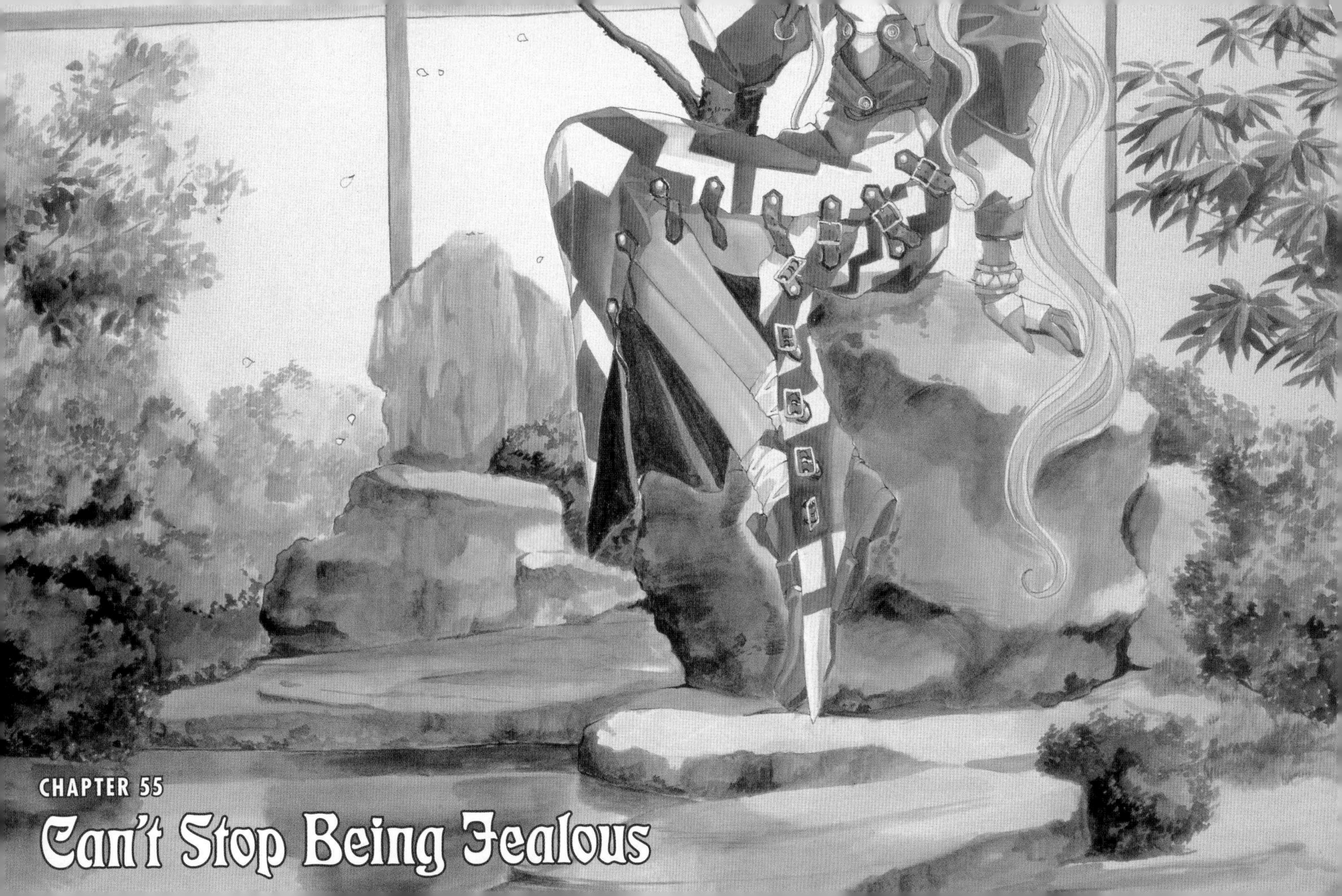
CHAPTER 55
Can't Stop Being Jealous

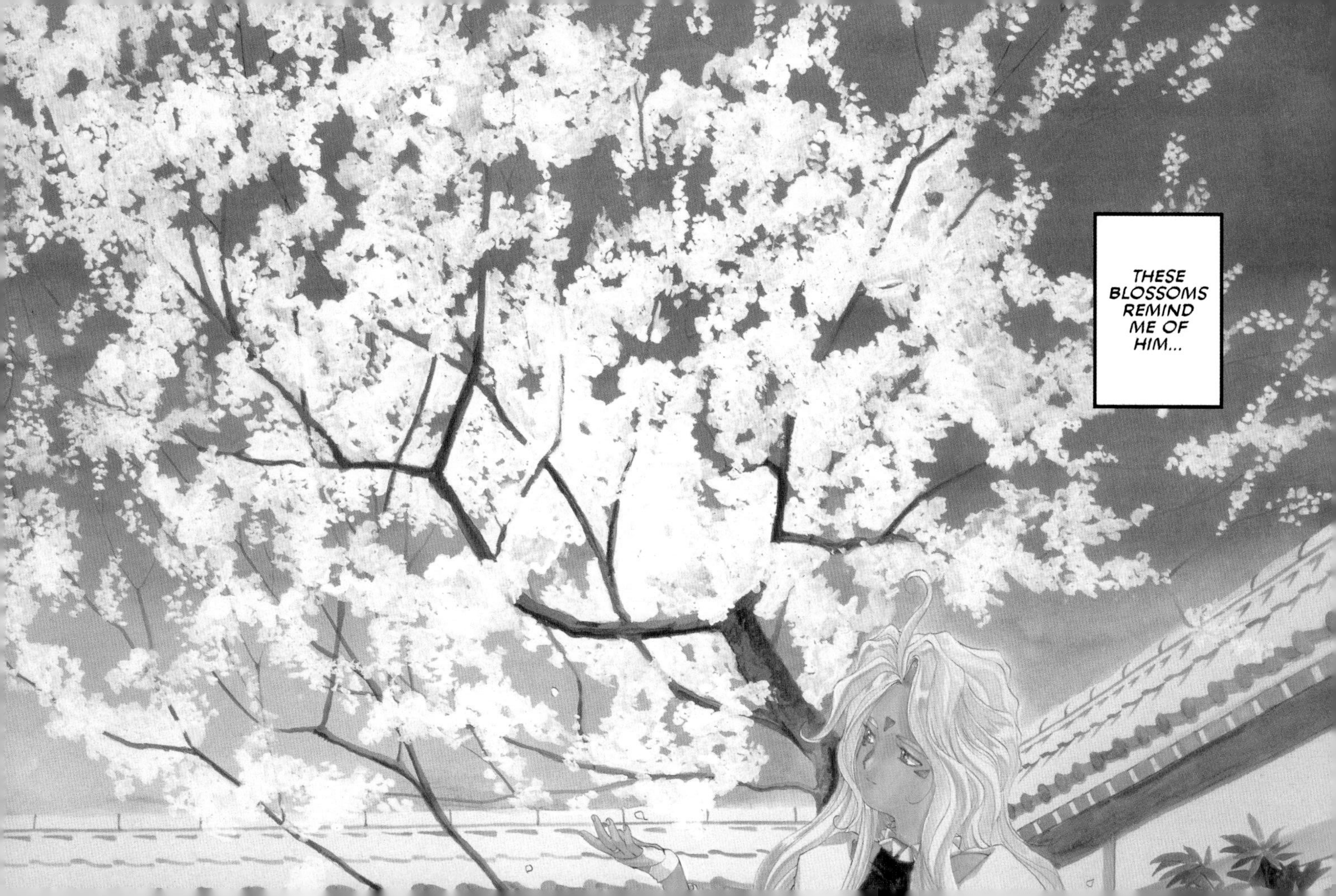
THESE BLOSSOMS REMIND ME OF HIM...

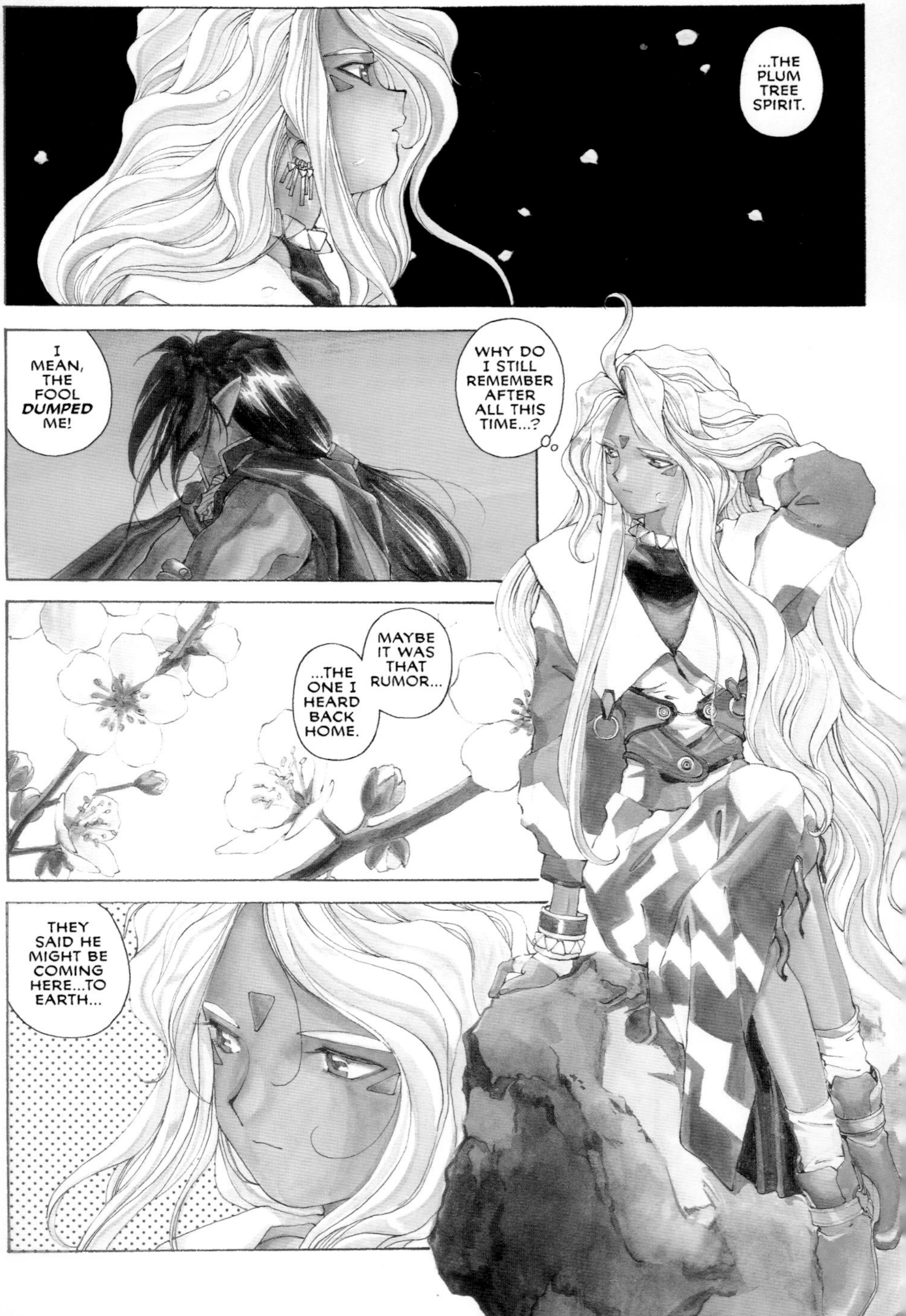
...THE PLUM TREE SPIRIT.
WHY DO I STILL REMEMBER AFTER ALL THIS TIME...?
I MEAN, THE FOOL *DUMPED* ME!
MAYBE IT WAS THAT RUMOR...
...THE ONE I HEARD BACK HOME.
THEY SAID HE MIGHT BE COMING HERE...TO EARTH...

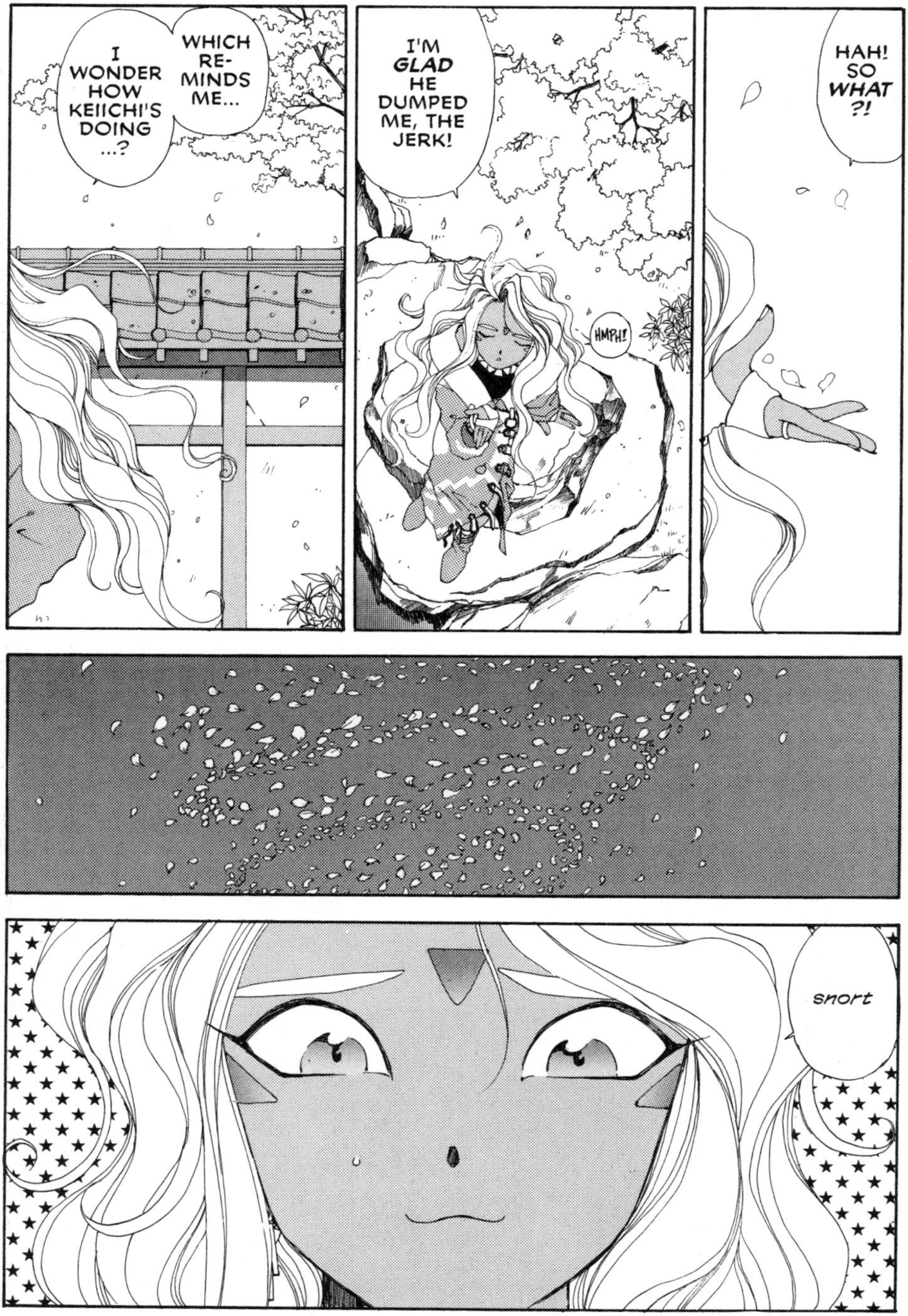
HAH! SO WHAT?!
I'M GLAD HE DUMPED ME, THE JERK!
HMPH!
WHICH RE-MINDS ME...
I WONDER HOW KEIICHI'S DOING...?
snort

YEAH, *SURE!* IT'S *NOT* LIKE YOU WENT INTO MY ROOM AND TOOK *MY* STUFF WITHOUT *MY* PERMISSION, RIGHT?!
WELL, UH... YOU'VE GOT A POINT THERE...
snort #2
C'MON-- IT WAS *YOUR* STUPID MEDICINE THAT DID THIS TO ME!
DON'T LAUGH...
...IT'S NOT *THAT* FUNNY.
OH, BUT IT IS! IT IS THAT FUNNY!
I'M SORRY, KEIICHI. I CAN'T REVERSE URD'S MEDICINE.
SHE USES A DIFFERENT SCHOOL OF MAGIC.
DON'T TELL ME...
M-MAYBE... I'LL BE THIS WAY...
...FOR THE REST OF MY *LIFE* ...?
HEY! YOU'RE UGLY...
...AND SKULD DRESS-ES YOU FUNNY!!

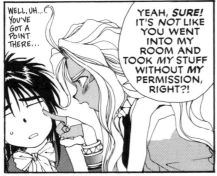

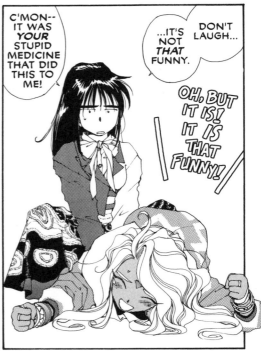

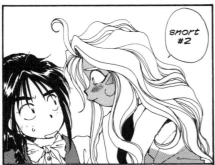

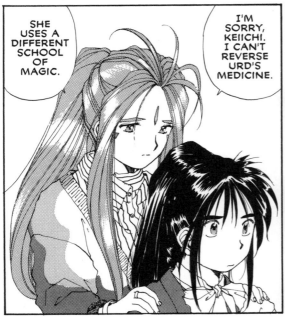

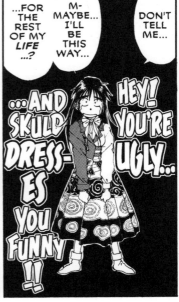

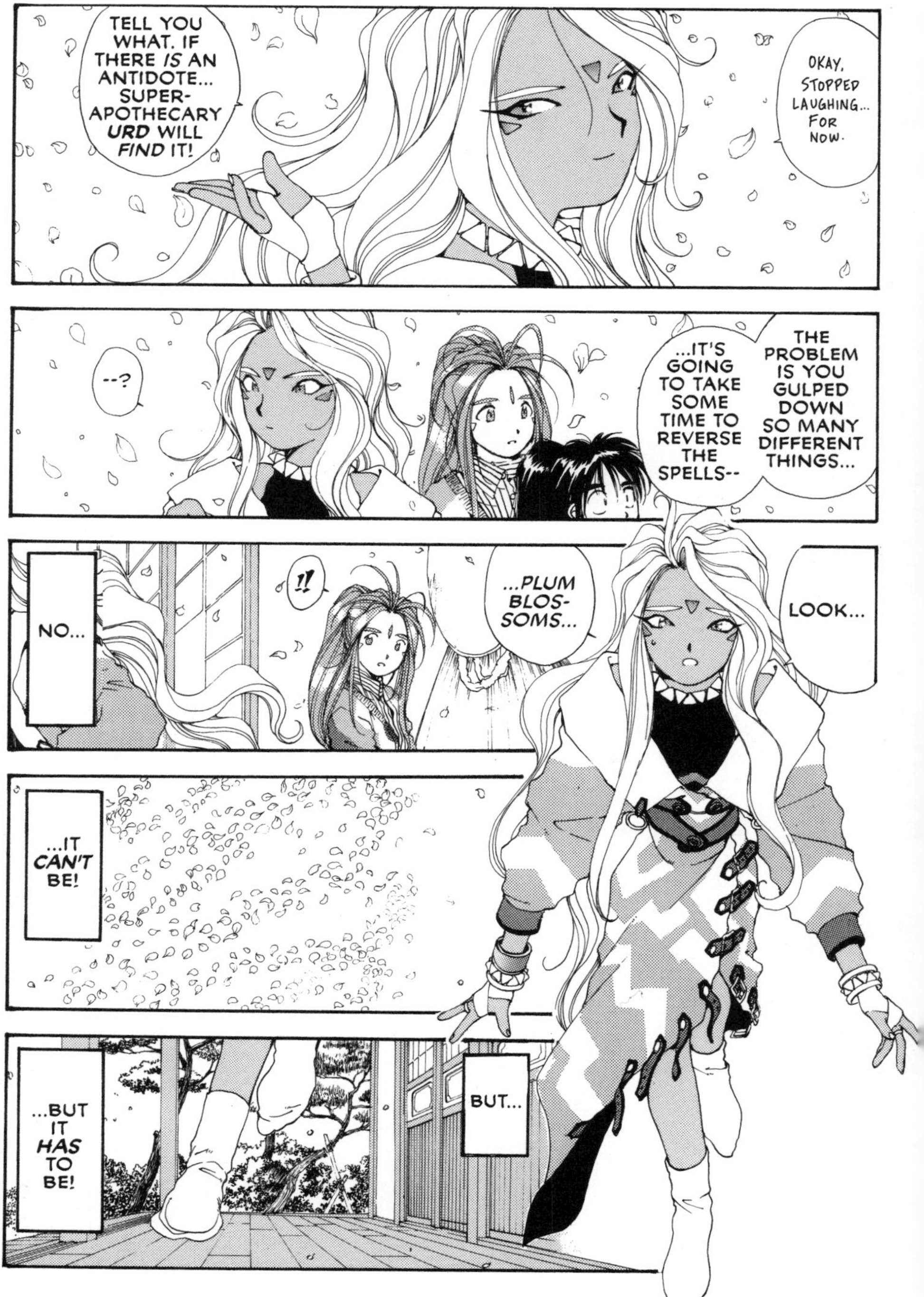
OKAY, STOPPED LAUGHING... FOR NOW.
TELL YOU WHAT. IF THERE *IS* AN ANTIDOTE... SUPER-APOTHECARY **URD** WILL ***FIND*** IT!
THE PROBLEM IS YOU GULPED DOWN SO MANY DIFFERENT THINGS...
...IT'S GOING TO TAKE SOME TIME TO REVERSE THE SPELLS--
--?
LOOK...
...PLUM BLOS-SOMS...
!!
NO...
...IT ***CAN'T*** BE!
BUT...
...BUT IT ***HAS*** TO BE!

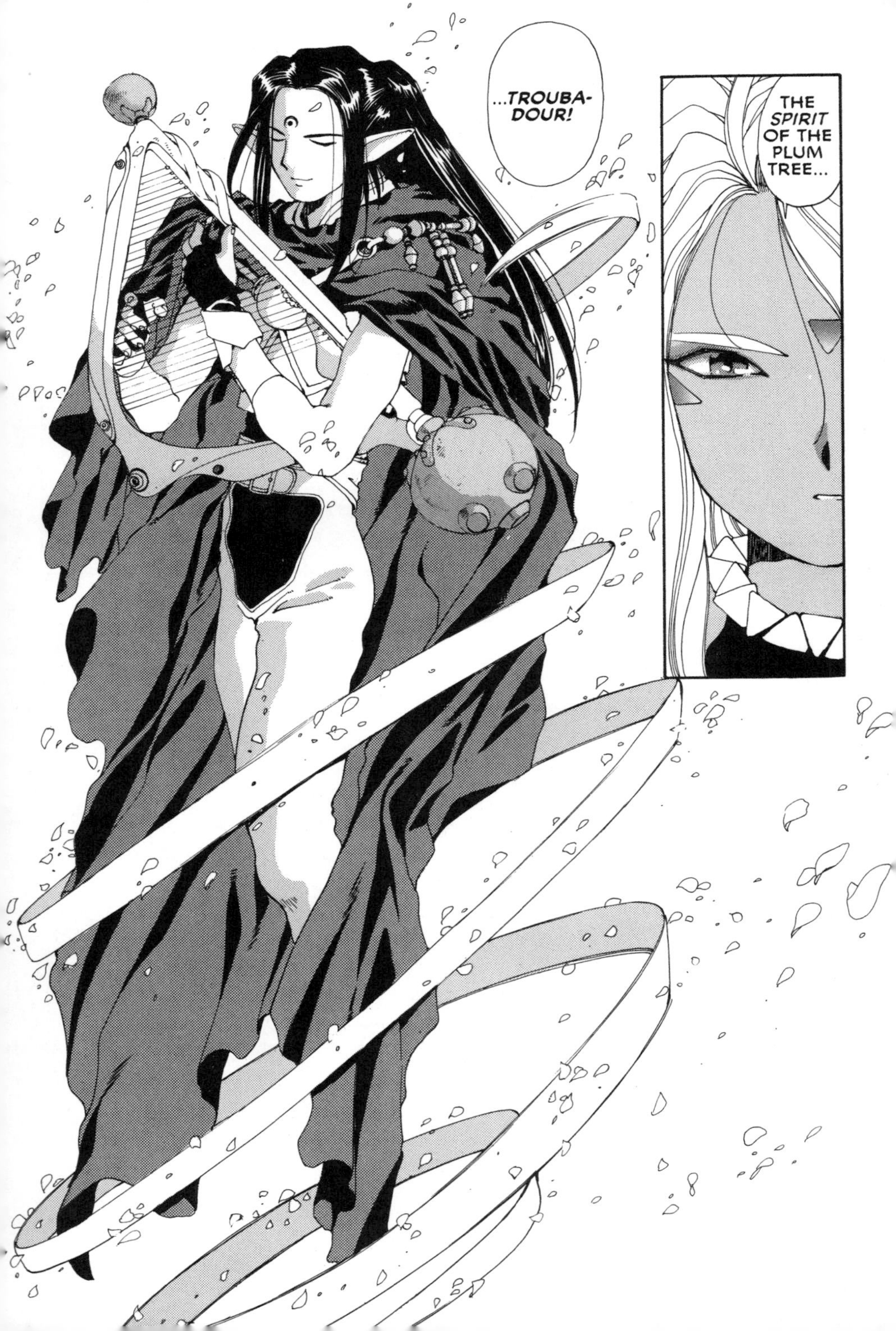
THE SPIRIT OF THE PLUM TREE...
...TROUBA-DOUR!

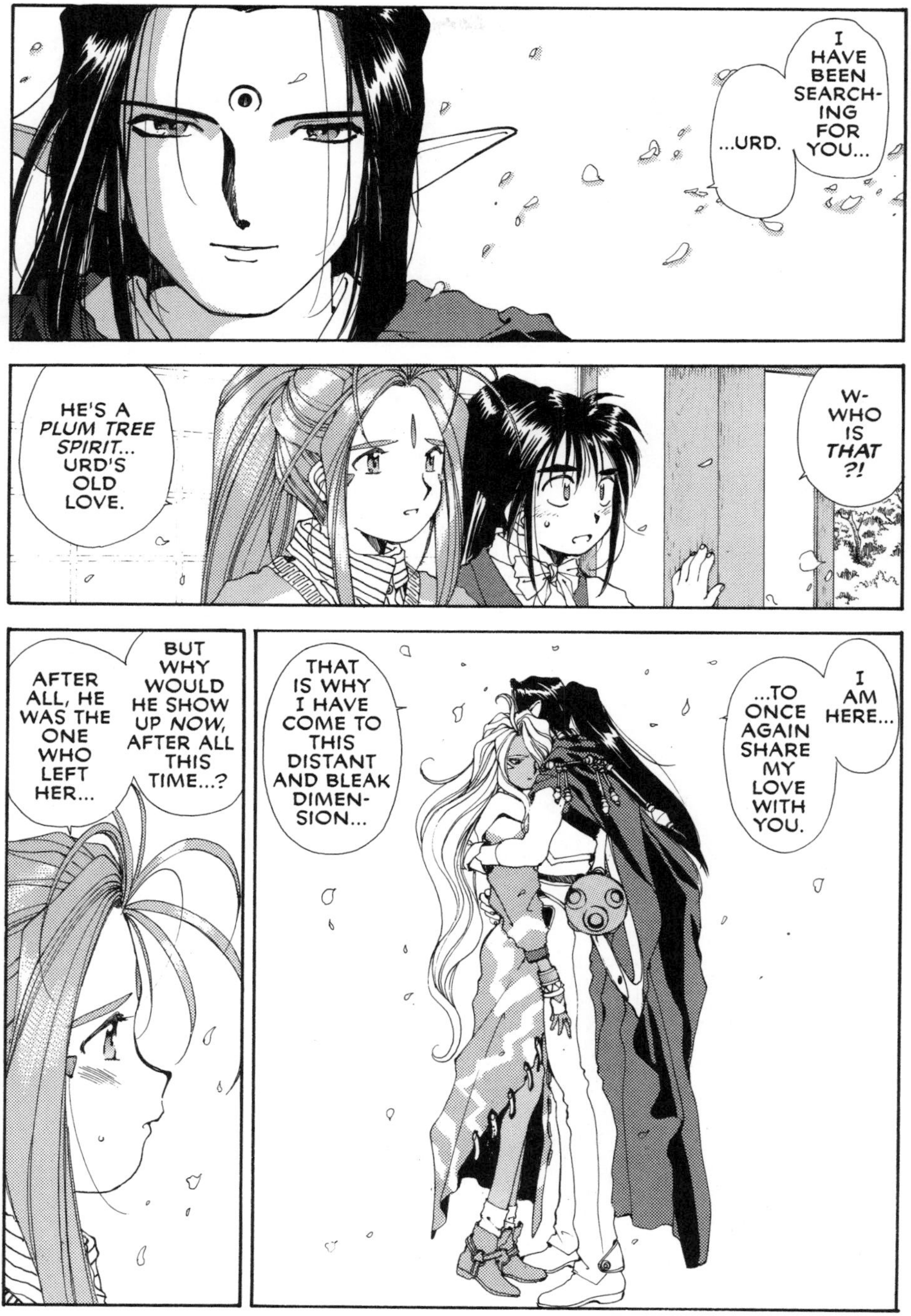
I HAVE BEEN SEARCHING FOR YOU...
...URD.
W-WHO IS *THAT* ?!
HE'S A *PLUM TREE SPIRIT*... URD'S OLD LOVE.
I AM HERE...
...TO ONCE AGAIN SHARE MY LOVE WITH YOU.
THAT IS WHY I HAVE COME TO THIS DISTANT AND BLEAK DIMENSION...
BUT WHY WOULD HE SHOW UP *NOW*, AFTER ALL THIS TIME...?
AFTER ALL, HE WAS THE ONE WHO LEFT HER...

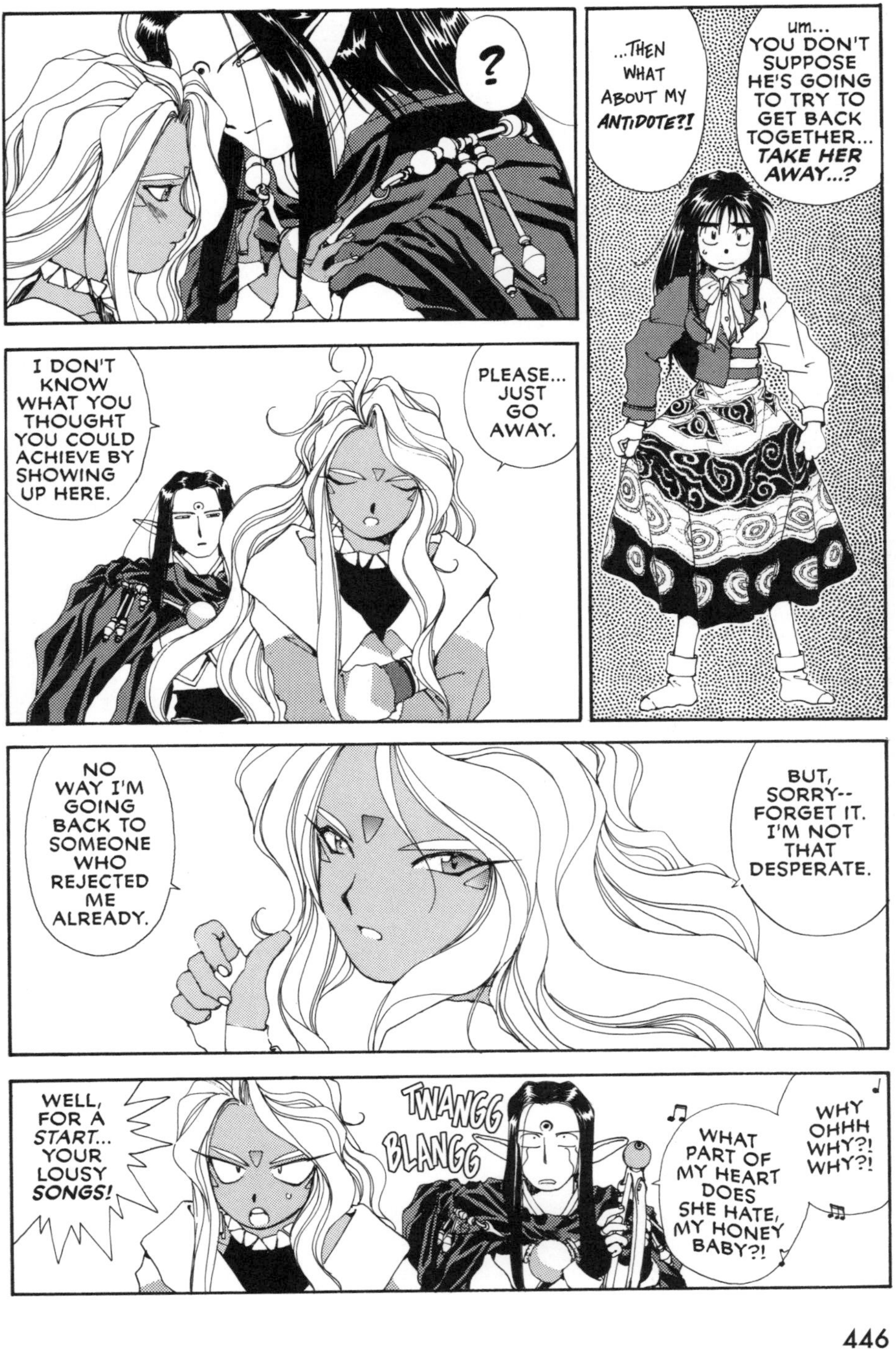
um... YOU DON'T SUPPOSE HE'S GOING TO TRY TO GET BACK TOGETHER... TAKE HER AWAY...?
...THEN WHAT ABOUT MY ANTIDOTE?!
?
PLEASE... JUST GO AWAY.
I DON'T KNOW WHAT YOU THOUGHT YOU COULD ACHIEVE BY SHOWING UP HERE.
BUT, SORRY-- FORGET IT. I'M NOT THAT DESPERATE.
NO WAY I'M GOING BACK TO SOMEONE WHO REJECTED ME ALREADY.
WHY OHHH WHY?! WHY?!
WHAT PART OF MY HEART DOES SHE HATE, MY HONEY BABY?!
TWANGG
BLANGG
WELL, FOR A START... YOUR LOUSY SONGS!

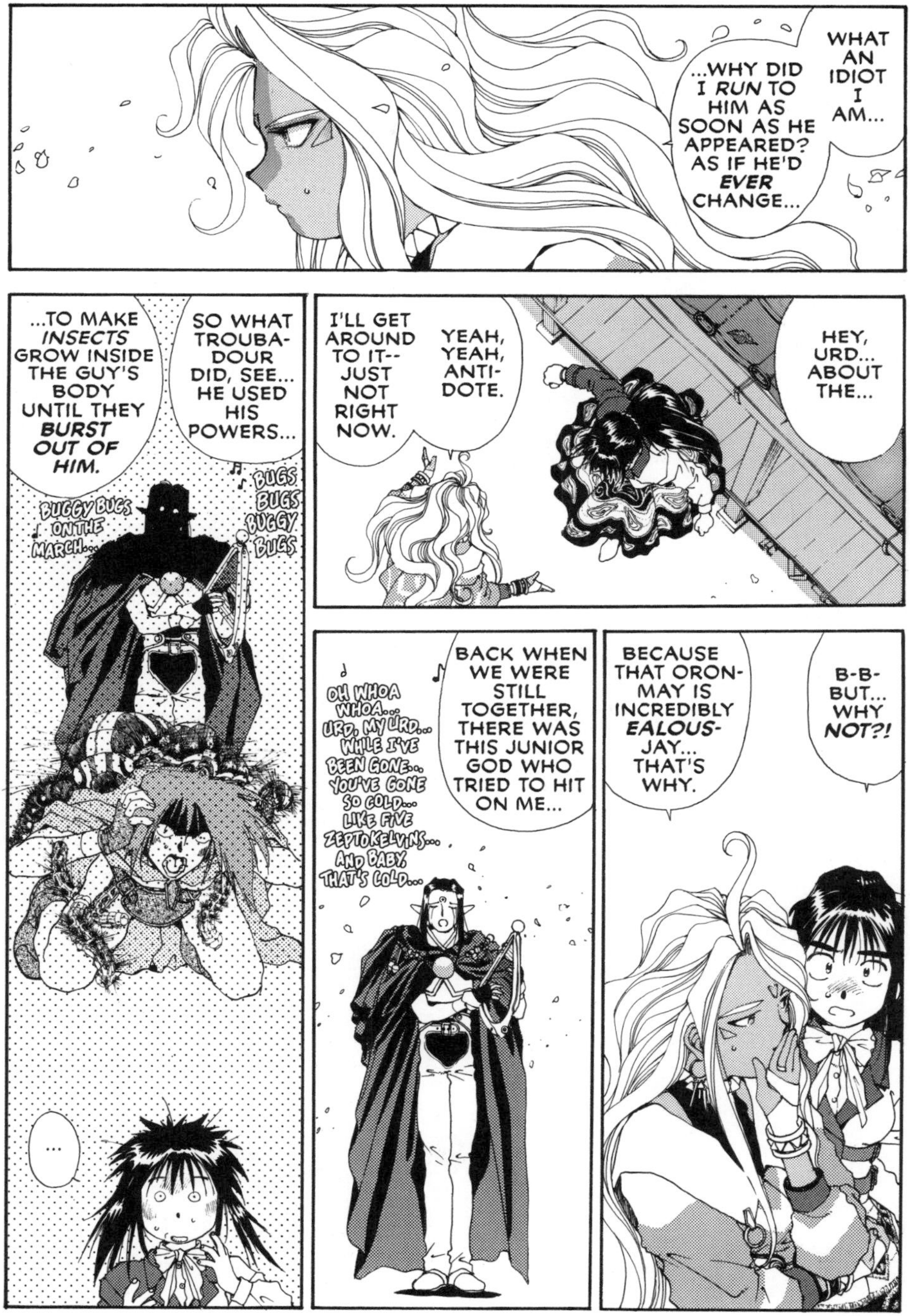
WHAT AN IDIOT I AM...
...WHY DID I *RUN* TO HIM AS SOON AS HE APPEARED? AS IF HE'D ***EVER*** CHANGE...
HEY, URD... ABOUT THE...
YEAH, YEAH, ANTIDOTE.
I'LL GET AROUND TO IT-- JUST NOT RIGHT NOW.
B-B-BUT... WHY ***NOT?!***
BECAUSE THAT ORON-MAY IS INCREDIBLY ***EALOUS-***JAY... THAT'S WHY.
BACK WHEN WE WERE STILL TOGETHER, THERE WAS THIS JUNIOR GOD WHO TRIED TO HIT ON ME...
OH WHOA WHOA... URD, MY URD... WHILE I'VE BEEN GONE... YOU'VE GONE SO COLD... LIKE FIVE ZEPTOKELVINS... AND BABY, THAT'S COLD...
SO WHAT TROUBADOUR DID, SEE... HE USED HIS POWERS...
...TO MAKE *INSECTS* GROW INSIDE THE GUY'S BODY UNTIL THEY ***BURST OUT OF HIM.***
BUGS BUGS BUGGY BUGS
BUGGY BUGS ON THE MARCH...
...

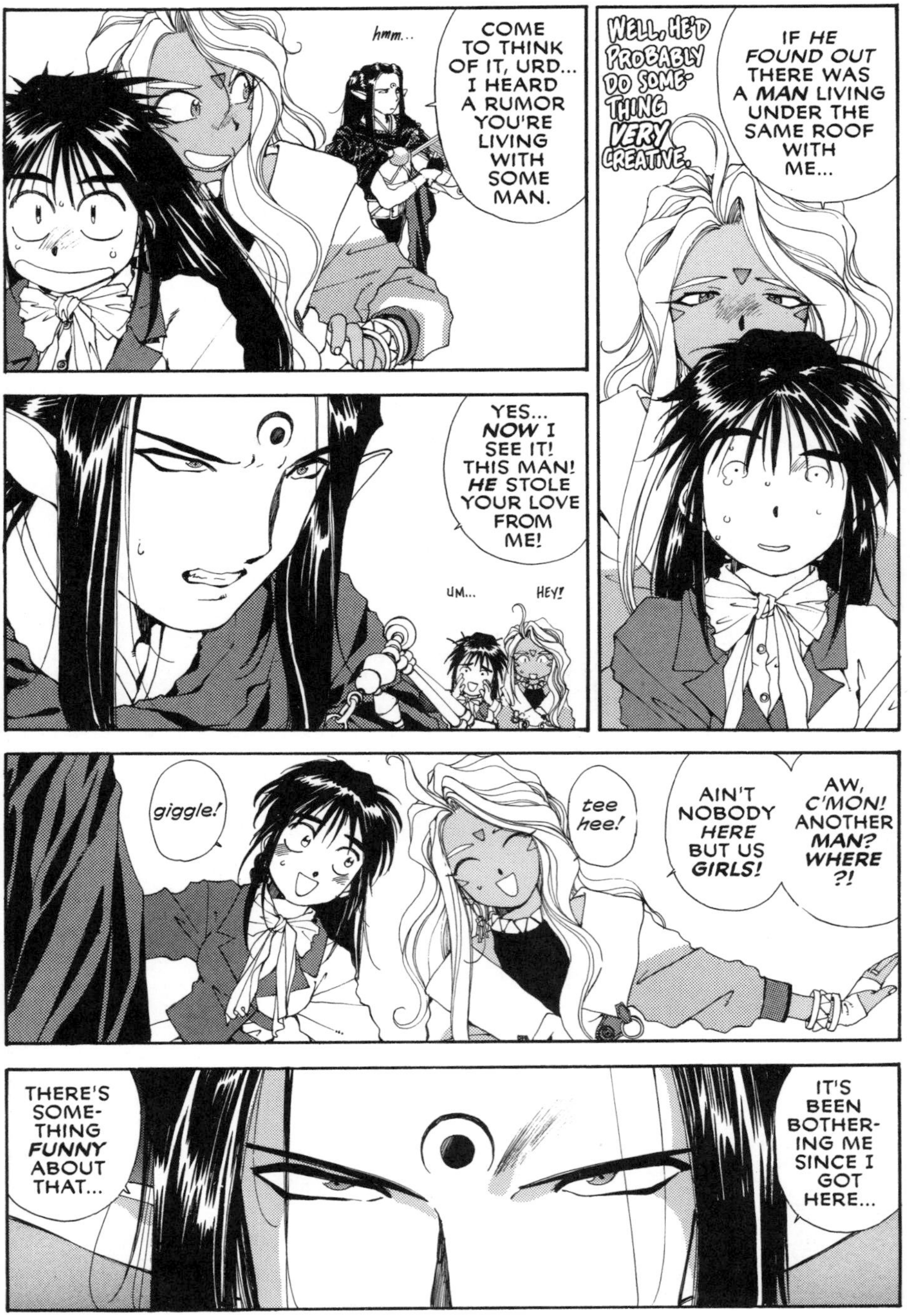
IF HE FOUND OUT THERE WAS A MAN LIVING UNDER THE SAME ROOF WITH ME...
WELL, HE'D PROBABLY DO SOMETHING VERY CREATIVE.
COME TO THINK OF IT, URD... I HEARD A RUMOR YOU'RE LIVING WITH SOME MAN.
hmm...
YES... NOW I SEE IT! THIS MAN! HE STOLE YOUR LOVE FROM ME!
HEY!
UM...
AW, C'MON! ANOTHER MAN? WHERE?!
AIN'T NOBODY HERE BUT US GIRLS!
tee hee!
giggle!
IT'S BEEN BOTHERING ME SINCE I GOT HERE...
THERE'S SOMETHING FUNNY ABOUT THAT...

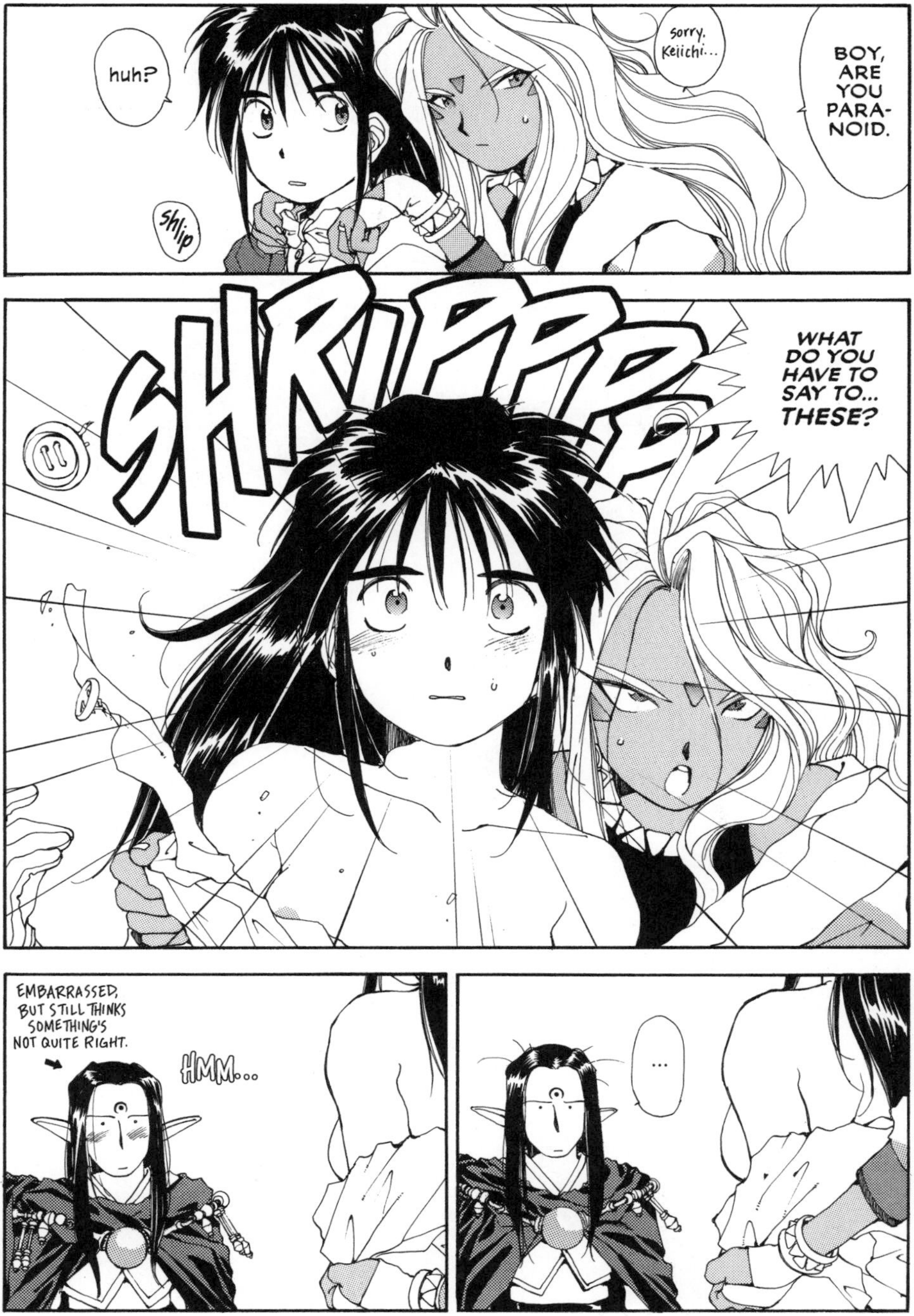
BOY, ARE YOU PARA-NOID.
Sorry, Keiichi...
huh?
shlip
WHAT DO YOU HAVE TO SAY TO... THESE?
SHRIPPP
...
EMBARRASSED, BUT STILL THINKS SOMETHING'S NOT QUITE RIGHT.
HMM...

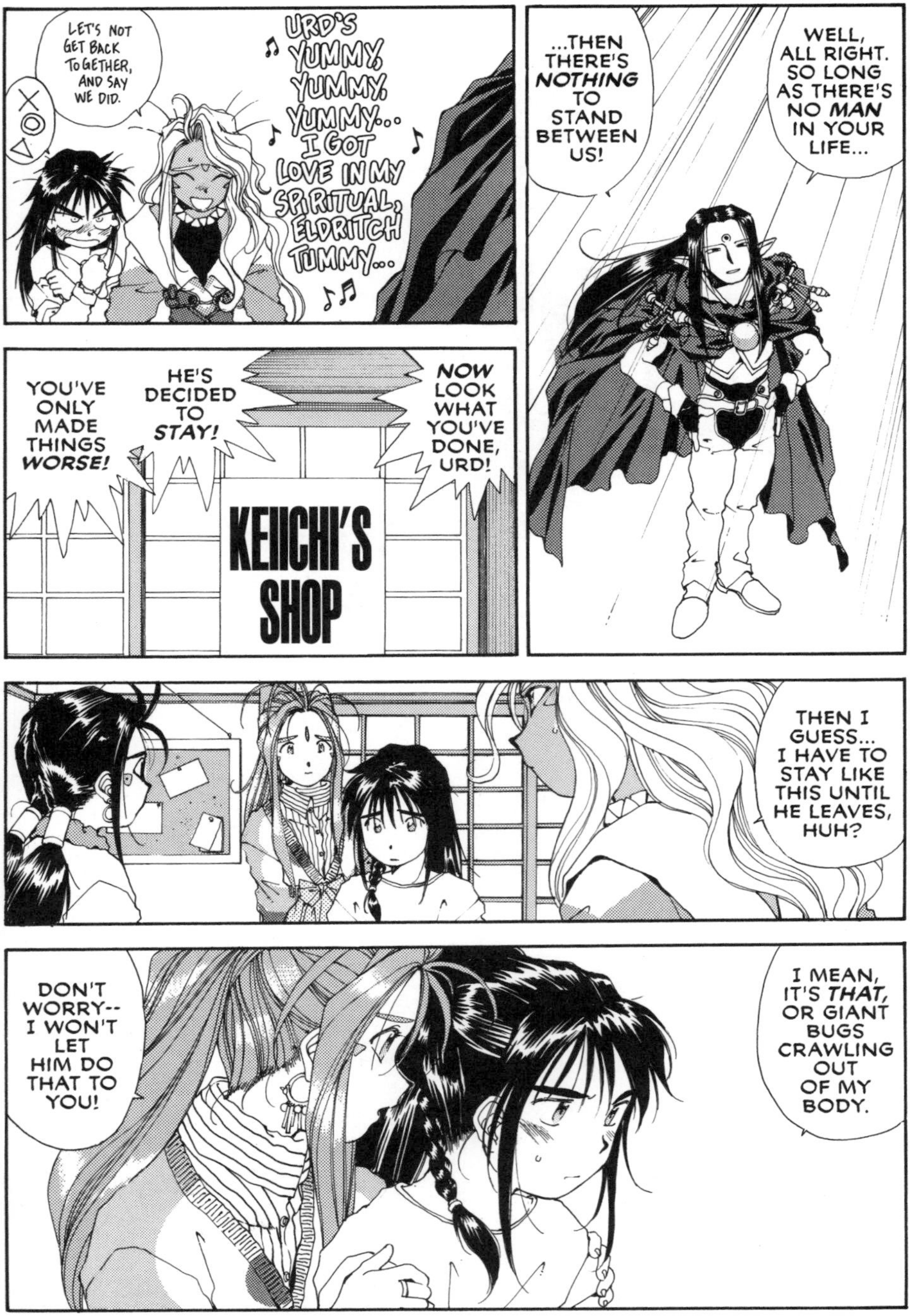
WELL, ALL RIGHT. SO LONG AS THERE'S NO MAN IN YOUR LIFE...
...THEN THERE'S NOTHING TO STAND BETWEEN US!
URD'S YUMMY, YUMMY, YUMMY... I GOT LOVE IN MY SPIRITUAL, ELDRITCH TUMMY...
LET'S NOT GET BACK TOGETHER, AND SAY WE DID.
NOW LOOK WHAT YOU'VE DONE, URD!
HE'S DECIDED TO STAY!
YOU'VE ONLY MADE THINGS WORSE!
KEIICHI'S SHOP
THEN I GUESS... I HAVE TO STAY LIKE THIS UNTIL HE LEAVES, HUH?
I MEAN, IT'S THAT, OR GIANT BUGS CRAWLING OUT OF MY BODY.
DON'T WORRY-- I WON'T LET HIM DO THAT TO YOU!

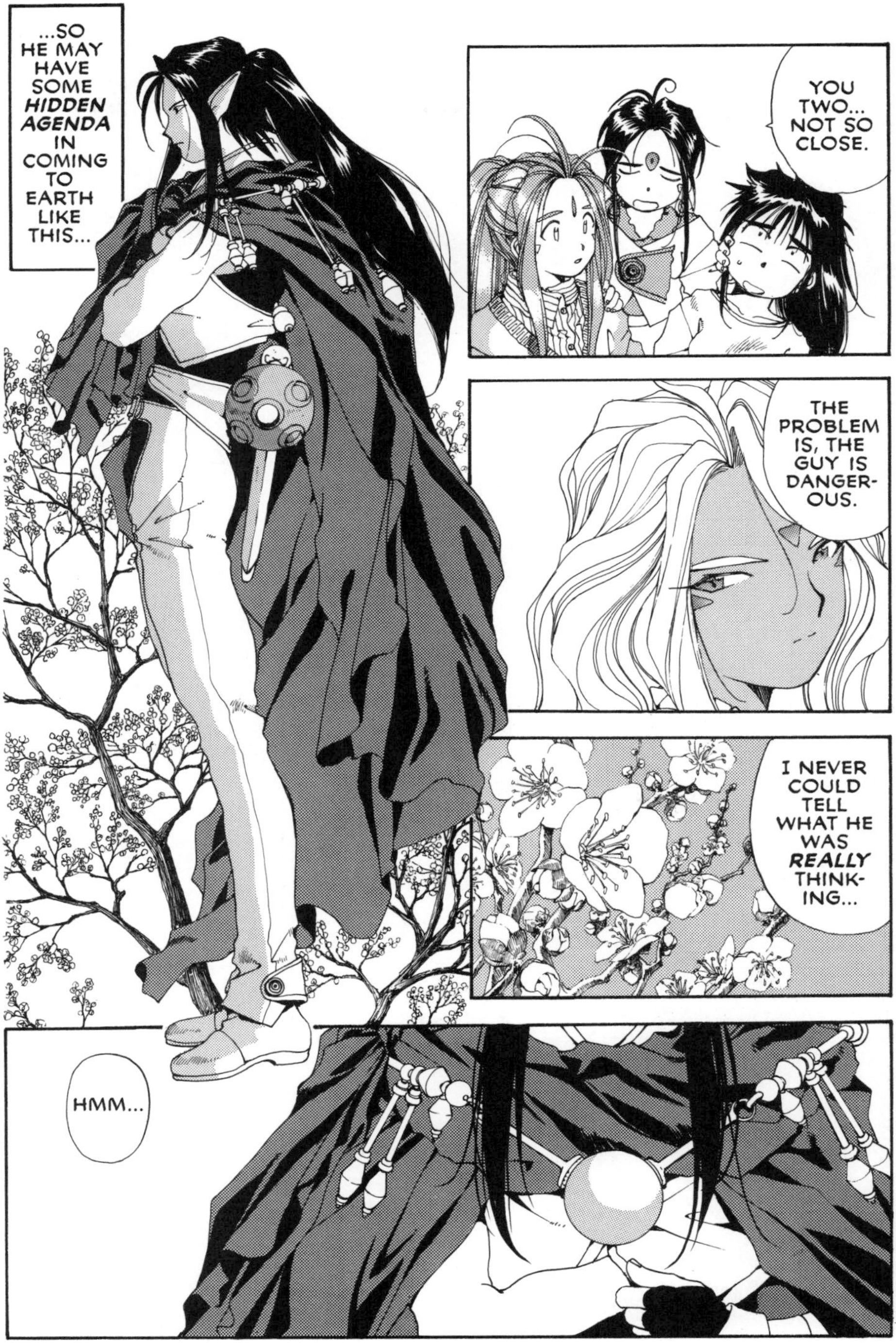
YOU TWO... NOT SO CLOSE.
THE PROBLEM IS, THE GUY IS DANGEROUS.
I NEVER COULD TELL WHAT HE WAS *REALLY* THINKING...
...SO HE MAY HAVE SOME *HIDDEN AGENDA* IN COMING TO EARTH LIKE THIS...
HMM...

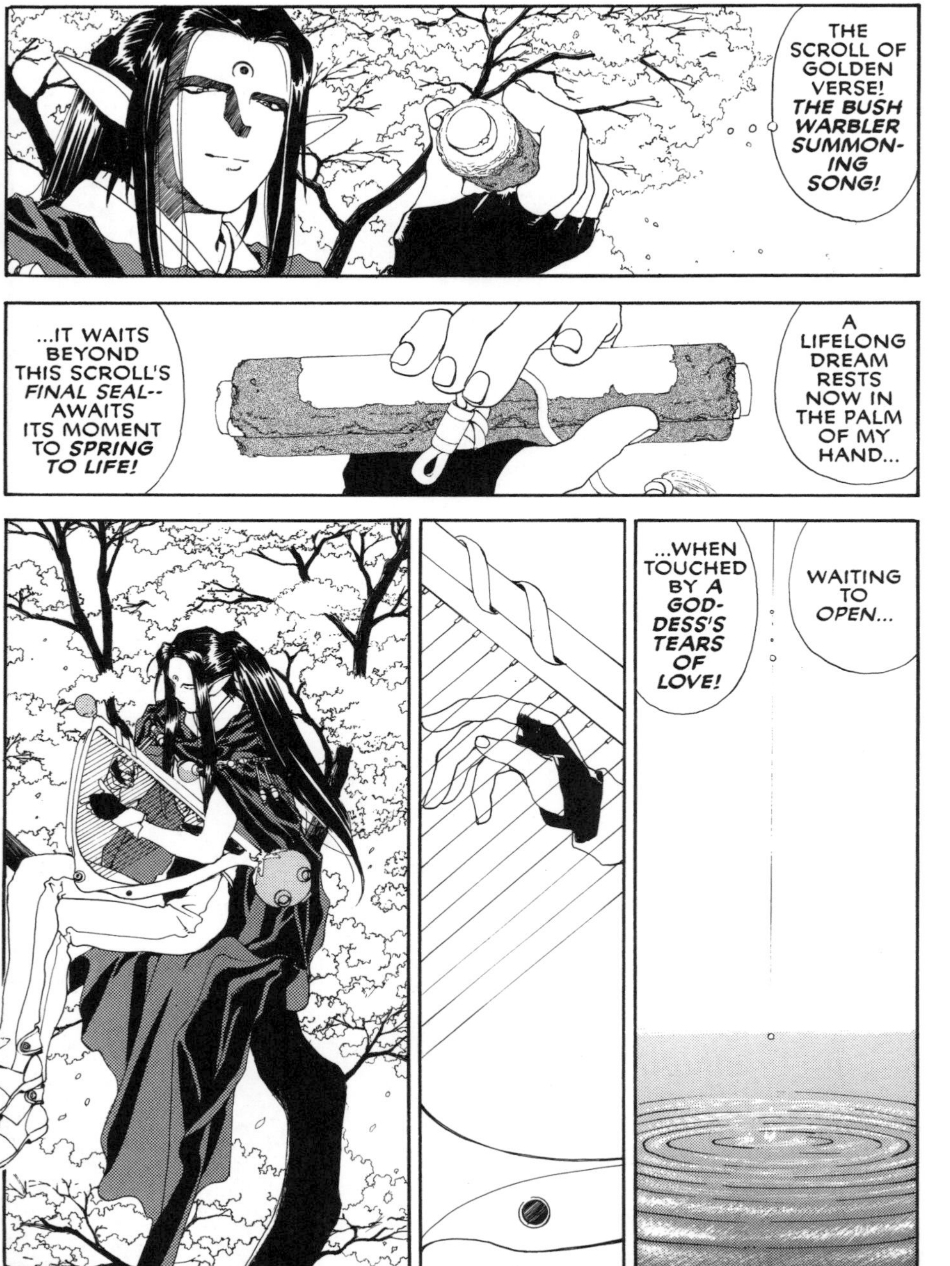
THE SCROLL OF GOLDEN VERSE! *THE BUSH WARBLER SUMMONING SONG!*
A LIFELONG DREAM RESTS NOW IN THE PALM OF MY HAND...
...IT WAITS BEYOND THIS SCROLL'S *FINAL SEAL*-- AWAITS ITS MOMENT TO *SPRING TO LIFE!*
WAITING TO *OPEN...*
...WHEN TOUCHED BY *A GODDESS'S* TEARS OF *LOVE!*

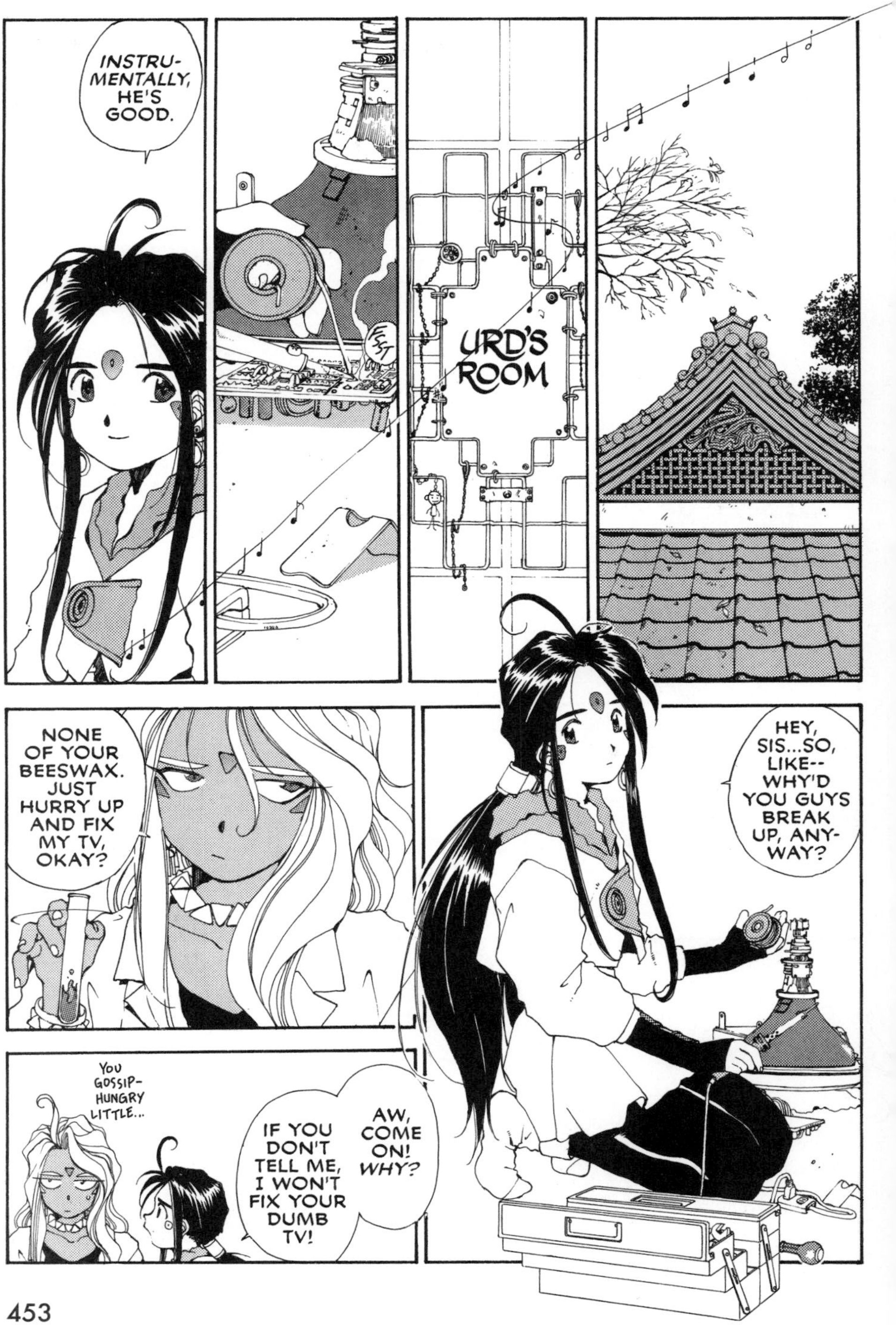
URD'S ROOM
INSTRUMENTALLY, HE'S GOOD.
HEY, SIS...SO, LIKE--WHY'D YOU GUYS BREAK UP, ANYWAY?
NONE OF YOUR BEESWAX. JUST HURRY UP AND FIX MY TV, OKAY?
AW, COME ON! *WHY?*
IF YOU DON'T TELL ME, I WON'T FIX YOUR DUMB TV!
YOU GOSSIP-HUNGRY LITTLE...

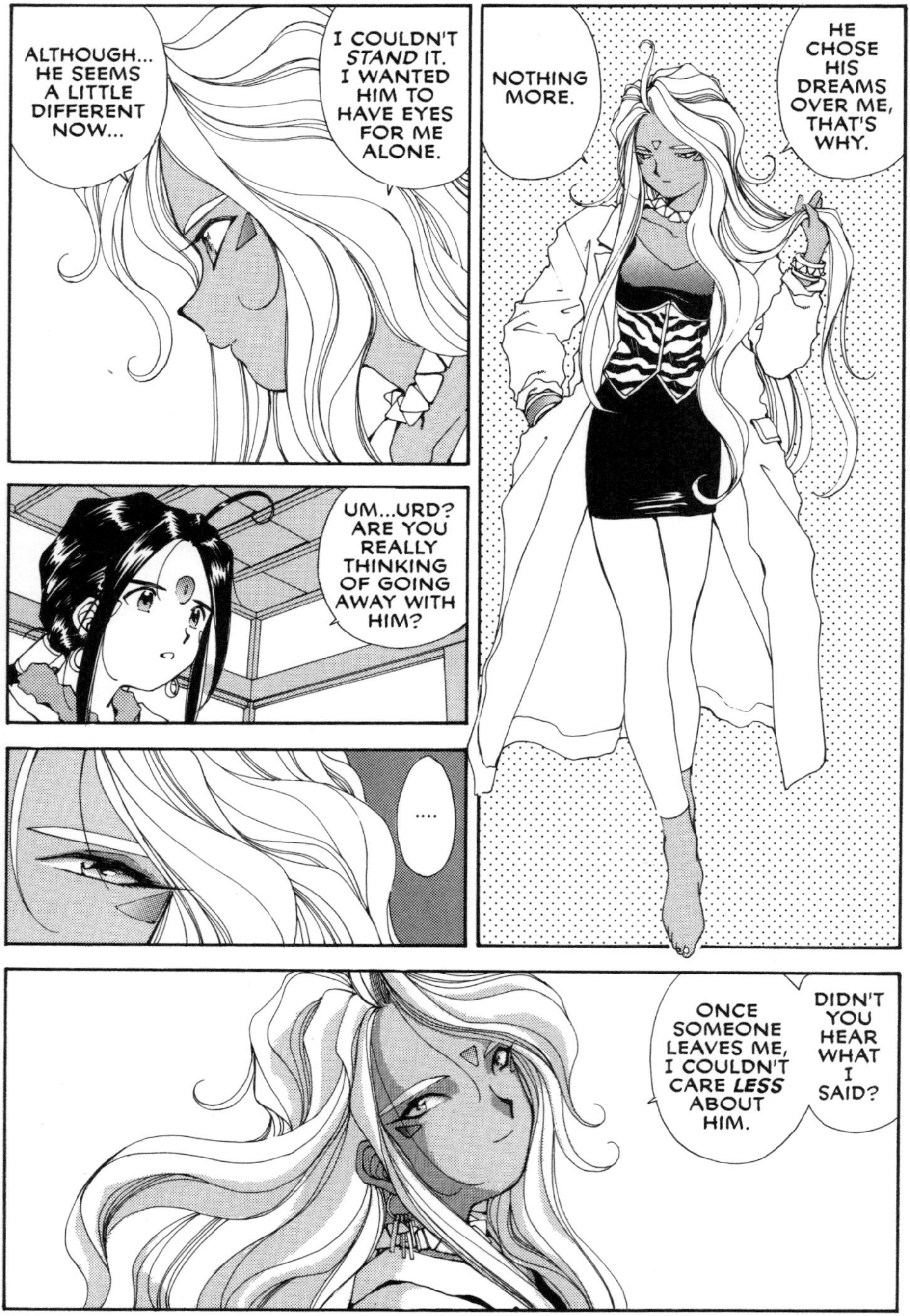
HE CHOSE HIS DREAMS OVER ME, THAT'S WHY.
NOTHING MORE.
I COULDN'T *STAND* IT. I WANTED HIM TO HAVE EYES FOR ME ALONE.
ALTHOUGH... HE SEEMS A LITTLE DIFFERENT NOW...
UM...URD? ARE YOU REALLY THINKING OF GOING AWAY WITH HIM?
....
DIDN'T YOU HEAR WHAT I SAID?
ONCE SOMEONE LEAVES ME, I COULDN'T CARE *LESS* ABOUT HIM.

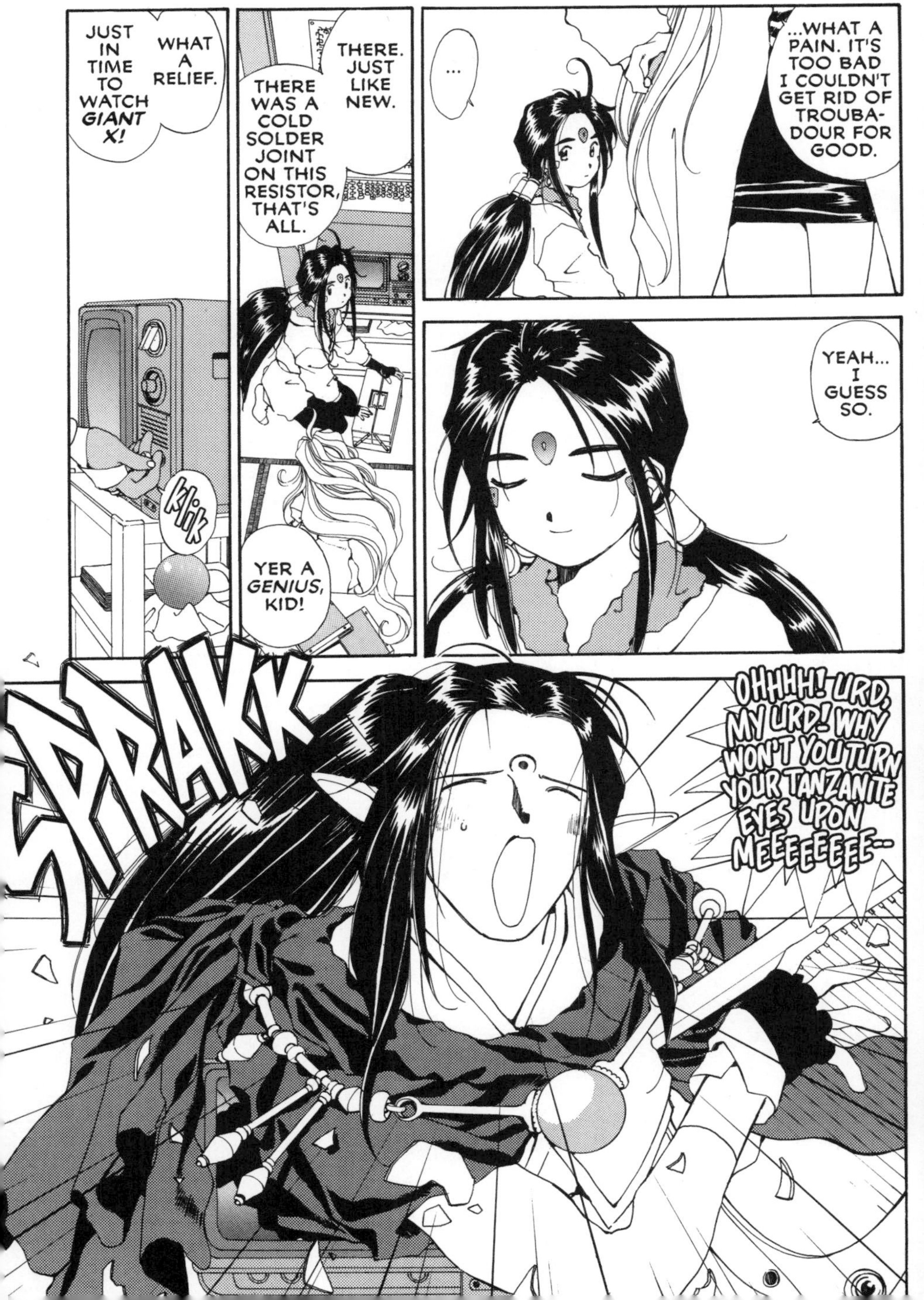
...WHAT A PAIN. IT'S TOO BAD I COULDN'T GET RID OF TROUBADOUR FOR GOOD.
...
YEAH... I GUESS SO.
THERE. JUST LIKE NEW.
THERE WAS A COLD SOLDER JOINT ON THIS RESISTOR, THAT'S ALL.
YER A *GENIUS*, KID!
WHAT A RELIEF.
JUST IN TIME TO WATCH *GIANT X!*
klik
OHHHH! URD, MY URD! WHY WON'T YOU TURN YOUR TANZANITE EYES UPON MEEEEEEEE--
SPRAKK

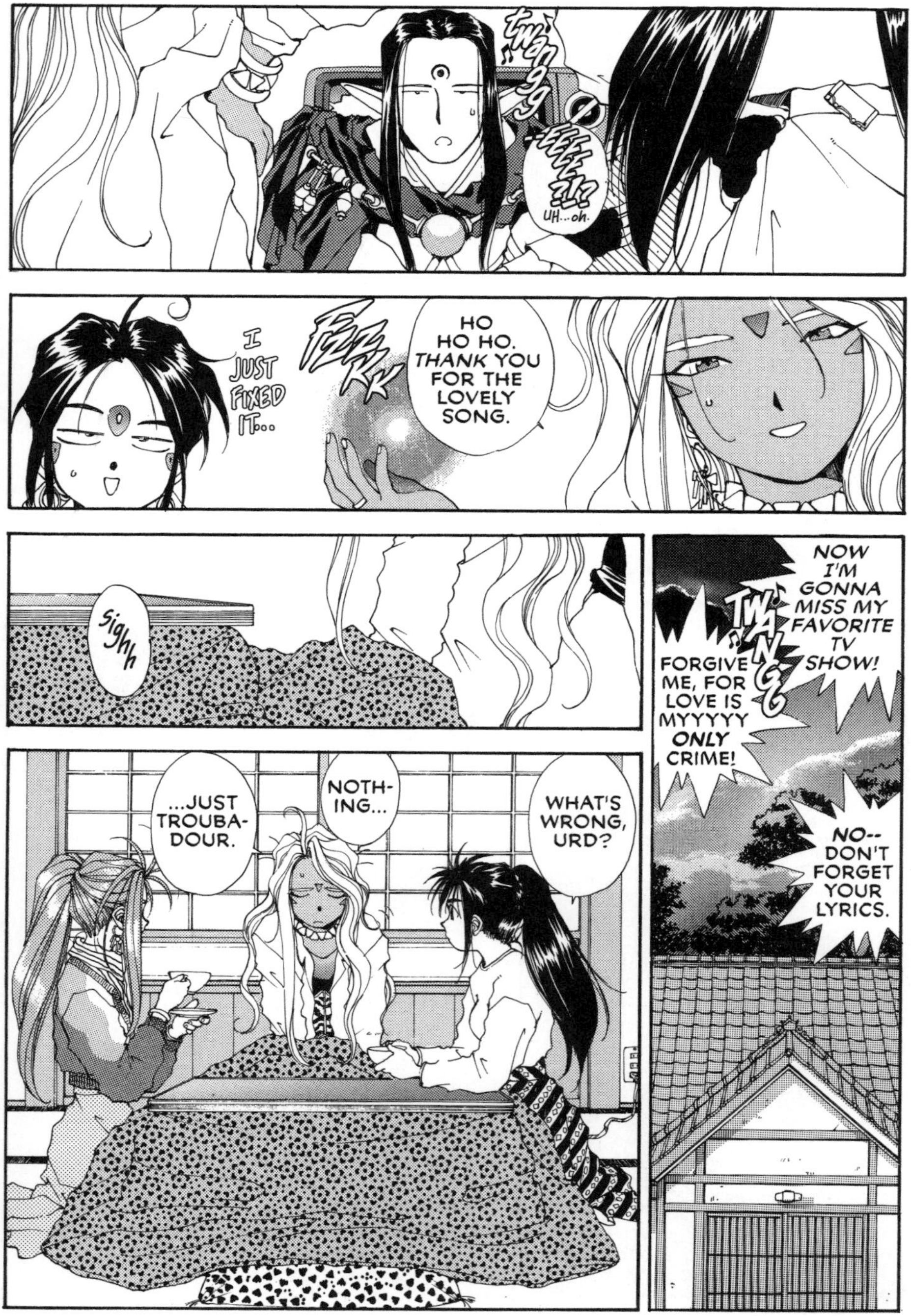
twanggg
EEEEE?!!?
UH...oh.
HO HO HO. *THANK* YOU FOR THE LOVELY SONG.
I JUST FIXED IT...
NOW I'M GONNA MISS MY FAVORITE TV SHOW!
TWANG
FORGIVE ME, FOR LOVE IS MYYYYY ***ONLY*** CRIME!
NO-- DON'T FORGET YOUR LYRICS.
sighh
WHAT'S WRONG, URD?
NOTHING...
...JUST TROUBADOUR.

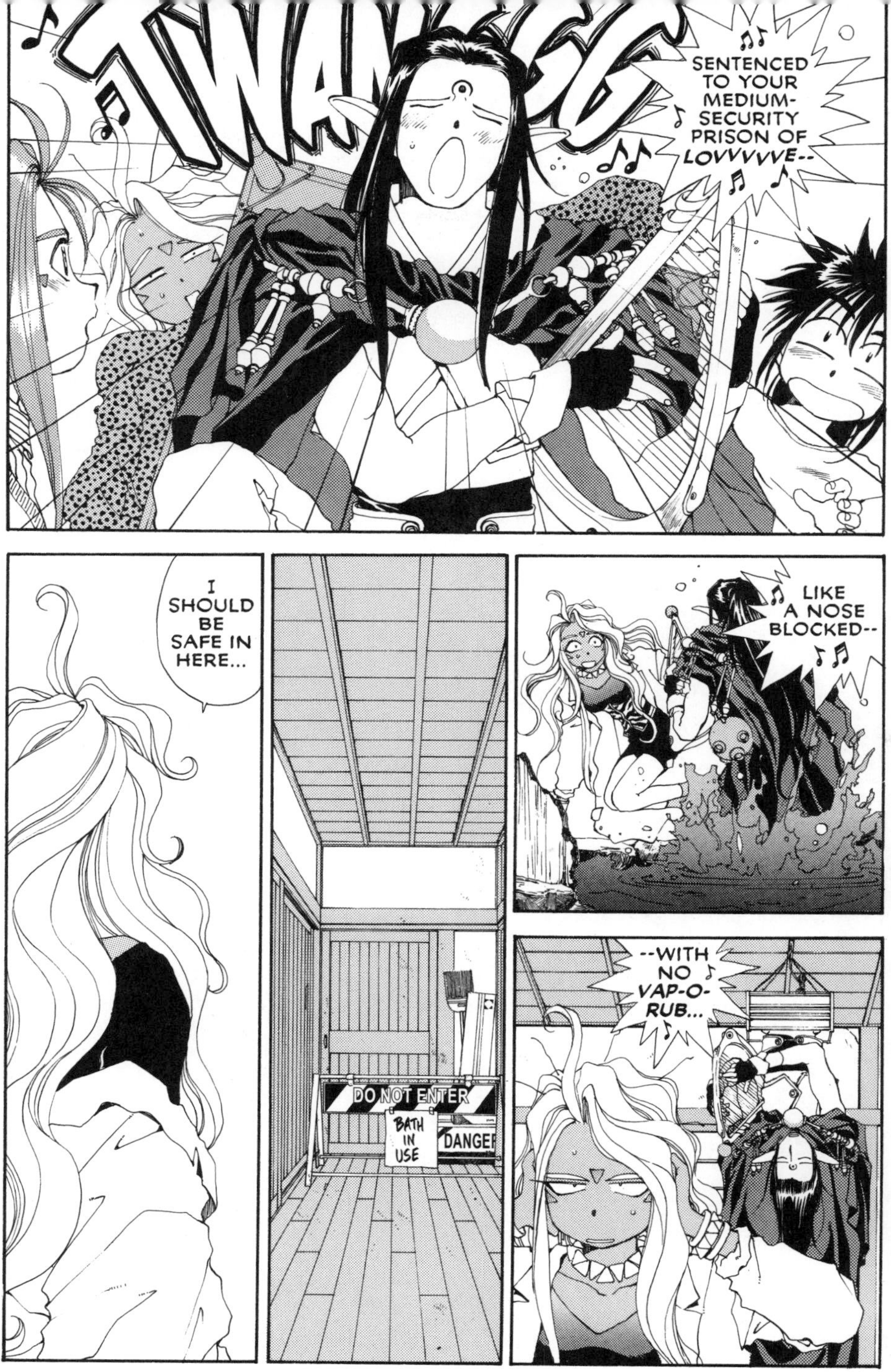
SENTENCED TO YOUR MEDIUM-SECURITY PRISON OF LOVVVVVE--
LIKE A NOSE BLOCKED--
--WITH NO VAP-O-RUB...
DO NOT ENTER
BATH IN USE
I SHOULD BE SAFE IN HERE...

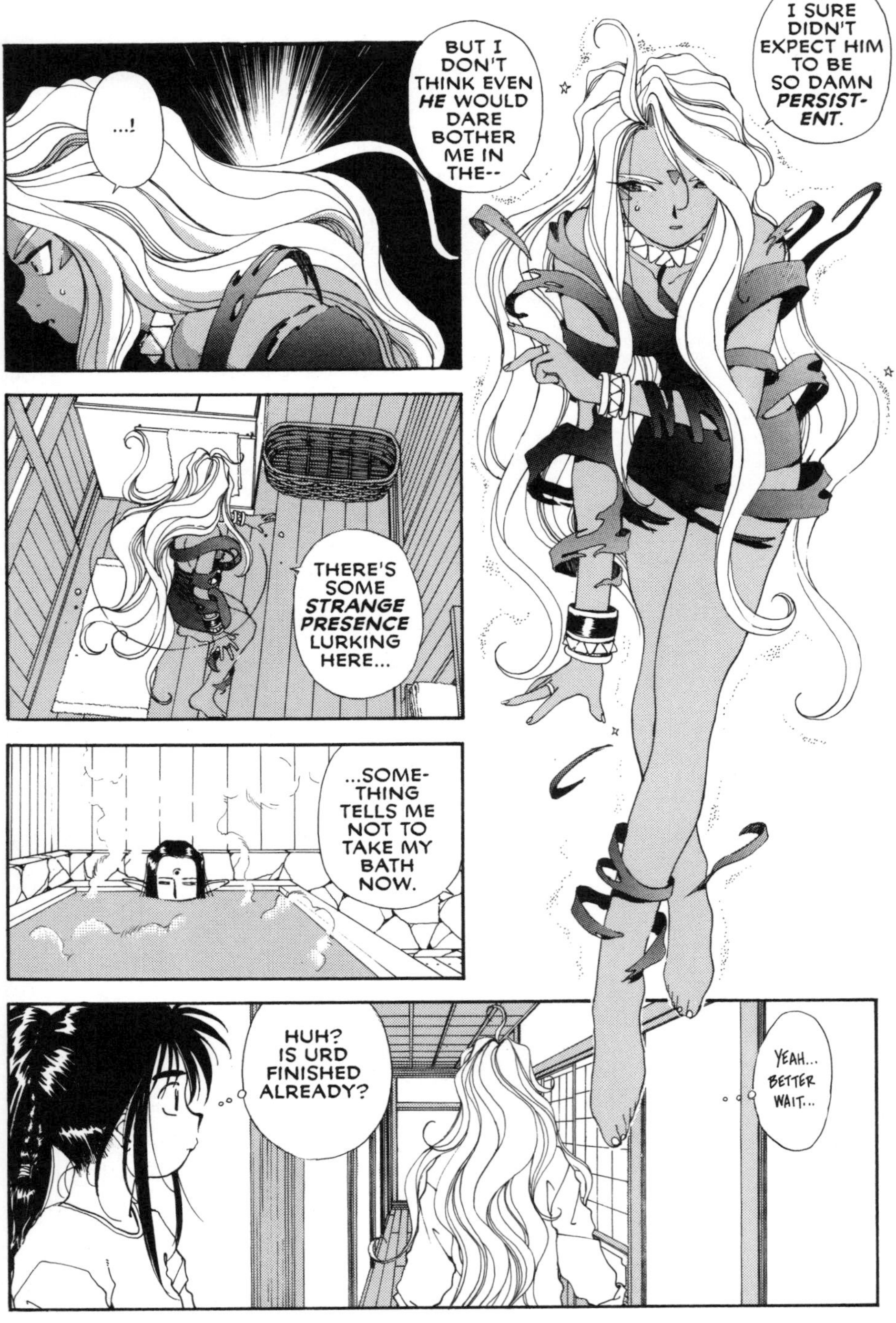
I SURE DIDN'T EXPECT HIM TO BE SO DAMN *PERSISTENT*.
BUT I DON'T THINK EVEN *HE* WOULD DARE BOTHER ME IN THE--
...!
THERE'S SOME *STRANGE PRESENCE* LURKING HERE...
...SOMETHING TELLS ME NOT TO TAKE MY BATH NOW.
YEAH... BETTER WAIT...
HUH? IS URD FINISHED ALREADY?

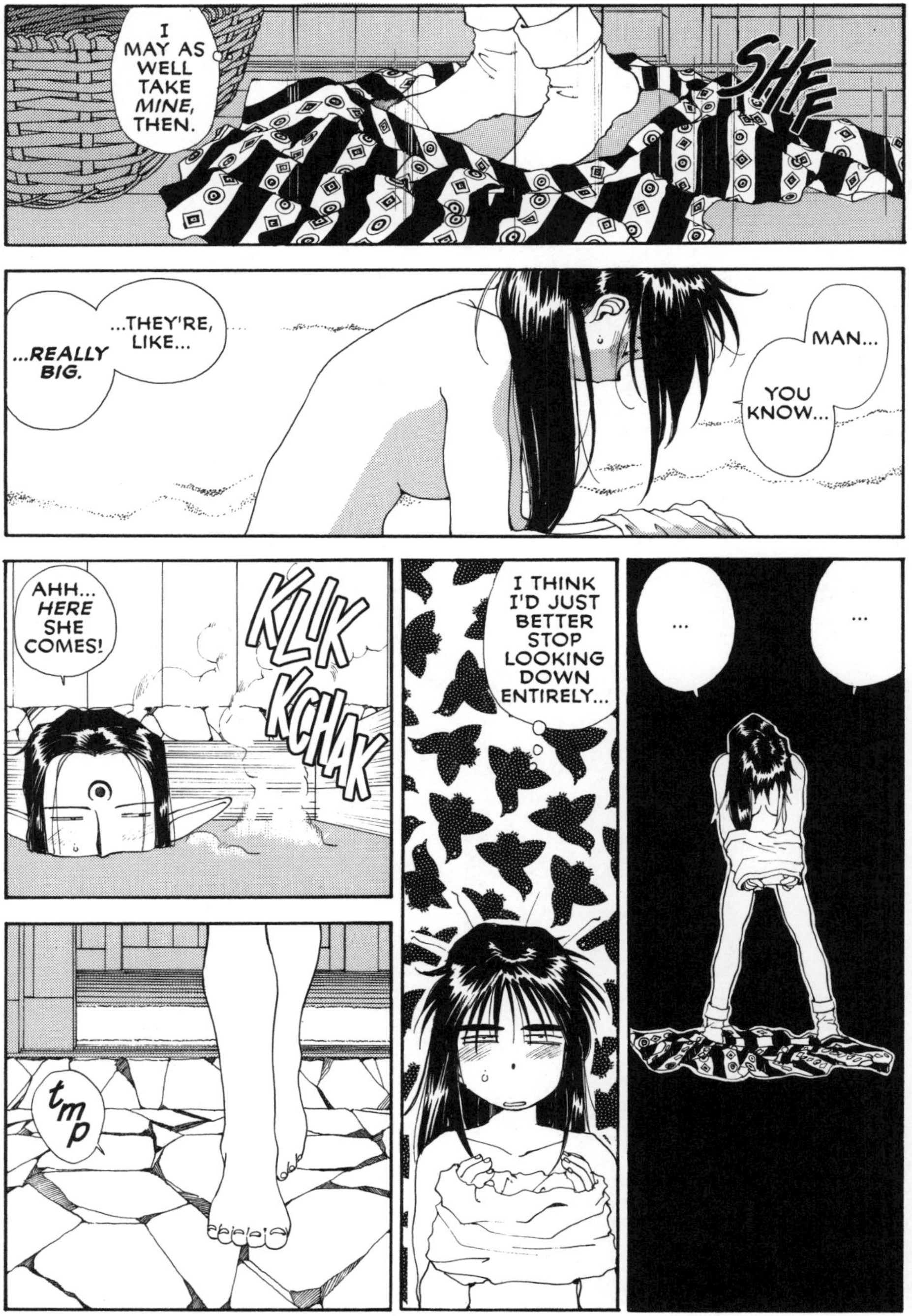
I MAY AS WELL TAKE *MINE*, THEN.
SHFF
MAN...
YOU KNOW...
...THEY'RE, LIKE...
...REALLY BIG.
...
...
I THINK I'D JUST BETTER STOP LOOKING DOWN ENTIRELY...
AHH... *HERE* SHE COMES!
KLIK
KCHAK
tmp

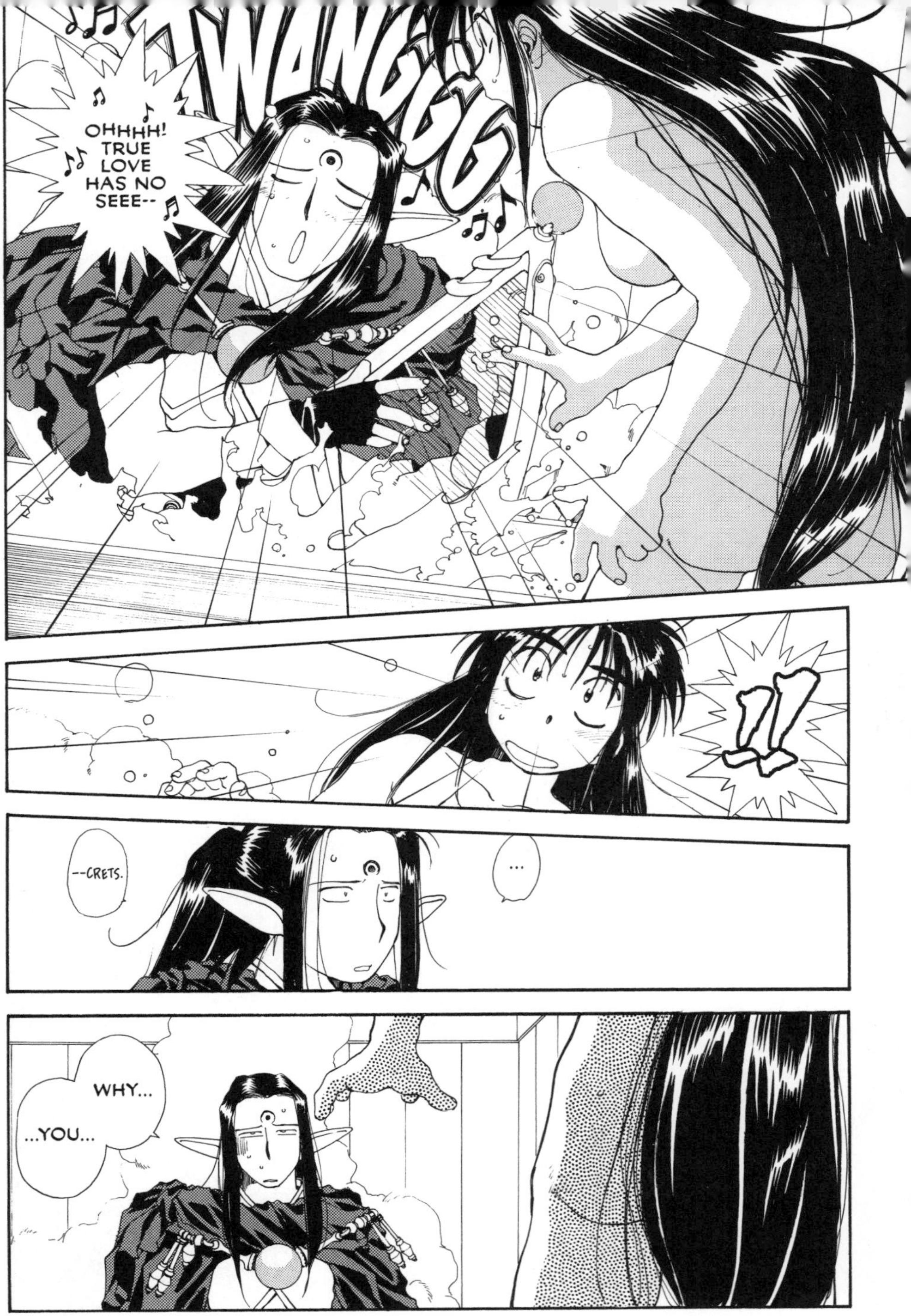
OHHHH! TRUE LOVE HAS NO SEEE--
!!
...
--CRETS.
WHY...
...YOU...

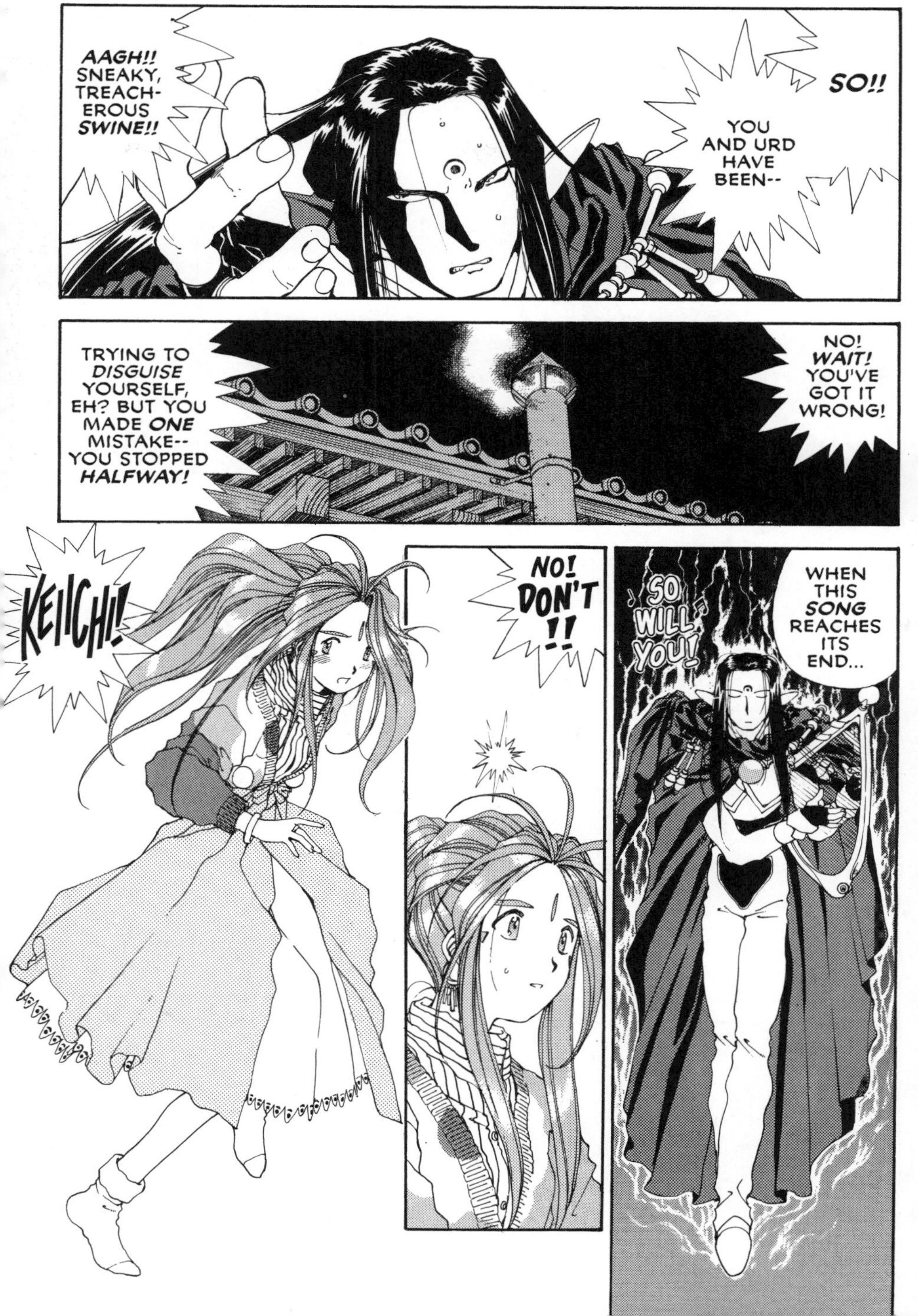
SO!!
YOU AND URD HAVE BEEN--
AAGH!! SNEAKY, TREACHEROUS SWINE!!
NO! WAIT! YOU'VE GOT IT WRONG!
TRYING TO DISGUISE YOURSELF, EH? BUT YOU MADE ONE MISTAKE-- YOU STOPPED HALFWAY!
WHEN THIS SONG REACHES ITS END...
SO WILL YOU!
NO! DON'T!!
KEIICHI!

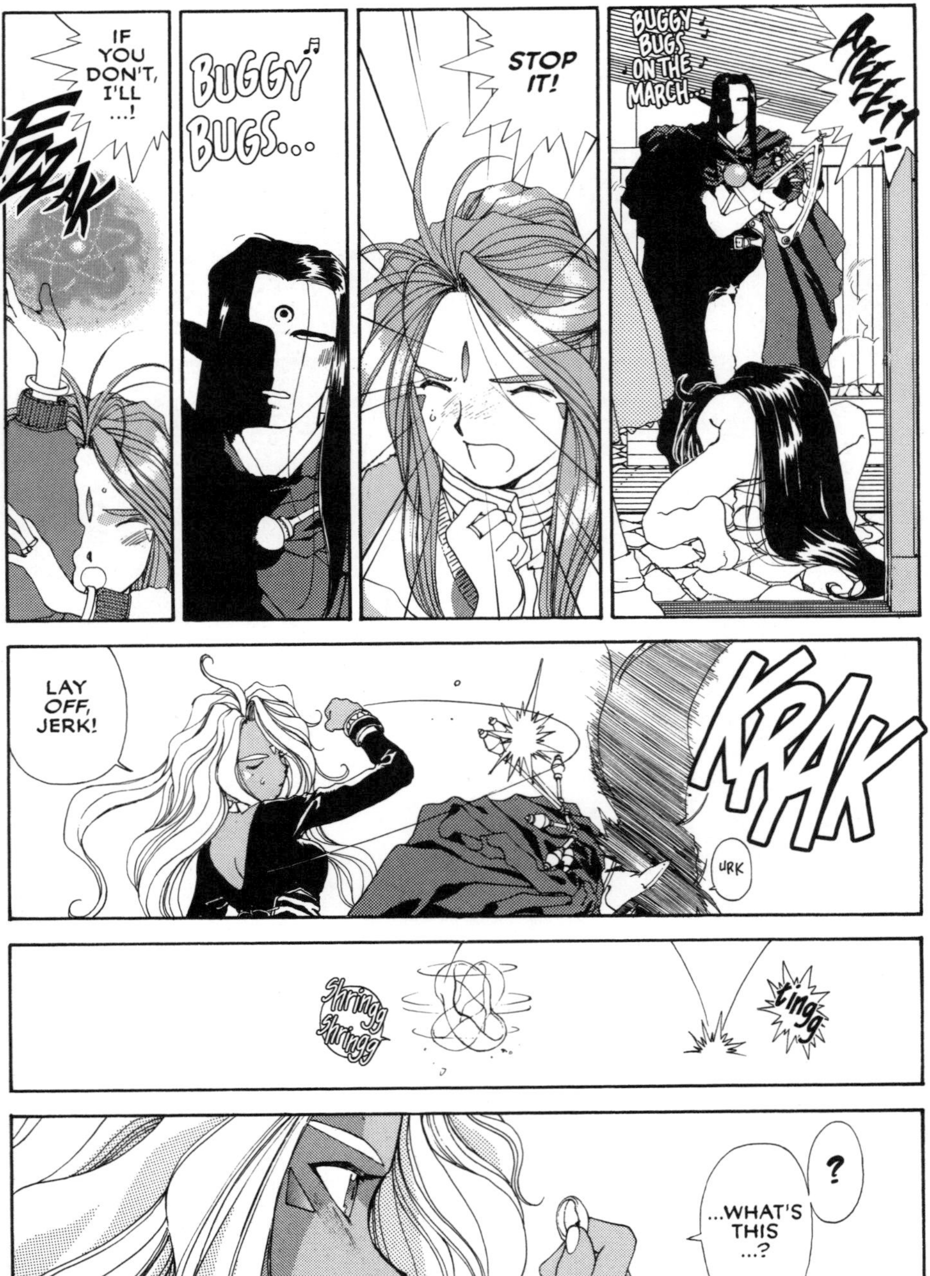
AIEEEE!!
BUGGY BUGS ON THE MARCH...
STOP IT!
BUGGY BUGS...
IF YOU DON'T, I'LL ...!
FZZZAK
KRAK
URK
LAY OFF, JERK!
tingg
Shringg Shringg
?
...WHAT'S THIS ...?

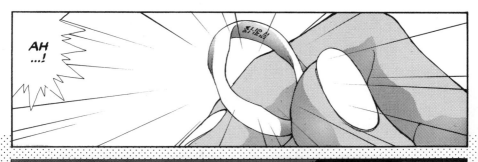

AH
...!

BACK
WHEN
WE FIRST
STARTED
GOING
OUT...

THE
TWO
OF
US...

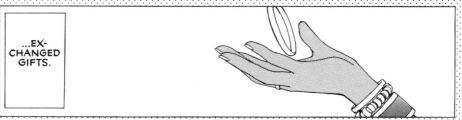

...EX-
CHANGED
GIFTS.

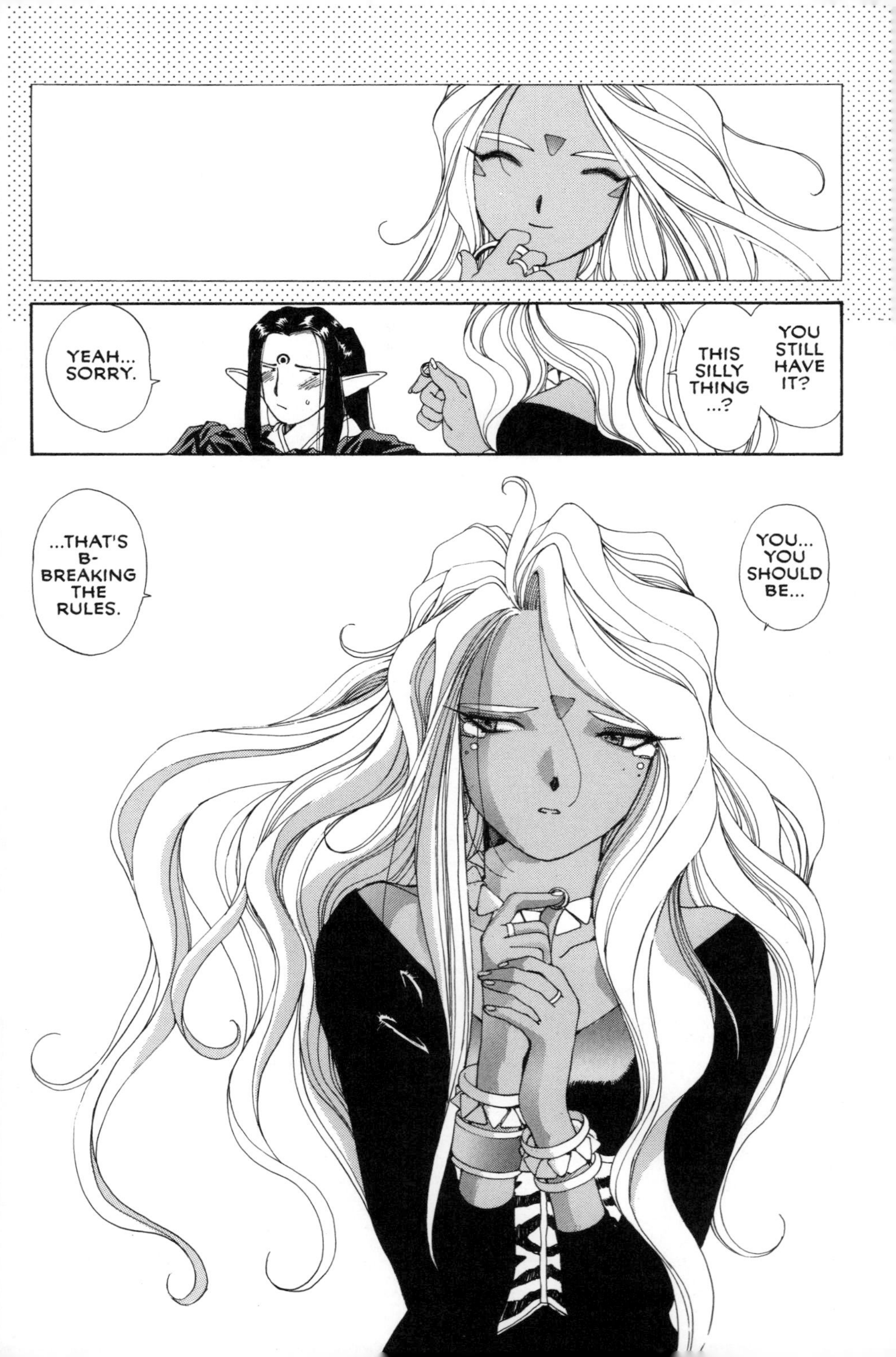
YOU STILL HAVE IT?
THIS SILLY THING ...?
YEAH... SORRY.
YOU... YOU SHOULD BE...
...THAT'S B-BREAKING THE RULES.

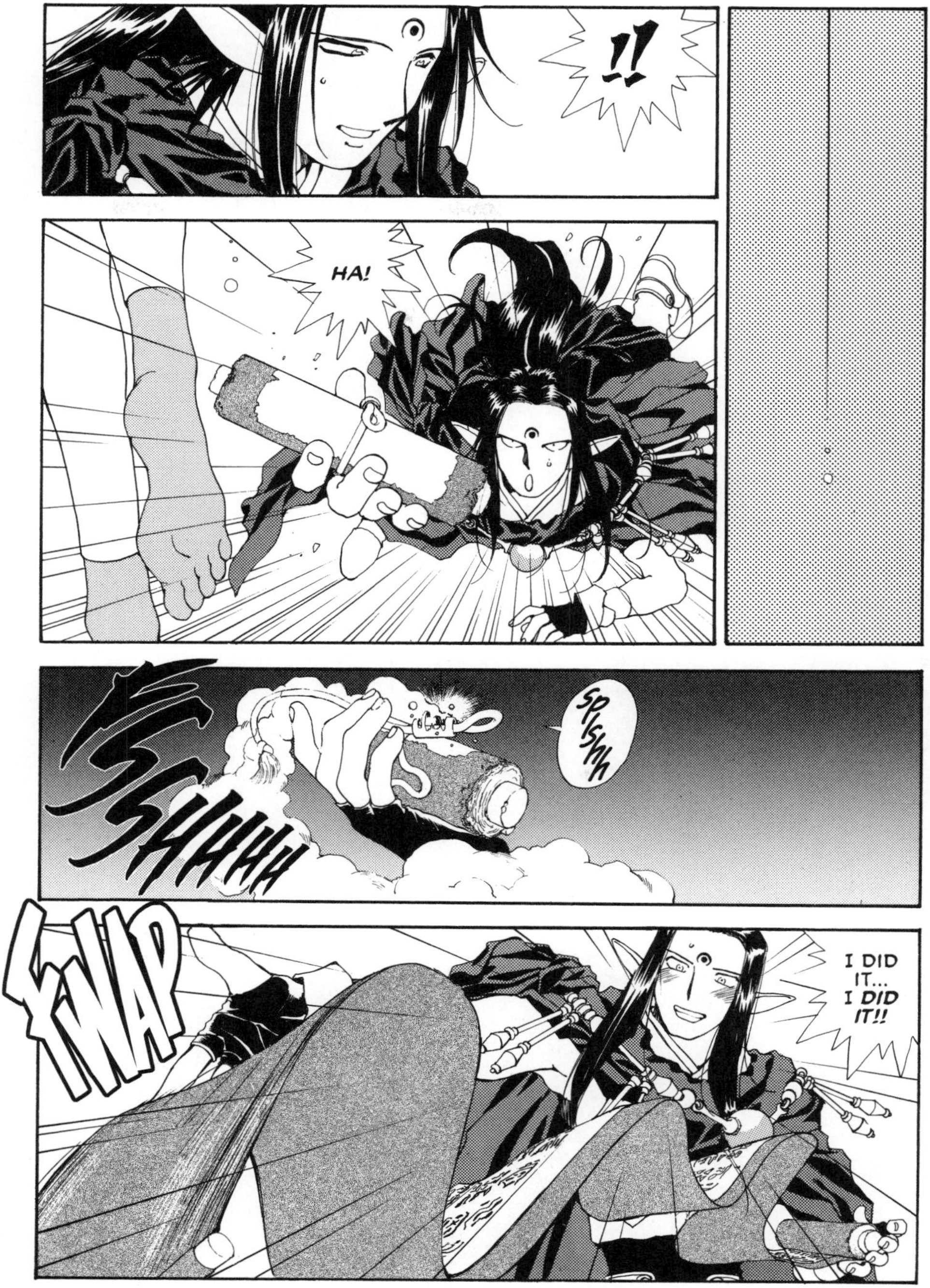
!!
HA!
SPISHH
I DID IT... I DID IT!!
FWAP

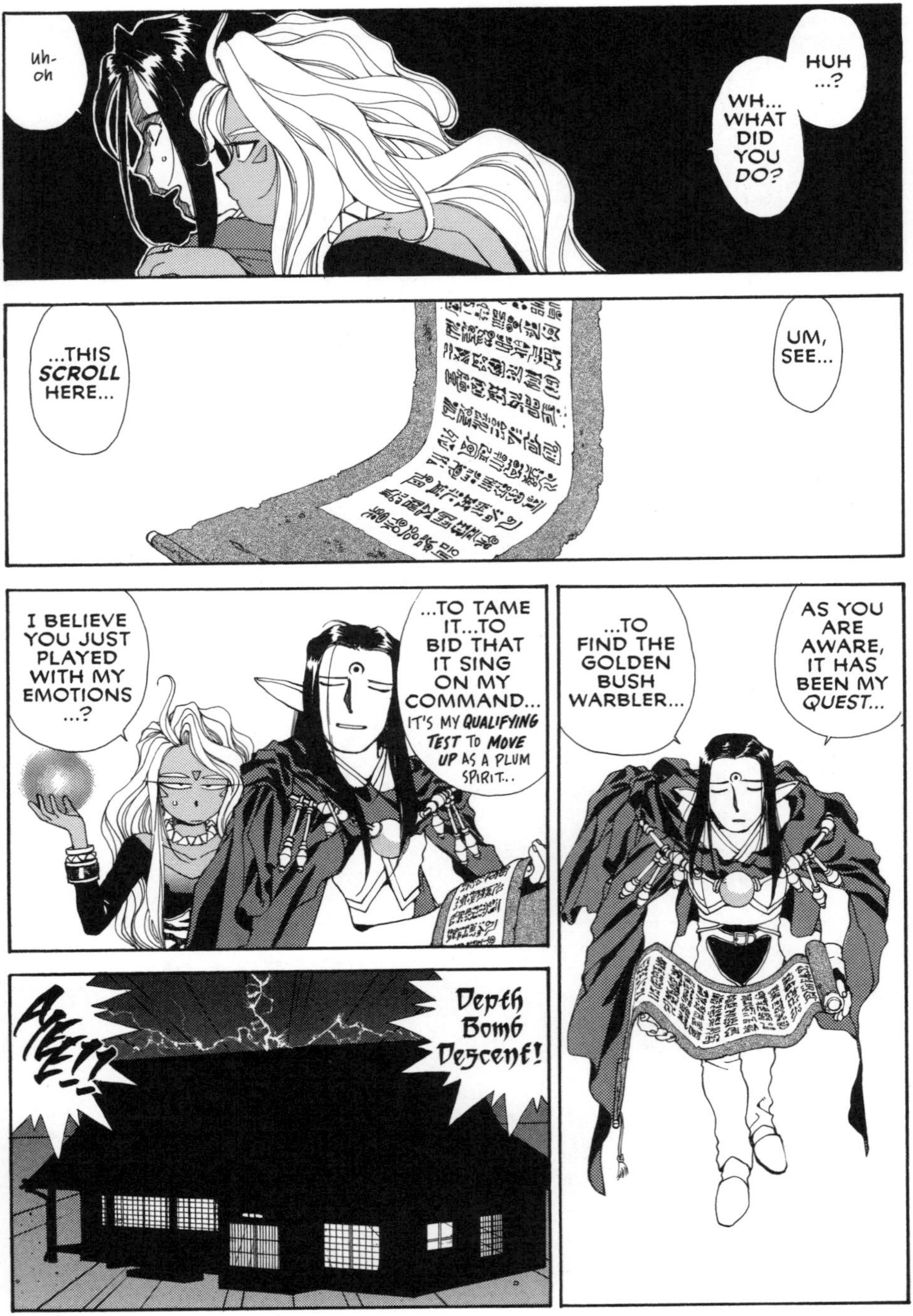
HUH ...?
WH... WHAT DID YOU DO?
uh-oh
UM, SEE...
...THIS SCROLL HERE...
AS YOU ARE AWARE, IT HAS BEEN MY QUEST...
...TO FIND THE GOLDEN BUSH WARBLER...
...TO TAME IT...TO BID THAT IT SING ON MY COMMAND...
IT'S MY QUALIFYING TEST TO MOVE UP AS A PLUM SPIRIT..
I BELIEVE YOU JUST PLAYED WITH MY EMOTIONS ...?
Depth Bomb Descent!

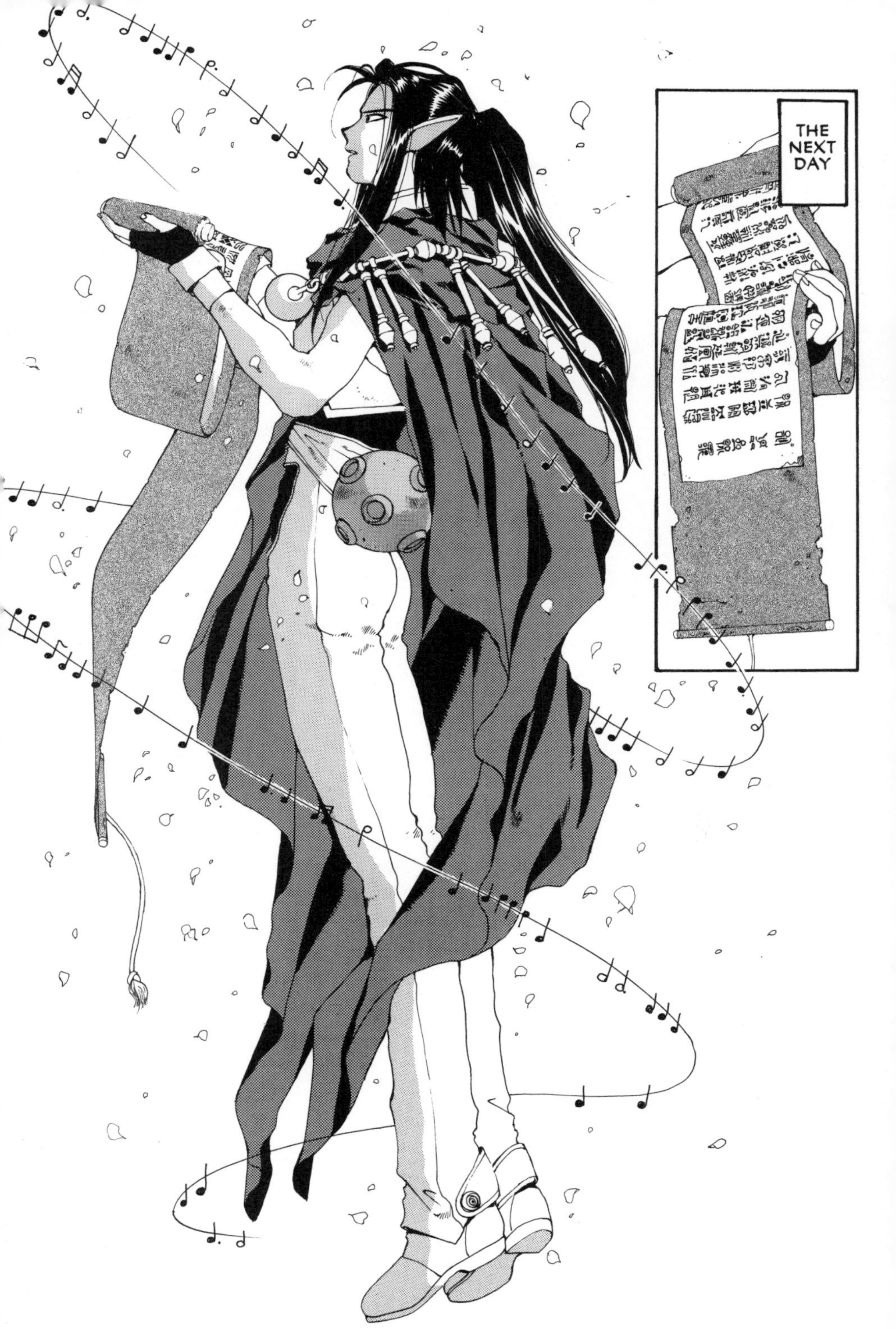
THE NEXT DAY

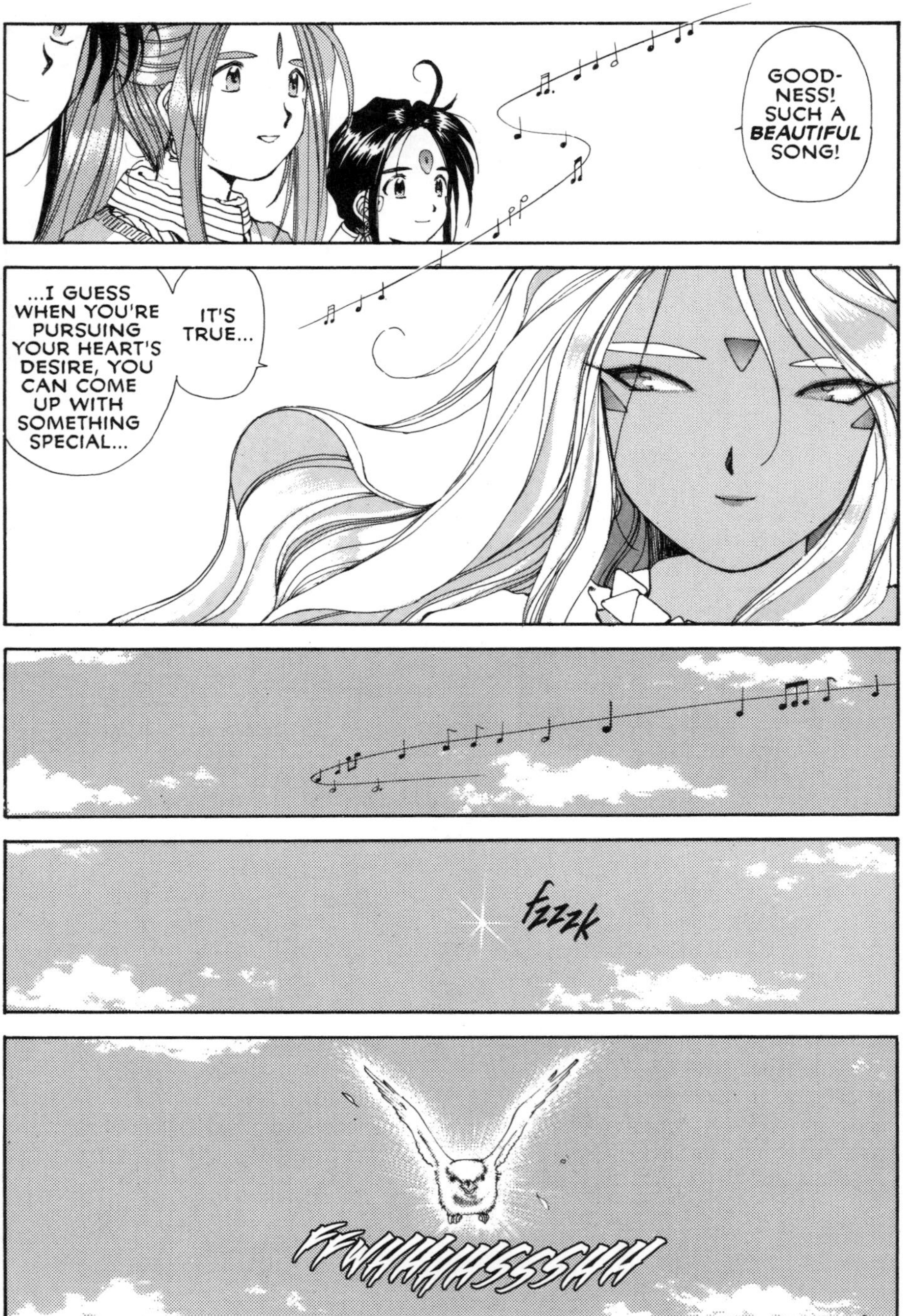
GOOD-NESS! SUCH A *BEAUTIFUL* SONG!
IT'S TRUE...
...I GUESS WHEN YOU'RE PURSUING YOUR HEART'S DESIRE, YOU CAN COME UP WITH SOMETHING SPECIAL...
fzzzk
FFWHHHHHSSSSHH

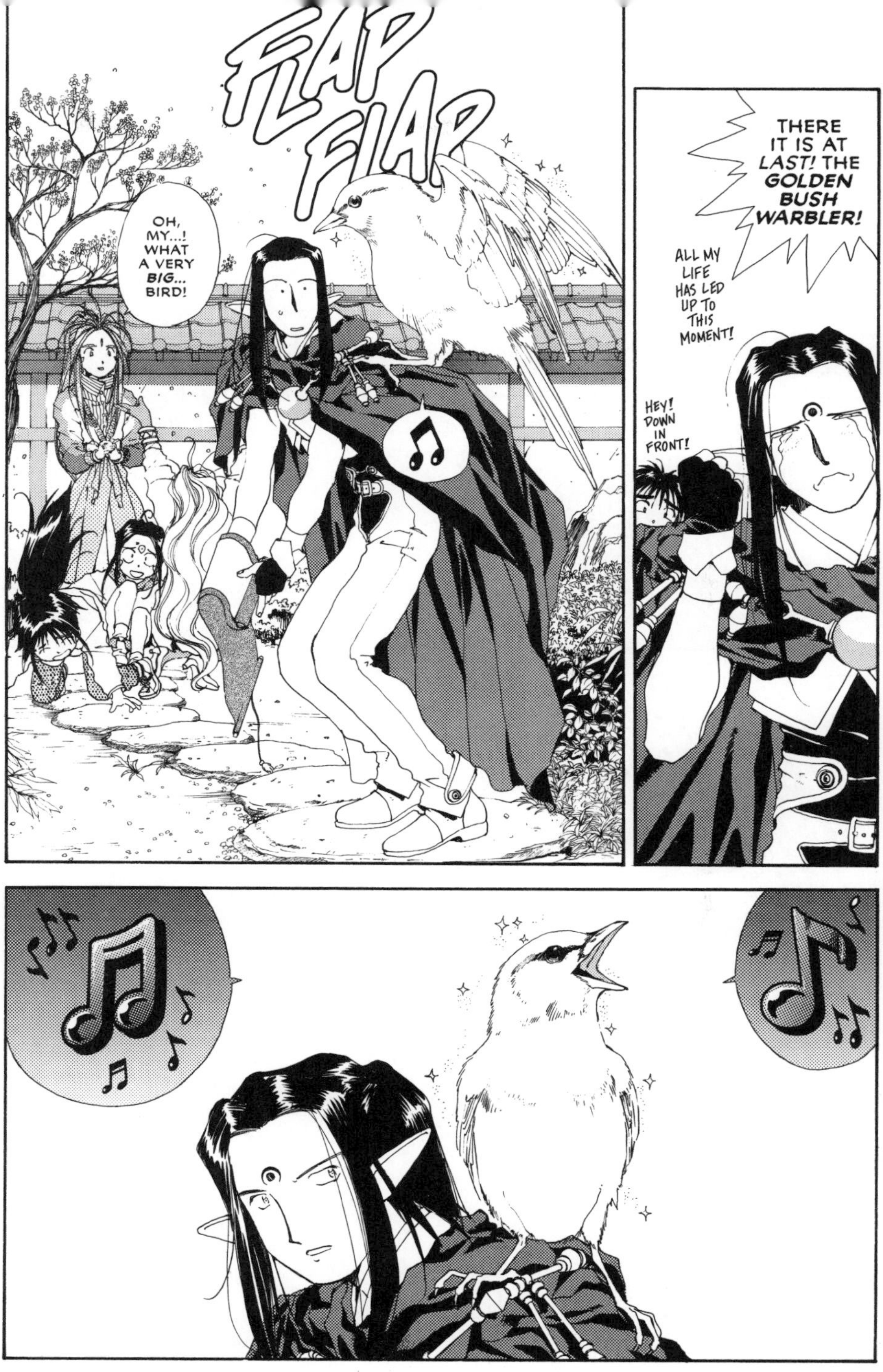
THERE IT IS AT LAST! THE GOLDEN BUSH WARBLER!
ALL MY LIFE HAS LED UP TO THIS MOMENT!
HEY! DOWN IN FRONT!
FLAP FLAP
OH, MY...! WHAT A VERY BIG... BIRD!

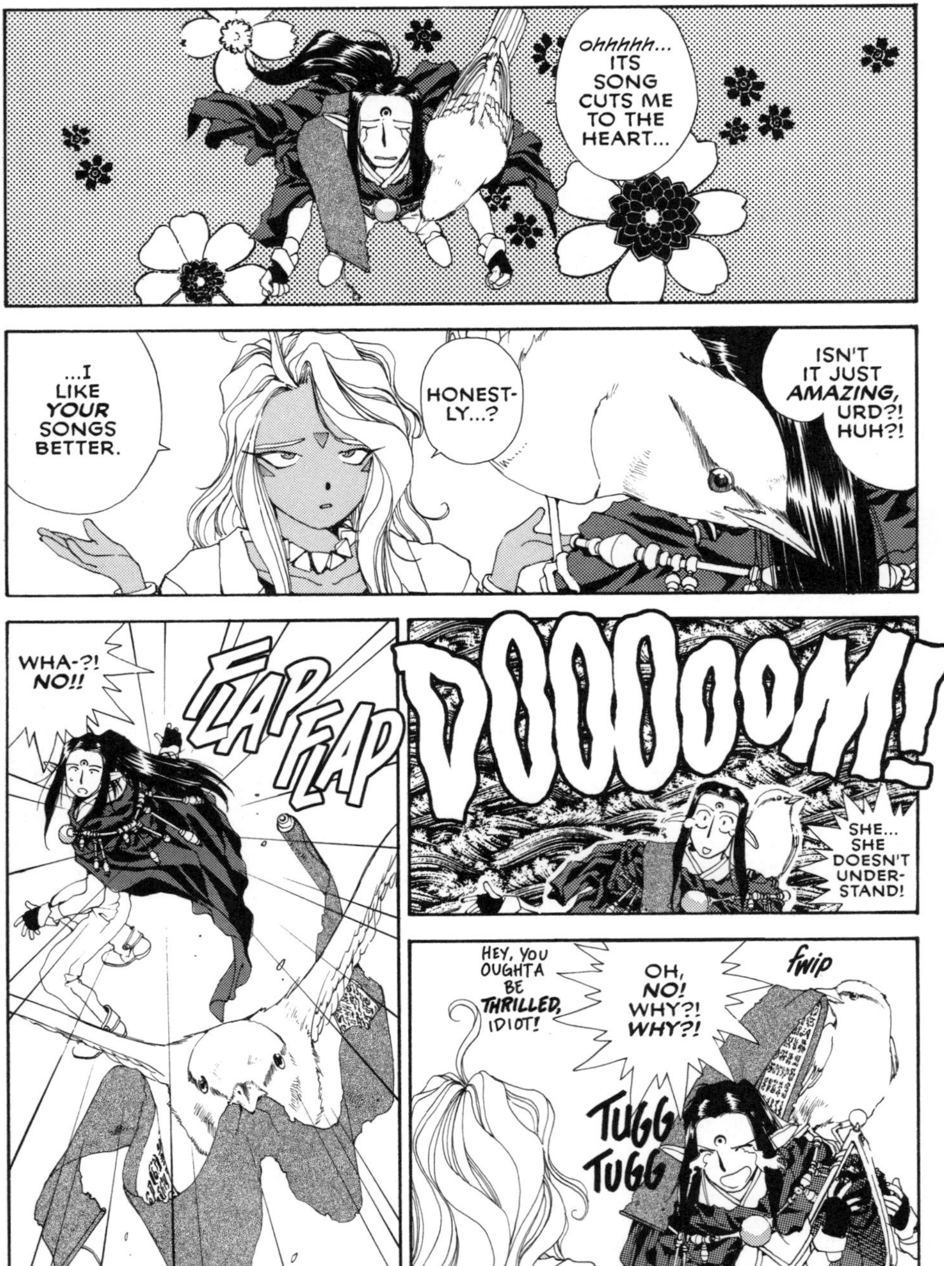
ohhhhh... ITS SONG CUTS ME TO THE HEART...
ISN'T IT JUST AMAZING, URD?! HUH?!
HONEST-LY...?
...I LIKE YOUR SONGS BETTER.
DOOOOOM!
SHE... SHE DOESN'T UNDER-STAND!
fwip
OH, NO! WHY?! WHY?!
HEY, YOU OUGHTA BE THRILLED, IDIOT!
TUGG TUGG
FLAP FLAP
WHA-?! NO!!

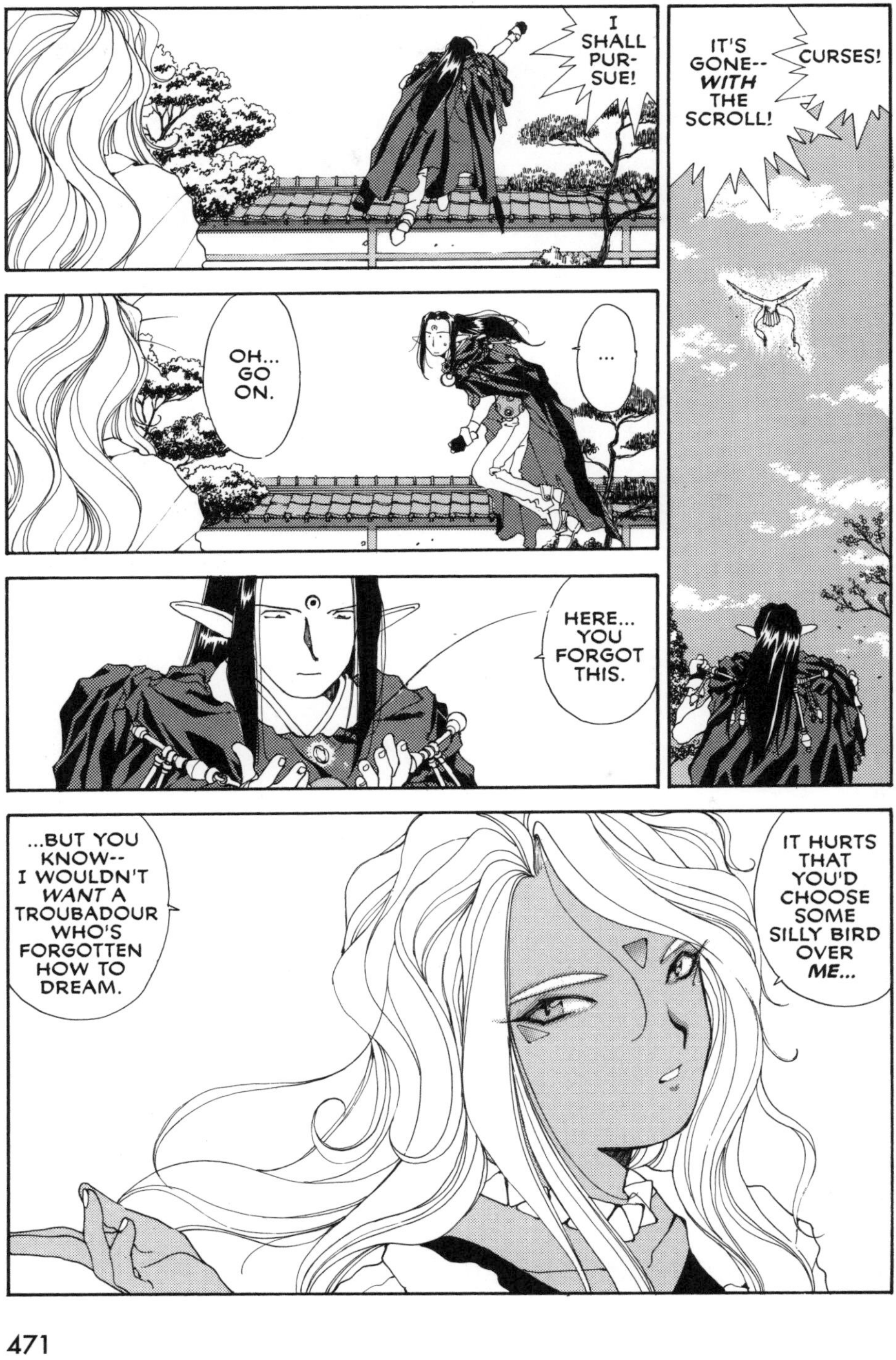
CURSES!
IT'S GONE--*WITH* THE SCROLL!
I SHALL PURSUE!
...
OH... GO ON.
HERE... YOU FORGOT THIS.
IT HURTS THAT YOU'D CHOOSE SOME SILLY BIRD OVER *ME...*
...BUT YOU KNOW-- I WOULDN'T *WANT* A TROUBADOUR WHO'S FORGOTTEN HOW TO DREAM.

...FOR-GIVE ME, URD!

YEESH... *WHAT AN IDIOT.*

HANG-ING ON TO THAT SILLY RING...

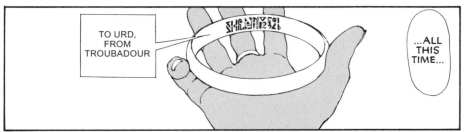

TO URD, FROM TROUBADOUR

...ALL THIS TIME...

OOPS! I FORGOT...

UH, ANTI-DOTE? PLEASE?

CHAPTER 56

It's Lonely at the Top

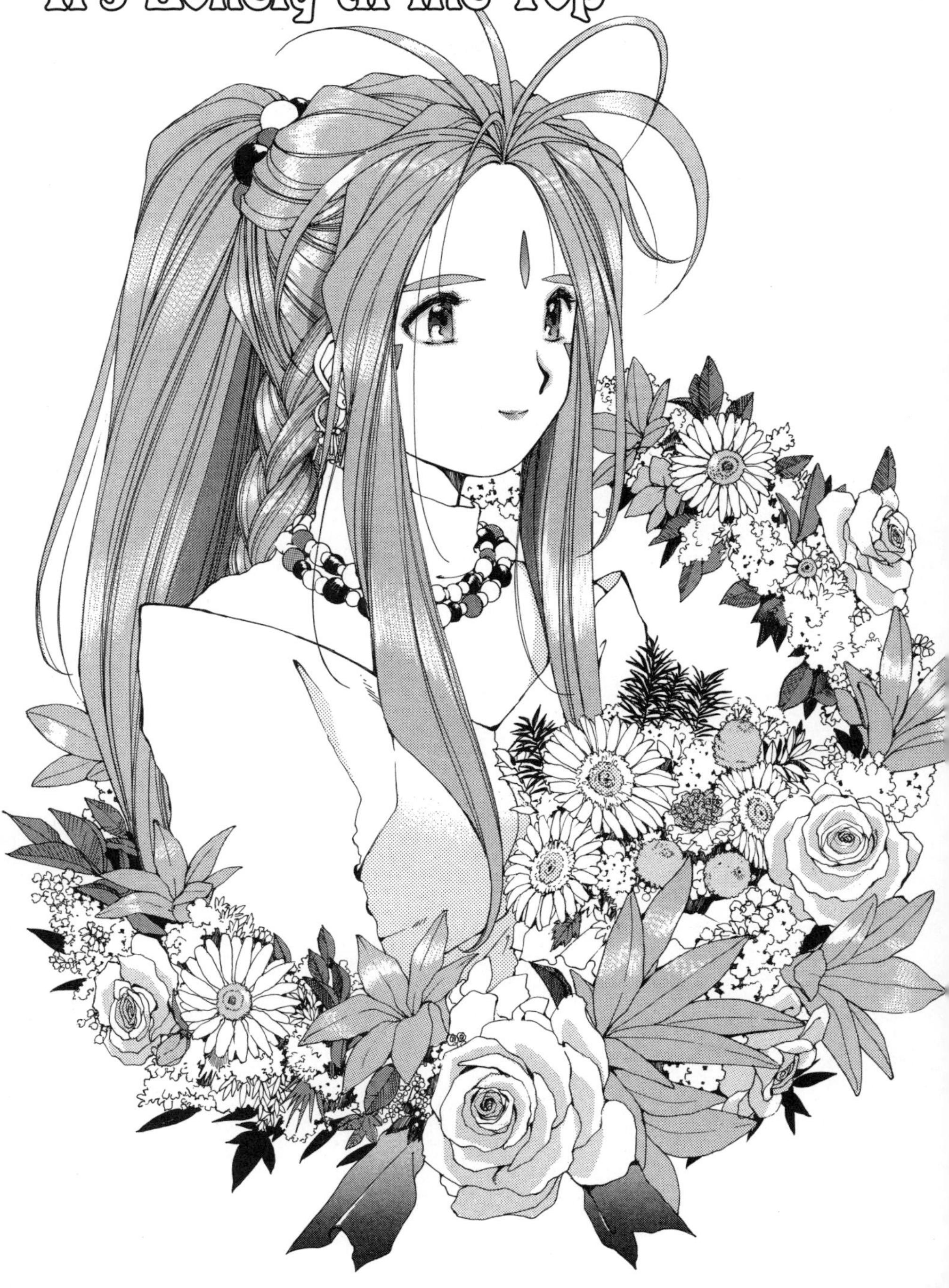

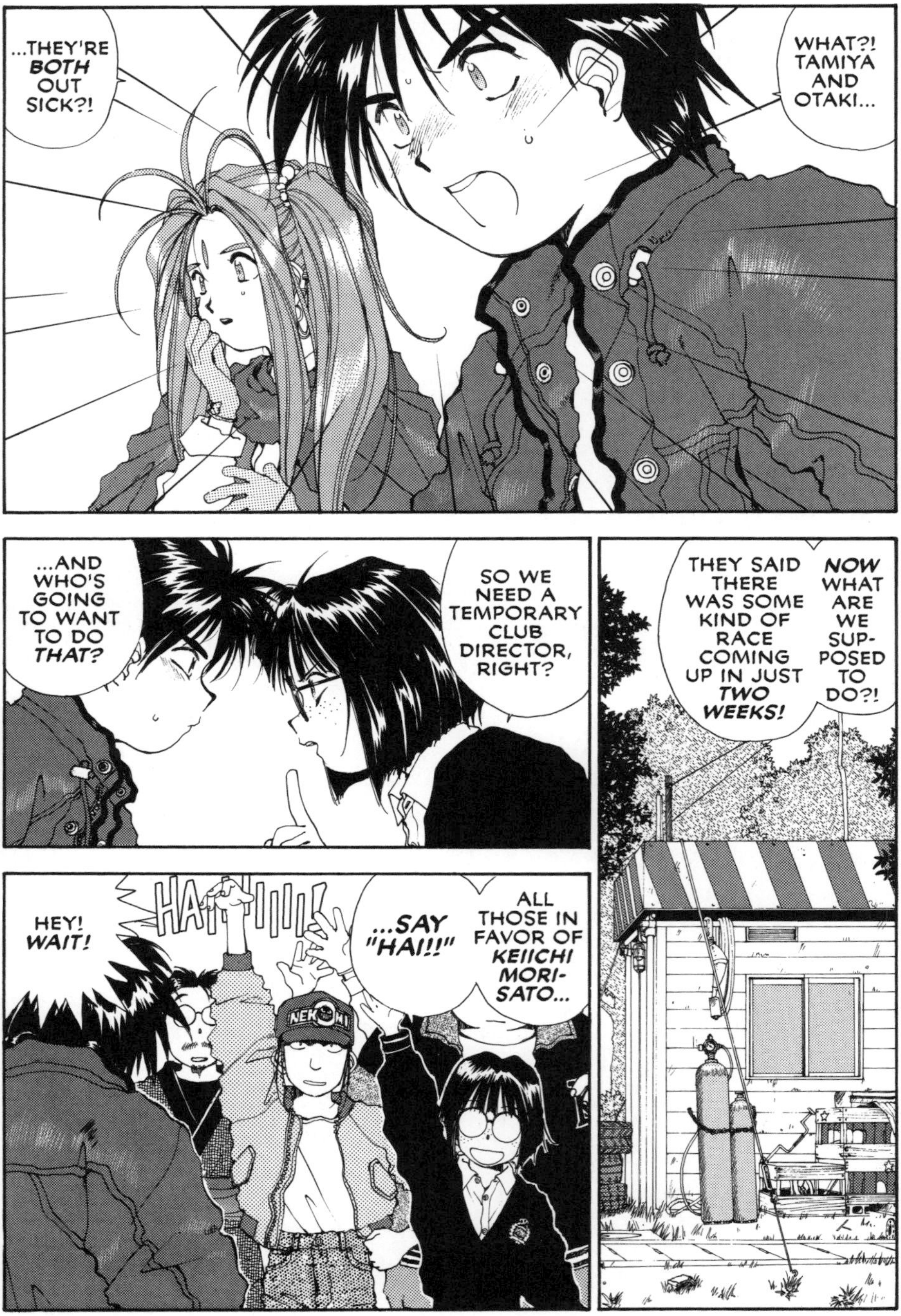
WHAT?! TAMIYA AND OTAKI...
...THEY'RE *BOTH* OUT SICK?!
NOW WHAT ARE WE SUP-POSED TO DO?!
THEY SAID THERE WAS SOME KIND OF RACE COMING UP IN JUST *TWO WEEKS!*
SO WE NEED A TEMPORARY CLUB DIRECTOR, RIGHT?
...AND WHO'S GOING TO WANT TO DO *THAT?*
ALL THOSE IN FAVOR OF *KEIICHI MORI-SATO...*
...SAY "HAI!!"
HAIIIIII!
HEY! *WAIT!*

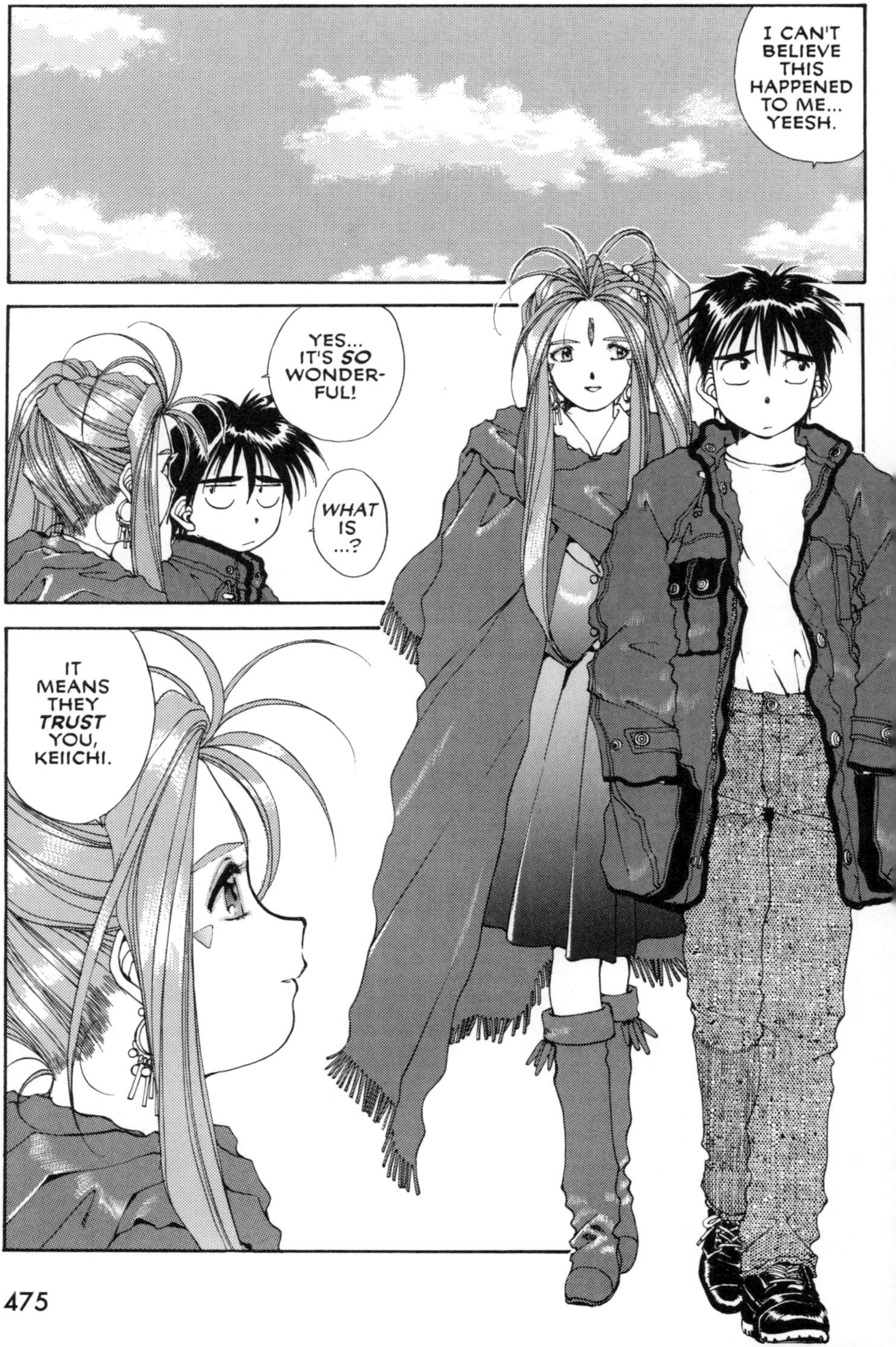
I CAN'T BELIEVE THIS HAPPENED TO ME... YEESH.
YES... IT'S *SO* WONDERFUL!
WHAT IS ...?
IT MEANS THEY *TRUST* YOU, KEIICHI.

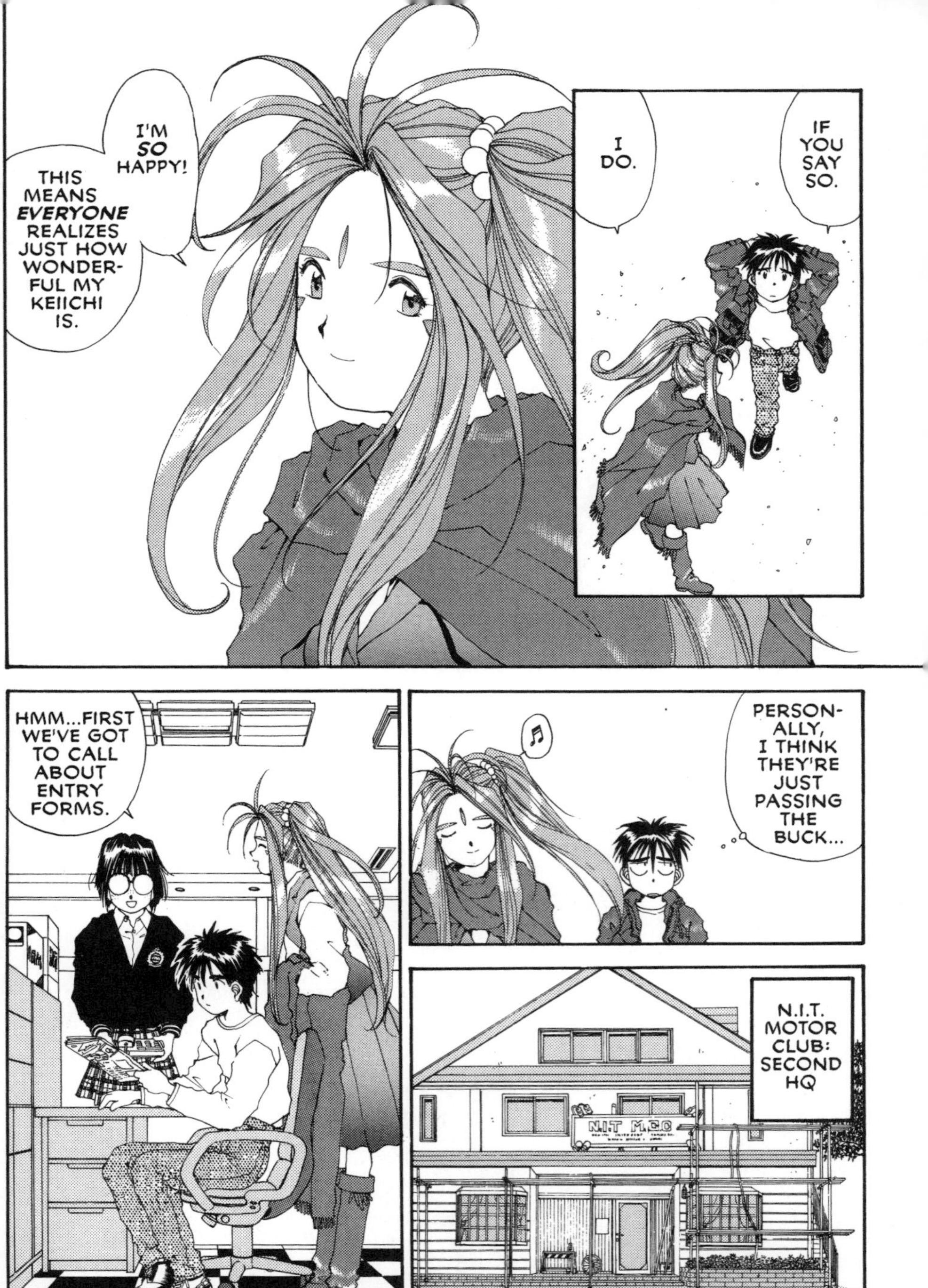
IF YOU SAY SO.
I DO.
I'M *SO* HAPPY!
THIS MEANS ***EVERYONE*** REALIZES JUST HOW WONDERFUL MY KEIICHI IS.
PERSONALLY, I THINK THEY'RE JUST PASSING THE BUCK...
♪
N.I.T. MOTOR CLUB: SECOND HQ
HMM...FIRST WE'VE GOT TO CALL ABOUT ENTRY FORMS.

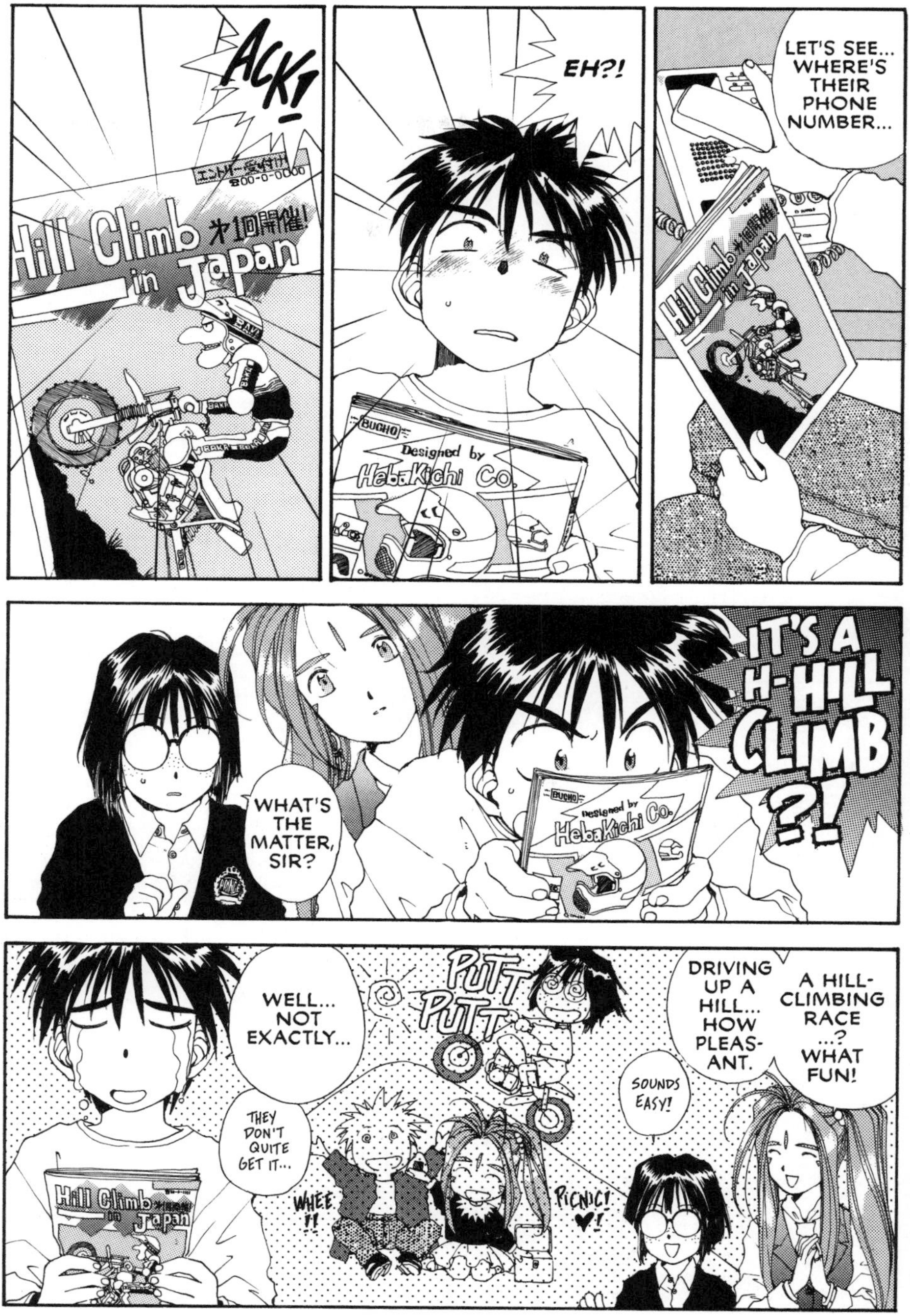
LET'S SEE... WHERE'S THEIR PHONE NUMBER...
Hill Climb in Japan
EH?!
BUCHO
Designed by HebaKichi Co.
ACK!
Hill Climb in Japan
IT'S A H-HILL CLIMB ?!
WHAT'S THE MATTER, SIR?
BUCHO
Designed by HebaKichi Co.
A HILL-CLIMBING RACE ...? WHAT FUN!
DRIVING UP A HILL... HOW PLEASANT.
SOUNDS EASY!
PICNIC! ♥!
PUTT PUTT
WHEE !!
THEY DON'T QUITE GET IT...
WELL... NOT EXACTLY...
Hill Climb in Japan

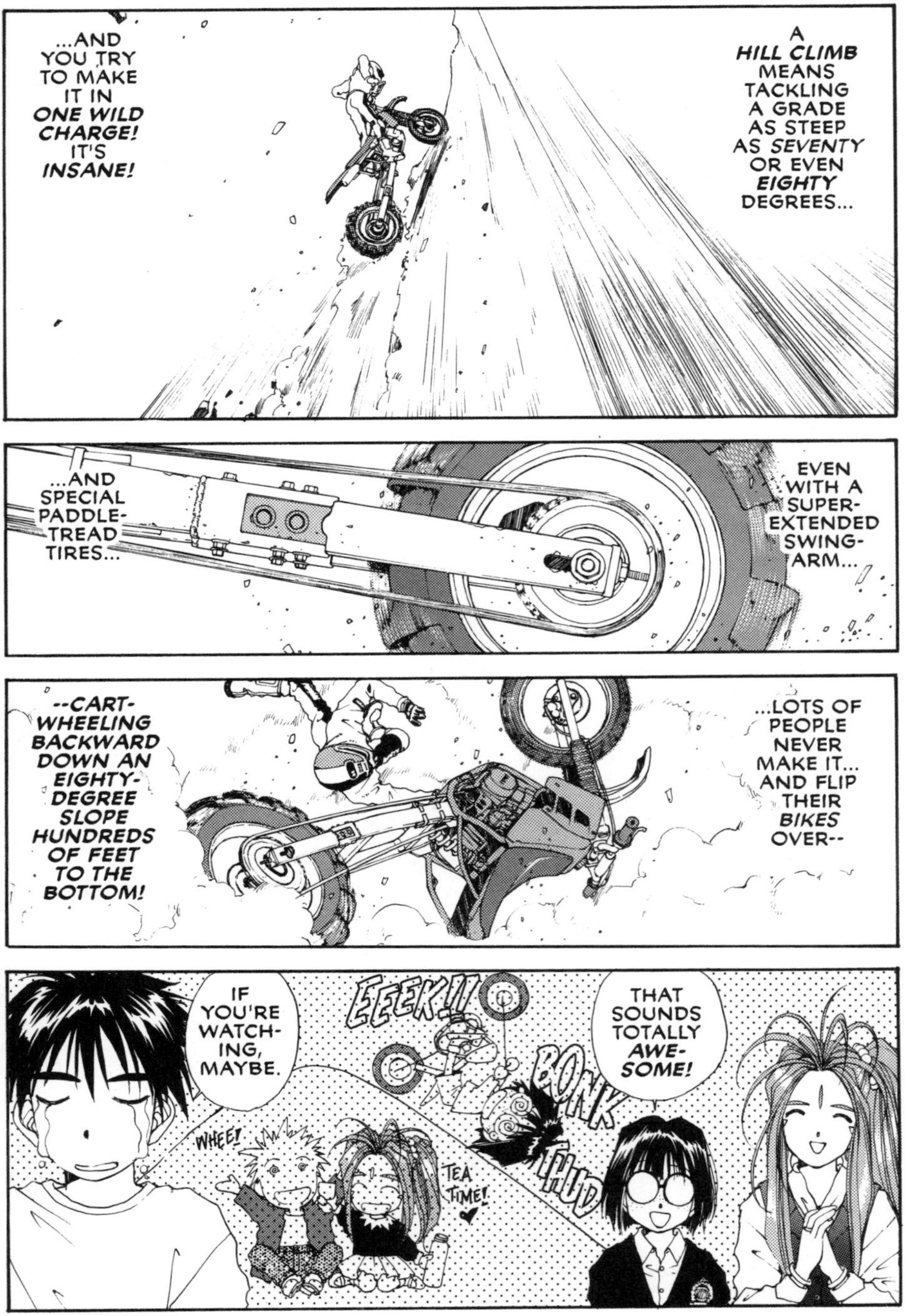
A HILL CLIMB MEANS TACKLING A GRADE AS STEEP AS SEVENTY OR EVEN EIGHTY DEGREES...
...AND YOU TRY TO MAKE IT IN ONE WILD CHARGE! IT'S INSANE!
EVEN WITH A SUPER-EXTENDED SWING-ARM...
...AND SPECIAL PADDLE-TREAD TIRES...
...LOTS OF PEOPLE NEVER MAKE IT... AND FLIP THEIR BIKES OVER--
--CART-WHEELING BACKWARD DOWN AN EIGHTY-DEGREE SLOPE HUNDREDS OF FEET TO THE BOTTOM!
THAT SOUNDS TOTALLY AWESOME!
BONK
THUD
TEA TIME!
EEEK!!
IF YOU'RE WATCHING, MAYBE.
WHEE!

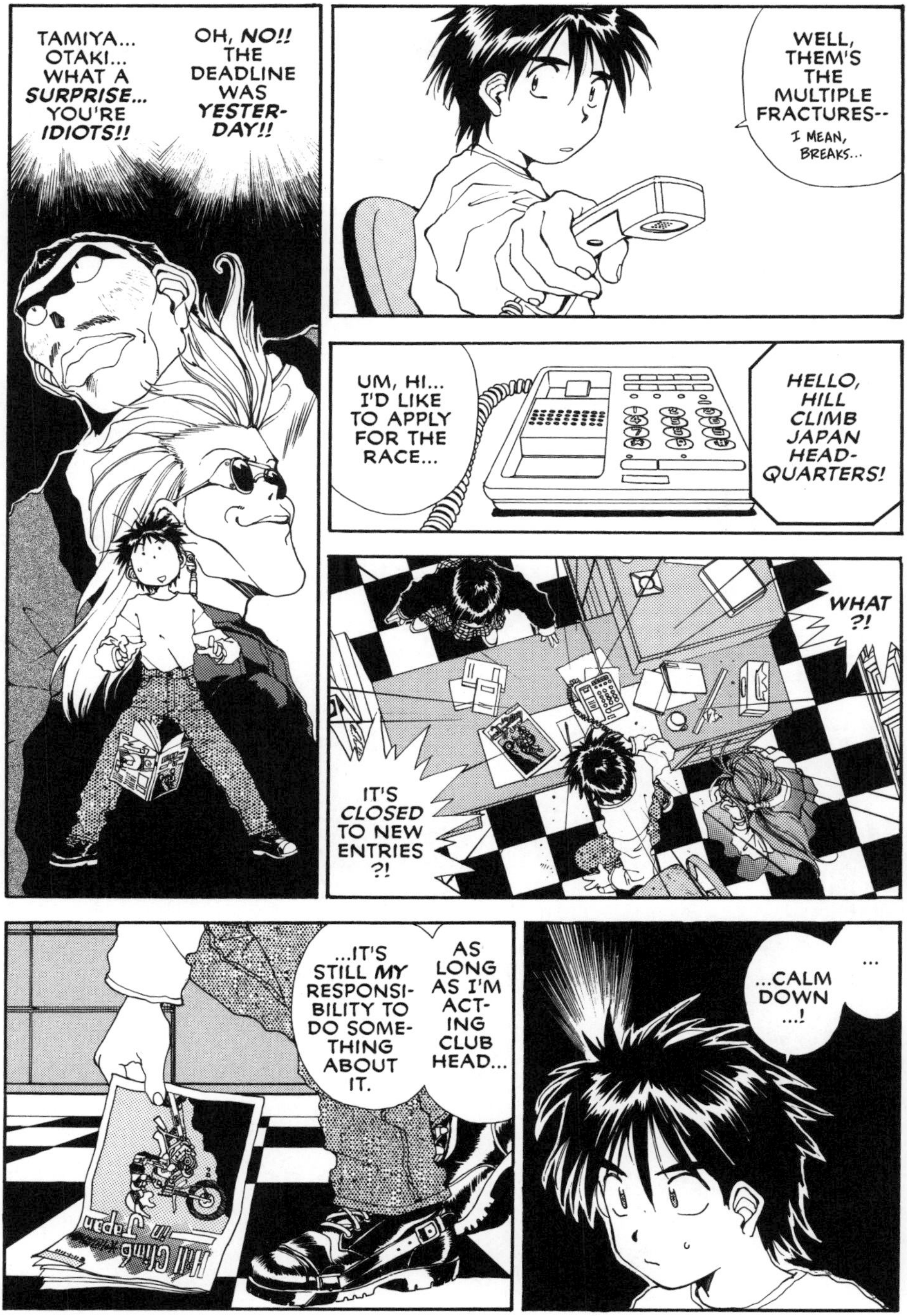
WELL, THEM'S THE MULTIPLE FRACTURES-- I MEAN, BREAKS...
HELLO, HILL CLIMB JAPAN HEAD-QUARTERS!
UM, HI... I'D LIKE TO APPLY FOR THE RACE...
WHAT ?!
IT'S CLOSED TO NEW ENTRIES ?!
OH, NO!! THE DEADLINE WAS YESTER-DAY!!
TAMIYA... OTAKI... WHAT A SURPRISE... YOU'RE IDIOTS!!
...
...CALM DOWN ...!
AS LONG AS I'M ACT-ING CLUB HEAD...
...IT'S STILL MY RESPONSI-BILITY TO DO SOME-THING ABOUT IT.

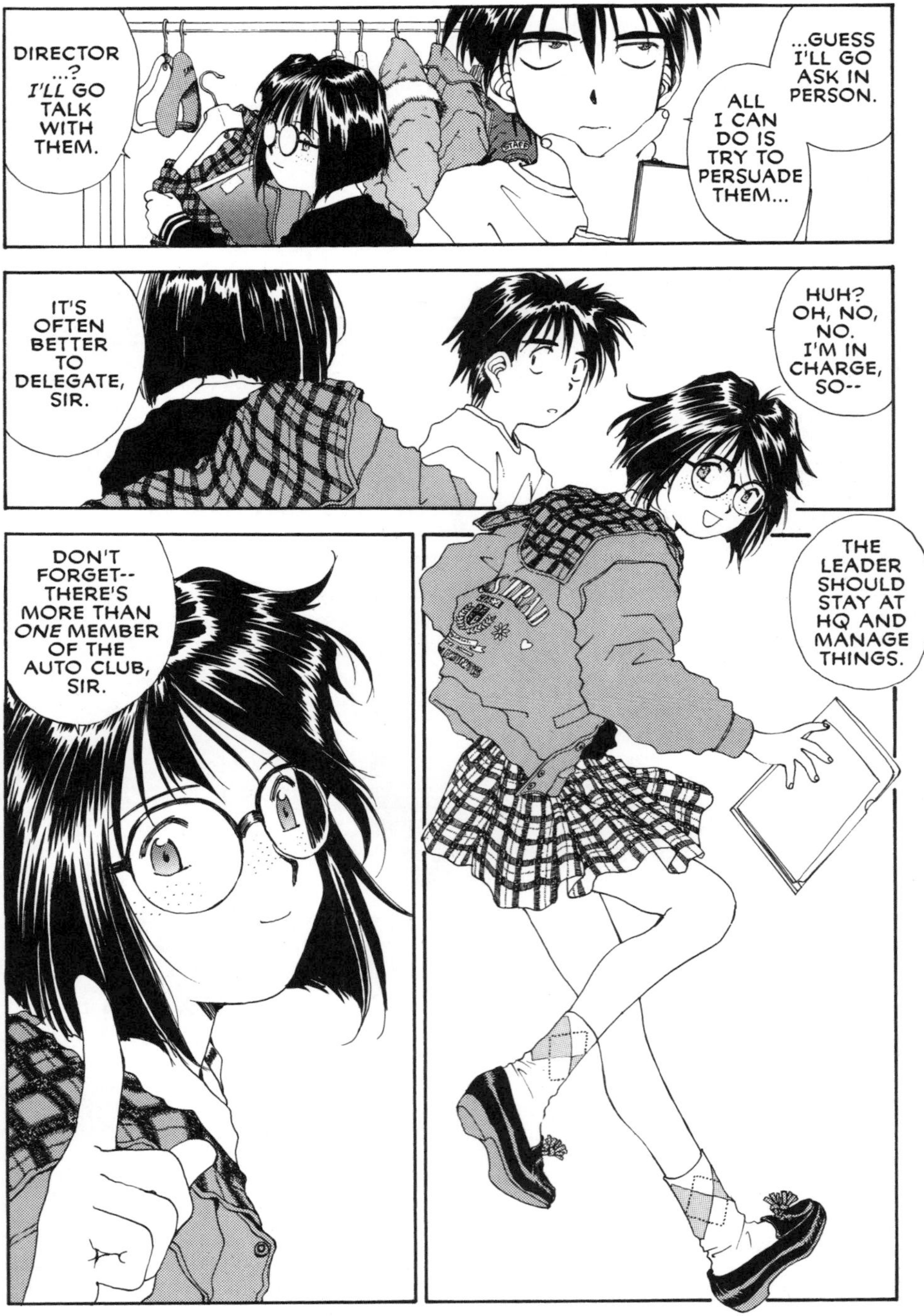
...GUESS I'LL GO ASK IN PERSON.
ALL I CAN DO IS TRY TO PERSUADE THEM...
DIRECTOR ...? *I'LL* GO TALK WITH THEM.
HUH? OH, NO, NO. I'M IN CHARGE, SO--
IT'S OFTEN BETTER TO DELEGATE, SIR.
THE LEADER SHOULD STAY AT HQ AND MANAGE THINGS.
DON'T FORGET-- THERE'S MORE THAN *ONE* MEMBER OF THE AUTO CLUB, SIR.

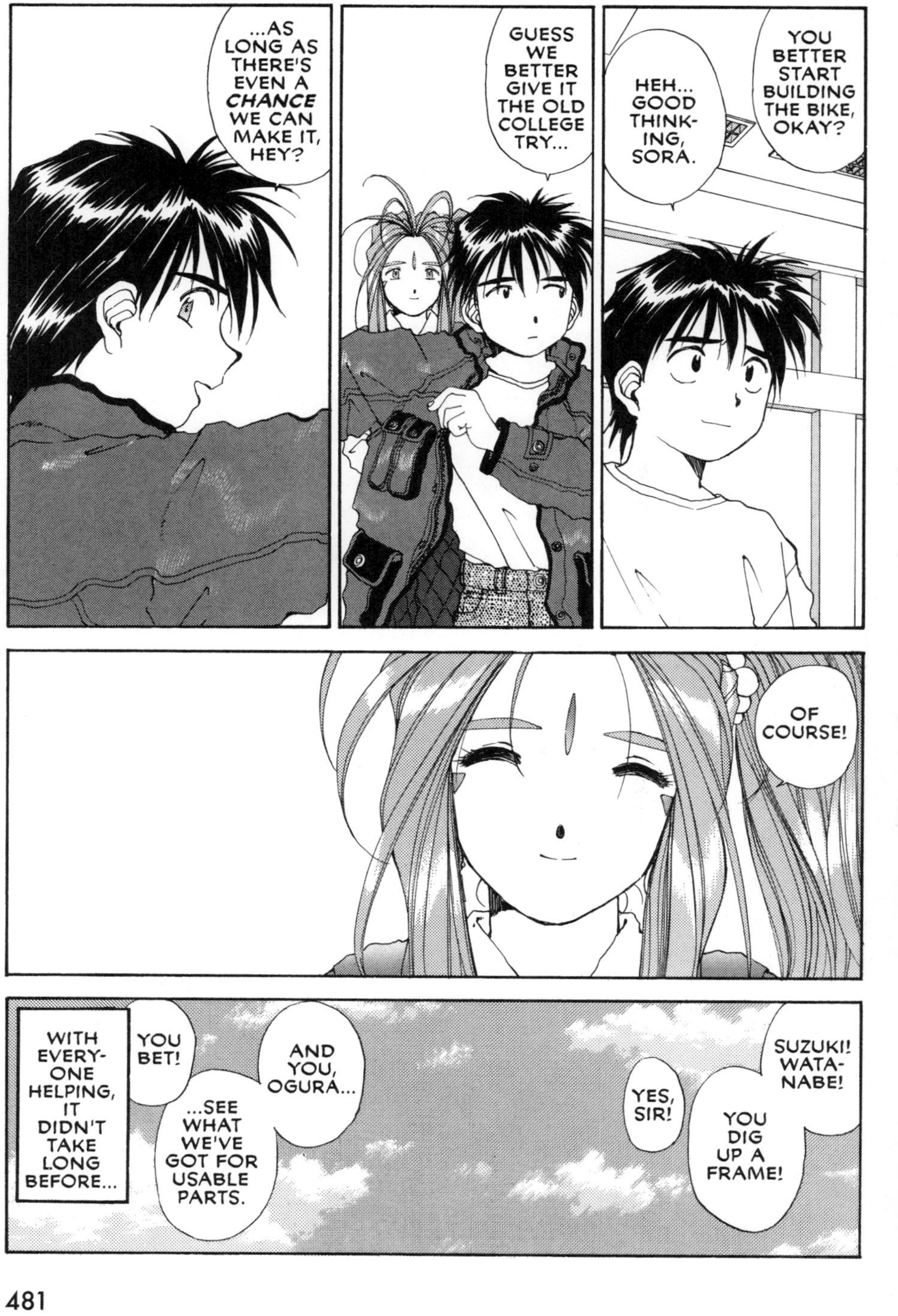
YOU BETTER START BUILDING THE BIKE, OKAY?
HEH... GOOD THINKING, SORA.
GUESS WE BETTER GIVE IT THE OLD COLLEGE TRY...
...AS LONG AS THERE'S EVEN A *CHANCE* WE CAN MAKE IT, HEY?
OF COURSE!
SUZUKI! WATANABE!
YOU DIG UP A FRAME!
YES, SIR!
AND YOU, OGURA...
...SEE WHAT WE'VE GOT FOR USABLE PARTS.
YOU BET!
WITH EVERYONE HELPING, IT DIDN'T TAKE LONG BEFORE...

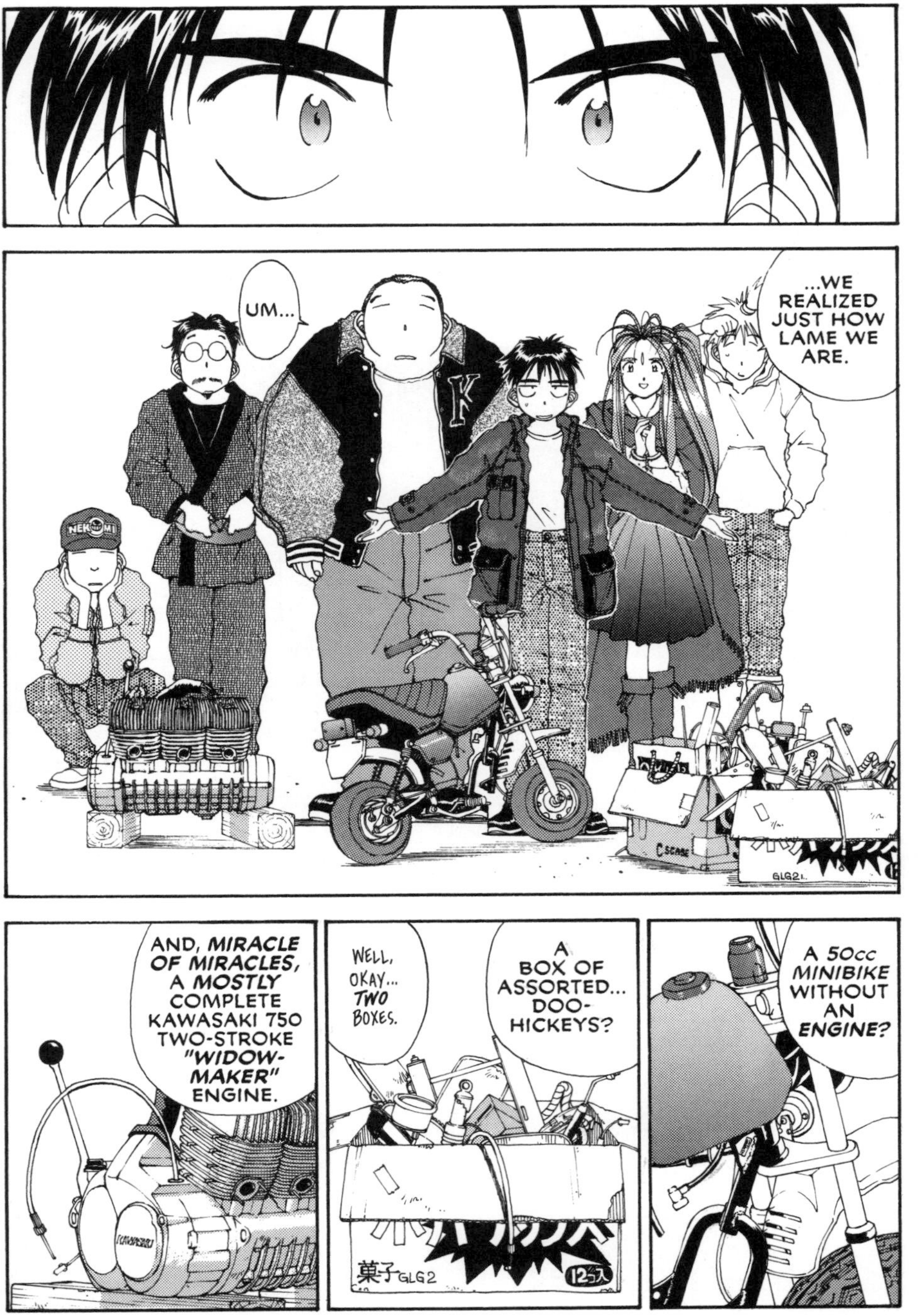
...WE REALIZED JUST HOW LAME WE ARE.
UM...
NEKOMI
A 50cc MINIBIKE WITHOUT AN ENGINE?
A BOX OF ASSORTED... DOO-HICKEYS?
WELL, OKAY... TWO BOXES.
菓子GLG2
12コ入
AND, MIRACLE OF MIRACLES, A MOSTLY COMPLETE KAWASAKI 750 TWO-STROKE "WIDOW-MAKER" ENGINE.

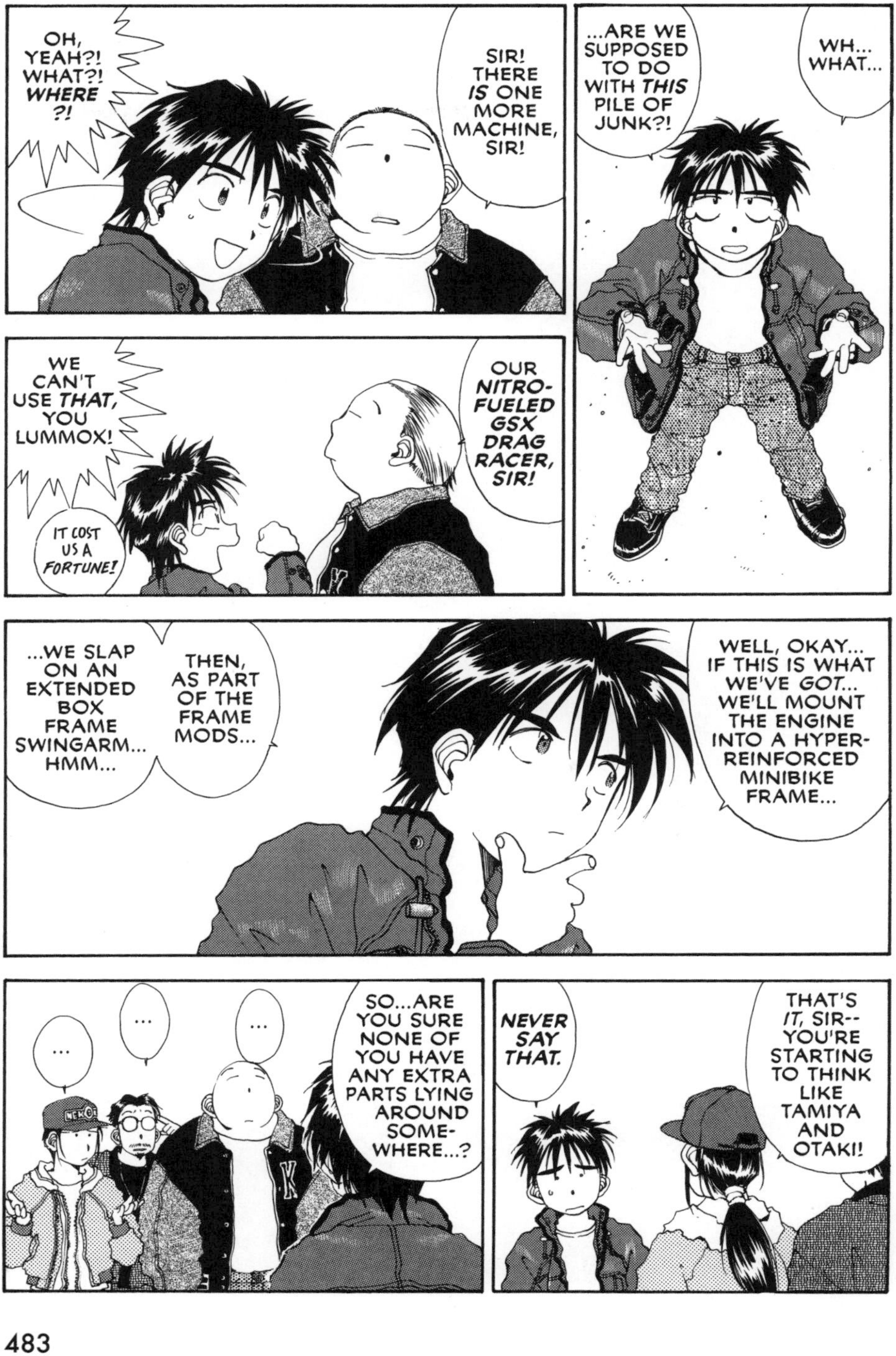
WH... WHAT...
...ARE WE SUPPOSED TO DO WITH *THIS* PILE OF JUNK?!
SIR! THERE *IS* ONE MORE MACHINE, SIR!
OH, YEAH?! WHAT?! *WHERE?!*
OUR *NITRO-FUELED GSX DRAG RACER, SIR!*
WE CAN'T USE *THAT,* YOU LUMMOX!
IT COST US A *FORTUNE!*
WELL, OKAY... IF THIS IS WHAT WE'VE *GOT*... WE'LL MOUNT THE ENGINE INTO A HYPER-REINFORCED MINIBIKE FRAME...
THEN, AS PART OF THE FRAME MODS...
...WE SLAP ON AN EXTENDED BOX FRAME SWINGARM... HMM...
THAT'S *IT,* SIR-- YOU'RE STARTING TO THINK LIKE TAMIYA AND OTAKI!
NEVER SAY THAT.
SO...ARE YOU SURE NONE OF YOU HAVE ANY EXTRA PARTS LYING AROUND SOME-WHERE...?
...
...
...

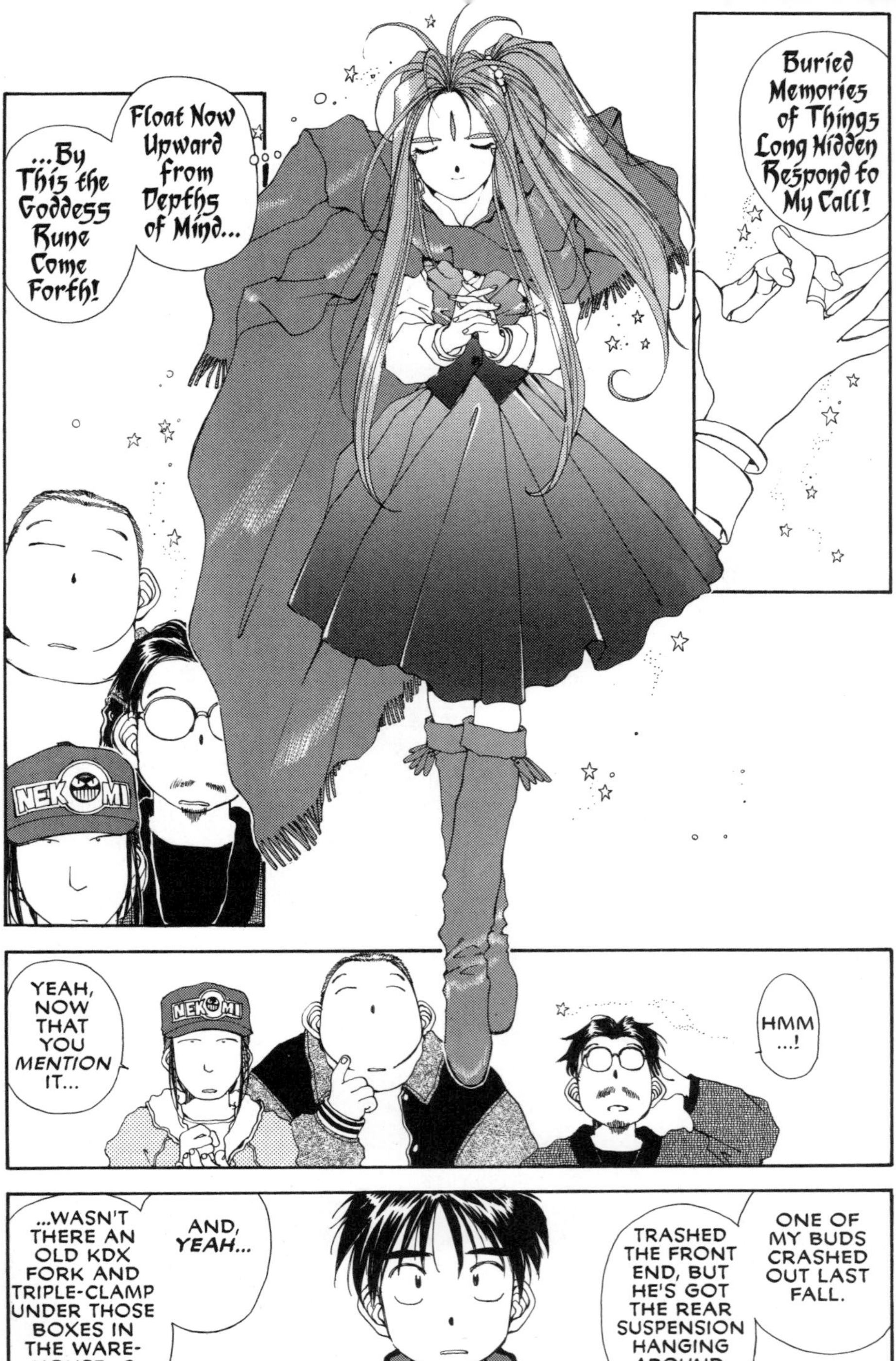
Buried Memories of Things Long Hidden Respond to My Call!
Float Now Upward from Depths of Mind...
...By This the Goddess Rune Come Forth!
NEKOMI
HMM ...!
YEAH, NOW THAT YOU *MENTION* IT...
NEKOMI
ONE OF MY BUDS CRASHED OUT LAST FALL.
TRASHED THE FRONT END, BUT HE'S GOT THE REAR SUSPENSION HANGING AROUND.
AND, *YEAH*...
...WASN'T THERE AN OLD KDX FORK AND TRIPLE-CLAMP UNDER THOSE BOXES IN THE WARE-HOUSE...?

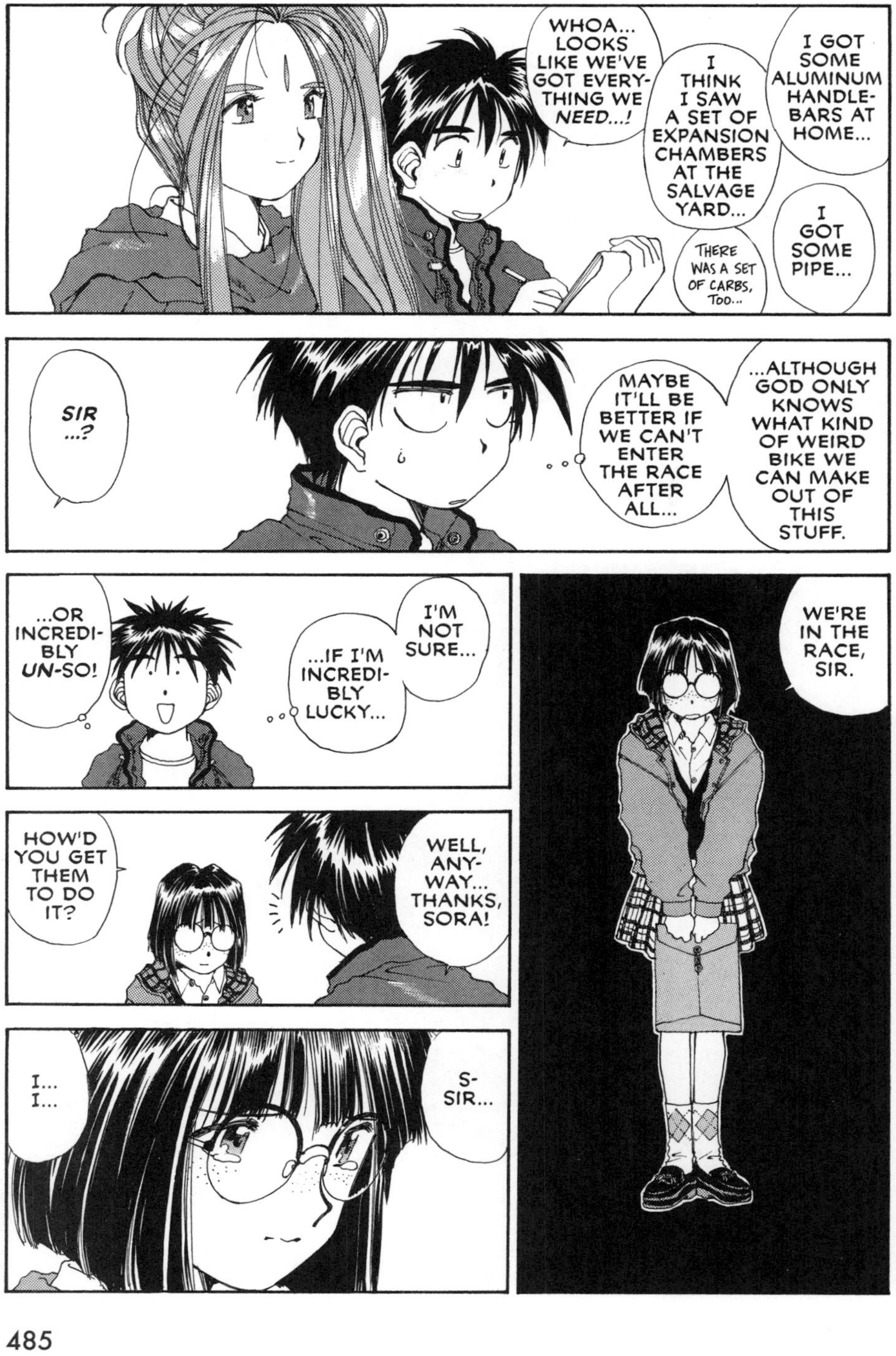
I GOT SOME ALUMINUM HANDLE-BARS AT HOME...
I GOT SOME PIPE...
I THINK I SAW A SET OF EXPANSION CHAMBERS AT THE SALVAGE YARD...
THERE WAS A SET OF CARBS, TOO...
WHOA... LOOKS LIKE WE'VE GOT EVERYTHING WE *NEED*...!
...ALTHOUGH GOD ONLY KNOWS WHAT KIND OF WEIRD BIKE WE CAN MAKE OUT OF THIS STUFF.
MAYBE IT'LL BE BETTER IF WE CAN'T ENTER THE RACE AFTER ALL...
SIR ...?
WE'RE IN THE RACE, SIR.
I'M NOT SURE...
...IF I'M INCREDIBLY LUCKY...
...OR INCREDIBLY *UN*-SO!
WELL, ANYWAY... THANKS, SORA!
HOW'D YOU GET THEM TO DO IT?
S-SIR...
I... I...

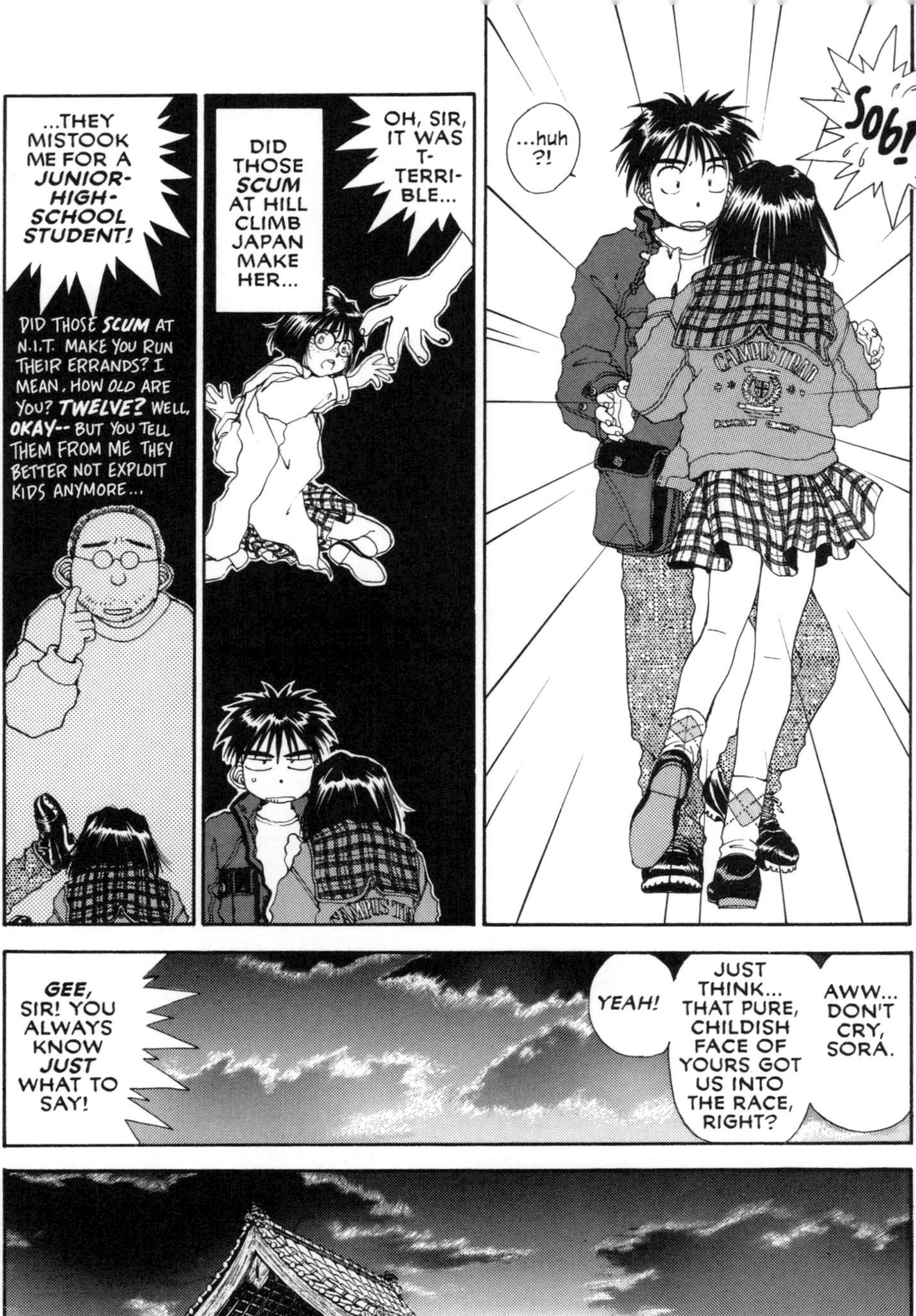
SOB!
...huh ?!
OH, SIR, IT WAS T-TERRIBLE...
DID THOSE SCUM AT HILL CLIMB JAPAN MAKE HER...
...THEY MISTOOK ME FOR A JUNIOR-HIGH-SCHOOL STUDENT!
DID THOSE SCUM AT N.I.T. MAKE YOU RUN THEIR ERRANDS? I MEAN, HOW OLD ARE YOU? TWELVE? WELL, OKAY-- BUT YOU TELL THEM FROM ME THEY BETTER NOT EXPLOIT KIDS ANYMORE...
AWW... DON'T CRY, SORA.
JUST THINK... THAT PURE, CHILDISH FACE OF YOURS GOT US INTO THE RACE, RIGHT?
YEAH!
GEE, SIR! YOU ALWAYS KNOW JUST WHAT TO SAY!

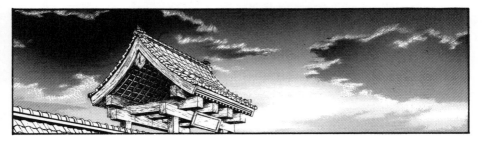

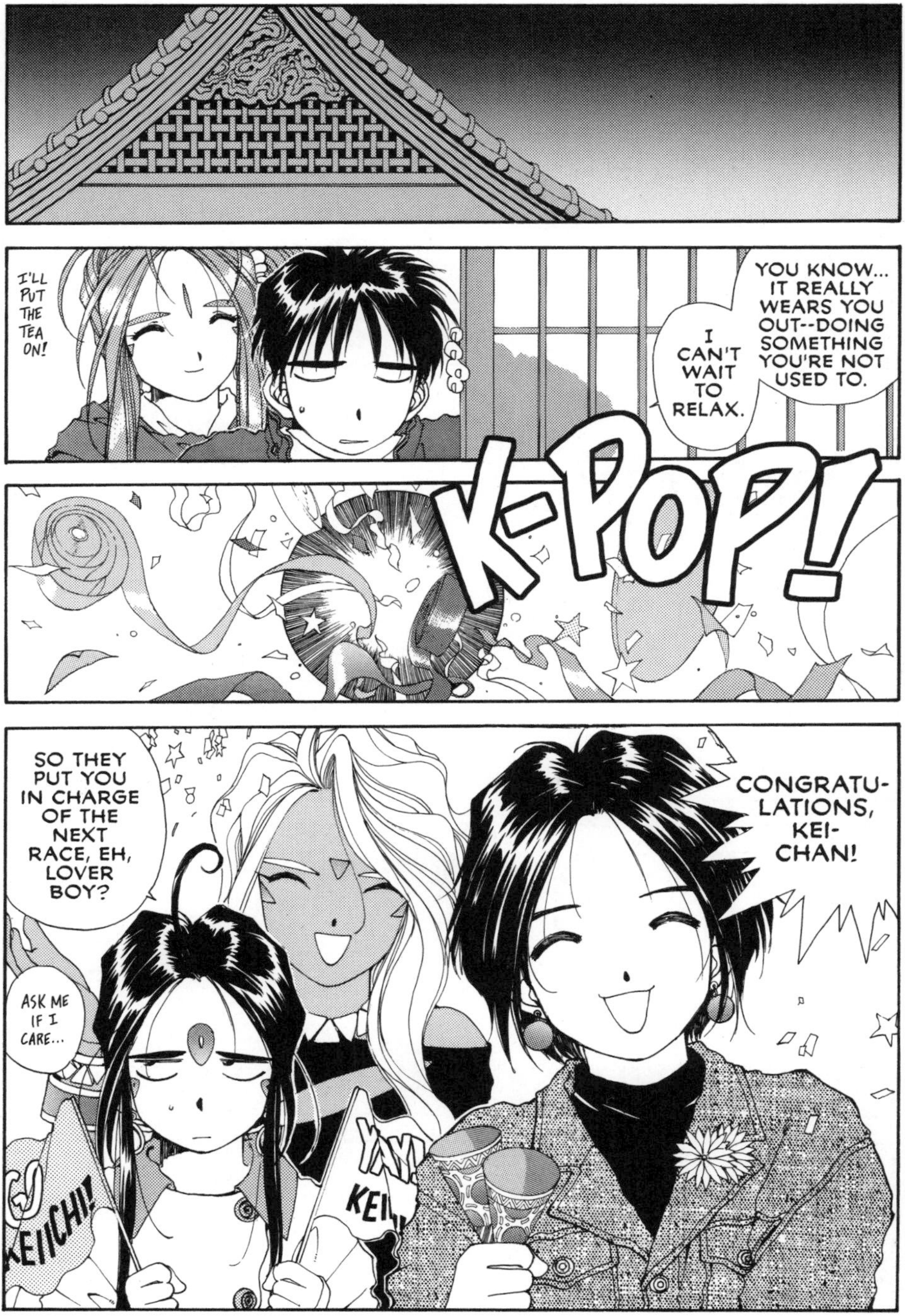
YOU KNOW... IT REALLY WEARS YOU OUT--DOING SOMETHING YOU'RE NOT USED TO.
I CAN'T WAIT TO RELAX.
I'LL PUT THE TEA ON!
K-POP!
CONGRATU-LATIONS, KEI-CHAN!
SO THEY PUT YOU IN CHARGE OF THE NEXT RACE, EH, LOVER BOY?
ASK ME IF I CARE...
KEIICHI!

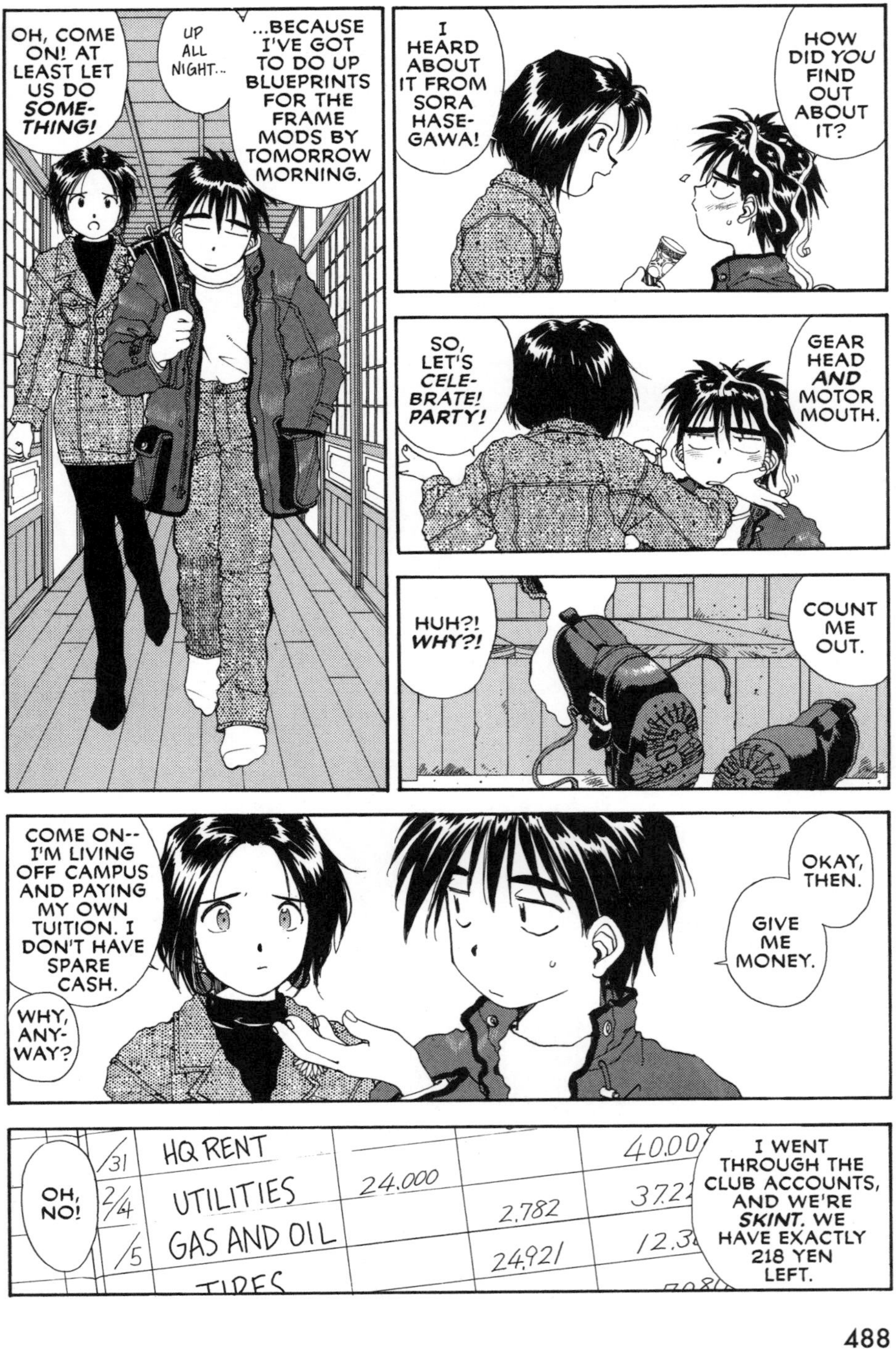
HOW DID *YOU* FIND OUT ABOUT IT?
I HEARD ABOUT IT FROM SORA HASE-GAWA!
GEAR HEAD ***AND*** MOTOR MOUTH.
SO, LET'S *CELE-BRATE! PARTY!*
COUNT ME OUT.
HUH?! ***WHY?!***
...BECAUSE I'VE GOT TO DO UP BLUEPRINTS FOR THE FRAME MODS BY TOMORROW MORNING.
UP ALL NIGHT...
OH, COME ON! AT LEAST LET US DO ***SOME-THING!***
OKAY, THEN.
GIVE ME MONEY.
COME ON-- I'M LIVING OFF CAMPUS AND PAYING MY OWN TUITION. I DON'T HAVE SPARE CASH.
WHY, ANY-WAY?
I WENT THROUGH THE CLUB ACCOUNTS, AND WE'RE ***SKINT.*** WE HAVE EXACTLY 218 YEN LEFT.
OH, NO!
/31 HQ RENT
2/4 UTILITIES 24.000
/5 GAS AND OIL 2.782
24.921

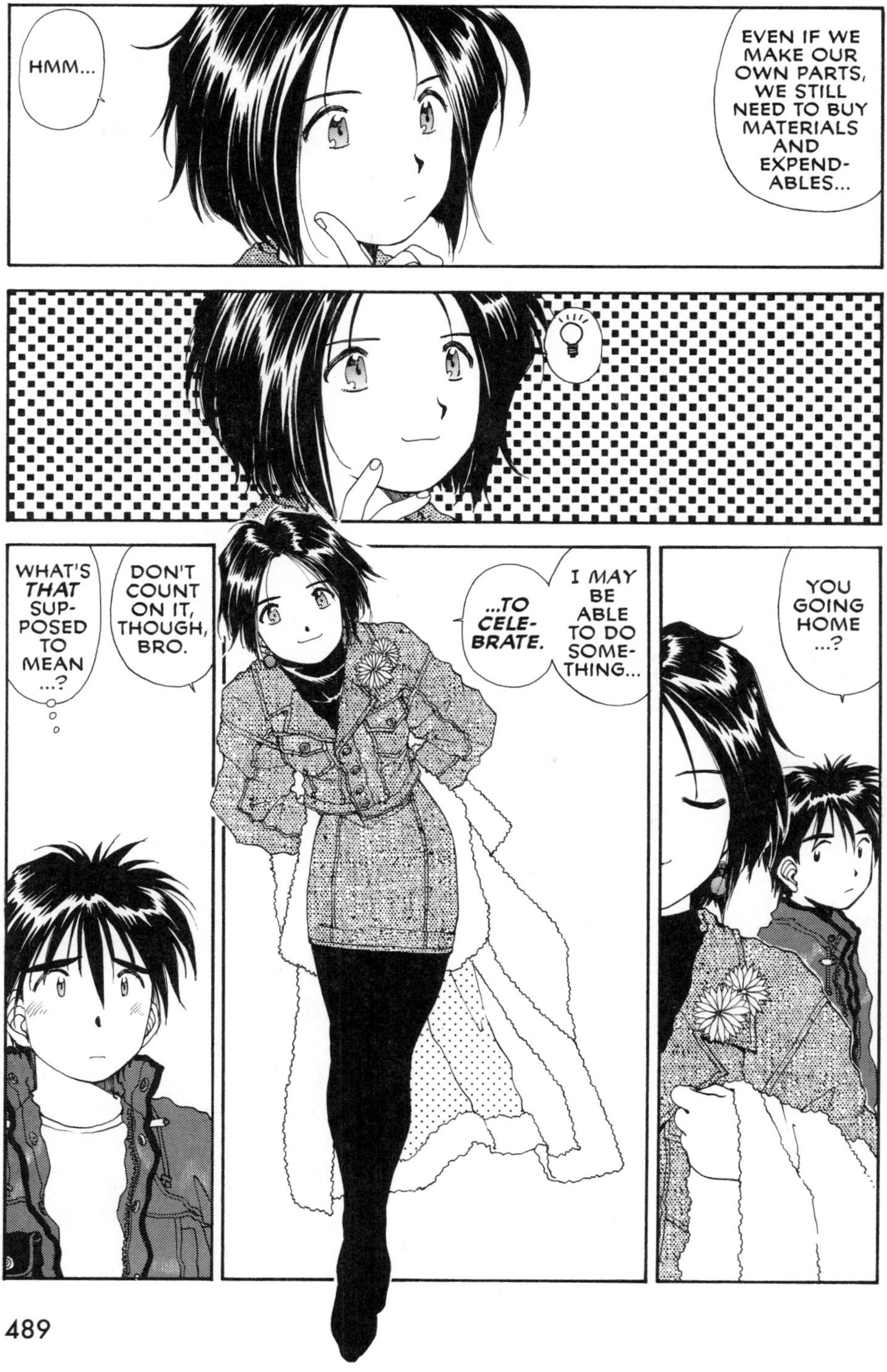
EVEN IF WE MAKE OUR OWN PARTS, WE STILL NEED TO BUY MATERIALS AND EXPEND-ABLES...
HMM...
YOU GOING HOME ...?
I *MAY* BE ABLE TO DO SOME-THING...
...TO CELE-BRATE.
DON'T COUNT ON IT, THOUGH, BRO.
WHAT'S *THAT* SUP-POSED TO MEAN ...?

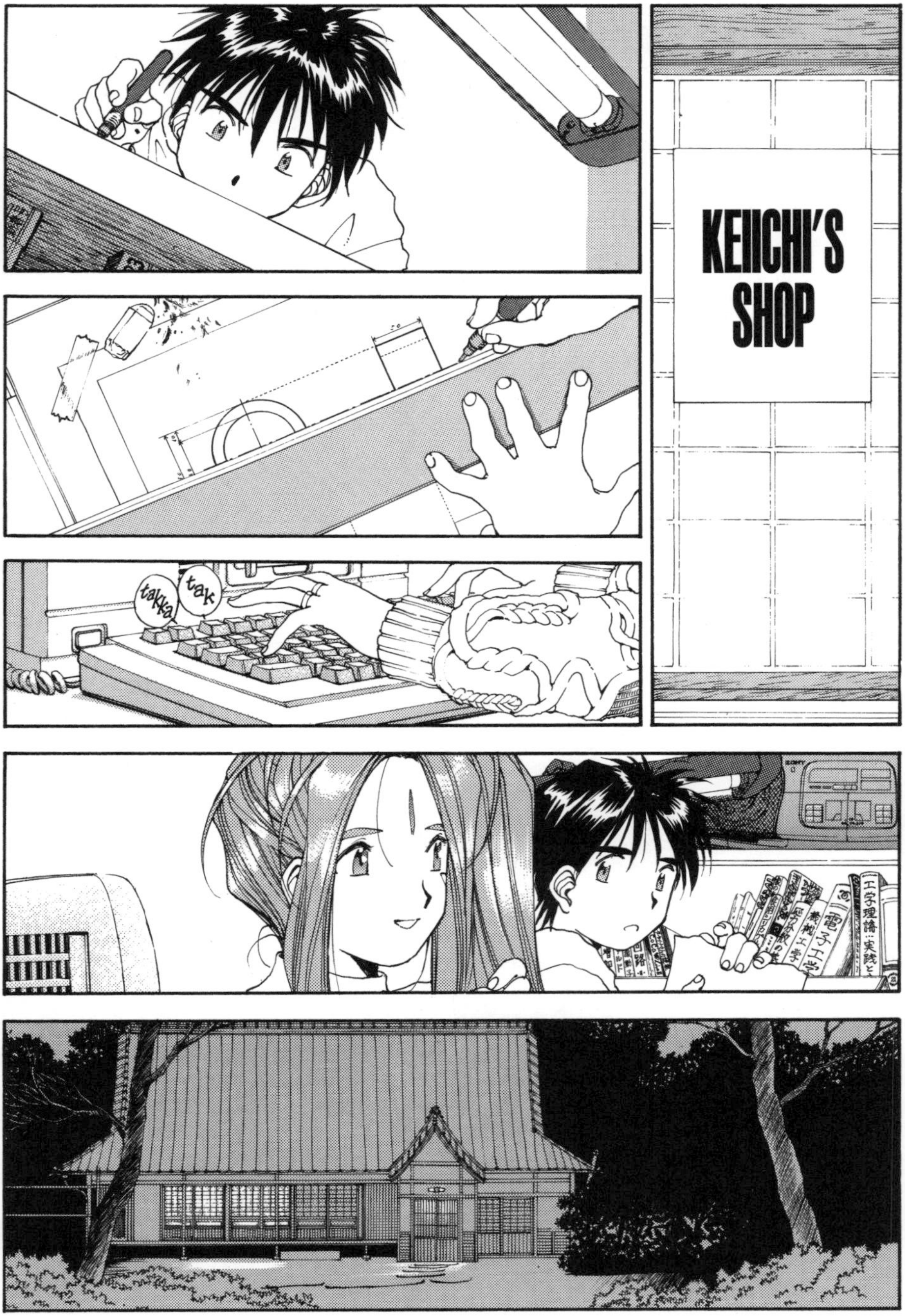
KEIICHI'S SHOP
tak
takka

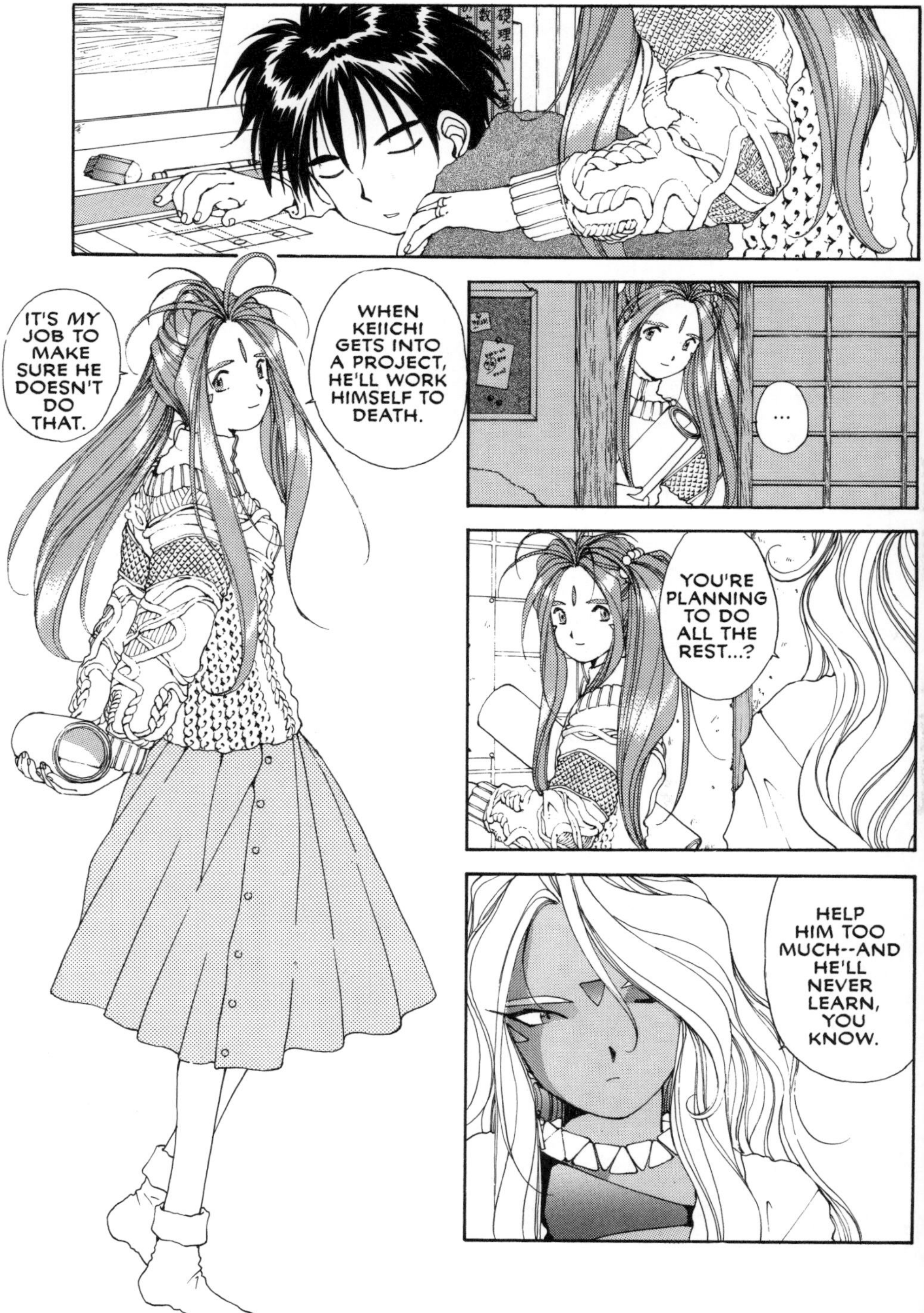
...
YOU'RE PLANNING TO DO ALL THE REST...?
HELP HIM TOO MUCH--AND HE'LL NEVER LEARN, YOU KNOW.
WHEN KEIICHI GETS INTO A PROJECT, HE'LL WORK HIMSELF TO DEATH.
IT'S MY JOB TO MAKE SURE HE DOESN'T DO THAT.

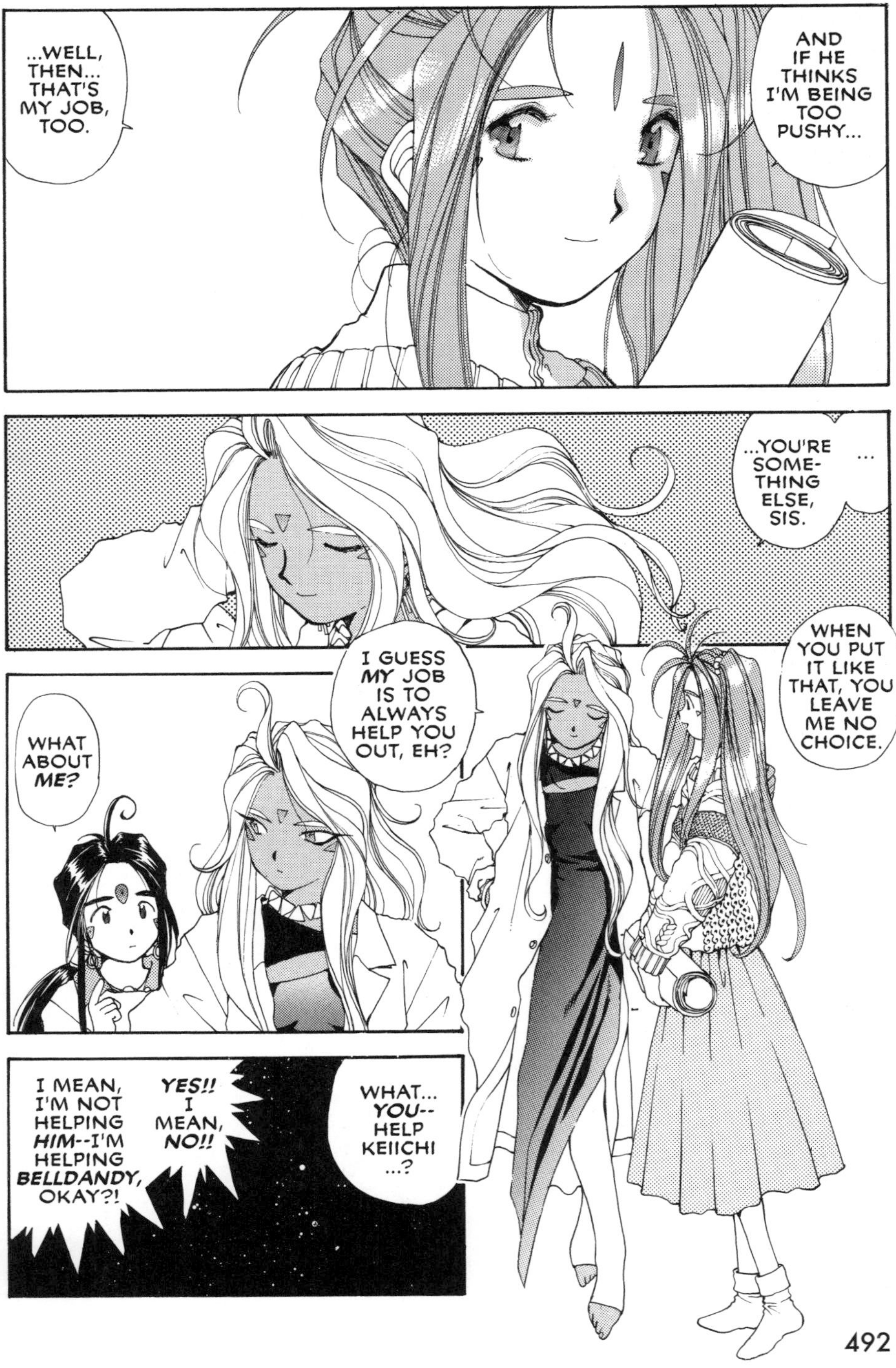
AND IF HE THINKS I'M BEING TOO PUSHY...
...WELL, THEN... THAT'S MY JOB, TOO.
...YOU'RE SOMETHING ELSE, SIS.
...
WHEN YOU PUT IT LIKE THAT, YOU LEAVE ME NO CHOICE.
I GUESS *MY* JOB IS TO ALWAYS HELP YOU OUT, EH?
WHAT ABOUT *ME?*
WHAT... *YOU*-- HELP KEIICHI ...?
YES!! I MEAN, *NO!!*
I MEAN, I'M NOT HELPING *HIM*--I'M HELPING *BELLDANDY*, OKAY?!

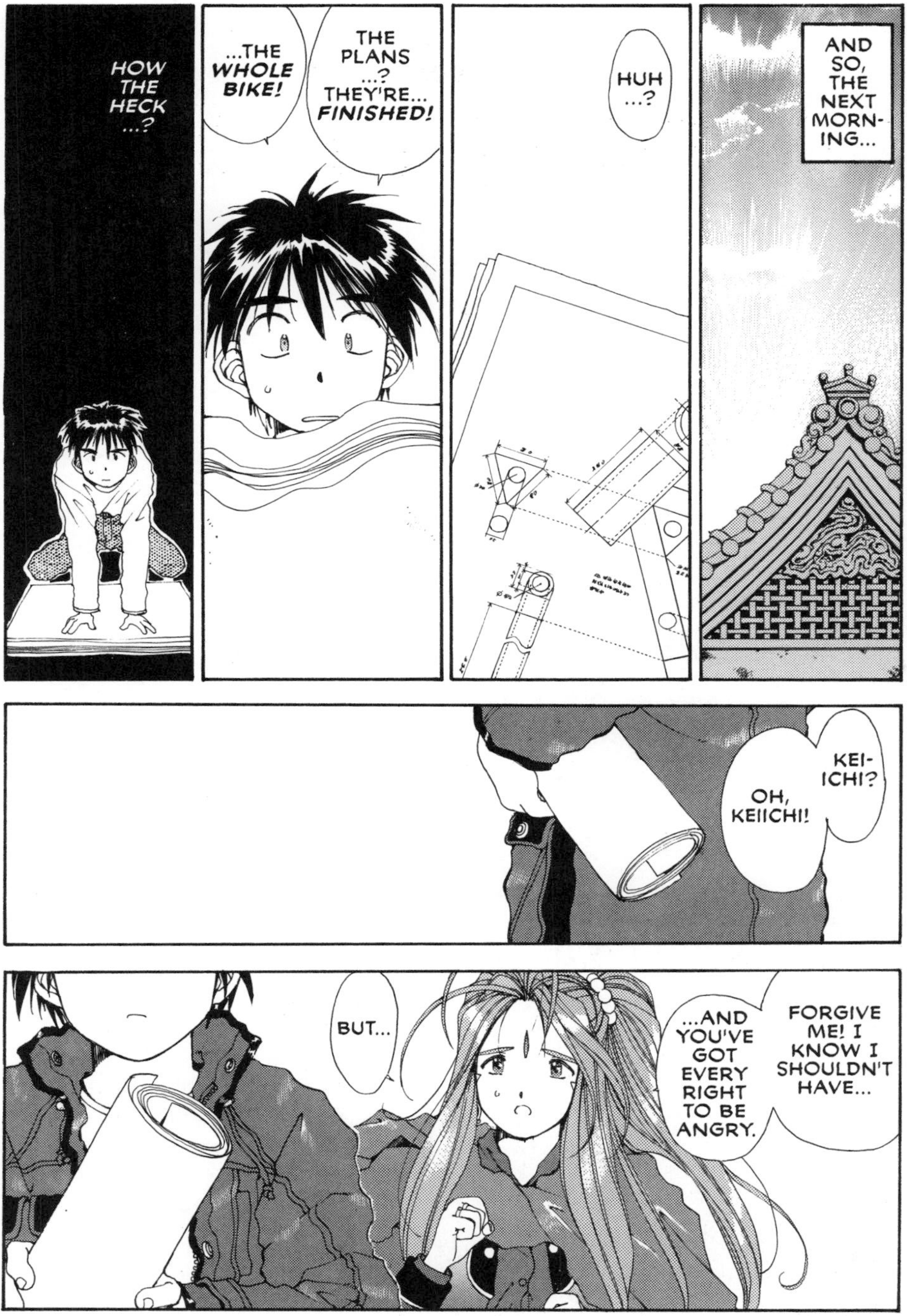
AND SO, THE NEXT MORNING...
HUH ...?
THE PLANS ...? THEY'RE... **FINISHED!**
...THE **WHOLE** BIKE!
HOW THE HECK ...?
KEI-ICHI?
OH, KEIICHI!
FORGIVE ME! I KNOW I SHOULDN'T HAVE...
...AND YOU'VE GOT EVERY RIGHT TO BE ANGRY.
BUT...

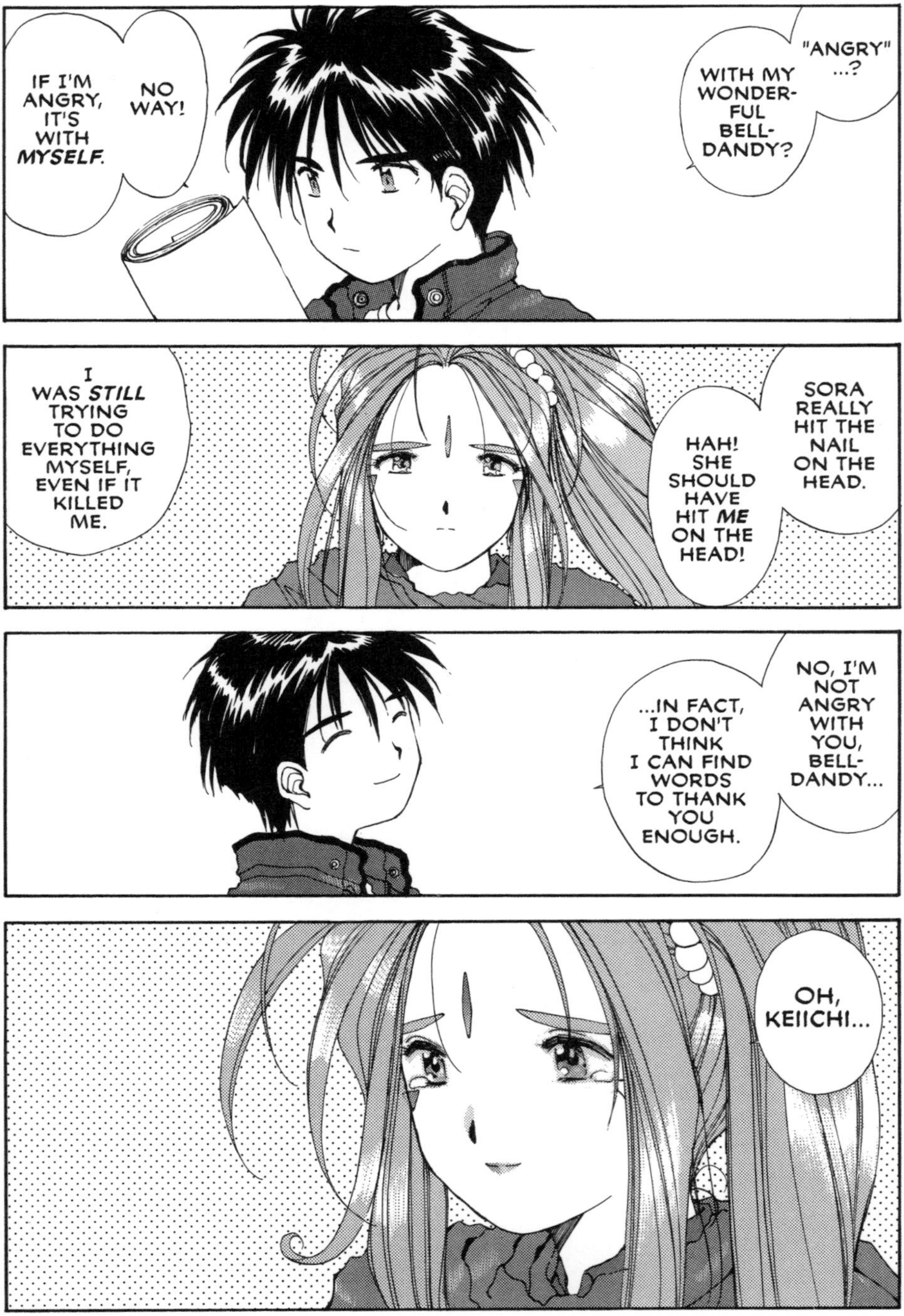
"ANGRY" ...?
WITH MY WONDERFUL BELLDANDY?
NO WAY!
IF I'M ANGRY, IT'S WITH *MYSELF*.
SORA REALLY HIT THE NAIL ON THE HEAD.
HAH! SHE SHOULD HAVE HIT *ME* ON THE HEAD!
I WAS *STILL* TRYING TO DO EVERYTHING MYSELF, EVEN IF IT KILLED ME.
NO, I'M NOT ANGRY WITH YOU, BELLDANDY...
...IN FACT, I DON'T THINK I CAN FIND WORDS TO THANK YOU ENOUGH.
OH, KEIICHI...

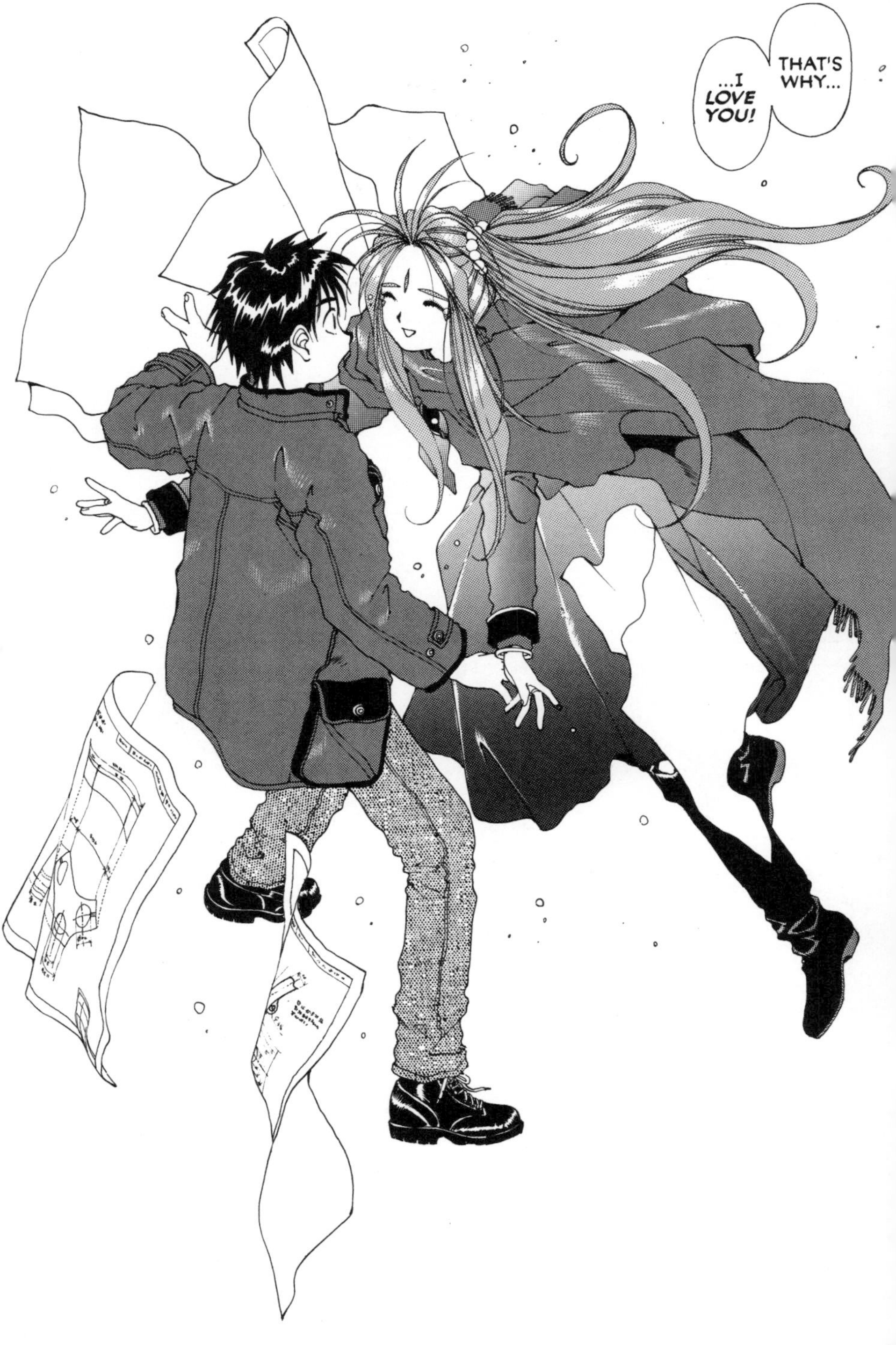
THAT'S WHY...
...I LOVE YOU!

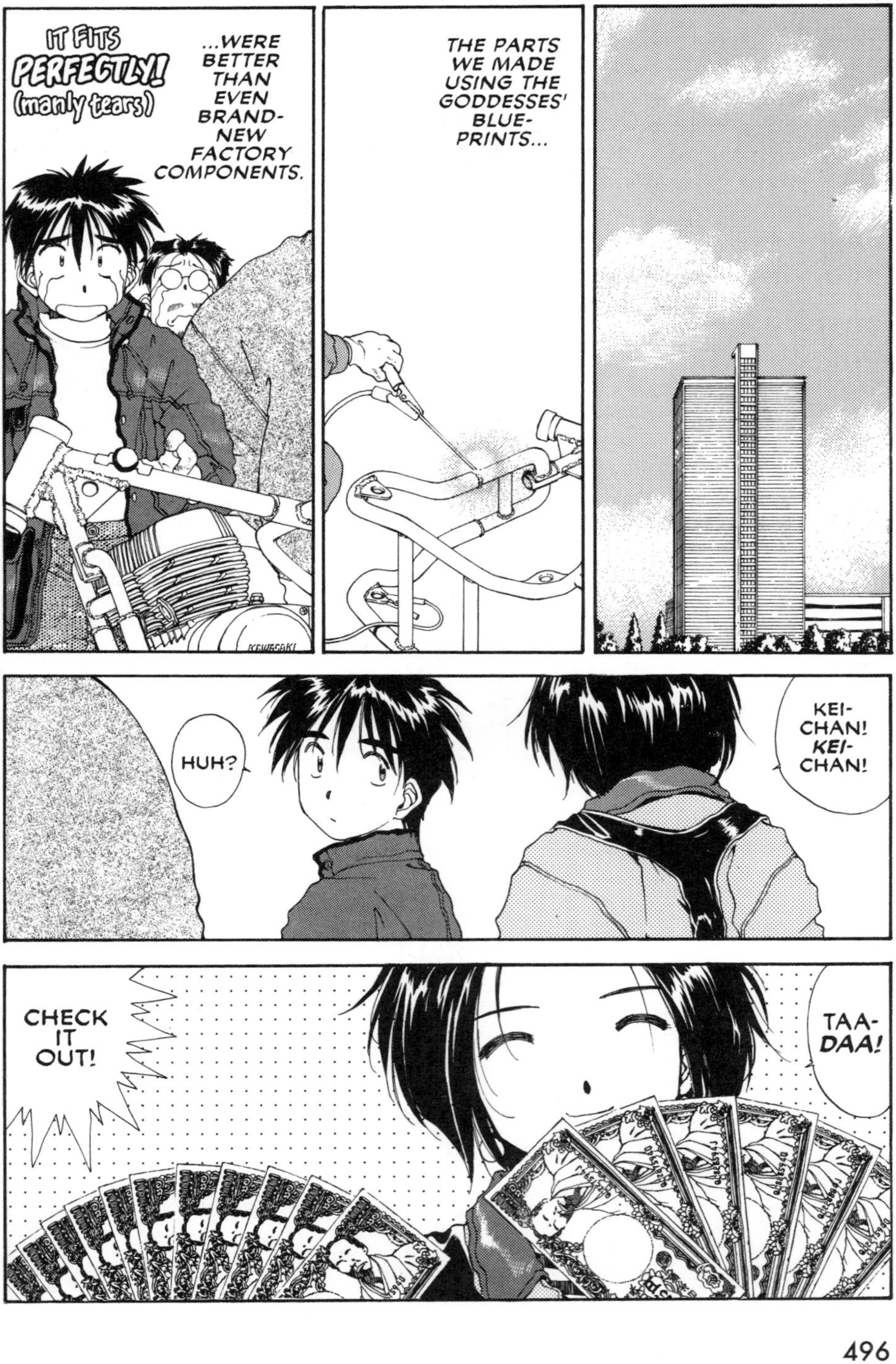
THE PARTS WE MADE USING THE GODDESSES' BLUE-PRINTS...
...WERE BETTER THAN EVEN BRAND-NEW FACTORY COMPONENTS.
IT FITS PERFECTLY! (manly tears)
KEI-CHAN! KEI-CHAN!
HUH?
TAA-DAA!
CHECK IT OUT!

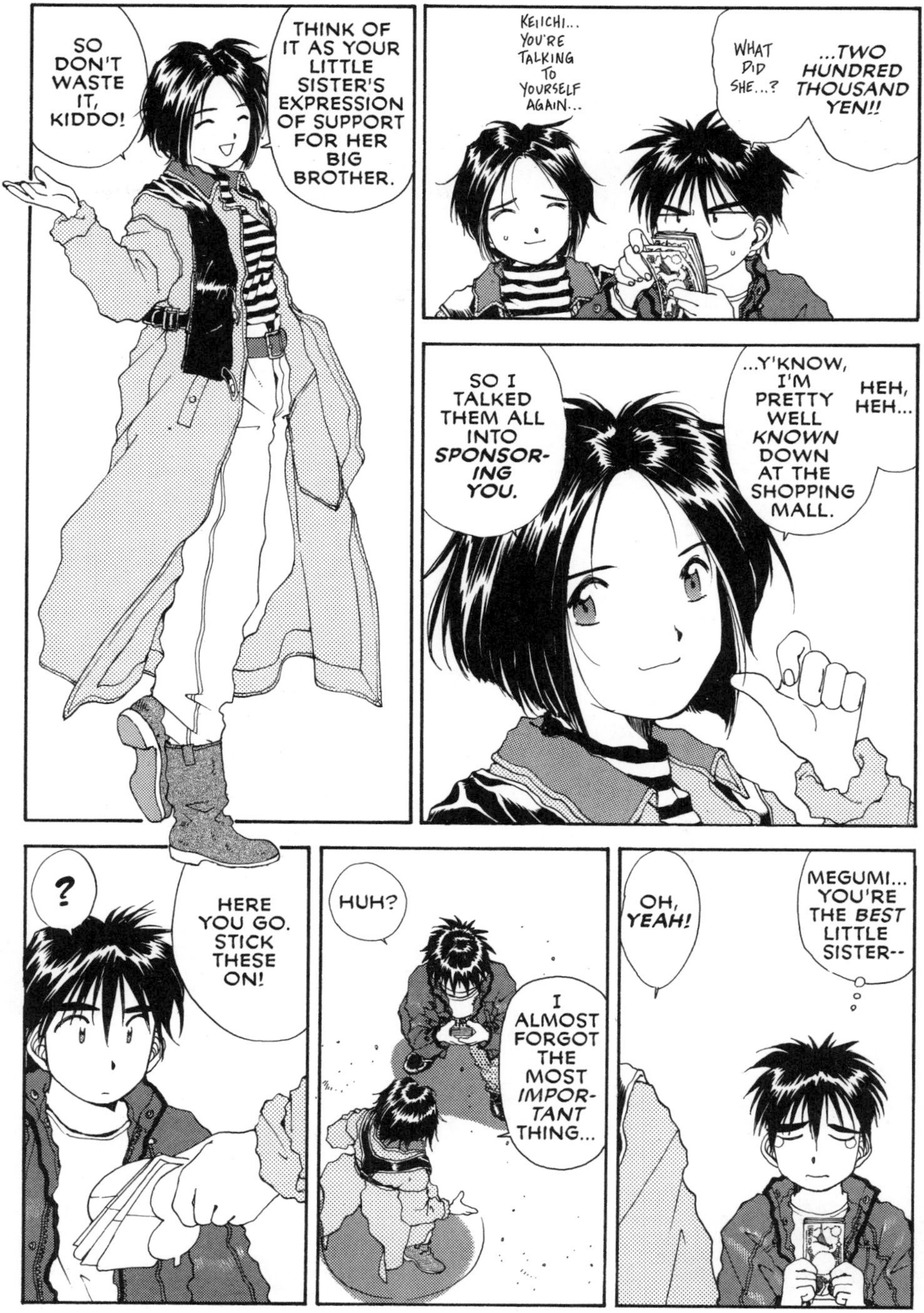
...TWO HUNDRED THOUSAND YEN!!
WHAT DID SHE...?
KEIICHI... YOU'RE TALKING TO YOURSELF AGAIN...
HEH, HEH...
...Y'KNOW, I'M PRETTY WELL *KNOWN* DOWN AT THE SHOPPING MALL.
SO I TALKED THEM ALL INTO *SPONSORING* YOU.
THINK OF IT AS YOUR LITTLE SISTER'S EXPRESSION OF SUPPORT FOR HER BIG BROTHER.
SO DON'T WASTE IT, KIDDO!
MEGUMI... YOU'RE THE *BEST* LITTLE SISTER--
OH, *YEAH!*
I ALMOST FORGOT THE MOST *IMPORTANT* THING...
HUH?
HERE YOU GO. STICK THESE ON!
?

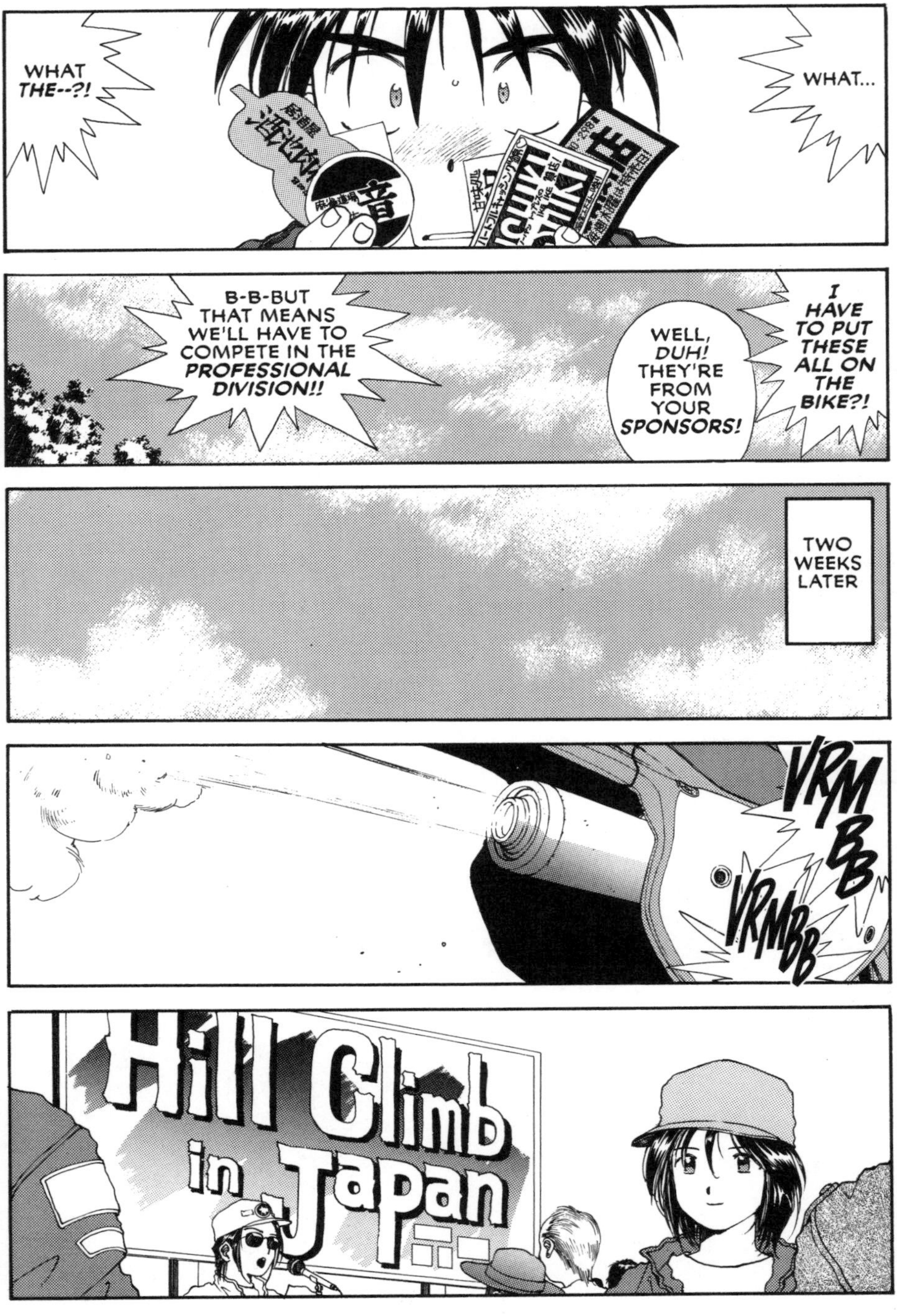
WHAT...
WHAT THE--?!
I HAVE TO PUT THESE ALL ON THE BIKE?!
WELL, DUH! THEY'RE FROM YOUR SPONSORS!
B-B-BUT THAT MEANS WE'LL HAVE TO COMPETE IN THE PROFESSIONAL DIVISION!!
TWO WEEKS LATER
VRMBB
VRMBB
Hill Climb in Japan

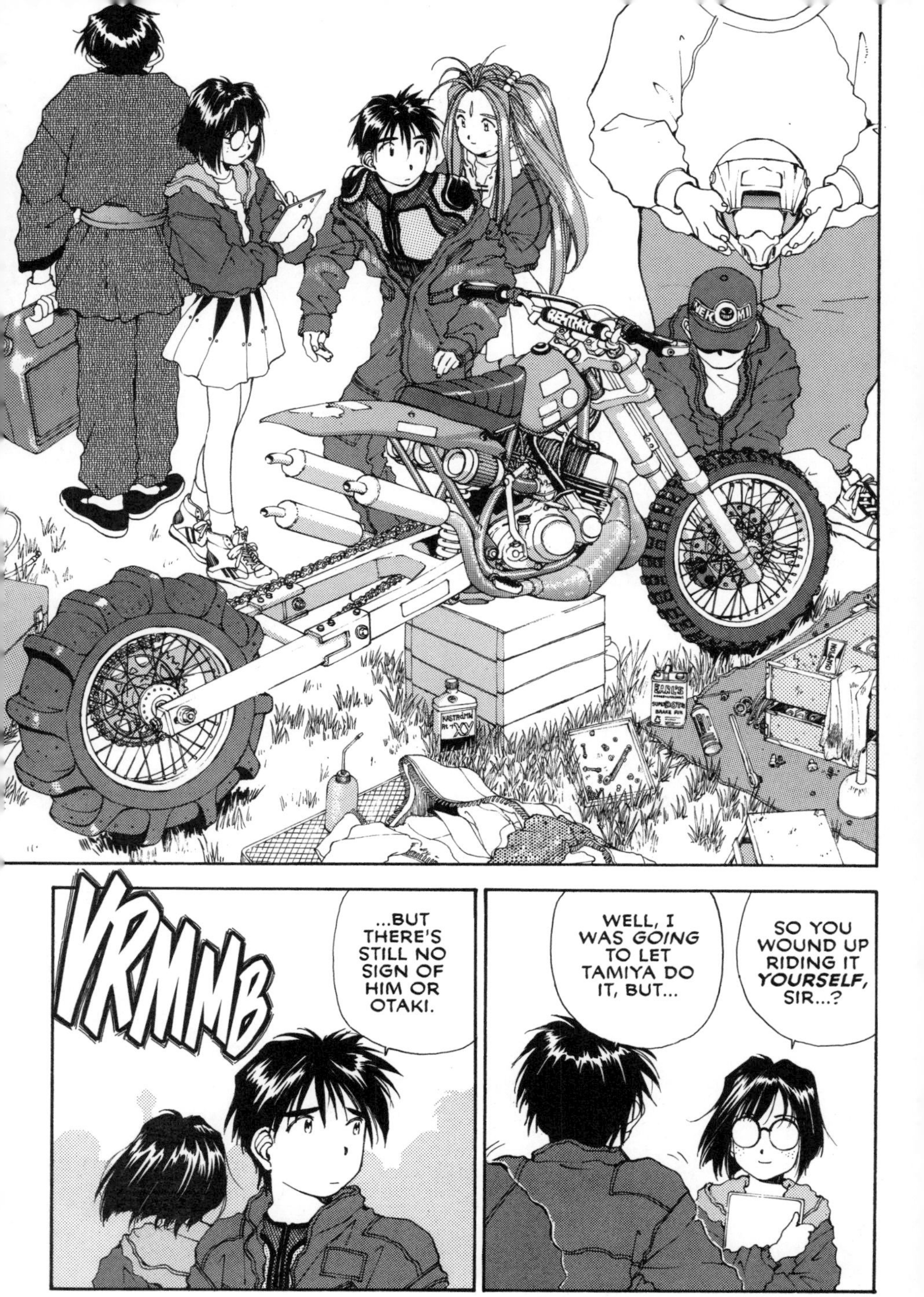
SO YOU WOUND UP RIDING IT *YOURSELF,* SIR...?
WELL, I WAS *GOING* TO LET TAMIYA DO IT, BUT...
...BUT THERE'S STILL NO SIGN OF HIM OR OTAKI.
VRMMB

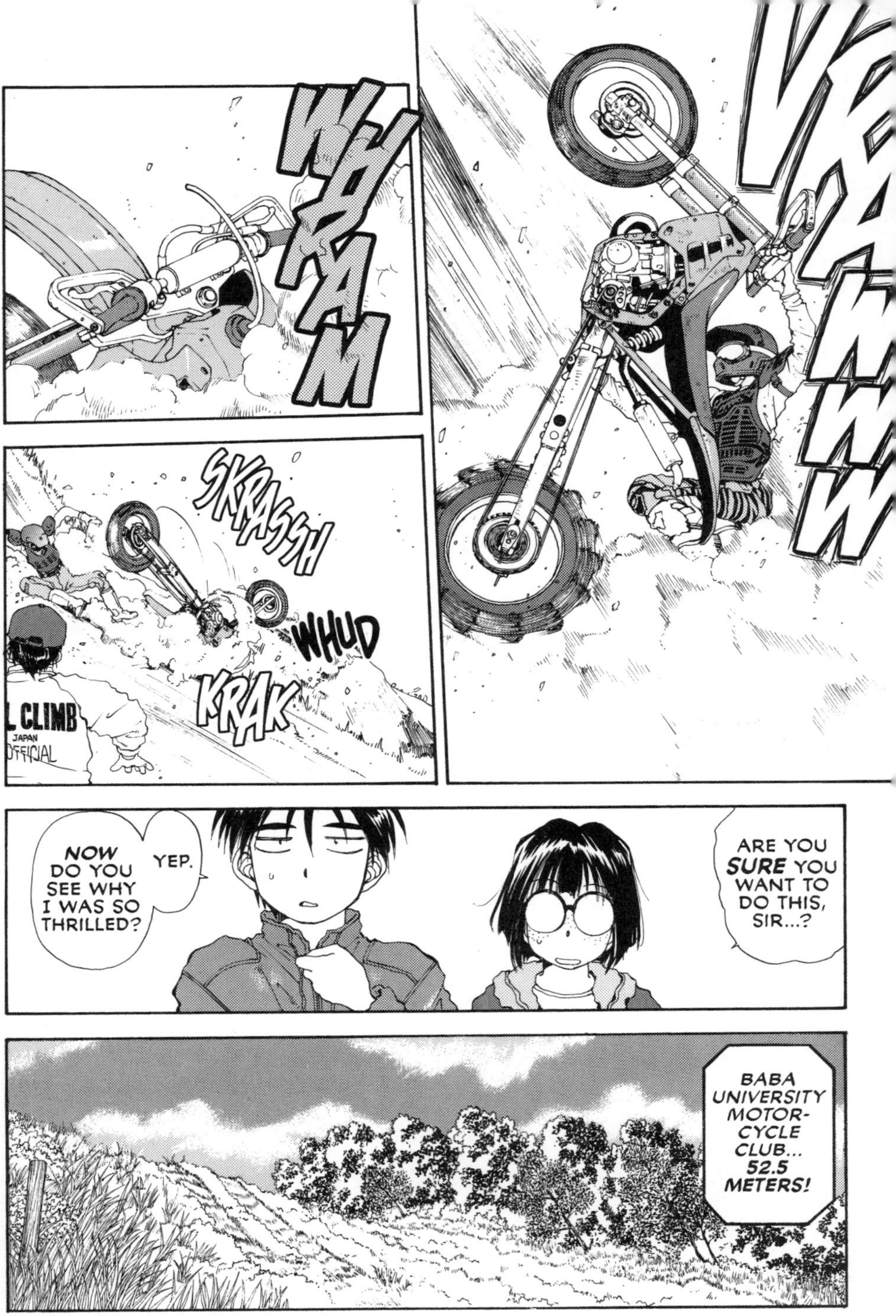
WHAM
SKRASSH
WHUD
KRAK
L CLIMB
JAPAN
OFFICIAL
ARE YOU SURE YOU WANT TO DO THIS, SIR...?
NOW DO YOU SEE WHY I WAS SO THRILLED?
YEP.
BABA UNIVERSITY MOTOR-CYCLE CLUB... 52.5 METERS!

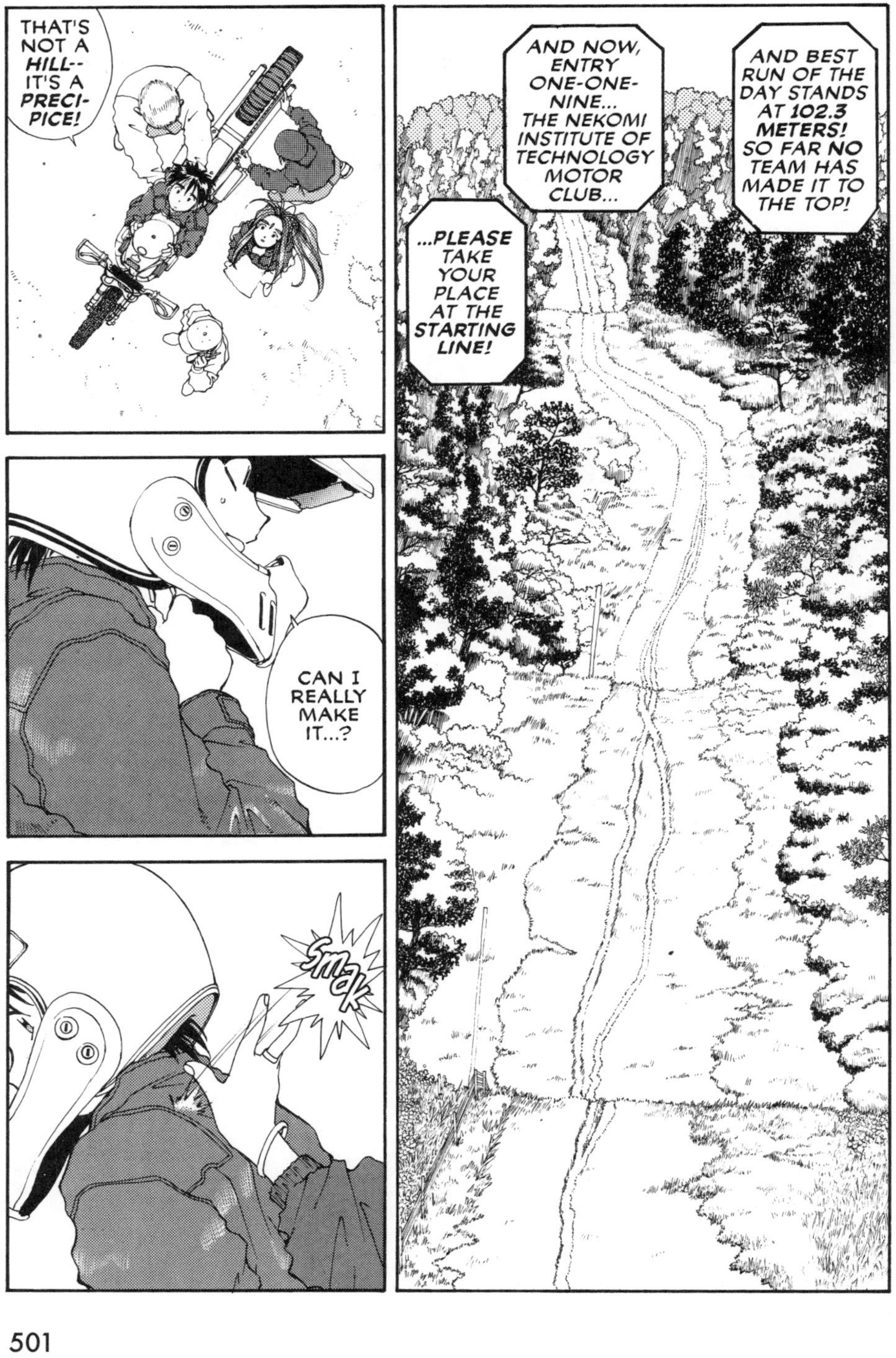
AND BEST RUN OF THE DAY STANDS AT 102.3 METERS! SO FAR NO TEAM HAS MADE IT TO THE TOP!
AND NOW, ENTRY ONE-ONE-NINE... THE NEKOMI INSTITUTE OF TECHNOLOGY MOTOR CLUB...
...PLEASE TAKE YOUR PLACE AT THE STARTING LINE!
THAT'S NOT A HILL-- IT'S A PRECIPICE!
CAN I REALLY MAKE IT...?
SMAK

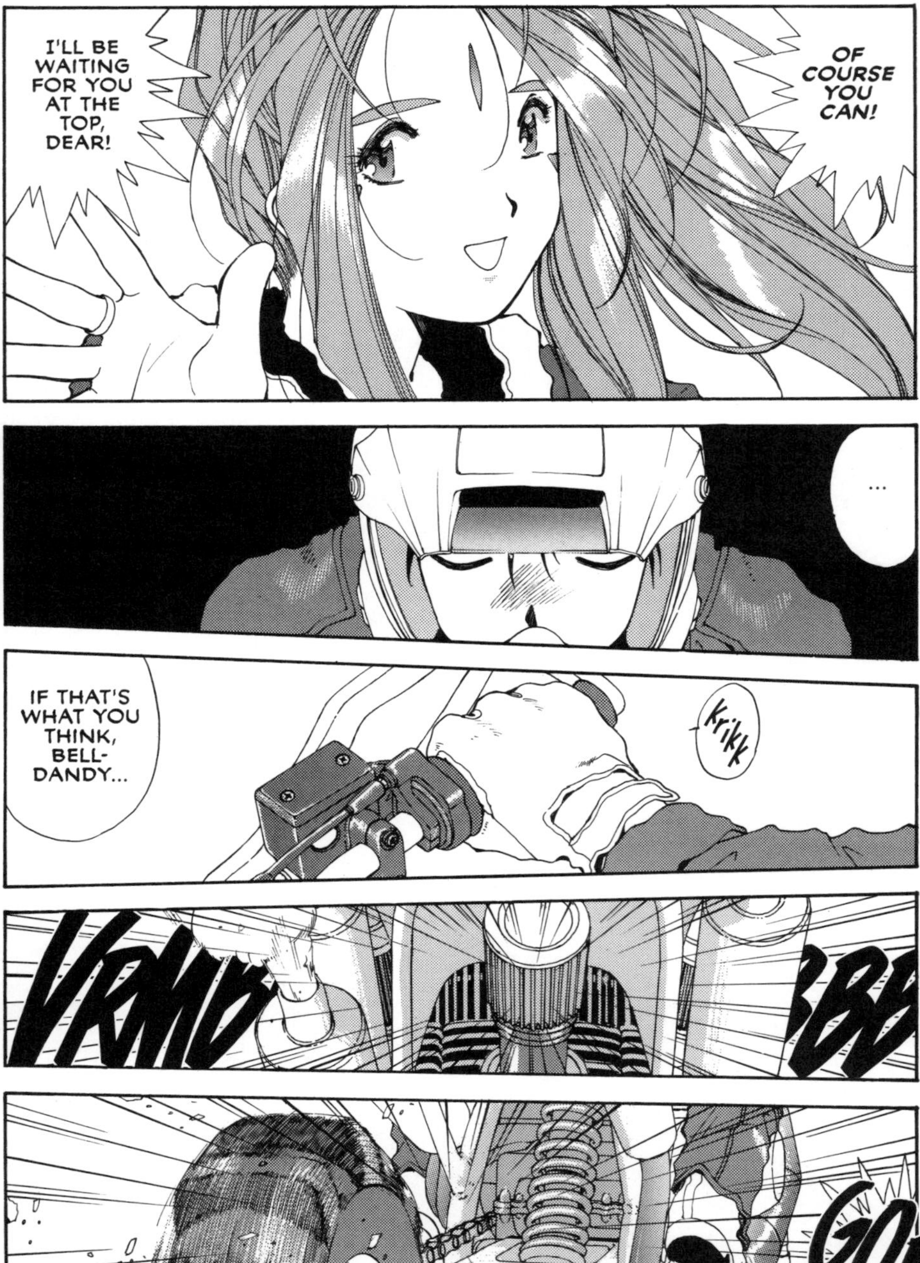
OF COURSE YOU CAN!
I'LL BE WAITING FOR YOU AT THE TOP, DEAR!
...
Krikk
IF THAT'S WHAT YOU THINK, BELL-DANDY...
VRMB
BBB
GO!!

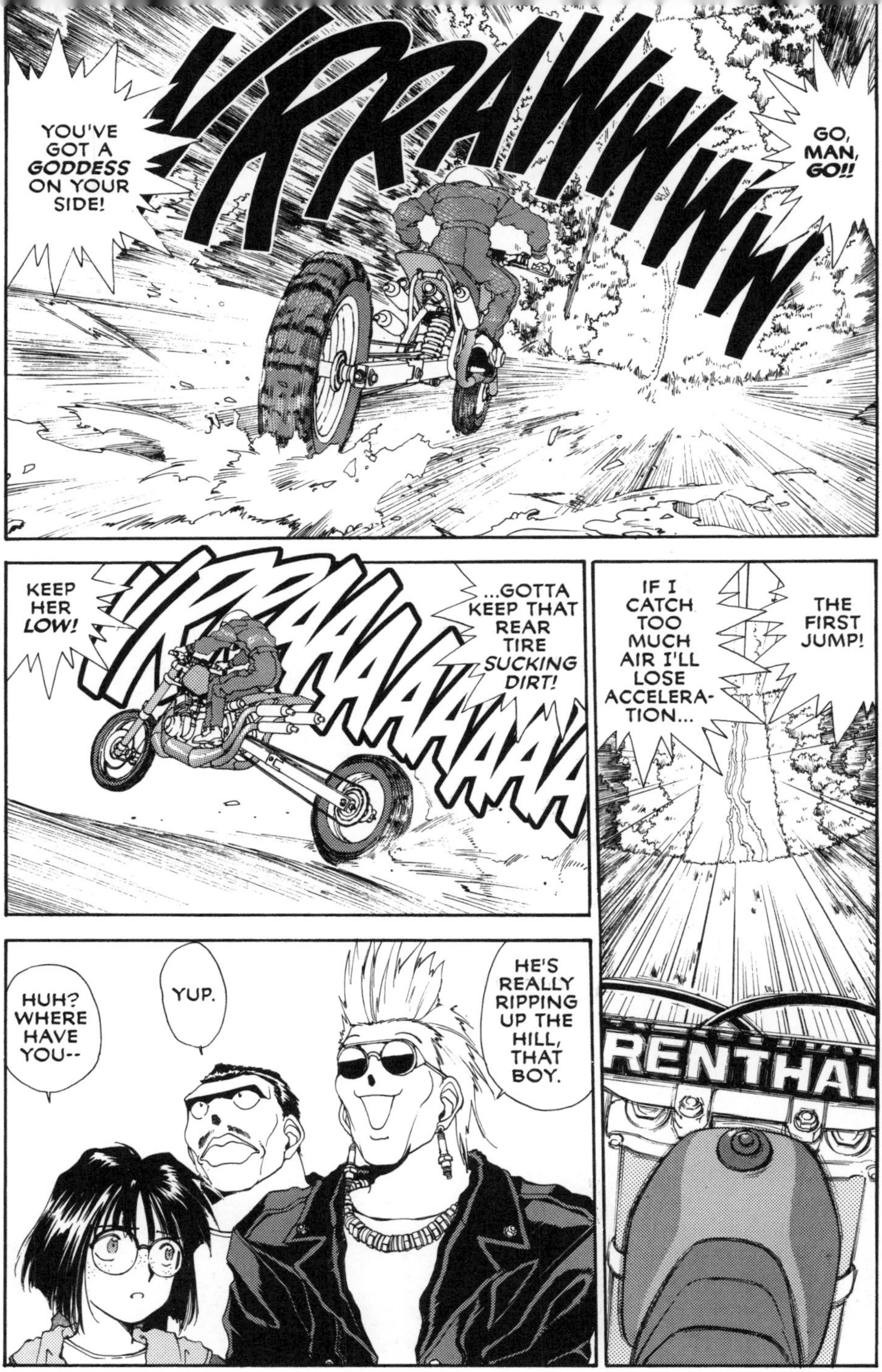
VRRAWWWWWW
GO, MAN, GO!!
YOU'VE GOT A GODDESS ON YOUR SIDE!
THE FIRST JUMP!
IF I CATCH TOO MUCH AIR I'LL LOSE ACCELERATION...
RENTHAL
VRRAAAAAAAAA
...GOTTA KEEP THAT REAR TIRE SUCKING DIRT!
KEEP HER LOW!
HE'S REALLY RIPPING UP THE HILL, THAT BOY.
YUP.
HUH? WHERE HAVE YOU--

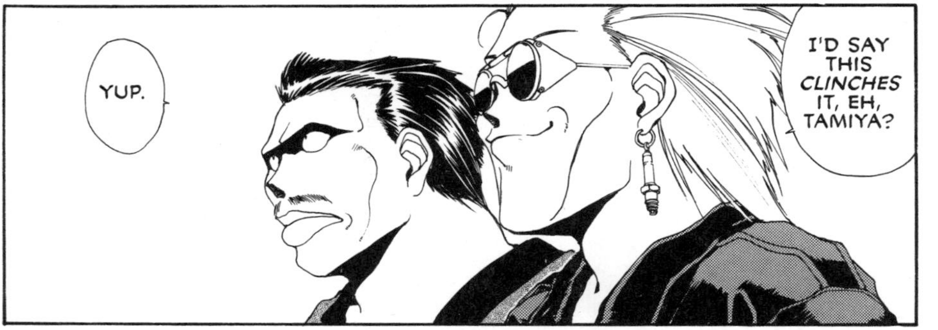
I'D SAY THIS *CLINCHES* IT, EH, TAMIYA?
YUP.

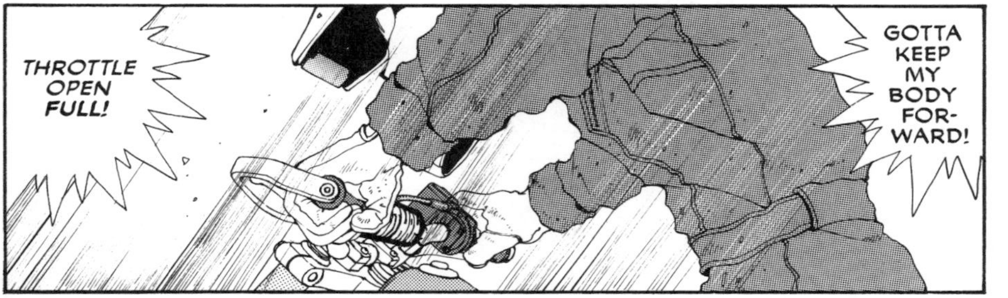
GOTTA KEEP MY BODY FOR-WARD!
*THROTTLE OPEN **FULL!***

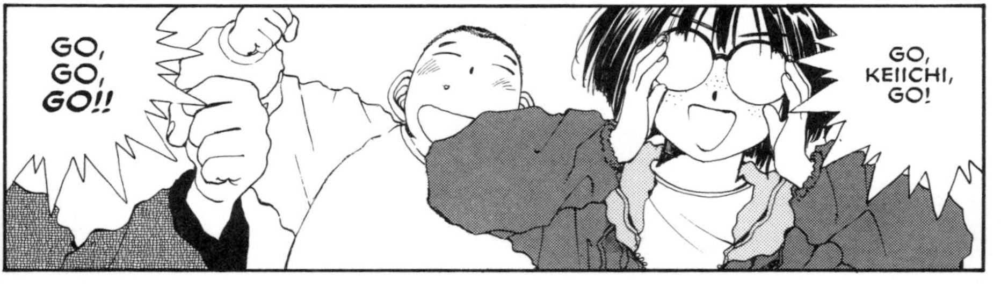
GO, KEIICHI, GO!
GO, GO, *GO!!*

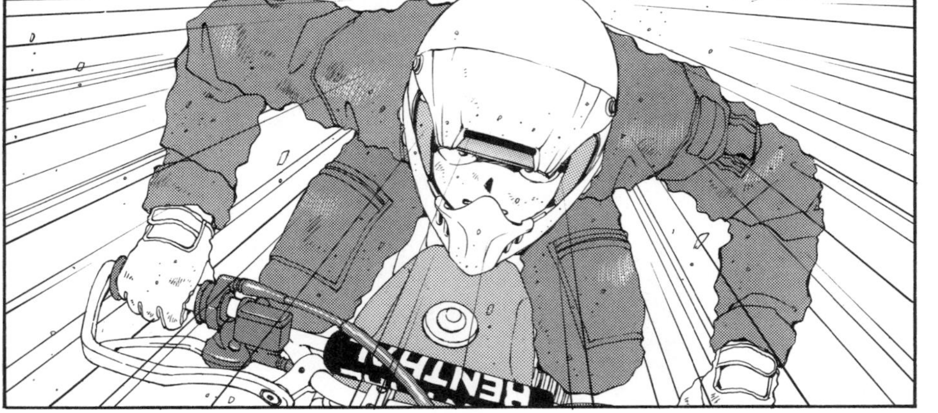

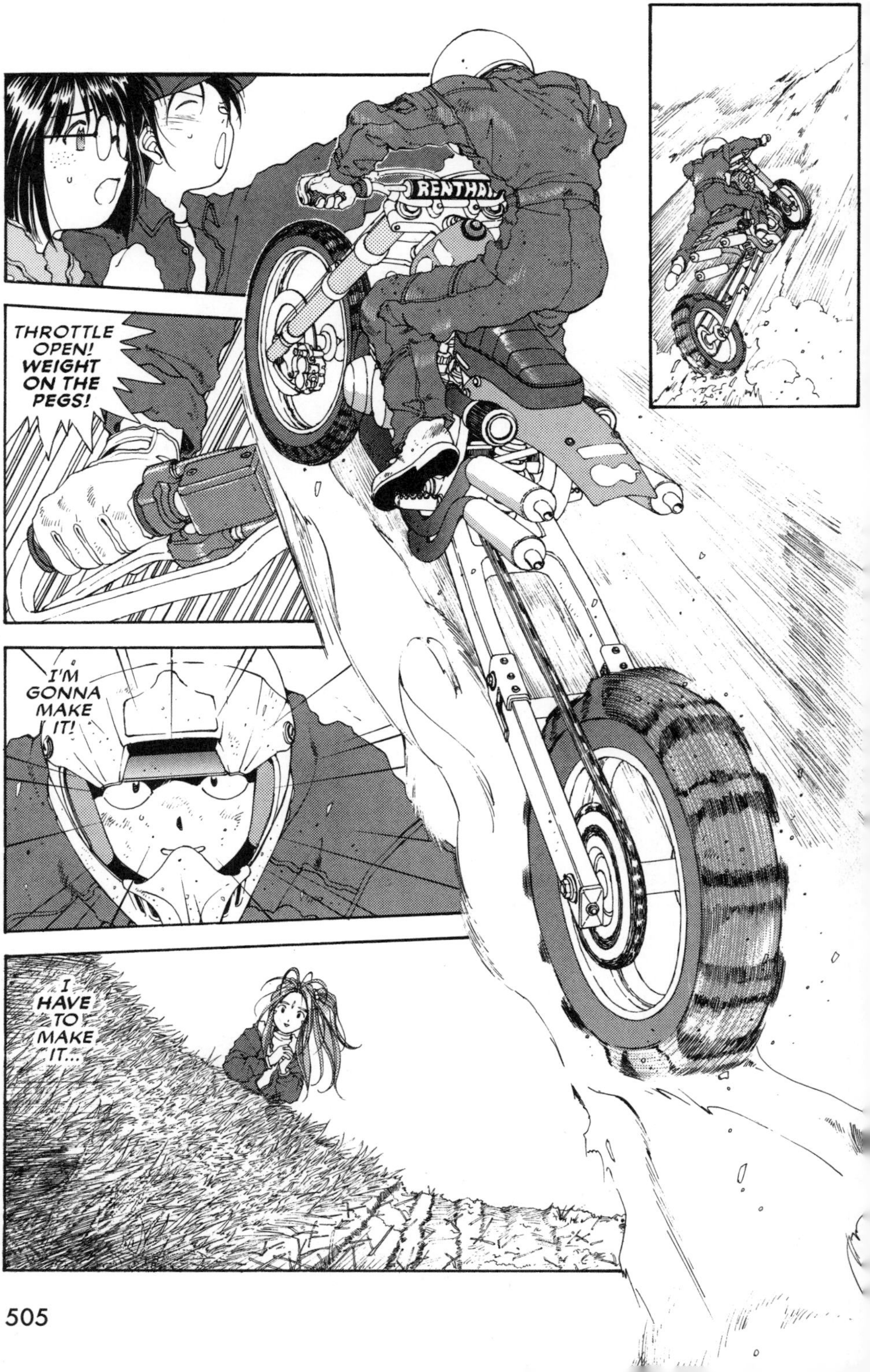
RENTHAL
THROTTLE OPEN! WEIGHT ON THE PEGS!
I'M GONNA MAKE IT!
I HAVE TO MAKE IT...

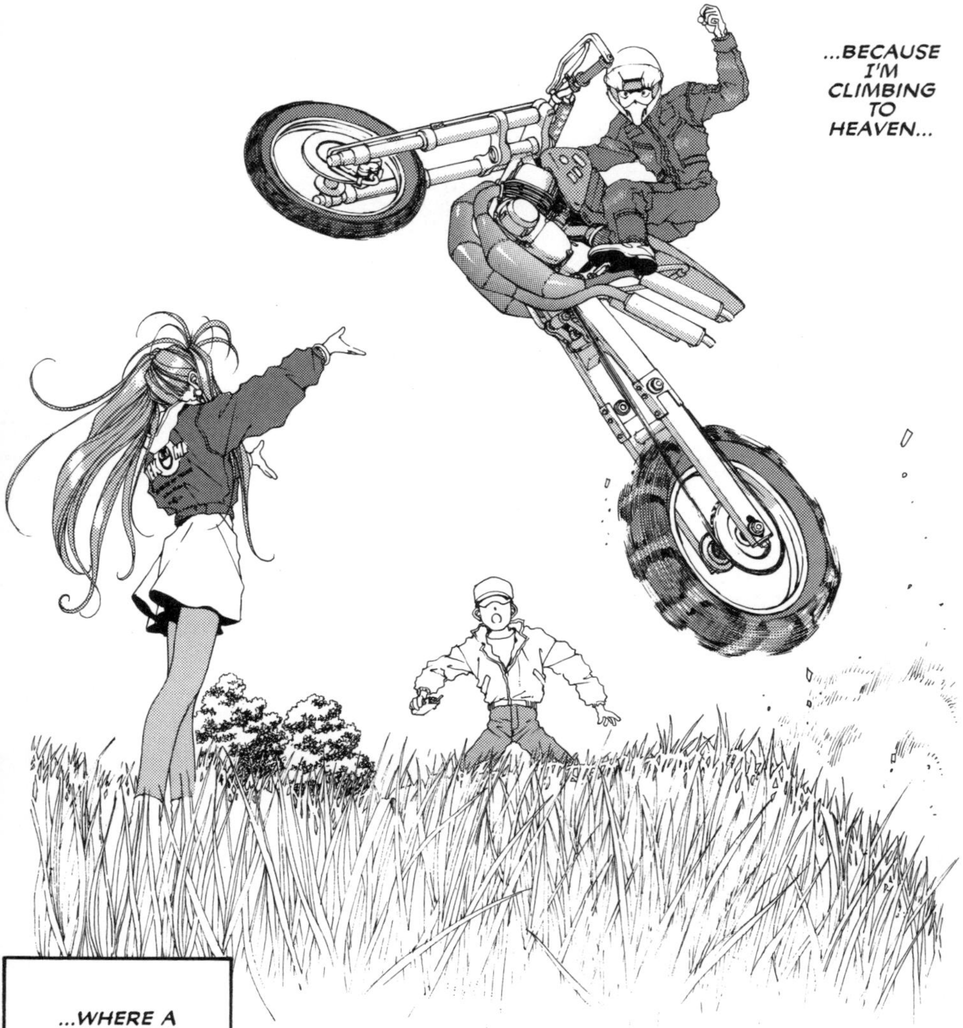
...BECAUSE I'M CLIMBING TO HEAVEN...

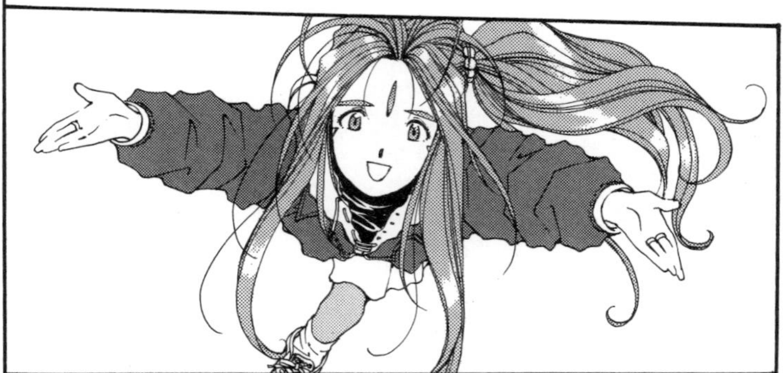

...WHERE A GODDESS IS WAITING FOR ME.

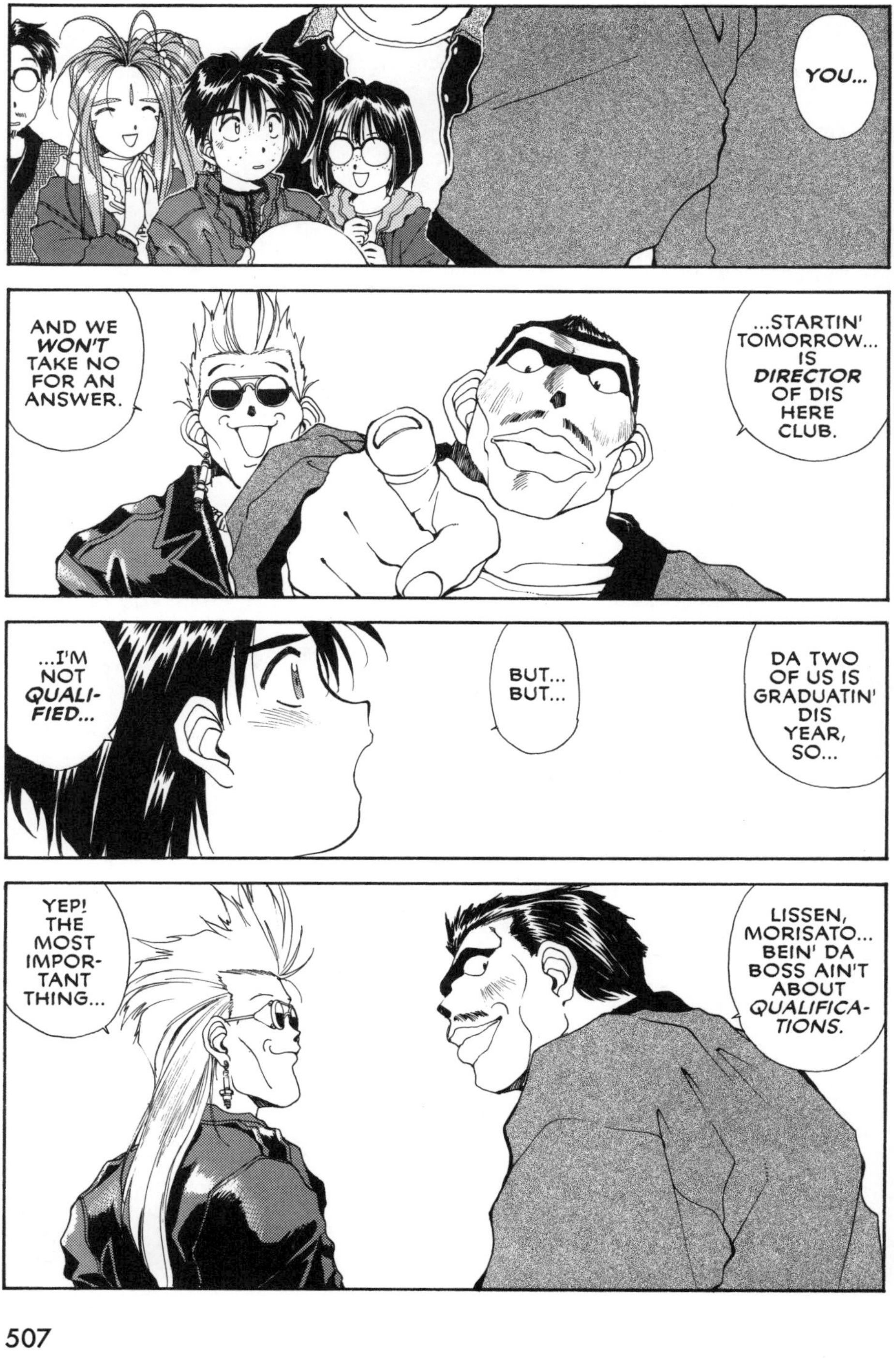
YOU...
...STARTIN' TOMORROW... IS *DIRECTOR* OF DIS HERE CLUB.
AND WE *WON'T* TAKE NO FOR AN ANSWER.
DA TWO OF US IS GRADUATIN' DIS YEAR, SO...
BUT... BUT...
...I'M NOT *QUALIFIED...*
LISSEN, MORISATO... BEIN' DA BOSS AIN'T ABOUT *QUALIFICATIONS.*
YEP! THE MOST IMPORTANT THING...

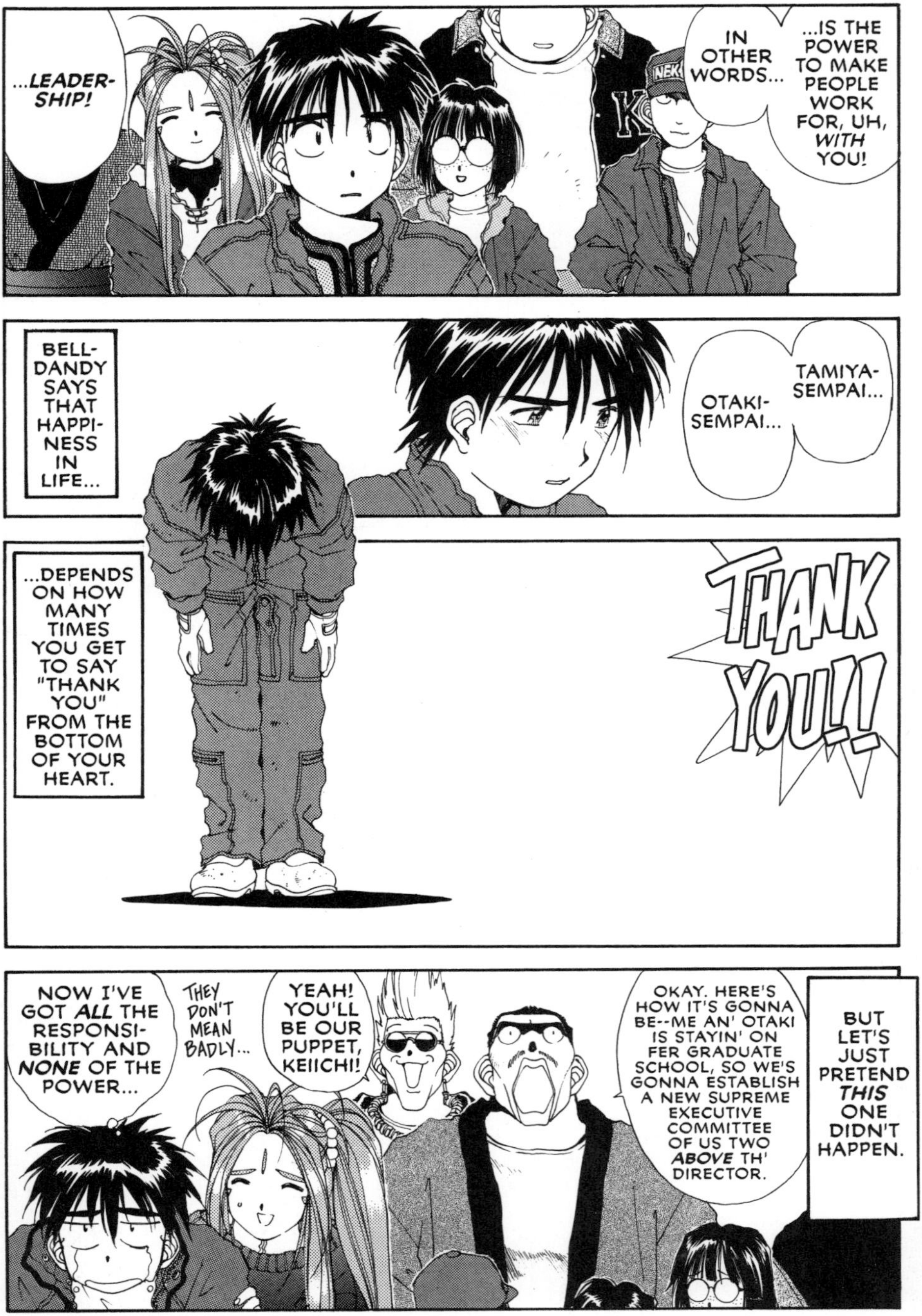
IN OTHER WORDS...
...IS THE POWER TO MAKE PEOPLE WORK FOR, UH, *WITH* YOU!
...*LEADERSHIP!*
TAMIYA-SEMPAI...
OTAKI-SEMPAI...
BELLDANDY SAYS THAT HAPPINESS IN LIFE...
THANK YOU!!
...DEPENDS ON HOW MANY TIMES YOU GET TO SAY "THANK YOU" FROM THE BOTTOM OF YOUR HEART.
BUT LET'S JUST PRETEND *THIS* ONE DIDN'T HAPPEN.
OKAY. HERE'S HOW IT'S GONNA BE--ME AN' OTAKI IS STAYIN' ON FER GRADUATE SCHOOL, SO WE'S GONNA ESTABLISH A NEW SUPREME EXECUTIVE COMMITTEE OF US TWO *ABOVE* TH' DIRECTOR.
YEAH! YOU'LL BE OUR PUPPET, KEIICHI!
THEY DON'T MEAN BADLY...
NOW I'VE GOT *ALL* THE RESPONSIBILITY AND *NONE* OF THE POWER...

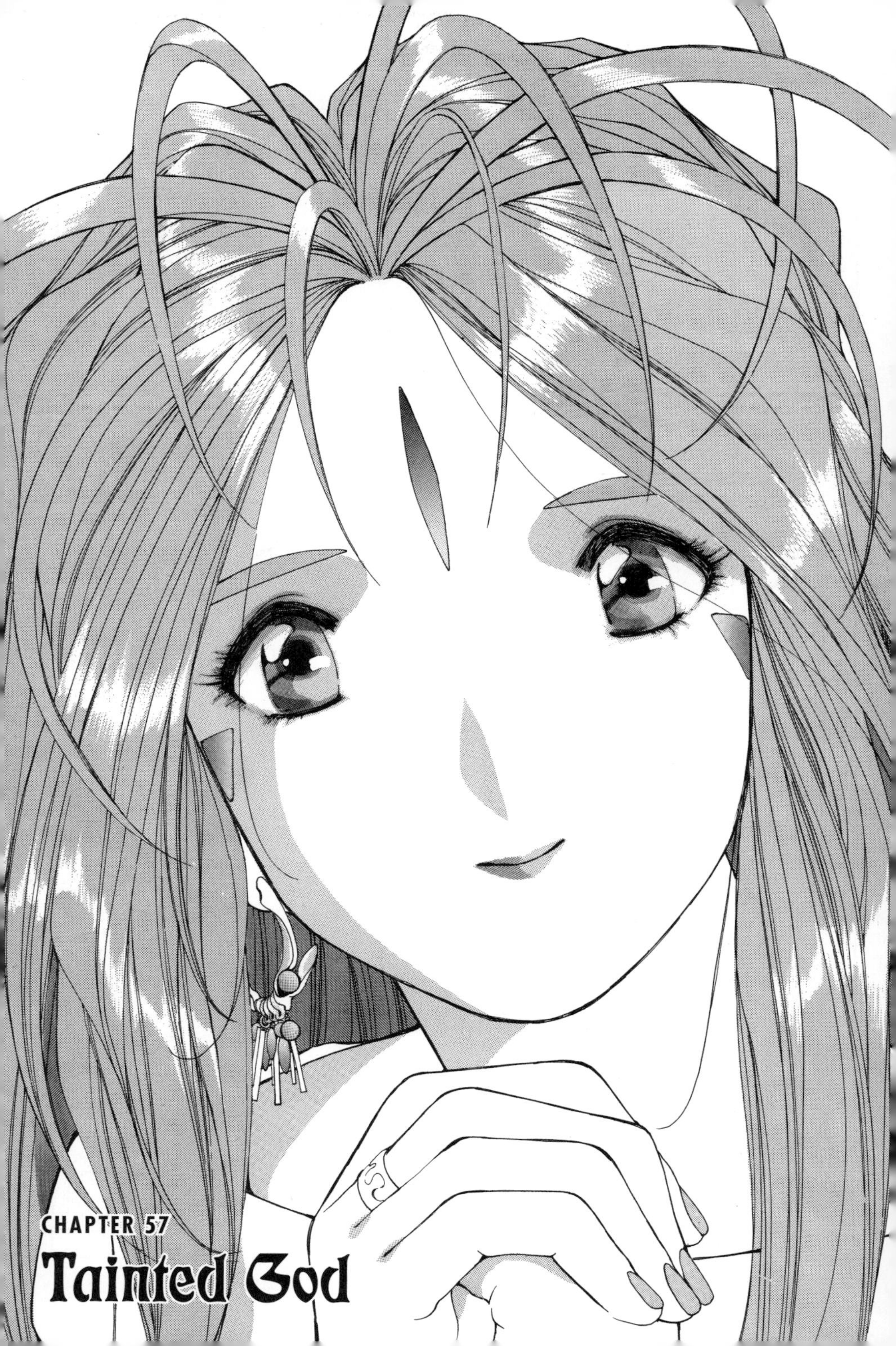

CHAPTER 57

Tainted God

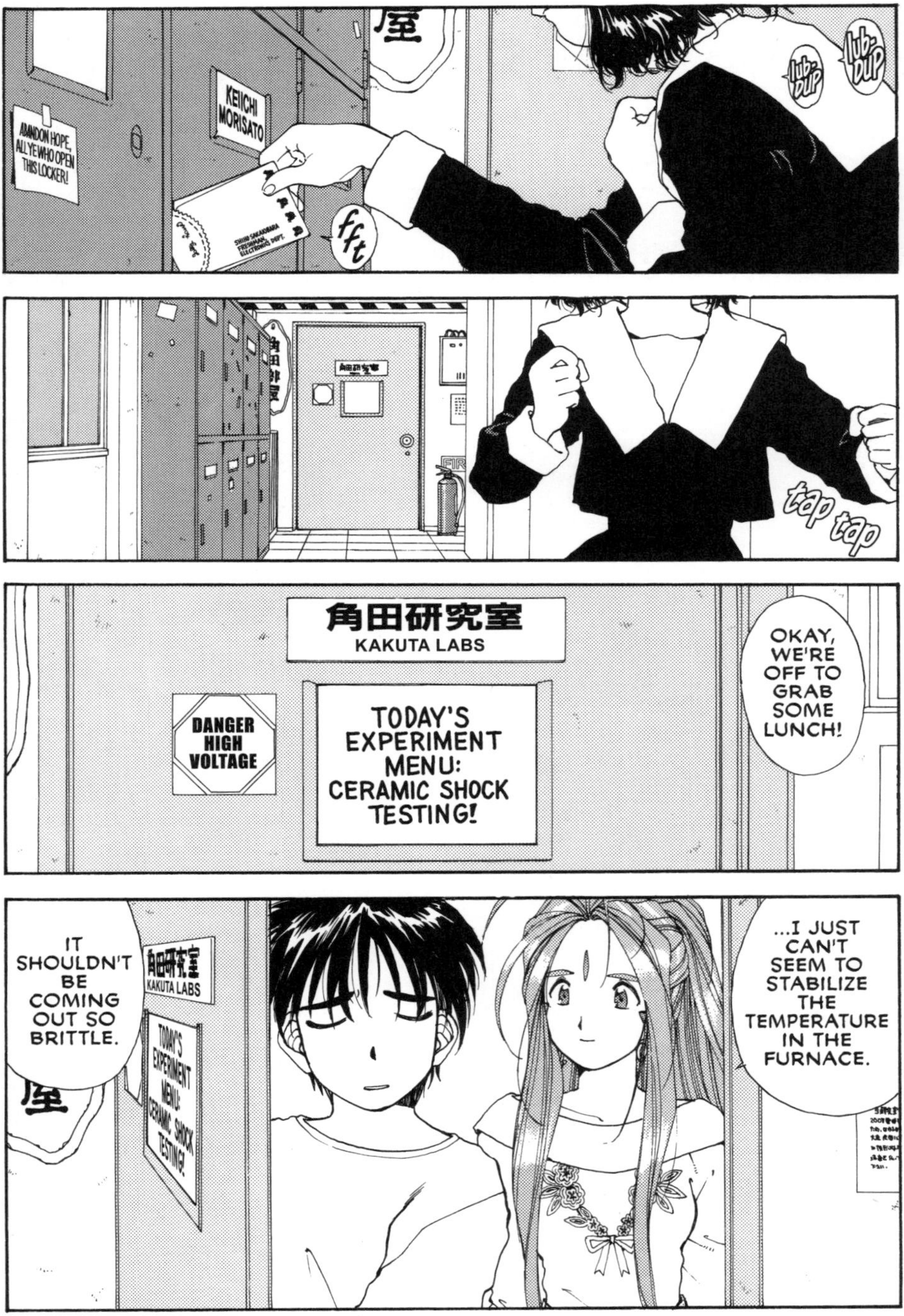
lub-DUP
lub-DUP
KEIICHI MORISATO
ABANDON HOPE, ALL YE WHO OPEN THIS LOCKER!
fft
SHIHO SAKAKIBARA FRESHMAN, ELECTRONICS DEPT.
tap tap
OKAY, WE'RE OFF TO GRAB SOME LUNCH!
角田研究室
KAKUTA LABS
TODAY'S EXPERIMENT MENU: CERAMIC SHOCK TESTING!
DANGER HIGH VOLTAGE
...I JUST CAN'T SEEM TO STABILIZE THE TEMPERATURE IN THE FURNACE.
IT SHOULDN'T BE COMING OUT SO BRITTLE.
角田研究室
KAKUTA LABS
TODAY'S EXPERIMENT MENU: CERAMIC SHOCK TESTING!

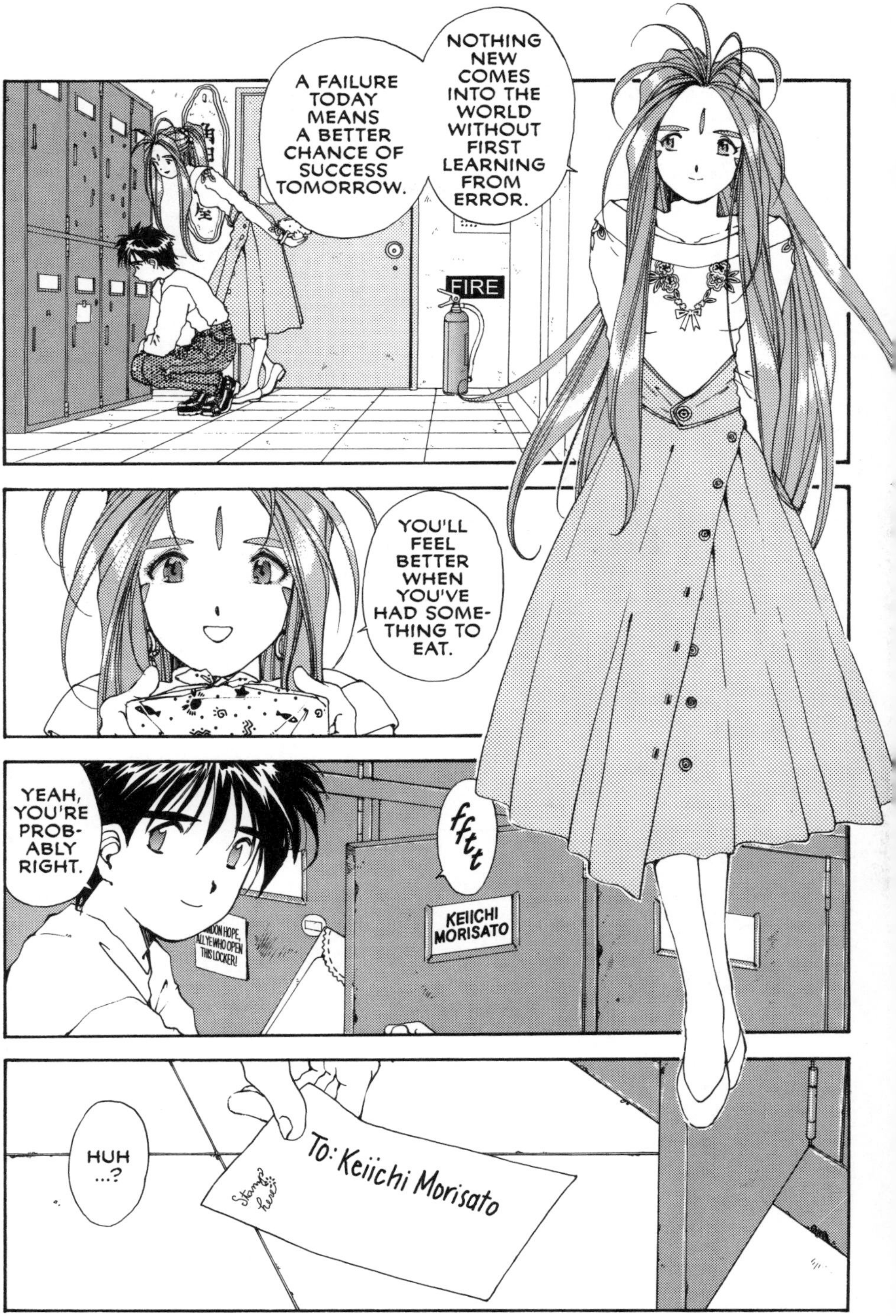
NOTHING NEW COMES INTO THE WORLD WITHOUT FIRST LEARNING FROM ERROR.
A FAILURE TODAY MEANS A BETTER CHANCE OF SUCCESS TOMORROW.
FIRE
YOU'LL FEEL BETTER WHEN YOU'VE HAD SOME-THING TO EAT.
fftt
KEIICHI MORISATO
YEAH, YOU'RE PROB-ABLY RIGHT.
To: Keiichi Morisato
Stamp here
HUH ...?

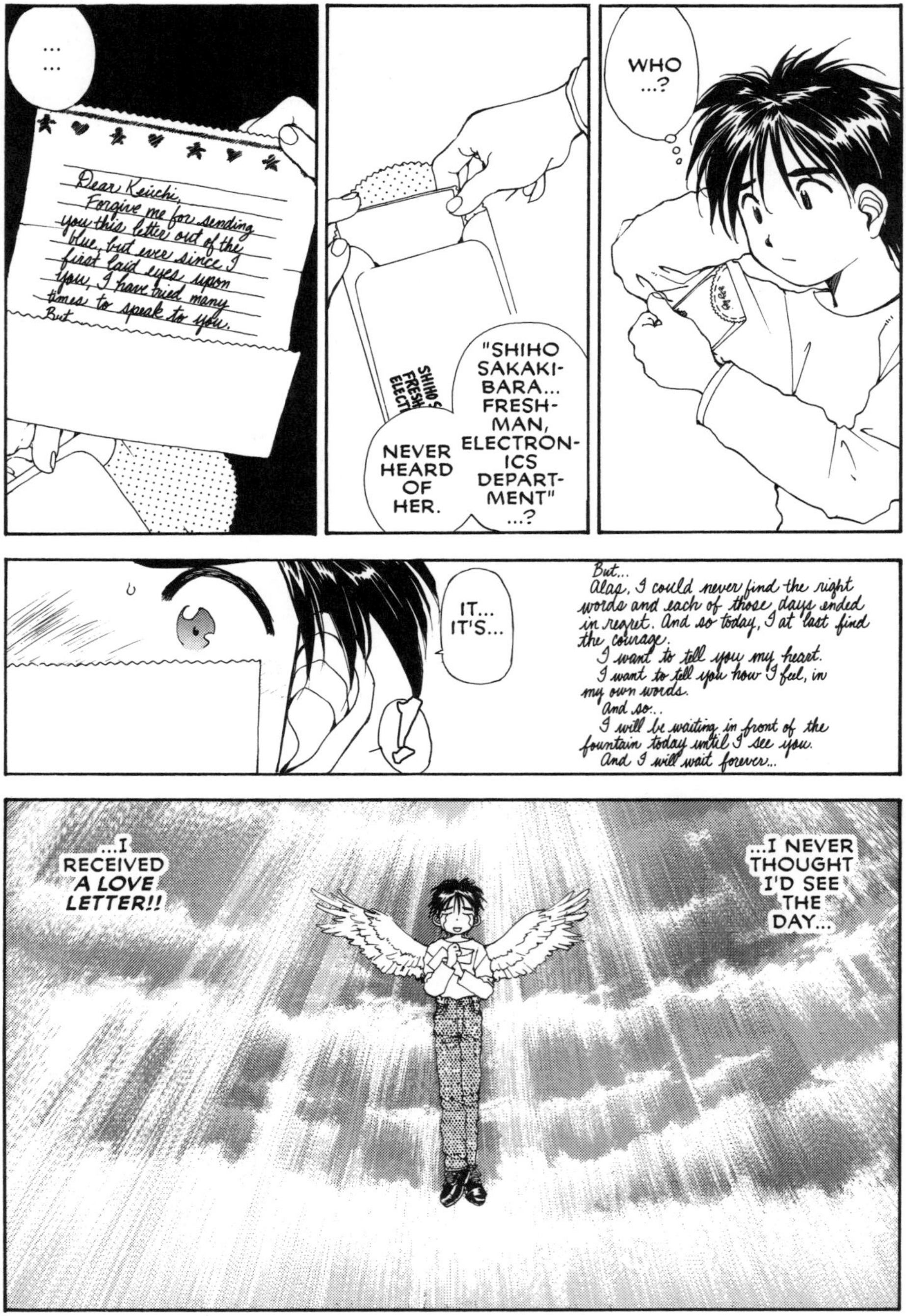
WHO ...?
"SHIHO SAKAKIBARA... FRESHMAN, ELECTRONICS DEPARTMENT" ...?
NEVER HEARD OF HER.
... ...
Dear Keiichi,
Forgive me for sending you this letter out of the blue, but ever since I first laid eyes upon you, I have tried many times to speak to you.
But
But...
Alas, I could never find the right words and each of those days ended in regret. And so today, I at last find the courage.
I want to tell you my heart.
I want to tell you how I feel, in my own words.
And so...
I will be waiting in front of the fountain today until I see you.
And I will wait forever...
IT... IT'S...
...I NEVER THOUGHT I'D SEE THE DAY...
...I RECEIVED A LOVE LETTER!!

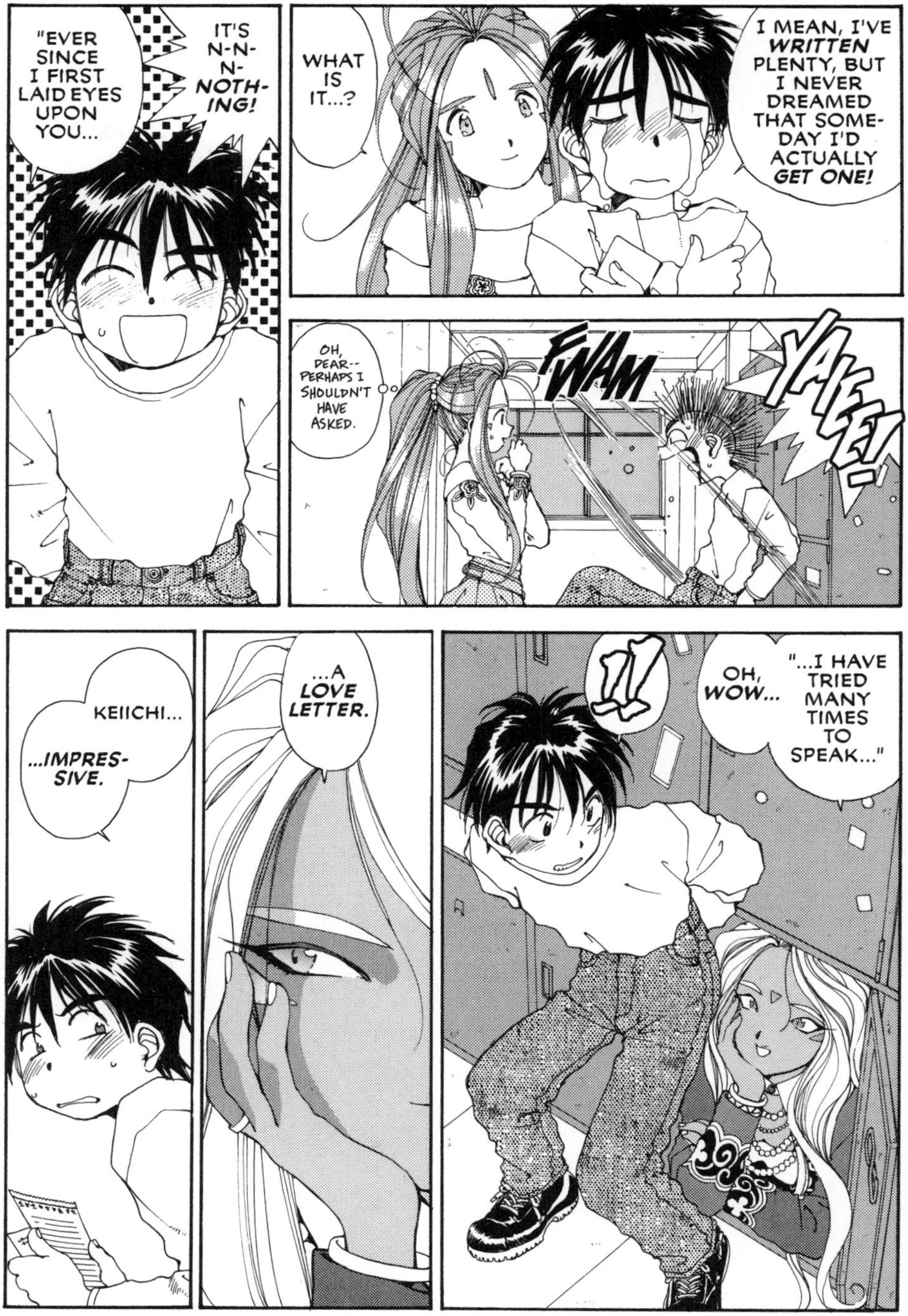
I MEAN, I'VE WRITTEN PLENTY, BUT I NEVER DREAMED THAT SOME-DAY I'D ACTUALLY GET ONE!
WHAT IS IT...?
YAEEE!
FWAM
OH, DEAR-- PERHAPS I SHOULDN'T HAVE ASKED.
IT'S N-N-N-NOTHING!
"EVER SINCE I FIRST LAID EYES UPON YOU...
"...I HAVE TRIED MANY TIMES TO SPEAK..."
OH, WOW...
...A LOVE LETTER.
KEIICHI... ...IMPRESSIVE.

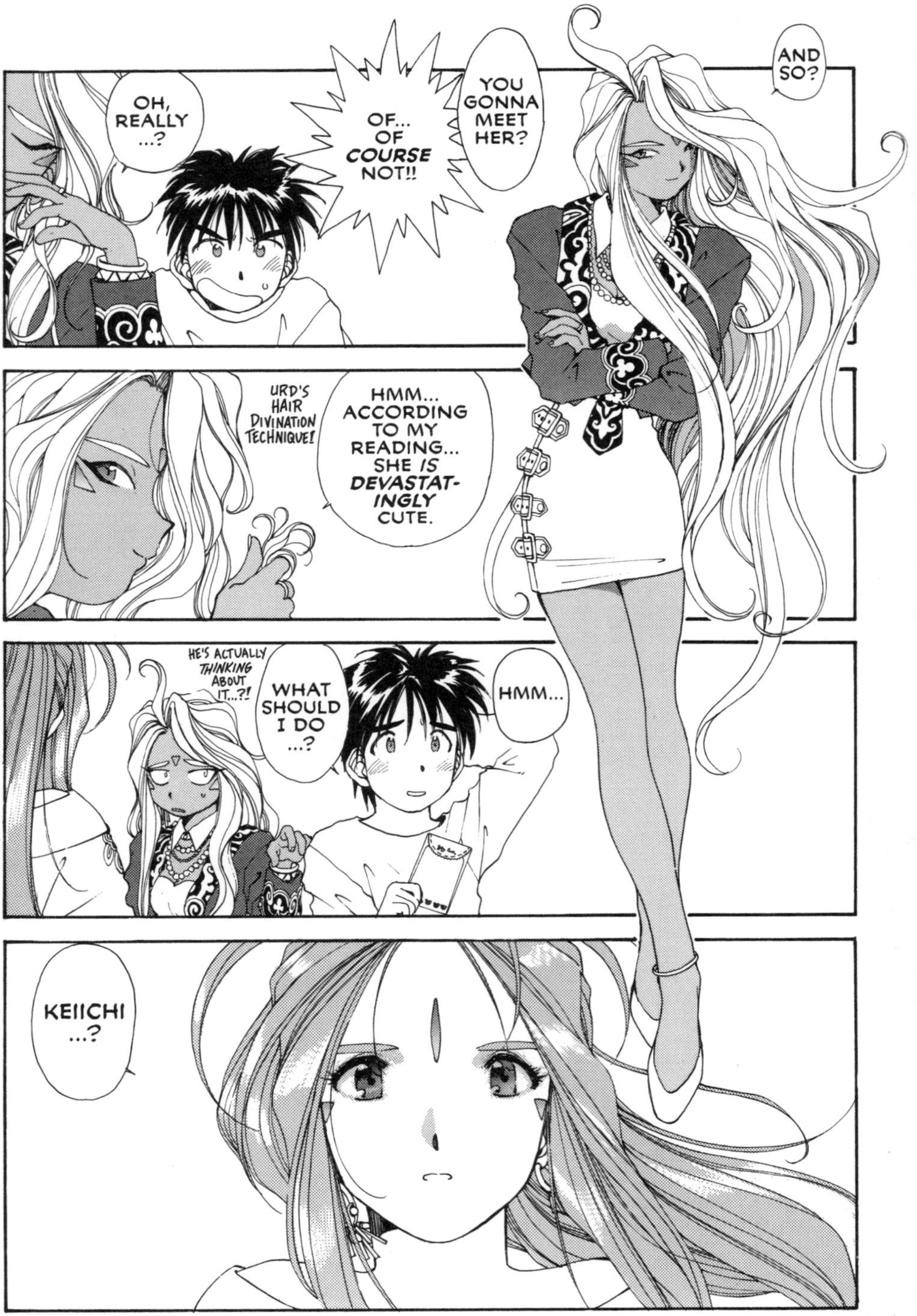
AND SO?
YOU GONNA MEET HER?
OF... OF COURSE NOT!!
OH, REALLY ...?
HMM... ACCORDING TO MY READING... SHE IS DEVASTATINGLY CUTE.
URD'S HAIR DIVINATION TECHNIQUE!
HMM...
WHAT SHOULD I DO ...?
HE'S ACTUALLY THINKING ABOUT IT...?!
KEIICHI ...?

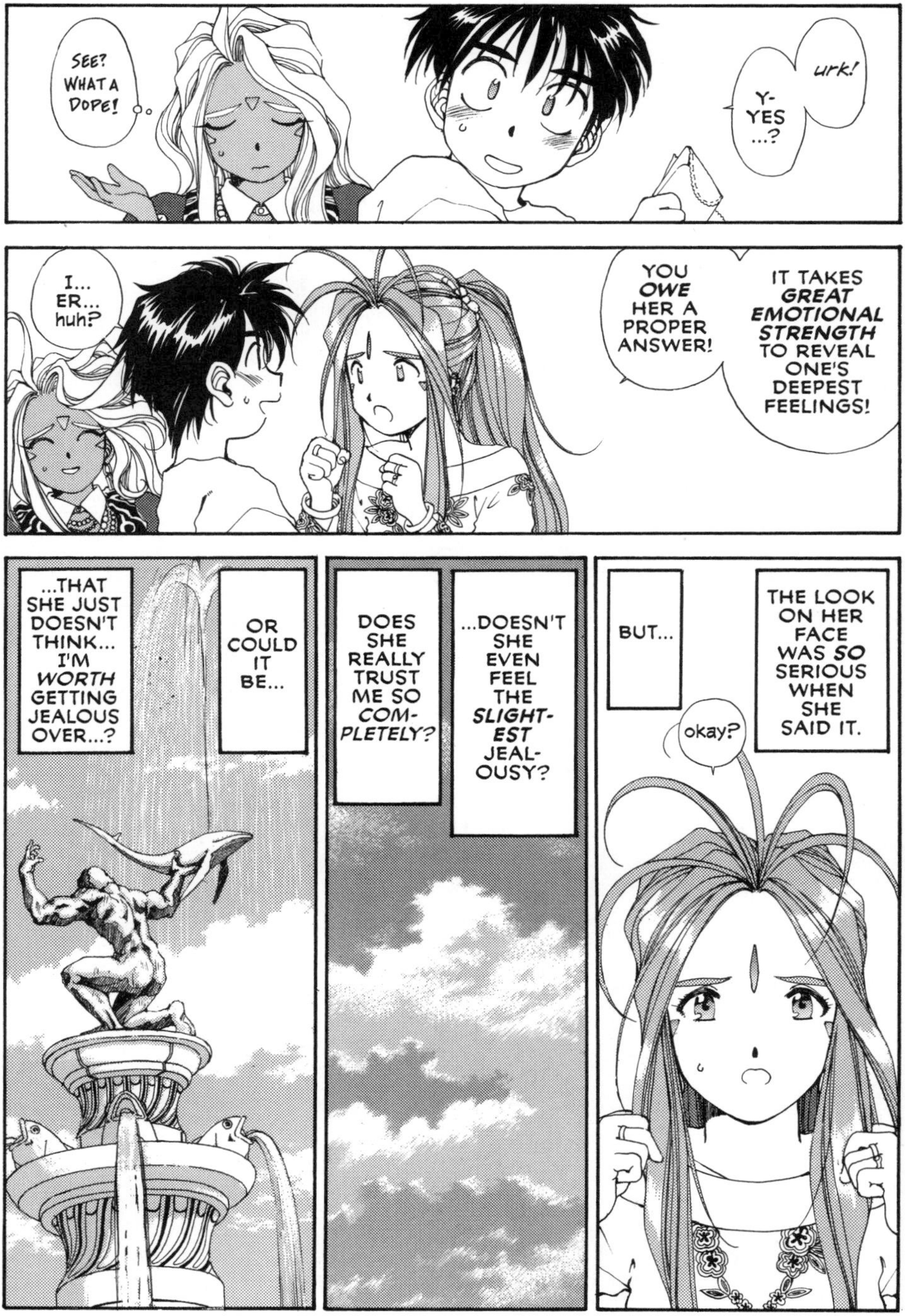
urk!
Y-YES ...?
SEE? WHAT A DOPE!
IT TAKES GREAT EMOTIONAL STRENGTH TO REVEAL ONE'S DEEPEST FEELINGS!
YOU OWE HER A PROPER ANSWER!
I... ER... huh?
THE LOOK ON HER FACE WAS SO SERIOUS WHEN SHE SAID IT.
BUT...
okay?
...DOESN'T SHE EVEN FEEL THE SLIGHTEST JEALOUSY?
DOES SHE REALLY TRUST ME SO COMPLETELY?
OR COULD IT BE...
...THAT SHE JUST DOESN'T THINK... I'M WORTH GETTING JEALOUS OVER...?

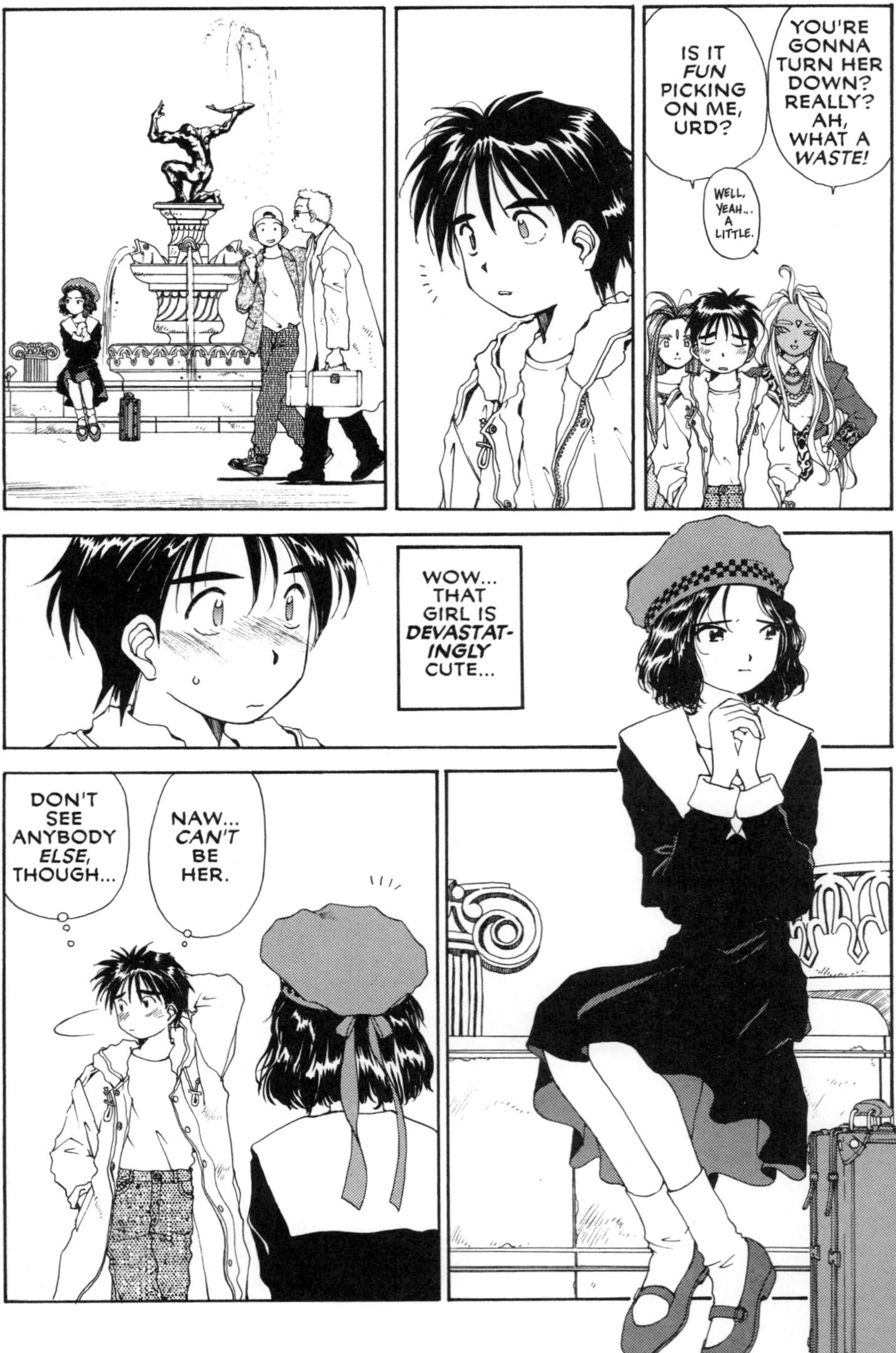
YOU'RE GONNA TURN HER DOWN? REALLY? AH, WHAT A WASTE!
IS IT FUN PICKING ON ME, URD?
WELL, YEAH... A LITTLE.
WOW... THAT GIRL IS DEVASTATINGLY CUTE...
NAW... CAN'T BE HER.
DON'T SEE ANYBODY ELSE, THOUGH...

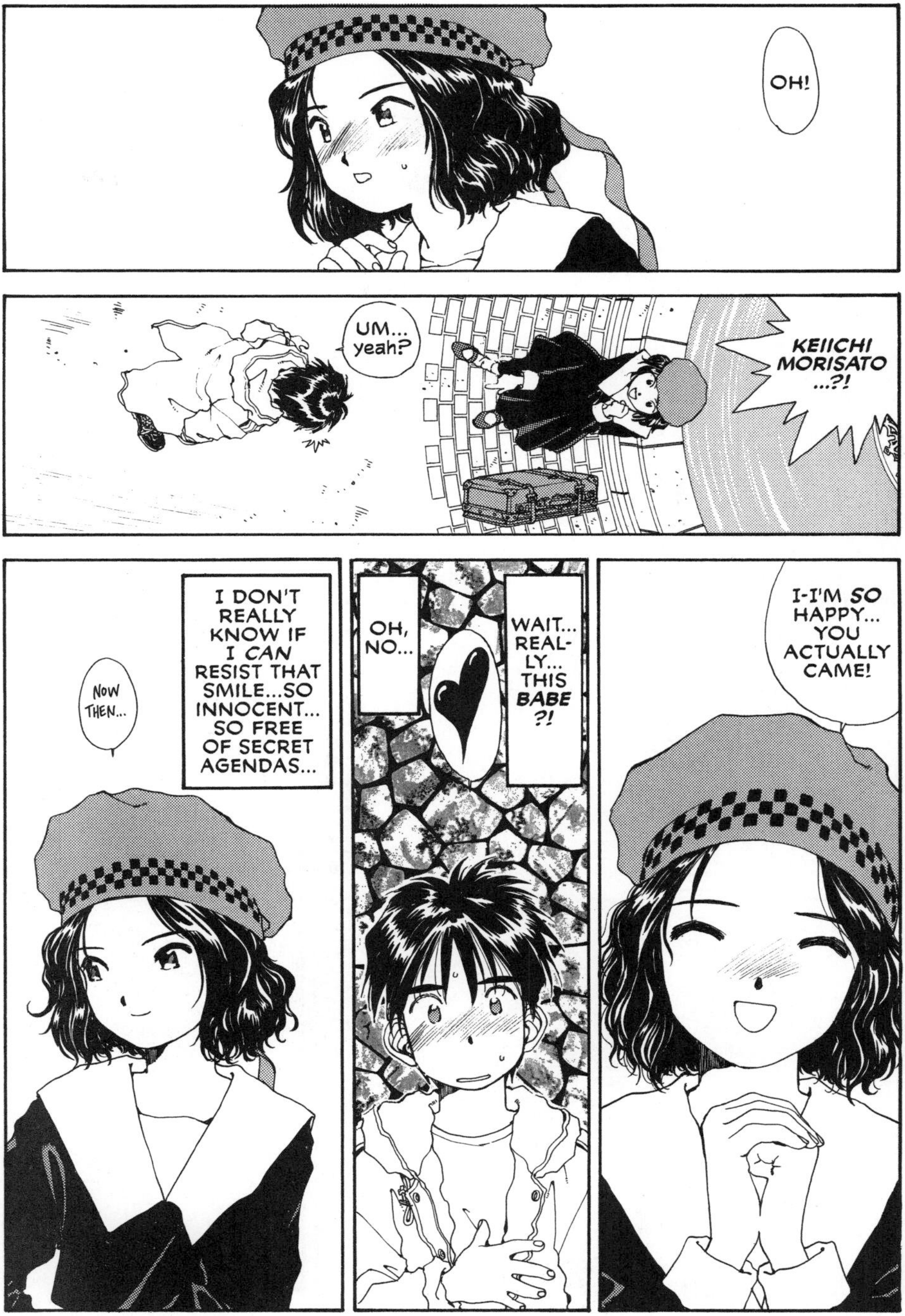
OH!
KEIICHI MORISATO ...?!
UM... yeah?
I-I'M *SO* HAPPY... YOU ACTUALLY CAME!
WAIT... REAL-LY... THIS *BABE* ?!
OH, NO...
I DON'T REALLY KNOW IF I *CAN* RESIST THAT SMILE...SO INNOCENT... SO FREE OF SECRET AGENDAS...
NOW THEN...

DON'T MOVE!

huh?

SORRY!

--BUT I JUST CAN'T--

I KNOW...

I'VE GOT IT...

THERE!

uh...?

wuh?

AH-HA!

I WAS RIGHT!

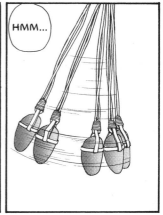

HMM...

518

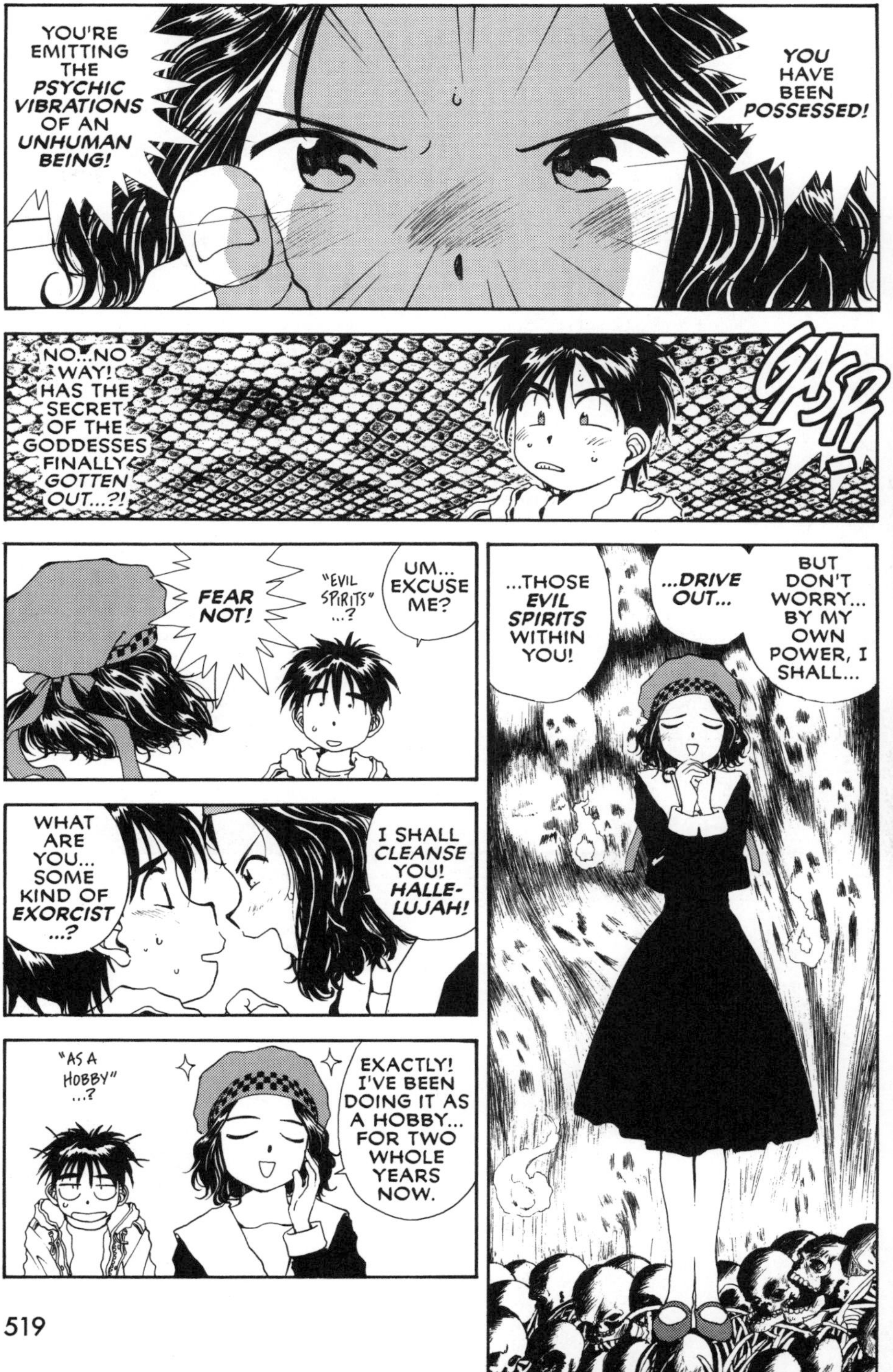
YOU'RE EMITTING THE PSYCHIC VIBRATIONS OF AN UNHUMAN BEING!
YOU HAVE BEEN POSSESSED!
GASP!
NO...NO WAY! HAS THE SECRET OF THE GODDESSES FINALLY GOTTEN OUT...?!
BUT DON'T WORRY... BY MY OWN POWER, I SHALL...
...DRIVE OUT...
...THOSE EVIL SPIRITS WITHIN YOU!
UM... EXCUSE ME?
FEAR NOT!
"EVIL SPIRITS" ...?
I SHALL CLEANSE YOU! HALLE-LUJAH!
WHAT ARE YOU... SOME KIND OF EXORCIST ...?
EXACTLY! I'VE BEEN DOING IT AS A HOBBY... FOR TWO WHOLE YEARS NOW.
"AS A HOBBY" ...?

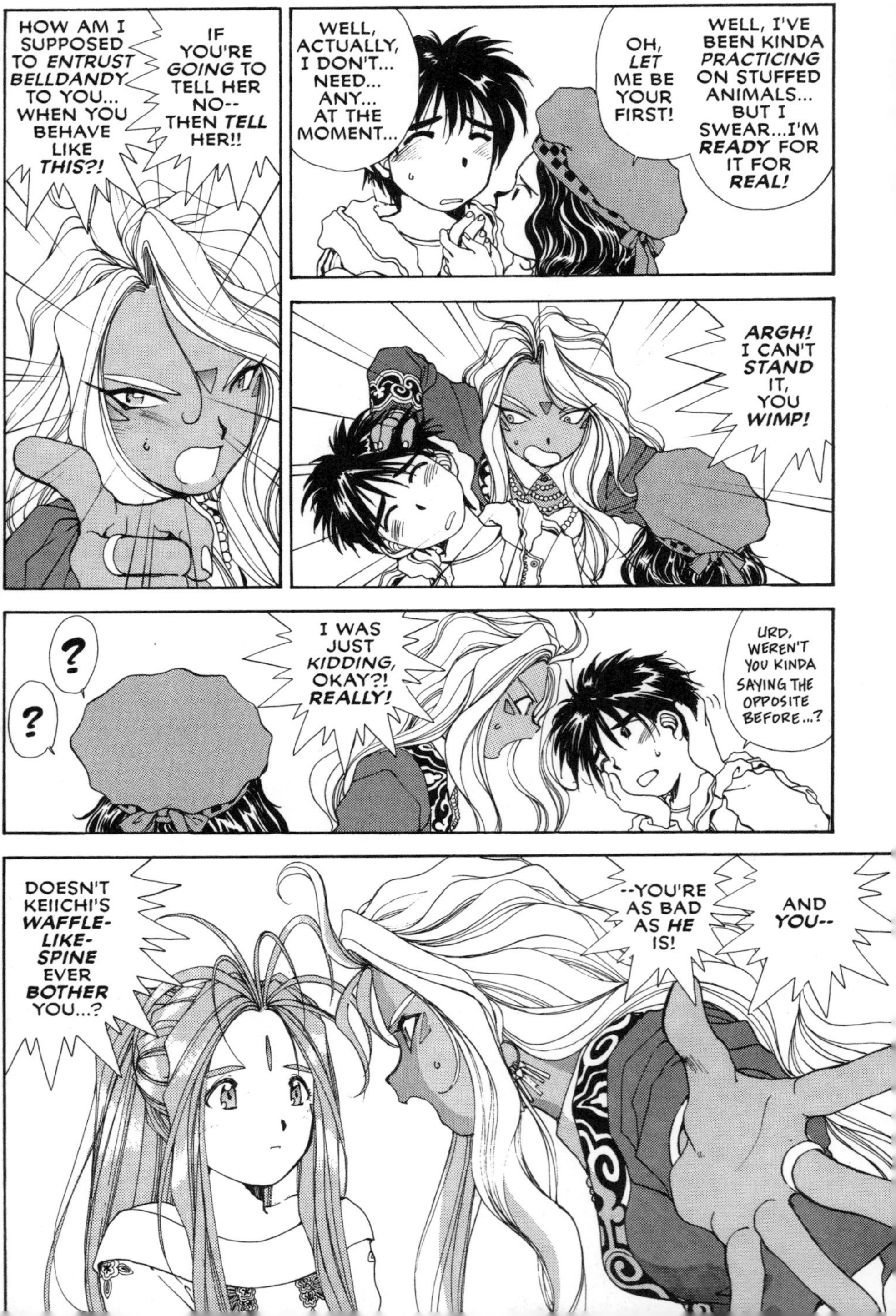
WELL, I'VE BEEN KINDA PRACTICING ON STUFFED ANIMALS... BUT I SWEAR...I'M READY FOR IT FOR REAL!
OH, LET ME BE YOUR FIRST!
WELL, ACTUALLY, I DON'T... NEED... ANY... AT THE MOMENT...
ARGH! I CAN'T STAND IT, YOU WIMP!
IF YOU'RE GOING TO TELL HER NO-- THEN TELL HER!!
HOW AM I SUPPOSED TO ENTRUST BELLDANDY TO YOU... WHEN YOU BEHAVE LIKE THIS?!
URD, WEREN'T YOU KINDA SAYING THE OPPOSITE BEFORE...?
I WAS JUST KIDDING, OKAY?! REALLY!
?
?
AND YOU--
--YOU'RE AS BAD AS HE IS!
DOESN'T KEIICHI'S WAFFLE-LIKE-SPINE EVER BOTHER YOU...?

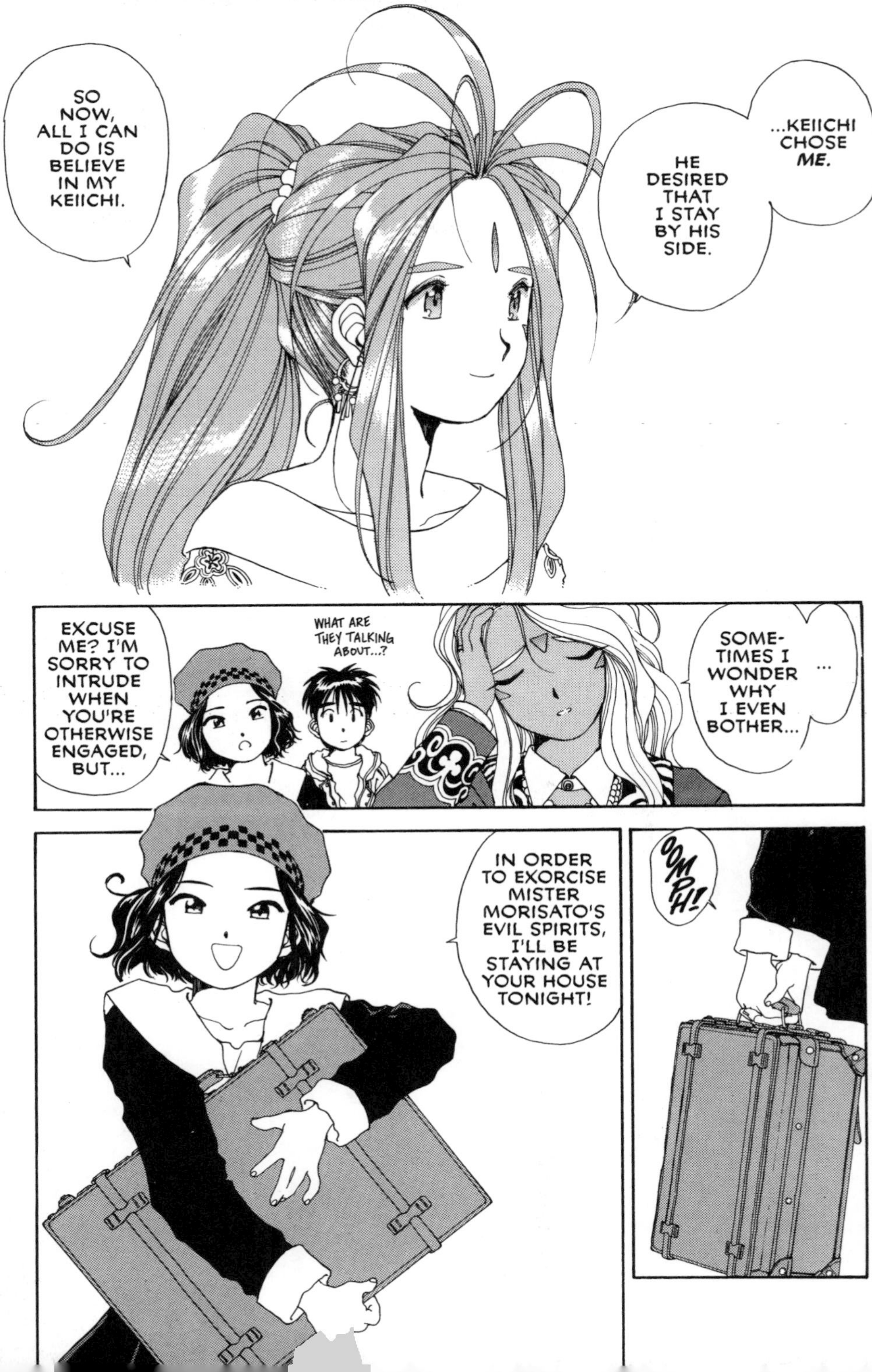
...KEIICHI CHOSE *ME.*
HE DESIRED THAT I STAY BY HIS SIDE.
SO NOW, ALL I CAN DO IS BELIEVE IN MY KEIICHI.
SOME-TIMES I WONDER WHY I EVEN BOTHER...
...
WHAT ARE THEY TALKING ABOUT...?
EXCUSE ME? I'M SORRY TO INTRUDE WHEN YOU'RE OTHERWISE ENGAGED, BUT...
OOMPH!
IN ORDER TO EXORCISE MISTER MORISATO'S EVIL SPIRITS, I'LL BE STAYING AT YOUR HOUSE TONIGHT!

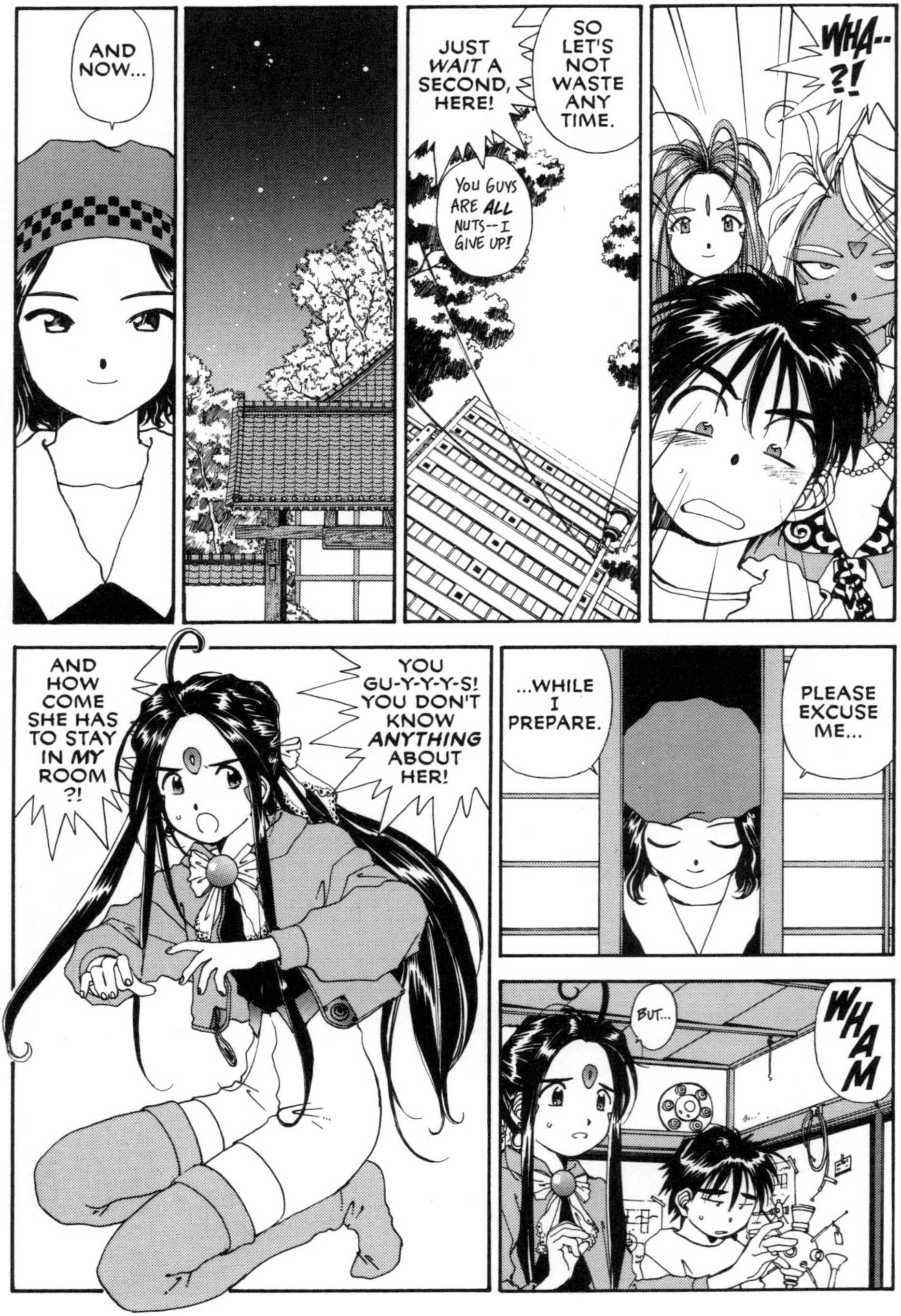
WHA-- ?!
SO LET'S NOT WASTE ANY TIME.
JUST WAIT A SECOND, HERE!
YOU GUYS ARE ALL NUTS-- I GIVE UP!
AND NOW...
PLEASE EXCUSE ME...
...WHILE I PREPARE.
WHAM
BUT...
YOU GU-Y-Y-Y-S! YOU DON'T KNOW ANYTHING ABOUT HER!
AND HOW COME SHE HAS TO STAY IN MY ROOM ?!

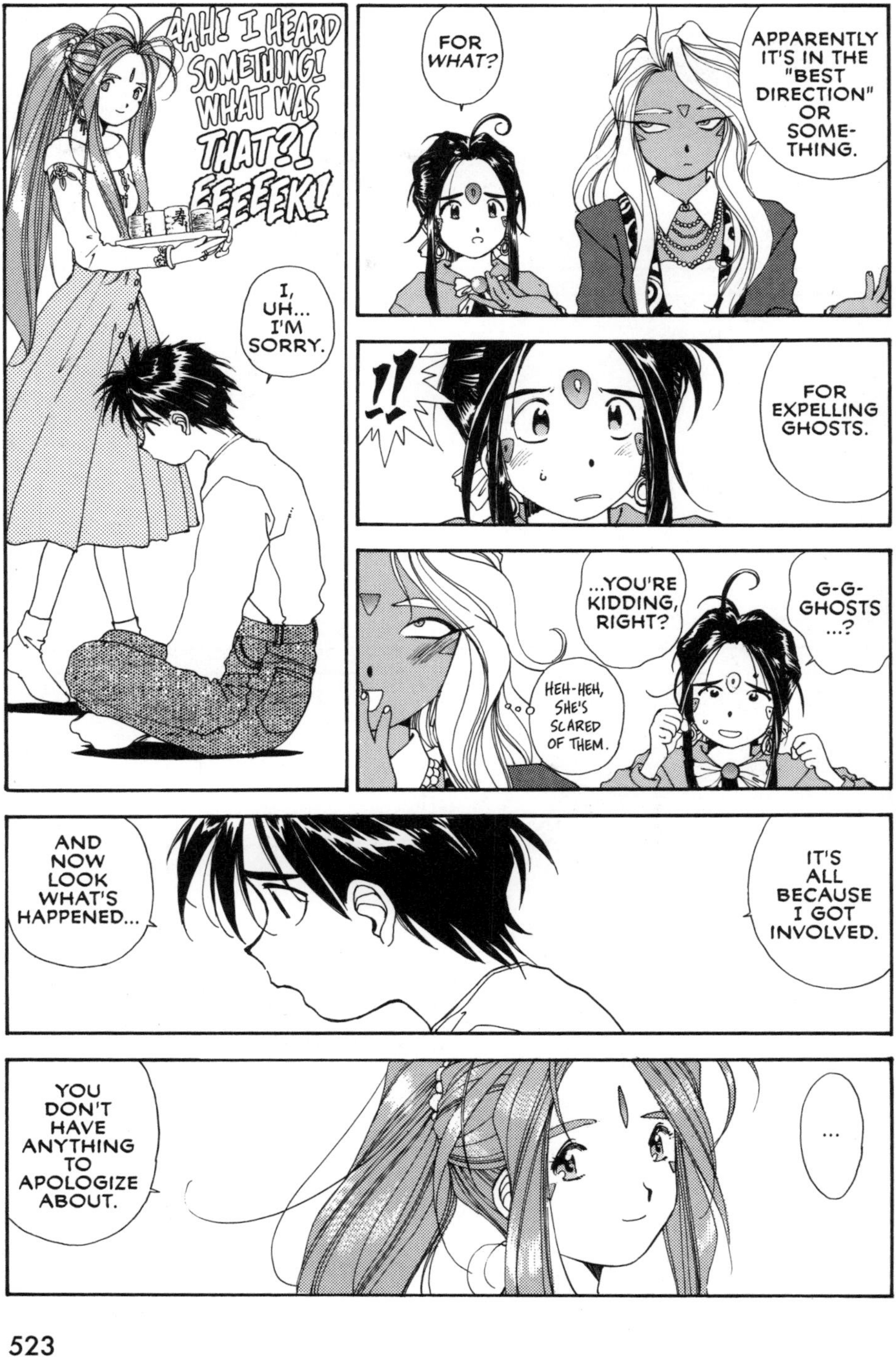
APPARENTLY IT'S IN THE "BEST DIRECTION" OR SOME-THING.
FOR WHAT?
FOR EXPELLING GHOSTS.
!!
G-G-GHOSTS ...?
...YOU'RE KIDDING, RIGHT?
HEH-HEH, SHE'S SCARED OF THEM.
AAH! I HEARD SOMETHING! WHAT WAS THAT?! EEEEEK!
I, UH... I'M SORRY.
IT'S ALL BECAUSE I GOT INVOLVED.
AND NOW LOOK WHAT'S HAPPENED...
...
YOU DON'T HAVE ANYTHING TO APOLOGIZE ABOUT.

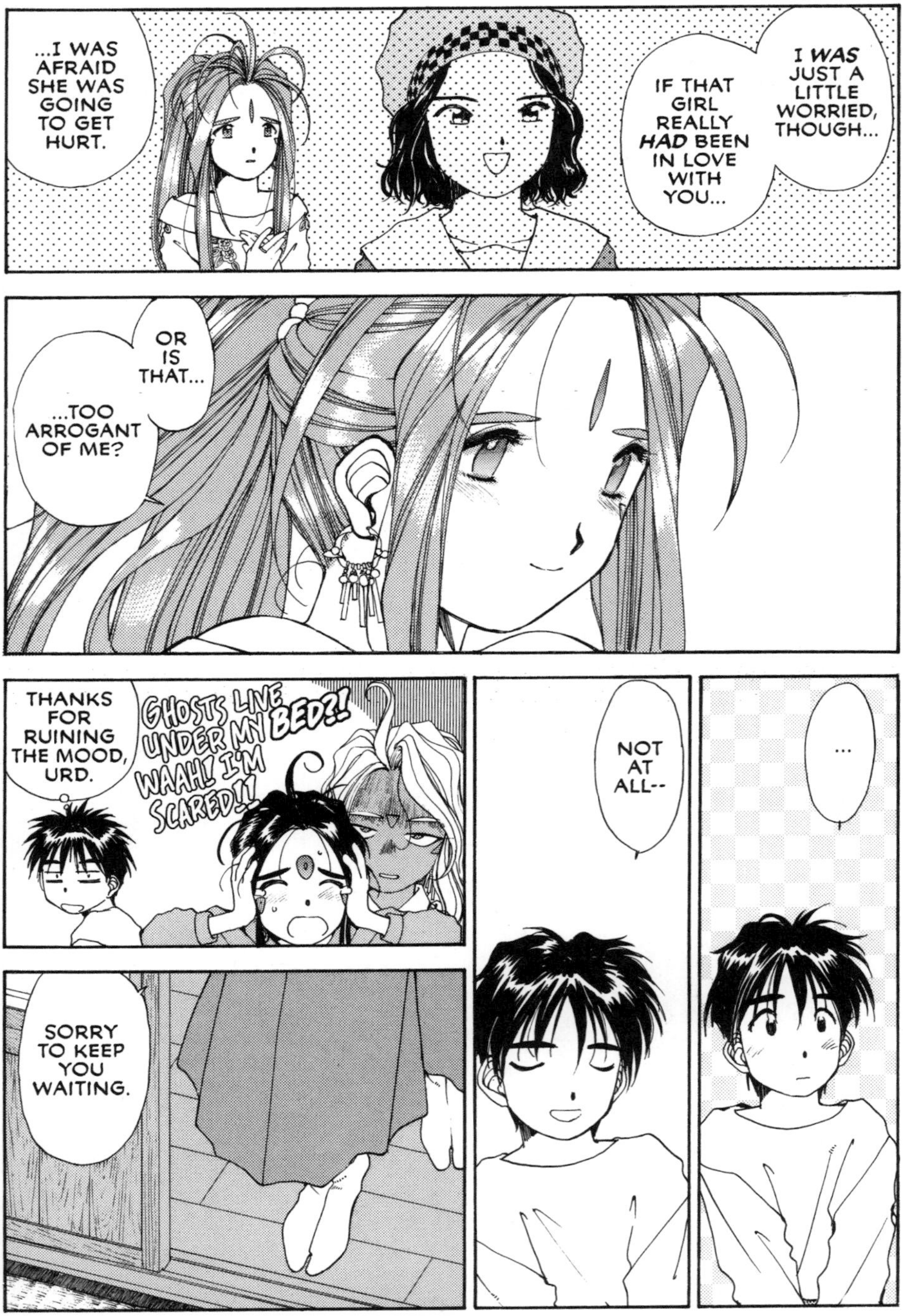
I WAS JUST A LITTLE WORRIED, THOUGH...
IF THAT GIRL REALLY HAD BEEN IN LOVE WITH YOU...
...I WAS AFRAID SHE WAS GOING TO GET HURT.
OR IS THAT...
...TOO ARROGANT OF ME?
...
NOT AT ALL--
GHOSTS LIVE UNDER MY BED?! WAAH! I'M SCARED!!
THANKS FOR RUINING THE MOOD, URD.
SORRY TO KEEP YOU WAITING.

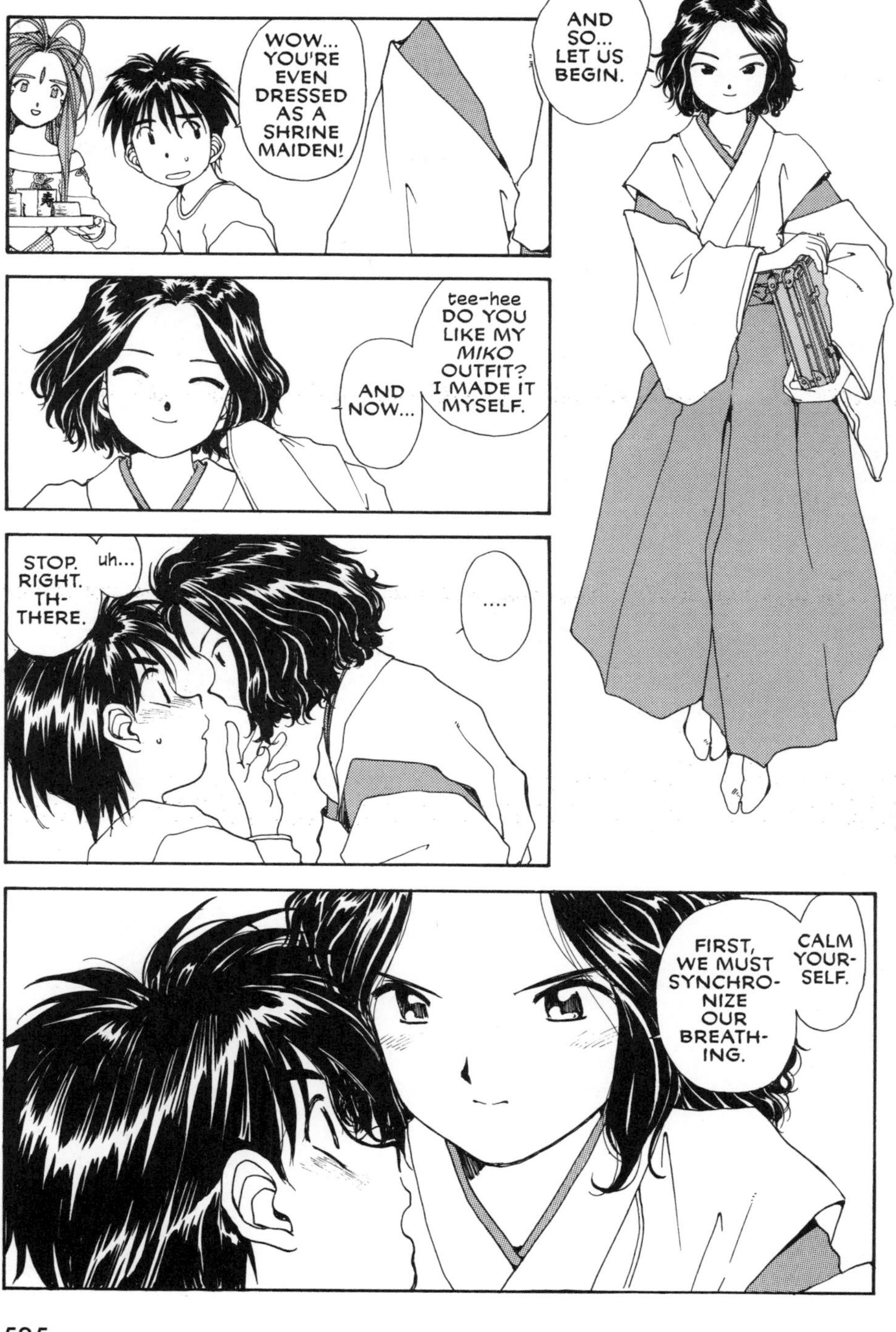
AND SO... LET US BEGIN.
WOW... YOU'RE EVEN DRESSED AS A SHRINE MAIDEN!
tee-hee DO YOU LIKE MY *MIKO* OUTFIT? I MADE IT MYSELF.
AND NOW...
....
uh...
STOP. RIGHT. TH- THERE.
CALM YOURSELF.
FIRST, WE MUST SYNCHRONIZE OUR BREATHING.

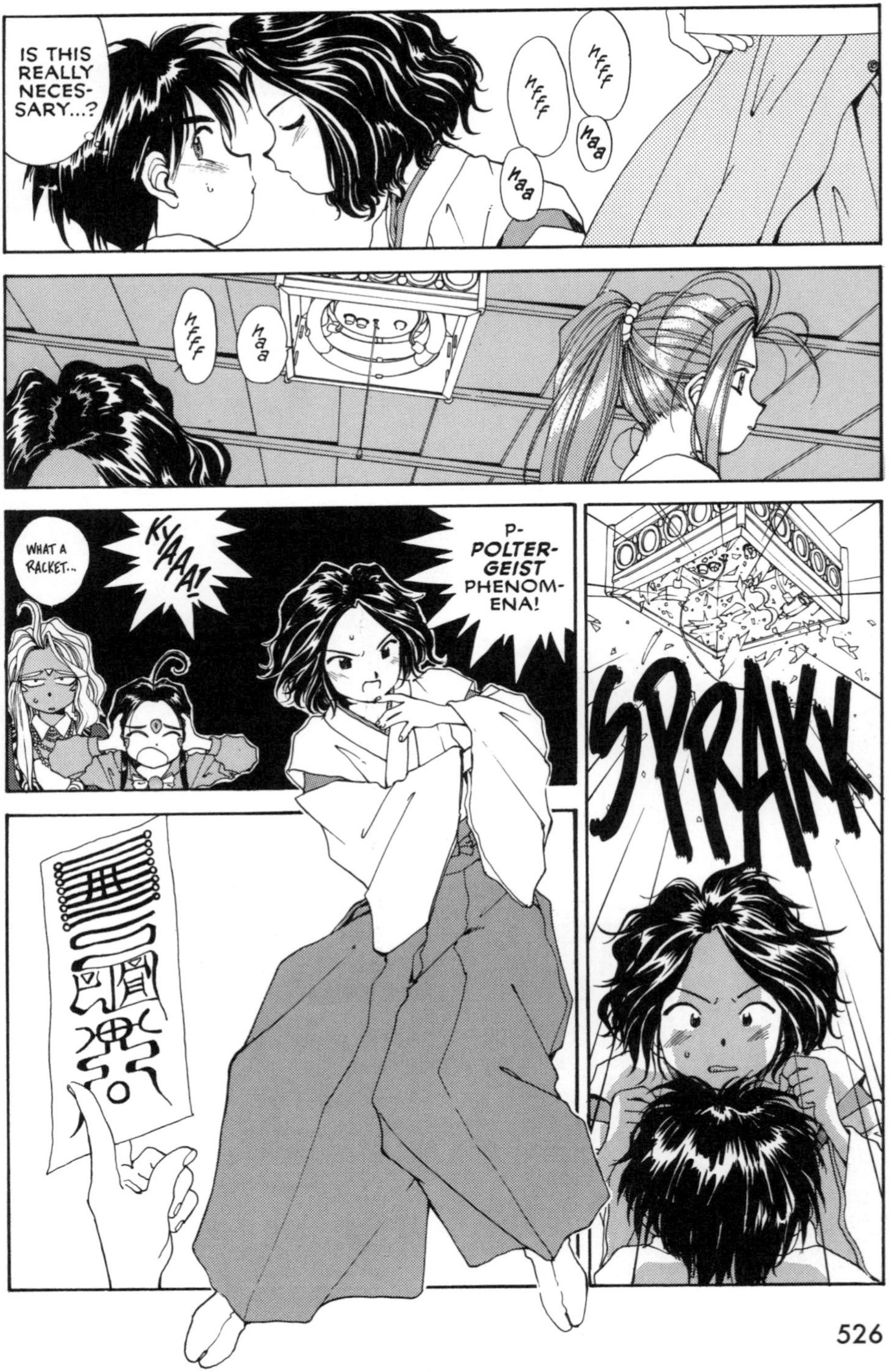
nfff
naa
nfff
naa
IS THIS REALLY NECES-SARY...?
naa
nfff
SPRAKK
P-POLTERGEIST PHENOMENA!
KYAAAA!
WHAT A RACKET...

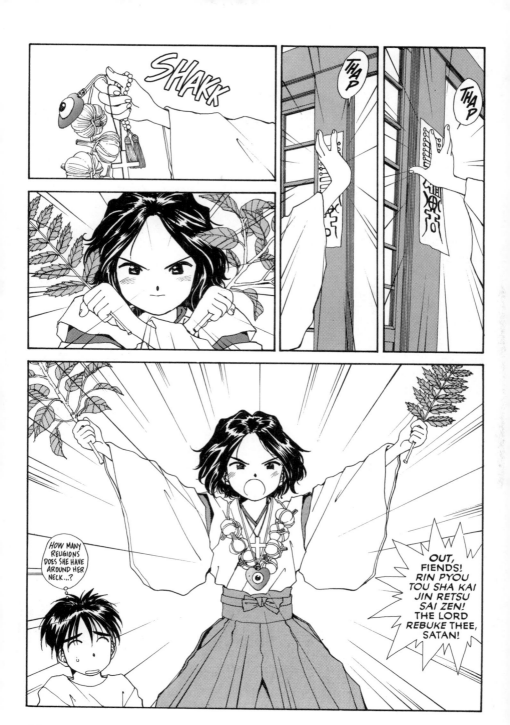

THAP
THAP
SHAKK
OUT, FIENDS! RIN PYOU TOU SHA KAI JIN RETSU SAI ZEN! THE LORD REBUKE THEE, SATAN!
HOW MANY RELIGIONS DOES SHE HAVE AROUND HER NECK...?

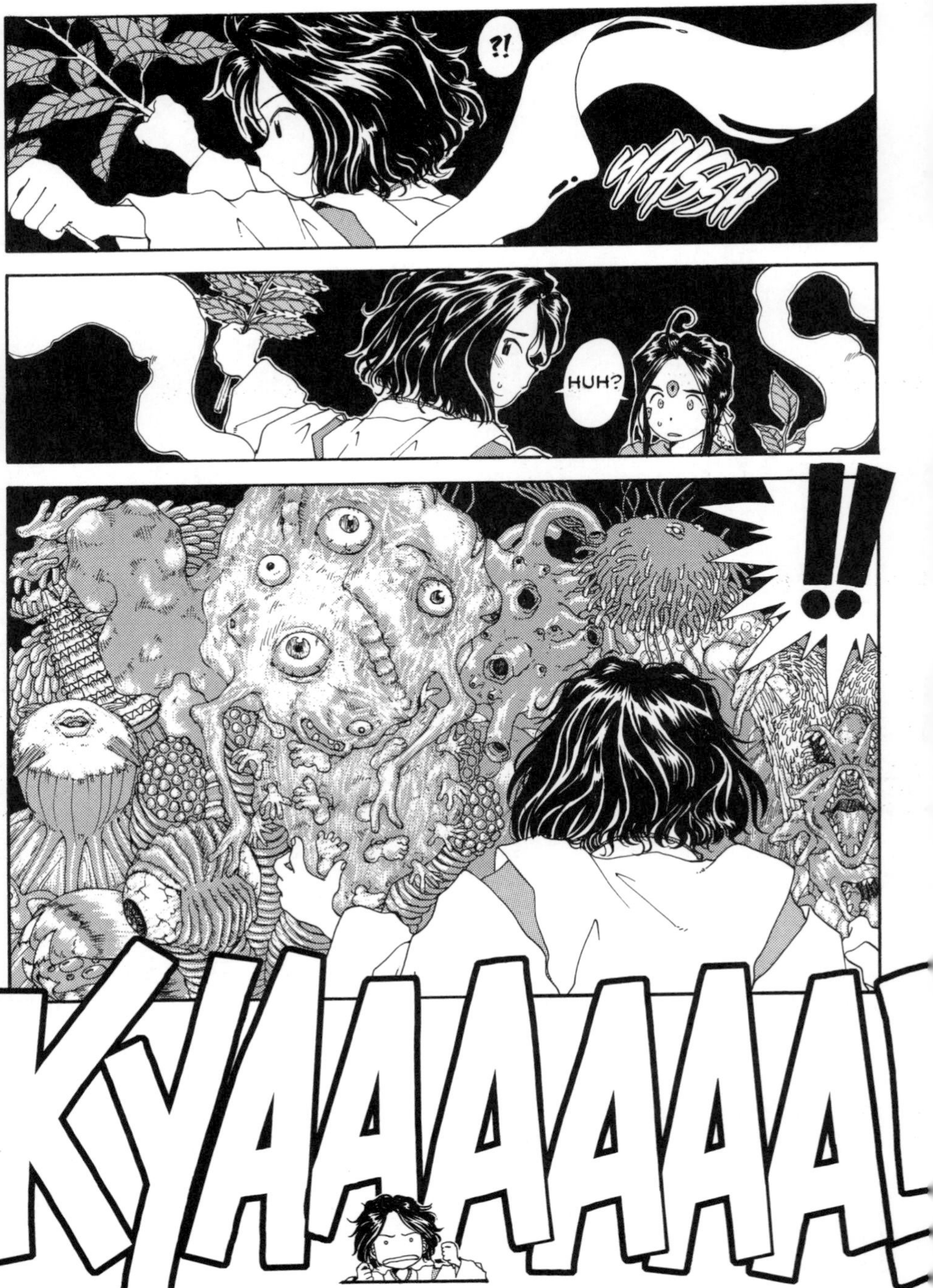
?!
WHSH
HUH?
!!
KYAAAAAA

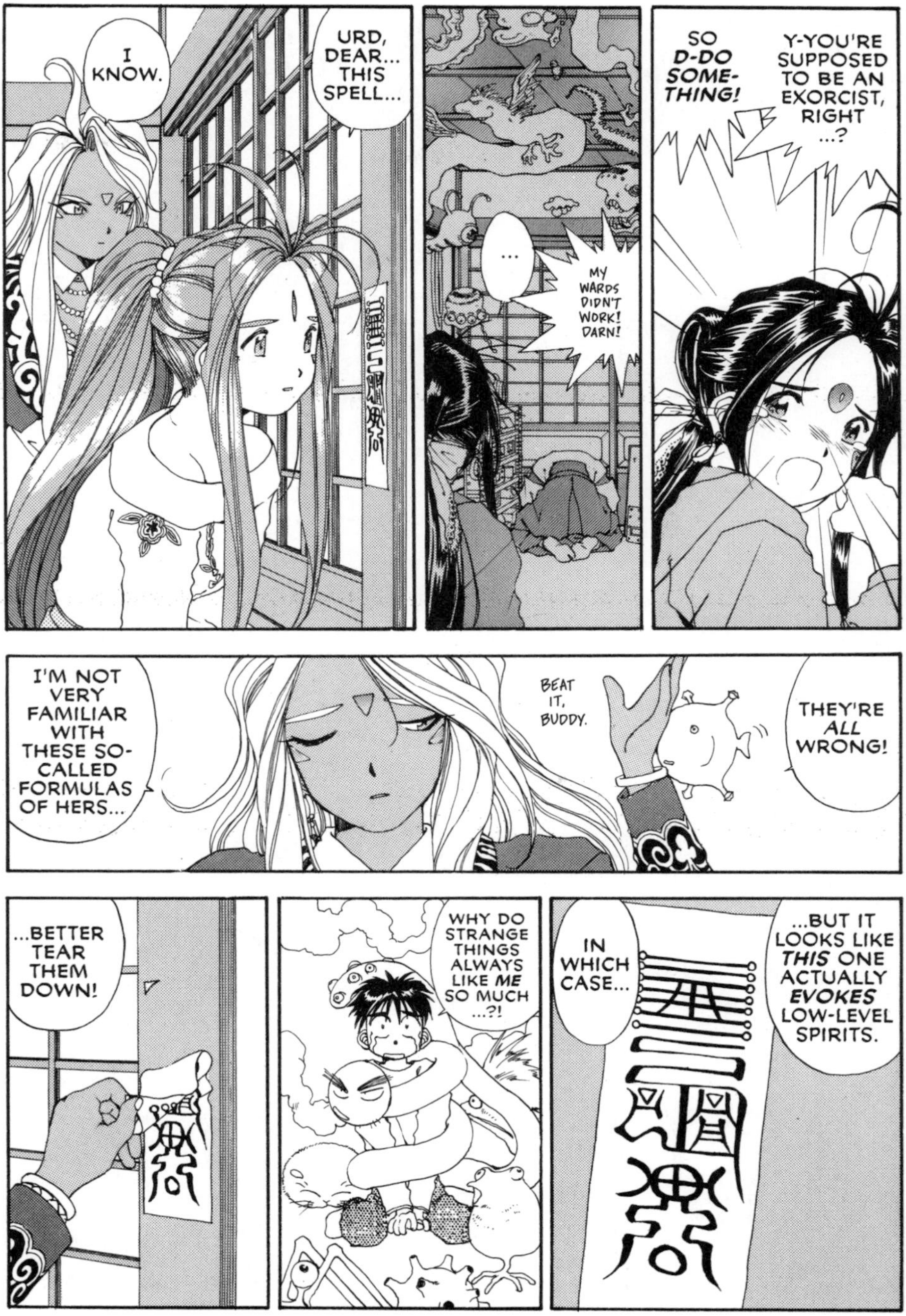
Y-YOU'RE SUPPOSED TO BE AN EXORCIST, RIGHT ...?
SO D-DO SOMETHING!
...
MY WARDS DIDN'T WORK! DARN!
URD, DEAR... THIS SPELL...
I KNOW.
THEY'RE ALL WRONG!
BEAT IT, BUDDY.
I'M NOT VERY FAMILIAR WITH THESE SO-CALLED FORMULAS OF HERS...
...BUT IT LOOKS LIKE THIS ONE ACTUALLY EVOKES LOW-LEVEL SPIRITS.
IN WHICH CASE...
WHY DO STRANGE THINGS ALWAYS LIKE ME SO MUCH ...?!
...BETTER TEAR THEM DOWN!

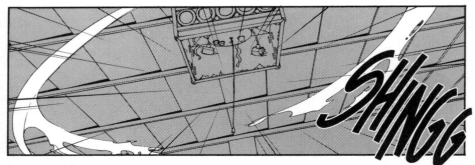

SHINGG

WHA--?

HUH?

I... I...

OH, HEY-- THEY JUST TOOK A MOMENT TO KICK IN!

?

THEY'RE... GONE?

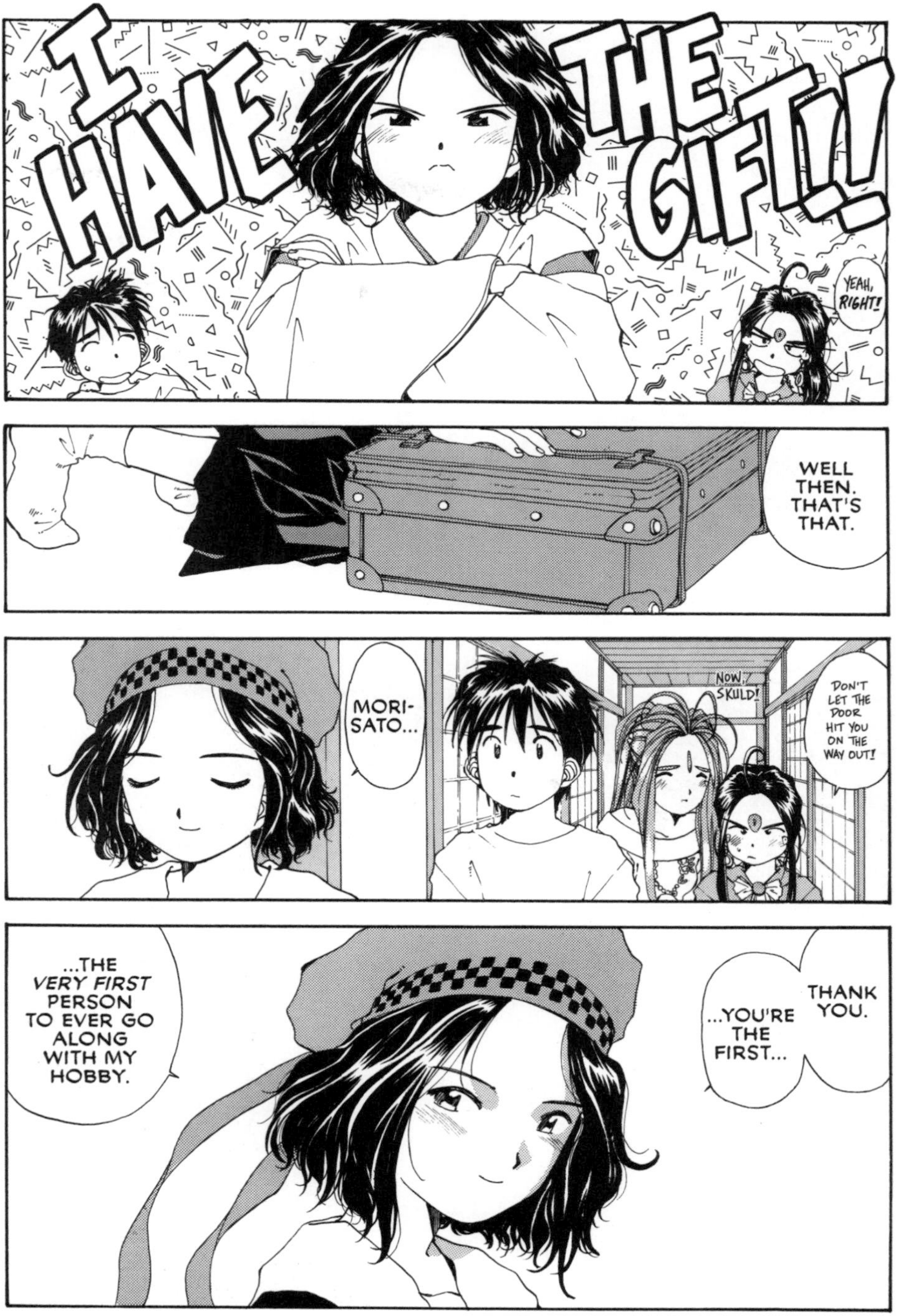
I HAVE THE GIFT!!
YEAH, RIGHT!
WELL THEN. THAT'S THAT.
DON'T LET THE DOOR HIT YOU ON THE WAY OUT!
NOW, SKULD!
MORI-SATO...
THANK YOU.
...YOU'RE THE FIRST...
...THE *VERY FIRST* PERSON TO EVER GO ALONG WITH MY HOBBY.

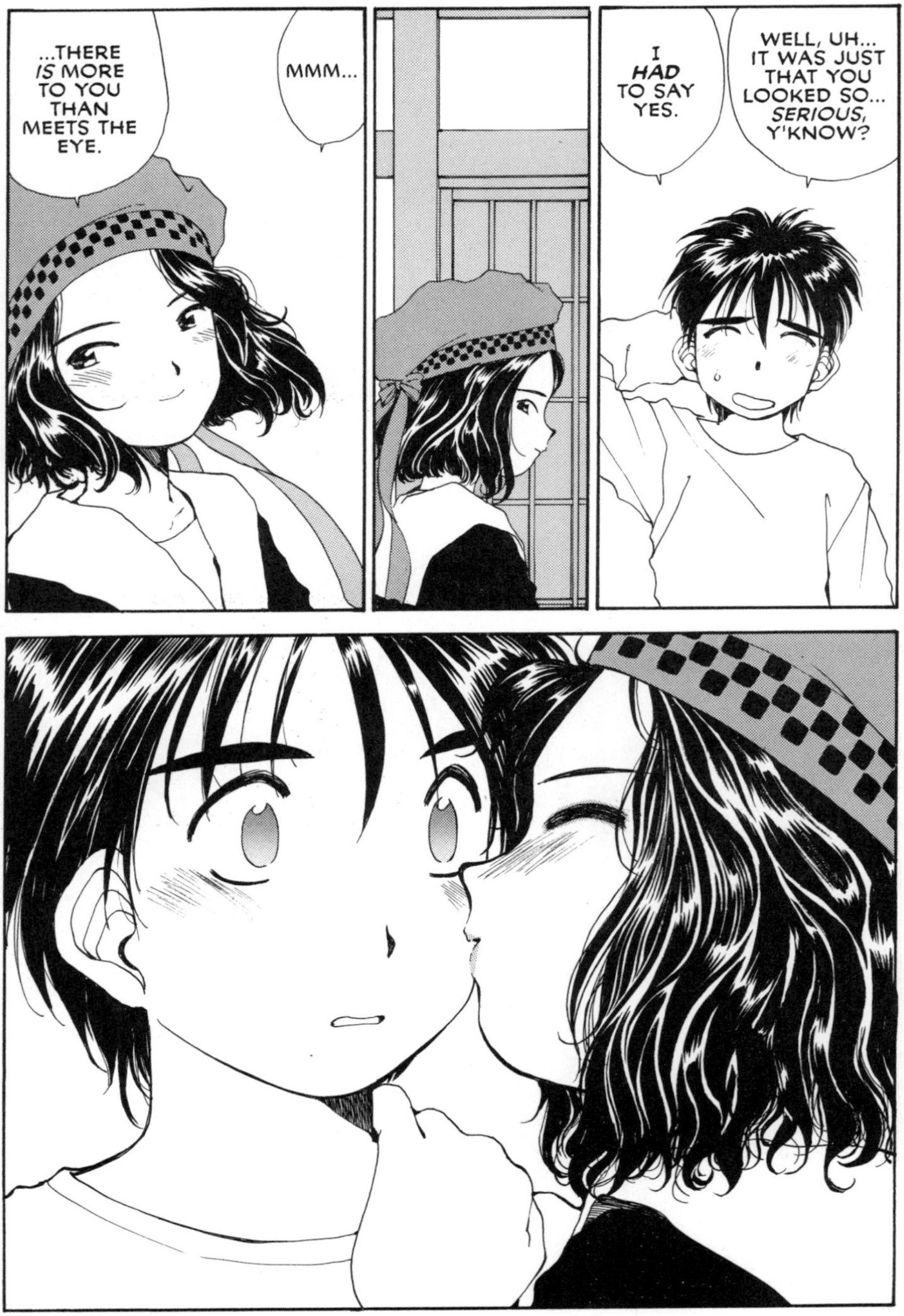
WELL, UH... IT WAS JUST THAT YOU LOOKED SO... *SERIOUS,* Y'KNOW?
I *HAD* TO SAY YES.
MMM...
...THERE *IS* MORE TO YOU THAN MEETS THE EYE.

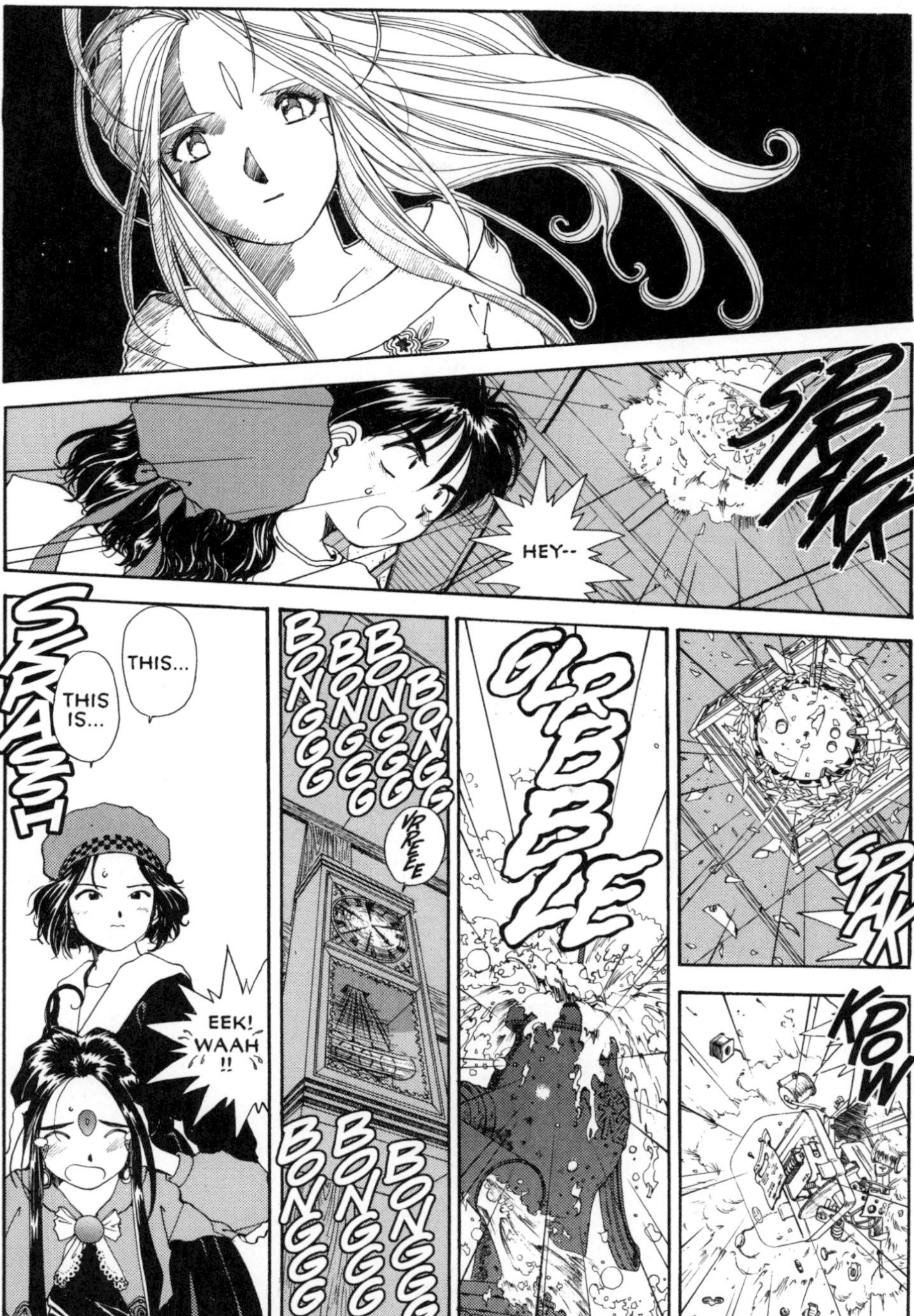
SPRAKK
HEY--
SPAK
KPOW
GLRBBLE
BONGGG BONNGGG BONNGGG BONGGG
BONGGG BONGGG BONGGG
THIS...
THIS IS...
EEK! WAAH!!

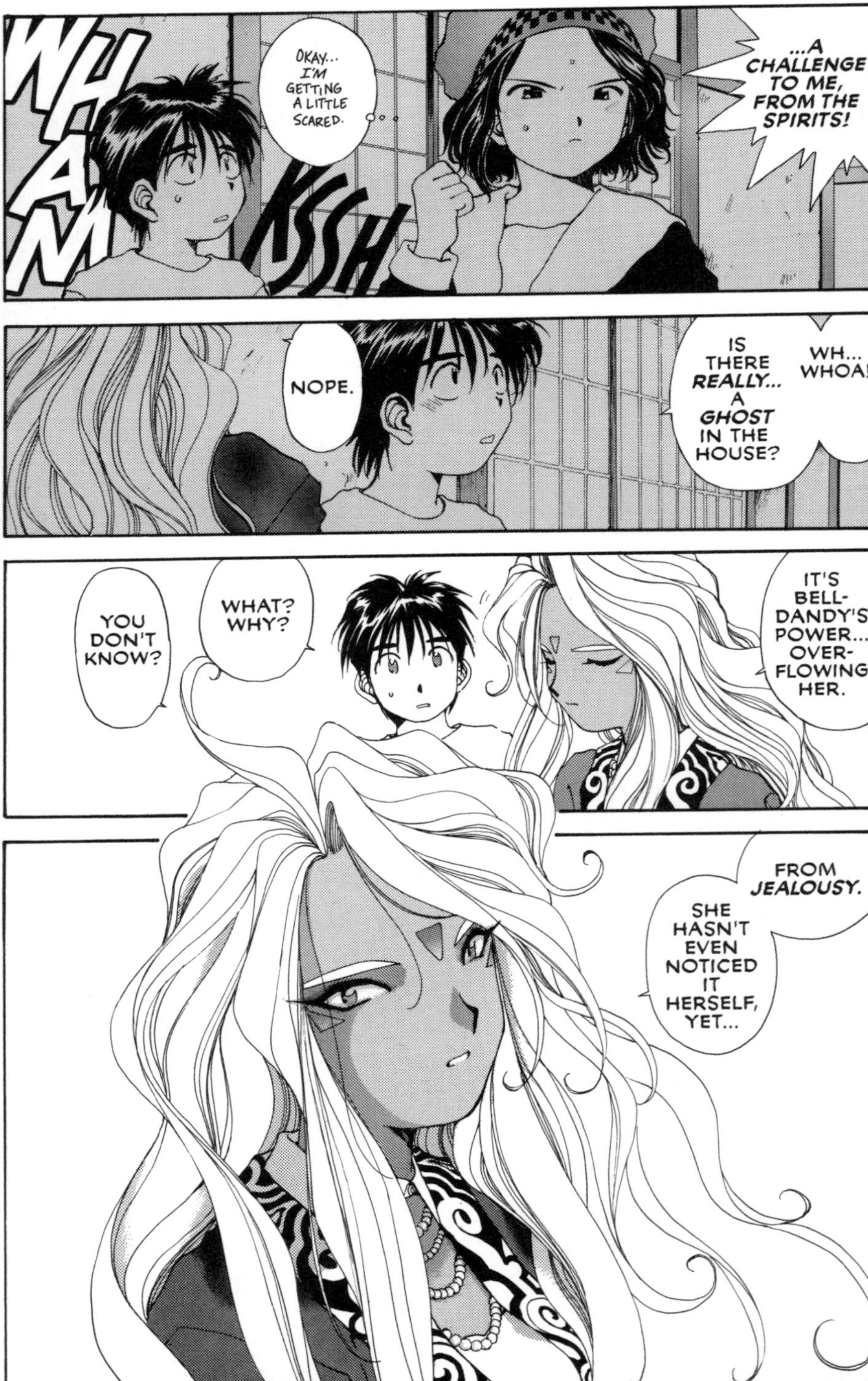
...A CHALLENGE TO ME, FROM THE SPIRITS!
OKAY... I'M GETTING A LITTLE SCARED.
KSSH
WHAM
WH... WHOA!
IS THERE REALLY... A GHOST IN THE HOUSE?
NOPE.
IT'S BELL-DANDY'S POWER... OVER-FLOWING HER.
WHAT? WHY?
YOU DON'T KNOW?
FROM JEALOUSY.
SHE HASN'T EVEN NOTICED IT HERSELF, YET...

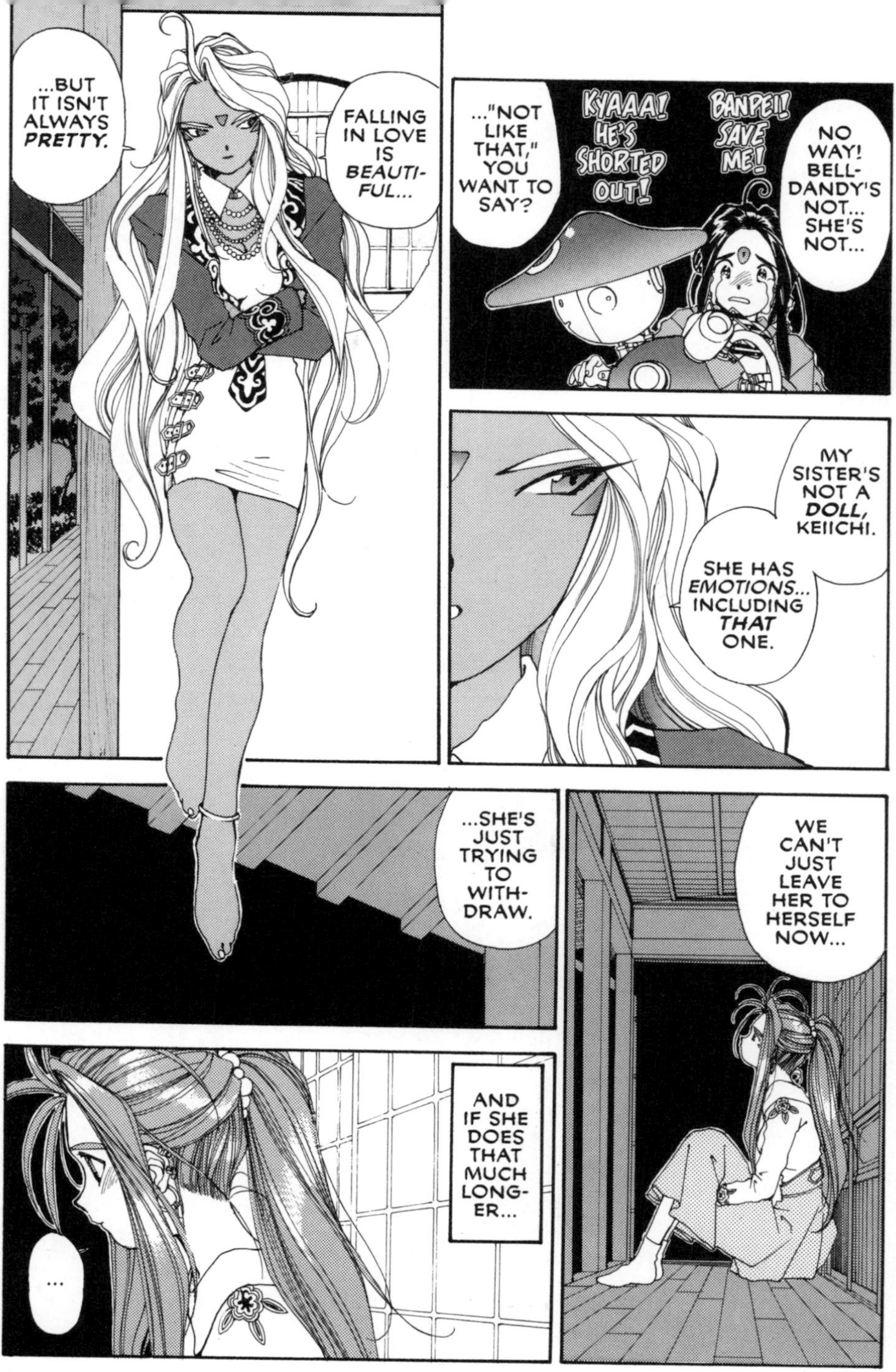
NO WAY! BELLDANDY'S NOT... SHE'S NOT...
BANPEI! SAVE ME!
KYAAA! HE'S SHORTED OUT!
..."NOT LIKE THAT," YOU WANT TO SAY?
MY SISTER'S NOT A *DOLL,* KEIICHI.
SHE HAS *EMOTIONS...* INCLUDING *THAT* ONE.
FALLING IN LOVE IS *BEAUTIFUL...*
...BUT IT ISN'T ALWAYS *PRETTY.*
WE CAN'T JUST LEAVE HER TO HERSELF NOW...
...SHE'S JUST TRYING TO WITHDRAW.
AND IF SHE DOES THAT MUCH LONGER...
...

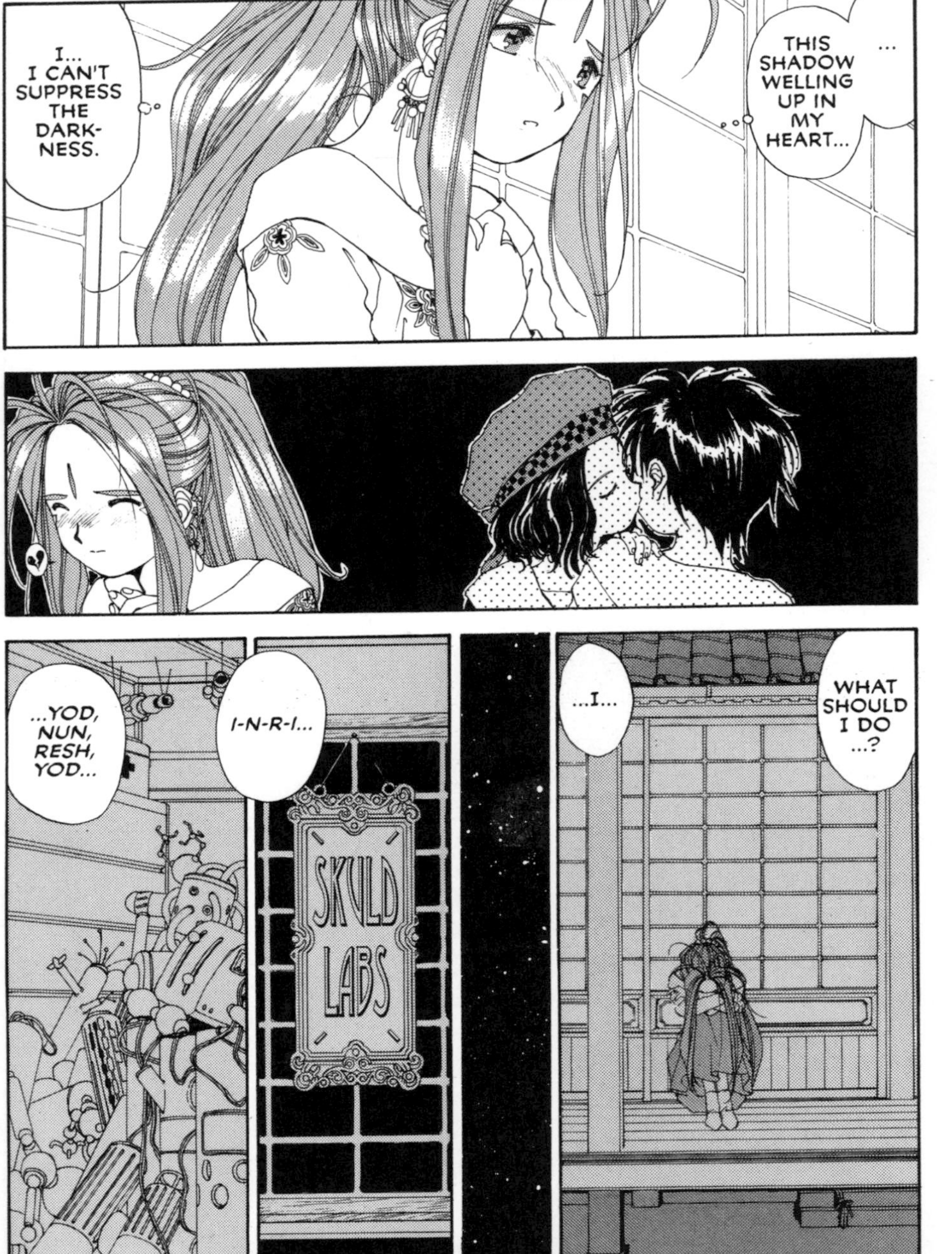
...
THIS SHADOW WELLING UP IN MY HEART...
I... I CAN'T SUPPRESS THE DARKNESS.
WHAT SHOULD I DO ...?
...I...
I-N-R-I...
SKULD LABS
...YOD, NUN, RESH, YOD...

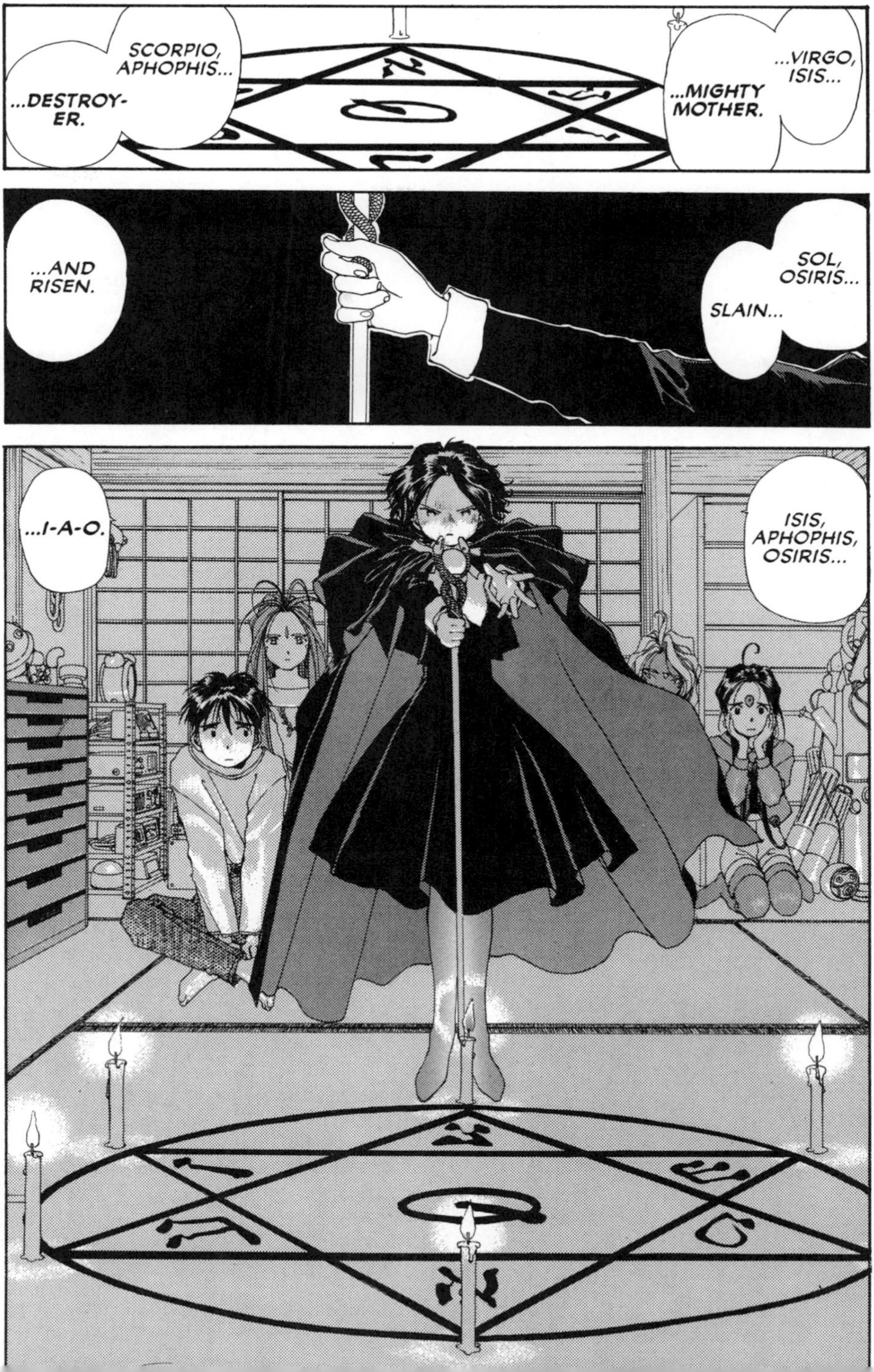
...VIRGO, ISIS...
...MIGHTY MOTHER.
SCORPIO, APHOPHIS...
...DESTROY-ER.
SOL, OSIRIS...
SLAIN...
...AND RISEN.
ISIS, APHOPHIS, OSIRIS...
...I-A-O.

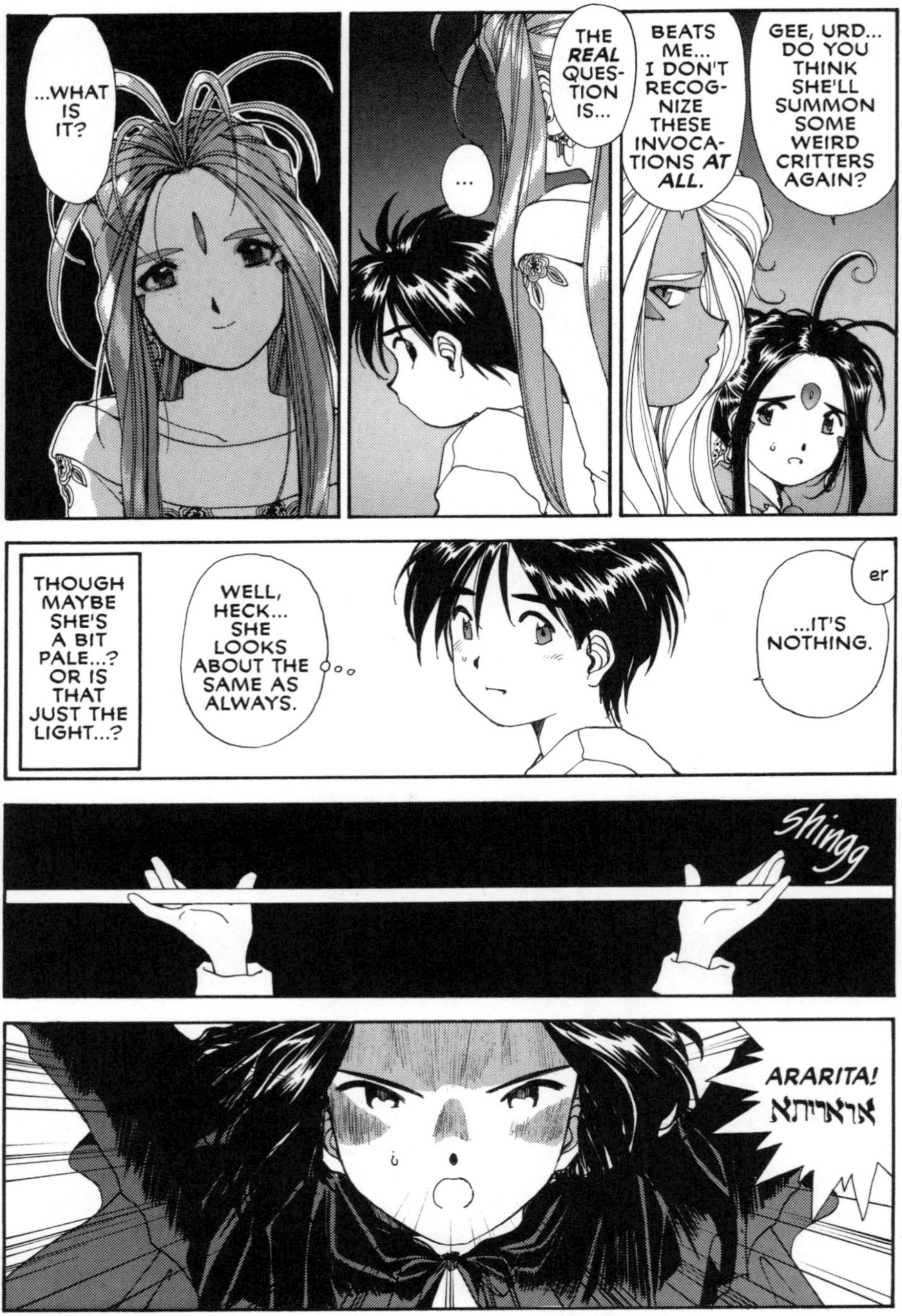
GEE, URD... DO YOU THINK SHE'LL SUMMON SOME WEIRD CRITTERS AGAIN?
BEATS ME... I DON'T RECOGNIZE THESE INVOCATIONS *AT ALL.*
THE *REAL* QUESTION IS...
...
...WHAT IS IT?
er
...IT'S NOTHING.
WELL, HECK... SHE LOOKS ABOUT THE SAME AS ALWAYS.
THOUGH MAYBE SHE'S A BIT PALE...? OR IS THAT JUST THE LIGHT...?
shingg
ARARITA!
אראריתא

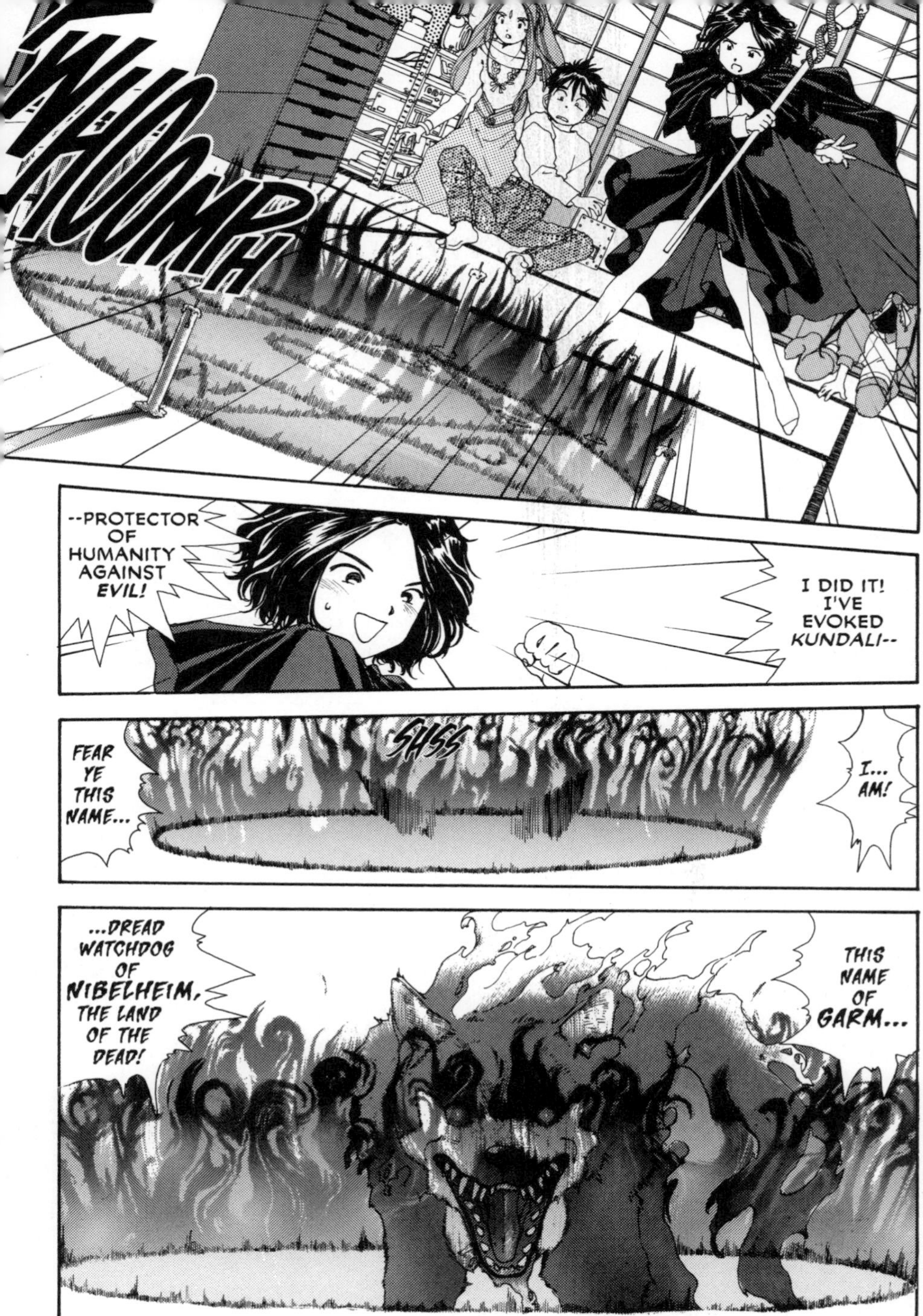
WHOOMPH
I DID IT! I'VE EVOKED KUNDALI--
--PROTECTOR OF HUMANITY AGAINST EVIL!
I... AM!
SHSS
FEAR YE THIS NAME...
THIS NAME OF GARM...
...DREAD WATCHDOG OF NIBELHEIM, THE LAND OF THE DEAD!

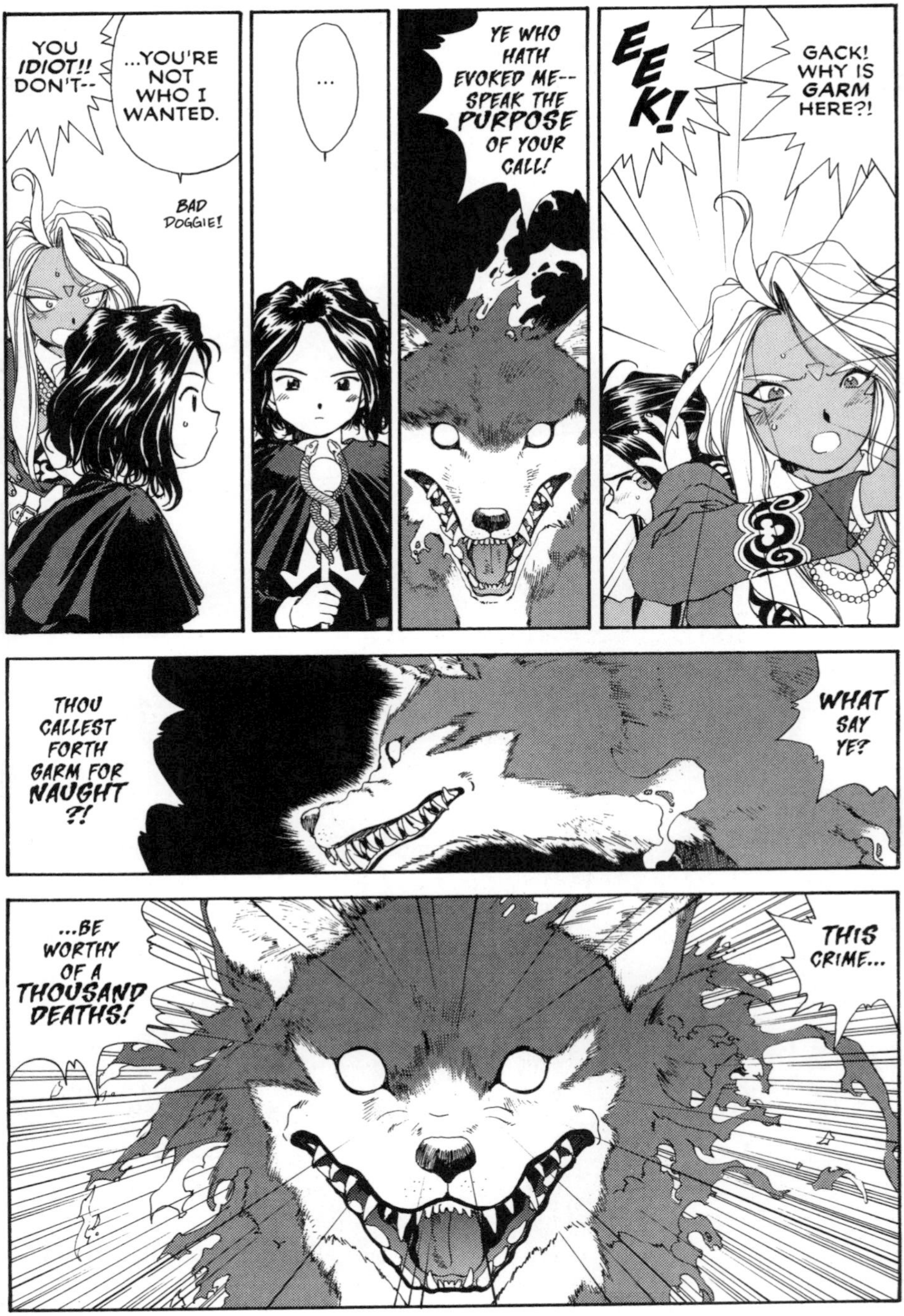
EEK!
GACK! WHY IS GARM HERE?!
YE WHO HATH EVOKED ME--SPEAK THE PURPOSE OF YOUR CALL!
...
...YOU'RE NOT WHO I WANTED.
YOU IDIOT!! DON'T--
BAD DOGGIE!
WHAT SAY YE?
THOU CALLEST FORTH GARM FOR NAUGHT?!
THIS CRIME...
...BE WORTHY OF A THOUSAND DEATHS!

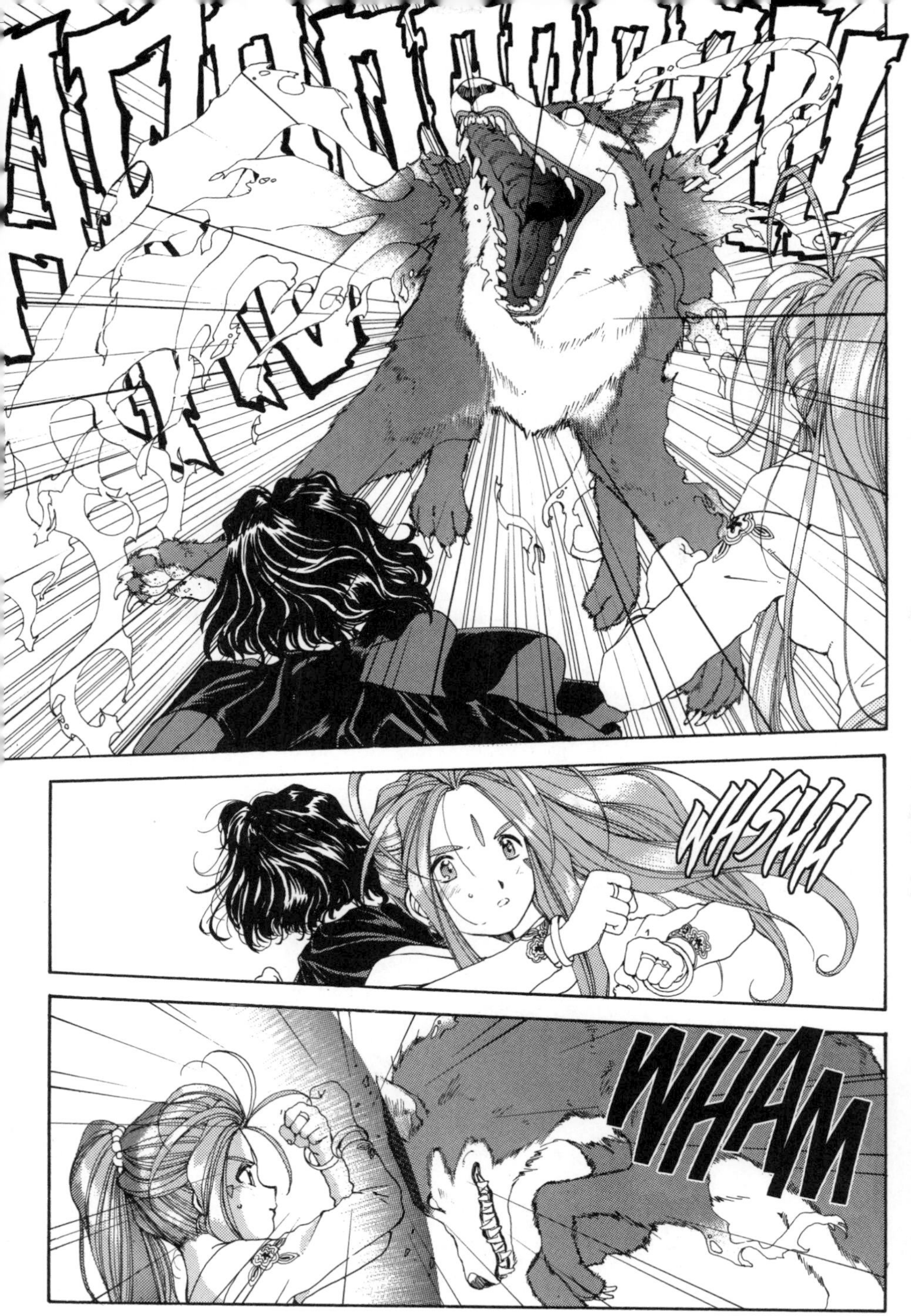
WHSHH
WHAM

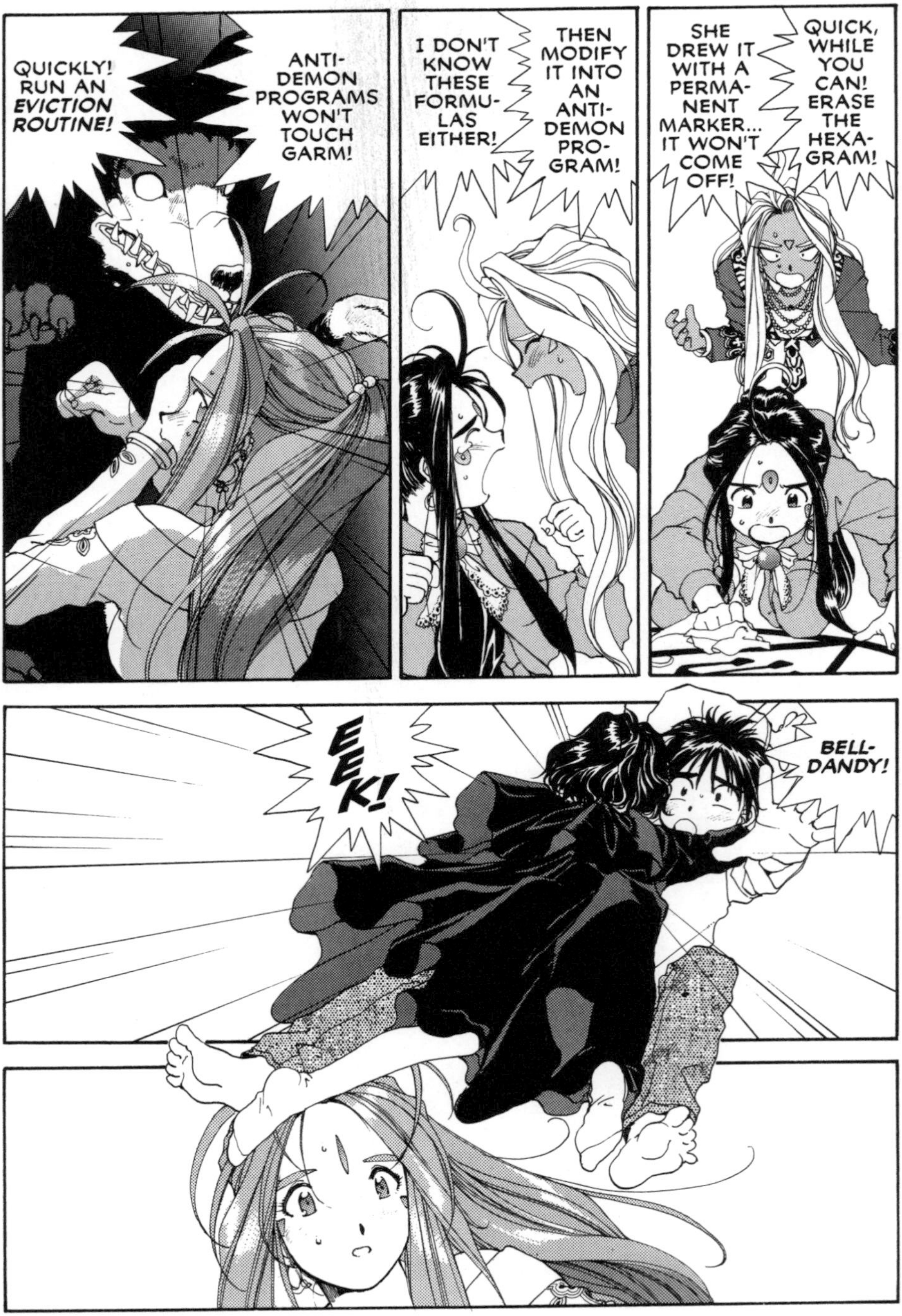
QUICK, WHILE YOU CAN! ERASE THE HEXA-GRAM!
SHE DREW IT WITH A PERMA-NENT MARKER... IT WON'T COME OFF!
THEN MODIFY IT INTO AN ANTI-DEMON PRO-GRAM!
I DON'T KNOW THESE FORMU-LAS EITHER!
ANTI-DEMON PROGRAMS WON'T TOUCH GARM!
QUICKLY! RUN AN *EVICTION ROUTINE!*
BELL-DANDY!
EEK!

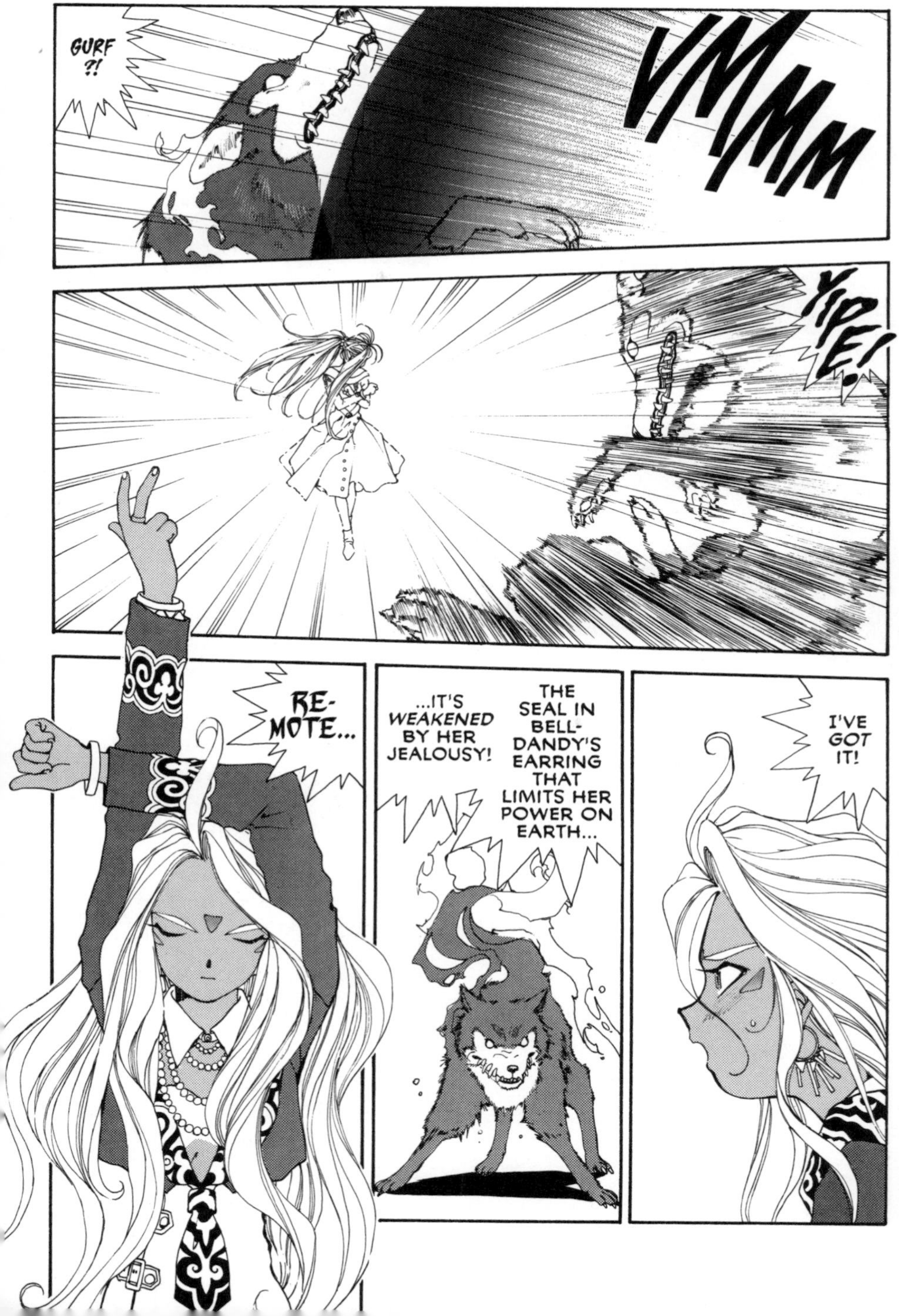
VMMMM
GURF ?!
YIPE!
I'VE GOT IT!
THE SEAL IN BELL-DANDY'S EARRING THAT LIMITS HER POWER ON EARTH...
...IT'S *WEAKENED* BY HER JEALOUSY!
RE-MOTE...

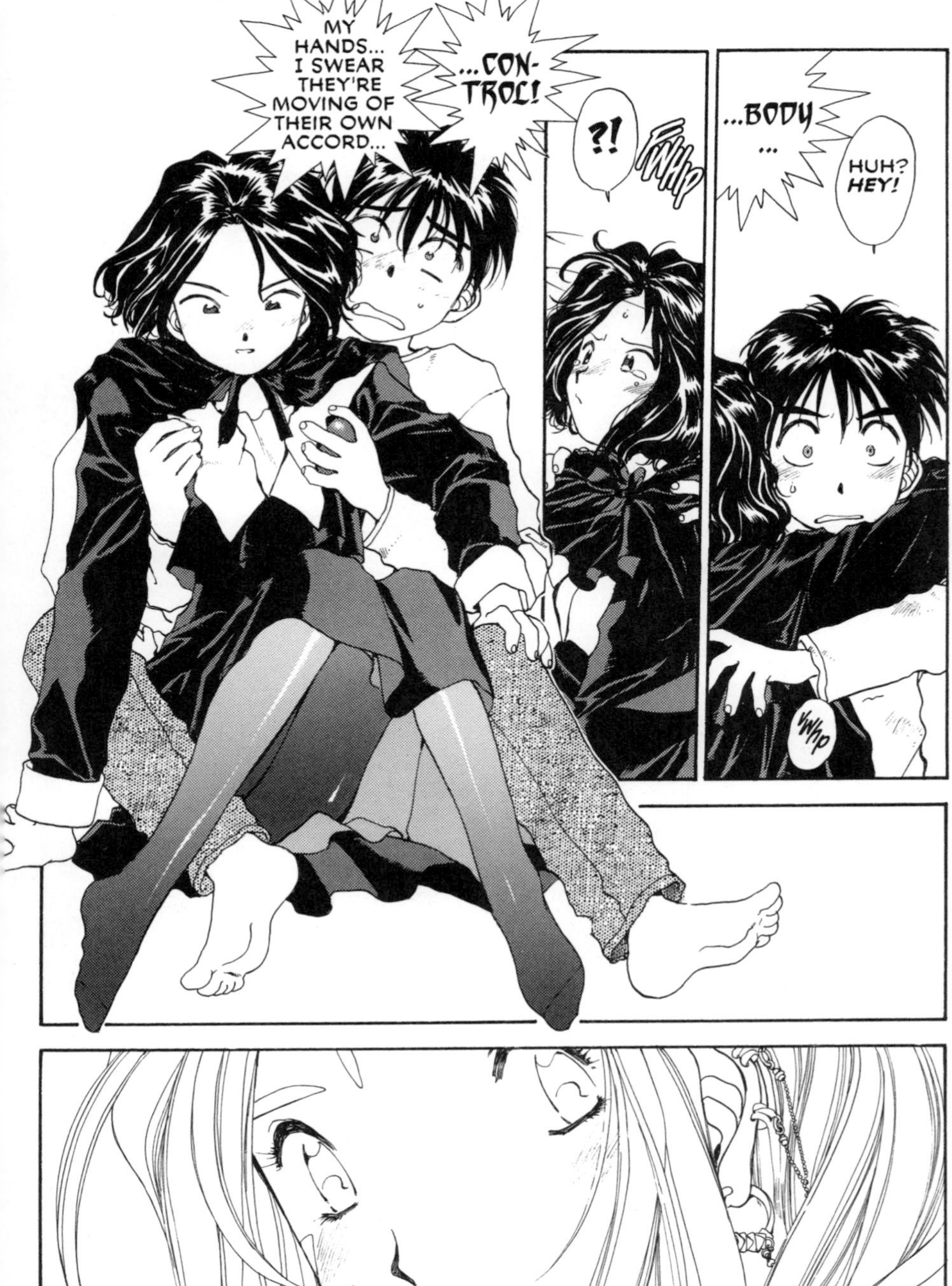

...BODY ...
HUH? HEY!
VWHP
?!
FWHP
...CON-TROL!
MY HANDS... I SWEAR THEY'RE MOVING OF THEIR OWN ACCORD...

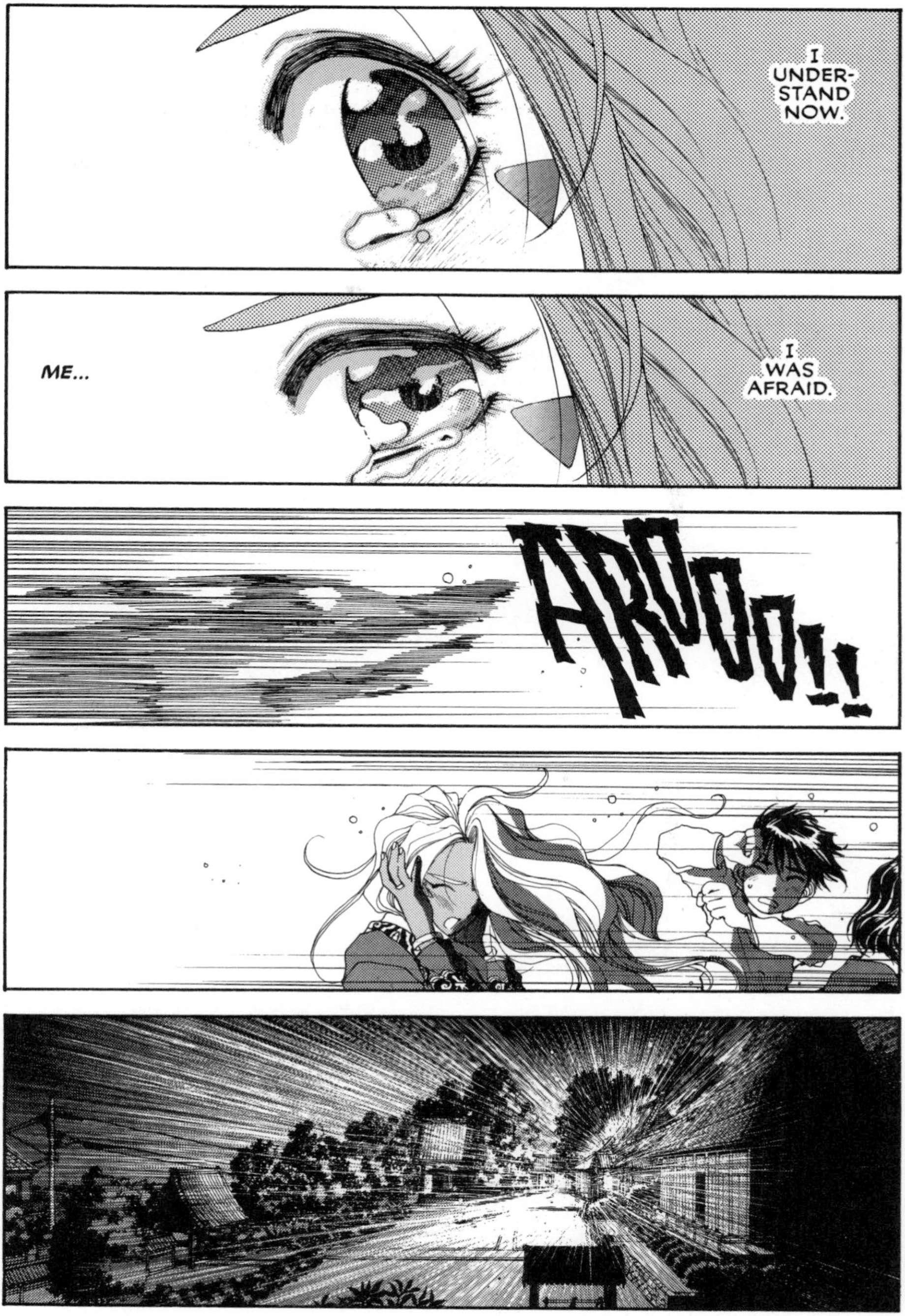

I UNDER-
STAND
NOW.
I
WAS
AFRAID.
ME...
AROOO!!

snff

snff

nng...

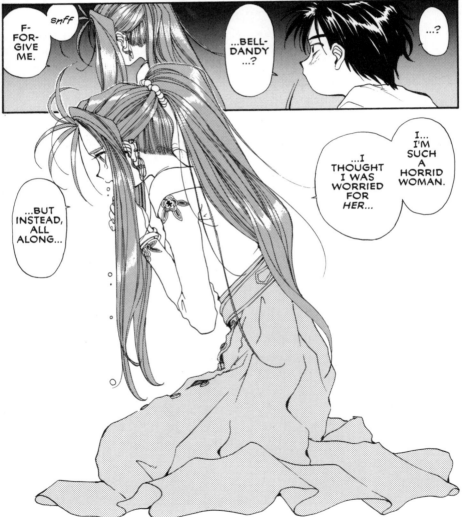

F-FOR-GIVE ME.

snff

...BELL-DANDY ...?

...?

I... I'M SUCH A HORRID WOMAN.

...I THOUGHT I WAS WORRIED FOR *HER*...

...BUT INSTEAD, ALL ALONG...

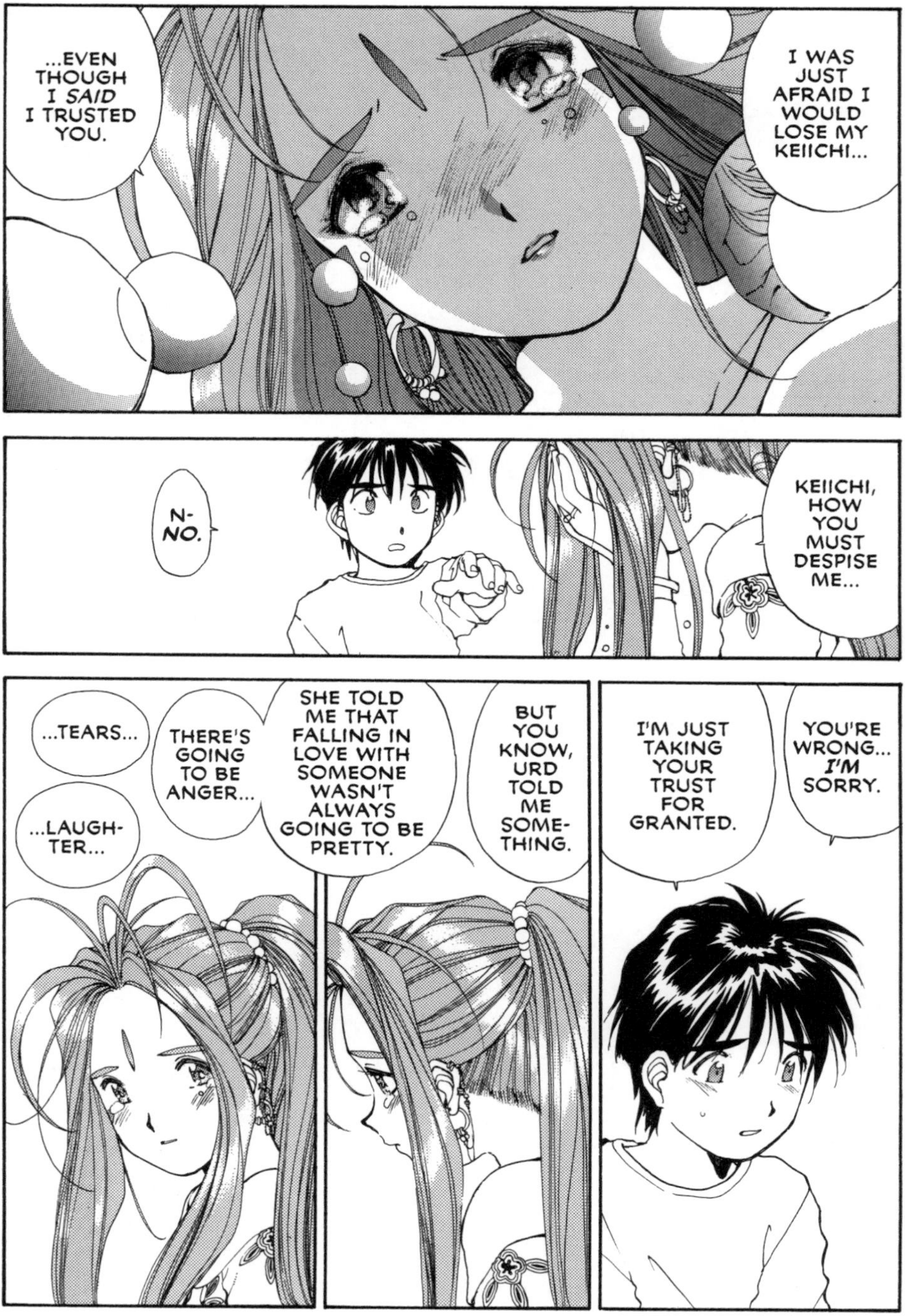
I WAS JUST AFRAID I WOULD LOSE MY KEIICHI...
...EVEN THOUGH I *SAID* I TRUSTED YOU.
KEIICHI, HOW YOU MUST DESPISE ME...
N- *NO.*
YOU'RE WRONG... *I'M* SORRY.
I'M JUST TAKING YOUR TRUST FOR GRANTED.
BUT YOU KNOW, URD TOLD ME SOMETHING.
SHE TOLD ME THAT FALLING IN LOVE WITH SOMEONE WASN'T ALWAYS GOING TO BE PRETTY.
THERE'S GOING TO BE ANGER...
...TEARS...
...LAUGHTER...

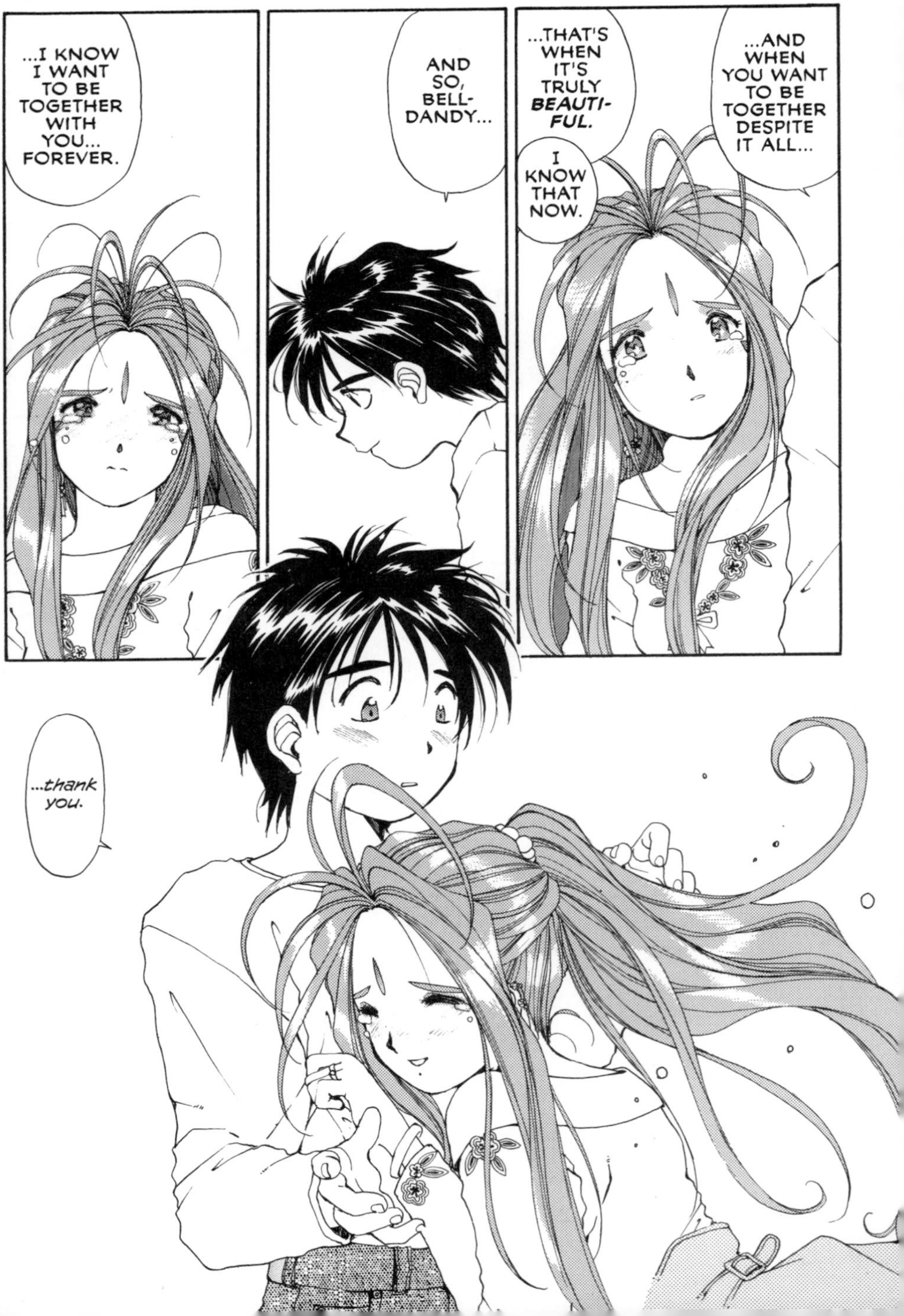
...AND WHEN YOU WANT TO BE TOGETHER DESPITE IT ALL...
...THAT'S WHEN IT'S TRULY ***BEAUTIFUL.***
I KNOW THAT NOW.
AND SO, BELL-DANDY...
...I KNOW I WANT TO BE TOGETHER WITH YOU... FOREVER.
...thank you.

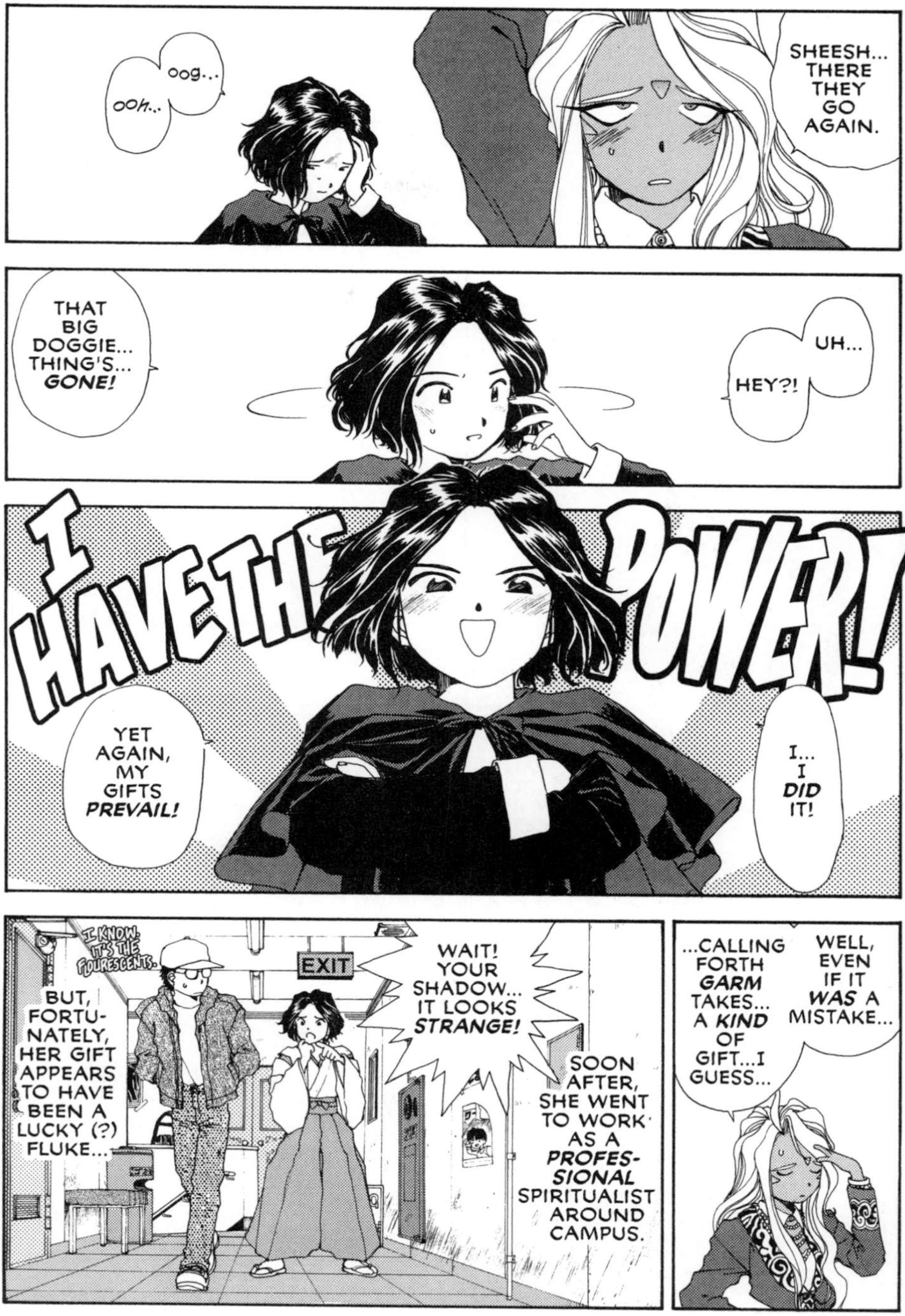
SHEESH... THERE THEY GO AGAIN.
oog... ooh...
UH... HEY?!
THAT BIG DOGGIE... THING'S... GONE!
I HAVE THE POWER!
I... I DID IT!
YET AGAIN, MY GIFTS PREVAIL!
WELL, EVEN IF IT WAS A MISTAKE...
...CALLING FORTH GARM TAKES... A KIND OF GIFT...I GUESS...
WAIT! YOUR SHADOW... IT LOOKS STRANGE!
SOON AFTER, SHE WENT TO WORK AS A PROFESSIONAL SPIRITUALIST AROUND CAMPUS.
I KNOW. IT'S THE FLOURESCENTS.
EXIT
BUT, FORTUNATELY, HER GIFT APPEARS TO HAVE BEEN A LUCKY (?) FLUKE...

THE ADVENTURES OF MINI-URD

NINJA-FORTIFIED

◇ IS THE MISO SOUP IN *YOUR* HOUSE SAFE? ◇

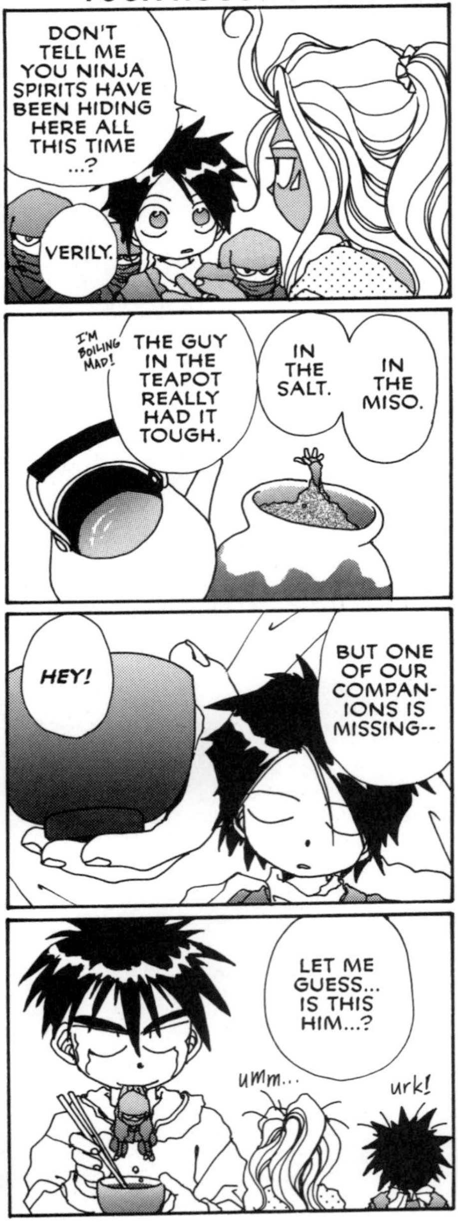
DON'T TELL ME YOU NINJA SPIRITS HAVE BEEN HIDING HERE ALL THIS TIME ...?
VERILY.
IN THE MISO.
IN THE SALT.
THE GUY IN THE TEAPOT REALLY HAD IT TOUGH.
I'M BOILING MAD!
BUT ONE OF OUR COMPANIONS IS MISSING--
HEY!
LET ME GUESS... IS THIS HIM...?
urk!
umm...

◇ WARNING: EXCESSIVE SUBDIVISION CAN BE HAZARDOUS TO YOUR HEALTH ◇

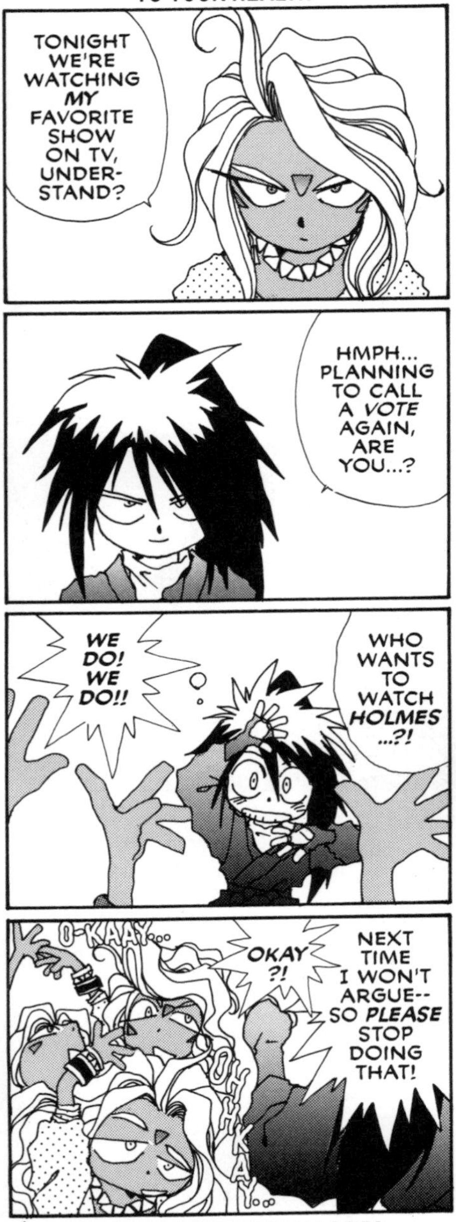
TONIGHT WE'RE WATCHING *MY* FAVORITE SHOW ON TV, UNDER-STAND?
HMPH... PLANNING TO CALL A *VOTE* AGAIN, ARE YOU...?
WHO WANTS TO WATCH *HOLMES* ...?!
WE DO! WE DO!!
NEXT TIME I WON'T ARGUE-- SO *PLEASE* STOP DOING THAT!
OKAY ?!
O-KAAY...
OHHKAY...

▲ SUBDIVIDED INTO TOO MANY COPIES...

Oh My Goddess!
ああっ女神さまっ
4
OMNIBUS
藤島康介
KOSUKE FUJISHIMA

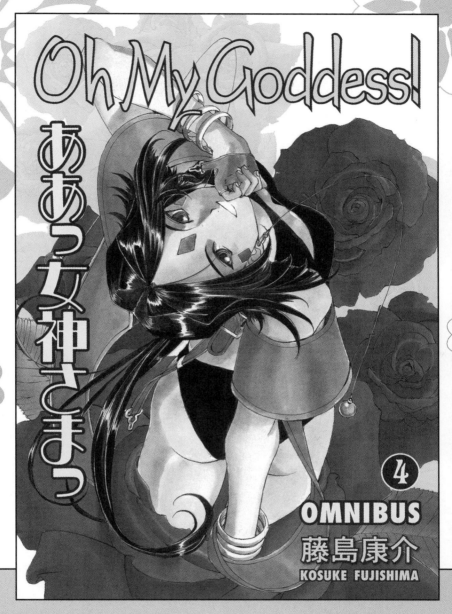

The fourth goddess, Peorth, arrives in Keiichi's life . . . to make it more complicated than ever! Peorth, mistress of roses, is in the same business as Belldandy—granting wishes to mortals. Keiichi thinks there must be some mistake, as he already has Belldandy in his life . . . but Peorth is certain he can't really be satisfied, or else how was he able to contact her? Now she's determined to stick around until Keiichi admits what he *really* wants . . . so she can grant it!

PRESIDENT AND PUBLISHER
Mike Richardson

EDITOR
Carl Gustav Horn

DESIGNER
Sarah Terry

DIGITAL ART TECHNICIAN
Christina McKenzie

English-language version
produced by Dark Horse Comics

OH MY GODDESS! Omnibus Book 3

Published by Dark Horse Manga
A division of Dark Horse Comics, Inc.
10956 SE Main Street
Milwaukie, OR 97222
DarkHorse.com

To find a comics shop in your area,
call the Comic Shop Locator Service
toll-free at 1-888-266-4226.

First edition: March 2016
ISBN 978-1-61655-895-6

1 3 5 7 9 10 8 6 4 2

Printed in China

東京 TOKYO BABYLON

CLAMP

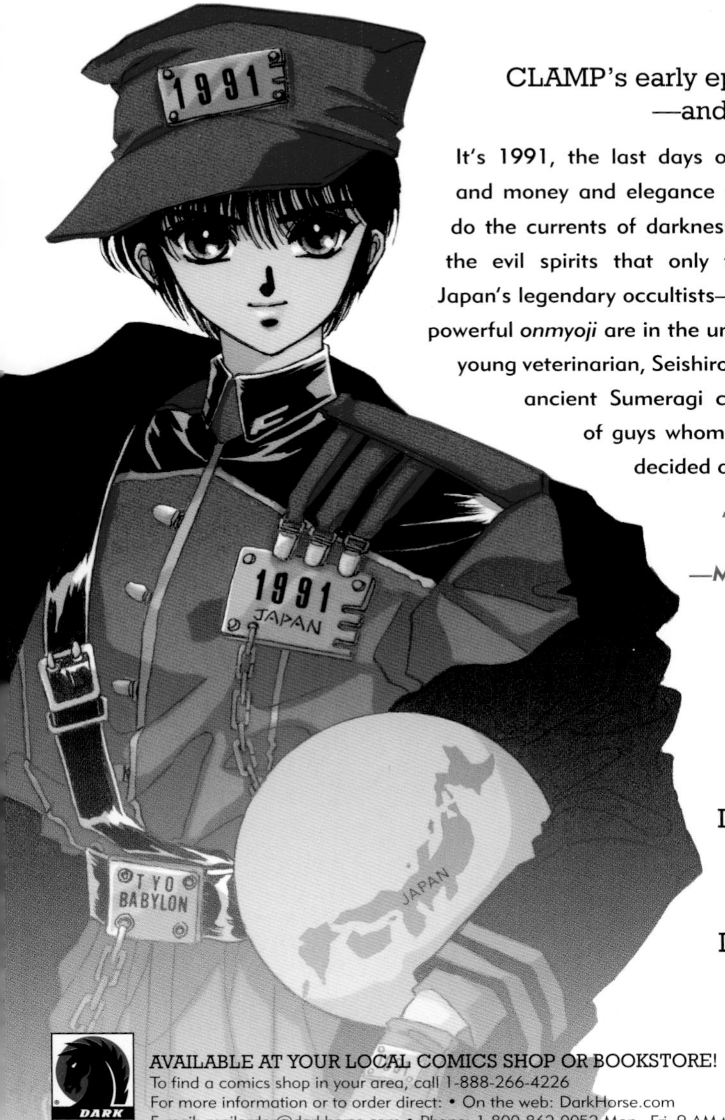
1991
1991
JAPAN
TYO
BABYLON
JAPAN

CLAMP's early epic of dangerous work —and dangerous attraction!

It's 1991, the last days of Japan's bubble economy, and money and elegance run through the streets. So do the currents of darkness beneath them, nourishing the evil spirits that only the arts of the *onmyoji*—Japan's legendary occultists—can combat. The two most powerful *onmyoji* are in the unlikely guises of a handsome young veterinarian, Seishiro, and the teenage heir to the ancient Sumeragi clan, Subaru—just a couple of guys whom Subaru's sister Hokuto has decided are destined to be together!

"Tokyo Babylon is CLAMP's first really great work."
—Manga: The Complete Guide

Each omnibus-sized volume features over a dozen full-color bonus pages!

VOLUME ONE
ISBN 978-1-61655-116-2
$19.99

VOLUME TWO
ISBN 978-1-61655-189-6
$19.99

DARK HORSE MANGA
DarkHorse.com

AVAILABLE AT YOUR LOCAL COMICS SHOP OR BOOKSTORE!
To find a comics shop in your area, call 1-888-266-4226
For more information or to order direct: • On the web: DarkHorse.com
E-mail: mailorder@darkhorse.com • Phone: 1-800-862-0052 Mon.–Fri. 9 AM to 5 PM Pacific Time

CLAMP オキモノ キモノ
Mokona's
OKIMONO
KIMONO

CLAMP artist Mokona loves the art of traditional Japanese kimono. In fact, she designs kimono and kimono accessories herself and shares her love in *Okimono Kimono*, a fun and lavishly illustrated book full of drawings and photographs, interviews (including an interview with Onuki Ami of the J-pop duo Puffy AmiYumi), and exclusive short manga stories from the CLAMP artists!

From the creators of such titles as *Clover*, *Chobits*, *Cardcaptor Sakura*, *Magic Knight Rayearth*, and *Tsubasa*, *Okimono Kimono* is now available in English for the first time ever!

ISBN 978-1-59582-456-1
$12.99

AVAILABLE AT YOUR LOCAL COMICS SHOP OR BOOKSTORE
To find a comics shop in your area, call 1-888-266-4226
For more information or to order direct: • On the web: DarkHorse.com
E-mail: mailorder@darkhorse.com • Phone: 1-800-862-0052 Mon.–Fri. 9 AM to 5 PM Pacific Time.

CLAMP MOKONA NO OKIMONO KIMONO © 2007 CLAMP Mokona. Original Japanese edition published by Kawade Shabo Shinsha, Publishers. English translation copyright © 2010 Dark Horse Manga. Dark Horse Manga™ is a trademark of Dark Horse Comics, Inc. All rights reserved. (BL 7078)

DARK
HORSE
MANGA
kHorse.com

ANGELIC LAYER

Story and Art by
CLAMP

YOUNG TEEN MISAKI SUZUHARA
has just arrived in Tokyo to attend the
prestigious Eriol Academy. But what really
excites her is Angelic Layer, the game where
you control an Angel—a miniature robot
fighter whose moves depend on your mind!
Before she knows it, Misaki is an up-and-
coming contender in Angelic Layer . . . and in
way over her not-very-tall head! How far can
enthusiasm take her in an arena full of much
more experienced fighters . . . and a game
full of secrets?

Don't miss the thrilling prequel to the
acclaimed CLAMP manga *Chobits*! These
omnibus-sized volumes feature not only the
full story of *Angelic Layer* but also gorgeous,
exclusive bonus color illustrations!

VOLUME ONE
978-1-61655-021-9

VOLUME TWO
978-1-61655-128-5

$19.99 each

From the creators of *Clover, Chobits,* and *Cardcaptor Sakura*!

Story and Art by
CLAMP

Umi, Hikaru, and Fuu are three schoolgirls out on a field trip to Tokyo Tower, whisked suddenly away by a strange voice and light to Cefiro, a world full of spirits and sorcery. Summoned by the beautiful Princess Emeraude, could they be the trio destined to become the legendary magic knights that can save her realm?

VOLUME ONE
ISBN 978-1-59582-588-9

VOLUME TWO
ISBN 978-1-59582-669-5

$19.99 each

CLAMP

IN NEAR-FUTURE JAPAN,

the hottest style for your personal computer, or "persocom," is in the shape of an attractive android! Hideki, a poor student, finds a persocom seemingly discarded in an alley. He takes the cute, amnesiac robot home and names her "Chi."

But who is this strange new persocom in his life? Hideki finds himself having to teach Chi how to get along in the everyday world, even while he and his friends try to solve the mystery of her origins. Is she one of the urban-legendary *Chobits*—persocoms built to have the riskiest functions of all: real emotions and free will?

CLAMP's best-selling manga in America is finally available in omnibus form! Containing dozens of bonus color pages, *Chobits* is an engaging, touching, exciting story.

BOOK 1
ISBN 978-1-59582-451-6
$24.99

BOOK 2
ISBN 978-1-59582-514-8
$24.99

AVAILABLE AT YOUR LOCAL COMICS SHOP OR BOOKSTORE
To find a comics shop in your area, call 1.888.266.4226. For more information or to order direct: •On the web: DarkHorse. com •E-mail: mailorder@darkhorse.com •Phone: 1.800.862.0052 Mon.–Fri. 9 AM to 5 PM Pacific Time.

CHOBITS © CLAMP. Publication rights for this English edition arranged through Pyrotechnist, Ltd. All rights reserved. Dark Horse Manga™ is a trademark of Dark Horse Comics, Inc. All rights reserved. (BL 7082)

arkHorse.com

MANGA BY
CLAMP

Fourth grader Sakura Kinomoto has found a strange book in her father's library—a book made by the wizard Clow to store dangerous spirits sealed within a set of magical cards. But when Sakura opens it up, there is nothing left inside but Kero-chan, the book's cute little guardian beast…who informs Sakura that since the Clow cards seem to have escaped while he was asleep, it's now her job to capture them!

With remastered image files straight from CLAMP, Dark Horse is proud to present *Cardcaptor Sakura* in omnibus form! Each book collects three volumes of the original twelve-volume series, and features thirty bonus color pages!

OMNIBUS BOOK 1
ISBN 978-1-59582-522-3

OMNIBUS BOOK 2
ISBN 978-1-59582-591-9

OMNIBUS BOOK 3
ISBN 978-1-59582-808-8

OMNIBUS BOOK 4
ISBN 978-1-59582-889-7

$19.99 each!

AVAILABLE AT YOUR LOCAL COMICS SHOP OR BOOKSTORE!
To find a comics shop in your area, call 1-888-266-4226
For more information or to order direct: • On the web: DarkHorse.com
E-mail: mailorder@darkhorse.com • Phone: 1-800-862-0052 Mon.–Fri. 9 AM to 5 PM Pacific Time

STOP! This is the back of the book!

This manga collection is translated into English, but arranged in right-to-left reading format to maintain the artwork's visual orientation as originally drawn and published in Japan. If you've never read comics this way before, take a look at the diagram below to give yourself an idea of how to go about it. Basically, you'll be starting in the upper right-hand corner, and will read each word balloon and panel moving right to left. It may take a little getting used to, but you should get the hang of it very quickly. Have fun! If this is the millionth manga you've read this way, never mind. ^_^

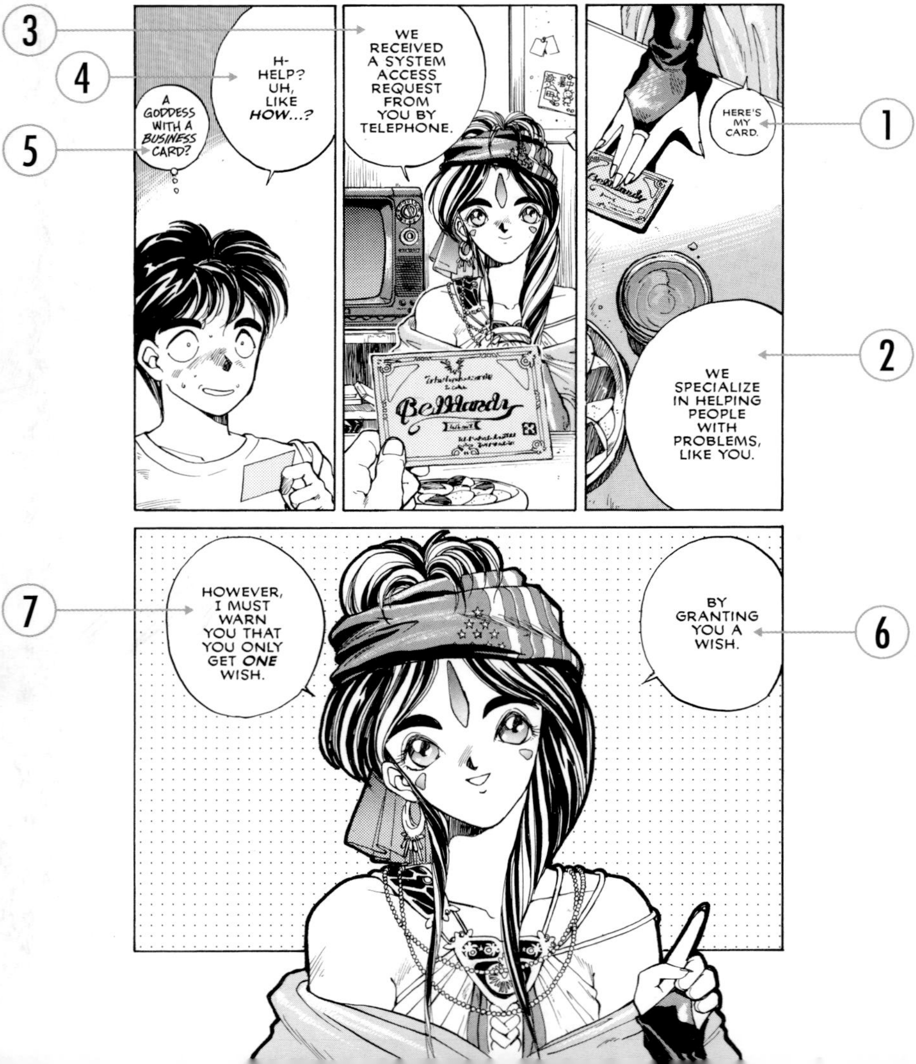
1
HERE'S MY CARD.
2
WE SPECIALIZE IN HELPING PEOPLE WITH PROBLEMS, LIKE YOU.
3
WE RECEIVED A SYSTEM ACCESS REQUEST FROM YOU BY TELEPHONE.
4
H-HELP? UH, LIKE HOW...?
5
A GODDESS WITH A BUSINESS CARD?
6
BY GRANTING YOU A WISH.
7
HOWEVER, I MUST WARN YOU THAT YOU ONLY GET ONE WISH.